Concordance to The Song Book of The Salvation Army

Concordance to The Song Book
of
The Salvation Army

Concordance to The Song Book of The Salvation Army

compiled
by
William Metcalf

The Salvation Army, United Kingdom Territory
101 Queen Victoria Street, London EC4P 4EP

First published 1992
ISBN 0 85412 525 6 (Hardback)
ISBN 0 85412 595 7 (Paperback)

WILLIAM METCALF, BA

Cover by Jim Moss Graphics

The photographs on the front and back covers were taken by
Robin Bryant at the 1990 international congress.

Typeset by
The Campfield Press, St Albans
Printed by Hartnolls Ltd, Bodmin, Cornwall

FOREWORD

Next to the Bible, no book is in more constant use by Salvationists than *The Song Book of The Salvation Army*. Its rich treasury of poetry and song lifts our hearts in worship, stills our minds in contemplation, and sounds the clarion call to action. It sets the gospel to music!

How valuable it is to have a companion volume that does for the Song Book what Cruden's Concordance has done for the Bible. Every student of the Scriptures owes much to Cruden. Every Salvationist stands indebted to William Metcalf. He has given us an inspired means by which to explore the hidden resources of the Song Book.

In an era when renewed emphasis is being given to putting words of Scripture to music, the *Concordance to the Song Book* will remind us that poets of every age have drawn lavishly from that source. Our Song Book breathes the Word of God. Hence the power of its songs.

May this volume prove a useful tool to all who lead worship. May it be a constant guide to the student. And may it bring new insights and fresh revelations to all seekers after truth.

John Larsson
Commissioner
TERRITORIAL COMMANDER

Key

Headings

EACH word concorded is indicated only once in bold, and is then subdivided where necessary. Each word is treated on merit, so there is no consistency of treatment, or order of sub-sections. In general however:

(a) all parts of a verb are included with the infinitive, eg, 'forgot', 'forgotten', and 'forgetting' will all be found under **forget**;

(b) frequently-used words are often classified as to whether they are 'divine' or 'human' attributes, or actions being performed by God or man. When neither is the case, the sections are headed 'general' or 'other'.

(c) In sub-headings, 'God' is used as an overall designation of the Godhead, and 'Jesus' includes references to 'Christ', 'Lord' and 'Saviour'. References to angels are usually classified under 'human' for the purposes of this concordance.

(d) Sub-headings often include other keywords, sometimes in round brackets. Where suitable, these words are indicated in the lines only by their initial letter. A word in square brackets is not found in every reference below, but is the main or biblical word of that set.

Bible references

A reference is given where:

(a) the lines that follow borrow clearly from that Scripture, *or*

(b) the text is the best-known scriptural use of the word being concorded.

An asterisk after a text indicates that the reference is only one of several that could have been quoted as containing the keyword.

References in brackets may not contain the keyword at all, but study would show the link between song and Scripture, and the reference offers a possible starting-point for that study. (MR) following a Bible reference indicates the marginal reading.

Cross-references

Each sub-section is separately numbered and lettered, to make cross-reference easier. Section 'a' is not normally lettered unless it needs a heading or scriptural reference, and the 'a' should be assumed. Cross-references appear at the end of numbered sections, and should be used when complete coverage of the

keyword is wanted. Cross-references in italics are to useful parallel words which will extend study of a theme.

An asterisk after a song number indicates that the reference is found in more than one verse of the song.

Abbreviations

(a) Traditional abbreviations of biblical books are used.

(b) Grammatical terms are used sparingly, and again without consistency. Use is made of n (noun), v (verb), adj (adjective), adv (adverb) and (prep) preposition. The most important is voc (vocative), indicating that the word (usually a person) is being addressed, as vocatives are not generally included, when they occur in quantity.

(c) The abbreviation 'nc' means that the word has not been fully concorded because of its frequency, and only useful sub-sections are included.

(d) The use of 'c' before a number indicates that the reference is found in the chorus section. When it follows the number the chorus appears as part of that song.

A

abased *(Matt 23:12)* . . . 159.2

Abba *(Rom 8:15)** . . . 106.5

abhorring 303.1

abide-ing
1 *[God] abides* *John 14:16*
Jesus, my Saviour, a. within . 315.2
he a. with us still . . . 397.1
he a., o'er all prevailing . . 539.3
b *prayers* *Luke 24:29*
o come to us, a. with us. . 86.4
come, a. for evermore . . 213.3
a., O gentle Spirit . . . 221.3
come quickly and a. . . 587.3
a. within me, and control . 619.2
a. with me; O Man of Galilee . 628.3
a. with me; fast falls . . 670.*
a. with me from morn . . 676.3
a. with me when night . . 676.3
come, Holy Spirit, and a. . c62
for evermore a. c102
2 *[Others] abide*
general
no thanks to them a. . . 1.4
joys that through all time a. . 112.4
not a sigh nor a tear, can a. . 397.2
content and calm . . . a.. . 551.2
star upon our path a. . . 716.2
a. all blameless, we believe . 785.5
I shall at his feet a. . . 884.*
everlasting spring a. . . 898.1
in thy garner to a. . . . 924.4
constantly a., Jesus . . . c36
b *abide (at/in side)*
heaven to a. at his s. . . 333.3
a. close sheltered in . . . s. . 424.3
at his s. I'll a. c154
close by his s., there I'll a. . c169
c *Luke 2:8*
shepherds in the field a.. . 75.2
d *John 12:24*
a. yet alone 923.2
it must a. alone . . . 923.3
e *John 15:4-7*
into thy blessèd will to a. . 300.3
where I ever would a. . . 320.1
I a. in his salvation . . . 330.c
if I in Christ a. . . . 361.2
a. in him always . . . 458.1
but let me still a. . . . 596.4
there I would always a. . . 639.3
fruitful, if in Christ a. . . 764.2
in him a., my all confiding . c176
f *abide (in love)* *John 15:10*
in his l. a., in the rock . . 341.2
as I in your l. a. . . . 552.1
I would in thy l. a. . . 627.1
in heavenly l. a. . . . 736.1
in his mighty l. a. . . 759.c
let me in thy l. a. . . . 837.2
g *1 John 2:17*
where saints a. for ever . . 934.4
h *abide (in faith)* *2 John 9*
with thee in f. a. . . . 595.3
constant still in f. a. . . 634.3
i *[word] abides* *1 Peter 1:23*
that word . . . no thanks . . . a. 1.4
God's truth a. still . . . 1.4
but still thy word a. . . . 6.4
Lord, thy word a. . . . 655.1
dwell, love (8b), *stay*

abiding (adj)
my heart is thy a. home . . 208.3
a fixed a.-place may find . 451.1
thy shadow for my a. place . 476.3
I dwell in thy a. care . . 644.c

ablaze 529.2

able
would you not like to be a. . 388.4
love that is a. to banish . . 443.3
b *2 Tim 1:12*
persuaded that he is a. . . 730.c
c *Heb 7:25*
a. to save, a. to keep, my Lord c1
he is a., abundantly a. . . c12
Jesus is a. . . . a. to save . c179

abode
the heart *John 14.23*
formed thee for his own a. . 157.1
make thine a. in me . . 209.1
fix in me his loved a. . . 214.3
their soul is Christ's a. . . 411.1
b *heaven*
veiled . . . his far a. . . 398.3
rise to that sublime a. . . 414.4
mount aloft to thine a. . . 559.5
place of thy people's a. . . 639.2
at our Father's loved a. . . 918.4

abound-ing
when darkness of sin is a. . 19.4
blessings a. where'er . . 160.3
streams of mercy are a. . . 239.1
love, unchanging love, a. . 254.4
let our songs a. . . . 314.3
true pleasures a. . . . 355.3
let strength divine a. . . 624.4
peace and gentleness a. . 664.1
daring when dangers a. . . 679.3
let the healing streams a. . 737.4
temptations, troubles a. . 773.1
with triumphant power a. . 815.2
in this world a. . . . 841.3
his a. goodness has been . c147
joy a. we are finding . . c195
b *(grace) abounds* *Rom 5:15-20**
God's grace did a. . . . 319.2
rivers of grace are a. . . 383.1
mercy and grace a. . . 384.2
that his grace doth a. . . 467.1
sin will a. till grace . . . 468.2
c *Phil 4:18*
must have all things and a. . 14.3

about
a. thee the gloom . . . 225.2
though tossed a. . . . 293.3
a wall of fire a. me . . . 344.3
God is round a. me . . 736.1
b *(concerning)*
what is divine a. my creed . 518.2
so sing a. it 544.1
have a fear a. their coming . 824.3
tell them all a. . . . 829.1
sing a. the mercy . . . 835.2
he talked a. a Kingdom . . 855.3
I want to tell you all a. . . c170
Jesus knows all a. . . . c182
c *about to*
to the souls a. to die . . 819.1

above
1 *preposition*
a. the din and toil . . . 31.1
among the fields, a. the sea . 41.1
all a. me mystery I see . . 52.1
a. thy deep . . . sleep . . 86.1
a. the rest this note . . 144.c
a. earth's lamentation . . 358.1
I see the blue a. it . . . 358.3
sing a. the toil . . . 393.3
far a. thy thought . . . 721.4
a. the things of . . . time. . 729.4
a. thee watching . . . 767.4
If Jordan a. me shall roll. . 771.3
live a. feeling . . . 773.4
a. the world-wide battle . 774.1
a. the storms of passion . 862.3
a. the waves . . . the ills. . 872.1
bright a. the sun . . . reign . 897.3
see it in the heaven a. me . c121
fly a. the clouds . . . c134
clear are the skies a. . . c152
a. our heads until we die . c240
b *above all*
a. all earthly powers . . . 1.4
high a. all praise . . . blessing. 20.2
good a. all other . . . 97.1
loved a. all earthly love . . 135.4
one . . . a. all others . . 377.1
all other names a. . . . 496.2
a. all other, earnestly . . 792.2
2 *adverb* nc, but *see*
Advocate, court, enthrone, home (3c), host (4b), lay (2c), leave (1a), Jerusalem (b), realm (b), rest (3), thing (1f), treasure (3b)
Heaven above
ye citizens of H. a.. . . 85.2
is our Lord in H. a.. . . 87.5
coming to me from H. a. . 114.c
in earth and H. a. . . . 178.2
I bring thee joy from H. a. . 229.4
travelling home to H. a. . . 275.1
no treasure had in H. a. . . 379.2
told my homecoming to H. a.. 388.3
trust for earth and H. a.. . 423.3
shine on my soul from H. a. . 446.1
fit me for life and H. a. . . 623.4
we lose ourselves in H. a. . 676.6
inspired from H. a. . . 781.1
H. a., where all is love . . c250
b *from above*
angels chanted f. a. . . 78.1
drops already f. a. . . 165.4
light and comfort f. a. . . 190.1
angels . . . bring f. a. . . 310.2
born . . . with life f. a. . . 371.2
blessing . . . I receive f. a. . 436.4
come, Saviour Jesus, f. a. . 480.1
thy likeness f. a. . . . 516.4
open the fountain f. a. . . 533.2
Lord, supply me f. a. . . 538.4
Spirit, breathing f. a. . . 545.1
pour the Spirit f. a.. . . 581.3
every blessing f. a.. . . 646.2
morning mercies f. a. . . 672.1
hearts inspirèd f. a. . . 704.4
full influence f. a. . . 942.4
c *(come) from above*
c. to me f. Heaven a. . . 114.c
O thou who c. f. a. . . 199.1
did he c. down f. a. . . 289.1
c. quickly f. a. . . . 444.5
thou who c. f. a. . . . 532.4
c. now, my Saviour, f. a. . 620.4
the joy that c. f. a.. . . c143

d *[Jesus] f. above* *John 8:23*
it brought my Saviour f. a. . 46.c
Jesus descended f. a. . . 140.2
descending f. a. . . . 221.1
Christ brought f. a.. . . 298.1

e *Jas 1:17*
wonderful gift from a. . . c197

send (1b), wisdom (1d)

f *general*
mountains high soaring a. . 8.2
hail thee as the sun a. . . 10.1
stars in their courses a. . . 33.2
glorious as the heaven a. . 40.2
or in the heavens a. . . 49.1
him on the cross a. . . 130.1
high as the heavens a. . . 383.2
O calm of hills a. . . . 567.3
and a. the sky is dark . . 805.1

Abraham
a *Ex 3:6**
The God of A. praise . 223.1, 2
hail A.'s God and mine! . . 223.5

b *Heb 11:8*
we obey, like A. of old . . 763.3

abroad
publish a. his . . . name . . 24.1
sound his power a. . . 26.2
spread through . . . earth a. . 64.2
spread a. the victor's fame . 147.3
thy work through . . . earth a. 198.3
must speak their joys a.. . 314.1
at home, a., by night . . 356.4
tell its rapture all a. . . 365.1
walk with thee a. . . . 656.3
sound his name a. . . . 939.4

b *Mark 1:45*
let us blaze his name a. . . 34.2

c *Rom 5:5*
shed it in my heart a. . . 214.4
our light be shed a. . . 688.4

absent *(2 Cor 5:6)* . . . 877.1

absolute 487.4

absolved 116.2

absorbing 666.3

abundance
grace and glory in a. flow . 452.4
needful blessings in a. . . 921.2

b *1 Kings 18:41*
sound of a. of rain . . . 637.2

abundant
like a river rolls a. . . . 254.2
fill us with a. power . . 622.3
gives to me a. peace . . 761.2
all our coasts a. stores . . 925.3
treasure in a. measure . . c249

b *(John 10:10)*
life . . . a., enduring . 553.1

c *2 Cor 4:15*
his a. grace is given . . 555.2

d *1 Peter 1:3*
again, by God's a. mercy . 173.1

abundantly
they shall drink a. . . . 95.1

b *Eph 3:20*
he is able, a. able . . . c12

abuse 123.1

abyss 746.2

accents
hear now his a. 235.3
pleading in a. meek . . . 299.3
those a. dear I languished . 398.2
tell me, in a. of wonder . . 848.3
in a. clear and still . . . 862.3

accept-ed-ing
a
a. me now, Lord . . . 108.3
he will a. for the name . . 183.4
a., sanctified in thee . . 287.3
gladly I a. the message . . 514.1
the Lord a. me . . . 514.4
a. burdens not his own . . 801.2
a. these simple tokens . . 922.2
a. each faithful vow . . 940.3
a. the gift we offer . . 943.1

b *accept (offering)*
a. my o. today . . . 786.c
a. our grateful o. . . . 870.4
stand . . . our o. a. . . 934.3

c *2 Cor 6:2*
in this a. hour . . . 196.1
O today is time a. . . . 241.3

acclaim
every land shall a. . . . 159.5
a. him with trumpet . . 537.4

acclamation
come with shouts of a. . . 37.4
hark, those bursts of a. . . 147.4

accomplish
not in my own strength . . . a. 501.3
God's will may be a. . . 833.2

accord
in sweet a. we wait . . 211.1
in a song with sweet a. . . 314.1
saints will sing in sweet a. . 368.4
in gladsome a. . . . 392.2
so that in full a. . . . 574.5

b *with one accord* *Acts 2:1*
let us all with o. a.. . . 90.6
tongue confess with o. a. . 174.5
we meet with o. a. . . 196.2
assembled here with o. a. . 216.2
with o. a. praise God . . 408.5
assembled here with o. a. . 638.2
we raise with o. a. . . 674.1
and all, with o. a. . . 784.1
we bring with o. a. . . 825.4

accorded
I am a. in Heaven a place . 906.2

according *Ps (119:25)**
a. to thy will and word . . 441.3
and that, a. to thy word. . 642.2

account-ing *Rom 14:12**
a strict a. to give . . . 472.3
for the great a. day . . c249

accursed/st *Deut 21:23*
hanging on the a. tree . . 120.4
bleeding on th' a. tree . . 548.2
lives are most by sin a. . . 919.2
cursed

accuse-r *(Rev 12:10)*
I may my fierce a. face . . 284.4
when the a. comes . . 724.3

ache-ing
sin that made it a. . . . 309.c
sorrow filled my a. heart . 363.3
they have left an a. void . 442.3
ease a. hearts with words . 529.3
my heart is a. here . . . 895.1
sowing . . . with an a. heart . 931.3

achieve-ments
forbid that man's a. . . . 6.2
nothing can I a. . . . 605.2

acquainted *Isa 53:3* . . . 137.2

acquit 652.2

across
flash a. the . . . sky . . 39.2
drifting dark a. the sky . . 40.3
ray a. to the garden . . 145.1
a. the field of battle . . 158.1
was born a. the sea . . 162.4
Jesus swept a . . . strings . 390.2
a gleam a. the wave . . 478.c
steal a. the sky . . . 673.1
flash a. its waters . . . 726.4
march a. death's . . . river . 902.3

act
in this dread act. . . . 121.5
my a. of faith and love . . 199.4
each a. thy approval . . 589.3
thought before the a. . . 863.4

action
turn my dreams to . . . a. . 32.2
beautiful a. of love . . . 114.2
a. bold/meek/brotherly . 212.1, 2
all my a. sanctify . . . 492.1
no spring of a. sure . . 508.2
by your a. too . . . 829.c
service bold, in a. kind . . 861.3

active
life into an a. quest . . 858.3
my hands for a. life . . 867.3

Adam *(Rom 5:14)*
a second A. to the fight. . 18.2
which did in A. fail . . 18.3
sinners lost of A.'s race . . 56.3
the tribes of A. boast . . 160.4
the worst of A.'s race . . 266.4
for A.'s helpless race . . 283.2

add-ed
a. more lustre to the day . 112.3
a. grace to . . . grace . . 423.4
so shall a. years fulfil . . 566.4
to a. afflictions he a. . . 579.1

addressed 93.5

admission 241.1

adopted/ion *Rom 8:15*
O Spirit of a., now . . 196.6
I've been a. 354.3

adoration
with true a. shall sing . . 16.6
praise him in glad a. . . 19.1
I will bow in humble a. . . 37.4
honour, praise, a. . . . 177.4
we yield thee a. . . . 185.4
in hymns of a. . . . 934.1

adore-d-ing
thine angels a. thee . . 8.4
joyful, we a. thee . . . 10.1
I triumph and a. . . . 14.4
in the heights a. him . . 17.4
all that is in me a. him . . 19.5
gladly for aye we a. him. . 19.5
the Lord your God a. . . 20.5
then let us a. and give . . 24.3
and to a. the Lamb . . 57.4
a. the all-atoning Lamb . . 62.1
a. the mystery of love . . 78.1
by highest Heaven a. . . 82.2
come let us a. him . . . 85.*
yet I love thee, and a. . . 110.6
I knelt to a. 111.1

our hearts a. move . . 135.4
all his works a. . . . 155.1
your Lord and King a. . . 164.1
the Father be by all a. . . 174.5
kneel and a. him . . 183.1, 5
we a. thee, . . . Father . . 192.c
to eternity love and a. . . 219.4
all the saints a. thee . . 220.2
I shall his powers a. . . 223.4
by your sacrifice a. him . . 242.5
I'll ever a. thee . . . 357.4
the lover of sinners a. . . 367.3
thou whom my soul a. . . 448.3
we a. thee, we a. thee . . 500.1
I praise and a. you . . . 506.4
thy name a. 526.3
with thanksgiving we a. . 576.4
we in Heaven a. thee . . 643.4
garden . . . for the Lord I a. . 647.3
he whom we a. shall keep . 767.4
we worship and a. thee . . 870.4
near the dear Lord I a. . . 906.1
our hearts to a. . . . 925.5
with your lives a. him . . 929.3
this is the God we a. . . 962
at thy feet I bow a. . . c35
'tis thee I a. c61
we would a. thee . . . c98
earth (e)

adorn-ing
a royal diadem a. 168.1
diadem . . . that his brow a. . 228.3
his bright crown a. . . . 852.c
robes . . . the fields a. . . 934.1
b *Titus 2:10*
as we the doctrine . . . a. . 656.4
c *1 Peter 3:3*
so truly a. the spirit . . 237.2
nor a., rich and gay . . 320.1
let this my a. be . . . 516.4
I want that a. divine . . 589.1
thy beauty a. c104

advance-ing
the mighty host a. . . . 804.2
let the foe a. 818.3

adventure
a road of high a. . . . 868.1
launched upon a high a. . 869.1

adversity 455.4

advocate *1 John 2:1*
hope . . . a. sure . . . 236.2
ask my a. above . . . 286.3
I have an a. above . . . 305.1
a. above; keeps me . . 347.2
an a. with God . . . 414.4
my a. appears . . . 762.1

afar
journeyed from the east a. . 80.3
but, a., his rising sun . . 145.1
commissioned from a. . . 163.2
hope is singing from a. . . 185.3
a. from Heaven . . . from God 225.1
glories gleam a. . . . 345.3
this land and lands a. . . 576.1
banner streams a. . . . 701.1
radiance from a. . . . 711.2
millions who are now a. . . 776.2
b *Matt 26:58*
by faith it sees a. . . . 742.1
c *Acts 17:27*
yet not a God a. . . . 6.1
d *Heb 11:13*
we can see it a. . . . 900.1
far

affection
a
I bring my whole a. . . 504.1
my warmest, best a. . . 520.2
my Saviour's a. . . . c207
b *Gal 5:24*
nail my a. to the cross . . 453.2

afflicted *Isa 53:4* 99.2

affliction
grievous a. has fallen . . 111.3
to added a. he addeth . . 579.1
the storm of deep a. . . 663.3
they who in a.'s woes . . 910.3
when stern a. clouds . . 911.4

afford
deliverance he a. to all . . 21.3
what joy the sight a. . . 147.4
place that Heaven a. . . 168.2
to lose the world I can a. . 513.3
can peace a. 587.1
love he only could a. . . 631.1
promises a. . . . light . . 657.1
his friendly aid a. . . . 662.1
which his smile doth a. . . 734.2
he doth his help a. . . . 915.2

affright
though . . . dangers a. . . 763.1
let . . . nothing a. thee . . 956

aflame
he has set my heart a. . . 63.c
our banners are a. . . . 163.1
set thou my zeal a. . . 574.3

afraid
faith is not a. of darkness . 555.3
love is not a. of hardness . 555.3
I am not a. 717.4
shall make my soul a. . . 726.1
thou shalt not be a. . . 739.2
of the dark a. . . . 740.1
b *Luke 2:9, 10*
and be ye not a. . . . 72.3

afresh
should strive a. 18.3
to revive thy work a. . . 201.c
fall a. on me c53
I feel a. thou canst heal . . c92

after
a. striving and praying . . 321.2
a. I'd wandered . . . 371.1
a. the passing of time . . 371.3
with him for ever a. all . . 399.2
a. thee my heart . . . 434.1
hard a. thee my soul . . 448.1
make me a. thy will . . 487.1
draw me a. thee . . . 630.1
a. battling through . . 663.1
ease which comes swift a. . 719.3
peace which follows a. . . 719.3
earnest strivings a. truth . 867.5
a. the seed is sown . . 923.2
b *after death*
a. d. its joys shall be . . 464.3
a. d. at thy right hand . . 917.5

again nc, but see
born (1b), once (4c), touch (1d)

against
a
railed they a. him . . . 130.1
close . . . a. the light . . 251.1
valiant be a. all disaster . . 685.1
a. the Church prevail . . 690.4
bring them up a. me . . 724.c
a. the host of Hell . . . 778.2
'tis a war a. Hell . . . 787.3
battling a. all evil . . . 859.2
a. the powers of evil . . 866.2
b *against sin*
wield his sword a. s. . . 583.4
speed the war a. s. . . 622.4
a. the forces of s. . . . 687.1
not a. the sinner, but s. . . 687.2
a. the powers of s. . . . 700.1
a. s. and darkness . . . 774.4
c *against day* *2 Tim 1:12*
unto him a. that d. . . . 730.c
a. the aweful . . . d. . . 885.1
fight (3), foe (g)

age
1 *(singular)*
the terrors of our a. . . . 5.4
your a.-long plan . . . 38.3
the a. of gold . . . 83.3
to serve the present a. . . 472.2
bends with a. . . . 544.3
in every a. the same . . 629.1
a light to every a. . . . 657.2
good news for this a. . . c210
b *age to age*
from a. to a. the same . . 1.2
shall from a. to a. endure . 3.4
a. to a. it never ends . . 55.2
a. to a. each nation grows . 146.1
a. to a. shall say . . . 155.1
never fails from a. to a. . . 157.2
from a. to a. goes on . . 198.3
2 *(plural)*
our help in a. past . . 13.1, 6
a thousand a. in thy sight . 13.4
God of a., God of grace . . 643.2
hopes of all the a. . . . 868.2
the saved of the a. . . . 908.2
b *[eternal] ages*
whilst endless a. roll . . 43.4
boundless as e. a. . . . 230.3
while e. a. roll . . . 514.2
through e. a. . . . ring . . 757.1
while e. a. run . . . 890.5
c *through(out) ages* *Eph 3:21*
t. this and . . . future a. . . 142.5
my joy t. the a. . . . 179.4
song t. a. all along . . . 187.5
undisturbed, t. the a. . . 539.3
this t. countless a. . . . 690.5
unchanging t. the a. . . 751.3
t. the a. . . . endure . . 755.c
t. eternal a. . . . ring . . 757.1
t. unending a. . . . sure . . 870.1
will t. the a. be Glory . . 906.1
rock (1b)

aglow
with the pure flame . . . a. . 443.3
with my heart all a. . . 469.1.c
hearts a. with . . . salvation . 704.2

ago
prophets long a. foretold . 72.4
on the hillside long a. . . 74.2
night in the long a. . . . 80.1
I was saved years a. . . 321.2
all with Jesus long a. . . 333.1
friends . . . loved long a. . 906.3

agony *Luke 22:44*
dies in grief and a. . . . 104.4
lest I forget thine a. . . 117.c
I shelter from such a. . . 122.2
to bear the cross and a. . . 125.3
by thy painful a. . . . 140.3
in that dark a. 486.3

agree
Spirit with mine doth a. . . 323.3
let us in our homes a. . . 661.4
all nature doth a. . . . c121
earth (1e)

ahead
nor . . . see the path a. . . 748.2
mighty are the tasks a. . . 789.3
conquer all the foes a. . . 858.2

aid
a. us in thy strife . . . 152.3
give us still thy . . . a. . . 202.3
thy mighty a. bestowing . 448.4
for thy mighty a. . . . 642.3
I will still give thee a. . . 653.2
each his friendly a. afford . 662.1
thy covenanted a. . . . 717.4
a. when . . . burdens press . 719.1
does come my certain a. . 767.1
he is willing to a. you . . 823.c
b *without aid*
w. our a. he did us make . 3.2
power, w. our a., made us . 4.2
not . . . one step w. thy a. . 726.1

ailing 456.2

aim
all selfish a. I flee . . . 461.c
in singleness of a. . . . 513.1
of all . . . be thou the a.. . 516.5
selfish a. do we forsake . . 532.1
our hopes, our a. are one . 660.2
one in our a. to vanquish . 692.2
the highest a. in view . . 801.1
keep us loyal to our a. . . 863.5
this is my a., my creed . . c107
I follow a purposeful a. . . c173

air
it breathes in the a. . . . 16.4
till the a., everywhere . . 73.1
as the a. we breathe . . 230.3
music fills the balmy a. . . 268.1
as the eagle cuts the a. . . 559.5
the Christian's native a. . . 625.5
there's music in the a. . . 664.2
in the open a. . . . prepare . 818.2
ampler is the a. . . . 878.4
they breathe on the a. . . 886.2
for ever fill the a. . . . 899.3
spring . . . embalms the a. . 925.2
I feel it in the a. around . . c121

alarm
I sink in life's a. . . . 508.1
shelter from the night's a. . 740.1
secure from all a. . . . 768.c

alas
a.! and did my Saviour . . 105.1
a., the duties left undone . 466.4
a.! a storm-tossed sea . . 749.2

alien *(Eph 2:12)*
an a. by birth . . . 354.3
a soldier on an a. shore . . 801.1

alike
a. at work and prayer . . 187.1
o'er all the earth a.. . . 362.1
each land . . . with him a. . 362.1
all scenes a. . . . prove . . 556.1
b *Ps 139:12*
dark and light are both a. . 674.3

alive
keeps my soul a. . . . 733.6
a. and quick to hear . . . 839.3
b *Gen 46:30*
and are we yet a. . . . 915.1
c *1 Cor 15:22*
a. in him, my . . . head . . 283.4
d *Rev 1:18*
Christ is a. . . . . 142.*
Jesus is a. in me . . . c177

all
1 *adjective nc, but see separate sections of many keywords*
all = adjective
the King, a. glorious . . 16.1
God of a.-redeeming grace . 23.5
the name a.-victorious . . 24.1
trust the a.-creating voice . 26.4
he, with a.-commanding might 34.3
by thine a.-wise command . 39.1
God is a.-loving 51.3
his a.-transforming might . 178.3
a.-powerful as the wind . . 200.3
a.-quickening fire . . . 207.1
a. sacred fire! . . . 208.1
thou a.-inspiring Spirit . . 210.1
Father a.-glorious . . . 219.1
his a.-constraining grace . 445.4
whose a.-searching sight . 453.1
the a.-prevailing name . . 481.4
this transport a. divine . . 545.1
his a.-discerning love . . 738.2
thou, a. conquering Lord . 742.3
a.-prevenient grace . . 762.1
in the a.-prevailing name . 791.2
atone (c), eye (k), important, redeeming, sufficient
2 *all [entirely]*
a. to be my Saviour . . 52.3
'tis a. my business here . . 60.5
gathered a. above . . . 86.2
a. meanly wrapped . . . 93.4
'tis mercy all, immense . . 283.2
he washed a. away sins. . 321.2
my spirit a. in a flame . . 360.c
bark a. in the dark . . . 375.1
when I am a. renewed . . 407.6
till spotless a. and pure . . 423.2
sometimes a. smile . . . frown. 468.1
with my heart a. aglow . . 469.1
my glory a. the cross . . 476.3
ever, only, a. for thee . . 525.6
I stand a. bewildered . . 542.1
a. of self . . . a. of thee . 548.1, 4
when sin is a. destroyed . 597.4
a. sacred to thyself . . 615.2
centre a. in thee . . . 630.2
confidence is a. in thee . . 714.3
his name is a. my trust . . 735.2
I am a. unrighteousness . . 737.3
a. for want of faith . . 770.1
abide a. blameless . . . 785.5
when a. alone I stand . . 837.3
saints a. immortal and fair . 886.1
prepared and a. furnished . 905.3
a. fruitful in good work . . 933.1
our work is a. in vain . . 943.2
'twas a. for me . . . c14
3 *all (pronoun)* nc, but
a *all who seek*
a. who s. shall . . . find . . 249.1
eternal life to a. who s. . . 277.c
unto a. who will s. . . . 329.3
the hope of a. who s. him . 334.3
a. who s. this . . . river . . 471.2
saying to a. who s. . . 724.1
b *[died] for all*
for a. my Saviour died . . 62.5
died . . . for a. who lift . . 181.3
do you know for a. he died . 243.1
Christ has died for a. . . 243.4
died for a. on Calvary's . . 381.2
who gave his life for a. . . 929.3
believe (b), free (1i), preach (a), but (1a)
4 *all (everything)* nc, but
a *know all*
thou k. a. so well . . . 421.4
a. is k. to thee, my Master . 522.2
a. is k., and that is why. . 522.2
he . . . k. a. you need . . 773.3
b *lay all*
a. . . . down at thy . . . feet I l.. 447.2
a. at thy feet now I l. . . 543.2
a. we l. before thee . . 643.3
c *all I am*
all I have, and a. I am . . 23.3
all I have and a. I am . . 492.1
a. that I am and have . . 524.4
bring a. thou hast and art . 864.3
d *Col 3:11*
till thou and thine art a. . . 181.3
my treasure and my a. . . 207.3
Christ, and a. with Christ . 214.2
be thou my a. . . . 468.3
from hence my a. shalt be . 498.1
e *[superlatives]*
of a. in earth . . . the dearest. 65.1
most impossible of a. . . 407.2
love thee best of a. . . 428.5
I have trusted least of a.. . 770.2
happy most of a. to know . 837.4
the sweetest place of a.. . c116
best of a., I know . . . c167
altar (e), beside (2), bring (2c), consecrated (b), conquer (2b), forsake (2b), give (1d, 2c), have (2g), leave (2c), need (3c), part (2d), resign (2b), surrender (a), take (2c), do (1c), have (2e), above (1b), around (a), more (2g), over (1a), Jesus (8e)
5 *all [everywhere]*
a. above me mystery . . 52.1
tell its rapture a. abroad . . 365.1
around (a)
6 *all [in phrases]*
Nowell, sing a. we may . . 72.c
to sinners, one and a. . . 94.2
thy raiment a. over . . . 111.2
for me, and once for a. . . 131.4
its sorrows a. too keen . . 267.2
a. you have to do . . . 403.3
I will obey at a. cost . . 513.c
a. through the night . . 635.3
trusting Jesus, that is a. . . 754.*
never laugh at a. . . . 830.1
b *all in all* *Col 3:11*
Saviour, art a. in a. to me . 325.2
My Christ is a. in a. . . 346.5
my a. in a. . . . . 489.*
my a. in a., I pray . . . 565.2
I am thy a. in a. . . . 571.1
them that find . . . a. in a. . 602.2
Christ is a. in a. to thee . . 718.4
my Saviour as my a. in a. . 757.4
own (3b, 4g), well (2b), while (a)

allegiance
our a. now we bring . . 532.1
pledge a fresh a. . . . 777.4
he is claiming youth's a. . 868.3

alleluia *(Rev 19:1)** 2*, 146*, 151*, 174*

allow
one doubt should I a. . . 385.2
his grace will sure a. . . 385.4
no sin-cursed thing . . . a. . 440.2

alloy
pure and free from sin's a. . 76.3
pardon, joy without a. . . 391.c

allure-ment
treasures no longer a. . . 640.4
earth's a. spurning . . . 803.3

almighty
by a. love anointed . . 109.2
come, thou a. King . . 219.1
Thou, who a. art . . . 219.3
o'erwhelmed at his a. grace . 223.3
thou, whose a. word . . 224.1
trust in that a. name . . 562.2
O Saviour, whose a. word . 569.2
a. to create . . . renew . . 596.1
beneath thine own a. wings . 671.1
where the one a. Father . . 765.6
watered by God's a. hand . 935.1
b *almighty (power)*
when Christ by his a. p.. . 149.1
Saviour . . . whose p. is a. . 640.1
I rest in thine a. p. . . . 714.3
c *Almighty* *Ps 91:1**
A., victorious, thy . . . name . 8.1
A., thy power hath founded . 16.3
praise to the Lord, the A. . 19.1
ponder . . . what the A. can do 19.2
d *Isa 63:1*
come, a. to deliver . . 438.2
thou art a. to keep! . . 454.5
blessed Lord, a. to heal . . 459.2
he is a. to deliver . . . 686.3
e *Rev 4:8**
how great is God A. . . 25.4
holy, Lord God A. . 220.1, 4
save (1h)

almost
your enemies a. prevail . . 537.2
when temptations a. win . 753.2
courage a. gone . . . 804.2
b *Acts 26:28*
a. persuaded . . . . 226.*

aloft 559.5

alone nc, but
a *God alone*
the Lord is G. a. . . . 4.1
G. a. the change . . . 338.4
to serve my G. a. . . . 505.2
b *Christ/Jesus alone*
faith in C. a. 46.3
C. a. . . . our portion . . 239.4
life is found a. in J. . . 240.4
to C. a. resolved . . . 480.4
in C. a. I'll boast . . . 521.3
stand for C. a. . . . 687.c
o'ercome through C. a. . . 695.5
my J. a. can set free . . 708.4
loving J. a. 893.2
trusting a. in J. . . . c119
c *thine alone*
the victory is t. a. . . . 163.1
thine, yea, t. a. . . . 293.6
thine ever, t. a. . . . 421.6
and t. a. I'll be . . . 538.c
the grace is t. a. . . . 571.2
talent and grace t. a. . . 589.3
t. a., throughout . . . 762.3
all my life . . . t. a.. . . 859.1
t. a., henceforth . . . c38
d *John 8:16*
a. with me . . . not a. . . 564.2
e *not alone*
n. . . . lip of praise a. . . 7.1
n. . . . temple crowd a. . . 7.2
n. on Calvary's height a. . 127.1
n. at Pentecost a. . . . 198.3
can't express by words a. . 215.3
n. a. the gift of life . . . 345.2
n. . . . years of time a. . . 349.c
leave (1d), stand (3d), walk (2b)

along nc, but see march (2b)

aloud
and he calls a. to thee . . 260.2
the Saviour cries a. . . 275.3
shout a. hosanna! . . . 698.c
we'll shout a. throughout . 782.1
shout a. salvation . . . 815.1
shout a. the victories . . 835.2
sing a. of Heaven . . . 835.3
sing a.: Hosanna . . . 853.2

already
promise . . . drops a. . . 165.4
I have a. come . . . 308.3

also
this mortal life a. . . . 1.4
them his glory a. show . . 2.4
a. for the winters tough . . 552.2
a. what must please thee . 925.5
beside (2), too (2), well (2d)

altar
saints before the a. . . 75.3
they have builded him an a. . 162.2
nothing from his a. . . 420.4
makes my heart his a. . . 495.2
my soul before thine a. . . 762.3
for the a. or the sword . . 769.2
bring an offering to the a. . 920.1
we toward thine a. move . 922.2
b *Lev 6:9*
thou art our a.-flame . . 648.2
c *Matt 23:19*
the a. sanctifies the gift . . 208.4
d *from the altar* *Isa 6:6*
f. his own a. brought . . 20.3
who f. his a. call . . . 56.4
f. thy a. blessings flow . . 528.1
a coal f. thine a. . . . c97
e *on/upon altar*
all . . . u. his a. lay . . 23.3
on Jewish a. slain . . . 120.1
on the mean a. of my heart . 199.1
see us on thy a. lay . . 203.4
until all on the a. we lay. . 397.4
u. the a. here I lay . . . 415.4
on the a. now we lay soul . 481.2
my all is on the a. . . . 511.c
my all u. thy a. laid . . 513.1
placing talents on thine a. . 863.4
heap on his sacred a. . . 929.3
u. thine a., Lord, we lay. . 934.2
on thine a. here I lay all . . c34

alter-ed
other things may a. . . 49.2
the joy that can a. never . 73.4
if my purposes have a. . . 522.1

alteration 865.3

although nc

always *nc, but see*
ever, lead (3c)

amaze-d-ing
a. pity, grace unknown . . 105.2
love so a., so divine . . 136.4
I stand a. in the presence . 179.1
O what a. words of grace . 254.1
a. love! how can it be . . 283.1
a. grace! how sweet the sound 308.1
thoughts of such a. bliss . 314.2
I am a. when I think . . 319.*
O love so a. that broke . . 331.3

ambition
this must be my life's a.. . 463.3
perish every fond a. . . 498.2
to sever from selfish a. . . 501.1
my highest a., my . . . delight. 640.4

this my hope, my life's a. . c38
only one intention, . . . a. . c48

amen
let the a. sound . . . 19.5
hallelujah to the lamb . . . a.!. 57.c
yea, a., let all adore thee . 161.4
light, and love, a. . . . 171.3
a., a., my soul replies . . 312.4
hallelujah, a.! . . . 322.c
send the glory! . . . a.! . . 355.c
for ever with the Lord! a. . 877.1
for ever and ever, A. . . 951.

(a)mid-st
helper he, a. the flood . . 1.1
see, a. the winter's snow . 88.1
a. flaming worlds . . . 116.1
a. rending rocks . . . 125.2
a. the crowd that gathered . 304.1
peace a. the tempest's roar . 330.c
unperceived a. the throng . 370.4
so a. the conflict . . . 396.3
'tis because, a. temptation . 404.3
is not the Christ a. . . . 527.2
a. earth's sin and sorrow . 529.1
growing right a. the weeds . 552.2
calm a. its rage . . . sleep . 569.2
rest a. life's conflicts . . 575.3
a. the encircling gloom . . 606.1
a. all the traffic . . . 615.1
a. the darkness and cloud . 641.2
smiling a. opposing legions . 686.2
a. the tempest and . . . storm. 687.c
a. the homes of want . . 697.3
a. the angry billows' roll. . 713.1
a. the tempest I have been . 713.2
sometimes a. scenes . . 725.2
like a rock a. . . . billows. . 750.2
a. the problems that . . 759.1
sing a. bliss unspoken . . 835.3
found a. the fields . . . 871.2
a. the noise of . . . strife. . 884.3
a. the hottest fire . . . 910.4
strife (c)

among
a. the fields . . . . . 41.*
parted a. the soldiers . . 126.2
one a. the ransomed throng . 514.4
Jesus, stand a. us . . . 599.1
Jesus was here a. men . . 794.1
sing a. the angels . . . 840.3
God resides a. his own . . 909.2

ample-r
God's a. grace for . . . man . 656.2
larger, a. is the air . . . 878.4

anchor *Heb 6:19*
will your a. hold . . . 280.*
we have an a. . . . 280.c
hope has dropped her a. . 333.3
our a. and our stay . . 654.3
a. within the . . . veil . . 733.4
its a. holds alone to thee . 742.3
my a. holds within the veil . 745.2
my soul's a. may remain . 746.1
this a. shall . . . sustain . . 746.5
I have a. my soul . . . c178

ancient
a
for still our a. foe . . . 1.1
its a. splendours fling . . 83.3
still its a. power . . . 558.5
b *Dan 7:9*
glorious, the A. of days . . 8.1
defender, the A. of days . . 16.1
reign over us, A. of days . 219.1
A. of everlasting days . . 223.1

anew
ponder a. what the Almighty . 19.2
make my heart a. . . 32.1, 3
a. this song we'll sing . . 118.5
and build it up a. . . 149.3
fill me with life a. . . . 189.1
and make it a. . . . 335.c
fashion lives a. . . . 335.3
bids nature smile a. . . 494.2
a soul . . . is born a. . . 550.2
with eyes that see a. . . 618.3
each morning a. God calls . 666.4

angel-ic *(adj)*
what a. tongue can tell?. . 55.4
as an echo of the a.-choir . 70.c
with the a. host proclaim . 82.1
beneath the a.-strain . 83.2
the song of the a. band . . 94.c
help, ye bright a. spirits . . 109.3
where bright a. feet . . 891.1
choir, face (1b), voice (2)

angel-s
a. in the heights adore . . 17.4
born the King of a. . . 85.1
a. are lingering near . . 226.2
a. can do nothing more . . 367.3
a. now are hovering round . 370.4
a. will attend 396.3
thee, whom a. praise . . 592.1
as a. do in Heaven . . . 624.2
there's an a. in the house . 664.c
b *all angels*
a. adore thee, all veiling . . 8.4
all the a. told the story . . 74.2
all the a. faces . . . 141.2
purer than all the a. . . 177.3
c *Gen 28:12*
a. descending, bring . . 310.2
a. to beckon me nearer . . 617.3
d *Ps 91:11, 12*
a. hold a charge divine . . 728.2
e *Matt 13:41*
give his a. charge at last. . 924.3
with all thine a., come . . 924.4
a. shout . . . harvest home . 932.c
f *Matt 26:53*
a. waited his command . . 130.3
g *Matt 28:2*
a. rolled the stone away. . 145.2
a. in bright raiment . . 152.1
h *Luke 2:13*
'twas by an a. told them . 72.2
all the a. told 74.2
a., shepherds, wise men . 74.2
a., from the realms . . 75.1
a. chanted from above . . 78.1
a. bending near the earth . 83.1
the a. keep their watch . . 86.2
we hear the Christmas a. . 86.4
with the a. let us sing . . 89.3
the first Nowell the a. . . 90.1
the a. of the Lord came . . 93.1
worshipped by the a. . . 96.1
tell how the a. in chorus. . 99.1
the a. proclaimed . . . 137.1
a. with rapture announce . 139.1
still the a. chant . . . 253.3
i *Luke 15:10*
let the a. bear the tidings . 259.4
glory, how the a. sing . . 550.c
a., swell the . . . strain . . 550.3
a. in their songs rejoice . . 625.4
j *John 20.12*
a. in robes of light . . . 117.2
k *Rom 8:38*
death, nor life, nor a. . . 554.3
l *1 Thess 4:16*
O trump of the a. . . . 771.4
m *1 Peter 1:12*
a. would the mystery scan . 439.2
n *Rev 5:11, 12**
thine a. adore thee . . . 8.4
a. delight to hymn thee . . 16.6
blessing, with a. above . . 24.3
let a. prostrate fall . . . 56.1
with a. round the throne . 57.1
a. crown him 147.2
a. with bright wings . . 268.1
with the a. I will sing . . 327.3
the harps of the a. . . . 406.2
to sing among the a. . . 840.3
a. will stand on . . . strand . 879.c
the a. are watching . . 883.3
bright (1c), choir, man (2d), saint (3b), sing (2b), song (2)

anger
men from strife and a. . . 833.1
b *Hos 14:4*
God's a. now is turned . . 317.1

angry
the waves in a. motion . . 96.2
trial . . . before the a. mob . 181.2
the a. waves . . . o'erflow . 280.2
out of the a. waves . . 336.3
loud and a. billows roar . . 478.2
bid its a. tumult cease . . 569.3
'midst the a. billows' roll . 713.1

anguish
mocking his a. and pain . . 99.3
how pale art thou with a. . 123.1
here tell your a. . . . 236.1
neither sighing nor a. . . 905.2
with what a. and loss . . c24

announce 139.1

annoy
hopes deceive and fears a. . 112.2
the cares of life a. . . . 462.2

anoint-ed
a *Ps 23:5*
thou dost with oil a. . . 54.4
b *Acts 4:27*
his dear a. one . . . 106.4
by almighty love a. . . 109.2
be my love-a. King . . 122.4
expects his own a. Son . . 150.4
c *Acts 10:38*
a. me with . . . Holy Ghost . 432.3

anointing (n) 527.2

another
we want a. Pentecost . . 203.1
o'er a. soul forgiven . . 259.4
a. touch, I ask a. still . . 628.2
dawn leads on a. day . . 677.3
we'll have a. song . . . 815.1
a. voice is calling . . . 864.2
share one with a. . . . 927.3
faithful through a. year . . 937.1

answer
1 *God*
down to a. all my need . . 91.3
a. to the blood . 106.4; c129
he a. our pitiful call . . 245.2
will a. when we call . . 270.c
Lord, a. these questions . . 289.4
a. now my soul's desire . . 479.2
Christ is the a. . . . c151
b *answer prayer*
a. thy prayerfulness . . 183.2
he plans to a. all your p.. . 238.1
triumph in a. to p. . . . 373.3
thou art a. my p. . . . 434.4
waits to a. p. 560.1
for a. p. we thank thee . . 576.4
hear, O hear, and a. p. . . 584.c
pray till the a. we get . . 608.2
thank thee, Lord, for a. p. . 642.1
shall be thy a. to our p. . . 642.1
place where God a. p. . . c67
I believe God a. p. . . . c70
never a p. he will not a.. . c87
c *Jesus answers prayer*
seat, where Jesus a. p. . . 284.1
Jesus loves to a. p. . . 563.1
Jesus a. p. c113
2 *(general)*
faith that a. firmly . . . 6.3
be swift . . . to a. him . . 162.3
I want to a. thee . . . 409.1
yea, Lord . . . my a. must be. 507.1
in vain, and proudly a. . . 548.1
grace to a. grace . . . 659.4
I a., life is fleeting . . 780.4
wave the a. back to Heaven . 804.c
hear then our a. . . . 864.c
swift obedience a. love . . 867.2
what shall the a. be . . c28
gladly be a. by me . . . c55
b *answer call*
love that a. every c. . . 426.2
living to a. thy c. . . . 786.2
like him to a. at thy c. . . 839.3

anthem
their loud a. thrilled . . 5.2
how the heavenly a. drowns . 156.1
a hundred a. rise . . . 163.3
a. of praise . . . eternally . 392.4
the a. of the free . . . 550.c
loud your a. raise . . . 690.2

anxiety . . . . . 246.*

anxious
bids all a. fears depart . . 68.2
with a., longing thirst . . 447.1
bid my a. fears subside . . 578.3
hear our a. prayer . . . 582.1
sad doubt and a. fear . . 746.3
how the a. shout it . . 815.2

any
have you a. room for Jesus . 241.1
make a. change in my mind . 318.3
could not see . . . a. grace . 353.1
glows in a. earthly sky . . 387.1
nor hold back . . . a. part . 422.1
depth, nor a. creature . . 554.4
free . . . on a. shore . . 556.2
let not self hold a. part . . 643.3
up against me a. more . . 724.c
nor a. . . . light refuse . . 871.3
b *any time*
in a. t. of trouble . . . 98.3
a. t. for Jesus? . . . 241.3
at a. t. and anywhere . . c71

any(body)
does a. know 274.2
grace . . . than a. is aware . 615.4

anything 422.4

anywhere
is it a. said 289.2
a., everywhere, . . . follow . 483.c
is there trouble a. . . . 645.2
at any time and a. . . . c71
fly above the clouds . . . a. . c134
I'll go a. c172

apace
the moments fly a. . . 255.3
when life sinks a. . . . 763.5

apart
when from thee I'm a. . . 448.3
thy sons, from earth a. . . 942.3
b *Ps 4:3*
I'm set a. for Jesus . . 495.1
to thy service set a. . . 865.3
c *Mark 6:31*
come ye yourselves a. . . 564.1

apostle 428.2

appal-ling
my spirit a. 237.1
then no tempest shall a.. . 285.3
no fear my heart a. . . 489.4
none a. us c239

appeal 434.2

appear
1 *[God] appears* *Col 3:4**
we see thee now a. . . 36.3
in his temple shall a. . . 75.3
now in flesh a. . . . 85.3
see the Lamb of God a. . . 88.1
sacrifice in my behalf a.. . 106.1
our captain did a. . . 163.3
a., desire of nations . . 167.3
let thy life in mine a. . . 212.2
in flowing wounds a. . . 368.2
within me doth a. . . . 370.2
in my heart a.. . . . 412.1
let my healing a. . . 647.2
relief will surely a. . . 712.1
his counsel shall a.. . . 721.4
my advocate a. . . . 762.1
b
God a. on earth . . . 161.1
God, whose might must . . . a. 871.4
2 *(human)*
and as I am a. . . . 415.2
let his (her) name a. . . 792.3
in thy temple we a. . . 925.1
love my sins, a saint a. . . 932.3
b *2 Cor 5:10*
bold shall they a. . . . 372.3
before the ineffable a. . . 414.3
triumphantly a. . . . 747.3
and in his sight a. . . 915.1
all before the judge a. . . 932.2
before thy throne a. . . 933.4
3 *general*
a. a shining throng . . . 93.5
how worthless they a. . . 460.2
there let my way a. . . 617.3
a flag . . . a. 774.1
near when foes a. . . 798.3
reinforcements now a. . . 804.1
thy golden gates a. . . 877.2
while Heaven a. in view. . 912.2
the full corn shall a. . . 924.2
when dark clouds a. . . c196
b *Acts 2:3*
no cloven tongues . . . a. . 198.1
c *[seem]*
precious did that grace a. . 308.2
a palace a toy would a. . . 318.3
makes each burden light a. . 320.2
let sin a. in thy . . . ray . . 446.1

appearing (n) *Titus 2:13*
the day of his a. . . . 334.2
ye who long for his a. . . 875.2

apple *(Prov 7:2)* 425.3

apply
feel thy power, a. Christ . 191.3
let perfect love a. . . . 446.1
a. them to this heart . . 446.2
when for healing they're a. . 471.2
Lord, thy grace a. . . . 479.3
b *apply blood*
the cleansing b. to a. . . 195.3
to my heart was the b. a. . 315.1
his b. was there a.. . . 348.1
I feel his b. a. . . . 361.2
a. thine own b.. . . . 436.2
the b. is a., I am whiter . . 436.4
freely his b. is a. . . . 535.4
'tis thine the b. to a. . . 756.2

appoint-ed *(Luke 22:29)*
into God's a. day . . . 145.2
in our a. place . . . 196.2
service which thy love a. . 485.4
in their a. days . . . 494.1
its own a. limits keep . . 569.1
where he a. we go . . . 659.2
to work he a. me to do . . 734.2
a. my soul a place . . 735.4
b *Heb 3:2*
precious Lamb by God a. . 109:2

appointment
where our a., Lord, may be . 688.3
by divine a. they stand . . 766.1

appraisal 618.2

approach-ing
a. with joy his courts . . 3.3
to see the a. sacrifice . . 150.3
bold I a. the . . . throne . . 283.4
a., my soul, the . . . seat . 284.1
heavy-laden I a. him . . 363.3
I want the first a. . . . 425.2
as hourly we a. the grave . 933.4

approval-ed *2 Tim 2:15*
each act thy a. to bear . . 589.3
his smile of a. my . . . gain . 640.3
strive to be a. of God . . 688.4

arc 27.2

arch-es-ing
like the a. of the heavens . 32.2
Heaven's eternal a. ring . . 81.4
Heaven's a. rang/ring . 101.2, 4
make the heavenly a. ring . 312.3

archangel *1 Thess 4:16*
hear the a.'s voice . . 164.c
highest a. in glory . . . 184.1

architect 827.3

ardent 660.2

argument 60.c

aright
love and serve a. . . . 466.5
guide my words a. . . 568.1
which thou wilt guide a. . 597.1
that we a. may learn . . 654.5
he always leads a. . . 759.2
near you, guiding a. . . 773.3
b *Prov 4:26 (MR)*
order all my steps a. . . 641.3

arise
1 *[God] arose*
he a. on Easter day . . . 96.4
we pray thee, Lord, a. . . 172.4
a., O morning Star, a. . . 172.6
in my life he may a. . . 619.4
from whence a. . . . 767.1
b *Mal 4:2*
we see thy light a. . . 185.3
sun of righteousness a. . . 412.1
sun of righteousness a. . . 452.3
c *Christ arose* *1 Cor 15:4**
up from the grave he a. . . 148.c
he a. a victor . . . Christ a. . 148.c
when Christ . . . a. and left . 149.1
but now hath Christ a. . . 153.c
2 *human*
a., my soul, a. . . . 106.1
a. all ye bondslaves . . 233.1
quickly a. and away . . 248.4
then may I a. pure . . . 673.4
soldiers of Christ, a. . . 695.1
soldiers of our God, a. . . 696.1
soldiers of the cross, a.. . 697.1
3 *general*
saw ye not the cloud a. . . 165.4
though . . . troubles a. . . 233.3
no earth-born cloud a. . . 676.1
ten thousand foes a. . . 812.1
when . . . temptations a. . 881.1

ark *(Ex 25:16)**
placed upon the sacred a. . 590.1
dim before the sacred a. . 839.1

arm-s
1 *(divine)*
sufficient is thine a. . . 13.2
thy conquering a. . . . 100.3
his a. extended wide . . 107.2
open thine a. and take me . 305.2
on my own beloved's a.. . 430.3
to thy dear a. . . . I flee . . 450.2
imprison me . . . thine a. . 508.1
held in thine a. I shall . . 543.3
whose a. hath bound . . 569.1
your a. to embrace . . 611.3
in his a. he'll take . . . 645.3
his a. are near . . . 718.4
trust his omnipotent a. . . 734.2
his a. enfolding . . . 884.1
safe in the a. of Jesus . . 889.*
put his a. unfailing round . 954.3
b *arms [of love]*
a. of love that compass . . 60.4
his loving a. receive us . . 66.3
a. outstretched in love . . 181.3
threw his loving a. around . 337.2
loving a. of Jesus . . . 792.2
in his a. of love enfolds . . c163
c *Isa 40:11*
in his a. he carries . . . 184.1
d *Isa 59:16*
a. shall bring salvation . . 819.2
e *Mark 10:16*
a. of Jesus . . . . 792.*
his a. had been thrown . . 794.1
shall crowd to his a. . . 794.3
bare (2), everlasting (b), faith (2i), lean (b), mighty (1f), short (b), strong (1c), throw (a)
2 *(human)*
from our mother's a. . . 12.1
in whose gentle a. he lay . 87.3
a. of flesh . . . fail . . . 699.3
comfort . . . shepherd's a. . 740.1
and a. are strong . . . 876.4
flesh (c)
3 *arm-ed (verb)*
a. with cruel hate . . . 1.1
a. hosts to meet . . . 158.2
a. me with jealous care . . 472.3
Lord, a. me with . . . might . 516.5
a. with jealous care . . 596.3
be a. with the power . . 679.3
a. you with the . . . sword . 813.1
a. with inward blessing . . 863.2
a. then, O youth! . . . 864.4
a. us with holy might . . 870.3
a. us . . . for the war . . 937.2
b *1 Peter 4:1*
O a. me with the mind . . 568.2
4 *arms [weapons]*
to a.! is the call . . . 684.1

to a., Salvation Army! . . 781.3
won't lay down our a. . . 822.1
I call to a. the soldiers . . 830.2

armour-ed *Eph 6:11*
a. with all . . . graces . . 577.4
makes the soldier's a. . . 646.3
may I find my a. there . . 658.6
I'll gird on the a. . . . 686.c
no a. is there 689.2
nor will we lay our a. . . 692.5
put your a. on . . . 695.1
to keep your a. bright . . 695.4
gird you with your a. . . 697.1
gird your a. on . . . 698.1
put on salvation a. . . . 699.3
all the a. of Heaven . . 703.3
buckle on the a. tight . . 809.2
nor lay thine a. down . . 812.3
don your a. 817.3
arrayed in a. bright . . 821.2
girding on salvation a. . . 869.4

armoury
from a secret a. . . . 176.2
thy word is like an a. . . 658.4

army
1 *[Salvation] Army*
in the S. A. so brave . . 321.3
o'er our A. send . . . 452.2
give thy blood-washed A. . 593.1
in the A. we will serve . . 593.2
the A. more thanksgiving . 622.3
heart of our A.'s need . . 648.1
the S. A. is marching . . 681.*
S. A. Jehovah has blessed . 684.4
S. A.'s the A. for me . . 684.4
thy A., we salute . . . 692.3
S. A. to victory must go . 703.2
who'll enlist in this A. . . 703.3
the A. chariot rolls . . . 775.1
to my Saviour in the A. . . 778.c
the A. banner 781.1, 2
to arms, S. A. 781.3
lift up the A. banner . . 783.c
one great A. make . . . 788.2
A. of salvation . . . the Lord . 803.c
joy in the S. A. . . . 807.*
gives the A. joy . . . 807.2
our A. we prepare . . . 818.2
ever true to the A. . . . 820.5
we're an A. . . . . 821.*
soldiers of the A. of S. . . 822.1
the A. that shall conquer . 822.c
to the beat of A. drums . . 829.2
pleasure in the A. . . . 869.1
in the A. . . . service . . 869.2
witness in the A. . . . 869.3
a future for the A. . . . 869.4
with all the A. there . . 901.2
the A. means to lead . . 901.5
since the A. opened fire . . 939.1
soldier in the A. brave . . c225
this is the A.'s call . . . c226
in the ranks of the A. . . c230
in the A. ranks are we . . c236
ranks of the dear old A. . . c237

b *[God's] Army*
joined the A. of the Lord . 402.c
in the A. of Jesus . . . 687.1
we're in God's A. . . . 705.1
thine A., Lord, prepare . . 774.4
flag of God's great A. . . 779.2
Salvation A., A. . . . 802.c
A. of salvation . . . the Lord . 803.c
joy! in the A. of the Lord . 807.*
soldiers in the A. . . . 866.c
power in the A. c51

c *join Army*
j. the A. of the Lord . . 402.c
come, j. our A. . . . 681.*
j. our happy A. . . . 902.5

bless (1c), flag (b), great (2c), soldier (b)

2 *army*
God's a., just hid . . . 537.2
'tis the ransomed a. . . 550.c
pillar at our a.'s head . . 682.1
like a mighty a. . . . 690.3
his a. he shall lead . . . 699.1
enter we the a. . . . 707.2
but the King's own a. . . 707.4

b *Rev 19:14*
a. of the ransomed saints . 167.1
all the a. of the sky . . 382.2
noble a., men and boys . . 701.4
back with their a. . . . 864.4

arose see *arise* (1c)

around *nc, but*
a *all around*
underneath me, a. a. me . 182.1
tidings a. the world a. . . 279.1
tell it to a. a. . . . 384.2
tell the message a. a. . . 393.1
that a. a. shall know . . 649.4
happiness beams a. a. . . 664.1
decay in a. a. I see . . . 670.2
when a. a. my soul . . 745.3
tell . . . to the nations a. a. . 809.1
tell it a. a. 835.1
a. a., many kinds . . . 841.3

b *(a)round earth/world*
let it echo r. the e. . . . 63.2
r. the wide w. let it ring . 158.2
tidings all the w. a. . . 279.1
in all the w. a. me I see . . 334.2
the spacious e. a. . . . 382.2
all r. the w. . . . . 775.*
r. the wide, wide w. . . 814.1
flying r. the w. . . . c242
bless our Army r. the w. . c244

c *Ps 34:7*
encamp a. the dwellings . 21.3
angels . . . hovering r. us . 370.4
God is r. about me . . . 736.1

everlasting (b), gather, rage, rally, shine (1e), throne (4h), throw (a), wall (c)

array-ed
in robes of white a. . . 72.3
in these a., with joy . . 116.1
in robes of light a. . . 117.2
orders in their great a. . . 141.2
join our glad a. . . . 693.3
a. in armour bright . . 821.2
legions . . . in dread a. . . 864.1
sweet fields a. . . . 887.2

b *Rev 7:13*
in robes of light a. . . 701.4
saints . . . in bright a. . . 876.5
who are these a. in white . 909.1

arrest 433.3

arrive
when we a. at home . . 312.1
safely to a. at home . . 313.2
our souls a. in peace . . 918.4
when we a. at the end . . c222

arrogant 300.3

arrow
oft Satan's a. wound . . 806.1
a mortal a. pierced . . 890.2

art
Lord of a. 30.3
knows the healing a. . . 311.2
O may I learn the a. . . 568.3
teach me the happy a. . . 597.3
commerce, industry or a. . 688.1
a. and power employing . 696.2
all the a. of Hell oppose . 747.1

as *nc, but see*
crimson (b), dew (b), dove, eagle, hart, heaven (1b), infinity, morning (1b), night (1c), ocean, rock (2b), scarlet, sea (1c), snow (b, c), sun (2b), thunder, wind (1d)

as [God]
pleased a. man . . . to dwell . 82.2
crown him a. your captain . 141.5
thou, a. Lord of hosts . . 163.3
Lord a. King to crown . . 169.1
hath he diadem a. monarch . 228.3
a. the bearer of sin . . 271.2
God a. man came down . . 274.*
a. a friend he can cheer . . 329.2
wandered . . . a. the poorest . 354.2
gladly own him a. my King . 405.3
a. Lord and Master . . 480.3
the Son a. man is known . 785.2
with Jesus a. our leader . . 810.1
come, a. thou didst of old . 827.2
now a. King he reigneth . . 853.2
a. King of all kingdoms . . 908.4

b *as [thou art]*
a. thou hast been . . . wilt . 33.1
see thee a. thou art . . 58.4
a. thou art thou dost . . 303.4
to see thee a. thou art . . 591.3
and see thee a. thou art . . 791.3
I would be a. thou art . . 793.5

c *as [I am]*
a. I am, before thy face . . 285.1
a. I am, so tired . . . 285.2
a. I am, for death or life . . 285.2
take me a. I am . . . 291.*
a. I am, O hear me pray . . 292.4
a. I am I come, believing . 303.4
I came to Jesus a. I was. . 332.1
and a. I am appear . . . 415.2

just (2b), long (4b), old (c), pray (2b), well (2e)

ascend
I shall . . . to Heaven a. . . 223.4
long shall my praises a. . . 454.5
our morning hymns a. . . 677.1
let our praise a. . . . 803.2
heartfelt thanks to thee a. . 933.3

b *ascend (hill)* *Ps 24:3*
now to a. my soul aspires . 461.1
let me now thy hill a. . . 461.4
in faith a. thy holy hill . . c72

ascended *John 20:17*
Jesus, our a. Lord . . . 198.2

ascent *(Rev 11:12)* . . . 701.4

ascertain 214.4

ascribe *(Deut 32:3)**
a. salvation to Jesus . . 24.2
to him all majesty a. . . 56.2
a. their conquest . . . 879.3

ashamed
a *Mark 8:38; Rom 1:16*
a. of thee 592.1
a. of Jesus . . . . . 592.*
Christ is not a. of me . . 592.4
I'm not a. to own my Lord . 735.1

b *2 Tim 2:15*
work I may not be a . . . 484.3
workmen, not to be a. . . 688.4

ashes *Isa 61:3* c148

aside
glories didst thou lay a. . . 135.1
all . . . shall be thrown a. . 188.c
come ye a. from all . . 564.2
stray from thee a. . . . 743.3

cast (e), lay (3d)

ask-ed-ing
1 *God asks*
my Father doth not a.• . . 48.3
love a. a sacrifice . . 128.2
the Saviour a. no tears . . 131.2
knocks and a. admission . 241.1
stoops to a. my love . . 307.2
and dost thou a. a gift . . 475.*
love . . . a. the gift of me . 504.1
a., for I cannot refuse . . 528.4
a. a quick . . . choice . . 749.1
b
a. what you will . . . 294.2
a. what thou wilt . . . 507.c
2 *[We] ask*
I a., but for a life . . . 7.1
humbly a. for more . . 23.1
I a. thee to stay close . . 77.3
to none who a. . . . denied . 121.6
eager I a., I pant . . . 207.2
if I a. him to receive . . 228.6
then a. for pardon . . . 270.2
a. my advocate above . . 286.3
only a. more and more . . 439.4
I a. no higher state . . 441.4
I dare not a. as though . . 456.3
I a. no other sunshine . . 476.3
I a. thee for . . . . . 485.*
I a. to serve thee here . . 560.4
do we a. our way to be . . 570.2
I do not a. thee, Lord . . 586.*
but O I a. today . . . 586.1
nor let me a. thee . . . 588.4
the gift divine I a. . . . 601.1
I do not a. to see . . . 606.1
I a. that thou my judge . . 618.1
I dare not a. to fly . . . 621.4
I a. another still . . . 628.2
all we ought to a. . . . 668.4
we a. . . . not wealth . . 791.2
we a. eternal life . . . 791.2
a. for a share in his love. . 794.2
I will a. Jesus to help . . 844.3
things I would a. him . . 848.1
not from . . . care . . . a.. . 916.1
what can I a. more . . . c61
love I a. for c83
b *Matt 7:7*
he gives to those who a. 44.c, 3
if every one that a. . . 216.3
grace . . . to those who a. . 324.4
to none that a. denied . . 485.3
a.! and it shall be given . . c5
c *John 15:7*
my soul, a. what thou wilt . 560.2
none can ever a. too much . 563.2
d *Eph 3:20*
more than we a. . . . 642.1, 2
e *James 1:6*
a. in faith, I receive . . 454.4
3 *[others] ask*
dost a. who that may be? . . 1.2
none will a. what they . . 170.1
if one should a. of me . . 323.3
to all who will a. him . . 329.3
you a. me how I know . . 334.c
sick, they a. for healing . . 682.2
a. the Saviour to help you . 823.c

asleep
Jesus a. on the hay . . . 77.1
soon will be a. . . . 673.2
a. within a manger bed . . 855.1

aspect 925.3

aspire
how great a flame a. . . 165.1
to thee our souls a. . . 216.4
Godward our spirits a. . . 351.2
vainly a. to reach . . . 456.2
to ascend my soul a. . . 461.1
all my powers to thee a.. . 616.3
my spirit a. to the things . 640.4
as to serve him you a. . . 790.3
unto thee our souls a. . . c101

assail
though Hell should me a. . 366.5
more than the foes which a. . 537.2
when doubts and fears a. . 574.2
scorn . . . a. his ways . . 577.2
when Hell a., I flee . . 746.3
storms of doubt . . . a. . . 757.2
when Hell a., I'll trust . . 761.3
though troubles fierce a. . . 763.1
temptations fierce a. . . 789.3
both earth and Hell a. . . 809.2
those who shall a. us . . 822.3
problems of life . . . a. . . c151

assemble-d
near thy cross a., Master . 197.1
here, Lord, a. in thy name . 581.1
a. in thy name . . . 603.1
martial hosts a. . . . 803.1
since we a. last . . . 915.2
b *Acts 4:31*
a. here with one accord . . 216.2
a. here with one accord . . 638.2

assign-ed
through every toil a. . . 744.3
my daily task thou shalt a. . 867.6

assist
a. me to proclaim . . . 64.2
a. by his grace . . . 78.3
he will a. you to conquer . 233.2
a. me with thy . . . grace . 480.1
do thou a., we . . . pray. . 747.2

assume . . . . . . 44.*

assurance
joy the blest/sweet a. . 144.1, 4
with a. seek his face . . 249.3
know, with a. . . . 271.4
blessed a., Jesus is mine . 310.1
in this a. . . . sweetest . . 323.5
endurance in this a. . . 724.3
in love's a. we confide . . 748.4
let this blest a. control . . 771.2
b *Heb 10:22**
be thou their full a. . . 948.2

assure-d
triumph over death a. . . 102.2
faith in my heart a. . . 176.3
thou dost my strength a. . 423.2
a., if I my trust betray . . 472.4
confide in thee, a. . . . 574.2
a. that thou . . . shalt save . 714.4
of this I am a. . . . 732.1
cheerful and our hearts a. 755.3
the Bible a. us . . . 763.1
he the vilest will a.. . . 819.2

astray *Isa 53:6*
when we went a. . . . 192.3
from my Saviour . . . far a. . 309.1
the sheep that went a. . . 337.2
my wandering and going a. . 394.2
when so far a. . . . 401.1
lead my captive soul a. . . 509.2
toiled . . . for the world a. . 680.2
seek us when we go a. . . 845.2
though you've gone a. . . c11

asunder
he burst them a. . . . 137.4
to lives now torn a. . . 529.3
when we a. part . . . 660.4

atom
God of a., God of mine . . 30.1
the a.'s hidden forces . . 38.2

atone-d-ing
who died for me . . . to a. . 116.3
for all our wrongs a. . . 127.1
all receive the grace a. . . 191.4
love's a. work is done . . 261.4
nor yet . . . for sin a. . . 269.3
all for sin could not a. . . 302.2
nothing can for sin a. . . 306.3
a. for a . . . world's sin . . 785.3
b *blood atone* *Lev 17:11**
his b. a. for all . . . 106.2
through a. b. outpoured . 135.1
wash us in the a. b. . . 210.1
b. that a. for the soul . . 271.3
the b. that did for me a.. . 303.3
ventured on the a. b. . . 361.2
the doctrine of a. b. . . 656.2
in Christ's a. b. . . . 943.4
c *atoning Lamb*
to adore the all-a. L. . . 62.1
thou loving, all-a. L. . . 140.3
Jesus, all-a. L. . . . 497.1

atonement *Rom 5:11*
his life an a. for sin . . 22.1
while Jesus doth a. make . 107.3
thou hast full a. made . . 109.2
full a. —can it be? . . . 118.3

attain *(Phil 3:12)**
by God's grace we may a. . 324.3
want to a. . . . likeness . . 589.2
nothing . . . achieve . . . a. . 605.2
shall a. that deepest joy . . 630.3
patient endurance a. . . 956

attempt 50.3

attend-ed-ing
here daily a. thee . . . 19.2
thousand saints a. . . . 161.1
a. the promised Comforter . 214.2
angels will a. 396.3
will he not a. to my cry?. . 459.2
thy love a. me . . . 516.5
nor will he . . . a. . . . 588.3
to a. the whispers . . . 636.4
a. with constant care . . 695.4
presence my steps shall a. . 734.1
when peace . . . a. my way 771.1
bade them still a. him . . 853.1
may thy grace . . . a. me . 865.2
b *attend prayer* *Ps 61:1**
Spirit . . . a. our p. . . . 217.1
Word . . . our p. a. . . 219.2
his ear a. the softest p. . . 715.4

attentive
waiting, like a. Mary . . 210.3
a. to thy holy word . . 613.1

attract-ion
many places a. me . . 119.1
wondrous a. for me . . 124.2
great the world's a. . . 461.2

attuned 583.3

aught
who a. to my charge . . 116.2
the touch of a. unreal . . 409.3
nor should I a. withhold . . 524.1
hearts that dare do a. . . 704.1
anything

author *Heb 12:2*
thou, of life the a. . . . 155.3
a. of the new creation . . 452.1
thou a. of all grace . . 946.3

autumn 925.3

avail-ed
his blood a. for me . . 64.4
nought but . . . can a. . . 91.2
almost cannot a. . . . 226.3
Christ's sacrifice a. . . 706.1
my strength of small a. . . 780.2

available c2

avenues c6

avow-ed
I dare a. that Jesus . . 440.4
his first a. intent . . . 685.1

await
greater things a. you . . 433.3
beyond a. the heights . . 711.3
the precious fruits a. . . 923.2

awake
a. life in cell 38.3
every soul from sin a. . . 43.1
constant with joy whilst a. . 51.1
the baby a. 77.2
our trumpets are a. . . 163.1
my heart a. cries . . . 187.1
a. my soul . . . still a. . . 425.3
blessed consciousness, a. . 632.2
serve my God when I a. . . 671.4
the fair, sweet morn, a. . . 896.1
b *Rom 13:11**
a., my voice, and sing . . 26.1
Christians, a. 78.1
a. from your dream . . . 233.1
a., a.! Fling off . . . 408.1
a. and rise . . . 408.2, 4
a. our souls . . . a. and run . 559.1
a., my soul, and with . . 665.1
O soldier, a. 689.1
a., happy song 818.c
rise (3d), sing (4d)

awakening 950.1

aware
make me a. of thee . . . 613.*
consistently a. of thee . . 613.3
more . . . than any is a. . . 615.4

awe-some
when I in a. wonder . . 37.1
kneel in a. and wonder . . 73.3

awe-ful
before Jehovah's a. throne . 4.1
can bear my a. load . . 297.2
beneath thine a. eye . . 466.2
in a. majesty unfolds . . 871.4
the trumpet's a. sound . . 875.1
the a. judgment day . . 885.1
O a. thought 885.3
most a. truth 932.2

awful 297.2

awhile
come and look a. . . . 121.1
desert garden bloom a. . . 333.2
come . . . apart and rest a. . 564.1
loved . . . and lost a. . . 606.3

aye
gladly for a. we adore . . 19.5
upward for a. on wings . . 300.3
thine for a. 643.4
but a. the fadeless morn . 895.1
and a. the dews of sorrow . 896.3
praise/blest/reign for a. . 897.*
by our side now and for a. . 955
always, ever

B

babe-baby
a *(divine)* *Luke 2:12**
b. who came from Glory . 74.2
the b. awakes . . . 77.2
trace we the b. . . . 78.3
a mother laid her b. . . 87.1
cam'st a little b. thing . . 91.1
the heavenly b. . . . find. . 93.4
the b. of Bethlehem . . 96.1
tell them of the b. . . . 829.c
b *(human)*
shield this b. small . . . 792.2
bless this b. dear . . . 792.3
bring their b. boy(girl) . . 795.1
as b. grows, discerning . . 795.2

Babel *Gen 11:9* 211.1

back
1 *(noun)*
turn not thy b. 689.2
2 *(adverb)*
let nothing draw me b. . . 59.4
world give b. the song . . 83.3
my soul looks b. to see . . 120.4
I will not go b. . . . 298.5
drew me b. into his way. . 337.2
echo b., ye ocean . . . 393.2
nor hold b. . . . any part. . 422.1
my fearful heart points b. . 440.3
I give thee b. thine own . . 492.3
b. on thy strength . . . throw. 507.3
I give thee b. the life . . 621.1
the thought comes b. . . 686.1
b. to the narrow way . . 691.4
it gives me b. my peace. . 714.1
no want shall turn me b. . 736.2
leads us b. to Pentecost. . 783.3
disciples drove them b. . . 797.1
wave the answer b. . . 804.c
bring them b. to God . . 822.c
b. with their armies . . 864.4
child of mine, come b. . . c6
he has come b. . . . c11
go b. to the old wells . . c40
bring (1i), keep (1b)

backslider
b., hear! God speaks . . 267.2
come, sinner and b. . . 269.2

backsliding *Hosea 14:4* . . 305.2

backward 828.2

bad
b. as I was he cleansed . . 380.2
b. language disdain . . 823.2

bade see bid

baits 596.2

balance 863.4

balm *(Jer 8:22)*
holy b. of peace . . . 200.2
a b. for each wound . . 252.3
out of . . . into thy b. . . 300.2
a soverign b. 382.1
pouring the b. then . . 457.2
soothe . . . with gentle b. . 479.2
thy coolness and thy b. . . 567.5
make known thy healing b. . 575.1
whose presence is b. . . 611.4
seek the heavenly b. . . 663.3
our b. in sorrow . . . 674.4

balmy 268.1

band
1 *(group)*
song of the angel b. . . 94.c
a glorious b., the chosen . 701.3
onward goes the pilgrim b. . 765.1
holy, blood-washed b. . . 781.3
come, join our b. . . . 798.2
a strong opposing b. . . 810.2
a b. that shall conquer . . 820.1
Daniel's b. . . . . 847.*
follow the children's b. . . 848.4
thy children, a holy b. . . 873.3
march upward with our b. . 901.1
ye happy praying b. . . 912.1
conquering (b)
2 *[musical] band*
clarion call of b. . . . 780.3
with a thousand b. . . 807.3
the music of the b. . . c230
3 *bands [ties]*
swathing b. 93.4
b *Isa 58:6*
mercy . . . loosed my b. . 23.4
c *(Col 2:19)*
thine eternal b. . . . 949.2

bane 112.4

banish
he came to b. death . . 274.c
O b. sadness, sing now . . 724.2
pleasures b. pain . . . 898.1
b *banish fear* *(1 John 4:18)*
his love has b. every f. . . 48.2
f. that I hate, O b. . . . 422.3
able to b. all f. . . . 443.3
gathered . . . b. all my f.. . 740.1

bank
on Jordan's stormy b. . . 887.1
when on Jordan's b. . . 911.5

banner
our b. are aflame . . . 163.1
see his b. go 690.1
raise your b. in the sky . . 697.2
rally round the b. . . . 698.c
shield and b. bright . . 698.2
his blood-red b. streams . 701.1
Christ's own b. leads . . 702.2
with b. floating high . . 705.3
beneath this glorious b. . . 781.3
would you of our b. know . 783.1
gathering 'neath our b. . . 803.2
see the glorious b. . . . 804.3
we'll raise our b. high . . 810.1
write it on your b. . . . 813.c
with shield and b. bright . 818.1
hold the gospel b. high . . 847.4
we'll serve beneath his b. . 853.2
b *Song 2:4*
salvation b. of love 382.c; 782.c
keep love's b. floating . . 954.4
lift (2b), unfurl

banquet *(Song 2:4)*
the b. of glory in Heaven . 373.4
in the b. hall on high . . 375.3

baptise
come and now b. us all . . 201.1
a soul b. with . . . energy . 426.3
b. us more and more . . 575.1
with thy power b. us all. . 622.1
with mighty power . . . b. . 649.3
wanted, hearts b. . . . 704.1
b *Acts 1:5*
b. us with the Holy Ghost . 609.2

bar
man's puny judgment b. . 185.3
so fast to b. the gate! . . 299.2

bars
he tore the b. away . . 148.3
b. from Heaven's . . . fell . 151.4

bards 83.3

bare
1 *[adjective]*
that manger rude and b. . 76.3
of self and sin swept b. . . 615.3
2 *bare arm* *Isa 52:10*
Jehovah, b. thine a. . . 575.1
thy mighty a. make b. . . 626.1
b
toward the child she b. . . 110.3

bark
waves your b. o'erflow?. . 280.2
my drifting b. . . . 375.1
whelm our tossing b. . . 654.3

barn *Luke 12:24* . . . 763.2

barren
from b. mountains rivers . 159.5
pilgrim through this b. . . 578.1
no more their b. aspect . . 925.3

barrenness *Gal 4:27* . . 217:4

barrier
love no b. could confine . 5.1
love . . . has broken every b.. 293.6
to try and scale the b. . . 510.2
breaks the b. down . . 749.1

base
emptied of every b. desire . 208.1
from b. desire . . . saves. . 401.2

based 827.1

baseness 409.3

bathe
b. and wash them . . . 140.4
we'll b. in the full ocean. . 239.4
I'll b. in its full ocean . . 368.1
his feet I'll b. 634.3

battalions
b. now are marching . . 169.2
our b. never shall waver. . 800.2
Hell's b. tremble . . . 803.1
our grand b. . . . abound . 815.2

battle
1 *noun*
the b. is not done . . . 42.3
strife is o'er, the b. done . 151.1
give courage for the b. . . 575.3
my King's in the b. . . 684.1
ten thousand b. . . . 684.2
forward into b. . . . 690.1
God and fiends are b. . . 693.1
when the b.'s done . . 698.3
this day the noise of b. . . 699.4
from the b.'s post . . . 702.1

through the b. . . . strife. . 731.3
the b.'s blazing heat . 749.3
when the b. rages fast . 769.2
O God of b. . 774.1
emblem of a thousand b. . 777.1
and the b. we are waging . 778.1
with his hosts in b. . 790.c
ours to press the b. here . 799.4
b. end in saving sinners . 802.4
the b. ne'er give o'er! . 812.2
I shall not fear the b. . 862.1
trusting in the b.'s fray . c119

b *fight battle*
b.'s fought, the victory's . 107.4
strengthen all who f. thy b. . 576.1
hard the b. ye must f. . 697.1
we will f. his b. . 866.3
b. fought, the victory . 890.1
the b. fought bravely . 893.3

c *go to battle*
join our Army, to b. we g. . 681.1
to b. undaunted we g. . 687.4
gird ourselves and g. to b. . 700.1
we will to b. g. . 775.3
we g. forth to b. . 789.2
to save, to b. we will g.. . 821.c

d *[win] battle*
he must win the b. . 1.2
the fight, the b. won . 143.2
we boast no b. ever won . 163.1
b. lost or scarcely won . 466.4
my last great b. won . 774.3
hardest b. have been won . 806.2
for the b. we have won . 899.1

fierce (b), Jesus (6c)

2 *adjective*
life's long b.-day . 658.4
may be our b. ground . 705.1
our universal b. song . 821.3
cross, it is thy b. sign . 864.2

battlefield, cry (4c), front

3 *verb*
first to b. in the fray . 400.2
b., conquering for thee . 643.4
b. through the long day . 663.1
b. for the right . 698.2
work for God and b. . 818.1
b. for God and the right . 820.4
b. 'gainst all evil . 859.2
we would b., Lord, for thee . c236

battlefield
far across the field of b.. . 158.1
stand upon our b. . 163.4
our Master's darkest b. . 705.2
above the world-wide b. . 774.1
march on . . . o'er the b. . 817.2

battleground . 801.1

beacon . 375.1

beam
sun with golden b. . 2.1
blooming in the sunlight b. . 39.3
leading onward, b. bright . 76.1
the sun of bliss is b. . 112.3
sheds its b. around me . 115.2
come . . . love is b. 232.1, 3
his bright rays come b. . 316.2
thy mercy's b. I see . 412.3
bear the uncreated b. . 414.3
brightly b. . . . mercy . 478.1
b. of heavenly day . 657.3
happiness b. all around . 664.1
Zion b. with light . 682.1
love b. through . . . eyes . 855.4
b. with radiance divine . 868.3
bright . . . b. every eye . 897.3

b
God of girder and of b. . 30.1

bear-ing/bore-ne
1 *(God) bears*
knows . . . b. my part . 68.2
b. with man his . . . lot . 102.1
five bleeding wounds he b. . 106.3
thou hast b. all for me . 117.4
b. shame and scoffing . 118.2
meekly b., that crown . 126.2
what pains he had to b.. . 133.2
faithfully he b. it . 141.3
b. it up triumphant . 141.4
his dazzling body b. . 161.3
high . . . he will b. it . 183.2
b. the lamp of grace . 224.3
I b. the cruel thorns . 229.2
felt the love he b. you . 242.2
all a loving Saviour b. . 276.c
came to b. in my place . 319.3
he . . . sin's curse did b.. . 363.4
but b. it all for me . 421.3
b. death, . . . defending . 500.1
my spirit to Calvary b. . 639.2
O b. me safe above . 743.4
pain and death to b. . 835.2
much he was willing to b. . c24
b. all my woe . c219

b *bear burden*
cross, my b. gladly b. . 37.3
how gently his b. he b. . 111.1
see the b. thou didst b. . 120.4
he b. my b. to Calvary . 179.3
the cross, each b. b. . 246.1
never a b. he cannot b. . 246.c
b. of shame he must b. . 708.2
he careth, each b. he b.. . c139

c *bear cross* *John 19:17*
to b. it to dark Calvary . 124.2
to b. the c. and agony . 125.3
the c. he b. is life . 168.6
to b. the c. and shame . 284.5
he b. for me . . . a heavy c. . 451.2

d *bear [grief]* *Isa 53:4*
yet he has b. our guilt . 108.2
thy shame and grief he b. . 126.c
guiltless, my guilt b. . 290.1
he has b. the strife . 402.3
our sins and griefs to b.. . 645.1

e *bear sin* *Isa 53:12, Heb 9:28*
who b. your load of s. . 241.1
he b. my s. and curse . 360.2
for all s.'s curse did b. . 363.4
our s. and grief to b. . 645.1

gently (b), sorrow (1b), witness (1b)

2 *(we) bear*
must b. the largest part . 11.2
helps me b. the pain . 204.2
pressing on and b. up . 212.4
this toiling flesh has b. . 297.1
can b. my awful load . 297.2
his name and sign who b. . 299.1
his glorious image b. . 370.2
on my naked spirit b. . 414.3
the truth, I will b. it . 457.1
b. tidings, precious . 500.2
help me b. the strain . 519.1
love is b. and forgiving . 544.4
what needless pain we b. . 645.1
give me to b. . . . yoke . 667.3
I'll b. the toil, endure . 678.4
b. shame for his . . . sake . 777.3
let us b. in mind . 805.c
help me patiently to b. . 837.5
do thy will, or b. it . 865.2
how . . . b. a last farewell . 874.2

b *bear cross* *Luke 14:27*
b. daily my c. for thee . 117.4
its shame . . . gladly b. . 124.3
c. b., dangers sharing . 197.3
the next his c. to b. . 278.1
c. . . . you are called to b. . 396.2
in his c.-b. now . . . share . 406.4
while we b. the c. . 452.3
while for thee my c. I b.. . 477.4
the c. I will gladly b. . 499.2
help me the c. to b. . 524.2
c. . . . seem light to b. . 551.3
helps to b. the c. . 555.3
each other's c. to b. . 662.1
who patient b. his c. . 701.1
hearts to b. with him the c. . 704.3
thy chosen c. to b. . 761.2
first the c. to b. . 777.3
with us the c. to b. . 825.4
they that b. the c. . 909.1
if the c. we boldly b. . c233

c *1 Cor 13:7*
all things I will . . . b. . 499.3

d *(Gal 6:17)*
the prophet's marks you b. . 95.3

burden (2f) help (1j)

3 *(general)*
time . . . b. all its sons . 13.5
joy that b. the soul . 70.4
that b. thee to Calvary . 101.3
the angels b. the tidings. . 259.4
b. the news to every land . 393.1
may b. the burning bliss. . 414.2
tidings, b. them far away . 550.3
act thy approval to b. . 589.3
wings shall my petition b. . 633.2
b. it onward; lift it high . 697.2
great the name they b. . 866.1
b. in a song to me . 889.1
will . . . b. evil or good . 928.3
power to do and grace to b. . 947.4

fruit (2b)

bearer *Heb 9:28*
b. of our sin and shame . 109.1
there as the b. of sin . 271.2
thou wonderful sin-b. . 448.1
b. of all pain . 628.2

b
b. of thy love and truth . 863.1
b. of a royal proclamation . c226

beast
from b. to brain of man . 38.3
thine humble b. pursues . 150.1
b. of prey come not there . 268.3
birds and b. and flowers . 673.2

b *(Heb 9:12)*
not all the blood of b. . 120.1

beat
heart forget to b. . 573.5
hearts that b. true ever . 704.2
heart . . . must b. . . . true . 779.2
though to b. us . 800.1

drum

beauteous
and every b. grace . 515.4
O b. world, how part . 874.2

beautiful
all things bright and b. . 25.c
b. actions of love . 114.2
bright and b. for thee . 205.1
b. stream . 252.*
b. words! wonderful words . 258.c
pierced on his b. brow 331.1.c
swift and b. for thee . 525.2
b. of earth . . . b. again . 551.1
b. are they and free . 555.3
b. place . . . to prepare . 794.2
my b. home . 872.c
b. land/theme/prospect/thought 873.*
O that b. city . 883.3
the b., the b. river . 891.c
b. Zion . . . b. city of God . 901.c
stand by the b. river . 908.3
b. flower, fairest . c54

b *beautiful [Jesus]*
b. the name of Jesus . 63.2
b. Jesus . . . Christ . 175.*
b. Saviour, Lord . 177.4
come, b. Christ . c61
shore (2b)

beautify . 923.1

beauty
1 *(divine)*
its b., truth and grace. 27.2
the b. of thy house . 36.6
the b. of your will. 38.4
b. in the name of Jesus. 70.1
thy b. to behold . 154.2
in b. glorified . 156.4
I love to sing of his b.. 178.2
more of their b. see . 258.1
words of life and b. . 258.1
his is b., purest, rarest. 343.1
love in its glory and b.. 383.2
the smile of love and b.. 462.2
the b. of the Lord. 494.2
soon his b. we'll behold. 892.4
b *beauty (face)*
the b. of thy f. behold. 59.3
b. shining from his . . . f. 242.4
the b. of thy f. . . . dawns. 353.1
mercy in the b. of thy f.. 595.2
c *(his beauty in us)*
a song of purest b. 70.c
my b. are, my glorious. 116.1
truth in its b.. 183.3
come with grace and b.. 221.2
that I may reveal thy b.. 435.c
thy b. be my chosen prize . 449.3
the b. of thy peace . 567.4
thy love, thy b. show . 656.3
shall shine in their b. . 852.c
touch my life into b. . c37
bloom in all thy b.. c43
my life thy b. show . c96
thy b. adorning . c104
d *Ps 96:9*
in the b. of holiness . 183.1, 5
e
let the b. of Jesus. c77
f *Isa 61:3*
b. for ashes . c148
King (2b)
2 *life*
b. of the earth . . . skies. 28.1
for the b. of each hour . 28.2
touchest earth with b. 32.1, 3
with b. shall be clad . 159.3
in the b. of the lilies . 162.4
all b. fades away . 494.1
a store of created b. 666.2
each gift of b. rare . 833.2
all b. we must share . 851.3

beauties . 545.2

because *nc, but*
because (love) *(John 3:16)*
all b. he loved me so. 134.c
carry b. he loveth so . 186.2
b. thou hast first loved . 357.2
just b. he loved me so . 389.c
just b. of love . 829.c
b. he loved me so . 840.*
save me b. he loved me so . c204

beckon-ing
let me see thy b. hand . 463.2
angels to b. me nearer . 617.3
the b. hills before me . 766.1
my comrades b. stand . 780.4

become-ing-became
for he b. my ransom . 65.2
b. the victor's brow . 147.1
host on earth b. blest . 217.5
on earth a man b. . 363.2
suffering servant he b. . 451.2
I would b. the servant . 451.4
till my will b. blended . 493.2
wiser, stronger still b. . 842.4
what will then b. of thee . 875.3
b. the house of God . 943.4

bed
that lowly manger b. . 76.2
no crib for a b. . 77.1
in a manger for his b. . 87.1
vainly they watch his b.. 148.2
flowery b. of ease . 678.2
asleep within a manger b. 855.1

bedewed . 564.3

bees . 41.1

befall
in thy hands whate'er b. 285.3
care not what b. me . 330.3
I am his whate'er b. . 399.2
serve . . . whate'er may b. 499.1
trusting him whate'er b. 754.c
whate'er b. . . . conquer all . c234
betide

before *nc, but see*
bow (2c), cast (j), cross (1b, 2c), face (2b), fall (2c), go (1), lie (4b), throne (3b)

befriend
he who with love doth b. 19.2
tell . . . and he'll b. thee. 225.4
do thou b. us . 845.2

befriender . 762.1

beg . 447.1

begin-began-begun
1 *(God) begins*
thy triumphs now b. 150.2
thy rule, O Christ, b. 172.1
the revolution now b. 203.2
perfect . . . grace has b.. 410.1
full giving is only b. 579.2
thou hadst b. to meet . 642.2
love perfecteth what it b. 741.4
b *begin work* *Phil 1:6*
when he first the w. b. . 165.2
now I feel your w. b. 206.3
be the w. of grace b. 251.4
thy w. b., thy w. complete . 291.4
some w. of love b. . 524.3
the gracious w. b. . 676.4
our outward w. b. . 863.2
c *[Heaven] begin*
feel that Heaven is now b. 312.2
glory b. below . 314.3
shall Heaven indeed b. . 630.3
2 *(general)*
so shall I b. on earth . 7.3
the morning stars b. 10.4
b. . . . some heavenly theme. 26.1
the joyful tidings first b.. 78.1
b. and never cease . 93.6
the song of praise b. 151.1
rivers shall b. to flow . 159.5
now in thee b. to live . 207.2
than when we first b. 308.4
where shall I . . . b. 370.1
to praise him I'll b. . 380.3
finish well what we've b. 462.3
with my burden I b. 563.3
stars b. to peep . 673.2
with thee b., with thee . 674.2
one the march in God b. 765.5
have you . . . just b. 806.2
proclaims its fight b. 869.4
yes, we truly have b. 869.4
and our warfare once b.. 869.4
ere the winter storms b.. 924.1
the fight so well b.. 939.3
real life is b. c106

beginning (noun)
I hungered to make a b.. 553.1
b *John 1:1*
from the b. was . . . Word . 141.1

begone . 712.1

begotten *Rev 1:5* . 149:2

begun see begin

behalf . 106.1

behaviour . 553.3

behest . 677.1

behind
b. a frowning providence . 29.4
not a look b. . 682.1
the past b. me . c152
we won't drag on b. . c224
don't stay b. . c228
cast (g), leave (2d)

behold
1 *(God) beholds*
b., to thee our souls . 216.4
b. me . . . at thy feet . 291.4
now b. me waiting . 477.1
b., we give our thoughts . 515.1
b., these walls we raise . 946.2
2 *(people) behold*
a *1st person*
I b. his hands no more . 129.1
thy beauty to b. . 154.2
but we b. thee stand . 163.4
thy cross b. . 185.1
cross of suffering I b. . 420.4
he found me; I b. him . 548.2
my Lord b. . 884.*
soon his beauty we'll b. 892.4
we b. our redeemer . 908.4
harvest time our eyes b.. 923.1
b *2nd person*
b., I bring good tidings . 78.2
late in time b. him come. 82.2
come and b. him . 85.1
b. his arms . . . hands . 107.2
b. him now on yonder tree . 108.1
b., he bows his . . . head . 108.2
b. his hands and side . 156.4
b. me standing . 229.1, c
will your eyes b. . 280.4
b. I freely give . 332.2
b. the throne of grace . 560.1
b., he sleepeth not . 767.2
b.! On a hill, Calvary . 830.*
c *3rd person*
ye b. him face to face . 17.4
did the guiding star b. . 76.1
men b. must confess . 494.2
they b. the mercy seat . 604.1
eye hath not b. them . 682.3
lead them to b. . . . light. 819.1
mysteries no man b. . 871.4
d *John 1:29*
cry: B. the Lamb . 60.5, 6
b.! b. the Lamb of God . 107:1
e
greater glories . . . yet b. . c44
f *Acts 9:11*
and cry: B., he prays . 625.4
face (2c), *see (4)*

being (noun)
thy b. and thy ways 7.1
let all my b. speak 7.3
take my undivided b. 477.2
hold o'er my b. . . . sway 487.4
Lord of all b. 506.5
b. thou art of love 509.3
with its glorified b. 883.3

believe-d-ing
offender who truly b. 22.2
I now b. in Jesus 67.3
I b. thy precious blood 116.4
b., we rejoice 120.5
he who dies b. 123.4
I do b., I will b. 132.c
we b. it was for us 133.2
yet we b. thee nigh 198.1
we b. to us and ours 216.1
praise God, I b. 222.*
I b. in God . . . Father/Son/Spirit 222.c
I b. in full salvation 222.c
I b. I'll receive a crown 222.c
b., a pardon have found 263.2
we do b. that Jesus can 267.3
but I b. in thee 282.2
as I am I come, b. 303.4
the hour I first b. 308.2
I have rest . . ., I b. 322.2
I b. that God 324.*
I, b., find indeed 351.c
living and b. 352.2
with my heart I b. 367.2
when at the cross I b. 371.3
that can in Jesus' name b. 407.1
I can, I do b. 407.1
look up just now, b. 413.2
he's saving, I'm b. 413.3
I can, I do just now b. 447.4
whereon I cry, b. 456.4
I, b., trust my soul 514.2
Lord, we b. 608.3
who its truth b. 655.1
we find it hard . . . to b. 748.3
we b., that we may know 748.4
and consciously b. 756.4
if we b. as they b. 760.4
we b. 785.*
I b. Jesus saves 808.c
I b. we shall win 820.c
content to die b. 874.3
I'm b. and receiving c42
I b. God answers prayers c70
this moment I b. . . . I do b. c128
I b. it, do you c130

b *all (that) believe*
gladness of all that b. 372.4
reward to all who dare b. 461.3
sure for all who dare b. 760.3

c *[appeal]* *Acts 16:31*
b., thou shalt prove 126:4
sinner, O won't you b. it 139.1
almost persuaded now to b. 226.1
b., and the light 233.1
b., and thou shalt live 255.2
repent, b., be born again 275.3
b. him! the holy one 410.1
dare you now b. 413.c
b. and take the blessing 433.c
now b. and enter in 433.2
only b., and . . . see 718.4
keep on b. 773.c
the glory of b. 790.3
keep on b., trust c63

d *believe promise*
because thy p. I b. 293.5
thy p. I dare to b. 437.2
I thy p. b. 469.2

e *believe word*
b. his w., and trust 633.2
nor how b. in his w. 730.2
I b. in the w. of God c130
his w. b., new life c176

f *believe on* *Rom 9:33*
b. on him without delay 231.3
they who b. on his name 248.4
thousands . . . Christ b. 381.3
who on Jesus . . . will b. 392.1
I b. on the Son 392.c
have you on the Lord b. 418.1
forgive if they on him b. 691.2

dare (c), know (3o)

believer
to every b. the promise 22.2
in a b.'s ear 58.1
redeem the weakest b. 372.1
grace to each b. gives 760.1
every true b. 943.4

believing *(adjective)*
b. souls, rejoicing go 46.4
whole through faith b. 232.3
heart, b., true and clean 444.3

b *John 20:27*
be not faithless but b. 693.c

bell
when heavenly b. . . . calling 39.4
sweet chiming b. 79.c
whene'er the . . . church b. 187.2
the death-b. will toll 237.3
b. of Heaven with harmony 342.c
ring all the b. of Heaven 383.c
ring the b. of Heaven 550.1
the music of church b. 780.3

belong
strength b. to gentleness 198.4
all God's children may b. 324.2
service, too, to him b. 336.2
Jesus b. to me 349.c

b *belong to [God]* *Ps 62:11*
glory unto the Lord b. 184.3
praise to Christ b. 370.4
to thee the praise b. 382.3
power unto God b. 724.1
to God the world . . . b. 782.3
to thee by every right b. 925.5
all praise b. . . . to thee 926.1

c *belong to [Jesus]* *Mark 9:41*
our song, who to Jesus b. 166.c
now I b. to him/Jesus 349.*
know that to thee I b. 437.4
I b. to Christ the Lord 514.1
Saviour, I b. to thee 514.c
and to Jesus Christ b. 514.4
and to him to b. 687.4
inspired . . . to Christ b. 825.3
little ones to him b. 843.1
world . . . b. to Christ 868.3

d *Luke 19:42*
b. to their peace 527.2

beloved
with my beloved ones 7.2
ring with thy b. name 81.4
thou, b. Saviour, art all 325.2
on my own b.'s arms 430.3
listen, b., he speaketh 542.4
closer . . . to his b. embrace 659.4

b *Matt 3:17*
Jesus, b. of God 175.2
Christ, his well b. Son 335.1

below nc, but
a *[Heaven] below*
foretaste, here b. 46.4
glory begun b. 314.3
'tis Heaven b. 355.4
Heaven b. my redeemer 367.3
his love makes my Heaven b. 535.4
life . . . enjoy here b. 640.5

b *serve below*
and s. him here b. 48.3
I ask to s. thee here b. 560.4
loved and s. the Lord b. 875.4

c *earth/world below*
echoed in the e. b. 80.1
born for us on e. b. 88.1
best thing . . . in the w. b. 451.c
a stranger in the w. b. 880.2
to leave the w. b. 901.1
this is the field, the w. b. 932.1
serve me while on e. b. 932.3

bend-ing-bent
saints before the altar b. 75.3
there to b. the knee 76.2
when the skies b. down 80.2
angels b. near the earth 83.1
Jesus now is b. o'er thee 259.2
not distrustingly b. I 296.1
b. this stubborn heart 445.1
b. with age but never dies 544.3
b. our pride to thy control 577.3
foes are b. 593.3
in lowliness I b. me 635.2
and b. its stubborn will 782.3
b. lower, lower still c35

beneath/neath *nc, but*
a *beneath [flag]*
fight b. its colours 382.c/782.c
b. thy standard . . . stay 692.5
as we fight b. its folds 774.1
'n. our colours, waving 774.c
b. thy shade enrolled 774.2
'n. the yellow, red and blue 778.*
b. this glorious banner 781.3
fight b. our flag unfurled 782.1
'n. the blood and fire 788.1
gathering 'n. our banner 803.2
we'll serve b. his banner 853.2
'n. the flag so dear c236
'n the yellow, red and blue c237
march b. the yellow c241

cross (2d) wings (1d)

benefits *Ps 68:19** 616.2

bequeathed 200.1

bereft 222.2

beseech-ing
our Father, we b. thee now 5.4
Lord, I come to thee b. 434.1

beset *Heb 12:1*
snares b. my path below 389.1
sore temptations may b. me 399.3
temptations my pathway b. 553.2
who so b. him round 685.2
foes b. and friends 780.2
though trials b. me c125

beside
1 *(preposition)*
with thee, dear Lord, b. me 53.4
on the road b. me now 59.2
b. thee as I walk 59.3
go on with thee b. us 97.5
b. the Syrian sea 567.2
we wait b. thee 595.3
to rest with thee b. me 635.1
break the loaves b. the sea 650.1
I kneel b. thy . . . cross 729.1
my shepherd is b. me 736.2
if b. you . . . waver 805.3
no place b. . . . thy grace 861.5
b. the crystal stream 901.4
b. the chilly wave 910.1

b *close beside*
God himself is c. b. you 238.1
that is flowing c. b. 462.1
c. b. my Saviour . . . keep 483.3
ceased from walking c. b. 534.2

knowing thou art c. b. me . 770.4
stay c. b. me 843.3
c *(except)*
there is none b. thee . 220.3
whom have I . . . b. thee . 301.4
2 *beside-s (adverb)*
with ten thousand b. . 33.3
even for the thorns b. . 552.3
all b. is vain endeavour . 555.4
with Christ, in all b. . 565.1
than all b. more sweet . 573.2
and nothing know b. . 659.3
than all the world b. . c216

bespeak 167.2

besprinkled *Heb 12:24** . 629.1

best
1 *(adjective)*
my b., my only friend . 14.1
all its b. giving . . 51.2
when the b. in this world . 51.2
love of every love the b.. 182.3
b. resolves I only break . 291.3
merits my soul's b. songs . 336.2
unto the true things, unto the b. 351.2
b. of blessings he'll provide . 377.4
all my b. works are naught . 416.3
thy new b. name of love . 444.5
the b. thing I know . 451.c
do his will my b. reward. . 451.4
his own b. evidence . 496.4
my warmest, b. affection . 520.2
b. bliss that earth imparts . 602.1
his way is b., you see . 732.c
sweetest and brightest and b.. 794.3
lay your b. at . . . feet . 920.1
while our b. we bring thee . 921.1
b *dearest and best*
cross where the d. and b. . 124.1
give/surrender the d. and b. . 507.*
bring your d. and your b. 920.c. 2
c *[do] best*
today have you done your b.. 666.3
do your b. in fighting . 805.3
we'll try our b. to please. . 849.3
d *[give] best*
love gives its b. . . 51.*
part with thy b. . . 923.3
I give thee my b. . . c41
in giving of my b. . . c208
2 *(adverb)*
guiding . . . as may b. . 183.2
thou . . . knowest me b.. . 675.3
who b. can drink his cup . 701.1
what b. for each will prove . 715.5
to be the b. that I can be . 860.3
as b. may seem to thee . . 917.2
learn how b. to do . . c72
b. of all, I know he's mine . c167
b *love best*
front I l. the b. . . 362.3
serve and l. thee b. . 428.5
when I'm l. thee the b. . 503.3
the one you l. the b. . 829.1
those I l. most and b. . 882.3
the thing I l. the b.. . c230
we l. it the b. of all. . c243
c *serve best*
they s. you b. who s. . 518.2
how I may s. thee b. . 571.4
may s. my neighbours b. . 838.4
d *(in phrases)*
my faith at b. is weak . 731.2
will be for the b. . . 755.2
I know are for the b. . 761.2

bestow-ed-ing
no learning can b. . . 6.3
the gifts he hath b. . 23.1
great gifts on him b. . 48.3
honours which Jesus will b. . 169.2
b. or canst withhold . 171.2
calm thy sweet presence b. . 209.1
and the glory b. . . 209.*
rich blessings to b. . 231.2
blessings God on man b. . 257.3
he can freedom b. . . 329.2
would you know the joy he b. 348.3
pardon and mercy b. . 383.3
and the joy he b. . . 397.4
a heart like this b. . . 426.1
Jesus, thy purity b. . 432.1
thy mighty aid b. . . 448.4
sanctifying power b. . 531.3
thine image, Lord, b. . 560.4
thyself b., for thee alone . 565.2
thou only . . . canst b. . 589.1
living water now b. . 601.1
armour . . . God will b. . 703.3
see the Kingdom I b. . 875.4
b *bestow grace* *1 Cor 15:10*
all thy g. on us b. . . 210.4
freely he his g. b. . . 418.3
Father, on me the g. b. . 601.3
the g. thou dost b. . 624.3
c *bestow love* *1 John 3:1*
Lord, a l. like this b. . 426.2
l. his Spirit only can b. . 465.1
new strength and l. b. . 675.2
d *bestow peace*
he waits . . . sweet p. to b. . 331.4
p. that he loves to b. . 443.2
cleanse from sin and p. b. . 528.1
p. unending . . . b. . 857.c

bestowal *(1 John 3:1)* . 493.2

Bethany *Matt 21:17** . 663.2

Bethel *Gen 28:19*
B. I'll raise . . . 617.4
O God of B. . . . 918.1

Bethlehem *Luke 2.4**
which said: Go ye to B. . . 72.3
sped to B. straightway . . 72.5
Christ is born in B. . . 82.1
O come ye to B . . 85.1
O little town of B. . . 86.1
O holy Child of B. . . 86.4
Christ is born in B. . . 88.c
o'er B. it took its rest . . 90.4
story of the babe of B. . . 96.1
in B.' home . . . no room . 101.1
a boy was born in B. . 855.1

betide
naught . . . shall e'er b. . . 377.4
run not . . . whatever b.. . 458.3
cheer me, whatever b. . 506.4
hope in him whate'er b. . . 738.1
secures us, whatever b. . . 763.1
Jesus, whate'er b. . . 955
befall

betray
if I my trust b. . . 472.4
however you b. him . 854.3

betrayal 750.1

better
your b. self deplores . 244.1
power to be a b. person. 244.1, c
there is a b. world . . 268.1
I feel something b. . 298.4
I want to love him b. . 369.2
how can I b. serve . . 488.1
the b. way . . . to spread . 529.2
'twere b. far to die. . 780.*
b. are these treasures . 849.3
'tis b. on before . . 911.*
how to serve thee b. . c105
I love him b. every day . c169
part (1c)

between
with not a cloud b. . 426.1
while Jordan rolled b. . 898.2

Beulah *Isa 62:4*
is not this the land of B.. . 320.c
come along to B. . . . land . c153

beware *Matt 16:6* . . 689.2

bewildered 542.1

beyond nc, but see
degree, far (e), grave (2b), *past*, river (b), sky (b)

Bible
word of B., faith of Church . 30.3
wonderful things in the B. . 323.1
I opened up my B. . . 403.1
holy B., book divine . 652.1, 4
the B. assures us . . 763.1
the B. tells us so . . 814.1
go with the Holy B. . 830.2
for the B. tells me so . 843.1

bid-bade
1 *(God) bids*
thy suffering b. me share . 138.3
since thou b. us leave . 154.5
b. the nations see . . 155.4
God hath b. all mankind . . 234.1
thou b. me come to thee . 293.1
b. me be thy child . . 303.1
b. me sin no more . . 305.3
and b. my struggling cease . 366.4
b. us dwell in safety . 377.3
b. me go and happy be . 402.2
banish, and b. me be whole . 422.3
found me and b. me be whole 467.3
which thou hast b. me tread . 529.2
b. me be every whit whole . 542.3
he himself has b. thee pray . 563.1
b. the mighty ocean deep . 569.1
b. my anxious fears subside . 578.3
b. our inmost souls rejoice . 603.5
since he b. me seek . 633.2
and b. my heart rejoice . 636.3
b. darkness turn to day . 743.3
speak again and b. me come . 749.2
he who b. us forward go . 772.1
what he b. us, that to do . 772.5
thy hand . . . b. us follow . 788.1
b. these children welcome . 797.3
he b. them still attend him . 853.1
he will b. us welcome . 930.3
b. thy cloud of glory rest . 942.1
b *[Jesus] bids*
the Saviour b. thee live . 256.3
for Jesus b. us come . 312.3
Jesus b. me go free . 322.1
Jesus has b. them to come . 794.3
for Jesus b. you come . 802.2
Jesus b. us shine . . 841.*
cease (b), depart (3c), rise (3b)
2 *(man) bids*
to b. their hearts rejoice. . 62.5
b. him enter in . . 227.2
b. him enter while you may . 241.c
b. sadness and sorrow . 537.1
b. me choose/mingle/try . 780.1
welcome (b)
3 *(other)*
shadows b. thee no longer . 250.5
past defeats would b. me . 285.2
dew b. nature smile anew . 494.2

b. me at my Father's throne . 633.1
the sun that b. us rest . . 677.4
b. us think of Christ . . 783.2
b. a soldier his warfare . . 894.1

bidders 796.2

bidding *(noun)* 808.4

big 29.3

billow *Ps 42:7*
sure while the b. roll . . 280.c
beneath thy blest b. . . 298.3
b. his will obey . . . 336.3
floods . . . like the sea b. . 394.c
when upon life's b. . . 396.1
loud and angry b. roar . . 478.2
when the stormy b. roll . . 627.2
'midst the angry b.' roll . . 713.1
a rock 'midst dashing b.. . 750.2
waves and b. are gone o'er . 762.1
sorrows like sea-b. roll . . 771.1
chided the b. 848.3
though the b. round me roll . c131

bind-bound
1 *bind to/by God*
mercy . . . hath b. me fast . 23.4
b. alone by love . . . 130.1
I b. myself to thee . . . 130.4
firmly b., for ever free . . 194.3
b. my wandering heart . . 313.4
I was bruised, and he b. me . 330.2
thus he b. me to him . . 345.1
by love he's b. me to serve . 706.c
b. . . . by love's cord . . 757.3
b *Isa 61:1*
the broken heart to b. . . 81.3
it b. up the wounds . . 237.2
came to b. the broken . . 274.c
to b. the broken-hearted . 832.1
2 *bind to/by sin*
b. and condemned to die . 45.1
I delivered thee when b.. . 110.2
fast b. in s. 283.3
they b. my poor soul . . 298.3
came to Jesus, b. and sad . 348.2
things that b. my heart . . 523.c
that souls who are b. . . 523.3
I was b., but now I'm free . 546.2
fears that long have b. us . 577.2
free each s.-b. slave . . 775.2
millions s.-b. lie . . . 780.2
the millions b. by evil . . 832.2
fetter (b), Satan (b)
3 *bind to each other*
brother-love b. man to man . 10.4
b. brave hearts together . 593.2
blest be the tie that b. . . 660.1
thou to them dost b. us . . 788.2
close-b. all mankind . . 826.2
as thou didst b. . . . 949.2
4 *bind [hands]* *John 18:24*
willing h. and feet are b. . 121.2
h. . . . b. fast with cords. . 129.1
h. of Jesus . . . b. for me . 129.c
b. them as to death they go . 129.2
would'st thou b. . . . h. . . 129.3
no longer b. to . . . years . 142.2
arm hath b. the . . . wave . 569.1

binding (adj) 249.2

bird
chanting b. and . . . fountain . 10.2
God speaks to us in b. . . 31.1
like the first b. 35.1
from flower to b. . . . 38.3
sweet b. and sweet flowers . 318.1
b. with gladder songs . . 545.2
when the b. waketh . . 632.1
b. . . . soon will be asleep . 673.2
as the b. homeward wend . 675.3
the b. beneath her feathers . 722.4
b *bird [sings]*
each little b. that s. . . 25.1
b. that soar while s. . . 32.3
hear the b. s. sweetly . . 37.2
over hill . . . the b. are s. . 39.3
among the s. of the b. . . 41.1
the b. their carols raise . . 42.2
days of joy when b. are s. . 711.1
c *(Matt 6:26)*
the b. without barn . . 763.2
by him the b. are fed . . 935.2

birth
1 *(divine)* *(Matt 1:18)*
now proclaim Messiah's b. . 75.1
tidings of a Saviour's b.. . 78.2
proclaim the holy b. . . 86.2
told us of a Saviour's b.. . 88.3
kindles to joy in his b. . . 92.2
from b. to dying cry . . 94.1
as they welcomed his b. . 99.1
of lowly b. cam'st thou . . 101.2
tender from moment of b. . 175.1
2 *(other)*
love which from our b. . . 28.1
gave the universe its b. . . 30.4
from b. to final issue . . 38.3
born to give them second b. . 82.3
an alien by b. 354.3
springs to glorious b. . . 682.2
to bring that day to b. . . 774.4

birthright 944.2

bit 169.3

bitter
bud may have a b. taste. . 29.5
manger to his b. cross . . 78.3
drinks for you the b. cup . 107.3
comprehend thy b. cry . . 122.2
with exceeding b. throes . 127.2
side by side with b. loss. . 145.1
sad, sad that b. wail . . 226.3
have caused him b. tears . 250.2
b. the tears of remorse . . 298.2
how to steal the b. . . 333.2
oft has caused you b. grief . 433.2
O the b. shame and sorrow . 548.1
the b. is sweet . . . 712.4
the cup . . . not more b.. . 758.2
that scene . . . of b. pain . 848.5

bitterness
and will not let old b. depart . 572.2
tears no b. 670.4
life is not all b. . . . c201

black
the b., the white . . . 170.2
sinful and b. though . . 437.1
b. as on the judgment day . 446.1

blackbird 35.1

blackest
b. darkness brought . . 448.2
crimes of b. dye . . . 697.4
b. stains brought to light . 893.1

blade *Mark 4:28* . . . 924.2

blameless *2 Peter 3:14**
make me b. in thy sight . . 601.3
abide all b., we believe . . 785.5

blaspheme 407.1

blast
shelter from the stormy b. . 13.1
through all the stormy b. . 334.2
the b. of discord cease . . 669.3
help us in the fiery b. . . 769.2
time's wild wintry b. . . 882.2

blaze
sets the kingdoms on a b. . 165.1
with inextinguishable b. . . 199.2
in thy sunshine's b. . . 621.2
b *Mark 1:45*
let us b. his name abroad . 34.2

blazing (adj)
make me a b. fire . . . 521.2
in b. light your cross . . 572.3
make my life one b. fire . . 620.3
in the battle's b. heat . . 749.3

bleed-bled
1 *(God) bled*
on the cross he b. for me . 125.1
b. for Adam's helpless race . 283.2
how he suffered and b. . . 289.2
b. on th' accursèd tree . . 548.2
b *bleed and die*
he b. and d., to take away . 37.3
did my Saviour b. . . . d. . 105.1
he suffered and b. and d. . 184.2
wondrous love, to b. and d. . 284.5
he b., he d. to save me . . 345.2
who for us did b. and d. . 481.3
how thou hast b. and d. . 521.2
b. and d., was crucified . . 798.1
since for me he b. and d. . c216
2 *(we) bleed*
when b., healed thy wound . 110.2
whate'er it cost, howe'er I b.. 440.2
even when my spirit b. . . 552.2
heart more deeply b. . . 586.3
though . . . hearts may b. . 923.3

bleeding (adj)
sacrifice . . . appears . . 106.1
five b. wounds he bears. . 106.3
Saviour, by thy b. form . . 138.3
let me kiss thy b. feet . . 140.4
hearts . . . broken and b. . 383.3
waiting at thy b. feet . . 477.1
lay me at thy b. feet . . 600.3
Jesus' feet were b. . . 903.2
b *bleeding Lamb* *(Rev 12:11)*
going to see the b. L. . . 275.2
glory to the b. L. . . . 360.*
salvation! O thou b. L. . . 382.3
O the L., the b. L. . . . c193
side (2c)

blend-ed-ing
in my soul are b. . . . 222.3
justice and his love do b. . 269.2
mind to b. with . . . life . 485.3
God and man in oneness b. . 540.4
scene where spirits b. . . 573.3
love with every passion b. . 607.3
b. with ours your voices. . 690.5
while the trumpets b. . . 803.2
b. my wakening thought . 871.2
our voices b. in song . . 888.1
new vows for war we b. . 933.3
with ours today are b. . . 934.4
b *blend will*
till my w. becomes b. . . 493.2
prevent me b. it with thine . 504.2
cleanse and b. my w. . . 555.4
renew my w. . . . b. it . . c95

bless-ed-ing
1 *(God) bless*
ever b., ever blest . . . 10.3
hath b. us on our way . . 12.1
swift to b. 17.2
hands outstretched to b. . 129.1
he lives to b. me . . . 144.2

contrite spirit he will b. . . 225.3
the cross which thou hast b. . 287.1
he alone can help and b. . 343.2
great delight to b. us . . 377.3
here to save and b. . . 434.2
thou shalt own . . . and b. . 473.2
b. me through good or ill . 539.3
his love and power can b. . 560.3
how can your pardon . . . b. . 572.2
so long thy power hath b. . 606.3
the waiting soul to b. . . 633.2
thou canst not fail to b. . . 642.3
with thee thy trials to b.. . 653.3
the humble meal he b. . . 663.2
with thee at hand to b. . . 670.4
Army Jehovah has b. . . 684.4
great creator's power to b. . 871.1
my service b. c84
ever near to b. and cheer . c154

b *(request)*
b. all the dear children . . 77.3
sweetly b. this . . . hour. . 217.4
come, and thy people b. . 219.2
my soul and body b. . . 431.1
come to our hearts and b. . 561.2
Saviour, richly b. us . . 575.1
b. us here today . . . 575.c
O b. me now, my Saviour . 587.c
b. our General/leaders, etc . 622.4
O come and b. us now . . 626.1
if the Holy Spirit b. . . 652.3
come near and b. us . . 676.6
thou wilt richly b. . . . 769.3
b. this baby 792.3
receive and b. our child . . 796.4
b. our sacrifice . . . 921.1
b. thou our labour . . . 927.2
b. me now, b. me now . . c58

c *bless Army*
the A. of salvation b. . . 609.1
b. our A. . . . . 622.*
God b. our A. round . . c244

d *Num 6:24*
the Lord b. thee . . . 961

e *Matt 14:19**
for him to b. and break . . 512.2
will b. me in the breaking . 631.4

2 *(we) bless*
a *bless [Lord]* *Ps 34:1**
all things their creator b. . 2.5
we b. the Lamb . . . 120.5
I b. the Christ of God . . 297.6
thee we would be always b. . 438.2
hearts are made to b. thee . 642.3
we stand to b. thee . . 674.1
I'll b. the hand . . . heart. . 896.3

b *Neh 9:5*
stand up and b. the Lord . 20.*

c *bless name*
praise, laud and b. his n. . 3.3
in one to b. the . . . n. . . 57.4
b. the sound of Jesus' n. . 62.1
bow and b. the sacred n. . 223.1
every day, b. his n. . . c126
b. his n., he sets me free . c149
b. his dear n., I'm free . . c189

d
that others I may b. . . 475.2
b. and being blest . . . 571.4
I b. the happy day . . . 798.c

3 *(other)*
sun may never rise to b. . 251.2

blessed-blest
1 *(passive)*
life's course, designedly b. . 51.c
the sons of want are b. . . 160.3
to be . . . welcomed and b. . 170.2
heart received and Spirit b. . 211.1
b. as the host above . . 217.5
and you are fully b. . . 231.3
and thou shalt be b. . . 248.2
b. with a sense of his love . 318.3
would you be b.? . . . 348.c
hardly more favoured or b. . 373.2
b. if we trust and obey . . 397.3
and finding, it is b. . . 420.1
there let my soul be b. . . 431.3
blessing and being b. . . 571.4
b. when our faith . . . 602.3
speak! and make me b. . . 614.3
all the nations are b. . . 708.3
in his presence b. . . . 740.c
feeling safe and b. . . . 792.1
crowd to his arms and be b. . 794.3
in Christ are fully b. . . 828.3
b. are thy children . . . 873.3
b. by God, are sanctified . 874.1
b., b. for aye 897.2
by which all toil is b. . . 942.1

b *how blest*
how b. are they, and only . 21.4
how b. the Lord's alone . . 317.2
how b. are they . . . abide . 424.3

c *I am blessed*
I . . . am happy and b. . . 310.3
I know I am b. . . . 323.5
I am perfectly b. . . . 367.4
obeying, I am b. . . . 475.1
none more blest than I . . 557.3

d *Matt 5:3-10*
b. are the . . . . 95.*
b. are the pure in heart . . 411.1

2 *(adjective)—general*
the Spirit's b. dower . . 15.4
b. rest from inbred sin . . 46.3
like him in this b. quest . . 51.3
was born this b. day . . 72.c
b. thought! for every one . 261.4
send the b. tidings . . 279.1
beneath thy b. billows . . 298.3
b., b. land of light . . 320.c
in his b. presence live . . 336.2
b. is the spot to me . . 348.2
but the b. word was spoken . 363.3
to his b. throne I move . . 365.2
sunshine, b. sunshine . . 387.c
does his b. presence cheer . 418.2
in thy b. hands I am . . 419.5
confirms the b. work . . 423.4
to get this b. washing . . 436.2
my all, this b. day . . . 447.2
'tis a b. way and holy . . 462.2
hasten thy b. news . . 523.2
at the b. mercy seat . . 524.2
naught but b. content . . 551.2
life seem as brief as b. . . 551.3
this b. consciousness . . 632.2
thine in b. reality . . . 649.4
b. be the dear . . . love . . 659.1
b. be the tie that binds . . 660.1
O what b., sweet communion 709.c
thank thee for the b. hope . 714.1
into thy b. hands receive . 720.4
leadeth me. O b. thought . 725.1
faith has . . . b. reward . . 748.4
round our b. standard . . 818.2
all the b. gifts . . . 861.5
fellowship as b., so sweet . 888.3
mansions bright and b. . . 892.1
in that b. land . . . 905.2
b. is that land of God . . 934.4
thrice b. . . . harvest song . 934.4

b *[ever] blessèd*
ever blessing, ever b. . . 10.3
thou ever b. morn . . . 88.c
with him for ever b. . . 190.3
sacred name forever b. . . 223.1
ever-b. heights above . . 711.1
name . . . be for ever b.. . 876.1

c *blessèd face*
I'll see his b. f. . . . 344.3
I saw his b. f. . . . 366.3
until thy b. f. I see . . . 612.7
cannot hide his b. f. . . 758.c
some day I'll see his b. f. . 884.c

d *blessèd name* *Ps 145:1*
sound than thy b. n. . . 61.2
thy n. . . . be for ever b.. . 876.1

e *blessèd peace*
and b. p. to cheer us . . 12.2
agree this b. p. to gain . . 661.4
I have b. p. with my Lord . 768.3

f *blessèd will*
understand thy b. w. . . 218.2
into thy b. w. to abide . . 300.3
by faith and do his b. w. . 344.3
to tell to all thy b. w. . . 620.2

g *Matt 25:34*
come near, ye b. . . . 875.4

assurance, command (d), gospel (c), hope (3g)

3 *divine*
most b., most glorious . . 8.1
freely with that b. one . . 15.3
O b. Holy Spirit . . . 221.3
b. Godhead, Three in One . 222.c
Christ, the b. one, gives. . 258.2
b. Spirit, . . . brought me . 504.3
b. and glorious King . . 561.1

b *blessèd Jesus*
sweetest carol . . . b. J.. . 67.c
b. J. thou art mine . . 128.3
b. J. wouldst thou know . 377.4
I'm thine, O b. J., washed . 511.4
b. J., teach me . . . 713.2
b. J., thou hast bought . . 845.1
over Jordan, with my b. J. . c247

c *blessèd Lamb*
b. L. of Calvary 205.1; 538.1; c69

d *blessèd Lord*
our b. L. refuses none . . 251.4
calm it, O b. L., but thine . 325.3
b. L., this is the gift . . 415.1
b. L., almighty to heal . . 459.2
b. L., who . . . was slain. . 473.1
draw me nearer . . . b. L. . 585.c
b. L., to see thee truly . . 591.3
b. L., in thee is refuge . . 713.1
O the b. L. of light . . . 819.2

e *blessèd Master*
now I said: B. M. come in . 373.1
but say: B. M., thy will . . 410.2
channels only, b. M. . . c60
b. M., walk with me . . c110

f *blessèd redeemer*
Jesus, our b. r. . . . 184.1
our b. r., ere he breathed . 200.1
thee will I sing, my b. r.. . 364.4
O to be like thee, b. r. . 623.1, c
nearer to thee, B. R. . . c45

g *blessèd Saviour*
I love the b. S.'s name . . 67.3
'tis because my b. S. . . 404.1
all to thee, my b. S. . . 474.c
b. S., now behold me . . 477.1
for our b. S.'s sake . . 481.3
O b. S., is thy love. . . 515.1
I am praying, b. S. . 584.1, 3
b. S., then in love . . . 743.4
I'm glad my b. S. . . . 840.2

Trinity

blessedly . . . . 321.*

blessedness
what a b., what a peace. . 768.1
the way to every b. . . 806.1

b *Gal 4:15*
where is the b. I knew . . 442.2

blessing-s
unfoldest b. on our way . . 2.4
lose the b. of our Lord . . 5.3
the b. of his Heaven . . 86.3
the prophets' b. share . . 95.3
bane and b. 112.4
and the b. waits for us . . 145.3
b. abound where'er . . 160.3
tribes . . . boast more b.. . 160.4
'tis an ocean vast of b. . . 182.3
rich b. to bestow . . . 231.2
missing the b. God on man . 257.3
you can have this b. . . 328.3
I have seen his face in b. . 330.1
what a b. to know . . . 355.1
riches eternal and b. . . 371.3
best of b. he'll provide . . 377.4
count your (many) b. . . 396.*
may ours this b. be . . 411.4
believe and take the b. . . 433.c
with thy b. make us thine . 452.1
will be a b. in disguise . . 455.4
let thy b. fill 470.3
how great the b. . . . 536.1
may my life a b. be . . 538.4
the b. that setteth me free . 542.2
and your b. on my way . . 552.1
as I reached out for the b. . 553.3
moment the b. was mine . 553.3
pressed . . . for the b. . . 610.2
we now for thy b. call . . 622.1
the b. shall be ours . . 626.3
sweet . . . rich in b. . . 634.1
may I still enjoy this b. . . 634.4
perpetual b. from thy hand . 672.3
with thy tenderest b. . . 673.3
enrich the poor with b. . . 676.5
with thy b. filling each . . 707.3
with numberless b. . . 710.3
for each b. 795.1
these parents, for your b. . 795.1
armed with inward b. . . 863.2
not a sigh for the b. . . 900.2
b. that hallow our days . . 900.3
b. from thy gracious hand . 918.5
then will thy b. reach . . 927.4
the first-fruits of thy b. . . 934.2
many years of b. . . . 939.1
the primal marriage b. . . 949.1
greater b. as the days . . c44
make me a channel of b. . c84
b *Mal 3:10*
wonder-working b. pour . 940.3
c *James 3:10*
for b. or cursing . . . 928.1
d *all blessing*
all the b. earth displays . . 15.2
b. all mine 33.3
all the b. of the light . . 671.1
e *Neh 9:5*
above all b. high . . . 20.2
f *Eph 1:3*
from thy altar b. flow . . 528.1
whence all my b. flow . . 616.1
from whom all b. flow 665.6; 959
g *Rev 5:12*
all honour and b. . . . 24.3
b. more than we can give . 57.3
honour, power and b. . . 109.3
h *each/every blessing*
Fount of every b. . . . 313.1
yet possessing every b. . . 607.1
brings every b. from above . 646.2
each b. you have granted . 795.1
claim (2b), give (1e), head (2c), more (2b), receive (2b), rest (1b), seek (2c), send (1c), shower (b)

blest
a see *blessed*
b *the blest*
for all the pure and b. . . 139.3
there, with the good and b. . 882.3
fly to the land of the b. . . 886.3
songs of the b. . . . 900.2
the realms of the b. . . 904.1
day when all the b. . . 940.4

blight-ed
saves . . . from evil's b.. . 30.4
broken hearts and b. hopes . 702.3
shame b. men's souls . . 789.4
free from the b. of sorrow . 889.2

blind-ed
b. unbelief is sure to err . . 29.6
sight to the inly b. . . . 224.2
room for the lame . . . b. . 266.2
if I am b. to human need . 518.2
too desolate, too b. . . 590.2
halt, the b., the great . . 590.3
for b. my own . . . 635.2
b., they grope for day . . 682.2
heal the sick, . . . the b.. . 737.3
b *John 9:25**
b. eyes made to see . . 257.c
came to make the b. to see . 274.c
canst make the b. to see . 295.3
was b. but now I see . . 308.1
once I was b. but now . . 347.c
Lord, I was b. . . . 353.1
thou hast made the b. . . 353.5
once I was b., but now . . 380.1
he made my b. eyes to see . 386.1
making the b. to see . . 724.1
c *Rev 3:17*
poor, wretched, b. . . 293.4
eye (2c)

blindly
mine to follow, even b. . . 510.2
guide me, or I b. rove . . 630.1

blindness *(Eph 4:18)**
Lord, upon our b. . . . pour . 40.3
forgive all my b. . . . 288.3
in my b. I thought . . . 395.2
in b. once I sacrificed . . 449.1
sight for my b. give . . 488.3
lest in our b. . . . stray . . 747.2
how much misery and b. . 770.1

bliss
to come from highest b. . . 88.4
when the sun of b. . . 112.3
what b. till now was thine . 123.2
partake the glorious b. . . 165.1
or fades my earthly b. . . 187.3
in Heaven's eternal b. . . 187.4
crowned with b. again . . 268.4
such amazing b. . . . 314.2
O b. of the purified . . 364.*
see the b. of thine own . . 372.4
O what b. complete . . 375.3
may bear the burning b. . 414.2
translate me to . . . b. . . 441.4
b. at thy side evermore . . 457.3
my b. shall never end . . 464.4
the fountain-head of b. . . 497.3
the rapturous b. to know . 540.2
with what a rest of b. . . 545.3
the b. till now unknown . . 547.1
rich to all intents of b. . . 565.4
best b. that earth imparts . 602.1
your b. in our hearts . . 611.1
what b. that one so vile . . 709.1
sing 'mid b. unspoken . . 835.3
b. . . . shall last . . . 880.2

blissful
b. as an echo . . . 70.c
now thy b. self impart . . 210.1
reached that b. shore . . 275.1
towards that b. shore . . 911.1

block 943.2

blood
1 *natural*
he sets in b. no more . . 143.2
his b.-red banner streams . 701.1
b *Heb 9:12, 13*
not all the b. of beasts . . 120.1
richer b. than they . . . 120.2
flesh (b)
2 *divine*
his b. can make . . . avails . 64.4
it is the b. that . . . 113.*
sealed my pardon with his b.. 118.2
word, by b. is sealed . . 126.3
a fountain filled with b. . . 132.1
in thy b. . . . to lave . . 135.4
b. insures the boon divine . 208.4
thy b. was freely given . . 221.2
his b. for thee streaming . 237.3
his the b. which paid . . 249.2
there is healing in his b.. . 265.4
pardon which thy b. . . 287.2
O pardon-speaking b. . . 290.3
by his life's b. he has . . 330.3
b. that can all sins erase. . 335.2
his heart the b. o'erflows . 348.3
that his b. cannot cure . . 364.3
feel in the life-giving b. . . 367.4
b. now fills the fountain. . 413.1
the b. is flowing there . . 434.4
'tis the b. 434.5
by thy b. thou dost claim . 473.1
b. that makes me clean . . 489.3
made holy by his b. . . 495.1
thy b. doth sin destroy . . 593.3
I have a token in the b. . . 724.3
make me holy by thy b. . . 727.3
oath, his covenant and b. . 745.3
witness with the b. . . 756.1
his b. makes me whiter . . 808.c
had . . . through the b. . . 808.2
through the b. of Calvary . 822.3
thy b. . . . is sufficient . . 883.2
b *[drops] of blood* *Luke 22:44*
sweat great d. of b. . . 137.2
thy sweat of b., thy grief . 140.3
sweat d. of b. for mine . . 179.2
thy sweat as b. falls . . 486.3
from thee fell d. of b. . . 586.2
c *John 19:34*
let the water and the b. . . 302.1
d *to the blood*
Spirit answers to the b. . . 106.4
I sacrifice them to his b. . 136.2
to the b. for refuge flee . . 240.3
drive me to the b. again. . 425.4
all who will come to the b. . c23
Spirit answers to the b. . c129
e *under the blood*
my sins are u. the b. . . 317.*
the past is u. the b. . . 542.c
f *blood [bought]* *(1 Cor 6:20)*
my b.-b. life I give him . . 65.3
with all the b.-b. throng . . 69.4
with his b. mankind hath b. . 90.6
why perish, b.-b. sinner . . 107.1
with his b. he purchased . 180.c
thy b.-b. gift today . . 203.1
with his precious b. he b. . 377.2
complete b.-b. redemption . 413.2
thou hast b. me with thy b. . 477.2
b. for me by b. divine . . 481.4
b. of Christ has b. me . . 504.3
thy b.-b. right maintain . . 563.4
the b.-b. souls destroying . 696.2
claim each b.-b. nation . . 828.4
O the b. that b. me . . c218
g *cleansing blood* *1 John 1:7*
find . . . c. through the b. . 46.2
the b. of Jesus c. me . . 176.1
the c. b. to apply . . . 195.3
flowed the sin-c. b. . . 271.2

whose b. can c. each spot . 293.2
Lord, let the c. b. . . . 296.4
c. b. has reached me 313.c; 520.c
his b. has c. me white . 359.2, 3
c. by thy b., bold shall . . 372.3
b. doth c. as white as . . 401.3
heart by b. made clean . . 415.5
soul-c. b. of the Lamb . 417.c
for c. in thy precious b. . . 423.1
wash me, c. me in thy b. . 423.c
to wash me in thy c. b. . . 424.1
c. in the b. that flows . . 427.c
and the b. now c. me . . 429.c
thy b. for my c. I see . . 454.4
the b. that makes me clean . 489.3
let the b. . . . c. my heart . 502.3
c. by thy b. I shall walk . . 543.3
c. in the b. for me . . . 757.5
b. of Jesus c. white . . 798.*
his b. will c. you from sin . c18
glad there is c. in the b.. . c47
the b. . . . it c. from . . c192
proud to tell of the c. b.. . c199

h *[through] blood* *Eph 1:7; Col 1:14*
redemption, the purchase of b. 22.2
the virtue of thy b. . . . 109.2
trust in his redeeming b. . 133.5
redemption through the b. . 222.c
b.-bought redemption . . 413.2
worthy through his b. . . 431.c
through the b. . . . 432.*
victory through the b. . . 750.3
conquer through the b. . . 809.c
through the b. . . . prevail . 809.2

i *blood of Christ* *Eph 2:13**
b. of C. so rich and free. . 295.4
let the b. of C. . . . flood. . 502.3
the b. of C. has bought me . 504.3
through the b. of C. . . 702.c
in C.'s atoning b. . . . 943.4

j *blood of Jesus* *1 John 1:7*
extol the power of J.' b. . 56.4
J., thy b. and righteousness . 116.1
the b. of J. cleanses me. . 176.1
hearts unwashed in J.' b. . 268.3
nothing but the b. of J. . . 306.*
for I am washed in J.' b. . 326.5
washed my robes in J.' b. . 359.c
the b. of J. fully saves . . 404.2
the brands in J.' b. . . 720.2
full confidence in J.' b. . . 733.1
J.'s b. and righteousness . 745.1
J.' b. . . . mercy . . . cries . 746.2
b. of J. whispers peace . . 752.1
b. of J. cleanses white . . 798.*
in J.' b. my heart . . . c168
O the b. of J. . . . cleanses . c192

k *blood of Saviour*
precious b. my S. spilt . . 108.c
the S.'s b. was shed . . 253.2
the S.'s b. can wash away . 253.3
b. of my S. . . . whole . . 273.3
an interest in the S.'s b. . 283.1
by the b. of their S. . . 392.2
the S.'s b. was spilt . . 403.1
S.'s b., the Holy Ghost . . 779.2
thy b., O my S. . . . for me . 883.2
cleansing in the S.'s b. . . c47
by the b. my S. shed . . c150

apply (b), atone (b), fire (4), flesh (b), flow (2b), interest, Lamb (2f), own (4d), power (4h), precious (b), redeem (c), save (1d), shed (2b), spilt, water (3d)

3 *blood—(adjective)*
by the b.-current swept . . 437.2
b.-besprinkled witnesses . 629.1
b.-red crimson tells . . 783.2

b *blood-washed*
in b.-w. hearts to rule . . 138.1
join the b.-w. throng . . 374.3
I join the b.-w. throng . . 375.3
Jesus, give thy b.-w. Army . 593.1

a holy, b.-w. band . . . 781.3
their robes surely b.-w. . . 893.3
the songs of the b.-w. . . 904.2

stain (d), wash (3b)

bloom-ed-ing
flowers are b. 39.3
b. a garden, passing fair . 145.1
b. in every meadow . . 155.2
the b. garb of spring . . 177.2
the flowers b. for ever . . 320.c
make the desert garden b. . 333.2
where the flowers are b. . 483.1
the b. on all I do . . . 591.2
where Eden's bowers b. . 725.2
content to b. in native . . 838.2
the deserts b. and spring . 929.2
b. in all thy beauty . . . c43
Rose of Sharon, b. for me . c54

blossom-ing
b. and flourish as leaves. . 8.3
b. meadow, flashing sea . 10.2
from the ground there b. . 621.4
b. and wood 927.1

blot 293.2

blow
and the wild winds b. . . 280.2
though the winds may b. . 341.1
when sin's tempests b. . . 347.2
heavenly breezes are b. . . 383.1
then winds may b. . . . 526.4
every stormy wind that b. . 573.1
hear the trumpet b. . . 804.3
tempers every wind that b. . c127
heavenly gales are b. . . c221

b
strike . . . a telling b. . . 801.1

blue
so b. and calm and fair . . 103.1
I see the b. above it . . 358.3
heaven above is softer b. . 545.2
b., . . . holy living . . . 777.3
heavenly b. suggests . . 783.4
the land beyond the b. . . 902.c
God's b. sky o'erhead . . c238

b *yellow, red and blue*
r. and b. and y. gleaming . 777.4
'neath the y., r. and b. . . 778.*
y. star and r. and b. . 779.c,2
the y., r. and b. . . 781.1
with its y. r. and b. . . 783.1
follow the y., r. and b. . . c228
flag, of the y., r. and b. . . c230
'neath the y., r. and b. . . c237
the y., r. and b. shall fly. . c240
beneath the y., r. and b. . c241

blush *(Ezra 9:6)*
whene'er I b., be this . . 592.2
or b. to speak his name . . 678.1

board 7.2

boast-ed-ing
thy victory, b. grave . . 143.4
where's all his b. pomp and show 157.3
the tribes of Adam b. . . 160.4
we b. no battle ever won . 163.1
the angels Heaven can b. . 177.3
let others b. of heaps . . 356.2
of which I once did b. . . 435.2
of greater love can b. . . 515.3
nor is the b. vain . . . 592.4
let not thy people b. . . 648.2

b *Ps 34:2*
his deliverance I will b. . . 21.2
soul shall make her b. . . 468.4

in Christ alone I'll b. . . 521.3
I'll b. the Saviour slain . . 592.4
'tis in him we b. . . . 803.4

c *Eph 2:9*
forbid . . . I should b. . . 136.2
I have no room to b. . . 468.4
we dare not b., O Lord . . 747.2

boat 848.3

body
1 *divine*
where thy b. lay . . . 152.1
we hail thy b. glorified . . 154.3
still his dazzling b. bears . 161.3

2 *human*
vigorous when the b. dies . 214.1
our b. may far off remove . 659.1
tryst that the b. must keep . 739.2
blight . . . their b. maim . . 789.4
gifts . . . of b., intellect . . 871.1

b *Matt 10:28*
the b. they may kill . . 1.4

c *Rom 8:11*
will raise our b. too . . 149.3

d *Rom 12:1*
I now present my b. . . 482.3

e *2 Cor 5:6*
here in the b. pent . . . 877.1

f *Eph 4:4*
all one b. we 690.3

g *1 Thess 5:23*
soul and b., thine to be . . 128.2
sanctify all my b., mind . . 188.2
soul and b. consecrating . 197.1
holiness of b., mind and . 204.3
give thee my b., mind and . 221.2
soul and b. . . . image bear . 370.2
my soul and b. bless . . 431.1
giving now my soul and b. . 470.3
now we lay soul and b. . . 481.2
my soul and b.' powers . . 492.2
take my b., spirit, soul . . 497.1
as I give thee soul and b. . 510.4
my b., soul . . . I give . . 511.1
we bring, b. soul and spirit . 532.1
consecration, b., mind and . 788.3

bold
b. shall I stand . . . 116.2
with actions b. and meek . 212.1
b. I touch thy . . . garment . 520.3
b. to take up 596.2
those martyrs b. and daring . 686.1
to meet the b. tempter . . 689.1
all be warriors b. . . . 829.3
in service b., in action . . 861.3
faithful, true and b. . . 876.3
b. they lifted high . . . 939.2

b *make bold*
need that m. us b. . . . 198.5
faith m. us b. . . . 763.3
success and joy to m. me b. . 860.4

c *Heb 4:16*
b. I approach . . . throne . 283.4
b. will I kneel . . . throne . 303.3
thou canst not be too b. . 560.2

d *1 John 4:17*
b. shall I stand . . . 116.2
b. shall they appear . . 372.3

bolder 298.5

boldly
all our foes we b. dare . . 722.4
b. trusted God's . . . word . 760.4
we'll b. march along . . 775.2
for Jesus b. stand . . . 810.2
renew it b. every day . . 812.2
our colours b. show . . 821.c

I may walk b. all my days . 867.3
b. have stood in . . . fire. . 910.4
that we may follow b. . . 944.2
if the cross we b. bear . . c233
b. the heroes tread . . c238

boldness
if you want b. 427.3
mark for pureness and for b. . 531.2

bond
1 *(fault)*
strong were the b. of fault . 176.1
break our b. . . . . release. . 185.2
burst every b. 419.3
O burst these b. 453.1
there are no b. for me . . 485.4
b., so long enchaining . . 539.2
every b. is riven . . . 546.2
b *1 Cor 12:13*
rich and poor, for b. and . 261.3
2 *(love)*
happy b. that seals . . 365.2
in a b. nor life . . . break. . 534.3
in b. of love eternal . . 781.3

bondage *Rom 8:15**
in Satan's b. held . . . 81.2
from sin's b. to reclaim . . 114.1
are you in b. 257.1
can this sore b. break . . 297.5
out of my b., sorrow . . 300.1
throwing off the b. . . 693.3
the slaves of sinful b. . . 776.2
b *(free from) bondage*
free from this terrible b. . . 459.1
your b. is freedom . . . 506.2
Now I am from b. freed . . 546.2
from all the b. . . . free . . 608.3
no longer in b., my freedom . 640.3
free from the b. and power . c157

bondsmen 130.1

bondslaves 233.1

book
shine thou on the b. . . 193.3
tells of his love in the b. . 323.1
in thy b. revealed I see . . 650.3
unseal the sacred b. . . 651.2
holy Bible, b. divine . 652.1, 4
the b. says: Whosoever . . 824.3
all about the dear old b. . . 829.1
for your holy b. we thank . 856.*
the b. of thy Kingdom . . 883.*

boon 208.4

borders 910.1

bore see *bear*

born
1 *general*
b. of this conviction . . . 6.2
b. of the one light . . . 35.3
good be b. 41.2
though b. of the dust . . 288.2
first-b. light . . . decline . . 545.3
no earth-b. cloud arise . . 676.1
b *born [again]* *John 3:3*
repent, believe, be b. a. . . 275.3
b. anew, a ransomed child . 550.2
precious soul is b. a. . . 550.3
chronicles of twice-b. men . 774.2
there I was b. a. . . . 946.4
witness that I'm b. a. . . c173
day when I was b. a. . . c175
c *born of God* *John 1:13*
I am b. of God . 106.4; c129
and I was b. of God . . 361.2
d *born of Spirit* *John 3:8*
b. of his S., washed . . 310.1
b. of the S. with life . . 371.2
e *(Gal 4:26)*
the land of the free-b. . . 895.1
2 *divine* *Isa 9:6*
a child this day is b. . . 72.1
King . . . was b. . . . 72.c
this day your Lord is b. . . 72.4
Christ is b.! their choirs . . 73.1
Saviour of the world was b. . 78.1
this day is b. a Saviour . . 78.2
b. to set thy people free. . 79.1
b. . . . to deliver . . . reign . 79.3
glory to the new-b. King . 82.1.c
Christ is b. in Bethlehem . 82.1
b. that man . . . b. to give . 82.3
b. the King of angels . . 85.1
b. this happy morning . . 85.3
Christ is b. of Mary . . 86.2
be b. in us today . . . 86.4
b. for us on earth below. . 88.1
Christ is b. in Bethlehem . 88.c
b. is the King of Israel . . 90.c
is b., of David's line . . 93.3
in a stable b. our brother . 97.1
when Jesus was b. . . 137.1
a Saviour was b. to save 137.1, c
Christ was b. across the. . 162.4
b. in a manger, so rude . . 175.1
a boy was b. in Bethlehem . 855.1
new-born

borne see *bear*

borrow
what language shall I b. . . 123.3
heart restores its b. ray . . 621.2
it gives, but b. none . . 657.2

bosom
1 *divine* *John 13:23*
with a glory in his b. . . 162.4
on thy b. it has leant . . 508.3
on thy b. reclined . . . 639.1
let me to thy b. fly . . . 737.1
on Jesus' b. . . . calm . . 752.3
fold them to my b. . . . 797.2
b *John 1:18*
from the Father's b. came . 116.3
opened his b. to pour out . 298.7
2 *other*
a longing fills my b. . . . 94.1
upon her b., could he see . 103.1
and every b. swell . . . 164.5

both
b. warmth and light . . . 2.3
to b. great and small . . . 8.3
continued b. day and night . 90.2
did b. stop and stay . . 90.4
b. the rich and the poor . . 170.1
lands b. near and far . . 172.6
stand b. pure and free . . 176.1
hinder . . . b. will engage . 233.2
b. to save and sanctify . . 479.3
b. instant and constant . . 527.3
dark and light are b. . . 674.3
b. earth and hell assail . . 809.2
meet b. east and west . . 826.4
I am b. weak and sinful . . 840.1
b. to work and pray . . 869.1
with b. work and war . . 933.3
proclaim b. loud and long . 940.2

bottomless 746.2

bough 155.2

bought
a *1 Cor 6:20*
he has b. with a price . . 322.1
he has b. for us salvation . 381.2
he b. me everlasting life . . 402.3
what a price my pardon b. . 503.2
Jesus, thou hast b. us . . 707.3
thou hast b. us, thine . . 845.1
for Christ who b. me . . c229
b *pleasure bought*
earth's p. . . . dearly b. . . 267.2
p. sought, dearly b. . . 379.1
blood (1f) *buy*

bound
1 *(noun)*
beyond the farthest b. . . 27.1
tell to earth's remotest b. . 43.2
his spirit, with a b. . . . 890.3
2 *(verb)*
a see *bind*
b *bound for*
I'm a soldier b. f. Glory . . 338.1
I'm b. f. Canaan's shore. . 375.c
b. f. the promised land . . 887.c
we're b. f. the land . . 905.1
c *bound to*
I'm b. to meet you . . . 312.4
in thy strength I'm b. . . 477.4
we're b. to win the day . . 782.2

bounding (adj) 362.2

boundary
the b. of endless space . . 52.c
his power no b. known . . 579.3

boundless
thou b. power, thou God . 146.3
b. as ocean tide . . . 224.4
b. as the . . . . . . 230.*
b. ocean, I would cast . . 439.1
from thine own b. store . . 646.4
blessings from thy b. store . 676.5
b *boundless cleansing*
b. c. to provide . . . 126.1
b. c. from all sin's . . . 230.3
c *boundless grace*
with b. stores of g. . . 58.3
b. is the g. to save us . . 230.4
what b. g., what . . . love . 253.2
g. of God so strong and b. . 295.4
thy g. is b. in its store . . 741.2
b. the g. that keeps me . . c152
d *boundless love*
God's l. is as b. and free . 47.2
is the b. l. of God . . . 52.c
passing understanding . . . b. l. 52.3
in his b. l. and mercy . . 180.2
vast, unmeasured, b., free . 182.1
b. l., unmeasured mercy . 225.4
is the b. l. of Jesus . . 230.1
of l., a b. store . . . 311.1
b. and free as the ocean. . 383.2
O his matchless, b. l. . . 418.c
b. compassion of God . . 527.1
with b. charity divine . . 720.5
his b. l. proclaim . . . 880.4
l. so b. and free . . . c184
e *boundless mercy*
thy b. m. yearn to save . . 135.4
b. m., making . . . whole . 230.1
streams of b. m. flow . . 261.4
his b. m. will provide . . 718.3
mercy, free, b. m. cries . . 746.2
f *boundless salvation*
is the b., full s. . . . 230.3
O b. s.! deep ocean . . 298.1
this sea of b. s. . . . 298.7
b. s. is coming to me . . 543.3

bounteous
O may this b. God . . . 12.2
thy b. grace hath given . . 667.4
has daily been thy b. hand . 933.2
thy b. hand confessing . . 934.2

bountiful *(Ps 145:17) (MR)*
thy b. care what tongue . . 16.4
flowing b. and free . . 40.1
wealth of God, more b. . . 796.2
to our b. Father above . . 900.3

bounty
Lord of all b. 506.4
freely by thy b. . . . 921.2

bow
1 *[God] bows*
in sorrow b. beneath . . 855.4
b *bow head* *John 19:30*
b. his sacred h. and dies . . 107.4
behold, he b. his sacred h. . 108.2
Saviour b. his h. and dies . 125.2
when he b. his h. and died . 128.4
b. thy meek h. . . . 150.5
thou didst b. thy sacred h. . 538.2
2 *[people] bow*
b. in humble adoration . . 37.4
on one b. in shame . . 129.3
I b. and bless . . . name . . 223.1
to him, thy Saviour b. . . 255.1
with broken heart I b. . . 282.1
b. down beneath . . . sin . 284.3
and b. me to the rod . . 305.1
all our souls we b. . . . 424.4
at thy footstool b. . . . 440.1
my will shall b. . . . 446.3
as I b. to thy command . . 463.2
in love my soul would b. . 524.1
while here to thee we b.. . 626.1
at thy throne we b. . . 638.2
all in penitence may b. . . 638.3
they b. their necks . . . 701.3
when your heart is b. . . 759.1
O God . . . to thee we b. . 947.1
while I b. I pray to thee . . c33
at the cross helpless I b.. . c68
b *bow at feet*
at thy f. they . . . b. . . 175.3
f. in reverence b. . . . 185.4
at his f. lowly b. . . . 248.3
come and b. at . . . f. . . 278.2
humbly at his f. I b. . . 474.2
for pardon, at thy f. I b.. . 727.2
at thy f. I b. adoring . . c35
c *bow before*
b. . . . throne, . . . b. . . 4.1
moon b. down b. him . . 17.4
b. b. the child . . . 74.2
b. down b. him . . 183.1, 5
b. your soul b. . . . 242.5
Lord, we b. b. thee . . 576.3
as we b. b. thee . . . 643.c
b. b. his face 835.3
d *bow [knee]* *Phil 2:10*
at the name of Jesus b.. . 66.4
every knee shall b. . . . 141.1
every knee to him shall b. . 147.1
b. to his command, and fall . 164.4
which all knees shall b. . . 174.4
the ransomed nations b. . 223.3
supplicant, I b. the knee . 613.2
humbly (b)

bower
where Eden's b. bloom . . 725.2
to bloom in native b. . . 838.2

boy-s
b. and girl, and friend . . 544.4
noble army, men and b. . . 701.4
bring their baby b.(girl) . . 795.1
a b. was born in Bethlehem . 855.1
a b. grew up in Nazareth . 855.2

brain
from beast to b. of man . . 38.3
b. and troubled breast . . 669.2

branch-ing
b. willows watch . . . 39.3
b *Matt 13:32*
spread their b. far . . . 159.4
c *Matt 21:8*
waving a b. of the palm . . 848.4
d *John 15:4*
as the b. from the vine . . c176

brandished 701.3

brands *Zech 3:2*
quench the b. in . . . blood . 720.2
plucked as b. from burning . 803.3

brass
a *Isa 45:2**
gates of b. . . . burst . . 81.2
b *1 Cor 13:1*
nought but sounding b. . . 530.1

brave
1 *verb*
dangers b., sinners saving . 819.c
b. sin's hostility . . . 939.2
2 *(adjective)*
so our b. forefathers sang . 158.1
Salvation Army so b. . . 321.3
I would be b. 491.1
bound b. hearts together . 593.2
harmless, patient and b. . 623.3
courageous and b. . . 679.3
stand like the b. . 684.c; 689*
our soldiers will be b. . . 775.1
foe may be mighty and b. . 820.3
we're an Army b. . . . 821.2
and hearts are b. again . . 876.4
quiet b. endurance . . 948.2
soldier in the Army b. . . c225
be a soldier b. and true . . c228
b.-hearted and true . . c231
b *make brave*
m. our weak hearts . . . b. . 203.4
thine to m. us b. . . . 799.4
when in danger m. me b. . 837.2
m. me true and b. . . . 859.2

braver 704.1

bravely
that b. takes the cross . . 619.3
b. fought till death . . . 686.1
to hoist the colours b. . . 704.c
foot it b., strong or weary . 716.1
b. fight and God will give . 805.1
b. o'er the battlefield . . 817.2
a cross to follow b. . . 868.1
of the battles fought b. . . 893.3
march on b. to victory . . c228

brazen 696.2

bread
there are souls without b. . 527.1
b. that satisfies for ever . . 631.2
O B. from God, I choose . 631.3
b. of our souls . . . 654.2
give us the b. eternal . . 934.2
b *[daily] bread* *Matt 6:11*
give me, Lord, my daily b. . 566.1
learn to trust for our b. . . 763.2
give us . . . our daily b. . . 918.3
milling for daily b. . . . 927.2
dost give us earthly b. . . 934.2
he gives our daily b. . . 935.2
c *Matt 14:19*
offered Christ their b. . . . 5.1
d *Luke 22:19*
Christ's broken b. . . . 512.1
in the breaking of b. . . 631.4
e *bread of life* *John 6:35*
b. of l. my soul to feed . . 342.3
hungering for the b. of l. . 626.2
break thou the b. of l. . . 650.1
thou art the b. of l. . . 650.2
f *bread of Heaven* *John 6:41*
feed me with the b. of H. . 531.4
b. of H., feed me . . . 578.1
thou art the b. of H. . . 631.1
g *living bread* *John 6:51*
still break . . . the l. b. . . 129.3
portions of the l. b. . . 277.2

breadth *Eph 3:18* . . 55.1, 3

break-ing-broken
b. in blessings . . . 29.3
. . . b. by thy suffering . . 122.4
nor Heaven nor earth can b. . 171.2
b. with thine iron rod . . 172.1
best resolves I only b. . . 291.3
love . . . b. my hard heart . 331.3
b. forth from . . . mountain . 350.2
I b. his laws 380.2
cannot b. the firm decree . 407.4
thraldom of evil is b. . . 410.3
b. like the thunder . . . 529.3
nor life nor death shall b. . 534.3
love that b. through . . 544.5
b. my selfish pride . . . 605.1
b. in him whose life . . 631.1
thou didst b. the loaves . . 650.1
glory b. upon my view . . 657.4
chords that were b. . . 691.3
b. the tempter's spell . . 693.1
loveliness b. on my sight . 719.4
b. me, melt me . . . c53
b. a light divine . . . c191
b. my heart, won my heart . c209
b *break [chains]*
b. the power of . . . sin . . 64.4
calls you, b. your chains . 75.4
b. the chains of death . . 149.1
b. our bonds . . . release . 185.2
Lion . . . b. every chain . . 233.c
can this sore bondage b. . 297.5
b. the chains . . . captivity . 353.5
b. every earthly fetter . . 894.2
c *break down*
b. every barrier d. . . . 293.6
b. d. every idol . . . 436.1
b. the barriers d. . . . 749.1
d *[day] break*
morning has b. . . . 35.1
at the b. of the day . . 611.1
pray, until the b. of day . . c76
e *Song 2.17*
Heaven's morning b. . . 670.5
b. . . . more glorious day . 876.5
b. on the golden shore . . 889.3
the dawn of Heaven b. . . 896.1
morning b., eternal . . 907.1
f *Isa 42:3*
nor . . . b. the bruisèd reed . 269.2
g *John 10:35*
whose word cannot be b. . 157.1
bread (d-g), break (2), fetter (c)

breaker
when the b. roar . . . 280.2
on the b. tossed . . . 375.1
and the fearful b. roar . . 598.3

breast
1 *human*
with sweetness fills my b. . 61.1
into this my longing b. . . 201.c
consecrate my b. . . . 207.1
within our hallowed b. . . 210.2
take possession of my b. . 214.3
without rest, in my b. . . 379.3

seal thou my b. 424.2
drove thee from my b. . . 442.4
for ever seal my b. . . . 450.2
pure love within my b. . . 480.5
calm within my b. abide . 551.2
take possession of my b. . 563.4
that trembles in the b. . . 625.1
loves fills every b. . . . 661.1
his zeal inspired their b. . 879.4
troubled (b)

2 *divine*
to the Father's b. . . . 141.4
force me to thy b. . . . 307.1
thy head upon my b. . . 332.1
sure haven of his b. . . 333.3
tears . . . dried on his b.. . 364.3
rise to be hid in thy b. . . 639.3
my home safe in thy b. . . 675.3
safe on his gentle b. . . 889.1

b *Saviour's breast*
for ever on my S.' b. . . 676.2
I look into my S.'s b. . . 746.3
on the loving S.'s b. . . 829.1
confusion to Jesus's b. . . c94
lean

breath
1 *breath [of God]*
breathe on me, B. of God . 189.*
breathe . . . O B. divine . . 211.3
send . . . thy quickening b. . 669.5
keen B. of Heaven . . . 827.2

2 *[other]*
with every fleeting b. . . 58.5
the b. of man bestow . . 171.2
soft as the b. of even . . 200.5
draw this fleeting b. . . 302.4
newborn soul found b. . . 343.1
while I've b. I mean . . 356.1
long as thou lendest me b. . 357.3
the Christian's vital b. . . 625.5
they, with united b. . . 879.3

b *Ps 150:6*
all that hath life and b. . . 19.5
latest

breathe
1 *[God] breathes*
b. on me, Breath of God . 189.*
b. into the music . . . 193.1
one soul, one feeling b. . . 196.3
ere he b. . . . farewell . . 200.1
b. in our souls, O Breath . 211.3
b. into us the life . . . 218.3
in thy mercy b. upon me 477.1, c
b. within my life . . . 479.2
b. through the heats . . 567.5
b. forgiveness o'er us . . 607.2
voice that b. o'er Eden . . 949.1

b *breathe Spirit* *John 20:22*
S., b. from above . . . 545.1
b. the Holy S. . . . 599.2
S. b. upon the word . . 657.1

2 *[we] breathe*
b. that holy name . . . 66.2
as the air we b. as free . . 230.3
b. out in faith . . . sigh . . 589.5
only b. to b. thy love . . 720.3
song that they b. . . . 886.2

3 *other*
it b. in the air 16.4
upon my cheeks are b. . . 39.3
b. each day nearness . . 632.2
sighing nor anguish can b. . 905.2

breathing (noun)
still with softest b. stir . . 202.4
at the b. of thy will . . 839.4

breeze
and feel the gentle b. . . 37.2
heavenly b. are blowing . . 383.1
unfurled by every b. . . 779.1
in the b. . . . streaming . . 783.1
singing coming on the b. . 803.1
banners unfurled to the b. . 808.5
banners unfurled to the b. . 820.4
winter's chilling b. . . . 930.2
the b. and the sunshine . . 935.1
catch the heavenly b. . . c116

brethren
b., come; from all . . . 73.2
our b. shield 569.4
is waking our b. . . . 677.4

bride *Rev 21:2*
hark! the b. and Spirit . . 261.3
with Christ's own b. . . 949.4

brief
life seem as b. as blest . . 551.3
the b. hours are not lost. . 564.4
b. is our journey . . . 874.1

bright
1 *(adjective)*
fire so masterful and b. . . 2.3
all things b. and beautiful . 25.c
treasures up his b. designs . 29.2
ways through mornings b. . 31.3
b. hope for tomorrow . . 33.3
O b. eternal One . . . 36.1
b. with hope is burning . . 73.3
stars in the b. sky . . . 77.1
all is calm, all is b. . . . 89.1
once was b. as morn . . 123.1
hold the vision b. . . . 154.4
b. and beautiful for thee . 205.1
his b. rays come beaming . 316.2
all thy days be b. . . . 332.3
your heart will be b. . . 373.c
more glorious and b. . . 387.1
with my heart so b. . . 402.1
show . . . and all is b. . . 498.4
moments calm and b. . . 602.4
b. with thy praise . . . 617.4
for such a b. display . . 657.3
the b. and better part . . 664.3
shield and banner b. . . 698.2
their b. faces glow . . . 703.4
safe in the b. day . . . 724.3
b. skies will soon be o'er . 736.3
we expect a b. tomorrow . 764.3
if all were b. 773.2
b. emblem of salvation . . 781.1
b. days shall dawn . . . 802.4
in b., happy homes . . . 807.3
weapons sharp and b. . . 809.2
with shield and banner b. . 818.1
sad ones or b. ones . . 848.5
all the b. ones 852.2
with b., unclouded eyes . . 855.5
written in b. letters . . 883.2
painful, dark or b. . . . 917.2
b. robes of gold . . . 934.1
all things b. and good . . 935.3
when . . . skies are b. . . 947.2

b *bright path-way*
b. sunshine . . . p. gild . . 277.1
makes my p. b. 379.4
a p., though thorny, b. . . 465.5
guide . . . make his p. b. . 658.3
O how b. the p. grows . . 768.2
makes your daily p. b. . . 790.3

c *bright [angels]*
voices of the angels b. . . 80.2
ye b. angelic spirits . . 109.3
angels in b. raiment . . 152.1
angels with b. wings . . 268.1
angels b. wear crowns . . 872.c
b. angel feet have trod . . 891.1
with angels b. and fair . . 895.2
b. angels whisper . . . 911.5

d *bright [re Heaven]*
death with thee is b. . . 40.4
in the heavenly country b. . 76.5
the crystal b. fountain . . 139.2
in sparkling raiment b. . . 167.1
its waters gleam b. . . . 252.1
where its b. waves roll . . 252.2
world . . . O so b. . . . 268.1
and the harbour b. . . . 280.4
the robes b. and shining . 406.3
where the heaven is b. . . 682.3
b. and sunny regions . . 686.2
like crystal b. shall be . . 726.4
his b. crown . . . b. gems . 852.c
the b. and pearly gates . . 872.3
saints . . . in b. array . . 876.5
b. inheritance of saints . . 877.2
how b. their glories be . . 879.1
that b. home far away . 881.c, 2
that b. . . . rapturous scene . 887.2
mansions b. and blessed . 892.1
saints . . . b., b. as day . . 897.1
b. in that happy land . . 897.3
b. above the sun reign . . 897.3
mansions b., . . . harps . . 902.1
the hills of b. Glory . . 905.4
b. and cloudless morning . 907.2
b. crowns laid up . . . 912.c

e *bright and fair*
with flowers b. and f. . . 658.1
the city b. and f. . . . 663.3
peaceful, b. and f. . . 872.1, 3
land, so b. and f. . . . 873.1
happy, glorious, b. and f. . 881.c
with angels b. and f. . . 895.2
the streets are b. and f. . . 901.3
country so b. and so f. . . 904.1
eternal, b. and f. . . . 907.1

armour, morning (2), reality, star (f), sunshine (2)

2 *bright-ly (adverb)*
leading onward, beaming b. . 76.1
b. burning . . . Fire . . 206.1
its waters gleam b. . . . 252.1
light shining clear and b. . 260.1
b. shining as the sun . . 308.4
b. beams . . . mercy . . 478.1
b. doth his Spirit shine . . 754.2
flame that burneth b. . . 838.1
mercies new . . . b. shine . 938.2

brighten-ing
that b. up the sky . . . 25.2
he b. our way 316.1
b. my path, so only . . 628.1
b. all the path we tread . . 765.3
will always others b. . . 805.2
b. earthly sorrow . . . 948.3

brighter
Jesus shines b. 177.3
b. than the morning star . 185.3
way grows b. every day. . 340.3
somebody's life . . . b. . . 384.c
b. than the morning star . 516.4
my way has b. grown . . 549.c
its day may b., fairer b. . . 621.2
in b. worlds above . . . 657.4
light . . . shines the b. . . 758.4
crown will shine the b. . . 899.1
b. than the noonday sun . 909.1
b. rays may shine . . . 916.2

brightest
spoil my b. days . . . 728.3
sweetest and b. and best . 794.3
b. realms of fadeless day . 888.1

brightness
show thy face in b. . . 155.4
b. fills the holy place . . 268.2
see my Saviour's b. . . 470.1
claims the b. of my youth . 867.5

bring-ing/brought
1 *[God] brings*
b. the knowledge . . . 102.1
all his ransomed home to b. . 118.5
pleading b. grace to me . . 129.c
b. it back victorious . . 141.3
b. us to the . . . land . . 163.3
to b. fire on earth . . . 165.1
from death to life has b.. . 180.4
who didst come to b. . . 224.2
he . . . b. hope again . . 238.2
rose . . . to b. us freedom . 242.c
b. me from the verge . . 330.2
b. me forth to walk . . 330.3
b. to me the living word. . 398.2
fire . . . b. to me liberty . . 420.4
light some pain is b. . . 434.4
Spirit, thou hast b. me . . 504.3
he b. me, and made me . . 535.2
b. me lower 548.3
b. the truth to sight . . 657.1
never b. them up . . . more . 724.c
victories he for us did b.. . 835.2
b. me out of darkness . . c160
b *[Jesus] brings*
Jesus' name b. joy . . 63.1
rich the trophies Jesus b. . 147.2
Jesus, . . . treasure you b. . 175.2
Christ b. from above . . 298.1
Jesus b. me sight of thee . 449.1
Christ b. us . . . homeland . 895.3
the Lord has b. us . . . 915.2
c *love brings*
b. my Saviour from above . 46.c
God's l. b. his Son down 47.2, 3
l. b. me down at . . . feet . 128.2
l. b. him down . . . redeem . 323.2
l. . . . b. me, dear Jesus. . 331.3
l. . . . that b. it down to man. 405.4
it b. the glory to my soul . c170
d *bring joy*
fulness of j. he b. . . . 227.1
I b. thee j. from Heaven . . 229.4
wash away . . . b. thee j. . 253.3
e *bring life* 2 *Tim 1:10**
light and l. to all he b. . . 82.3
immortal l. to b. . . . 149.2
died eternal l. to b. . . 156.2
l. . . . his empire shall b.. . 166.1
our l. and peace to b. . . 411.2
f *bring pardon*
no other name b. p. . . 71.c
I b. thee p., peace . . . 229.4
p. which thy blood has b. . 287.2
that he might p. b. . . 798.1
g *bring peace*
b. p. in endless flow . . 74.2
for wonderful p. he b. . . 227.c
I b. thee pardon, p. . . 229.4
b. holy p. and liberation . . 702.3
h *bring salvation* *Titus 2:11**
thou didst free s. b. . . 109.1
life and s. . . . shall b. . . 166.1
b. near thy great s. . . 167.3
O b. thy free s. nigh . . 291.1
Jesus came . . . to b. me s. . 349.2
who did for me s. b. . . 356.1
he hath b. s. near . . . 370.2
doth to me deliverance b. . 401.1
his arm shall b. s. . . . 819.2
when, his s. b., to Zion . . 853.1
precious blood s. b. . . c30
i *bring back*
b. it b. victorious . . . 141.3
the way to b. me b. . . 305.3
b. to the Father he b. . . 384.2

j *bring in*
b. the glorious fulness in . 46.3
he b. his Kingdom in . . 195.2
b. the light and glory in . . 203.2
let thy Spirit b. me in . . 419.4
b. thy glorious Kingdom in . 692.2
b. the power of God within . 733.6
k *bring nigh* *Isa 46:13**
blood that brings us n. . . 113.3
b. thy soul to Heaven n.. . 269.3
flame once more b. n. . . 440.3
l *(request)*
b. me at last to see . . 59.4
b. our ransomed souls . . 76.4
thy gracious Kingdom b. . 79.3
b. me to thy holy place . . 102.4
b. its scenes before me . . 115.3
b. us safe through Jordan . 152.3
b. again our daylight . . 155.4
b. to every thankful mind . 191.1
b. in the calm . . . 209.1
b. the glorious liberty . . 441.1
b. her bud to . . . flower. . 577.1
b. the vilest 919.2
b. thy final harvest home . 924.4
m *Ps 43:3*
b. me to thy holy hill . . 457.2
fold (c), home (2b), safe (b)
2 *[we] bring*
a *bring [others to God]*
b. the power to others . . 435.3
slaves of sin to b. . . . 499.3
I would b. peace . . . 529.3
such ever b. thee . . . 604.2
to b. men back to . . . way . 680.2
claims . . . will b. . . . 687.2
helpers other lives to b. . . 707.1
b. God's . . . kingdom in . 760.2
b. that day to birth . . 774.4
lost ones to b. . . . 786.4
b. sinners of every kind . . 814.c
we b. the jubilee . . . 815.c
sinners to Jesus shall b.. . 820.1
to his feet we shall b. . . 820.5
the world to Christ we b. . 825.*
we'll b. . . . duties . . . 849.3
hope one day to b. to you . 851.3
b *bring [to God]*
costliest treasures b. . . 76.3
though we b. them . . 183.4
we b. the need that makes . 198.5
I b. thee my cares . . . sins . 288.1
b. my heart/life/sins all to Jesus 420.*
b. my sins/grief/joys/life . 421.*
I b. them . . . all to thee. . 421.1
I b. my whole affection . . 504.1
Lord, to thy feet I b. . . 523.c
some offering b. thee now . 524.1
our allegiance now we b. . 532.1
love must b. its offering. . 591.1
b. a worthier gift . . . 618.3
whate'er I am I b. . . . 631.4
our requests . . . we b. . . 642.1
what can I b. to thee . . 675.2
my help from thee I b. . . 737.2
dearest treasures . . . b.. . 777.4
little child . . . we b. . . 796.1
what shall we children b. . 849.1
child may b. . . . 849.2, 3
to his cause we b. . . . 866.c
while our best we b. thee . 921.1
our labour we b. to serve . 927.2
grateful hearts . . . we b. . 938.1
c *bring all*
I b. my all to Jesus . . 420.4
I b. them . . . all to thee. 421.1, 5
b. thee . . . Jesus, my all . 422.1
Saviour, my all I will b. . . 457.c
all I have I am b. . . . 473.c
I b. thee all my . . .. . 486.*
freely all to Christ I b. . . 514.3
Saviour, my all I'm b. . . 523.1

more than all I do or b. . . 591.2
b. all our talents . . . 833.2
I b. to thee all . . . gifts . . 861.5
b. all thou hast and art . . 864.3
all I b. to thee . . . c34
b *bring care*
come, b. thy sin . . . care . 126.4
all your c., b. . . . leave . . 246.c
I b. thee my c. and my . . 288.1
to thee I b. my c. . . . 421.3
daily b. . . . his daily c. . . 580.1
when we b. our c. to Jesus . 759.3
b. to him my c. . . . c113
e *bring heart*
here b. your wounded h. . 236.1
I b. my h. to Jesus . . . 420.1
my h. to thee I b. . . . 421.2
h., my life, my all I b. . . 421.6
I b. thee all my h. . . . 486.2
I b. to thee my h. to fill . . 489.1
we'll b. him h. that love . . 849.2
grateful h. to thee we b. . 938.1
gladly would we b. h. . . c213
f *bring nothing*
no! no! n. do I b. . . . 292.c
n. in my hand I b. . . . 302.3
g *bring [praise]* *Jer 33:11**
to his feet thy tribute b.. . 17.1
earth their praises b. . . 43.1
b. your sweetest . . . lays . 109.3
b. peculiar honours . . 160.5
Heaven its tribute b. . . 171.1
boundless praises . . . b. . 230.4
to his feet my praises b.. . 343.2
to thee our praise we b.. . 561.1
b. him thankful praise . . 849.2
b. sacrifice of praise . . 934.1
h *bring sin*
b. thy s., thy sorrow . . 126.4
I b. thee the s. . . . 288.1
I b. my s. to Jesus . . . 420.3
I b. my s. to thee . . . 421.1
I b. thee all my s. . . . 486.1
i *Ps 126:6*
b. in the sheaves . . . 930.*
j *Rom 10:6*
b. the Lord Christ down . . 496.3
that cry will b. thee down . 586.3
nothing (h) offering (2b)
k *brought (passive)*
from his own altar b. . . 20.3
he was b. to Pilate . . . 137.3
hither by his help I'm b. . . 338.4
into subjection b. . . . 415.5
we, out of trial b. . . . 466.5
through sleep . . . b. . . 668.1
millions . . . shall be b. . . 776.2
fain I would . . . be b. . . 793.2
sin to full fruition b. . . 885.3
blackest stains b. to light . 893.1
3 *(others) bring*
love song which they b.. . 83.2
eastern wise men b. gifts . 89.2
who is he to whom they b. . 104.3
no other name . . . can b. . 269.3
angels descending, b. . . 310.2
parents . . . b. their baby . 795.1
their children b. to Jesus . 797.1
wise/rich/some/may b. . 849.1
tidings
b *(appeal)*
b. forth the royal diadem . 56.1
b. your wounded hearts . . 236.1
b. him thy burden . . . 248.2
your every burden b. . . 254.4
large petitions with thee b. . 563.2
forts . . . b. them down . . 696.c
b. all thou hast and art . . 864.3
b. an offering to the altar . 920.1
b. your dearest . . . best. . 920.c

bring . . . time/gift/best . 920.2
b. it to Jesus . c31
c *Mal 3:10*
b. your tithes . 920.1
4 *general*
such . . . punishment to b. . 108.1
b. the fire just now . 201.3
every effort b. me nearer . 369.2
if faith but b. the plea . 423.5
darkness b. into my soul . 448.2
rise again to b. you care. . 471.3
the shame my sin has b. . 503.2
my weariness b. pain . 528.2
suffering b. thee victory . 586.2
b. all Heaven . 604.3
b. every blessing . 646.2
each day b. . . . challenge . 666.1
road to b. us daily nearer . 668.4
trust that b. the triumph . 713.3
sins that b. you pain . 806.3
employment b. enjoyment . 869.2
whate'er the future b. . 916.2
b. me nearer to thee . c45
b. sadness to your heart . c139

brink
b. of . . . life-giving flood . 298.5
I on the b. of ruin fell . 380.1
linger, shivering on the b. . 898.2

broad-er *(Eph 3:18)*
b. and deep and glorious . 40.2
b. than the boundaries . 52.c
the love of God is b. . 265.6
fields spread far and b. . 934.4
b *Matt 7:13*
the b. road of folly . 905.1

broadening . 519.4

broken
1 see *break*
2 *(adjective)*
our b. years are mirrored . 131.2
b. peace might be restored . 135.1
across the b. strings . 390.2
Christ's b. bread . 512.1
b. pledges uncovered . 893.1
cisterns
b *broken heart-ed* *Luke 4:18**
blessed are the b. -h. . 95.1
a b. and a contrite h. . 121.6
a b. h. love's dwelling is. . 121.6
b. h. the Lord will favour . 225.3
is there a h. that is b. . 247.2
with b. h. I bow . 282.1
lost, despairing, b. -h. . 369.3
h. that were b. . 383.3
b. h. and blighted hopes . 702.3
for the poor and b. -h. . 824.3
it b. my h., won my h. . c209
bind (1b), heal (1d), Spirit (6c)

brood-ing
thick darkness b. yet . 172.6
the b. of the gentle dove . 202.2
Holy Spirit, who didst b. . 569.3
heart that b. on wrongs . 572.2
b. o'er our nature's night . 651.3

brook
hear the b. . 37.2
b. by the traveller's way. . 654.1
hills, and b. and vales . 887.3
b *(John 18:1)*
beyond the b. his winepress . 512.2

brother
the Father, Christ our b. . 10.3
treat their foes as b. . 50.2
he did for you, my b. . 96.3
in a stable born our b. . 97.1
men as b. shall embrace . 170.3
trim your . . . lamp, my b. . 478.3
feel his b.'s care . 662.1
lightened my b.'s load . 675.2
b., lift your voices . 690.2
b., we are treading . 690.3
courage, b., do not stumble . 716.*
b. clasps the hand of b. . 765.2
join hands then, b. . 826.3
our b. may know thy care . 927.3
into your soul, my b. . c223
b *Prov 18:24*
love beyond a b.'s . 377.1
brethren, sister

brother-ly *Heb 13:1*
b.-love binds man to man . 10.4
and with actions b. . 212.2

brought see *bring*

brow
1 *(divine)*
lest I forget thy . . . b. . 117.1
become the victor's b. . 147.1
the mighty victor's b. . 168.1
glory crowns thy sacred b. . 185.4
diadem . . . his b. adorns . 228.3
have you seen his . . . b. . 243.1
thorns thy b. encircle . 299.2
pierced on his beautiful b. . 331.1
his b. was pierced . 339.3
the thorns on thy b. . 357.2
thorn-crown pressed thy b. . 586.2
b *(general)*
on Calvary's b. . 125.1
soothe the troubled b. . 129.2
cold on my b. . 357.3
glittering crown on my b. . 357.4
wipe from your b. . 564.1

bruised
a *Isa 42:3; Matt 12:20*
break the b. reed . 269.2
b *Luke 4:18*
I was b., and he bound me . 330.2
b. but Jesus healed me . 337.3
c *Rom 16:20*
b. Satan's head . 60.3

buckle . 809.2

bud
b. of Heaven . 28.5
b. may have a bitter taste . 29.5
bring her b. to . . . flower . 577.1

buffet . 771.2

build-t
and b. it up anew . 149.3
they have b. him an altar . 162.2
they're b. a palace for me . 354.4
help us to b. each other. . 662.2
longs to b. thy house . 720.1
b. on nothing less . 745.1
. . . b. in righteousness . 827.1
may b. . . . a Kingdom meet . 827.3
b. a glad new world . 827.4
help to b. the city . 833.2
b. upon God's promise sure . 833.3
the Lord will surely b. . 868.2
hands to b. my city . 868.2
b. a grand tomorrow . 869.2
on him alone we b. . 940.1
we have b. this house . 941.1
this temple, Lord, we b. . 945.1
b *Ps 127:1*
he that without thee b. . 605.2
except you b. the house . 943.2
c *build on rock* *Matt 7:24*
the r. on which I b. . 58.3
b. on the r. . 738.1
d *Ps 104:2, 3*
that which b. the skies . 26.3

builder
b. of sun and the cross . 288.2
the master -b. calleth . 868.2

building (n) *(Psalm 127:1)* . 827.3

bulwark *Isa 26:1* . 1.1

burden
1 *(general)*
b. of the fruitful vine . 512.3
the b. of a sigh . 625.2
b *Gal 6:2, 5*
carry all our b. gladly . 462.3
accepting b. not his own . 801.2
day (2j)
2 *(spiritual)*
the b. nigh o'ercame . 59.1
never a care or b. . 186.3
your b. shares . 238.c
place to leave your b. . 246.2
come with thy b. today . 247.1
bring him thy b. . 248.2
your every b. bring . 254.4
tell the b. of thy heart . 261.1
makes each b. light . 320.2
then my b. took from me . 379.c
though my b. pressed me . 391.2
my cross a b. deem . 400.1
from me my b. did roll . 467.3
losing b. that need never . 471.3
life's b. they are easy . 503.1
with my b. I begin . 563.3
as our b. grow greater . 579.1
come with b., joy . 595.1
he taketh my b. away . 710.2
it will your b. lighten . 805.2
dost all our b. share . 827.4
you've carried your b. . c31
though . . . b. distress us . c122
sadness . . . and b., too. . c139
b *Ps 38:4*
the b. is too great for me . 421.1
c *cast burden* *Ps 55:22*
on him your b. c. . 236.3
c. my b. on the Saviour . c166
d *burden (of sin)*
saved from the b. of sin. . 166.4
free from your b. of sin . 281.1
lifted sin's great b. . 386.2
e *(lay) burden (down)*
lay thy b. of carefulness. . 183.2
next to lay every b. . 278.2
I laid my b. down . 366.2
sinners, lay your b. down . 369.3
till I have laid my b. . 551.3
lay we every b. down . 891.3
f *Gal 6:2*
nor of b. hard to bear . 320.2
not a b. we bear . 397.3
some . . . bear heavy b. . 576.2
our mutual b. bear . 660.3
each the other's b. share . 663.3
hasten their b. to share . 679.2
life's heaviest b. bears . 733.3
we bear the b. of the day . 934.3
bear (1b), every (a), heavy (b), lift (1b), light (8b), roll (2d)

burdened
b. with sorrow . 257.1
load of sin that b. me . 340.3
are you ever b. . 396.2
b. by my guilt . 403.1
ye heart -b. ones . 905.2
b *burdened souls*
thou callest b. s. to thee . 284.2

sins which have b. my s. . 288.1
when my s. was b. . . 348.1
my b. s. found liberty . . 405.c
till each sin-b. s. knows . . 708.3
b. s., . . . humbly kneeling . 802.3

burdening *(adj)* 947.4

burn-ing
1 *[God] burns*
b. all my dross and sin . . 201.4
Christ of b., cleansing . . 203.1
to b. up every trace . . 203.2
b. out every . . . thought . 205.2
b., brightly/deeply/gently . 206.*
the fire doth surely b. . . 415.4
b. in me, . . . overthrowing . 448.4
a holy fire to b. within . . 541.2
b *Isa 4:4*
always b., Holy Spirit . . 206.c
come, thou b. Spirit . . 481.1
2 *[we] burn*
flame b. where'er I go . . 447.3
let the lower lights be b.. . 478.c
b. love is my need . . . 527.c
ablaze with holy b. . . 529.2
thy b. charity . . . 594.1
deep, b. love for souls . 649.1, c
oft thy light b. low . . . 723.2
b. strains are telling . . 802.1
flame that b. bright . . 838.1
like a little candle b. . . 841.1
b *Lev 6:9*
let it for thy glory b. . . 199.2
3 *(other)*
b. sun with golden beam . 2.1
bright with hope is b. . . 73.3
b. . . . glorious . . . star . . 80.3
desires which in thee b. . . 256.1
fast fell the b. tears . . 326.2
may bear the b. bliss . . 414.2
b. of the noontide heat . . 476.1
b. the fiery pillar . . . 682.1
b. the guiding light . . 765.2
the lamp was b. dim . . 839.1
can't stop fire from b. . . 854.2
remorse and vain desire b. . 885.3
b *Amos 4:11*
plucked as brands from b. . 803.3

burnished 905.3

burst
1 *[God] burst*
gates . . . before him b. . . 81.2
he b. them asunder for me . 137.4
Christ hath b. the gates . . 143.3
had Christ . . . ne'er b. . . 153.c
might b. e'en the grave . . 532.4
b *Nah 1:13*
b. every bond . . . 419.3
O b. these bonds . . . 453.1
2 *(other)*
heart b. forth to sing . . 39.c
those b. of acclamation . . 147.4
. . . b. on our vision . . 173.2
visions of rapture b. . . 310.2
joy -b. of singing . . . 724.2
b. from the furrowed soil . 923.2

bury-ied
who was b. in the tomb. . 96.4
rise, O b. Lord . . . 155.3
the gift of b. grain . . . 512.3
feelings lie b. . . . 691.3
deep b. in the earth . . 923.2
b., he carried my sins . . c185

bus 544.1

business
room for b. 241.2
b *(Luke 2:49)*
all my b. here below . . 60.5
my sole b. be thy praise. . 516.5

busy
far past my b. hands . . 416.3
life's b. mart 664.3
b. my hands this day . . 675.1

but nc, but
a *all but*
emptied . . . of a. b. love . 283.2
ever closed to a. b. thee. . 424.2
a. b. thee far hidden . . 647.2
none nothing

buy
which riches cannot b. . . 277.2
wealth can never b. them . 555.4
bought

by and by
meet him b. and b. . . 94.*
b. and b. he'll call me . . 352.3
home in Heaven b. and b. . 354.2
victory's coming b. and b. . 810.*
in the sweet b. and b. . . 900.c
b. and b. we'll strike . . 903.3
b. and b. the harvest . . 930.2
sweet, sweet b. and b. . . c237

bygone 91.3

byway
called me from the b. . . 463.1
thank you, too, for b. . . 552.2
highways, in the b. . . 832.c

C

cable
Lord of c., Lord of rail . . 30.2
when . . . the c. strain . . 280.1

call-ed-ing
1 *[God] calls*
c. order and delight . . 36.1
heavenly bells . . . are c. . 39.4
mercy c. you 75.4
ungrateful . . . slight thy c. . 114.3
mercy's tender c. rings . . 131.4
still he doth c. today . . 139.2
c. from . . . mountain . . 139.2
who . . . c. to sacrifice . . 204.2
who . . . c. to holiness . . 204.3
as in grace he c. again . . 241.3
he c. aloud to thee . . 260.2
would not hearken . . . c. . 286.2
I hear the loud c. . . . 298.6
others thou art c. . . 301.1, c
c. me still to seek . . . 307.2
mercy . . . c. for song . . 313.1
c. me, long before . . . 339.2
out of my darkness he c. . 378.*
heard him gently c. . . 391.1
still he c. 428.4
c. me from the byway . . 463.1
rise when thou dost c. . . 510.1
who c. forth our love . . 533.2
c. to thy service . . . 543.2
he c. me closer to him . . 549.2
the promise c. me near . . 560.1
c. into thy fold of peace. . 630.2
c. me to seek thy face . . 636.4
to c. me when I rove . . 652.2
when . . . I c. thee to go. . 653.3
follow thou me, he c. . . 680.c
making the Master's c. . . 680.2
c. to men . . . self-same way. 680.3
great God who c. you . . 703.2
heights . . . are ever c. . . 711.2
thine is the c. . . . 744.4
listening . . . Spirit's c. . . 757.4
when he c. us, why delay . 772.4
where he c. us, . . . go . . 772.5
how he c. little children . . 794.1
sound a nobler c. . . . 827.2
c. upon us in our youth . . 863.1
the master-builder c. . . 868.2
heed the c. today . . . 869.2
c. you now from Calvary . 885.4
who for help dost c. . . 921.1
c. me by my own name . . c6
his service c. us . . . c239
b *God calls*
out of my darkness G. c. . 378.1
each morning anew G. c. . 666.4
when thou art c. of G. . . 816.1
c *Jesus/Saviour calls*
hark! the voice of J. c. . . 240.1
still the S. c. to thee . . 240.2
J. is tenderly c. . . . 248.*
sweetly echo the S.'s c.. . 258.3
tenderly J. is c. . . . 264.1, c
what is the c. of J. . . 276.2
still J. c. me on . . . 423.3
J. c. us 428.1, 3, 5
when J. from Calvary c. . 553.1
obey when J. c. . . . 575.2
J. is c. you and me . . 680.c
J. c. for men of war . . 686.4
summon all, at J.' c. . . 693.c
J. c. us to . . . peace . . 752.7
work till J. c. . . . . 818.*
our S. c. all to him . . . 831.2
J. is c., c. me c6
while the S. now is c. . . c8
J. is c., open . . . wide . . c15
d *John 11:28*
S. is c., is c. for thee . . 263.c
Jesus is c., is c. . . . 273.c
my King's . . . c. for me. . 684.1
e *[obey] call*
obedient to thy c. . . . 108.3
fain would now o. the c. . 307.3
daily I o. his c. . . . 399.1
obedient to thy . . . c. . . 422.1
surrender all to o. thy c.. . 482.c
all in obedience to thy c. . 532.1
his c. we o. like Abraham . 763.3
saints of old o. the c. . . 789.5
as I o. the c. c33
f *call [to heaven]*
when thou comest and c. . 101.c
fighting till he c. me . . 330.3
by and by he'll c. me . . 352.3
c. us, O Lord, to . . . peace . 674.4
until the Master c. . . . 703.c
c. to go from the ranks . . 894.c
home (2d)
g *John 15:15*
who hast c. me friend . . 675.3
answer (2b), hear (2c), today (b), voice (1b)
2 *[we] call*
a *(to God)*
Holy Ghost, for thee we're c. 213.2
answered our pitiful c. . . 245.2
will answer when we c.. . 270.c
loving . . . when sinners c. . 296.4
to thee for help I c. . . 489.1
for thy blessing c. . . . 622.1
if in danger, for him c. . . 754.3
b *(to others)*
on all the world to c. . . 62.5
sent . . . on you I c. . . 234.2
we will every nation c. . . 243.4
a voice to c. men . . . 706.3
we'll send the c. . . . 802.3
I c. to arms the soldiers . . 830.2
this is the Army's c. . . c226
c *call [to mean 'name']*
I joy to c. thee mine . . 123.2
we should c. him Lord . . 141.1
I c. this Saviour mine . . 297.6
naught . . . my own I c.. . 345.2
Christ, what shall I c. . . 346.5
c. him my Saviour . . . 388.4
c. the path of duty . . . 462.1
path that we c. duty . . 462.2
little strength to c. . . . 489.3
d *Acts 2:21; Rom 10:13*
as on Jesus we c. . . . 637.4
on the Saviour c. . . . 693.3
my soul has c. upon thee . 762.2
e *called (passive)*
c. and commissioned . . 163.2
cross . . . you are c. . . 396.2
c. by thy great name . . 516.5
c. to thy service . . . 543.2
c. by thee to fight . . . 692.2
youth is c. upon . . . 869.2
c. to go from the ranks . . 894.c
f *Matt 5:9*
his children shall be c. . . 95.2
hear (1b), name (1i), save (1k)
3 *(others)* call
a *(people)*
who from his altar c. . . 56.4
on thee I'll c. 226.1
you may c. in vain . . . 241.3
for pardon c. 269.2
thy grace for every c. . . 561.3
on the Saviour c. . . . 693.3
hears his father c. . . . 740.3
those I love . . . are c. . . 895.3
souls . . . yet are c. . . 922.1
b *(general)*
bird and . . . fountain c.. . 10.2
never c. retreat . . . 162.3
c. me from a world . . 633.1
deep is c. unto deep . . 641.1
voices of evening c. . . 675.1
where duty c. 699.3
it c. to deeds of valour . . 781.2
the roll is c. up yonder . . 907.*
dear old drum . . . c. . . c230
clarion, trumpet

calling *(noun)* *(Eph 4:4)**
my c. to fulfil . . . 472.2
take me, and my c. seal. . 529.3
gracious c. of the Lord . . 567.2
let youth obey your c. . . 943.3

calm
thunder, fire and c. . . 36.2
c. the troubled breast . . 58.2
all is c. 89.1
so blue and c. and fair . . 103.1
that c. each fear . . . 200.5
bring in the c. . . . 209.1
soothe and hush and c. . . 325.3
in the c., sure haven . . 333.3
my inmost c. 358.2
with c. delight can live . . 414.1
through the tempest . . . c. . 430.3
a c. and heavenly frame. . 442.1
c. and serene my frame . . 442.6
c. in the peace . . . 443.2
all is c. and joy . . . 453.4
be c. in thy soul . . . 458.4
source of c. unfailing . . 539.3
blest content and c. . . 551.2
I can be c. and free . . 556.2
O c. of hills above . . . 567.3
still small voice of c. . . 567.5
with c. and tempered zeal . 568.2
a c., a sure retreat . . . 573.1
one that in c. repose . . 574.1
all our moments c. . . 602.4
Lord of all c. 611.4
obtain that inward c. . . 613.2
c. and order all my days. . 630.2
c. and sweet repose . . 673.3
voice will c. my fears . . 740.3
naught but c. is found . . 752.3
found in Jesus c. repose . 910.3
c. all earthly strife . . . 948.3
b *calm [in storm]* *Matt 8:26**
to c. this tossing sea . . 194.4
storms . . . into thy c. . . 300.2
no storm can shake . . . c. . 358.2
thou makest c. the storm . 502.2
c. amid its rage . . . 569.2
make the storm a c. . . 663.3
c. succeeds the storm . . 911.6

calming *(adj)* 39.2

calm(ly)
c. we wait thy . . . grace . 216.2
c. ordering the whole . . 479.3
c. amid its rage . . . 569.2
fighting, trusting c. . . 593.1
I want a c. fervent zeal . . 720.2
I c. sojourn here . . . 880.2

Calvary *(Luke 23:33)*
by the C. track . . . 59.4
by Christ of C. . . . 65.*
they bore thee to C. . . 101.3
a hymn of C.'s road . . 103.3
wounds . . . received on C. . 106.3
lead me to C. . . . 117.*
the seal . . . in C. I see . 119.c
speak to my heart of C. . 125.c
that dread hour on C. . 125.3
humbling thyself . . . on C . 174.3
bore my burden to C . 179.3
our guilt made his C. . 245.c
power in the blood of C. . 257.c
come . . . to C.'s tide . 281.2
from Glory to C. he came . 319.3
C. is proof enough . 324.1
load . . . rolled away at C. . 340.3
O C., the thorn . . 368.2
flowing freely from C. . 383.1
at/to/of/on C. . . . 405.*
come, with me visit C. . 413.1
C.'s stream is flowing . 413.c
that flowed on C. . 423.1, c
to C.'s holy feast . 431.3
kept . . . by C.'s tide . 443.1
thou on C. . . . didst part . 475.4
light my way to C. . . 486.1
that lead me to my C. . 488.2
by the sight of C. . 503.2
When Jesus from C. called . 553.1
wash . . . in C.'s fountain . 593.4
C'. great salvation fame . 609.2
heritage of C. and Easter . 613.3
my spirit to C. bear . 639.2
gave its all on C. . . 741.1
through the blood of C. . 822.3
shall hear of C.'s stream . 828.2
behold! on a hill, C. . 830.*
he calls you now from C. . 885.4
C., so dear, so sweet . c7
wonderful place called C. . c29
Lord, make C. real to me . c81
greatest proof . . . is C. . c121
Jesus of C. . . . c214

b *Calvary's love*
C.-l. has made the stair . 369.3
fully through C.'s l. . 371.2
red reveals the l. of C. . 777.2

c *Calvary's mountain*
who died on M. C. . 57.c
flows from C.'s m. . 115.1
not on C.'s height alone . 127.1
calling from C.'s m. . 139.2
the lost to C.'s height . 188.3
but I came to C.'s m. . 309.1
forth from C.'s m. . . 350.2
died for all on C.'s m. . 381.2
more sacred . . . C.'s hill . 590.1
died for me on C.'s m. . 811.c

d *Calvary's tree*
on C.'s t. . . . languished . 126.1
this cry from C.'s t. . 128.4
purchased . . . on C.'s t. . 357.2
hung on C.'s . . . t. . c19
on C.'s t. he suffered . c161

e *cross of Calvary*
on the c. of C. . . 128.*
bright from the c. of C. . 260.1
left . . . for the c. on C. . 337.1
through the c. of C. . 539.1
from C.'s rugged c. . 700.2
to the c. of C. . . . fly . 810.c

f *died on Calvary*
from above, to d. on C. . 46.c
who d. on Mount C. . 57.c
that Jesus d. on C. . 108.c
on C.'s brow my Saviour d. . 125.1
the Christ who d. on C. . 327.2
d. for all on C. . . 381.2
for me he d. on C. . . 405.1
d. . . . on C.'s mountain. . 811.c
on C. a young man d. . 855.4

g *Lamb of Calvary*
blessed L. of C. 205.1; 538.1
thou L. of C. . . . 743.1
bleeding L., the L. of C. . c193

dark (b)

came—see *come*

camps 162.2

can(not) nc, but
a *Matt 27:42*
himself he c. save . . 130.1, 2
b *Titus 1:2*
God speaks, who c. lie . 385.2

fail (1a, b, 2d), fall (2d), how (1d), see (3l), what (1b)

Canaan *(Gen 17:8)**
in C. we will sing again . 43.4
nearer C.'s shore . . 369.2
C.'s happy shore . . 375.c
safe on C.'s side . . 578.3
C.'s fair and happy land . 887.1
old C. stood . . . 898.2
see the C. that we love . 898.3
march . . . to C.'s shore. . 902.5
reach fair C.'s land . 912.1

cancelled
the power of c. sin . 64.4
now our c. sin reveal . 210.2

candle 841.1

canopy 16.2

canticle 187.5

captain *Heb 2:10*
crown him as your c. . 141.5
our c. did appear . . 163.3
the c. took me in . . 375.1
to Jesus, our c. . . . given . 681.2
by our c. led . . . 682.1
thy c. is near . . . 689.3
to your . . . c. cleaving . 693.c
walking in your c.'s sight . 695.4
Christ is c. . . . 698.c
mighty C. of the host . 789.6
c. . . . will protect us . 818.3
Jesus is our c. . . 866.2
thou, Lord, their c. . 876.2

captive
a c. to love's victories . 122.4
brought c. to thee . . 416.1
make me a c., Lord . 508.1
the c. of thy grace . 723.4
b *Isa 61:1; Luke 4:18*
lead my c. soul astray . 509.2
c.'s fetters . . . rending . 593.3
c. to Jesus we'll win . 687.1
from our c. chain . . 803.3
the c. are set free . . 832.2
to free the c. . . . c25
c *Eph 4:8*
triumphs . . . o'er c. death . 150.2

captivity (Luke 4:18) . . 353.5

care
1 (divine) *1 Peter 5:7**
his c. our souls will feed. . 9.3
on thy c. depend . . 14.1
thy bountiful c. . . 16.4
wants shall be his c. . 21.5
see the c. . . . dost render . 39.1
God plans . . . he still c.. . 44.c
ourselves out of his c. . 49.c
have we a name for c. . 71.3
someone c. . . . 238.c
the spring of his c. . 378.2, 4
keep . . . 'neath thy c. . 582.1
my soul to thy c. . . 589.5
I bring into thy c. . . 631.4
every token of thy c. . 642.1
make us thy c. . . 648.1
c. for our eternal good . 656.2
to thy continual c. . . 714.4
ever watchful is his c. . 722.3
one who c. and understands . 732.1
thine the c. . . . 744.4
thy providential c. . . 761.2
in his holy c. . . . 767.2
in your c. and shelter . 792.1
his wondrous love and c. . 907.3
leave entirely to thy c. . 917.1
softened by thy c. . . 925.3
brother may know thy c. . 927.3
watchful c. . . . 938.2
I know he c. for me . c133
I'm not beyond his c. . c134
surely he will c. for you . c139
the c. of love divine . c176

guardian, loving (1c), take (1c), tender (b)

2 *(human)*
a woman's tender c. . 110.3
a love that c. for all . 426.2
compassion that will c. . 463.3
there are those who c. . 491.1
prayer to . . . sweeten c. . 604.3
c. for the dying . . 691.1
attend with constant c. . 695.4
spirits need thy c. . . 702.3
go, c. for the dying . 703.4
the objects of her c. . 722.4
gifts are in my c. . . 871.1
will be then in other c. . 941.3

jealous

b *(not) care*
no one . . . really c. . 238.1
I c. not what befalls me . 330.3
why should I c. . . 354.4
c. not my Lord was crucified . 405.1
nor c. that we are loved . 466.3
c. to find an easier way . 619.3
all those who do not c. . 851.3
Lord, I c. not for riches . 883.1

3 *care [worry]*
the troubled brow of c. . 129.2
never a c. or burden . 186.3
life weighed down by c. . 246.1
weighed down with c. . 257.1
somebody's c. . . . lighter . 384.c
burdened with a load of c. . 396.2
my life . . . with its c. . 420.2
in c. and pleasures . 428.4
coming with my life of c. . 470.2
rise again to bring you c. . 471.3
times with c. is crowded . 534.2
calm and free from c. . 556.2
to live exempt from c. . 566.5
c. sweep o'er my spirit . 583.2
with burdens, joy and c. . 595.1
no c. could destroy . 611.1
from a world of c. . . 633.1
I forget all . . . c. . . 636.2
cumbered with a load of c. . 645.3
our comforts and our c. . 660.2
feel his brother's c. . 662.1
his hosts free from c. . 708.1
self-consuming c. . . 715.4
cast c. aside . . . 718.3
leaving cumbering c. . 728.1
sea of c. and doubt . 749.2
heart is bowed with c. . 759.1
bear . . . toil and c. . 837.5
safe from corroding c. . 889.2
cause . . . a needless c. . 917.3
joy or burdening c. . 947.4

place of freedom from c. . c67
earthly c. increase . . . c143
c. my soul would flurry . . c145
b *all care*
all the c. of what men . . 437.4
thou who knowest all my c. . 584.c
bid c. all cease . . . 635.2
from all temptation . . . c. . 872.2
c *every care*
tells me e. c. . . . roll . . 344.1
love will lighten e. c. . . 503.3
peace with e. c. . . . 551.3
I'll cast on him my e. c. . . 633.2
dawn on e. cross and c.. . 668.3
d *care and sorrow*
bring thee my c. and my s. . 288.1
when c. and s. meet me. . 343.2
c. and doubting, gloom . . 540.5
away from my s. and c.. . 886.3
from s., temptation and c. . 904.3
not from s., pain, or c. . . 916.1
e *cares of life* *Luke 21.34*
and the c. of l. annoy . . 462.2
the c. of l. and fashion . . 832.3
the ills and c. of l. . . . 872.1
bring (2d) cast (i) fret

careful 555.1

carefulness 183.2

careless
c. of our loneliness . . 238.2
I can no more be c. . . 482.2
no c. slumber . . . close . . 767.2
c. sinner 875.3

caressing 330.1

carnal *2 Cor 10:4* . 701.c; 705.c

carol
the birds their c. raise . . 42.2
sweetest c. ever sung . . 67.c
a c. to my King . . . 387.2

carry-ied
1 *[God] carries*
c. his lost one again . . 111.1
c. me from height to height . 641.3
he will c. you through . . 823.*
it c. consolation . . . 828.3
b *Isa 40:11*
in his arms he c. them . . 184.1
c *carried sin* *Isa 53:4*
he c. our sin 245.4
c. my sins with him there . c24
h. c. my sins far away . . c185
2 *(other)*
Jesus will help to c. . . 186.2
when c. to the cross . . 186.3
I c. a heavy burden . . 340.c
c. all our burdens gladly . . 462.3
c., Lord, to please thee . . 503.1
c. everything to God . . 645.1
must I be c. to the skies. . 678.2
c. truth's unsullied ray . . 697.4
c. with the fire . . . 822.c
it c. consolation . . . 828.3
to c. and to help . . . 851.2
you've c. your burden . . c31
faith will c. us through . . c239

case
to every sinner's c. . . 254.1
one who knows my c. . . 311.2
Jesus pitied our c. . . . 687.3

cast
c., like a mantle, the sea . 16.3
my idols I c. at thy feet . . 454.3
c. down mountains . . 593.4
our changeful lot is c. . . 602.3
its light . . . be c. . . . 620.4
c. a wistful eye . . . 887.1
he c. my record . . . c190
b *Luke 21:2*
c. it in God's treasury . . 920.3
c *Matt 13:30*
in the fire the tares to c.. . 924.3
d *cast [on God]*
come, c. in thy sorrow . . 237.3
Lord, I c. myself on thee . 292.6
c. thy poor soul . . . 315.4
my soul I c. 415.1
I would c. myself on thee . 439.1
c. my load on . . . grace. . 449.3
e *cast (aside)*
c. care aside 718.3
c. aside all other gods . . 827.2
realm deserted, c. aside . . 885.3
f *cast (away)*
I c. them all away . . . 41.2
c. away thy every fear . . 261.1
you he will not c. away . . 331.4
c. foreboding fears away . 566.2
c. sloth away . . . 683.4
c. their evil chains away. . 776.2
strive to c. away the load . 816.1
g *cast (behind)*
my sins behind him c. . . 366.2
c. behind the baits . . . 596.2
h *Neh 9:26*
or c. his words behind . 784.3
i *cast (care)* *1 Peter 5:7*
O Lord, I c. my care . . 14.4
will you c. . . . your care. . 242.5
on thee I c. my care . . 596.1
c. on him my every care. . 633.2
c. all your care on him . . 759.c
j *cast (crown)* *Rev 4:10*
c. down their . . . crowns . 220.2
till we c. our crowns . . 438.3
at thy feet to c. it down. . 860.5
c. their crowns before . . 949.4
k *cast (down)* *2 Cor 4:9*
sometimes c. down . . 468.1
why c. down, my soul . . 557.4
c. down, but for thy grace . 747.1
though often c. down . . 823.3
l *cast (out)*
c. out our sin 86.4
c. every evil passion out. . 432.2
c. out every foe . . . 436.1
m *John 6:37*
he will not c. you out . . 267.3
thou didst not c. me out . 331.3
n *1 John 4:18*
love c. out your fears . . 243.2
all fear c. out 541.3
burden (2c)

catch-caught
that all might c. . . . 165.1
c. the wandering of my will . 425.2
I c. its radiant glory . . 726.3
we have c. the vision . . 833.1
c. the heavenly breezes . . c116

cattle
the c. are lowing . . . 77.2
stood a lowly c. shed . . 87.1

caught see *catch*

cause
1 *(undertaking)*
lead us . . . to thy holy c. . 181.1
Jesus undertook my c. . . 380.2
our c. defending . . . 500.1
fear to own his c. . . . 678.1
thy c. shall . . . sway . . 692.5
rest your c. upon . . . word . 698.1
our c. we know must prevail . 698.2
to him commend thy c. . . 715.4
or to defend his c. . . . 735.1
onward in the c. of Jesus . 776.1
honoured in the c. . . . 776.3
fresh allegiance to the c. . 777.4
we dedicate to Heaven's c. . 796.3
to his c. we bring . . . 866.c
in his c. enlisted . . . 866.2
in thy c. contending . . c48
b *cause of right*
vanguard for the c. of r.. . 787.2
in the c. of r. . . . stand. . 817.3
battling . . . the c. of r. . . 859.2
c *Ps 140:12*
he will our c. maintain . . 9.2
d *plead cause* *Isa 51:22**
he lives to p. my c. above . 144.2
lives to p. our c. above . . 242.c
need him to p. your c. . . c11
2 *(reason)*
when you have c. to fear . 98.4
c. of endless exultation . . 161.3
see the c. in Jesus' face. . 286.3
c. for grief and pain . . 618.3
give them c. . . . to praise . 620.3
in his righteous c. . . . 909.1
b *(verb)*
c. our faith to wane . . 6.2
c. all day his course to run . 34.4
c. him bitter tears . . . 250.2
me who c. his pain . . 283.1
oft has c. you bitter grief . 433.2
no more to c. my heart . . 536.2
human design may c. me pain 644.3
I'll . . . c. thee to stand . . 653.2
c. thy needless fear . . 721.4
dangers may c. you to fear . 817.1
never c. . . . needless care . 917.3

caves 393.2

cease
when rolling years shall c. . 4.4
c. toward the child . . 110.3
that wars may c. . . . 156.3
when shall all hatred c. . . 172.2
works of darkness . . . c. . 198.4
soon that voice will c. . . 240.3
your Saviour's pleading c. . 241.4
I c. from my striving . . 410.2
if you want sorrow . . . to c.. 427.1
grief and pain shall c. . . 453.4
have I c. from walking . . 534.2
Jesus spake, dissension c. . 539.2
till all our strivings c. . . 567.4
when all his labours c. . . 580.3
we c. to fight . . . 646.3
ere our worship c. . . . 674.1
realms where sorrows c. . 697.5
when other friendships c. . 709.2
'twill c. before long . . 712.4
soon shall the warfare . . . c.. 813.4
labour and sorrow c. . . 890.4
your sorrow shall c. . . c31
b *bid cease*
b. them c. 19.3
that b. our sorrows c. . . 64.3
b. my doubts . . . all c. . . 549.2
b. its angry tumult c. . . 569.3
b. resentment c. . . . 572.4
b. cares all c. . . . 635.2
b. thou . . . discord c. . . 669.3
b. our conflict c. . . . 674.4
at his b. to c. 808.4
b. a soldier his warfare c. . 894.1
c *never/not cease*
begin and n. c. 93.6
streams of mercy, n. c. . . 313.1
love and peace, n. to c. . . 420.2
questioning cries do n. c. . 527.2
love that n. c.. . . . 534.c, 3

a love which cannot c. . . 545.1
n.-c. music rolls . . . 887.5
joy that will n. c. . . . c46
d *1 Thess 2:13*
thanks n.-c. 24.3
loudest praises without c. . 109.3
n. once they c. to sing . . 158.1
praise thee without c. . . 438.2
in n.-c. prayer 714.4
e *cease from sin* *1 Peter 4:1*
sin shall c. 185.2
I e'er from s. should c. . . 407.2
where the life of s. c. . . 429.2
c. that moment from s. . . 553.1
from s. for ever c. . . . 714.1
struggle (b), wandering (1)

ceaseless
this my c. song shall be . . 360.4
in c. rest I roam . . . 362.3
let them flow in c. praise . 525.1
Father, thy c. love . . . 715.5
in c. love for men be shown . 796.4

celebrate
to c. with me 62.1
this day in faith we c. . . 198.1

celebration 943.1

celestial
with food c. feedeth . . . 53.2
pure c. fire to impart . . 199.1
a deep c. spring . . . 254.4
c. fruit on earthly ground . 314.3
expand thy wings, c. Dove . 651.3
c. radiance from afar . . 711.2

cell 38.3

centre
c. of unbroken praise . . 10.2
c. all in thee 630.2

central 141.4

certain
sure and c. as God's love . 49.1
c. poor shepherds . . . 90.1
the sure, the c. seal . . 214.4
I am c. that Jesus loves me . 323.2
'tis c., though impossible . 407.3
in danger I'm c. . . . 684.2
from God . . . my c. aid . . 767.1

chain
bound with Satan's c. . . 155.4
leaps to lose his c. . . . 160.3
as steel the binding c. . . 249.2
fettered and bound by c. . 257.3
one more c. must . . . riven . 434.3
thou hast wrought its c.. . 508.2
cast their evil c. away . . 776.2
freed us from our captive c. . 803.3
the captive from his c. . . c25
b *Acts 12:7*
my c. fell off 283.3

challenge 666.1

challenged 705.1

chamber 208.2

chance
a shining new c. to live . . 666.1
God gives to you c. . . . 773.2
all the past with its c. . . 893.2
every c. will soon be past . 913.2

change
1 *(external)*
a *divine* *Mal 3:6*
but naught c. thee . . . 8.3

thou c. not 33.1
c. never, nevermore . . . 182.2
thou who c. not, abide . . 670.2
he c. not 718.4
nothing c. here . . . 736.1
we may c., but Jesus never . 750.c
God never c. 956
b *(other)*
through all the c. years . . 6.1
the c. scenes of life . . 21.1
everything is c. . . . 49.2
no c. of season or place. . 318.3
c. that will surely come . . 485.1
no c. can harm me . . . 536.3
c. and decay in all around . 670.2
no c. my heart shall fear. . 736.1
2 *(internal)*
is there a name to c. men . 71.1
c. earthly craving . . . 197.2
till our faith is c. . . . 230.2
power that can c. the heart . 257.2
darkness he has c. to day . 317.1
any c. in my mind . . . 318.3
God can c. the hearts . . 324.2
O wondrous c. . . . 541.3
faith that c. fighting . . 713.3
my c. moods do not control . 717.4
darkness c. to shining day . 719.2
fire that c. fearing . . . 830.3
sinners c. to saints may be . 919.2
prayer c. things . . . c114
clouds will c. to sunshine . c115
b *change wrought*
God along the c. has w.. . 338.4
it was love w. the c. . . 340.2
c. in my life has been w. . 394.1
glory (2c)

changeful
such c. feelings had . . 549.1
where'er our c. lot is cast . 602.3

changeless
by a c. decree 16.3
the sinner's c. friend . . 282.3
love . . . so pure and c. . . 295.4
strong, c., free . . . 571.3
pure, warm and c. be . . 743.2
free and c. is his favour . . 764.1
thy c. shade 767.3
love so true and c. . . . 938.1

channel
c. only, blessed Master . . c60
make me a c. of blessing . c84

chant-ing
c. bird and flowing fountain . 10.2
c. this sacred lay . . . 72.5
angels c. from above . . 78.1
to c. Immanuel's praise . . 109.3
angels c. the strain . . . 253.3

chaos *(Gen 1:2)**
c. and darkness heard . . 224.1
didst brood upon the c. . . 569.3

character 928.2

charge-ing
c. me to preach thy power . 303.4
'tis thy divine c. to me . . 786.1
give his angels c. . . . 924.3
b *Lev 8:35**
a c. to keep I have . . . 472.1
c *Ps 91:11; Matt 4:6*
angels hold a c. divine . . 728.2
d *Rom 8:33*
aught to my c. shall lay . . 116.2

chariot
the Army c. rolls . . . 775.1
roll the old c. along . . c224

b *Ps 104:3*
his c. of wrath . . . 16.2

charity *1 Cor 13*
fill . . . with c. divine . . 181.3
found with perfect c. . . 568.2
thy burning c. . . . 594.1
one in c. 690.3
boundless c. divine . . 720.5
one in perfect c. . . . 769.3
assurance of tender c. . . 948.2

charm-ed
a *(spiritual)*
c. their griefs to rest . . 21.2
the name that c. our fears . 64.3
the c. of the cross . . . 119.c
c. to confess the voice . . 365.3
breathe . . . thy c. . . . 479.2
no fairer c. I see . . . 565.1
ten thousand c. . . . c167
b *(secular)*
c. all their own . . . 119.1
vain things that c. me most . 136.2
from folly's c. . . . 401.2
I sacrifice their c. . . . 461.2
not in joy to c. me . . . 498.5
phantom c. 630.1

chart
God of map . . . and c. . . 30.3
c. and compass . . . 598.1
c., wherein we read . . 654.2

chase
a *(noun)*
when heated in the c. . . 557.1
b *(verb)*
c. the horrors of night . . 19.4
c. our gloom away . . . 196.5
glory shall c. . . . gloom. . 465.4
c. my fears away . . . 502.1
c. the dark night of sin . . 602.4
c. its gloom away . . . 669.1
c. far the gloom . . . 765.3
all their sorrows c. . . . 909.3

chasten 862.3

chastening *2 Sam 7:14* . . 939.4

check
that c. each fault . . . 200.5
do not c. that falling tear . 259.1

cheeks 39.3

cheer
blessèd peace to c. us . . 12.2
as a friend he can c. . . 329.2
I hear his voice of c. . . 334.1
a song of c. is ringing . . 340.1
c. us while we bear . . 452.3
the world's delight and c. . 460.2
let thy love my spirit c. . . 563.5
light to c. the darkness . . 575.3
for thy voice that c. . . 614.1
c. the fainting . . . 623.2
then thy word doth c. us . 655.2
with comfort to c. . . . 689.3
what can I say to c. . . 706.1
a friend to help and c. . . 709.3
victory's ringing c. . . . 713.3
c. the faint 737.3
c., my comrades, c. . . 804.4
to c., to comfort . . . 851.4
no other friend to . . . c. me . 857.2
and c. the vine . . . 925.2
ever near to bless and c. . c154
no one like Jesus can c.. . c207
b *cheer heart/spirit*
his promises our s. c. . . 43.3
the drooping h. to c. . . 67.1

never fails my h. to c. . . 68.3
let thy love my s. c. . . 563.5
thy willing h. to . . . c. . . 683.3
thine it is our h. to c. . . 799.4

c *cheer with hope*
c. it with h., with love . . 516.2
without a h. to c. the tomb . 683.5
h. c. him with her . . . note . 911.4

presence (b)

cheerful
sing . . . with c. voice . . 3.1
our c. banners are unfurled . 5.5
let us join our c. songs . . 57.1
bless . . . with c. voice . . 120.5
rests my c. will . . . 208.2
c. praises fill his house . . 365.2
put a c. courage on . . 559.1
wait in c. hope . . . 738.2
let us then be c. . . . 755.3
c. be, . . . burdens lighten . 805.2
valiant and c. . . . 813.3
sings with c. heart . . . 911.1
c. homage paid . . . 925.4

cheerfully *2 Cor 9:7* . . . 920.3

cheerfulness c201

cheerily 837.5

cheering
soul -c. presence restore . 318.4
c. ray of hope to dim . . c166

cheerless 412.3

cherish-ed
thee . . . with heed I'll c. . 73.4
c. the old rugged cross . . 124.c
thee will I c., . . . honour . 177.1
c. all things good . . . 212.5
hope each . . . soul may c. . 363.4
let this promise still be c. . 753.3
what my love should c. . . 842.2
c. every laden hour . . 874.1
thy word . . . may be c.. . 941.3

cherubim 220.2

chide-d-ing
slow to c. 17.2
the kindly c. of the Spirit . 192.2
Master . . . c. the billows . 848.3

chief
it is my c. complaint . . 110.6
your c. concern . . . 343.3
c. delight his . . . employ . 451.3
c. desire . . . to dedicate . 517.1

b *chief of sinners* *1 Tim 1:15*
room for the c. of s. . . 266.3
me, the c. of s., spare . . 286.1

child
1 *(divine)* *Luke 1:32**
a c. this day is born . . 72.1
a c. of high renown . . 72.1
bowed before the c. sublime . 74.2
born a c. and yet a King. . 79.3
O holy C. of Bethlehem . . 86.4
Jesus Christ her little c. . 87.1
that c. so dear and gentle . 87.5
teach us, holy C. . . . 88.5
virgin mother and c. . . 89.1
gentle c. of gentle mother . 97.1
a helpless, homeless c. . . 274.1
thou wast once a little c. . 793.4
Christ, the holy c., in me . 793.6
Saviour was once a c. . . 840.2
thou hast been a c. . . 842.3

2 *(literal)*
brother, sister, parent, c. . 28.4
toward the c. she bare . . 110.3
where a c. of loving lies. . 544.3
as a mother stills her c. . 598.2
like to a c. who . . . hears . 740.3
take/shield/bless this c. . 792.*
as they raise this c. . . 795.2
receive and bless our c. . 796.4
his watch the temple c. . 839.2
the poorest c. may bring . 849.2
yet these a c. may bring. . 849.3
brother, sister, c. . . . 938.4

b *little child*
as to a l. c. 98.1
take this l. c. 792.1
look upon a l. c. . . . 793.1
give a l. c. a place . . . 793.2
our l. c. . . . we bring . . 796.1
let his l. c. come in . . 843.2

3 *(figurative)*
c. of sorrow and of woe. . 66.1
the lowest c. of man . . 439.2
the penitent c. to receive . 691.2
grieved for every c. of man . 855.4

4 *(spiritual)*
he owns me for his c. . . 106.5
bid me be thy c. once more . 303.1
as his own c. . . . named me. 330.3
I'm the c. of a King . 354.c, 4
thy c. shall obey . . . 507.3
his weary, wandering c.. . 550.1
born anew, a ransomed c. . 550.2
some poor wandering c. . 676.4
thou dost keep thy c. . . 741.1
be thy loving c. below . . 837.6
evermore thy c. to be . . 837.6
happy every c. of grace . . 880.1
cause his c. . . . care . . 917.3
c. of mine, come back again . c6

b *child of God* *Gal 3:26**
a c. of G. am I . . . 59.2
the c. of G. shall sever . . 555.1

childhood 87.3, 4

childlike *Mark 10:15*
in c. faith I pray . . . 285.2
thoughts in c. speech . . 398.1
in c. faith . . . stretch . . 437.3
from a c. heart within me . 522.3
trust, ever c. 611.1
turn with simple, c. hearts . 654.5
the c., praying love . . 720.1
may read with c. eyes . . 839.5
c. trust that fears not . . 948.2

children
1 *(literal)*
respond when c. cry . . 50.3
bless all the dear c. . . 77.3
Christian c. all must be . . 87.3
c. early lisp his fame . . 661.2
we for our c. plead . . 791.1
the c. thou hast given . . 791.1
many dear c. are gathering . 794.2
I see forsaken c. . . . 830.1
c. too of modern days . . 834.1
while c.'s voices sing . . 834.c
c., sing for gladness . 835.1, c
what shall we c. bring . . 849.1
there are hundreds of c.. . 850.4
little c., who love . . . 852.3
retaineth his love for c. . 853.2
let . . . c. see your face . . 943.3

b *Matt 19:13, 14*
how he called little c. . . 794.1
c. . . . crowd to his arms . 794.3
suffer/teach little c. to come . 797.*
Jesus, friend of little c. . 842.1
c. stood around his knee . 848.2

c *Matt 21:15*
c. of Jerusalem sang . . 834.1
I'd follow the c.'s band . . 848.4
the c. all stood singing . . 853.1

2 *(spiritual)*
frail c. of dust . . . 16.5
he leads his c. on . . . 87.5
how could thy c. fear . . 146.3
none but Zion's c. know . 157.3
Jesus will guard his c. . . 184.1
I died for you, my c. . . 299.3
makes thy c. free . . . 485.4
whereso'er thy c. are . . 576.1
thy c.'s warring madness . 577.3
let me seek thy erring c.. . 612.1
as with thy c. I unite . . 613.3
keep thy c. free . . . 674.3
sees all thy c.'s wants . . 715.5
so the Lord his c. gathers . 722.4
nor death can pluck his c. . 723.3
Jesus loves his c. . . . 836.4
Saviour bestow on his c. . 857.c
blest are thy c. . . . 873.3
all thy c. gladly give . . 921.3
providing food for thy c. . 927.3
much more to us, his c.. . 935.2

b *[God's] children*
all God's c. may belong . . 324.2
make friends of God's c. . 458.1
where the Father's c. are . 776.2

c *Matt 5:9*
they his c. shall be called . 95.2

chill-ing-ly
flood has lost his c. . . 153.3
when the waters cold c.. . 280.3
with a deathly c. ensnaring . 303.2
beside the c. wave . . 910.1
winter's c. breeze . . . 930.2

chime-ing
where holy voices c. . . . 7.2
sweet c. bells 79.c
heaven's music c. . . . 744.6
when joybells c. . . . c123

choice
ye people of his c. . . . 20.1
day that fixed my c. . . 365.1
a quick yet lasting c. . . 749.1
the c. is yours . . . 885.1
share thy cross . . . my c. . c108

b *make choice*
m. his will your c. . . . 227.3
let us freely m. him our c. . 235.2
my unchanging c. is m. . . 356.1
ye that have m. him your c. . 537.1
m. the . . . call their c. . . 680.2

choicest 564.3

choir
an echo of the angel -c. . . 70.c
their c. are singing . . . 73.1
sing, c. of angels . . . 85.2
when . . . her c. shall sing . 101.4
angel c. are crying: Glory . 370.3

choose-chose-n
1 *[God] chooses*
man of God's own c. . . . 1.2
dark Calvary he c. to know . 134.c
he c. out a lowly way . . 398.1
c. the pure in heart . . 411.3
whene'er he shall c. . . 443.2
power as thou shalt c. . . 525.4
for what you c. to hide . . 552.1
in the way he shall c. . . 640.3
him who c. us for his own . 738.2
c. not, Lord, this house . . 945.4

b *Matt 20:16*
glorious band, the c. few . 701.3
his c. ones shall gather . . 907.2

c *1 Cor 1:27*
thou didst c. and use . . 163:2

d *2 Tim 2:4*
c. to be a soldier . . . c225
2 *[we] choose*
help us . . . c. the right . 193.5
c. and cherish all things . 212.5
c. to gain through loss . 429.2
thy beauty be my c. prize . 449.3
I c. thee now with gladness . 631.3
thy c. cross to bear . 761.2
c. them to pursue . . 795.2
c. to heed thy voice . 796.3
thou shalt be our c. God . 918.5
c. the right and refusing . c210
b *choose [path/way]*
know and c. thy way . 190.2
feet ran in self -c. ways . 422.2
fruitless . . . way of my c. . 501.2
thy way I c. 605.3
I loved to c. . . . my path . 606.2
as we take our c. way . 688.1
bid me c. an easier path . 780.1
thy c. path to tread . 944.2
c *Luke 10:42*
let me c. the better part . 497.2
many c. the better part . 832.3

chords
those loud triumphant c. . 147.4
stirred the slumbering c. . 390.2
c. that were broken . 691.3

chorus
join the mighty c. . . . 10.4
how the angels in c. sang . 99.1
singing the rapturous c. . 139.3
who'll swell the c. . . 278.3
swell the heavenly c. . 902.2

chose—see *choose*

Christ—see *Jesus*

Christian *(Acts 11:26)*
C., awake, salute . . . 78.1
C. children all must be . . 87.3
let C. sing . . . 142.1
shame on us, C. people . 299.1
every C. may be Christlike . 324.3
rejoice, rejoice, O C. . 334.3
C., follow me . . . love me 428.1, 3
C.'s vital breath . . . air . 625.5
our hearts in C. love . 660.1
we, as C. truly named . 688.4
onward, C. soldiers . 690.1, c, 2
say I can a C. be . . 780.3

Christless 545.2

Christlike
every Christian may be C. . 324.3
armoured with all C. graces . 577.4

Christly 826.4

Christmas
this happy C. day . . . 74.1
we hear the C. angels . . 86.4

Christward 776.2

chronicles 774.2

Church
the c. with psalms must shout 11.2
word of Bible, faith of C. . 30.3
let his C. with gladness . 152.2
fulfil thy C.'s story . . 577.1
thy C. unsleeping . . 677.2
moves the C. of God . 690.3
C. of Jesus . . . will remain . 690.4
'gainst the C. prevail . 690.4
bell

circle-ing
lines and c., planes and arcs . 27.2
with the ever-c. years . . 83.3
a hundred c. camps . . 162.2
their everlasting c. run . 559.3
crowns the c. year . . 925.1

cisterns *Jer 2:13*
I tried the broken c. . 547.3
though c. be broken . 712.2

citizens *(Eph 2:19)* . . . 85.2

city
1 *(literal)*
without a c. wall . . 133.1
into the c. I'd follow . 848.4
b *Luke 2:11*
royal David's c. . . . 87.1
2 *(figurative)* *(Heb 11:16)**
that c. fair 59.4
the c. of gold . . . 280.4
to dwell in that c. . . 394.4
way to that c. of light . 406.1
threshold of the c. bright . 663.3
there's a c. of the future . 868.2
hands to build my c. . 868.2
O that beautiful c. . . 883.3
the c. we shall see . . 901.2
to the hallelujah c. . . 902.c
b *city of God*
Zion, c. of our God . . 157.1
build the c. of our God . 833.2
that beautiful c. of God . 901.c

clad 159.3

claim-ed-ing
1 *[God] claims*
c. mankind by grace divine . 30.4
his death's a c. . . 114.3
never raised to seek or c. . 129.2
to c. the here and now . 142.2
mocking . . . Saviour's c. 147.3
c. the Kingdom for thine own. 161.4
who is it c. the heart of me . 204.3
c. us for thy habitation . 210.2
art thou its c. denying . 276.1
let . . . thy grace c. me . 285.1
by . . . blood he has c. me . 330.3
Love, for ever c. my eyes . 449.3
by thy blood thou dost c. . 473.1
my life's purpose c. . 484.3
c. me for thy service, c. all . 492.1
thou art c. every feeling . 503.1
c. it, take it . . . 504.1
I own thy lawful c. . . 509.1
c. of our King . . . will bring . 687.2
love that c. lives . . 707.2
he c. me for his own . 730.1
c. each blood-bought nation . 828.4
when we urge his c. . 832.3
I own his c. on heart . 867.1
He c. my heart/hands/lips . . . 867.*
he is c. youth's allegiance . 868.3
our . . . leader c. our praise . 879.5
gospel that c. all . . . c210
2 *[we] claim*
by faith I c. him mine . . 46.2
c. my mansion in the skies . 116.5
faith presents her c. . 198.2
thy . . . gift today we c.. . 203.1
no one has c. . . . denied . 257.4
c. the crown through Christ . 283.4
I have no c. on grace . 290.1
rivers of thy grace I c. . 303.4
c. a mansion there . . 312.4
liberty I c. from my sin . 348.2
from the Saviour we c. all . 351.3
that his pardon I might c. . 363.2
thy righteousness c. . 372.3
reach now . . . now c. . 413.2
c. . . . complete deliverance . 433.2

I c. cleansing from thee . . 437.1
none need fail . . . to c. . . 456.3
in faith, thy mercy c. . . 460.3
by faith the gift I c. . . 481.4
c. a closer communion . . 501.1
c. the power to make me whole 513.2
I c. victory for me . . . 543.1
no other can I c. or own. . 556.4
thy help we c.. . . . 581.1
I c. an entrance there . . 619.1
naught of our own we c.. . 648.2
ends shall c. no right . 702.1
c. the blessing now. . . 742.1
no . . . goodness we c. . . 763.4
they c. the victory God's. . 774.2
pardon c., O guilty one . . 831.4
at the cross I c. it mine . . c48
love I c. c83
all c. the same cleansing. . c112
b *claim blessing*
this b. now I c. . . . 413.3
we c. thy promised b. now . 638.2
lifts . . . and c. the b. now. . 742.1
c *claim promise*
c. the Father's p. mine . . 208.4
thy p. just now I c.. . . 450.4
thy p. now I c. . 511.2; 562.2
thy p. presence c. . . . 603.1
we c. thy p. blessing now. . 638.2
3 *(other)*
seeking my soul to c. . . 724.3

clarion
c. call of band. . . . 780.3
loud rings the c. call. . 781.3
tell it with a c. voice. . 829.3

clashing 508.3

clasp
c. thy hand in mine . . 725.3
c. the hand of brother . . 765.2

class
help him save all c. . . 704.3
every c. and race . . 705.2

clay
left its encumbering c. . . 890.3
b *Job 10:9*
power . . . made us of c. . 4.2
c *Ps 40:2*
lifted me from the miry c. . 335.c
d *Jer 18:4; Rom 9:21*
c. on the wheel am I . . 416.4
potter, I am the c. . . . 487.1
as the potter handles the c. . 501.c

clean
provided . . . robes are c. . 170.1
now I know I'm c. within . 201.4
my soul desireth to be c. . 420.4
where we may be pure and c.. 429.1
c. as thou . . . art c. . . 453.2
can I not at this moment be c. 459.2
love that's pure and c. . . 779.2
c. my mind 861.3
till every part be c. . . . c72
b *clean heart* *Ps 51:10*
a h. by blood made c. . . 415.5
a c. h. within me create . 422.3
a h. that's true and c. . 426.1
h., believing, true and c. . 444.3
in life and h. entirely c. . . 629.3
he claims my h. to keep it c. . 867.2
who can make my h. quite c.. c13
c *keep clean* *(1 John 1:7)*
power to k. us . . . c. . . 230.4
what can k. me always c. . 306.1
saves me and k. me c. . . 315.3
O make and k. me c. . . 494.3

he k. his temple c. . . . 495.2
k. now, and every instant, c. . 540.3
the soul k. c. 541.3
claims my heart, to k. it c. . 867.2
d *make clean* *(Isa 1:16)*
come and wash and m. you c. 232.2
Lord, m. me c. 296.3
knew not how to m. them c. . 359.1
from every stain m. c. . . 415.1
a heart by blood m. c. . . 415.5
the Spirit m. me c. . . 447.4
that can m. the foulest c. . 471.1
the blood that m. me c. . . 489.3
O m. and keep me c. . . 494.3
stream to m. the foulest . . . c. 700.2
who can m. my heart quite c.. c13

cleanse-d-ing
have we a name for c. . . 71.3
for whose c. he came . . 245.c
come then for c. . . . 281.2
welcome, pardon, c., relieve . 293.5
thy waters can c. me . . 298.2
for my c. this I see. . . 306.2
what joy to know he c. me . 317.2
I am c., I am whiter . . 322.3
all I need to c. and make me . 344.1
fully saves and c. me . . 404.2
c. by the crystal flow . . 416.1
c., thou refining flame, all . 416.2
that I may c. be . . . 421.1
wash me, c. me . . . 423.c
dost my vileness fully c.. . 423.2
down at his feet you'll be c. . 427.4
pass me through the c. . . 430.1
the power of perfect c. show. 432.1
love that c. every stain . . 439.3
the faith receiving c. . . 456.4
perfect c. gaining there . . 471.3
c. me and fill me . . . 501.c
c. and make me whole . . 511.3
through a sterner c. . . 522.1
Jesus has c. even me . . 535.1
c. and blend my will . . 555.4
shed to c. our fallen race . 590.2
c. thou the wounds . . 647.2
all I require to c. me . . 647.3
I am trusting thee for c. . 727.3
healing, c., setting free . . 777.3
doth c. and make it whole . 798.1
c. and healing for all . . 808.2
grace to c. and power to free. 845.3
our lives be c. for service . 943.4
let the waves c. me . . c78
wash me and c. me . . c111
all claiming the same c. . . c112
b *cleanse from*
c. f. all its guilt . . . 108.c
c. f. every stain . . . 268.4
c. me f. its guilt . . . 302.1
f. all the guilt . . . c. . . 437.*
c. f. all evil, ... 443.1
that I might be c. f. guilt . 538.2
c. . . . f. sin's hidden stain . 610.3
c *cleanse (from) sin* *1 John 1:7*
blood . . . that c. from all s. . 113.1
c., O c. my heart from s. . 128.3
c. from all sin's impurity. . 230.3
where for c. from s. I cried . 315.1
c. me from s. that I may live . 431.1
c. from s. and peace bestow . 528.1
plunge in the s.-c. wave. . 535.c
c. my soul from s. . . . 562.1
hearts completely c. from s. . 704.1
his blood will c. you from s. . c18
blood of Jesus c. from all s. . c192
he'll c. your soul from s. . c203
d *cleanse heart*
c., O c. my h. from sin . . 128.3
c. my h. as white as snow . 347.1
c. my hands, and c. my h. . 461.c
flood and c. my h. within . 502.3
my h. he hath c. . . . 640.1
he. completely c. from sin . 704.1
c. my h. and make me pure . 914.3
my h. its waves are c. . . c42
e *cleanse soul*
s. to c. from all its guilt . . 108.c
Spirit . . . c. thou our s.. . 218.3
I have reached this s.-c. sea . 298.5
c. the s., making it whole . 329.c
bad as I was he c. my s.. . 380.2
c. my s. from fear . . . 493.c
come in and c. my s. from sin 562.1
c. the depths within our s. . 572.4
c. our s. this very hour . . 638.1
he'll c. your s. from sin . . c203
boundless (b), sin (1e)

cleanser 257.4

cleansing *(adjective)*
O the c. stream does flow . 128.1
Christ of burning, c. flame . 203.1
been . . . for the c. power . 417.1
thirst thy c. grace to prove . 440.1
all who seek this c. river. . 471.2
the c. stream is flowing . . c221
blood (2g), flood (1b), flow (2c)

clear
1 *(verb)*
heavy load . . . the Father c. . 127.4
wake my spirit, c. my sight . 194.1
start this moment, c. the way. 275.4
he gently c. thy way . . . 721.2
2 *clear-er (adjective)*
flowing water, pure and c. . 2.3
dim past and present c. . . 31.2
music . . . echo c. and strong. 32.3
c. and plain that the love . 49.2
its c. unfolding . . . 70.1
came upon the midnight c. . 83.1
c. than ever I see . . . 99.3
c. to faith's vision . . . 114.2
with wisdom kind and c. . 212.2
fountain flows divinely c. . 232.2
abundant, free and c. . . 254.2
make the message c. and plain 262.c
song of cheer is ringing c. . 340.1
Jesus came with message c. . 398.2
O vision c. 398.4
thy word is c. . . . 449.2
speak out thy wishes still c. . 513.c
some c., winning word . . 519.2
conscience as the noonday c. 665.2
singing, if my way be c.. . 754.3
a clarion voice so c. . . 829.3
in accents c. and still . . 862.3
lamp of c. and living flame . 869.3
voice inaudible, but c. . . 874.2
c. are the skies above me . c152
b *clear light*
with c. l. thy witness bear . 207.4
l. shining c. and bright . . 260.1
the l. is growing c.. . . 696.1
c. . . . burns the guiding l. . 765.2
shine with a c., pure l. . . 841.1

clearest 452.4

clearly
know their duty c. . . . 704.c
more c. would I realise . . 717.2
nor c. see the path ahead . 748.2

cleave-ing *Rom 12:9**
ever c. to thee . . . 497.2
my spirit c. to thee . . 517.3
joyful wing, c. the sky . . 617.5
closer let us c. . . . 659.4
conquering captain c. . . 693.c

cleft *Ex 33:22*
Rock of ages, c. for me . 302.1, 4
thy side be c. in vain . . 440.4
concealed in the c. . . . 639.3
the c. of the rock . . 710.1, c

clever 824.2

climb-ed-ing
love c. the green hill . . 51.c
c. to my homestead . . 369.1
c. the ladder 369.2
getting others to c. . . 369.3
I'm c. up the golden stair . 369.c
c. the steeps 393.1
c. the heavenly steeps . . 496.3
they c. the steep ascent. . 701.4
my soul doth c. . . . 729.4
higher than the loftiest c. . 766.2
to c. the highest heights . 858.2
c. where Moses stood . . 898.3
c. up to the mountain top . c116
ascend, ladder

clime
we'll tell in every c. . . 326.4
abounding in every . . . c. . 383.1
my country is in every c. . 556.2
lift . . . in every land and c. . 781.2
children of every c. . . 794.3

cling-ing
ever to him I'll c. . . . 336.2
while to that refuge c. . . 358.2
sinners to Jesus now c. . . 383.c
to thy promises I'm c. . . 434.4
I c. to thy word . . . 454.2
closer to thee I'll c. . . 523.c
b *cling to cross*
c. to the old rugged c. . . 124.c
by faith I'm c. to thy c. . . 292.c
to thy c. I c. 302.3
holiness, c. to the c. . . 427.4

close
1 *[close] end*
he c. the yawning gates. . 151.4
life's evening is c. . . . 237.3
he has not c. the gate . . 267.2
outside the fast-c. door . . 299.1
c. to all but thee . . . 424.2
I cannot c. my heart to thee . 621.3
swift to its c. 670.2
at the c. of day I come . . 675.1
life's long warfare c. . . 890.4
b *Matt 13:15*
c. thine eyes 251.1
eye (2d), eyelids
2 *close-r (near)*
c. walk with God . . 442.1, 6
claiming a c. communion . 501.1
in c. dearer company . . 519.3
for c. communion I pine . . 639.1
3 *close-ly (adverb)*
stay c. by me for ever . . 77.3
if I still hold c. to him . . 228.5
round my heart still c. twine . 345.1
c. sheltered in thy . . . side . 424.3
c. to thee I'll c. . . . 523.c
he called me c. to him . . 549.2
I must more c. dwell . . 618.c
a life more c. linked . . 618.2
c. and c. let us cleave . . 659.4
c. walk with thee to Heaven . 667.4
gathered me c. . . . 740.1
while I follow c. . . . 740.c
cord c.-binding all mankind . 826.2
ever keep me c. to thee . . 842.1
ever keeping c. to thee . . 846.3
c. knit in holy vow . . . 947.1
c. by his side, . . . abide. . c169
beside (1b), draw (1c)

clothe-d
heavens are c. . . . 107.2
kept the folded grave c. . . 152.1

c. herself for spring 155.2
c. us with the Spirit's might 593.2
b *1 Peter 5:5*
c. me with wisdom 516.4
to be c. upon with meekness 584.2
majesty (b)
c *Ps 132:9*
c. in righteousness divine 283.4

clothing *1 Tim 6:8* 921.2

cloud
1 *[literal]*
c. that sail in heaven 2.2
c. which are fountains 8.2
deep thunder-c. form 16.2
winds that drift the c. along 31.1
when the c. are threatening 39.2
c. and darkness veiled 128.4
points the c. their course 715.2
by him the c. drop fatness 929.2
above the c. of the dawning c134
b *Ex 34:5*
bid thy c. of glory rest 942.1
c *1 Kings 18:44*
saw ye not the c. arise 165.4
d *Rev 1:7*
he comes with c. descending 161.1
pillar (a), witness (2b)
2 *[figurative]*
melt the c. of sin 10.1
drive the c. of doubt 10.1
c. ye so much dread 29.3
no more shall darkness c. 277.4
when the c. unfold 280.1
the c. grows thin 358.3
not a shadow-c. ... obscuring 369.1
not a c. in the skies 397.2
with not a c. between 426.1
joy grows dim and c. 534.2
'mid the darkness and c. 641.2
even through c. skies 648.3
through c. and sunshine 670.3
may no earth-born c. arise 676.1
when c. hang low 719.4
waves and c. and storms 721.2
no c. can spoil 728.3
c. may over-spread the sky 892.2
when stern affliction c. 911.4
fearing neither c. 930.2
c. have gathered round 938.3
c. will change to sunshine c115
through c. and sunshine c132
b *dark clouds*
when c. are drifting d. 40.3
drive these d. c. 318.4
no d. c. of doubt . . . obscure 394.3
makes the d. c. withdraw 646.2
and d. c. before us 655.3
though d. c. may gather round 732.1
where the d. c. have been 736.3
trusting when d. c. appear c196
c *no clouds [in Heaven]*
no c. thy glory hide 76.4
no c. e'er pass along 268.2
where . . . c. are no more 318.4

cloudless
dwells in c. light 465.2
have won to c. day 878.1
bright and c. morning 907.2
earth with c. day 942.4

cloudy
let the fiery, c. pillar 578.2
c. or fine, Lord, I am thine c49

cloven *Acts 2:3* 198.1

clover 41.2

cloy 607.3

coal *Isa 6:6*
touch my lips with living c. 528.c
touch us with the living c. 609.3
touch my lips with a c. c97

coast 925.3

coffers 354.1

cold
c. wind in the winter 25.3
c. my warmest thought 58.4
on a c. winter's night 90.1
we learn that love grown c. 172.5
faithless hearts are c. 202.1
soon your heart be c. 241.4
when the waters c. chill 280.3
death-dew lies c. 357.3
tongue be silent, c. 573.5
e'en death's c. wave 725.4
death's c. sullen stream 743.4
ice from being c. 854.2
nor death's c. flood 898.3

coldly 466.3

coldness 531.2

colour-s
he made their glowing c. 25.1
c., scorn or wealth divide 142.4
your c. will not matter there 170.2
sombre the c. are and gay 644.2
b *colours [flag]*
fight beneath its c. 382.c; 782.c
true to our c. 681.3
my c. I'll show 684.2
hoist the c. bravely 704.c
'neath our c. waving 774.c
around our c. . . . rally 775.1
have our c. waving 775.c
proudly we salute the c. 777.1
true to my c. 778.c
with all its c. mean 779.2
its c. so resplendent 781.1
our c. still are flying 800.1
will our c. boldly show 821.c

combat 803.2

combined 202.2

come
1 *[God] comes*
a *(in incarnation)*
to the rescue c. 18.2
he c., to release/to bind 81.2, 3
late in time behold him c. 82.2
thou c. a little baby thing 91.1
a light c. out of darkness 94.1
thou c. . . . with the living 101.3
out of the Father's heart he c. 114.1
he c., he died, for you 114.2
from the Father's bosom c. 116.3
c. ruined sinners to reclaim 118.1
was it for me he c. to die 134.1
sinners unto whom he c. 141.3
to bring fire . . . he c. 165.1
thou c. to us in lowliness 174.2
c. to share our human life 181.1
thou who c. from above 199.1
thou who didst c. to bring 224.2
c. to be . . . Saviour/friend 225.3
he c. as the light 245.1
for whose cleansing he c. 245.c
he c. to give/bind/make . . . 274.c
Son of God as man c. down 274.*
did he c. down from above 289.1
he c. to set his people free 468.c
from thy throne again c. down 532.4
King of glory c. down 840.1
heal the broken heart he c. c25
that ever he c. to the cross c217
earth (1c), glory (3b), save (1c)
b *[Jesus] came*
Jesus came the world to save 62.2
Jesus . . . c. to earth 74.1
hark! . . . the Saviour c. 81.1
Joy . . .! the Lord is c. 84.1
till Jesus c. from heaven 94.1
whom Jesus c. to save 98.3
Jesus c. down my ransom 114.1
one day Jesus c. 245.1
we wonder why Christ c. 274.*
Jesus c. to save me 347.1
Saviour c. seeking his sheep 388.1
Saviour of men c. to seek 527.1
for such our Saviour c. 789.4
save the world the Saviour c. 831.1
the Lord c. down to save me 840.1
holy Jesu, c. from God 871.2
Christ, the Lord, is c. c27
c *[during life of Jesus]*
she knew her Lord had c. 304.2
when . . . to Zion Jesus c. 853.1
on Easter morning Jesus c. 855.5
Jesus went to the cross c24
d *[came at Pentecost]*
he c. in semblance of a dove 200.2
c. in tongues . . . as the wind 200.3
c. sweet influence to impart 200.4
God's Holy Spirit c. 215.c
on whom the Spirit c. 701.3
e *[comes today]*
c. down . . . stair . . . to answer 91.3
c. to succour, help 104.5
c. to claim the here and now 142.2
Jesus c.! 159.*
may I c. in 229.*
God is c. very near 259.1
the Spirit will c. 410.1
prayed that Christ would c. 541.1
if Christ c. in to reign 541.2
the Lord will c., revealing 591.1
you c. yourself each one 748.3
you c. to us, our God 748.4
in thee, O Jesus, c. near 871.4
he has c. back to your heart c11
thou art c. to meet my need c86
f *[testimony]*
thou dost this moment c. 208.3
Spirit c. in like a flood 321.2
in loving kindness Jesus c. 339.1
J. came down to bring me 349.2
Christ c. to me 376.c
Jesus c. with peace to me 379.c
he c. a-seeking, he pitied 388.2
since Jesus c. into my heart 394.*
he c. right down to me 398.c
Jesus c. with message clear 398.2
the Spirit has c. 410.3
thou again to live hast c. 513.3
now Christ has c. to reign 541.3
grace that he should c. 541.4
my Lord, thou dost c. in 562.3
c. the love of Jesus c140
g *come [request]* nc, but
c. like dew . . . shower 213.2
c. as a mighty rushing wind 216.3
c. great Spirit 217.1
c. as the light/fire/dew/dove 217.*
c. as of old . . . to sanctify 218.1
c., as thou didst of old 827.2
haste (c), heart (7j), quickly (b), revealing (c), Spirit (1a)
h *come (again)*
when Christ shall c. 37.4
when thou c. and callest 101.c
when he c., our glorious King 118.5
lo! He c. with clouds 161.1
everlasting God, c. down 161.4
Jesus the judge shall c. 164.6
the King who is c. to reign 166.1

Prince and Saviour, c. . . 167.3
c. in thy great might . . 172.4
Christ is c., . . . victorious . 184.3
hold the fort, for I am c. . 804.c
onward c. our great commander 804.4
shout till the Master c. . . 807.3
till Jesus c. again . . . 828.4
the Lord our God shall c. . 924.3
even so, Lord, quickly c. . 924.4
till the reapers c. . . . 931.3
the reaping time will c. . . 932.c
one day he's c. . . . c185

i *Mal 3:17*
c. to make up his jewels. . 852.1

2 *[people] come*
a *(biblical)*
three wise men c. 90.3
when wise men c. seeking . 92.1
the angel of the Lord c. down 93.1
Mary . . . c. with a gift . . 117.3
shepherds c. thither to see . 137.1
I c. as the prodigal c. . . 288.3
she c. in fear and trembling . 304.2
shepherds c. to worship him . 855.1
the sower c. to sow . . 932.1

b *Luke 13:29*
c. from the east . . . west . 170.*

c *Matt 19:14*
suffer me to c. to thee . . 793.1
let the little ones c. . . 794.1
suffer little children to c. . 797.*

d *[general]*
like a warrior I shall c. . . 338.5
bring thee where they c. . 604.2
forth from thy heart we c. . 648.2
to tell me whence I c. . . 652.1
grant that I may c. . . . 675.3
compel the wanderer to c. . 683.6
when we c. to die . . . 798.3

e *Ps 121:8*
thy going out, thy c. in . . 767.4

rejoice (f)

3 *coming to God*
c. we to the joy supernal . 185.2
Saviour who would have us c. 265.2
thou bid'st me c. to thee . 293.1
my lifeless soul to c. . . 353.4
though c. weak and vile. . 423.2
c. to the mercy seat . . 646.1
c. unto the healing waters . 647.1
filling each who c. to thee . 707.3
speak again and bid me c. . 749.2
the little children to c. . . 797.3
pardon is for all who c. . . 831.4
let his little child c. in . . 843.2

b *John 14:6*
I can c. no other way . . 292.4
thou by whom we c. to God . 625.6

4 *coming to God—invitation*
a *to consecration*
c., with me visit Calvary. . 413.1
c. to him without delay . . 433.1
c., let us use the grace . . 784.1

b *come to Jesus*
c., sinners, to Jesus . . 233.1
ye all may c. to Christ . . 234.3
c. to the Saviour . . . 235.*
c. to Jesus while you may . 239.2
c. to the Saviour who offers . 247.2
Jesus is waiting, O c. . . 248.3
c. to the Saviour now pleading 263.1
c. to Christ . . . confessing . 328.3
O sinner, c. to Jesus . . 403.3
O sinner, c. to Jesus . . 913.c
are you c. home to Jesus . c4
if you c. to him . . . c203

c *'come to me'* *Matt 11:28*
c. to me, saith one . . 228.1
c., ye guilty, c. to me . . 240.1
c., ye laden, c. to me . . 240.2

c., and he will give you rest . 262.2
c. to me, the Saviour said . 277.1
c. unto me and rest . . 332.1

d *John 4:14*
he who c. . . . never thirst . c16

e *to reward*
c. on, my comrades dear . 312.3
c. and take thy crown . . 352.3
c. at his bidding to cease . 808.4
who will c. and go with me . 887.c
c. to this happy land . . 897.2
angels whisper: C. away . 911.5

blessed (1g) higher (c)

f *to salvation*
c. and be saved by . . . grace. 56.3
brethren, c. 73.2
c., sinners, see him lifted . 107.3
c., bring thy sin . . . 126.4
O wanderer, c. 226.2
c. with me where love/light . 232.1
c. with all thy sins . . . wash. 232.2
c. . . . to the gospel feast . 234.1
c., all the world . . . 234.2
tenderly saying: C. . . . 235.1
do not delay, but c. . . 235.2
c., ye disconsolate . . . kneel. 236.1
burden cast, trustfully c. . 236.3
c., cast in thy sorrow . . 237.3
c. and wash your sins away . 239.2
c. with thy burden today . 247.1
c. to thy only redeemer/love . 247.2
c. with thy sins . . . delay . 248.3
c. where its . . . waves roll . 252.2
c., thirsty souls . . . 254.3
c. then, with all . . . wounds. 254.4
c., and thy sin confessing . 255.1
c., he waits for thee . . 255.c
why not c. and say . . 255.4
c. . . . there is refuge . . 257.1
c. to the waters . . . 257.3
c. away to him . . . who died. 260.3
c. enter the door . . . 263.3
c., and go with me . . 266.c
leave your sin and c. . . 267.3
c., sinner and backslider . 269.2
c. and bow at his . . . feet . 278.2
c. then for cleansing . . 281.2
c. . . . make a full surrender . 343.3
broken-hearted, all may c. . 369.3
wanderer, c. in . . . 391.1
c. this very moment . . 403.3
c., plunge in 535.c
c., guilty souls . . . 802.2
who c. . . . never disappointed 824.c
c. then to him who has laid . 881.3
c. along, for Jesus is strong . c3
child of mine, c. back . . c6
c. with thy sin . . . c9
c. ye who still are dry . . c16
let the dear Master c. in. . c18
pardon for all who will c. . c23

cross (2g), delay (b), home (2c), sin (1b), today (c), whoever

g *to service*
c., join our Army . . . 681.*
c. and join our . . . band. . 694.c
c. and join our ranks . . 818.c

h *Acts 16:9*
c. and help us 922.1

i *to [worship]*
c. ye before him and rejoice . 3.1
c. now with praise before him 19.5
c. to the Father through Jesus 22.c
c., let us join our . . . songs . 57.1
c. then, let us hasten yonder. 73.3
c. and worship Christ . . 75.*
c., all ye faithful . . . 85.1
c. ye to Bethlehem . . . behold 85.1
c. let us adore him . . . 85.*
c. and look awhile on him . 121.1
c. let us sing: Praise . . 166.c

c. comrades dear . . . 312.1
c., ye that love the Lord. . 314.1
c. and hear me tell . . . 338.1
all who love the Saviour, c. . 338.1
c. and praise the Lord . . 360.1
c., my soul, thy suit prepare . 563.1
thou art c. to a King . . 563.2
c. ye aside from all . . 564.2
c., tell me all 564.3
c., shout and sing . . . 798.1
c. with happy faces . . 836.*
c. with hearts sincere . . 836.3
c., ye thankful people, c. . 924.1
c. to God's own temple, c. . 924.1

apart

j *Luke 15:5*
c. and rejoice with me . . 311.*

5 *[testimony]*
I c. to Jesus with my sin . 52.2
I have already c. . . . 308.3
I c. to Calvary's mountain . 309.1
hither by thy help I'm c.. . 313.2
I know, when I c. . . . 331.3
I c. to Jesus . . . 332.1, 2
there I c. to Jesus, bound . 348.2
I c., and ever since . . 359.2
when as a sinner I c. . . 371.2
when I c. to him Christ c. . 376.c
c. to the mercy seat pleading. 383.3
to the cross then I c. . . 395.1
I c. to him so sinful . . 403.2
they shall c. forth to tell. . 893.3

b *Rev 7:14*
out of great distress they c. . 909.2

6 *[commitment]*
now I c., before thee fall . 114.3
in penitence we c. to thee . 131.4
c. and now baptise us all . 201.1
I c. to thee for rest. . . 284.3
Lord, I will c. . . . let me c. . 285.*
Christ crucified, I c. . . 287.*
I c. as the prodigal came . 288.3
O Lamb of God, I c. . . 293.*
not despairingly c. I . . 296.1
Jesus, I c. to thee . . . 300.*
naked, c. to thee for dress . 302.3
as I am I c., believing . . 303.4
I'm c., dear Jesus . . . 368.3
I am c., Lord, c. now to thee. 423.c
though c. weak and vile. . 423.2
Lord, I c. to thee beseeching . 434.1
as I c. thou wilt . . . receive . 437.2
with . . . thirst I c. . . . 447.1
c. once more to thee . . 448.2
I c. to thee with quiet mind . 449.c
spotless Lamb, I c. . . 450.1, c
I am c., dear Saviour . . 469.*
I am c., Lord, to thee . . . 470.1
helpless . . . I c. . . . 488.c
I am c., dear Saviour . . 493.1
Lord, I c. to thee for rest . 563.4
bless me now . . . I c. . . 587.c
we c. to hail thee . . . 595.1
c. to seek . . . with burdens . 595.1
which here we c. to prove . 603.2
I c., thy life in mine . . 631.4
at the close . . . I c. to thee . 675.1
we c., and from thee never . 693.2
Jesus Christ, I c. . . . 860.1
with first-fruits we c. . . 936.1
I am c. to the Saviour . . c13
to thy cross I c., Lord . . c109

b *Ps 126:6*
we shall c. rejoicing . . 930.*

7 *[general]*
a *come [from God]*
joy c. again 146.2
from whom the promise c. . 198.2
his bright rays c. beaming . 316.2
the wrath that's to c. . . 321.4
heaven c. down and Glory . 371.c

crystal flow c. from thee . 416.1
till grace c. in . . . 468.2
joy which c. 534.1
glory c. thrilling . . . 542.3
boundless salvation is c. . 543.3
Heaven c. down . . . to greet. 573.4
salvation . . . shall surely c. . 596.4
chart and compass c. . . 598.1
c. with the morning star. . 641.2
tell of joys to c. . . . 652.4
a deeper joy c. . . . 711.1
ease which c. swift . . 719.3
whence their victory c. . . 879.3
strength that c. from thee . 938.3

peace (2d)

b *Ps 121:1*
thence my help is c. . . 766.2
whence . . . my salvation c. . 767.1

c *general*
our hope for years to c. . .13.1, 6
all . . . c. to an ending . . 39.4
it c. upon the midnight . . 83.1
c. round the age of gold. . 83.3
gain c. not except by loss . 211.3
doom c. at last . . . 226.3
beasts of prey c. not there . 268.3
bright rays c. beaming . . 316.2
days of darkness still c. . . 337.4
c. joy or c. sorrow . . . 473.c
sorrow that c. with tomorrow 473.3
changes that will surely c. . 485.1
when nightfall c. . . . 628.3
thought c. back to me . . 686.1
c. the plains . . . days of joy . 711.1
when the accuser c. . . 724.3
the hour has c. to die . . 753.4
sounds . . . c. on the breeze . 803.1
whence have c. these legions. 803.2
building c. to naught . . 827.3
spring from c. in . . . 854.1
no evil thing c. to despoil . 883.3
the heavenly summons c. . 890.2
death may c. when least . 913.2
and its shadow c. . . . 916.3
to thy hand shall c. . . 921.3
whence have c. these fields . 923.1
rest c. for the weary . . 934.3
for all that's to c. . . . 962
c. this way, a mighty revival . c63
drum with its c., c., c. . . c230

d *[last things]*
when c. the promised time . 172.3
victory will c. . . . 681.4
wide world shall c. . . 700.3
the day of victory's c. . . 810.*

day (3h), kingdom (1d)

8

a *come and/or go*
a love to c. or go . . . 426.2
charms, they c. and go . . 630.1
kings and nations c. and go . 799.1

b *come what may*
fears of what may c. . . 41.2
trust him, c. what may . . 333.3
day by day, c. what may . 499.c
I trust him, c. what may. . c132

comeliness *Eze 16:14*
true c. renew . . . 494.2
thy c. put upon me . . 589.2

comfort
1 *(divine)*
from mine example c. take . 21.2
it will joy and c. give . . 66.1
c. in the name of Jesus . . 70.3
c. thy sorrows . . . 183.2
my c. still is this . . . 187.3
light and c. from above . . 190.1
my peace, my life, my c. thou 207.3
the spring of all my c. . . 301.4
my only hope and c. . . 325.1
in sorrow he's my c. . . 344.1
O what c. 350.3
what a c. divine . . . 355.1
help and c. give you . . 396.3
solid c. when we die . . 464.2
thank you . . . for precious c. 552.3
not suffice my c. to restore . 565.3
thy mighty c. feel . . . 603.4
supplying c. to the dying . 655.5
with c. to cheer . . . 689.3
gently falling for our c. . . 711.2
with heavenly c. fraught . 725.1
whisper words of c. . . 731.2
still support and c. me . . 737.2
doth keep and c. me . . 741.3
grace shall c. us through . 763.5
fold him (her) in your c. . . 792.1
c., strengthen and keep you . 823.c
Spirit, stay to c. me . . 958

b *sweet comfort*
the s. c. and peace . . 367.1
that s. c. is mine . . . 367.2
for thy s. c. in distress . . 719.1
with his own s. c. . . . c113

c *Ps 23:4*
thy rod and staff my c. . . 53.4
rod and staff me c. . . 54.3
c. and protects me . . 583.3

d *Matt 9:22*
daughter, be of good c. . . 304.3

e *2 Cor 1:3*
God of c. and compassion . 576.1

2 *(human)*
speak the word of c. . . 706.1
longing for c. . . . 740.1
seeking the c. of a . . . hand . 740.2
every c. be withdrawn . . 746.4
song that c. the sad . . 838.3
to cheer, to c. and to tell . 851.4

b *comforts*
though my joys and c. die . 358.2
our c. and our cares . . 660.2
helpers fail, and c. flee . . 670.1

distress (2b), people (1b)

comforter
time of trouble a c. . . 98.3

b *John 14:16*
Jesus . . . gives the C. . . 195.1
draw near, O promised C. . 198.5
a guide, a C. bequeathed . 200.1
Holy Ghost, the C. . . 202.4
attend the promised C. . . 214.2
O that the C. would come . 214.3
come, holy C. . . . 219.3
here speaks the C. . . . 236.2
Spirit of peace, my C. . . 647.1
now the C. guides thee . . 739.3

comfortless *Matt 5:4* . . . 95.1

coming
1 *(noun)*
no ear may hear his c. . . 86.3
how gracious his c. to earth . 92.2
at thy c. to victory . . . 101.4
glory of the c. of the Lord . 162.1
we celebrate thy c. . . 198.1
at his c. heavenly music. . 227.3
to hinder your c. . . . engage. 233.2
never . . . fear about their c. . 824.3
heralding the c. of the King . c226

b *1 Cor 1:7**
for thy c. we pray . . . 166.5
for thy c. we wait . . . 771.4

2 *(adjective)*
waiting the c. day . . . 148.1
soon our c. King . . . 347.3
through the c. night . . 674.3

command
a *(over nature)*
wide as the world is thy c. . 4.4
he, with all-c. might . . 34.3
thy voice c. light . . . 36.1
thine all-wise c. . . . 39.1
angels waited his c. . . 130.3
bow to his c. 164.4
oceans move at thy c. . . 171.2
waiting his c. . . . 333.4
who Heaven and earth c. . 715.1
flowery spring at thy c. . . 925.2

b *(over man)*
to sanctify, to take c. . . 163.3
teach us love's c. . . . 218.2
at whose supreme c. . . 223.2
I'm at his c. 321.3
to die fulfilling thy c. . . 362.2
as I bow to thy c. . . . 463.2
freely flows at love's c. . . 520.3
if thy c. ordain . . . 629.2
weave at thy c. . . . 644.4
labour on at thy c. . . . 667.2
yield my powers to thy c. . 672.3
received the royal c. . . 702.2
freely follows his c. . . 732.2
he gives the word of c. . . 734.3
redeem the time at thy c. . 747.3
we obey divine c. . . . 785.5
who will heed the great c. . 868.1

c *[God's] commands*
onward! 'tis the Lord's c. . 393.1
the Lord's c. to go . . 700.1
we fight at God's c. . . 798.2
forward, 'tis the Lord's c. . 817.3
heeding God's c. . . . 847.1
obey thy Lord's c. . . . 923.3

d *blest command*
heed now his b. c. . . . 235.3
thy b. c. were laid upon me . 534.1
keeps the b. c. by Jesus . 580.3
at thy b. c., I sail . . . 628.4

commander *Isa 55:4*
but by our c. led . . . 789.3
onward comes our great c. . 804.4

commenced 338.3

commend *Luke 23:46*
my soul . . . I faithfully c. . 714.4
to him c. thy cause . . 715.4

commerce 688.1

commission
called and c. from afar . . 163.2
when the fire of thy c. . . 463.2
would stain my c. . . . 786.1
his glorious c. . . . 864.3

commit
a *Ps 37:5*
c. thou all thy griefs . . 715.1
I c. my way to thee . . c33

b *2 Tim 1:12*
everything to him c. . . 514.2
in thy ministry c. . . . 528.3
keep that which I've c. . . 730.c
what I've c. to his hands . 735.3
to love c. all their loves . . 874.3

c *1 John 3:9*
without c. sin shall live . . 714.2

common
the c. words I speak . . 7.2
life's c. looks and tones . . 7.2
around one c. mercy seat . 573.3
in the midst of c. days . . 618.1
trivial round, the c. task . . 668.4

commune
with thee, my God, I c. . . 585.3
with him c. like him . . . grow 640.5

communion *2 Cor 13:14*
in sweet c. talk . . . 59.3
claiming a closer c. . . 501.1
sharing in the new c. . . 595.3
for closer c. I pine . . 639.1
O what blessed, sweet c. . 709.c
true hearts . . . c. find . 826.2

companion
Holy Spirit, c. divine . . 209.2
my old c., fare you well . . 275.4
Christ . . . c. is of mine . . 400.1
be c., friend and shepherd . 576.1
shun evil c. 823.2

company
in closer, dearer c. . . . 519.3
in your c. we'll wait . . 748.1
marching forth a c. grand . c236

compare
what love can c. . . . 119.c
c. with Christ, in all beside . 565.1
can e'er c. with thine . . 870.2
I can't c. it c170

compass
chart and c. come from thee . 598.1
b *Ps 32:7*
arms of love that c. me . . 60.4
hands that c. . . . relief . . 129.3

compassion
human hands c. show . . 50.1
how tender his c. . . . 94.2
thy grief and thy c. . . 123.2
with c. pure and sweet . . 212.3
out of love and c. for me 289.1, c
Jesus, thou art all c. . . 438.1
the boundless c. of God . . 527.1
God of comfort and c. . . 576.1
to be like thee! full of c. . 623.2
his nature is c. . . . 854.2
b *deep compassion*
give me a c. d. . . . 205.3
re-create a d. c. . . . 463.3
true holiness, c. d. . . c208
c *heart of compassion*
serving thee with a h. of c. . 493.3
h. o'erflowing with c. . . 704.2
O for a h. of c. . . . 786.4
d *Ps 86:15**
he is of great c. . . . 272.2
in great c. Jesus watches . 341.2
e *Matt 9:36*
moved by thy divine c. . . 370.1
except I am moved with c. . 527.c
f *compassions* *Lam 3:22*
thy c. they fail not . . 33.1

compassionate
what a tender, c. friend . . 371.1
lack in c. zeal . . . 527.2

compel
his love is mighty to c. . . 234.4
sink, by dying love c. . . 307.4
b *Luke 14:23*
c. the wanderer to come in . 683.6

complaint
Lord, it is my chief c. . . 110.6
tell my true c. . . . 290.2
love has silenced all c. . . 926.1

complete
when our journey is c. . . 66.4
asks a sacrifice c. . . . 128.2
Christ's c. mission . . . 173.2
pardon, precious, sure, c. . 259.3
thy work c. 291.4
what bliss c. 375.3
finding c. relief . . . 383.3
c. in me thy perfect plan . 398.4
our hearts and lives c. . . 413.1
c. bloud-bought redemption . 413.2
c. deliverance . . . 433.2
this moment the work is c. . 454.3
b *make complete*
it m. my joys full and c. . . 68.1
m. the sacrifice c. . . . 199.4
plunge in today and be m. c. . 315.4
m. me for thyself c. . . 477.1
m. your sacrifice c. . . 920.1
c *stand complete* *Col 4:12*
and s. c. at last . . . 695.5
before his throne we'll s. c. . 888.3
sacrifice (2b)

completely
Jesus c. saves . . . 336.3
hearts c. cleansed from sin . 704.1
trusting thee c. . . . 947.3

completeness 35.2

compose-ed
c. so rich a crown . . . 136.3
sharper than c. his crown . 758.2

comprehend
I cannot c. such love . . 48.1
more than I can ever c. . . 52.3
or c. thy bitter cry . . . 122.2
whence it came and c. love . 496.2
b *Eph 3:18*
I now can c. the wonders . 215.2
O Lord, I shall now c. . . 454.5
with the saints, I am now c. . 493.3

comrade
c. faint amid the strife . . 70.3
do you, c., feel at times . . 169.3
come, c. dear . . . 312.1, 3
c. there in love I share . . 375.3
c. and kindred will shout . 543.4
every c., Lord, we pray . . 769.3
my c. beckoning stand . . 780.4
c. here remind us . . . 788.2
my c., see the signal/cheer 804.1, 4
if beside you . . . c. waver . 805.3
sing it as our c. sang it . . 815.1
rejoin our conquering c. . . 819.3
who once were c. . . . 878.1
c. has found release . . 894.1
wider fields our c. reap . . 922.1
c., let us be true . . . c239

concealed
c. in the cleft of thy side . 639.3
truth c. within thy word . . 650.3

conceive
no heart c. how dear . . 69.3
nor heart c. the glory . . 878.4

concern
great c. shall be to love . . 14.4
pleasing him your chief c. . 343.3

concerning 218.2

concrete 30.1

condemn-ed
don't assume that God c. . 44.3
bound and c. to die . . 45.1
in my place c. he stood . . 118.2
a sinner, c., unclean . . 179.1
we stand all c. before God . 245.4
c. in thought and deed . . 290.1
for sinners c., what way . 319.2
let holy truth c. each sham . 446.2
mine to judge, c., acquit . 652.2

condemnation *Rom 8:1*
no c. now I dread . . . 283.4
I fear no c. 361.3
in dread c. I pine . . . 364.2
washing stains of c. . . 540.2
troubled with much c. . . 553.2

condescend-ing
thy c. grace., freely move . 307.2
to c. to be my friend . . 398.c
King of love so c. . . . 500.1

condition 498.2

conduct 458.2

confer-ing
on each waiting soul c. . . 198.5
with evil everywhere c. . . 864.1

confess-ed-ing
1 *[witness]*
earth with joy c. . . . 155.2
two wonders I c. . . . 476.2
let our ordered lives c. . . 567.4
my love for thee I will c.. . 719.1
for this flag our love c. . . 777.1
in silent worship I c. . . 871.1
to those who have c. . . 875.4
oft are its glories c. . . 904.1
thy bounteous hand c. . . 934.2
b *Matt 10:32; Phil 2:11*
every tongue c. him . . 141.1
let every tongue c. . . 174.5
by earth and Heaven c. . . 223.1
charmed to c. the voice . . 365.3
men beholding must c. . . 494.2
outward lips c. the name . 496.2
until men c. Christ's Kingdom 776.3
God's mighty love c. . . 833.3
faith before the world c. . 876.1
all men c. thy . . . hand . . 927.4
2 *[admit]*
to him c. my deepest need . 52.2
all I must forsake, c. . . 434.2
I here c. is small . . . 489.3
now as to God we're c. . . 637.4
b *James 5:16*
hear us, Lord, our faults c. . 863.2
c *confess sin* *1 John 1:9*
stand and here c. my s. . . 120.3
come, and thy s. c. . . 255.1, c
come away . . . and c. thy s.. 260.3
I c. to thee sadly my s. . . 296.3
to that heart, its s. c. . . 303.3
come to Christ, your s. c. . 328.3
there are s. my lips c. . . 460.2
find peace from s. c. . . 590.3
their s. c. truly . . . 831.4

confide-ing
in our own strength c. . . 1.2
they, who in his truth c.. . 21.4
help me c. in thee . . . 574.2
safe is such c. . . . 736.1
in love's assurance we c. . 748.4
in his promises c. . . . 759.c
happy, still in God c. . . 764.2
my heart is longing to c. . c62
c. to the care of love . . c176

confidence
with c. I now draw nigh . . 106.5
by . . . fellowship c. give . 209.2
c. unshaken 222.2
with humble c. look up . . 596.1
there is c. in him . . . 711.3
my c. is all in thee . . . 714.3

full c. in Jesus' blood . 733.1
full of c. while he is near . c132
dwell with him in c. . c143
b *Isa 30:15*
then quietness and c. . 717.6

confident
of this I'm c. . 732.2
with c. and humble mind . 744.3

confine-d
love no barrier could c. . 5.1
thou, within no walls c. . 604.2

confirm-ed *1 Cor 1:8*
Jesus, c. my heart's desire . 199.3
c. the blessed work . 423.4
c. our hope . 662.2
c. his good pleasure . 712.3
all our works c. by thee . 863.3
registered, c. by thee . 865.3

conflict
a *(outer)*
while in c. we engage . 249.4
so amid the c. . 396.3
'tis because in every c. . 404.4
in the toils and c. . 499.3
though in the c. for right . 537.2
present though the c. rages . 539.3
rest amidst life's c. . 575.3
voice shall bid our c. cease . 674.4
all your c. past . 695.5
forth to the mighty c. . 699.2
in the c. men are wanted . 702.1
fierce may be the c. . 707.4
c. which faith will require . 734.3
one the c., one the peril . 765.5
nor weary in the c. . 781.3
on to the c., soldiers . 813.1
soon . . . the c. cease . 813.4
then forward to the c. . 814.3
in the mighty c. never yield . 817.2
in c. he always is near . 820.3
c. and dangers are over . 894.1
they who in the c. dire . 910.4
what c. we have passed . 915.2
the last great c. won . 939.3
b *(inner)*
peace instead of inner c. . 244.2
many a c., many a doubt . 293.3
every c., without and within . 640.2

conform-ity *Rom 8:29, 12:2*
that full divine c. . 419.1
all my will c. to thine . 445.1
c. my will to thine . 560.5
whate'er c. not to thy love . 565.4

confound-ed-ing
all virtue c. . 19.4
do but themselves c. . 685.2
storms . . . threaten to c. me. 732.1
enemies we shall c. . 809.3
not a foe can e'er c. . 822.2
the sinner's heart c. . 875.1
perils thick c. you . 954.3
b *Isa 50:7**
nor shall I be c. . 361.3

confusion *(1 Cor 14:33)*
men have wrought c. . 6.4
give, for wild c., peace . 569.3
from earth's c. . c94

congregation *Ps 35:18** 24.2

conquer-ed-ing
1 *[God] conquers* *Rev 6:2*
because he c., we shall win . 5.5
thy wondrous love has c. me. 108.3
c. every place and time . 142.2
darkness is c., death . 146.1
Jesus shall c., lift up . 173.c
Jesus . . . hath c. for you . 233.2
Christ hath c. there . 465.4
thy love at last has c. . 548.4
2
grace to c. in the fight . 203.3
he will assist you to c. . 233.2
I shall c. still . 391.3
none but the soul who has c.. 406.4
the faith that c. doubt . 432.2
help me to c. Satan's host . 432.3
I'm bound to c. . 477.4
loath are my feet to c. . 488.2
they may c. in the strife. . 582.5
that I may c. in the fight. . 620.1
battling, c. for thee . 643.4
determined to c. . 686.c
sing and c. every nation. . 696.3
he would desire to c. . 760.3
onward to c. the world . 802.c
c. through the blood . 809.c
with blood and fire we'll c. . 810.2
how the weakest c. . 815.2
we have c. in . . . past . 820.2
the Army that shall c. . 822.c
be c. through the blood . 822.3
through faith . . . c. . 823.3
b *conquer all*
the faith that c. all . 756.5
I c. all while hiding . 761.3
I shall surely c. all . c234
c *conquer (die)*
by thee we'll c. or we'll d. . 692.3
we'll c. if we d. . 694.c
determined to c. or d. . 800.2
d *conquer foe*
can I not . . . c. every f.. . 447.3
c. every f. . 620.*
help us to c. the f. . 681.1
we shall c. the f. . 687.4
I can c. every f. . 758.c
band that shall c. the f. . 820.1
who . . . c. every f. . 835.3
c. all the f. ahead . 858.2
e *conquer sin*
captive death and c. s. . 150.2
power to c. inbred s. . 214.1
c. over Hell and s. . 532.2
c. s. that bring you pain. . 806.3
daily c. s. and wrong . 816.4
wrong (b)

conquering *(adjective)*
a *(divine)* *Rev 6:2*
proclaims thy c. arm . 100.3
risen c. Son . 152.1, c
his c. love consent . 234.4
O c. Jesus, Saviour thou . 424.4
live a c. Christ within . 447.2
by thy c. name, victory . 543.1
power to speak thy c. word . 609.3
to your c. captain cleaving . 693.c
thou, all c. Lord . 742.3
in the c. name of Jesus . 787.3
follow our c. Saviour . 800.2
with the c. Son of God . 819.c
b *(human)*
come and join our c. band . 694.c
glory crown our c. band . 702.c
rejoin our c. comrades . 819.3
the c. host above . 894.c
a c. band to be . c236

conqueror
1 *(divine)*
'tis finished! . . . c. cries . 107.4
own thee c. . 307.4
thy love shall be the c. . 410.2
be thou c. of each heart. . 643.3
2 *(human)*
o'er death I shall c. be . 137.5
as c. meet him there . 242.5
I shall c. be . 508.1
singing . . . shall c. be . 543.3
pleasant the c.'s song . 712.4
I may sing the c.'s song. . 719.5
evermore we shall c. be . 800.1
we'll be c. for ever . 800.3
c. at last . 802.4
b *more than conqueror* *Rom 8:37*
make us m. t. c. . 152.3
fire that makes us m. t. c. . 197.3
yet m. t. c. am I . 385.3
I m. t. c. shall stand . 468.3
we shall m. t. c. be . 554.2
who . . . trusts is m. t. c. . 695.2
m. t. c. in every fight . 811.3

conquest
great the c. to be won . 158.2
delights in the c. . 799.3
ascribe their c. . 879.3

conscience
give the guilty c. peace . 120.1
King within my c. reign . 194.3
how to ease my c. . 303.2
c. keen to feel . 409.3
quick . . . my c. make . 425.3
sin-stained c. smart . 446.3
c. free from guilt . 563.3
c. as the noonday clear . 665.2

conscious-ly
c. believes . 756.4
c. you are very near . 795.1

consciousness 632.1, 2

consecrate-ing *1 Chr 29:5**
soul and body c. . 197.1
come and c. my breast . 207.1
c. to thee alone . 492.3
residue of days I c. . 505.1
c. me now to thy service . 585.2
to thee I c. my days . 672.3
heart, mind and will c. . 786.3
c. myself to thee . 860.1
come . . . c. this place . 946.1

consecrated *(adjective)*
bless this c. hour . 217.4
seek that c. spot . 261.2
divide this c. soul . 480.3
a c. offering . 511.1
life, and let it be c.. . 525.1
serve thee, every c. hour . 591.c
sustain the c. cross . 596.2
gleams a c. sword . 799.2
by our c. giving . 922.1
each . . . c. unto thee . 941.2
upon this c. ground . 942.1
b *all consecrated*
my all c. to thee . 469.4
my all is c. . 495.1

consecration
draw me . . . in deeper c. . 493.c
I sought the path of c. . 534.1
prayer . . . for a perfect c. . 584.3
fit us for full c. . 622.1
thine in c. . 788.3
may this solemn c. . 865.3

consent
c. to languish . 135.1
his conquering love c. . 234.4

consider
a *Ps 8:3*
in awesome wonder, c. . 37.1
when I thy works c. . 39.1
b *Prov 6:6*
O soul, c. and be wise . 885.1

consistently . . . 613.3

consolation *Luke 2:25*
all thy people's c. . . 79.2
may I thy c. share . . 633.3
word of c. . . 655.2
it carries c. . . 828.3

console . . . 486.3

conspire . . . 382.2

constancy . . . 685.1

constant
love thee with a c. mind . 5.4
instant and c. with joy . 51.1
this my c. theme shall be . 107.5
my wise and c. friend . 144.3
c. the vigil I must keep . 176.2
fix in me his c. home . 214.3
should c. joys create . 314.2
that c. cleansing flow . 350.2
I want thy c. presence . 455.4
through c. watching, wise . 485.2
instant and c. for thee . 527.3
still, by c. mercy fed . 566.1
my c. prayer shall be . 584.3
thy c. goodness . 616.1
this is my c. longing . 623.1
c. still in faith abiding . 634.3
my c. delight . 640.4
Church . . . c. will remain . 690.4
attend with c. care . 695.4
one . . . c. will remain . 750.1

constantly
shall c. partake . 277.3
c. witnessing . 323.3
c., faithfully working . 484.c, 2
c. to know fellowship . 630.1
obey . . . and c. believe . 785.5
c. abiding . c36

constellation . . . 38.1

constrain-ed-ing *2 Cor 5:14*
let thy love my heart c. . 140.5
his love your hearts c. . 234.3
his love's c. power . 234.4
when shall thy love c. . 307.1
daily I'm c. to be . 313.4
his all-c. grace . 445.4
love of Christ doth me c. . 526.1
his love c. us . c239

consume-ing
thy dross to c. . 653.4
gain by self-c. care . 715.4
give to my soul c. fire . 830.3
b *Lev 9:24*
c. my humble offering . 511.3

contact . . . 613.2

contemplate . . . 595.2

contempt . . . 136.1

contend *(Jude 3)*
powers of Hell c. . 694.2
in thy cause c. . c48

content-ed *Phil 4:11*
c. with beholding his face . 318.3
I pass c. by . 461.2
c. to let the world go by. . 476.3
c. to fill a little space . 485.3
blest c. and calm . 551.2
c. to trust my way to thee . 644.c
c., whatever lot I see . 725.3
a favoured and c. guest . 728.2
c. to take whate'er . 738.2
c. . . . wounds be theirs. . 774.2
c. to bloom . . . bower . 838.2
c. to die believing . 874.3
we will be c. . 921.2
I've been c. to dwell . 482.2

contentment
real c. has . . . laws . 244.3
whose voice is c. . 611.4
in giving . . . I find c. . c208

contest
fiercer gets the c. . 499.4
and give the c. o'er . 911.3

continent . . . 677.3

continual . . . 714.4

continuance . . . 785.5

continue-d
c. both day and night . 90.2
prayer for him (her) c. . 795.3

contrast . . . 446.2

contrite
c. sinner's voice . 625.4
b *contrite heart* *Ps 51:17*
hope of every c. h. . 61.3
broken and a c. h. . 121.6
my c. h. is drawn to thee . 122.1
lowly, c. h. . 444.3
yield . . . their c. h. . 802.3
c *contrite spirit* *Ps 34:18*
c. spirit he will bless . 225.3
lowly, c. s. . 259.3

contrition . . . 301.2

control
wants to take c. . 204.3
sensitive to thy c. . 209.3
all my life wilt thou c. . 479.3
c. my every thought . 568.1
firm in thy strong c. . 571.1
bend our pride to thy c. . 577.3
c. the wanderings . 619.2
come, O Spirit, take c. . 630.2
direct, c., suggest . 665.5
all my life thou shalt c. . 713.1
changing moods do not c. . 717.4
blest assurance c. . 771.2
to chasten or c. . 862.3
b *under control*
u. thy supreme c. . 208.2
I'm u. his c. . 362.1
beneath his c. . 458.4

convenient *Acts 24:25* . 226.1

converse-ing
c. . . . never known . 564.2
c. with your Lord . 564.4
with thee c., I forget . 636.2
prospect, c. sweet . 873.3
b *2 Cor 1:12**
let all thy c. be sincere . 665.2
purest word in all my c. . 867.4

convert-ing
thou only canst c. . 290.2
since I have been c. . 309.2
souls . . . c. to thee . 608.3

converts *(noun)*
bless our c. . 622.4
hark! c. are singing . 703.4
fresh c. still we gain . 815.3

convey . . . 565.2

convict
sinner c., Lord . 608.1
c. us by . . . power . 638.3

conviction . . . 6.2

convince-ing *(John 16:8)*
teach, c., subdue . 200.3
c. men of sin . 730.3

cool-ing
c. waters touched his feet . 103.3
a c. shading rock . 288.4
the hart for c. streams . 557.1

coolness . . . 567.5

copious . . . 940.3

copy . . . 444.4

cord
bound fast with c. . 129.1
service is the golden c. . 826.2
by the c. of service . 833.3
b *cords of love* *Hos 11:4*
drew me . . . c. of love . 345.1
bound . . . by love's strong c.. 757.3

cordial . . . 382.1

corn
the hushing of the c. . 41.2
raise the c. . 925.2
valleys . . . thick with c. . 934.1
full (g)

corner
in every c. sing . 11.*
come and every c. fill . 481.2
you in your small c. . 841.*
b *Eph 2.20**
Christ is our c.-stone . 940.1

corroding . . . 889.2

corruption . . . 499.1

cost-ing
salvation . . . highest c. . 46.1
empty glory is c. me . 98.4
fearless of the c. . 197.2
at such tremendous c. . 325.1
paid sin's fearful c. . 335.2
whate'er it c. . 440.2
c. thee such a price . 507.2
I will obey at all c. . 513.c
fight . . . c. thy life. . 816.2
redeemed at countless c. . 825.2
gift which c. you pain . 920.2
b *count cost* *Luke 14:28*
hast thou counted the c. . 263.3
nor count the c. . 798.3

costliest . . . 76.3

cot
so rude was thy c. . 175.1
lowly c. or stately home. . 705.1

cottage . . . 354.4

counsel
fulfil thy sovereign c. . 526.3
his c. shall appear . 721.4
b *Ps 73:24*
your c. to guide . 506.4
his c. guide . 954.1

counsellor *Isa 9:6*
so wise a C. and guide . 345.4
my C. thou art . 597.2

count
c. your (many) blessings . 396.*
sins I cannot c. . . 421.1
c. it an honour to die . 684.3
fight nor c. the odds . 774.2
c. good through peace . 874.3
c., dear Lord, on thee . c145
c. it a privilege here . c172
though men c. thee poor . c249
b *1 Tim 1:12*
he may c. me faithful . 522.c
c *count [loss]* *Phil 3:7, 8*
richest gain I c. but l. . 136.1
gladly c. all but dross . 320.2
c. . . . earth but dross . 427.c, 4
c. it gain to suffer l. . 489.2
c. . . . my life as dross . 729.1
cost (b), tear (2b)

countenance *Num 6:26* . 961

countless
who holds the c. stars . 6.1
c. gifts of love . 12.1
c. souls are gathered in . 266.1
through c. years my song . 400.3
thy c. benefits demand . 616.2
treasures still of c. price. 668.2
through c. ages . 690.5
c. hosts he leads . 790.1
redeemed at c. cost . 825.2

country
a *(literal)*
came from c. far . 90.3
c. is in every clime . 556.2
meets a c.'s need . 923.1
b *(figurative)* *Heb 11:14-16*
in that heavenly c. bright . 76.5
c. far from mortal sight . 880.1
c. so bright . 904.1

courage
fresh c. take . 29.3
we seek thy c. . 181.2
a song of . . . c. . 186.c
though . . . my c. failed . 391.2
tempest can my c. shake . 489.4
put a cheerful c. on . 559.1
increase my c., Lord . 678.4
God will your c. renew . 679.1
c! onward . 693.3
let c. rise with danger . 699.2
c., brother, do not stumble . 716.*
c. and zeal shall inspire . 734.3
c. almost gone . 804.2
mighty was their c. . 866.1
faith and dauntless c. . 866.c
flushing with the c. . c238
b *give/grant courage*
g. me holy c. . 499.3
g. c. for the battle . 575.3
g. thy fortitude and c. . 576.3
g. us wisdom . . . c. . 577.*
Lord, g. me c.. . 719.5
hope will g. us c. . 755.3
fire that g. the c. . 830.3
Jesus, g. me c. . 859.2
g. us c. when we falter . 863.4
g. . . . c. for the fight . 870.3

courageous *Josh 1:7*
c. and brave in the fight. 679.3
be more c. still . 782.3
God's soldier must c. be . 801.2

courageously . 570.1

course
stars in their c. above . 33.2
love planned our life's c. . 51.c
the stars their c. make . 171.2
on my onward c. . 345.3
our daily c. . 668.2
clouds their c. . 715.2
b *run course*
all day his c. to r. . 34.4
way my c. may r. . 536.3
r. my c. with even joy . 667.4

court(s)
see the c. of God . 59.4
upward to the c. of Heaven . 259.4
seal it for thy c. above . 313.5
when the c. of Heaven ring . 327.3
the temple c. were dark . 839.1
the c. above echo . 873.2
the c. of Heaven are filled . 940.1
sing . . . in the c. above. c222
b *Ps 100:4*
approach . . . his c. unto . 3.3
fill thy c. with . . . praise . 4.3
fear not to enter his c. . 183.3

covenant-ed
I renew my c. with thee. 534.c
plead fresh c. to make . 534.3
let me my c. renew . 618.3
control thy c. aid . 717.4
his oath, his c. and blood . 745.3
the c. we this moment make . 784.3
the c. is ratified . 785.4
b *Jer 50:5*
in a perpetual c. join . 784.1
c *Heb 8:6*
when, in solemn c. . 774.3

cover
c. my defenceless head . 737.2
the Army flag shall c. . 774.3
spread thy c. wings around . 918.4
b *Ex 33:22*
c. me there with his hand . 710.c
c *cover sin* *Ps 32:1; Rom 4:7*
the cross now c. my sins . 542.c
grace to c. all my sin . 737.4
c. is my unrighteousness . 746.2
never a sin . . . cannot c. . c87

covet
what can I c. more . 361.3
'tis thyself I c. most . 435.2
I c. to rest . 639.3

coward . 805.2

cradle-d
his c. was a stall . 87.2
a manger his c. . 92.1
Jesus, c. in a manger . 97.2
for his c. and his throne. 411.3
love that gazes at the c.. 544.3

craft . 1.1

craftsman
a c.'s tools . . . excellence . 688.2
my toil, my c.'s skill . 867.5

crag . 606.3

crave
thy guidance we c. . 209.3
heart for mercy c. . 393.3
faith . . . Lord, I would c. . 488.3
freedom to serve I c. . 571.4
no good to c. . 592.3

craving
fire that changes earthly c. . 197.2
Lord, fill my c. heart . 649.1, c

create-d-ing
he can c. and he destroy . 4.1
hands all things c. . 6.1
thy hands c. me . 23.4
I trust the all-c. voice . 26.4
should constant joys c. . 314.2
re-c. a deep compassion . 463.3
thee, almighty to c. . 596.1
c. soul-thirst for thee . 626.2
c. faith in him . 730.3
b *create (heart)* *Ps 51:10*
a clean h. within me c. . 422.3
within me a new h. c. . 436.3
hand (1c)

created *(adjective)*
all. c. streams are dried . 14.2
need they no c. light . 76.5
a store of c. beauty . 666.2

creation
the humbler c. . 16.6
the King of c. . 19.1
love is as wide as c. . 47.2
whole c. join in one . 57.4
ye who sang c.'s story . 75.1
e'en from the dawn of c. . 139.2
c. sprang at once to sight . 141.2
till all c. lives . 142.5
new song thy c. shall sing . 166.5
day, for which c. . . . made . 167.2
theme that thrills all c. . 178.2
Lord of c., . . . all praise . 506.1
shakes the vast c. round . 875.1
b *new creation 2 Cor 5:17; Gal 6:15*
that hails a n. c. . 358.1
finish then thy n. c. . 438.3
author of the n. c. . 452.1
lo, a n. c. dawning . 520.5

creator
all things their c. bless . 2.5
their true c. . . . adore . 155.1
O Father and C. . 221.1
C., we believe . 785.1
my great c.'s power . 871.1

creature
no good in c. can be found . 14.3
stamped your image on your c. 38.4
died for man, the c.'s, sin . 105.3
nor depth, nor any c. . 554.4
the c. of thy hand . 616.2
b *(all/every) creature*
all c. of our God . 2.1
all c. great and small . 25.c
through all ranks of c. . 141.4
let every c. rise . 160.5
high exalted o'er all c. . 174.4
praise him, all c. . 665.6; 959
till all thy c. own . 677.5
though . . . c. all fail . 712.2
all thy c.'s daily need . 933.2

creed
what is divine about my c. . 518.2
this is my c. . 529.1
deeds must ever match our c. 760.4
this is my aim, my c. . c107

creep-ing
the foes that round me c. . 176.2
the past o'er me c. . 237.1

crib . 77.1

cried see *cry*

crime
justly suffers for his c. . 108.1
lust, oppression, c. . 172.3
c. of blackest hue . 697.4
struggle with c. and want . 830.2

crimson
raiment . . . with c. is dyed . 111.2
into the c. flood . . . 231.2
have you felt the c. flow . 243.1
this great c. sea . . . 298.2
plunge in the c. tide . . 364.1
vanished in the c. flow . . 389.2
endless c. tide . . . 540.1
cleansing in the c. flood . . 727.3
its c. glory streaming . . 783.1
blood-red c. tells . . . 783.2
b *Isa 1:18*
sin's deep c. stains . . 237.1
though they be red like c. . 272.1
iniquity c. hath been . . 296.2
my sin was red like c. . . 386.3

crooked *Isa 45:2* . . . 446.2

crops 936.2

cross
1 *cross [of Jesus]*
to his bitter c. 78.3
his c. and sorrow see . . 94.3
c. where they nailed him . 99.3
could he see a c. reflected . 103.1
behold! . . . on the c. . . 107.*
never shall the c. forsake . 112.2
from the c. the radiance. . 112.3
by the c. are sanctified . . 112.4
c. reveals beautiful actions . 114.2
the charm of the c. . . 119.c
the love of his c. . . . 119.3
love upon a c. impaled . . 122.1
the old rugged c. . . . 124.*
I love that old c. . . . 124.1
c. in mystery veiling . . 126.3
upon a world-wide c. . . 127.2
railed . . . on the c. above . 130.1
all for me—the c. . . . 134.3
from thy c. irradiates . . 135.3
survey the wondrous c. . . 136.1
his c. stands empty . . 142.1
speed the c. 158.3
thy c. beholding . . . 185.1
in the c. we triumph . . 185.4
builder of sun and the c. . 288.2
glorious gain of thy c. . . 300.2
by the c. . . . crown . . 315.2
the c. is saying . . . 324.1
his c. of suffering . . . 420.4
c. now covers my sins . . 542.c
your c. reveals the truth. . 572.3
seek the healing of thy c. . 590.4
c. that liftest up my head . 621.4
glorious c. surrounding . . 693.c
a c. of love and light . . 705.2
his c. for ever stands . . 723.3
power of the c. we'll show . 800.3
make known . . . the c. . . 830.2
the c. where my Saviour . . 848.5
go with the c. 864.2
Jesus went to the c. . . c24
ever he came to the c. . . c217
b *cross before*
his c. b., his joy within . . 5.5
thy c. b. to guide me . . 53.4
c. b. my closing eyes . . 670.5
c. . . . going on b. . . 690.1, c
c *cross of Jesus*
in the c. of Christ I glory. . 112.1
tarry . . . at the c. of Jesus . 348.c
beneath the c. of Jesus . . 476.1
upon that c. of Jesus . . 476.2
with the c. of Jesus . 690.1, c
Saviour's c. . . . share . . 818.2
d *[Jesus died on] cross*
on the c. . . . he bled and d. . 37.3
bows . . . and d. on the c. . 107.4
on the c. he bled for me. . 125.1
on the c. he shed his blood . 125.c
on the c. of Calvary Jesus d. 128.1
Jesus d. on the c. . . 128.1, 4
on the c. he shed . . . 132.c
on the c. . . . didst redeem . 138.4
on the cruel c. he suffered . 180.1
on the c. he sealed . . 180.c
c. where my Saviour d. . . 315.1
upon the c. . . . salvation . 341.3
on the c. his life did Jesus . 363.c
d. for me on the c. . . . 395.3
there on the c. he d. . . 884.2
on the c. Jesus suffered . . c20
Calvary (e), endure (d), glory (2d), kneel (2b), nail (b), passion (1a), rugged, shadow (c), shame (1b), soldier (c)
2 *(ourselves at the cross)*
on the c. my Lord I saw. . 326.2
standing by his c. . . . 352.3
b *at the cross*
at the c. there's room . . 261.*
down at the c. . . . died. . 315.1
when at the c. the Saviour . 371.c
at the c. I believed . . . 371.3
at the c. . . . saw the light . 395.*
at the c. myself . . . 434.4
here at the c. . . . hour . . 488.c
at the c. I seek . . . sever . 502.c
room at the c. . . . c21
at the c. I claim . . . c48
at the c. helpless I bow . . c68
humbly at thy c. I bow . . c69
c *before the cross*
b. thy c. my soul I cast . . 415.1
while b. thy c. I'm seeking . 502.1
which b. the c. I spend . . 634.1
d *beneath the cross*
I shelter . . . b. thy c. . . 122.2
'neath his c. I'll live . . 343.c
b. the shade of the c. . . 427.c
b. the c. of Jesus . . . 476.1
with thee 'neath the c. . . 532.3
e *near the cross*
Jesus, keep me n. the c. . 115.1
'tis n. the c. . . . be seen. . 138.4
the garden n. the c. . . 145.*
n. thy c. assembled . . 197.1
f *to the cross*
lift their faces to thy c. . . 181.3
when carried to the c. . . 186.3
drawn to the c. . . . 287.1
weary sinners to the c. . . 399.3
draw me nearer . . . to the c.. 585.c
to the c. . . . they will fly . 810.c
g *come to the cross*
c. unto the c. . . . fountain . 232.2
c. to the c., each burden . 246.1
c. to his c., and . . . learn . 256.3
c. away, to the c. . . . flee . 260.c
to the c. then I c. . . . 395.1
c. to the c. . . . nailed him . c89
to thy c. I c., Lord . . . c109
cling (b)
3 *cross (for man)*
ours the c., the grave . . 143.5
to them the c., . . . is given . 168.4
empower . . . sustain our c. . 211.3
not a frown nor a c. . . 397.3
I my c. a burden deem . . 400.1
though I mount the c. . . 489.2
take up thy c. . . . a living c.. 490.1
the pathway of the c. . . 522.1
no c. I shun 526.2
the consecrated c. . . 596.2
e'en though it be a c. . . 617.1
dawn on every c. . . . 668.3
whate'er my c. may be . . 678.c
mocked the c. and flame . 701.3
cries: no c., no crown . . 749.1
the c. is not greater . . 758.c
where would the c. be . . 773.2
seek a lighter c. . . . 780.1
there's a c. to follow . . 868.1
now the glory for the c. . . 894.2
if thou callest to the c. . . 916.3
bear (1c, 2c), heavy (c), share (2b), take (3b)
4 *cross (verb)*
since Jesus c. the river . . 153.3
when I c. the river . . . 309.3
climb . . . c. the waves . . 393.1
when I have c. . . . flood . 583.5
till I c. the narrow sea . . 585.4
river thou didst c. for me . 726.4
I'll c. old Jordan's tide . . 884.*
shrink to c. this . . . sea. . 898.2
shadows deep have c. . . 938.3

crowd
1 *(noun)*
not in the temple c. alone . 7.2
with the c. . . . joined I . . 129.1
with the c. we passed . . 135.2
a c. of frightened sheep . . 265.1
c. of fears obstruct . . 285.2
amid the c. that gathered . 304.1
the Christ 'midst the c. . . 527.2
2 *crowd-ed*
we'll c. thy gates . . . 4.3
saints and angels c. around . 147.3
heart . . . with care is c.. . 534.2
c. to his arms . . . 794.3
c. the Saviour from the heart. 832.3

crown
1 *crown of Jesus*
a sceptre and a c. . . . 72.1
throne and thy kingly c. . . 101.1
c. become the . . . brow. . 147.1
a kingly c. to gain . . . 701.1
bright c. adorning . . . 852.c
bright gems for his c. . . 852.c
b *crown him*
c. h. Lord of all . . . 56.*
c. h., ye martyrs . . . 56.4
in Heaven we'll c. h. . . 66.4
c. h., c. h. Lord of all . . 104.c
King of my life, I c. thee. . 117.1
c. h. as your captain . . 141.5
c. h., c. h. . . . . 147.*
sinners in derision c. h. . . 147.3
c. h. with many crowns . . 156.1
c. h. the Lord . . . . 156.*
Lord as King to c. . . . 169.1
c. h.! Prophet and priest . 184.3
King of my heart to c. . . 415.4
I c. thee . . . Lord of all . 499.1, 4
c *crown with glory* *Heb 2:9*
c. with g. now . . . 168.1
g. c. thy sacred brow . . 185.4
c. with g. and dominion . . 776.3
d *John 19:5*
than composed his c. for me . 758.2
thorn (d)
2 *crown for man*
some day for a c. . . . 124.c
a c. and a kingdom . . . view. 233.3
claim the c. . . . my own . 283.4
come and take thy c. . . 352.3
an heir to . . . a c. . . . 354.3
glittering c. on my brow. . 357.4
started for the c. . . . 366.2
the c., and the palm . . 406.3
lose I all, the c. I'll gain . . 528.4
I'll win the promised c. . . 678.c
the victor's c. shall gain. . 686.2
we exchange it for a c. . . 692.5
not for c. and palm . . 707.2
cries: no cross, no c. . . 749.1
till the c. . . . seize. . . 808.5
till thou obtain the c. . . 812.3
to a glorious c. . . . 818.4
c. will shine the brighter. . 899.1
till we the c. obtain . . 915.3
fit us for the promised c. . 937.4
a palace and c. . . . c189

b *win crown*
I a c. shall w. . . 315.2
till the c. be w. . 483.1
w. . . . the victor's c. . 876.3
be a c. and kingdom w. . 897.3
c *1 Peter 5:4*
c. of fadeless glory . 777.3
d *crown of life* *Rev 2:10*
I'll receive a c. of l. . 222.c
you shall gain the c. of l. . 266.c
the c. of life are wearing . 686.1
a c. of l. shall be . 699.4
where c. of l. . . . given. . 761.4
God giveth a c. . 823.3
e
come and take thy c. . 352.3
f *crown-ed*
to c. the offering . 203.4
we may be c. with bliss. . 268.4
thy faithful mercies c. . 438.1
glory c. the mercy seat . . 573.4
whom God will c. . 580.3
with glory c. our . . . band . 702.c
each moment he c. . 710.3
c. with glory we shall be . 809.4
Jesus shall c. you . 813.2
c. our labours with success . 833.3
c. by the hand of Jehovah . 894.1
will all our labours c. . 943.2
cast (j), gold (2b), joy (1c), lay (2e), receive (2i), wear (b)
3 *(other)*
our c. of peace is gone . . 268.4
it must its c. resign . 508.3
c. and thrones may perish . 690.4
evil c. and deified . 885.3
b *Ps 65:11*
goodness c. the . . . year . 925.1
he c. the year with goodness. 929.2

crowning *(adjective)*
the c. day is coming . 169.c
to hail thy c. day . 171.1
keep . . . till the c. day . . 787.c
story my c. glory . c212

crucify-ied
1 *[Jesus] crucified*
a *(as title)*
the temple of the c. . 121.6
take thy throne. O C. . 122.4
we worship thee, O C. . 135.1
my love, the c., hath sprung . 153.1
have you seen the c.? . 243.1
a look at the c. one 271.1, c
blood of the c. one . 392.c
do you rest . . . in the c.. . 417.2
blood of the c. one . 427.2
b *Matt 27:35*
for all my Lord was c. . 62.5
why should Christ be c.. . 108.1
Jesus, our Lord, is c. . 121.*
'twas there my Lord was c. 125.1, c
when the Lord was c. . 128.4
where the dear Lord was c. . 133.1
lives, though ever c. . 142.4
though men c. their Saviour . 324.1
caring not my Lord was c. . 405.1
for they c. my Lord . 758.3
who bled and died, was c. . 798.1
c *1 Cor 2:2*
thought . . . is of Christ c. . 119.1
hail him! Jesus the c. . 184.2
but for Christ, the c. . 241.2
Christ c. I come . 287.*
yield to Jesus c. . 343.3
O Jesus the c., thee . 364.4
for my Lord c. 448.c, 4
hang on a c. God . 639.2
nothing esteem, but Jesus c. 659.3
hope . . . through Jesus c. . 761.4
to serve . . . Christ, the c. . 866.1
2 *Gal 6:14*
the world is c. to me . 138.3
come, and self now c. . 188.2
c. to the world . 469.3

cruel
armed with c. hate . 1.1
c. thorns . . . piercing . 96.3
that crown of c. thorn . 126.2
c. thorns, the mocking jeer . 134.1
on the c. cross he suffered . 180.1
bore the c. thorns . 229.2
lamb to c. slaughter led . 253.2
Satan's c. fetters . 328.1
hands by c. nails were torn . 339.3
enduring c. reproaches . 623.3
my c. sins had pierced . 917.4
c. death did follow . c14

crumble . 416.4

crusade . 859.3

crush-ed-ing
c. defeats I have seen . 437.1
c. by the tempter . 691.3
some would try to c. . 810.3

cry
1 *(literal)*
respond when children c. . 50.3
no c. he makes . 77.2
that made a woman c. . 91.1
2 *(divine)*
birth to dying c. . 94.1
forgive, they c. . 106.3
hear his all-important c. . 107.1
now the conqueror c. . 107.4
comprehend thy bitter c. . 122.2
repeat the Saviour's c. . 127.3
the Father clears, and c. . 127.4
it is finished was his c. . 128.4
this c. from Calvary's tree . 128.4
weep not for me, he c. . 131.2
that strange expiring c. . 140.1
hearing thy expiring c. . 185.1
the Saviour c. aloud . 275.3
faithful, hear him c. . 694.4
free, boundless mercy, c. . 746.2
c.: no cross, no crown . 749.1
finish (b)
3 *(human)*
a *cry (to mean 'appeal')*
Abba Father! c. . 106.5
me forgive! I instant c. . 122.3
all within me c. . 131.3
Jesus . . . to thee I c. . 291.1
for cleansing from sin I c. . 315.1
heard my despairing c. . 336.1
still I c.: . . . Jesus. . 343.2
show thyself to me, I c.. . 435.1
thee to know is all my c. . 439.4
my hungry soul c. out . 450.2
none can c. . . . unheeding . 456.3
the name whereon I c. . 456.4
will he not attend to my c. . 459.2
for earth . . . this is my c. . 489.1
the c. of need? That c. . 586.3
unto thee will I c. . 641.1
lifting my heart, I c. . 647.1
c., with joy unspeakable . 756.3
now to God be c. . 913.1
b *Ps 39:12*
give ear to my c. . 454.2
c *(others) cry*
long for the waters, and c. . 351.1
who the c. will heed . 351.c
none can c. . . . unheeding . 456.3
questioning c. do not cease . 527.2
poured out c. and tears . 879.2
hear (1c), help (2c)
4 *cry (to mean 'proclaim')*
business here below to c. . 60.5
preach him to all, and c. . 60.6
c. the news from . . . hill . 127.c
all the tribes hosanna c.. . 150.1
c. to Zion: See thy God . . 159.2
my heart awaking c. . 187.1
hail Father . . . they ever c. . 223.5
with c., entreaties, tears . 526.1
dumb sound joyful c. . 590.3
we'll still be c. . 693.2
salvation full . . . our c. . 782.2
we'll raise the joyful c. . 813.4
we'll send the c. along . 814.1
earth, he c., . . . my place . 880.1
and c.: it shall be done . c118
b *[angels] cry*
worthy the Lamb . . . they c.. 57.2
angel choirs are c. . 370.3
angels . . . c.: Behold . 625.4
c *battle cry*
sound the b. c. . 698.1
I hear their b. c. . 780.4
to do or die, our b. c. . 798.2
we'll shout our b. c. . 798.3
they shout their b. c. . 799.2
blood and fire gives the b. c.. 807.2
salvation . . . our b. c. . 810.3
d *war cry*
their holy w. c. rang . 158.1
saved . . . is our w. c. . 681.3
to the w! . . . sounds the c. . 703.1
who'll the w. c. obey? . 703.2
to the war louder rings . . . c. 703.3
ever is the w. c. . 813.c
ring (b), stone (2d)

crystal
make me c. pure . 32.1
watch by c. streams . 39.3
b *Rev 4:6; 22:1*
c. bright fountain . 139.2
gathered by the c. sea . 337.c
cleansed by the c. flow . 416.1
open thou the c. fountain . 578.2
wave like c. bright . 726.4
c. rivers . . . strand . 873.1
c. tide for ever flowing . 891.1
beside the c. stream . 901.4
where flows the c. river. . 934.4

cultivate . 485.5

cumbered-ing *Luke 10:40*
c. with a load of care . 645.3
leaving c. cares with him . 728.1

cunning . 801.1

cup
a *Ps 23:5*
my c. overflows . 54.4
my c. is overflowing . 343.2
a c. o'erfilled . 512.1
b *Ps 116:13*
sacred c. of saving grace . 23.2
c *Matt 20:23*
his c. of pain and grief . 5.3
thy c. of grief to share . 117.4
drink (c)

cure
wounded soul to c. . 81.3
no sorrow . . . cannot c. . 236.2
be of sin the double c. . 302.1
no wound . . . cannot c. . 364.3
trust thee for a perfect c. . 419.5
c. for my soul's ailing . 456.2
is there no thorough c. . 459.1
c. thy children's . . . madness 577.3
self and temper c. . 914.3

current
the c. of thy love . . . 182.1
by the blood-c. swept . . 437.2
see the cleansing c. flow . 540.2
love's resistless c. . . . 540.3

curse *Gal 3:13, Rev 22:3*
feel the c. remove . . . 120.5

c. are known no more . . 160.4
from the c. to set me free . 180.1
vast the c. 243.4
he bore my sins and c. . . 360.2
for all sin's c. did bear . . 363.4

cursed *(Deut 13:17)*
no sin-c. thing . . . allow . 440.2

I renounce the c. thing . . 448.2

cursing *(noun)* *(James 3:10)*
for blessing or c. . . . 928.1

curtain *Isa 40:22* . . . 672.2

cut 559.5

D

daily
d. attend thee 19.2
d. sending forth new life . 63.1
scarred by d. fret . . . 129.2
d. . . . with the Father reigns. 142.3
help us d., by thy might. . 193.5
live d. his praises to sing . 281.4
d. I'm constrained to be. . 313.4
his purpose d. learn . . 343.3
their d. delight . . . 372.3
are you walking d. . . 417.2
d. refreshed by . . . dews . 443.2
Saviour, in my d. striving . 463.1
in his presence d. live . . 474.1
d. the Saviour is showing . 553.4
supply each d. need . . 561.2
d. strength for d. needs. . 566.2
thou my d. task shalt give . 566.4
d. brings . . . d. care . . 580.1
d., hourly, I may do . . 628.2
and d. . . . increase . . 629.1
thy d. stage of duty run. . 665.1
my d. labour to pursue . . 667.1
if on our d. course . . . 668.2
bring us d. nearer God . . 668.4
live d. your duty to do . . 679.1
we d. find in his mercy . . 724.1
overcoming d. . . . 757.3
d. strive to lead them . . 790.2
makes your d. pathway . . 790.3
d. conquering sin . . . 816.4
d. task shalt thou assign . 867.6
d. walk with thee in white . 919.3
thy creatures' d. need . . 933.2
d. been thy bounteous hand . 933.2
d. manna still provide you . 954.2
b *Luke 9:23*
bear d. thy cross . . . 117.4
d. I obey his call . . . 399.1
bread (b), grow (3e), strength (2e)

dale 884.3

damp 162.2

dance
like thy d. waves . . . 32.2
b *Ps 28:7 (MR)*
d. his glad heart for joy . . 62.3
my heart it doth d. . . . 355.2

danger
flee from woe and d. . . 73.2
crosses bearing, d. daring . 197.3
to rescue me from d. . . 313.3
he freed my soul from d. . 361.1
fear no d., he is with you . 433.3
d. cannot fright me . . 483.2
trust till the d. is past . . 537.3
shield in d.'s hour . . . 569.4
endeavour, failure, d. . . 570.3
from harm and d. . . . free . 674.3
daring when d. abound . . 679.3
whatever thy d. take heed . 689.2
let courage rise with d. . . 699.2
where duty calls or d. . . 699.3
nor shrink from the d. . . 734.1
though . . . d. affright . . 763.1
when . . . d. surround . . 773.1
where . . . deadly d. lurk . 801.2
d. braving, sinners saving . 819.c
d. and sorrow stand . . 882.1
conflicts and d. are over . 894.1
d. may threaten . . . c132
b *all/every danger*
for us facing every d. . . 97.2
at last, all d. past . . . 375.3
trust, in all d. . . . 763.3
c *in danger*
souls in d., look above . . 336.3
when in sorrow, . . . in d. . 582.3
in d. I'm certain . . . 684.2
if in d., for him call . . 754.3
when in d. make me brave . 837.2
d *many dangers*
through m. d., toils . . 308.3
from the m. d. threatening . 792.2
m. d. may cause . . . fear . 817.1

Daniel . . . . 847.*

dare
crosses bearing, danger d. . 197.3
there is much to d. . . 491.1
love will d. 503.3
as more for thee we d. . . 642.3
eager to do and to d. . . 679.2
d. or die for Jesus . . 696.2
hearts to d. and do . . 704.c
all our foes we boldly d.. . 722.4
things . . . impossible I d. . 744.4
with us reproach to d. . . 825.4
b *dare (with verb)*
d. we . . . deride . . . 121.3
Christ, who d. to stand . . 181.2
d. to leave it there . . . 415.1
I d. avow that Jesus . . 440.4
who shall d. to separate. . 554.1
faith that d. to die . . . 619.3
I d. step out to thee . . 628.3
d. ye still lie fondly. . . 693.1
hearts that d. do aught . . 704.1
d. thy word receive . . 714.2
I d. to trust in thee. . . 749.3
d. to be/stand/have/make . 847.c
in him they d. depart . . 874.3
c *dare believe*
d. you now b. . . . receive . 413.c
thy promise I d. to b. . . 437.2
O Saviour, I d. to b. . . 454.4
reward to all who d. b. . . 461.3
there is a place, I d. b. . . 536.2
d. b. thy precious word . . 638.2
sure for all who d. b. . . 760.3
in him they d. b. . . . 874.3
d *dare not*
scarcely d. to think . . 399.2
I d. not hope 403.1
I d. not ask as though . . 456.3
none other d. I follow . . 529.1
I d. not ask to fly . . . 621.4
without thee I d. not die. . 676.3
ye d. not trust your own. . 699.3
I d. not walk alone . . 717.1
I d. not take one step . . 726.1
I d. not walk alone . . 731.1
I d. not trust . . . frame . . 745.1
we d. not boast . . . 747.2
men . . . d. not to stand. . 847.2

daring
be d. when dangers abound . 679.3
martyrs bold and d. . . 686.1
scorn of my foes may be d. . 758.3
Pentecostal d. . . . 830.3

dark
1 *(noun)*
through the d. . . . beaming . 316.2
bark all in the d. . . . 375.1
d. and light . . . alike . . 674.3
of the d. afraid . . . 740.1
through the d. . . . ringing . 802.2
2 *dark-est*
life is d. without thee . . 40.4
in thy d. streets shineth . . 86.1
victor from the d. domain . 148.c
in the fight all looks d. . . 169.3
the d., the fair . . . 170.2
in earth's d. place . . . 224.3
none can be too d. . . 232.3
d. shadows were falling . . 237.1
d. . . . the past has been . 292.3
my soul of one d. blot . . 293.2
this d. unrest . . . 297.4
over d. sorrow . . . radiance . 329.2
grief and d. distress . . 343.2
sin's d. sepulchre . . . 353.4
my heart's d. door . . . 373.1
when my heart was d. . . 402.2
d. and cheerless is the morn . 412.3
native sphere is d. . . . 414.3
the d. halls of thought . . 416.1
failures in d. days . . . 440.3
e'en a d. adversity . . 455.4
the d. waters flow . . . 483.2
in that d. agony . . . 486.3
from sin's d. hold . . . 534.1
naught of d. tomorrow . . 540.5
chaos d. and rude . . . 569.3
what if d. and lonely days . 586.3
fire through watches d. . . 654.3
our Master's d. battlefield . 705.2
safe in the d. day . . . 724.3
life's d. maze I tread . . 743.3
d. and deadly dangers . . 801.2
the sky is d. and stormy. . 805.1
d. passions subdue . . 823.1
the temple courts were d. . 839.1
earth's d. shadows flee . . 888.1
d., d. . . . the midnight . . 896.1
painful, d. or bright . . 917.2
may its d. story . . . dwell . c7
one d. thought . . . retaineth . c72
b *dark Calvary*
to bear it to d. C. . . . 124.2
O Calvary, d. C. . . . 125.c
d. C. he chose to know . . 134.c
c *dark (death)*
in death's d. vale . . . 53.4
walk in death's d. vale . . 54.3
death's d. swelling river. . 338.5
in death's d. valley . . 523.4
d *dark despair*
redeem . . . from sin and d. d. 138.4
gloom has spread of d. d. . 225.2
the day of its d. d. . . 245.1
countless cost from d. d. . 825.2
e *dark hour*
not only . . . in the d. h.. . 717.2
temptation's d. h. . . . 790.c
hope for the d. h. . . . c46
cheer in the d. h. . . . c154
f *dark night*
speaks to us in d. n. . . 31.3
steep . . . and d. was the n. . 388.2
d. the n. of sin . . . 478.2
chase the d. n. of sin . . 602.4
the n. is d. 606.1
world's d. n. is hastening . 683.4
though thy path be d. as n. . 716.*
shadows fall and d. the n. . 719.4
no fears can wake my d. n. . 728.3
courage in the d. n. . . 755.3
sin's d. n. be past . . . 802.4

turned the d. n. to day . . c1
even in the d. n. . . . c134

g *dark path*
d. is his p. on the wings. . 16.2
though the p. be d. . . 391.3

h *dark way*
he lights the d. w. . . . 48.3
the world's d. w. . . . 173.1
in w. d. and wild . . . 175.3
though d. be my w. . . 712.2
the w. is d. before me . . 726.3
sin's d. w. forsaking . . 788.1
reclaimed from sin's d. w. . 825.3

clouds (2b), world (2b)

darken-ed-ing
across the d. sky . . . 39.2
rending rocks and d. skies . 125.2
sorrows d. all our skies . . 127.1
doubt shall not d. . . . 166.4
in our d. hearts . . . shine . 174.1
doubts that have d. my soul . 422.3
all lesser light will d. . . 551.1
d. clouds may gather . . 732.1
though . . . d. be the sky . 761.1
a d. ruin lay 890.3
'neath d. skies . . . 923.2

b *Gen 1:2*
the waters' d. face . . 202.1

darkly
gathered round so d. . . 938.3

darkness
1 *(literal)*
the sun in d. hide . . . 105.3
d. descends . . . veiling . . 126.3
clouds and d. veiled . . 128.4
through sleep and d. . . 668.1
now the d. gathers . . 673.2
d. falls at thy behest . . 677.1

b *Gen 1:2*
chaos and d. heard . . 224.1

2 *(figurative)*
into d. spread his fame . . 63.3
his word dispel the d. . . 126.4
d. is conquered . . . 146.1
tread the path of d. . . 155.3
thick d. broodeth yet . . 172.6
though the d. hide thee . . 220.3
in d. living 253.1
came to banish . . . d. . . 274.c
no more shall d. cloud . . 277.4
turning our d. . . . away. . 316.2
in the d., just before me. . 330.1
days of d. still come . . 337.4
wandered in d. away . . 371.1
made all the d. depart . . 371.1
out of . . . d. . . . called. . 378.*
in my d. and shame . . 395.1
blackest d. brought . . 448.2
own thy d. passed away . 465.3
all is d. here below . . . 470.1
though by d. . . . veiled . . 473.4
in the d. may be lost . . 478.3
where the d. is deep . . 527.1
though d. surround you . . 537.3
faith is not afraid of d. . . 555.3
d. be over me . . . 617.2
'mid the d. and cloud . . 641.2
the d. deepens . . . 670.1
forward through the d. . . 682.2
men die in d. . . . 683.5
man's d. and loss . . . 708.2
out of the d. hears . . . 740.3
d. seems to veil . . . 745.2
clear . . . through the d. . 765.2
sinks the reign of d. . . 776.2
onward through the d. . . 777.1
in the world is d. . . . 841.1
many kinds of d. . . . 841.3
though . . . through d. . . 859.3
out in the d. . . . falling . . 864.2
multitudes in d. . . . 868.3
the d. . . . draws near . . 874.2
souls in d. . . . calling . . 922.1

gather (a) world (2b)

b *Isa 42:7.**
those who sit in d. . . 830.1
souls who dwell in d. . . c236

c *Matt 8:12*
to final d. hurled . . . 799.4
back . . . into d. hurled . . 864.4

d *Acts 26:18**
d. he has changed to day . 317.1
d. . . . sunshining day . . 378.3
d. changed to shining day . 719.2
bid d. turn to day . . . 743.3

e *Col 1:13*
the prince of d. grim . . 1.3
no powers of d. me molest . 671.3
legions of d. o'erthrow . . 689.2
all the powers of d. . . 695.6
storm the forts of d. . . 696.c
hosts of Hell and d. . . 822.2

f *1 John 1:5*
whose life no d. knows . . 408.3
in whom no d. is . . . 465.2

g *darkness (with light)*
light came out of d. . . 94.1
in d. the light of thy face . 288.4
d. shineth as the light . . 453.1
give light to cheer the d. . 575.3
in the d. . . . true light . . 876.2
sown in the d. or . . . light . 931.c

light (4i)

h *darkness and sin*
d. of s. is abounding . . 19.4
bear . . . s. d. 319.3
from d., from s. . . . 535.2
'gainst s. and d. . . . 774.4

gather (a), light (4b), work (3b), world (2b)

dart *Eph 6:16*
shields when d. are hurled . 495.3
the venomed d. should pierce 532.2

dashed-ing
rock 'midst d. billows . . 750.2
the foes of God are d. . . 864.4
d. up its silver spray . . 891.2

daughter
well supply thy sons and d. . 157.2

b *Matt 9:22*
d., be of good comfort . . 304.3

dauntless
d., untired, I'll follow . . 453.3
need of d. soldiers . . . 787.2
faith and d. courage . . 866.c

David *Luke 2:11*
once in royal D.'s city . . 87.1
to you, in D.'s town . . 93.3
is born, of D.'s line . . 93.3
to D.'s royal Son . . . 853.2

dawn-ing
a *(literal)*
fairer than daylight d. . . 632.4
d. leads on another day . . 677.3
sweet with every d. . . 751.2
where the d. glows . . . 776.1
d. till setting sun . . . 907.3
by the d.-light fair . . . 931.1
the clouds of the d. . . c134

b *(figurative)*
redemption's happy d. . . 88.c
glory is d. on my soul . . 98.4
from the d. of creation . . 139.2
hasten . . . the d. . . . 166.5
d. upon this soul . . . 194.1
in radiant vision d. . . . 353.1
thou art the d. . . . 486.1
a new creation d. . . . 520.5
watching for the d. . . 599.3
d. the sweet consciousness . 632.1
d. on every cross . . . 668.3
bright days shall d. . . 802.4
d. the welcome day . . 813.4
one golden d. 888.1
the d. of Heaven breaks. . 896.1
d. upon eternal love . . 948.3

day
1 *(past)*
a *(re Jesus)*
a child this d. is born . . 72.1
born this blessed d. . . 72.c
this d. your Lord is born. . 72.4
this happy Christmas d. . . 74.1
this day . . . fulfilled . . 78.2
this day is born . . . 78.2
in David's town this d. . . 93.3
he arose on Easter d. . . 96.4
the d. that he passed . . 99.2
once, on a d. . . . 129.1
that fountain in his d. . . 132.2
the third d. he rose . . 137.4
God's appointed d. . . 145.2
waiting the coming d. . . 148.1
the three sad d. . . . sped . 151.3
his three-d. prison . . . 153.c
small and feeble . . . d. . . 165.2
the d. of Pentecost . . 196.1
of a d. long past . . . 198.2
one d. Jesus came/gave/died . 245.*
he wept . . . one d. . . 331.2
at their tasks each d. . . 680.1

b *(general)*
d. of its . . . despair . . 245.1
dark d. gone by . . . 440.3
to think of happier d. . . 557.3
in d. long past . . . 590.1
loved the garish d. . . . 606.2
in their youthful d. . . . 910.2
earliest wedding d. . . 949.1

c *(day of conversion)*
wonderful d. . . . never forget 371.1
night was turned to d. . . 371.c
because of that . . . d. . . 371.3
on that wonderful d. . . 386.*
never . . . forget the d. . . 401.1
d. when I was born again . c175

ancient (b), glad (c), happy (2b), yore

2 *(present)*
a *(special day)*
this d. . . . we celebrate. . 198.1
give us a d. of wonders . . 575.1
this is the d. of . . . . 669.*
this thanksgiving d. . . 934.2
this celebration d. . . . 943.1

b *(general)*
make of these d. . . . sign . 173.3
in this their d. . . . 561.3
the living of these d. . . 577.2
children, too, of modern d. . 834.1
bright, bright as d. . . . 897.1
to the present d. . . . 938.1

c *this day*
our all, t. very d. . . . 203.4
wash thou . . . t. d. . . . 296.3
my all, t. blessèd d. . . 447.2
control, suggest, t. d. . . 665.5
I t. d. have done . . . 671.2
busy my hands t. d. . . 675.1
t. d. the noise 699.4
let me from t. d. . . . 743.1
thy presence here t. d. . . 941.1

d *John 9:4*
while it is d. 683.4
fight while 'tis d. . . . 703.2

e *day by day*
d. unfoldest blessings . . 2.4
d. like us he grew . . . 87.4
keep me spotless d. . . 303.c
leave it all with Jesus d.. . 333.3
love that keeps me d. . . 342.2
d. this pathway smooths . 358.3
d. his sweet voice . . . 428.1
may we d. prepare . . 466.5
d. my devotion to prove. . 493.3
d., come what may . . 499.c
planning for me, d. . . 501.3
d. his tender mercy . . 548.3
d. the manna fell . . 566.1, 2
d. to thee I live . . 566.4
praise thee d. . . . 582.4
Father, lead me d. . . 837.1
Saviour, teach me d. . . 846.1
follow Jesus d. . . . c26
time and talents, d. . . c34
d. to grow like thee . . c38

f *day to day*
help me walk from d. . . 115.3
hearts and minds from d. . 192.1
lighting our pathway from d. . 316.1
give grace from d. . . . 575.3
I may live, from d. . . 618.2
thy grace from d. . . . 761.1
the path grows from d. . . 768.2
renew my will from d. . . c95

g *each day*
kept e. d. from sinning . . 328.2
rolls o'er my soul e. d. . . 375.2
use e. d. 408.5
my life e. d. proclaim . . 494.3
e. departing d. . . . 524.3
help us e. returning d. . . 532.3
e. d. its heavy toll . . 534.2
die to self e. d. . . . 619.3
breathe e. d. nearness . . 632.2
prove his death e. d. . . 634.4
e. d. is a . . . . . . 666.*
at their tasks e. d. . . 680.1
e. d. in dedication . . 787.4
e. d. your pathway easy. . 817.c
shine for him e. d. . . 844.1
we have to do e. d. . . 849.3
he uses us e. d. . . . 851.1
e. d. glorify thy name . . 916.c
give us e. d. . . . bread . 918.3
e. d. that we live . . 928.2
henceforth e. d. . . . 933.3
joy is mine, I live e. d. . . c196

h *every day*
e. d. it's new 49.3
Jesus! e. d. the same . . 68.c
Holy Jesus! e. d. keep us . 76.4
I'll serve him e. d. . . . 326.1
way grows brighter e. d. . 340.3
live rejoicing e. d. . . 365.c
e. d. it seems . . . strive. . 369.2
he saves me e. d. . . . 374.2
full victory e. d. . . . 432.1
intense e. d. 527.3
this and e. d. 668.5
with e. d. that starts . . 724.2
strength sufficient e. d. . . 740.2
simply trusting e. d. . . 754.1
we're rising e. d. . . . 810.3
renew it boldly e. d. . . 812.2
trusting, serving e. d. . . 892.3
serve thee better e. d. . . c105
through e. d. c124
the Christ of e. d. . . . c126
I love him better e. d. . . c169
following Jesus e. d. . . c206
true devotion e. d. . . . c213

hour (2d)

i *all day long*
carries them all d. l. . . 184.1
praising my Saviour all the d. 310.c
him all d. l. 356.4
we'll be happy all the d.. . 367.c
I am happy all the d. . . 395.c
singing all the d. . . . 811.c
praise my Saviour all d. l. . 858.1
all the happy, golden d. . 891.2
a glory song all d. l. . . c175

j *burden of day* *Matt 20:12*
for the b. of the d. . . . 462.3
burning . . . and b. of the d. . 476.1
from the heat of the d. . . 639.1
through the long d. . . 663.1
we bear the b. of the d.. . 934.3

k *by day* *Ps 121.6*
our sun and shield by d.. . 43.3
surround you by d. . . 537.3
radiant cloud by d. . . 654.3
no sun by d. . . . smite . . 767.3

fairer (a), some (2b), strength (2e), *today*

3 *(future)*
d. are hastening on . . 83.3
speed the d. when men . . 135.4
unmeasured d. to be . . 350.3
the d. I cannot see . . . 732.c
all we are for d. to be . . 789.1
bright d. shall dawn . . 802.4
hope one d. to bring . . 851.3

b *[all] my days*
gladly dedicate my d. . . 290.3
all thy d. be bright . . . 332.3
attend me all my d. . . 516.5
all my d. be thine . . . 616.3
calm and order all my d. . 630.2
I consecrate my d. . . . 672.3
all my happy d. . . . 793.6
thank you all our d. . . 795.1
serve thee all my d. . . 861.1
walk boldly all my d. . . 867.3
all my d. and . . . hours . . c32

c *rest of my days*
hallelujah, the r. of my d. . 298.7
spend all the r. of my d. . 422.2

length (a), residue

d *endless/eternal day*
before us to the e. d. . . 40.4
last through e. d. . . . 48.3
Heaven's joys and e. d. . . 125.2
one e. d. of glory spend. . 309.3
glory shines through e. d. . 592.1
the dawning of e. d. . . 599.3
to the land of e. d. . . . 627.3
shines one e. d. . . . 887.4

e *(in Heaven)*
exchange it some d. . . 124.c
he'll call me some d. . . 124.3
no less d. to sing . . . 308.4
one d. to be shared . . 682.3
won to cloudless d. . . 878.1
some d. I'll cross . . . 884.*
some d. the gates . . . 884.*
realms of fadeless d. . . 888.1
all the happy, golden d. . . 891.2
what a d. of rejoicing . . 892.c
infinite d. excludes . . 898.1
in the realms of d. . . . 946.4

f *(judgment) day*
that all-important d. . . 356.3
d. that tries by fire . . . 522.c
own us in that d. . . . 875.2
in that d. all offences . . 924.3
that great j. day . . . c11

great (2d), judgment (b)

g *day (of Christ)*
his d. is marching on . . 162.2
not yet we hail the d. . . 163.4
hasten . . . the dawn of the d. 166.5
d., for which creation . . 167.2
remember that d. coming . 169.3
seal us to that d. . . . 195.3
tell of that glad d. . . . 335.3
live in Christ's new d. . . 408.1
the d. is drawing nearer . . 696.1
bring that d. to birth . . 774.4
to the Saviour's d. . . . 776.2
in that d. thy foes . . . 799.4
praise him . . . in that d.. . 808.1
d. of lasting peace . . . 813.4
d. when all the blest . . 940.4

glorious (2c) perfect (2b)

h *day coming*
there is c. on a great d. . . 169.1
the crowning d. is c. . . 169.c
remember that d. c. on . . 169.3
soon the d. is c. . . . 250.4
d. of his appearing . . 334.2
d. of victory's c. . . . 810.*

i *2 Tim 1:12*
unto him against that d.. . 730.c

win (2b)

4 *(time in general)*
a *(life-span)*
thought his d. was done . 145.1
end of mortal d. . . . 171.3
d. be few or many . . . 477.3
trust through . . . the d. . 484.2
in their appointed d. . . 494.1
my moments and my d. . . 525.1
weakness half their d. . . 806.2
new-born souls, whose d. . 825.3
glad morning of my d. . . 860.2
fleeting . . . longest d. . . 874.1
guide till the d. is done . . c182

b *day (literal)*
dies at the opening d. . . 13.5
caused all d. his course . . 34.4
re-creation of the new d. . 35.3
joyless is the d.'s . . . 412.3
give us a d. of wonders . . 575.1
ere the d. is half-done . . 579.2
break/noon/eve/of the d. . 611.*
midst of common d. . . 618.1
Christ of working d. . . 618.2
one single d. 635.1
the evening of the d. . . 663.2
the d.'s closed door . . 666.4
now the d. is over . . . 673.1
busy my hands this d. . . 675.1
now at the close of d. . . 675.1
leads on another d. . . 677.3
keep the d. from dawning . 854.1
d.'s march nearer home . . 877.1
months and weeks and d. . 925.4

c *(time in general)*
mighty have their d. . . 6.4
more lustre to the d. . . 112.3
some more convenient d. . 226.1
God's d. of grace . . . 241.4
waited, d. and years . . 250.2
honours perish in a d. . . 356.2
d. fresh triumphs win . . 413.4
that hallow our d. . . . 900.3
as the d. unfold . . . c44

d *[good] days*
for . . . healthful d. . . 15.2
come in the d. of joy. . 711.1, 3
spoil my brightest d. . . 728.3
golden d. 730.4
chimes the glad d. in . . 744.6
the glad d. of youth . 857.1, c
these glad d. of youth . . 870.3
d. . . . with pure delight. . 947.2

e *[bad] days*
never a d. so dreary . . 186.1
d. of mourning ever gone . 275.2
in d. of tribulation . . 555.1
d. of woe 711.3
find him in the evil d. . . 738.1
through d. of sorrow . . 764.3
for my d. of despair . . c148

f *[dark] days*
d. of darkness still come . 337.4

failures in dark d. 440.3
d. of darkness . . . for me 473.3
dark and lonely d. 586.3
safe in the dark d. 724.3

g *[working] days*
d. of toil and hours 428.4
till fighting d. are o'er 575.3
Christ of working d. 618.2
d. of labour 833.2

h *days go by*
keep singing as the d. 396.2
in d. gone by my Lord 732.3
trusting as the d. go by 754.c

i *day and night*
no part of d. or n. 7.4
beauty . . . of the d. 28.2
continued both d. and n. 90.2
abroad, by n., by d. 356.4
I am climbing d. and n. 369.c
d. and n. to feast 480.2
serve thee d. and n. 593.2
rests not now by d. or n. 677.2
I'll labour n. and d. 685.3
keeps us safe by d. and n. 722.2
by n., by d., art . . . near 742.3
faith in the n. . . . the d. 773.c
watches . . . by d. and n. 839.4
serve their Master d. 909.2
ever with us d. and n. 938.2
guides me n. and d. c132

j *one day*
one d. Jesus came/gave/died 245.*
one eternal d. of glory 309.3
wept over sinners one d. 331.2
one d. kind, the next 377.1
leave me one . . . d. 635.1
one d. to be shared 682.3
hope one d. to bring 851.3
shines one eternal d. 887.4
one d. he's coming c185

k *Ps 42:3*
night and d. my meat 762.1

end (2f), life (6c), travelling

5 *spiritual light*
fill us with . . . d. 10.1
d. returns with thee 155.4
where the gospel d. 224.1
once obscured is d. 277.4
into his sunshining d. 378.3
live in Christ's new d. 408.1
its d. may brighter 621.2
beams of heavenly d. 657.3
blind, they grope for d. 682.2
soon end in joyous d. 721.2
until the break of d. c76
to the light of the d. c159

b *Acts 26:18*
Spirit turned our night to d. 43.2
where night is turned to d. 257.c
my night was turned to d. 371.c
the darkest night to d. c1
night will turn to d. c115

darkness (2d)

daylight
bring again our d. 155.4
work till d. softens 564.4
lovelier than d. 632.1
fairer than d. dawning 632.4

dayspring *Luke 1:78*
d. from in high, be near 412.1
d. rise upon our night 669.1
but d. is at hand 896.1

daystar *2 Peter 1:19* 412.1

dazzle-ing
still his d. body bears 161.3
see the sights that d. 862.2

dead
1 *(re Jesus)*
vainly they seal the d. 148.2
glorious from the d. 151.3
lives who once was d. 249.4
who mourned him d. 855.5

2 *(other)*
a *figurative*
watched at d. of night 88.3
Lord, I was d. 353.4
love . . . may ne'er be d. 529.2
in dust life's glory d. 621.4
though joys be . . . d. 746.4

b *John 11:25**
life into the d. 60.3
d., his Spirit gave 330.2
rise up from the d. 408.4
wake d. souls to love 669.5

live (2d), raise (1b)

c *Rom 6:2*
to be d. unto sin 469.3
d. to self, we . . . live 922.3

d *1 Thess 4:16*
wake the d. in number 153.2
voice that wakes the d. 626.1
life from the d. 877.1
d. in Christ shall rise 907.2

e *Rev 1:5*
first-begotten of the d. 149.2

deadly
thine the d. pain 123.2
dark and d. dangers 801.2
d. is the strife 813.2

deaf
Lord, I was d. 353.2
the d. to hear 353.5
nor d. thine ear 604.4

deal 291.4

dear
1 *(general)*
d. mother earth 2.4
friends most d. 31.2
bless all the d. children 77.3
his d. disciples 96.2
rise from hearts so d. 226.2
though d. it may be 263.1
comrades d. 312.1, 3
things I held so d. 460.2
as d. as a right eye. 481.3
all the world holds d. 564.2
the d. uniting love 659.1
thou art d. 718.4
bless this baby d. 792.3
many d. children 794.2, 3
baby boy (girl) so d. 795.1
many d. to my heart 886.4
'neath the flag, so d. c236

b *too dear*
costing me too d. 98.4
count the cost too d. 798.3

old (b)

2 *(re divine)*
thy own d. presence 33.3
no heart conceive how d. 69.3
d. desire of every nation 79.2
child so d. and gentle 87.5
our King most d. 97.2
his d. anointed one 106.4
the d. Lamb of God 124.2
d. hands of Christ 129.2
d. dying Lamb 132.3
d. tokens of his passion 161.3
praise my d. redeemer 180.3
all thy words and d. 353.2
to those d. wounds 368.2
still with his presence d. 373.4
those accents d. 398.2

why he is so d. to me 404.*
to thy d. arms . . . flee 450.2
how precious, d. redeemer 520.4
Jesus! that d. friend 592.2
parents hold him d. 661.2
to thy d. self 726.2
with thy d. love 729.1
safe by thy d. side 837.2
my heart's d. refuge 889.3
Calvary, so d. c7
led the d. Master come in c18
mine, this friend so d. c167

b *dear Jesus/Christ*
the d. C. enters in 86.3
brought me, d. J., to thee 331.3
I'm coming, d. J. 368.3
I bring thee, d. J. 422.1
J., so d. to us 955

c *dear Lord*
with thee, d. L., beside 53.4
the d. L. was crucified 133.1
O save me, d. L. 288.c
d. L., if . . . I am thine 318.4
before thy face, d. L. 409.1
I want, d. L. 426.*
at last, d. L., translate 441.4
thine all the glory, d. L. 457.3
d. L., no more to part 470.3
dost thou, d. L. request 475.1
d. L., I do surrender 482.1
speak . . . d. L. to me 490.2
more of thy power, d. L. 523.1
d. L., to thy feet I bring 523.c
give me more love, d. L. 523.2
d. L., my vows were given 534.1
speak, d. L., O speak 534.2
d. L. and Father 567.1
subdue/save/ d. L. 638.3
d. L., I lift my heart 717.1
all the praise, d. L. 741.3
which calls, d. L., to thee 749.1
yield, d. L. . . . hearts 802.3
d. L., give . . . fire 830.3
just to be near the d. L. 906.1
by right, d. L. to thee 926.1
shall be thine, d. L. c32
d. L. . . . I still linger c37
left one treasure, d. L. c55
I count, d. L., on thee c145

d *dear name*
d. n., the rock 58.3
Jesus, the n. to sinners d. 60.2
his d. n. shineth 63.3
sake of that d. n. 127.4
for the n. that is d. 183.4
O praise his d. n. 371.2
again, to thy d. n. 674.1
bless his d. n. I'm free c189
I'll praise his d. n. c217

e *dear Saviour*
d. S. I can ne'er repay 105.4
d. S., enter, enter 299.3
just now, d. S., let it be 468.2
coming, d. S. to thee 469.*
d. S., I will follow thee 473.c
I am coming, d. S. 493.1
Saviour, d. S., draw nearer 513.c
d. S., richly bless us 575.1
sun of my soul, thou S. d. 676.1
yes, d. S., I will trust 770.4
d. S. has shown me the way 881.1
d. S., I know thou art mine c186

f *dear Son* *Col 1:13*
d. S. of God 398.4
forgive . . . for thy d. S. 671.2
the train of thy d. S. 799.1
think how thy d. S. 916.3

sake (1c)

dearer
Jesus has been growing d. 343.1

no one now to me is d. . . 399.1
in closer, d. company . . 519.3
d. still my faith to hold . . 860.4

dearest
d. name to me . . . 65.1
d. name of names to me . 70.c
to thank thee, d. Friend . . 123.3
d. that Jesus loves me . . 323.1
d. idol I have known . . 442.5
one thing needful, d. Lord . 565.1
d. treasures to him bring . 777.4
bring . . . d. treasure . . 920.2
d., the fairest is Jesus . . c217
best (1b)

dearly
O d., d., has he loved . . 133.5
pleasures . . . too d. bought . 267.2
sought, d. bought . . . 379.1

death
1 *(spiritual)*
from d. to life hast brought . 180.4
to lose him would be d. . . 343.1
b *John 8:51-55*
o'er d. . . . conqueror be . 137.5
before we taste of d. . . 154.4
lives, that d. may die . . 156.2
d. . . . known no more . . 160.4
sin and d. and Hell . . . 180.3
pain and d. defies . . . 214.1
man can triumph over d. . 652.3
fears nor pain nor d. . . 948.2
2 *(human)*
d. with thee is bright . . 40.4
from the dust of d. . . 116.5
till d. . . . mercies seal . . 199.4
in d.'s glad hour . . . 504.3
at the gates of d. . . . 625.5
I from d. shall wake . . 665.3
bravely fought till d. . . 686.1
d.'s cup I should drink . . 686.3
bowed . . . the d. to feel. . 701.3
when d. draws near . . 709.3
with d. there's a tryst . . 739.2
hope soars beyond d. . . 744.6
d. shall o'ertake me . . 751.4
d. is in view 763.5
all that d. can seize . . 774.3
d. stands at the door . . 911.4
d. . . . least expected . . 913.2
till d. we fought . . . 933.4
b *Ps 23:4*
in d.'s dark vale . . . 53.4
walk in d.'s dark vale . . 54.3
then in d.'s dark valley . . 523.4
peace, d. shadowing us . 752.6
the vale of d. . . . tread . . 874.3
c *(death as river)*
d.'s cold, sullen stream . . 743.4
d., like a narrow sea . . 898.1
flood (3), river (2b), wave (2)
d *Song 8:6*
faithful, strong as d. . . 110.4
stronger than fear of d. . . 724.3
e *in death*
refresh my soul in d. . . 58.5
preach . . . cry in d. . . 60.6
eyes shall close in d. . . 302.4
triumph in d. 364.4
victorious be in d. . . 560.5
f *death life* *Rom 8:38*
shall l. or d.? . . . No! . . 345.4
than d., l. or duty . . . 383.2
neither l. nor d. can part . 444.3
nor l. nor d. shall break . . 534.3
d., nor l., nor angels . . 554.3
nor l. nor d., can part . . 659.5
neither l. nor d. can . . 723.3
d. will never sever . . . 891.4

g *Phil 1:20*
know, in l. and d. . . . 181.4
in l. and d. our guide . . 196.6
as I am, for d. or l.. . . 285.2
love thee in l. . . . in d. . . 357.3
and l. or d. is gain . . . 424.1
l. or d., to save . . . 522.2
in l. in d., O Lord, abide . . 670.5
let us in l., in d. . . . 721.5
in d. as in l. . . . peace . . 771.3
resigned . . . in l. and d.. . 839.5
h *1 Cor 15:54, 55*
victorious when from d. . 141.3
final victory over d. . . 171.3
rose victorious over d. . . 181.4
he came to banish d. . . 274.c
with thee, can d. destroy . 362.3
fear of d. has gone . . 536.2
in d. . . . victory for me . . 684.3
after (b), sting (b), taste (d, e)
3 *death of Jesus*
his d.'s a claim . . . 114.3
as to d. they go . . . 129.2
save in the d. of Christ . . 136.2
when from d. he passed . 141.3
humbling thyself to d. . . 174.3
who him to d. pursued . . 283.1
bearing d. . . . defending . 500.1
pain and d. to bear . . 835.2
cruel d. did follow . . . c14
b *(death defeated)* *Acts 2:24**
risen Master, d. defying . 97.3
triumph over d. assured . 102.2
dispelling fear and d. . . 134.2
but d. . . . could not hold . 137.4
love in d. . . . never die . . 142.1
d. in vain forbids . . . 143.3
conquered, d. undone . . 146.1
d. cannot keep his prey . 148.3
captive d. and . . . sin . . 150.2
powers of d. have done . 151.2
thou o'er d. hast won . 152.1, c
broke through d. . . . 544.5
lives through d. . . . 631.2
Vanquisher of d. . . . 669.5
Jesus has vanquished d. . 752.6
c *(purpose of death)* *Romans 5:10**
redemption by his d. . . 46.2
by d. our ransom . . . paid . 108.2
from d. returning . . . 130.2
purpose of thy d. . . . 138.1
thy precious d. and life . . 140.3
d. didst undergo . . . 155.3
shame and d. to him . . 168.6
by thy d. . . . salvation . . 174.2
d. your life might win . . 242.3
by his d. . . . Jesus saves . 393.3
by his d. he bought . . 402.3
provide by thy d. . . . 543.1
life deriving from his d. . . 634.3
his d. . . . more healing . . 634.4
passion and d. on the tree . 639.2
their triumph to his d. . . 879.3
d *sin and death* *Rom 5:12, 21*
in vain do s. and d. . . . 9.3
from s. and d. we flee . . 100.1
to vanquish s. and d. . . 134.c
fight with d. and s. . . 167.1
the d. of s. remove . . 603.5
e *Rev 1:18*
nor d. nor Hell . . . harm . 100.3
chains of d. and Hell . . 149.1
the keys of d. and Hell . . 164.3
over sin and d. and Hell . . 180.3
life and d. are waiting . . 333.4
d. of d. and H. . . . 578.3
f *Rev 21:4*
ruthless d. . . . not there . 268.3
I shall escape from d. . . 877.4
pains of d. are past . . 890.4
no d. in the homeland . . 895.3
no d., no weeping . . . 899.3

taste (e)
4 *death (adjective)*
d.-bell will toll . . . 237.3
d.-dew lies cold . . . 357.3

deathless
through thy d. love . . 152.3
d. it shall reign . . . 508.2
given in d. love . . . 631.1
sing the d. story . . . 828.4

deathly 303.2

debt
d. of love I owe . . . 105.4
how small the d. men owe . 572.3
how great the d. to you . . 572.3
b *pay debt*
sin's d. to p. 126.1
paid the d. and made . . 180.c
dying thy d. had not paid . 271.2
my every d. to p. . . . 303.c
gave himself my d. to p. . 342.1

debtor *Rom 8:12* . . . 313.4

decay-ing
best in this world is d. . . 51.2
death and fierce d. . . 268.3
my portion never can d. . . 356.2
cannot know d. . . . 494.1
change and d. in all . . 670.2
heart fail and flesh d. . . 746.5
love that never can d. . . 808.1
though earth d. . . . 873.4
life beyond d. . . . 895.3

deceive-ed-ing
hopes d. and fears annoy . 112.2
they all have been d. . . 338.3
one day kind, the next d. . 377.1
hearts and looks d. . . 498.3
b *1 John 1:8*
I, self-d., felt stronger . . 553.2

December 318.1

decide
d. the destiny of man . . 6.4
experience will d. . . . 21.4
what has thy heart d. . . 255.3

decisive 735.3

declare
a *[God] declares*
thou to man the truth d. . 97.4
till thou all thy mind d. . . 210.4
glorious gospel word d. . . 385.1
pardon d. 605.1
thy word d. 642.1
d. in Christ for every . . 760.2
so the word of God d. . . 932.1
b *[others] declare*
d. their maker's praise . . 42.2
thy wondrous love d. . . 524.2
though in d. Christ . . 530.1
thy love for a sinner d. . . 639.2
how shall we that truth d. . 656.3
thy steadfast truth d. . . 721.5
thy truth . . . works d. . . 926.3
I really must d. it . . . c170

decline 545.3

decree
a changeless d. . . . 16.3
wounds my sin d. . . . 122.1
cannot break the firm d. . 407.4
a place by God's d. . . 850.3

dedicate-d-ing
in their d. hands . . . 238.2

gladly d. my days . . . 290.3
d. myself to thee . . . 517.1
my all to thee d. . . . 786.c
we would d. to thee . . 789.1
we d. to Heaven's cause . 796.3
Father, let me d. . . . 916.1
we d. ourselves to thee . 919.1
I d. my all c33

dedication
did my d. seal . . . 463.2
in this hour of d. . . . 787.1
as each day in d. . . . 787.4
in this d. hour . . . 795.3

deed
by many d. of shame . . 172.5
memories of d. gone by . 303.2
by loving d. expressed . 518.1
every loving d. of mine . 518.3
to hallow every d. . . . 619.4
d. must every match . . 760.4
grace . . . hallow ever d. . 760.4
calls to d. of valour . . 781.2
noble d. and worthy strife . 867.3

b *do deeds*
by faith the d. is done . 513.3
d. of kindness done . . 524.3
d. of valour we'll do . . c239

c *thought and deed*
who led in d. and t. . . 5.2
condemned in t. and d. . 290.1
offering each t. and d. . 493.1
ruin man in d. and t. . . 760.3
in t. and d. . . . freed . . 861.3
in every t. and d. . . . c107

d *word and deed* *Col 3:17**
wrought in w. and d. . . 287.2
nor sin in d. or w. . . 407.4
nor guarded d. and w. . 466.2
in w. and d. . . . holy . . 521.1
in w. and in d. . . . love . 527.c
he proved by w. and d. . 555.2
need . . . for w. and d. . 561.2
w. . . . d. full of grace . 848.2
by w. and by d. . . . 928.3

mighty (1g)

deem-ed
my cross a burden d. . . 400.1
things d. impossible . . 744.4

deep-er-est
1 *sea (literal)*
dyed the lovely d. . . . 103.2
the mighty ocean d. . . 569.1
walkedst on the foaming d. . 569.2

2 *water (figurative)*
its fountains are d. . . 252.2
a d. celestial spring . . 254.4
the fountain, 'tis d. . . 413.1
d. and swelling flood . . 583.5
through the d. waters . . 653.3
though the sea be d. . . 772.2
the wild stormy d. . . . c178

b *Ps 42:7*
d. is calling unto d. . . 641.1

c *Rom 10:7*
search the lowest d. . . 496.3

deep (3c), launch (b), well (1b, c)

3 *(general)*
d. thunder-clouds form . 16.2
d. in unfathomable mines . 29.2
d. and dreamless sleep . 86.1
yet d. do I ponder . . . 94.3
who is he in d. distress . 104.2
thy wounds they are d. . 111.2
d. thunders roll . . . 126.3
sunk in d. despair . . . 253.2
grounded firm and d. . . 280.c
. . . in d. contrition . . 301.2
gloom fell d. as night . . 330.1
d. poverty or wealth . . 356.3
he saw my d. dismay . . 386.2
torrent so rushing and d. . 388.1
a d. truth I see . . . 434.3
in d. consecration . . . 493.c
where the darkness is d. . 527.1
flowers with d. beauties . 545.2
in d. reverence, praise . 567.1
d. homage now I give . . 600.3
attain that d. joy . . . 630.3
sanctify . . . d. distress . 653.3
like a d., d. mine . . . 658.2
storm of d. affliction . . 663.3
the shadows d. lie . . . 697.4
a d. joy comes . . . 711.1
scenes of d. gloom . . 725.2
O for a d. . . . trust. . . 770.c
in d. submission I pray . 786.c
d. secrets of the flower . 871.2
d. buried in the earth . . 923.2
shadows d. have crossed . 938.3

b *deep [heart]*
d. stamp thyself . . . 207.4
thy heart's d. grief . . . 225.4
not hide thy d. emotion . 259.1
strange d. longings . . 325.3
my spirit's d. desire . . 379.3
satisfy my d. longings . . 531.3
with purpose pure and d. . 534.3
the regions d. within . . 540.3
grace, d. as need . . . 571.2
image d. on my heart . . 623.c
heart's d. fountain . . . 749.1
d. in our hearts . . . 864.2

c *deep [love]*
broad and d. and glorious . 40.2
God's l. is as d. as . . . 47.1
such l., so great, so d. . . 48.1
it's as d. as the sea . . 49.c
d. than the depths . . . 110.4
the d., d. love of Jesus . 182.*
l. unbounded . . . d. . . 184.2
a l. so true and d. . . . 265.1
d. ocean of l. . . . 298.1
a d., strong l. . . . 426.2
wisdom's d., clearest sea . 452.4
mercy so high and so d.. . 454.5
d. depths of thy l. . . . 493.3
d. than the d. sea . . . 548.4
d., burning l. for souls . 649.1, c
more d. I'll drink above . 896.2
tokens of our d. . . . love . 922.2

compassion (b)

d *deep need*
confessed my d. n. . . 52.2
knows your d. n. . . . 238.c
have their d. n. supplied . 471.2
grace, d. as n. . . . 571.2

e *deep sin/stains*
purge our d. s. . . . 121.4
d. were the scarlet s. . . 176.1
sin's d. crimson s. . . 237.1
their s. are so d. . . . 298.2
I was sinking d. in s. . . 336.1
from s. d. mire . . . 401.2
soul sunk d. in s. . . . 700.2
souls in s. d. sleep . . 875.3

deepen-ing
earth's d. shades descend . 595.3
d. in me thy work . . . 649.2
the darkness d. . . . 670.1
time but d. their delights . 799.3

deeply
d. wailing 161.2
d. burning holy fire . . 206.2
very d. stained within . . 336.1
heart more d. bleed . . 586.3

defeat-ed-ing
disciples in despair, d. . . 96.4
past d. would bid me stay . 285.2
nor suffer a d. . . . 366.5
crushing d. I have seen . 437.1
thine to gladden my d. . . 510.3
hell to d. is my endeavour . 686.3
no retreating, hell d. . . 702.c
when d. seems . . . near. . 713.3
knowing not d. or fear . . 713.3
d., were it not for thee . . 747.1
story of my life's d. . . 770.1
all our enemies d. . . . 778.3
not in sorrow to d. me . . c166

defence *Ps 62:2**
our d. is sure 13.2
trusting in thy sure d. . . 595.2
my strength, my sure d. . 717.6
Jehovah thy d. . . . 767.3

defenceless 737.2

defend
prosper thy work and d. . 19.2
our cause d. 500.1
let thine eyes d. me . . 635.2
Lord, thou dost d. us . . 685.3
or to d. his cause . . . 735.1
from sin d. us . . . 845.2

defender
our shield and d. . . . 16.1
our maker, d., redeemer . 16.5
so mighty a d. . . . 345.4
still my soul's d. . . . 762.1

defiant 869.4

defiled-ing
helpless and d. . . . 98.1
the tainted and d. . . . 274.1
from all d. taint of sin . . 867.2

defy-ing
risen Master, death d. . . 97.3
pain and death d. . . . 214.1
every doubt d. . . . 222.1
wilt thou as rebel d. . . 276.2
thy power d. 303.2
the foe we d. . . . 681.3
hell and God d. . . . 693.2
enlist . . . all Hell to d. . . 703.3
our every foe d. . . . 810.2
Satan and his host d. . . 847.4

degradation
I was sunk in d. . . . 309.1
lost in sin's d. . . . 349.2
slaves of sin and d. . . 702.3

degree
proclaiming thy royal d. . 101.2
love beyond d. . . . 105.2
love for me, beyond d. . . 340.2

deified 885.3

deign
thou d. to have dwelling . 6.1
that he should d. to hear . 48.1
if he d. thy willing heart . 683.3

deity 82.2

delay-ing
believe on him without d. . 231.3
rise at once d. no more . . 267.3
haste . . . no more d. . . 412.2
why still d. 471.4
working, I will not d. . . 484.2
to the front! no more d. . . 702.3
often, therefore, we d. . . 748.2
when he calls us, why d. . 772.4

d. not to follow . . . 805.2
d. its sure returning . . 854.2
join us then without d. . . 869.2
sinners, don't d. . . . c17
make haste, do not d. . . c30

b *(come, no) delay*
c. sinners . . . no longer d. . 233.1
c. . . . make no d. . . . 235.1
do not d., but c. . . . 235.2
c., then, at once; d. . . 246.3
c., and no longer d. . . 248.3
whosoever c. need not d. . 279.2
c., without d., let us go . 348.3
c. to him without d. . . 433.1
c. . . . and do not d. . . 681.4
and no d. . . . I c. . . . 860.2

delight
1 *(divine)*
in me d. to rest . . . 207.1
his great d. to bless us . . 377.3
thine own supreme d. . . 601.3
God doth in his saints d. . 909.2

2 *(human)*
angels d. to hymn thee . . 16.6
make . . . service your d. . 21.5
hearts that know d. . . 27.5
heart and mind's d. . . 28.3
called order and d. . . 36.1
be all my heart's d. . . 178.3
perfect d. 310.2
rivers of d. . . . flow . . 344.3
Glory and endless d. . . 357.4
height of the holy d. . . 367.4
our hearts d. to hear . . 377.3
the d. of his love . . . 397.4
with calm d. can live . . 414.1
the world's d. and cheer . 460.2
may no profane d. divide . 480.3
the saints' d. . . . 880.1
rivers of d. 887.2
its ten thousand d. . . 905.4

b *I delight* *Ps 40:8**
Lord, I will d. in thee . . 14.1
as I walk, I will d. . . . 59.3
my soul d. to hear . . . 67.4
in the war d. . . . 309.2
I run with d. . . . 321.1
I fight with d. . . . 321.4
their daily d. . . . 372.3
my chief d. . . . employ . 451.3
I shall d. in thy will. . . 457.2
I d. in his ways . . . 640.2
my constant d. . . . 640.4
victory will be your d. . . 679.3
in this warfare we're d. . 778.2
time but deepens their d. . 799.3
we are filled with d. . . 808.3
fighting is our great d. . . 809.2
we d. to walk . . . c195

c *pure delight*
p. d. of a single hour . . 585.3
a land of p. d. . . . 898.1
days are filled with p. d.. . 947.2

delightfully 667.4

deliver *Matt 6:13; Gal 1:4*
born thy people to d. . . 79.3
I d. thee when bound . . 110.2
my passing soul d. . . 153.3
bolder, d. I'll be . . . 298.6
from every sin to d. . . 384.3
the blood that doth d. . . 434.5
from all self and sin d. . . 452.2
from all ills its waves d.. . 471.2
d. by thy mighty power . 624.4
grace our spirits will d. . 891.3
abundantly able to d. . . c12

b *strong/almighty to deliver*
so s. to d., so good . . 372.1
come, almighty to d. . . 438.2
Jesus is s. to d. . . . 467.c
he is almighty to d. . . 686.3

deliverance *Luke 4:18*
of his d. I will boast . . 21.2
d. he affords to all . . . 21.3
a name for . . . d. . . . 71.1
do you want d. . . . 257.1
beneath . . . d. I see . . 298.3
he doth to me d. bring . . 401.1
claim . . . complete d. . . 433.2
is there no d. for me . . 459.1
can full d. find . . . 590.2
there is perfect d. . . . 808.2

b *Ps 32:7*
a song of d. 186.c

Deliverer
wondrous D. . . . 257.4
their guide, and their D. . 576.2
strong D. 578.2

dell 187.2

deluded 251.2

deluge 620.4

demand
give what he'll d. . . . 44.3
d. my soul, my life . . . 136.4
sins d. that I should die . . 282.2
fulfil thy law's d. . . . 302.2
sinners yet d. my love . . 463.3
the whole of love's d. . . 512.2
its heavy toll d. . . . 534.2
make thy d. on me . . 605.3
thy countless benefits d. . 616.2
d. perpetual songs . . . 672.3
duty d. it 691.4
the law of love's d. . . 732.3
continuance . . . d. . . 785.5
as thy great love d. . . 861.4
his d. I would fulfil . . . 867.1
d. successive songs . . . 925.4

demons 1.3

denial see *self* (2d)

deny-ied-ing
art thou its claims d. . . 276.1
for those that you d. . . 552.3
shall ne'er be d. . . . 763.2
a passage seem d. . . . 772.2

b *Matt 16:24*
myself in all things to d.. . 509.1
room to d. ourselves . . 668.4

c *Matt 26:35*
can I my Lord d. . . . 94.3
men d. those hands . . 129.1
follow . . . d. thee never. . 490.c
have I d. thee . . . 534.2

d *(none) deny* *2 Tim 2:13**
wants supply, and none d. . 50.c
none who ask will be d. . 121.6
no one has . . . been d. . 257.4
no seeking soul . . . d. . . 303.3
to none that ask d. . . 485.3
that none may be d. . . 521.2
self (2d)

depart-ed-ing
1 *[God] departs*
ne'er from us d. . . . 219.3
do not let thy Lord d. . . 251.1
friendship . . . never d. . . 273.2
O never, Lord, d. . . . 597.3
thy glory never hence d. . 945.4

2 *[we] depart*
we from God may ne'er d. . 190.2
or from thy paths d. . . 597.2
let me not unheard d. . . 614.3
never a moment d. . . 639.3

3 *other*
my fear has all d. . . . 169.3
made all the darkness d. . 371.1
where all sins d. . . . 383.3
let old bitterness d. . . 572.2

b *depart [to heaven]*
they dare d. . . . 874.3
with d. friends to stay . . 902.2
and at my d. 953

c *bid depart*
b. all anxious fears d. . . 68.2
b. all my fear d. . . . 363.3
b. sadness and sorrow d. . 537.1
b. . . . from each soul d. . 599.2
disciples . . . b. them d.. . 797.1

departing *(adjective)* . . . 524.3

depend-ing
on thy care d. . . . 14.1
faith on love d. . . . 222.3
I on his oath d. . . . 223.4
my hopes of Heaven d. . . 592.2
in all things to d. . . . 597.3
often . . . our faith d. on sight 717.5
none will on himself d. . . 799.3

deplore 244.1

depth
ocean-d. of happy rest . . 10.3
in the d. be praise . . 18.1, 4
what d. of human grief . . 135.1
is the d. of my devotion. . 591.2
in thine ocean d. . . . 621.1
d. of his salvation plan . . 656.2
hidden in its mighty d. . . 658.2

b *Ps 130:1*
out of the d. of ruin . . 300.4
heart's most secret d. . . 311.4
from the d. of sin . . . 339.1
out of the d. of my night . 378.1
into the d. of mind . . . 416.3
in the d. of my soul . . 493.1
Lord, cleanse the d. . . 572.4
d. of many a heart . . . 612.4
from the d. my soul . . 762.2

c *Rom 8:39*
from d. to height reply . . 187.4
for him no d. can drown . 496.3
nor d., nor any creature . 554.4

d *depth of [love]* *Eph 3:18*
d. of sovereign grace . . 55.1
d. of all-redeeming love . . 55.4
deeper than the d. beneath . 110.4
d. of mercy 286.1
none its d. can ever tell . 363.1
d. of love and mercy . . 368.2
deeper d. of thy love . . 493.3
d. of his grace . . . 535.3
there are d. of love . . 585.4
d. of love divine . . . 651.4
hideth . . . in the d. . . 710.c
the d. of God's design . . 858.3

deride *Luke 16:14*
dare we the sinless one d. . 121.3
let the world d. or pity . . 157.3

derision *Luke 23:35* . . . 147.3

derive-ing
life . . . do thence d. . . 424.3
life d. from his death . . 634.3

descend-ed-ing
1 *(God) descends*
suddenly, the Lord, d. . . 75.3
d. to us, we pray . . . 86.4
Jesus d. from above . . 140.2

b *Rev 1:7*
he comes with clouds d. 161.1

c *(Matt 3:16)*
d., O Holy Spirit . . . 211.1
d. and make me whole . . 215.1
d. with . . . gracious powers . 217.1
Spirit . . . on us d. . . . 219.2
d. from above . . . 221.1
d. the heavens . . . 448.3
let thy touch now d. . . 493.1
life immortal, Heaven d. . 540.4
here on our souls d. . . 590.4
Spirit of our God, d. . . 607.3
d., O gracious Lord, d. . . 626.1
let thy power d. on me . . c93

fire (2c)

2 *(other)*
d. to the plain . . . 16.4
storms are on my head d. . 39.2
darkness d. . . . veiling . . 126.3
deepening shades d. . . 595.3
mercies shall on you d. . 920.4

b *Gen 28:12*
angels d. with songs . . 160.5
angels d., bring . . . 310.2

descent 216.4

desert-ed
1 *general*
through the d. mark . . 159.1
soon the d. will be glad . . 159.3
in the d. ways I sing . . 194.5
make the d. garden bloom . 333.2
in the d. and the strife . . 499.2
redeem the d. places . . 647.3
forward through the d. . . 682.1
earth is a d. drear . . . 882.1
passage through a d. lies . 911.2
d. bloom and spring . . 929.2
d. or the star-lit north . . c238

b *Isa 35:1, 6*
streams in d. dreary . . 448.1
d. lands rejoice . . . 583.2
stream in the d. . . . 689.3

c *Matt 4:1, 2*
fasting alone in the d. . . 99.2
in temptation's d. . . . 288.4
through the d. . . . go . . 607.2

2 *(verb)*
devil's ranks d. . . . 309.2
will not d. to its foes . . 653.5
a realm d., cast aside . . 885.3

deserve-ing
though we don't d. it . . 49.3
'tis of thanks d. . . . 276.3

design-ed
all things to thy d. . . . 6.2
his bright d. 29.2
Lord of sequence and d. . 30.3
your life he'll re-d. . . 44.2
your d. is my desire . . 206.2
searching the plan d. . . 416.3
shatter my own d. . . 605.2
human d. may cause me pain 644.3
d. thy dross to consume . 653.4
the depths of God's d. . . 858.3
whose love d. to frame . . 944.1

designedly 51.c

designers 95.2

desire
1 *(divine)* *Hag 2:7*
dear d. of every nation . 79.2
d. of nations . . . 167.3

b
what thou most d. . . . 935.3

2 *[good] desires* *Ps 73:25*
faith d. no more . . . 26.4
kindle every high d. . . 194.2
craving into pure d. . . 197.2
your design is my d. . . 206.2
the lure of strong d. . . 207.1
gav'st the enlarged d. . . 210.2
new d. which in thee burn . 256.1
eager and longing d. . . 351.2
meet my spirit's deep d.. . 379.3
make my d. secure . . 416.2
see thee now, d. thee . . 449.2
nothing on earth do I d. . . 480.5
henceforth my chief d. . . 517.1
serving Christ my one d. . 522.3
the heats of our d. . . 567.5
teach our faint d. . . 604.3
nothing d. . . . but Jesus . 659.3
an even, strong d. . . 720.2
he would d. to conquer . . 760.3
filled with new d. . . 788.1
when his will is your d. . . 790.3
my d. is now to love him . 857.3
love's unquenchable d. . . 939.1

b *soul's desire*
none can quench my s. d. . 351.c
how my s. d. to be clean . 420.4
answer now my s.'s d. . . 479.2
satisfy our s.'s d. . . . 481.c
the s.'s sincere d. . . . 625.1

c *heart's desire* *Ps 37:4*
confirm my h.'s d. . . 199.3
he is all my h.'s d. . . 522.c
pure and fervent h.-d. . . 620.3
joy and d. of my h. . . 639.1

d *Ps 51:6*
given us minds d. truth . . 27.5

3 *[bad] desires*
wrong d. destroy . . . 408.4
pride or fond d. . . . 425.2
dread remorse and vain d. . 885.3

base

desolate
joy of the d. 236.2
no one . . . too d. . . . 590.2

despair
1 *(divine)*
don't think . . . he d. . . 44.c

2 *(human)*
mourned . . . in d. . . 96.4
dispel the darkness of d. . 126.4
though sunk in deep d. . . 253.2
there is refuge from d. . . 257.1
out of d. into raptures . . 300.3
leave my soul d. . . . 303.2
heard my d. cry . . . 336.1
lost, d. broken-hearted . . 369.3
out of . . . doubt, . . . d. 378.2, 4
in d. my heart . . . sink . 399.2
darkness, from sin and d. . 535.2
owning . . . my d. . . . 605.1
d. or doubt would seize . . 722.1
all is d., everything sad . . 773.1
for joy or d. 928.1
for my days of d. . . . c148

dark (d)

b *2 Cor 4:8*
I never will d. . . . 334.2
hearts need not d. . . 363.4
press on then, never d. . 773.4
you must not d. . . . 817.2

despairingly 296.1

despise-d-ing
the d., the distressed . . 170.1
escape . . . sins I d. . . 459.1
friends and foes d. . . 482.3
though I be d., forsaken . 498.1

let the world d. . . . 498.3
see thy love, d. . . . 503.2
friends d., forsake thee . 645.3
forbid that we d. it . . . 944.2

b *Isa 53:3*
he was d. and afflicted . . 99.2
hail, thou once d. Jesus . . 109.1
so d. by the world . . . 124.2
past the reach of all d. . . 185.3
once d., rejected . . . 347.3

c *Zech 4:10*
thou wilt not d. . . . 921.1

despoil 883.3

destiny 6.4

destroy
would thy hopes d. . . 253.3
with thee, can death d. . 362.3
the devil can't d. . . . 402.c
no cares could d. . . . 611.1
blood-bought souls d. . . 696.2

b *[nothing] can destroy*
peace n. can d. . . . 243.3
joy which . . . n. can d. . 352.2
n. can our peace d. . . 607.3
peace n. can d. . . . c184

c *destroy [wrong]* *1 John 3:8*
hate and greed d. . . . 71.1
fire d. fear 197.2
fetters . . . he d. . . . 348.2
sting of death has been d. . 375.2
wrong desires d. . . . 408.4
vice d. or virtue spread . . 581.2

d *destroy sin* *Rom 6:6*
shall all our s. d. . . . 164.5
d. the works of s. . . . 448.4
thy blood doth s. d. . . 593.3
when s. is all d. . . . 597.4

work (3c)

e *Gen 6:7*
he can create, and he d. . 4.1

destruction *(Hos 13:14)*
and Hell's d. 578.3

determined
d. to conquer . . . 686.c
d. to conquer or die . . 800.2
d. in thy strength to go . . 933.3
I'm d. my voice I'll raise. . c194

devil
Jesus does with d. fight. . 107.2
d.'s ranks deserted . . 309.2
the d. can't destroy . . 402.c
though the d. says, no . . 608.2
pull down the d.'s kingdom . 696.c
in spite of men and d. . . 810.1

b *James 4:7*
d. fear and fly . . . 60.1
thy name makes d. fly . . 593.3

devote-d
did he d. that sacred head . 105.1
wholly to thyself d. . . 210.3
d. solely to thy will . . 516.3
thy d. servant make me . . 865.1
to thy service d. . . . c52

devotion
sweeter than human d. . . 383.2
day by day my d. . . . 493.3
ask . . . my d. to test . . 507.c
depth of my d. . . . 591.2
offer him our heart's d. . . 777.4
may his d. to thy word . . 796.4
just a true d. c213

devour
wolves d. thy fold . . 172.5
my simple soul d. . . 720.1

dew
sweetly distils in the d. . 16.4
evening d. and damps . . 162.2
the death-d. lies cold . . 357.3
by the heavenly d. . . 443.2
still d. of quietness . . 567.4
thy freshening d. . . . 669.2
soft d. of kindly sleep . . 676.2
aye the d. of sorrow . . 896.3
b *as/like dew*
as d. upon the spirit . . 70.3
like d. from Heaven . . 213.2
come as the d. . . . 217.4
as gently falling d. . . . 494.2
sins as morning d. . . . 665.4
early (c)

dewfall 35.2

dewy 930.1

diadem *Isa 62:3*
bring forth the royal d. . 56.1
royal d. adorns . . . 168.1
hath he d. as monarch . . 228.3
life-blood for thy d. . . 707.3

diamonds 354.1

dictate 692.4

did see *do*

die-d-ing
1 *(man) dies*
be near me . . . when d. . 123.4
could thy children fear to d. . 146.3
saints like him shall d. . . 149.2
vigorous when the body d. . 214.1
d. fulfilling thy commands . 362.2
happier . . . if thine I d. . . 492.3
though as a martyr d. . . 530.3
d. if thou shouldst will . . 532.3
I dare not d. . . . 676.3
honour to d. in the field . . 684.3
we will fight and d. . . 693.2
dare or d. for Jesus . . 696.2
who fears not to d. . . 703.1
the hour has come to d.. . 753.4
we hope to d. shouting . . 763.5
'twere better far to d. . . 780.*
do or d., our battle cry . . 798.2
gloriously they d. . . . 866.1
content to d. believing . . 874.3
b *live and/or die* *Phil 1:20*
l. to thee . . . with thee d. . 73.4
make us fit to l. or d. . . 203.2
l. and d. for thee . . . 210.3
his cross I'll l. and d. . . 343.c
thine we will d. . . . l. . . 424.4
thine I'll l. and . . . d. . . 439.4
to suffer, l. or d. . . . 448.c
l. d., sacrificing . . . 452.3
thine to d., thine to l. . . 469.3
l., d., thine to be . . . 470.3
joy or grief, to l. or d. . . 489.1
this moment, l. or d. . . 505.2
thine, to l. and d. . . . 509.1
or in l., or in d. . . . 764.3
for God to l. and d. . . 784.2
for Christ to l. or d. . . 830.3
l., d., testifying . . . 869.3
c *(till) I die*
shall be till I d. . . . 132.4
fight . . . till we d. 382.c; 782.c
glorify thee till I d. . . 589.5
we will fight until we d.. . 593.3
we'll fight till we d. . . 681.3
fight for God until we d. . 782.2
fight until we d. . . . 810.c
above our heads until we d. . c240
d *(when) I die*
near me, Lord, when d. . 123.4
go to Heaven when you d. . 256.c
solid comfort when we d. . 464.2
when I d. . . . my share . . 477.4
when we come to d. . . 798.3
if I love him, when I d. . . 843.3
e *die [in sin]*
bound and condemned to d. . 45.1
nor let . . . sinner d. . . 106.3
Jesus have the sinner d. . 140.1
to d. with no hope . . . 263.3
to d. out of Christ . . . 263.3
sins demand that I . . . d. . 282.2
unless thou help . . . d. . . 291.1
wash me . . . or I d. . . 302.3
I shall for ever d. . . . 472.4
multitudes are d. . . . 482.2
precious souls are d. . . 499.4
droop and d. 559.4
men d. in darkness . . 683.5
to a world of rebels d. . . 693.2
heedless millions d. . . 696.1
many d. in sin . . . 708.4
souls about to d. . . . 819.1
help them lest they d. . . 922.1
f *(never) die* *John 6:50; 8:51*
man no more may d. . . . 82.3
so shall I never d. . . . 189.4
where pleasures never d. . 266.c
thou need'st never d. . . 271.4
he shall never d. . . . 277.1
joys that never d. . . . 375.3
love that never d. . . . 432.3
where pleasure never d. . . 818.4
g *John 12:24*
unless it d. . . . abide . . 923.3
h *die to self* *(1 Cor 15:31)*
who d. with thee . . . 512.3
dares to d. to s. . . . 619.3
we'll conquer if we d. . . 694.c
in my service fight and d. . 694.4
fight that s. may d. . . 705.3
conquer (2c), fight (2e)
2 *(Jesus) dies*
God . . . sent him to d. . . 37.3
give his Son to d. for me . 48.c
worthy the Lamb that d. . 57.2
d. in grief and agony . . 104.4
to d. for me on a cross . . 114.1
he came, he d., for you . . 114.2
d. for me . . . to atone . . 116.3
the hill where he d. . . 119.1
who for us d. . . . 121.1
this I know: he d. for me . 131.3
for me he came to d. . . 134.1
did not feel thee d. . . 135.2
the Prince of Glory d. . . 136.1
witness thou hast d. . . 140.2
ride on to d. . . . 150.2, 5
sing of him who d. . . 156.1
for thou hast d. for me . . 156.4
camest thou to earth to d. . 185.1
look to him who d. . . 239.1
the heart for which he d. . 241.2
left him to d. 245.3
O be saved, he d. for thee . 259.c
come to him who d. . . 260.3
gained thy salvation by d. . 276.1
d. he for me who caused . 283.1
thou, my God, shouldst d. . 283.1
tell him thou hast d. . . 284.4
since there d. a Lamb . . 290.1
I d. for you, my children . 299.3
d. for me . . . his enemy . 363.c
he d. from sin to sever . . 413.1
thou who didst d. loving . 443.c
for his friend to d. . . 515.3
cross where thou hast d. . . 585.c
name of him who d. . . 678.c
lives for whom he d. . . 707.2
as thou hast d. for me . . 743.2
did for every sinner d. . . 756.2
hath surely d. for me . . 756.2
made as he d. there . . . c89
d., he saved me . . . c185
b *Christ died* *1 Cor 15:3*
C. . . . d. for . . . sin . . 105.3
C. led forth to d. . . . 129.1
C., who d. with arms . . 181.3
live for C. hath d. . . 239.3
C. should have to d. . . 274.2
my only plea C. d. for me . 291.c
I love the C. who d. . . 327.2
story of the C. who d. . 337.1, c
thou art the C. who d. . . 529.1
C. who d. for the sins . . 783.2
c *Jesus died*
J. who d. . . . satisfied . . 42.3
enough that J. d. . . 60.c
wonder why J. d. for me . 94.3
J., for thy people d. . . 97.3
that J. d. on Calvary . . 108.c
J. hath lived, hath d. . . 116.5
J. d., a . . . sacrifice . . 126.3
on the cross . . . J. d. . . 128.1
believe that J. d. for me . 132.c
J. d., O wondrous love . . 242.c
J. Christ has d. for all . . 243.4
is it nothing . . . one day J. d. 245.3
sinners everyone, J. d. . . 268.4
remember J. d. on the tree . 276.c
J. hath d. for me . . . 296.1
J. d. that none . . . perish . 363.4
sinner, but J. d. for me . . 368.*
J. d. for you and me . . 381.2
J. has d. to redeem us . . 384.1
J. . . . d. for our race . . 687.3
for the world, J. d. . . 821.c
J. loves me, he who d. . . 843.2
J. has d. that . . . free . . 881.3
J. has d. for me . . . 889.3
J. d. for all mankind . . c22
believe that J. d. for me. . c128
d *Lord died*
fight for the L. who d. . . 188.3
L. . . . in his love d. . . 395.3
e *Saviour died*
for all my S. d. . . . 62.5
see your S. d. . . . 107.1
on Calvary's brow my S. d. . 125.1
S. bows his head and d. . 125.2
on every hill our S. d. . . 127.1
our S. willing d. . . . 131.4
Calvary where the S. d. . . 260.1
cross where my S. d. . . 315.1
that the S. should d. . . 319.c
there where the S. d. . . 366.*
tell . . . a S. has d. . . 691.4
f *died that/to*
d. to save us all . . . 133.1
d. that we . . . forgiven . . 133.3
d. to make us good . . 133.3
once he d. . . . to save . . 143.4
he who d. . . . to save . . 149.3
d. eternal life to bring . . 156.2
he d. to make men holy . . 162.4
d. to call them all . . 182.2
d. that I might live . . 221.1
I d. to ransom thee . . 229.3
friend who d. to save . . 259.2
d. that no seeking soul . . 303.3
he bled, he d. to save me . 345.2
d. my heart to win . . . 370.1
d. our souls to free . . 383.2
Jesus has d. to redeem . . 384.1
d. from sin to sever . . 413.1
the souls he d. to save . . 929.3
g *Rom 5:8*
did for every sinner d. . . 756.2

h *Gal 2:21*
nor suffer him to d. in vain . 234.3
all (3b), bleed (1b), bow (1b), Calvary (f), cross (1d), lift (3b), rise (2c), sheep (2c), suffer (2c), tree (2d)
3 *(other)*
as a dream d. . . . 13.5
ill thoughts can d. . . 41.2
his love . . . never d. . . 49.3
his love . . . shall never d. . 142.1
lives, that death may d. . . 156.2
my joys and comforts d. . 358.2
bends with age but never d. . 544.3
that never will d. out . . 609.3
nor d. the strain of praise . 677.3
thy mercy never d. . . 746.4
prospects droop and d. . . 761.1
praises never d. . . . 887.5
love cannot d. . . . 897.3
b
the ready ground to d. . . 923.1
on the rocks to d. . . 931.2

difference 824.4

diffused 283.3

dim-med
from the d. past . . . 31.2
nor is d. by . . . time . . 63.1
his pitying eye is d. . . 121.2
the d. and flaring lamps . . 162.2
d. the eye 185.1
find earth's glitter d. . . 267.1
sun shines but d. . . 318.1
each d. recess of mine . . 325.3
eyes were d. with tears . . 330.1
whose mind is d. . . . 414.3
treasures, poor and d. . . 420.2
his sight is never d. . . 736.2
though the path be d. . . 740.2
lamp was burning d. . . 839.1
if our light is d. . . . 841.2
cheering ray of hope to d. . c166
b *grow dim*
that early joy g. d. . . 534.2
earth's joys g. d. . . 670.2
nevermore . . . shall g. d. . 773.4

dimension c173

dimly 572.3

din 31.1

dire 910.4

direct *Prov 3:6*
d. and safely lead . . . 561.2
then its light d. . . . 655.3
d., control, suggest . . 665.5
he shall d. thy . . . feet . . 715.2
may every word . . . d. . . 943.3

direction 376.3

disappear-ed
earth's sorrow . . . then d. . 169.1
at his word Hell d. . . 243.2
all d. in the fountain . . c189

disappointed 824.c

disappointment 246.3

disaster
valiant be 'gainst all d. . . 685.1
in each trial and d. . . 751.2

discard-ed
sceptre-reed d. . . . 126.2
soul d. thy fears . . . 249.3

discern-ing
we may d. the beauty . . 38.4
your perfect plan d. . . . 206.2
quick-d. eye 596.3
O that we, d. . . . 655.6
his all-d. love . . . 738.2
as baby grows, d. . . . 795.2

disciples
to his dear d., tossing . . 96.2
mourned by his d. . . . 96.4
thy d. teach us . . . 452.3
d. turned and ran . . . 544.5
when his first d. heard . . 700.1
those first d. of the Lord . 760.1
those first d. heard . . 760.4
stern d. drove them back . 797.1

disclose
souls, your wants d. . . 254.3
d. thy lovely face . . . 412.2

disconsolate 236.1

discontented 376.3

discord
d. filled my heart . . . 390.2
blasts of d. cease . . . 669.3

discouraged
d., thinking all is lost . . 396.1
we should never be d. . . 645.2
yet never be d. . . . 810.2

discouragement . . . 685.1

discover-ed
d. the true source . . . c210
d. that God is his goal . . c210

disdain-ing
here I stand, myself d. . . 460.2
bad language d. . . . 823.2

disease
whole of sin's d. . . . 441.2
health that overcomes d. . 631.2
b *Ps 103:3*
healed my d. 380.2

disguise 455.4

disheartened 396.3

disillusion 544.2

dismal 685.2

dismay-ed *(Isa 41:10)*
filled us with d. . . . 192.1
Satan d. . . . doth flee . . 323.5
he saw my deep d. . . 386.2
let nothing your spirit d. . 537.3
final judgment with d. . . 618.2
O be not d. 653.2
can I be d. 736.1

dismissed 44.1

disobedience 433.2

disobey 854.3

disordered 651.3

disown
myself, my all I still d. . . 362.2
If e'er I d. you . . . 506.5

dispel-ling
his word d. the darkness . 126.4
my presence shall d. . . 277.4
shadows d. 371.1
Christ, our woes d. . . . 558.3
Jesus there d. the sadness . 663.2
sin's sorrows to d. . . . c7
b *dispel fear*
his name d. my guilt and f. . 67.4
d. f. and death . . . 134.2
trembling soul, d. thy f. . 269.1

disperse-d
their legions hath d. . . 151.2
his presence d. my gloom . 318.2
d. my sins as . . . dew . . 665.4

display-ed
the blessings earth d. . . 15.2
to human view d. . . . 93.4
now thy might d. . . . 188.1
light of truth to us d. . . 190.2
heavenly life d. . . . 195.3
more and more thyself d. . 412.4
hast my spirit, there d. . . 516.2
such a bright d. . . . 657.3
saving sign d. . . . 697.4
d. for all to view . . . 781.1
thy power . . . here d. . . 945.1
b *display power*
thy p. . . . . universe d. . . 37.1
he d. his healing p. . . 160.4
Spirit . . . d. thy p. . . 561.1
thou hast d. thy p. . . 629.3

dissension. 539.2

distance 740.3

distant
d. years in Palestine . . 142.2
ours is not a d. God . . 238.2
loved ones, now far d. . . 582.1
to see the d. scene . . 606.1
the d. hills before me . . 766.1
the d. triumph song . . 876.4
b *distant lands*
from far d. l. battalions . . 169.2
e'en to the most d. l. . . 243.3
I see in l. far d. . . . 830.1

distil *Deut 32:2*
sweetly d. in the dew . . 16.4
gently d. like early dew . . 672.1

distracting 630.3

distress-ed-ing
1 *(divine)*
who is he in deep d. . . 104.2
gaze upon thy sore d. . . 122.2
this was his d. . . . 129.1
2 *(human)* *Isa 25:4; Rom 8:35*
to our fathers in d. . . . 17.2
till all that are d. . . . 21.2
the despised, the d. . . 170.1
art thou sore d. . . . 228.1
gifts for souls d. . . . 287.1
whence my soul's d. . . 290.2
out of d. to . . . psalm . . 300.2
grief and dark d. . . . 343.2
nor comfort a people d. . . 527.3
not d. or persecution . . 555.1
seasons of d. and grief . . 633.1
sanctify . . . thy deepest d. . 653.3
the problems that d. you . 759.1
war . . . may prove d. . . 805.1
out of great d. they came . 909.2
in our weakness and d. . . 937.3
burdens d. us c122
b *comfort distressed* *1 Thess 3:7*
help me to c. the d. . . 518.1
look down and c. their d. . 582.3
mine, to c. in d. . . . 652.3
thy sweet c. in d. . . . 719.1

distribute 530.3

distrust
why should we d. 377.3
fear and d. remove 743.4

distrustingly 296.1

disturb
d. this faith of ours 554.3
let no ill dreams d. 671.3
let nothing d. thee 956

divers *Matt 4:24* 558.1

divide-d-ing
in a world d. 6.3
hate shall ne'er d. us 97.5
scorn or wealth d. 142.4
no profane delight d. 480.3
love and grief my heart d. 634.3
we are not d. 690.3
like a narrow sea, d. 898.1
Jesus will the waves d. 902.3

divine
a *(with title)*
sacred Infant, all d. 88.4
thou, O King d. 174.1
come, remembrancer d. 191.3
brightly burning Fire d. 206.1
Spirit, companion d. 209.2
breathe . . . O Breath d. 211.3
fill me, Radiancy d. 412.4
Saviour d., to whom else 443.c
Jesus, Saviour, Christ d. 447.1
thine, precious Saviour d. 469.4
heal me, Saviour d. 487.3
who dies . . . O Word d. 512.3
weaver d. 644.1
Saviour d.; now hear me 743.1
thou art the Christ d. 870.2
b *(general)*
graces human and d. 28.5
the pattern be d. 44.2
one so holy, so d. 108.1
through that heart d. 131.2
my canticle d. 187.5
glows with thy fire d. 189.3
truth/love/right/peace/joy d. 194.*
insures the boon d. 208.4
foretaste of glory d. 310.1
what a comfort d. 355.1
now the favour d. 367.2
moved by thy d. compassion 370.1
God's family d. 371.2
full d. conformity 419.1
a heart d. 426.1
bought . . . by blood d. 481.4
for that blessing d. 493.2
what is d. about my creed 518.2
this transport all d. 545.1
thou majesty d. 557.2
I want that adorning d. 589.1
the gift d. I know/ask 601.1
shaping a plan d. 605.2
with strength d. 616.3
let strength d. abound 624.4
Bible, book d. 652.1, 4
might d. . . . our stay 702.2
fellowship d. 709.c
filled with his goodness d. 710.3
sunlight of thy face d. 726.3
hold a charge d. 728.2
by d. appointment 766.1
that we obey d. commands 785.5
'tis thy d. charge to me 786.1
help d. implore 812.2
beams with radiance d. 868.3
clothed in majesty d. 875.2
test ourselves, by help d. 926.4
d. protection 938.2
abiding, rapture d. c36
in the ocean d. c137
breaks a light d. c191
c *joy divine*
lift us to the j. d. 10.3
Holy Spirit, j. d. 194.5
what j. d. 340.3
fellowship, what a j. d. 768.1
d *love divine*
l. so amazing, so d. 136.4
Holy Spirit, l. d. 194.2
the signature of l. d. 214.4
light and l. d. 232.1
I rest on l. d. 297.6
in l. d. he took my place. 341.3
marked by l. d. 400.1
l. like thine, a l. d. 426.2
l. d., all l. excelling 438.1
l. d., from Jesus flowing 439.1
full of l. d. 444.4
l. and power d. 445.4
fill my life with l. d. 463.c
fill me with l. d. 521.1
fill me with thy l. d. 531.4
l. d. shall be my guard 556.5
the depths of l. d. 651.4
the story of l. d. 831.3
gracious gifts of l. d. 858.3
enfold within thy l. d. 861.2
fill my soul with l. d. 865.1
the care of l. d. c176
e *power divine* *2 Peter 1:3*
we sense a p. d. 27.1
receive honour and p. d. 57.3
light and love and p. d. 445.4
preserved by p. d. 915.1
p. d. . . . be it mine c93
charity, grace (2q), life (2c), loveliness, spirit (1b), voice (1d)

divinely
fountain flows d. clear 232.2
d. joined in one 948.1

divinity
words . . . echo thy d. 211.1
in tune with thy d. c72

dizzy 766.2

do-ing-done-did
1 *(we) do*
it is seemly so to d. 3.3
sins that I have d. 105.2
d. what thou wouldst d. 189.1
to d. and to endure 189.2
not what I feel or d. 297.2
naught . . . that I have d. 306.3
I could not d. without 325.*
what he says we will do 397.5
what the world may d. 402.c
all you have to d. 403.3
love that would anything d. 422.4
to d. whate'er I know 426.3
self-salvation will not d. 430.1
say there's naught to d. 482.2
the ill that I . . . have d. 671.2
eager to d. and to dare 679.2
them that d. the wrong 701.2
dare d. aught for him 704.1
what can I d. 706.*
whate'er I d. . . . be 725.1
what he bids us, . . . d. 772.5
d. or die, our battle cry 798.2
d. some witnessing 832.c
tempted to d. wrong 837.3
may I d. the good I know 837.6
power to d. 947.4
cries: It shall be d. c118
b *do works*
try his w. to d. 133.5
not by the w. that we d. 319.c
a w. of lowly love to d. 485.5
men may see the w. I d. 518.3
thy w. to d., thy help 581.1
so shall thy w. be d. 715.3
to w. he appoints me to d. 734.2
we love his w. to d. 851.5
our w. on earth is d. 907.3
c *all I do*
'tis a. that I can d. 105.4
a. that I can d. is vain 292.5
that a. I d. is right 441.3
a. that ye have . . . d. 564.3
the bloom on a. I d. 591.2
d *Eph 6:13*
having all things d. 695.5
e *Phil 4:13*
'tis fixed, I can d. all 526.4
till I can all things d. 596.1
f *(what) do*
no matter what you d. 44.1
tells me what to d. 204.1
what these hands have d. 297.1
what to d. to be pure 459.1
but it's not what you d. 467.2
what I've d. . . . is small. 489.3
teach you what to d. 664.3
what I ought to d. 837.1
g *what . . . do?*
w. shall I d. . . . to love 55.1
w. shall I d. to make it 62.4
w. shall I d. . . . to praise 372.1
w. could I d. but obey 378.3
w. will you d. with Jesus c28
best (c), deed (b), duty (b), part (1b), right (3c), service (c), think (2c), well (2j), will (1b)
2 *(God) does*
what the Almighty can d. 19.2
for all mankind hast d. 62.4
this he d. for you 96.3
d. what thou wouldst d. 189.1
d. so much for me 488.1
all thy love has d. 503.2
what thy grace can d. 571.2
he will d. the same 790.1
thou for us hast d. 919.1
for all thy power hast d. 936.2
all thy grace can d. c74
think of what he's d. c211
b *[Lord] has done*
tell what God has d. 335.1
what the L. has d. for me 335.c
praise God for what he's d. 380.1
for what the L. has d. 380.c
surprise . . . L. has d. 396.1, c
see what God has d. 396.c
what a work the L. has d. 769.1
c *things done* *Ps 126:3; Luke 1:49*
wondrous t. hath d. 12.1
great t. he has d. 22.*
d. great t. for me 538.1
d *work done*
the w. of grace is d. 110.5
love's redeeming w. is d. 143.2
let thy w. in me be d. 188.c
love's atoning w. is d. 261.4
saved by the w. he has d. 319.c
Lord, this w. must d. 581.2
what a w. the Lord has d. 769.1
the w. . . . will not be d. 812.3
well (2j)
3 *(other)*
no other name will d. 71.c
death have d. their worst 151.2
sin and woe are d. away 268.1
angels can d. nothing more 367.3
what the world may d. 402.c
never mind what others d. c26
b *done [finished]*
the battle is not d. 42.3
thought his day was d. 145.1

oppressed . . . d. n. 558.2
earth and Heaven d. n. 669.4
we now d. n. 933.1

3 *(other)*
let nothing d. me back 59.4
this star d. near 90.4
d. from Immanuel's veins 132.1
d. forth the cry of need 586.3
night is d. nigh 673.1
the day is d. nearer 696.1
when death d. near 709.3
the darkness . . . d. n. 874.2
harvest home d. near 926.4

dread
clouds ye so much d. 29.3
mighty d. had seized 93.2
in this d. act 121.5
that d. hour on Calvary 125.3
from death's d. sting 151.5
no condemnation now I d. 283.4
fear and d. of the tomb 300.4
in d. condemnation 364.2
no d. of ill 726.1
what have I to d. 768.3
forth in d. array 864.1
nor sigh, nor d. 874.3
d. remorse and vain desire 885.3

dreadful *Mal 4:5* 161.2

dream
reach the way we d. 27.6
turn my d. to noble action 32.2
awake from your d. 233.1
never think or d. 551.1
yet in my d. I'd be 617.2
let no ill d. disturb 671.3
who shall d. of shrinking 682.1
still lie fondly d. 693.1
ends life's transient d. 743.4
with many d. of fame 860.4

b *Job 20:8*
fly forgotten, as a d. 13.5

dreamless 86.1

drear-y
the d. night had paled 145.2
never a day so d. 186.1
when all else seems d. 316.1
in the d. wilderness 340.2
streams in desert d. 448.1
lone and d., faint 607.2
road be long and d. 716.1
sin's mountain d. 740.1
praying, if the path be d. 754.3
long the fight and d. 802.4
the way is long and d. 817.1
thou in the darkness d. 876.2
earth is a desert d. 882.1
often toil seems d. 934.3
so many lives are d. c200

dress-ed
my glorious d. 116.1
come to thee for d. 302.3
stand d. in living green 898.2

drew see *draw*

drift-ing
winds that d. the clouds 31.1
when clouds are d. dark 40.3
anchor d. or firm remain 280.1
my d. bark all in the dark 375.1
the millions who're d. 703.1
a world at random d. 868.3

drink-ing-drank
a *Ex 15:23*
kneel and d. of Marah 510.3
b *(Jer 2:13)*
e'en as I stooped to d. 547.3

c *Matt 20:22; John 18:11*
d. for you the bitter cup 107.3
death's cup I should d. 686.3
d. his cup of woe 701.1
cup which I d. 758.2
than he d. in Gethsemane 758.2

d *John 4:14; 7:37*
they shall d. abundantly 95.1
d. with thankful hearts 254.3
d. the gushing streams 268.2
let me d. and live 282.3
d. endless pleasures in 314.2
I am d. at the fountain 320.1
stoop down and d. 332.2
I came to Jesus, and I d. 332.2
yet invites to d. again 439.3
d. and find refreshing 462.3
shall d. a fresh supply 559.4
thee let me d. 601.2
more deep I'll d. above 896.2
d. the pure joys 905.4
come and d. a full supply c16

e *1 Cor 10:4*
Christ is my d. 346.4

f *1 Cor 12:13*
let me d. of thy Spirit c75

dried see *dry*

drive-n-ing
d. the fearful shades 145.2
d. these dark clouds 318.4
d. me to the blood 425.4
d. thy foes from out 440.2
d. me from the track 440.3
d. thee from my breast 442.4
sin that d. thee from me 448.2
the foe must be d. 681.2
disciples d. them back 797.1
d. sin from our land 798.2
we never shall be d. 800.2

b *drive away*
d. the clouds . . . a. 10.1
d. a. his fear 58.1
d. a. my fears 366.4
smile quickly d. it a. 397.2
he d. my foes a. 495.3
d. them not a. 797.2

c *driven snow*
robe as white as d. s. 389.3
whiter than the d. s. 540.2
whiter than the d. s. c42
as white as d. s. c168

droop-ing
the d. heart to cheer 67.1
in every d. sinner's ear 140.4
quicken all my d. powers 412.2
melt away and d. and die 559.4
lift my head when d. 713.1
lifts my d. spirit up 714.1
lifts its d. eyes to thee 742.1
prospects d. and die 761.1

drop-ped
promise of a shower d. 165.4
a d. my store 207.2
no tear-d. glisten 268.2
hope has d. her anchor 333.3
d. thy still dews 567.4
d. of finite happiness 601.2
mercy d. round us 637.c
sowing . . . tear-d. start 931.3
blood (2b)

dross *Isa 1:25*
burning all my d. and sin 201.4
beyond earth's fading d. 429.2
thy gifts for d. 449.1
purify from sinful d. 452.3
refine its d. 453.2
cleanse . . . fear and d. 493.c

gold be mixed with d. 522.1
earthly things are d. 532.3
thy d. to consume 653.4
a little of earth's d. 780.1
count (c)

drove see *drive*

drown-ing
the heavenly anthem d. 156.1
strive to d. the thought 267.2
I was d. in tears 376.2
for him no depth can d. 496.3

drowsing-y
where d. poppies nod 41.2
quickens all my d. powers 672.2

drum
the d. and clarion call 780.3
beat the d. 807.1
a thousand d. 807.3
to the beat of Army d. 829.2
I love the dear old d. c230

dry-ied
all created streams are d. 14.2
tears attempt to d. 50.3
its music d. the . . . tear 68.3
lips with thirst are d. 121.2
haste to d. those tears 249.3
seeing . . . d. my tears 294.1
that never will run d. 312.2
every tear be d. 314.3
tears of the mourner be d. 364.3
a d. thirsty land 710.c
work seems hard and d. 837.5
come ye who still are d. c16

due *Ps 96:8* 7.3

dull
d. are my ears to hear 488.2
shake off d. sloth 665.1

dumb *Ps 38:13**
Lord, I was d. 353.3
the d. to speak 353.5
let sense be d. 567.5
d. sound joyful cry 590.3

dungeon 283.3

dust *(Gen 3:19); (Ps 103:14)*
frail children of d. 16.5
though born of the d. 288.2
sweat and d. of toil 564.1
lay in d. life's glory 621.4
d. of earthly striving 647.2
b *Ps 22:15*
from the d. of death 116.5

duty
love and not in d. 242.4
teach me faith and d. 258.1
pathway of d. 320.c; 462.*; 868.c
stronger than . . . d. 383.2
daily stage of d. run 665.1
each day . . . round of d. 666.3
d. demands it 691.4
where d. calls 699.3
know their d. clearly 704.c
thronging d. pressed 752.2
from his d. never flee 801.2
where joy and d. meet c40
b *do duty*
larger d. to be done 158.2
alas, the d. left undone 466.4
live daily your d. to do 679.1
do your d., shirk it never 750.3
little d. we have to d. 849.3

dwell-t-ing
1 *(God) dwells*
Jesus would d. with me . 318.3
with God . . . d. the Son . 785.2
where Jesus d. . . . 888.2
b *dwell with [men]* *John 1:14*
pleased as man . . . to d. . 82.2
Christ drew near to d. . . 102.1
d. in lowliness with men . 411.2
came down on earth to d. . 840.1
c *dwell in us* *Eph 3:17; Rom 8:9*
God, through Jesus, d. . 176.4
bequeathed with us to d. . 200.1
mighty Spirit, d. with me . 212.4
O come and d. in me . 441.1, c
know in me thou wilt d.. . 459.3
God, by grace, shall d. . . 465.5
in thy fulness d. with me . 502.2
in the . . . humble you d. . 506.1
live, d. and move in me . 516.3
how d. thy Spirit in me . . 527.c
and d. with me alone . . 562.1
in me thy Spirit d. . . . 594.2
come and d. therein . . 615.1
d. with us . . . manifest . . 941.2
d *dwell within*
d. w. for evermore . . 128.3
d. w. our hallowed breast . 210.2
I pray thee, d. w. . . . 221.3
from him that d. w. . . 444.3
d. w., that men may see . 479.1
the Christ who d. w. . . 494.3
cleansed, he is d. w. . . 640.1
d. w. the hearts of all . . 827.4
O d. w. my glowing heart . c96
e *Ps 85:9*
glory d. in . . . land . . 896.*
2 *(we) dwell*
a *(literal)*
that on earth do d. . . . 3.1
where'er they d. . . . 556.1
b *(figurative)*
d. on his love . . . 160.2
on a higher plane I d. . . 339.4
I've been content to d. . 482.2
c *Ps 91.1*
thy saints have d. secure . 13.2
pure in heart may d. . . 591.1
d. within the secret place . 728.1
d *dwell in/with* *1 John 3:24**
then let us d. in him . . 36.5
men shall d. in his . . . light . 166.2
to d. in thy love . . . 300.3
those who w. him d. . . 363.1
to d. within thy wounds. . 424.1
let me d. w. thee . . . 461.c
they d. in thee . . . 556.1
must more closely d. w. . 618.c
I d. in thy abiding care . . 644.c
wonderful to d. w. him . . c143
e *dwell [in Heaven]*
friends . . . Heaven shall d. . 146.2
joy of all who d. above . 168.3
must take to d. with God . 190.3
with Jesus Christ to d. . 275.4
I'll . . . d. in thy sight . . 357.4
to d. in that city . . . 394.4
may d. in that land . . 406.4
d. in the eternal light . . 414.5
d. in cloudless light . . 465.2
receive me to d. alway . . 635.1
f *dwell for ever* *Ps 23:6*
shall d. with thee for e. . . 73.4
e. we shall d. . . . 899.3
d. with Jesus . . . for e. . c233
safety (b)
3 *(other)*
there d. a song . . . 70.c
d. upon our tongues . . 382.3
power that d. in thee . . 620.2
such power did d. to speed . 760.1
nevermore to d. within . . 783.4
ever in my memory d. . . c7
souls who d. in darkness . c236
b *Col 3:16*
word richly in us d. . . 533.4

dwellers 17.4

dwelling
deignest to have d. . . . 6.1
the d. of the just . . . 21.3
him whose d. is above . . 36.5
broken heart love's d. . . 121.6
fit to be thy d. . . . 188.c
fix in us thy humble d. . . 438.1
make thy d. there . . . 615.4
temple meet for thy d. . . 623.4
heart of the Father thy d. . 739.3
make my poor heart thy d. . c104
b *dwelling-place* *Ps 90:1*
God's house . . . my d.-p. . 54.5
make our hearts thy d.-p. . 200.7
d.-p. is the Most High . . 362.1
thy d.-p. to be . . . 455.c
my d.-p. art thou alone . . 556.4
while in his d.-p. I stay . . 728.2
prepare us a d.-p. there . . 900.1
in heaven thy d.-p. . . 945.2

dye-d
sunrise d. the lovely . . 103.2
with crimson is d. . . 111.2
crimes of blackest d. . . 697.4

dying
1 *(verb)* see *die*
2 *(noun)*
by thy d., Prince . . . 185.2
thou Witness of his d. . . 191.3
his d. thy debt . . . paid . 271.2
by his d. on the tree . . 554.2
let the d. live 575.c
comfort to the d. . . . 655.5
care for the d. . . . 691.1
stoop to help the d. . . 702.3
go, care for the d. . . . 703.4
the sad, the sick, the d.. . 828.3
lost and d. I may help . . 859.2
the d. of Jesus . . . c209
3 *(adjective)*
a *(re Jesus)*
from birth to d. cry . . 94.1
thy d. groans . . . 105.c
he turns his d. eyes . . 107.4
for this, his d. sorrow . . 123.3
dear d. Lamb . . . 132.3
the Saviour's d. merit . . 191.1
purchase of our d. Lord . . 216.2
the very d. form . . . 476.2
sinner's d. friend . . . 634.1
d. Lord who found us . . 702.2
followers of the d. God . . 909.1
b *dying love*
we . . . sing his d. l. . . 120.5
such wondrous, d. l. . . 128.2
sing the Saviour's d. l. . . 275.1
I sink, by d. l. . . . 307.4
Saviour, thy d. l. . . . 524.1
knowledge of thy d. love . 565.2
possessed with d. l. . . 704.4
a d. l. like thine . . . c83
his d. l. has won my heart . c174
c *(re man)*
the d. thief rejoiced . . 132.2
who saved the d. thief . . 266.3
never-d. soul to save . . 472.1
d. men to save . . . 499.c
from the d. millions . . 702.2
d. sinners pray to live . . 945.2
d *dying world*
live a d. w. to save. . . 203.4
to a d. w. . . . show . . 521.2
preaching Christ to a d. w. . 811.4

E

each
1 *(pronoun)*
a *re people*
e. . . . sweet music make 43.1
give us e. a lowly mind 193.4
grant us e. a seat 195.4
balm . . . on e. to shed 200.2
kindle in e. the . . . fire 216.4
e. his friendly aid afford 662.1
Heaven in e. we see 668.3
e. who comes to thee 707.3
knows what best for e. 715.5
e. upon his Lord relies 799.3
there's a robe for e. 899.1
e. rejoicing say 946.4
e. as we pray 955.1
b *re objects*
e. has a place 850.3
2 *(adjective)* nc, but
a *each heart*
make e. h. thy home 218.c
his praise e. h. o'erflow 381.1
solemnise e. waiting h. 638.3
be thou conqueror of e. h. 643.3
make e. h. a living stone 941.2
b *each one*
come yourself e. o. 748.3
help us, Lord, e. o. 941.2
c *each soul*
on e. waiting s. confer 198.5
hope e. guilty s. 363.4
sorrows from e. s. depart 599.2
till e. sin-burdened s. 708.3
day (2g), fear (2e), feeling, moment (b), other (1d), thought (2e)

eager
e. to reclaim 129.3
e. I ask, I pant 207.2
e. and longing desire 351.2
thine e. praises wake 353.3
e. eyes are watching 478.2
stretch my e. hand 520.3
may young, e. spirits 575.2
e. to do and to dare 679.2
we are e. to obey 789.2
e. to express our praise 795.1
heard with e. mind 871.2

eagerness 611.2

eagle *Ex 19:4; Isa 40:31*
on e.'s wings upborne 223.4
as the e. cuts the air 559.5
there, there on e. wings 573.4
martyr first, whose e. eye 701.2
mount up with wings as e. c66

ear
1 *Mark 4:28*
the blade and then the e. 924.2
fruitful e. to store 924.3
2 *(divine)*
tell it . . . Saviour's e. 261.1
nor deaf thine e. 604.4
e. attends . . . prayer 715.4
nor . . . a quicker e. 717.3
b *give ear* *Ps 17:1*
give e. to my cry 454.2
Jesus, give e. to us 955
3 *(human)*
joy of e. and eye 28.3
to my listening e. 42.1
with my quickened e. 48.2
in a believer's e. 58.1
no e. may hear his coming 86.3
what pleasure to our e. 382.1
dull are my e. 488.2
sweet to every e. 661.2
give me Samuel's e. 839.3
open e., O Lord 839.3
steals on the e. 876.4
ringing in my e. 895.2
b *sinner's ear*
music in the s.'s e. 64.3
every drooping s.'s e. 140.4
in every s.'s e. 828.3
hear (3d, f), music (b)

earliest 949.1

early
e. in the morning our song 220.1
inspired my e. zeal 463.2
e. joy grows dim 534.2
children e. lisp his fame 661.2
b *Ps 63:1*
may he (she) e. choose 796.3
let us e. turn to thee 845.3
e. let us seek/do 845.4
found Jesus e. 910.2
in life's e. splendour c213
c *Hos 6:4*
the e. dew of morning 98.2
gently distil like e. dew 672.1

earn 869.4

earnest
1 *(noun)* *Eph 1:14**
e. of love . . . larger e. 207.3, 4
2 *(adjective)*
how e. his entreaty 94.2
with e. tones and grave 98.3
thy heart in e. prayer 253.3
let my e. zeal 568.2
give me an e. mind 574.3
hear our e. intercession 576.1
this, my e. prayer 618.c
the e. looking forward 765.4
be thoughtful and e. 823.2
e. strivings after truth 867.5
make us more e. 933.4

earnestly
e. . . . Jesus is calling 264.c
e. seeking/working 484.1, c
plead with them e. 691.2
I promised God most e. 774.3
e. we pray 792.2
e. seek him below 794.2

earth
1
a *(vocative)*
dear mother e. 2.4
thou e., reply 143.1
sing, O e. 184.1
b *(general)*
e. . . . shall fill thy courts 4.3
the e. is not too low 11.1
e. received her frame 13.3
the blessings e. displays 15.2
e., with its store 16.3
let the e. hear his voice 22.c
touchest e. with beauty 32.1, 3
wealth . . . to e. restoring 70.4
echoed in the e. below 80.1
bending near the e. 83.1
let e. receive her King 84.1
to the e. . . . great light 90.2
on e. though a stranger 92.2
theirs the e. by right 95.1
ring the e. with . . . flame 127.c
e. with joy confesses 155.2
e. prolong the . . . strain 160.5
the e. first you sought 175.2
I all on e. forsake 223.2
e. shall keep her jubilee 393.2
e. around is sweeter 545.2
bliss that e. imparts 602.1
tread this e. before us 607.2
here o'er e. I rove 636.1
how could e. be trod 654.4
e. has ne'er a spot 663.1
while e. rolls onward 677.2
self nor e. . . . sever 693.2
friend when e. is past 709.4
till e. be past 754.4
King o'er e. shall reign 816.4
the whole wide e. 826.1, 4
sweep through the e. 827.2
headlong to the e. 847.3
though e. decay 873.4
e. . . . is not my place 880.1
e. is a desert drear 882.1
buried in the e. it lies 923.2
sons, from e. apart 942.3
rejoice the e. 942.4
c *come to earth*
c. to e. with gifts 74.1
he c. down to e. 87.2
gracious his c. to e. 92.2
when thou c. to e. for me 101.1
c. thou, Lord, on e. 101.2
c. thou to e. to die 185.1
joy . . . to e. c. down 438.1
c. down on e. to dwell 840.1
d *Heaven and earth*
e. and h. reflect thy rays 10.2
e. and H. be one 42.3
sing, ye h.: thou e. 143.1
he rules o'er e. and H. 164.3
one accord in H. and e. 174.5
creation in e. and H. 178.2
by e. and H. confest 223.1
e. has no sorrow that H. 236.*
trust for e. and H. above 423.3
H. and e. salvation 452.4
H., in e., or on the sea 556.1
who H. and e. commands 715.1
H. and e. and Hell 721.3
my e. a present H. 729.4
make e. and H. ring 940.2
joy of e. and hopes of H. 941.1
e *earth adore* *Ps 69:34*
whom e. and H. adore 12.3
H. and e. . . . praises 43.1
let e. and H. agree 62.1
him whom H. and e. adore 76.2
let H. and e. adore 509.3
let H. and e. agree 562.3
e. and H. draw near 669.4
f *made earth* *Ps 121:2*
made H. and e. of naught 90.6
who H. and e. hath made 767.1
g *2 Peter 3:10*
e. and . . . H. pass away 228.6
h *Rev 20:11*
H. and e. may fade 545.3
e.'s vain shadows flee 670.5
when H. and e. are fled 746.1
i earth or Heaven
on this e. or in the h. 49.1
of all in e. or H. 65.1
nor H. nor e. can break 171.2
for e. or H. . . . my cry 489.1

j *from earth to Heaven*
saves from e. to H. . . 733.2
all the way from e. to H. . 753.c
all the way from e. to H. . c110

k *earth and/or Hell*
in H. or e. or sky . . 60.1
shall e. or H? No, I am . 345.4
though e. and H. . . . gainsay 407.3
e. and H. may strive . 533.4
e. and H. proclaim God . 721.3
both e. and H. assail . 809.2

l *all earth*
all e.'s . . voices . . 40.1
spread through all the e. . 64.2
flight o'er all the e. . . 75.1
hope of all the e. . . 79.2
over all the e. . . . fling . 83.3
fills all the e. and sky . 167.2
work through all the e. . 198.3
o'er all the e. alike . . 362.1
salt of all the e. . . 682.2
faint through all the e. . 864.1
around (b), sea (1b), sky (1c)

2 *earth's (possessive)*
not thirst for e. reward . 5.3
the silent paths of e. . . 7.2
e. telescopes . . . 27.3
for the beauty of the e. . 28.1
flowers of e. . . . 28.5
all e. sorrow and its sin . 169.1
bright star of the e. . . 175.1
in e. darkest place . . 224.3
find e. glitter dim . . 267.1
out of e. sorrows . . 300.2
above e. lamentation . . 358.1
to leave e. vanity . . 461.1
things of e. have filled . 466.1
'mid e. sin and sorrow . 529.1
beautiful of e. . . . 551.1
e. deepening shades . . 595.3
e. vain shadows flee . . 670.5
like e. proud empires . . 677.5
e. trifles leaving . . 693.c
e. foundations melt away . 746.5
e. struggles . . . cease . 752.7
passing gains of e. . . 796.3
e. allurement spurning . 803.3
goal of e. strait race . . 878.2
e. dark shadows flee . . 888.1
saved of e. shall gather . 907.1
from e. confusion . . c94

b *joy/hope of earth* Ps 48:2
the joy of e. and Heaven . 62.2
hope of e. and joy . . 66.c
hope of all the e. . . 79.2
joy of Heaven, to e. . . 438.1
joys of e. and hopes . . 941.1
bound, dross, end (2g), glory (4d), joy (5b), Jesus (8d), pleasure (1b), son (2b), treasure (1)

3 *on earth*
on e. is not his equal . . 1.1
people that on e. do dwell . 3.1
so shall I begin on e. . . 7.3
friends on e. . . . 28.4
sweetest name on e. . . 69.1
no saint on e. . . . 69.3
all the nations on the e.. . 78.2
lived on e. our Saviour . 87.2
God appears on e. . . 161.1
on e. to hold the sway . . 171.1
presence on our e. . . 181.4
let thy host on e. . . 217.5
I all on e. forsake . . 223.2
once wandered on e. . . 354.2
on e. a man became . . 363.2
life's pilgrimage on e. . . 400.3
O love, revealed on e. . . 449.1
on e. I'll crown thee . . 499.4
we meet on e. . . . 603.3
hearts on e. but filled . . 704.4
when my task on e. is done . 725.4

strife on e. is done . . . 819.3
no power on e. . . . sever . 854.3
streams on e. . . . 896.2
our work on e. is done . . 907.3
below (c)

b Ps 73:25
whom have I on e. . . 301.4
nothing on e. do I desire . 480.5

c Matt 6:10
on e. to do thy will. . 624.2
thy kingdom come on e. . 774.4

d Luke 12:49
to bring fire on e. . . 165.1

e Heb 11:13
a stranger on e. . . . 354.3
no home on e. have I . 362.1
no place on e. I own . 362.2
peace (2g)

earth-born 676.1

earthen 2 Cor 4:7
my e. vessel is stored . 457.3
fill the e. vessel . . c65

earthly
word above all e. powers . 1.4
with man his e. lot . . 102.1
loved above all e. love . 135.4
or fades my e. bliss . . 187.3
this e. part of me . . 189.3
changes e. craving . . 197.2
from all e. passions free . 210.3
all our e. pilgrimage . . 249.4
fruit on e. ground . . 314.3
e. friends may fail . . 377.1
glows in any e. sky . . 387.1
empty my heart of e. love . 480.1
the taste of e. gain . . 631.3
dust of e. striving . . 647.2
throughout our e. life . . 674.4
e. loss is heavenly gain . 683.2
shadows on the e. pathway . 711.2
where e. forces fail . . 744.2
away from e. slumber . . 766.3
e. kingdoms rise and fall . 799.1
the waves of e. strife . . 872.1
the noise of e. strife . . 884.3
from e. struggles . . 894.1
broken every e. fetter . . 894.2
give us e. bread . . 934.2
brightens e. sorrow . . 948.3
calms all e. strife . . 948.3
e. cares increase . . c143
when e. skies are grey . . c206

b 2 Cor 5:1
this e. house shall fail . 149.3
fill this e. temple now . 208.1

c 2 Peter 3:10
when e. things are past . 76.4
all e. things that bind . 523.c
e. things are dross . . 532.3
e. things are paltry show . 630.1
joy (5b), pleasure (1b)

earthquake 1 Kings 19:12 . 567.5

ease
can e. this weight of sin . 297.3
how to e. my conscience . 303.2
e. aching hearts . . 529.3
e. life's heavy burdens . 706.2
e. which comes swift . 719.3
let him e. the load . . c126

b (Amos 6:1)
hours of e. . . . 428.4
too long at e. in Zion . 482.2
love of e. and . . show . 500.2
not for e. that prayer . 570.1
flowery beds of e. . . 678.2

wrapped in e. . . . 693.1
seek not worldly e. . . 816.3

east
trump from e. to west . . 153.2
north, south, e. and west . 243.4
with thee the e., the west . 362.3
from e. to west, unfurled . 779.1
in Christ . . . e. nor west 826.1, 4
tell them in the e. . . 829.1
love the best in the . . . e. c230

b Matt 2:1
journeyed from the e. . . 80.3
shining in the e. . . . 90.2

c Luke 13:29
they shall come from the e. . 170.*

Easter-tide
loosed . . . with E.'s might . 30.4
he arose on E. day . . 96.4
this joyful E. . . . 153.1
in my soul an E. morning . 520.5
Calvary and E. light . . 613.3
on E. morning Jesus came . 855.5

eastern 89.2

easy
life's burdens they are e. . 503.1
an e. . . . pleasant path . 586.1
if all were e. . . . 773.2
each day your pathway e. . 817.c
yoke

easier
to find an e. way . . . 192.2
cares to find an e. way . 619.3
choose an e. path . . 780.1

eat Luke 22:30 . . . 650.2

ebb-ing
life's e. and flow . . . 390.1
a never-e. sea . . . 496.1
e. out life's little day . . 670.2

Ebenezer 1 Sam 7:12
here I raise my E. . . 313.2
here I raise my E. . . 338.4
each sweet E. . . . 712.3
singing E. . . . c147

echo
the e. shall prolong . . 7.4
e. clear and strong . . 32.3
let love's sweet e. . . 51.3
let it e. round the earth . 63.2
e. of the angel-choir . . 70.c
e. in the earth below . . 80.1
e. thy divinity . . . 211.1
e. the Saviour's call . . 258.3
e. of mercy . . . 310.2
e. in my soul . . . 358.1
let the e. fly . . . 382.2
e. back, ye ocean waves . 393.2
living e. of thy tone . . 612.1
e. to thy voice . . . 636.3
laughter e. in the street . . 664.2
joy is but an e. . . . 711.1
its e., loudly ringing . . 802.2
e. with redeeming love . 873.2
e. the glad refrain . . c226

eclipse 143.2

ecstasy 728.2

Eden Gen 2:15*
E. saw play . . . 35.3
our loss of E. . . . 140.2
E.'s bowers bloom . . 725.2
the E. above . . . 905.*
voice that breathed o'er E. . 949.1

edged *Heb 4:12* . . . 609.3

effectual *James 5:16*
they pour e. prayers . . 106.3
their e. pleading . . . 129.c

e'en see *even*

efficacious
O cleansing, e. flood . . 131.1
a cleansing, e. flood . . 638.1

effort
weak is the e. . . . 58.4
every e. brings me nearer . 369.2

elate
yet e. with gratitude . . 566.5
when e. with joy . . . 939.4

elation
praise with e. . . . 35.3
let sanctified e. . . . 828.1

elements 19.3

Eli *1 Sam 1:9** 839.2

Elijah
where Moses and E. stood . 154.2
God of E., hear our cry . . 203.2

else
when no one e. is nigh . . 256.2
when all e. seems dreary . 316.1
to whom e. shall I go . . 443.c
more than all e. . . . 451.4
all things e. but loss . . 694.1
none e. to be my guide . . 857.2
b *nothing else*
have n. e. to fear . . . 21.5
in n. e. my soul . . . 107.5
n. e. will meet . . . 830.1
c *what else*
pleasure, and w. e. . . 480.4
w. e. can he withhold . . 560.2

embalms 925.2

emblem
e. of suffering and shame . 124.1
e. of purity, e. of good . . 175.2
e. of a thousand battles . . 777.1
bright e. of salvation . . 781.1
yellow, e. of the Spirit . . 783.3
Jesus, it is an e. of thee. . c54

embrace-ing
would all mankind e. . . 60.4
world-e. heart is wrung . . 127.2
as brothers shall e. . . 170.3
held our sorrows in e. . . 242.4
feel love's warm e. . . 269.1
his warm e. 335.2
thy Kingdom's cause e. . . 500.1
live in his loving e. . . 535.3
your arms to e. . . . 611.3
to his beloved e. . . . 659.4
b *Heb 11:13*
all his promises e. . . . 23.2

emotion
do not hide thy deep e. . . 259.1
with each e. sanctified . . 861.2

empire
his e. shall bring . . . 166.1
like earth's proud e. . . 677.5
none thine e. . . . o'erthrow . 799.1

employ(ment)
1 *(noun)*
chief delight his . . . e. . . 451.3
keep me yet in thy e. . . 522.1
engaged in his sacred e. . 553.4
full e. brings enjoyment . . 869.2
rest from thy loved e. . . 890.1
praise be thy new e. . . 890.5
2 *(verb)*
my heart and tongue e. . . 21.1
new songs . . . his lips e. . 62.3
his songs our tongues e. . 66.3
let men their songs e. . . 84.2
pursuits my time e. . . 517.2
my every hour e. . . . 636.5
for thee delightfully e. . . 667.4
their art and power e. . . 696.2
our grateful songs e. . . 828.1
how shall I my life e. . . 846.2
to e. my every skill . . . 871.1
thy praise our lips e. . . 925.1

empower 211.3

emprise 799.2

emptiness 217.2

empty-ied
this world's e. glory . . 98.4
show . . . the e. tomb . . 117.3
his cross stands e. . . . 142.1
fill this e. soul of mine . . 206.1
e. of every base desire . . 208.1
my e. heart to fill . . . 221.2
e. himself of all . . . 283.2
e. . . . and worthless . . 399.2
e. hands I'm stretching . . 435.1
e. . . . world's enjoyment . 470.1
e. . . . of earthly love . . 480.1
all my e. nature fill . . . 520.2
without love 'tis e. show . 530.2
e. are we 648.2

encamp *Ps 34:7* . . . 21.3

enchain-ing
the bonds, so long e. . . 539.2
fetters that e. . . . 827.1

encircle-ing
thy brow e. 299.2
amid the e. gloom . . . 606.1

encompass 48.2

encounter
meet and e. the foe . . 734.3
each e. with evil . . . 893.2

encumber-ing
may naught my way e. . . 766.3
left its e. clay . . . 890.3

end
1 *(purpose)*
selfish e. . . . no right . . 702.1
2 *(finish)*
the e. of all . . . love . . 146.2
speak his sorrows e. . . 155.2
wrong shall be e. . . . 166.2
e. of our resources . . 579.2
till the war shall e. . . 799.3
battles e. in saving . . 802.4
b *end of sin* *Dan 9:24*
'tis the e. of my s. . . . 119.2
to make an e. of s. . . 195.2
c *no/never/without end*
grace . . . it n. e. . . . 55.2
thy pity without e. . . 123.3
my bliss shall n. e. . . 464.4
worship without e. . . 785.6
joys will e., no n. . . . 899.2
which n. hath an e. . . 934.4
love which knows no e. . . 948.1
his favours n. e. . . . c146
d *Luke 1:33*
reign shall know no e. . . 156.3
e *John 13:1*
loves me to the e. . . 144.3
a love that will not e. . . 215.2
loves me without e. . . 311.4
love me to the e. . . . 597.3
love that never will e. . . c251
f *end of day*
watch that e. the night . . 13.4
peace . . . at the e. . . 611.4
with thee shall e. the d. . . 674.2
the d. . . . Lord, is e. . . 677.1
g *ends of earth*
e. of the e. we will go . . 700.c
to the e. of the e. . . . 800.3
h *end (of life)*
keep me . . . to the e. . . 309.3
at the e. of the race . . 389.3
faith in sight shall e. . . 504.3
to the e. of the way . . 506.5
trusting to the e. . . . 544.4
we know we at the e. . . 685.3
its e. far out of sight . . 716.1
soon e. in joyous day . . 721.2
evils in a moment e. . . 880.2
God be at mine e. . . . 953
i *Ps 37:37*
his e. untroubled peace . . 580.3
j *Isa 40:2*
e. is thy warfare . . . 352.3
k *Matt 10:22*
thine to follow to the e. . 510.c
and to the e. endure . . 574.4
serve thee to the e. . . 862.1, 4
l *end (of time)*
how firm to the e. . . . 16.5
real comes to an e. . . 39.4
the e. of mortal days . . 171.3
the same unto the e. . . c163
to the e. of the world . . c243
m *Matt 28:20*
with me to the e. . . . 389.1
journey (c) life (6d)

endeavour
my faint e. 345.3
the limit of human e. . . 501.3
all besides is vain e. . . 555.4
through e., failure . . . 570.3
my weak e. 635.3
hell should e. to shake . . 653.5
hell to defeat is my e. . . 686.3
with high e. 863.1
all our life's e. . . . 863.5

endless
boundaries of e. space . . 52.c
peace in e. flow . . . 74.2
doomed . . . to e. pains . 75.4
e. is the victory . . . 152.1, c
cause of e. exultation . . 161.3
death thy e. mercies seal . 199.4
might . . . and e. praise . . 223.5
drink e. pleasures in . . 314.2
my e. theme in Glory . . 327.3
glory and e. delight . . 357.4
life flows on in e. song . . 358.1
with thee is e. joy . . . 362.3
an e. crimson tide . . . 540.1
how e. is thy love . . . 672.1
hell's e. woe 703.1
redemption's e. song . . 828.4
in e. paradise . . . 949.4
b *endless life* *Heb 7:16*
e. l. in Heaven . . . 46.4
his death and e. l. . . . 393.3
l. that shall e. be . . . 621.4
I may of e. l. partake . . 665.3
prize . . . is e. l. . . . 813.2
age (2b), day (3d), glory (2f), year (d)

endue-ing *Luke 24:49*
with grace our souls e. 38.5
with the Spirit's power e. 408.2

endurance
our store of e. 579.2
e. in this assurance 724.3
quiet brave e. 948.2
patient e. attaineth 956

endure-d-ing
his rage we can e. 1.3
a peace that e. 33.3
secure, whatever I e. 45.2
the soul's e. worth 181.4
to do and to e. 189.2
for ever shall e. 279.3
hope that will surely e. 371.3
this short-e. world 480.4
abundant, e. and free 553.1
things which e. 640.4
which through eternity e. 885.1
while this fabric shall e. 941.3
b *Ps 100:5**
age to age e. 3.4
his mercies shall e. 34.*
thy grace and truth e. 419.5
power . . . firm e. 559.3
shall their truth e. 755.c
and ever shalt e. 870.1
c *Matt 10:22*
to the end e. 574.4
by his grace we shall e. 722.1
faith that will e. 733.4
grace . . . that we may e. 755.1
men of faith who will e. 760.2
help us to e. 937.4
d *Heb 12:2*
cross . . . e. so patiently 515.2
e. cruel reproaches 623.3
e. the pain 678.4

enemy
in vain our e. oppose 9.2
your e. almost prevail 537.2
sin the e. of Christ 583.4
so the e. shall know 686.c
God's e. strong 687.4
mighty are your e. 697.1
we own no man as e. 705.1
all our e. defeating 778.3
e. we shall confound 809.3
b *Rom 5:10*
me who was his e. 363.c
for thine e. wast slain 515.3

energy
its mighty e. fulfil 38.2
a Holy Spirit's e. 414.4
baptised with heavenly e. 426.3
by the e. of prayer 566.5
my various e. to use 871.3

enfold-ing
let his will e. you 141.5
thy realm e. the universe 171.1
thy power e. me 534.c, 3
e. within thy love divine 861.2
his arms e. 884.1
arms of love e. me c163

enforce 568.2

engage-d-ing
they both will e. 233.2
while in conflict we e. 249.4
all my power e. 472.2
heart whose love e. 522.2
e. in his . . . employment 553.4
all scenes alike e. prove 556.1
e. the waiting soul 633.2
every ransomed power e. 693.1
power and thought e. 702.2
'neath our standard . . . e. 778.1

engraving 207.3

enjoy-ed-ing
I now e. his fellowship 48.3
shall e. his favour 309.3
sweetly be e. 375.2
e. a full salvation 427.c
peaceful hours I once e. 442.3
those e. on high 461.2
still e. this blessing 634.4
life everlasting e. here 640.5
hearts e. God's . . . favour 704.1
we who God's gifts e. 828.1
but more e. them there 880.4

enjoyment
empty is the world's e. 470.1
I have fullest e. 553.4
full employment brings e. 869.2

enlarge-d-ing
he his kingdom is e. 159.3
b *Ps 119:32*
thou gav'st the e. desire 210.2
give me a . . . soul, e. 619.2
e. . . . and fill my heart 720.5

enlist-ed-ing
time for e. is passing 681.4
will you not e. with me 686.4
who'll e. in this Army 703.3
in his cause e. 866.2

enough
it is e. that Jesus died 60.c
no other good e. 133.4
Calvary is proof e. 324.1
thou art e. for me 450.4
nothing less can be e. 549.3
one step e. for me 606.1
labour on., e. while here 683.3
thou art e. for me 729.c
e. . . . struggles cease 752.7
grace e. is given 755.1
in our Saviour strength e. 805.c

enrich *(2 Cor 8:9)*
e. the humble poor 81.3
e. the poor 676.5

enrol-led
will eternal years e. 70.1
beneath thy shade e. 774.2
of thy grace are we e. 799.1

enshrined 465.2

enslave-d
by their pride e. 130.1
sin that long had e. me 349.3
e. it with thy . . . love 508.2

ensnaring 303.2

ensure
peace and happiness e. 277.3
e. for me an even mind 728.1

enter-ed
the dear Christ e. in 86.3
e. in those wise men 90.5
bid him e. in 227.2
bid him e. while you may 241.c
not a place that he can e. 241.2
no human heart could e. 325.3
this is the life that I e. 457.3
he e. Heaven with prayer 625.5
e. we the army 707.2
let all who e. here 943.1
b *(request)*
cast out our sin, and e. 86.4
e. every longing soul 218.c
dear Saviour, e. 299.3
e. every longing heart 438.1
e. and speak me pure 450.3
with power, Lord, e. in 575.2
e. right into my heart c64
c *John 10:9*
Heaven with him I e. in 262.3
come e. the door 263.3
e. within the door 266.1
e. while you may 279.2
I have e. in 315.3
the Holy Spirit e. 361.2
I would e. the fold 883.1
d *Heb 4:11*
believe and e. in 433.2
e. now the land of rest 433.3
e. into rest 551.3
court (b), joy (3c)

enthralled 553.1

enthrone-d
e. in heavenly glory 6.1
who reigns e. on high 72.6
the sins that men e. 129.2
in your hearts e. him 141.5
seat of power e. him 147.2
who reigns e. above 223.1
risen One, e. on high 435.1
Lord, in me thy love e. 530.c
thou Christ e. above 561.1

entice-ing *James 1:14**
his the love doth now e.. 249.2
the world's e. 500.2

entirely
do his will e. 343.3
e. all my sins remove 419.6
life and heart e. clean 629.3
thine e., thine for ever 693.2
I leave e. to thy care 917.1

entrance
my powers thine e. feel 207.4
I claim an e. there 619.1

entreat
soft and sweet, doth e. 73.2
hear a voice that e. you 272.2

entreaty
how earnest his e. 94.2
heed his e. 246.3
with cries, e., tears 526.1

equal
on earth is not his e. 1.1
O sin that hath no e. 299.2
e. joy to go or stay. 556.3

equip
e. me for the war 568.1
e. for joyful service 870.3

equipment 324.4

erase 335.2

err-ing
unbelief is sure to e. 29.6
I was e., and he sealed 330.2
thy e. children lost 612.1
weep o'er the e. one 691.1

errand 851.2

error
forward, out of e. 682.2
thy word, from e. free 941.3
let sin and e. pass 942.4

escape-d
we can't e. his love 49.c

no e. from the sins . . 459.1
oft e. the tempter's snare . 633.1
shall e. from night . . . 809.4
I shall e. from death . . 877.4
none e. from his sight . . 893.1
b *Gen 19:17*
O e. to yonder mountain . 239.2

(e)stablish
s. by the Lord . . . 159.4
e. thy gardens of grace . . 288.4
not with might to e. . . 527.3
s. our place 648.3
b *Ps 148:6*
hath s. it fast 16.3

estate *(Phil 4:11)*
in whatsoe'er e. . . . 485.5
b *Luke 1:48*
how my lost e. to save . . 180.2
regarded my helpless e. . . 771.2

esteem
e. the Saviour's name . . 135.2
love e. it Heaven . . . 333.3
nothing e., but Jesus . . 659.3

estimate
none can e. the treasure . 363.1
none can e. their measure . 922.2

eternal
1 *(with title)*
e. God, our song we raise . 5.1
e. God, unchanging . . 6.1
the one e. God . . . 12.3
O bright e. One . . . 36.1
by the power of God e. . . 96.4
is it thus, O Christ e. . . 185.2
the heart of the e. . . . 265.6
my heart is fixed, e. God . 356.1
e. Father, strong to save . 569.1
through his e. Son . . 695.1
King (2f), Spirit (2e)
2 *(general)*
sing the new e. song . . 69.4
Heaven's e. arches ring . . 81.4
whose joys e. flow . . 100.4
by God's e. purpose . . 174.4
in Heaven's e. bliss . . 187.4
e. praises be 219.4
soul's e. prize . . . 266.c
sing e. hallelujahs . . . 334.3
riches e. and blessings . . 371.3
translate me to e. bliss . . 441.4
health's e. spring . . . 557.4
his care for our e. good . . 656.2
still to things e. look . . 667.3
to thine e. peace . . . 674.4
on the far e. shore . . . 765.6
its message is e. . . . 781.1
shall we gain e. joy . . 785.6
can gain e. praise . . . 806.2
welcomes . . . to e. peace . 894.1
the morning breaks, e. . . 907.1
e. calm succeeds . . . 911.6
e. source of every joy . . 925.1
give us the bread e. . . 934.2
thine e. goodness . . . 939.5
sacred to thine e. name . . 946.2
in thine e. bands . . . 949.2
b *eternal home* *2 Cor 5:1*
and our e. h. 13.1
to their e. h. 164.6
gather . . . in our e. h. . . 235.c
in the h. e. 711.3
c *eternal life* *John 3:15*
died e. l. to bring . . . 156.2
I freely give e. l. . . . 277.1
e. l. to all who seek . . 277.c
'tis e. l. to know him . . 377.2
they e. l. may obtain . . 523.2
l. e. I shall gain . . . 552.3
gift of love, e. l. . . . 576.2
we ask e. l. 791.2
escape . . . and l. e. gain . 877.4
for thy gift of l. e. . . . 922.3
dawns upon e. love and l. . 948.3
d *eternal love* *(Jer 31:3)*
shines . . . his e. l. . . . 40.2
springing from e. l. . . 157.2
sweeter . . . is his e. l. . . 383.2
through the e. l. . . . 414.5
Spirit of e. l. 630.1
e. l. made manifest . . 728.4
in bonds of l. e. . . . 781.3
homeland of his e. l. . . 895.3
O God of l. e. . . . 943.1
dawns upon e. l. . . . 948.3
e *eternal throne*
high on thy e. t. . . . 161.4
approach the e. t. . . . 283.4
nearest the e. t. . . . 909.1
ages (2b), day (3d), gain (c), glory (2f), light (2d), rest (2c), salvation (e), song (1i), Spirit (2e), year (d)

eternally
saved, to serve him e. . . 114.2
he lives, e. the same . . 144.4
there to live e. . . . 328.3
anthem . . . shall e. be . . 392.4
spring and flow e. . . . 456.1
that will stand e. . . . 538.5
e. held in thy heart . . 639.3
shall reign e. 699.4
thy joy and crown e. . . 718.1
bound to him e. . . . 757.3
e. shall last 880.2
sealed by thy Spirit, e. . . c52

eternity
stars that reach e. . . . 52.c
our glory . . . through e.. . 61.5
heard in God's e. . . . 127.3
perfect life of thine e. . . 189.4
to e. love and adore . . 219.4
that could see, from e. . . 319.1
shall my song in e. be . . 323.4
praise him through e. . . 380.c
I'll sing it in e. . . . 401.3
flowing from e. . . . 439.1
parent of e. 452.4
throughout e., I am his . . 545.3
silence of e. 567.3
through e. expanding . . 751.1
which through e. endures . 885.1
b *all eternity*
King through all e. . . 156.1, 4
bathe . . . to all e. . . . 368.1
thine for all e. . . . 514.c
through all e. . . . for thee . 524.4
worship . . . to all e. . . 624.5
love . . . through all e. . . 660.5
rise to all e. 737.4
salvation . . . to all e. . . 781.2
Lord God o'er all e. . . 957
c *as eternity*
vast as e. thy love . . . 4.4
lasting as e. 464.3
time (1b)

eve
Lord, at the e. of the day . 611.3
abide . . . from morn till e. . 676.3
b *Ecc 11:6*
at e. stay not thy hand . . 923.3
the dewy e. 930.1

even
1 *(noun)*
soft as the breath of e. . . 200.5
daylight softens into e. . . 564.4
b *Mark 1:32*
at e., ere the sun . . . 558.1
2 *(adjective)*
run my course with e. joy . 667.4
an e., strong desire . . 720.2
ensures for me an e. mind . 728.1
3 *(adverb)* nc, but
a *even me*
from me, e. me, receive . . 7.3
e. me that Jesus died . . 108.c
by grace e. I may be . . 114.2
for me, e. me, to atone . . 116.3
I, e. I, have mercy found . 140.4
e. me with all my sin . . 262.3
fall on me, e. me . . . 295.*
bought with a price e. me . 322.1
Jesus loves e. me . . . 323.c
that e. I may know . . 385.1
breathe upon me, e. me . . 477.c
Jesus has cleansed e. me . 535.1
thou hast pardoned e. me . 538.3
Lord, use e. me . . . 612.7
thus supported, e. I . . 630.3
e. I may go to sing . . . 840.3
unworthy me, e. me . . c109

evening
lights of e., find a voice . . 2.2
like an e. gone . . . 13.4
shadows fall with e. light . 31.3
the e. dews and damps . . 162.2
morning of joy give for e. . 183.4
life's e. is closing . . . 237.3
this solemn e. hour . . 558.5
in this quiet e. hour . . 576.1
in the e. of the day . . 663.2
each e. . . . will question . 666.3
every e. new 672.1
shadows of the e. . . . 673.1
voices of e. call . . . 675.1
in the e. while shadows . . 675.c
hushed was the e. hymn . 839.1
light and e. shade . . . 925.4
he lights the e. star . . 935.2
whisper a prayer in the e. . c114
changes things in the e.. . c114
e., when lights are low . . c123

eventide
when in the hush of e. . . 103.3
the star at e. 486.1
once more 'tis e. . . . 558.2
fast falls the e. . . . 670.1

ever-forever nc, but
a *ever thine* *Song 2.16*
we e. will be his . . . 9.4
and he is mine for e. . . 53.1
be, Lord, for e. thine . . 57.3
O make me thine for e. . . 123.3
wholly thine, for e. . . 128.3
his for e. . . . . 345.*
let me be thine e. . . . 421.6
Saviour, I am thine for e. . 439.4
his life is mine for e. . . 495.2
thine for e. now . . . 504.2
offering, thine e. to be . . 511.1
seal me e. thine . . . 521.1
his for e., only his . . . 545.3
entirely, thine for e. . . 693.2
Saviour, always thine . . 707.c
e. thy child to be . . . 837.6
thou art mine for e. . . 859.1
thine I am, O Lord, for e. . 865.3
e. thine, thine alone . . c38
b
with e.-joyful hearts . . 12.2
like an e.-rolling stream . . 13.5
e. faithful, e. sure . . . 34.*
with the e.-circling years . 83.3
hail, thou e. blessèd morn . 88.c
the e.-thrilling story . . 96.3
e. mighty to prevail . . 165.2

firmly bound, for e. free . . 194.3
why not now be free for e. . 471.4
immortal love, for e. full. . 496.1
e. new, and e. young . 559.3
the e.-flowing spring . . 559.4
power e. present to heal . 589.4
trust, e. childlike . . . 611.1
e. watchful is his care . . 722.3
the world is e. near . . 862.2
my foes are ever n. me . . 862.2

c *Ps 23:6*
within thy house for e. . . 53.5
in God's house for e. . . 54.5

d *Ps 89.2*
his mercy is for e. sure . . 3.4

e *Ps 145:1*
name . . . be for e. blessed . 876.1

f *Matt 28:20*
Jesus . . . to be e. with me . 352.1
he is e. by my side . . . 389.1
e. with us day and night. . 938.2
grace . . . be with us e. . . 940.4

g *1 Thess 4:17*
in Glory, for e. with . . 368.4
for e. with the Lord . . . 877.*

h *Rev 11:15*
to reign in us for e. . . . 79.3

i *if ever*
if e. I loved thee . . . 357.*
if e. I disown you . . . 506.5
if e. I fear to fall . . . 571.1

abide (1b, 2g), dwell (2f), feed (c), feel (2b), full (1b), ground (2b), keep (2b, 3c, 3f), lead (3c), live (3b), near (2c), plead (1b), realise, reign (1d), shine (1b), since (b), sing (3b), stay (1d, 2b), true (2b), trust (3e), kingdom (1b), live (1c), same (1c)

everlasting
make thine e. throne . . 55.5
their e. theme . . . 168.6
make . . . an e. sign . . 173.3
present e. Heaven . . . 210.4
ancient of e. days . . . 223.1
their e. circles run . . . 559.3
to gain the e. prize . . . 633.3
let e. thanks be thine . . 657.3
in his e. might . . . 700.*
the e. throne of love . . 711.1
my e. friend 714.4
thy e. truth 715.5
sing the e. song . . . 880.4
there e. spring abides . . 898.1

b *everlasting arms* *Deut 33:27*
leaning on the e. a. . . 768.*
e. a. are round . . . 809.3

c *everlasting fire* *Matt 18:8*
from the e. f. 401.2

d *everlasting God* *Heb 1:12*
from e. thou art G. . . . 13.3
Christ, the e. Lord . . . 82.2
e. G., come down . . . 161.4
thou art from e. . . . 870.1

e *everlasting life* *John 3:16*
l. e. he gives 271.4
'tis l. e. 355.4
he bought me e. l. . . . 402.3
l. e. enjoy here below . . 640.5
believing . . . Jesus, e. l. . 874.3

f *everlasting light* *Isa 60:19*
shineth the e. l. . . . 86.1
onward . . . to the e. l. . . 777.1
darkness into e. l. . . . 938.4

g *everlasting love* *Jer 31:3*
sovereign, e. l. . . . 140.5
loved with e. l. . . . 545.1
thy name is . . . e. l. . . 603.2
from the e. throne of l. . . 711.1
loved with an e. l. . . . 746.5

h *everlasting name* *Isa 56:5*
Jesus' n. is e. 63.1
their n. an e. n. . . . 168.4

King (2f), song (1i), Spirit (2e)

evermore see *ever,* henceforth (1c)

every nc, but
a *every burden*
come . . . e. b. bring . . 254.4
lay e. b. down . . . 278.2
lay we e. b. down . . . 891.3

b *every foe*
cast out e. f. 436.1
show thy power to e. f. . . 620.3
learn to fight with e. f. . . 658.6
till e. f. is vanquished . . 699.1
triumph over e. f. . . . 804.3
our e. f. defy 810.2
e. f. shall quit the field . . 813.3
live . . . 'gainst e. f. . . 933.3

conquer (d)

c *every need*
he knows our e. n. . . . 9.3
will meet our e. n. . . . 203.3
he supplies my e. n. . . 317.4
love supplies my e. n. . . 342.3
reveal my e. n. . . . 502.1
grace for e. time of n. . . 539.2
Jesus e. n. supplying . . 764.3
why not speak my e. n. . . 770.3
answer to my e. n. . . . c151

d *every soul*
let e. s. from sin awake . . 43.1
e. fallen s. of man . . . 140.5
applying Christ to e. s. . . 191.3
enter e. longing s. . . . 218.c
e. s. by sin oppressed . . 231.1
e. s. be Jesus' guest . . 234.1
tell e. sin-sick s. . . . 384.3
kindle fire in e. s. . . . 609.3
e. s. of man made known . 656.1
shows the way to e. s. . . 700.2
fill up e. s. with love . . 909.3

e *every word*
e. w. of grace is strong . . 26.3
write on my heart e. w. . . 99.1
to follow e. w. . . . 614.4
may e. w. here spoken direct 943.3

see separate sections of many keywords

everybody
sets e. free 71.c
e. should know c155

every/one
he made them e. o. . . . 25.3
e. o. that asks may find . . 216.3
for e. o. . . . there's room . 261.4
we're sinners e. o. . . . 268.4
e. who seeks may pluck. . 658.1
stand firm e. o. . . . 698.1
reveals God's sword to e. . 705.2
let us praise him e. o. . . 769.1
his power to e. is shown . 829.2
but God knows e. o. . . 850.*
show his love to e. . . . 851.1
all gone, yes e. o. . . . c188

everything
e. rejoices 40.1
e. is changing 49.2
he's e. to me 344.1
e. for Jesus 352.c
I've given to Jesus e. . . 405.3
removing e. that mars . . 494.3
e. to him committed . . 514.2
Jesus, thou art e. to me. . 600.*
e. to God in prayer . . . 645.1
all is despairing, e. sad . . 773.1
he's e. to me c174
tender care is e. to me . . . c212

b *1 Thess 5:18*
give thanks for e. 408.5

everywhere
banner . . . e. unfurled . . 40.2
he speaks to me e. . . . 42.2
his love is e. 49.c
for always, e. 71.3
e., now with joy is ringing . 73.1
e. he leads me . . . follow 483.1, c
e. we'll still be crying . . 693.2
fight for the Lord e. . . 708.*
standard . . . uplifted e. . . 774.4
follow Jesus gladly e. . . 817.2
true hearts e. 826.2
hearts of all men e. . . 827.4
spread the tidings e. . . 835.1
sound out the praises e.. . 835.c
for your people e. . . . 856.*
with evil e. conferring . . 864.1
tokens . . . are e. . . . 870.1
God is with us e. we go. . c123

evidence *Heb 11:1* . . . 496.4

evil
saves . . . from e.'s blight . 30.4
e. forces seem . . . sway . 171.1
e. shall perish . . . 173.c
o'er e. a victory win . . 281.1
refine the e. nature . . 324.2
thraldom of e. . . . 410.3
an e. heart indeed . . . 421.2
cast every e. passion out . 432.2
cleansed from all e. . . 443.1
all the e. passions slay . . 481.2
from e. separated . . . 495.1
every e. way forsaking . . 502.2
the hosts of e. round us. . 577.2
make all e. natures good . 593.4
the e. days of yore . . . 724.c
cast their e. chains away . 776.2
e. tempers, pride . . . 783.4
where e. reigns . . . 801.1
shun e. companions . . 823.2
millions bound by e. . . 832.2
battling 'gainst all e. . . 859.2
e. with e. . . . conferring . 864.1
its e. in a moment end . . 880.2
e. crowned and deified . . 885.3
each encounter with e. . . 893.2
bear e. or good . . . 928.3

b *Matt 6:13*
deliver . . . when e. . . 624.4
from every e. . . . keep . . 767.4
keep his (her) heart from e. . 792.2
keep . . . from all that's e. . 795.3

c *evil thing* *1 Cor 10:6*
let no e. t. prevent me . . 504.2
where no e. t. cometh . . 883.3

d *powers of evil* *Rom 8:35-39*
no p. of e. can sever . . 349.1
by e. p. possessed . . . 590.3
the p. of e. have sought. . 760.3
'gainst the p. of e. . . . 866.2

e *Ecc 12:1*
find him in the e. days . . 738.1

evoke 728.3

exalt-ed *Phil 2:9*
to be e. thus 57.2
e. the name of Jesus . . . 68.3
now in Heaven, e. high . . 118.4
following our e. head . . 143.5
thou art high e. . . . 174.4
e. thy precious name . . 626.2
there my e. Saviour stands . 880.3

example *1 Peter 2:21*
from mine e. comfort . . 21:2
and his e. too . . . 580.2
thou shalt my e. be . . 793.4

exceeding
with e. bitter throes . . 127.2
b *Matt 5:12*
be e. glad—rejoice . . 95.3

excellence 688.2

excellent *Ps 8:1**
tell of his e. greatness . . 184.c
in his e. word . . . 653.1

excelling
all loves e. 438.1
treasure e. in power . . c65

except
comes not e. by loss . . 211.3
e. I am moved . . . 527.c
b *Ps 127:1*
e. you build . . . fill. . . 943.2

exchange
e. it some day . . . 124.c
e. thy throne 448.3
till we e. it for a crown . . 692.5

exclaim 407.4

excludes
it ne'er e. his face . . . 758.1
infinite day e. the night . . 898.1

excuse 409.3

exempt 566.5

exercise *1 Tim 4:7* . . . 646.2

exert
e. the virtue of thy name . 629.1
I all my strength e. . . . 720.5

exhausted 579.2

exile-d
e. long for home . . . 167.3
though e. from home . . 354.4

expand-ing
for all the race e. . . . 539.1
e. thy wings 651.3
through eternities e. . . 751.1
his mercy doth e. . . . 896.2

expect-ed
come, thou long-e. Jesus . 79.1
e. his own anointed Son . 150.4
e. his fulness to receive . . 659.4
we e. a bright tomorrow . 764.3
come when least e. . . 913.2

expectation *Phil 1:20* . . 765.1

expel 445.2

experience 21.4

expiring
that strange e. cry . . . 140.1
hearing thy e. cry . . . 185.1

explain 544.2

explanation 894.2

explore
no future to e. 44.2
Spirit of light e. . . . 196.5
may I e. the mine . . . 658.5

expose 408.3

express-ed
language by the heart e. . 211.1
can't e. by words alone . . 215.3
O this joy, who can e. . . 328.2
tongue can never e. . . 367.1
no tongue can e'er e. . . 406.c
by loving deed e. . . . 518.1
more than they can e. . . 560.3
Scriptures' . . . words e. . 656.2
tongue fails to e. . . . 728.4
eager to e. our praise . . 795.1
love e. in service . . . c208

extend-ed-ing
sovereign grace to all e. . . 55.2
behold his arms e. wide . . 107.2
flowers of Paradise e. . . 156.3
art thou his fame e. . . 276.4
still e. his . . . hands . . 880.3
those wide e. plains . . 887.4

extol *Isa 52:13**
name . . . of Jesus e. . . 24.1
e. the power of . . . blood . 56.4
passing time can ne'er e. . 70.1
I may e. thy name . . . 574.3

exultant 916.2

exultation
sing in e. 85.2
cause of endless e. . . 161.3
with shouts of e. . . . 934.1

exulting 364.1

eye
1 *(divine)*
he turns his dying e. . . 107.4
his pitying e. is dimmed . . 121.2
mirrored in his e. . . . 131.2
thine e. diffused . . . ray. . 283.3
beneath thine aweful e. . . 466.2
through his suffering e. . . 855.4
b *Ps 32:8*
let thine e. defend me . . 635.2
guide thee with mine e. . . 753.*
c *eye [see]* *Ps 33:18*
thine e. doth see . . . 416.3
sight of the all-seeing e. . . 459.1
e. pervadeth space . . . 517.3
thy kind but searching e. . 522.2
for God's all-seeing e. . . 665.2
e. my inmost purpose see . 667.2
sinless in thy holy e. . . 673.4
e. is on the sparrow . . c139
2 *(human)*
a *literal*
he gave us e. to see . . 25.4
the joy of ear and e. . . 28.3
with sad and wondering e. . 150.3
the heart and dim the e. . . 185.1
the e. of sinful man . . 220.3
glisten in the e. . . . 268.2
when my e. were dimmed . 330.1
glad my e. 412.3
wipe the weeping e. . . 485.2
still e. that weep . . . 527.1
Christless e. . . . never . . 545.2
upward glancing of an e. . 625.2
with e. and hand perceive . 748.3
e. may scan the . . . height . 766.2
my e. look to the skies . . 766.3
fall from women's e. . . 830.1
with bright, unclouded e. . 855.5
e. are filled with tears . . 895.2
bright . . . beams every e. . 897.3
at harvest time our e. . . 923.1
God be in mine e. . . . 953
lift (2c)
b *figurative*
like searching e. 27.3
e., new faith receiving . . 123.4
will your e. behold . . . 280.4
for ever claim my e. . . 449.3
mine e. at times can see. . 476.2
eager e. are watching . . 478.2
no other light my e. . . 490.1
quick-discerning e. . . . 596.3
all Heaven before our e. . . 604.3
frank and unaverted e. . . 618.1
with e. that see anew . . 618.3
that he may touch my e. . 650.3
slumber from your e. . . 696.1
martyr . . . whose eagle e. . 701.2
my e. have never seen . . 713.2
e. the sight is given . . 729.4
draw from my timid e. . . 744.2
give us e. to see . . . 756.2
read with childlike e. . . 839.5
c *blind eyes*
b. e. made to see . . . 257.c
b. e., weary sighs . . . 379.1
he made my b. e. to see. . 386.1
my sightless e. received . . 547.4
d *eyes close*
c. thine e. against . . . 251.1
when mine e. shall c. . . 302.4
its c. e. looks up . . . 632.3
thy cross before my c. e. . 670.5
e *open eyes* *John 9:30*
o. mine e. to see victory. . c81
o. mine e., illumine me . . c99
o. my e. to the light . . c159
f *(Prov 7:2)*
as the apple of an e. . . 425.3
g *Matt 5:29*
as dear as a right e. . . 481.3
h *1 Cor 2:9*
what e. hath not seen . . 506.3
e. hath not beheld them . . 682.3
e. cannot see nor heart . . 878.4
i *Rev 1:7*
our e. at last shall see . . 87.5
every e. shall now behold . 161.2
j *Rev 7:17; 21:4*
wipe from mine e. the tear . 48.1
no tears within their e. . . 878.5
k *Luke 2:30*
mine e. have seen . . . 162.1
hide (b) longing (2b)

eyelids
sleep mine e. close . . 671.4
may their e. close . . . 673.3
e. gently steep . . . 676.2
shall his e. close . . . 767.2

F

fabric
within thy f. of thy will . . 644.1
this f. shall endure . . . 941.3

face
1 *(general)*
all who lift their f. . . . 181.3
with our f. to the sun . . 462.3
smile in f. of failure . . 510.3
turns his f. to Heaven . . 580.3
smile on every f. 664.1
f. at the door are sweet . . 664.2
with thy f. to the foe . . 689.*
their bright f. glow . . 703.4
come with happy f. . . 836.*
wipe . . . from every f. . . 909.3
affliction clouds his f. . . 911.4
see each other's f. . . . 915.1
b *angel faces*
all the a. f. 141.2
those a. f. smile . . . 606.3
set (f), water (1b)
2 *(divine)*
by thy f. so meek . . . 88.5
unveil thy f. 102.4
I gaze upon thy f. . . . 138.2
that suffering f. . . . 138.2
provoked him to his f. . . 286.2
tears thy f. have marred. . 299.2
disclose thy lovely f. . . 412.2
search his f. and find . . 449.2
look into thy f. 615.3
sunlight of thy f. divine . . 726.3
seems to veil his f. . . . 745.2
ne'er excludes his f. . . 758.1
cannot hide his blessèd f. . 758.c
through his glowing f. . . 855.2
b *before (thy) face*
shall flee thy f. before . . 172.3
as I am before thy f. . . 285.1
before my maker's f. . . 290.1
before thy f., dear Lord . . 409.1
proclaim, before thy f. . . 415.3
before thy f., each vow . . 534.3
wear . . . before thy f. . . 698.3
may stand before thy f. . . 791.3
bowed before his f. . . 835.3
c *behold face* Ps 17:15
beauty of thy f. b. . . . 59.3
I shall b. his f. 223.4
ever thy glorious f. to b.. . 300.4
content with b. his f. . . 318.3
till we b. thy f. . . . 515.4
when shall I b. thy f. . . 557.2
may we b. thy f. . . . 590.4
d *see face*
when his f. I do not s. . . 176.3
s. his f. in blessing . . . 330.1
I s. his blessèd f. . . . 366.3
nor could I s. . . . f. . . 398.3
we long to s. your f. . . 748.1
and children s. your f. . . 943.3
I can s. my pilot's f. . . c131
e *see face [in Heaven]* Rev 22:4
soon I shall s. his f. . . 45.3
sweeter for thy f. to s. . . 61.1
they shall s. the f. . . . 95.2
his f. I at last shall s. . . 179.4
to s. his glorious f. . . . 195.4
s. the Father's f. . . . 290.3
there we shall s. his f. . . 314.2
I'll s. his blessèd f. . . . 344.3
I'll s. my Saviour's f. . . 389.3
f. of God I shall s. . . . 459.3
feebly longed thy f. to s. . 466.3
s. thy f. and serve thee . . 466.5
when thy f. I s. 524.4
until thy blessed f. I s. . . 612.7
before his f. I s. . . . 730.4
no shadows . . . s. thy f. . 878.2
how I'd like to s. his f. . . 884.1
some day I'll s. . . . f. . . 884.c
I shall look on his f. . . 906.c
just . . . to look on his f.. . 906.2
until thy f. I shall s. . . c49
f *see face to face* Gen 32:30
ye behold him f. to f. . . 17.4
to see him f. to f. . . . 583.5
f. to f. we then shall s. . . 809.4
I shall s. him f. to f. . . c245
g *seek thy face* Ps 27:8
with assurance s. his f. . . 249.3
s. thy Father's f. . . . 256.1
would I s. thy f. . . . 301.3
I s. thy f. 305.2
still to s. thy f. . . . 307.2
s. a Father's f. . . . 581.4
he bids me s. his f. . . 633.2
callest me to s. thy f. . . 636.4
lift up . . . and s. his f. . . 718.2
to all who s. his f. . . . 724.1
thy people s. thy f. . . 945.2
h *face shine* Num 6:25; Matt 17:2
f. and garments . . . s. . . 154.1
beauty s. from his . . . f.. . 242.4
the sunshine of his f. . . 476.3
thy f. of love s. evermore . 741.2
I trust the s. of thy f. . . 762.1
the Lord make his f. s. . . 961
i *show face*
s. thy f. in brightness . . 155.4
Jesus s. his smiling f. . . 387.c
s. thou thy f., and light . . 486.1
s. thy f. and all is bright . 498.4
s. me thy f. . . . . . 551.*
Jesus s. a smiling f. . . 560.1
s. us thy f. 648.3
j *[Jesus'] face*
before the Saviour's f. . . 223.3
smile of Jesus' lovely f. . . 253.1
gaze upon the Saviour's f. . 268.2
see the cause in Jesus' f. . 286.3
Saviour's f. obscuring . . 369.1
I'll see my Saviour's f. . . 389.3
love-light of Jesus' f. . . 848.2
mirror of the Saviour's f. . 891.4
in the f. of Jesus Christ . . c158
beauty (1b), blessed (2c), Father (2c), light (4j), smile (1b)
3 *face (verb)*
for us f. every danger . . 97.2
my fierce accuser f. . . . 284.4
for the f. of this hour . . 577.1
trust must f. its trial . . 717.5
the storms I f. 732.1
f. up to sternest fact . . 863.4
foe (e)

fact 863.4

fade-d-ing
sun's last rays are f. . . . 63.3
lasts when youth has f. . . 544.3
by the f. light 931.1
b Isa 24:4; James 1:11
f. . . . worldling's pleasure . 157.3
or f. my earthly bliss . . 187.3
when all other lights f. . . 237.2
f. are its treasures . . . 420.2
beyond earth's f. dross . . 429.2
its honours f. and fall . . 489.2
all beauty f. away . . . 494.1
Heaven and earth may f. . . 545.3
earthly joys . . . f. . . . 711.3
though joys may f. . . . 761.1
c *not fade* 1 Peter 1:4; 5:4
never f. the name of Jesus . 63.1
joys that will not f.. . . 227.1
one that f. not away . . 320.1
kindness can ne'er f. . . c207

fadeless (1 Peter 1:4; 5:4)
the crown of f. glory . . 777.3
realms of f. day . . . 888.1
but aye the f. morn . . 895.1

fail
1 *(God) not fail* (Josh 1:5)*
nor find thee to f. . . . 16.5
think that God will f. . . 44.3
he will not f. to keep . . 48.1
never f. . . . to cheer . . 68.3
his Kingdom cannot f. . . 164.3
canst thou f. to give . . 303.3
he who never f. . . . 341.1
never f. to strengthen . . 521.3
thou . . . shalt never f. . . 532.2
Jesus cannot f. . . . 749.3
never will he f. us . . . 755.2
cannot f. the way to show . 772.1
God in man can never f.. . 809.2
God who ne'er will f. us. . 822.3
a never-f. friend . . . c146
b 1 Kings 8:56
word of God can never f. . 407.3
word . . . canst not f. . . 642.3
promise . . . cannot f. . . 690.4
promises that cannot f. . . 757.2
thy promise never f. . . 761.3
c Lam 3:22
thy compassions they f. not . 33.1
mercies new and never-f. . 938.2
d Luke 12:33
my never-f. treasury . . 58.3
e (1 Cor 13:8)
mines of never-f. skill . . 29.2
whose/thy goodness f. never 53.1, 5
never f. from age to age. . 157.2
thy power cannot f. . . 459.2
love never f. 530.c
thy grace can never f. . . 574.2
thine can never f. . . . 727.5
fruits that never f. . . . 887.3
2 *(we) fail*
which did in Adam f. . . 18.3
because you've f. him . . 44.c
earthly house shall f. . . 149.3
works of darkness f. . . 198.4
unaided man must f. . . 212.4
almost is sure to f. . . 226.3
though you have f. him . . 270.3
knowing my f. 294.1
earthly friends may f. . . 377.1
my courage f. 391.2
heart . . . has f. to take . . 415.3
myself for ever f. . . . 456.2
the waters f. 547.3
I've f. to obtain . . . 610.2
when other helpers f. . . 670.1
the arm of flesh will f. . . 699.3
where men have sorely f. . 706.1
friend when others f. . . 709.2
creatures all f. . . . 712.2
tongue f. to express . . 728.4
where earthly forces f. . . 744.2
friends should all f. . . 763.1
my faith must surely f. . . 780.2
should we f. proclaiming . 853.3

b *strength fail*
when our s. has f. . . 579.2
and what if s. should f. . . 586.3
our f. s. renew . . . 669.2

resources

c *heart fail* *Ps 73:26*
though my h. f. . . . 746.5

d *not/never fail*
thy praise . . . shall n. f. . 156.4
you can n. f. 280.3
none need f. . . . to claim . 456.3
f. n. man nor thee . . . 577.4
we n. can f. 698.2
faith that cannot f. . . 733.4
then can I n. f. . . . 877.3
with Christ . . . n. f. . . c151

failure
out of my shameful f. . . 300.2
through the past of f. . . 415.1
points back to f. . . . 440.3
smile in face of f. . . . 510.3
only with f. I met . . . 553.2
f. every work of mine . . 555.4
your victories and your f. . 564.3
through endeavour, f. . . 570.3
f. I cannot hide . . . 605.1

fain
f. would I hide . . . 131.3
I f. would now obey . . 307.3
I f. would take my stand . 476.1
f. . . . great name record . 533.1
Jesus, I f. would find . . 594.1
f. I would pour out . . 762.1
f. I would . . . be brought . 793.2

faint-ing-est
f. whisper of my heart . . 48.1
f. amid the strife . . . 70.3
my love is weak and f. . . 110.6
and should I f. be . . . 123.3
f. . . . from many a fall . 337.3
nerve my f. endeavour . . 345.3
some poor f. . . . seaman . 478.c
teach our f. desires . . 604.3
lone and dreary, f. . . . 607.2
cheering the f. . . . 623.2
raise . . . cheer the f. . . 737.3
my faith so weak, so f. . . 742.2
the f. and overborne . . 825.1

b *faint heart* *Deut 20:8*
my f. h. rejoice . . . 26.4
for when my f. h. . . . 59.1
when f. my h. . . . 635.2
shame on our f. h. . . . 724.2
strength to my f. h. . . 743.2
men's h. grow f. . . . 864.1

c *fainting soul* *Ps 107:5; Jonah 2:7*
sinful, thirsting, f. s. . . 254.2
s. that are weary, f. . . 351.1
gasps my f. s. for grace. . 412.2
with my f. weary s. . . 469.1
spirits tire and f. . . . 559.2
then my spirit f. . . . 877.2

d *not faint* *Isa 40:31*
who can f. while such . . 157.2
toil on, f. n. 683.6
f. n., nor fear 718.4
make thee . . . f. or quail . 816.2
shall walk and n. f. . . c66

faintly 548.2

fair
shines in all that's f. . . 42.2
blue and calm and f. . . 103.1
a garden, passing f. . . 145.1
trees . . . strong and f. . . 159.4
white, the dark, the f. . . 170.2
f. are the meadows . . . 177.2
f. is the sunshine . . . 177.3
ne'er a spot so f. . . . 663.1
world is f. 711.1
flowers f. the meadows . . 850.2
with its pages . . . f. . 883.1, c
if on life serene and f. . . 916.2
by the dawn-light f. . . 931.1

b *re Heaven*
that city f. 59.4
f. flowers of paradise . . 156.3
harps . . . mansion f. . . 268.1
a home, a mansion f. . . 811.c
city . . . wondrous f. . . 833.2
a Kingdom f. 855.3
a Kingdom f. to gain . . 868.1
to despoil what is f. . . 883.3
all immortal and f. . . . 886.1
f. and happy land . . . 887.1
f., sweet morn, awakes . . 896.1
f. land of promise . . . 908.3
reach f. Canaan's land . . 912.1

bright (2e)

fairer
f. the woodlands/moonlight . 177.*
to f. worlds on high . . 314.3
may brighter, f. be . . 621.2
f. than morning/daylight 632.1, 4
home that is f. than day. . 881.1
land that is f. than day . . 900.1

b *Ps 45:2*
Jesus is f. 177.2
f. than the sons of men . . 497.3
no f. charm I see . . . 565.1

fairest
pluck the f. flower . . . 145.3

b *Song 5.9, 10*
f. of thousands . . . 175.c
f. Lord Jesus . . . 177.1
of friends the f. . . . 343.1
f. of ten thousand . . 344.1, c
flower, f. that grows . . c54
the f., is Jesus to me . . c217

faith
1 *faith for salvation*
f. would lay her hand . . 120.3
f. can hear his invitation. . 240.2
my f.'s growing bolder . . 298.6
reach out f.'s hand . . 413.2
mine the f., receiving . . 456.4
my f. reward 461.c
know not how this . . . f. . 730.2
creating f. in him . . . 730.3
my f. looks/takes/holds . . 742.*
my f. looks up . . . Lamb . 743.1

b *by/in faith* *Rom 3:28**
by f. I claim him . . . 46.2
when by f. I trusted . . 52.2
by f. I saw the stream . . 132.4
by f. through Christ . . 269.1
who seeks in f. . . . 277.3
in childlike f. I pray . . 285.2
but by f. I'm clinging . . 292.c
there by f. I washed . . 348.1
by f. they see and know. . 359.4
by f. I received my sight. . 395.c
blessing by f. I receive . . 436.4
in childlike f. . . . stretch . 437.3
while I'm waiting in f. . . 457.1
by f. the gift I claim . . 481.4
by f. the deed is done . . 513.3
by f. put in my plea . . 562.2
with f. I plunge me . . 746.3
washed their robes by f. . 909.2
would in f. ascend . . . c72

c *through faith* *Eph 2:8*
t. f. in Christ 46.3
t. f. believing . . . 232.3

d *Matt 9:22*
f. hath made thee whole . 304.3

e *have faith* *Mark 11:22**
fear not, h. f. 583.1
h. f. in God . . . . 723.*

2 *faith for living*
cause our f. to wane . . 6.2
f. to match our time . . 6.2
f. that answers firmly . . 6.3
f. desires no more . . . 26.4
my f. . . . can see fulfilled . 39.4
f. . . . assures my mind . . 176.3
f. presents her claim . . 198.2
f. is heard replying . . . 222.1
teach me f. and duty . . 258.1
from f. and hope . . . grow . 314.3
f. can firmly trust him . . 333.3
if f. but brings the plea . . 423.5
f. for my doubtings . . 488.3
f. knows naught . . . 540.5
f. is not afraid . . . 555.3
free our hearts to f. . . 577.2
power . . . to strengthen f. . 604.3
f. that says, yes . . . 608.2
strength of f. that dares. . 619.3
test my f. through doubt . 644.3
f. again is upward led . . 711.2
f. that changes fighting . . 713.3
f. triumphant . . . 713.3
because my f. is high . . 717.3
my f. is firm 732.2
unwavering f. shall rely . . 734.1
conflicts which f. . . . 734.3
but f. has . . . blest reward . 748.4
if our f. is pure . . . 755.2
the f. that conquers all . . 756.5
f. makes us bold . . . 763.3
f. can sing 764.3
all for want of f. . . . 770.1
when my f. could most . . 770.2
f. will make them all . . 770.3
our f. shall grow dim . . 773.4
with f. and feeling . . . 775.3
my f. must surely fail . . 780.2
f. . . . proudly flies . . . 799.2
sweet unmurmuring f. . . 839.5
f. and dauntless courage . 866.c
f. will carry us through . . c239

b *by/in faith*
in f. we celebrate . . . 198.1
sundered far, by f. . . . 573.3
with thee in f. abiding . . 595.3
constant still in f. . . . 634.3
in f. keep holding on . . 806.3
through f. . . . conquer . . 823.3
stone . . . in f. we lay . . 945.1
if I by f. . . . rely . . . c120

c *live by faith* *Gal 2:20*
while I l. by f. and do . . 344.3
help me to l. by f. . . . 445.3
bought me . . . by f. I l. . . 504.3
teach me to l. by f. . . 560.5
l. by f. and not by sight . . 770.4

d *faith and love* *1 Thess 5:8*
my acts of f. and l. . . 199.4
f. on l. depending . . . 222.3
on wings of l. and f. . . 369.1
to perfect f. and l. . . . 423.3
out of all the l. and f. . . 440.2
f. . . . and l. its Galilee . . 496.5
exercise to f. and l. . . 646.2
increase our f. and l. . . 646.4
f. shouts . . . l. must win . 744.6
f. and l. will make . . . 755.3

e *living faith*
now the l. f. impart . . 191.2
in l. f. be heard . . . 626.3
mine, to show by l. f. . . 652.3
inspire the l. f. . . . 756.4

f *[weak] faith* *Rom 14:1*
my feeble f. looks up . . 524.2
my f. at best is weak . . 731.2
my f. so weak, so faint . . 742.2

g *hold faith* Heb 3:14
f. . . . not loose its h. . 198.5
f. lays h. of . . . promise. 201.3
my hand in f. takes h. . 450.4
glory of the f. we h. . 656.4
my f. takes h. of thee . 742.2
f. undimmed to h. . 799.1
dearer still my f. to h. . 860.4

h *hold faith fast* Heb 10:23
when our f. can h. thee f. . 602.3
my f. h. fast on thee . 742.3

i *arms of faith*
rise in the a. of f. . 585.1

j *fight of faith* 1 Tim 6:12
fight the f. of f. with me. 694.3
lose the f. of f. 701.c; 705.c
good fight is the f. of f.. 705.4
marching with a f. f. . c136

k *[men] of faith*
men of f. whose power . 5.1
more heroes of f. . 684.4
I have read of men of f.. 686.1
men of hope and f. . 702.1
men of f. who will endure . 760.2

l *[work] of faith* 2 Thess 1:11
my acts of f. and love . 199.4
the work of f. . . . wrought . 407.4
work that keeps f. sweet . 519.3
work of f. will not be done . 812.3

m Rom 3:3
Lord of all f. . 611.2
I want the f. of God . 733.1

n 1 Cor 13:2
though great my f. be . 530.2

o 2 Cor 4:13
Spirit of f., come down . 756.1

ask (2e), give (1g), increase (c), keep (2e), see (3j), sight (2c), small (e), stand (3f), steadfast (c), strong (2c), trial (2b), victory (2i), wing (b), work (1h)

3 *faith for future*
wait in f. to hail . 171.1
in f. my last sigh . 589.5
by f. I catch . . . glory . 726.3

b *[see] by faith* Heb 11:13
by f. I saw him . 333.1
its heights by f. I see . 461.1
by f. it sees afar . 742.1
by f., I see the land . 880.1
by f. we can see it afar . 900.1
mighty f., the promise s. . c118

4 *shared faith*
f. of Church . 30.3
disturb this f. of ours . 554.3
laid for your f. in . . . word . 653.1
who thee by f. . . . confessed. 876.1

b *[one] faith* Eph 4:13
one the f. . . . never tires . 765.4
one in f. and harmony . 769.3
brothers of the f. . 826.3
one in our f. . c226

saint (1b), vain (d)

faithful
1 *(divine)*
ever f., ever sure . 34.*
free and f. . 110.4
this f. guide . 343.3
all thy f. mercies crown . 438.1
find a friend so f. . 645.2
f. through another year . 937.1
our f. . . . friend . 962

b 1 Cor 1:9
spare not, f. God . 446.3
f. God of love . 714.3

c *faithful word* Titus 1:9
lean upon his f. word . 729.2
promise of that f. word . 877.3

d *True and Faithful* Rev 3:14
come then, T. and F. . 155.3
so f. and t. . 372.1

just (1d)

2 *(human)*
O come, all ye f. . 85.1
only f. souls can hear . 214.2
f., loving service, too . 336.2
fixed and f. it may be . 421.2
a loving, f. heart . 475.4
f. I will be . 499.3
give me a f. heart . 524.3
thy f. witness will I be . 526.4
hold my soul f. to thee . 571.1
his f. follower I will be . 725.c
f. I stand in rule . 744.5
in f. love remember thee . 762.3
each f. vow now renewing . 786.2
f. be, delaying not . 805.2
art thou f.? . 816.3
honour them, the f. few . 847.1
soldiers, f., true . 876.3
Lord's true f. soldier . 894.c
we as f. soldiers keep . 922.1
f. who have striven . 939.3
accept each f. vow . 940.3

b *ever faithful*
shine, and ever f. be . 649.4
for ever f. to thy love . 714.1

c *keep faithful*
k. me f. at my post . 432.3
k. us . . . thy f. soldiers . 787.c
k. us f., keep us pure . 937.4

d Rev 2:10
if f. to my Saviour . 309.3
be thou f., hear him cry . 694.4
crowns of life to f. ones. 761.4
let us then be . . . f. . 892.3

count (b)

faithfully
f. he bore it spotless . 141.3
f. working . 484.c, 3
f. your weapons yield . 694.5
my soul . . . I f. commend . 714.4
do thine own part f. . 738.3
led us onward f. . 769.1
teach us f. to share . 796.2

faithfulness Lam 3:23*
glorious in his f. . 17.2
tell of his wondrous f. . 26.2
great is thy f. . 33.*
Jesus, look to thy f. . 407.2
speak the f. of God . 939.4

b Rev 3:14
f. engage . . . to bless . 633.2

faithless
when our f. hearts . 202.1
love the f. sinner still . 305.2
a f., wandering thing . 421.2
o'er a f., fallen world . 697.2

b John 20:27
be not f., but believing . 693.c

fall
1 *(Spirit) falls* Acts 8:17*
as dew upon the spirit f. . 70.3
hallelujah! it is f. . 201.4
like dew from Heaven f.. 213.2
thou dost on sinners f. . 216.3
let some showers f. on . 295.1
Heaven's ray f. today . 379.4
as gently f. dew . 494.2
let the light now f. . 502.1
no word . . . fruitless f. . 558.5
the fire from Heaven f. . 622.1
drops round us are f. . 637.c
O that today they might f. . 637.4
on our . . . way is gently f. . 711.2
as it f. on paths . 758.4
while the light . . . is f. . 893.c
f. afresh on me . c53

Spirit (4b)

2 *(we) fall*
I f. . . . upon my knees . 122.1
don't f. out and rest . 817.c
he f., but felt no fear . 890.2

b *(spiritual)* Ps 145:14
ruined by the f. . 46.1
partakers of the f. . 56.3
to those who f. . 61.3
sees me when I f. . 204.2
great the f. . 243.4
all who linger . . . f. . 262.1
by a thousand f. . 286.2
in sin when I f. . 329.1
faint . . . from many a f.. . 337.3
on the brink of ruin f. . 380.1
I stumble and f. . 506.5
if e'er I fear to f. . 571.1
trembling feet should f. . 726.2
can I be surprised to f. . 770.2
thousands who wander and f. 794.3
men around us f. . 804.2
men are thickly f. . 864.2

c *fall (at feet)*
let angels prostrate f. . 56.1
we at his f. may f. . 56.5
men before him f. . 60.1
f. prostrate at his f. . 66.4
at whose f. the shepherds f. . 104.1
at his f. we humbly f. . 104.c
I come, before thee f. . 114.3
f. beneath his f. . 164.4
Master, at thy f. we f. . 197.1
at thy f. just now we f. . 201.1
seraphim f. down before . 220.2
f. before his throne . 269.2
humbly f. before his f. . 284.1
Lord, at thy f. I f. . 307.3
than to f. at his f. . 367.3
at thy f. I f., yield . 448.c
when at his f. ye f.. . 929.3

d *not fall* 2 Peter 1:10
surely I shall never f. . 468.3
never let me f. . 727.6
while he leads . . . not f.. . 754.2
standing . . . I cannot f.. . 757.4

e *fallen* Rev 2:5
to save a f. race . 62.4
that every f. soul of man . 140.5
all that now is f. . 155.4
my f. spirit to restore . 305.3
grace for a f. race . 341.3
a f. world like this . 414.2
to cleanse our f. race . 590.2
grace for f. man . 656.2
lift up the f. . 691.1
o'er a faithless, f. world. . 697.2
raising the f. . 724.1
raise the f. . 737.3

3 *other*
sweet the rain's new f. . 35.2
affliction has f. on thee . 111.3
discarded where it f. . 126.2
the bars . . . f. . 151.4
sorrow on my heart may f. . 399.3
its honours fade and f. . 489.2
a tempest . . . was f. . 490.1
day by day the manna f.. . 566.1
fast f. the eventide . 670.1
d. falls at thy behest . 677.1
when the night may f. . 740.3
kingdoms rise and f. . 799.1
can't stop rain from f. . 854.1
we'll never let . . . f. . c243

b *tears fall*
music dries the f. t. . 68.3
do not check that f. t. . 259.1
fast f. the burning t. . 326.2

the f. of a t. 625.2
I see the t. that f. . . . 830.1
though t. may f. 923.3

c *Luke 10:18*
Satan's power shall f. . . 499.4
the foe before us f. . . 693.3
down shall f. at last . . 802.4
to the earth would f. . . 847.3

d *blood fell* *Luke 22:44*
sweat as b. f. down . . 486.3
f. drops of b. 586.2

e *John 12:24*
there f. the tiny seed . . 923.1

f *Acts 12:7*
my chains f. off . . . 283.3

shadow (b)

fallen see *fall (2e)*

false
f. limits of our own . . 265.5
baseness of a f. excuse . . 409.3
f. and full of sin . . . 737.3

falter-ed-ing
never once they . . . f. . . 158.1
f. hearts may now be strong . 249.1
f. and weak my labour . . 488.1
if my feet have f. . . . 522.1
can I wonder I have f. . . 770.2
do not lag or f. . . . 817.1
courage when we f. . . 863.4

fame
forsake its wisdom, f. . . 223.2
health and f. consecrate . 492.3
not wealth or f. . . . 791.2
the flight of f. . . . 854.2
with many dreams of f. . . 860.4
now the rest and f. . . 894.2

b *fame of Jesus* *Matt 9:31**
into darkness spread his f. . 63.3
spread . . . the victor's f. . 147.3
art thou his f. extending. . 276.4
O God of pentecostal f. . . 447.3
way thy f. to spread . . 529.2
spread . . . great salvation f. . 609.2
children early lisp his f. . . 661.2
spread his f., . . . sing . . 696.3

familiar 874.1

family *Eph 3:15*
to the f. of Jesus . . . 324.2
into God's f. divine . . 371.2

fan 205.2

fancy-ied
my f. ways why . . . heed . 91.3
then f. flee away . . . 685.3
I shall f. his blessing . . 848.2

far
left him f. behind . . . 44.1
came from country f. . . 90.3
in the Temple f. away . . 96.1
on a hill f. away . . . 124.1
a green hill f. away . . 133.1
f. across the field . . . 158.1
for the f. future . . . 294.3
brought me safe thus f. . . 308.3
must be near, not f. away . 335.3
veiled . . . his f. abode . . 398.3
f. down the future's . . . way. 519.4
bear them f. away . . . 550.3
though sundered f. . . 573.3
dark . . . f. from home . . 606.1
meet at life's f. end . . 618.2
from all but thee f. hidden . 647.2
its end f. out of sight . . 716.1
peace, with loved ones f. . 752.4
chasing f. the gloom . . 765.3
f., f. away, like thunder . . 802.3
a little will go so f. . . . c200

b *(to mean 'afar)*
star that from f. 73.3
seeking for Jesus from f. . 92.1
sweet though f.-off hymn . 358.1
bodies may f. off remove . 659.1
strayed f. on the mountain . 740.1

c *[by] far*
sweeter f. thy face to see . 61.1
happiness . . . f. outweighs . 399.3
more precious f. . . . 516.4
greater f. than . . . think. . 642.2
better f. to die . . . 780.*

d *far away (re Heaven)*
call . . . to my home f. a. . 124.3
on the f. eternal shore . . 765.6
country f. from . . . sight . 880.1
my home f. a. . . . 881.*
happy land f. f. away . . 897.1

e *far beyond/past*
east b. them f. 90.2
f. p. my busy hands . . 416.3
f. b. . . . fading dross . . 429.2
f. b. all understanding . . 751.1
f. b. . . . sight . . . 871.4

f *far and near*
speaks to us in f. and n.. . 31.2
as I hear, f. and n. . . . 73.1
o'er lands both n. and f.. . 172.6
ring out f. and n. . . . 829.3
of all things n. and f. . . 935.2
scatter it f. and n. . . . c200

g *far and wide*
their branches f. and w.. . 159.4
the world, f. and w. . . 224.4
to sinners f. and w. . . 393.2
fields spread f. and broad . 934.4

h *far too*
a present f. too small . . 136.4
f. too many there must be . 850.1

distant (b, c)

fare-ing
f. forth in robes of light . . 145.2
soldiers . . . are f. forth . . c238

farewell
his tender last f. . . . 200.1
companions, f. you well . 275.4
f. to . . . pleasure/self . . 502.3
how . . . bear a last f. . . 874.2

farmland 544.1

farther 248.1

farthest 27.1

fashion
his power can f. lives . . 335.3
crumble, then f. me . . 416.4
cares of life and f. . . . 832.3
flight of fame or f. . . . 854.2

fast
hath stablished it f. . . . 16.3
hath bound me f. to thee . 23.4
bound f. with cords . . 129.1
lay f. bound in sin . . . 283.3
outside the f.-closed door . 299.1
so f. to bar the gate . . 299.2
when the battle rages f.. . 769.2

b *hold fast* *1 Thess 5:21*
I lay f. h. on . . . name . . 290.1
faith can h. thee f. . . . 602.3
my faith h. f. on thee . . 742.3
rock . . . h. f. its place . . 750.2

c *fast [quickly]*
his purposes will ripen f. . 29.5
years are fleeting f. . . 325.4
f. fell the . . . tears. . . 326.2
I was sinking f. . . . 375.1
f. falls the eventide . . 670.1
life is fleeting f. . . . 780.4

2 *(verb)* *Matt 4:2*
f. alone in the desert . . 99.2
f. in the wilderness . . 104.2

fastened 280.c

faster
power to send us f. . . 197.1
climb the ladder f. . . . 369.2
that I may follow f. . . 614.2

fateful 162.1

Father *(vocative nc)*
1 *(divine)*
F.-love is reigning . . . 10.4
F.-like he tends and spares . 17.3
O come to the F. . . . 22.c
my F. doth not ask that I . 48.3
word of the F. . . . in flesh . 85.3
the F. hears him pray . . 106.4
the F. clears, and cries . . 127.4
Saviour with the F. reigns . 142.3
F. on his sapphire throne . 150.4
to be met by their F. . . 170.2
'tis the loving F. calls . . 279.c
our F. art thou . . . 288.2
my F. is rich in houses . . 354.1
back to the F. he brought . 384.2
made known the F.'s grace . 398.3
O the grace the F. shows . 418.3
come to seek the F. . . 595.1
our F. keeps us safe . . 722.2
our F. never slumbers . . 722.3
in the heart of the F. . . 739.3
one almighty F. reigns . . 765.6
who serves my F. as a son . 826.3
my F. loves me so . . . 837.4
our bountiful F. above . . 900.3

b *Father (God)* *Eph 4:6*
our God our F. is . . . 9.4
faithfulness, O God my F. . 33.1
much more shall God our F. . 50.c
God the F. be . . . adored . 174.5
I believe that God the F.. . 324.1
if our God our F. be . . 607.1
my God, my F., make me . 744.1

c *Father (in Trinity)* *2 Cor 13:14*
praise the F. . . . Son . . 2.5
thanks to God the F. . . 12.3
I believe in God the F. . . 222.c
hail, F. Son and 223.5
praise F., Son . . 665.6; 959
with God the F. dwell . . 785.2
when the F., Son and . . . 833.3
F., Son and Spirit . . . 939.5
O F., let thy love . . . 958

d *[heavenly] Father* *Matt 6:9, 14*
we adore thee, h. F. . . 192.c
promise of our h. F. . . 213.1
glad that our F. in H. . . 323.1
h. F., now we pray . . 576.2
lead us, h. F., lead us . . 607.1
our F., who in H. art . . 624.1
our h. F. poured . . . grace . 777.2
our h. F. has inspired . . 785.1
we praise thee, h. F. . . 870.1
h. F., thou hast brought . 938.1
to your loving h. F. . . c4
h. F., bless me now . . c58
trust my F. in H. . . . c133
the praises of your h. F.. . c223

e *Matt 7:11*
F. in love forgive/wants supply 50.c

f *John 14:6*
he who would the F. seek . 100.1

g *John 14:9*
the F. is shown . . . 739.1

h *John 15:26*
from the F. and the Son . 481.1

i *John 16:32*
alone . . . with my F. . 564.2
with . . . my F. not alone . 564.2

j *Phil 2:11*
'tis the F.'s pleasure . 141.1
F. be by all adored . . . 174.5

k *(Heb 7:25)*
interceding with his F. . 242.3
in the F.'s presence . 347.2

abba, forgive (1e), praise (3j)

2 *Father's*
this is my F. world . . 42.*
through our F. land . 252.1
the F. mercy seat . . 278.2
my F. own Son . . 354.2
my F. wrath is o'er . 361.3
my F. grand domain . 362.1
our F. full giving . . 579.2
back to the F. way . . 680.2
win my F. smile . . 706.3
F. kindness share . . 722.3
where the F. children . 776.2
glorify our F. name . 863.5
their F. kingdom . . 932.4
F. eye is on the sparrow. c139

b *Father's bosom* *John 1:18*
out of the F. heart . . 114.1
from the F. bosom came . 116.3
to the F. breast . . 141.4

c *Father's face*
seek the F. f. . . . 256.1
and see the F. f. . . 290.3
seek a F. f. . . . 581.4
before his F. f. . . 735.4

d *Father's hand*
I hold my F. h. . . . 48.2
F. h. still holds . . 446.3
kept by a F. h. . . 897.3
F. h. will never . . 917.3

e *Father's house* *John 14:2*
my F. h. on high . . 877.2
F. waits . . . to prepare . 900.1
at our F. loved abode . 918.4

f *Father's love* *1 John 3:1**
the F.-l. of God . . 218.3
F. of l., of justice . . 486.1
on our F. l. relying . . 764.3
F. l. forbids all fear . . 926.3

g *Father's throne*
at his F. t. . . . 70.2
he left his F. t. . . 283.2
bids me at my F. t. . 633.1
before our F. t. . . 660.2

h *Father's will* *John 5:30*
to pardon is the F. w. . 127.c
not my own, my F. w. . 566.4
to do the F. w. . . 683.1

mercy (j) promise (3e)

3 *father (human)* *(Acts 3:13)*
to our f. in distress . 17.2
than their f. lost . . 160.4
hears his f. call . . 740.3
hast all our f. led . . 918.1
God of our f. . . . 918.2

fatherland 882.1

fatness *Ps 65:11* . . . 929.2

fault
strong . . . bonds of f. . 176.1
that checks each f. . . 200.5
past of failure, f. . . 415.1

b *James 5:16*
Lord, our f. confessing . 863.2

faultless *Jude 24* . . . 70.2

faulty 459.2

favour-ed
for his grace and f. . . 17.2
to know thy f. sure . . 26.4
once for f. sinners . . 161.1
broken heart . . . will f. . 225.3
I shall enjoy his f. . . 309.3
now the f. divine . . 367.2
manifests his pardoning f. 370.2
could be hardly more f. . 373.2
for the f. he shows . . 397.4
while I seek for f. . . 420.3
nothing but thy f. . . 503.c
enjoying God's full f. . 704.1
a f. and contented guest . 728.2
changeless is his f. . 764.1
fear not to lose men's f.. 805.3
early let us seek his f. . 845.4
the f. to the last . . 950
his f. never end . . c146
of his f. I'm determined . c194

b *Acts 7:46**
by thy merits we find f. . 109.1

fear
1 *fear of God*
a *Ps 34:9**
f. him, ye saints . . 21.5
taught my heart to f. . 308.2
we have not f. thee . 466.2
f. and love . . . aright . 466.5
Lord, may love and f. . 655.6
never will throw off his f. 784.4

b *Heb 12:28*
plant holy f. . . . 190.2
the grace of holy f. . 466.2

c *Rev 11:18*
not f. his holy name . 20.2

godly

2 *human fears*
you have cause to f. . 98.4
hope for our f. . . 183.4
when our f. had filled us . 192.1
in the straits of f. . . 280.2
crowds of f. obstruct . 285.2
knowing my failings . . . f. 294.1
haunted with f. . . 298.4
heart was torn by f. . 330.1
f. possessed me . . 337.3
why should we . . . f. him 377.3
the past of failure . . . f.. 415.1
f. what men may think . 415.2
my heart . . . with its f. . 420.1
the f. that I hate . . 422.3
a host of haunting f. . 433.1
if e'er I f. to fall . . 571.1
filled with sorrow, f. . 576.2
f. that long have bound . 577.2
spite of f., pride ruled . 606.2
the stress of secret f. . 647.2
caused thy needless f. . 721.4
f. the perils of . . . way . 740.2
the storm that I f. . . 758.1
sin rampant, f. . . 789.4
earth's joys and f. . . 795.3
watch . . . through f. . 816.4
dangers may cause . . . f. 817.1
too long mistrust and f. . 827.2
f. to launch away . . 898.2

b *Mark 5:33*
she came in f. . . 304.2

c *2 Cor 7:5*
war without and f. within 284.3
fightings within and f. . 293.3
fightings without and f. . 915.2

d *hope and fear*
watching long in h. and f. 75.3
h. and f. of all the years. 86.1
h. deceive and f. annoy . 112.2

with its f., its h. . . 420.1
your failures, h. and f. . 564.3
our f., our h. . . . one . 660.2
provoke my h. or f. . 880.2

e *all/each/every fear* *Ps 34:4**
so shall e. f. . . . 7.4
love has banished e. f. . 48.2
all their guilty f. . . 60.2
bids all anxious f. depart . 68.2
to silence all my f. . . 144.2
all f. of want remove . 157.2
my f. has all departed . 169.3
that calms e. f. . . 200.5
cast away thy e. f.. . 261.1
turning . . . f. all away . 316.2
saved from e. f. . . 352.2
bidding all my f. depart . 363.3
I lost all my f. . . 376.2
all the f. that . . . point . 437.3
all my f. I let go . . 507.3
through e. f. . . . climb . 729.4
from e. f. set free . . 749.2
lay aside all f. . . 805.1
love forbids all f. . . 926.3
gone is e. f. . . . c191

f *[save from] fear*
drives away his f. . . 58.1
name that charms our f. . 64.3
scatters f. and gloom . 152.2
grace my f. relieved . 308.2
from f. . . . freedom bestow . 329.2
drove away my f. . . 366.4
a cordial for our f. . . 382.1
cleanse my soul from f. . 493.c
chase my f. away . . 502.1
away, our f. . . . 559.1
cast foreboding f. away . 566.2
bid my anxious f. . . 578.3
bid the f. . . . depart . 599.2
will calm my f. . . 740.3
f. and distrust remove . 743.4
save us from our f. . 769.2
fire that changes f. . 830.3
love for my f. . . c148

g *sins and fears*
from our f. and s. release . 79.1
victory over s. and f. . 102.2
absolved . . . from s. and f. . 116.2
liberty from . . . f. and s. . 441.1
by f. and s. no more . 454.1
wrestled . . . with s. and . . . f. 879.2

banish (b), cast (n), dispel (b), doubt (f), quell

3 *[not] fear*
not f., for God has willed . 1.3
bids all . . . f. depart . 68.2
shake off thy guilty f. . 106.1
I can no longer f. . . 106.5
not f. a disappointment . 246.3
discard thy f. . . 249.3
yet why should I f.. . 303.3
thou needst not f. . . 320.3
I f. no more . . . 375.1
no f. my heart appal . 489.4
f. and shame . . . no more . 540.5
f. shall vanish . . 702.1
knowing not defeat or f. . 713.3
faint not, nor f. . . 718.4
give to the winds thy f. . 721.1
no f. can wake . . 728.3
I shall not f. . . 732.1
it doth not, cannot f. . 742.1
what have I to f. . . 768.3
not meet that we . . . f.. . 772.3
with him we shall not f.. . 798.3
lay aside all f. . . 805.1
fell, but felt no f. . . 890.2

b *(specific fears)*
nor f. the terrors . . 5.4
f. of what may come . 41.2
shall I f. to own him . 94.3
f. no threatening rod . 95.2

thy children f. to die . . 146.3
not f. a disappointment . . 246.3
the f. . . . of the tomb . . 300.4
I f. no condemnation . . 361.3
from f. of man . . . 401.2
f. no danger 433.3
from ever f. to speak . . 437.4
changes . . . I do not f. . . 485.1
I f. no shame 526.2
f. of death has gone . . 536.2
I f. no foe, with thee . . 670.4
shall I f. to own his cause . 678.1
I'll f. not what men say . . 685.3
who f. not to die . . . 703.1
stronger than f. of death . 724.3
no change my heart shall f. . 736.1
f. not to lose . . . favour. . 805.3
I shall not f. the battle . . 862.1
f. not shame or loss . . 866.3
f. neither clouds . . . 930.2
f. nor pain nor death . . 948.2

c *fear no evil* *Ps 23:4*
I f. no ill 53.4
yet will I f. no ill . . . 54.3
valley I'll have no f. . . 523.4
my soul shall f. no ill . . 731.c

d *fear [not]* *Isa 41:10; Lk 12:32*
f. not to enter his courts . 183.3
f. not, I am with thee . . 390.1
f. not, have faith, 'tis I . . 583.1
f. not, I will pilot . . . 598.3
f. not, I am with thee . . 653.2

e *Luke 2:10*
f. not! said he 93.2

f *never fear*
n. f., only trust . . . 397.5
I will n., n. f. 483.2
near, I will n., n. f. . . . 770.4
yet we will n. f. . . . 814.2
we'll n. n. f. 818.3
they need n. have a f. . . 824.3
threaten but I n. f. . . . c132

g *nothing to fear*
have n. else to f. . . . 21.5
n. to wish or to f. . . . 318.2
I've n. now to f. . . . 344.3
and now I have n. to f. . . 467.4
believing, there's n. to f. . 773.c
peace . . . I've n. to f. . . c196

h *without fear* *Luke 1:74*
serve thee w. f. . . . 407.5
mine w. a doubt or f. . . 447.1
him to follow w. f. . . . 772.5
w. a doubt or f. . . . 914.2

fear (2e-f)

4 *(others) fear*
yet men f. them so . . 129.2
routing the foe in f. . . 686.4
f. shall oppress them . . 813.3

b *James 2:19*
devils f. and fly . . . 60.1

fearful
ye f. saints 29.3
the f. shades of loss . . 145.2
f. soul discard thy fears . . 249.3
paid sin's f. cost . . . 335.2
my f. heart points back . . 440.3
no f. shade shall wear . . 465.4
the f. breakers roar . . 598.3

fearfulness *Ps 55:5* . . . 183.4

fearless-ly
f. of the cost 197.2
f. stretch my eager hand . 520.3
go, f. go 689.1
f. through the night . . 765.2
f. let us still proceed . . 772.2
f. in thy name we go . . 789.2
may we follow f. . . . 789.5

feast *Luke 14:13,17*
come . . . to the gospel f. . 234.1
to the heavenly f. . . . 355.5
then he spread a f. . . 373.2
he will f. me still . . . 373.4
at the heavenly f. . . . 375.3
f. on the riches . . . 390.3
Calvary's holy f. . . . 431.3
day and night to f. . . . 480.2
upon his love I f. . . . 495.1
spread the f. today . . 550.3

feathers *Ps 91:4* . . . 722.4

features 38.4

fed see *feed*

feeble-y *(Isa 16:14; 35:3)*
f. as frail 16.5
though f. their lays . . 16.6
our f. frame he knows . . 17.3
judge not . . . by f. sense . 29.4
small and f. was his day. . 165.2
f. longed thy face to see . 466.3
trim your f. lamp . . . 478.3
my f. faith looks up . . 524.2
my f. steps I stay . . . 597.1

feed
a *(spiritual)*
he doth us f. 3.2
the multitudes were f. . . 5.1
with food celestial f. . . 53.2
in my pastures f. . . . 277.4
whose fruits do f. . . . 346.3
abide . . . f. on his word. . 458.1
f. me with the bread . . 531.4
God . . . f. the strength . . 559.2
by constant mercy f. . . 566.1
keep us, f. us . . . 607.1
are f., on thy bosom . . 639.1
bread . . . whereon we f. . 654.2
in thy . . . pastures f. us. . 845.1
thy people still are f. . . 918.1

b *feed souls*
his care our s. will f. . . 9.3
bread of life my s. to f. . . 342.3
the s. of men are f. . . 934.2

c *ever feed*
f. me now and evermore . 578.1
his saints for e. f. . . . 909.3

d *[feed others]* *1 Peter 5:2**
souls, refreshed and f. . . 512.1
quick to f. the hungry . . 518.1
f. me . . . that I may f. . . 612.2
f. by saints unnumbered . 869.3

e *feed [providence]*
all things . . . he doth f. . . 34.5
all who live may f. . . . 39.1
that . . . we may be f. . . 927.2
f. and watered by God's . 935.1

birds (c)

feel-ing-felt
1 *(God) feels*
he f. for our sadness . . 87.4
f. its keenest woe . . . 607.2

2 *(we) feel*
f. the gentle breeze . . 37.2
f. the curse remove . . 120.5
f. . . . a bit downhearted . 169.3
f. . . . the thrill of life . . 173.3
to f. thy greatness . . . 181.4
now thy influence I f. . . 207.2
thine entrance f. . . . 207.4
f. the crimson flow . . 243.1
thou canst f. . . . pardon . 259.3
not what I f. or do . . . 297.2
I have f. his hand . . . 330.1
I f. his blood applied . . 361.2
holy delight which I f. . . 367.4

keen to f. the baseness . . 409.3
the first approach to f. . . 425.2
I f. the precious blood . . 440.4
I f. the sacred flame . . 474.5
I f. how weak I am. . . 489.1
all I know and all I f. . . 492.2
men . . . hatred f. . . . 529.3
I f. the sacred fire . . . 546.1
self-deceiving, f. stronger . 553.2
not f. what I say . . . 588.4
great need I am f. . . . 610.1
bowed . . . the death to f. . 701.3
f. our interest in his blood . 756.3
when you f. weakest . . 773.1
f. safe and blest . . . 792.1
from all we f. and see . . 874.2
fell, but f. no fear . . . 890.2

b *[always] feel*
which for thee we ever f. . 210.2
that always f. the blood. . 444.1

c *feel love*
I've f. God's l. . . . 215.1
l. consent to f. . . . 234.4
have you f. the l. . . . 242.2
f. l.'s warm embrace . . 269.1
f. and know the l. . . . 466.3
f. the kindling of thy l. . . 636.1
all the l. I f. and owe . . 846.4

d *feel power*
let us f. thy p. . . . 191.3
I've f. God's . . . p. . . 215.1
thy mighty comfort f. . . 603.4
f. thy Spirit's p. . . . 613.1
endeavour f. not thy might . 635.3
let us f. its quickening p. . 638.1
to f. thy p., to hear . . c108
I can f. his p. c154

e *feel presence*
make thy p. f. in me . . 531.2
let us f. thy p. now . . 638.3
I must f. his p. near me . . 731.1

f *feel [thee]*
did not f., thee die . . . 135.2
now I f. him mine . . . 361.1
have you f. the Saviour . 418.2
know and f. thee mine . . 447.1
f. thee gently leading . . 463.2
f. thy Spirit indwelling . . 589.4
joy to f. him there . . . 759.1
let me f. thee near me . . 862.2

g *feel [for]*
f. each other's sadness . . 50.3
f. his brother's care . . 662.1
can for others f. . . . 704.2
f. for all the world . . . c83

h *feel it*
prone to wander. . . I f. . . 313.5
do I f. it pain 409.4
a pain to f. it near . . . 425.1
I f. it in my soul . . . 562.3
I f. it in the air . . . c121

i *feel like*
I f. l. singing 326.1
f. l. giving in 790.1

j *feel [that]*
I f. your work begin . . 206.3
f. that no one . . . knows . 238.1
f. something better . . 298.4
she f. that . . . virtue . . 304.2
we f. that Heaven . . . 312.2
'twas done, for I f. . . . 395.2
f. by right they're thine . . 475.3
f. that . . . in me . . . live . 523.3
f. I shall conqueror be . . 543.3
I f. 'tis saving me . . . 546.3
f. the promise is not vain . 621.3
f. afresh thou dost heal . . c92
f. I really must declare . . c170

know (3e), long (1g), touch (1b)

feeling *(noun)*
one soul, one f. breathe . . 196.3
each wish and f. brought . 416.1
with its hopes and f. . . 420.1
every f. of my soul . . . 503.1
each human f. 528.c
such changeful f. had . . 549.1
f. lie buried 691.3
live above f. 773.4
with faith and f. . . . 775.3

feet-foot
1 *(human)*
may we with willing f. . . 76.2
thy f. have wandered . . 225.1
f. have found sin's way . . 225.2
snares . . . for my f. . . 400.2
my f. . . . the open door. . 400.3
my f. . . . self-chosen ways . 422.2
loath are my f. . . . 488.2
wayward f. to stay . . 519.2
if my f. have faltered . . 522.1
wandering . . . wavering f. . 612.2
smooth for little f. . . 664.2
trembling f. should fall . . 726.2
though his f. may roam . . 740.3
human f. stand on it . . 766.2
lest my f. . . . should run . 842.2
angel f. have trod . . . 891.1
b *1 Sam 2:9*
hold thou my f. . . . 529.2
keep thou my f. . . . 606.1
c *Ps 40:2*
set our f. on . . . places . . 577.4
Lord, plant my f. . . . c80
d *Ps 119:105*
lest my f. should stray . . 342.2
mine . . . to guide my f.. . 652.2
lamp of our f. 654.1
direct thy wandering f. . . 715.2
paths . . . marked for my f. . 734.1
e *Ps 121:3*
suffer that thy f. . . . 767.2
suffer not our f. to stray. . 789.6
f *Ps 91:11,12*
keep my f. in ways . . 728.2
g *Rom 16:20*
beneath my f. . . . my foe . 401.2
h *Isa 52:7; Eph 6:15*
be jubilant my f. . . . 162.3
take my f. . . . swift . . 525.2
joy . . . winged my f. . . 534.1
we are the f. of Christ . . 851.2
swift be my f. to stay . . 861.4
he claims my f. . . . 867.3
2 *(divine)*
a *feet of Jesus (literal)*
cool waters touched his f. . 103.3
hands and f. are bound . . 121.2
head, his hands, his f. . . 136.3
round his pierced f. . . 156.3
in his f. . . . wound-prints . 228.2
Jesus' f. were bleeding . . 903.2
those wounds in his . . . f. . c89
b *(figurative)*
to his f. . . . tribute bring . 17.1
where his f. pass . . . 35.2
to his f. draw near . . . 260.3
gather round his f. . . . 265.2
while before thy f. . . . 303.1
to his f. my praises . . 343.2
Lord, to thy f. I bring . . 523.c
to thy f. I am pressing . . 610.2
the world to his f. . . . 820.5
c *at his feet*
low at his f. . . . burden. . 183.2
a needy sinner at thy f. . . 282.1
behold me . . . at thy f. . . 291.4
Jesus, see me at thy f. . . 292.1
those living at his f. . . 413.1
seek for favour at his f. . . 420.3
down at his f. . . . cleansed . 427.4
at thy precious f. I lay . . 447.2
idols I cast at thy f. . . 454.3
waiting at thy bleeding f. . 477.1
down at thy f. . . . let go . 507.3
all at thy f. now I lay . . 543.2
at thy f. to cast it down. . 860.5
shall at his f. abide . . . 884.*
at thy f. I still linger . . c37
I am listening at thy f. . . c100
d *Saviour's feet*
down at Jesus' f. . . . 128.2
happy at the S.'s f. . . 210.3
lead the lost to Jesus' f.. . 212.3
kneeling at the S.'s f. . . 259.3
cast . . . at the S.'s f. . . 315.4
Jesus' f. were bleeding . . 903.2
lay your best at Jesus' f. . 920.1
till we meet at Jesus' f.. . 954.c
bow (2b), fall (2c)
3 *(other)*
with such light f. . . . 551.3
at the f. of the rock . . 639.3

fell see *fall*
little word shall f. him . . 1.3

fellowship
a *with God* *1 John 1:3*
all . . . be f. with thee . . 7.4
I now enjoy his f. . . . 48.3
by thy rich f. 209.2
then in f. sweet . . . 397.5
give me f. with thee . . 429.c
in f. with him to be . . 536.1
O what f. is mine . . . 540.4
constantly to know f. . . 630.1
f. divine 709.c
what a f. 768.1
no sin can sever a f. . . 888.3
walk . . . in f. and love . . c143
b *with each other* *1 John 1:7*
f. at hearth and board . . 7.2
know that f. of love . . 465.1
f. with hearts to keep . . 485.5
friend . . . f. with friend . . 573.3
f. of kindred minds . . 660.1
as in f. we meet . . . 748.3
one great f. of love . . 826.1

felt see *feel*

fen 606.3

fertile 931.2

fertilising 217.4

fervent-ly
a *Rom 12:11*
f. heart-desire 620.3
I want a . . . f. zeal. . . 720.2
in f. manner . . . praise . . 803.2
b *James 5:16*
prayer and f. praise . . 199.2
at the mercy seat f. . . 236.1
we bring with f. prayer . . 825.2

fervour
with little f. wrought . . 466.4
f. of my zeal 594.2

fetch 851.2

fetter
grace, Lord, like a f. . . 313.4
broken every earthly f. . . 894.2
b *fetters bound* *Mark 5:4*
f. and b. by chains . . . 257.3
b. by Satan's cruel f. . . 328.1
f. which had b. me . . . 348.2
c *(Luke 4:18)*
Jesus . . . f. breaks . . . 60.3
iron f. yield 81.2
will snap every f. . . . 273.3
snapped sin's f. . . . 347.c
from my soul . . . every f. . 439.4
break thou each f. . . . 501.1
captive's f. . . . rending . . 593.3
f. that enchain . . . 827.1

few
the moments are f. . . . 273.1
talents are f. 294.2
should my days be f. . . 477.3
Lord, we are f. 604.4
though f. the gifts . . . 605.3
honour them the faithful f. . 847.1
b *few more*
f. m. fleeting hours . . 368.3
only a f. m. trials/tears . . 889.2
c *Matt 20:16**
the chosen f. 701.3
labourers

field
1 *(literal)*
f. and forest, vale . . . 10.2
among the f. 41.1
out in the f. of God . . 41.2
while f. and floods . . . 84.2
f. strive in vain . . . 318.1
no f., no house be mine . . 362.2
village, farmlands, f. . . 544.1
office, f. or mart . . . 688.3
found amid the f. . . . 871.2
these f. of gold . . . 923.1
harvest of sown f. . . . 927.1
gold the f. adorn . . . 934.1
we plough the f. . . . 935.1
b *Luke 2.8*
shepherds in the f. . . 75.2
in f. as they lay . . . 90.1
2 *(figurative)*
a *field of battle*
sent us in the f. . . . 593.2
to die in the f. . . . 684.3
and rush to the f. . . . 686.c
and win the f. . . . 694.5
take the f. for Jesus . . 696.1
victory waits us on the f. . 809.3
every foe shall quit the f. . 813.3
scattered . . . from the f. . 820.2
taken the f. for God . . c243
battlefield
b *(Heaven)*
to the radiant f. . . . 818.4
sweet f. arrayed . . . 887.2
over the f. of glory . . . 889.1
f. beyond the . . . flood . . 898.2
f. where the glorified . . 905.2
golden f. spread far . . 934.4
c *Matt 13:38*
world is God's own f. . . 924.2
from his f. . . . purge . . 924.3
this is the f., the world . . 932.1
d *John 4:35*
f. are white to harvest . . 482.2
f. where the labourers . . 527.1
wider f. . . . reap . . . 922.1

fiends
let men . . . f. repine . . 407.4
God and f. . . . waging . . 693.1

fierce-r-est
when . . . the foe seems f. . 169.3
f. decay come not there . . 268.3
I may my f. accuser face . 284.4
when f. temptations try . . 326.3
f. gets the contest . . . 499.4
fight be doubly f. . . . 532.2

f. may be the conflict . . 707.4
when temptations f. assail . 789.3
our warfare may be . . . f. . 806.1
f. our foes and hard . . 937.2
b *fierce battle*
f. is the b., but victory . . 681.4
though the b. be f. . . 703.2
f. . . . the b. rages . . . 804.4
though f. the b. be . . 814.3
c *fierce strife*
last and f. s. is nigh . . 150.4
if the s. . . . f. grow . . 805.2
Satan's f. s. . . . quail . . 816.2
and when the s. is f. . . 876.4

fiercely 813.2

fiery
the f. heavens scan . . 27.3
filled with f. orbs . . . 230.2
the f. flag 779.1
f. yellow, emblem . . . 783.3
b *1 Peter 4:12*
when through f. trials . . 653.4
in the f. blast 769.2
pillar (a)

fifty 477.3

fight-ing-fought
1 *(God) fights*
a second Adam to the f. . 18.2
Jesus does with devils f. . 107.2
in the battle's f. . . . 107.4
f. the f., the battle . . . 143.2
rejoice, the f. is won . . 146.1
from the f. . . . victorious . 147.1
he f. for your release . . 242.2
f., and I must prevail . . 877.3
2 *spiritual fight*
in the f. all . . . dark . . 169.3
strengthens us to f. . . 197.3
grace to conquer in the f. . 203.3
I f. with delight . . . 321.4
in the glorious f. . . . 338.2
in the f. I am today . . 338.3
life given up to the f. . . 422.4
take part in the f. . . . 427.3
nerve me for the f. . . . 499.4
the f. be doubly fierce . . 532.2
keep me f. all the way . . 586.1
in the field to f. . . . 593.2
we cease to f. . . . 646.3
learn to f. with every foe . 658.6
must f. if I would reign . . 678.4
brave in the f. . . . 679.3
through the toil and f. . . 682.1
I'll f. to the last . . . 684.3
though he with giants f. . . 685.2
join at once the f. . . . 686.3
men of war who will f. . . 686.4
to f. 'gainst the forces . . 687.1
not to f. 'gainst the sinner . 687.2
called by thee to f. . . . 692.2
forward to the f. . . . 693.c
f. round the cross . . . 694.1
wrestle and f. and pray . . 695.6
fear shall vanish in the f. . 702.1
to the front! the f. . . . 702.2
f. while 'tis day . . . 703.2
to share the hardest f. . . 704.c
in God's Army and we f. . 705.1
makes me love to f. . . 733.5
how many f. I've lost . . 770.1
giving victory in the f. . . 770.4
and where the f. . . . 773.2
f. nor count the odds . . 774.2
we f. at God's command . 798.2
seasoned in a hundred f. . 799.3
keeping his soldiers f. . . 800.1
long the f. and dreary . . 802.4
in the f., say, . . . weary. . 805.1

bravely f. 805.1
our victory in the f. . . 807.2
march forward to the f. . . 810.1
conqueror in every f. . . 811.3
watch and f. and pray . . 812.2
arm . . . and march to f.. . 813.1
f., though it may cost . . 816.2
we're praying while we f. . 819.1
if we f. in the strength . 820.1, c
f. in the name of the King . 820.5
suffer for the f. . . . 830.3
f. nor resting 864.c
f. in days of yore . . . 866.1
how to . . . f. and pray . . 869.1
proclaims its f. begun . . 869.4
courage for the f. . . . 870.3
f. as the saints . . . f. . . 876.3
hard the f. 937.2
who have striven in the f. . 939.3
one in our f. c226
f. on the narrow way . . c227
is to f. in the ranks. . . c230
we're in this war to f. . . c243
b *fight (for)*
f. for his glory . . . 352.3
and for thee f. . . . 424.3
quick to f. for thee . . . 446.4
for thee to toil . . . to f.. . 466.4
f. for his overthrow . . 532.2
f. . . . for a . . . jubilee . . 593.1
for thy glory we will f. . . 593.3
to f. well for thee . . . 608.3
f. for right and opposing . 681.1
join the f. for the right . . 700.*
in the cause we f. for . . 776.3
we will f., f. for thee . . 788.c
f. . . . for thy Kingdom . . 788.2
c *fight [for God]*
strong to f. for the Lord . . 188.3
for Jesus I've been f. . . 309.2
f. for God ever since . . 321.3
for Jesus now I f. . . . 374.c
f. for the King of kings . . 402.c
wonderful . . . f. for God . 583.4
I am f. for Jehovah . . 686.c
f. for your Lord . . . 694.*
f. for the Lord everywhere . 708.*
for our Saviour . . . f. . . 778.2
we'll f. for God until . . 782.2
f. the f. for God . . . 798.3
rise and f. for Christ . . 799.2
we for Christ will f. . . 803.3
in f. for your Saviour . . 805.3
yes, we will f. for Jesus. . 814.3
soldier, f. for your Lord . . 817.3
we'll f. for the King . . 820.2
f. for a glorious King . . 821.1
f. for Christ who bought . c229
d *fight (un)til*
I'm f. till he calls me . . 330.3
f. till . . . latest day. . . 543.2
f. . . . till f. days . . . 575.3
we will f. until we die . . 593.3
bravely f. till death . . . 686.1
f. until the Master calls . . 703.c
f. for God until we die . . 782.2
we'll f. until we die . . 810.c
till death we f. for thee . . 933.4
e *fight and die*
thine . . . we will f. and d. . 693.2
in my service f. and d. . . 694.4
f. that self may d. . . . 705.3
f *fight on*
f. on, with the blood . . 703.c
salvation soldiers, f. on . . 782.3
f. on! salvation makes us . 815.c
f. manfully onward . . 823.1
g *Ps 144:1*
teach me how to f. . . 205.3
teach my hands to f. . . 568.1
teach us how to f. . . . 787.2
trained to f. 919.3

teach our . . . fingers to f. . c236
h *good fight 1 Tim 6:12; 2 Tim 4:7*
fought the f. 143.2
when I have fought the f. . 583.5
the g. f. is the f. . . . 705.4
f. the g. f. 718.1
f. the f. for God . . . 798.3
warrior, f. the g. f. . . . 859.2
in the well-fought f. . . 876.2
i *2 Tim 4:7,8*
finished, their f. . . . 167.1
to cease from the f. . . 808.4
once the f., now the rest . 894.2
battle (b), beneath, faith (2j), name (1m), passage, trust (2b), well (2f), win (2c)
3 *(other) Acts 5:39*
f. against your God . . 234.4

fighting *(noun, adjective)*
for every f. year . . . 163.3
rough be the f. . . . 233.3
are you tired of f. . . . 244.2
inflame thy f. host . . . 609.2
faith that changes f. . . 713.3
the f. is too hard . . . 780.2
the f. may be tough . . 805.c
your f. just begun . . . 806.2
f. is our great delight . . 809.2
f. be hard and severe . . 820.3
through all the f. . . . 822.3
marching with a f. faith . . c136
b *fighting over*
when f. here is o'er . . 374.3
till f. days are o'er . . . 575.3
when our f. here is over. . 899.c
till at last, f. past . . . c154
fear (2c)

fill-ed-ing
1 *(general)*
content to f. a . . . space . 485.3
we'll f. the ranks . . . 700.2
we're going to f. the world . 801.c
b
world, with demons f. . . 1.3
with sweetness f. . . . 61.1
longing f. my bosom . . 94.1
fountain f. with blood . . 132.1
hallelujahs f. . . . earth . . 167.2
does sadness f. my mind . 187.3
fears had f. us with dismay . 192.1
music f. the balmy air . . 268.1
f. with grief 303.1
soul . . . f. full of woe . . 348.1
sorrow f. my . . . heart . . 363.3
discord f. my heart . . 390.2
f. my life with woe. . . 401.2
heart's f. with . . . music . 406.2
blood now f. the fountain . 413.1
doubts . . . f. me with gloom. 437.3
the world can never f. . . 442.3
things of earth have f. . . 466.1
world so f. with sorrow . . 576.2
my eyes are f. with tears . 895.2
songs . . . f. the air . . 899.3
lives . . . f. with work . 933.2, 3
courts of Heaven are f. . . 940.1
days are f. with . . . delight . 947.2
we want to f. the world. . c220
glory (4d), presence (c)
2 *(God) fills us*
the Saviour must f. . . 119.3
f. it with the glory . . . 141.4
f. my spirit with gladness . 178.1
f. me with life anew . . 189.1
f. and saves us higher . . 197.2
f. this empty soul . . . 206.1
f. this earthly temple . . 208.1
f. every chamber . . . thoughts 208.2
f. our spotless souls . . 210.1

brightness f. . . . place . . 268.2
f. shall ever be . . 277.2
f. with his goodness . . 310.3
my hungry soul shall f. . . 344.3
f. my every longing . . 390.c
f. me, Radiancy divine . . 412.4
with himself me f. . . 413.3
f. me now, so shall . . 479.2
every corner f. . . 481.2
cleanse me and f. me . . 501.c
f. with messages from thee . 525.3
my needy soul to f. . 586.3
f. me with thy fulness . . 612.6
with thyself my spirit f. . . 665.4
with thy blessing f. . . 707.3
f. with his goodness . . 710.3
f. with new desire . . 788.1
f. us with thy inspiration. . 863.3
mould me, f. me . . . c53
f. the earthen vessel . . c65
f. us with life divine . . c101

b *grace fill*
f. with . . . stores of g. . . 58.3
f. me with g. divine . . 188.4
with g. . . . heart to f. . . 221.2
f. . . . with g. and power . 795.3

c *Heaven fill*
f. with the H. of God . . 367.4
f. my heart with H. . . 534.1
on earth but f. with H. . . 704.4

d *light fill*
f. us with the l. of day . . 10.1
f. the . . . world with l. . . 34.3
f. with fiery orbs of l. . . 230.2

e *love fill*
wonderful l. . . . f. me . . 114.c
f. . . . with charity divine . 181.3
f. us with his l. . . 215.c
soul f. with Jesus' l. . . 367.1
l. that f. to overflowing . . 439.3
f. . . . with perfect l. . . 441.c
f. with the l. . . . true . 443.3
f. my soul with l. . . 445.2
f. my life with l. divine . . 463.c
f. me with thy l. . . 474.4
the l. that f. my soul . . 520.4
f. me with l. divine . . . 521.1
f. me with thy l. divine . . 531.4
f. with thy l. . . . win . . 543.3
f. . . . with l. and praise. . 576.4
I need thy l. . . . to f. . . 620.2
pour . . . f. with thy l. . . 623.4
l. for souls, Lord, f. . . 649.1
l. f. every breast . . . 661.1
f. . . . boundless charity. . 720.5
f. my soul with l. divine . . 865.1
f. up every soul with l. . . 909.3

f *[joy] fill* *Rom 15:13*
what j. will f. my heart . . 37.4
f. my spirit with gladness . 178.1
shall be with gladness f.. . 277.1
with gladness f. her soul . 304.3
f. my soul with j. . . . 309.c
f. my heart with happiness . 340.2
my soul f. with rapture . . 364.4
whole nature f. with j. . . 408.4
thought shall f. . . . j. . . 517.2
bliss Christ can f. . . . 545.3
f. . . . with heavenly j. . . 607.3
we are f. with delight . . 808.3

g *peace fill*
with his p. . . . has f. . . 539.3
f. . . . with perfect p. . . 549.2
thy p. our spirits f. . . . 669.3

h *power fill*
f. our hearts with p. . . 201.2
f. us with abundant p. . . 622.3
f. us with thy mighty p. . . 638.2
with thy p. come f. . . 643.2
f. him . . . with p. . . 795.3
God will f. me with his p. . 858.c

i *praise fill* *Ps 71:8*
f. . . . with sounding p. . . 4.3
f. . . . every part with p.. . 7.1, 3
joyful heart is f. with p. . . 134.3
f. our hearts with . . . p.. . 201.2
let cheerful p. f. . . 365.2
f. our hearts with . . . p.. . 576.4
ever f. my soul with p. . . c194

j *Spirit fill* *Acts 2:2, 4; Eph 5:18**
f. with thy S. till all . . 487.4
loving S. . . . nature f. . . 520.2
f. with the Holy Ghost . . 521.3
f. us with thy Holy S. . . 622.2
f. us with the Holy Ghost . 643.c
f. us with the Holy Ghost . 789.6
Holy S., f. this place . . 941.2
f. with thy S. every heart . 942.3
except your S. f. it . . 943.2

fulness (d), heart (4b), life (4b), soul (2f), Spirit (6b)

final
from birth to f. issue . . 38.3
f. victory over death . . 171.3
our f. rest 190.3
f. judgment with dismay . 618.2
proof of f. victory . . . 777.4
down to f. darkness . . 799.4
the f. victory's won . . 819.3
bring thy f. harvest . . 924.4

find-ing-found
1 *(God) finds*
where he can f. . . . heart . 200.4
Saviour . . . a ransom f.. . 253.1
f. me, keeping me . . . 388.c
when thou dost f. first . . 416.3
abiding-place may f. . . 451.1
f. fulfilment in me . . . 553.4
purer lives thy service f.. . 567.1
tell me all thou f. . . . 618.c
f. amid the fields . . . 871.2

b *found me* *Luke 15:4, 5*
love and mercy f. me . . 115.2
the grace that f. out me. . 140.5
my God, it f. out me . . 283.2
lost, but now am f. . . 308.1
wandering, and he f. me . 330.2
lost, but Jesus f. me . . 337.2
f. me in . . . wilderness . . 340.2
the love that f. us . . . 370.4
Saviour sought and f. me . 386.1
he f. me, he f. me . . . 386.c
f. me, keeping me . . . 388.c
in my sorrow he f. me . . 467.3
yet he f. me; I beheld . . 548.2
dying Lord who f. us . . 702.2
and since he f. me . . . 706.c
God in love . . . f. us . . 722.2
so Jesus f. me . . . 740.1
he who f. and freed us . . 803.3

2 *(we) find*
nor can the memory f. . . 61.2
you there shall f. . . . 93.4
we f. favour 109.1
I, have mercy f. . . . 140.4
a solace here I f. . . . 187.3
thought to f. an easier . . 192.2
but only sorrow f. . . . 257.3
we f. in life's wilderness. . 288.4
I have f. a treasury. . . 311.1
f. a mighty arm . . . 311.3
men of grace have f. glory . 314.3
f. a richer treasure . . . 320.1
I f. in him my star . . . 332.3
all who trust . . . f. him true . 335.3
newborn soul f. breath . . 343.1
f. it hath Paradise f. . . 355.3
f. the narrow way . . . 366.3
burdened soul f. liberty . . 405.c
thy will to f. 449.c
man's knowledge to f. . . 506.3
until it master f. . . . 508.2

I can f. this in thee. . . 527.c
secret of victory I f. . . 553.2
I fain would f. thy zeal . . 594.1
can I f. liberation . . . 610.3
I may f. myself . . . 615.2
nor cares to f. . . . way . . 619.3
here . . . I f. my Heaven. . 634.2
f. my Heaven in thee . . 636.5
f. . . . needful weapons . . 658.4
to f. at last my home . . 675.3
daily f. . . . themes . . 724.1
freedom . . . I would f. . . 744.3
I have f. the ground . . 746.1
we may always f. . . . 805.c
I've f. the secret . . . 806.1
high communion f. . . 826.2
we shall f. him there . . 836.1
we f. pleasure . . . 869.1
comrade has f. release . . 894.1
higher . . . than I have f.. . c80
life has a new-f. theme . . c173
I've f. out the reason . . c202

b *find [that]*
nor f. thee to fail . . . 16.5
f. my name is written . . 59.4
f. ourselves . . . presented . 70.2
f. my fear . . . departed . . 169.3
f. sin's way is thorny . . 225.2
f. its pleasures vain . . 225.2
f. soon the joys . . . flown . 267.1
f. earth's glitter dim . . 267.1
f. that from fear . . . 329.2
to f. my soul was free . . 348.2
f. indeed that Christ . . 351.c
f. thy love unheeding . . 456.3
f. our needs supplied . . 462.1
f. thy heart made . . . his . 465.2
f. that his grace . . . 467.1
f. him in the evil days . . 738.1
f. it hard, Lord, to believe . 748.3
f. the cross is heavy . . 790.1
f. that trusting Jesus . . 790.3
f. your path is rough . . 805.1
f. the way is long . . . 817.1
f. each day your pathway . 817.c
we're f. that the trail . . 903.1
f. if you take Jesus . . c22

c *found (passive)*
no good . . . may be f. . . 14.3
but may be f. in thee . . 14.3
no other help is f. . . . 62.2
was there f. no room . . 101.1
balm . . . in its waters is f. . 252.3
wherever man is f. . . . 279.1
what way could be f. . . 319.2
my earnest zeal be f. . . 568.2
f. beneath the mercy seat . 573.1
place is f. . . . in prayer . . 619.1
sustenance be f. in thee. . 631.3
in whom my springs are f. . 647.1
within its pages f. . . . 656.1
wherever wrong is f. . . 705.1
goes where sin is f. . . 801.1
land where man is f. . . 831.3
Saviour may by all be f. . . 835.1
his soul is f. in peace . . 890.4
gain is f. . . . sacrifice . . 922.3
in whom alone is f. . . 942.1
may we be f. above . . . 950

d *find [seek]* *Matt 7:7*
what to those who f. . . 61.4
every one that asks may f. . 216.3
if I f. him . . . follow . . 228.4
f. by those who seek it . . 324.4
the help of all who f. . . 334.3
to them that f. thee . . 602.2
where'er they seek . . . f. . 604.1

e *find all*
all I need in thee to f. . . 293.4
all I want I f. in thee . . 517.4
all we need in thee to f.. . 576.3
hallow all we f. . . . 668.2

more than all in thee I f.. . 737.3
f. in Jesus all the help . c166

f *find friend*
I have f. a f. who knows. . 311.4
I've f. a f. in Jesus . . 344.1
I've f. a f., O such . . 345.1
I f. a f. to walk/stand . 376.1, 2
we have f. a f. in Jesus . . 377.3
for I've f. a loving f. . 389.1
can we f. a f. so faithful. . 645.2

g *find [God]*
f. . . . the Saviour of men . 92.1
f. this faithful guide . . 343.3
what a Saviour I have f.. . 363.c
I . . . f. thee near . . 449.2
on to f. my Saviour . . 470.2
may the sinner f. thee . . 575.2
wake and f. thee there . . 632.3
of the Saviour we have f. . 809.1
when the Saviour . . . f.. . 815.2
f. Jesus early . . 910.2
I'm glad I f. thee . . c54
f. such a wonderful Saviour . c155

h *find [joy]*
joy . . . only f. in Jesus . . 244.3
sweetest j. I f. . . 399.3
no j. I f. when . . . apart. . 448.3
to f. thy gladness . . 470.1
were that j. not f. . . 498.5
my soul hath f. . . . the j. . 547.1
lasting j. . . . f. in thee . 547.c
whatever betide in j. . 458.3
all my lasting joys are f.. . 600.c
perfect j. to f. . . 788.3
greatest j. is f. . . 857.1, c
j. abounding we are f. . c195
j. you will f. . . c228

i *find life*
f. the l. supreme . . 27.6
l. is f. alone in Jesus . 240.4
f. in thee my l. . . 287.1
f. in thee its l. . . 508.3

j *find [pasture]* *John 10:9*
store he ever f. in me . 277.2
drink and f. refreshing . 462.3
pastures I languish to f. . 639.1
f. my soul's refreshment . 644.c

k *find peace*
p. is f. but under . . . wings . 227.2
f. p. at the mercy seat . . 246.3
f. in thee alone the p. . . 547.1
f. p. from sins confessed . 590.3
all f. our p. restored . . c112

m *find rest* *Matt 11:29*
let us f. our r. in thee . . 79.1
raptured soul shall f. r. . . 115.c
weary f. eternal r. . . 160.3
in the Saviour f. thy r. . . 261.2
f. in thee my life, my r. . . 287.1
I f. sweetest r. . . 323.5
f. in him a r.-place . . 332.1
hope has . . . f. her r. . . 333.3
shall in Jesus f. r. . . 364.3
when shall my soul f. her r. . 454.1
I can f. in thee my r. . 503.3
my soul has f. a r.-place. . 536.c
naught but calm is f. . . 752.3
in him f. perfect r. . . 828.3
how to f. the sweetest r. . 829.1
f. in Jesus calm repose . . 910.3
f. in thee eternal r. . . 940.4

n *find no rest* *Jer 45:3*
no r., no joy I f. . . 448.3
soul f. happiness in none . 556.3

o *find salvation*
I have f. a great s. . . 63.c
before I f. s. . . 309.1
I've f. this great s. . . 320.2
I have f. a great s. . . 328.1
can full deliverance f. . . 590.2
can I f. full s. . . . 610.3
many f. s. free . . 939.2

p *find pardon*
thou mayest f. . . . a p. . . 253.2
believing, a p. have f. . . 263.2
where the sinner f. p. . . c67

q *find redemption*
in Christ we have r. f. . . 43.2
r. by his death I f. . . 46.2

r *find [others]*
desire the lost to f. . . 620.3
the wandering sinner to f. . 623.2

grace (2l), pearl (a), refuge (b), relief, solace

3 *(other)*
lights . . . f. a voice . . 2.2
it f. an echo in my soul . . 358.1
have now their meaning f. . 894.2
sickle work has f. . . 926.3
no ill power f. place . . 949.3

finding *(noun)* 351.3

fine c49

fingers *Ps 144:1* . . . c236

finish-ed
f. then thy new creation. . 438.3
f. well what we've begun . 462.3
f., Lord, this work . . . 531.4
f. my work . . . 543.4

b *it is finished* *John 19:30*
'tis f. . . . conqueror cries . 107.4
it is f.! was his cry . . 118.4
it is f.! was his cry . . 128.4
it is f! he cried . . 137.3
'tis f.! all is f. . . . 167.1

finite 601.2

fire
1 *(general)*
thou f. so masterful . . 2.3
seen him in the watch-f. . 162.2
can't stop f. from burning . 854.2
made ripe by golden f. . . 936.2
since the Army opened f. . 939.1

b *1 Kings 19:12*
through thunder, f. . . 36.2
speak through the . . . f. . 567.5

2 *(spiritual)* *Matt 3:11**
glows with thy f. . . 189.3
perish . . . in thy pure f.. . 194.2
f. that changes/turns . . . 197.2, 3
brings the f. just now . 201.3
f. we want . . . for f. . 203.3
f. will meet . . . need . 203.3
burning F. divine/within 206.1, 3
come . . . all-quickening f. . 207.1
come as a f. . . . 217.3
Spirit's hallowed f. . . 379.3
f. doth surely burn . . 415.4
a soul on f. for thee . . 426.3
faith and f. I need . . 440.2
the f. of thy commission . 463.2
trust thee for the f. . . 481.c
the f. of thy indwelling . . 493.c
I'm waiting for the f. . . 511.c
make me a blazing f. . . 521.2
love with principle and f. . 522.3
be all flames of f. . . 561.4
set us all on f. . . 609.2
my life one blazing f. . . 620.3
motion of a hidden f. . . 625.1
living flame of f. . . 649.3
old prophetic f. . . 651.1
hearts baptised with f. . . 704.1
want the faith that f. . . 733.5
yellow stands for f. . . 777.3
the f. that gives . . 830.3

b *holy/sacred fire*
guard the h. fire . . 199.3
deeply burning holy F.. . . 206.2
come . . . all s. f. . . . 208.1
Spirit's hallowed f. . . 379.3
h. f. to burn within . . 541.2
now I feel the s. f. . . 546.1

c *1 Kings 18:38; 2 Kings 1:10*
let the f. descending . 201.2
f. descending . . . liberty . 420.4
let the f., descending . . 511.3
f. from Heaven fall . . 622.1

d *living fire* *(Isa 6:6)*
kindle . . . the l. f. . . 216.4
changeless be, a l. f. . . 743.2
with l. f. touch 942.3

e *wall of fire* *Zech 2:5*
a wall of f. about me . . 344.3
walls of f. . . ., surround. . 809.3
wall of f. around us . . 814.2

f *Luke 12:49*
Jesus' love the nations f. . 165.1
to bring f. on earth . . 165.1
send this f. on me . . . 197.3
celestial f. to impart . . 199.1
send the f. . . . . 203.*

kindle (b), pillar (a), refine (b), tongue (1e)

3 *(hardship)*
f. and tempest rage . . 5.4
tempest, f. and foe . . 569.4
amid the hottest f. . . 910.4

b *Zech 3:2*
save . . . out of the f. . . 720.2

c *Matt 13:42*
from the everlasting f. . . 401.2
like an unconsuming f. . . 885.3
in the f. the tares . . 924.3

d *James 3:5*
quench the kindling f. . . 425.2
f. of passion roll . . 630.2

e *1 Peter 1:7*
day that tries by f. . . 522.c

4 *blood and fire*
win with f. and b. . . 593.4
his b. and f. soldier . . 684.2
march with b. and f. . . 696.3
march with the b. and . . . f.. 700.c
with the b. and f. . . 703.c
saving . . . by b. and f. . . 774.c
b. and f., thy kingdom . . 774.4
with b. and f., with faith . 775.3
b and f., through . . 779.c
b. and f., lift it higher . . 783.c
'neath the b. and f. . . 788.1
conquer . . . with f. and b. . 802.c
b. and f. is/gives/makes . 807.2
b. and f. . . . conquer . . 810.2
with the f. and b. . . 820.5
by b. and f. made strong . 821.3
flag of b. and f. . . 822.1
with the f. and the b. . . 822.c
soldiers of the b. and f. . . 830.2
with b. and f. unfurled . . 901.5
with b. and f. 'neath . . c240

5 *(verb)*
Jesus' love the nation f.. . 165.1

fireside 663.1

firm *(Heb 3:6)*
f. as a rock thy truth . . 4.4
how f. to the end . . . 16.5
anchor . . . f. remain . . 280.1
grounded f. and deep . . 280.c
f. decree 407.4
f. endures 559.3
f. in thy strong control . . 571.1
f. as a rock, and sure . . 574.4
f. to sustain 596.2
f. on the rock . . . 612.3
with a step more f. . . 614.2

how f. a foundation 653.1
stand f. every one 698.1
hearts that will be f. 704.1
my faith is f. 732.2
f. as his throne 735.3
we shall stand f. 833.3
dare to have a purpose f. 847.c
f. on the rock of ages 889.3

firmly
at all times f. stood 3.4
faith that answers f. 6.3
f. bound, for ever free 194.3
faith can f. trust him 333.3
with you we will f. stay 748.2
f. shall . . . stand 873.4

first
1 *(general)*
like the f. morning/bird 35.1
like the f. dewfall/grass 35.2
joyful tidings f. begun 78.1
man's f. heavenly state 78.3
the f. Nowell 90.1
f. approach to feel 425.2
f.-born light . . . decline 545.3
his f. avowed intent 685.1
his f. disciples heard 700.1
the martyr f. 701.2
those f. disciples 760.1, 4
our f. parents strayed 785.3
f. the blade 924.2
reaching f. . . . end 938.4
b *first-fruits* *Ex 22:29**
the f.-f. of thy blessing 934.2
while with f.-f. we come 936.1
c *Matt 28:1*
this is the f. of days 669.5
2 *(personal)*
our f. pure vow 5.4
f. let me hear 31.4
the hour I f. believed 308.2
than when we f. begun 308.4
when I f. commenced 338.3
f. I learned to love it 358.3
f. saw the light 395.*
when f. I saw the Lord 442.2
f. to know thee 591.3
guard my f. springs 665.4
f. the cross to bear 777.3
f. let me hear how 848.2
f., in true submission 864.3
b *first of all*
find f. of all, thee 416.3
obey thee f. of all 839.3
shine f. of all for him 841.2
3 *(re divine)*
when he f. the work begun 165.2
the earth f. you sought 175.2
Christ . . . was f. to lead. 400.2
he was f. to battle 400.2
b *first loved* *1 John 4:19*
thou hast f. l. me 357.2
who f. l. me 846.*
c *Rev 1:5*
f.-begotten of the dead 149.2
d *first and last* *Rev 1:11*
my Christ is f. . . . l. 346.5
him f. and l. him all 356.4
let love be f. . . . l. 620.4
near from f. to l. 938.2
Jesus, the f. and the l. 962

fisher-men *Matt 4:19*
the f. toiled 680.1
make you f. of men 680.c
f. heard by Galilee 680.3
I will make you f. of men c232

fit-ted
f. us for Heaven 77.3
f. to be thy dwelling 188.c, 4
to make us f. to live 203.2
f. for our heavenly rest 210.2
f. to be indwelt 416.4
f. it for the sky 472.1
I am f. for the task 528.3
f. us . . . consecration 622.1
f. me for life . . . above 623.4
f. us for perfect rest 668.5
f. us for the fray 787.1
f. us for . . . crown 937.4
b *fit for service*
f. for s. above 458.4
for thy s., f. me 488.c
vessel f. for thy s. 501.c
f. me for yet wider s. 531.4

fit-ting *(adjective)*
f. temples for thy grace 202.3
what is f. . . . denied 763.2
raiment f. provide 918.3
shall we f. praises sing 938.1

fittest 473.3

fitful 298.3

five 106.3

fix-ed
f. thy sacred presence 207.1
f. to live . . . for thee 210.3
f. in me . . . home/abode 214.3
day that f. me choice 365.1
f. the intention sure 416.2
f. in us thy . . . dwelling. 438.1
f. abiding-place may find 451.1
f. on thee alone 504.1
my hopes are f. on thee 517.2
'tis f., I can do all 526.4
f. on his work thy . . . eye 715.3
f. on this ground 746.5
f. thy throne 945.4
b *heart fixed* *Ps 57:7*
f. in every h. 216.4
my h. is f., eternal God 356.1
f. and faithful 421.2
f. my frail . . . h. 517.1

flag
f. of many victories 774.1
f. unhindered flies 774.1
f. of hallowed memories 774.2
keep every f. unfurled 775.c
for this f. our love 777.1
the f. again is lifted 777.4
cannot leave . . . f. 780.*
fight beneath our f. 782.1
f. shall wave for ever 800.1
f. shall have the sway 810.3
with the f. unfurled 811.4
seen the f. of blood 822.1
and with f. unfurled 829.c
under the f. we stand c226
follow the f. c228
'neath the f., so dear c236
only one f. for me c241
never let . . . f. fall c243
our f.'s unfurled c243
b *Army flag*
the A. f. shall cover all 774.3
wave our A. f. for Jesus 775.2
A. f.! thy . . . glory 776.1
A. f.! we too will follow 776.3
f. of the dear old A. 779.c
f. of God's great A. 779.2
if you follow the A. f. c228
love the dear old A. f. c230
fly (d)

flame-d-ing
1 *(general)*
'midst f. worlds 116.1
they kindle to a f. 223.3
the dungeon f. 283.3
quell my f. heart 303.2
floods and f. surrounded 361.3
f. shall not hurt thee 653.4
mocked the cross and f. 701.3
land of the ice or f. c238
2 *(spiritual)*
how great a f. aspires 165.1
all might catch the f. 165.1
a f. of sacred love 199.1
Christ of . . . cleansing f. 203.1
fan my love into a f. 205.2
like sacrificial f. 217.3
sets my spirit all in a f. 360.c
my heart is in a f. 413.3
cleanse, thou refining F. 416.2
track of heavenly f. 440.3
pure f. of the Spirit 443.3
kindling, f., glowing 546.1
the pure f. of love 594.2
to light the holy f. 624.1
thou art our altar-f. 648.2
little f. that burneth 838.1
b *sacred flame*
ring . . . with sacred f. 127.c
now I feel the sacred f. 474.5
c *living flame* *(Isa 6:6)*
O for the l. f. 20.3
in tongues of l. f. 200.3
touched with l. f. 353.3
can I not have that l. f. 447.3
every tongue a l. f. 609.2
a l. f. of fire 649.3
lamp of clear and l. f. 869.3
d *Heb 1:7*
let us . . . be all f. 561.4
tongue (e)

flaring 162.2

flash-ing
f. sea 10.2
when lightnings f. 39.2
heavenly light may f. 726.4

flawless 416.4

flax *Isa 42:3* 269.2

flee-fled
1 *flee away/from*
sinfulness before him f. 63.2
shall f. thy face before 172.3
Satan . . . now doth f. 323.5
the care I cannot f. 421.3
all selfish aims I f. 461.c
heaven and earth may . . . f. 545.3
as I stopped . . . they f. 547.3
when other . . . comforts f. 670.1
then fancies f. a. 685.3
Satan's host doth f. 690.2
cold wave I will not f. 725.4
Heaven and earth are f. 746.1
when . . . friends are f. 780.2
saw them ere they f. 797.1
from his duties never f. 801.2
tremble and prepare to f. 803.1
truth shall make them f. 813.3
at his look, prepare to f. 875.3
doubts and fears will f. c116
b *Matt 3:7*
f. from woe and danger 73.2
from sin and death we f. 100.1
warning sinners to f. 321.4
shadow (h)
2 *flee to*
to thee in . . . trouble f. 14.1
to those dear wounds I f. 368.2
to thy dear arms . . . I f. 450.2
hither . . . I f. 746.3

b *flee for refuge* *Heb 6:18*
there for r. f. . 237.c
to the blood for r. f. . 240.3
to him for safety f.. . 253.3
to the cross for r. f. . 260.c
for r. to Jesus have f. . 653.1

fleet-ing
with every f. breath . 58.5
while . . . this f. breath . 302.4
for years are f. fast . 325.4
few more f. hours . 368.3
f. is its glittering show . 470.1
the years will f. . 551.3
life is f. fast . 780.4
f. are our longest days . 874.1

flesh
my f. in hope shall rest . 153.2
this toiling f. has borne . 297.1
through my f. and spirit . 430.4
soul and f. receive . 516.1
thou hast my f. . 516.3
let f. retire . 567.5
put off this robe of f. . 633.3
heart fail and f. decay . 746.5
while in the f. . 880.3
b *flesh and blood*
that f. and b. . . . fail . 18.3
'tis hard for f. and b. . 729.3
f. and b. would quail . 749.3
c *2 Chr 32:8*
the arm of f. will fail . 699.3
d *John 1:14*
veiled in f. . 82.2
now in f. appearing . 85.3
God's Word made f. . 181.1

flickering . 621.2

flight
Lord of f. . 30.2
wing your f. . 75.1
took their f. . 224.1
speed forth thy f. . 224.3
faith, in mystic f. . 766.2
up to glory wing our f. . 809.4
f. of fame or fashion . 854.2
b *put to flight*
all be put to f. . 722.2
we'll put the foe to f. . 810.1

fling-ing-flung
its ancient splendours f.. . 83.3
f. wide life's portals . 130.3
f. a quenchless ray . 145.1
f. open wide the . . . gates . 167.1
f. off the night . 408.1
at thy cross . . . I'm f. . 434.4
widely the doors now I f. . 457.c
thine to f. an open door . 510.2

float-ing
let it f. there . 697.2
with banners f. high . 705.3
keep love's banner f. . 954.4

flock *Isa 40:11; 1 Peter 5:2**
we are his f. . 3.2
shepherd leads the f. . 614.2
with the lambs of thy f.. . 639.3
forward, f. of Jesus . 682.2
b *Luke 2:8*
watching o'er your f. . 75.2
watched o'er their f. . 80.2
shepherds watched . . . f. . 93.1
keep (3l)

flood
1 *(salvation)*
plunged beneath that f. . 132.1
with pentecostal f. . 218.3
Spirit came in like a f. . 321.2
joy f. my soul . 349.3
f. of joy o'er my soul . 394.c
send a great salvation f.. . 452.2
f. and cleanse my heart . 502.3
send a great salvation f.. . 593.4
f. of salvation and power . 608.3
wash in the life-giving f.. . 808.2
b *cleansing flood*
O c., efficacious f. . 131.1
the c. f. will flow . 413.2
pour on me the c. f. . 440.4
c., efficacious f. . 638.1
I'm trusting in the c. f. . c149
crimson (a), giving (b)
2 *(difficulty)*
helper he, amid the f. . 1.1
f. and flames surrounded . 361.3
o'er my spirit like a f. . 583.2
when f. o'erwhelm . 628.3
must I not stem the f. . 678.3
in the 'whelming f. . 745.3
3 *(death)*
death's f. has lost . 153.3
anchor hold in the f. . 280.3
when death's f. I see . 401.3
death's . . . swelling f. . 583.5
beyond the swelling f. . 898.2
nor death's cold f. . 898.3
4 *(literal)*
while fields and f. . 84.2

flourish-ed
we blossom and f. . 8.3
where thorns have f. . 159.4
freedom shall f. . 166.3
these f. and remain . 198.4

flow-ed-ing
1 *(general)*
happy light is f. . 40.1
peace in endless f. . 74.2
my life f. on . 358.1
life's ebb and f. . 390.1
the dark waters f. . 483.2
so shall my moments f. . 521.3
let them f. in . . . praise . 525.1
its f. may richer . . . be . 621.1
Jordan f. before us . 682.1
from a pure heart f. . 910.3
power, f. through me . c60
b *tears flow*
could my t. for ever f. . 302.2
that t. may never f. . 586.2
f. the sympathising t. . 660.3
2 *(salvation)* *(Rev 22:1)**
whose joys eternal f. . 100.4
it f. from the throne . 252.2
f. for all nations/thee . 252.3
now f. for all men . 298.1
the tide is now f. . 298.6
O precious is the f. . 306.c
cleansing flood will f. . 413.2
cleansed by the crystal f. . 416.1
f. the cleansing river . 471.c
it f. from the throne . 471.c
from the heart of Jesus f. . 539.1
cleansing current f. . 540.2
f. through my soul . 647.3
f. from out the mountain . 762.2
f. by the throne . 891.1, c
where the full tides f. . c137
b *blood flows*
f. the b. that sets us free . 260.1
f. the sin-cleansing b. . 271.2
b. from thy . . . side . . . f. . 302.1
feel his b. f. . 355.4
b. that f. on Calvary . 423.c
cleansed in the b. that f. . 427.c
for the b. is f. there . 434.4
b. for . . . sinner f. . 638.1
the b. f. from his side . 783.2
the precious b. is f. . c8
c *cleansing flow*
let the c., healing f. . 205.1
that constant c. f. . 350.2
I saw the c. f. . 366.c
now I know the c. f. . 375.2
see the c. current f. . 540.2
'neath the c. f. . c198
d *fountain flows*
f., free to all . . . f.. . 115.1
a f. f. divinely clear . 232.2
there's a f. f. . 417.3
f. of life . . . f. eternally . 456.1
healing f., freely f. . 520.3
where the healing f. f. . 777.2
e *grace flows*
I take the g. that f.. . 122.3
g. is f. . . . still it f.. . 239.3
where g. and mercy f. . 257.3
g. and glory . . . f. . 452.4
redeeming g. shall f. . 775.3
while redeeming g. is f. . 893.c
f. *love flows*
sorrow and l. f. . 136.3
l. in its fulness is f.. . 383.3
l. without a limit, f. . 439.1
l. . . . for ever f. free . 496.1
l. must rule . . . f. forth . 522.3
l. like a stream . . . will f.. . 689.3
l. of Jesus freely f.. . 833.1
g *mercy flows*
widely as his m. flows . 17.3
where grace and m. f. . 257.3
streams of boundless m. f. . 261.4
God's m. that is f. . 462.1, 3
all the streams of m. f. . 601.3
h *water flows*
its w. so free are f.. . 252.c
where still w. f. . 341.1
life-giving w. are f. . 383.1
where . . . sweet w. f. . 483.1
where healing w. f. . 590.1
healing w. f. . 647.c
when the w. f. . 647.2
blessing (f), crimson (a), giving (b), honey, river (1b, 2c), stream (2a), water (3e)

flowing *(adjective)*
thou f. water . 2.3
chanting bird and f. fountain . 10.2
thy f. wounds supply . 132.4
in f. wounds appears . 368.2
thee, the ever-f. spring . 559.4

flower
1 (literal)
f. and fruits . 2.4
hearts unfold like f. . 10.1
each little f. that opens . 25.1
vale and tree and f. . 28.2
from f. to bird . 38.3
and f. are blooming . 39.3
sweet birds and sweet f. . 318.1
f. with deeper beauties . 545.2
for fragrant f. growing . 552.2
birds and beasts and f. . 673.2
hundreds . . . millions of f. . 850.2
deep secrets of the f. . 871.2
he paints the wayside f.. . 935.2
2 *(figurative)*
f. of earth and buds . 28.5
but sweet will be the f. . 29.5
pluck the fairest f. . 145.3
where the f. are blooming . 483.1
bud to glorious f. . 577.1
spring to f. . 656.4
with f. bright and fair . 658.1
its fragrant f. glean . 658.5
make my life a little f. . 838.2

my feet for poison f. . . 842.2
beautiful f., fairest . . . c54

b *flowers (in Heaven)*
fair f. of paradise . . . 156.3
where the f. bloom . . 320.c
never-withering f. . . . 898.1

flowery
f. beds of ease . . . 678.2
f. spring 925.2

flown see *fly*

flung see *fling*

flurry c145

flushed-ing
f. with victory . . . 803.1
f. with the courage . . . c238

fly-ing-flown
his praise may thither f. . . 11.1
they f. forgotten . . . 13.5
for my succour f. . . . 123.4
then to Glory I'll f. . . . 137.5
moments f. apace . . . 255.3
the joys of sin are f. . . 267.1
I to the fountain f. . . . 302.3
let the echo f. . . . 382.2
every doubt will f. . . . 396.2
dare not ask to f. . . . 621.4
let me to thy bosom f. . . 737.1
when . . . watchers f. . . 753.2
as the moments f. . . . 754.c
make my pulse f. . . . 780.3
all nations they will f. . . 810.c
f. to the land 886.3
your time is swiftly f. . . 913.1

b *Jer 48:40*
on wings . . . I upward f. . 369.1
on wings . . . souls shall f. . 559.5
on joyful wings . . . f. . . 617.5
f. on the wings of morning . 776.1
on the wings . . . we'll f.. . 819.1
f. above the clouds . . . c134

c *devils fly* *James 4:7*
devils fear and f. . . . 60.1
thy name makes devils f. . 593.3
sees the tempter f. . . 596.3
hell's legions shall f. . . 800.2
makes the foe to f. . . 807.2
sin shall f. before us . . 815.3

d *flag fly*
our f. unhindered f. . . 774.1
f. o'er all the nations . . 777.1
f. o'er lands and seas . . 779.1
her standard proudly f. . . 799.2
our colours still are f. . . 800.1
red and blue shall f. . . c240
keep the old f. f. . . . c242

foaming 569.2

foe
a *foes (of God)*
God is stronger than his f. . 9*
in spite of his f. . . . 137.4
triumph o'er his f. . . . 148.c
all his f. shall quell . . . 164.5
drive thy f. from . . . soul . 440.2
with thee 'gainst thy f. . . 532.2
strength thy f. to slay . . 575.3
f. of God around us . . 778.1
till the f. of God . . . 864.4

b
still our ancient f. . . . 1.1
in presence of my f. . . 54.4
king to slay their f. . . . 91.1
war with the f. of truth . . 373.3
f. at every hand I meet . . 400.2
to f. without . . . within. . 468.1
he drives my f. away . . 495.3
than the f. which assail . . 537.2
f. are bending . . . 593.3
will not desert to its f. . . 653.5
the f. must be driven . . 681.2
f. may surround us . . 681.2
the f. we defy . . . 681.3
routing the f. in fear . . 686.4
f. before us falling . . . 693.3
strong to meet the f. . . 698.2
sin is our challenged f. . . 705.1
the scorn of my f. . . . 758.3
never from the f. retreating . 778.3
near when f. appear . . 798.3
thy f. shall be . . . hurled . 799.4
cunning f. to overthrow . . 801.1
makes the f. to fly . . . 807.2
we'll put the f. to flight . . 810.1
let the f. advance . . . 818.3
scattered the f. . . . 820.2
fierce our f. 937.2

c *(Rom 16:20)*
beneath my feet . . . my f. . 401.2

d *all foes*
rescues us from all our f. . 17.3
smile at all thy f. . . . 157.1
till all his f. submit . . . 164.4
he all his f. shall quell . . 164.5
all our f. we . . . dare . . 722.4
f. all unite 763.1
f. all subdued . . . 813.4

e *face foe*
no f. for me to f. . . . 678.3
thy f. to the f. . 684.c/689.*
who will f. the f. . . . 707.1

f *foe (friend)*
treat their f. as brothers . . 50.2
f. shall be friend . . . 166.3
friends and f. despise . . 482.3
friend of all—the f. . . 491.2
f. may hate and friends . . 498.4
friends . . . fail, and f. . . 763.1
f. beset and friends . . 780.2
f. may scoff and friends . . 790.2

g *against the foe*
strive afresh a. their f. . . 18.3
a. the f. to march . . . 432.2
we are with thee g. thy f. . 532.2
leads a. the f. . . . 690.1
a. unnumbered f. . . . 699.2
to battle g. the f. . . . 789.2
live for thee g. every f. . . 933.3

h *no foe*
let no f. . . . arrest . . . 433.3
I fear no f. 670.4
no f. for me to face . . 678.3
no f. shall stay . . . 685.2
not a f. . . . confound . . 822.2

i *strong foe*
although our f. be s. . . . 9.1
f. seems fierce and s. . . 169.3
s. are the f. that round . . 176.2
though mighty the f. . . 703.2
s. may be the f. . . . 707.4
mighty is the f. . . . 787.3
our f. may be mighty . . 820.3

conquer (2d), every (b), near (1b), prevail (e), refuge, thousand (2b)

foil 670.3

fold
watching o'er their f. . . 72.2
f. him in your comfort . . 792.1
f. them to my bosom . . 797.2

b *John 10:16*
wolves devour thy f. . . 172.5
peace of thy sheltering f. . 300.4
wandering . . . f. of God . 313.3
call into thy f. of peace . . 630.2
from the f. has strayed . . 740.1
as lambs to his f. . . . 794.1
the Shepherd and the f. . . 829.3
for our use thy f. . . . 845.1
I would enter the f. . . 883.1

c *brought to fold* *Jer 23:3*
he b. us to his f. . . . 4.2
to his f. . . . b. us . . . 377.2
with his sheep securely f. . 954.1
grace that b. me to the f. . c218

d *fold-ed (re cloth)*
kept the f. grave clothes. . 152.1
fight beneath its f. . . . 774.1
its f. hung over me . . 774.3
f. lies the blood and fire . . 774.4

folk 71.c

follow-ed-ing
1 *(God) follows*
his love still f. you . . . 44.1
light that f. all my way . . 621.2

b *Ps 23:6*
shall surely f. me . . . 54.5

2 *(we) follow*
a *(general)*
to f. the star 90.3
more to f. . . . . 418.*
peace which f. after . . 719.3
into the city I'd f. . . . 848.4
reading it, and f. . . . 856.2
long patience f. toil . . 923.2
when cruel death did f. . . c14
f. the flag c228

b *(spiritual)*
f. truth as he knew . . 27.6
f. our exalted head . . 143.5
fire that f. 197.2
if I find him, if I f. . . 228.4
let me hear and I will f. . . 502.2
love . . . will f. . . . 503.3
thine to f. to the end . . 510.c
mine to f. . . . blindly . . 510.2
none other dare I f. . . 529.1
guide us as we f. . . . 595.2
that I may f. faster. . . 614.2
still to f. every word . . 614.4
f. in his/their train . . . 701.*
freely f. his commands . . 732.2
f. the light of his word . . 734.1
just to trust and f. him . . 755.2
him to f. without fear . . 772.5
f. where the Saviour goes . 776.1
we too will f., f. . . . 776.3
may we f. fearlessly . . 789.5
delaying not to f. . . . 805.2
a cross to f. bravely . . 868.1
giving up my all to f. . . c35
f. a purposeful aim . . . c173
very narrow but I'll f. . . c205

c *follow (lead)*
where Christ has l., f. . . 143.5
and f. where I l. . . . 277.4
where he l. me I will f. . . 321.3
l. me I would f. on . . 483.1, c
he'll l. and I will f. . . . 491.c
where Jesus l. I'll f. . . 687.c
f. closely where . . . l. . . 740.c
f. where Christ l. . . . 805.2
f. boldly where . . . l. . . 944.2
where he l. me I will f. . . c57
I'll f. where he l. . . . c180

d *follow footsteps* *1 Peter 2:21*
I would f. in thy f. . . . 470.3
in thy steps I will f. . . 473.c
f. the f. of the Lord . . 580.2
and his f. f. still . . . 731.c
if I try to f. his f. . . . 840.2
f. thy f., ever unafraid . . 859.3
in his steps we f. . . . 866.c
I will f. in the f. . . . c205

e *follow Jesus*
they f. J. in the light . . . 5.2
the next to f. J. . . . 278.*
I love to f. J. 320.2
still f. thy Lord . . . 458.3
f., I will f. J. 483.c
take up thy cross and f.. . 490.2
in constancy f. the Master . 685.1
we f. J., Son of God . . 705.1
f. our conquering Saviour . 800.2
f. J. all the way . . . 817.c
f. J. gladly 817.2
f. their incarnate God . . 879.4
f. J. day by day . . . c26
joy in f. J. c206

f *'follow me'* *Matt 4:19; 16:24*
take up thy cross and f.. . 275.3
he says: F. m. . . . 276.4
Christian, f. m. . . . 428.1
take up thy cross and f.. 490.1, 2
f. thou me, he calls . . 680.c
leave . . . nets and f. m.. . 680.3
fishers of men if you f. . . c232

g *follow thee* *Matt 8:19*
I f. him to f. t. . . . 449.c
untired, I'll f. t. . . . 453.3
to f. t. unblamable . . . 455.3
Saviour, I will f. t. . . . 473.c
I'll f. t., of life 490.c
from this hour I'll f. t. . . 490.2
all to leave, and f. t. . . 498.1
f. t., my Saviour . . . 498.c
lowly manger I will f. t. . . 499.2
where'er . . . to f. t. . . 509.1
bids us f. t. 788.1
to all who f. t. . . . 862.4
give me grace to f. . . 862.4
reckon on me f. t. . . . c49
from this hour will f. t. . . c109

h *follow on* *Hos 6.3*
drew me, and I f. o. . . 365.3
my soul doth f. o. . . . 448.1
he leads me I . . . f. o. . 483.1, c
Jesus leads I'll f. o. . . 687.c
rise (3c)

follower
his faithful f. I will be. . . 725.c
trembling f. as well . . 893.3
f. of the dying God . . 909.1
b *Rev 14:4*
f. of the Lamb . . . 678.1

folly
all my blindness and f. . . 288.3
from f.'s charm . . . 401.2
turn from sin and f. . . 704.4
pride, and worldly f. . . 783.4
in the broad road of f. . . 905.1

fond-ly
name I f. love to hear . . 68.3
of pride or f. desire . . 425.2
perish every f. ambition . . 498.2
these f. pursuits . . . 509.2
still lie f. dreaming . . 693.1

food
with f. celestial feedeth . . 53.2
bitter . . . medicine f. . . 712.4
f. for thy children . . . 927.3
life, our health, our f. . . 935.3
b *1 Tim 6:8*
having f. and clothing . . 921.2

foolish
f. fears of what may come . 41.2
perverse and f. oft . . . 53.3
f. hearts! why . . . wander . 265.1
forgive our f. ways . . 567.1
b *1 Cor 2:14*
we were that f. thing . . 163.2

foot
1 *(verb)* 716.1
2 *(noun)* see *feet*

footprints
I saw thy f. on my road . . 59.1
see thy f., Lord . . . 628.1

footsteps
walking in his f. . . . 483.1
in all thy f. tread . . . 568.3
follows the f. of the Lord . 580.2
with quickened f. . . . 599.3
our f. guideth . . . 655.1
still in Jesus' f. tread . . 659.2
f. that he trod . . . 879.4
wandering f. guide . . 918.3
gently leading on our f. . . 938.1
in the Master's f. . . . c195
follow in the f. of my Lord . c205
b *Ps 77:19*
plants his f. in the sea . . 29.1
follow (2d)

footstool *Ps 99:5**
before his f. leave it . . 420.2
see me at thy f. bow . . 440.1
to bring to thy f. . . . 786.4
still to his f. in prayer . . 794.2

forbear
his wrath f. 286.1
if the preacher f. . . . 527.2

forbid-den
f. that man's achievements . 6.2
death in vain f. his rise . . 143.3
f. me not thy service . . 522.1
love . . . f. me to think . . 712.3
Father's love f. all fear . . 926.3
f. that we despise it . . 944.2
b *Mark 10:14*
gracious Lord, f. it not . . 793.2
c *Gal 6:14*
f. it, Lord, . . . boast . . 136.2

forbidden 630.2

force
1 *(noun)*
the atom's hidden f. . . 38.2
evil f. seem . . . sway . . 171.1
'gainst the f. of sin . . 687.1
when our invading f. . . 705.2
Kingdom cometh not by f. . 705.3
where earthly f. fail . . 744.2
Hell's f. may be mighty . . 810.2
b *Matt 11:12*
Kingdom . . . it takes by f. . 742.2
2 *(verb)*
they f. me to wrong . . 298.3
f. me to thy breast . . . 307.1
f. me to render . . . sword . 508.1

fording 388.1

foreboding 566.2

forefathers 158.1

forehead
cruel thorns his f. . . . 96.3
b *Rev 7:3*
thy seal in my f. to wear. . 589.3

foremost 909.1

foreseeing 877.2

forest
field and f., vale . . . 10.2
woods and f. glades . . 37.2

foretaste
glorious f. here below . . 46.4
what a f. of glory . . . 310.1

foretold *Acts 3:24*
prophets long ago f. . . 72.4
by prophet bards f. . . 83.3

forever—see *ever*

forfeit
f. your soul 273.4
gladly I'll f. all . . . 623.1
what peace we often f. . . 645.1

forged 874.1

forget-ing-forgot-ten
1 *(we) forget*
fly f. as a dream . . . 13.5
for I f. so soon . . . 98.2
lest I f. . . . . . 117.*
canst thou . . . f. the mercy . 250.3
f. in nothing his blessing . 458.1
giving, and f. the gift . . 491.2
I shall f. the weary days. . 551.2
they f. the mighty God . . 559.2
sun, moon and stars f. . . 617.5
though we may f. them . . 928.1
f. how hard the way . . c208
b *never forget*
O let me n. f. 42.3
day I will n. f. . . . 371.1
I n. shall f. the day. . . 401.1
n. once f. be 865.3
c *Gen 41:51*
I f. all time and toil. . . 636.2
d *Ps 137:5*
let my hand f. her skill . . 573.5
f. to beat, if I f. . . . 573.5
2 *(God) forgets*
don't assume that God's f. . 44.1
b *Isa 49:15*
he will not f. you . . . c122
he cannot f. me . . . c125

forgetful *Isa 49:15* . . . 110.3

forgetfulness c190

forgive-n-ing
1 *(God) forgives*
thou art giving and f. . . 10.3
Father in love f. . . . 50.c
me f.! I instant cry . . . 122.3
Father clears, and cries: f. . 127.4
thy love f. 146.3
learn how freely he'll f. . . 256.3
f. all my blindness . . . 288.3
f., and bid me sin no more . 305.3
Jesus lives and f. . . . 420.3
f. our foolish ways . . . 567.1
f. me, Lord . . . the ill . . 671.2
f. if I should roam . . . 675.3
he will f. if . . . believe . . 691.2
Saviour's goodness who f. . 835.1
b *1 Kings 8:30*
when thou hearest . . . f. . 945.2
c *Matt 6:12*
f. our sins as we f.. . . 572.1
trespasses, O Lord, f. . . 624.3
d *Mark 2:7*
none can f. but thee . . 486.1
e *Luke 23:34*
f. him, O f., they cry . . 106.3
f.! I hear thee plead . . 122.3
f. them. Father, O f. . . 140.1
heard him pray, F. them . . 548.2
f *forgiven (passive)*
healed, restored, f. . . 17.1
all thy people are f. . . 109.2

that we might be f. . . . 133.3
another soul f. . . . 259.4
f., he lifted me . . . 339.2
past was long f. . . . 434.3
all may be washed and f. . 535.1
by his grace f. . . . 740.c
all who are washed and f. . 794.2

g *sins forgiven* *1 John 1:9*
souls redeemed, for s. f. . 15.5
your many s. may be f. . . 67.2
my s. in Christ f. . . . 207.3
peace, the seal of s. f. . . 210.4
do you know your s. f. . . 243.2
s.-f. Saviour . . . 257.4
faithful and just . . . f. . . 296.4
I know my s. are all f. . . 360.3
my s. are all f. . . . 361.2
I knew my s. f. . . . 366.1
though you know your s. f. . 433.3
all my s. thou hast f. . . 477.2
f. our s. as we f. . . . 572.1
their many s. he will f. . . 814.1
who knows his s. f. . . 880.1
must have your s. f. . . 913.1
yet he will thy s. f.. . . c3
f. is all s. c106
f. my s. and bearing all . c219

h *Luke 7:47*
love I much? I'm much f. . 634.2

ready (b), transgression (b)

2 *(we) forgive*
love is bearing and f. . . 544.4
forgive our sins as we f.. . 572.1
loving f., tender . . . 623.2

forgiveness
laid in f. on one bowed . . 129.3
free f. are for thee . . . 225.4
breathe f. o'er us . . . 607.2

forgo 436.2

forgot-ten see *forget*

forlorn
my guilt and grief, f. . . 339.3
to the outcast and f. . . 697.5

form
deep thunder-clouds f. . . 16.2
by thy bleeding f. . . . 138.3
very dying f. of one . . 476.2
if thy f. we cannot see . . 558.2
the simplest f. of speech . 625.3
his sacred f. would rest . . 663.2
we could not see thy f. . . 938.3

b *Gen 2:7*
f. us men 4.2
works . . . thou hast f. . . 39.1
f. thee for his own . . . 157.1

c *(Eph 2:10)*
when . . . I am f. again . . 407.6

former 167.2

forsake-ing-n/forsook
1 *(God) forsakes Josh 1:5; Heb 13:5*
never . . . cross f. me . . 112.2
never . . . f. me here . . 344.3
I'll never . . . never f. . . 653.5
God never yet f. . . . 738.3
never once . . . f. me . . 762.3
he never will f. me . . . 840.2

b *Matt 27:46*
God-f. loneliness . . . 122.2
lonely, f., our sinbearer . . 130.4

2 *(we) forsake*
when bereft. f. . . . 222.2
worldly honours all f. . . 320.2
though all the world f. me . 344.2
all I must f. . . . 434.2

though I be despised, f. . . 498.1
though all the world f. . . 498.c
selfish aims do we f. . . 532.1
for the lonely and f. . . 555.2
do thy friends despise, f. . 645.3
will no more our God f. . . 784.3
I see f. children . . . 830.1
tempted to f. his God . . 911.3
pleasures we'll f. . . . 912.2

b *forsake all* *Matt 19:27*
I all on earth f. . . . 223.2
I've all for him f. . . . 344.2
worldly pleasures all f. . . 474.2

c *Isa 55:7*
every evil way f. . . . 502.2
sin's dark ways f. . . . 788.1

fort
storm the f. of darkness. . 696.c
hold the f. 804.c

forth *nc, but*
go (2d), lead (3e), show (2d)

forthtell 856.1

forthwith 93.5

fortify 695.3

fortitude
grant thy f. and courage . 576.3
finding f. and grace . . 595.2

fortress *2 Sam 22.2**
a mighty f. is our God . . 1.1
my secret f. 631.2
thou wast their . . . f. . . 876.2

forward
f.! be our watchword . . . 682.1
f. to the fight . . . 693.c
f., O ye sons of God . . 696.2
onward, f., shout . . . 698.c
earnest looking f. . . . 765.4
f. with the sword . . . 809.3
then f. to the conflict . . 814.3
f., 'tis the Lord's . . . 817.3
f., O youth 864.3

b *go forward*
command to go f. . . . 321.3
I'll boast and f. go . . . 521.3
f. . . . see his banners go . 690.1
he who bids us f. go . . 772.1
f. go the lost to save . . 814.2
go marching f. . . . 817.3
you'll wish you'd gone f. . 893.2

march (2c)

fought see *fight*

foul-est
can make the f. clean . . 64.4
f., I to the fountain fly . . 302.3
can make the f. clean . . 471.1
from sin's f. corruption . . 499.1
make the f. sinner clean. . 700.2

found see *find*

foundation
Hell's f. quiver . . . 690.2
when earth's f. melt . . 746.5

b *2 Tim 2:19*
firmly shall thy f. stand . . 873.4
to thee, the sure f. . . . 944.1

c *Rev 13:8*
before the world's f. . . 746.1

lay (1d)

founded
a *Ps 102:25*
thy power hath f. of old. . 16.3

b *Matt 7:25*
on the rock of ages f. . . 157.1
f. on the rock of ages . . 833.3

fount-ain
1
thy clouds which are f. . . 8.2
chanting bird and flowing f. . 10.2
heart's deep f. springs . . 749.1

2 *[re salvation]* *Zech 13:1*
a f. filled with blood . . 132.1
crystal bright f. . . . 139.2
invites you to the f. . . 239.2
its f. are deep . . . 252.2
I know a f. 257.c
from the f.-head . . . pure . 277.3
foul, I to the f. fly . . . 302.3
no other f. I know . . . 306.c
plunged into the f. . . . 309.1
thou F. of every blessing . 313.1
come to this f., so rich . . 315.4
I am drinking at the f. . . 320.1
come to the f. today . . 331.4
living in the f. . . . 352.1
a f. ever springing . . . 358.3
blood now fills the f. . . 413.1
plunge in the f. . . . 427.2
led . . . to f. of love . . 458.4
wash . . . in Calvary's f.. . 593.4
in that healing f. . . . 647.3
f. of light and love . . . 651.1
f. of heavenly grace . . 654.1
I'm living in the f. . . . 811.c
Christ! He is the f. . . . 896.2
of light and wisdom the f. . c98
disappeared in the f. . . c189

b *living fountain* *Rev 7:17*
now a l. f. see . . . 261.3
march to see the l. f. . . 902.4
to the l. f. lead . . . 909.3

c *precious fountain*
there a p. f., free . . . 115.1
O p. f. that saves . . . 315.3
where the p. f. springs . . 348.3
p. f. which to open . . . 439.3

d *(Ps 42:1)*
hart that panteth for the f. . 762.2

e *fountain of life* *Rev 21:6*
the f. of l. unsealèd . . 456.1
thou, Lord, of l. the f. . . 601.1
thou f. of l., thou light . . 602.1
thou of l. the f. art . . . 737.4

f *Jer 2:13*
the f.-head of bliss . . . 497.3

flow (2d), open (c), see (3e)

fragment c32

fragrance
their f. ever sweet . . . 156.3
f. of purity 383.1
nothing . . . keep the f. . . 591.2

fragrant
thank you . . . f. flowers. . 552.2
its f. flowers glean . . . 658.5

frail *Ps 39:4*
f. children of dust . . . 16.5
my f., inconstant heart . . 517.1
f. am I 762.1

frailties 288.2

frame
1 *(noun)*
a calm and heavenly f. . . 442.1
calm and serene my f. . . 442.6

the sweetest f. . . . 745.1
arrow pierced his f. . . 890.2
know (1d)
2 *(verb)*
nor heart can f. 61.2
whose love designs to f. . 944.1

frank 618.1

frankincense *Matt 2:11* . . 90.5

fraught 725.1

fray
first to battle in the f. . . 400.2
lead us forth into the f. . . 769.3
fit us for the f. . . . 787.1
send us . . . into the f. . . 789.2
marching to the f. . . . 817.1
trusting in the battle's f.. . c119

free
1 *(people) free*
that we might be f. . . 174.3
I stand both pure and f. . . 176.1
firmly bound, for ever f. . . 194.3
a f. and pardoned slave . . 303.4
thou, too, shalt be f. . . 304.c
happy and f. 321.c
Jesus bids me go f. . . 322.1
bliss of the f. 364.1
every sinner may be f. . . 381.2
dying our souls to f. . . 383.2
spotless and f. . . . 416.1
shout and be f. . . . 427.3
why not now be f. . . . 471.4
then I shall be f. . . . 508.1
lowly paths of service f.. . 519.1
I am from bondage f. . . 546.2
just as f. as Heaven . . 546.2
the anthem of the f. . . 550.c
step more firm and f. . . 614.2
my path to life is f.. . . 736.3
f. each sin-bound slave . . 775.2
valiant, f. and strong . . 803.2
grace . . . and power to f. . 845.3
ever serving, ever f. . . 846.4
young, strong and f. . . 860.3
now in Jesus I am f. . . c149
ransomed me, I am f. . . c157
grace that keeps me f. . . c164
bless . . . name, I'm f. . . c189
b *free heart/soul*
thy s. he waits to f. . . 253.1
fell off, my h. was f. . . 283.3
gone and my s. is f. . . 317.c
to find my s. was f. . . 348.2
my s. was f. at last . . 366.2
dying our s. to f. . . . 383.2
to loyal h. and f. . . . 423.5
my f. s. may run the race . 449.3
with a glad h. and f. . . 505.1
f. our h. to faith . . . 577.2
thy s. shall be f. . . . 739.1
other s. to f. 788.c
c *make free John 8:32, 36; Gal 5:1**
m. me glad and f. . . . 32.2
reign again to m. men f.. . 63.2
let us live to m. men f. . . 162.4
paid the debt and m. me f. . 180.c
lead . . . and m. me f. . . 419.3
cleansed and m. f. . . . 427.4
m. my spirit f. . . . 441.c
that m. thy children f. . . 485.4
thou hast m. me f. . . . 529.1
Jesus m. me f. indeed . . 546.2
till thou hast m. us f. . . 662.3
thou hast m. us f. . . . 707.3
where Christ m. f. . . . 757.5
salvation m. us f. . . . 815.c
loyal service m. me f. . . 867.6
d *set free* *Luke 4:18*
he sets the prisoner f. . . 64.4
sets everybody f. . . . 71.c
come, Lord, to set me f. . 123.4
now he sets me f. . . . 132.c
for service sets me f. . . 178.1
from the curse to s. me f. . 180.1
by the fire set f. . . . 197.3
that I might be set f. . . 221.2
the blood that set us f. . . 260.1
from my guilt, O set me f. . 292.6
I long to be set f. . . . 307.3
the Saviour set me f. . . 328.1
snapped . . . and set me f. . 347.c
power has set me f. . . 389.2
him who s. the prisoner f. . 400.3
he will set you f. . . . 403.3
break . . . now set me f.. . 450.1
burst . . . and set it f. . . 453.1
the blessing that s. me f. . 542.2
set my conscience f. . . 563.3
the fight to set men f. . . 577.4
Jesus alone can set f. . . 708.4
from every fear set f. . . 749.2
healing, cleansing, s. f. . . 777.3
saved us, set us f. . . . 788.1
the captives are set f. . . 832.2
all's well, he sets me f. . . 960
bless his name, he s. me f. . c149
now he sets me f. . . . c174
the power that sets us f. . c199
e *set [soul] free*
thy s. to set f. . . . 276.3
set my sad heart f.. . . 282.2
and set my spirit f.. . . 297.4
set my shackled spirit f.. . 303.1
happy . . . heart is set f.. . 372.2
set my longing spirit f. . . 480.2
break . . . set my soul f.. . 501.1
suffer my soul to set f. . . 543.1
f *set free from sin* *Rom 6:18*
from s. have set me f. . . 23.4
from s. to set me f. . . 45.1
is from s. set f. . . . 62.3
from s. may be set f. . . 69.2
from s. he'll set thee f. . . 260.3
witness, from all s. set f. . 407.6
from every s. set f. . . 415.1
a heart from s. set f. . . 444.1
from s. . . . shame set f.. . 447.3
all stains of s. set f. . . 536.1
hearts from s. set f. . . 561.4
all . . . from s. set f. . . 932.4
now from s. set f. . . . c150
g *free from*
f. sacredness be f. . . . 7.4
f. us f. all ills 12.2
f. all . . . you are f. . . 73.2
f. men f. remorse . . . 102.2
f. . . . sting thy servants f. . 151.5
f. its penalty I'm f. . . . 188.1
f. all . . . passions f. . . 210.3
would you be f. f. . . . 281.2
he f. me f. them all . . 337.3
f. my soul f. danger . . 361.1
f. self I am not f. . . . 434.3
f. all pollution f. . . . 445.2
calm and f. f. care . . . 556.2
f. harm . . . children f. . . 674.3
keeps us f. f. doubting . . 700.3
his hosts f. f. care . . . 708.1
f. us f. our . . . chain . . 803.3
f. . . . selfishness are f. . . 833.1
f. f. the fret 878.3
f. f. the blight/doubts . . 889.2
f. sorrow . . . are f. . . 908.2
thy word, f. error f. . . 941.3
to f. the captive . . . c25
h *free from sin* *Rom 6:18*
f. s. and sorrow f. . . . 69.4
f. f. s.'s alloy 76.3
f. s. we might be f. . . 128.1
f. s. . . . pure and f. . . 235.c
f. f. your burden of s. . . 281.1
f. me f. s. that long . . 349.3
when f. all s. . . . f. me . . 457.2
s. we shall be f. . . . 660.5
f. f. the power of s. . . 857.3
f. s. be ever f. . . . 861.3
f. s. and sorrow f. . . . 897.2
f. f. sorrow, . . . s.. . . 924.4
f. f. the power of s. . . c152
f. f. . . . sense of s. . . c157
i *free to all*
he offers f. to all . . . 46.1
f. to a., a healing stream . 115.1
all the world . . . go f. . . 128.4
f. to all who thither go . . 261.4
to all . . . just as f.. . . 329.3
salvation f. to all men . . 810.3
we all may be f. . . . 881.3
j *Gal 3:28**
for bond and f. . . . 261.3
k *Gal 4:31*
the land of the f.-born . . 895.1
bondage (b), indeed (b), people (2b)
2 *(other)*
light . . . bountiful and f. 40.1
f. and faithful, strong . . 110.4
hands no more were f. . . 129.1
love for every sinner f. . . 140.5
as the air . . . as f.. . . 230.3
wondrous, rich and f. . . 250.1
its waters so f. . . . 252.c
flows for all nations f. . . 252.3
blood . . . so rich and f.. . 295.4
so rich and so f. . . . 298.1
wonderful, matchless and f. . 319.1
flowing so f. for you . . 413.c
waters rich and f. . . . 439.1
life is lovely, f. . . . 544.1
abundant, enduring and f. . 553.1
beautiful are they and f.. . 555.3
strong, changeless, f. . . 571.3
f. and changeless . . . 764.1
Christ . . . rich and f. . . c146
b *free grace* *Rom 3:24*
g. for all is rich and f. . . 239.1
be saved, his g. is f. . . 259.c
so f., so infinite his g. . . 283.2
his g. so rich and f. . . 403.2
g. was f.. . . . . 405.c
thy g., so rich and f. . . 470.1
g. for every sinner f. . . 533.3
what matchless g. . . . f. . 831.2
c *free mercy*
God's f. m. streameth . . 40.2
'tis m. all, immense and f. . 283.2
in thy m., rich and f. . . 538.3
f., boundless m. cries . . 746.2
call for m. full and f. . . 802.3
d *free [salvation]*
purchased . . . pardon f.. . 125.1
f. forgiveness are for . . 225.4
s. . . . abundant, f. . . 254.2
chorus of f. redemption . . 278.3
bring thy f. s. nigh . . . 291.1
Jesus spoke a pardon f.. . 402.2
life and s. are f. . . . 535.1
s.! for every sinner f. . . 781.2
s. f. to all men . . . 810.3
many found s. f. . . . 939.2
full (b, i), gift (2d)

freedom
in f. I rejoice 48.2
have we a name for f. . . 71.1
f. shall flourish . . . 166.3
rose again to bring us f.. . 242.c
into thy f., gladness . . 300.1
he can f. bestow . . . 329.2
f., friends and health . . 492.3
your bondage is f. . . . 506.2

I walk in your f. 506.5
f. to serve I crave 571.4
my f. I'll use 640.3
f. in service . . . find 744.3
f. we proclaim 866.2
place of f. from care c67

b *freedom from sin*
f. here from s.'s dominion 433.3
the f. from all sin 471.1
f. from self, from . . . sin 541.2
cleansing and f. from sin 610.3
speak of its f. from sin 904.3

freely
1 *(re divine)*
he f. suffers in our stead 108.2
souls are f. welcome here 254.2
flowing f. from Calvary 383.1
so f. spilt for me 444.1
thy blood shed so f. 469.2
f. flows at love's command 520.3
f. his blood is applied 535.4
f. flows from sea to sea 833.1
f. by thy bounty 921.2

b *Hos 14:4*
f. my backslidings heal 305.2

c *Rom 3:24*
mercy he f. offers thee 255.c
how f. he'll forgive 256.3
grace . . . did f. move 307.2
mercy bestowing f. 383.3
f. Jesus pardoned me 403.2
f. he his grace bestows 418.3
justified, f. for ever c185

d *freely give* *Rom 8:32; Rev 21:6*
f. . . . thou g. all 15.3
to our race so f. g. 28.5
his salvation f. g. 74.3
he the ransom f. g. 180.2
thy blood was f. g. 221.2
all so f. g. 258.2
to him I f. g. 277.1
behold I f. g. 332.2
love he so f. hath g. 373.4
grace . . . hast f. g. 603.3
whose life was f. g. 631.1

2 *(human)*
f. all I give to thee 201.3
f. make him our choice 235.2
all to him I f. give 474.1
f. give up all the rest 480.5
it cannot f. move 508.2
f. follow his commands 732.2

b *Matt 10:8*
f. all to Christ I bring 514.3

c *Rev 22:17*
f. let me take of thee 737.4

freeman *1 Cor 7:22*
he was the f., bound 130.1
a f., once a slave 571.4

fresh
f. courage take 29.3
f. from the Word 35.1
it flows as f. as ever 239.3
peace of Christ makes f. 358.3
my days f. triumphs win 413.4
f. covenant to make 534.3
shall drink a f. supply 559.4
f. from converse 564.4
f. and solemn splendour 632.2
arise pure and f. 673.4
f. lips are making 677.4
peace, f. and sweet 751.2
pledge a f. allegiance 777.4
f. converts still we gain 815.3

freshening 669.2

freshness 277.3

fret-ed-ing *Ps 37:1**
so shall each fear, each f. 7.4
little cares which f. me 41.1
scarred by daily f. 129.2
bear . . . the f. of care 519.1
f. ghosts of vain regret 551.2
the f. of mortal years 878.3

friend
1 *(divine)*
my best, my only f. 14.1
redeemer and f. 16.5
thank thee, dearest f. 123.3
my wise and constant f.. 144.3
to the f. who died 259.2
f. before the throne 305.1
as a f. he can cheer 329.2
f., of friends the fairest 343.1
would you gain this f. 343.3
tender, compassionate f. 371.1
f. will never leave 377.1
condescend to be my f. 398.c
be the living God my f. 464.4
he is my f. 491.c
be companion, f. 576.1
our Master and our f. 590.4
Jesus! that dear f. 592.2
pardoner . . . f. indeed 600.1
O F. of mine 600.2
a f. of Jesus when . . . 709.*
my everlasting f. 714.4
be a f. to me 842.1
f. of the young 860.1
my Master and my f. 862.1, 4
faithful, unchangeable f. 962
my great unchanging f. c163
mine, this f. so dear c167

b *no other friend*
n. o. f. so keen . . . quick 246.2
n. o. f. can read 325.3
n. o. f. to help 857.2
not a f. like . . . Jesus c182

c *friend/Saviour* *John 15:13*
all to be my S. and my f. 52.3
'tis because my f. and S. 404.5
he is my S. and my f. 728.4
he is our maker, S., f. 785.6
wonderful S., wonderful f. c251

d *friend of sinners* *Matt 11:19*
came to be the s.'s f. 225.3
strong f. of s. 282.2
s.'s changeless f. 282.3
from the s.'s dying f. 634.1
publishing the s.'s f. 720.4
Jesus is the s.'s f. 814.1

e *friend of Jesus* *John 15:15*
never a f. like J. 246.c
J. is a f. of mine 326.1
found a f. in J. 344.1
found a f. in J. 377.3
what a f. . . . in J. 645.1
who hast called me f. 675.3
name of Christ, your f. 694.2
a f. of J.! . . . bliss 709.1
J. is a f. of mine 709.c
J., f. of . . . children 842.1
we are the f. of Christ 851.5
never-failing f. is Christ c146
he is my f. indeed c151

find (2f) guide (b) loving (1d)

2 *(human)*
peace . . . f. most dear 31.2
earthly f. may fail 377.1
make f. of God's children 458.1
thy f. . . . shall see. 458.2
freedom, f. and health 492.3
boy and girl, and f. 544.4
f. holds fellowship 573.3
commune as f. with f. 585.3
do thy f. despise 645.3
old f., old scenes 668.3
world a f. to grace 678.3
prove a f. indeed 706.2
though . . . f. be gone 746.4
to hail the f. 855.5
my life, my f. . . . leave 917.1
sister, child and f. 938.4
into your soul, my f. c223

b *friends [in Heaven]*
f. on earth, and f. above. 28.4
f. severed now 146.2
I shall not lose my f. 880.4
f. I shall see 881.2
think of the f. over there 886.2
and f. are at rest 886.3
with departed f. to stay 902.2
f. will be there 906.3
all our f. we'll see 912.3

c *John 15:13*
for his f. to die 515.3

foe (f)

friendless 491.2

friendly 662.1

friendship
f. of Jesus will never 273.2
in him perfect f. indeed 553.4
perfect love and f. 660.5
f. with Jesus 709.c
when other f. cease 709.2
his f. is so wonderful 851.5
f. forged . . . purified 874.1

frighten-ed
a crowd of f. sheep 265.1
dangers cannot f. me 483.2
coward's soul may f. 805.2
f. us from the shore 898.3

from *nc, but*
a *from . . . to*
f. death t. life 180.4
f. depth t. height reply 187.4
f. the uttermost t. 249.c
f. Glory t. Calvary 319.3
f. shades . . . t. plains 339.c
f. glory into glory 438.3
f. height t. height 641.3
f. morn till eve 676.3
f. strength t. strength 695.6
f. victory unto victory 699.1
on f. door t. door 802.1
f. darkness into l. 821.2
flows f. sea t. sea 833.1
f. the dawn till . . . sun 907.3
near f. first t. last 938.2

age (1b) day (2f) east pole

front
battle's f. I love 362.3
to the f.! 702.*
battle f. increases 864.4

frontiers 864.4

frown-ing
behind a f. providence 29.4
never a murmur . . . a f.. 388.3
not a f. nor a cross 397.3
sometimes all f. 468.1
smile and not f. 801.c

fruit
1 *(literal)*
flowers and f. . . . grow. 2.4
ripe f. in the garden 25.3
the precious f. await 923.2
gather f. from tree 926.3
f. of the orchard 927.1
the f. thy generous soil 933.1

b *Ps 107:37*
f. unto his praise 924.2

2 *(spiritual)*
celestial f. 314.3
whose f. do feed . . . 346.3
f. of . . . hour of prayer . . 633.3
gain . . . the f. of prayer. . 646.4
f. of today 675.2
f. that never fail . . . 887.3

b *bear fruit* *John 15:2*
may I b. much f. in thee. . 538.5
test . . . what f. we b. . . 926.4
f. they must b. . . . 928.1

c *John 15:16*
let our gracious f. . . . 533.4

d *Rom 6:22*
rich f. of holiness . . . 936.3

e *Gal 5:22; Eph 5:9*
f. of love and joy . . . 198.4
f. of truth and goodness . 408.2
Spirit whose f. is love . . 561.1
the f. of the Spirit . . . c46

first (1b)

fruitful *(Col 1:10)*
for the f. years . . . 5.2
strong and fair and f. . . 159.4
burden of the f. vine . . 512.3
the f. summers . . . 552.2
f., if in Christ abiding . . 764.2
f. ears to store . . . 924.3
f. the land 927.4
seasons in f. order move . 929.1
all f. in good work . . . 933.1

fruition 885.3

fruitless
f. . . . way of my choosing . 501.2
no word . . . can f. fall . . 558.5

frustrate-d *Gal 2:21*
longings . . . have been f. . 760.3
must not God's plan f. . . 801.2

fulfil-l-ed-ing
its mighty energies f. . . 38.2
hope can see f. . . . 39.4
within my heart . . . f. . . 138.1
f. thy love's . . . plan . . 167.3
intention I would f. . . 294.2
die f. thy commands . . 362.2
thy pleasure . . . to f. . . 422.2
your tasks to f. . . . 506.2
my heart f. its vow . . 524.1
f. thy Church's story . . 577.1
his demands I would f. . . 867.1
hopes . . . stand f. . . . 868.2

b *Ps 20:4*
f. thy sovereign counsel . . 526.3

c *Col 4:17*
my calling to f. . . . 472.2

d *fulfil promise*
the p. . . . wilt in me f. . . 419.2
every p. is f. if faith . . 423.5
in me thy p., Lord, f. . . 446.4
thy rich p. in me f. . . . 587.4
God will f. . . . each p. . . 723.1
rich p. . . . shall be f. . . 738.3
the p. . . . here in me f. . . 877.3

e *fulfil will* *2 Thess 1:11*
thy w. f. in me, Lord . . 531.c
years f. . . . Father's w. . . 566.4
stormy winds f. thy w. . . 947.3

f *fulfil word* *Col 1:25*
God f. his promised w. . . 78.2
now f. thy w. . . . 155.3

law (b)

fulfiller 154.3

fulfilment 553.4

full
1 *(adjective)*
his f. hand supplies . . 34.5
bathe in the f. ocean . . 239.4
f. equipment for the task . 324.4
his coffers are f. . . . 354.1
bathe in its f. ocean . . 368.1
'tis deep, 'tis f. . . . 413.1
f. divine conformity . . 419.1
give me f. victory . . . 432.1
he gives f. strength . . 495.3
f. and perfect peace . . 545.1
so that in f. accord . . 574.5
our Father's f. giving . . 579.2
can f. deliverance find . . 590.2
fit us for f. consecration. . 622.1
enjoying God's f. favour . 704.1
f. confidence in . . . blood . 733.1
mercy's f. power . . . 746.5
by his f. grace salvation . . 785.4
when to f. stature . . . 796.4
f. employment . . . 869.2
to f. fruition brought . . 885.3
truth's f. influence . . . 942.4
drink a f. supply . . . c16
where the f. tides flow . . c137

b *full and free*
a pardon f. and f. . . . 253.2
scattering f. and f. . . . 295.1
his power f. and f. . . . 406.c
for ever f. . . . flowing f.. . 496.1
so great, so f., so f. . . 515.1
f. and f. for evermore . . 540.5
healing, helping, f. and f. . 548.3
call for mercy f. and f. . . 802.3

c *full of*
hands f. of power . . . 129.3
f. of guilt 291.2
heart is f. of singing . . 328.2
filled f. of woe . . . 348.1
my heart is f. of music . . 369.1
f. of love divine . . . 444.4
heart so f. of sadness . . 470.1
f. of sin I am . . . 737.3
my heart is f. of glee . . 837.4
words f. of kindness . . 848.2
I'm f. of confidence . . c132
life is f. of hopefulness . . c201

d *John 1:14*
Jesus, f. of . . . grace . . 305.2
more f. of grace . . . 305.2
thou art f. of truth and g. . 737.3
deeds f. of grace . . . 848.2
sturdy lad and f. of grace . 855.2

e *Ps 86:15*
like thee! f. of compassion . 623.2

f *Heb 6:11; 10:22*
be thou their f. assurance . 948.2

g *Mark 4:28*
eyes behold f. sheaves . . 923.1
f. corn shall appear . . 924.2

h *full salvation*
s. f., at highest cost . . 46.1
lead me on to f. s. . . . 188.1
longing for a f. s. . . . 197.1
seal us heirs of f. s. . . 210.2
I believe in a f. s. . . . 222.c
f. s. Jesus purchased . . 230.3
still longing for a f. s. . . 257.2
his touch will f. s. give . . 267.3
promise . . . f. s. to give. . 392.1
to purchase a f. s. . . . 427.1
enjoying a f. s. . . . 427.*
with f. s. might . . . 431.2
seek just now a f. s. . . 433.1
O thou God of f. s. . . 452.1
O the joy of f. s. . . . 474.5
and I now have f. s. . . 504.c
joy which came with f. s. . 534.1
all f. s. may know . . . 535.c
full salvation, f. s. . . . 540.*
seeking for God's f. s. . . 553.2
in thee can I find f. s. . . 610.3
hearts aglow with f. s. . . 704.2
ours is such a f. s. . . . 764.2
s. f. shall be our cry . . 782.2
it tells of f. s. 783.c
on to f. s. 788.3
if f. s. you would gain . . 806.3
preserved . . . to f. s. . . 915.1

i *full and free salvation*
a free, f. s. is offered . . 233.1
shout s. f. and free . . 393.4
God's great, free, f. s. . . 413.2
s., f., present and free . . 454.4
s., now I know 'tis f. . . 546.3
f. s., great and free . . 727.1
with a free and f. s. . . 800.3

atonement, joy (2d), surrender (b)

2 *(adverb)*
f. reverently 90.5

fuller-est
rolling in f. pride . . . 224.4
f. know redemption's plan . 439.2
I have f. enjoyment . . 553.4
its flow may richer, f. be . 621.1
f., sweeter is that life . . 878.4
that f. life to share . . . 880.4

fully
trusted f. in his name . . 52.2
f. absolved through these . 116.2
you are f. blest . . . 231.3
my all I f. give . . . 282.3
I am f. his 352.c
justified f. 371.2
f. saves and cleanses . . 404.2
I will surrender f. . . . 413.3
are you f. trusting . . . 417.1
my vileness f. cleanse . . 423.2
sanctify each moment f. . . 463.c
from being thine f. . . 473.2
take the life I f. yield . . 531.1
when I had f. yielded . . 549.2
himself more f. know . . 634.4
f. on them . . . prove . . 720.3
when f. he . . . wrought. . 721.4
than thou canst f. know. . 723.2
in Christ are f. blest . . 828.3
make us f. thine . . . 870.4
f. trusting c119

whole (2c)

fulness *John 1:16; Eph 3:19*
thy f. is the same . . . 14.2
love brings the glorious f. . 46.3
f. of his power to give . . 102.3
in its f. over me . . . 182.1
f. of love, of Heaven . . 214.4
come now in all thy f. . . 221.1
life in all its f. . . . 274.c
O f. of mercy . . . 298.1
that is the f. . . . 355.5
love in its f. is flowing . . 383.3
his f. you shall know . . 413.2
Jesus, thy f. give . . . 431.1
in thy f. dwell with me . . 502.2
in f. of thy love . . . 562.1
O fill me with thy f. . . 612.6
come in thy f. . . . 623.c
expect his f. to receive . . 659.4
his f. . . . shall supply . . 734.1
my need and . . . f. meet . 741.4
there to an ocean f. . . 896.2

b *prove fulness*
all his f. . . . ever prove . . 239.4
all his f. would prove . . 535.3
proved the f. of his grace . 910.2

c *Ps 16:11*
f. of joy he brings . . . 227.1
f. of joy in thy presence . . 457.3
now in the f. of joy . . c159

d *Ps 24:1*
he filleth with his f. . . 929.2

furious 911.2

furnish-ed
my table thou hast f. . . 54.4
made ready and f. for me . 289.3
f. all we ought to ask . . 668.4
prepared and all f. . . . 905.3
b *2 Tim 3:17*
f. with all that I need . . 553.4

furrow-ed
it smooths all its f. . . . 237.2
bursts from the f. soil . . 923.2

further
f. from the light 379.1
a f. triumph win 885.2

fury 19.3

future
don't assume . . . no f. . . 44.2
this and every f. age . . 142.5
make the f. in the present . 158.3
all my f. thou canst see . . 285.3
far f. I cannot see . . . 294.3
I have a f. in Heaven . . 371.3
my f. is veiled 473.4
let my f. be for God . . . 477.2
I am leaving the f. . . . 501.2
the f.'s broadening way . . 519.4
doubts . . . for f. years . . 551.2
nor things f. can disturb . . 554.3
though the f. is veiled . . 739.2
peace, our f. all unknown . 752.5
a city of the f. 868.2
there's a f. for the Army . . 869.4
must to our f. . . . give . . 928.2
in the f. bear evil or good . 928.3
veiled the f. 937.2
and the f. is with him . . c166
b *(whatever) future*
w. my f. may require . . 385.4
w. the f. holds 732.c
w. the f. brings 916.2

G

gaily 724.2

gain-ed-ing
the sacred g. of toil . . 5.2
grief . . . for sinners' g. . . 123.2
I should g. an interest . . 283.1
glorious g. of thy cross . . 300.2
would you g. this friend . . 343.3
part . . . thy power to g.. . 513.1
no progress . . . had g. . . 553.3
resemblance to g. . . . 589.2
his smile . . . infinite g. . . 640.3
g. from thine . . . store . . 646.4
this blessèd peace to g. . . 661.4
no profit canst thou g. . . 715.4
grief means others' g. . . 729.3
to g. the topmost plain . . 766.3
converts still we g. . . 815.3
a Kingdom fair to g. . . 868.1
joy and g. . . . sanctified . 874.1
g. . . . through sacrifice . . 922.3
may we g. from Heaven. . 940.4
may I thy likeness g. . . 958
b *gain [crown]* *Rev 2:10*
shall g. the c. of life . . 266.c
lose I all, the c. I'll g. . . 528.4
g. the everlasting prize . . 633.3
the victor's c. will g. . . 686.2
a kingly c. to g. . . . 701.1
c *eternal gain*
life eternal I shall g. . . 552.3
shall we g. eternal joy . . 785.6
lead us to eternal g. . . 803.3
can g. eternal praise . . 806.2
and life eternal g. . . . 877.4
but now the eternal g. . . 894.2
d *gain [loss]* *Matt 16:26; Phil 3:7*
richest g. I count but l. . . 136.1
g. comes not except by l. . 211.3
prepare me for g. or for l. . 288.2
choose to g. through l. . . 429.2
teach us how to g. by l.. . 452.3
to know no g. or l. . . 476.3
count it g. to suffer l. . . 489.2
g. in every l. 551.3
earthly l. is heavenly g. . . 683.2
trust through g. or l. . . 704.3
l. now turned to g. . . 719.3
from worldly l. and g. . . 872.2
all things l. . . . Jesus g.. . 915.3
turning all my g. to l. . . 916.3
e *gain [salvation]*
g. thy s. by dying . . . 276.1
perfect cleansing g. there . 471.3
if full s. you would g. . . 806.3
f *Matt 16:26*
the taste of earthly g. . . 631.3
passing g. of earth . . 796.3
g *Phil 1:21*
life or death is g. . . . 424.1

gainsay 407.3

gainst see *against*

gale
every high and stormy g. . 745.2
heavenly g. are blowing . . c221

Galilean
hail, thou G. King . . . 109.1
by the G. lake . . . 428.2

Galilee *(Matt 15:29)**
tossing on the waves of G. . 96.2
when Jesus looked o'er G. . 103.1
and love its G. . . . 496.5
Sabbath rest by G. . . 567.3
man who walked by G. . . 618.2
O Man of G. . . . . 628.*
shores of G. 680.1
heard by G. 680.3
days by G. 680.c
a tempest on G. . . . 848.3
man walked by G. . . . 855.3
Jesus of G. c214

galling 693.3

gaping 526.1

garb 177.2

garden
1 *(literal)*
ripe fruits in the g. . . . 25.3
sweetness of the wet g.. . 35.2
thy word is like a g. . . 658.1
b *John 18:1*
love won in the g. . . . 51.c
in the g. he prayed . . 137.2
it was in the g. . . 179.2
praying in the g. . . 486.3
that scene, in the g. . . 848.5
the g. and the morrow . . c14
c *John 19:41*
a g., passing fair . . . 145.1
the g. near the cross . . 145.*
2 *(figurative)* *Isa 51:3; 58:11**
our hearts a watered g. . . 210.1
thy g. of grace . . . 288.4
desert g. bloom awhile . . 333.2
in God's g. grows . . . 346.3
the g. of my heart . . . 600.1
make a g. there . . . 647.3
in the g. of my heart . . c43

garish 606.2

garland 658.1

garment
a *Isa 61:3*
g. of praise for my days. . c148
b *Matt 9:20, 21*
touch the hem of his g. . 304.1, c
I touch thy sacred g. . . 520.3
I touched but . . . his g.. . 542.3
c *Matt 17:2*
thy face and g. . . . 154.1
d *Matt 21:8*
palms and scattered g. . . 150.1
e *Dan 7:9; Rev 7:13*
washed . . . and g. new. . 335.1
are your g. spotless . . 417.c
g. that are stained . . . 417.3
wash our g. in thy blood. . 452.2
in those g. to shine . . 589.1
walk . . . in g. of white . . 640.4
robed in their g. of white . 708.1
in pure g. of white . . . 883.3
robed in their g. of white . 886.1
g. must be white . . . 914.1

garner *Matt 3:12*
ears to store in his g. . . 924.3
in thy g. to abide . . . 924.4
for the g. of God . . . 928.3

gasp
may but g. his name . . 60.6
g. my fainting soul . . 412.2

gate
mercy's g. open wide . . 126.1
he has not closed the g.. . 267.2
so fast to bar the g. . . 299.2
watches at thy g. . . . 839.4
b *Ps 100:4*
enter then his g. . . . 3.3
we'll crowd thy g. . . . 4.3
c *Isa 60:18*
her g. to tell thy praise . . 944.1
d *Matt 7:13*
g. that is leading . . . 247.2
e *gates of Hell* *Matt 16:18*
burst the g. of H. . . . 143.3
the yawning g. of H. . . 151.4
the trembling g. of H. . . 165.2
g. of H. can never . . . 690.4
f *gates [of Heaven]* *Gen 28:17; Rev 21:12*
opened the life g. . . . 22.1
it leads to H.'s g. . . . 462.1
watchword at the g. . . 625.5
H.'s g. to open wide . . 843.2
thy golden g. appear . . 877.2
its g. . . . are burnished . . 905.3
sweeping through the g. . 910.c
brass (a), open (d), pearly

gather-ed-ing
power to g. souls . . . 63.1
if temptations . . . g. . . 66.2
g. round its head . . . 112.*
the g. shadows . . . 250.5
amid the crowd that g. . . 304.1
the shadows g. o'er me . . 330.1
the darkness g. round . . 358.2
now the darkness g. . . 673.2
darkened clouds may g. . . 732.1
darkness round you g. . . 759.2
g. 'neath our banner . . 803.2
all is safely g. in . . . 924.1
g. fruits from tree . . . 926.3
g. in time or eternity . . 931.c
clouds have g. round . . 938.3
b *Matt 23:37*
g. round his feet . . . 265.2
g. you under my wing . . 331.2
the Lord his children g. . . 722.4
g. me close 740.1
c *(in Heaven)* *Matt 13:30; 24:31*
g. all above 86.2
all the ransomed shall g. . 169.1
we shall g., Saviour . . 235.c
countless souls are g. in. . 266.1
g. by the crystal sea . . 337.c
g. on the hills of God . . 483.3
children are g. there . . 794.2
he will g. the gems . . 852.2
g. at the river . . . 891.*
saved of earth shall g. . . 907.1
chosen ones shall g. . . 907.2
when we g. at last . . . 908.1
g. thou thy people in . . 924.4
g. the harvest home . . 931.3

gave see *give*

gay
strive in vain to look g. . . 318.1
nor adorning, rich and g. . 320.1
sombre . . . and g. . . . 644.2

gaze
1 *(divine)*
thy penetrating g. . . . 201.2
teach . . . to meet thy g. . . 618.1

2 *(we) gaze* *(Acts 1:11)*
ever g. and wonder . . 94.3
g. upon thy sore distress . 122.2
I g. upon thy face . . 138.2
with what rapture g. we. . 161.3
g. upon the Saviour's face . 268.2
g. on the ocean of love . . 542.1
love that g. at the cradle . 544.3
upon the Lamb I g. . . 634.2
in true happiness g. . . 639.2
g. over the fair land . . 908.3

gem
not with gold or g. . . . 707.3
bright g. for his crown . . 852.c
the g. for his Kingdom . . 852.2

gender 211.2

General 622.4

generation 941.3

generous
g. fruits 887.3
fruits thy g. soil . . . 933.1

gentle
1 *(re Jesus)* *2 Cor 10:1*
child so dear and g. . . 87.5
g. child of gentle mother . 97.1
Jesus, so g. and mild . . 175.3
more like Jesus, g. . . 193.4
pleading . . . with g. voice . 229.1
waits the Saviour, g. . . 236.3
half so g., half so sweet. . 265.2
soothe . . . with g. balm. . 479.2
g. arms of Jesus . . 792.1
g. Jesus, meek and mild . 793.1
loving Jesus, g. Lamb . . 793.3
thou art g., meek . . . 793.4
safe on his g. breast . 889.1, c
b *(re Spirit)* *Gal 5:22*
g. soothing of thy Spirit . . 192.1
his that g. voice we hear . 200.5
brooding of the g. dove . . 202.2
abide, O g. Spirit . . 221.3
g. power of righteousness . 705.3
2 *(re people)*
for all g. thoughts . . . 28.4
in whose g. arms he lay . . 87.3
g. child of g. mother . . 97.1
3 *(re objects)*
feel the g. breeze . . . 37.2

gentleness *Gal 5:22*
strength belongs to g. . . 198.4
in the g. of Jesus . . . 324.1
Lord of all g. 611.4
peace and g. abound . . 664.1
fruit of the Spirit is g. . . c46

gently
g. burning Fire within . . 206.3
I heard him g. calling . . 391.1
a voice so g. calling . . 490.1
as g. falling dew . . . 494.2
g. distil like early dew . . 672.1
wearied eyelids g. steep . . 676.2
plead with them g. . . 691.2
pilgrim way is g. falling . . 711.2
prayer g. lifts me . . . c94
b *Isa 40:11*
he g. bears us . . . 17.3
on his shoulder g. laid . . 53.3
g. his burden he bore . . 111.1
me . . . he g. did lay . . 388.1
my Saviour bears me g. . . 549.3
he g. clears thy way . . 721.2
lead (3k)

get-ting
all the saints g. home . . 312.3
shout . . . when I g. there . 369.c
joy of g. others to climb. . 369.3
to g. this blest washing . . 436.2
fiercer g. the contest . . 499.4
till the answer we g. . . 608.2
g. more smiles than tears . 806.1
mine when I g. there . . 811.c
g. it on your knees . . . 813.c
when we all g. to Heaven . 892.c
when the glory g. into . . c223

Gethsemane *Matt 26:36*
Jesus praying in G. . . 96.3
lest I forget G. . . . 117.c
than he drank in G. . . 758.2

ghastly 696.2

ghost see *Spirit (1-5)*
fretting g. of vain regret. . 551.2

giants *(Gen 6:4)*
though he with g. fight . . 685.2
many g. great and tall . . 847.3

gift
1 *(to God)*
great g. on him bestow . . 48.3
come with a g. to thee . . 117.3
is it so? a g. 475.1
dost thou ask a g. . . . 475.*
g. of passing time . . . 475.3
giving, and forget the g. . 491.2
love . . . asks the g. of me . 504.1
few the g. I have . . . 605.3
bring a worthier g. . . . 618.3
my talents, g. and graces . 720.4
each g. of beauty rare . . 833.2
these are g. that even . . 849.2
than richest g. without . . 849.3
bring . . . all the blest g.. . 861.5
what wondrous g. . . . 871.1
g. which costs you pain . . 920.2
g. our hearts outpouring . 922.1
laying now our g. before . 922.2
accept the g. we offer . . 935.3
accept the g. we offer . . 943.1
b *Matt 2:11*
as they offered g. . . . 76.3
wise men bring g. . . . 89.2
rich g. to greet him . . 92.1
c *Matt 7:11*
where g. are spurned . . 50.2
d *Matt 23:19*
altar sanctifies the g. . . 208.4
2 *(from God)*
the g. he hath bestowed . 23.1
his g. of grace to me . . 52.1
his g. to all mankind . . 74.3
thy blood-bought g. . . 203.1
his g. . . . has squandered . 225.1
with healing g. for souls. . 287.1
now the g. I receive . . 322.2
the priceless g. . . . now. . 403.3
reject the g. no longer . . 410.2
this is the g. . . . promised . 415.1
failed to take . . . the g.. . 415.3
sacrificed thy g. . . . 449.1
by faith the g. I claim . . 481.4
the g. of buried grain . . 512.3
though all thy g. remove . 562.1
Jesus, the g. divine . . 601.1
thy gracious g. be given. . 624.2
each day is a g. supernal . 666.1
g. are every evening new . 672.1
thy wondrous g. . . . sees . 742.1
we dedicate . . . thy g. . . 796.3
build, with all thy . . . g.. . 827.3
gave thy greatest g. . . 861.1
the g. his goodness gave . 929.3
wonderful g. from above . . c197

b *gift of life* *(John 3:15,16)*
yieldeth up the g. of l. . . 5.3
the wondrous g. is given . 86.3
not alone the g. of l. . . 345.2
g. of love, eternal life . . 576.2
thy g. of l. eternal . . . 922.3
c *gift of love*
countless g. of love . . 12.1
love's g. is God's g. . . 51.3
g. of l., eternal life . . . 576.2
gracious g. of l. divine . . 858.3
glorious g. of his l. . . . 900.3
peace, the g. of God's l. . c197
d *free gift* *Rom 5:18*
g. of God, sent free . . 240.4
thy g. so free . . . 524.4
e *1 Cor 12:1*
Spirit and the g. are ours . 1.4
all the g. of Heaven . . 555.3
g. of the Spirit is healing . c46
f *2 Cor 9:15*
prove the g. unspeakable . 55.4
g *Eph 2:8; John 4:10*
the g. most wonderful . . 52.1
is his g. of grace to me . . 52.1
all thy g. of grace . . . 398.4
lavishing thy g. of grace. . 500.1
g. of his infinite grace . . 906.2
with g. of grace supernal . 934.2
h *Eph 4:11*
came to earth with g. . . 74.1
i *2 Tim 1:7*
I want the g. of power . . 214.1
j *James 1:17*
each perfect g. of thine . . 28.5
all good g. around us . . 935.c
God (3c), stir (b), wondrous (b)

gild
when morning g. the skies . 187.1
g. its holy pages . . . 193.3
shall his pathway g. . . 277.1
g. the teardrop . . . 333.2
glory g. the sacred page . 657.2

gird-ed-ing *Eph 6:14*
g. with praise . . . 16.1
g. on thy mighty sword . . 219.2
g. our lives 577.4
I'll g. on the armour . . 686.c
g. you with your armour . 697.1
g. your armour on . . . 698.1
let us g. ourselves . . . 700.1
g. on salvation armour . . 869.4

girder 30.1

girl
boy and g., and friend . . 544.4
bring their baby boy (g.) . 795.1

give-ing-n/gave
1 *(God) gives*
a *material blessings*
to all life thou g. . . . 8.3
he g. us eyes to see . . 25.4
have g. us minds . . . 27.5
to our race so freely g. . . 28.5
g. the universe its birth . . 30.4
g. such rich resources . . 38.2
life is great and . . . g. . . 544.1
g. the weary . . . repose. . 673.3
the day thou g. . . . ended . 677.1
the children thou hast g. . 791.1
the gifts his goodness g. . 929.3
b *(spiritual blessings)*
thou art g. and forgiving . 10.3
g. a purpose and a way . . 36.4
g. a glorious foretaste . . 46.4
born to g. . . . second birth . 82.3
the wondrous gift is g. . . 86.3

all hope of good is g. . . 127.4
the cross . . . is g. . . 168.4
morning of joy g. . . . 183.4
a larger earnest g. . . . 207.4
confidence g. . . . 209.2
if thou g. the . . . desire. . 210.2
g. thy word success . . 219.2
he g. his healing . . . 238.2
the book he has g. . . . 323.1
g. me Jesus . . . 343.c, 2
will g. me a home . . . 354.2
g. triumph in answer . . 373.3
g. what can . . . be enjoyed . 375.2
help and comfort g. you . 396.3
the happiness he g. me . . 399.3
he the witness g. . . . 423.5
g. me fellowship with thee . 429.c
Jesus, thy fulness g. . . 431.1
Lord, g. the zeal . . . might . 466.4
to us he g. the keeping . . 478.1
naught . . . thou didst not g. . 532.1
thou canst g. no more . . 565.3
g. us a day of wonders . . 575.1
g. courage for the battle . 575.3
g. light to cheer . . . 575.3
g. and g. and g. again . . 579.3
commands by Jesus g. . . 580.3
Jesus, g. . . . liberty . . 593.1
Lord, g. us souls . . . 608.*
g. us, we pray, your bliss . 611.1
g. . . . more holy living . . 622.3
g. . . . more thanksgiving . 622.3
thy gracious gifts be g. . . 624.2
g. refreshing showers . . 626.3
will still g. thee aid . . . 653.2
whate'er . . . grace hath g. . 667.4
g. me heat and light . . 733.5
g. us eyes to see . . . 756.2
crowns of life . . . are g.. . 761.4
God g. to you chances . . 773.2
g. a little child a place . . 793.2
loves to g. the better . . 806.3
g. . . . consuming fire . . 830.3
fire that g. the courage . . 830.3
for his own pattern g. . . 879.5
who can g. you hope . . 885.4
as thy hand hath g. . . 921.3
g. his angels charge . . 924.3

c *give . . . to*
Jesus, g. to us t. know . . 145.3
g. us quietly t. tarry . . 210.3
g. thy servant t. possess . 419.4
g. me on thee t. wait . . 596.1
g. me constantly t. know . 630.1
g. me to eat and live . . 650.2
g. me to bear . . . yoke . . 667.3

d *give all*
thee, who g. a. . . . . 15.*
a. you need . . . surely g. . 73.2
who g. thine a. for me . . 221.2
g. . . . measureless a. . . 245.2
a. I return thee, who g. . . 454.3
a. . . . in mercy g. . . . 617.3
g. its a. on Calvary . . 741.1
thou hast g. a. . . . 921.1
a. this my Lord g. to me . c184
he g. a. to save us . . . c213

e *give blessing*
fail to g. a b. 303.3
the b. the Lord g. to me. . 329.3
for b. which he g. me now . 387.3
the b. . . . to me hast g.. . 415.5
g. b. without number . . 575.1
God will g. his b. . . . 805.1
for the b. thou hast g. . . 941.1

f *give [Comforter]* *John 14:16*
g. the Spirit's . . . dower . 15.4
glorified and g. the C. . . 195.1
Holy Ghost to man is g.. . 195.*
g. us still . . . aid . . . 202.3
g. us the . . . Holy Ghost . 203.1
like thy Spirit, gladly g. . . 211.3

g *give faith*
g. us f. to know . . . 466.2
g. f. to fight 575.3
g. us the f. that will not. . 608.2
g. me the f. which can . . 720.1
the f. . . . by Jesus g. . . 733.2
g. us f., O Lord, we pray . 769.c
g. me the wings of f. . . 879.1

h *give grace* *James 4:6*
g. . . . g. for every task . 44.c, 3
he'll g. me needful g. . . 45.3
g. us g. to persevere . . 97.1
he hath g. the word of g. . 165.3
g. is g. to those who ask . 324.4
the Lord g. g. and glory . . 410.3
g. me but g. for this . . 441.4
his abundant g. is g. . . 555.2
g. that the Lord has g. . . 555.3
g. g. from day to day . . 575.3
he g. more g. 579.1
that g. and strength be g. . 586.1
the g. . . . freely g.. . . 603.3
to us may g. be g. . . . 701.4
g. enough is g. . . . 755.1
g. to each believer g. . . 760.1
he will g. you g. . . 790.1, c
O g. me g. to follow . . 862.4
may that g., once g. . . 940.4
g. me grace . . . power . . c1

i *give heart/soul*
g. us h. and tongues . . 196.4
g. us a pure and lowly h. . 411.4
g. me a h. that is true . . 422.4
g. me a h. . . . whiter . . 443.c
g. a pure and loving h. . . 466.3
g. me a faithful h. . . . 524.3
g. me a self-denying s. . . 619.2
g. me an obedient h. . . 793.5
O g. me Samuel's h. . . 839.4
g. me a h. like thine . . c39

j *give [himself]* *Gal 2:20**
love . . . for my soul he g. . 130.4
g. me thyself, for ever g. . 207.2
he g. himself . . . to pay. . 342.1
his own self he g. me . . 345.2
g. thyself to me . . . 435.c
O g. thyself to me . . . 486.c
thyself to me be g. . . 562.1
thou g. me thy heart . . 741.2

k *give joy*
it will j. and comfort g. . . 66.1
what j. . . . assurance g. 144.1, 4
O what j. he g. . . . 352.c
the j. thy love has g. . . 421.5
g. me full j. and peace . . 431.3
friend who g. me j. . . 709.2

l *give life* *(Gal 2:20)*
who g. his l. for me . . . 69.2
God's l. for rebels g. . . 113.3
shouldst g. thy l. for me. . 125.3
but his l. he g. . . . 130.2
Saviour who g. his l. . . 178.1
blood was freely g. . . 221.2
I for thee l. g. . . . 260.2
sacrifice that Jesus g. . . 269.3
he g. his l. to ransom . . 349.1
blood he g. to redeem . . 349.3
his l. did Jesus g. for me . 363.c
love for him who g. his l. . 400.3
whose l. was freely g. . . 631.1
in mercy he g. his l. . . 831.1
g. the greatest gift . . . 861.1
who g. his l. for all. . . 929.3
there his l. he g. . . . c7

m *give eternal life* *John 10:28, 17:2*
l. is g. through thy name . 109.1
the l. everlasting he g. . . 271.4
he came to g. us l. . . . 274.c
I freely g. e. l.. . . . 277.1
will g. e. l. to all . . . 277.c
shall g. new l. to thee . . 304.c

his Spirit g. me l. . . . 330.2
g. me a holy l. . . . 416.1

n *give love*
g. me a compassion deep . 205.3
l. he so freely hath g. . . 373.4
g. me the l. that never . . 432.3
g. me more l., dear Lord . 523.2
dying l. thou g. me . . 524.1
g. me more soul-saving l. . 609.1
g. us, we pray, your l. . . 611.3
g. me the childlike . . . l.. . 720.1
give me a l. like thine . . c83

o *give mind*
g. us each a lowly m. . . 193.4
g. me a . . . mind . . . 574.*
O g. me Samuel's m. . . 839.5

p *give peace* *John 14:27*
can g. me p. within . . 297.3
he has g. p. to my heart. . 348.1
the p. which Jesus g. . . 348.3
he g. me p. and pardon . . 391.c
wonderful . . . p. Jesus g. . 406.c
g. me full joy and p. . . 431.3
g. me thy perfect p. . . 450.3
p. that only thou canst g. . 519.4
his p. Jesus g. unto me . . 542.2
my p. I will g. unto thee. . 542.4
O the p. my Saviour g. . . 549.c
for the p. you g. me . . 552.2
g., for wild confusion, p. . 569.3
g. p. when lions roar . . 575.3
g. us, we pray, your p. . . 611.4
friend who g. me . . . p.. . 709.2
it g. me back my p. . . 714.1
g. to me abundant p. . . 761.2
the Lord . . . g. thee p. . . 961

q *give [power]* *John 1:12*
fulness of his p. to g. . . 102.3
g. me the p. to master . . 432.2
Lord, . . . g. the might . . 466.4
thy p. now g. me . . . 490.2
g. me more p. . . . 523.3
g. p. to speak . . . word. . 609.3
g. p. unto thy word . . 626.3
g. you grace and p. . 790.1, c
g. me grace, g. me p. . . c1

r *give promise* *2 Peter 1:4*
precious p. were g. . . 216.1
precious p. God hath g. . . 753.1
but a p. he has g. . . . 824.1

s *give rest* *Matt 11:28*
he will surely g. you r. . . 231.1
come, and he will g. you r. . 262.2
with the wise to g. r. . . 527.3
g. r. amidst . . . conflicts . 575.3
g. thine own sweet r. . . 612.5
g. to me abundant . . . r. . 761.2

t *give [salvation]*
his s. freely g. . . . 74.3
break . . . and g. release. . 185.2
his s. g. to you . . . 232.3
touch will full s. g. . . 267.3
readily he g. it . . . 348.2
promise . . . full s. to g.. . 392.1
rose . . . his pardon he g. . 687.3

u *give song* *Job 35:10*
g. my heart a s. . . . 32.3
a s. that Jesus g. me . . 327.1
s. in the night he g. . . 358.2

v *give strength* *Ps 29:11*
g. full s. for trial . . . 495.3
g. me thy s., O God . . 526.4
g. s. and happiness . . 561.2
g. s. thy foes to slay . . 575.3
that grace and s. be g. . . 586.1
g. us, we pray, your s. . . 611.2
g. me the s. of faith . . 619.3
he g. me s. as my day . . 710.2

w *give [task]*
g. me heavy loads . . . 204.2
the t. that thou hast g. . . 528.3

thou my daily t. shalt g.. . 566.4
t. that thou . . . hast g. . . 618.3
the cross that he g. . . 758.1

x *give water* *John 4:10*
g. the living water . . . 332.2

y *give word*
g. thy word success . . 219.2
words . . . all so freely g. . 258.2
words . . . shalt g. me . 727.5
he g. the word of command . 734.3

z *2 Cor 4:6*
to g. the light . . . c158

ask (2b), bread (a, b), courage (b), ear (2b), freely (1d), measure (b), name (1j), ransom (c), sight (2b), son (1e), spirit (4c), victory (2h)

2 *(we) give*
a *(general)*
sometimes g. where gifts . 50.2
can g. me peace . . 297.2
I would be g. 491.2
g. to the winds thy fears . 721.1
help each g. the other . 938.3
wait to g. us welcome . . 938.4

b *give [to God]*
adore and g. him his right . 24.3
assume you cannot g. . . 44.3
whatever I can be g. . . 212.5
room and time now g. . . 241.4
g. him . . . rightful place. . 249.3
what . . . I will not g. . . 447.2
thine own I will g. thee . 473.1
I have not much to g. . . 475.c
my hours I'll g. . . . 475.3
now I g. thee back . . . 492.3
I g. you my will . . . 506.2
I'll g. thee the dearest . 507.1
love's demands to g. . . 512.2
what offering shall I g. . 516.1
when . . . my vows were g. . 534.1
perfect service g. . . . 788.3
g. our time, bring all . . 833.2
we have g. little . . . 921.1
gladly g. thee more . . 921.3
nothing . . . but that we g. . 922.3
the years so gladly g. . . 939.3
what have we to g. . . c213

c *give (up) all*
I g. myself, I g. up all . . 114.3
freely all I g. to thee . . 201.3
my all to thee I g. . . . 221.1
my all I fully g. . . . 282.3
g. up all to thee . . . 307.3
g. to Jesus everything . . 405.3
all to thee now I g.. . . 469.3
all to him I freely g. . . 474.1
freely g. up all the rest . . 480.5
I have g. my all to God . . 504.c
thus my all to thee I g. . . 504.3
I g. you my all . . . 506.5
behold we g. . . . our all. . 515.1
all that I have to g.. . . 666.1
who g. to thee our all . . 675.c
at thy word they g. up . . 789.5
all I have I g. thee . . . 859.c
g. up my all to follow . . c35
I g. my all, I trust . . . c88

d *give heart*
now thy h. O g. to me . . 260.2
all my h. to him I g. . . 336.2
our h. and hands we g. . . 424.4
g. our h. to thy obedience . 428.5
I g. my h. to thee . . . 455.c
let me g. thee all my h. . . 497.2
all my h. I g. thee . . . 499.c
Lord . . . I g. you my h.. . 506.4
behold we g. . . . our h.. . 515.1
Jesus, all my h. I g. . . 520.1
h. that unto thee are g. . . 704.4
if their h. to me they g. . . 797.2
I g. my h. I'll do . . . 830.c
all my h. I g. to thee . . c33

e *give life*
blood-bought l. I g. him . . 65.3
a l. g. up to the fight . . 422.4
to thee my l. is g. . . . 482.3
all my l. I g. thee . . . 499.c
behold we g. . . . our l. . . 515.1
I g. thee back the l. . . 621.1
will g. to thee all my l. . . 859.1
my l. to g., my vows . . 860.2

f *give [praise]*
all p. . . . now be g. . . 12.3
all p. to thee be g. . . . 15.5
blessings . . . we can g.. . 57.3
loudest p. . . . for us to g. . 109.3
strength and honour g. . . 184.1
songs of p. . . . ever g. . . 578.3
homage now I g. to thee . 600.3
in thy temple I g. p. . . 613.1
more p. than I can g. . . 616.2
we g. him worship . . . 785.6
p. for all to God be g. . . 834.2
glory and p. to Jesus g. . . 915.1

g *give [self]*
here . . . I g. myself away . 105.4
I g. myself, I g. up all . . 114.3
here I g. myself to thee . . 128.2
gladly . . . g. myself away . 255.4
g. thyself this moment . . 377.4
Lord, I g. myself to thee. . 474.4
Lord, now myself I g. . . 523.3
g. up ourselves . . . 784.2

h *give [soul]*
teach me how to g. thee . 221.2
g. now my s. and body . . 470.3
I g. you my will/mind/heart/all 506.*
as I g. thee s. and body . . 510.4
my body, s. . . . Jesus, I g. . 511.1

i
such as I have I g. . . . 475.2
such as I have, Lord, g. . . c103

account, best (1d), cheerfully, glory (4e), joy (4), power (4m), receive (2g), thanks (c)

3 *(general)*
a *give in*
you feel like g. in . . . 790.1
we never will g. in . . . 800.*
do not g. in but strive . . 817.1

b *give o'er*
pursuits I all g. o. . . . 509.2
fight and ne'er g. o. . . 686.4
the battle ne'er g. o. . . 812.2
g. the contest . . . 911.3

c *give up sin*
unwilling to g. u. thy s. . . 263.2
g. u. your s. and . . . win . c146

4 *(other)*
g. man both warmth . . 2.3
love g. its best . . . 51.*
world g. back the song . . 83.3
to the earth it g. . . . 90.2
g. . . . conscience peace . 120.1
the lamp to pilgrim g. . . 176.4
g. the winds a . . . voice. . 393.4
'tis religion that can g. . . 464.1
this . . . world can g. . . 480.4
splendour still is g. . . 632.2
g. exercise to faith . . . 646.2
word of mercy, g. . . . 655.5
it g. a light to every age. . 657.2
it g. but borrows none . . 657.2
it g. us inward pain . . 660.4
the world shall be g. . . 681.2
all around . . . g. way . . 745.3
g. the battle cry . . . 807.2
must . . . its character g. . 928.2

cause (2a)

giver
g. of immortal gladness . . 10.1
like the Lord, the g. . . 157.2

I hold it for the g. . . . 345.2
g. of the freedom . . . 471.1
thee, of life the g. . . . 490.c

giving
a *(noun)*
voiced in its g. . . . 51.1
all its best g. 51.2
Father's full g. . . . begun . 579.2
Saviour's g. to mankind . . 777.2
by our consecrated g. . . 922.1

b *life-giving*
l.-g., holy dove . . . 224.3
lost in its l.-g. flow . . . 281.3
healing, l.-g. flood . . . 296.4
wonderful, l.-g. flood . . 298.5
drank of that l.-g. stream . 332.2
feel in the l.-g. blood . . 367.4
l.-g. waters are flowing . . 383.1
'neath the l.-g. flow . . 443.1
O thou l.-g. one . . . 448.1
wash in the l.-g. flood . . 808.2
shade of the l.-g. tree . . 908.3

glad *(Ps 126:3)*
praise him in g. adoration . 19.1
hark the g. sound . . . 81.1
our g. hosannas . . . 81.4
the great g. tidings tell . . 86.4
g. tidings of great joy . . 93.2
the desert will be g. . . 159.3
hear the g. message . . 247.1
I tell you: I'm g. . . . 376.1
to meet the g. . . . 485.2
hear . . . g. well done . . 500.3
sworn in g. service . . 506.5
the g., triumphant strain . 550.3
g. hymns of praise . . . 569.4
ever sing g. praise . . . 574.5
g. when thy . . . smile . . 602.3
obedience g. and steady . 614.4
join our g. array . . . 693.3
life of trust, how g. . . 741.4
nothing seems g. . . . 773.1
g. trophies won . . . 774.2
till g. voices rend . . . 807.3
build a g. new world . . 827.4
the g. morning of my day . 860.2
at last, with g. surprise . . 871.3
house of g. remembrance . 944.1
echo the g. refrain . . . c226

b *make glad* *Ps 92:4*
make me g. and free . . 32.2
he has made me g. . . 332.1
so g. was my heart then m. . 348.2
makes the singer g. . . 838.3

c *glad day*
tell of that g. d. . . . 335.3
chimes the g. d. in . . . 744.6
the g. d. of youth . . 857.1, c
in these g. d. of youth . . 870.3
some g., sweet d. . . . 884.c

d *glad heart* *Ps 16:9*
dances his g. h. for joy . . 62.3
g. was my h. then made . 348.2
with a g. h. and free . . 505.1
one g. h. . . . brighten . . 805.2
g. h. . . . rise by faith . . 916.2
now my h. is g. . . . c191

e *glad [hour]*
bear, in this g. h. . . . 219.3
till, in death's g. h. . . 504.3
we bring in this g. h. . . 561.1
in this g. moment . . . 692.3

f *glad song*
taught the g. new s. . . 326.4
I'll sing the g. new s. . . 375.3
birds with g. songs . . . 545.2
in g. s. my voice to raise . 613.1
my new g. s. I raise . . 741.2
there are g. s. singing . . c153
in my heart is a g. new s. . c157

g *glad that/to*
g., so g. to tell you. . 96.1, 2
so g. I have entered in . . 315.3
I am so g. that our Father . 323.1
so g. that Jesus loves me . 323.c
g. that the blessings . . 329.3
g. to join our holy song . . 370.4
I am so very g. . . . 403.c
g. my Lord has offered . . 403.2
g. to take . . . part . . . 776.3
I'm g. my blessèd Saviour . 840.2
g. there is cleansing . . c47
I'm g. I've found thee . . c54
h *Matt 5:12*
be exceeding g. 95.3
i *Ps 32:11*
be g. in the Lord . . . 537.*

gladden-ed
g. thou this heart . . . 194.5
g. my eyes and warm . . 412.3
g. when thou dost find . . 416.3
thine to g. my defeat . . 510.3

gladder-st
I am g. when I'm loving . . 503.3
birds with g. songs . . 545.2

gladly
g. for aye we adore . . . 19.5
g. we welcome thee . . 175.c
like thy Spirit, g. given . . 211.3
g. to thee . . . I give . . 255.4
g. dedicate my days . . 290.3
g. be spent in promoting . 298.7
g. counting all but dross . 320.2
g. his love proclaim . . 383.c
g. own him as my King . . 405.3
g. I sacrifice 461.2
g. now no longer mine . . 504.2
g. I accept the message . . 514.1
thy service, I g. obey . . 543.2
g. I'll forfeit all . . . 623.1
follow Jesus g. . . . 817.2
as we g. march along . . 818.c
we g. learn to share . . 818.2
g. then shall I obey . . 865.2
g. we . . . tribute pay . . 869.1
g. reckon all things loss . . 915.3
children g. give thee . . 921.3
g. to gather the harvest . . 931.3
years so g. given . . . 939.3
work, . . . we g. share . . 941.3
g. I give thee . . . best . . c41
shall g. be answered . . c55
g. would we bring hearts . c213
b *gladly [bear]*
my burdens g. b. . . . 37.3
shame and reproach g. b. . 124.3
carry all our burdens g. . . 462.3
sufferings . . . I will g. b.. . 499.2
all things I will g. b. . . 499.3
g. life's . . . burden b. . . 733.3
c *gladly yield*
our lives we g. y. . . . 692.1
g. I y. thee my all . . . 786.2
our lives we g. y. thee . . 870.4
that I would not y. g. . . c55

gladness
giver of immortal g. . . 10.1
if men . . . share their g.. . 50.3
as with g. men of old . . 76.1
he shareth in our g. . . 87.4
let his Church with g. . . 152.2
he fills my spirit with g. . 178.1
life . . . with g. filled . . 277.1
into thy freedom, g. . . 300.1
with g. filled her soul . . 304.3
full of music and of g. . . 369.1
g. of all that believe . . 372.4
g. in my soul today . . 387.3
great was the g. . . . 388.3
our wanton selfish g. . . 577.3
choose thee now with g. . 631.3
grant me in pain or g. . . 635.2
worshipped him with g. . . 663.2
sing now for g. . . . 724.2
one the g. of rejoicing . . 765.6
a g. which increases . . 790.3
children, sing for g. . 835.1, c
with what g. . . . sing . . 859.1
unceasing songs of g. . . 899.3
our g. . . . will spring . . 928.2
hills leap up in g. . . . 929.2
to the home of g. . . . 949.4
b *Isa 51:3; Luke 1:14**
name brings joy and g. . . 63.1
had such joy and g. . . 309.2
oil (b)

gladsome
let us with a g. mind . . 34.1
there's a g. melody . . 340.1
sing . . . in g. accord . . 392.2

glades 37.2

glance-ing
thy kind but searching g. . 558.4
upward g. of an eye . . 625.2
'neath your g. so mild . . 792.1

glare 931.1

glassy *Rev 4:6* 220.2

gleam-ing
silver moon with softer g. . 2.1
and his banner g. . . . 40.2
hope is g. still . . . 126.c
g. of its glory . . . 173.2
its waters g. bright . . 252.1
eternal glories g. afar . . 345.3
send a g. across the wave . 478.c
transient g. of loveliness . 551.1
shall be the sacred g. . . 591.3
some softening g. of love . 668.3
banner . . . g. in the light . 698.2
g. and burns the . . . light . 765.2
red and blue . . . g. . . 777.4
g. a consecrated sword . . 799.2
any g. of light refuse . . 871.3
ever in the sunlight g. . . 894.2

glean 658.5

glee 837.4

glimpse 590.4

glisten 268.2

glitter-ing
find earth's g. dim . . . 267.1
g. crown on my brow . . 357.4
fleeting its g. show . . 470.1
g. starlight stands watch . 666.4

gloom
was mourned . . . in g. . . 96.4
lead . . . through the g. . . 117.3
dispelling fear and . . . g. . 134.2
scatters fear and g. . . 152.2
the g. . . . of dark despair . 225.2
g. that once obscured . . 277.4
presence disperses my g. . 318.2
g. fell deep as night . . 330.1
out of my g. to his glory. . 378.3
softly through the g. . . 393.3
the g. had all passed . . 395.3
pierce the g. of sin . . . 412.4
doubts . . . filled me with g. . 437.3
g. and sorrow . . . no more . 540.5
light in g. decline . . . 545.3
amid the encircling g. . . 606.1
shine through the g. . . 670.5
time's thickest g. . . . 683.5
scenes of deepest g. . . 725.2
though it be the g. . . . 772.3
chase (b)

gloomy
all the way seems g. . . 316.c
g. thoughts that rise . . 898.3

glorify-ied
1 *(we) glorify*
a *glorify God* *Rom 15:6*
my days my God to g. . . 290.3
I have, a God to g.. . . 472.1
content . . . if thou be g. . 485.3
it g. our Lord 494.2
g. thee till I die . . . 589.5
b *Phil 3:21*
we hail thy body g. . . 154.3
in beauty g. 156.4
c *glorify name* *2 Thess 1:12*
his name to g. . . . 784.2
g. our Father's n. . . . 863.5
g. thy name . . . . 916.*
d *2 Thess 3:1*
Jesus' word is g. . . . 165.3
Jesus is g. and gives . . 195.1
2 *(we) are glorified* *John 17:10*
thy life in me be g.. . . 861.2
b *(Rom 8:17)*
I shall be g. 761.4
the g. ever shall roam . . 872.c
I shall be g. 882.3
with its g. beings . . . 883.3
robes which the g. wear . 904.2
fields where the g. rove . . 905.2

glorious
1 *(re divine)*
most blessed, most g. . . 8.1
he rose, our g. head . . 149.2
g. Prince of Life . . . 152.3
Father all-g. 219.1
g. Trinity 224.4
will of his g. Son . . . 654.4
g. Saviour, thee I praise . . 741.2
our g. leader claims . . 879.5
b *glorious King*
worship the K., all g. . . 16.1
when he comes, our g. K. . 118.5
lives again our g. K. . . 143.4
call him my . . . g. K. . . 388.4
blessed and g. K. . . . 561.1
fighting for a g. K. . . . 821.1
c *glorious Lord* *Isa 33:21*
we our g. L. will bring . . 230.4
crown thee g. L. of all . . 499.4
d *glorious name*
bless his g. n. . . . 20.5
proclaim . . . that g. n. . . 940.2
e
to see his g. face . . . 195.4
thy g. face to behold . . 300.4
thy g. eye pervadeth . . 517.3
f *Phil 3:21*
he rises g. from the dead . 151.3
then his g. image bear . . 370.2
rise . . . in g. majesty . . 870.2
2 *(general)*
g. in his faithfulness . . 17.2
broad and deep and g. . . 40.2
love brings the g. fulness . 46.3
a g. foretaste 46.4
his g. righteousness . . 60.5
a g. guiding star . . . 80.3
my beauty . . . g. dress . . 116.1
look, . . . the sight is g. . . 147.1
O g. hour 149.1

those g. scars 161.3
rejoice in g. hope 164.6
all partake the g. bliss 165.1
my g. rest above 182.1
his the g. sacrifice 249.2
g. gain of thy cross 300.2
in the g. fight to start 338.2
more g. and bright 387.1
sent his g. light 408.1
wonder of his g. love 476.2
love thee for the g. worth 515.2
O the g. revelation 540.2
bring . . . to g. flower 577.1
shall rise the g. thought 632.4
springs to g. birth 682.2
his g. cross surrounding 693.c
a g. band, the chosen few 701.3
joys of that g. time 794.3
a g. crown beyond 818.4
take . . . his g. commission 864.3
this great and g. war 869.4
all will be happy, g. 881.c
one g. morning 888.1
g. gift of his love 900.3
what a g. shout there'll be 912.3
the g. harvest home 924.4
the g. unknown morrow 948.3
saved, O g. thought c30
show . . . radiance g. c102
g. victory that overcomes c117

b *glorious [banner]*
raise the g. standard 696.3
beneath this g. banner 781.3
see the g. banner waving 804.3

c *glorious day*
hasten to thy g. day 667.3
in this his g. day 699.2
darkness, to thy g. day 859.3
breaks a yet more g. day 876.5
he's coming, O g. day c185

d *glorious [gospel]* *1 Tim 1:11*
sheds not its g. ray 224.1
I have g. tidings of Jesus 329.1
the g. gospel word 385.1
spread the g. news 499.4
let the g. message roll 546.3
sing out the tidings g. 828.2

e *glorious Kingdom* *Ps 145:12*
his Kingdom is g. and rules 24.1
bring thy g. Kingdom in 692.2
bring God's g. Kingdom in 760.2

f *glorious liberty* *Rom 8:21*
bring the g. liberty 441.1
g. news, liberty 499.4
'tis a g. liberty 546.2

g *glorious song*
the angels' g. s. 74.3
that g. song of old 83.1
the angels sing a g. s. 326.5
a song with g. harmony 327.3
a g. symphony of song 858.1

h *glorious things* *Ps 87:3*
g. t. of thee are spoken 157.1
'tis a g. t. to know 375.2

i *glorious throne* *Isa 22:23*
raise us to thy g. t. 79.4
a g. t. of sovereign grace 269.1

gloriously
he hath saved us g. 769.1
g. they died 866.1

glory
1 *(general)*
this world's empty g. 98.4
shut his g. in 105.3
all lower g. wane 551.1
I lay in dust life's g. 621.4
a g. gilds the . . . page 657.2
earth's . . . g. pass away 670.2
not for weight of g. 707.2
spread their g. o'er me 766.1
flag! thy threefold g. 776.1
its crimson g. streaming 783.1

2 *(spiritual glory) (man's)*
Jesus, be thou our g. now 61.5
when that world's g. 98.4
where his g. . . . I'll share 124.3
thou my soul's g. 177.1
to bring the light and g. 203.2
rekindle . . . the g. bestow 209.*
foretaste of g. divine 310.1
found g. begun below 314.3
my g. and my plea 325.1
my g. and my wealth 346.4
G. filled my soul 371.c
what a g. he sheds 397.1
the rays of g. shine 400.1
all the g. I possess 406.c
g. in thy perfect love 438.2
highest g. his reproach 451.4
g. came thrilling my soul 542.3
g. crowns the mercy seat 573.4
may this my g. be 592.4
g. of . . . well done 628.4
g. of the faith we hold 656.4
g. in Christ, the Lord 724.2
a life . . . of g., too. 787.4
the g. of believing 790.3
how bright their g. be 879.1
now the g. for the cross. 894.2
it brings the g. c170
story my crowning g. c212
when the g. gets into c223

b *glory (name)* *Ps 105:3*
may I . . . g. in thy n. 14.2
I will g. in thy n. 157.3

c *2 Cor 3:18*
changed from g. into g. 438.3
from g. unto g. changed 515.4
g. upon g. . . . prepared 682.3

d *glory (in cross)* *Gal 6:14*
in nothing else . . . g. 107.5
in the cross of Christ I g. 112.1, 5
cross, be my g. ever 115.c
cross has wondrous g. 320.3
my g. all the cross 476.3
the g. of his cross 735.1

e *crown of glory* *1 Peter 5:4*
with g. crown . . . band 702.c
c. of fadeless g. 777.3
c. with g. we shall be 809.4
a c. laid up in G. 899.1

f *[eternal] glory* *1 Peter 5:10*
one eternal day of g. 309.3
eternal g. gleam afar 345.3
the realms of endless g. 381.1
his eternal g. won 916.3

prepare (b)

3 *Glory [Heaven]* *Ps 73:24*
then to G. I'll fly 137.5
g. of that perfect rest 141.4
it lifts me up to G. 182.3
lights our way up to G. 316.c
a soldier bound for G. 338.1
sweeping up to G. 344.3
with G. in my view 361.3
wending on to G. 368.1
the golden stair to G. 369.c
banquet of g. in Heaven 373.4
safe to G. . . . guide 377.4
all the way to G. 430.c
till g. breaks 657.4
up to g. wing our flight 809.4
marching to G. 815.*
soon we in realms of G. 828.4
on, then, to g. run 897.3
marching home to G. 902.1
a golden harp in G. 902.c
the hills of bright G. 905.4
through the ages be G. 906.*
marching along to G. c229
all the way to G. c231

b *(John 17:5)*
babe who came from G. 74.2
mild he lays his g. by 82.3
left his g. above 124.2
what g. . . . lay aside 135.1
didst yield the g. 174.1
from G. to Calvary he came 319.3
how he left his home in G. 337.1
left the realms of G. 363.2

c *in Glory* *Col 3:4*
with the ransomed in G. 179.4
highest archangels in g. 184.1
may we in g. see 219.4
my endless theme in G. 327.3
with the saints in G. 337.c
in G., in G., for ever 368.4
then in G. shine 560.5
soldier in G. I'll be 684.3
with me in G. live 797.2
where thou art in G. 862.4
we'll sing in G. . . . story 888.3
one glimpse of him in G. 892.3
where saints in g. stand 897.1
crown/harp/mansion in G. 899.*
a golden harp in G. 902.c
we shall up in G. meet 902.4
robes . . . and harps of g. 902.5
ransomed in G. we see 908.1

gloryland, leave (1a), mansion (c), realm (2b)

4 *divine glory*
let them his g. also show 2.4
enthroned in heavenly g. 6.1
the g. of thy love 36.6
the g. of my God and King 64.1
have we a name for g. 71.2
no clouds thy g. hide 76.4
g. of his righteousness 84.3
of Jesus and his g. 98.1
his g. now we sing 156.2
praise and g. . . . not fail 156.4
with a g. in his bosom 162.4
gleams of its g. bursting 173.2
g. crowns thy . . . brow 185.4
and the g. shall stream 233.1
high in heavenly g. 240.2
send the g. 355.c
my gloom to his g. 378.3
love in its g. 383.2
g. shall chase away 465.4
there display thy g. 516.2
thy joy, thy g. share 612.7
in thy sole g. may unite 665.5
the glory of . . . presence 711.3
catch its radiant g. 726.3
seeking to mirror thy g. 786.2
with g. stand fulfilled 868.2
untold g. linger there 873.1
my love and g. know 875.4
nor heart conceive the g. 878.4
at the throne of g. 894.1
oft are its g. confessed 904.1
towers with g. . . . burnished. 905.3
g. of his resurrection 907.2
make thy g. known 942.2
the g. of your presence 943.2
thy g. never thence depart 945.4
I'm singing a g. song c175
his g. showing . . . growing c176
the g. of his face c187

b *for [God's] glory*
God's great g. . . . revealing 159.2
let if for thy g. burn 199.2
for all thy g. meet 210.3
fighting for his g. 352.3
for thy g. make me thine 463.c
for the g. of my King 514.3
for thy g. we will fight 593.3

c *[Lord] of glory* *1 Cor 2:8*
great Father of g. 8.4

God of g., Lord of love . . 10.1
God of g. and of grace . . 102.4
O Lord of life and g. . . 123.2
the Prince of G. died . . 136.1
Christ of G., Prince . . 479.1
thou art holy, Lord of G. . 528.1
God of grace and . . . g.. . 577.1
Lord of all g. 957

d *fill with glory* *Ps 72:19*
whose g. fills the earth . . 30.4
thy g. fills the night . . 154.1
G. filled my soul . . 371.c
whose g. fills the skies . . 412.1
fill the world with g. . . 801.c
thy g., Lord, fill . . . space . 946.1

e *give glory due*
Ps 96.8; (Matt 5:16)
receive the g. due . . . 7.3
give him the g. . . . 22.c
to thee be g. given . . 85.3
his g. proclaim . . 183.1, 5
give the g. all to you . . 518.3
all g. to Jesus be given . . 535.1
give the g. all to God . . 809.c
give to Jesus g. . . 831.*/952
g. and praise to Jesus g. . 915.1

f *grace and glory* *Ps 84:11*
God of g. and of g. . . 102.4
the g. and g. of thy name . 353.3
the Lord gives g. and g.. . 410.3
g. and g. in abundance . . 452.4

g *live to glory*
and to his g. live . . . 23.2
may to thy great g. live . . 492.1
me to thy g. live . . . 720.4

h *Matt 6:13*
thine shall the g. be . . 117.1
thine is the g. . . 152.1, c
take the power and g. . . 161.4
thine is the g., Lord . . 171.3
power and g. . . . belong . 184.3
thine all the g. . . . 457.3
g. and might are beyond us . 506.1
the g. shall be all thine . . 626.3
thine is the g. for ever . . 951

i *Luke 2:32*
eyes have seen the g. . . 162.1

j *see his glory* *John 17:24*
thou shalt see my g. . . 110.5
thy g. may not see . . . 220.3
let us now thy g. see . . 481.1
in Heaven shall see his g. . 514.4
in his g. I'll see . . . 543.4
till I thy g. see . . . 636.5
King in his g. we see . . 808.5
his g. unclouded we see . 908.4
we may thy g. see . . . 933.4
greater g. . . . yet behold . c44
all men thy g. may see . . c59

k *2 Cor 4:6*
knowledge of the g. of God . c158

cloud (1b), crown (1c, 2c), dwell (1e), honour (c), King (2h), Lamb (2e), reveal (f), shine (1d), show (1j)

5 *glory! [exclamation]*
what a g., he is mine . . 74.*
all g. to our risen head . . 151.3
g., g., hallelujah . . . 162.c
go singing glory! home . . 338.5
g. to the great I AM . . 370.3
G.! Praise ye 383.c
g. for evermore . . . 413.4
O g., my soul . . . perfect . 436.4
g., g., hallelujah! . . . 504.c
g., g., g., ... 546.*
g., g., how . . . sing/ring . 550.c

b *glory [to God]* *Luke 2:9, 14*
all g. be to G. 72.6
all g. in the highest . . 80.c
g. to the new-born King . 82.1, c
g. to G. in the highest . . 85.2
g. shone around . . . 93.1
all g. be to G. on high . . 93.6
g. to God in the highest . . 99.1
g. be to G. on high . . 326.c
g. to God . . . . 328.*
all g. to G., I'm the child . 354.4
g. to G., I'm out of Hell . . 380.1
shines the g. of the Lord . 555.1
g. to G. on high . . . 562.3
g. to G. for such . . . 710.3
g. in the highest . . . sing . 757.1
give the g. all to G. . . 809.c
g. to G., he has ransomed . c157
I am a soldier, g. to G. . . c229

c *glory (to name)* *Ps 105:3*
he lives, all g. to his n. . . 144.4
g. to his name . . . 315.*
g., g. to his n. . . . 474.5
g. to his name . . . 750.c

d *Eph 3:21*
to God be the g., great . . 22.1
to God be the g., . . . mine . 640.1
g. to thee, my God . . 671.1

e *Rev 5:12**
all g. and power . . . might . 24.3
g. for ever to Jesus . . 99.3
g. to Jesus, the Lamb . . 166.1
g. to Jesus, to Jesus . . 166.c
g. to Jesus, I know . . 323.3
g. to the Lamb . . . 520.c
g. . . . unto Christ . . . 690.5
unto Jesus g. . . . 803.4
to Jesus be the g. . . . 828.1
g., honour and salvation . c27

Lamb (2e), sing (3d)

Gloryland
when we reach the G. land . 94.c
in that l. of G. reign . . 268.4
before, the G. . . . c152
glow of the G. . . . c153

glow-ing
he made their g. colours . 25.1
summer suns are g. . . 40.1
g. with peace and joy . . 112.2
this earthly part of me g. . 189.3
rekindle the g. . . . 209.*
till it g. with grace . . . 324.2
my path his light doth g. . 347.3
g. in any earthly sky . . 387.1
light of life . . . must g. . 408.2
the sacred fire . . . g. . . 546.1
o'er flow in . . . g. word. . 612.6
their bright faces g. . . 703.4
where the dawning g. . . 776.1
beyond the g. skies . . 818.4
within the world to g. . . 838.1
through his g. face . . 855.2
bright letters that g. . . 883.2
we see the golden g. . . c153

b *glow (in heart)*
g. within this h. . . . 194.2
my h. with joy is g. . . 343.2
may this g. h. rejoice . . 365.1
dwell within my g. h. . . c96
bring h. g. and tender . . c213

go-ing/gone/went
1 *(God) goes*
g. thou still before us . . 40.4
the place where he is g.. . 87.5
as to death they g. . . 129.2
from age to age g. on . . 198.3
g. on from . . . hour . . 201.c
where the Saviour would g. . 316.c
thine . . . to g. before . . 510.2
my Saviour g. before . . 540.5
desert thou didst g. . . 607.2
the way the Master w. . . 683.1
cross of Jesus g. on . . 690.1, c
the Son of God g. forth . . 701.1
where the Saviour g. . . 776.1
way which thou didst g. . 846.3
g. through my heart . . c50
if Jesus g. with me . . c172

b *John 14:2*
place he is g. to prepare . 794.2
home he's g. to prepare . . c251

2 *(we) go*
a *(re salvation)*
opened . . . that all may g. . 22.1
world may now g. free . . 128.4
my heart . . . g. out . . 138.2
to all who thither g. . . 261.4
I will g. . . . let me g. . . 275.4
I will not g. back till . . 298.5
without delaying, let us g. . 348.3
all my fears I let g.. . . 507.3
with what joy they w. . . 558.1
in all need to Jesus g. . . 634.4
in prayer I may g. . . . 794.2
while I to the river g. . . c42
beneath its waves I am g. . c221

b *go [to Heaven]*
those who've g. before . . 45.3
those who've g. on before . 139.3
all the righteous g. . . 217.2
will you g. . . . . 275.*
will not g. . . . to Hell . . 275.4
shall g. there to dwell . . 394.4
g. . . . to the promised land . 817.3
rejoin . . . comrades g. . . 819.3
Heaven, there the holy g. . 835.3
that even I may g. . . . 840.3
who will come and g. . . 887.c
called to g. from the ranks . 894.c
step by step we mean to g. . 901.1
O say, will you g. . . . 905.*

c *go [to service]*
we'll g. on with thee . . 97.5
g. singing all the time . . 326.4
where he sends we will g. . 397.5
bade me g. and happy be . 402.2
down in the valley . . . g. . 483.*
we obey thy word to g. . 500.2
g. where thou canst use . 528.4
where I ought to g. . . 531.3
g. . . . thy will pursuing . . 534.3
where we ought to g. . . 622.3
when . . . I call thee to g. . 653.3
where he appoints we g. . 659.2
to the rescue we g. . . 687.1
let the . . . herald g. . . 697.3
marching on we g. . . 698.2
ends of the earth . . . g.. . 700.c
g., care for the dying . . 703.4
to the war we will g. . . 703.4
hearts that will g. . . . 704.1
like heroes g. before . . 704.1
safe shalt thou g. on . . 715.3
g. without a murmur . . 731.c
suffer and triumph I'll g. . 734.3
calls us, there to g. . . 772.5
to the ends . . . we will g. . 800.3
God's soldier g. . . . 801.1
determined . . . to g. . . 933.3
I'll g. with him . . . c57
everywhere we go . . . c123
if Jesus goes . . . I'll g. . . c172
singing we g. . . . c220

d *go forth*
I rose, w. forth . . . 283.3
forth in thy name . . . I g. . 667.1
g. forth into . . . highway . 683.6
we g. forth not to fight . . 687.2

e *as I go*
singing as I g. . . . 390.c
as onward I g. . . . 394.4
upon me as I g. . . . 586.2
as to the war we g. . . 705.1
as through . . . we g. . . 814.3
as we g. marching . . . 815.*

onward, singing as we g. . 818.c
as we g. to seek . . 822.c
singing as we g., g. home . 903.c

f *go or .*
with him to g. or stay . 451.3
equal joy to g. or stay . 556.3
witness, to g. or remain . 640.3

g *go [to death]*
through the vale I g. . 709.3
you'll have to g.; prepare . 914.1

h *go (imperative)*
rejoicing g. . . 46.4
g. ye to Bethlehem . 72.3
g.! cry the news . . . ring . 127.c
come, and g. with me . 266.c
in Jesus' ways g. on . 312.1
g., labour on . . . 683.*
g. forth into . . . highways . 683.6
g., fearlessly g. . 689.1
from strength . . . g. on. . 695.6
never mind, g. on . . 805.*
g. with . . . Bible/songs . 830.2
g. with the cross . . 864.2
g. back to the old wells . c40

i *Acts 24:25*
g., Spirit, g. thy way . 226.1

j *Ps 121:8*
shall preserve thy g. out. . 767.4

k *Matt 28:19*
command to g. . . 700.1

l *John 6:68*
to whom shall I g. . . 289.4
to whom else shall I g. . . 443.c
where shall we g. . . 791.1

astray, battle (c), forward (b),
Heaven (2l), home (3c), let (1c, d),
more (5e), onward (b), peace (2h),
strength (2d), victory (2b), wash
(2c), wherever (b), who (c)

3 *(general)*
goods and kindred g. . . 1.4
like an evening g. . . 13.4
wherever it w. . . 90.3
all our griefs . . . g. . 131.2
our crown of peace is g. . 268.4
my guilt is g. . . . 317.c
sight was g. and fears . 337.3
thraldom of evil is . . . g. . 410.3
fear of death has g. . 536.2
trembling thought be g. . 559.1
wishes . . . g. with the words. 588.1
g. take thee . . 604.2
till the night is g. . . 606.3
the war will g. on . . 684.4
courage almost g. . . 804.2
tide that's g. out . . 854.2
g. is my burden . . c159
they are all g. . . c188
g. is every fear . . . night . c191
every sin had to g. . . c198
a little will g. so far . . c200

b *go by*
the silent stars g. by . 86.1
memories of deeds g. by . 303.2
singing as the days g. by . 396.2
in dark days g. by . . 440.3
to let the world g. by . 476.3
in days g. by . . . sufficient . 732.3
grave of years g. by . 753.3

c *go down*
it's sun which g. not d. . 76.5
sun . . . no more g. d. . 275.2
the sun g. d. . . 617.2
ere the sun g. d. . 913.*

d *go over* Ps 38.4
sin hath g. over me . 296.1
storms g. o'er my head . 746.4
billows are g. o'er me . 762.1

day (4h)

4 *going to*
we're g. to see . . 275.2
thou art g. to save . . 608.3
we're g. to fill/smile . . . 801.c
I'm g. to make my life . . . 858.*
I'm g. to march beneath . c241

goal
lead me to that g. . . 204.3
on toward the g. . . 309.2
safely reach the g. . . 344.2
miss thy Kingdom's g. . 577.3
not the grave, is our g. . 771.4
this shall be our g. . . 788.3
g. of earth's . . . race . 878.2
lures them from the . . . g. . 885.2
God is his g. . . c210

God *voc n c, but see*
almighty (e), eternal (1a), everlasting
(d), grace (3e), gracious (b), great
(1b), incarnate, living (3b), mighty
(1b), pardoning (a), wise (e)

l
may this bounteous G. . 12.2
G. moves in a . . . way . 29.1
don't assume that G. . 44.*
this day hath G. fulfilled. . 78.2
so G. imparts to . . . hearts . 86.3
G.-forsaken loneliness . 122.2
cry to Zion: See thy G. . 159.2
G. appears on earth . 161.1
G. is marching on . 162.3, 4
that G. . . . dwells in me. . 176.4
I believe in God . . 222.c
G. hath bidden all mankind . 234.1
all condemned before G. . 245.4
our G. in pity lingers . 251.3
blessings G. on man . 257.3
flax G. will not quench . 269.2
can my G. . . . forbear . 286.1
who never know our G. . 314.1
G. can change the hearts . 324.2
gulf that G. did span . 405.4
G. has sent . . . light . 408.1
G. . . . shall dwell in thee . 465.5
whom G. will crown . 580.3
G. planned . . . to show . 590.1
hang on a crucified G. . 639.2
G. . . . we then shall know . 651.4
bring us daily nearer G. . 668.4
glories hath our G. prepared . 682.3
strength which G. supplies . 695.1
triumphant G. will make . 702.1
armour . . . G. will bestow . 703.3
G. hears thy sighs . . 721.1
G. shall lift up . . 721.1
G. sitteth on the throne . 721.3
G. will fulfil . . . promise. . 723.1
G. will remember them no more 724.c
leave G. to order all . 738.1
G. never yet forsook . 738.3
scoffed and mocked my G. . 758.3
the hope our G. inspires. . 765.4
while our G. is saving . 774.c
I promised G. . . 774.3
G. judges, we believe . 785.6
G. is keeping his soldiers . 800.1
story of our G.-made host . 803.4
G. loves to give . . 806.3
God in man can never fail . 809.2
Army . . . that G. is raising . 822.1
without G. as architect . 827.3
G. our thought is reading . 836.3
G. make my life . . 838.*
G. knows every one . 850.*
you can't stop G. . . 854.*
G. smiled . . . glowing face . 855.2
G. will fill me . . 858.c
saints whom G. has led . 858.2
G. reliant, Hell defiant . 869.4
still G. . . . yet appear . 871.4

G. stoops from Heaven . . 885.4
G. resides among his own . 909.2
G. . . . in his saints delight . 909.2
tempted to forsake his G. . 911.3
G. shall say: Well done . 912.3
G. is pledged to multiply . 923.3
G. sends his reapers . 928.2
G. be in my head . . . 953
G. never changeth . 956
who G. possesseth . 956
alone G. sufficeth . 956
more hath G. in store . c44
that G. may use me . c71
G. can and will . . . supply . c120
I know G. can . . c120
G. will take care of you . c124
G. bless our Army . . c244

alone (a), answer (1b), appear (1b),
born (1c), call (1b), can (b), do (2a),
fail (1a), fight (2c), forsake (1),
glorify (1a), glory (5b), high (3c),
lead (3a, e), mediator, meet (3f),
mercy (f), pardon (2a), praise (3k),
provide (c), reside, see (3b, 5d),
serve (1b), speak (1b), thanks (c),
trust (3d), will (3b)

b *God gives*
G. g. his Son for me . 45.1
G. g. . . . equipment . 324.4
promise G. hath g. . 753.1
G. g. to you chances . 773.2
G. will g. his blessing . 805.1
G. g. a crown . . 823.3

c
while G. is G. to me . . 14.3
of gods he is the G. . 34.2
him who is thy G. . . 557.4
I am thy G. . . . 653.2
he still is G. . . 785.2
thou shalt be our . . . G.. . 918.5
this is the G. we adore . 962

d *God is . . .*
mighty fortress is our G. . 1.1
yet not a G. afar . . 6.1
G. is stronger . . 9.*
our G. our Father is . 9.4
G. is our strength . 20.4
G. is the ruler yet . 42.3
himself is close . . 238.1
ours is not a distant G. . 238.2
G. is our light . . 316.1
G. is over all . . 396.3
shore, since G. is there . 556.2
happy . . . when G. is there . 661.1
who is a G. like unto thee . 724.2
G. . . . is one who cares. . 732.1
G. is round about me . 736.1
G. is your wisdom . . 773.3
this G. is mine . . 875.2
where G. is not . . 885.3
G.! is so good and kind . c5
G., is not far away . . c115
G. is still on the throne . c122
G. is there . . . c134
G. is his goal . . . c210

e *Matt 1:23*
G. is with us . . . 158.*
G. is with . . . soldiers . 381.3
G. be with you till . 954.*
G. is with us all the time. . c123

f *2 Cor 4:6*
God hath shined . . . c158
light (2b), love (2b), near (2b)

God of
G. of concrete . . . 30.1
G. of pentecostal fame . 447.3
coming to the G. of prayer . 470.2
show . . . O G. of power . 504.3
strength, O G. of power. . 526.4
G. of comfort . . . wisdom . 576.1
thou G. of every nation . 621.1
O thou G. of all . . 698.3

90

G. of battles 774.1
G. of our fathers . . . 918.2
Abraham, Bethel, Elijah, glory (4c), grace (3e), Heaven (4b), host (2b), Jesus (8e), light (2b), love (2c), peace (2j), salvation (1c)

3 *God's (possessive)*
G. truth abideth . . . 1.4
the hosts of G. encamp . . 21.3
ye servants of G. . . . 24.1
G. re-creation of . . . day . 35.3
out in the fields of G. . . 41.2
in G. house for evermore . 54.5
ye martyrs of our G. . . 56.4
to see the courts of G. . . 59.4
our G. inspiring voice . . 95.3
G. remedy for sin . . . 98.2
the mercy seat of G. . . 116.4
heard in G. eternities . . 127.3
ransomed host of G. . . 132.3
G. appointed day . . . 145.2
trump of G. shall sound . . 164.c
G. eternal purpose . . 174.4
temple of indwelling G. . . 214.3
G. day of grace . . . 241.4
days to sing G. praise . . 308.4
purchase of G. . . . 310.1
from the fold of G. . . 313.3
G. strong arm . . . embrace . 335.2
in G. garden grows . . 346.3
into G. family divine . . 371.2
in the presence of G. . . 372.3
saints of G., lift up . . . 381.1
Jesus, Light of G. . . . 429.3
the voice of G. obey . . 433.1
a holy hill of G. . . . 461.1
the voice of G. obey . . 471.4
on the hills of G. . . . 483.3
boundless compassion of G. . 527.1
the temple of our G. . . 533.5
G. armies, just hid . . . 537.2
the ways of G. . . . record . 656.1
perceive the mind of G. . . 656.3
G. all-seeing eye . . . 665.2
G. trumpet is sounding . . 684.1
G. enemies strong . . . 687.4
moves the Church of G. . . 690.3
enjoying G. full favour . . 704.1
G. hand that leadeth me . . 725.1
the guest of G. . . . 728.*
I want the faith of G. . . 733.1
G. glorious Kingdom . . 760.2
claim the victory G. . . 774.2
foes of G. around us . . 778.1
wealth of G. . . . bountiful . 796.2
G.'s soldier . . . . 801.*
not G. plan frustrate . . 801.2
the sacrifice of G. . . . 830.2
a place by G. decree . . 850.3
written on G. memory . . 850.4
depths of G. design . . 858.3
in the palace of G. . . . 886.2
G. tomorrow 888.c
servant of G., well done . . 890.1
followers of the dying G. . 909.1
cast it in G. treasury . . 920.3
work out G. sentence . . 928.1
blessed is that land of G. . 934.4
G. almighty hand . . . 935.1
the faithfulness of G. . . 939.4
become the house of G. . 943.4
keep the touch of G. . . c76
this G. moment . . . c106
live in G. sunshine . . . c116
present shows G. mercy . . c166
G. blue sky o'erhead . . c238
in G. great name . . . c238

b *God's face*
they shall see the f. of G. . 95.2
the f. of G. I shall see . . 459.3
repent before G. f. . . . 785.4

c *God's gift*
love's gift is G. g. . . . 51.3
grandest g. G. . . . impart . 119.2
'tis the g. of G. . . . 240.4
g. of G. unto his own . . 539.1
we who G. g. enjoy . . 828.1

d *God's life*
G. life for rebels given . . 113.3
living in the life of G. . . 330.3

e *God's will*
may know the w. of G. . . 451.1
doing the w. of G. . . . 451.c
the w. of G. be all my joy . 451.3
G. will be done . . . 536.3
my will is the w. of my G. . 542.c
G. w. may be accomplished . 833.2

anger (b), approval, Army (1b), breath (1), child (4b), children (2b, c), city (2b), command (c), field (2c), garner, grace (2h), Lamb (2b), love (2e), mercy (i), name (1d), own (4c), power (4n), promise (3d), salvation (g), soldier (e), son (1c, 2c), Spirit (3b), sword (2d), thing (1c), throne (4i), wisdom (1c), word (1b)

4
[by/of] God
Lamb by G. appointed . . 109.2
Jesus, beloved of G. . . 175.2
when blessed by G. . . 874.1
chosen by G. . . . c225

b *[for] God*
a highway for our G. . . 159.1
let my future be for G. . 477.2
thy zeal for G. in me . . 594.1
for G. to live and die . . 784.2
we will work for G. . . 818.1
the world for G. . . . 830.*
for G. had been a host . . 847.2

fight (2c), right (3b)

c *[from] God*
from G. may ne'er depart . 190.2
afar from G. . . . strayed . 225.1
message as from G. . . 234.3
wandering from my G. . . 305.1
Bread from G. I chose . . 631.3
parents strayed from G. . . 785.3
holy Jesus, come from G. . 871.2
for ever separate from G. . 885.2
ye wanderers from G. . . 905.1

d *[in] God*
rejoice in G. sent down . . 195.*
have faith in G. . . . 723.*
rest thou in G. . . . 729.2
still in G. confiding . . 764.2
one the march in G. begun . 765.5

e *[(un)to] God*
render to my G. . . . 23.1
wooing them to G. again . 212.3
to G. draw near . . . 269.1
return ye unto G. . . . 272.2
brought me home to G. . . 347.1
I was to G. a stranger . . 361.1
things are possible to G. . 407.6
given my all to G. . . . 504.c
a sacrifice to G. . . . 511.4
speaks to G. in prayer . . 580.1
take me home to G. . . 597.4
by whom we come to G. . 625.6
as to G. we're confessing . 637.4
carry everything to G. . . 645.1
to help me on to G. . . 678.3
sing to G. 807.1
true to the Army and G. . . 820.5
bring them back to G. . . 822.c
now to G. be crying . . 913.1
sinners home to G. . . c25

belong (b), glory (5b, d), lead (3d), live (2j)

f *[with] God*
must take to dwell with G. . 190.3
fill . . . souls with G. . . 210.1
an advocate with G. . . 414.4
with my G. to guide . . 556.3
walk with G. 583.1
wonderful . . . talk with G. . 583.2
wonderful . . . live with G. . 583.5
leave the rest with G. . . 750.3

peace (i) reconcile walk (2d)

5 *God and . . .*
gracious Master and my G. . 64.2
G. and sinners reconciled . 82.1
leads to Heaven and G. . . 113.2
fulness of . . . Heaven, of G. . 214.4
G. and Heaven . . . my own . 498.2
leads to G. and Heaven . . 586.1
Heaven . . . and G. defying . 693.2

Father (1b), Jesus (7), King (2k), man (2g), right (3b)

b *Lord God*
bless the L. your G. . . 20.1
the L. your G. adore . . 20.5
the L. G. made them all . . 25.c
for my L. and G. I own . . 116.3
saith the L. your G. . . 272.3
from G. the L. . . . come . 767.1
the L. our G. shall come . 924.3

c *Ps 100:3, 5*
the Lord . . . is G. indeed . 3.2
the Lord our G. is good . . 3.4
know that the Lord is G. . 4.1

Godhead *Col 2:9*
veiled in flesh the G. . . 82.2
to the throne of G. . . 141.4
blessed G., Three in One . 222.c
make to us the G. known . 756.1
the G., we believe . . . 785.2

godless 19.4

godly *Heb 12:28*
of jealous, g. fear . . . 425.1
I want a g. fear . . . 596.3
g. fear redeem the time . . 747.3

gods *Ex 20:3*
of g. he is the God . . . 34.2
worship g. of stone . . 588.2
cast aside all other g. . . 827.2

Godward
G. our spirits aspire . . 351.2
Christward, homeward, G. . 776.2

gold-en
1 *(general)*
sun with g. beam . . . 2.1
he the g.-tressèd sun . . 34.4
comes round the age of g. . 83.3
with g. of obedience . 183.1, 5
the vain world's g. store . 428.3
each day is a g. treasure . 666.2
days of . . . g. sunshine . . 711.3
weary ways or g. days . . 730.4
service is the g. cord . . 826.2
these fields of g. . . . 923.1
g. sheaves of harvest . . 929.3
robes of g. the fields . . 934.1
g. fields spread far . . . 934.4
made ripe by g. fire . . 936.2
reapers return with g. sheaves 936.4
the path with g. light . . 938.2

b *silver and gold*
of s. and g., his coffers . . 354.1
take my s. and my g. . . 525.4
care not for . . . s. nor g. . 883.1

c *Ex 25:17*
mercy seat . . . purest g. . 590.1

d *Mal 3:3*
g. be mixed with dross . . 522.1
thy g. to refine . . . 653.4
mingle with Heaven's g. . 780.1

e *Matt 2:11*
their g. and myrrh . . . 90.5

f *1 Peter 1:7*
boast of heaps of g. 356.2
your g. will waste 356.2
g. . . . more precious far 516.4
dreams of fame and g. 860.4

g *1 Peter 1:18*
not with g. or gem 707.3

2 *(re Heaven)*
I reach the g. strand 115.4
ripple o'er g. sand 252.1
behold . . . the city of g. 280.4
strike those g. strings 368.4
climbing up the g. stair 369.c
one g. dawning 888.1
break on the g. shore 889.3
all the happy, g. day 891.2
g. glow of the Gloryland c153

b *golden crown* *Rev 4:4**
casting down their g. c. 220.2
climbing with my g. c. 369.c
a robe . . . a c. of g. 811.c
the victor's c. of g. 876.3

c *Rev 21:18, 21*
thy g. gates appear 877.2
tread the streets of g. 892.4
march to tread the g. street 902.4

harp (b)

good
1 *(noun)*
all hope of g. is given 127.4
emblem of g. 175.2
a point my g. 207.2
more graces for the g. 265.4
naught but g. . . . betide 377.4
souls . . . lost to the g. 527.1
give . . . every g. 561.2
no g. to crave 592.3
care for our eternal g. 656.2
longings for the . . . g. 760.3
do the g. I know 837.6
with the g. and blest 882.3
bear evil or g. 928.3

b *Ps 14:3*
no g. in creatures 14.3

c *Rom 8:28*
thread . . . for my g. 644.4
shall work for my g. 712.4
all counted g. 874.3

ill (b)

2 *(adjective re divine)*
Jesus, g. above all 97.1
no other g. enough 133.4
none other is so . . . g. 334.3
so g. to redeem 372.1
through God's g. grace 718.2
we have a g. guide 763.3
God! is so g. and kind c5

b *Ps 100:5*
the Lord our God is g. 3.4
g. to those who seek 61.3
g. in all thy ways 576.4
seek thee thou art g. 602.2

shepherd (1c)

3 *(adjective—general)*
all must be . . . g. as he. 87.3
go on from this g. hour 201.c
cherish all things g. 212.5
holy, all are g. 268.3
nought of g. . . . done 306.3
right, and pure and g. 444.4
they'll be g. for me 499.3
life is lovely . . . g. 544.1
'twould not be g. for me 586.1
scatter the g. seed 935.1
all g. gifts around us 935.c
all things bright and g. 935.3
this is g. news c210

b *make good*
he died to m. us g. 133.3
with thy nature m. us g. 452.2
m. all evil natures g. 593.4
he will m. g. his right 685.2
all things . . . thou m. g. 927.1

c *Matt 17:4*
'tis g., Lord, to be here 154.*

d *Luke 10:42*
secure the g. part 469.2

e *Col 1:10*
nor yet g. works . . . atone 269.3
fruitful in g. work 933.1

f *Rom 12:2*
while we do his g. will 397.1

comfort (1d), fight (2h), pleasure (3b), report, seem (b), tidings (c)

goodness
clouds . . . fountains of g. 8.2
they who thirst for g. 95.1
filled with his g. 310.3
g. o'er my sin prevailed 391.2
fruits of truth and g. 408.2
Lord, thy g. show 409.c
his g. I have seen 495.2
would contemplate thy g. 595.2
constant g. is the spring 616.1
all thy g. tell 622.4
all thy g. prove 646.4
filled with his g. divine 710.3
tell . . . Saviour's g. 835.1
thank him for his g. 836.c
how to grow in g. 842.3
ever reflecting his g. 844.3
thine eternal g. praising 939.5
power and g. here display 945.1
g. has been all my song c147

b *(Ps 14:3)*
no strength or g. 325.2
no . . . g. we claim. 763.4

c *Ps 23:6*
g. and mercy . . . attend 19.2
g. faileth never 53.1, 5
g. and mercy all my life 54.5

d *Ps 65:11*
thank . . . for all your g. 552.1
g. crowns the . . . year 925.1
thy g., Lord, we see 926.1
crowns the year with g. 929.2
gifts his g. gave 929.3
making thy g. known 936.4

goods *(Luke 12:19)*
g. and kindred go 1.4
take . . . all my g. 492.2
rich in g. and poor 577.3

goodwill *Luke 2:14*
g. to men and peace 72.6
on earth, g. to men 80.c
on the earth, g. to men 83.1
g. . . . Heaven to men 93.6

gory 701.3

gospel
g. day sheds not 224.1
sinners, to the g. feast 234.1
the g. news is sounding 239.1
grace . . . in the g. found 254.1
trip in the g. ship 375.c
g. sounding, summon all 693.c
sing the g. story 801.c
hold the g. banner high 847.4
g. that matches/claims c210
g. of life . . . love c226

b *Mark 16:15**
as we tell the g. 832.2

c *blessèd gospel* *Rom 1:9*
thy b. g. may . . . be heard 626.3
proclaim the b. g. 945.3

glorious (2d), preach (a)

grace-s
1 *(human)*
g. human and divine 28.5
more g. for the good 265.4
no special g. 294.2
with all Christlike g. 577.4
each talent and g. thine 589.3
take every virtue . . . g. 695.3
my talents, gifts and g. 720.4

2 *(divine)*
keep us in his g. 12.2
g. our souls enduing 38.5
sovereign g. to all 55.2
have we a name for g. 71.2
Lord . . . thy g. supplying 97.3
amazing pity, g. unknown 105.2
for g. to love thee more 110.6
pleading brings g. to me 129.c
may taste the g. 140.5
g. which . . . never fails 157.2
thy g. might shine 174.1
with an inward g. 202.1
for g. to conquer 203.3
we wait the promised g. 216.2
almighty g. for ever new 223.3
ready . . . his g. to reveal 236.3
in g. he calls again 241.3
what is his g. . . . to thee 276.3
I have no claim on g. 290.1
hope . . . from thy g. 290.2
O soul-renewing g. 290.3
look to thee for g. 302.3
g. . . . every debt to pay. 303.c
thy condescending g. 307.2
amazing g. 308.1
to g. how great a debtor 313.4
till it glows with g. 324.2
g. for a fallen race 341.3
took of the offer of g. 371.2
his g. will sure allow 385.4
Christ made known . . . g. 398.3
perfect . . . what g. 410.1
gasps my . . . soul for g. 412.2
O the g. the Father shows 418.3
to keep thy g. . . . show me 440.3
I cast . . . on timeless g. 449.3
helpless . . . until thy g. 456.2
Lord, thy g. apply 479.3
seek . . . the g. to obey 501.3
thank you, Lord, for g. 552.1
and thy refreshing g. 557.1
the g. is thine . . . deep 571.2
thy g. can never fail 574.2
his g. has no measure 579.3
g. that we . . . inspired 581.1
g. that they may conquer 582.5
ask thee for thy g. 588.4
redemption's g. to show 590.1
little place of mystic g. 615.3
lead us to g. 648.3
bounteous g. hath given 667.4
world a friend to g. 678.3
with g. to support 689.3
unworthy of such g. 730.1
his g. as my shield 734.3
plenteous g. . . . is found 737.4
g. to cover . . . sin 737.4
thy g. upholdeth me 741.4
rest on his unchanging g. 745.2
cast down, but for thy g. 747.1
it ne'er outweighs his g. 758.1
not greater than his g. 758.c
all-prevenient g. 762.1
for g. that I . . . remember 762.3
the g. that sealed us 764.1
to g. there is no limit 770.3
of thy g. are we enrolled 799.1
g. our spirits will deliver 891.3
proved the fulness . . . g. 910.2
with thy pentecostal g. 941.2
g. that rescued/keeps c164
ponder his sweet g. c187
the g. that brought me c218

abound (b), bestow (b), boundless (c), fill (2b), flow (2e), free (2b), full (1d), give (1h), glory (4f), grant (b), great (2e), grow (3e), heavenly (b), impart (b), more (2c), plenteous, receive (2c), redeeming (b), saving (b), sing (3e), Spirit (3d), trust (4b)

b *all grace* *2 Cor 9:8*
the source of all g.. . 119.2
with all its g., is given . 168.4
the Spirit of all g. . 196.2
all thy g. on us bestow . 210.4
gratitude for all his g. . 533.1
Lord of all g. . 611.3
all the g. your word imparts . 856.4
thou author of all g. . 946.3

c *let/may grace* let thy g.
let that g. . . . bind. . 313.4
let thy g. my will incline. . 460.3
let me share that g. . 512.3
let thy g. . . . cleanse . 555.4
let thy g. inspire . 616.3
may that same g. inspire . 760.1
may thy g. . . . attend me . 865.2
may that g., once given . 940.4

d *grace can*
g. alone . . . can pardon. . 297.5
of what thy g. can do . 571.2
what but thy g. can foil . 670.3
feelings . . . g. can restore . 691.3
all thy g. can do in me . c74

e *[reject] grace*
rejecting offered g. . 253.1
long withstood his g. . 286.2
could not see . . . any g. . 353.1
g. I long have slighted . 361.1
I spurned his g. . 380.2

f *John 1:16*
adding g. to welcomed g. . 423.4
and every beauteous g. . 515.4

g *under grace* *Rom 6:15*
kept low by g. . 468.4
I am . . . under g. . c164

h *grace of God* *1 Cor 15:10*
God's rich g. was granted . 52.2
g. of God so strong . 295.4
when I think of God's g. . 319.2
God's g. did abound . 319.2
by God's g. we may attain . 324.3
made known the Father's g. . 398.3
the saving g. of God . 494.2
God's ample g. for . . . man . 656.2
through God's good g. . 718.2
why God's wondrous g. . 730.1
kept by the g. of God . c199

i *sufficient grace* *2 Cor 12:9*
more than s. God's g. . 319.2
my g. all-s. shall be . 653.4
s. is thy g. from day . 761.1

j *grace of Jesus* *2 Cor 13:14*
be saved by J.' g. . 56.3
the g. of J. strengthens . 176.2
they are talking of J.' g.. . 372.2
partakers . . . Saviour's g. . 659.5
strong in the g. of the L. . 679.*
by J.' g. we stand . 781.3

k *2 Tim 2:1*
in the strength of g. . 505.1
be strong in the g. . 679.*

l *find grace* *Heb 4:16*
f. fortitude and g. . 595.2
plenteous g. . . . is f. . 737.4
striving saint f. g. . 943.3

m *by grace*
assisted by his g. . 78.3
kindled by his g. . 256.1
by his all-constraining g. . 445.4
made worthy by thy g. . 461.4
God, by g., shall dwell . 465.5
kept low by g. . 468.4
by thy g. I'll follow . 490.c
by thy g. I'll follow . 498.c
by thy life and g. we live . 532.1
overcoming by limitless g. . 640.5
help us . . . by thy g. . 698.3
by his g. we shall endure . 722.1
when by thy g. . . . won. . 725.4
promise ratified by g. . 760.2
by thy g. we will . 804.c
by his g. I shall look . 906.c
by thy g. I will be thine . c10

n *Gal 1:15*
led by g. . . . to know . 545.1
draws thee by his g. . 816.1

o *[saved] by grace* *Eph 2:5*
be s. by Jesus' g. . 56.3
by g. . . . may be when s. . 114.2
a sinner s. by g. . 266.4
s. me by thy g. . 301.3
s. . . . kept by thy g. . 431.4
hearts renewed by g. . 704.2
by his g. forgiven . 740.c
by his saving g. . 769.1
b. his full g., salvation . 785.4
we by g. are justified . 785.4
who s. us by his g. . 888.2
s. and kept by the g. . c199
tell the story s. by g. . c245

p *through grace*
I t. g. a member am . 157.3
t. what thy g. . . . work. . 287.3
t. g. he lifted me . 339.1
t. thy . . . g. . . . stand . 437.3
now, t. heavenly g. at peace . 536.c
t. g. I'll win . . . crown . 678.c
run . . . t. God's good g. . 718.2
t. g. I shall be glorified . 761.4

q *grace divine*
claims mankind by g. d.. . 30.4
filling me with g. d. . 188.4
fit temples for thy g. d. . 202.3
thy g. divine . 571.2
by the power of g. d. . 584.2
by the power of g. d. . 585.2
whose g. is d. . 640.1
hearts renewed by g. d.. . 704.2
by thy g. divine . 707.c
it speaks of g. d. . 781.2
let us use the g. d.. . 784.1

abound (b)

3 *of grace*
for means of g. . 15.5
the triumphs of his g. . 64.1
the treasures of his g. . 81.3
kindled by a spark of g. . 165.1
bearing the lamp of g. . 224.3
pass God's day of g. . 241.4
gushing streams of g. . 268.2
let the merits of thy g. . 285.1
thy gardens of g. . 288.4
the men of g. have found . 314.3
the whispers of thy g. . 636.4
the captive of thy g. . 723.4
in the Kingdom of thy g. . 793.2
happy every child of g. . 880.1

b *[throne] of grace* *Heb 4:16*
sprinkles now the t. of g. . 106.2
t. of sovereign g. . 269.1
before the t. of g. . 286.3
g. for every time . 539.2
behold the t. of g. . 560.1
thy g. for every call . 561.3
before thy t. of g. . 918.2

c *[wonder] of grace*
O the w. of thy g. . 52.c
touched by the w. of thy g. . 138.2
sing the w. of his g. . 223.4
O wondrous g. that he . 541.4
know not why God's w. g. . 730.1
such w. g. . . . provided. . c62
w. g. that brought me . c218

d *word of grace* *Acts 20:32*
every w. of g. is strong . 26.3
given the w. of g. . 165.3
what amazing w. of g. . 254.1
sound this w. of g. . 262.1
w. of his g. shall comfort . 763.5
all the g. your w. imparts . 856.4

e *[God] of grace*
praise . . . the God of g.. . 17.4
God of all-redeeming g. . 23.5
God of wisdom, g. . 576.1
God of g. and . . . glory. . 577.1
God of ages, God of g. . 643.2
Lord of all . . . g. . 957

depth (d), gift (2g), miracle, promise (3c), rich (2d), river (2c), Spirit (3d), treasure, work (1f)

4 *grace and . . .*
for his g. and favour . 17.2
come with g. and beauty . 221.2
no more his love and g. . 249.3
g. and peace o'ershadow . 576.4
thy g., thy love . . . show . 656.3
missed the joy and g. . 748.1
poured his tenderness and g.. . 777.2
present g. and joys above . 940.1
his love and g. I've seen. . c173

b *grace and power*
learned thy wisdom, g. and p. 466.1
for g. and p. to win . 541.1
his g. and p. are such . 563.2
God of wisdom, g. and p. . 576.1
will give you g. and p. . 790.1
fill . . . now with g. and p. . 795.3
g. to cleanse and p. . 845.3
p. to do and g. to bear . 947.4
giving me g., . . . p. . c1
wonderful p., by thy g. . c39

glory (4f), mercy (c), truth (b)

gracious

1 *(divine titles)*
heaven's all-g. King . 83.1
a g., willing guest . 200.4
pass me not, O g. Father . 295.2
my g. redeemer . 357.1
plan our life, O g. Saviour . 863.1
g. Saviour, own us . 875.2
be present, g. Saviour . 949.2
Jesus, so . . . loving, so g. . c7

b *gracious God* *Jon 4:2**
g. Master and my God . 64.2
daily need . . . most g. God . 561.2
here, g. God . . . draw nigh . 940.3

b *gracious Lord* *1 Peter 2:3*
come quickly, g. Lord . 55.5
most g. Lord, may we . 76.1
nature, g. Lord, impart . 444.5
g. Lord, thy grace apply . 479.3
every hour, most g. Lord . 587.1
descend, O g. Lord . 626.1
g. Lord, forbid it not . 793.2
g. Lord . . . hearts now fill . 845.4

Spirit (3d)

2 *(general)*
thy g. Kingdom bring . 79.3
how g. his coming . 92.2
g. guiding of the Spirit . 192.2
with all thy g. power . 217.1
heed the g. message . 240.3
plead thy g. name . 284.5
let our g. fruit remain . 533.4
how g. his presence . 553.4
g. calling of the Lord . 567.2
vindicate thy g. will . 568.2
glad when thy g. smile . 602.3
thy g. gifts be given . 624.2
the g. work begin . 676.4
whate'er his g. will . 738.2
the g. promises of God . 755.c, 3

thy g. riches to prove . . . 786.4
g. gifts of love divine . . . 858.3
b *gracious hand*
into thy g. h. . . . placed . . 362.2
my g. omnipotent h. . . . 653.2
in thy g. h. I am . . . 793.3
blessings from thy g. h. . . 918.5
confessing thy g. h. . . . 927.4
c *Luke 4:22*
g. lips with thirst . . . 121.2
waiting for thy g. word . . 614.1
d *Num 6:25*
be g. unto thee . . . 961
e *Isa 30:19*
he g. will be 329.3

graciously *Hos 14:2*
g. he heard me . . . 348.1
g. he pardoned me . . . 386.2

grain
the gift of buried g. . . . 512.3
sheaves of ripened g. . . 923.1
wholesome g. . . . may be . 924.2
warmth to swell the g. . . 935.1

grand
is not this salvation g. . . 243.3
my Father's g. domain . . 362.1
by thy g. redemption . . 707.c
hear their hallelujahs g. . . 780.4
a message g. and true . . 783.1
forth to g. emprise . . . 799.2
how g. the truths . . . 802.1
our g. battalions . . . 815.2
was e'er so g. a theme . . 828.2
on to victory g. . . . 847.4
build a g. tomorrow . . . 869.2
songs . . . and music g. . . 873.2
we march to victory g. . . 901.5
songsters' song so g. . . c230
a company g. . . . c236
reward will be a g. one . . c237

grandest 119.2

grandeur
rocks of towering g. . . . 32.1
the g. of the universe . . 871.4

grandly 802.3

grant
g. us, by . . . knowledge . . 6.3
g. us . . . illumination . . 38.1
g. us that way to know . . 100.4
g. his name to know . . . 168.3
g. us . . . greater revelations . 173.3
g. me . . . marks of thy zeal . 484.1
g. me patience to wait . . 493.2
g. that thy servant may be . 527.3
g. . . . my spirit's longing . 548.4
for the prayers you've g. . 552.3
he always g. more . . . 560.3
g. us wisdom, g. us courage . 577.*
g. me . . . earnest prayer . 618.c
g. us to worship . . . 624.5
g. that thy blessèd gospel . 626.3
g. . . . now a refreshing . . 637.3
g. me to feel thy touch . . 644.3
g. that we . . . may learn . 654.5
g., Lord, when I . . . wake . 665.3
g. that I may come to find . 675.3
g. that . . . we labour . . 688.3
g. me no resting place . . 723.4
each blessing you have g. . 795.1
g. them strength . . . 795.2
g. the pledges . . . making . 795.2
g. us understanding . . . 922.3
Lord of harvest, g. . . . 924.2
g. . . . whate'er may be . . 941.3
g. them the joy . . . 948.3

b *grant grace*
God's rich g. was g. . . . 52.2
g. the g. of holy fear . . 466.2
g. to thy people all thy g. . 561.3
you alone can g. us g. . . 572.1
g. us g. to show . . . 624.3
c *grant peace*
g. . . . thy perfect p. . . 635.2
g. us thy p. . . . . . 674.*
g. us thy p. who give . . 675.c
g. our souls thy p. . . . 942.4
g. them the p. which calms . 948.3
d *Rev 3:21*
g. us each a seat . . . 195.4
courage (b)

grapes 162.1

graph 30.3

grass
dewfall on the first g. . . 35.2
clover-scented g. . . . 41.2
in the rustling g. . . . 42.2

grateful-ly
g. sing his power . . . 16.1
g. learn how freely . . 256.3
our g. songs employ . . 828.1
with a g. spirit . . . 836.c
accept our g. offerings . . 870.4
from each g. home . . . 921.3
a song of g. love . . . 929.1
with g. hearts . . . nigh . . 933.1
filled up with g. work . . 933.2
g. hearts to thee we bring . 938.1
g. for thy loving care . . 941.1
with g. hearts imploring . . 950

gratitude
in g. for all his grace . . 533.1
elate with g. 566.5

grave
1 *noun (re Jesus)*
g. where they laid him . . 99.3
who is he who from the g. . 104.5
through an open g. . . . 130.3
all for me—the . . . g. . . 134.3
g. could not hold him . . 137.4
triumphant o'er the g. . . 144.1
not for long the g. . . . 145.2
low in the g. he lay . . 148.1
up from the g. he arose . . 148.c
arose and left the g. . . 149.1
the folded g. clothes . . 152.1
triumphed o'er the g. . . 156.2
Christ is risen from the g. . 242.1
might burst e'en the g. . . 532.4
know you risen from the g. . 748.1
up from the g. he rose for me. 884.2
2 *noun (general)*
lies silent in the g. . . . 132.5
ours the cross, the g. . . 143.5
no . . . tremble at the g.. . 149.3
master o'er my sin . . . the g.. 303.4
shout o'er the g. . . . 364.4
from the gaping g. . . . 526.1
from sin and the g. . . . 691.1
surround my lowly g. . . 751.4
the g. of years gone by . . 753.3
the sky, not the g. . . . 771.4
borders of the silent g. . . 910.1
in the g. . . . be lying . . 913.1
hourly we approach the g. . 933.4
b *beyond grave*
pierce b. the g. . . . 701.2
show thyself b. the g. . . 714.4
what hope . . . b. the g.. . 885.4
victory (2g)
3 *(adjective)*
with earnest tones and g. . 98.3

great
1 *(with title)* *Ps 96:4*
g. Father of glory . . . 8.4
g. Lord of nature . . . 38.5
the g. physician . . . 67.1
come, g. Spirit, come . . 217.1
come, g. Spirit, come . . 218.c
to the g. One in Three . . 219.4
come, O come g. Spirit . . 481.c
O thou g. Jehovah . . . 578.1
g. Guardian of my . . . hours . 672.2
comes our g. commander . 804.4
my g. creator's power . . 871.1
my g. unchanging friend . . c163
b *great God*
how g. is God Almighty . . 25.4
g. God of universal love . . 140.2
God is g.! 544.5
the g. God who calls . . 703.2
bless our child, g. God . . 796.4
c *great redeemer*
our g. r. liveth still . . . 5.5
sing my g. r.'s praise . . 64.1
ocean of the g. r.'s love . . 239.4
my g. r.'s throne . . . 444.2
our g. r.'s praise . . . 853.3
I AM, King (2b)
2 *(general)*
craft and power are g. . . 1.1
henceforth my g. concern . 14.4
the g. congregation . . . 24.2
g. gifts on him bestow . . 48.3
g. glad tidings tell . . . 86.4
it gave g. light . . . 90.2
and in g. humility . . . 101.2
orders in their g. array . . 141.2
g. the heritage/conquests . 158.2
God's g. glory . . . 159.2
come in thy g., might . . 172.4
g. the fall 243.4
thou g. crimson sea . . 298.2
God in g. mercy . . . 347.c
g. transaction's done . . 365.3
his g. delight to bless . . 377.3
lifted sin's g. burden . . 386.2
g. was the gladness . . 388.3
mercy there was g. . . 405.c
though g. . . . attractions . 461.2
to thy g. glory live . . 492.1
though g. my faith be . . 530.2
life is g.! 544.1, 2
love is g.! 544.3
a g., mighty shower . . 608.1
though our trials be g. . . 687.4
g. mountains to remove . . 733.1
need and thy g. fulness . . 741.4
trusted God's g. word . . 760.4
last g. battle won . . . 774.3
telling of that g. war . . 802.1
fighting . . . g. delight . . 809.2
one g. fellowship . . . 826.1
giants, g. and tall . . . 847.3
in the g. crusade . . . 859.3
thy g. love demands . . 861.4
g. the name they bore . . 866.1
heed the g. command . . 868.1
g. and glorious war . . 869.4
his g. judgment throne . . 893.*
harvest rich and g. . . 923.2
last g. conflict won . . 939.3
to thy g. truth . . . rear . . 942.2
at the g. awakening . . . 950
b *how great*
how g. is God Almighty . . 25.4
how g. thou art! . . . 37.c, 4
see how g. a flame . . 165.1
to grace how g. a debtor . 313.4
how g. the blessing . . 536.1
how g. our debt to you . . 572.3
how g. their joys . . . 879.1
c *great Army*
g. A. of salvation . . . 696.3

flag of God's g. A. . . . 779.2
one g. A. make . . . 788.2

d *great day* *Rev 16:14**
bold . . . in thy g. d. . 116.2
a g. d. of rejoicing . . . 169.1
not only . . . on that g. d. . 618.1
for the g. accounting d. . . c249

e *great grace* *Acts 4:33*
g. g. . . . upon us all . . 216.3
g. g. would hallow . . 760.4

f *great love* *Eph 2:4*
such l. so g., so deep . . 48.1
in his g. l. . . . whole . . 273.4
whose l. was so g. . . 331.1
thy g. l. and power . . 409.5
that g. l. which made . . 475.c
thy l., so g. and tender . . 504.1
is thy l. so g. 515.1
only . . . in thy g. l. . . 668.5
l. so g. that men . . . 827.2
tell of his g. l. . . . 851.4
as thy g. l. demands . . 861.4
hopes . . . on his g. l. . . 940.1
whose l. is as g. . . . 962

g *great name* *Ezek 36:23*
thy g. n. we praise . . 8.1
my vows . . . to his g. n. . 23.3
but unto thy g. n. . . . 163.1
I trust in thy g. n. . . . 415.4
I trust in thy g. n. . . . 511.2
called by thy g. n. . . . 516.5
we his g. n. record . . 533.1
the Saviour's g. n. . . . 763.4
thy g. n.! 916.c
in thy g. n. we place . . 942.2
the power of his g. n. . . 945.3
forth in God's g. n. . . c238

h *great need*
the world's g. n. I see . . 482.1
my g. n. I am feeling . . 610.1
millions . . . n. is g. . . 801.2
my g. n. are known . . c74

i *great salvation* *Heb 2:3*
I have found a g. s. . . 63.c
bring near thy g. s. . . 167.3
to sing of his g. s. . . . 178.3
now reveal his g. s. . . 191.2
I've found this g. s. . . 320.2
I have found a g. s. . . 328.1
he wrought so g. s. . . 341.3
God's g., free, full s. . . 413.2
let us see thy g. s. . . . 438.3
send a g. s. flood . . . 452.2
send a g. s. flood . . . 593.4
Calvary's g. s. fame . . 609.2
full s., g. and free . . . 727.1
swell the g. s. theme . . 901.4

j *great [tribulation]* *Rev 7:14*
out of g. t. to triumph . . 170.3
out of g. distress . . . 909.2

blood (2b), compassion (d), do (2b, c), faithfulness (a), king (2b), price, promise (3i), rejoice (k), reward (c), small (b), tidings (c), too (1b)

greater
g. will be our wonder . . 22.3
use unto thy g. praise . . 163.2
still g. revelations . . . 173.3
as our burdens grow g. . . 579.1
g. victories every hour . . 622.3
more than we can ask, and g. 642.2
the cross is not g. . . . 758.c
O for a g. . . . trust. . . 770.c
g. glories/blessings c44

b *John 15:13*
no man of g. love . . . 515.3

c *greater things* *John 1:50*
g. t. await you still . . . 433.3
even/prove g. things . . 769.*

greatest
the g., the grandest gift . . 119.2
the pearl of g. price . . 346.1
my soul's g. longing . . 493.1
g. joy is found . . . 857.1
gave thy g. gift . . . 861.1
pay love's g. price . . . 922.3
g. proof of his love . . c121

b *1 Cor 13:13*
love's the g. way . . . 544.4

greatly
we g. need thee . . . 213.3
how g. I needed . . . 553.3

greatness *Ps 150:2*
the g. and the praise . . 171.3
his g. and his love . . . 178.2
feel thy g. till we know . . 181.4
tell of his excellent g. . . 184.c
I now have seen his g. . . 215.2

b *Eph 1:19*
the g. of thy power . . 533.5

c
some may bring their g. . . 849.1

greed
hate and g. destroy . . 71.1
g. and selfishness are free . 833.1

green
love climbed the g. hill . . 51.c
there is a g. hill . . . 133.1
earth . . . is sweeter g. . . 545.2
arrayed in living g. . . 887.2
dressed in living g. . . 898.2

pasture

greet
yea, Lord, we g. thee . . 85.3
with rich gifts to g. him . . 92.1
lovingly he g. thee . . . 152.2
g. with life reviving . . 155.2
lift thy voice and g. . . 159.2
Heaven comes down . . . to g. 573.4
g. them with this . . . song . 744.1
come . . . each one to g. . 748.3
g. the rising of the sun . . 776.1
souls each other g. . . 873.3

greeting
peace, is the g. . . . 751.2
with a heavenly g. . . . 908.2

grew—see grow

grey c206

grief
1 *(divine)* *Isa 53:3*
his cup of pain and g. . . 5.3
dies in g. and agony . . 104.4
thy cup of g. to share . . 117.4
with g. and pain weighed . 123.1
thy g. and thy compassion . 123.2
his g. for all . . . atone . . 127.1
thy g. and shame . . . 140.3
no tears for his own g. . . 179.2
remember all my g. . . 229.3
bore for me in g. . . . 451.2
solace in thy g. is found. . 486.3

2 *(human)* *Isa 53:4*
charm their g. to rest . . 21.2
knows all my g. . . . 68.2
all our g. . . . surging . . 131.2
thy heart's deep g. . . 225.4
my heart . . . torn with g. . 292.2
filled with g., my soul . . 303.1
he can cheer one in g. . . 329.2
from my guilt and g. . . 339.3
he all my g. has taken . . 344.2
g.-laden did I wander . . 379.1
torn by remorse and g. . . 383.3
I bring my g. to thee . . 421.4
the g. I cannot tell . . . 421.4
caused you bitter g. . . 433.2
out of my stony g. . . . 617.4
seasons of distress and g. . 633.1
love and g. . . . dividing . . 634.3
commit thou all thy g. . . 715.1
if my g. means . . . gain. . 729.3
g. around me spread . . 743.3
my life's defeat and g. . . 770.1
there is no g. above . . 895.3
in our g. alone to be . . 938.3

b *grief and joy*
in j. or g., to live . . . 489.1
'tis not in g. to harm . . 498.5
in j., in g., through life . . 524.4
j. or pain, . . . g. . . . 544.2
nor j., nor g. . . . part . . 659.5
toil and g., or j. . . . 874.1

c *grief and pain*
p. and g. and dark distress . 343.2
g. and p. shall cease . . 453.4
in my hours of g. and p.. . 552.3
inured to p., . . . g. . . 596.2
cause for g. and p. . . 618.3

d *grief and sin*
depth of human g. and s. . 135.1
the gloom of s. and g. . . 412.4
all our s. and g. to bear . . 645.1

bear (1d), loss (b), river (2d)

grieve-d
from all doth g. you . . 73.2
look on him . . . and g. . . 191.4
though we've g. thee . . 213.3
g. him by . . . falls . . . 286.2
I will not g. thee more . . 409.5
I may never more g. . . 437.2
to g. thee . . . never more . 502.3
have I g. thee . . . 534.2
cause my heart to g. . . 536.2
he g. for every child . . 855.4
our spirit often g. . . . 930.3

grievous
this g. affliction . . . 111.3
how g. man's darkness . . 708.2

grim 1.3

grip 733.3

groan-ing
thy dying g. 105.c
bond through which I g. . 419.3
victims g. 696.2

b *Rom 8:22*
let us g. thine inward g. . 191.4

grope 682.2

ground
1 *(literal)*
all seated on the g. . . 93.1
sweat . . . upon the g. . . 486.3
fruits from tree and g. . . 926.3
this consecrated g. . . 942.1

b *Ex 3:5*
every place is hallowed g. . 604.1

c *John 12:24*
into the ready g. to die . . 923.1

2 *(figurative)*
fruit on earthly g. . . . 314.3
through Immanuel's g. . . 314.3
have I that g. maintained . 409.2
from the g. there blossoms . 621.4
may be our battle g. . . 705.1
all other g. is . . . sand . . 745.c
at sunrise, on the g. . . 890.3
plant . . . on higher g. . . c80

b *stand ground*
s. your g., and win . . 694.5
s. your g., today . . 750.3
we will s. our g. for ever. . 800.2
s. your g. and never yield . 809.3
c *1 Tim 3:15*
the truth, . . . the g. . . 656.1
now I have found the g.. . 746.1
fixed on this g. . . . remain . 746.5

grounded *Eph 3:17* . . . 280.c

grow-ing-n/grew
1 *Jesus (grew)*
day by day like us he g.. . 87.4
a boy g. up in Nazareth . . 855.2
2 *(general)*
fruits that in thee g. . . 2.4
scattered seed has g. . . 926.2
b
as baby g., discerning . . 795.2
to full stature . . . g. . . 796.4
daily as I g. 842.3
c
the journey g. longer . . 553.2
3 *(spiritual)*
praises there may g. . . 11.1
the verdant pastures g. . . 53.2
trees . . . be seen to g. . . 159.4
it spreads and g. . . . 165.2
celestial fruit . . . may g. . 314.3
in God's garden g. . . . 346.3
the tree of life does g. . . 374.c
g. light my g. need . . 534.1
for fragrant flowers g. . . 552.2
the life . . . is g. . . . 553.4
Kingdom stands, and g. . . 677.5
on trees immortal g. . . 887.3
flower, fairest that g. . . c54
b *grow (adjective)*
love g. cold 172.5
my faith's g. bolder . . 298.6
the way g. brighter . . 340.3
Jesus has been g. dearer . 343.1
the cloud g. thin . . . 358.3
ever deeper, richer g. . . 539.1
my way has brighter g. . . 549.c
as our burdens g. greater . 579.1
the light is g. clearer . . 696.1
toil . . . will g. lighter . . 758.4
how bright the path g. . . 768.2
unceasing war g. wise . . 799.3
strife should fiercer g. . . 805.2
men's hearts g. faint . . 864.1
stars g. pale 873.4
c *Matt 13:25-30*
unto joy or sorrow g. . . 924.2
to g. with wheat . . . 932.3
tares and wheat . . . g. . . 932.3
d *Eph 4:15*
each nation g. more like . . 146.1
g. like him . . . pattern . . 443.4
like him I shall g. . . . 640.5
in all things g. . . . 662.3
day by day to g. like thee . c38
e *2 Peter 3:18*
in that knowledge daily g. . 748.4
as he (she) g. in knowledge . 792.3
how to g. in goodness . . 842.3
men in grace have g. . . 936.3
I'm daily g. c176
dim (b), multiply (a), weary (e)

grudgingly *2 Cor 9:7* . . 475.3

guard-ed-ing
1 *(God) guards*
thou our g. while life . . 13.6
angels . . . g. thee . . . 117.2
Jesus will g. his children . 184.1
all power . . . to g. me . . 345.3
g. thou thine own . . . 516.2
love divine . . . my g. . . 556.5
my guide, my g. my friend . 563.5
g. us, guide us . . . 607.1
g. my first springs . . . 665.4
g. thou the lips . . . 674.2
thou hast the g. . . . 717.4
as the bird . . . g. . . . 722.4
his wisdom shall g. me . . 734.2
now my g. and guide . . 917.4
2 *(we) guard*
let me g. . . . holy fire . . 199.3
nor g. deed and word . . 466.2
speak to g. the tempted. . 581.4
standing on its g. . . . 596.3
my soul, be on thy g. . . 812.1
writing, g. and translating . 856.1

guardian
be thou our g. 190.1
great G. of my . . . hours . 672.2
thy love and g. care . . 721.5
g. care evokes my praise . 728.3
be the g. of our way . . 845.2
thou G. of my soul . . 862.3

guess 666.2

guest *(Luke 19:7)*
a gracious, willing g. . . 200.4
thou g. of the soul . . . 209.1
nor visit as a . . . g. . . 214.3
every soul be Jesus' g. . . 234.1
made me his own happy g. . 373.2
the g. of God! . . . . 728.*

guidance
thy g. we crave . . . 209.3
for g. kneel 408.3
we seek thy . . . g.. . . 576.3
our hope of g. . . . light . . 692.4

guide-d-ing
1 *(divine)* *Ps 48:14/John 16:13*
presence to cheer . . . g. . 33.3
is there a name to g. . . 71.3
be thou . . . our g. . . . 190.1
in life and death our g. . . 196.6
a g. a Comforter . . . 200.1
if he be my g. . . . 228.2
find this faithful g. . . . 343.3
so wise a Counsellor and g. . 345.4
since I made him my g. . . 376.3
let him be thy g. . . . 458.3
with my God to g. . . . 556.3
in our wanderings . . . g. . 570.3
be their g. . . . Deliverer. . 576.2
be their light and g. . . 582.2
my patient spirit g. . . 596.4
my wisdom and my g. . . 597.2
provided, pardoned, g. . . 607.3
who . . . my g. and stay. . 670.3
there is light to g. us . . 711.3
since he is my g. . . . 712.2
lean on thy g. 718.3
trusting thee to g. me . . 727.4
wherever he may g. me . . 736.2
thy all-sufficient . . . g. . . 738.1
be thou my g. 743.3
we have a good g. . . . 763.3
he's your g. and shield . . 817.2
none else to be my g. . . 857.2
if thou wilt be my g. . . 862.1
bless the hand that g. . . 896.3
now my guard and g. . . 917.4
I have a pilot who g. . . c132
he will g. till . . . done . . c182
b *friend and guide*
unfailing f. and g. . . . 257.4
g. and helper, lover, f. . . 510.c
as my g. . . . my f.. . . 563.5
f. and g. and King . . . 859.1
f. and g. . . . long journey . 938.1
Jesus, be f. and g. . . 955
c *(request)*
g. us when perplexed . . 12.2
in all our doings g. . . . 97.5
g. me . . . great Jehovah . 578.1
teach us, g. us . . . 595.2
guard us, g. us . . . 607.1
g. me, or I . . . rove . . 630.1
take . . . hand and g. me 635.1, 3
g. us that we too may g. . 796.2
only do thou g. . . . 865.2
g. us . . . Morning Star . . 937.2
d *Ps 32:8*
g. thee with mine eye . . 753.*
e *guide [steps]* *Ps 37:23*
g. thy s. as may best . . 183.2
feeble s. . . . g. aright . . 597.1
g. my steps and keep . . 641.1
our footsteps g. . . . 655.1
wandering footsteps g. . . 918.3
f *guide feet* *Luke 1:79*
he g. me lest my f.. . . 342.2
mine . . . to g. my f. . . 652.2
g *[Spirit] guides* *John 16:13*
gracious g. of thy Spirit . . 192.2
the Comforter g. thee . . 739.3
through the Spirit's g. . . 764.2
whose Spirit shall g. us . . 962
aright (a), counsel (b), safe (c)
2 *(other)*
a *(Scripture)*
our g. and chart . . . 654.2
and our footsteps g. . . 655.1
seen, to g. the traveller . . 658.3
its message be our g. . . 856.3
b
thy cross before to g. me . 53.4
need no star to g. . . . 76.4
g. . . . where the Saviour . 316.c
I need no other g. . . . 374.2
there's a star to g. . . . 716.*
c *(we) guide*
teach me . . . g. them . . 519.2
my life may g. men . . 529.1
g. the wandering . . . 581.4
that we too may g. . . 796.2
star (e)

guiding
a *(noun)*
safest g. 716.2
b *(adjective)*
left his g. light . . . 267.1
I trust thy g. hand . . . 628.4
comfort of a g. hand . . 740.2
gleams . . . the g. light . . 765.2
let your g. presence . . 792.3
his g. voice we hear . . 818.3
thy wisdom g. teaches . . 927.3
star (e)

guile 6.3

guilt
his name dispels my g. . . 67.4
doomed for g. to . . . pains . 75.4
cleanse from all its g. . . 108.c
knows her g. was there . . 120.4
our g. made his Calvary . . 245.c
guiltless, my g. bore . . 290.1
helpless . . . full of g. . . 291.2
from my g., O set . . . 292.6
stained with g. . . abhorring . 303.1
my g. is gone . . . 317.c
from my g. and grief . . 339.3
burdened by my g. . . 403.1
from all the g. of my sins . 437.1
might be cleansed from g. . 538.2

set . . . free from g. . . 563.3
take all my g. away . . 743.1
nor spot of g. remains . . 746.2

b *guilt and [power]*
the g. and p. of sin . . 230.4
cleanse me from its g. . . 302.1
from the g. and p. of sin . 540.3
g. and strength of sin . . 629.3

c *guilt and shame*
absolved . . . from g. and s. . 116.2
knew our g. and s. . . 135.2
all our g. and s. unfolding . 185.1

guiltless 290.1

guilty
a g. rebel I 45.1
all their g. fear . . . 60.2
shake off thy g. fear . . 106.1
g., vile and helpless . . 118.3
give the g. conscience . . 120.1
lose all their g. stains . . 132.1
g. past is washed away . . 188.1
come, ye g., come . . 240.1
pardon claim, O g. one . . 831.4
for me, the g. one . . . c211

b *guilty sinner*
there is never a g. s. . . 186.4
making g. s. whole . . 230.1
and g. s. unrenewed . . 268.3
g. s., such as I . . . 284.5
I was a g. s., but Jesus . . 368.*
for every g. s. flows . . 638.1
brings g. s. home . . . c25

c *guilty soul*
g. s. for mercy plead . . 269.2
can save this g. s. . . . 297.1
each g. s. may cherish . . 363.4
till my g. s. . . . turned . . 405.2
come, g. s., for Jesus . . 802.2
g. s. rise alone . . . 893.1

gulf *Luke 16:26* . . . 405.4

gushing *Ps 78:20* . . . 268.2

H

habit 748.3

habitation *Eph 2:22* 210.2

hail-ed
h. thee as the sun above . 10.1
h. the star 73.3
with joy they h. its light . . 76.1
we h. thy body glorified . . 154.3
h. his triumph now . . 155.2
not yet we h. the day . . 163.4
h. thy crowning day . . 171.1
h. a new creation . . . 358.1
we come to h. thee . . . 595.1
Jesus came to h. . . . 855.5
b *(exclamation)* *Matt 27:29*
h. the incarnate Deity! . . 82.2
h. the . . . Prince . . . Sun . 82.3
h. . . . blessed morn/dawn . 88.c
h. . . . Jesus/King/Saviour . 109.1
h. him as . . . King . . . 156.1
h. him! highest archangels . 184.1
h. him! Jesus the crucified . 184.2
h. Immanuel 185.3
h. Father, Son . . . God . . 223.5
c *all hail*
all h. the power . . . 56.1
all h., redeemer, h. . . . 156.4
all h. reproach . . . 526.2
all h., I'm saved! . . . 694.c
all h. to Daniel's band . . 847.1
all h. the power . . . c175

hair 103.2

half
shepherd h. so gentle . . 265.2
tell not h. the story . . 333.4
ere the day is h.-done . . 579.2
mourn . . . h. their days . . 806.2

hall
the banquet h. on high . . 375.3
purge the dark h. . . . 416.1
tell it in the h. . . . 829.2

hallelujah
1 *(exclamation)* nc, but see amen
2 *(adjective)*
stand on the h. strand . . 879.c
h. city/music/Heaven . . 902.*
3 *(noun)* *Rev 19:1**
sing h. to our King . . . 76.5
let us sing h. 89.3
what rush of h. . . . 167.2
sing eternal h. . . . 334.3
the loud h. prolong . . 537.4
I hear their h. grand . . 780.4
world with h. ring . . . 821.1
with . . . your h. raise . . 929.1

hallow-ed
dwell within our h. breast . 210.2
yearning for the . . . h. fire . 379.3
h. each thought . . . 453.2
thy h. shrine 516.3
within these h. walls . . 575.2
h. now our mercy seat . . 590.3
time . . . be a h. hour . . 599.1
every place is h. ground . . 604.1
arise to h. every deed . . 619.4
to h. all we find . . . 668.2
grace would h. every deed . 760.4
flag of h. memories . . 774.2
blessings that h. our days . 900.3
h. path they trace . . . 949.3
stay . . . h. this hour . . c98
name (1g)

halt
1 *(noun)* *Luke 14:21*
room for the lame, the h. . 266.2
the h., the blind . . . 590.3
2 *(verb, adjective)*
in perplexity we h. . . . 711.2
h. the progress . . . 854.2
b *1 Kgs 18:21*
held by my h. behaviour . 553.3

hand
1 *(divine)*
a *(physical—re Jesus)* *John 20:27**
behold his bleeding h. . . 107.2
h. and feet are bound . . 121.2
h. my pride has nailed . . 122.1
sacred h. of Jesus . . . 129.c
from his head, his h. . . 136.3
behold his h. and side . . 156.4
in . . . h. are wound-prints . 228.2
pierced his h. through . . 245.c
with his outstretched h. . . 260.c
with his wounded h. . . 260.2
spreads his h. 286.4
lo! that h. is scarred . . 299.2
his h. . . . were torn . . 339.3
the print . . . in his h. . . 364.1
whose human h. were quick . 518.1
strong h. were skilled . . 611.2
h. swift to welcome . . 611.3
you do not show your h. . 748.4
I wish that his h. . . . 794.1
tiny h. and downy head . . 855.1
extends his wounded h. . . 880.3
h. my . . . sins had pierced . 917.4
those wounds in his h. . . c89
by the print . . . in his h.. . c248
b *(figurative)*
thy h. still holds . . . 6.4
all . . . thy h. hath provided . 33.c
his full h. supplies . . . 34.5
feed from out thy h. . . 39.1
in his strong h. . . . trust. . 48.1
gift . . . God's own h. . . 52.1
acclaim his powerful h. . . 159.5
the h. of Jesus reaches me . 176.3
felt his h. caressing . . 330.1
I see his h. of mercy . . 334.1
with tender h. he lifted . . 339.c
the wealth . . . in his h. . . 354.1
from his precious h. . . 371.3
take from thy own h. . . 415.3
let thy h. support me . . 453.3
see thy beckoning h. . . 463.2
touch me . . . healing h.. . 531.1
thy tender h. had healed . 534.1
he laid his h. on me . . 542.3
I trust thy guiding h. . . 628.4
thy loving h. will bless . . 631.4
the workings of thy h. . . 644.2
thy loving h. doth thread . 644.4
blessings from thy h. . . 672.3
I would clasp thy h. . . 725.3
comfort of a guiding h. . . 740.2
at whose hand . . . appears . 762.1
h. of strength . . . 762.1
place thy h. upon me . . 762.3
we from his h. shall take . 777.3
now thy h. upon us . . 788.1
from his h. we shall seize . 808.5
take from his h. . . . 864.3
crowned by the h. of Jehovah 894.1
bless the h. that guided . . 896.3
God of Bethel, by whose h. . 918.1
as thy h. hath given, to thy h.. 921.3
thy h. in autumn . . . pours . 925.3
thy h. unfailing, strong . . 926.2
daily . . . thy bounteous h. . 933.2
thy bounteous h. confessing . 934.2
kept in thy h. c144
c *Job 10:8*
h. all things created . . 6.1
thy h. created me, thy h. . 23.4
the worlds thy h. have made . 37.1
his h. the wonders wrought . 42.1
worlds . . . hanging on his h.. 333.4
the creature of thy h. . . 616.2
planted by omnipotent h. . 766.1
d *Ps 91:12*
in his h. he gently bears . . 17.3
e *Ps 139:10*
his h. doth lead . . . 317.4
by his h. . . . led . . . 337.4
with his h. to lead me . . 483.2
with thy powerful h. . . 578.1
God's h. that leadeth me . 725.*
held by his mighty h. . . c152
f *[palm] of hand* *Isa 49:16*
name is written on his h. . 106.1
name's on the p. of his h. . c125
g *Luke 23:46*
trust my all in thy h. . . 285.3
into thy gracious h. . . 362.2
in thy blessèd h. I am . . 419.5
into thy h., Lord, take me . 501.c
all is in the Master's h. . . 512.2
commit . . . into his h. . . 715.1
into thy blessèd h. receive . 720.4
I'm in his h. . . . . . 732.*
I've committed to his h. . . 735.3
in thy gracious h. I am . . 793.3
within thy h. they lie . . 922.2
h *mighty hand* *1 Peter 5:6**
flung . . . with his m. h.. . 130.3
shield me with thy m. h. . 837.3
watered by God's a. h. . . 935.1
held by his m. h. . . . c152
cover (b), Father (2d), gracious (2b), pluck (c), stretch (1b), strong (1d), time (3b), uphold (a)
2 *(human)*
human h. compassion show . 50.1
faith would lay her h. . . 120.3
thy h. has squandered . . 225.1
in their dedicated h. . . 238.2
not what these h. . . . 297.1
not the labours of my h.. . 302.2
nothing in my h. I bring . . 302.3
reach out faith's h. . . 413.2
willing mind, a ready h. . . 426.3
my h. . . . takes hold . . 450.4
slow are my h. to work . . 488.2
strong shall be my h. . . 508.1
weak, o'erladen h. . . . 534.2
holds my h. and calls . . 544.2
wash from my h. . . . dust . 647.2
a sword in thy h. . . . 689.1
touched by a loving h. . . 691.3
hold thou my h. . . . 726.*
lifts its trembling h. . . 742.2
with eye and h. perceive . 748.3
clasps the h. of brother . . 765.2
join h. then, brothers . . 826.3
branch . . . high in my h. . 848.4
we are the h. of Christ . . 851.1
he claims my h. . . . 867.3
h. are wanted . . . youthful . 868.2
join their loving h. . . . 949.2

if on my h. a stain . . . c72
h. in h. under the flag . . c226

b *hands and hearts*
with h. and h. and voices . 12.1
here's my h. . . . my h. . . 312.4
our h. and h. we give . . 424.4
with mind and h. and h. . . 688.3

c *1 Kings 18:44*
little as a human h. . . 165.4

d *Ps 24:4*
Lord, cleanse my h. . . 461.c

e *Eph 6:17*
sword of God in h. . . 686.2
a sword in thy h. . . . 689.1
sword of truth in my h. . . 734.3
in each h. . . . sword . . 799.2
the sword of God in h. . . 819.1

busy, forget (1d), outstretched, right (4c-g), stay (2c), stretch (2b), take (2d), teach (1f)

3 *(in phrases)*
condemns you out of h. . . 44.3
spread on every h. . . . 243.3
foes at every h. I meet . . 400.2
with thee at h. to bless . . 670.4
the strife is at h. . . . 689.1
round me on every h. . . 882.1
dayspring is at h. . . . 896.1

handle 501.c

hang
thief h. on each side . . 108.1
h. o'er all . . . land . . . 165.4
when clouds h. low . . 719.4
its folds h. over me . . 774.3

b *Job 26:7*
worlds on worlds are h. . . 333.4

c *(Luke 19:48)*
believer that h. upon him . 372.1
h. on a crucified God . . 639.2
h. my helpless soul on thee . 737.2

d *Acts 5:30*
h. on the accursèd tree . . 120.4
upon a . . . cross is h. . . 127.2
he h. and suffered there. . 133.2
sentenced to h. on a tree . 137.3
why h. he then on . . . tree . 140.1
h. on Calvary's . . . tree. . c19

Hannah *1 Sam 1:20f* . . 839.2

haply 726.2

happen 544.2

happiness
as songs of h. I raise . . 134.3
shall peace and h. ensure . 277.3
I've a life of h. . . . 328.2
filled my heart with h. . . 340.2
O the h. he gives me . . 399.3
stoop to worldly h. . . 497.3
I sighed for rest and h. . . 547.2
the soul finds h. in none. . 556.3
give strength and h. . . 561.2
drops of finite h. . . . 601.2
saints in true h. gaze . . 639.2
h. beams all around . . 664.1
guest of God! such h. . . 728.4
lasting h. and peace . . 857.c
nor can its h. or woe . . 880.2
on the road of h. . . . c195
sing a song of h. . . . c201
true h. is love expressed . c208

happy
1 *re people*
h., if with . . . breath . . 60.6
h. at the Saviour's feet . . 210.3
take it now and h. be . . 240.*
wish that you were h. . . 244.3
no mortal so h. as I . . 318.2
h. and free, Jesus with me . 321.c
your life shall h. be . . 328.3
with Jesus we'll be h. . . 367.c
I am h., so h., as onward . 394.4
now I am h. all the day . . 395.c
bade me go and h. be . . 402.2
h. people, h. in his love . . 722.1
h., still in God confiding . . 764.2
h. in his wondrous love . . 811.c
h. most of all to know . . 837.4
how pleasant and h. . . 844.2
O we shall h. be . . . 897.2
the home of the h. . . . 905.1
you'll be h. all the time . . c116
always h. are we . . . c199

b *happy (in Jesus)*
I, in my Saviour, am h. . . 310.3
when I am h. in him . . 318.1
way to be h. in Jesus . . 397.c
h. we who trust in Jesus . 722.1
I'm h., I'm h. in Jesus . . c159

c *(how) happy*
how h. is our portion . . 43.3
O how h. are they . . . 367.1
how h. the man whose heart . 372.2
how h. every child . . . 880.1

d *thrice happy*
in that t. h. place . . . 195.4
in . . . Lamb t. h. I am . . 355.2
thine I live, t. h. I . . . 492.3

2 *(general)*
ocean-depth of h. rest . . 10.3
h. light is flowing . . . 40.1
redemption's h. dawn . . 88.c
h. bond that seals . . . 365.2
his own h. guest . . . 373.2
Canaan's h. shore . . . 375.c
joined the h. throng . . 381.3
peaceful, h. moments roll . 387.c
hope for a h. return . . 388.2
h. is my lot indeed . . . 539.2
teach me the h. art . . 597.3
h. the home when/where . . . 661.*
join our h. throng . . . 690.5
his h. people march . . 705.3
h. we who trust . . . 722.1
sing the h. song . . . 807.1
shout with the h. throng . 807.1
praise . . . in bright, h. homes. 807.3
then awake, h. song . . 818.c
come with h. faces . . 836.*
all will be h., glorious . . 881.c
join our h. Army . . . 902.5
march on, h. soldiers . . 905.4
ye h. praying band . . 912.1
this h. heart of mine . . c176
life's a h. song . . . c201

b *happy day*
on this h. Christmas d. . . 74.1
'twas a h. d. 309.c
burden rolled away, h. d. . 333.1
O what a h. d. . . . 335.c
what a h., h. d. . . . 340.1
O h. d. that fixed . . . 365.1
h. d., when Jesus washed . 365.c
O h., h. d. when old . . 366.1
serve thee all my h. d. . . 793.6
I bless the h. d. . . . 798.c
all the h. golden d. . . 891.2
in tenderness, h. d. . . c171

c *happy land*
no clouds . . . h. l. . . . 268.2
to the h. l. we'll march . . 807.1
Canaan's fair and h. l. . . 887.1
there is a h. l. . . . 897.1
Zion's h. l. 901.1, 5

d *happy morning*
salute the h. m. . . . 78.1
born this h. m. . . . 85.3
welcome, h. m. . . . 155.1, c

happier
h. still if thine I die . . . 492.3
I sigh to think of h. days. . 557.3

happiest
show me that h. place . . 639.2
hope . . . with her h. note . 911.4

harbour
city . . . and the h. bright . 280.4
trying now to make the h. . 478.3
until, the h. won . . . 628.4

hard
nor of burdens h. to bear . 320.2
if leaning h. on thee . . 325.2
broke my h. heart . . . 331.3
when my heart was so h. . 395.1
h. the battle ye must fight . 697.1
at times 'tis h. . . . 729.3
tasks . . . seem h. and long . 744.1
we find it h., Lord . . . 748.3
the fighting is too h. . . 780.2
our warfare may be h. . . 806.1
hosts . . . are pressing h. . 812.1
the fighting be h. . . . 820.3
when my work seems h. . 837.5
they wrestled h., as we . . 879.2
fierce . . . and h. the fight . 937.2
makes it h. to say . . . c95
forget how h. the way . . c208

b *Ps 63:8*
h. after thee my soul . . 448.1

c *Jer 32:17*
nothing is too h. for thee . 407.2

harden *Ps 95.8; Heb 3:8*
h. not thy heart . . . 251.1

hardest
to share the h. fight . . 704.c
the h. battles . . . won . . 806.2

hardly
h. more favoured or blest . 373.2
how h. souls are wooed. . 564.3

hardness
melt the h. . . . coldness . 531.2
love is not afraid of h. . . 555.3
in the h., God gives . . 773.2

hardship
h., grief, or disillusion . . 544.2
soul inured to . . . h. . . 596.2
share my neighbour's h. . 706.2
help . . . bear pain and h. . 837.5

hark
h! . . . from yonder manger . 73.2
h. the glad sound . . . 81.1
h! the herald angels . . 82.1
h. my soul! it is the Lord . 110.1
h., those loud . . . chords . 147.4
h., all the tribes . . . 150.1
h! . . . heavenly anthem . . 156.1
O h. to what it sings . . 187.2
h! the gospel news . . 239.1
h.! the voice of Jesus . . 240.1
h.! . . . cross there's room . 261.3
h. to this pleading . . . 457.1
h.! I hear the warriors . . 693.3
h.! from ruin's . . . road . . 696.2
h.! converts are singing . . 703.4
h.! . . . their battle cry . . 799.2
h., h., my soul . . . 802.1
h.! the sounds of singing . 803.1
h., h., h. . . . infant voices . 834.c
h. the trumpet's . . . sound . 875.1
h.! . . . voice of angels . . 889.1

harm *1 Peter 3:13*
death nor Hell shall h. . . 100.3
not in grief to h. me . . 498.5

no change can h. me 536.3
from h. and danger keep 674.3
shall guard me from h. 734.2
no moon shall h. thee 767.3
sin cannot h. me there 889.2
I know they cannot h. me c145

harmless *Matt 10:16* 623.3

harmony
for the mystic h. 28.3
melody with Heaven's h. 327.c
song with glorious h. 327.3
bells . . . with h. are ringing 342.c
life may be in joyful h. 561.3
one in faith and h. 769.3
in sweet peace and h. 833.1

harps *Rev 5:8**
ringing of a thousand h. 167.2
I'll tune my h. 368.4
you may talk of the h. 406.2
how the loud h. ring 550.c
a h., a home, a mansion 811.c
robes . . . h. of glory 902.5

b *harps [of gold]*
angels . . . their h. of g. 83.1
h. of g. and . . . fair 268.1
heavenly h. of g. 829.3
there's a g. h. in Glory 899.2
g. h. are playing/to play 902.*

hart *Ps 42:1*
as pants the h. for streams 448.1
as pants the h. . . . streams 557.1
as the h. that panteth 762.2

harvest
1 *(literal)* *Gen 8:22*
winter, and springtime and h. 33.2
at h. time our eyes 923.1
before the h. rich 923.2
the h. is thy work indeed 926.2
help us at this h. time 926.4
h. of sown field 927.1
h., milling 927.2
the golden sheaves of h. 929.3
the seed time and the h. 935.3

2 *(figurative)*
waiting for the h. 930.1
by and by the h. 930.2
what shall the h. be? 931.*
sure, will the h. be 931.c

b *Jer 8:20*
almost . . . h. is past 226.3

c *Matt 9:38*
Lord of h., grant 924.2
sing to the Lord of h. 929.1

d *Matt 13:39*
we shall reap . . . the h. 500.3
must all . . . the h. know 932.2
for the h., O prepare 932.2
blessèd is that h. song 934.4

e *John 4:35*
fields are white to h. 482.2

f *harvest home*
the song of h. h. 924.*
when h. h. draws near 926.4
gather the h. h. 931.3
angels shout the h. h. 932.c
and shout the h. h. 936.*

haste-n/-ed-ing
the days are h. on 83.3
h. now, his word obey 241.c
seeker h. to dry 249.3
h. thee . . . tarry not 261.2
yet onward I h. 355.5
march with bounding h. 362.2
lay your burden . . . h. home 369.3
h., my Lord, no more delay 412.2
h. . . . news to proclaim. 523.2
h. their burdens to share 679.2
dark night is h. on 683.4

b *Luke 2:16*
while with joy they h. on 72.5
let us h. yonder 73.3

c *make haste* *Luke 19:5*
m. h. to receive him 273.1
m. h., Lord, and come 410.2
m. h., do not delay c30

d *2 Peter 3:12*
h., O Father, the dawn 166.5
h. to thy glorious day 667.3

hate
1 *(verb)* *Rom 7:15*
thy sins, long h. 250.2
I h. my pride 415.2
shame . . . fears that I h. 422.3
I h. the sins . . . mourn 442.4
learn . . . to h. the sin 568.3

b *Ps 5:5*
thou h. all iniquity 568.3

c *John 15:18*
foes may h. 498.4
they'll h. me . . . living 758.3
world should h. us 805.3

2 *hate-hatred (noun)*
armed with cruel h. 1.1
h. at last must yield 63.2
their h. and greed destroy 71.1
h. shall ne'er divide us 97.5
when shall all h. cease 172.2
men rise . . . h. feel 529.3
rest, and h. of sin 541.3
hurts that h. can send 544.4
love . . . shall vanquish h. 705.4

haunt-ed-ing
then h. with fears 298.4
a host of h. fears 433.1
shall h. my soul no more 551.2
h. of sin and shame 832.1

have-ing/has/had
1 *[God] has*
a *(to mean 'possess')*
deignest to h. dwelling 6.1
Jesus' name h. . . . worth 63.2
he shall h. his own again 169.c
he h. no tears 179.2
all thou h. and . . . art 210.4
h. he marks to lead me 228.2
h. he diadem as monarch 228.3
I h. rest and peace 240.1
he h. mercy and pardon 264.3
he h. riches untold 354.1
thou shalt h. them all 477.3
thou, who h. the right 480.3
h. thine own way, Lord 487.*
thou shalt h. . . . way 507.3
more shouldst thou h. 516.1
thou h. my soul . . . spirit 516.2
thou h. my flesh 516.3
thy touch h. . . . power 558.5
nor h. thou . . . quicker ear 717.3
thou h. the guarding 717.4
my Saviour h. my treasure 736.3
thou h. mercy to relieve 845.3
let God h. his own again 920.2
much more h. God in store c44
thou h. my treasure c144

b *(to mean 'desire')*
would Jesus h. the sinner die. 140.1
who would h. us come 265.2
what thou wouldst h. me be 287.3
what h. thou to say 614.1
pure as thou wouldst h. 863.3
thou wilt h. me be 916.1

2 *[we] have*
his presence we h. 24.2
h. we a name for . . . 71.*
we h. a message 273.*
I h. an advocate above 305.1
we've no less days 308.4
I've h. such joy 309.2
I h. rest in his word 322.2
I h. a song that Jesus 327.1
I h. glorious tidings 329.1
naught that I h. my own 345.2
while I've breath I mean 356.1
I . . . h. a sight of Heaven 366.1
now I've a hope . . . future 371.3
I h. light in my soul 394.1
I h. pleasure 399.1, c
h. I a truthful heart 409.3
h. I the zeal I h. 409.4
can I not h. . . . flame 447.3
a charge to keep I h. 472.1
I h. a fellowship 485.5
more . . . if I h. more 516.1
though I h. wisdom 530.2
naught h. we . . . not give 532.1
such changeful feelings h. 549.1
I h. fullest enjoyment 553.4
few the gifts I h. 605.3
let me h. . . . strength 620.1
h. we trials 645.2
we h. Christ's . . . promise 690.4
Ebenezer I h. in review 712.3
I h. a token . . . the word 724.3
witness in himself he h. 756.4
what h. I to dread . . . fear 768.3
let me h. thy . . . mind 793.5
we'll h. another song 815.1
strength and health I h. 838.4
I h. a home 881.1
h. a hallelujah Heaven 902.3
h. food and clothing 921.2
we h. a gospel c210
what h. we to give c213

b *have [Jesus]*
whom h. I on earth beside 301.4
I've a friend . . . the fairest 343.1
Christ I h., . . . Christ h. I 346.1
h. for my portion Jesus 352.2
I only want to h. thee 415.4
not give to h. thee 447.2
more . . . I cannot h. 565.3
what a friend we h. 645.1
I must h. the Saviour 731.*
we h. a good guide 763.3
while I've Christ within 811.2
I h. a pilot c132
I h. a Saviour . . . mighty c165

c *have peace*
struggles cease, I h. p. 379.4
I h. wondrous p. 413.4
I h. blessèd p. 768.3

d *have salvation*
by which we can s. h. 62.2
I now h. full s. 504.c
floods of s. . . . shall h. 608.3
if we would h. . . . s. 785.4

e *all I have*
a. I h. . . . I am 23.3
a. I h., by thy blood 473.*
but a. I h. is thine 475.c
claim a. I h. and . . . am. 492.1
a. I h. I yield to thee 504.1
a. I h. and . . . hope for 514.c
a. that I am and h. 524.4
a. that I h. to give 666.1
a. that I h. . . . thine 786.3
a. I h. I give thee 859.c
bring a. thou h. and art 864.3

f *have (no-t)*
we h. n. other argument 60.c
n. light, n. hope h. we 94.1
I h. n. claim . . . no right 290.1
I h. n. secrets 294.2
n. home on earth h. I 362.1
n. wound h. the soul 364.3
I n. treasure h. 379.2

I h. n. room to boast . . 468.4
I h. n. much to give . . 475.c
h. n. other will . . . 480.2
I've little strength . . . 489.3
it h. n. spring . . . sure . . 508.2
then . . . I'll h. n. fear . . 523.4
to h. n. will but thine . . 584.2
when I've n. sin . . . 592.3
we h. n. help but thee . . 607.1
other refuge h. I none . . 737.2
need never h. a fear . . 824.3
we h. n. wealth or learning . 849.1

g *Phil 4:18*
I must h. all things . . . 14.3
I h. all in thee . . . 741.4

faith (1e), give (2i), life (2j), must (2c), place (1c), such (2c), victory (2c)

3 *(others) have*
the mighty h. their day . . 6.4
will h. part in the honours . 169.2
h. you h. a taste . . . 243.2
h. you peace . . . destroy . 243.3
you can h. this blessing . . 328.3
lost the love they h. . . 558.3
voices h. a kindly sound . . 664.1
bidders h. to spare . . 796.2
all h. need of God's . . 824.1
h. no hope of liberty . . 832.2
dare to h. a purpose firm . 847.c
what hope h. you . . . 885.4
each saint h. a mansion . . 905.3
he that h. ears . . . 932.4
man h. no meaning . . c210

4 *(general)*
bud may h. a bitter taste . 29.5
h. a wondrous attraction . 124.2
hell h. no terrors . . . 166.4
real contentment h. . . . laws. 244.3
life h. point and purpose . 376.3
faith h. still its Olivet . . 496.5
shall h. power to separate . 554.4
earth h. ne'er a spot . . 663.1
ills h. no weight . . . 670.4
faith h. . . . reward . . 748.4
joy to be h. 808.2
flag shall h. the sway . . 810.3
trials . . . h. now . . . 894.2
song . . . never h. an ending . 934.4
life h. . . . intention/theme . c173

b *love has*
l. h. a language . . . 51.1
his l. h. a plea . . . 114.3
his l. h. no limits . . . 579.3

5 *have to*
what pains he h. to bear . 133.2
Christ should h. to die . . 274.2
all you h. to do . . . 403.3
soldier h. to stand alone . . 801.2
duties we h. to do . . . 849.3
throne you'll h. to go . . 914.1
every sin h. to go c198

haven *Ps 107:30*
'tis a h. sweet of rest . . 182.3
sure h. of his breast . . 333.3
safe into the h. guide . . 737.1
anchored . . . in the h. . . c178

hay
among the new-mown h. . 41.2
asleep on the h. . . . 77.1
h. from the mown field . . 927.1

head
1 *(divine)*
laid down his sweet h. . . 77.1
gathers round its h. . . 112.1,5
that meek h. of thine . . 120.3
my Saviour bows his h. . . 125.2
when he bowed his h. . . 128.4
his h., his hands, his feet . 136.3
bow thy meek h. to . . . pain. 150.5
the h. that once . . . crowned. 168.1
tiny hands and downy h. . 855.1

b *sacred head*
did he devote that s. h. . . 105.1
bows his s. h. and dies . . 107.4
behold, he bows his s. h. . 108.2
O s. h. once wounded . . 123.1
thou didst bow thy s. h.. . 538.2

c *Eph 1:22**
following our exalted h. . . 143.5
he rose, our glorious h. . . 149.2
all glory to our risen h. . . 151.3
alive in him, my living h.. . 283.4
in one spirit to our h. . . 659.2
into thee, our living h. . . 662.3
looked upon their living h. . 855.5

2 *(human)*
storms are on my h. . . 39.2
lay down thy h. . . . 332.1
oil of gladness on our h.. . 573.2
cover my defenceless h. . 737.2
storms go o'er my h. . . 746.4
his hands . . . on my h. . . 794.1
God be in my h. . . . 953
shall fly above our h. . . c240

b *lift head* *(Ps 110:7)*
with joy . . . l. up my h.. . 116.1
cross that l. up my h. . . 621.4
power to l. my h. . . . 713.1
God shall l. up thy h. . . 721.1

c *Prov 10:6*
in blessings on your h. . . 29.3

anoint (a)

3 *(general)*
from the fountain-h. . . 277.3
leave the fountain-h. . . 497.3
at our army's h. . . . 682.1

b *Gen 3:15/Rom 16:20*
bruises Satan's h. . . . 60.3

headed 25.2

headlong 847.3

heal-ed-ing
1 *(God) heals*
ransomed, h., restored . . 17.1
have we a name for h. . . 71.1
potent and h., eager . . 129.3
no sorrow . . . cannot h. 236.1, 3
there is h. in his blood . . 265.4
with h. gifts for souls . . 287.1
riches, h. of the mind . . 293.4
virtue had h. her . . . 304.2
bruised, but Jesus h. me . 337.3
his light will . . . h.. . . 408.3
here to seek thy h.. . . 434.2
receiving cleansing and h. . 456.4
the balm . . . that h. . . 457.2
Lord, almighty to h. . . 459.2
when for h. they're applied . 471.2
touch me and h. me . . 487.3
come . . . with tender h. . 528.c
thy tender hands had h.. . 534.1
laid his hand . . . and h.. . 542.3
h., helping, full . . . 548.3
in thy mercy h. us all . . 558.5
thy power to help and h. . 571.3
power ever present to h. . 589.4
seek the h. of thy cross . . 590.4
long to feel thy . . . h. . . 610.1
let my h. appear . . . 647.2
the blood that h. us . . 764.1
h., cleansing, setting free . 777.3
cleansing and h. for all . . 808.2
afresh thou canst h. . . c92

b *healing [wings]* *Mal 4:2*
risen with h. in his w. . . 82.3
with h. in thy train . . . 218.1
on thy redeeming w. h. . . 224.2
with h. in his w. . . . 346.2

c *heal sick* *Matt 10:8*
feed the hungry, h. the s. . 518.1
s., they ask for h. . . . 682.2
h. the s. . . . the blind . . 737.3
sin-s. . . . Christ doth h.. . 825.1

d *heal (broken)* *Luke 4:18*
his tender touch can h. . . 126.4
broken hearts . . . be h. . . 269.1
h. my . . . broken spirit . . 301.3
to h. the broken heart . . c25

e *Rev 22:2*
flows . . . to h. the nations . 232.2
whose leaves do h. . . . 346.3

backsliding, disease (b), servant (2c), stripes, wound (2d)

2 *(we) heal*
words that help and h. . . 212.1
men he gives his h. . . 238.2
seeking to save and to h. . 484.1
words that soothe and h. . 529.3

healer *Jer 30:17**
wonderful H., touch me . 610.*
h. of wounds and bearer . 628.2
my Comforter and h. . . 647.1

healing *(adjective)*
what thy h. name . . . 59.1
displays his h. power . . 160.4
the cleansing, h. flow . . 205.1
h., life-giving flood . . 296.4
knows the h. art . . . 311.2
virtue, like a h. fountain . . 520.3
with thy h. hand, Lord . . 531.1
make known thy h. balm . 575.1
where h. waters flow . . 590.1
his death each day more h. . 634.4
unto the h. waters . . . 647.1
h. waters flow . . . 647.c
in that h. fountain . . . 647.3
love, my h. power . . . 729.1
where the h. fountains flow . 777.2
gift of the Spirit is h. . . c46

b *healing stream*
free to all, a h. s. . . . 115.1
whence the h. s. . . . 578.2
a h. s. for human woes . . 638.1
let the h. s. abound . . 737.4

health
h. that pain . . . defies . . 214.1
h. to the sick in mind . . 224.2
out of my sickness into thy h. 300.1
pining sickness or in h. . . 356.3
to . . . h. restore my soul . 419.6
Spirit of h., remove . . 441.2
freedom, friends and h. . . 492.3
though . . . h. and friends . 746.4
time, h. and talents . . 786.3
strength and h. . . . serve . 838.4
some bring strength and h. . 849.1
our life, our h., our food . 935.3

b *Ps 42:11*
he is thy h. and salvation . 19.1
'tis life and h. and peace . 64.3
cross he bore is . . . h. . . 168.6
my medicine and h. . . 346.4
thy h.'s eternal spring . . 557.4
name is . . . h. and peace . 603.2
inward h. that overcomes . 631.2
life and h. and peace . . 634.1

healthful
peaceful homes and h. days . 15.2
gift of . . . h. mind . . . 214.1

heap
let others boast of h. . . 356.2
h. on his sacred altar . . 929.3

hear
1 *(God) hears*
music for thy Lord to h.. . 2.3

he h. the waves repeat . . 103.3
Holy Spirit, h. us . . . 193.1
h. us, we humbly pray . . 224.1
he will h. thy tale . . 225.c
no other . . . quick to h.. . 246.2
speak, and he will h. . . 261.1
Saviour, h. me . . . 303.1
graciously he h. me . . 348.1
h. us as with joy . . . 532.4
h. in this . . . hour . . 558.5
h., O h., and answer . . 584.c
the Lord will never h. . . 588.3
wondrous doings h. on high . 677.4
always to see and h. . . 742.3
who h. our solemn vow . . 784.4
I know he h. my praise . . 840.3
h. us, Lord, . . . confessing . 863.2
h. then our answer . . 864.c
in the quiet Temple h. . . 871.2
h. thou in Heaven . . . 945.2

b *hear call*
h., Lord, while we c. . . 197.1
h. me while I'm c. . . . 502.1
h. us when we c. . . . 698.3

c *hear cry* *Ps 102:1*
God of Elijah, h. our c. . . 203.2
strong Friend . . . h. my c. . 282.2
h. my humble c. . . 301.1, c
h. my despairing c. . . 336.1
h. us when we c. to thee . 569.*
Jesus, Saviour, h. my c. . 620.1
our c. was h. 642.2

d *hear plea(ding)*
my p. is h. by thee . . . 188.4
h. my p., Lord, make . . 441.c
h. my humble p. . . . c74

e *hear (pray)*
the Father h. him p. . . 106.4
h. us, we humbly p. . . 224.1
as I am, O h. me p. . . 292.4
Lord, h. us while we p. . . 575.c
now h. me while I p. . . 743.1
Saviour, h. us as we p. . . 787.c
h. us when we p. . . . 845.2
Spirit of God, O h. us p.. . c101

f *hear prayer* *(1 John 5:14)*
for h. . . . our p. repeat . . 127.3
God himself will h. . . . p. . 238.c
no other one to h. your p. . 246.2
my all . . . laid, O h. my p. . 513.1
Father, h. the p. we offer . 570.1
h. our anxious p. . . . 582.1
know thou h. p. . . . 596.1
Shepherd, h. my p. . . . 641.*

g *hear song*
Master surely h. the s. . . 103.4
Jesus . . . can h. the s. . . 387.2
smiled to h. their s. . . 853.1
h. our s. of thankfulness . 937.1
forgive (1b), intercession, sigh (b), vow (b), whisper (1)

2 *(we) hear*
a *(literal)*
I h. the rolling thunder . . 37.1
h. the birds . . . brook . . 37.2
I h. him pass 42.2
let me h. how the children . 848.2

b *(figurative)*
first let me h., then sing. . 31.4
my soul delights to h. . . 67.4
let us h. again the story . . 74.3
h. again the message . . 74.3
we h. the Christmas angels . 86.4
help us . . . truth to h. . . 97.4
shall we refuse to h. him . 121.3
forgive! I h. thee plead . . 122.3
h. thy expiring cry . . . 185.1
no . . . wind we h. . . . 198.1
only faithful souls can h. . 214.2
faith is h. replying . . . 222.1
h. the Lord's: Well done . 222.c
could I h. some sinner . . 275.4
I have h. how he suffered . 289.2
I h., and bow me . . . 305.1
h. his loving whisper . . 333.1
now I h. thee and rejoice . 353.2
I h. the . . . hymn/music . 358.1
hearts delight to h. him . . 377.3
h. the welcome from the King 389.3
only Christ is h. to speak . 444.2
let me h. . . . pleading . . 463.2
h. the . . . glad well done . 500.3
let me h. and I'll obey . . 502.1
h. him pray: Forgive . . 548.2
I h. thy words, my Saviour . 562.3
wonderful . . . to h. him say . 583.1
may I h. thee say to me . . 598.3
h. thy whispered love . . 600.3
make thy people h. . . 626.1
h. thee inly speak . . . 636.4
hark! I h. the warriors . . 693.3
we have h. the cry . . . 702.2
h. him whisper: All is well . 759.3
I h. their hallelujahs . . 780.4
I h. their battle cry . . . 780.4
see him and h. him above . 794.2
alive and quick to h. . . 839.3
O let me h. thee speaking . 862.3
I h. him talking . . . 884.3
the heavenly music h. . . 901.2
let . . . pleadings be h. . . c55

c *hear call*
I h. the loud c. . . . 298.6
c. me long before I h. . . 339.2
yet I h. him gently c. . . 391.1
Saviour, may we h. thy c. . 428.5
I've h. the c. for workers . 482.1
then let me h. thee c. . . 571.1
h. this mighty c. . . . 700.1
h. thy . . . leader c. . . 753.4

d *hear voice*
let the earth h. his v. . . 22.c
h. the music of his v. . . 48.2
O h. the v. of Jesus . . 67.1, 2
h. . . . sweetest angel v.. . 73.1
h. the angelic herald's v. . 78.2
his pardoning v. I h. . . 106.5
h. the archangel's v. . . 164.c
his that gentle v. we h. . . 200.5
when . . . h. that inward v. . 214.2
come . . . O h. his v. . . 235.2
h. a v. that entreats you. . 272.2
I h. the v. of Jesus say . . 332.*
I h. his v. of cheer . . . 334.1
I could not h. . . . v. . . 353.2
v. divine . . . had not h.. . 398.2
I h. thy welcome v. . . 423.1
dull . . . to h. thy v. . . 488.2
I h. a v. so gently . . . 490.1
I h. his v. . . . saying . . 490.2
let me h. thy v. now . . 502.1
wonderful . . . to h. his v. . 583.2
I have h. thy v. . . . 585.1
Master, let it now be h. . . 614.1
when thy v. is truly h. . . 614.4
let me h. thy v. afar . . 641.2
thy reassuring v. to h. . . 644.3
left . . . when they h. his v. . 680.2
self-same v. is h. today . . 680.3
oft have I h. thy . . . v. . . 749.1
his guiding v. we h. . . 818.3
I'll h. the music of his v.. . 884.c
he h. a v. which says . . 911.3
to feel . . . h. thy v. . . c108

e *hear of*
I h. o. the blood . . . 237.1
I have h. o. . . . love . . 289.1
Lord, I h. o. showers . . 295.1
I h. o. a Saviour . . . 331.1
I'll h. no more o. . . . yore . 724.c

f *Isa 40:21*
have we not h. it . . . 724.1
love (7k), servant (2b), sound (f), word (1d)

3 *(others) hear*
h. by listening man . . 27.3
his name the sinner h. . . 62.3
h. the angels sing . . . 83.*
man . . . h. not the love song. 83.2
no ear may h. his coming . 86.3
have you ever h. . . . 96.*
sweetest that ever was h. 99.1. c
h. me pleading evermore 229.1. c
faith can h. his invitation . 240.2
have you h. the angels . . 242.1
have you h. him . . . 242.3
some have h., but tell . . 243.4
have you not h. of . . . stream 252.1
h. the songs that resound . 263.2
all would h. . . . Spirit . . 324.3
made . . . the deaf to h.. . 353.5
winds and waves . . . h.. . 569.2
make thy people h. . . 626.1
home where prayer is h. . 661.3
let the voice of hope be h. . 697.3
h. his father call . . . 740.3
thousands . . . never h. . . 794.3
thousands . . . never h. . . 797.3
the world shall h. . . . 802.2
all the world shall h. us . . 815.3
till every nation shall h. . . 828.2
men seldom h. his name . 832.1
make salvation's story h. . 832.c
purest word . . . may be h. . 867.4
he started up to h. . . . 890.2

b *(imperative)*
h. his all-important c. . . 107.1
thy Saviour, h. his word . 110.1
h. now his accents . . 235.3
h. him today 248.4
backslider, h. 267.2
come and h. me tell . . 338.1
be thou faithful, h. him . . 694.4
h. the trumpet blow . . 804.3
hands are wanted, h. him . 868.2

c *(historical)*
these tidings shepherds h. . 72.2
song that the shepherds h. . 80.2
as of old apostles h. it . . 428.2
trust like theirs who h. . . 567.2
when his first disciples h. . 700.1
those first disciples h. . . 760.4

d *Matt 11:15**
all ye who h. 19.1
whosoever h.! shout . . 279.1
he that hath ears . . . h.. . 932.4

e *Rom 10:14*
how shall they h. . . . 527.3

f *1 Cor 2:9*
what ear has not h. . . 506.2
ear hath never h. . . . 682.3

g
chaos and darkness h. . . 224.1
hear (2d), message (b), sound (f)

hearken *Ps 81:11* . . . 286.2

heart
1 *(divine)*
our names are on his h. . . 9.4
him whose h. knows all . . 68.2
out of the Father's h. . . 114.1
his world-embracing h. . . 127.2
go surging through that h. . 131.2
thy loving h., so rent . . 138.3
more like the h. of him . . 146.1
high on his h. . . . bear . . 183.2
carries...on his own loving h. 245.4
the h. of the eternal . . 265.6
from the h. of Jesus . . 539.1
eternally held in thy h. . . 639.3
h. of the Army's need . . 648.1
forth from thy h. we came . 648.2
in the h. of the Father . . 739.3
thou givest me thy h. . . 741.2
I'll bless the h. that . . 896.3

2 *(vocative)*
h. of sin, may I come in . . 229.1

say, weary h., oppressed . 229.c
foolish h.! why . . . wander . 265.1
have faith in God, my h. . 723.1

3 *(as subject)*
h. unfold like flowers . . 10.1
our h. and lips shall prove . 36.6
to thee our h. . . . move. . 135.4
my h. in love goes out . . 138.2
my h. awakening cries . . 187.1
thy h. has found . . . vain . 225.2
what has thy h. decided. . 255.3
the h. that once has . . . known 267.1
h. unwashed . . . come not there 268.3
how our h. delight to hear . 377.3
when the h. for mercy craves. 393.3
in despair my h. would sink . 399.2
my h. . . . has failed to take . 415.3
my h. shall obey . 422.c/589.c
my h. is reaching . . . 434.1
O for a h. to praise. . . 444.1
a h. that always feels . . 444.1
my h. . . . sinning no more . 454.1
wants my h. is telling . . 460.1
my h. fulfils its vow . . 524.1
how shall h. move . . . 527.2
cause my h. to grieve . . 536.2
h. more deeply bleed . . 586.3
until my very h. o'erflow . 612.6
my h. restores . . . ray . . 621.2
my h. has slowly trusted . 713.2
until I rest, h. . . . and soul . 723.4
no change my h. shall fear . 736.1
though my h. fail . . . 746.5
with our gifts our h. . . 922.1
though . . . h. may bleed . 923.3
our h. to adore . . . 925.5
my h. is longing to confide . c62

dance, man (2f), must (2b), rejoice (b), reply, sing (3c)

4 *as object*
a
my h. and tongue employ . 21.1
give my h. a song . . . 32.3
or turn my h. from thee . . 59.4
my h. reveal . . . seal . . 102.4
thy love my h. constrain. . 140.5
melt the h. and dim . . 185.1
gladden thou this h. of mine . 194.5
nor leave the h. that once . 202.3
who is it claims the h. . . 204.3
his love your h. constrain . 234.3
for thy h. he's waited . . 250.2
grace that taught my h. . . 308.2
temptations try my h. . . 326.3
powers stained my h. . . 379.2
glad . . . warm my h. . . 412.3
sever our h. and lives . . 413.1
prepare my h. for him . . 448.4
let my h. be sealed . . 460.c
treasures . . . my h. possessing 460.2
this . . . my h. shall move . 463.3
empty my h. of . . . love. . 480.1
help my h., so unbelieving . 503.2
things that bind my h. . . 523.c
test the h. that . . . sealed . 531.1
no more . . . my h. to grieve . 536.2
my h. attuned to sing . . 583.3
quicken our h. . . . 608.1
I cannot close my h. . . 621.3
grief my h. dividing . . 634.3
unite our h. in love . . 661.4
lift up our h. to seek . . 669.4
guard . . . the h. from shame. 674.2
earth our h. shall sever . . 693.2
wanted, h. . . . . . 704.*
let it my h. o'erpower . . 720.1
cheerful and our h. assure . 755.3
no power . . . h. can sever . 854.3
this h. of mine enfold . . 861.2
while my h. is tender . . 865.1
I would yield that h. . . 865.1
he claims my h. . . . 867.2
the sinner's h. confound . 875.1

shrouding h. and home . . 916.3
your h. lay down . . . 929.3
our h. we raise in hymns . 934.1
it broke . . . won my h. . . c209

b *fill heart*
what joy will f. my h. . . 37.4
joyful h. is f. with praise. . 134.3
let the fire . . . f. our h. . . 201.2
my emptied h. to f. . . 221.2
f. my h. with happiness . . 340.2
sorrow f. my aching h. . . 363.3
he f. my h. with melody. . 386.3
discord f. my h. with pain . 390.2
my h.'s f. with . . . music . 406.2
f. and overflow my h. . . 470.3
I bring . . . my h. to f. . . 489.1
f. my h. with Heaven . . 534.1
with his peace my h. has f. . 539.3
Christ can f. the loving h. . 545.3
f. our h. with heavenly joy . 607.3
need thy love my h. to f. . 620.2
Lord, f. my craving h. 649.1. c
h. on earth but f. . . . 704.4
inflame, and f. my h. . . 720.5
with thyself our h. now f. . 845.4
f. with thy spirit every h. . 942.3

c *keep heart*
k. my h. in purity . . . 455.5
k. thou my h. ablaze . . 529.2
k. her h. from evil . . . 792.2
to k. my h. from sin . . 844.3

d *make heart*
m. my h. anew . . . 32.1, 3
peace . . . m. fresh my h. . 358.3
m. my h. whiter than snow . 535.4
h. are m. to bless thee . . 642.3

heart (6c) home (2e)

e *set heart*
he has s. my h. aflame . . 63.c
s. my sad h. free . . . 282.2
he s. my h. a-singing . . 342.c
man whose h. is s. free . . 372.2
s. my h. at liberty . . . 419.3
a h. from sin s. free . . 444.1
and h. from sin s. free . . 561.4
s. my h. on things above . 630.1

bind (3a), bring (2e), cheer (b), cleanse (d), create (b), fix (b), give (1i, 2d), harden, incline, inspire (b), lift (2e), make (4e), open (b), overflow (a), purge (b), renew (b), search (2c), stir (c), take (2e), tune, win (1b)

5 *(described)*
a *as subject*
trembling h. need not . . 363.4
the sorrowing h. find rest . 364.3
have I a trustful h. . . . 409.3
the h. I cannot read . . 421.2
a sunlit h., with not . . 426.1
a h. as white as snow . . 426.1
my fearful h. points back . 440.3
a h. resigned, submissive . 444.2
a h. from all pollution . . 445.2
my wistful h. said faintly . 548.2
this throbbing h. forget . . 573.5
true h. everywhere . . . find . 826.2
where nobler h. have led . 944.2

b *as object*
still this restless h. . . . 194.4
raise my sinking h. . . 303.1
quell my flaming h. . . 303.2
bind my wandering h. . . 313.4
look on this sin-stained h. . 440.1
turn my wandering h. . . 445.3
bless the unforgiving h. . . 572.2
teach my yearning h. . . 586.3
solemnise each waiting h. . 638.3
thy restless h. keep still . . 738.2
a lowly h., that waits . . 839.4
unwashed h. are rejected . 893.1

c *hearts (are)*
that e'er our h. should be . 135.2

soon your h. be cold . . 241.4
is your h. now full of joy. . 243.3
is there a h. o'erbound . . 246.1
is there a h. that is/has . . 247.*
when my h. was torn . . 330.1
my h. my strength . . . are his. 345.2
your h. will be bright . . 373.c
when my h. was so hard . 395.1
when my h. was dark . . 402.2
my h. is in a flame . . . 413.3
O for a h. that is whiter . . 443.*
h. at leisure from itself . . 485.2
my h. . . . with care is . . 534.2
that h. and life . . . united . 561.3
home when h. are holy . . 663.1
my h. may low be laid . . 736.1
let thy h. be at rest . 739.1, 2
when your h. is bowed . . 759.1
h. are brave again . . . 876.4
my h. and soul, are there . 880.3
my h. is washed as white . c168
so many h. are lonely . . c200

aching, broken (b), clean (b), compassion (c), contrite (b), faint (b), fixed (b), free (1b), full (h), glad (d), glowing (b), human (b), humble (b), joyful (c), longing (2c), loving (2b), new (e), poor (3b), pure (2c), secret (e), simple (b), sincere, sinful (b), slow (c), strong (2b), stubborn, tear (1b), tender (c), thankful (b), true (1c), upright (b), weary (b), whole (1c), willing (2b)

6
a *all heart*
a. my h. this night . . . 73.1
a. our h. rejoice . . . 74.1
rule in a. our h. . . . 79.4
he is a. my h.'s desire . . 522.c
hate . . . with a. my h. . . 568.3
seek with a. their h. . . 806.3
love with a. thy h. . . . 816.3
with a. my h., I come . . 860.2

b *every heart*
joy of e. longing h. . . 79.2
let e. h. prepare a throne . 81.1
let e. h. prepare him room . 84.1
e. h. will . . . own . . . 169.1
plant holy fear in e. h. . . 190.2
come . . . into e. longing h. . 210.1
fix in e. h. thy seat. . . 216.4
now rule in e. h. . . . 219.3
let e. h. leap forth . . . 235.2
bestowing freely on e. h. . 383.3
enter e. longing h. . . . 438.1
when e. h. was tuned . . 557.3
breathe . . . into e. h. . . 599.2
let e. waiting h. . . . feel. . 603.4
let e. h. . . . be set. . . 608.2
Kingdom come to e. h. . . 624.1
there's joy in e. h. . . . 664.1
fill . . . e. h. 942.3
Kingdom come to e. h. . . 945.4

each (2a)

c *hearts [his]*
my h. shall be thine . . 111.3
make our h. thy dwelling . 200.7
my h. thy temple make . . 285.1
make my h. a house . . 305.3
thy h. made truly his . . 465.2
my h. is thine now . . . 490.2
he makes my h. his altar . 495.2
my h. thy temple making . 502.2
my h. the Spirit's shrine . . 540.4
make a thousand h. thine . 604.4
let my youthful h. be thine . 865.1
h. and will . . . are thine. . 867.6
make each h. a living stone . 941.2
make . . . h. thy dwelling . c104

home (2e), throne (2)

d *heart like/as*
h. like thine . . . as white . 426.1

h. like heroes . . . 704.1
wanted, h. like thine, Lord . 704.4
give me a h. like thine . . c39

e *no heart* *1 Cor 2:9*
nor h. can frame . . . 61.2
no h. conceive how dear . 69.3
no human h. could enter . 325.3
nor h. conceive the glory . 878.4

7
a *by heart*
by the h. expressed . . 211.1
by h. received . . . 211.1
led by valiant h. . . . 939.1

b *from heart*
prayers rise from h. . . 226.2
from my h. . . . rolled away . 309.1
Jesus from my h. did take . 309.c
from my h. the burden . . 333.1
idols torn from my h. . . 344.2
from my smitten h. . . 476.2
from a childlike h. within . 522.3
lift as from the h. of one. . 765.5
don't turn . . . from your h. . c11
springing from this . . . h. . c176

c *in heart*
strong in h., with purpose . 534.3
in life and h. . . . clean . . 629.3
we still are one in h. . . 659.1
the same in mind and h.. . 659.5
still be joined in h. . . . 660.4

pure (2c), upright (b)

d *in/into/within heart*
each in his h. . . . make . . 43.1
room in my h. 101.c/282.c/444.c
within my h. . . . fulfil . . 138.1
in your h. enthrone him . . 141.5
kindled in some h. it is . . 165.1
in the h. he implanteth . . 186.c
glow within this h. . . . 194.2
thrice welcome in our h. . 213.1
hid in my h. . . . stains . . 237.1
in my h. I read it so . . 359.3
ringing in my h. today . . 389.*
in my h. appear . . . 412.1
within my h. . . . stay . . 432.1
want thee ever in my h.. . 455.c
for ever in my h. to be . . 455.2
all in my h., Lord . . . 507.c
if, in my h., . . . unwilling . 507.2
within my h. to reign . . 541.1
in the meek and lowly h. . 555.4
find thee in my h. . . . 601.1
plant thy nature in my h. . 601.3
give us . . . in our h. . . 611.*
whisper softly in your h. . 664.3
down in the human h. . . 691.3
so in my h. . . . find . . 729.2
peace within my h. . . 730.2
spring . . . within my h.. . 737.4
may its message in our h. . 856.4
deep in our h. . . . voice. . 864.2
God be in my h. . . . 953
not in my h. . . . treasure . c55
enter . . . into my h. . . c64
in my h. . . . new song . . c157
with Jesus in the h. . . c220

e *dwell/live in*
in my h. there d. a song. . 70.c
rose . . . and l. in my h.. . 125.c
he l. within my h. . . . 334.c
Jesus l. in my h. . . . 375.2
which in the h. resides . . 494.1
in the h. . . . you dwell . . 506.1
to l. . . . within my h. . . 513.3
Spirit indwelling my h. . . 589.4
l. thyself within my h. . . 793.3
come . . . d. within the h. . 827.4
d. within my glowing h.. . c96

melody, place (3a), rule (2b), shed (2d), shine (1f)

f *on heart*
touch upon my h. and soul . 215.1
sorrow on my h. may fall . 399.3
a tempest on my h. . . 490.1
on thy h. has been laid . . 739.2
I own his claim in h. . . 867.1
lay some soul upon my h. . c79

g *Jer 31:33/Heb 8:10*
engraving pardon on my h. . 207.3
stamp . . . on my h. . . 623.c
seal thine image on my h. . 865.3

write (b)

h *through heart*
through my h., . . . flesh . 430.4
fire, go through my h. . . c50

i *to heart*
speak to my h. of Calvary . 125.c
preach his gospel to my h. . 191.2
to my h. thyself reveal . . 207.2
speak to our h. today . . 209.3
to that h., . . . confessing . 303.3
to my h. . . . blood applied 315.1, c
given peace to my h. . . 348.1
apply them to this h. . . 446.2
thy love to my h. . . . known. 459.3
will he not show to the h. . 527.2
to the h. where strife . . 539.2
given to the h. resigned . . 555.2
speak to my h. and let me . 636.1
many dear to my h. . . 886.4
bring sadness to your h. . c139

j *come to heart*
c. t. my h., Lord 101.c/282.c/444.c
c. t. my h. today . . . 209.1
c. . . . into every longing h. . 210.1
since Jesus c. into my h. . 394.*
c. t. our h. and bless . . 561.2
c. t. this h. of mine . . 605.2
Kingdom come t. every h. . 624.1
Kingdom come t. every h. . 945.4
c. back t. your h. again . . c11

k *with heart*
w. my h. I believe . . 367.2
w. my h. so bright . . 402.1
w. my h. all aglow . 469.1, c
coming w. my h. . . . 470.2
I have a fellowship w. h. . 485.5

hand (2b), mind (2c), soul (2k), voice (3b)

l *(other)*
round my h. . . . twine . . 345.1
words without the h. . . 588.3

8 *of heart*
Cleanser of h. . . . 257.4
King of my h. to crown . . 415.4
King of my h. to reign . . 541.4
conqueror of each h. . . 643.3

b *(possessive)*
faintest whisper of my h. . 48.1
weak . . . effort of my h. . 58.4
be all my h.'s delight . . 178.3
the mean altar of my h. . 199.1
thy h.'s deep grief . . . 225.4
tell the burden of thy h. . 261.1
outcrying pains of my h. . 288.3
my h.'s most secret depths . 311.4
he met the need of my h. . 371.1
burden of my h. rolled . . 395.c
with joy of h. . . . sing . . 401.1
prayer of my h. . . . prevail . 459.2
knows a h.'s refreshment . 580.1
do the wishes of my h. . . 588.1
hidden depths of many a h. . 612.4
all the yearning of my h. . 614.3
serve with singleness of h. . 688.1
offer him our h.'s devotion . 777.4
my h.'s dear refuge . . 889.3
earthen vessel of my h. . . c65
burden of my h. rolled away . c198

desire (2c), door (2d), garden (2)

9 *(in phrases)*
in your h. of h. . . . 244.1
once so sick at h. . . . 311.2
walking . . . h. in h. . . 420.1
in my h. of h. . . . denied . 534.2

b
beseeching for a h.-renewing . 434.1
pure and fervent h.-desire . 620.3
ye h.-burdened ones . . 905.2

hearted
be . . . kind-h. and true . . 823.2
brave-h. and true . . . c231

broken (b)

heartfelt 933.3

hearth
in fellowship at h. . . . 7.2
there's sunshine on the h. . 664.2

heat-ed
when h. in the chase . . 557.1
breathe through the h. . . 567.5
gives me h. and light . . 733.5
the battle's blazing h. . . 749.3

b *Matt 20:12*
burning of the noontide h. . 476.1
screened from the h. . . 639.1

heaven
1 *the sky (heavens)*
clouds that sail in h. . . 2.2
the h. are not too high . . 11.1
the fiery h. scan . . . 27.3
like the arching of the h. . 32.2
fall sunlit from h. . . . 35.2
rainbows span the h. high . 39.2
when the h. above . . . rang . 80.1
the h. are clothed . . . night . 107.2
show in the h. . . . sign . . 167.3
of whom the h. . . . symbol . 486.2
h. above is softer blue . . 545.2
higher than the highest H. . 548.4
where the h. is bright . . 682.3
to the h. our praises ring . 700.3
I see it in the h. above me . c121

b *as the heavens*
high as the h. . . . raise . . 4.3
glorious as the h. above. . 40.2
love is as high as the h.. . 47.1
boundless as the . . . h.. . 230.2
high as the h. above . . 383.2

earth (1d, i, j, l), rend (b)

2 *(Glory)*
H., H., for evermore . . 45.3
fit us for H. to live . . . 77.3
hail the H.-born Prince . . 82.3
H. and nature sing . . . 84.1
H. its tribute brings . . 171.1
all the angels H. can boast . 177.3
speaks of H. 200.5
earth has no sorrow that H. . 236.*
had a taste of H. . . . 243.2
h. with him I enter in . . 262.3
told of a H. on high . . 289.3
there's a Saviour and H. . 289.4
H. came down and Glory . 371.c
to lift me nearer H. . . 421.5
God and H. are . . . my own . 498.2
I'll make H. ring . . . 543.4
just as free as H. . . . 546.2
bring all H. before . . . 604.3
fit me for life and H. . . 623.4
he enters H. with prayer . 625.5
or H. itself be won . . . 654.4
reach H. just as surely . . 700.3
make H. ring with praises . 798.1
sing aloud of H. . . . 835.3
I seek my place in H. . . 880.1
H. is my fatherland . . 882.1
I would make sure of H.. . 883.1

have a hallelujah H. . . 902.3
for H. our spirits prepare . 904.4
while H. appears in view . 912.2
when H. at last is won . . 912.3

b *1 Kgs 8:27*
'tis a H. of h. to me . . 182.3
Christ, he is the H. of h.. . 346.5
remove to the H. of h. . . 355.6

c *Heaven and (Hell)*
he turns their Hell to H. . . 60.2
Hell . . . vanquished, H. . . 155.1
H. and Hell and God defying . 693.2
'tis H. or Hell, the choice . 885.1

d *Heaven (home)*
give me a home in H. . . 354.2
towards my home in H. . . 761.4
my home is in H. . . . 881.c
H. is my home . . . 882.*

e *highest Heaven*
with them in h. H. . . . 12.3
Christ, by h. H. adored . . 82.2
higher than the h. H. . . 548.4
lifts me to h. H. . . . c94

f *Heaven [now]*
present everlasting H. . . 210.4
H. to abide at his side . . 333.3
had a sight of H. . . . 366.1
what a H. in Jesus' name . 367.2
H.'s peace is in God's will . 539.3
thyself . . . will make my H. . 562.1
H. comes down . . . to greet . 573.4
here it is I find my H. . . 634.2
find my H. in thee . . . 636.5
Jesus makes our home a h. . 663.1
more of H. in each we see . 668.3
my earth a present H. . . 729.4
'tis H. to me wherever . . c172

begin (1c), below (a), fill (2c)

g *from Heaven*
goodwill . . . from H. to men . 93.6
when from H.'s splendour . 175.2
come like dew from H. . . 213.2
afar from H. . . . wandered . 225.1
inspired from H. above . . 781.1
he looks down from H. . . 841.2
God stoops from H. . . 885.4
light from H. is falling . . 893.c
here may we gain from H. . 940.4
seek the truth from H. . . 942.3

h *[came] from Heaven* *John 6:38*
brought his Son . . . from H. 47.2, 3
he c. down . . . from H.. . 87.2
till Jesus c. from H. . . 94.1
c. to me from H. above . . 114.c
joy from H. above . . . 229.4
the Lord, who left the h. . 411.2
shine . . . from H. above . 446.1
descend the h., thou whom . 448.3
cometh H.'s peace to me . 539.1
life immortal, H. descending . 540.4
H. comes down . . . to greet . 573.4
rend the h., c. quickly . . 604.4

i *2 Kgs 1:10*
let the fire from H. fall . . 622.1
stands for fire from H. . . 777.3

j *1 Peter 1:12*
God sent down from H. . . 195.*
Holy Ghost sent . . . from H. . 216.1
it was sent from H. above . 327.1
sent from H. above . . 829.c
things . . . sent from H. . . 935.c

above (2b), holiness (b), send (1b, f)

k *to Heaven*
wing to H. our thought . . 20.3
way for travellers to H. . . 36.4
to H. he turns . . . eyes . . 107.4
leads to H. and God . . 113.2
fighting my passage to H. . 137.5
hands to H. I lift . . . 208.4
lead men to . . . joy and H. . 211.3
to H. ascend 223.4
wooing us to H. . . . 258.2
bring thy soul to H. nigh . 269.3
we're travelling home to H. . 275.1
the way to H. is straight. . 275.3
bring me safe to H. . . 345.3
told my homecoming to H. . 388.3
wayward men to lead to H. . 528.3
turns his face to H. . . 580.3
leads to God and H. . . 586.1
steps unto H. . . . 617.3
a worthier gift to H. . . 618.3
nearness unto thee and H. . 632.2
walk with thee to H. . . 667.4
I lift my heart to H. . . 766.3
wave the answer back to H. . 804.c
taught the way to H. . . 834.2
shows the same path to H. . 879.5
who will journey to H. . . 881.3
when we all get to H. . . 892.c

earth (1j), way (2c)

l *go to Heaven*
go . . . in peace to H. . . 67.2
we might go at last to H. . 133.3
or you can't go to H. . . 256.c
I shall go to H. . . . 361.2
if you wish to go to H. . . 913.1

3 *in Heaven*
a *(people)*
endless life in H. . . . 46.4
ransomed hosts in H. . . 63.3
in H. with all . . . throng. . 69.4
in H. are now installed . . 95.2
friends . . . in H. shall dwell . 146.2
this is my passport into H. . 176.4
and in H. . . . a mansion . 328.3
I have a future in H. . . 371.3
banquet of glory in H. . . 373.4
in H. we take our place . . 438.3
till in H. I crown thee . . 499.1
with thee in H. . . . wear . 499.2
reap in H. the harvest . . 500.3
in H. shall see his glory . . 514.4
place . . . in H. for me . . 536.2
they dwell in thee, in H.. . 556.1
more of . . . rest in H. . . 564.4
that we may meet in H. . . 603.3
in H. with thee receive me . 635.1
we in H. adore thee . . 643.4
lose ourselves in H. above . 676.6
in H. they never suffer . . 911.6
in H. above . . . no sorrow . c250

place (4), treasure (3b)

b *(divinity)*
King of kings in H. . . 66.4
is our Lord in H. above . . 87.5
in H. he was known . . 92.2
Lord in H., thy grace . . 97.3
now in H., exalted high . . 118.4

c *1 Kgs 8:30*
hear thou in H. . . . 945.2

d *Ps 73:25*
whom in H. but thee . . 301.4

e *Matt 5:12*
great is your reward in H. . 95.3

f *Matt 6:9*
our Father in H. tells . . 323.1
our Father, who in H. art . 624.1
as angels do in H. . . . 624.2
I'll trust my Father in H.. . c133

4 *of Heaven (possessive)*
buds of H. 28.5
all the wealth of H. . . 70.4
all ye citizens of H. above . 85.2
the blessings of his H. . . 86.3
H.'s joys and endless day . 125.2
the vault of H. rings . . 147.2
H.'s high portals . . . 151.4
H.'s eternal light . . . 168.2
in H.'s eternal bliss . . 187.4
pledge of H. 207.3
of H. a larger earnest . . 207.4
fulness of love, of H. . . 214.4
melody with H.'s harmony . 327.c
H.'s ray falls today . . 379.4
the host of H. rejoices . . 381.1
H.'s peace is in . . . will. . 539.3
all the gifts of H. . . . 555.3
H.'s bright . . . regions . . 686.2
the steep ascent of H. . . 701.4
all the armour of H. . . 703.3
H.'s victories are won . . 705.4
a friend . . . on H.'s shore . 709.4
H.'s music chimes . . . 744.6
H.'s perfect peace . . . 752.7
mingle with H.'s gold . . 780.1
dedicate to H.'s cause . . 796.3
keen Breath of H. . . . 827.2
to reveal H.'s glory . . 835.2
the dawn of H. breaks . . 896.1
by faith on H.'s tableland . c80
the rays of H. shine . . c176

arch, bell, bread (f), court, gate (f), hope (2c), Jesus (8d), joy (1b), King (2i), light (4l), such (1b), window

b *Neh 2:4*
hear, thou God of H. . . 482.3
but to the God of H. . . 791.1

heavenly
enthroned in h. glory . . 6.1
begin . . . some h. theme . 26.1
when h. bells . . . calling . 39.4
triumph with the h. throng . 43.4
man's first h. state . . 78.3
praises to our h. Lord . . 90.6
the h. babe . . . find . . 93.4
Christ, the h. Lamb . . 120.2
all the h. orders . . . 141.2
his h. love to me . . . 180.4
h. portals . . . ring . . . 184.3
the h. life display . . . 195.3
peace and h. joys . . . 214.2
I join the h. lays . . . 223.5
though high in h. glory . . 240.2
h. joy imparts . . . 254.3
who the h. pathway leave . 262.1
make the h. arches ring . . 312.3
O word with h. sound . . 319.2
receiving h. wages here . . 352.2
in the h. Lamb . . . happy . 355.2
haste to the h. feast . . 355.5
the least at the h. feast . . 375.3
h. breezes are blowing . . 383.1
I know in that h. throng . . 392.3
he gives me h. measure . . 413.4
baptised with h. energy . . 426.3
the track of h. flame . . 440.3
a calm and h. frame . . 442.1
refreshed by the h. dews . 443.2
climb the h. steeps . . 496.3
tire along the h. road . . 559.5
spring up . . . in h. power . 601.2
fill our hearts with h. joy . 607.3
to its h. teaching turn . . 654.5
with beams of h. day . . 657.3
let us seek the h. balm . . 663.3
praise . . . h. host . . 665.6/959
brings a h. challenge . . 666.1
with h. thoughts supply . . 671.3
earthly loss is h. gain . . 683.2
words with h. comfort . . 725.1
anchored within the h. veil . 733.4
in h. love abiding . . . 736.1
h. blue suggests . . . 783.4
in your h. Kingdom . . 792.3
the h. harps of gold . . 829.3
Zion's h. hill 853.2
lures them from the h. goal . 885.2
the h. summons came . . 890.2
with a h. greeting . . . 908.2
catch the h. breezes . . c116
the h. gales are blowing . . c221

b *heavenly grace*
I do the h. g. receive . . 447.4
assist me with thy h. g. . 480.1
h. g. our souls sufficing . 500.2
O Lord, thy h. g. impart . 517.1
through h. g., at peace . 536.c
the fount of h. g. . . . 654.1

c *heavenly King*
to thee, our h. K. . . . 76.3
Prince . . . the h. King . 108.1
soldiers of the h. King . 314.1
the mercy of our h. King . 835.2

d *heavenly light*
bright in the h. l. . . . 252.1
bright with the h. l. . . 373.c
so bright in the h. l. . . 402.1
my night into h. l. . . . 467.3
h. l. may flash . . . 726.4

e *heavenly [music]*
how the h. anthem drowns . 156.1
at his coming h. m. rings . 227.3
heart's filled with h. m. . 406.2
the h. m. hear . . . 901.2
swell the h. chorus . . 902.2

f *heavenly peace*
rests in h. p. 89.1
rejoicing with a h. p. . . c31

g *heavenly rest*
fitted for our h. r. . . . 210.2
one their h. r. . . . 661.1

h *heavenly [land]*
in the h. country bright . . 76.5
safe by the h. shore . . 280.4
meet you in that h. l. . . 312.4
never heard of that h. home . 794.3
divides this h. l. . . . 898.1

dove, Father (1d), race (2b)

heavy-iest
its h. toll demands . . . 534.2

b *heavy burden* *Ps 38:4*
my h. b. is rolled away . . 340.1
I carried a h. b. . . . 340.c
some we love bear h. b.. . 576.2
to ease life's h. b. . . . 706.2
for aid when h. b. press. . 719.1
life's h. b. bears . . . 733.3
will make the h. b. light . . 755.3

c *heavy cross*
never a c. so h. . . . 186.2
tell me not of h. c. . . . 320.2
does the c. seem h. . . 396.2
crown of thorns, a h. c. . 451.2
the h. c. . . . light to bear . 551.3
the c. . . . may be h. . . 758.1
when you find the c. is h. . 790.1

d *heavy load*
our h. l. of sin . . . 127.4
who is it gives me h. l. . . 204.2
shared with men their h. l. . 398.3

laden (b)

heed-ing
a *(God) heeds*
why shoulds't thou h. . . 91.3
h. . . . pains of my heart. . 288.3
one . . . the cry will h. . . 351.c
thou takest h. to all . . 933.2

b *(we) heed*
thee . . . with h. I'll cherish . 73.4
h. now his blest commands . 235.3
sinner, h. the . . . message . 240.3
h. his entreaty . . . 246.3
why . . . h. not his mercies . 264.2
speak, and I will h. . . 502.1
men h. thee . . . not . . 683.2
take h. and beware . . 689.2
ours if we will h. . . . 760.2
choose to h. thy voice . . 796.3
h. God's command . . . 847.1
who will h. the . . . command. 868.1
if we h. the call today . . 869.2

heedless
h. passed by 245.3
while the h. millions die . . 696.1

height-s
not on Calvary's h. alone . 127.1
to the central h. . . . 141.4
point . . . to Calvary's h. . 188.3
its h. by faith I see. . . 461.1
Mount Pisgah's lofty h. . . 633.3
rugged are the h. . . . 641.1
carry me from h. to h. . . 641.3
upon a lonely h. . . . 705.2
from the ever-blessèd h. . 711.1
h. of truth . . . calling . . 711.2
beyond, await the h. . . 711.3
scan the dizzy h. . . . 766.2
to climb the highest h. . . 858.2

b *Ps 148:1*
angels in the h. adore . . 17.4
holiest in the h. . . . 18.1, 4

depth (c)

c *Eph 3:18*
breadth and h. to prove . . 55.1
higher than the h. above . 110.4
rapturous h. of . . . delight . 367.4
higher h. . . . of thy love. . 493.3
rapturous h. of his love . . 535.3
h. . . . I may not reach . . 585.4
what h. of joy . . . mine. . 726.3

heightened 878.3

heir
God, mark out thine h. . . 207.4
an h. to a mansion . . . 354.3
he . . . made me an h. . . 535.2

b *Heb 1:14**
h. of full salvation . . . 210.2
h. of salvation, purchase . 310.1

held-see *hold*

Hell
H. hath no terrors . . . 166.4
at his word H. disappears . 243.2
will not go with you to H. . 275.4
glory . . . I'm out of H. . . 380.1
sinking into H. . . . 482.2
conquer over H. and sin . . 532.2
all H.'s legions rout . . 609.3
war 'gainst sin and H. . . 622.4
H. should endeavour . . 653.5
H. to defeat . . . endeavour . 686.3
H.'s foundations quiver . . 690.2
streaming downwards into H. 693.1
with the powers of H. . . 694.2
no retreating, H. defeating . 702.c
H.'s endless woe . . . 703.1
enlist . . . all H. to defy . . 703.3
the arts of H. oppose . . 747.1
stronger than . . . H. . . 751.3
'tis a war 'gainst H. . . 787.3
H's dominions storming . . 788.c
H.'s legions shall fly . . 800.2
tear H.'s throne to pieces . 800.3
H.'s battalions tremble . . 803.1
H.'s forces may be mighty . 810.2
H. be backward hurled . . 828.2
God reliant, H. defiant . . 869.4

b *Rev 20:14*
death and H.'s destruction . 578.3

assail, death (3e), earth (1k), gate (e), heaven (2c), host (5b), verge

helm 628.4

helmet *Eph 6:17* . . . 689.1

help-ed-ing
1 *(God) helps*
Jesus will h. to carry . . 186.2
Jesus lives to h. . . . 242.1
Jesus will h. me . . . 491.c
Jesus will h. . . . conquer . 681.1
h. us save the lost . . . 783.3
ask the Saviour to h. you . 823.c
I will ask Jesus to h. me. . 844.3
his Spirit h. me . . . c107
in Jesus all the h. I need. . c166

b *Ps 10:14*
h. of the helpless . . . 670.1

c *Ps 22:11**
no other h. is found . . 62.2
no other . . . keen to h. . . 246.2
no one but Christ could h. . 336.c
we have no h. but thee . . 607.1
no other friend to h. . . 857.2

d *Ps 46:1*
our h. in ages past . . . 13.1
our h., our hope . . . 43.3
a present h. is he . . . 496.5

e *Ps 121:1*
all my h. from thee . . 737.2
thence my h. is coming . . 766.2

f *help and . . .*
comes to . . . h. a. save . 104.5
he alone can h. a. bless . 343.2
power to h. a. heal . . 571.3
strengthen thee, h. thee . 653.2
a friend to h. a. cheer . . 709.3
Lord, h. us, and inspire . . 827.3

g *(general)*
h. us while we sing . . 193.1
unless thou h. me . . . die . 291.1
the h. of all who find . . 334.3
weary, h. me I pray . . 487.3
to thee for h. I call . . . 489.1
h. us each . . . day. . . 532.3
h. by thy Spirit's sword . . 561.4
thy h. we claim . . . 581.1
thou canst h. me now . . 586.2
h. you in life's . . . mart. . 664.3
h. us one and all . . . 698.3
to h. me quite through . . 712.3
h. us in the fiery blast . . 769.2
h. us save the lost . . . 783.3
our h. is near 804.4
h. divine implore . . . 812.2
he doth his h. afford . . 915.2
test . . . by h. divine . . 926.4

h *Mark 9:24*
h. my unbelief . . . 301.2
h. . . . so unbelieving . . 503.2

i *help [to]*
you h. us tread . . . 38.5
h. us . . . truth t. hear . . 97.4
h. me walk from day t. day . 115.3
h. me point the lost . . 188.3
h. us . . . wrong t. conquer . 193.5
h. me t. obey . . . 204.1
h. me take the strain . . 204.2
h. me bear the pain . . 204.2
h. us thy name t. sing . . 219.1
h. us t. praise . . . 219.1
h. me t. conquer . . . host . 432.3
h. me t. tear it . . . 442.5
h. me t. watch and pray . 472.4
h. me spread . . . news . . 499.4
h. me t. comfort . . . 518.1
h. me the slow . . . move . 519.2
h. me in thee . . . trust . . 523.4
h. me confide in thee . . 574.2
h. us t. pray 608.2
h. me t. . . . sacrifice . . 619.4
h. us on earth to do . . 624.2
h. us . . . to prove . . . prayer 642.3
h. us t. help each other . . 662.1
h. us t. build each other . 662.2
h. me t. remember thee . 837.4

h. us . . . t. test ourselves . 926.4
h. us t. endure . . . 937.4
h. us . . . t. be consecrated . 941.2

j *help (bear)*
h. me b. the strain of toil . 519.1
h. me the cross to b. . . 524.2
patience h. to b. the cross . 555.3
h. me . . . b. pain . . . 837.5

k *help (live)*
h. me to l. and do . . . 431.2
h. me to l. by faith . . . 445.3
h. me to l. a spotless life . 649.2
h. us . . . l. more nearly . . 668.5

l *help [see]*
h. us to s. 'tis only . . . 8.4
h. us to recognise . . . 27.4
h. us to trace . . . 38.3

2 *(we) help*
with words that h. and heal . 212.1
h. those who are weak . . 458.1
speak to . . . h. the weak . 581.4
h. the helpless . . . 623.2
help us to h. each other . . 662.1
warriors are wanted to h. . 684.1
stoop to h. the dying . . 702.3
hearts to h. him save . . . 704.3
to h. mankind in need . . 706.2
we would h. to build . . 833.2
that h. others to be strong . 838.3
to carry and to h. . . . 851.2
dying I may h. to save . . 859.2
we will h. to lead them . . 866.3
who for h. dost call . . 921.1
love for h. is seeking . . 921.3
h. each gave the other . . 938.3

b *(other)*
h., ye bright . . . spirits . . 109.3
h. to sing . . . chant . . 109.3
angels . . . h. and comfort . 396.3
h. me on to God . . . 678.3
each victory will h. you . . 823.1

c *Acts 16:9*
heard the cry for h. . . 702.2
come and h. us . . . cry . . 922.1

d
I cannot h. but love him . . 65.2

helper *Ps 54:4*
our h. he, amid the flood . 1.1
h. of men in their . . . need . 351.c
guide and h., lover, friend . 510.c
when other h. fail . . . 670.1
who will be his h. . . . 707.1
thou wilt my h. be . . . 714.3
he's a h. and a stay . . c126

helpless
h. and defiled 98.1
guilty, vile and h. we . . 118.3
a h., homeless child . . 274.1
Adam's h. race . . . 283.2
h. I am and full of guilt . . 291.2
h., look to thee . . . 302.3
see! h. I cling . . . 454.2
h. am I until thy grace . . 456.2
h. indeed, I come . . . 488.c
serve the h. and oppressed . 518.2
helping the h. . . . 623.2
help of the h., O abide . . 670.1
my h. soul, rest . . . 729.2
hangs my h. soul on thee . 737.2
regarded my h. estate . . 771.2
at the cross h. I bow . . c68
weak (c)

helplessness 717.1

hem *Matt 9:20*
she only touched the h. . . 304.1
touch the h. of his garment . 304.c
I touched but the h. . . 542.3

hence
glory never h. depart . . 945.4

b *hence(forth)*
h. my great concern . . 14.4
goodwill h. from Heaven . 93.6
let me h. be like Jesus . . 188.2
that h. my life . . . 205.*
h. I live for thee alone . . 208.3
h. is he thy Master . . . 276.2
yet h. shall he live . . . 277.1
thy pleasure h. to fulfil . . 422.2
h. may no profane delight . 480.3
from h. my all shalt be . . 498.1
h. my chief desire . . . 517.1
my sweetest thought h. . . 517.4
each departing day h. . . 524.3
h. earthly things . . . 532.3
go h. thy will pursuing . . 534.3
be it Christ h. to live . . 771.3
want h. our lives to be . . 933.1
h. each day our lives . . 933.3
thine alone, h., Saviour . . c38

c *henceforth evermore*
his glorious name h. for e. . 20.5
praises be, h. e. . . . 219.4
shall keep thee h., yea, for e.. 767.4

her-self
Jesus Christ h. little child . 87.1
fold him (her) 792.1
love . . . surround him (her) . 795.3

b *(general)*
earth, with h. . . . tongues . 4.3
or earth received h. frame . 13.3
let earth receive h. King . . 84.1
clothes h. for spring . . 155.2
greets . . . h. returning King . 155.2
faith presents h. claim . . 198.2
soul . . . to h. eternal rest . 307.1
when . . . soul find h. rest . 454.1
hand forget h. skill . . 573.5
the objects of h. care . . 722.4
soul shall h. vigour renew . 734.2
youth obeys h. . . . call . . 799.2
h. walls . . . h. gates . . 944.1

herald-ing
angelic h.'s voice . . . 78.2
the h. angels sing . . . 82.1
let the Saviour's h. go . . 697.3
one of his h. 848.4
h. here thy truth proclaim . 946.2
h. the coming of the King . c226

herd 41.1

here
nc, but

a *here and now*
to claim the h. and n. . . 142.2
offered h. and n. . . . 413.2
h. and n. it makes me . . 434.5
surrender, h. and n. . . 446.3
h. and n. I know . . . 459.2
begin h. and n. in me . . 630.3
power is h. and round me n. . 744.5

heritage
great the h. they left . . 158.2
the meek their h. possess . 198.4
share that wondrous h. . . 613.3

heroes
fire that turns men into h. . 197.3
more h. of faith . . . 684.4
hearts like h. gone before . 704.1
fire that makes men h. . . 830.3
boldly the h. tread . . . c238

hesitate-d-ing
when we h. on the way . . 192.3
delay no more, nor h. . . 267.3
you have long been h. . . 433.2

hide-ing-/hid-den
splendour of light h. . . . 8.4
he h. a smiling face . . . 29.4
the atom's h. forces . . . 38.2
where could we h. 49.c
no clouds thy glory h. . . 76.4
the sun in darkness h. . . 105.3
sorrow h. beneath her wings . 145.3
though the darkness h. thee . 220.3
do not h. . . . emotion . . 259.1
h. not the worst . . . 457.1
God's armies, just h. . . 537.2
what you choose to h. . . 552.1
wounds that shame would h.. 558.4
h. rocks and . . . shoal . . . 598.1
failure I cannot h. . . . 605.1
reach the h. depths . . 612.4
the motion of a h. fire . . 625.1
from all but thee far h. . . 647.2
jewels rich and rare are h. . 658.2
the storm cannot h. . . 758.c
when your path seems h. . 759.2

b *hide (eyes)*
in light . . . h. from our eyes . 8.1
would I h. mine eyes . . 131.3
to h. thee from . . . eyes. . 676.1

c *hide [sin]*
for h. . . . sin's . . . stains . 237.1
I would not h. my sin . . 415.2
my sins in thee to h. . . 486.1
sin's h. stain 610.3
no surviving h. sin . . . 630.3

d *hide [in God]* *Ps 17:8*
let me h. myself in thee . 302.1, 4
in the tempest he h. me . . 467.4
he h. my soul . . . 710.1, c
spreads . . . h. us there . . 722.4
h. me . . . Saviour, h. . . 737.1
I conquer all while h. . . 761.3
for safety we h. . . . 763.4
'neath his wings . . . h. you . 954.2

e *hiding-place* *Ps 32:7**
my shield and h.-p. . . . 58.3
be thou my shield and h.-p. . 284.4
O what a h. p. . . . precious . 341.c
a h.-p. thou art . . . 761.3
I have found my h.-p. . . c164

f *Hab 3:4*
in the h. of thy power . . 591.c

g *Col 3:3*
h. my life in thee . . . 630.2
to be h. in thy breast . . 639.3
he h. my life in . . . love. . 710.c
tower that h. my life . . 714.3
he . . . h. our life above . . 915.2
rock (2c), wise (d)

high
1 *(re divine)*
h. above all praise . . . 20.2
above all blessing h. . . 20.2
the name h. over all . . 60.1
a child of h. renown . . 72.1
now in Heaven, exalted h. . 118.4
not . . . remotely h. . . 142.3
h. on thy eternal throne . . 161.4
thou art h. exalted . . . 174.4
h. on his heart . . . 183.2
h. in heavenly glory . . 240.2
my merciful h. priest . . 880.3

b *Most High* *Ps 91.9**
dwelling-place is the M. H. . 362.1
Son of God m. h. . . . 590.3

2 *(general)*
heavens are not too h. . . 11.1
rainbows span the heavens h. 39.2
Heaven's h. portals . . 151.4
kindle every h. desire . . 194.2
sins . . . rise mountains h. . 253.3
no . . . name, however h. . 269.3
though the waves roll h. . 325.4

when the noontide is h. . . 351.1
mercy so h. and so deep . 454.5
with banners floating h. . . 705.3
because my faith is h. . . 717.3
while the tempest . . . is h. . 737.1
every h. and stormy gale . 745.2
their h. communion find . 826.2
hold the gospel banner h. . 847.4
waving . . . h. in my hand . 848.4
with h. endeavour, bearers . 863.1
h. in Heaven . . . never suffer. 911.6
seed by the wayside h. . . 931.2
adventure

b *high as/like*
h. as the heavens . . . raise . 4.3
justice like mountains h. . 8.2
love . . . h. as the heavens . 47.1
it's as h. as the sky . . 49.c
h. as the heavens above . 383.2
rose as h. as a mountain . c189

c *lift high*
to slay . . . l. them h. . . 91.1
bear it onward; l. it h. . . 697.2
blood and fire, l. it h. . . 783.c
in each hand uplifted h. . . 799.2
lift (2b)

d *raise high*
r. your . . . triumphs h. . . 143.1
r. the standard h. . . . 698.1
we'll r. our banner h. . . 810.1
nailed him, r. h. . . . c89

3 *on high*
lift up the banner on h. 382.c/782.c

b *(re Heaven)*
secrets of your work on h. . 38.1
they saw a host on h. . . 72.3
reigns enthroned on h. . . 72.6
for ever up on h. . . . 73.4
died, and rose on h. . . 156.2
his treasure is on h. . . 277.1
told of a Heaven on h. . . 289.3
Jesus' throne on h. . . 312.2
fairer worlds on h. . . . 314.3
take me . . . up on h. . . 318.4
reigning for ever on h. . . 354.2
the banquet hall on h. . . 375.3
enthroned on h. . . . 435.1
those enjoyed on h. . . 461.2
lead to realms on h. . . 590.2
reach the majesty on h. . . 625.3
doings heard on h. . . 677.4
take me home on h. . . 843.3
live with him on h. . . 844.4
my Father's house on h. . . 877.2
crowns laid up on h. . . 912.c

c *God on high*
God ruleth on h. . . . 24.2
power, thou God on h. . . 146.3
give thanks to God on h. . 223.5
glory (5b)

d *from on high* *Luke 1:78*
thy coming from on h. . . 198.1
dayspring from on h. . . 412.1
true manna from on h. . . 654.2

higher
purer and h. and greater . 22.3
h. than the stars . . . 52.c
fills and saves us h. . . 197.2
now on a h. plane I dwell . 339.4
lead me h. up the mountain . 429.c
h. up where light increases . 429.2
I ask no h. state . . . 441.4
h. still, and rising h. . . 546.1
raise the . . . standard h. . 696.3
h. than the loftiest climb . 766.2
h. and yet h. rise . . . 834.3
lift thy praises h. and h. . . 936.2
h. plane than I have found . c80
plant my feet on h. ground . c80

b *Ps 103:11*
h. than the highest Heaven . 548.4

c *Luke 14:10*
says: Come up h. . . . 910.4
depth (c)

highest
salvation full, at h. cost . . 46.1
to come from h. bliss . . 88.4
Jesus takes the h. station . 147.4
the h. place that Heaven . 168.2
h. archangels in glory . . 184.1
all h. strength . . . 202.2
my h. glory his reproach . 451.4
my h. ambition . . . 640.4
on the h. summit . . . 766.3
keep the h. aims in view. . 801.1
to climb the h. heights . . 858.2
glory (5b), heaven (2e)

highway
a *Isa 40:3*
make a h. for our God . . 159.1
on the King's h. . . . c26

b *Matt 22:9*
placed me on the h. . . 463.1
forth into the world's h. . 683.6
in the h. and the byways . 832.c

hill
1 *Calvary*
love climbed the green h. . 51.c
the h. where he died . . 119.1
on a h. far away . . . 124.1
from that sacred h. . . 126.c
there is a green h. . . . 133.1
sacred now is Calvary's h. . 590.1
from a h. I know . . . 647.c
behold! on a h., Calvary . . 830.*

2 *Heaven*
gather on the h. of God . . 483.3
on Zion's heavenly h. . . 853.2
the h. of bright Glory . . 905.4

3 *(general)*
it streams from the h. . . 16.4
h. and plains repeat . . 84.2
on every h. our Saviour . . 127.1
cry the news from every h. . 127.c
make this h. our home . . 154.4
O calm of h. above . . 567.3
the distant h. before me. . 766.1
found amid the fields and h. . 871.2
rocky h., and brooks . . 887.3

b *hill and [vale]*
h. and v. and tree . . . 28.2
when over h. and v. . . 39.3
peals over h. and dell . . 187.2
tidings over v. and h. . . 279.c
over the h. and the valleys . 637.2
the h. and dales of life . . 884.3

c *[holy] hill* *Ps 43:3*
lead me to thy h. h. . . 453.3
bring me to thy h. h. . . 457.2
there is a h. h. of God . . 461.1
let me now thy h. ascend . 461.4
in thy h. h. stablish . . 648.3
from the h. shall make . . 762.2
ascend thy h. h. . . . c72

d *Ps 65:12; 68:16*
h. leap up in gladness . . 929.2
h. with joy are ringing . . 934.1

e *Ps 121:1*
to the h. I lift my eyes . . 766.1
unto the h. around . . . 767.1

f *Prov 8:25*
before the h. in order . . 13.3

hillside
on the h. long ago . . . 74.2
marching up the h. . . . 903.1

hinder-ed
all that h. . . . aside . . 188.c
to h. your coming . . . 233.2
joy which none can h. . . 352.2
those doubts that h. . . 399.1
h. by your unbelief . . 433.2
cursèd thing that h. . . 448.2
loss and pain shall not h. . 473.2
from all that h. . . . 543.2
load that would h. . . . 816.1

hindrance 646.1

hireling *John 10:12, 13* . . 522.2

hither *1 Sam 7:12*
h. by thy help I'm come. . 313.2
h. by his help I'm brought . 338.4
h., when Hell assails . . 746.3

hoarded 579.2

hoist 704.c

hold-ing/held
1 *(God) holds*
who h. the countless stars . 6.1
thy hand still h. the plan. . 6.4
h. our sorrows in embrace . 242.4
arm which h. me evermore . 311.3
he h. the wealth . . . 354.1
the salvation h. up . . . 395.1
hand still h. the rod . . 446.3
h. . . . absolute sway . . 487.4
h. in your keeping . . . 506.2
h. thou my feet . . . 529.2
never ceased to h. me . 534.c, 3
h. in thy arms . . . live . 543.3
h. me with thy . . . hand. . 578.1
eternally h. in thy heart . . 639.3
h. thou thy cross . . . 670.5
confidence in him who h. . 711.3
God's mercy h. . . . plan . 723.2
h. thou my hand . . . 726.*
knowing that you h. him (her) 792.1
h. by the power of a love . c48
mighty power he h. me . . c163

b *Ps 66:9*
h. my soul faithful . . . 571.1

c *Ps 119:117*
he h. me up 710.2
hand (1e)

2 *(we) hold*
I h. my Father's hand . . 48.2
might we h. the vision . . 154.4
if I still h. closely . . . 228.5
I can h. out no more . . 307.4
I h. it for the giver . . . 345.2
the treasure h. by those. . 363.1
not h. back . . . any part. . 422.1
things I h. so dear . . . 460.2
if someone . . . h. my hands . 544.2
parents h. him dear . . 661.2
for ever be h. true . . . 795.2
secret . . . h. on . . . 806.*
God's name h. in reverence . 823.2
h. the gospel banner high . 847.4
or h. the tide 854.2
naught we h. . . . surrender . 922.3
faith (2g), fast (1b), lay (3c)

3 *(general)*
h. . . . by undying love . . 126.1
but death . . . could not h. . 137.4
will your anchor h. . . 280.*
all the world h. dear . . 564.2
friend h. fellowship . . 573.3
angels h. a charge divine . 728.2
whate'er the future h. . . 732.c
anchor h. alone to thee . . 742.3
anchor h. within the veil . 745.2
h. the fort 804.c

b *hold of [sin]*
in Satan's bondage h. . . 81.2
evil forces . . . h. the sway . 171.1
but from the h. of sin . . 290.2
when from sin's dark h. . . 534.1
h. by my halting behaviour . 553.3
let not self h. any part . . 643.3
where'er he h. dominion . 696.c
mistrust and fear have h. . 827.2

holier-st *Ps 148:1*
praise to the h. . . 18.1, 4
O for a h. walk . . . 445.2
within the h. place . . . 590.1

holiness
lead us to h. 190.3
every thought of h. . . 200.6
who is it calls to h.. . . 204.3
for the sight of h. . . . 414.5
that h. I long to feel . . 419.1
if you want h., cling . . 427.4
may live the life of h. . . 431.1
rest . . . in a spotless h.. . 446.4
reflex of thy h. . . . 455.2
may we glimpse thy h. . . 590.4
point the way to h. . . 656.2
one in h. 769.3
emblem . . . of h. and love . 781.1
our motto shall h. be . . 808.5
true h., compassion . . c208
b *holiness and Heaven*
nigh to h. and H. . . . 113.3
from h. and H. we never . 800.2
c *Ps 96:9*
the beauty of h. . . 183.1, 5
d *Luke 1:75*
with righteousness and h. . 609.1
e *Rom 1:4*
Spirit of h. . . . descend. . 219.2
Spirit of perfect h. . . . 441.2
f *Rom 6:22*
rich fruits of h. we see . . 936.3
perfect (2c)

hollow 379.3

holy
1 *re divinity*
h. Jesus! every day . . 76.4
proclaim the h. birth . . 86.2
lived . . . our Saviour h. . . 87.2
the one so h., so divine . . 108.1
the h., meek . . . Lamb . . 116.3
come, h. Comforter . . 219.3
life-giving, h. dove . . 224.3
h. and blessèd Three . . 224.4
the h. one is waiting . . 410.1
return, O h. Dove . . . 442.4
Christ, the h. Christ . . 479.2
h. Father, in thy mercy . . 582.1
h. Jesu, come from God . 871.2
h., blessèd Trinity . . . 939.5
b *[holy child]* *Acts 4:27*
O h. Child of Bethlehem . 86.4
teach us, h. Child . . . 88.5
h. infant, tender and mild . 89.1
Christ, the h. child, in me . 793.6
c *Rev 4:8; 15:4*
h., h., h.! Lord God . . 220.*
thou art h., Lord of Glory . 528.1
Holy Ghost/Spirit—see Spirit
2
to serve your h. will . . 38.2
so may we with h. joy . . 76.3
silent night! h. night . . 89.*
room for thy h. nativity . . 101.1
subdue all that is not h. . . 141.5
let shouts of h. joy . . . 151.2
loud their h. war cry . . 158.1
lead . . . to thy h. cause. . 181.1
thy h. balm of peace . . 200.2
sing with h. rapture . . 259.4
the h. delight which I feel . 367.4
glad to join our h. song . . 370.4
in the h. war 373.3
Calvary's h. feast . . . 431.3
with h. valour make me . . 432.2
let h. truth condemn . . 446.2
a blessed way and h. . . 462.2
the h., mighty . . . river . . 471.c
give me h. courage . . 499.3
ablaze with h. burning . . 529.2
with h. motives may . . . obey 581.3
lead us to his h. presence . 595.1
shed . . . thy h. light . . 602.4
thy h. laws fulfil . . . 649.2
sinless in thy h. eyes . . 673.4
h. peace and liberation . . 702.3
'neath his h. roof . . . 728.3
keepeth . . . in his h. care . 767.2
would be thy h. temple . . 786.1
to walk in h. ways . . . 849.2
arm us with h. might . . 870.3
closely knit in h. vow . . 947.1
how best to do thy h. will . c72
b *holy [Bible]*
gild its h. pages . . . 193.3
attentive to thy h. word. . 613.1
thy h. word the truth . . 650.2
h. Bible, book divine . 652.1, 4
discerning . . . h. learning . 655.6
rest . . . upon his h. word . 698.1
go with the H. Bible . . 830.2
for your h. book we thank . 856.*
c *holy name*
fear his h. n. 20.2
breathe that h. n. . . . 66.2
honour give to his h. n. . . 184.1
praise ye his h. n. . . . 383.c
just and h. is thy n. . . 737.3
captain, h. is his n. . . 866.2
d *holy place* *Heb 9:12**
bring me to thy h. p. . . 102.4
brightness fills the h. p. . . 268.2
serve within the h. p. . . 461.4
within the h. p. God . . 590.1
if still the h. p. is found . . 619.1
refuge . . . within the h. p. . 747.1
praise him . . . in his h. p. . 769.1
e *Rom 12:1*
a h., living sacrifice . . 516.1
f *(re people)*
where h. voices chime . . 7.2
say, ye h. shepherds, say . 88.2
the wise and h. men . . 96.1
there all are h. . . . good. . 268.3
road that h. men have trod . 583.1
a h., blood-washed band . 781.3
Heaven, where the h. go . 835.3
thy children, a h. band . . 873.3
land of the pure . . . h. . . 905.1
strains of . . . h. throng . . 934.4
fear (1b), fire (2b), flame (2b), hill (3c)
3 *(desire to be holy)*
I myself would h. be . . 212.5
h. and pure and perfect . . 407.5
give me a h. life . . . 416.1
wills that I should h. be . . 419.1
kept pure and h. . . . 443.1
keep me h. here . . . 447.1
take time to be h. . . . 458.*
in word . . . h. to be . . 521.1
h. and harmless, patient . 623.3
home when hearts are h. . 663.1
hearts like thine . . . h. . . 704.4
h., through . . . guiding . . 764.2
suggests we may be h. . . 783.4
to show how pure and h. . 840.2
b *make holy*
as he died to m. men h.. . 162.4
he shall now m. me h. . . 413.3
Jesus, m. me h. . . . 430.c
to redeem and m. you h. . 433.c
m. us h.: with thy blessing . 452.1
for thy mission m. me h. . 463.c
m. h. by his blood . . . 495.1
trusting thee to m. me h. . 727.3
c *holy living*
h. l. . . . we may attain . . 324.3
give us all more h. l. . . 622.3
hate me for my h. l. . . 758.3
blue, the sign of h. l. . . 777.3
on to h. l. 788.3

homage
bring gifts and h. . . . 89.2
deepest h. now I give . . 600.3
be the cheerful h. paid . . 925.4

home
1 *(literal)*
for peaceful h. and . . . days . 15.2
in peace of h. and friends . 31.2
Bethlehem's h. . . . no room . 101.1
let streets and h. . . . ring . 142.1
no h. on earth have I . . 362.1
with thee, my God, is h.. . 362.3
turned from h. and toil . . 428.2
take thee to their h. . . 604.2
be there at our h. . . . 611.3
happy the h. . . . . 661.*
let us in our h. agree . . 661.4
home is 663.1
love at h. . . . . 664.*
'mid the h. of want . . 697.3
lowly cot or stately h. . . 705.1
shining lights of h. . . . 740.3
in bright, happy h. . . . 807.3
in the h. and in the mart. . 832.3
shrouding heart and h. . . 916.3
from each grateful h. . . 921.3
b *at home*
at h., abroad, by night . . 356.4
at h., at school, at play . . 844.1
please him at h. . . . 849.3
2 *(spiritual)*
make this hill our h. . . 154.4
thine exiles long for h. . . 167.3
sinner . . . hasten h. . . 369.3
a h. within the wilderness . 476.1
I am far from h. . . . 606.1
lead the wretched . . . h. . 802.2
b *bring home*
h. rejoicing b. me . . . 53.3
b. me h. to God . . . 347.1
gladness when he b. me h. . 388.3
b. guilty sinners h. . . . c25
c *come home*
ye who are weary, c. h.. . 264.c
room: O c. h. . . . 333.4
are you c. h . tonight . . c4
c. h., never more to roam . c10
d *call home*
let thy voice c. me h. . . 101.4
he'll c. me . . . to my h.. . 124.3
in love he c. thee h. . . 225.1
tenderly c. thee h. . . . 248.1
his love . . . c. thee h. . . 250.5
c. the wanderer h. . . . 279.c
e *(heart) home*
my heart is thy abiding h. . 208.3
fix in me his constant h.. . 214.3
make this house thy h. . . 217.1
make each heart thy h. . . 218.c
make my heart thy h. . . 447.1
make my heart thy h. . . 562.1
3 *(Heaven)*
a *for Jesus*
he left his h. in Glory . . 337.1
b *for us*
his ransomed h. to bring . 118.5

we're travelling h. . . . 275.1
joy and light of thy h. . . 300.4
when we arrive at h. . . 312.1
safely to arrive at h. . . 313.2
though exiled from h. . . 354.4
I shall be at h. . . . 368.3
till . . . I view my h. . . 633.3
heard of that heavenly h. . 794.3
a harp, a h., a mansion . . 811.c
my h. is there . . . 872.*
h. of the soldier . . . 873.*
day's march nearer h. . . 877.1
h. of my soul . . . 877.2
I have a h. . . . fairer . . 881.1
h. far away . . . . 881.*
think of the h. . . . 886.1, c
their h. in the palace . . 886.2
soon be at h. over there. . 886.4
summoned h.! the call . . 894.1
we are marching h. . . 902.1
the h. of the happy . . 905.1
shall gather to their h. . . 907.2
till to the h. of gladness . . 949.4
shall guide us safe h. . . 962
wonderful h. . . . prepare . . c251

c *[go] home [above]*
bring . . . to thy h. above . 152.3
I'm a soldier going h. . . 338.1
go singing glory! h. . . 338.5
go to our h. above . 382.c/782.c
at last go h. to reign . . 686.2
then at last go h. to thee . 837.6
singing, going h. . . . 903.c

d *take home*
come . . . to t. me h. . . 37.4
t. me h. to God . . . 597.4
he will t. me h. on high . . 843.3
he will t. me h. . . . c154

e *welcome home*
Saviour shall w. us h. . . 808.4
sing their w. h. . . . 879.c
Jesus . . . will w. sinners h. . c17

eternal (2b), harvest (2f), heaven (2d), last (3c), lead (3f)

homecoming 388.3

homeland
the homeland! . . . 895.*
leading to the h. . . . 903.2

homeless
living as a h. stranger . . 97.2
h., rejected and poor . . 99.2
a helpless, h. child . . . 274.1

homestead 369.1

homeward
as h. he carried . . . 111.1
leading onward . . . h. . . 182.1
gate that is leading h. . . 247.2
guide them in the h. way . 519.2
peace upon our h. way . . 674.2
as the birds h. wend . . 675.3
Christward, h., Godward . 776.2
we're on the h. trail . . 903.c

honest
h. labour sanctified . . . 688.2

b *Phil 4:8*
h., just and lovely, too . . c56

honey *Ex 3:8**
with milk and h. flow . . 887.3
here the milk and h. flow . c153

honour-ed
he would h. and obey . . 87.3
now h. thy word . . . 637.3
maintain the h. of his word . 735.1

b *John 12:26*
will have part in the h. . . 169.2

h. to die in the field . . 684.3
h. in the cause . . . 776.3
h. them, the faithful . . 847.1
h. at the throne of glory. . 894.1

c *Rev 5:12,13**
all h. and blessing . . . 24.3
worthy to receive h. . . 57.3
spread . . . h. of thy name . 64.2
worship, h., power . . 109.3
bring peculiar h. . . . 160.5
thee will I h. 177.1
glory and h. . . . be thine . 177.4
strength and h. give . . 184.1
glory, laud and h. . . . 690.5
glory, h. to the Lamb . . 696.c
here let your Son be h. . . 943.4
glory, h. and salvation . . c27

d *(worldly honour)*
worldly h. all forsaking . . 320.2
your h. perish in a day . . 356.2
wealth, h., pleasure . . 480.4
its h. fade and fall . . . 489.2

hope
1 *(human hopes)*
brings h. again . . . 238.2
would thy h. destroy . . 253.3
all my sanguine h. . . . 566.3
broken . . . blighted h. . . 702.3
oft our h. were vain . . 750.1
secret h. have perished . . 753.3
provoke my h. or fear . . 880.2
human h. may vanish . . c143

fear (2d)

2 *(Jesus our hope)*
1 Tim 1:1; 1 Thess 2:19
our h. for years to come. .13.1, 6
h. of every contrite heart . 61.3
h. of all the earth thou . . 79.2
our light and h. to be . . 94.1
his people's h. . . . 168.6
h. of the penitent . . . 236.2
as the light of new h. . . 245.1
my only h. and comfort . . 325.1
the h. of all who seek . . 334.3
my h., my solace . . . 356.4
the h. of every nation . . 381.2
my every h. I stay . . . 400.2
the h. of my tomorrow . . 529.1
Jesus, my strength, my h. . 596.1
our h. of guidance . . . 692.4
my h., my joy, my all . . 726.2
nor let my h. be lost . . 735.2
here is my h. my joy . . 746.3

b *all hope*
cross . . . is all our h. . . 121.4
from which all h. of good . 127.4
human h. are all in thee . . 135.4
this is all my h. . . . 306.4
all my h. are fixed . . . 517.2
all my h. and stay . . . 745.3

c *hope (of Heaven)*
means of grace and h. or H. . 15.5
h. of earth and joy of H.. . 66.c
on whom my h. of H. depend. 592.2
joys of earth and h. of H. . 941.1

righteousness (e), stay (1b), steadfast (b)

3 *(spiritual hope)*
bright h. for tomorrow . . 33.3
bright with h. is burning. . 73.3
all our . . . h. thou sharest . 97.4
h. is gleaming still . . . 126.c
my flesh in h. shall rest . . 153.2
h. for our fear . . . 183.4
h. is singing from afar . . 185.3
ever by a mighty h. . . 212.4
a message of h. . . . 273.2
for thee, not without h. . . 305.1
h. . . . soul may cherish . . 363.4
h. that will surely endure . 371.3
h. my soul is swelling . . 460.1

in h. that sends . . . ray. . 519.4
shed thy light of h. . . 576.2
look up with a . . . h. . . 585.2
of all our h. the ground . . 656.1
let the voice of h. . . . 697.3
my h. I cannot measure . . 736.3
this h. is mine . . . Jesus . 761.4
that brings . . . new h. . . 779.1
for the poor . . . a h. . . 824.3
inspired with h. and praise . 825.3
the h. of all the ages . . 868.2
h. for whosoever will . . 919.2
our h. we place . . . 940.1
this is my h. . . . ambition . c38
h. for the darkest hour . . c46
this h. possesseth me . . c107
the cheering ray of h. . . c166
the h. of youth . . . c238

b *hope (faith and love)* *1 Cor 13:13*
f. and h. can see fulfilled . 39.4
from f. and h. may grow . 314.3
h. and praise and l. . . 387.3
on to perfect f. . . . h. . . 423.3
cheer it with h., with l. . . 516.2
h. will triumph . . . l. . . 555.3
confirm our h. 662.2
men of h. and f. . . . 702.1
h. soars . . . f. shouts . . 744.6
h. will give us courage . . 755.3
my h. and l. . . . are there . 880.3
steadfast f., of patient h. . 948.2
one in our f., one in our h. . c226

c *no hope* *Eph 2:12*
no light, no h. had we . . 94.1
to die with no h. . . . 263.3
without a h. to cheer . . 688.5
how bring back h. . . . 706.1
have no h. of liberty . . 832.2
what h. have you . . . 885.4
who can give you h. . . 885.4

d *one hope* *Eph 4:4*
our fears, our h. . . . one . 660.2
one in h., in doctrine . . 690.3
one the h. our God inspires . 765.4
one in our faith . . . h. . . c226

e *[rejoice] in hope* *Rom 5:2*
r. in glorious h. . . . 164.6
inmost souls r. in h. . . 603.5
wait in cheerful h. . . . 738.2

f *2 Cor 9:10*
sowing in h. 931.3

g *blessèd hope* *Titus 2:13*
thank thee for the b. h. . . 714.1
b. h., blessèd rest . . . 771.4

h *hope (anchor)* *Heb 6:19*
h. has dropped her anchor . 333.3

know (2f), remove (d)

4 hope *(verb)*
I h. the stains . . . 359.3
I could not h. for . . . 388.2
I dared not h. that . . . 403.1
all I've sought or h. . . 498.2
all I have . . . h. for . . 514.c
h., trusting to the end . . 544.4
love that suffered, h. . . 544.5
take what I h. to be . . 605.3
we h. to die shouting . . 763.5
h. one day to bring . . 851.3

b *hope [in God]* *Ps 42:5**
h., trusting ever . . . 115.4
we h. to meet above . . 239.4
h. . . . safely to arrive . . 313.2
h. still, and . . . sing . . 557.4
h. to meet again . . . 660.4
h., and be undismayed . . 721.1
h. in him whate'er betide . 738.1

hopeful-ness
Lord of all h. 611.1
nothing seems h. . . . 773.1
life is full of h. . . . c201

hopeless
to weary, h. nations . . 63.2
to the h. souls . . . 620.2

horrors 19.4

hosanna *Matt 21:9, 15*
our glad h., Prince . . . 81.4
all the tribes h. cry . . . 150.1
proclaim their young h. . . 160.2
shout aloud h. . . . 698.c
till h. reach the skies . . 834.3
children . . . singing h. . . 853.*
b *loud hosannas*
l. with h. ring 184.3
l. h. shout 807.1
l. h. to our King . . . 834.c
I would sing l. h. . . . 848.4

host
1 *(general)*
twinkling starry h. . . . 177.3
a h. of haunting fears . . 433.1
word is like a starry h. . . 658.3
2 *re divinity*
that he my h. should be . . 728.1
but more he is than h. . . 728.4
b *Lord of hosts* *Ps 24:10*
strong in the Lord of h. . . 695.2
trusting in the God of h.. . 700.2
3 *(angels)*
the h. of God encamp . . 21.3
all the h. of light . . . 141.2
the whole triumphant h. . 223.5
the host of H. rejoices . . 381.1
praise . . . heavenly h. . 665.6; 959
b *Luke 2:13*
they saw a h. on high . . 72.3
h. of angels chanted . . 78.1
with the angelic h. . . . 82.1
angel (f)
4 *(the Church)*
the ransomed h. in Heaven . 63.3
all the ransomed h. of God . 132.3
swelling the h. that . . . go . 169.2
feel through thine h. . . 173.3
see this waiting h. . . . 203.1
let thy h. on earth . . . 217.5
inflame thy fighting h. . . 609.2
we the people of thy h. . . 643.1
martial and mighty h. . . 648.2
the Lamb leads his h. . . 708.1
mighty Captain of the h. . 789.6
countless h. he leads . . 790.1
with his h. in battle . . 790.c
martial h. assemble . . 803.1
story of our God-made h. . 803.4
for God has been a h. . . 847.2
the ransomed h. we see . . 908.c
b *host above*
blest as the h. a. . . . 217.5
the shining h. a. . . . 367.c
serve thee as thy h. a. . . 438.2
the conquering h. a. . . 894.c
5 *host of [Satan]*
armèd h. to meet . . . 158.2
help . . . conquer Satan's h. . 432.3
the h. of evil round us . . 577.2
Satan's h. doth flee . . 690.2
though Satan's h. surround . 722.2
mighty h. . . . Satan leading . 804.2
through the h. of sin . . 811.2
the h. of sin are pressing . 812.1
Satan and his h. defy . . 847.4
b *hosts of Hell*
the h. of H. we're routing . 693.3
see the brazen h. of H. . . 696.2
'gainst the h. of H. uniting . 778.2
the h. of H. are uniting . . 800.1
h. of H. and darkness . . 822.2

hostility 939.2

hottest 910.4

hour
1 *(particular)*
that dread h. on Calvary . 125.3
in the sacrificial h. . . . 145.3
glorious h. when Christ . . 149.1
the h. I first believed . . 308.2
that soul-transporting h. . 350.1
days of toil and h. of ease . 428.4
my h. of grief and pain . . 552.3
shield in danger's h. . . 569.4
strength in h. of weakness . 570.3
delight of a single h. . . 585.3
be a hallowed h. . . . 599.1
weary ones in needful h. . 612.5
in that h., fairer . . . 632.4
sweet h. of prayer . . . 633.*
d *hour of death*
till, in d.'s glad h. . . . 504.3
till the decisive h. . . . 735.3
the h. has come to die . . 753.4
dark (2e), temptation (b)
2 *(general)*
how tasteless . . . the h.. . 318.1
a few more fleeting h. . . 368.3
idle h., mis-spent . . . 379.2
peaceful h. . . . enjoyed . . 442.3
trifles of the passing h. . . 466.1
my h. I'll give 475.3
brief h. are not lost . . 564.4
Guardian of my . . . h. . . 672.2
h. by h. fresh lips . . . 677.4
gospel that matches the h. . c210
b *all hours*
all my goods . . . h. . . 492.2
all my days and all my h. . c32
c *(each/every) hour*
the beauty of each h. . . 28.2
unfolding every h. . . . 29.5
he'll keep me every h. . . 389.2
can keep me every h. . . 415.3
to be kept every h. . . . 469.4
together every h. . . . 495.2
every h. I'll serve . . . 499.1
keep through every h. . . 513.2
dost keep me every h. . . 538.3
to praise him every h. . . 583.3
I need thee every h. . 587.1, c
every consecrated h. . . 591.c
greater victories every h. . 622.3
this my every h. employ. . 636.5
presence every passing h. . 670.3
he triumphs every h. . . 705.3
cherish every laden h. . . 874.1
by thy grace every h. . . c39
hallow each h. c98
walking each h. with Jesus . c152
d *(every day) and hour*
guide us . . . and every h. . 71.3
every d. and h. supplying . 727.4
right to rule each d. and h. . 867.1
use me every d. and . . . h. . c60
e *(this) hour*
in this accepted h. . . . 196.1
in this most vital h. . . 198.5
go on from this good h. . . 201.c
bless this consecrated h. . 217.4
in his grace this h. . . . 417.1
in this sacred h. . . . 488.c
from this h. I'll f. . . . 490.2
hear this h. . . . vow . . 504.2
this solemn evening h. . . 558.5
in this quiet evening h. . . 576.1
for the facing of this h. . . 577.1
convict, Lord, this h. . . 608.1
invade my soul this h. . . 613.1
satisfy my soul this h. . . 729.1
promise in this sacred h. . 784.2
in this h. of dedication . . 787.1
in this sacrificial h. . . . 789.1
in this dedication h. . . 795.3
from this h. manifest . . 941.2
from this h. will follow . . c109
f *(this very) hour*
saving power, this v. h. . . 304.c
save this v. h. 562.2
cleanse our souls this v. h. . 638.1
save, dear Lord, this v. h. . 638.3
yes, from this v. h. . . 814.2
glad (e)

hourly
h., I may do thy will . . 628.2
as h. we approach . . . 933.4

house
the beauty of thy h. . . 36.6
make this h. thy home . . 217.1
rich in h. and lands . . 354.1
no field, no h. be mine . . 362.2
praises fill this h. . . . 365.2
this h. . . . presence fill . . 516.3
an angel in the h. . . . 664.c
that in this h. have called . 674.2
longs to build thy h. . . 720.1
where in thy h. thou art . . 839.4
in this h. may worship . . 941.3
become the h. of God . . 943.4
h. of glad remembrance . . 944.1
not, Lord, this h. alone . . 945.4
b *Ps 23:6*
within thy h. for ever . . 53.5
in God's h. for evermore . 54.5
c *Ps 127:1*
except you build the h. . . 943.2
d *Matt 21:13*
my heart a h. of prayer . . 305.3
built this h. of prayer . . 941.1
e *2 Cor 5:1*
this earthly h. shall fail . . 149.3
ere from this small h. . . 905.3
Father (2e)

household *Eph 2:19* . . . 589.1

hovering 370.4

how
n c, but
a *(as question)*
h. shall we show . . . 15.1
you ask me h. I know . . 334.c
h. shall I . . . appear . . 414.3
h. shall they hear . . . 527.2
h. shall hearts move . . 527.2
h. shall we . . . declare . . 656.3
h. shall I my life employ . . 846.2
h. shall we bear . . . part . 874.2
h. shall we . . . sing . . 938.1
b *how (can/could)*
Jesus, Lord, h. can it be . 125.3
h. could thy children fear . 146.3
amazing love! h. can it be . 283.1
ask, h. could I tell . . . 323.3
h. can I keep from singing . 358.*
h. can I offer thee less . . 457.c
h. can I better serve . . 488.1
h. couldst thou smile . . 507.2
h. can your pardon reach . 572.2
h. could earth be trod . . 654.4
h. bring back hope . . . 706.1
h. can I quit my post . . 780.2
h. can I be sad . . . c191
c *how (much/many)*
h. much more shall God . . 50.c
think h. much we owe him . 377.2
h. much misery 770.1
h. many fights I've lost . . 770.1
h. much he was willing . . c24

d
h. or why, I cannot tell . . 339.4
great (2b), happy (1c), pleasant, show (1g)

however
no other name, h. high . . 269.3
h. I bleed 440.2
home is home, h. lowly . . 663.1
h. steep the way and long . 719.5
h. you betray him . . . 854.3

howling 757.2

hue 545.2

human
seek in h. wisdom . . . 6.2
graces h. and divine . . 28.5
wider than the h. mind . . 49.3
if h. hearts/minds/love . . . 50.1
by every h. tie . . . 59.2
to h. view displayed . . 93.4
what depth of h. grief . . 135.1
h. hopes are all in thee . . 135.4
with its h. light . . . 141.4
unmoved by h. pains . . 142.3
little as a h. hand . . 165.4
came to share our h. life . 181.1
who doth know h. frailties . 288.2
the limit of h. endeavour . 501.3
Lord, whose h. hands . . 518.1
if I am blind to h. need . . 518.2
sanctify each h. feeling . . 528.c
healing stream for h. woes . 638.1
h. design may cause me . 644.3
making h. toil thine own . 688.2
more than h. tongue . . 696.2
in h. wisdom, or in might . 747.2
and h. feet stand on it . . 766.2
h. thought transcending . 948.1
h. hopes may vanish . . c143
b *human heart*
if h. h. are often tender . . 50.1
so God imparts to h. h. . . 86.3
no h. h. could enter . . 325.3
h. h. and looks deceive . . 498.3
down in the h. h. . . . 691.3
the h. h. can sever . . . 854.3
c *human [love]*
for the joy of h. love . . 28.4
if h. love is touched . . 50.1
sweeter than h. devotion . 383.2

humble-r
1 *(adjective)*
h. creation, though feeble . 16.6
the hearts of h. men . . 36.2
bow in h. adoration . . 37.4
enrich the h. poor . . . 81.3
thine h. beast pursues . . 150.1
return in h. prayer . . . 199.2
he hears thy h. sigh . . 256.2
hear my h. cry . . 301.1, c
fix . . . thy h. dwelling . . 438.1
that h. saints receive . . 461.3
I would be h. 491.2
consume my h. offering . . 511.3
h. in spirit I kneel . . . 513.c
with h. confidence look up . 596.1
inhabitest the h. mind . . 604.2
the h. meal he blessed . . 663.2
star to guide the h. . . 716.*
confident and h. mind . . 744.3
our h. prayers implore . . 918.5
hear my h. pleading . . c74
b *humble hearts*
he can find one h. h. . . 200.4
a h., lowly, contrite h. . . 444.3
in the heart of the h. . . 506.1
our h., thankful h. . . 935.3
c *Mic 6:8*
O for a h. walk with God . 445.1
2 *(verb)*
most I'm saved I'm h. most . 468.4
I am praying to be h. . . 584.2
b *Phil 2:8*
h. for a season . . . 141.3
h. thyself to death . . . 174.3

humbleness *Col 3:12* . . 2.5

humbly
h. offered Christ . . . bread . 5.1
h. ask for more . . . 23.1
at his feet we h. fall . . 104.c
I h. kneel before thee . . 221.1
hear us, we h. pray . . 224.1
h. fall before his feet . . 284.1
h. I seek . . . grace. . . 501.3
h. my all . . . now I lay . . 543.2
h. I may possess . . . 666.2
assist, we h. pray . . . 747.2
by thousands h. kneeling . 802.3
I would be h. questioning . 871.3
may I h. do my part . . c79
b *humbly bow*
h. at his feet I bow. . . 474.2
in thy presence h. I bow. . 487.2
h. at thy throne I bow . . 638.2
h. at thy cross I bow . . c69

humility
in thy sweet h. . . . 88.5
and in great h. . . . 101.2

humming 41.1

hundred
a h. circling camps . . 162.2
a h. anthems rise . . . 163.3
seasoned in a h. fights . . 799.3
there are h. of . . . . . 850.*

hung see *hang*

hunger-ed-ing
I h. to make a beginning . 553.1
fear and h., pain . . . 576.2
may feed thy h. ones . . 612.2
h. for the bread of life . . 626.2
meet the h. of my soul . . 830.1
b *John 6:35*
soul shall never h. more . 277.2
no man will h. . . . 927.4

hungry *Ps 107:5; (Luke 1:53)*
manna to the h. soul . . 58.2
he my h. soul shall fill . . 344.3
my h. soul cries out . . 450.2
quick to feed the h. . . 518.1
the h. and oppressed . . 830.1

hurled
shields when darts are h. . 495.3
foes shall be . . . h. . . 799.4
Hell be backward h. . . 828.2
back . . . into darkness h. . 864.4

hurt *(Luke 10:19)*
wolves have sore h. thee . 111.2
let men h. him so . . . 274.2
soothe the h. with . . . balm . 479.2
forgiving all the h. . . 544.4
all things that may h. us . 554.2
flames shall not h. thee . . 653.4

hush-ed
the h. of the corn . . . 41.2
h. the noise, ye men . . 83.2
when in the h. of eventide . 103.3
soothe and h. and calm it . 325.3
thou canst h. the ocean . 598.2
chided . . . h. the wind . . 848.3

hymn
angels delight to h. thee . 16.6
a h. of Calvary's road . . 103.3
h. of triumph sing . . . 152.2
sweet though far-off h. . 358.1
our morning h. ascended . 677.1
hushed was the evening h. . 839.1
our hearts we raise in h. . 934.1
b *hymn of praise*
let h. of p. . . . tell . . . 151.4
glad h. of p. 569.4
parting h. of p. . . . 674.1

I

I AM *Ex 3:14; John 8:58*
Jehovah, great I AM . . 223.1
glory to the great I AM . . 370.3
b *[affirmations]*
I am this dark world's light . 332.3
Fear not, I am with thee . 390.1
Fear not, I am with thee . 653.2

ice
you can't stop i. . . . 854.2
land of the i. or flame . . c238

idle-y
i. hours, mis-spent powers . 379.2
sit no longer i. by . . . 696.1

idol *(1 John 5:21)*
renounce every i. . . . 263.1
I've all my i. torn . . . 344.2
each i. that would keep . 428.3
break down every i. . . 436.1
dearest i. . . . whate'er . . 442.5
my i. overthrowing . . 448.4
my i. I cast at thy feet . . 454.3

if nc, but see what (1c)

ignorance 414.5

ignore
Don't think . . . he'll i. . . 44.2
none . . . Christ i. . . . 270.2

ill
of mortal i. prevailing . . 1.1
free us from all i. . . . 12.2
from i. . . . soul deliver . . 153.3
all i. its waves deliver . . 471.2
resigned to mortal i. . . 532.3
with an i.-kept vow . . 534.2
oppressed with various i. . 558.2
baits of pleasing i. . . 596.2
i. have no weight . . . 670.4
i. that I this day have done . 671.2
let no i. dreams disturb . . 671.3
no dread of i. . . . afraid. . 726.1
conquest over i. . . . 799.3
above the i. and cares . . 872.1
no i. power find place . . 949.3
b *good and/or ill*
i. thoughts . . . g. be born . 41.2
blessing . . . g. or i. . . 539.3
may to us in g. and i. . . 624.2
know not what of g. or i. . 730.4
g. seems turned to i. . . 947.3
fear (3c)

illumin-e-ate-ation *Heb 10:32**
your Spirit's true i. . . . 38.1
i. my soul c50
open mine eyes, i. me . . c99

illusions 780.1

image
a *Gen 1:26*
you . . . have stamped your i. 38.4
though they mar that i. . . 38.4
stamp thine own i. . . 623.c
b *Rom 8:29*
shall in thine i. shine . . 407.4
thine i., Lord, bestow . . 560.4
that in thine i. shine . . 704.4
seal thine i. on my heart . 865.3
c *1 Cor 15:49*
his glorious i. bear . . . 370.2

Immanuel *Isa 7:14; Matt 1:23*
Lord is born, by name I. . 72.4
Jesus, our I. 82.2
abide with us, our Lord I. . 86.4
help to chant I.'s praise . . 109.3
drawn from I.'s veins . . 132.1
hail I., brighter . . . 185.3
marching . . . I.'s ground . 314.3
almighty . . . I. and thee. . 562.2
O rise, I.'s tide . . . 647.c
marching . . . to I.'s land . 866.2
glory . . . in I.'s land . . 896.*
spirit of I. c91

immense
sovereign grace . . . i. . . 55.2
mercy all, i. and free . . 283.2
this i. salvation . . . 546.3

immortal
giver of i. gladness . . 10.1
wake the i. strain . . . 139.1
joy i.! Alleluia . . . 146.3
rise to that i. state . . . 314.2
i. love, for ever full . . 496.1
no i. soul to save . . . 592.3
saints all i. and fair . . 886.1
on trees i. grow . . . 887.3
where saints i. reign . . 898.1
b *immortal life* *Rom 2:7/2 Tim 1:10*
rose . . . i. l. to bring . . 149.2
life i., Heaven descending . 540.4
life i. I receive . . . 546.1
c *1 Tim 1:17*
i., invisible, God 8.1

immortality *(2 Tim 2:10)**
the road to life and i. . . 38.5
portent of i. 176.4
that word, 'tis i. . . . 877.1

impaled 122.1

impart-ed
God i. to human hearts . . 86.3
true wisdom can i. . . 100.2
grandest gift God could i. . 119.2
living faith i. 191.2
celestial fire to i. . . . 199.1
sweet influence to i. . . 200.4
now thy blissful self i. . . 210.1
new words i. that echo . . 211.1
heavenly joy i. . . . 254.3
salvation to i. . . . 334.c
he doth himself i. . . . 411.3
till thou inward light i. . 412.3
thy nature . . . i. . . . 444.5
strength . . . Lord, i. . . 488.3
praise . . . for all you i. . . 506.4
newness of life to i. . . 589.4
i. . . . thy nature . . . 601.3
best bliss that earth i. . . 602.1
things thou dost i. . . 612.4
learn the wisdom it i. . . 654.5
by thy word i. . . . 655.4
faith to me he did i. . . 730.2
b *grace imparts*
thy heavenly g. i. . . . 517.1
nor a single g. i. . . . 555.4
may thy rich g. i. . . . 743.2
all the g. your word i. . . 856.4
c *love imparts*
joy and perfect l. i. . . 210.4
liberating l. i. . . . 274.c
faith reward, thy l. i. . . 461.c
to me thy l. i. . . . 649.1
for all thy l. i. . . . 935.3
to me thy l. i. c96

impassioned 530.1

implant 186.c

implore-ing
O come, we i. 263.3
guilty soul i. turned . . 405.2
we as one i. thee . . . 643.1
send it, we i. thee . . . 643.c
tender touch now we i. . . 675.c
help divine i. 812.2
our humble prayers i. . . 918.5
grace which we i. . . . 940.4
with grateful hearts i. . . 950

important
hear this all-i. cry . . . 107.1
in that all-i. day . . . 356.3

impossible/ities *Matt 19:26*
most i. of all 407.2
certain, though i. . . . shall . 407.3
things deemed i. I dare . . 744.4
laughs at i. c118

impressed 556.1

imprison-ed
long my i. spirit lay . . 283.3
i. me within thine arms . . 508.1

improve 662.2

impulse
move with one i. . . . 196.3
at the i. of thy love . . 525.2
i. of his will obey . . . 581.3
moved at the i. of love . . 786.4

impurity 230.3

inaccessible 8.1

inaudible 874.2

inbred
blessed rest from i. sin . . 46.3
power to conquer i. sin . . 214.1
land of rest from i. sin . . 419.4
weary I am of i. sin . . 450.3
freedom . . . from i. sin . . 541.2
purified from i. sin . . 783.4

incarnate
of God i. 78.1
hail the i. Deity . . . 82.2
come, thou i. Word . . 219.2
following their i. God . . 879.4

incense 183.1, 5

incline *Ps 119:36**
to thy truth my heart i. . . 429.3
let thy grace my will i. . . 460.3

includ-ed-ing
all our griefs, i. mine . . 131.2
i. me, i. me still . . . 359.2

inconstant 517.1

increase
freedom . . . and wisdom i. . 166.3
higher up where light i. . . 429.2
strength as our labours i. . 579.1
i. my courage, Lord . . 678.4
there's a gladness which i. . 790.3
make for life's i. . . . 827.4

the battle front i. 864.4
earthly cares i. c143

b *Ps 67:6*
all things with large i. . . 929.2

c *increase faith* *Luke 17:5*
i. the f. that conquers . . 432.2
i. our f. and love . . . 646.4
i. our f., confirm . . . 662.2

d *Acts 6:1*
i. thy . . . witnesses . . 629.1

e *Col 2:19*
let thy life in mine i. . . 479.1
his life in me i. . . . 495.1

incredible 49.1

indeed
Lord, ye know is God i. . . 3.2
grace was granted me i. . 52.2
thou only canst convert i. 290.2
dark, i., the past . . . 292.3
Lord, if i. I am thine . . 318.4
he i. is a . . . Saviour . . 329.2
I, believing, find i. . . . 351.c
an evil heart i. . . . 421.2
helpless i., I come . . . 488.c
knowest I love thee i. . . 507.c
happy is my lot i. . . . 539.2
perfect friendship i. . . 553.4
pardoner . . . and friend i. . 600.1
make me blest i. . . . 614.3
thus shall Heaven i. begin . 630.3
Christ is Lord i. . . . 699.1
prove a friend i. . . . 706.2
soul that trusted him i. . . 738.3
God wills, i., . . . so . . 760.3
life for them is life i. . . 878.2
harvest is thy work i. . . 926.2
he is my friend i. . . . c151

b *John 8:36*
Jesus makes me free i. . . 546.2
thou hast made us free i. . 662.3

indicate 27.2

induced 338.2

indulgence 257.3

industry 688.1

indwelling
fitted now for thy i. . . 188.4
temple of i. God . . . 214.3
thraldom of i. sin . . . 459.1
the fire of thy i. . . . 493.c
thy Spirit i. my heart . . 589.4

indwelt
fit to be i. by thee . . . 416.4
sacred and i. by thee . . 786.1

ineffable
measureless Might! I. Love . 16.6
before the i. appear . . 414.3

inextinguishable . . . 199.2

infant
yonder shines the i. light . 75.2
sacred I., all divine . . 88.4
holy i. tender and mild . . 89.1
i. voices shall proclaim . . 160.2
of speech that i. lips . . 625.3
like i. slumbers, pure . . 676.5

infinite
so free, so i. his grace . . 283.2
out of his i. riches . . . 579.3
his smile . . . my i. gain . 640.3
i. day excludes the night . 898.1
gift of his i. grace . . . 906.2

b *infinite love*
thanks . . . and i. l. . . 24.3
come to his i. l. . . . 247.2
worth of l. . . . i. . . . 497.4

c *Job 22:5*
i., i. sin 296.2

infinity 55.3

infirmity *Luke 13:12* . . 456.1

inflame
with love i. 516.2
zeal i. thy fighting host . . 609.2
love for thee and thine i. . 626.2
i. and fill my heart . . . 720.5

influence
came sweet i. to impart . . 200.4
if now thy i. I feel . . . 207.2
let us thine i. prove . . 651.1
till truth's full i. . . . 942.4

inform 100.2

inhabit 604.2

inherit *Matt 19:29* . . . 685.3

inheritance *Col 1:12* . . 877.2

iniquity *Job 22:5**
thy weight of i. roll . . 271.3
mine i. crimson hath been . 296.2

b *Ps 5:5*
thou hatest all i. . . . 568.3

c *Mic 7:18*
who can pardon i. . . . 724.2

inly
sight to the i. blind . . 224.2
hear thee i. speak . . . 636.4

inmost
no storm . . . my i. calm. . 358.2
bid our i. souls rejoice . . 603.5
eyes my i. purpose see . . 667.2
our i. wants are known . . 738.2

inner *(Eph 3:16)*
instead of i. conflict . . 244.2
quicken each i. wish . . 493.2
these, my i. life . . . 867.4

inscribe 944.1

insistent 864.2

inspiration
Christ our i. 803.c
fill us with thy i. . . . 863.3

inspire-d-ing
our minds i. 20.3
our God's i. voice . . . 95.3
old i. with wisdom . . . 196.4
come, thou all-i. Spirit . . 210.1
your love to i. me . . . 506.4
i. by purest love . . . 581.1
i. the living faith . . . 756.4
may that same grace i. . . 760.1
the hope our God i. . . 765.4
i. from Heaven above . . 781.1
i. with hope and praise . . 825.3
his zeal i. their breast . . 879.4
their lives our own i. . . 939.1

b *inspire hearts*
salvation shall i. our h. . . 382.3
my longing h. i. . . . 649.3
Holy Ghost, our h. i. . . 651.1
h. i. from above . . . 704.4
Lord, help us, and i. our h. . 827.3
i. our h. to serve thee . . 944.2

c *inspire souls*
our panting s. i. . . . 210.2
by thy . . . sword . . . s. to i. 561.4
let thy grace i. my s. . . 616.3
all my s. with zeal i. . . 733.5

Scripture zeal (2b)

installed 95.2

instant-ly
forgive! I i. cry . . . 122.3
now and every i. clean . . 230.4
I was i. released . . . 539.2
now, and every i. clean . . 540.3

b *Rom 12:12*
i. and constant with joy . . 51.1
both i. and constant for thee . 527.3
meet i. in prayer . . . 648.1

instead 244.2

instructed *Phil 4:12* . . 425.4

insult 142.4

insure 208.4

intellect
take my i., and use . . 525.4
of body, i. and will . . 871.1

intense 527.3

intent
seek . . . was their i. . . 90.3
i. on pleasing thee . . 485.1
rich to all i. of bliss . . 565.4
his first avowed i. . . . 685.1

intention
your i. I would fulfil . . 294.2
fix the i. sure 416.2
only one i. c48
life has a new-found i. . . c173

intercede-ing
with thee we i. . . . 648.1

b *Heb 7:25*
lives . . . for me to i. . . 106.2
thy wounds shall i. . . . 122.3
ever i., mercy 129.c
how for them he i. . . 182.2
have you heard him i. . . 242.3
liveth . . . to i. for me . . c193

intercession 576.1

interest
i. in the Saviour's blood . 283.1
feel our i. in his blood . . 756.3

interposed 313.3

interpreted-ing
i. its need 325.3
eternity, i. by love . . . 567.3

interpreter 29.6

intervene-ing
his love i. will pardon . . 237.3
where no shadows i. . . 878.2

inured 596.2

invade-ing
come, i. my soul . . . 613.1
when our i. forces march . 705.2

invest 127.3

invisible *1 Tim 1:17**
immortal, i., God 8.1

O Word i., we see thee now . 36.3
O Love, i. before . . . 449.2

invitation
the i. is to all . . . 234.2
faith can hear his i. . . 240.2

invite
Jesus i. you here . . . 226.2
Christ i. you . . . fountain . 239.2
Saviour i. you just now . . 273.4
yet i. to drink again . . 439.3

inward *(2 Cor 4:16)*
grant us, by i. knowledge . 6.3
keeps the i. witness right . 113.1
groan thine i. groaning . . 191.4
word of God and i. light . 194.1
stir them with an i. grace . 202.1
genders i. strife . . . 211.2
shall I hear the i. voice . . 214.2
till thou i. light impart . . 412.3
give . . . eternal i. rest . . 431.3
obtain that i. calm . . 613.2
the i. health that overcomes . 631.2
gives us i. pain . . . 660.4
speaks of i. purity . . . 777.3
armed with i. blessing . . 863.2
b *inward peace*
in joy of i. p. 496.4
possessing i. p. . . . 580.1
i. p. and i. light . . . 716.2

iron
a *Ps 107.16*
the i. fetters yield . . . 81.2
b *Rev 2:27**
break with thine i. rod . . 172.1

irradiate 135.3

island
sing, ye i. of the sea . . 393.2
each continent and i. . . 677.3

Israel
should ransom I. . . . 72.4
the priest of I., slept . . 839.2
b *Ps 80:1*
thou Shepherd of I. . . 639.1
c *Ps 121:4*
born is the King of I. . . 90.c
keepeth I. in . . . care . . 767.2

issue
from birth to final i. . . 38.3
it i. from . . . throne . . 312.2

itself
heart at leisure from i. . . 485.2
Heaven i. be won . . . 654.4
shall time i. outstay . . 869.1

J

Jacob *Gen 28:10-12** . . . 646.2

jasper *Rev 21:18**
till within the j. wall . . . 754.4
over the j. sea 889.1

jealous *2 Cor 11:2*
j., godly fear 425.1
arm me with j. care . . . 472.3
armed with j. care . . . 596.3

jeer 134.1

Jehovah
before J.'s aweful throne . 4.1
J., great I AM . . . 223.1
from the throne of J. . . 252.2
J.'s voice doth sound . . 253.1
J., bare thine arm . . . 575.1
guide me, . . . great J. . . 578.1
Army J. has blessed . . 684.4
I am fighting for J. . . 686.c
who in the name of J. . . 703.1
who in the might of J. . . 703.3
faith . . . that can J. see. . 733.3
J. . . . thy keeper/defence . 767.3
J. shall preserve . . . 767.4
while J.'s mighty power . 822.2
crowned by the hand of J. . 894.1
b *Isa 12:2*
J. is our strength . . . 9.1

Jerusalem
sing through all J. . . . 88.c
children of J. sang . . 834.1
b *Gal 4:25, 26*
inheritance . . . J. above . 877.2
to that J. above . . . 880.3
c *new Jerusalem* *Rev 21:2*
in the new J. appoint . . 735.4
gates of the new J. . . 910.c
a crown in the new J. . . c246
Salem

Jesus (Christ/Lord/Saviour)
1 *Vocative nc, but see*
beautiful (b), blessed (3c, e, g, h), conquering (a), dear (2b, c, e), divine (a), dying (3a), everlasting (d), gentle (1a), glorious (1c), gracious (1a, c), holy (1a), loving (1b, e), meek (1a), mighty (1c), precious (e), wonderful (b)
2 *Jesus yesterday*
brought my S. from above . 46.c
J. shed his blood . . . 125.c
J. descended from above . 140.2
C. hath burst the gates . . 143.3
C. hath . . . dispersed . . 151.2
J. crossed the river . . 153.3
J. mighty to redeem . . 165.3
salvation J. purchased . . 230.3
J. shed . . . blood . . . 231.2
S. hath a ransom found . 253.1
'twas C. made room . . 266.2
sacrifice that J. gave . . 269.3
loving S. bore for thee . . 276.c
song that J. gave me . . 327.1
C. has paid sin's 335.2
bruised, but J. healed me . 337.3
in loving kindness J. came . 339.1
J. has been growing . . 343.1
life did J. give . . . 363.c
S. made me whole . . . 371.c
it was J. knocked . . . 373.1
I came to him C. came . . 376.c
J. came with peace . . 379.c
J. undertook my cause . . 380.2
J. swept . . . strings . . 390.2
C. released me . . . 391.2
C. made known the grace . 398.3
freely J. pardoned me . . 403.2
blessèd S. . . . ransomed . 404.1
J. has cleansed even me . 535.1
J. . . . my heart has filled . 539.3
graces . . . L. has given . . 555.3
J. there dispelled . . . 663.2
L. has always proved . . 732.3
J. has vanquished death . 752.6
L. to Hannah's son . . 839.2
happiness . . . the S. bestow 857.c
dear S. has shown me . . 881.1
b *historical*
The little L. J. . . . . 77.*
J. C. her little child . . 87.1
over the place where J. . . 90.4
and did my S. bleed . . 105.1
J. does with devils fight. . 107.2
J. doth atonement make . 107.3
they laid the S. there . . 145.1
where J. knelt to share . . 567.3
J. loved to wend his way . 663.2
when J. was here . . . 794.1
children brought to J. . . 797.1
how kind was our S. . . 797.3
S. was once a child . . 840.2
c *Luke 24:15*
when C. drew near . 102.1, 2
J. himself drew near . . c135
3 *Jesus today*
for J. C. is here . . . 36.3
still the dear C. enters . . 86.3
J. C. is here . . . 89.2, 3
when C. draws near . . 102.3
'tis the L.! O wondrous . . 104.c
it is the L. . . . S. . . 110.1
place . . . the S. must fill . 119.3
that J. . . . sets me free. . 131.2
Lo! the C. is living . . 155.1
the C. is marching . . 159.3
J. the S. reigns . . . 164.2
J. shines brighter/purer . 177.3
J., S., reigneth for ever . . 184.3
J. is passing this way . . 247.1
blessed L. refuses none . . 251.4
C. . . . gives to all . . . 258.2
J. now is bending o'er . . 259.2
C. receiveth sinful men . . 262.*
the S. who would have us . 265.2
the S. cries aloud to . . 275.3
there's a S. and Heaven. . 289.4
J., my S., abides within . 315.2
how sweetly J. whispers . 320.3
the blessings the L. gives . 329.3
J. completely saves . . 336.3
L. of life is he . . . 341.2
Jesus, watches, . . . 341.2
J. belongs to me . . . 349.c
J. whispers sweet and low . 390.1
'Tis J. who confirms . . 423.4
J. sanctifies me now . . 440.4
only C. is heard to speak . 444.2
L. almighty to heal . . 459.2
the C. who dwells within . 494.3
the L. accepts me . . 514.4
O is not the C. midst . . 527.2
if C. came in to reign . . 541.*
J. makes me free indeed . 546.2
my S. bears me gently . . 549.3
daily the S. is showing . . 553.4
J. shows a smiling face . . 560.1
J. sheds the oil . . . 573.2
C. is not ashamed of me . 592.4
J. makes our home . . 663.1
there's J. in the midst . . 664.3
the S. shows the way . . 700.2
my L. has placed me . . 706.c
he whom J. nameth . . 707.2
L. his children gathers . . 722.4
S. has my treasure . . 736.3
may change but J. never . 750.c
what the L. ordaineth . . 755.2
where C. makes free . . 757.5
J. then . . . is watching . . 759.2
J. every need supplying . 764.3
the L. himself is there . . 772.3
C. has need . . . soldiers . 787.2
J. signals still . . . 804.c
whom C. doth heal . . 825.1
J. wants me . . . . 844.*
L. retaineth his love . . 853.2
my S. is now over there. . 886.3
C. brings us all to the . . 895.3
J. always recognises . . 920.3
long our S. triumph here . 942.2
the L. bless thee . . . 961
to keep, yes, my L. is able . c1
C. the L. is come to reign . c27
the C. of every day . . c126
beauty . . . my L. doth prepare c148
my S. tells me I am his . . c191
b *Jesus can*
C. c. make you whole . . 232.3
J. c. restore his work . . 267.3
J. c. make them whole . . 384.3
J., listening, c. hear . . 387.2
C. c. fill the loving 545.3
J. cannot fail 749.3
J. c. keep us so near . . 773.4
c *Jesus is (*adjective)*
J. is worthy to receive . . 57.3
C. is alive! . . . . 142.*
J. is fairer . . . purer . . 177.2
J. is glorified . . . 195.1
J. now is bending o'er . . 259.2
J. is strong to deliver . . 467.c
J. is the same . . . 750.c
come along for J. is strong . c3
J. so patient, so loving . . c7
J. is able, . . . to save . . c179
the fairest, is J. to me . . c217
d *Jesus is (*noun)*
C. our brother . . . 10.3
J. is the wondrous theme . 70.c
J. is the word of life . . 70.3
the L. is his name . . 183.1, 5
J. is the truth, the way . . 231.3
the proof is J., so look . . 270.3
J. is the true, the only . . . 279.2
my C. he is . . . . 346.*
C. is the water of life . . 351.c
still C. is my salvation . . 361.3
J. shall be all our song . . 381.3
J. is my light and song . . 400.*
more than life is J., love . 420.2
the L. is my stay . . . 467.4
thou art a mighty S. . . 538.c
J., thou art everything to me 600.*
C. is captain of the . . 698.c
C. is thy strength/path/etc . 718.*
J. is in all life's . . . 750.2
the L. is our power . . 763.4
C. our inspiration . . . 803.c
J. is our captain . . . 866.2
J., the wheat . . . 932.1
never-failing friend is C. . c146
C. is the answer . . . c151
J. is all I need . . . I'll . . c180
J. is all I need, my . . . c181

e *Jesus is mine*
blessèd Jesus, thou art m. . 128.3
all with C. are m. . . . 214.2
J., and all in him, is m. . . 283.4
I call this S. m. . . . 297.6
blessèd assurance, J. is m. . 310.1
I'll sing: J. is m. . . . 326.3
blessing to know . . . J. is m.. 355.1
O bliss . . . J. is m.. . . 364.2
I am thine, O L. . . . 510.c
I am C.'s, and C. is m. . . 520.5
a S. is m., whose power . 640.1
abiding, J. is m.; . . . c36
wonderful S., he's m. . . c162
S. for you and me . . . c214

f *Jesus is Lord* *(Phil 2:11)*
L. Sabaoth his name . . 1.2
that child . . . is our L. . . 87.5
C. is living, God . . . 155.1
confess . . . that J. C. is L. . 174.5
J., our ascended L. . . 198.2
the L., my S. liveth! . . 358.2
and C. is L. indeed . . 699.1
for J. is our L. . . . 701.c
for J. is our L. . . . 705.c
till C. is L. of all . . . 781.3

g *Christ is King*
now C. is K., my heart . . 541.4
hosannas: J. is K. . . . 848.4
make J. K. c220

h *Jesus is Saviour*
J. is the S.'s name . . 127.c
J., for he's the S. . . . 270.c
a wonderful S. is J. . . 329.c
I love J., he's my S. . . 338.c
J. is my S., this I know . . 348.1
my S. art thou . . . 357.1
while J. is my S. I can . . 402.c
a wonderful S. is J. . . 710.1
for J. is my S., he's . . 811.c
to J. be the glory, our S. . 828.1
J. . . . my light, my S. . . c181

i *Jesus loves*
J. lives and l. me still . 286.c, 4
that J. l. me . . . . 323.*
J. smiles and l. me too . . 338.c
J. l. to answer prayer . . 563.1
J. l. his children . . . 836.4
J. l. me! This I know . . 843.1

able (c), all (3b), drink (e), first (3d), friend (1b, c, d), leader (1), light (2c), peace (2j), refuge (a), save (1g), shepherd (1a), stone (1)

4 *Jesus—in eternity*
C. will triumph over wrong . 74.3
the L. . . . shall appear . 75.3
the L. will open fountains . 159.5
the L. will surely pour . . 165.4
honours which J. will bestow. 169.2
J. will guard his children . 184.1
J., S., reigneth for ever . . 184.3
J. in love will lighten . . 186.3
heart the L. will favour . . 225.3
the S. now will give . . 277.c
J. my L. will love me . . 349.1
C. his light . . . will shed. . 408.4
the L. will never hear . . 588.3
the L. will come . . . 591.1
the L. will question . . 666.3
S. shall welcome us home . 808.4
J. shall crown you . . . 813.2
J., he will carry you . . 823.3
C. shall be victorious . . 828.2
the L. will surely build . . 868.2
soon will the L. . . . prepare . 887.5
J. will the waves divide . . 902.3
J. will be with me . . . 903.3
J. will . . . welcome sinners . c17

Other references under 2-4
alone (1b), answer (1c), arise (1c), bid (1b), born (2a), bring (1b), burst (1), call (1c), come (1b), cross (1d), crucified (1b, c), die (2b-e), do (2b), dwell (1a), find (1b), give (1p), glorify (1b), glory (4f), have (1a), help (1a), ignore, invite, know (1a, 3i, j), lead (3a), leave (1a), live (1b), mercy (f), nothing (d), only (1b), overcome (c), pardon (2a), plead (1c), praise (3m, p, v), provide (b), regard (b), rise (2d, e), save (1b, c), say (1a), seek (1a), slain (1a), smile (1), speak (1c), stand (1b), suffer (2a, b), take (1a), taste (e), victory (2h), wait (1a), whole (2e)

5 *human response to Jesus*
they humbly offered C. . . 5.1
judge not the L. . . . 29.4
loosed the C. with Easter's . 30.4
to welcome C. the . . . King . 79.c
let us adore him, C. the L. . 85.*
men came seeking for J. . 92.1
can I my L. deny . . . 94.3
we should call him L. . . 141.1
crown the S. King of kings . 147.2
grace which, like the L. . . 157.2
greet the L. 159.2
will the S. then own . . 169.1
love to sing of the S. . . 178.1
applying C. to every soul . 191.3
be my L., and I shall be . . 194.3
would for C., my S. speak . 212.1
hear the L.'s: Well done . 222.c
persuaded C. to receive . 226.1
praises we our . . . L. will . 230.4
do not let thy L. depart . . 251.1
to die out of C. . . . 263.3
I bless the C. of God . . 297.6
J. no longer I see . . . 318.1
soul rejoices in . . . S. . . 341.3
take . . . but give me J. . . 343.c
cry: O give me J. . . . 343.2
yield to J. crucified. . . 343.3
happy are they . . . the S. obey 367.1
J. my S. I met! . . . 371.1
complete when my L. I meet . 375.3
call him my S. . . . 388.4
now I live for C. my S. . . 391.3
I'll never leave my S. . . 399.2
if you want J. to reign . . 427.2
when first I saw the L. . . 442.2
to bring the L. C. down . 496.3
they have left my S. too . 498.3
though in declaring C. . . 530.1
but while I passed my S. . 547.2
greatly I needed the S. . . 553.3
evil round us scorn thy C. . 577.2
his S. sees and his example . 580.2
ashamed of J! Yes, I may . 592.3
to the front! thy L. obeying . 702.3
revealing J. through the . 730.3
I'm not ashamed to own my L. 735.1
I met my L. 740.2
saves whoe'er on J. call. . 756.5
until men confess C.'s . . 776.3
ask the S. to help you . . 823.c
show C. in loving kindness . 830.2
we are witnesses for J. . . 832.*
my L. beholding . . . 884.*
near the dear L. I adore . . 906.1
so we may J. gain . . . 915.3
don't turn the S. away . . c11
take J. to all the world . . c22
we're all seeking the same S. c112
we're all seeking...self-same L. c112

b *Phil 1:21*
for me be it C., be it C. . . 771.3
for C. to live or die. . . 830.3

bless (2a, b), follow (2e), have (2b), know (3i, j), love (7c, d), part (2b), preach (b), prove (3b), rest (2d), see (3c, 5a), serve (1b), thank (c), trust (3b), worship (b, c)

6 *possessive*
lose the blessing of our L. . 5.3
the angel of the L. came. . 93.1
prayers repeat the S.'s cry . 127.3
dear hands of C.! and yet men 129.2
mocking thus the S.'s claim . 147.3
glory of the coming of the L. 162.1
J.'s word is glorified . . 165.3
Kingdom of C., for thy . . 166.5
C.'s completed mission . . 173.2
the hand of J. reaches me . 176.3
amazed in the presence of J. 179.1
wait the promise of our L. . 196.2
speak my L.'s sincerity . . 212.2
promises of J. for the soul . 230.2
every soul be J.'s guest. . 234.1
wounds of C. are open . . 237.c
your S.'s pleading cease . 241.4
you must be a lover of the L. 256.c
taste the sweets of J.'s word 312.1
from J.'s throne on high . 312.2
to the family of J. . . . 324.2
promises of J. are unchanged 324.4
the S.'s loving kindness . . 338.2
the peace of C. makes fresh . 358.3
who live in C.'s new day . 408.1
secret of the L. is theirs. . 411.1
their soul is C.'s abode . . 411.1
and do my S.'s will . . 413.3
daily by the S.'s side . . 417.2
to all my S.'s . . . will . . 419.1
in J.' steps my steps . . 449.c
servant of my servant-L. . 451.4
see my S.'s brightness . . 470.1
beauty of the L. . . . renew . 494.2
hear the S.'s glad well done . 500.3
J.'s reign has now begun . 500.3
C.'s broken bread . . . 512.1
from the heart of J. . . 539.1
when I let the S.'s pity . . 548.1
'gainst sin, the enemy of C. . 583.4
ye saints of the L. . . 653.1
forward, flock of J. . . 682.2
leaning on my S.'s might . 686.3
our warfare's the L.'s . . 687.4
we have C.'s own promise . 690.4
let the S.'s herald go . . 697.3
are the Kingdom of the L. . 697.6
the promise of our S. . . 700.3
beneath the sway of C. . . 700.3
around the S.'s throne . . 701.4
for me C.'s sacrifice . . 706.1
glory in the S.'s presence . 711.3
for the peace of the L. . . 739.*
wounds of J. for my sin . 746.1
to do the will of J. . . 752.2
on J.' bosom . . . calm . . 752.3
standing on the promises of C.757.1, 3
first disciples of the L. . . 760.1
onward in the cause of J. . 776.1
yielding to the S.'s day . . 776.2
men confess C.'s kingdom . 776.3
richness of our S.'s giving . 777.2
allegiance to the cause of C. . 777.4
gentle/loving/sacred arms of J. 792.*
saved by J.'s might . . 803.3
love . . . C.'s ways . . 816.3
tell . . . of the S.'s goodness. 835.1
stories of J. . . . 848.1, 5
we are the hands of C. . . 851.1
we are the feet/eyes of C. 851.2, 3
we are the lips/friends of C.851.4, 5
at my S.'s side, Heaven . . 882.3
safe in the arms of J. . . 889.*
soldier of C., well done . 890.5
trumpet of the L. . . . 907.1
let the beauty of J. . . c77
lean on the S.'s arm . . c138
'neath my S.'s smile . . c196
my S.'s affections . . . c207
'twas the suffering of J. . c209

b *Lord's*
how blest the L.'s alone. . 317.2
I am my L.'s and he is mine . 365.3
they, too, shall be the L.'s . 853.3

c *(1 Sam 17:47)*
the battle of the L.. . . 658.6
our warfare's the L.'s . . 687.4
Army (1b), birth (1), blood (2i, j, k), breast (2b), bride, call (1c), command (c), cross (1c), ear (2a), face (2j), feet (2a, d), footsteps (a), friend (1e), friendship, gentleness, grace (2j), keeping, lip (1), love (2d, f, g), merit (1b), mind (1), name (1b, c, j, k), own (4b), power (4g), sake (1d), secret (c), side (2a, b), soldier (d), strength (2b, d), sword (2d), voice (1c)

7 *place in Godhead*
sings my soul, my S. G. to thee 37.c
who is G. and L. of all . . 87.2
the death of C., my G. . . 136.2
C. is living, G. for evermore . 155.1
I bless the C. of G. . . 297.6
my S. and my G. . . 365.1
J., my G.! I know his name . 735.2
promises of God my S. . . 757.c
through the love of G. our S.. 764.1

b *Mark 8:29*
thou art the C. divine . . 870.2

c *John 20:28*
thou art my L., my G. . . 756.3

d *1 Cor 1:24*
C., the power of G. in man . 407.6

e *1 Tim 2:5*
one G. and one mediator...C. J. c156
God (5b, c), Jesus (9h), King (2, 1, m, n), Master (1d), Prince (1), Son (1a), Spirit (3a)

8 *Jesus for*
C. for me . . . . 356.*
C. for the world . . . 825.*
C. for the whole wide world . 829.*

b *Jesus of*
the C. of Calvary . . . 65.*
thou C. of burning, cleansing. 203.1
S. of the lost . . . 325.1
C. of pure and perfect love . 440.1
the C. of working days . . 618.2
C. of the loom . . . 644.4
C. of self denial . . . 921.1
C. of the mount . . . c98
the C. of every day . . c126
J. of Galilee . . . of Calvary . c214

c *Lord of*
L. of cable, L. of rail . . 30.*
L. of . . . constellation . . 38.1
great L. of nature . . . 38.5
the L. of truth and might . 145.2
L. of creation/power/wisdom 506.*
L. of my youth . . . 861.*

d *Lord of Heaven* *Acts 17:24*
O L. of H. and earth . . 15.1
C. is L. of H. and earth . . 358.2
the L. of earth and skies . 516.1
O L. of earth and sky . . 933.1
L. of H. and earth . . 941.1

e *Lord of all* *Acts 10:36*
and crown him L. of all . 56.*
who is God and L. of all . 87.2
crown him L. of all . . 104.c
King and L. of all . . 499.1, 4
L. of all hopefulness, . . 611.*
O thou God of all . . 698.3
till C. is L. of all . . 781.3

f *Lord of lords* *Rev 19:16*
crown him . . . L. of l. . . 147.4
L. of l. and Heaven's . . 168.2
Christ, he is the L. of l. . 346.2
glory (4c), harvest (2c), host (2b), life (5c), light (2c), love (2c), mercy (j), nation (d), nature (1b), peace (2j)

g *Saviour of* *John 4:42*
S. of the world was born . 78.1
came to be the lost one's S. . 225.3

h *Saviour of men* *1 Tim 4:10*
blest name, O S. of mankind . 61.2
celebrate . . . S. of mankind . 62.1
in a stable the S. of men . 92.1
the S. of men, once wandered 354.2
S. of men came to seek/touch 527.1,3
a S. he to all would be . . 831.2

i *Jesus in me* *Gal 2:20*
C., the holy C., in me . . 479.2
C. only, always, living in me . 487.4
C. that liveth in me . . c177

j *Jesus with*
happy and free, J. with me . 321.c
the S. still is with me . . 337.4

9 *by Jesus*
the path by J. shown . . 5.3
stablished by the L. . . 159.4
sent by my L., on you I call . 234.2
of my S. possessed . . 367.4
my heart, by my S. possessed 454.1
not my own, but saved by J.. 514.1
blest commands by J. given . 580.3
faith . . . to saints by J. given 733.2
peace, left with us by C. . 751.1

b *for Jesus*
make music f. thy L. . . 2.3
takes its stand f. J. . . 197.2
have you any room f. J. 241.1, c
have you any time f. J. . 241.3
would you do service f. J. . 281.4
witnessing f. J. . . . 352.c
everything f. J. . . . 352.c
I'm set apart f. J. . . . 495.*
garden there f. the L. . . 647.3
salvation soldier f. J. . . 684.1
I'll stand f. C. . . . alone . 687.c
take the field f. J. . . 696.1
dare and die f. J. . . . 696.2
raise the standard . . . f. the L. 698.1
stand up, stand up f. J. . 699.*
wave our Army flags f. J. . 775.2
cross to bear f. J. . . 777.3
f. J. boldly stand . . . 810.2
make a thoroughfare f. J. . 815.3
we are witnesses f. J. . . 832.*
I'll be a sunbeam f. J. . . 844.4
once the loss of all f. J. . 894.2
I'm living my life f. J. . . c173
work f. J. c215
fight (2c), win (2e)

c *from Jesus*
f. J. a pardon receives . . 22.2
eyes . . . f. J. shall not move. 123.4
learn f. J. God loves you . 270.3
take with rejoicing f. J. . . 271.4
we have a message . . . f. J.. 273.*
f. my S. wandered far . . 309.1
f. the S. we claim all we. . 351.3
though I wandered far f. J. . 391.1
love divine, f. J. flowing . 439.1
blessing f. the L. . . . 461.3
sent f. the S. above . . 637.1
command f. our dying L. . 702.2
just a smile f. my S. . . 906.3

d *in Jesus*
his love in C. proclaimed . 20.4
in C. we have redemption . 43.2
I now believe in J. . . 67.3
seal of my sin in C. . . 207.3
love divine, in C. . . . 232.1
all things in C. are ready . 234.2
joy . . . it's only found in J. . 244.3
in the S. find thy rest . . 261.2
soul rejoices in this . . . S. . 341.3
heart shall in J. find rest . 364.3
when I in C. am formed . 407.6
there is victory in J. . . 433.1
raised in C. to life divine. . 540.4
in C. he loved us . . . 544.5
infinite riches in J. . . 579.3
come for my need in J. . . 631.1
resting in my S. as my all . 757.4
grace, declared in C. . . 760.2
in our S. strength enough . 805.c
in C. . . . east . . . west. 826.1, 4
the dying, in C. are fully. . 828.3
lead us now to see in J. . 856.4
die believing still in J. . . 874.3
found in J. calm repose . 910.3
there is mercy in J. . . c23
to see victory in C. for me . c81
now in J. I am free . . c149
in J. I'm safe evermore . . c178
abide (2e), alone (b), dead (2d), glad (i), happy (1b), one (3b), trust (3b)

e *like Jesus* *1 John 3:2*
I long to be l. J. . . . 94.2
let me henceforth be l. J. . 188.2
make us more l. J. . . 193.4
never a friend l. J. . . 246.c
only l. J. I long to be . . c68
to be l. J.! This hope . . c107
not a friend l. the lowly J. . c182
there's no one l. J. . . c207

f *of (about) Jesus*
have you ever heard of J. . 96.*
I love to sing of the S. . . 178.1
love to sing of J. . . . 178.c
I have . . . tidings . . . of J. . 329.1
'tis of J. I would sing . . 343.2
tell them of J. the mighty . 691.1
whenever I think of J. . . c187
story (1)

g *on Jesus*
if on J. thy sins were not . 271.2
now as on J. we call! . . 637.4
the soul that on J. hath . . 653.5
thou on the L. rely . . 715.3
on C., the solid rock, I stand . 745.c
each upon his L. relies . . 799.3
cast my burden on the S. . c166
believe (f), wait (2c)

h *through Jesus*
God, t. J., dwells in me . 176.4
by faith t. C. to God . . 269.1
claim the crown, t. C., . . 283.4
t. C. I know the love of God . 290.3
what God has done t. C. . 335.1
t. J. . . . reach the goal . . 344.2
praise God t. J. C. our L. . 408.5
claim t. C. complete . . 433.2
conquerors be, t. the C. . 554.2
hope is mine, t. J. crucified . 761.4
justified t. J., we believe . 785.4

i *to Jesus*
sing t. the L. with cheerful . 3.1
lift up our eyes t. C. . . 38.4
when I came t. J. with my sin 52.2
hate . . . must yield t. J. . . 63.2
sing praises t. our heavenly L. 90.6
keys of death . . . t. our J. . 164.3
t. J. I repair 187.1
room and time now give t. J.. 241.4
only a step t. J. . . . 255.*
if faithful t. my S. . . . 309.3
hallelujah t. my S. . . . 322.c
sing . . . hallelujahs t. J. C. . 334.3
soul is now united t. C., . 361.1
sinners t. J. now clinging; . 383.c
now I've given t. J. . . 405.3
all sin expose t. C. . . 408.3
have you been t. J. for . . . 417.1
I bring my heart/life/sins t. J. 420.*
my soul t. my S. draws nigh . 454.2
all t. J. I surrender . . 474.*
t. C. my S. . . . trust . . 514.2
all t. C. I bring . . . 514.3
what shall we offer t. our L. . 533.1
devotion t. my S., Lord and . 591.2
in all need t. J. go . . 634.4
take it t. the L. in prayer . 645.*
who for refuge t. J. . . 653.1

t. J., our captain, the world . 681.2
captives t. J. we'll win . . 687.1
voice t. call men to the S. . 706.3
bring our cares t. J. . . 759.3
true t. my S. in the Army . 778.c
join ourselves t. C. . . 784.1
take your weakness . . . t. J.. 790.1
pointing them unto the S. . 790.2
children brought t. J. . . 797.1
t. J. we will bring sinners . 814.c
we sinners t. J. shall . . 820.1
the world t. C. we bring . 825.*
bring all . . . t. C., . . . 864.3
I am coming t. the S. who . c13
turn t. the L. and seek . . c27
burden . . . bring it t. J. . c31
if t. J. you'll be true . . c237

belong (b, c), come (4b), glory (5e), look (2f), turn (2b)

j *with Jesus*
wear a crown w. J. . . 67.2
they suffer w. their L. . . 168.5
there is mercy w. the S.. . 265.4
I mean w. J. C. to dwell. . 275.4
I left/leave it all w. J. . . 333.*
w. J. my S., I'm the child . 354.c
and w. J. we'll be happy . 367.c
I live w. J. all the time . . 402.1
speak oft w. thy L. . . 458.1
much time in secret w. J. . 458.2
in the valley w. my S. . 483.1, 2
service w. our L. to take . 532.1
w. my L. unbroken faith . 534.3
my meeting w. J. to show . 553.1
from converse w. your L. . 564.4
needful, . . . L., . . . one w. thee 565.1
battles w. J. I'll go . . . 684.2
w. C. in the vessel . . . 712.1
satisfied . . . w. J. here . . 758.c
w. C. on our side, we hope . 763.5
peace w. my L. so near . . 768.3
w. C. forever! No sin . . 888.3
who shall w. J. reign . . 946.4
what will you do w. J.? . . c28
w. C. my S. I shall never . c151
I'm satisfied w. J. here . . c174
w. J. in the heart . . . c220
when we dwell w. J. there . c233
Jordan, w. my blessèd J. . c247

ever (g), friendship, side (1b), talk (2), walk (2e, f)

10 *what a Saviour*
Hallelujah! W. a S.! . . 118.*
a S., and w. a S. . . 270.1
O w. a S., and Jesus . . 319.3
O w. a C. have I . . 346.1
w. a precious S. . . 347.3
w. a S.! Hallelujah! . . 363.c
w. a S. I have found . . 363.c
w. a loving S. may . . . found 835.1
O w. a wonderful S. . . c156
O w. a loving S. . . . c194
O w. a S. c194
w. a redeemer is J. my S. . c219

Jew-ish
beasts on J. altars slain . . 120.1
to the J. old Canaan . . 898.2

jewel
counting the j. of earth . . 427.c
j. rich and rare . . . 658.2

b *Mal 3:17*
claimed me as a j. . . . 330.3
to make up his j. . . . 852.1
children are his j. . . . 852.3

join-ed-ing
a *(to Christ)*
thy name is j. with mine . 59.2
j. . . . to our head . . . 659.2
j. ourselves to Christ . . 784.1

b *(with others)*
j. the mighty chorus . . 10.4
j. with all nature . . . 33.2
j. those who've gone . . 45.3
whole creation j. in one . 57.4
angels and men be j. . . 62.1
j. the triumph of the skies . 82.1
with the crowd . . . j. I . . 129.1
who'll be the next to j. . . 278.4
j. the heavenly race . . 366.3
to thy people j. . . . more . 629.3
still be j. in heart . . . 660.4
steps and voices j. . . . 682.1
I will j. at once . . . 686.3
j. our glad array . . . 693.3
j. our conquering band . . 694.c
j. the fight for the right . . 700.*
come, j. our band . . . 798.2
come and j. our ranks . . 818.c
j. hands, then, brothers . 826.3
by j. Daniel's band . . . 847.2
j. us then without delay . . 869.2
in Jesus' praise shall j. . . 880.4
in Jesus' praise we j. . . 915.1
j. with us in self-denial . . 920.c

c *Matt 19:6*
divinely j. in one . . . 948.1
j. their loving hands . . 949.2

d *join [song]*
j. in the everlasting s. . . 56.5
whole creation j. in one . . 57.4
j. our voices singing . . 74.*
we j. our s. of thankfulness . 173.1
I j. the heavenly lays . . 223.5
j. in a s. with sweet . . 314.1
glad to j. our holy s. . . 370.4
if you'd j. in the s. . . 406.3
j. in the s. of the Lamb . . 808.3
j. to sing . . . praise . . 834.1

Army (1c), throng (c)

Jordan *(Josh 3:8)**
bring us safe through J. . 152.3
labour ended, J. past . . 228.5
J.'s rolling tide . . . 278.4
sing of the joys over J. . . 406.1
tread the verge of J. . . 578.3
J. flows before us . . . 682.1
God through J. leadeth me . 725.4
if J. above me shall roll . . 771.3
some day I'll cross old J. . 884.*
on J's stormy banks . . 887.1
while J. rolled between . . 898.2
not J.'s stream . . . 898.3
gather at last over J. . . 908.1
when on J.'s bank he stands . 911.5
away over J. c247

journey-ed-ing
when our j. is complete . . 66.4
as they j. from the east . . 80.3
with thee I will j. . . . 111.3
doth his successive j. run . 160.1
as the j. grew longer . . 553.2
lead me all my j. through . 578.2
he has j. before thee . . 739.3
one the object of our j. . . 765.4
brief is our j. 874.1
friends . . . who have j. . . 881.2
who will j. . . . with me . . 881.3
before us the j. have trod . 886.2
we are marching on our j. . 903.2
we're j. together . . . c195

b *(life as a journey)*
life is a j.; long . . . 351.1
life a weary j. seem . . 400.1
lifelong though the j. be . 510.1
varied way of life we j. . . 711.1
through life's long j. . . 938.1
onward through life's j. . . 949.3

c *journey's end*
give you to your j.'s e. . . 396.3
lead me to my j.'s e. . . 563.5
till my j. shall e. . . . 734.1
the e. of my j. I see . . 886.4
reaching first their j.'s e. . 938.4
arrive at the e. of our j. . . c222
the e. of our j. . . . crown . c246

joy
1 *Jesus, our joy*
O j. of all the meek . . 61.3
Jesus, our only j. be thou . 61.5
is there a name for j. . . 71.1
j. of every longing heart . 79.2
j. to the world! . . . 84.*
j. to the nations when Jesus . 166.1
j. of all . . . above/below . 168.3
Holy Spirit, j. divine . . 194.5
j. of the desolate . . . 236.2
Jesus, thou j. of . . . hearts . 602.1
Lord of all j. 611.1
O J. that seekest me . . 621.3
the j. and desire of my heart . 639.1

b *joy of Heaven* *Ps 48:2*
j. of earth and H. . . . 62.2
hope of earth and j. of H. . 66.c
their j. the j. of H. . . 168.4
j. of H., to earth . . . 438.1

c *joy and crown* *Phil 4:1*
thou its light, its j. . . . 76.5
my soul's glory, j. and c. . 177.1
my peace . . . my j., my c. . 346.4
thy j. and c. eternally . . 718.1

d *1 Thess 2:19*
my hope, my j., my all . . 726.2
here is my hope, my j. . . 746.3

e *Luke 15:7*
there is j. today . . . 550.*

2 *spiritual joy (general)*
cross before . . . j. within . 5.5
the j. of living . . . 10.3
all their j. are one . . . 57.1
j. that bears . . . above . . 70.4
repeat the sounding j. . . 84.2
to j. in his birth . . . 92.2
I j. to call thee mine . . 123.2
lives and learns his j. . . 142.5
j. comes again . . . 146.2
shouts of holy j. outburst . 151.2
O j. . . . thousandfold . . 167.2
come we to the j. supernal . 185.2
can wash . . . bring thee j. . 253.3
heavenly j. imparts . . 254.3
let your j. be known . . 314.1
should constant j. create . 314.2
this j., who can express . . 328.2
j. floods my soul . . . 349.3
the j. of getting others . . 369.3
their j. is to walk . . . 372.2
in my j. I thought . . . 373.2
floods of j. o'er my soul . . 394.c
a well of j. within . . . 413.4
my j. I bring to thee . . 421.5
will of God be all my j. . . 451.3
that early j. grows dim . . 534.2
love and life and lasting j. . 547.c
equal j. to go or stay . . 556.3
attain that deepest j. . . 630.3
I j. in his will 640.2
there's j. in every heart . . 664.1
thy j. to do . . . will . . 683.1
a deeper j. comes . . . 711.1
j.-bursts of singing . . 724.2
in j. which his smile . . 734.2
j.! j.! j.! . . . . . 807.*
fire gives the Army j. . . 807.2
love will be my only j. . . 846.2
ever new that j. will be . . 846.2
greatest j. . . . in serving 857.1, c
eternal source of every j. . 925.1
j. that cometh from above . c143
pure are the j. within . . c152
singing, for j. is springing . c176
j. is mine, I live . . . c196
there's j. in following . . c206
go, our j. to show . . . c220

b *joy of salvation* Ps 51:12
O the j. of full s. . . . 474.5
j. which came with full s. . 534.1
may the j. of thy s. . . . 582.4

c John 15:11
I bring thee j. . . . 229.4
know the j. he bestows . . 348.3
Jesus and his j. . . . 352.2
gave . . . j. without alloy . 391.c
the j. he bestows . . . 397.4
the j. thy love has given. . 421.5

d *full/perfect joy* John 15:11; 16:24
it makes my j. f. . . . 68.1
p. j. and p. peace . . . 188.4
fulness of j. he brings . . 227.1
heart now f. of j. . . . 243.3
my soul is f. of j. . . . 402.c
give me f. j. and peace . . 431.3
p. j. to find 788.3
till the world is f. of j. . . 807.3
p. deliverance and j. . . 808.2
now in the fulness of j. . . c159

e John 16:22
j. which none can hinder . 352.2
j. that none can take away . 601.2

f *joy and . . .*
praise and j. to God . . . 74.1
source of victory and j. . . 113.3
raise your j. and triumphs . 143.1
solid j. and . . . treasure. . 157.3
their profit and their j. . . 168.5
light and j. receiveth . . 655.1
missed the j. and grace . . 748.1
brings new life . . . new j. . 779.1
for j. or despair . . . 928.1
your love and j. to share . 943.1
where j. and duty meet . . c40

g *joy (peace/love)*
Rom 14:17/Gal 5:22
it glows with p. and j. . . 112.2
perfect j. and perfect p. . . 188.4
p., righteousness and j. . . 195.2
fruits of love and j. and p. . 198.4
j. and perfect l. impart . . 210.4
p. and heavenly j. . . . 214.2
p. and j. unending . . . 222.3
what p. is mine! what j. . . 340.3
give me full j. and p. . . 431.3
all is calm and j. and p. . . 453.4
'tis a path of p. and j. . . 462.2
in j. of inward p. . . . 496.4
j., p. and rest 541.3
thee alone, the p., the j. . 547.1
gives me j. and p. . . . 709.2
there is p. . . . and a j. . . 759.3
p. . . . and j. . . . never cease. c46
wonderful j., p. . . . c184

h *joy and sorrow* (John 16:20)
seeking for j. but only s. . 257.3
over dark s. j.'s radiance . 329.2
for s. . . . j. shall receive. . 372.4
by his s. j. revealed . . 402.3
in our j. and in our s. . . 428.4
in j. or in s. . . . follow . . 458.3
come j. or come s. . . . 473.c
the j. or the s. that comes . 473.3
j. to share thy s. . . . 502.2
unto j. or s. grown . . . 924.2
j. which brightens . . . s. . 948.3

i *for joy*
dances his glad heart f. j. . 62.3
my heart doth sing f. j. . . 346.1
sing f. j. in his presence . 392.2
sing f. j., and use . . . 408.5
lame man leap f. j. . . 590.3
shout f. j., as we gladly . 818.c

j *what joy*
w. j. the . . . assurance . 144.1, 4
O w. j. the sight affords. . 147.4
w. j. to know he cleanses . 317.2
O w. j. he gives . . . 352.c
w. j. I receive . . . 367.2
with w. j. they went away . 558.1
O w. j. to feel him there. . 759.1

k *with joy*
approach w. j. his courts . . 3.3
nations bow w. sacred j. . . 4.1
works w. j. surround thee . 10.2
instant and constant w. j. . 51.1
thrills our souls w. j. . . 66.3
while w. j. they hasten . . 72.5
now w. j. is ringing . . . 73.1
w. j. they hailed . . . 76.1
so may we w. holy j. . . 76.3
w. j. we'll persevere . . 97.5
w. j. shall I lift up . . . 116.1
earth w. j. confesses . . 155.2
swell w. pure . . . j. . . 164.5
adorning the spirit w. j. . . 237.2
heart w. j. is glowing . . 343.2
w. j. I remove 355.6
w. j. I am telling . . . 371.1
w. j. . . . I now can sing . 401.1
as w. j. we sing . . . 532.4
run my course w. even j. . 667.4
w. . . . j. they serve . . 878.3
w. j. . . . thy glory see . . 933.4
hills w. j. are ringing . . 934.1

l 1 Peter 1:8
cry, with j. unspeakable . 756.3
elate with j. unspoken . . 939.4

depth (c), divine (c), fill (2f), find (2h), fulness (c), give (1k), gladness (b), height (c), morning (1c), pain (2b), pure (2d), receive (2e), seek (2d), share (2c), tidings (c)

3 *joy of Heaven*
Heaven's j. and endless . . 125.2
my j. through the ages . . 179.4
truth and j. and Heaven . . 211.3
the j. at his right hand . . 223.2
j. and light of thy home . . 300.4
for j. laid up above . . . 387.3
for j. in his presence . . 392.2
then, my j. 'twill be . . 401.3
the j. over Jordan . . . 406.1
all is calm and j. . . . 453.4
after death its j. . . . 464.3
there are heights of j. . . 585.4
thy j., thy glory share . . 612.7
to tell of j. to come . . 652.4
j. of that glorious time . . 794.3
j. untold . . . there . . . 811.c
how great their j. . . . 879.1
that will be my j. . . . 881.2
j. beyond the sky . . . 887.5
j. of the Eden above . . 905.4
j. like a river . . . flow . . 906.3
present grace and j. above . 940.1

b *[everlasting] joy* Isa 61.7
where j. are never stilled . 39.4
j. that can alter never. . . 73.4
whose j. eternal flow . . 100.4
j. that . . . abide . . . 112.4
j. immortal! Alleluia! . . 146.3
with thee is endless j. . . 362.3
the j. that never die . . 375.3
eternal j. or lasting pain . 785.6
our j. will end, no never . . 899.2

c *enter joy* Matt 25:21
e. into my Master's j. . . 636.5
e. thy Master's j. . . . 890.1
rest in thy Saviour's j. . . 890.5

4 *joy to others*
if I may but give thee j. . . 522.1
that giveth j. to all . . . 838.2

5 *human joy*
in trouble and in j. . . . 21.1
the j. of ear and eye . . 28.3
the j. of human love . . 28.4
j. and comforts die . . . 358.2
no rest, no j. I find . . . 448.3
in the world I see no j. . . 489.2
not in j. to charm me . . 498.5
in j. or pain 587.3
come with . . . j. and care . 595.1
nor j., nor grief . . . part. . 659.5
the other's j. possessing . 663.3
come the days of j. . . . 711.1
all other j. is . . . echo . . 711.1
days of j., or . . . woe . . 711.3
j. be withered all . . . 746.4
though j. may fade . . 761.1
j. to make me bold . . . 860.4
my j., my toil 867.5
its j. as soon are past . . 880.2
j. that yet are mine . . 916.2
for j. or despair . . . 928.1
quickening j. or . . . care . 947.4

b *joys [of earth]*
the j. of sin are flown . . 267.1
hollow j., worldly toys . . 379.3
in the world . . . no j. . . 489.2
all the j. of earth . . . 600.2
earth's j. grow dim . . 670.2
all earthly j. . . . fade . . 711.3
choice 'twixt earthly j. . . 749.1
earth's j. and fears . . 795.3
j. of earth and hopes . . 941.1

grief (2b)

joybells
morning when j. chime . . c123
there are j. ringing . . c153

joyful-ly
j., j., we adore thee . . . 10.1
j. music lifts us . . . 10.4
shepherds j. sped . . . 72.5
with j. steps they sped . . 76.2
j. tidings first begun . . 78.1
j., all ye nations, rise . . 82.1
j. and triumphant . . . 85.1
this j. Eastertide . . . 153.1
earth prolong the j. strain . 160.5
j. will the meeting be . . 235.c
sounding j. all the time . . 383.1
meet the glad with j. smiles . 485.2
pathway of j. obedience . 501.2
in j. obedience . . . fulfil . 506.2
to be used in j. service . . 514.3
sometimes j. . . . sad . . 549.1
tell the j. tidings . . . 550.3
may be in j. harmony . . 561.3
or if on j. wing . . . 617.5
j. rise to pay 665.1
they j. shout: to the war . 703.4
to serve him j. . . . 706.c
j. our little child . . . 796.1
be j. all the way . . . 807.1
raise the j. cry . . . 813.4
equip for j. service . . . 870.3
let me j. remove . . . 880.4
soon shall we j. know . . 904.4

b Ps 5:11
people that can be j. . . 372.2

c *joyful heart*
with ever-j. h. 12.2
my j. h. is filled . . . 134.3
with j. h. we worship . . 795.1
with j. h. and voices . . 929.1

d *joyful songs*
addressed their j. s. . . 93.5
ever in j. s. 184.c
loud, j. s. of praise . . 807.1
we bring with j. s. . . . 825.3
thankful hearts need j. s. . 926.1
in j. s. we will proclaim . . 940.2

news (b) sound (b)

joyless
my life has been j. . . . 298.4
j. is the day's return . . 412.3

joyous-ly
as j. it rings 187.2
soon end in j. day . . . 721.2
j. tidings we proclaim . . 789.4
solemn, yet j. and new . . c106

jubilant
be j. my feet 162.3
out of distress to j. psalm . 300.2

jubilee *Lev 25:9*
earth shall keep her j. . . 393.2
for a world-wide j. . . . 593.1
march on! we bring the j. . 815.c

Judah *Rev 5:5* 233.c

judge
1 *(noun)* *Acts 10:42**
Jesus the j. shall come . . 164.6
the j. upon the throne . . 265.5
thou my j. shalt be . . . 618.1
j., our nature wearing . . 875.2
all before the j. appear . . 932.2
2 *(verb)*
j. not the Lord 29.4
light will j., and j., heal . . 408.3
mine to j., condemn . . 652.2
God j., we believe . . . 785.6

judgment
brought to Pilate for j. . . 137.3
man's puny j. bar . . . 185.3
thy final j. with dismay . . 618.2
if thy j. make me quail . . 618.3
the accuser comes to the j. . 724.3
with mercy and with j. . . 896.3
b *judgment day* *Acts 17:31**
as black as on the j. d. . . 446.1
d. of j.! D. of wonders . . 875.1
against the aweful j. d. . . 885.1
c *judgment seat/throne* *Rom 14:10*
sifting . . . before his j. s. . 162.3
see thee on thy j. t. . . 302.4
light of his great j. t. . . 893.1

just
1 *(adjective)*
the dwellings of the j. . . 21.3
b *Acts 3:14*
j. and holy is thy name . . 737.3
c *Phil 4:8*
honest, j. and lovely . . c56
d *1 John 1:9*
faithful and j. art thou . . 296.4
thee . . . merciful and j. . . 714.2
2
a *(adverb)*
strand j. beyond the river . 115.4
guiding, j. where . . . go . 316.c
when I j. tell him . . . 323.5
in the darkness, j. before . 330.1
j. the time I need him . . 334.1
j. to do his will 343.3
j. what seemeth thee good422.c/589.c
j. outside the land . . . 433.1
will j. be the fittest . . 473.3
God's armies, j. hid . . 537.2
j. remember prayer . . 663.3
j. where I am/he needs . . 706.*
j. to trust and follow . . 755.2
your fighting j. begun . . 806.2
life j. for a look . . . 829.1
j. to be near/there/a smile . 906.*
j. on the borders . . . 910.1
j. to do my Master's will . c35
if you will j. remember . . c115
j. lean on the . . . arm . . c138
j. a true devotion . . . c213
b *just as*
j. as I am . . . . . 293.*
to all . . . are j. as free . . 329.3
j. as I am . . . struggling. . 415.2
Jesus makes . . . j. as free . 546.2
j. as thou wilt . . . 612.7
j. as true today . . . 700.1
reach Heaven j. as surely . 780.3
j. as I am, thine . . . strong 860.1, 3
c *just now*
met the good shepherd j. n. . 111.1
save such j. n. . . . 175.3
at thy feet j. n. we fall . . 201.1
brings the fire j. n. . . . 201.3
Saviour invites you j. n. . . 273.4
look up j. n., believing . . 413.2
j. n. a full salvation . . 433.1
I do j. n. believe . . . 447.4
promises j. n. I claim . . 450.4
j. n. . . . let it be . . . 468.2
Lord, wash me j. n. . . 487.2
mine . . . thine j. n. . . 510.4
fire descending j. n. . . 511.3
seal me j. n. 523.1
all my need j. n. supply . . 620.1
I look j. n. to thee . . . 628.1
can he come j. n. . . . c8
j. n. as I say to thee . . c33
to meet my need j. n. . . c86
O come j. n. to me . . . c88
d *just the same*
love of God is j. the s. . . 49.2
he is j. the s. today . . 96.*
j. the s. unto the end . . c163
because (a)

justice
thy j. like mountains . . 8.2
truth and j. reign again . . 63.2
j. now revokes the sentence . 75.4
learns his joy, his j. . . 142.5
j. . . . from his sceptre . . 166.2
a kindness in his j. . . . 265.3
j. and his love do blend . . 269.2
Father of love, of j. . . 486.1

justify-ied
what can I do to j. . . . 706.3
b *Rom 5:9**
j. fully through . . . love . . 371.2
we by grace are j. . . . 785.4
rising, he j. c185

justly *Luke 23:41* . . . 108.1

K

keen-est
no other friend so k. . . . 246.2
its sorrows all too k. . . 267.2
conscience k. to feel . . 409.3
feel its k. woe . . . 607.2
I need thy k. appraisal . . 618.2
k. breath of Heaven . . 827.2
far beyond our k. sight . . 871.4

keep-ing/kept
1 *(general)*
no door can k. them out . 11.2
death cannot k. his prey . 148.3
earth shall k. her jubilee . 393.2
own appointed limits k. . . 569.1
k. me tender . . . true . 591.2
tryst that the body must k. . 739.2
b *keep [back]*
what k. thee back . . . 263.1
each idol that would k. us . 428.3
what is it k. me out . . 440.2
I'll k. back no longer . . 473.2
2 *(we) keep*
a *personal*
that truth to k. 100.4
the vigil I must k. . . . 176.2
shame . . . to k. him standing 299.1
to k. thy grace . . . how. . 440.3
I'll k. back no longer . . 473.2
while k. at thy side . . 485.3
fellowship . . . to k. . . 485.5
one with vows to k. . . 522.2
grieved . . . ill-k. vow . . 534.2
as faithful soldiers k. . . 922.1
nothing k. but . . . give . 922.3
b *[ever] keep*
close . . . soul ever k. . . 483.3
k. . . . through the whole . 484.2
k. him for ever in his view . 580.2
be ever k. in mind . . . 784.3
ever k. close to thee . . 846.3
c *(other)*
angels k. their watch . . 86.2
lay k. their sheep . . . 90.1
k. the . . . grave clothes. . 152.1
and you will k. singing . . 396.2
her watch is k. . . . 677.2
the little Levite, k. . . . 839.2
or k. the day from dawning . 854.1
they k. perpetual tryst . . 878.5
d *(advice)*
may we k. and ponder . . 78.3
k. the blest commands . . 580.3
k. watch, and pray . . 683.6
to k. your armour bright . 695.4
restless heart k. still . . 738.2
k. on believing . . . 773.c
k. waving, k. every flag . . 775.c
k. the highest aims . . 801.1
k. holding on . . . 806.3
k. your weapons sharp . . 809.2
k. in step all the time . . 817.*
k. on believing, trust . . c63
k. the touch of God . . c76
k. on marching . . . faith . c136
k. a-marching on . . . c153
k. the old flag flying . . c242
e *2 Tim 4:7*
k. faith sweet . . . 519.3
unbroken faith to k. . . 534.3
charge (b)
3 *(God) keeps*
he will not fail to k. . . 48.1
k. the inward witness right . 113.1
anchor that k. the soul . . 280.c
power to k. me spotless . 303.c
it is love that k. me . . 342.2
Jesus lives to k. me . . 347.2
k. me when . . . blow . . 347.2
finding me, k. me . . . 388.c
he'll k. me every hour . . 389.2
can k. me every hour . . 415.3
blood does purge and k. . 440.4
thou art almighty to k. . . 454.5
grace . . . to k. me fighting . 586.1
k. us free from doubting . 700.3
Master, thou wilt k. us . . 707.c
faith . . . k. my soul alive . 733.6
thou dost k. thy child . . 741.1
right hand doth k. . . . me . 741.3
shall he k. thy soul . . 767.4
Jesus can k. us so near . . 773.4
God is k. his soldiers . . 800.1
comfort, strengthen and k. . 823.c
k. love's banner floating . 954.4
the grace that k. me . . c152
it is grace that k. me . . c164
Saviour who's mighty to k. . c165
b *(request)*
k. us in his grace . . . 12.2
k. us in the narrow way . . 76.4
k. us to thy presence near . 97.3
k. me near the cross . . 115.1
urge us on, and k. us . . 202.3
wash and k. me white . . 205.1
k. us from the world . . 210.3
k. it still awake . . . 425.3
k. me holy here . . . 447.1
k. me till . . . faith . . 504.3
k. me yet in thy employ . . 522.1
k. thou my heart ablaze . . 529.2
k. our loved ones . . . 582.1
k. them, in their weakness . 582.2
k. us fighting, trusting . . 593.1
guide us, k. us, feed us . . 607.1
k. me, King of kings . . 671.1
k. thy children free . . 674.3
k. us loyal to our aim . . 863.5
k. us true for ever . . . c244
c *ever keep*
k. me ever by thy Spirit . . 32.3
k., ever k. neath . . . flow . 443.1
make me and k. me ever . 445.4
k. us ever in the vanguard . 787.2
ever k. me close . . . 842.1
k. us evermore thine own . 937.4
d *kept (passive)*
k. by thy grace secure . . 431.4
k. low by grace . . . 468.4
safely k. by thy protection . 504.1
k. by his precious blood . 782.1
k. by thy Spirit . . . 785.5
k. by a Father's hand . . 897.3
k. . . . to sin no more . . c144
e *kept by power* *1 Peter 1:5*
k. by the p. of his might . 321.1
now he k. me by his p. . . 344.2
k. . . . by . . . wondrous p. . 469.4
k. . . . Holy Spirit's p. . . 538.3
f *save and keep*
Saviour, s. and k. for ever . 258.3
blessedly s. . . . k., yes . . 321.c
he s. and k. for ever . . 413.1
s. . . . k. by thy grace . . 431.4
s. . . . k. me from sinning . 640.2
he has s. . . . surely k. me . 857.3
able to s., able to k. . . . c1
able to s. and to k.. . . c179
s. and k. me, hallelujah . . c183
s. and k. by the grace . . c199
g *keep safe*
he will k. me safely . . 309.3
safely k. by thy protection . 504.1
safe hast k. . . . refreshed . 665.3
our Father k. us safe . . 722.2
k. me safe by . . . side . . 837.2
h *keep pure*
your heart must be k. p. . 406.3
with love my heart k. p. . 416.2
k. p. and holy . . . tide . . 443.1
k. my heart in purity . . 455.5
presence k. me p. . . . 742.3
to k. us p. within . . . 747.2
keep us faithful, k. us p. . 937.4
i *Num 6:24*
the Lord bless thee and k. . 961
j *1 Sam 2:9*
k. thou my feet . . . 606.1
guide my steps and k. . . 641.1
k *keep in peace* *Isa 26:3*
in perfect p. he k. . . . 317.3
k. . . . in perfect p.. . . 513.2
thou wilt k. him in p. p. . c142
l *Jer 31:10*
k. thy flock, from sin . . 845.2
m *John 17:12*
all his own to k. . . . 130.2
n *2 Tim 1:12*
he is able to k. . . . 730.c
able to save, able to k. . . c1
Jesus is able . . . to k. . . c179
o *Jude 24*
power to k. from sinning . 257.2
k. each day from sinning . 328.2
k. me from sinning . . 640.2
k. my heart from sin . . 844.3
clean (c), evil (b), faithful (2c), feet (1f), Israel (c), make (4f), power (4f)

keeper
k. of the garden . . . 600.1
b *Ps 121:5*
Jehovah is himself thy k. . 767.3

keeping (n)
the k. of the lights . . . 478.1
held in your k. . . . 506.2
in Jesus' k. we are safe . . 752.4
shall dwell in Jesus' k. . . 899.3

kept see *keep*

key
thyself the k. . . . 651.2
faith . . . turns the k. . . 733.2
b *Rev 1:18*
k. of death and hell . . 164.3

kill *Matt 10:28* 1.4

kin 826.3

kind
1 *(noun)*
God's love is for all k. . . 47.1
poor sinners of all k. . . 331.4
bring sinners of every k. . 814.c
many k. of darkness . . 841.3

in every k. of way . . . 851.1
ransomed sinners of all k. . 893.3
2 *(adjective)*
a *re divinity* *(Luke 6:35)*
praise the Lord for he is k. . 34.1
God's forgotten to be k. . 44.1
to those who fall, how k. . 61.3
entreaty, k. and sweet . . 246.3
most wonderfully k. . . 265.6
loving and k. art thou . . 296.4
none other . . . good and k. . 334.3
friend, so k., so true . . 345.4
his k. Spirit did yearn . . 388.2
k. is the light that . . . 457.2
thy k. but searching eye . 522.2
k. but searching glance . 558.4
thou art merciful and k. . 576.3
thou art pitiful and k. . . 793.5
seen his k. look . . . 794.1
how k. was our Saviour . 797.3
the Master, ready and k. . 848.3
God! is so good and k. . . c5
whispers, O so k. . . . c36
b *re people*
like Jesus, gentle . . . k. . 193.4
with wisdom k. and clear . 212.2
one day k., the next . . 377.1
forgiving, tender and k. . 623.2
be . . . k.-hearted and true . 823.2
loving and k. to all I see. . 844.2
in action k. 861.3

kindest 265.2

kindle-d-ing
stars at night do k. . . 486.2
k. thought and glowing . . 612.6
b *Luke 12:49*
his love my love k. . . . 92.2
k. by a spark of grace . . 165.1
k. in some hearts it is . . 165.1
k. every high desire . . 194.2
k. a flame of sacred love . 199.1
k. in each . . . living fire. . 216.4
they k. to a flame . . . 223.3
desires . . . k. by his grace . 256.1
fire, k., flaming . . . 546.1
k. fire in every soul . . 609.3
feel the k. of thy love . . 636.1
c *James 3:5*
quench the k. fire . . . 425.2

kindliness 611.3

kindly
k. chiding of the Spirit . . 192.2
lead, k. Light . . . 606.1
voices have a k. sound . . 664.1
soft dews of k. sleep . . 676.2
misinterpret . . . k. words . 790.2
sweetly smiled and k. said . 797.1

kindness
a k. in his justice . . . 265.3
since his k. drew me . . 343.1
some deed of k. done . . 524.3
wakened by k., chords . . 691.3
who the Father's k. share . 722.3
words full of k. . . . 848.2
sowing seeds of k. . . 930.1
k. can ne'er fade away . . c207
b *loving-kindness* *Ps 36.7**
thy l. k. make us love thee . 40.3
Saviour's l. k. overcame . 338.2
in l. k. Jesus came . . . 339.1
by thy l.-k. so unfailing . . 762.3
show Christ in l. k. . . 830.2
watchful care and l. k. . . 938.2

kindred
let goods and k. go . . 1.4
turned from home and . . . k. 428.2
comrades and k. will shout . 543.4
fellowship of k. minds . . 660.1
k. souls each other greet . 873.3
k. and friends are at rest . 886.3
b *Rev 5:9*
let every k., every tribe . . 56.2

king
1 *(human)*
all were looking for a k. . . 91.1
k. and nations come and go . 799.1
king (2j) priest (2b)
2 *(divine)*
sing hallelujahs to our K. . 76.5
a child and yet a K. . . 79.3
glory to the new-born K. 82.1, c
let earth receive her K. . . 84.1
gifts and homage to our K. . 89.2
hallelujahs to our K. . . 89.3
to seek for a K. . . . intent . 90.3
make we thee our K. . . 97.2
be my love-anointed K. . . 122.4
triumph with their K. . . 149.2
greets . . . her returning K. . 155.2
peculiar honours to our K. . 160.5
O K. divine, didst yield . . 174.1
King within my conscience . 194.3
I'm the child of a K. . . 354.c
a carol to my K. . . . 387.2
hear the welcome from the K. 389.3
such a mighty, mighty K. . 402.c
their pattern and their K. . 411.2
holy courage, mighty . . . K. . 499.3
for the glory of my K. . . 514.3
sing always . . . for my K. . 525.3
thou art coming to a K. . . 563.2
my Maker and my K. . . 616.1
my K.'s in the battle . . 684.1
the claims of our K. . . 687.2
we salute our K. . . . 692.3
warriors of the risen K. . . 696.3
who will serve the K. . . 707.1
the K.'s own army . . . 707.4
the strength of the K. 820.1, c
K. is the mighty to save. . 820.3
in the name of the K. . 820.4, 5
sing . . . hosannas to our K. . 834.c
sing . . . for your K. . . 835.c
offer to the K. . . . 849.*
thou art my . . . K.. . . 859.1
soldiers of the K. . . . 866.c
my K. may please . . . 867.4
earn the K.'s: Well done . 869.4
the K.'s highway . . . c26
heralding . . . the K. . . c226
b *[see] King [in beauty]* *Isa 33:17*
in his b. I s. the great K.. . 323.4
marching to meet the great K. 406.2
reign with the K. in his b. . 406.4
till in his b. my K. . . . s.. . 443.4
I'll s. my great K. . . . 543.4
K. in his glory we s. . . 808.5
c *King comes* *Zech 9:9*
when he c., our glorious K. . 118.5
sing we the K. who is c. . 166.1
c., thou almighty K. . . 219.1
soon our c. K. . . . 347.3
d *Zech 14:9*
K. o'er earth shall reign . . 816.4
e *hail, King* *Matt 27:29*
h., thou Galilean K. . . 109.1
h. him as thy matchless K. . 156.1
f *Jer 10:10/1 Tim 1:17*
praise the everlasting K. . 17.1
name of our eternal K. . . 26.1
g *King of . . .*
Almighty, the K. of creation . 19.1
the K. of love my shepherd . 53.1
born the K. of angels . . 85.1
K. of my life, I crown . . 117.1
K. of my heart to crown. . 415.4
K. of righteousness divine . 452.1
K. of love so condescending . 500.1
K. of my heart to reign . . 541.4
led on by Zion's K. . . 901.4
h *King of Glory* *Ps 24:7*
'tis the Lord, the K. of G. . 104.c
the K. of G. languished . . 126.1
confess him K. of G. now . 141.1
K. of G., camest thou . . 185.1
room for Jesus, K. of G. . 241.c
K. of G. a pardon offers . 250.1
tell of the K. and his g. . . 384.1
he with the K. of G. . . 699.4
how once the K. of G. . . 840.1
the K. of G. passes . . 876.5
i *King of Heaven*
praise . . . the K. of H. . . 17.1
H.'s all-gracious K. . . 83.1
mercy moves the K. of H. . 555.2
j *King of kings* *Rev 19:16**
K. of k. . . . we'll crown him . 66.4
because the K. of all k. . . 72.c
crown the Saviour K. of k. . 147.2
K. of k. and Lord of lords . 147.4
the K. of k. and Lord . . 168.2
thou art the K. of k. . . 171.1
swing wide . . . to the K. of k. 227.*
he is the K. of k. . . . 346.2
fighting for the K. of k. . . 402.c
keep me, K. of k. . . . 671.1
K. of all kingdoms . . . 908.4
k *God and King*
all creatures of our G. . . . K. 2.1
sing: My G. and K. . . 11.*
glories of my G. and K. . . 64.1
praises sing to G., the K. . 86.2
redeemer, my G. and my K. . 364.4
praises to our G. and K. . 809.1
l *King (with Jesus/Christ)*
salvation to J. our K. . . 24.2
Christ, the new-born K. . 75.*
welcome C., the . . . K. . . 79.c
C. . . . shall reign as K. . . 158.c
when Jesus is K. . . . 166.*
room for J., K. of Glory . . 241.c
do service for J. your K. . 281.4
hallelujahs to J. C. our K. . 334.3
now C. is K., my heart . . 541.4
honour unto C. the K. . . 690.5
yet one in C., the K. . . 705.2
the promises of C. my K. . 757.1
to the cause of C., our K. . 777.4
loudest hosannas: J. is K. . 848.4
soldiers of K. J. . . . 866.1
make J. K. c220
praises of our L. and K. . . c243
m *King and Lord* *(Psalm 10:16)**
'tis the L., the K. . . . 104.c
rejoice, the L. is K.! . . 164.1
your L. and K. adore . . 164.1
their L. as K. to crown . . 169.1
crown thee K. and L. . . 499.1
devotion to my . . . L. and K.. 591.2
promise of our . . . L. and K.. 700.3
the L. is K.! I own . . . 867.1
O L., my K., I turn . . . 867.6
n *King and Saviour*
crown the S. K. of kings . 147.2
our S.-K. shall reign . . 169.c
this is the blessing, S.-K. . 415.5
thee, my S. and my K. . . 421.6
unto thee, O S.-K. . . 532.1
we are with thee S.-K. . . 532.4
I hear thy words, my S.-K. . 562.3
devotion to my S. . . . and K. 591.2
S.-K., we wait . . . 595.3
promise of our S. . . . and K.. 700.3
the S.-K. has . . . overthrown. 829.2

worthy is our S.-K. . . . 897.1
hearts . . . to our S.-K. . . c213

fight (2c), glorious (1b), heavenly (c), Israel (c), praise (3n), priest (1)

kingdom
1 *(of God)*
thy gracious K. bring . . 79.3
he his K. is enlarging . . 159.3
his K. stretch from shore . 160.1
claim the K. for thine own . 161.4
his K. cannot fail . . . 164.3
ascertains the K. mine . . 214.4
a place in that K. for you . 392.4
thy K.'s cause embrace . . 500.1
take thy K. . . . crown . . 532.4
miss thy K.'s goal . . . 577.3
brought into the K. . . . 776.2
men confess Christ's K. . 776.3
serving for thy K.'s sake. . 788.2
in your heavenly K. . . . 792.3
a K. meet for thee . . . 827.3
o'er his K. reign . . . 828.4
the gems for his K. . . . 852.2
talked about a K. fair . . 855.3
a K. fair to gain . . . 868.1
in the book of thy K. . . 883.*
be a crown and k. won . . 897.3
seed for his K. sown . . 923.3
their Father's K. . . . see . 932.4
thy K. of light may see . . c236

b *Dan 2:44*
his K. is for ever . . . 1.4
thy K. stands, and grows . 677.5

c *Matt 5:3*
they the K. shall possess . 95.1

d *Kingdom come* *Matt 6:10*
we see thy K. c. . . . 154.4
K. of Christ, for thy c. . . 166.5
thy k. c., O God . . . 172.1
thy K. c. to every heart . . 624.1
his K. c. not by force . . 705.3
thy K. c. on earth . . . 774.4
thy K. c. to every heart . . 945.4

e *Matt 6:13*
thine is the K., Lord . . 171.1
k. of the world are thine. . 624.5
for thine is the K. . . . 951

f *Matt 25:34*
k. you shortly shall view. . 233.3
made me an heir to k. . . 535.2
see the K. I bestow . . 875.4

g *Mark 12:34*
so near to the K. . . . 263.*

h *Rom 14:17*
well in his K. of peace . . 166.3
brings his K. . . . peace . . 195.2
the K. of thy love . . . 742.2
in the K. of thy grace . . 793.2
the home . . . the K. of love . 905.1

i *Rev 11:15*
k. of the world are thine . 624.5
till . . . the K. of the Lord . 697.6
all the world his K. . . . 866.3

glorious (2e), restore (e), sit (c), such (1b)

2 *(of Satan)*
Satan's k. overthrow . . 622.2
pull down the devil's k. . . 696.c
Satan's k. down shall fall . 802.4
storm the k., but prevail . 816.2
the k. of Satan we'll seize . 820.4

3 *(of people)* *(Rev 11:15)*
sets the k. on a blaze . . 165.1
k. of the world are thine . 624.5
k. rise and wane . . . 690.4
till the k. of the world . . 697.6
earthly k. rise and fall . . 799.1
to all k. and all peoples . . 824.4

o'er the k. he shall reign . 833.2
as King of all k. . . . 908.4

kingly
leave thy . . . k. crown . . 101.1
a k. crown to gain . . . 701.1

kingship 250.4

kiss *Luke 7:38* 140.4

knee
bend the k. before him . . 76.2
reverently upon their k. . . 90.5
fall . . . upon my k. . . 122.*
not . . . bend I the k. . . 296.1
weakest saint upon his k. . 646.3
get it on your k. . . . 813.c
stood round his k. . . 848.2

bow (2d)

kneel-ing-knelt
1 *(Jesus) kneels* *(Luke 22:41)*
where Jesus k. to share . 567.3

2 *(we) kneel*
here let all . . . k. in awe . 73.3
I k. to adore 111.1
k. and adore him, the Lord 183.1, 5
when we k. to pray . . 193.2
I humbly k. before thee . . 221.1
at the mercy seat . . . k. . 236.1
k. at the Saviour's feet . . 259.3
k. there in . . . contrition . 301.2
boldly will I k. . . . 303.3
where I k. to thank him . . 348.2
k. before thee . . . praying . 501.1
mine to k. and drink . . 510.3
I, unworthy, k. before . . 528.1
when I k. in prayer . . 585.3
I may as well k. down . . 588.2
k. in penitence . . . 605.1
lowly k., wait thy word . . 674.1
before thine altar k. . . 762.3
as we k. to pray . . . 787.1
thousands humbly k. . . 802.3
lowly we k. in prayer . . 948.1

b *kneel at cross*
at the c. as I k. . . . 395.2
c. for guidance k. . . . 408.3
humble . . . I k. at thy c. . 513.c
here before thy c. I k. . . 649.1
repentant, he k. at the c. . 708.2
I k. beside thy sacred c. . 729.1

knew—see *know*

knit 947.1

knock-ed-ing
a *Matt 7:8*
k.! and the door will open . c5

b *Rev 3:20*
he k. and asks admission . 241.1
pleading, k., let him in . . 250.c
O Jesus, thou art k. . . 299.2
it was Jesus k. . . . 373.1
love for help is . . . k. . . 921.3
he's k. once more . . . c18

know-ing-n/knew
1 *(God) knows*
a *(with title)*
Jesus k. . . . weakness . . 645.2
God k. everyone . . . me . 850.*
Jesus k. all about . . . c182

b *(general)*
truth as he k. truth . . 27.6
he k. you by your name . . 44.c
k. all my griefs . . . 68.2
smiles like us he k. . . 87.4
Calvary he chose to k. . . 134.c
his reign shall k. no end . . 156.3
all my past is k. to thee . . 285.3
k. my failings . . . fears . . 294.1
k. my case . . . healing art . 311.2

k. my heart's . . . depths . 311.4
k. how to steal the bitter . 333.2
life no darkness k. . . . 408.3
yea, Lord, thou k. . . . 507.1
weary, I k. it 564.1
I k. how hardly souls . . 564.3
k. all the yearning . . . 614.3
thou . . . k. me best . . 675.3
k. what best for each . . 715.5
well he sees and k. it . . 841.2
surely thou dost k. . . . 842.3
k. neither measure nor end . 962
he k., the storms . . . c127
he k., he careth . . . c139

c *knows way* *Job 23:10*
k. the w. to bring me back . 305.3
he k. the w. he taketh . . 736.2
he k. the w. and I will . . 740.2
he alone can k. the w. . . 857.1

d *Ps 103:14*
our feeble frame he k. . . 17.3
doth k. human frailties . . 288.2
who k. all my weakness/care. 584.c
our weakness thou dost k. . 607.2

e *knows [need]* *Matt 6:8*
he k. our every n. . . . 9.3
someone k. your deepest n. . 238.c
k. all its truest n. . . . 614.3
our inmost wants are k. . 738.2
understands . . . k. all you n. 773.3
my great n. are k. to thee . c74

all (4a), love (7i)

2 *(others) know*
human minds can pity k. . 50.1
its breadth is k. . . . 55.3
in Heaven he was k. . . 92.2
hearts that k. him not . . 102.1
death . . . k. no more . . 160.4
k. the mystery of his love . 168.5
no one truly k. you . . 238.1
wanderer, k. not the smile . 253.1
k. . . . thou need'st never die. 271.4
she k. her Lord had come . 304.2
let your joys be k. . . . 314.1
who never k. our God . . 314.1
they see and k. their robes . 359.4
his fulness you shall k. . . 413.2
never k. a fallen world . . 414.2
you k. your sins forgiven . 433.3
k. that fellowship of love . 465.1
the world has never k. . . 564.2
no boundary k. unto men . 579.3
k. a heart's refreshment . . 580.1
who that k. the worth . . 646.1
that nature truly k. . . 656.3
so the enemy shall k. . . 686.c
hearts that k. their duty . . 704.c
hearts to k. no way . . 704.4
each . . . soul k. thy rest . 708.3
than thou canst fully k. . . 723.2
the Son as man is k. . . 785.2
k. that you hold him (her) . 792.1
k. the sweetness of his rest . 819.2
we'll let the millions k. . . 821.c
k. now thy perfect will . . 878.3
who k. his sins forgiven . . 880.1
they may k. there's mercy . 919.2
thy purpose more may k. . 919.3
our brother may k. . . . 927.3

b *(question)*
do you k. the song/story . 80.*
do you k. for all he died . . 243.1
do you his salvation k. . . 243.1
do you k. your sins forgiven . 243.2
does anybody k. . . . 274.2
would you k. the peace/joy . 348.3
Jesus, wouldst thou k. him . 377.4
would you k. why I love. . 404.*
would you . . . k. the meaning 783.1

c *all know*
a. may k. thou livest . . 138.1
that a. the world might k. . 261.4

a. may k. . . . I belong . . 437.4
a. the world may Jesus k. . 500.2
a. full salvation may k. . . 535.c
the world may k. I'm thine . 538.5
a. around shall k. I'm . . 649.4
k. there is room for them a. . 794.3
a. the world the harvest k. . 932.2
everybody should k. . . c155

d *Luke 19:42*
that your Saviour you k. . 331.2
the hearts that would k. . 527.2

e *Luke 23:34*
they k. not that by me . . 140.1

f *Eph 1:18*
their hope they k. . . . 701.3

God (5c)

3 *(I/we) know*
rejoice to k. thy favour . . 26.4
hearts that k. delight . . 27.5
seek until we k. . . . 36.5
k. thy mercies manifold . . 59.3
k. her guilt was there . . 120.4
not till we k. our guilt . . 135.2
give to us to k. . . . 145.3
grants his name to k. . . 168.3
feel . . . until we k. . . 181.4
loved me ere I k. him . . 345.1
loved ones I k. . . . 392.3
to do whate'er I k. . . 426.3
dearest idol I have k. . . 442.5
that I may k. the will . . 451.1
give us faith to k. . . . 466.2
all I've . . . hoped or k. . . 498.2
O to k. that thou art mine . 520.1
the heart longs to k. . . 527.3
full measure to k. . . . 553.1
peace and refreshment k. . 574.1
teach . . . to k. . . . thy will . 586.3
to k. fellowship with thee 630.1, c
k. thee for ever nigh . . 630.3
long . . . to k. you risen . . 748.1
make me k. . . . canst save . 837.2
happy most of all to k. . . 837.4
do the good I k. . . . 837.6
teach . . . thy steps to k. . 846.3
only to k. that the path . . c45

b *let me know*
Saviour, let me k. . . . 409.c
let me . . . fuller k. . . . 439.2
let me k. it is to me . . 614.2
let me k. . . . art nigh . . 618.1
let me now thy nature k. . c96

c *(positive testimony—I)*
this I k.: he dies for me . . 131.3
I k. I'm clean within . . 201.4
I k. a fount . . . a place . . 257.c
joy to k. he cleanses me . 317.2
this I k., this I k. . . . 322.3
I k. I love him . . . 323.2
Glory to Jesus, I k. . . 323.3
I k. I am blest . . . 323.5
I k. thou wilt be near . . 325.4
I k. it's there to stay . . 327.2
can cheer . . . this I k. . . 329.2
I k. . . . not cast me out. . 331.3
I k. that he is living . . 334.1
you ask me how I k. . . 334.c
I k. that he is leading . . 334.2
I k. 'tis well 339.4
I have k. . . . him long . . 343.1
my Saviour, this I k. . . 348.1
what a blessing to k. . . 355.1
I k. thou art mine . . . 357.1
ever since I k. his blood . . 359.2
I k. my sins . . . forgiven . 360.3
I k. my sins forgiven . . 366.1
a glorious thing to k. . . 375.2
no strength is mine, I k. . . 385.3
ever by my side, I k. . . 389.1
keep me every hour, I k. . . 389.2
welcome from the King, I k. . 389.3
for he pardoned me I k. . 389.c

sweetest name I k. . . . 390.c
I k. I am washed . . . 402.1
I k. it shall 407.2
this moment I k. the blood . 436.4
the best thing I k. . . . 451.c
I k. . . . power cannot fail . 459.2
now I k. to me . . . in me . 459.3
I k. thou wilt take me . . 473.1
I k. thou dost save me . . 473.4
Father, I k. that all . . . 485.1
I k. thou . . . all-in-all . . 489.4
I k. my weakness . . . 491.2
I k. I can find this . . . 527.c
since I have k. his mercy . 536.3
the rapturous bliss to k. . . 540.2
I k. as now I k. . . . 545.2
I k. 'tis full and free . . 546.3
k. thou hearest prayer . . 596.1
the gift divine I k. . . . 601.1
from a hill I k. . . . 647.c
I k. his name 735.2
I am satisfied to k. . . . 758.c
I k. are for the best . . 761.2
k. thou art close beside . . 770.4
hast taught me to k. . . 771.1
white as snow, yes, I k. . . 798.c
this I surely k. . . . 840.1
I k. he hears my praise . . 840.3
Jesus loves me! This I k. . 843.1
just a smile . . . I k. . . 906.3
I k. that you will find . . c22
I k. God can c120
I k. he cares for me . . c133
'tis wonderful to k. . . c143
I k. they cannot harm me . c145
I k. my sins are washed . . c149
I k. he's mine . . . c167
I k., yes, I k. . . . washed . c168
mine, I k. thou art mine . . c186

d *(positive testimony—we)*
we k. thou art not far . . 198.2
present we k. thou art . . 603.4
we k. thou art . . . same. . 629.1
we k. we at the end . . 685.3
our cause we k. . . . prevail . 698.2
we k. the promises . . . sure . 755.2
we k. God wills . . . 760.3
since we have k. . . . name . 763.4
we k. that we shall see . . 769.3
we k., we sinners . . . bring . 820.1
we k. that not a foe . . 822.2
we k. . . . salvation . . . see . 822.3
k. we that the sun . . . 874.2
for this we k., with Jesus . c220

e *know and feel*
God is love, I k., I f. . 286.c, 4
my Jesus to k., and f. . . 355.4
when shall I k. and f. . . 447.1
now I k., yes, I f. . . . 459.2
all I k. and all I f. . . . 492.2
we k. and f. . . . here . . 558.2
joyfully k. and f. . . . 904.4

f *Isa 40:21*
have we not k. . . . heard it . 724.1

g *Mark 1:24*
I k. thee who thou art . . 59.1

h *know way* *John 14:5*
grant us that way to k. . . 100.4
that we may k. . . . thy way . 190.2
not wish to k. the way . . 644.2
I cannot k. the way . . 732.2
we do not k. the way . . 748.2
not k. our way . . . 763.3

i *1 Cor 2:2*
no other fount I k. . . . 306.c
all who . . . k. thee. . . 429.3
pray that I may k. thee . . 435.1
only as I truly k. thee . . 435.3
thee to k. is all my cry . . 439.4
thyself to k., thy will . . 449.c

we have not k. thee . . 466.1
when shall we k. thee . . 466.5
k. no other will . . . 509.2
first to k. thee . . . 591.3
himself more fully k. . . 634.4
God . . . we then shall k. . 651.4
nothing k. beside . . . 659.3
only thee, resolved to k. . 667.1
I shall k. him c248

j *know Jesus*
once has J. k. . . . 267.1
that your Saviour you k. . 331.2
my J. to k. 355.4
all the world may J. k. . . 500.2
not yet my Saviour k. . . 720.3
J. we k. . . . the throne . 752.5
strength in k. J. . . . 759.1

k *John 17:3*
eternal life to k. him . . 377.2

l *1 Cor 13:2*
I may all things k. . . . 530.2

m *1 Cor 13:12*
k. as I am known . . . 877.4

n *Eph 3:19*
none but his loved ones k. . 61.4
none but Zion's children k. . 157.3
I k. the love of God . . 290.3
I may k. redeeming love . . 385.1
I want thy love to k. . . 455.1
k. the love thou art . . 466.3
led by grace that love to k. . 545.1
love that I cannot k. . . 585.4
believe, that we may k. . . 748.4
k. your love and . . . care . 856.2
shall my love and glory k. . 875.4

o *2 Tim 1:12*
I k. whom I have believèd . 730.c

p *(not know)* *Heb 11:8**
we may not k. . . . tell . . 133.2
I k. not how to make . . 359.1
k. not it was for me . . 405.1
to k. no gain nor loss . . 476.3
peace I never k. before . . 549.c
k. not defeat or fear . . 713.3
I k. not why/how/how/what 730.*
to tell . . . I k. not how . . c82

blessedness (b), greatness (b), one (4c), redeemer (c), truth (f)

4 *(general)*
peace . . . k. no measure . 112.4
my zeal no respite k. . . 302.2
it never k. an ending . . 328.2
cannot k. decay . . . 494.1
love only k. whence . . 496.2
faith k. naught of dark . . 540.5
our trust has k. betrayal . . 750.1
let it k. no alteration . . 865.3

5 *make/made known*
a *(God) makes known*
m. k. the blessed rest . . 46.3
Holy Spirit m. him k. . . 102.3
secret . . . soon be m. k. . 372.4
Christ m. k. . . . grace . . 398.3
thy love . . . is m. k. . . 459.3
to seeking ones m. k. . . 539.1
grace, deep as need, m. k. . 571.2
m. k. thy healing balm . . 575.1
love of God to us m. k. . . 595.1
for every soul of man m. k. . 656.1
to me he hath m. k. . . 730.1
Master whose work is m. k. . 739.1
m. to us the Godhead k. . 756.1
m. thyself k., Lord . . . c85

b *(we) make known—to God*
m. all my wants . . . k. . . 633.1

c *(we) make known—to others*
what . . . do to m. it k. . . 62.4
can I m. thee truly k. . . 435.3
to . . . souls m. k. the power. 620.2
shall m. thy praises k. . . 762.2
to the beat . . . m. k. . . 829.2
m. k. the sufferings . . 830.2
let us m. k. the story . . 831.3
dare to m. it k. 847.c
m. thy goodness k. . . 936.4
may they m. thy glory k. . 942.2
adore thee, m. k. thy power . c98

knowledge
grant us, by inward k. . . 6.3
the k. of thy dying love . . 565.2

b *2 Cor 4:6*
brought the k. of the Lord . 102.1
to give the light of the k. . c158

c *Eph 3:19*
love that passeth k. . . 299.2
surpasses man's k. to find . 506.3
peace which passes k. . . 759.3

grow (3e)

L

labour
the years of his l. 99.2
speed us to l. 173.2
many a sorrow, many a l. . 228.4
not the l. of my hands . . 302.2
weak my l. has been . . 488.1
as I l. and pray . . . 527.3
strength as our l. . . . 579.1
be there at our l. . . . 611.2
l. is rest 636.2
my daily l. to pursue . . 667.1
l. on at thy command . . 667.2
toil is done, l. is o'er . . 675.c
go, l. on . . . . 683.*
I'll l. night and day . . 685.3
honest l. sanctified . . 688.2
l. as we would for thee . . 688.3
strength for thy l. . . . 691.4
fully . . . my l. prove . . 720.3
days of l., nights . . . 833.2
crown our l. with success . 833.3
let us l. for the Master . . 907.3
bless thou our l. . . . 927.2
will all our l. crown . . 943.2
b *Ps 127:1*
he . . . l. in vain . . . 605.2
c *Rev 14:13*
l. ended, Jordan past . . 228.5
trials . . . their l. o'er . . 275.1
when all his l. cease . . 580.3
who from their l. rest . . 876.1
l. and sorrows cease . . 890.4
l. and trials are o'er . . 906.1
by and by . . . l. ended . . 930.2
when our l.'s over . . . 930.3
l. ends with sunset ray . . 934.3

labourers *Matt 9:37, 38*
white . . . l. are few . . 482.2
where the l. are few . . 527.1

labouring *(Matthew 11:28)* . 240.1

lack
l. in compassionate zeal . 527.2
b *Matt 19:20*
what dost thou l. . . . 263.1
c *lack nothing* *1 Thess 4:12*
nothing l. if I am his . . 53.1
nothing can I l. . . . 736.2

lad 855.2

ladder *Gen 28:12*
strive to climb the l. . . 369.2
climbs the l. Jacob saw . . 646.2

laden
we cherish every l. hour . 874.1
b *Matt 11:28*
come, ye l. come to me . 240.2
are you heavy l. . . . 257.1
heavy l., sore oppressed . 261.2
heavy-l. I approached him . 363.3
grief-l. did I wander . . 379.1
with weak, o'erl. hands . . 534.2
are we weak and heavy l. . 645.3

lag 817.1

laid—see *lay*

lake 428.2

lamb
1
with the l. of thy flock . . 639.3
like to a l. 740.1
called little children as l. . 794.1
a shepherd to these l. . . 797.2
b *Isa 53:7*
as a l. to cruel slaughter . 253.2
2 *(re divinity)*
hallelujah to the L. . . 57.c
and to adore the L. . . 57.4
Christ, the heavenly L. . . 120.2
since there died a L. . . 290.1
wondrous story of the L. . 326.4
in the heavenly L. . . . I am . 355.2
leads me to the L. . . 442.1, 6
with the mind, meek L. . . 568.2
while upon the L. I gaze . 634.2
a follower of the L. . . 678.1
the L. leads his hosts . . 708.1
loving Jesus, gentle L. . . 793.3
ascribe . . . to the L. . . 879.3
b *behold Lamb (of God)* *John 1:29*
cry: B. the L. . . . 60.5, 6
see the L. of God appears . 88.1
b.! b. the L. of God . . 107.1
L. by God appointed . . 109.2
near the cross! O L. of God . 115.3
spotless L. of God was he . 118.3
L. of God left his glory . . 124.2
to thy cross, O L. of God . 292.c
O L. of God, I come . . 293.*
blood of the L. of God . . 296.4
thy blood alone, O L. of God . 297.3
thou wounded L. of God . 424.1
O L. of God . . . sin-bearer . 448.1
thou L. of God . . . blood . 638.1
L. of God, I look to thee. . 793.4
c *[spotless] Lamb* *1 Peter 1:19*
holy, meek, unspotted L. . 116.3
s. Lamb of God was he . . 118.3
O s. L., I come to thee . . 450.1
thy blood, O Jesus, s. L. . 590.2
d *Rev 5:6*
the L. upon his throne . . 156.1
the L. . . . before his throne . 899.2
e *[glory] to Lamb* *Rev 4:11; 5:12*
worthy the L. that died . . 57.2
all g. to the risen L. . . 67.3
bless the L. with . . . voice . 120.5
g. to Jesus, the L. . . 166.1
sound . . . Worthy the L. . 223.3
g., g. to the L. . 313.c/520.c
g. to the bleeding L. . . 360.*
g., g. to the L. . . . 370.3
g., honour to the L. . . 696.c
f *blood of Lamb* *Rev 7:14; 12:11*
l., thy precious b. . . . 132.3
power in the b. of the L. . 281.c
b. of the L. of God . . . 296.4
thy b. alone, O L. of God . 297.3
saved by the b. of the L. . 321.c
washed in the b. of the L. . 321.4
received . . . b. of the L.. . 367.2
soul-cleansing b. of the L. . 417.c
washed in the b. of the L. . 417.*
b. of the L. that was slain . 437.1
wash me in the b. of the L. . 459.c
b. of the L. . . . . victory. . 468.c
b. of the L. who was slain . 808.1
the b. of yonder L. . . 909.2
washed in the b. of the L. . 910.*
g *song of the Lamb* *Rev 15:3*
join in the s. of the L. . . 406.3
join in the s. of the L. . . 808.3
s. of Moses and the L. . . 880.4
atone (c), bleeding (b), blessed (3d), Calvary (g), praise (3o), slain (1b)

lame
room for the l., the halt . . 266.2
b *Isa 35:6*
the l. man leap for joy . . 590.3

lamentation 358.1

lamp
dim and flaring l. . . . 162.2
the l. to pilgrim given . . 176.4
bearing the l. of grace . . 224.3
like a l. of . . . flame . . 869.3
b *1 Sam 3:3*
the l. was burning dim . . 839.1
c *Ps 119:105*
l. of our feet . . . 654.1
d *Matt 25:7*
trim your feeble l. . . 478.3

land
1 *(figurative)*
rich in houses and l. . . 354.1
through this barren l. . . 578.1
the desert l. rejoice . . 583.2
fruitful the l. . . . 927.4
b *(Heaven)*
through our Father's l. . . 252.1
meet . . . that heavenly l. . 312.4
blessèd l. of light . . . 320.c
may dwell in that l. . . 406.4
perfect in the l. of light . . 466.5
the l. of endless day . . 627.3
forward to Immanuel's l. . 866.2
l. where the glorified . . 872.c
beautiful l. . . . . 873.*
reach the l. I love . . . 877.2
fly to the l. of the blest . . 886.3
Canaan's fair . . . l. . . 887.1
the l. of the free-born . . 895.1
dwelleth in Immanuel's l. . 896.*
a l. of pure delight . . 898.1
divides . . . l. from ours . . 898.1
no weeping in that l. . . 899.3
l. that is fairer than day . . 900.1
the l. beyond the blue . . 902.c
we're bound for the l. . . 905.1
reach fair Canaan's l. . . 912.1
blessed is that l. of God. . 934.4
c *land of promise* *(Heb 11:9)*
bring us to the p. l. . . 163.3
just outside the l. of p. . . 433.1
marching to the p. l. . . 765.1
view the long-p. l. . . 766.3
forward to the p. l. . . 817.3
as we go, to the p. l. . . 818.c
bound for the p. l. . . . 887.c
the fair l. of p. . . . 908.3
d *land of rest*
l. of r. . . . perfect holiness . 419.4
enter now the l. of r. . . 433.3
l. of r., . . . delight . . . 880.1
Beulah, giant, gloryland, happy (2c), thirsty (b)
2 *(literal)*
l. both near and far . . 172.6
in this l. and l. afar . . 576.1
pilgrim in an unknown l. . 740.2
aloud throughout the l. . . 782.1
drive sin from our l. . . 798.2
swelling through all the l. . 802.1
sweeping through the l. . 819.1, c
in l. beyond the sea . . 832.c, 2
embalms . . . paint the l. . . 925.2
fruitful the l. . . . 927.4
the good seed on the l. . . 935.1
l. of the ice or flame . . c238

b *land and sea*
glowing over l. and s. . . 40.1
each l. and s. . . . alike . . 362.1
hymns . . . from l. and s. . 569.4
fall o'er l. and s. . . . 675.1
on l. and on water . . . 684.2
o'er l. and s. the Saviour . 700.2
flies o'er l. and s. . . . 779.1
winging over l. and s. . . 803.1
soon o'er every l. and s.. . 810.3
praises over every l. and s. . 815.c
over us, on s. or l. . . . 933.2

c *each/every land*
as he passes, e. l. . . . 159.5
abounding in e. land . . 383.1
bear the news to e. l. . . 393.1
to e. l. the ocean laves . . 393.4
streams through e. l. . . 540.1
in e. l. and clime . . . 781.2
in e. l. where man is . . 831.3
the youth of e. l. . . . 868.1
flying in e. l. unfurled . . c242

d *Isa 32:2*
rock within a weary l. . . 476.1

distant (b)

3 *land (verb)*
l. me safe on Canaan's side . 578.3
friends . . . l. safe . . . 881.2
safely l. there . . . 901.3

landscape 898.3

language
love has a l. 51.1
what l. shall I borrow . . 123.3
love's l. . . . expressed . . 211.1
bad l. disdain . . . 823.2

languid 228.1

languish-ed
how does that visage l. . . 123.1
the King of Glory l. . . 126.1
didst thou consent to l. in . 135.1
l. for thy sight . . . 172.4
l. thy descent to meet . . 216.4
where'er ye l. . . . 236.1
he l. and died . . . suffered . 289.2
why do I l. and pine . . 318.4
accents dear I l. for . . 398.2
pastures I l. to find . . 639.1
ones, who in misery l. . . 905.2

large-r-st
must bear the l. part . . 11.2
l. duties to be done . . 158.2
of Heaven a l. earnest . . 207.4
wake us . . . to l. life . . 211.2
l. petitions with thee . . 563.2
l., ampler is the air . . 878.4
filleth . . . l. increase . . 929.2

last
1 *(verb)*
guard while life shall l. . . 13.6
l. through endless day . . 48.3
summer would l. all the year . 318.2
love that l. when . . . faded . 544.3
trusting . . . life shall l. . 754.4
bliss . . . eternally shall l. . 880.2

2 *(adjective)*
sun's l. rays are fading . . 63.3
l. and fiercest strife . . 150.4
his tender, l. farewell . . 200.1
breathe . . . my l. sigh . . 589.5
be my l. thought . . . 676.2
thou, its l. resource . . 742.2
l. great battle won . . . 774.3
how . . . bear a l. farewell . 874.2
this may be the l. . . . 913.2
since we assembled l. . . 915.2
l. great conflict won . . 939.3

(first 3d)

3 *at last*
a *(re Jesus)*
yet was triumphant at l. . . 99.2
love at l. has conquered . 548.4
he'll leave me at l. . . . 712.3

b *[death]*
bring me at l. to see . . 59.4
at l. presented . . . 70.2
bring our . . . souls at l.. . 76.4
eyes at l. shall see him . . 87.5
trophies at l. I lay down . . 124.c
might go at l. to Heaven . 133.3
face I at l. shall see . . 179.4
what hath he at l. . . . 228.5
at l., all dangers past . . 375.3
at l., dear Lord, translate . 441.4
when at l. I near the shore . 598.3
lead me, lead at l. . . . 627.3
so shall it be at l. . . . 632.4
receive my soul at l. . . 737.1
so at the l. the music . . 740.3
at l. death . . . o'ertake . . 751.4
conquerors at l. . . . 802.4
warfare closed at l. . . 890.4
when we gather at l. . . 908.1
when at l. we behold . . 908.4
Heaven at l. is won . . 912.3
at l. our labour's o'er . . 934.3
at l. our journey's over . . 938.4

c *home at last*
find a. l. my h. . . . 675.3
a. l. go h. to reign . . . 686.2
friend when h. a. l. . . 709.4
a. l. go h. to thee . . . 837.6
shall reach h. a. l. . . . 882.2
a. l. . . . he will take me h. . c154

d *(spiritual peace)*
my soul was free at l. . . 366.2
rejoicing at l. . . . 395.3
by God's word at l. . . 405.2
to . . . arms at l. I flee . . 450.2
at l., I willing am . . . 509.1
all . . . at l. I will part . . 543.2
thy way at l. I see . . . 605.3
stand complete at l. . . 695.5
shall live to God at l. . . 714.2
at l., with glad surprise . . 871.3

e *(judgment)*
hate at l. must yield . . 63.2
doom comes at l. . . . 226.3
day . . . will come at l. . . 334.2
love at l. shall vanquish . . 705.4
Satan's kingdom . . . fall at l.. 802.4
give his angels charge at l. . 924.3
God's sentence upon us at l.. 928.1

4 *to the last*
spotless to the l. . . . 141.3
I'll fight to the l. . . . 684.3
we'll fight . . . to the l. . . 820.2
thy favour to the l. . . . 950

lasting
calling, to l. rest . . . 39.4
solid joys and l. treasure . 157.3
seeking . . . l. pleasure . . 227.1
l. as eternity 464.3
love and life and l. joy . . 547.c
all my l. joys . . . in thee. . 600.c
a quick yet l. choice . . 749.1
eternal joy or l. pain . . 785.6
welcome day of l. peace . 813.4
l. happiness and peace . . 857.c

late
l. in time behold him . . 82.2
it is not yet too l. . . . 267.2
see you, soon or l. . . 748.1

latent 463.3

latest
if with my l. breath . . . 60.6
chill your l. breath . . . 280.3
fighting till life's l. day . . 543.2
publish with our l. breath . 721.5
safe till my l. breath . . 724.3
my l. breath shall rend . . 877.4

lately 59.1

lathe 611.2

laud *Rom 15:11*
l. . . . his name always . . 3.3
who would not . . . l. . . 20.2
glory, l. and honour . . 690.5

laugh-ed
would look up and l. . . 491.2
now never l. at all . . . 830.1
he l. and ran 855.2
the valleys l. and sing . . 929.2
l. at impossibilities . . . c118

laughter
have we a name for l. . . 71.2
l. echoes in the street . . 664.2
l. for tears c148

launch-ed
l. upon a high adventure . 869.1

b *Luke 5:4*
fear to l. away . . . 898.2
l. out into the deep . . c137

laurels
l. of victory are waiting . . 233.3
l. are bedewed with tears . 564.3

lave
sin's wounds to l. . . . 135.4
to each land the ocean l. . 393.4

lavishing 500.1

law
a special set of l. . . . 244.3
I broke his l. 380.2
I trembled at the l. . . 405.2
my l., my love . . . 556.4
the l. it will provide . . 856.3

b *fulfil law* *(Gal 6:2)*
can f. thy l.'s demands . . 302.2
thy holy l. f. 649.2
the l. of love's demands. . 732.3

c *Rom 6:15*
I am not under l. . . . c164

d *Jer 31:33; Heb 8:10*
thy l. upon my heart . . 446.3

lawful 509.1

lay
1 *(noun)*
though feeble their l. . . 16.6
they chant this sacred l. . . 72.5
bring your . . . noblest l. . 109.3
I join the heavenly l. . . 223.5

2 *(God) lays/is laid*
l. down his sweet head . . 77.1
mild he l. his glory by . . 82.3
hands . . . l. in forgiveness . 129.3
glories didst thou l. aside . 135.1
he l. his hand on me . . 542.3
his love l. hold on me . . 547.2
Lord, l. some soul . . . c79

b *sins laid (on God)* *Isa 53:6*
every s. on him was l. . . 108.2
all our s. on thee were l. . 109.2
all my s. . . . l. upon thee . 119.c
on him our s. are l. . . 121.3
if . . . thy s. were not l. . . 271.2

c *laid [in tomb]* *John 19:42*
the grave where they l. him . 99.3
t. where thou wast l. . . 117.2
they l. the Saviour there . 145.1
d *1 Cor 3:11*
foundation . . . l. for your . 653.1
e *2 Tim 4:8*
joys l. up above . . . 387.3
l. up for you a crown . . 881.3
a crown l. up in Glory . . 899.1
bright crowns l. up . . 912.c
manger, shoulder (b)
3 *(we) lay/are laid*
a mother l. her baby . . 87.1
my faith would l. her hand . 120.3
my trophies . . . I l. down . 124.c
low at his feet l. . . . 183.2
the offerings to l. . . . 183.3
l. down, thou weary one . 332.1
l. thy weapons down . . 352.3
down at thy . . . feet I l.. . 447.2
my life I l. before thee . . 504.2
all at thy feet . . . l. . . 543.2
here I l. me at . . . feet . . 600.3
I l. . . . life's glory dead . . 621.4
all we l. before thee . . 643.3
nor will we l. our armour . 692.5
we l. all . . . weapons 701.c, 705.c
nor l. thine armour down . 812.3
won't l. down our arms . . 822.1
l. your best at Jesus' feet . 920.1
l. now our gifts before . . 922.2
your hearts l. down . . 929.3
this stone to thee . . . we l. . 945.1
b *Matt 6:20*
l. up their treasure . . . 367.1
l. up treasure in Heaven . . c249
c *lay hold* *1 Tim 6:12*
faith l. h. of . . . promise . 201.3
I l. fast h. on . . . name . . 290.1
only my need l. h. . . . 456.3
l. h. on life 718.1
d *lay aside* *Heb 12:1*
l. a. the garments . . . 417.3
l. a. all fear 805.1
e *laid [on us]*
bring the sorrow l. on me . 421.4
commands were l. upon me . 534.1
when sickness l. me low . 709.3
my heart may low be l. . . 736.1
peace of the Lord . . . l.. . 739.*
altar (e), burden (2e), charge (d), life (1c), see *lie* for *lay* as past tense

lead-ing-led
1 *(general)*
l. onward, beaming bright . 76.1
l. by a star 92.1
slowly they l. him . . . tree . 129.1
l. only further . . . 379.1
it l. to Heaven's gate . . 462.1
steeps that l. . . . Calvary . 488.2
no more shall l. . . . astray . 509.2
l. step by step to thee . . 510.1
dawn l. on another day . . 677.3
l. onward . . . to the . . . light. 777.1
Satan l. on 804.2
2 *(we) lead*
souls who l. in deed . . 5.2
l. men to truth . . . 211.3
l. the lost to Jesus' feet. . 212.3
l. weary sinners . . . 399.3
can I not l. lost souls . . 447.3
straying sheep to be l. . . 527.1
men to l. to Heaven . . 528.3
I may l. the wandering . . 612.2
leader of those who l. . . 648.1
l. them to thy open side . 720.5
daily strive to l. them . . 790.2
shall l. the wretched . . 802.2
we'll l. them to behold . . 819.1
we will help to l. them . . 866.3
the Army means to l. . . 901.5
l. by valiant hearts . . 939.1
where nobler hearts have l. . 944.2
3 *(God) leads*
a *(with title)*
soar . . . where Christ has l. . 143.5
Christ . . . first to l. . . 400.2
walk where Christ would l. . 619.4
where Jesus l. I'll follow . 687.c
Christ, the royal Master, l. . 690.1
the Lamb l. his hosts . . 708.1
God . . . l. me . . 725.3, 4
where my Lord may l. . . 740.c
God our way will truly l. . 760.4
the Lord vouchsafes to l. . 772.2
follow where Christ l. . . 805.2
saints whom God has l. . 858.2
Christ is l. us; comrades . c239
b *(general)*
he l. his children on . . 87.5
l. me to Calvary . . . 117.*
l. me, like Mary . . . 117.3
l. us in service . . . 181.1
l. me on to full salvation. . 188.1
l. us to holiness . . . 190.3
stir . . . and l. us right . . 202.4
l. me to that goal . . . 204.3
hath he marks to l. me . . 228.2
way that l. you into rest . 231.3
I know that he is l.. . . 334.2
l. me to Calvary's . . . feast . 431.3
l. me to my journey's end . 563.5
let the . . . pillar l. me . . 578.2
l. to realms on high . . 590.2
l. us to his . . . presence . 595.1
l. kindly Light . . . on . . 606.*
l. us, heavenly Father . . 607.1
l. us to grace 648.3
his army he shall l. . . 699.1
trusting in the God . . . to l. . 700.2
to l. me to the sky . . . 709.1
he/hand/God l. me! . . 725.*
thou alone shalt l. . . . 727.4
l. me where he will . . 731.c
heal the sick, and l. . . 737.3
while he l. I need not fall . 754.2
l. us back to Pentecost . . 783.3
countless hosts he l. . . 790.1
surely he shall l. us . . 803.3
and to l. us there . . . 835.2
l. us now to see in Jesus . 856.4
he alone can . . . l. me . . 857.1
thou wilt l. me upward . . 859.3
Lord, l. us on . . . 864.c
to the living fountains l. . 909.3
hast all our fathers l. . . 918.1
his providence has l. me . c147
c *always lead*
ever more be l. to thee . . 76.1
thou wilt l. me ever . . 635.3
he always l. aright . . . 759.2
l. me day by day, ever . . 837.1
d *lead to God*
way that l. t. . . . G. . . 113.2
l. us t. G., our . . . rest . 190.3
l. me to the Lamb . . 442.1, 6
the way that l. t. G. . . 462.2
all the way that l. t. G. . . 586.1
e *lead forth*
will l. his soldiers f. . . 312.2
alone can l. me f. . . . 419.3
Lord, l. us f. 708.3
l. me f. with . . . rod . . 762.2
l. us f. into the fray . . 769.3
f *lead [home]*
l. onward, l. h.ward . . 182.1
gate that is l. h.ward . . 247.2
grace will l. me h. . . 308.3
the trail l. h. . . . . 903.*
g *lead way*
Christ . . . first to l. the w. . 400.2
'tis I who l. the w.. . . 583.1
banner l. the w. . . . 702.2
God our w. will truly l. . . 760.4
h *led (passive)*
l. by grace that love . . 545.1
by our captain l. . . . 682.1
faith again is upward l. . . 711.2
by our commander l. . . 789.3
l. on by Zion's King . . 901.4
i *Ps 23:3; Rev 7:17*
ransomed soul he l. . . 53.2
l. me the quiet waters . . 54.1
l. us in those paths . . 217.2
l. me where . . . waters flow. 341.1
j *Ps 43:3*
l. me up the mountain . . 429.1
l. me higher 429.c
l. me to thy holy hill . . 453.3
thy light, let it l. me . . 457.2
l. kindly Light . . . 606.1
k *Isa 40:11*
feel thee gently l. . . . 463.2
where the shepherd l. . . 614.2
Saviour, l. me lest . . . 627.*
gently l. me all the way . . 627.1
l. me safely there . . . 641.3
like a shepherd l. us . . 845.1
gently, l. on our footsteps . 938.1
follow (2c) hand (1e) onward (c) safely (d) slaughter spirit (4d)

leader
1 *(divine)* *Isa 55:4*
share their l.'s victory . . 149.2
while I live be thou my l. . 477.4
l. of those who lead . . 648.1
hear thy trusted l. calling . 753.4
in our l.'s name . . . triumph . 804.3
with Jesus as our l. . . 810.1
with Jesus as our l. . . 814.2
proud to serve their l. . . 866.1
l. claims our praise . . 879.5
2 *(human)*
bless our l. 622.4

lean-ed-ing
if l. hard on thee . . . 325.2
weakness l. on his might . 333.2
on thy promise . . . I l. . . 437.1
on thy strength . . . I l. . . 489.3
soul that on Jesus hath l. . 653.5
l. on my Saviour's might . 686.3
l. on thy guide . . . l. . . 718.3
l. upon his faithful word. . 729.2
wholly l. on Jesus' name . 745.1
b *lean on arm*
teach me on thy a. to l. . . 713.2
l. on the everlasting a. . . 768.*
l. on his a. . . . Saviour's a. . c138
c *John 13:23; 21:20*
on thy bosom it has l. . . 508.3
while l. on thy breast . . 598.3
shall l. upon his breast . . 819.2
l. on the . . . Saviour's b. . 829.1

leap-ing
prisoner l. to lose . . . 160.3
let every heart l. forth . . 235.2
l. the frontiers . . . 864.4
b *Ps 65:12*
hills l. up in gladness . . 929.2
c *Isa 35:6*
the lame man l. for joy . . 590.3

learn-ing-t
story that the wise men l. . 80.3
creation . . . l. his . . . justice 142.5
we l. that love grows cold . 172.5

from your love . . . is l. . . 206.3
grateful l. how freely . . 256.3
since . . . l. to love it . . 358.3
'twas there I l. to pray . . 366.3
at last my sin I l. . . 405.2
nor l. thy wisdom, grace . 466.1
I would be ever l. . . . 529.2
mankind shall l. thy name . 533.3
since I l. to trust him . . 549.c
l. more of your Master . . 564.4
O to l. this lesson well . . 566.1
O may I l. the art . . . 568.3
l. of our Father's mercy . . 595.2
that we aright may l. . . 654.5
I'll l. to fight . . . foe . . 658.6
from them let us l. . . . 763.2
as he (she) l. earth's joys . 795.3
cross we gladly l. to share . 818.2
O shall we never l. . . . 827.3
l. the words of truth . . 836.4
l. both to work and pray. . 869.1
youth is l. how to pray . . 869.1
l. how best to do . . . will . c72

b *Matt 11:29*
l. from Jesus God loves . 270.3
his purpose daily l. . . 343.3

learned *(adj)*
he taught the l. doctors . 96.1
not the rich or l. or clever . 824.2

learning *(noun)*
no l. can bestow . . . 6.3
discerning its most holy l. . 655.6
wise may bring their l. . . 849.1
we have no wealth or l. . . 849.1

least
may the l. omission pain . 425.4
I have trusted l. of all . . 770.2
come when l. expected . . 913.2

b *Eph 3:8**
with the l. at . . . feast . . 375.3
though l. and lowest . . 614.3
to me, of saints the l. . . 880.3

leave-ing/left
1 *(God) leaves*
Jesus . . . l. his throne . . 52.3
thou didst l. thy throne . . 101.1
dear Lamb . . . l. his glory . 124.2
Christ . . . arose and l. . . 149.1
he l. his Father's throne . . 283.2
thou might'st l. me . . 295.2
how he l. his home in Glory . 337.1
Jesus l. the realms . . 363.2
Lord, who l. the heavens . 411.2
Jesus l. his throne above . 433.c
thou didst l. thy throne . . 538.1
how he l. his throne above . 835.2

b *John 14:27*
peace, l. with us . . . 751.1

c *not leave* *John 14:18/Heb 13:5*
n. l. us in the night . . 135.3
we were n. l. . . . to stray . 135.3
nor l. the hearts that once . 202.3
me unpardoned do not l. . 292.2
l. us nevermore . . . 299.3
thou wilt never l. me . . 325.4
he'll never, never l. me . . 344.3
this friend will never l. . . 377.1
never more thy temples l. . 438.2
while thy love is l. to me . 498.5
Saviour, do n. l. me . . 635.1
forbids me to think he'll l. . 712.3
I will never l. thee . . . c36

d *not leave alone*
l., ah! l. me n. alone . . 737.2
never l. us . . . alone to be . 938.3
he never l. me lonely . . c36
he never will l. us alone . . c122

2 *(we) leave*
a *leave [God]*
canst thou l. his pardon . . 250.3
the heavenly pathway l. . . 262.1
then l. his guiding light . . 267.1
prone to l. the God . . 313.5
I'll never l. my Saviour . . 399.2
l. the fountain-head . . 497.3
they have l. my Saviour . 498.3
never let me l. thy side . . 597.2
I cannot l. . . . flag . . 780.*
suffer me to l. thee never . 865.3
old wells, l. them no more . c40

b *leave [sin]*
consecrating, l. every s. . 197.1
anxiety . . . l. it there . 246.1, c
no other place to l. . . 246.2
if you but l. your s. . . 267.3
I l. it all with Jesus . . 333.*
dare to l. it there . . . 415.1
before his footstool l. it . 420.2
to l. earth's vanity . . . 461.1
earth's trifles l. . . . 693.c
who will l. the world's . . 707.1
l. cumbering cares . . 728.1
to l. the world below . . 901.1

c *leave all* *Mark 10:28*
l. a. for his dear sake . . 428.2
l. a. the world . . . doubts . 470.2
a. to l., and follow thee . . 498.1

net

d *leave behind*
think . . . l. him far b. . . 44.1
need not one be l. b. . . 234.1
l. b. the night . . . 682.2
weakness l. b. . . . 788.3
l. the world b. us . . . 836.2

3 *(general)*
wherefore have ye l. . . 88.2
bidst us l. the mount . . 154.5
the heritage they l. us . . 158.2
scorned him and l. him . . 245.3
they would l. my soul . . 303.2
friends may fail or l. us . . 377.1
they have l. an aching void . 442.3
the duties l. undone . . 466.4
let the world . . . l. me . . 498.3
l. the future with thee . . 501.2
l. no unguarded place . . 695.3
l. God to order all . . . 738.1
l. the rest with God . . 750.3
l. its encumbering clay . . 890.3
my friends, my soul I l. . . 917.1
many that we loved have l. . 938.4
not in my heart l. one . . c55

4 *leaves (noun)*
flourish as l. on the tree. . 8.3
l. on every bough . . . 155.2

b *Rev 22:2*
whose l. do heal . . . 346.3

led—see *lead*

left—see *leave*

legions
their l. hath dispersed . . 151.2
all hell's l.'s rout . . . 609.3
smiling amid opposing l. . 686.2
l. of darkness o'erthrow . 689.2
Hell's l. shall fly . . . 800.2
whence have come these l. . 803.2
summons its l. forth . . 864.1

leisure
heart at l. from itself . . 485.2
turning l. into treasure . . 869.1

lend
l. thy light 89.2, 3
long as thou l. me breath . 357.3

warriors l. their strength . 799.3
blest gifts thou l. me . . 861.5

length
a *Ps 21:4*
all the l. of days . . . 53.5
thine alone . . . my l. of days. 762.3
preserver through our l. . . 785.1

b *Eph 3:18*
l. and breadth and height . 55.1

c *at length*
thou, at l., decideth . . 6.4
we shall o'ercome at l. . . 9.1
renounce at l. thy . . . will . 251.3

less-er
we've no l. days to sing. . 308.4
how can I offer thee l. . . 457.c
l. of self and more . . . 548.3
all l. light will darken . . 551.1
l. than thyself will not . . 565.3

b *nothing less*
n. l. than perfect love . . 433.c
my soul can rest in n. l. . . 446.4
it shall be n. l. . . . 473.2
n. l. can be enough . . 549.3
n. l. . . . tender . . . true . 591.2
hope is built on n. l. . . 745.1
this and n. l. than this . . 774.4
give thee my best, n. l. . . c41

lesson
O to learn this l. well . . 566.1
love's sweet l. to obey . . 846.1
sweeter l. cannot be . . 846.1

lest
l. I forget . . . . 117.1, c
l. my feet should stray . . 342.2
l. we miss thy . . . goal . . 577.3
lead me, l. I stray . . 627.1, c
l. haply I should wander . 726.2
l. in our blindness . . 747.2
l. my feet for poison . . 842.2
help them l. they die . . 922.1

let
(as request) nc, but see
earth (1e), grace (2c), know (3b), light (2b, 4e, 5b), mind (1b), nothing (b), praise (3b), rejoice (c), sing (2b), soul (2c)

God's love l. him die . . 47.3
l. men hurt him so . . . 274.2
content to l. the world . . 476.3
when I l. the Saviour's pity . 548.1
will not l. . . . depart . . 572.2
we'll l. the millions know . 821.c
thou dost l. us live . . . 921.2
l. him ease the load . . c126
l. the storms pass o'er me . c145
never l. the old flag fall . . c243

b *let in*
unlock the gate . . . l. us in . 133.4
l. the victors in . . . 167.1
sinner will you l. him in . . 241.1
waiting . . . l. him in . . 250.c
l. the Master in . . . 373.c
l. in the light 408.3
mighty to save: l. him in. . 467.1
l. his little child come in . . 843.2
open . . . and l. him in . . c15
l. the dear Master come in . c18

c *let go*
all my fears I l. go . . . 507.3
Love that wilt not l. me go . 621.1
l. the shoreline go . . . c137

d *Gen 32:26*
we will not l. thee go . . 210.4
faith . . . not l. thee go . . 608.2

letters 883.2

Levite 839.2

liberated-ing
he l. love imparted 274.c
I was l. there and then 376.c

liberation
from my sins I've l. 328.1
in thee can I find l. 610.3
bring holy peace and l. 702.3

liberty
kindness . . . more than l. 265.3
l. I claimed from my sin 348.2
burdened soul found l. 405.c
struggling soul for . . . l. 415.2
fire . . . brings to me l. 420.4
if you want l., shout 427.3
healing, life and l. 456.4
life . . . is one of l. 485.4
Jesus, give . . . universal l. 593.1
no hope of l. 832.2
b *Isa 61:1; Luke 4:18*
set my heart at l. 419.3
set my soul at l. 446.4
their l. proclaim 832.1
proclaiming my l. c219
c *Gal 5:1*
in l. rejoice 324.3
l. where Christ makes free 757.5

lie-lay-lying
1 *Titus 1:2*
God speaks, who cannot l. 385.2
2
looked down where he l. 77.1
in whose . . . arms he l. 87.3
the place where Jesus l. 90.4
low in the grave he l. 148.1
where thy body l. 152.1
3 *(people) lie*
in fields as they l. 90.1
this . . . tongue l. silent 132.5
my imprisoned spirit l. 283.3
a child of loving l. 544.3
the sick . . . around thee l. 558.1
l. at the foot of the rock 639.3
if . . . I sleepless l. 671.3
let him no more l. down 676.4
still l. fondly dreaming 693.1
millions sin-bound l. 780.2
let him (her) l. at rest 792.1
a darkened ruin l. 890.3
in the grave . . . soon be l. 913.1
b *Ps 23:2*
he makes me down to l. 54.1
4 *(other)*
over and around us l. 28.1
world in . . . stillness l. 83.1
how still we see thee l. 86.1
deep crimson stains l. 237.1
when the death-dew l. cold 357.3
in me has dormant l. 463.3
thy pathway shall l. 653.4
feelings l. buried 691.3
where the shadows . . . l. 697.4
folded l. the blood and fire 774.4
in this . . . safety l. 885.1
where my possessions l. 887.1
passage through a desert l. 911.2
within thy hands they l. 922.2
deep buried . . . it l. 923.2
b *lie before*
life . . . b. us l. 718.2
the way that l. b. me 732.2
never mind what l. b. c26

life
1 *re divinity*
O L., awaking life 38.3
L. triumphant! Alleluia 146.1
O perfect L. . . . assurance 948.2
b *life of Jesus*
yielded his l. an atonement 22.1
by his l. we . . . live 102.3
pours out his l. for me 131.1
thy precious death and l. 140.3
sprung to l. this morrow 153.1
came to share our human l. 181.1
poured out his limitless l. 245.2
by his l.'s blood 330.3
whose l. no darkness knows 408.3
by thy l. . . . we live 532.1
through thy l. his l. 595.1
thine own l.-blood 707.3
living thy l. for others 870.2
c *John 10:15*
that he laid down his l. 331.1
give (1l)
d *John 14:6*
the true l. of all 8.3
find the l. supreme 27.6
thou art the l. 100.3, 4
that l. to win 100.4
thou art l., and light 171.3
l. is found alone in Jesus 240.4
the l., the truth, the way 625.6
you are . . . the l., the way 748.2
Christ, the l. and way 760.1
e *Eph 4:18*
living in the l. of God 330.3
give (1l, m), increase
2 *spiritual life*
opened the l. gate that all 22.1
road to l. and immortality 38.5
love's l. is always . . . giving 51.2
flung wide l.'s portals 130.3
raise to l. again 155.4
live with thee the . . . l. 189.4
the heavenly l. display 195.3
wake us . . . to larger l. 211.2
breathe into us the l. 218.3
death your l. might win 242.3
struggling . . . l. and liberty 415.2
l. . . . do thence derive 424.3
live the l. of holiness 431.1
receiving . . . l. and liberty 456.4
the l. that I enter 457.3
the l. . . . enthralled me 553.1
the l. . . . is growing 553.4
sorely stricken soul of l. 827.1
make for l.'s increase 827.4
seed . . . thy l. receives 936.4
real l. is beginning c106
b *[Christ] our life*
'tis l. and victory 62.3
his love is l. to me 65.3
a name for l. and light 71.2
the cross he bore is l. 168.6
find in thee my l. 287.1
more than l. to me 301.4
more than l. is Jesus 420.2
found in thee its l. 508.3
love and l. and . . . joy 547.c
my love, l.'s only sweet 556.4
Christ is thy l. . . . love 718.3
c *life divine*
the thrill of l. d. 173.3
aspire to reach the l. d. 456.2
lo, I rise to l. d. 520.5
raised in Christ to l. d. 540.4
fill us with l. d. c101
d *word of life* *John 1:1*
Jesus is the w. of l. 70.3
w. of l., supplying 655.5
e *life and light* *John 1.4**
a name for l. and l. 71.2
l. and l. to all 82.3
in that l. of l. 332.3
into the l. of his l. 378.1
the l. of l. . . . must glow 408.2
l. of l., within us 452.1
l. of my l., so surely 628.1
l., l. and love are in 647.3
gospel of l. . . . of l. c226
f *John 3:16*
'tis l. for evermore 279.3
which offers l. to all 568.2
l. which shall . . . stay 601.2
g *John 6:68*
wonderful words of l. 258.*
its words are peace and l. 830.2
h *give life* *John 10:28*
yieldeth up the gift of l. 5.3
to all l. thou givest 8.3
l. is given . . . thy name 109.1
he came to give us l. 274.c
his Spirit gave me l. 330.2
i *John 11:25*
speaks . . . l. into the dead 60.3
from death to l. has brought 180.4
l. from the dead is in 877.1
j *John 20:31*
l. . . . through thy name 109.1
we have l. in his name 351.3
k *[new] life* *Rom 6:4*
daily sending forth n. l. 63.1
fill me with l. anew 189.1
power . . . shall give n. l. 304.c
power can fashion l. anew 335.3
with a n. l. within 469.3
newness of l. to impart 589.4
flower in l. renewed 656.4
brings n. l., new hope 779.1
n. l. receiving c176
l *2 Cor 3:6*
Spirit of l. and love 15.4
his Spirit gave me l. 330.2
born of the Spirit with l. 371.2
m *1 Tim 6:12*
lay hold on l. 718.1
bring (1e), crown (2d), death (2f, g), endless (b), eternal (2c), everlasting (e), find (2i), fount (2e), gift (2b), give (1m), giving (b), immortal (b), path (c), peace (2c), river (2e), tree (2b), water (3c)
3 *life in Heaven*
fit me for l. and H. 623.4
l. from the dead is in 877.1
l. for them is l. indeed 878.2
fuller, sweeter is that l. 878.4
that fuller l. to share 880.4
the l. beyond decay 895.3
4 *individual life*
a l. made up of praise 7.1
love planned our l.'s course 51.c
King of my l., I crown 117.1
henceforth my l. may 205.*
power within our l. remain 211.2
to sever our hearts and l. 413.1
I bring my l. to Jesus 420.2
I want my l. . . . like thine 440.1
what a l. my l. must be 460.1
coming with my l. of care 470.2
my life's purpose claimed 484.3
l. of self-renouncing love 485.4
O that my l. may tell 488.1
so shall my l. . . . proclaim 494.3
my l. I lay before thee 504.2
my l. may guide men 529.1
so shall our l. . . . proclaim 533.3
may my l. a blessing be 538.4
may it be a l. of love 538.4
in purer l. thy service 567.1
let our ordered l. confess 567.4
live our l. courageously 570.1
l. will spread your peace 572.4
gird our l. . . . armoured 577.4
abide, or l. is vain 587.3
this shall rule my l. 591.3
l. that only seeks thy ways 618.2
l. more closely linked 618.2

make my l. one blazing fire . 620.3
help . . . live a spotless l. . 649.2
inspire our hearts and l. . . 827.3
God make my l. . . . . 838.*
how shall I my l. employ . 846.2
I'm going to make my l. . . 858.*
plan our l., O . . . Saviour . 863.1
I that l. to thee resign . . 865.2
my inner l. . . . may please . 867.4
will and l. are thine . . . 867.6
let my l. . . . glorify . . . 916.c
my l., my friends . . . leave . 917.1
our l. to serve 925.5
we want henceforth our l. . 933.1
l., our health, our food . . 935.3
thine . . . our l. shall be . . 939.5
our l. be cleansed . . . 943.4
touch my l. into beauty . . c37
l. possessing . . . blessing . c84
my l. thy beauty show . . c96

b *fill life*
f. thou my l., O Lord . . . 7.1
f. . . . l. with charity . . 181.3
l. shall be with gladness f. . 277.1
from sins that f. my l. . . 401.2
henceforth our l. . . . f. . 933.2, 3

c *take life*
t. my l. and let it . . . 525.1
t. the l. I fully yield. . . 531.1
t. thou my l., Lord . . . 786.c
l. and time . . . t. them all . 859.c
shouldst thou t. my l. . . 865.2

d *[testimony]*
my l. has been joyless . . 298.4
I've a l. of happiness . . 328.2
my l. flows on . . . 358.1
my l. is ever placed . . 362.2
in the ruins of my l. . . 376.2
discontented with . . . l. . 376.3
l. has point and purpose . 376.3
wonderful change in my l. . 394.1
what would now be l. . . 399.2
I lay in dust l.'s glory . . 621.4
l. surrounded is by love . . 728.3
count . . . my l. as dross . 729.1
this l. of trust, how glad . 741.4
story of my l.'s defeat . . 770.1
ours a l. of self denial . . 787.4
l. has . . . theme/intention . c173

e *life, all*
demands . . . my l., my a. . 136.4
our l., our a., this very day . 203.4
my l. my a. are his . . . 345.2
my l., my a., I bring . . 421.6
my l., my a., this blessèd . 447.2
render thee my l., my a. . 503.1
we give . . . our l. our a. . 515.1

f *all [my] life*
a. my l. . . . be fellowship . 7.4
through a. our l. be near . 12.2
goodness and mercy a. my l. . 54.5
a. my l. was wrecked . . 390.2
l. shall be wholly for thee . 473.4
a. my l. wilt thou control . 479.3
a. my l. is portioned out . 485.1
a. my l. I give thee . . 499.c
till a. my l. be love . . 516.3
do not ask . . . that a. my l. . 586.1
light o'er a. my l. be cast . 620.4
a. my l. thou shalt control . 713.1
. . . a. my l. and treasure . 859.1
for my whole l., I come . . 860.4
a. our l.'s endeavour . . 863.5

g *in my life*
wonderful change in m. l. . 394.1
in m. own l. is shown . . 435.3
his power in m. l. . . . shown 459.3
breathe within m. l. . . 479.2
in m. l. . . . thine own way . 507.3
in m. l. he may arise . . 619.4
flower in l. renewed . . 656.4
in m. l. please be . . . c85

h *[Christ's] life in me* (*Gal 2:20*)
l. in mine reveal/appear . 212.1, 2
live thy l. in me . . . 455.*
thy l. and not my own . . 479.1
his l. is mine for ever . . 495.2
share his l. through mine . 512.1
thy l. in mine is waking . . 631.4
thy l. in me be glorified . . 861.2
scatter thy l. . . . sanctify . c50

i *through life*
t. all our l. be near us . . 12.2
in joy, in grief, t. l. . . . 524.4
walk thou t. l. with me . . 628.c
throughout our earthly l. . 674.4
thou t. l. shalt save . . 714.4
grace t. l. attend me . . 865.2
throughout their l. . . . joined. 948.1

ambition, give (2e), hide (g), lose (c), spend (b), yield (2d)

j *your life*
y. l. he'll re-design . . . 44.2
is there a l. weighed down . 246.1
you may . . . live a l. . . 257.2
l. in my service be spending . 276.4
y. l. shall happy be . . . 328.3
he can take y. l. . . . 335.c
l. has been o'erclouded . . 433.1
it may cost thy l. . . . 816.2
with y. l. adore him . . 929.3

k *[his/their] life*
this mortal l. also . . . 1.4
somebody's l. . . . brighter . 384.c
would bring peace to l. . . 529.3
l. . . . in joyful harmony . . 561.3
his l. upright, his end . . 580.3
teaching sanctify their l. . 582.5
in l. and heart . . . clean. . 629.3
other l. to bring . . . 707.1
love that claimeth l. . . 707.2
other l. to win . . . 755.1
in their l. such power . . 760.1
guiding presence in his (her) l. 792.3
l. are most . . . accurst . . 919.2
their l. our own inspire . . 939.1
whate'er in l. . . . share . . 947.4
so many l. are drear . . c200

5 *life (as being)*
a *in nature*
to all l. . . . in all l. . . . 8.3
all that hath l. and breath . 19.5
awaking l. in cell . . . 38.3
greets with l. reviving . . 155.2
quickened into l. the seed . 926.2

b *in us*
be this, while l. is mine . . 187.5
restored to l. and power. . 668.1

c *Lord of life* (*Acts 3:15*)
L. of l. and glory . . . 123.2
glorious Prince of L. . . 152.3
thou, of l. the author . . 155.3
crown him the L. of l. . . 156.2
source o. l. and power . . 213.1
L. o. l. is he . . . 341.2
follow thee, o. l. the giver . 490.c
source o. l., live, dwell . . 516.3
L. o. my l., I dare . . . 628.3
L. o. l. and love . . . 789.1
L. o. my l., I come . . . 860.3

6 *life in general*
l.'s common looks and tones . 7.2
the changing scenes of l. . 21.1
daily, in the midst of l. . . 142.3
l. is a seeking . . . finding 351.2, 3
l.'s ebb and flow . . . 390.1
to blend with outward l. . 485.3
l. seem as brief as blest . . 551.3
l.'s busy mart . . . 664.3
to make this l. worthwhile . 706.3
the onward march of l. . . 731.3
trusting . . . while l. . . 754.4
l. is fleeting fast . . . 780.4

for every rule of l. . . . 785.1
tread the road of l. . . 857.2
he claims . . . for active l. . 867.3
hills and dales of l. . . 884.3
l. will pass away . . . c249

b *way of life*
walk with me in l.'s w. . . 209.2
along l.'s narrow w. . . 334.c
the varied w. of l. . . . 711.1
l. with its w. . . . lies . . 718.2
l.'s rugged w. . . . 761.1
guides me along l.'s w. . . c132

c *life's day*
till l.'s latest d. . . . 543.2
when ended l.'s short d. . 643.4
l.'s long battle-d. . . . 658.4
ebbs out l.'s little d. . . 670.2
to l.'s d. . . . unknown morrow 948.3

d *[end] of life*
e'en if l. be taken . . . 222.2
l.'s evening is closing . . 237.3
l.'s pilgrimage . . . is o'er . 400.3
follow till l.'s very end . . 491.c
the toils of l. are over . . 500.3
meet at l.'s far end . . 618.2
l.'s shadows flee . . . 632.4
guide me till l. be o'er . 635.1, 3
l.'s short race be o'er . . 709.4
when ends l.'s . . . dream . 743.4
shades of l. are falling . . 753.4
when l. sinks apace . . 763.5
l.'s long warfare closed . . 890.4
when all of l. is over . . 907.3

e *life's [difficulties]*
l. is dark without thee . . 40.4
the woes of l. o'ertake me . 112.2
we find in l.'s wilderness . 288.4
the bitter from l.'s woes . 333.2
when upon l.'s billows . . 396.1
l.'s wild, restless sea . . 428.1
l.'s burdens they are easy . 503.1
I sink in l.'s alarms . . 508.1
rest amidst l.'s conflict . . 575.3
l.'s tempestuous sea . . 598.1
in l.'s tempest . . . remember. 663.3
walking l.'s toilsome road . 675.2
ease l.'s heavy burdens . . 706.2
l.'s heaviest burden bears . 733.3
l.'s pathway runs steep . . 739.2
l.'s dark maze I tread . . 743.3
tasks of l. seem hard . . 744.1
will the toils of l. repay . . 892.3
l.'s troubles share . . . 899.1
each perplexing path of l. . 918.3
when l.'s perils . . . confound 954.3
over l.'s troubled sea . . c141
problems of l. . . . assail . c151

care (3e), sorrow (2b), storm (2b)

f *life's [pleasures]*
the triumph song of l. . . 10.4
the l. of sinning ceases . . 429.2
l. is great! . . . . 544.*
l. is lovely, free . . . 544.1
makes of l. a living psalm . 613.2
if on l. serene and fair . . 916.2
l. is . . . hopefulness . . . song c201
l.'s early splendour . . c213
l. is a song when you . . c215

life (4d)

lifeboat 375.1

lifelong 510.1

lifeless 353.4

lifetime c212

lift-ed-ing
1 *(God) lifts*
l. us to the joy divine . . 10.3

l. my thoughts above . . 32.2
to . . . l. them high . . 91.1
l. me up to Glory . . . thee . 182.3
l. me up again . . . 204.2
l. me from the miry clay . 335.c
he will l. you by his love . 336.3
he l. me . . . . 339.*
l. me up from sorrow . . 349.2
l. me from shame . . . 403.2
l. me nearer Heaven . . 421.5
thou canst l. me up again . 528.2
l. up valleys 593.4
l. up our hearts to seek . . 669.4
l. my drooping spirit up . 714.1
Lord, l. me up . . . c80
prayer gently l. me . . c94

b *lift burden*
burdens are l., blind eyes . 257.c
he l. sin's great burden . . 386.2
for burdens l. when I pray . 719.2
place for the l. of burdens . c67

c *Num 6:26*
l. . . . smile of his face . . 364.2
Lord l. up his countenance . 961

2 *(we) lift*
l. up the strain 173.c
all who l. their faces . . 181.3
hands to Heaven I l. . . 208.4
I would look up . . . and l. . 491.2
l. up the fallen . . . 691.1
l. its trembling hands . . 742.2
l. as from the heart of one . 765.5
we'll l. thy praises . . . 936.2

b *lift [banner]*
l. up the b. on high 382.c; 782.c
l. the blood-stained b. . . 696.1
bear it onward; l. it high . 697.2
l. high his royal b. . . . 699.1
the flag again is l. . . . 777.4
l. high the Army b. . . 781.2
l. up the Army b. . . . 783.c
bold they l. high their b. . 939.2

c *lift eyes* *Ps 121:1*
l. up our e. to Christ . . 38.4
l. l. mine e. 358.3
l. up thine e. and seek . 718.2
it l. its drooping e. . . 742.1
to/o'er the hills I l. my e. . 766.*
unto the hills . . . l. up . 767.1

d *lift voice* *Isa 24:14*
l. up your v. and with us . 2.1
l. thy v. and greet . . . 159.2
l. up your heart . . . v. . 164.c
Christian, l. up your v. . 334.3
saints of God, l. up your v. . 381.1
brothers, l. your v. . . 690.2

e *lift heart* *Lam 3:41*
l. up your h. . . . voice . . 164.c
l. thy h. in earnest prayer . 253.3
l. up your h. . . . accord . 408.5
l. my h., I cry . . . 647.1
Lord, I l. my h. to thee . . 717.1
I l. my h. to Heaven . . 766.3

head (2b) high (2c)

3 *(general)*
joyful music l. us 10.4
when the storm tides l. . . 280.1
till the veil be l. . . . 682.3

b *John 3:14*
see him l. up 107.3
l. up was he to die . . 118.4
once l. up to die . . . 590.2

light-ing lit
1 *natural light*
ye l. of evening 2.2
givest . . . warmth and l. . . 2.3
whose robe is the l. . . . 16.2
it shines in the l. 16.4
sun . . . and stars of l. . . 28.2
shadows fall with evening l. . 31.3
happy l. is flowing . . . 40.1
the morning l., the lily . . 42.2
with joy they hailed its l. . 76.1
we saw a wondrous l. . . 88.3
star, lend thy l. . . . 89.2, 3
it gave great l. 90.2
the l. of that same star . . 90.3
with fiery orbs of l. . . 230.2
first-born l. . . . decline . . 545.3
all the blessings of the l. . 671.1
word restores the l. . . 672.2
earth rolls onward into l. . 677.2
opening l. and evening shade. 925.4

b *Gen 1:3*
pure Father of l. 8.4
filled . . . world with l. . . 34.3
born of the one l. . . . 35.3
thy voice commanded l. . . 36.1

c *[darkness]/light* *Ps 139:12*
the d. shineth as the l. . . 453.1
d. and l. are both alike . . 674.3
where he is . . . all is l. . . 772.4

ray (b)

2 *[God] as light*
though thou veil thy l. . . 40.4
l. of l., shine o'er us . . 40.4
yonder shines the infant l. . 75.2
thou its l., its joy . . . 76.5
now we see thy l. arising . 185.3
quench thy sevenfold l. . . 202.4
l. of life, within us . . . 452.1
be thou the l. the stars . . 486.2
lead, kindly L. 606.1
O L. that followest . . . 621.2
yonder shines the l. . . . 641.3

b *1 John 1:5*
pure Father of l. 8.4
Spirit of l. explore . . . 196.5
God is our l. . . . sunshine . 316.1
O God of l., . . . love . . 446.1
God himself is l. . . . 465.5

c *[Jesus] as light*
a L. came out of darkness . 94.1
Jesus . . . our l. and hope . 94.1
l. of the sinner in ways . . 175.3
Jesus is my l. 387.1
Jesus is my l. and song . . 400.*
be their l. and guide . . 582.2
Jesus . . . sure, unerring l. . 597.1
Saviour of l., I look . . 628.1
dare not boast, O Lord of l. . 747.2
O the blessèd Lord of l. . . 819.2
thou art of l. . . . fount . . c98
my l., my Saviour, Jesus . c181

d *everlasting light* *Isa 60:19*
shineth the e. l. 86.1
Heaven's eternal l. . . . 168.2
Eternal L.! Eternal L.! . . 414.1
may dwell in the eternal l. . 414.5
leading . . . to the e. l. . . 777.1

e *light of* *John 8:12*
l. of the straying . . . 236.2
came as the l. of new hope . 245.1
I am this dark world's l. . . 332.3
Jesus, L. of God, now show . 429.3
fount . . . l. of men . . 602.1
shed . . . thy holy l. . . 602.4
the l. of the world is Jesus . c203

life (2e), shed (2c), true (d)

3 *(figurative)*
silent as l. 8.2
the l. of sacred story . 112.1, 5
shine with unborrowed l. . 154.1
l. of . . . victory . . . 173.1
come as the l. . . . reveal . 217.2
through the morning l. . . 280.4
dungeon flamed with l. . . 283.3
shades . . . to plains of l. . 339.c
a thousand rays of l. . . 658.3
forward into l. 682.2
gleaming in the l. . . . 698.2
shining l. of home . . . 740.3
stains brought to l. . . 893.1
sowing . . . by the fading l. . 931.1
sown in the l. . . . 931.c
strew . . . with golden l.. . 938.2
evening when l. are low . . c123

b *Ps 104:2*
in l. inaccessible hid . . 8.1
the splendour of l. hideth . 8.4
who reigns in l. above . . 465.1
dwells in cloudless l. . . 465.2

c *(re Heaven)*
need they no created l. . . 76.5
angels in robes of l. . . 117.2
all the hosts of l. . . . 141.2
forth in robes of l. . . . 145.2
up the steeps of l. . . . 167.1
joy and l. of thy home . . 300.4
blessèd land of l. . . . 320.c
way to that city of l. . . 406.1
perfect in that land of l. . . 466.5
Zion beams with l. . . . 682.1
in robes of l. arrayed . . 701.4
march by the river of l. . . 708.1
mansions of glory and l.. . 808.4
sing . . . ye saints of l. . . 809.4
angels . . . wear crowns of l.. 872.c
with its mansions of l. . . 883.3
side of the river of l. . . 886.1
foremost of the sons of l. . 909.1

4 *spiritual light*
fill us with the l. of day . . 10.1
though thou veil thy l. . . 40.4
gild . . . with the l. we need . 193.3
word of God and inward l. . 194.1
then left his guiding l. . . 267.1
there were tokens of his l. . 330.1
leaneth . . . all is l. . . . 333.2
on my path his l. . . . 347.3
let me see the l. . . . 374.1
leading . . . from the l. . . 379.1
I have l. in my soul. . . 394.1
where I first saw the l. . . 395.*
God has sent his glorious l. . 408.1
let in the l. 408.3
his l. will judge . . . 408.3
till thou inward l. impart. . 412.3
up where l. increases . . 429.2
'tis for l. . . . I'm appealing . 434.2
l. some pain is bringing . . 434.4
l. to shine upon the road . 442.1
purer l. shall mark . . . 442.6
pour . . . Spirit's pure l. . . 457.1
give l. to cheer . . . 575.3
Calvary and Easter l. . . 613.3
its l. o'er all my life . . 620.4
our hope of guidance . . . l. . 692.4
l. to guide us here below . 711.3
inward peace and inward l. . 716.2
lead them to . . . precious l. . 819.1
nor any gleam of l. refuse . 871.3
while the l. . . . is falling. . 893.c
let thy l. guide us . . . 937.2
opened my eyes to the l. . c159
breaks a l. divine . . . c191
thy Kingdom of l. may see . c236

b *light and . . .*
enfold . . . its l. and power . 141.5
l. and comfort from above . 190.1
bring the l. and glory in . . 203.2
l. and the glory . . . stream . 233.1
into thy . . . gladness and l. . 300.1
glorious news, liberty and l. . 499.4
new power I want . . . and l.. 620.1
l. and joy receiveth . . 655.1
gives me heat and l. . . 733.5

c *light and love*
bliss is beaming l. and l. . 112.3
thou art . . . l. and l. . . 171.3
l. and love divine . . . 232.1

from above with l. and love . 445.4
I sought for love . . . and l. . 541.1
l., life and l. are in . . . 647.3
fountain of l. and love . . 651.1
a cross of l. and l. . . 705.2

d *in light*
followed Jesus in the l. . . 5.2
dwell in his marvellous l. . 166.2
I am climbing in the l. . . 369.c
I'm living in the l. . . . 374.c
while in thy l. I stand . . 415.3
in thy l. I see 429.c
in thy l. seems poor . . 435.2
in the l. of God . . . 464.*
marching on in the l. . . 811.1
stand in the l. . . . 893.*
into . . . wondrous l. of God . c160

e *Gen 1:3*
let there be l. . . . 224.*
let there now be l. . . 651.3
let there be l. today . . 669.1

f *light and truth* *Ps 43:3*
the l. of t. . . . display . 190.2
send out thy l. . . 457.1, 2
give us l. thy t. to see . . 466.1
l. would be ours his t. . . 760.4

g *Ps 119:105*
in the l. of his word . . 397.1
then its l. directeth . . 655.3
afford a sanctifying l. . . 657.1
gives a l. to every age . . 657.2
follow the l. of his word. . 734.1

h *John 3:19*
we shunned the l. . . . 135.3
and close . . . against the l. . 251.1

i *darkness/light* *Acts 26:18; 1 Peter 2:9*
turned thy d. into l. . . 110.2
my d. he's turned into l.. . 322.4
my d. was turned into l.. . 395.2
from d. . . . into the l. . . 535.2
turn . . . its d. into l. . . 674.3
turns your d. into l. . . 790.3
turn . . . from d. into l. . . 821.2
through the d. into . . . l. . 938.4
coming . . . out of d. into l. . c4
brought me . . . d. into l. . . c160

j *2 Cor 4:4*
gospel of life . . . l. . . c226

k *2 Cor 4:6*
darkness the l. of thy face . 288.4
walk in the l. of thy face. . 372.2
l. hath on thee shone . . 465.3
let thy l. for ever shine . . 516.3
the l. of his face is on me . 542.4
worship . . . l. of his face . 640.5
may l. upon me shine . . 658.5
the l. of his love shines . . 758.4
love-l. of Jesus' face . . 848.2
give the l. of the knowledge . c158

l *Rev 21:23*
Heaven's eternal l. . . . 168.2
within the l. of Heaven . . 415.5
searching l. of Heaven . . 434.3

m *[no] light*
no l., no hope had we . . 94.1
no beacon l. before . . 375.1
no ray of l. 719.4
no l. may shine . . . 761.1
though . . . no ray of l. . . 772.3
l. may never shine . . . 868.3
clear (2b), fill (2d), heavenly (d),
reveal (e), stream (2b), walk (2f)

5 *(people as light)*
with its human l. . . . 141.4
oft thy l. burns low . . 723.2
make my life a little l. . . 838.1
shine with a clear, pure l. . 841.1
if our l. is dim . . . 841.2

b *Matt 5:16*
spread thy l. wherever . . 426.3
let my l. shine that souls . 523.3
Lord, let my l. so shine . . 538.5
so shall our l. be shed . . 688.4

c *Luke 12:35*
l. along the shore . . . 478.*

6 *(other)*
when all other l. fade . . 237.2
no other l. . . . could see . 490.1
all lesser l. will darken . . 551.1

7 *light-ing (verb)*
wisdom l. all mysteries . . 530.2
to l. the holy flame . . 624.1
torch that l. . . . gloom . . 683.5
he l. the evening star . . 935.2

b *light way*
he l. the darkest w. . . 48.3
l. our pathway from day . 316.1
Jesus l. our way up . . 316.c
l. the w. that leads. . . 462.2
l. my w. to Calvary . . 486.1

8 *(adjective)*
with such l. feet . . . 551.3
slumbers, pure and l. . . 676.5

b *Matt 11:30*
makes each burden l. . . 320.2
cross . . . seem l. to bear . 551.3
make the heavy burden l. . 755.3

lighten
Jesus in love will l. . . 186.3
love will l. every care . . 503.3
l. my brother's load . . 675.2
l. his load, and prove . . 706.2
it will your burdens l. . . 805.2

lighter
somebody's care will be l. . 384.c
my work will grow l. . . 758.4
bid me . . . seek a l. cross . 780.1

lighthouse
like a l. evermore . . . 63.3
from his l. evermore . . 478.1

lightning
Lord of l.'s livid line . . 30.2
when l. flash 39.2
l. rend the skies . . . 126.3
loosed the fateful l. . . 162.1

like
1 *re objects*, nc, but
a *like sheep* *Isa 53:6*
when l. . . . s. we strayed . 4.2
l. a crowd of frightened s. . 265.1
l. to a lamb . . . strayed. . 740.1

b *like a river*
grace is flowing l. a r. . . 239.3
salvation l. a r. rolls . . 254.2
when peace l. a r. . . . 771.1
joy l. a r. . . . will flow . 906.3
see refs listed under *as*

2 *re people*
l. a warrior . . . come . . 338.5
rise, l. men renewed . . 408.2
thou art not like them . . 498.3
simple trust l. theirs . . 567.2
let us, l. them, rise up . . 567.2
though l. a wanderer . . 617.2
stand l. the brave . 684.c; 689.*
l. to those martyrs . . 686.1
l. them, will take my stand . 686.2
l. a mighty army . . . 690.3
hearts l. heroes . . . 704.1
l. to a pilgrim/child . 740.2, 3
l. him to answer . . . 839.3
Abraham (b) Mary

b *(personal)*
who l. thee . . . should sing . 17.1
folk l. me and you . . . 71.c
l. us he grew/knew . . 87.4
saved a wretch l. me . . 308.1
pardon . . . rebel l. me . . 331.*
sinners lost l. me and you . 335.1
once a child l. me . . . 840.2
save (1)

c *like [God]*
we can be l. him . . . 51.3
made l. him, l. him we rise . 143.5
saints l. him shall die . . 149.2
grace which, l. the Lord . . 157.2
l. thy Spirit, gladly given . 211.3
a heart l. thine . . . divine . 426.1
a heart l. this bestow . . 426.1
want my life to be l. thine . 440.1
l. him thou shalt be . . 458.2
none do I love l. thee . . 486.2
none can console l. thee . 486.3
make us l. thee . . . 515.4
more l. thee . . . 584.1, 3
no tender voice l. thine . . 587.1
O to be l. thee . . . 623.*
who l. thyself my guide . . 670.3
l. him, with pardon . . 701.2
ever have a friend l. this. . 709.1

d *Ps 103:13*
Father-l. he tends . . . 17.3

e *Isa 46:9*
who is a God l. unto thee . 724.2

f *love like*
a love l. this . . . bestow . 426.2
I in love may be l. thee . . 455.1
O may I love l. thee . . 568.3
love . . . a zeal l. thine . . 720.5
from love l. this no power . 854.3
power of a love l. thine . . c48
dying love l. thine . . . give . c83
feel (2i), grow (3d), heart (6d),
Jesus (9e), shepherd (1b)

3 *(verb)*
would you l. some peace . 244.2
l. to be able to say . . . 388.4
l. to have been with them . 794.1
l. them to know . . . 794.3
how I'd l. to see . . . take . 884.1

likeness *Ps 17:15; Rom 6:5*
his l. shall see . . . 458.2
send down thy l. . . . 516.4
faithful heart, l. to thee . . 524.3
attain more l. . . . to thee . 589.2
thy perfect l. to wear . . 623.1
O Son, may I thy l. gain. . 958.1

lily
a *Song 2.1*
he's the l. of the valley . 344.1, c
Jesus, l. of the valley . . c43

b *(Matt 6:28)*
morning light, the l. white . 42.2
in the beauty of the l. . . 162.4

limit-s-less
poured out his l. life . . 245.2
false l. of our own . . . 265.5
wondrous love without a l. . 439.1
the l. of human endeavour . 501.3
own appointed l. keep . . 569.1
his love has no l. . . . 579.3
overcoming by l. grace . . 640.5
to grace there is no l. . . 770.3

line
beyond the ocean's l. . . 27.1
the l. and circles . . . 27.2
Lord of lightning's . . . l. . 30.2
ways of God its l. record . 656.1

b *Isa 28:17; Amos 7:7,8*
thy plummet and thy l. . . 446.2

c *Luke 2:4*
born, of David's l. . . . 93.3

linger-ing
angels are l. near . . . 226.2
our God in pity l. still . . 251.3
all who l., all who fall . . 262.1
why should we l. . . . 264.2
the glory l. near . . . 320.3
in perplexity we . . . l. . . 711.2
untold glories l. there . . 873.1
we . . . l. o'er familiar ways . 874.1
l. shivering on the brink . . 898.2
at thy feet I still l. . . . c37

linked-ing
l. sense to sound . . . 28.3
more closely l. with thee . 618.2

lion *Heb 11:33; 1 Peter 5:8*
give peace when l. roar . . 575.3
the l.'s gory mane . . . 701.3
where furious l. roar . . 911.2
Judah

lip
1 *re Jesus*
l. with thirst are dried . . 121.2
from thy l. his word . . 595.1
we are the l. of Christ . . 851.4
2 *(general)*
l. that we might tell . . 25.4
hearts and l. shall prove . . 36.6
songs do now his l. employ . 62.3
from the l. of sinners . . 141.3
unfaltering l. and heart . . 297.6
sins my l. confessing . . 460.2
outward l. confess . . 496.2
take my l. and let them . . 525.3
nor . . . to those l. attend . 588.3
than all my l. may utter . . 591.2
that infant l. can try . . 625.3
guard thou the l. . . . 674.2
l. are making . . . heard . . 677.4
that l. of thousands lift . . 765.5
tell them with your l. . . 829.c
he claims my l. . . . 867.4
Jesus' name upon their l. . 874.3
praise (3d), touch (c)

lisp-ing
poor l. stammering tongue . 132.5
children early l. his fame . 661.2

list-en/ed-ing
music . . . heard by l. man . 27.3
to my l. ears 42.1
O l. to his voice . . . 248.4
l. to the loving call . . . 258.2
if they l. to his voice . . 324.3
Jesus, l. can hear . . . 387.2
l., belovèd, he speaketh . . 542.4
I am l., Lord, for thee . 614.1, 4
l. every moment to . . . call . 757.4
speak to make me l. . . 862.3
I am l. at thy feet . . . c100

little
a *re Jesus*
the l. Lord Jesus . . . 77.*
Jesus Christ her l. child . . 87.1
he was l., weak . . . 87.4
cam'st a l. baby thing . . 91.1
thou wast once a l. child . 793.4
b *(general)*
one l. word shall fell him . 1.3
each l. flower . . . bird . . 25.1
the l. cares which fretted . 41.1
O l. town of Bethlehem . . 86.1
with l. fervour wrought . . 466.4
content to fill a l. space . . 485.3
l. strength to call my own . 489.3
a l. shrine . . . a l. place. 615.2, 3
our l. stock improve . . 662.2
to a l. home in Bethany . . 663.2
smooth for l. feet . . . 664.2
ebbs out life's l. day . . 670.2
a l. of earth's dross . . 780.1
God make my life a l. . . 838.*
the l. Levite, kept . . . 839.2
like a l. candle . . . 841.1
we'll bring the l. duties . . 849.3
we have given l. . . . 921.1
scatter a l. sunshine . . c200
c *little all*
I yield to thee my l. all . . 108.3
though your all is very l.. . 920.3
d *little ones*
let the l. o. come . . . 794.1
how pure . . . his l. o. . . 840.2
l. o. to him belong . . . 843.1
how . . . happy his l. o.. . 844.2
child (2b), children (1b), hand (2c)

live-est-s-eth-d-ing
1 *(God) lives*
in all life thou l. . . . 8.3
he l. for our salvation . . 96.4
l. as a homeless stranger . 97.2
tell how he l. again . . 99.3
all may know thou l. still . 138.1
l., though ever crucified . 142.4
l. again our . . . King . . 143.4
he l. . . . . . . 144.*
he l., I know . . . 149.c
and l., that death may die . 156.2
l. to plead our cause . . 242.c
he l. who once was dead . 249.4
I know that he is l.. . . 334.1
ask me how I know he l. . 334.c
l. and died and rose . . 445.3
thou again to l. hast come . 513.3
he rose and now l. . . . 687.3
l. thy life for others . . 870.2
l., he loved me . . . c185
b *[Jesus] lives*
l. on earth our Saviour . . 87.2
the Lord shall l. again . . 103.4
Jesus hath l., hath died . . 116.5
Jesus, my redeemer, l. . . 144.4
for her Lord now l. . . 152.2
lo! the Christ is l. . . . 155.1
Jesus l. to help and save . 242.1
Jesus, thy righteousness, l. . 271.4
Jesus l. and loves me . 286.c, 4
Christ Jesus l. today . . 334.c
Jesus l. to keep me . . 347.2
the Lord, my Saviour, l. . . 358.2
Jesus l. and forgives . . 420.3
tell to all . . . Jesus l. . . 760.1
c *ever lives* *Heb 7:25*
O e.-l. Lord 36.6
he e. l. above . . . 106.2
l. for e. with his saints . . 148.c
and e. l. to save . . . 149.1
word of the e.-l. God . . 654.4
l. again to intercede . . c193
d *live [with] in* *(Gal 2:20)*
rose . . . l. in my heart . . 125.c
more sensibly within me l. . 207.4
he l. within my heart . . 334.c
want thee . . . to l. in . . 436.1
have thee ever with me l. . 447.2
l. thy life in me . . . 455.*
Christ only . . . l. in me . . 487.4
l., dwell and move in me . 516.3
in me thou dost l. . . . 523.3
for lo! he l. with me . . 562.3
he l. with me . . . ever near . c167
Christ that l. in me . . . c177
e *love lives*
l. will l. on . . . . 51.*
l. the . . . way of l. . . 544.4
l. that l. through death . . 631.2
heart (7e), redeemer (c)
2 *(we) live*
that all who l. may feed . . 39.1
till all creation l. . . . 142.5
all with whom we . . . l.. . 624.3
a shining new chance to l. . 666.1
as we have l., so . . . gain . 785.6
when the nations l. . . 833.1
each day that we l. . . 928.2
b *(without Christ)*
could not l. w. him . . 65.3
no longer . . . l. from thee . 108.3
in darkness l. all the while . 253.1
not worth l. w. him . . 420.2
w. thee I cannot l. . . 676.3
c *(with Christ)*
a name to l. by . . . 71.1
all may come . . . and l.. . 234.3
believe, and thou shalt l. . 255.2
thy Saviour bids thee l. . . 256.3
l. a life that's true . . . 257.2
look and l. 271.c
let me drink and l. . . . 282.3
stoop down and drink and l. . 332.2
l. and believing . . . 352.2
l. rejoicing every day . . 365.c
I'm l. in the light . . . 374.c
I l. a moment at a time . . 385.4
l. with Jesus all the time . 402.1
those l. at his feet . . . 413.1
can l. and look on thee . . 414.1
l. beneath the shade . . 427.c
l. the life of holiness . . 431.1
help me to l. and do . . 431.2
while I l. . . . my leader . . 477.4
thine I l., thrice happy . . 492.3
shall rise and l. again . . 512.3
O to l. exempt from care . 566.5
l. our lives courageously . 570.1
to l. the words we say . . 572.1
let me thy witness l. . . 597.4
on thee alone I l. . . . 616.2
I may l., from day to day . 618.2
to l. a spotless life . . . 649.2
l. more nearly as we pray . 668.5
l. above feeling . . . 773.4
make it l. again. . . . 827.1
dead to self we truly l. . . 922.3
joy is mine, I l. each day. . c196
devotion every day we l. . c213
d *John 11:25*
dead . . . yet shall he l. . . 277.1
hast made . . . dead to l. . 353.5
I was dead, but now I l.. . 546.1
let the dying l. . . . 575.c
dying sinners pray to l. . . 945.2
e *Phil 1:21*
be it Christ hence to l. . . 771.3
f *1 John 4:9*
by his life we all may l. . . 102.3
know not that by me they l. . 140.1
all the world . . . may l.. . 140.2
to die that I might l. . . 221.1
all may l. for Christ . . 239.3
we l. by thee . . . 648.2
by thee we l., on thee . . 692.3
by thy bounty . . . l. . . 921.2
g *live for*
men can l. f. others . . 50.2
I l. f. thee alone . . . 208.3
fixed to l. and die f. thee . 210.3
now I l. f. Christ . . . 391.3
f. thee, O Master, . . . l. . 519.4
l. but f. the skies . . . 661.3
longer l. f. this alone . . 720.3
inspire . . . l. f. Christ . . 760.1
l. f. thee 'gainst . . . foe . 933.3
every moment to l. f. thee . c33
h *live to/that*
l. t. make men free . . 162.4
l. a dying world t. save . . 203.4
l. daily . . . t. sing . . . 281.4

l. t. do his will 391.3
l. daily your duty t. do . . 679.1
l. t. preach thy word . . 720.4
l. t. answer thy call . . 786.2
l. . . . thy servant t. be . . c49
l. t. all men . . . see . . c59
l. right t. God may use . . c71
l. t. men may see thyself . c72

i *live in [Christ]*
all who l. i. love are thine . 10.3
now i. thee begin to l. . . 207.2
l. i. the life of God . . 330.3
now I l. i. him . . . 332.2
i. his . . . presence l. . . 336.2
l. i. the fountain . . . 352.1
we who l. i. . . . new day . 408.1
fight, and i. thee l. . . 424.3
l. i. him for lost mankind . 451.1

j *Gal 2:19*
may l. and sing to thee . . 151.5
to Christ . . . resolved to l. . 480.4
day by day to thee I l. . . 566.4
joy, l. unto thee . . . 630.3
shall l. to God at last . . 714.2

k *Gal 2:20*
though I l. may it be . . 479.1
by thy life and grace we l. . 532.1
it's no longer I that l. . . c177

die (1b), faith (2c), glory (4g), help (1k), sight (1d)

3 *live in Heaven* *1 Thess 5:10*
fit us for Heaven to l. . . 77.3
l. with thee the . . . life . . 189.4
wonderful 'twill be to l. . . 583.5
eat and l. with thee above . 650.2
shall with me in Glory l. . . 797.2
then l. with him on high . . 844.4
Lord, we shall l. with thee . 897.2

b *live [for ever]* *John 6:51*
I'll l. with him f. e. . . 309.3
there to l. eternally . . 328.3
l. with him f. e. after . . 399.2
if . . . they'd l. f. e. . . 824.1

4 *(general)*
love will l. on . . . . 51.*
something l. in every hue . 545.2

lives (noun) see *life* (6e, f)

livid 30.2

living
1 *(noun)*
the joy of l. 10.3
there is mission in my l. . 463.1
for the l. of these days . . 577.2
succour to the l. . . . 655.5
what . . . to justify my l. . 706.3

holy (3c)

2 *(adjective)*
all things l. he doth feed. . 34.5
l. streams of . . . worth . . 312.2
a l. cross this was to be. . 490.1
in l. echoes of thy tone . . 612.1
makes of life a l. psalm . . 613.2
arrayed in l. green . . . 887.2
stand dressed in l. green . 898.2
all things l. . . . good . . 927.1

bread (g), coal, faith (2e), fire (2d), flame (2c), fountain (2b), sacrifice (2c), stone (2e), water (3e), way (1f), word (1e)

3 *re divinity*
O loving, l. Lord . . . 36.4
O ever-l. Lord . . . 36.6
to loose thy l. presence . . 181.4
Christ, the l. vine . . . 361.1
see . . . l. Christ, in me . . 479.1
praise that loving, l. man . 544.5
pants for thee, O l. Word . 650.1
precious, l., loving Lord . . 729.c
l. Christ, who . . . share. . 827.4
a l. bright reality . . . c90

b *living God* *Ps 42:2**
be the l. God my friend . . 464.4
consecrated unto the l. G. . 495.1
thee, my God, the l. God . 557.2
as offer to the l. God . . 588.2
word of the ever-l. God . . 654.4
long for thee, the l. God . 762.2

c *2 Cor 3:3*
thou Spirit of the l. God . . 198.3
Spirit of the l. God, fall afresh c53

head (1c)

lo nc, but
a *Matt 28:20*
lo, I am with you, keeps us . 700.3

load
who . . . gives me heavy l. . 204.2
can bear my awful l. . . 297.2
faint 'neath their l. . . 351.1
burdened with a l. of care . 396.2
shared . . . their heavy l. . 398.3
bring the l. that wearies . . 421.3
cast my l. on . . . grace . . 449.3
cumbered with a l. of care . 645.3
lightened my brother's l. . 675.2
groan beneath their l. . . 696.2
lighten his l., and prove . . 706.2
strive to cast away the l. . 816.1
let him ease the l. . . . c126
when . . . oppressed by my l. c135

b *load of sin*
our heavy l. of s. . . . 127.4
he who bore your l. of s. . 241.1
bowed . . . beneath a l. of s. . 284.3
did take the l. of s. . . 309.c
the l. of s. that burdened . 340.3
remove this l. of s. . . 563.3

loath 488.2

loaves *Matt 14:19* . . . 650.1

lofty-iest
look down from l. mountain . 37.2
set our feet on l. places . . 577.4
Mount Pisgah's l. height . 633.3
higher than the l. climb . . 766.2

lone-ly
a *re Jesus*
l., forsaken, our sinbearer . 130.4
l. and dreary, faint . . 607.2
upon a l. height . . . 705.2
l. river thou didst cross . . 726.4

b *(general)*
guiding l. . . . seamen . . 63.3
on the l. mountain steep . 88.2
for the l. and forsaken . . 555.2
what if dark and l. days . . 586.3
erring children lost and l. . 612.1
to tread a l. way . . . 719.2
l. work he cannot shirk . . 801.2
tell the . . . sad and l. . . 829.2
he never leaves me l. . . c36
so many hearts are l. . . c200

lone(li)ness
cry of God-forsaken l. . . 122.2
though in l. we sow . . 145.3
careless of our l. . . . 238.2
soon in solemn l. . . . 325.4
l. and loss he bore for me . 451.2
when in l. . . . look down . 582.3

long-ed-ing
1 *(verb)*
oft l. I've stood . . . 298.5

b *long for*
thine exiles l. f. home . . 167.3
heart . . . l. f. pardon . . 247.1
l. f. the waters . . . 351.1
all we have l. f. . . . 351.3
you may l. f. the robes . . 406.3
eager eyes are . . . l. . . 478.2
l.-f. resemblance . . . 589.2
l. f. thy voice . . . 614.1
l. f. comfort of . . . arm . 740.1
I l. f. the joys . . . 794.3

c *Ps 42:1*
so l. my soul, O Lord . . 557.1
I l. for thee . . . God . . 762.2

d *Ps 119:174*
l. for a full salvation . . 197.1
still l. for . . . salvation . . 257.2

e *2 Tim 4:8*
ye who l. for his appearing . 875.2

f *long to*
l. t. be like Jesus . . . 94.2
l. perfect peace t. win . . 227.2
I l. t. be set free . . . 307.3
Jesus, I l. t. be . . . whole . 436.1
feebly l. thy face t. see . . 466.3
l. t. sever 501.1
wholly thine, I l. t. be . . 509.1
I l. t. be nearer to thee . . 521.1
the heart l. t. know . . 527.3
I l. t. rise in the arms . . 585.1
bread . . . I l. t. share . . 631.4
I l. t. reside 639.1
l. t. build thy house . . 720.1
we l. t. see your face . . 748.1
heart is l. t. confide . . c62
only like Jesus I l. t. be . . c68

g *long to feel*
powerful stamp I l. t. f. . . 214.4
that holiness I l. t. f. . . 419.1
I l. t. f. thy . . . touch . . 610.1

2 *(adjective)*
why are my winters so l. . 318.4
l. is the road 351.1
life's l. battle-day . . . 658.4
battling through the l. day . 663.1
the strife will not be l. . . 699.4
let the road be l. . . . 716.1
tasks of life seem . . . l.. . 744.1
l. and warring years . . 774.1
l. the fight and dreary . . 802.4
fierce and l. the battle . . 804.4
when the . . . warfare l.. . 876.4
the l. cloud of witnesses . 879.5
life's l. warfare closed . . 890.4
l. patience follows toil . . 923.2
through life's l. journey . . 938.1

b *long way*
o'er the l. w. . . . my stay . 467.4
however steep the w., and l.. 719.5
you may find the w. is l.. . 817.1
forget how hard the w. and l. c208

3 *(adverb)*
watching l. in hope . . . 75.3
the Saviour promised l. . . 81.1
the world has suffered l. . 83.2
souls l. prisoned . . . 155.4
races l. severed . . . 166.2
I waited l. and patiently . . 229.2
sins, l. hated 250.2
l. my imprisoned spirit . . 283.3
l. withstood . . . provoked . 286.2
I have . . . proved him l.. . 343.1
sin that l. had enslaved . . 349.3
grace I l. have slighted . . 361.1
light . . . I l. had sought. . 394.1
you have l. been hesitating . 433.2
past was l. forgiven . . 434.3
l. shall my praises ascend . 454.5
l. my heart possessing . . 460.2
l. thou . . . pleaded in vain . 473.1
fears that l. have bound. . 577.2

powers . . . l. have sought . 760.3
l. may they make . . 942.2
l. our Saviour triumph . . 942.2
you've carried it l. . . . c31
b *long-*
thou l.-expected Jesus . . 79.1
bless thy l. deluded sight . 251.2
view the l.-promised land . 766.3
loud (b)
4 *(in phrases)*
your age-l. plan . . . 38.3
not for l. the grave . . 145.2
of a day l. past we speak . 198.2
called me l. before . . 339.2
in days l. past . . . seat . . 590.1
I have loved l. since . . 606.3
'twill cease before l. . . 712.4
b *[as] long as*
as l. as thou lendest . . 357.3
so l. as 'tis written . . . 763.2
c *so long*
never a night so l. . . . 186.1
waiting so l. . . . set free . 276.3
talents, so l. withheld . . 482.1
bonds, so l. enchaining . . 539.2
the joy, I sought so l. . . 547.1
so l. thy power hath blest . 606.3
d *too long*
too l. at ease in Zion . . 482.2
too l. mistrust and fear . . 827.2
ago, day (2i)

longer-st
as the journey grew l. . . 553.2
l. live for this alone . . 720.3
fleeting are our l. days . . 874.1
why l. in your sin remain . 885.4
b *no longer*
I can n. l. fear . . . 106.5
n. l. can I live from thee . 108.3
n. l. bound to distant . . 142.2
bid thee n. l. roam . . 250.5
when Jesus n. l. I see . . 318.1
n. l. in dread . . . I pine . . 364.2
reject the gift n. l. . . 410.2
n. l. on the threshold . . 433.2
from thee n. l. can I stay . 450.1
I'll keep back n. l. . . . 473.2
I n. l. will doubt thee . . 473.4
n. l. in bondage . . . 640.3
treasures n. l. allure . . 640.4
sit n. l. idly by . . . 696.1
it's n. l. I that liveth . . c177
c *no longer mine*
gladly, now n. l. mine . . 504.2
mine n. l., thine just now . 510.4
n. l. mine, but thine . . 516.2
it shall be n. l. mine . . 525.5
n. l. shall they be mine . . 786.3
delay (b)

longing
1 *(noun)*
may no l. of our own . . 5.3
a l. fills my bosom . . . 94.1
spirit's strange deep l. . . 325.3
fills my every l. . . . 390.c
my soul's greatest l. . . 493.1
satisfy my deepest l. . . 531.3
grant me now my spirit's l. . 548.4
this is my constant l. . . 623.1
his l. for the true . . . 760.3
2 *(adjective)*
into this my l. breast . . 201.c
eager and l. desire . . . 351.2
with anxious, l. thirst . . 447.1
b *longing eyes*
revive our l. e. . . . 172.4
whispered words and l. e. . 544.3
I lift up my l. e. . . . 767.1
c *longing heart*
my l. h. vouchsafe to make . 55.5
joy of every l. h. . . . 79.2
come . . . into every l. h. . 210.1
enter every l. h. . . . 438.1
exchange . . . my poor l. h. . 448.3
my l. h. shall own thy sway . 636.3
my l. h. inspire . . . 649.3
d *longing soul/spirit* *Ps 107:9*
l. s. is all thine own . . 208.3
enter every l. s. . . . 218.c
set my l. s. free . . . 480.2

look-ed-ing
1 *(God) looks*
Jesus l. o'er Galilee . . 103.1
Jesus is l. for thee . . . 247.c
Jesus, l. to thy faithfulness . 407.2
l. on this . . . heart. . . 440.1
l. upon a little child . . 793.1
his kind l. when he said . . 794.1
at his l., prepare to flee . . 875.3
b *look down*
l. down from the sky . . 77.2
l. down and see . . . host . 203.1
in thy love l. down . . . 582.3
God, l. down, . . . crown . 702.c
he l. down from Heaven . 841.2
2 *(general)*
life's common l. . . . 7.2
l. down from . . . mountain . 37.2
the stars . . . l. down . . 77.1
they l. up and saw a star . 90.2
they all were l. . . . 91.1
my soul l. back to see . . 120.4
come and l. awhile on him . 121.1
cries to l., and l. again . . 131.3
l., ye saints! . . . 147.1
squadrons of the sky l. . . 150.3
in the fight all l. dark . . 169.3
fields strive . . . to l. gay. . 318.1
human hearts and l. deceive . 498.3
I l. for thy salvation . . 511.2
I may l. into thy face . . 615.3
l. into my Saviour's breast . 746.3
the earnest l. forward . . 765.4
my eyes l. to the skies . . 766.3
l. not for reward or praise . 816.3
l. to my home far away . . 881.1
God be in . . . my l. . . 953
l. to that alone . . . c118
b *look above*
watching and waiting, l. a. . 310.3
souls in danger, l. a. . . 336.3
lean on his arm l. up a. . . c138
c *look on* *Zech 12:10; John 19:37*
l. o. his smiling face . . 390.3
can live and l. o. thee . . 414.1
l. upon their living head . . 855.5
when . . . l. o. his face . 906.2, c
pierce (c)
d *look (un)to* *Isa 45:22*
there is life for a l. . . 271.1, c
l. unto him and be saved . 271.1
l. and live 271.c
l. unto me, ye people . . 272.3
there is life just for a l. . . 829.1
e *2 Cor 4:18*
still to things eternal l. . . 667.3
f *look to Jesus* *Heb 12:2*
l. t. him who died for thee . 239.1
l. at J. 270.c, 3
helpless, l. t. thee . . . 302.3
l. unto me, thy morn . . 332.3
I l. t. J., and I found . . 332.3
l. up t. J. who died . . 427.1
by l. t. J., like him . . 458.2
l. t. J., still trust . . . 458.3
l. t. thee when sin is near . 596.3
J., we l. t. thee . . . 603.1
I l. just now t. thee . . 628.1
Lamb of God, I l. t. thee . 793.4
l. away t. J. . . . 805.3
l. ever t. J. . . . 823.*
g *look up*
l. u. just now, believing . . 413.2
I would l. u. and laugh . . 491.2
my feeble faith l. u. . . 524.2
let my soul l. u. . . . 585.2
with humble confidence l. . 596.1
its closing eye l. u. . . 632.3
my faith l. u. to thee . . 742.1
my faith l. u. to thee . . 743.1
voice which says: L. u. . . 911.3
h *Gen 19:17*
not a l. behind . . . 682.1

loom 644.4

loose-d
l. the Christ with . . . might . 30.4
l. the fateful lightning . . 162.1
l. thy living presence . . 181.4
faith that will not l. . . 198.5
b *Ps 146:7; Acts 16:26*
mercy hath l. my bands . . 23.4
l. the souls . . . prisoned . 155.4
infirmity

Lord—*see* God (5b, c), Jesus

lose-ing-lost
our striving would be l. . . 1.2
l. the blessing of our Lord . 5.3
I l. them yesterday . . 41.1
l. all their guilty stains . . 132.1
blood shall never l. . . 132.3
death has l. its sting . . 152.2
flood hath l. his chill . . 153.3
prisoner leaps to l. . . 160.3
more blessings than . . . l. . 160.4
we l. the tender shepherd . 265.5
to l. him would be death . 343.1
I l. all my fears . . . 376.2
have I l. . . . mission . . 463.2
battles l. or scarcely won . 466.4
sorrows l. their sting . . 503.1
pleasures l. I . . . mourned . 547.4
some have l. the love . . 558.3
brief hours are not l. . . 564.4
temptations l. their power . 587.2
loved . . . and l. awhile . . 606.3
we shall not l. the fight 701.c/705.c
how many fights I've l. . . 770.1
fear not to l. . . . favour. . 805.3
many mighty men are l. . 847.2
I shall not l. my friends . . 880.4
death has l. its sting . . 894.1
b *Luke 17:33*
l. ourselves to save . . 5.4
l. I all, the crown . . . 528.4
l. ourselves in Heaven . . 676.6
c *John 12:25*
loving life . . ., we l. it . . 922.3
d *Phil 3:7, 8*
to l. the world I can afford . 513.3
passing gains of earth to l. . 796.3
e *lost in*
sin stains are l. in . . . flow . 281.3
l. in his love 310.3
l. in wonder, love . . . 438.3
let my all be l. in thee . . 509.3
my will be l. in thine . . 585.2
doubt and sorrow, are l.. . c94
find (1b)

loss
side by side with bitter l. . 145.1
the fearful shades of l. . . 145.2
out of my shameful . . . l. . 300.2
whether it be l. . . . 352.3
outweighs the toil and l. . 399.3

in loneliness and l. 451.2
l. and pain shall not hinder 473.2
hope will triumph over l. 555.3
man's darkness and l. 708.2
what to me are l. and pain 729.3
fear not shame or l. 866.3
the l. sustained . . . grieves 930.3
with what anguish and l. c24

b *grief and loss*
never a g. or l. 186.3
not a g. nor a l. 397.3
hardship, g. and l. 596.2

c *Phil 3:7, 8*
thine are all, and self is l. 181.3
once the l. of all for Jesus 894.2

gain (d), reckon, retrieve, suffer (3b)

lost

1 *(verb)* see lose

2 *(noun)*
point the l. to Calvary 188.3
lead the l. to Jesus' feet. 212.3
O Saviour of the l. 325.1
the l. and the outcast 687.2
the need of the l. 708.4
lead the wretched, l. 802.2
the wayward and the l. 825.2
the l. and dying I may help 859.2
may the l. find refuge 943.3

b *[seek] lost* *Luke 19:10*
s. and saves the l. 197.2
preach . . . and s. the l. 409.4
s. thy erring children l. 612.1
the l. to find, the low 620.3
go, s. for the l. 703.4
to help him s. the l. 704.3
to help us save the l. 783.3
forward go the l. to save 814.2
as we go to s. the l. 822.c

3 *(adjective)*
in saving l. mankind 78.3
my l. estate to save 180.2
almost—but l. 226.3
l., despairing . . . come 369.3
thinking all is l. 396.1
live in him for l. mankind 451.1
in the darkness may be l. 478.3
for the l. world's sake 482.3
erring children l. and lone 612.1
to save a l. world 687.3
nor let my hope be l. 735.2
a l. and sinning race 777.2

b *Luke 15:4, 24*
I once was l. . . . found 308.1
I was l., but Jesus found 337.2
once I was l. in sin's 349.2
once I was l., . . . tossed 375.1

c *lost ones*
carried his l. o. again 111.1
to be the l. o.'s Saviour 225.3
how to win the l. o. 531.3
l. o. to bring 786.4
chosen . . . l. o. to save c225

d *lost sinners*
the world of s. l. 46.1
s. l. of Adam's race 56.3
for a world of l. s. 124.1
will for l. s. weep 205.3
s. l. like me and you 335.1
I want to tell to s. l. 335.2
to proclaim to all l. s. 523.2

e *lost souls*
die . . . thy s. to be l. 263.3
when . . . my s. was l. 402.2
can I not lead l. s. 447.3
s. who were l. to the good 527.1

lot *(Phil 4:11)*
Son of man, to right my l. 91.2
bear with man his . . . l.. 102.1

though lowly thy l. 175.1
wheresoe'er my l. may be 517.3
happy is my l. indeed 539.2
where'er our changeful l. 602.3
whatever l. I see 725.3
whatever my l. . . . well. 771.1

loud-er-est
their l. anthems thrilled 5.2
shall be our l. strain 43.4
l. praises without ceasing 109.3
those l. triumphant chords 147.4
l. their holy war cry 158.1
I hear the l. call 298.6
songs of l. praise 313.1
l. and angry billows roar. 478.2
the l. hallelujahs prolong 537.4
in l. rapture . . . ring 543.4
how the l. harps ring 550.c
where the tempest is l. 641.2
l. your anthems raise 690.2
l. rings out the cry 703.3
l. rings the clarion call 781.3
l. joyful songs of praise 807.1
l. than a thousand thunders 875.1
l. let his praises ring 897.1

b *loud and long*
proclaim it l. and l. 700.3
l. and l. sounds the cry 703.1
proclaim both l. and l. 940.2

hosanna (b)

loudly 802.2

love

1 *general statements*
all the world of l. is thine 30.4
l. brings . . . fulness in 46.3
l. stands the test . . . gives 51.*
a broken heart l.'s dwelling 121.6
the end of all . . . is l. 146.2
l. can soothe . . . breast 261.2
l. only knoweth . . . 496.2
l. will soften/lighten 503.3
l.'s value . . . l.'s test 507.1
l.'s resistless current 540.3
l. is great! 544.3
l. is giving and receiving. 544.4
l. is bearing and forgiving 544.4
l.'s the greatest way 544.4
l. is not afraid of hardness 555.3
l.'s meaning to unfold 590.1
let l. be first . . . last 620.4
l. at last shall vanquish 705.4
l. perfecteth what it begins 741.4
in l's assurance we confide 748.4
l. will triumph over sin 760.2
where l. alone can reign. 855.3
l.'s sun is shining 888.2
l. cannot die 897.3
l. for help is seeking 921.3
Heaven . . . where all is l. c250

b *1 Cor 13:1f*
if l. impassioned . . . 530.1

have (4b), live (1e), make (3h), never (1b), suffer (3c), victory (2e), way (3f), win (1c)

2 *God as love*
ineffable L.! 16.6
O L. upon a cross impaled 122.1
my l., the crucified 153.1
fulness of l., . . . of God 214.4
L. of l. so wondrous 250.1
emptied . . . of all but l.. 283.2
O L., revealed . . . . 449.*
immortal l., for ever full 496.1
O L. that wilt not let 621.1
thou art . . . l. that lives 631.2
O L., thou bottomless abyss 746.2
O perfect L., . . . transcending 948.1

b *1 John 4:8*
unite to sing: God is l. 43.*

God is all l. 51.3
God is l., I know 286.c, 4
God is l., the cross is saying 324.1
feel and know the l. thou art 466.3
for thou art l. 650.2
God is l., I feel it c121

c *(God) of love*
God of glory, Lord of l. 10.1
the King of l. my shepherd 53.1
great God of universal l.. 140.2
crown him the Lord of l. 156.4
the God of truth and l. 164.2
thou God of perfect l. 221.1
Ancient . . . and God of l. 223.1
O God of light . . . of l. 446.1
Father of l., of justice 486.1
God of wisdom, l. and might 498.4
King of l. so condescending 500.1
with thee, Christ of l. 532.4
thou God of peace and l. 561.1
Spirit whose fruit is l. 561.1
the faithful God of l. 714.3
Lord of life and l. 789.1
show thyself a God of l. 797.3
O God of l. eternal 943.1
O God of l. . . . we bow. 947.1

d *love of Christ* *(2 Cor 5:14)*
none the l. of C. can 363.1
the l. of C. doth me constrain 526.1
separate us from the l. of C. 554.1, 4
O the l. of C., my Lord c19

e *love of God*
the l. of G. to me 46.c
G.'s l. is . . . 47.*
G.'s l. to me is wonderful 48.*
certain as G.'s l./love of G. 49.*
is the boundless l. of G. 52.c
G.'s wondrous l. in saving 78.3
'tis the word of G.'s l. 119.2
O l. of G.! O sin of man! 121.5
O sin of man! O l. of G. 131.1
I've felt G.'s l. 215.1
the l. of G. is broader 265.6
I know the l. of G. 290.3
l. of G. so pure 295.4
when I think of G.'s l. 319.1
l. of G. to us made known 595.1
who trusts in G.'s . . . l. 738.1
through the l. of G. 764.1
G.'s mighty l. confess 833.3
peace, the gift of G.'s l. c197

f *love of Jesus*
the l. of J., what it is 61.4
song of J.' l. to me 69.4
story . . . of J. and his l. 98.1, c
J.' l. the nations 165.1
O the deep, deep l. of J. 182.*
is the boundless l. of J. 230.1
the l. of my J. will snap 273.3
what is the l. of J. to thee 276.1
in the l. of J. . . . a refuge 341.1
hiding place in the l. of J. 341.c
Heaven of heavens in J.'s l. 355.6
a soul filled with J.' l. 367.1
unmoved by J.' . . . l. 379.2
with the Master's own l. 527.2
shown in the l. of our Master. 739.1
in the l. of J. . . . is all 740.c
the pardoning l. of J. 833.1
sing the wondrous l. of J. 892.1
comes the l. of J. c140
l. of J. . . . brings the glory c170

g *love of Saviour*
it tells me of a S.'s l. 69.2
is my S.'s l. for me 179.c
the l. of my S. . . . precious 273.2
to sing the S.'s dying l. 275.1
grounded . . . in the S.'s l. 280.c
I have heard of a S.'s l. 289.1
I heard of a S. whose l. 331.1
the l. of my precious S. 342.*
mine, to show a S.'s l. 652.2

S.'s l. will be the theme . 700.c
come and reveal a S.'s l. . 946.3

h
though they mar . . . l. them . 38.4
think how God l. you . . 49.1
his l. is everywhere . . 49.c
stay . . . and l. me, I pray . 77.3
l. . . . the lowly mother . . 87.3
dearly, dearly, has he l. . . 133.5
suffers . . . yet l. the more . 142.4
wonder how he could l. me . 179.1
to speak his l. for men . . 181.1
how he l., ever l. . . . 182.2
failed him, God l. you . . 270.3
learn from Jesus God l. you . 270.3
yet l. me without end . . 311.4
tells of his l. in the book. . 323.1
he l. me ere I knew him . . 345.1
Jesus my Lord will l. me . 349.1
O how he l.! . . . . 377.*
l. me, seeking me . . . 388.c
in Christ he l. us . . . 544.5
Christ who proved he l. . . 554.2
who l. me evermore . . 571.3
it told thy l. to me . . . 585.1
thou hast l. us, l. us still. . 845.4
the Lord retaineth his l. . . 853.2
can't stop God from l. . . 854.*
friend . . . who l. me . . 860.1
thee who l. me my best . . c41
l. me, I cannot tell why . . c161
his l. . . . still the same . . c175
living, he l. me . . . c185

i *loved world* *John 3:16*
so l. he the w. that he gave . 22.1
God l. the w. of sinners lost . 46.1
l. for all the w. is shown. . 324.1
moved for the w. which he l. 527.1
that God so l. the w. . . 828.2

j *love to*
peace that he l. to bestow . 443.2
Jesus l. to wend his way . 663.2
God l. to give the better part . 806.3

because, Calvary (b), end (e), Father (2f), Jesus (3i), so (3b), Spirit (3e)

3 *God's love in action*
his l. sustains us . . . 5.5
with l. doth befriend thee . 19.2
l. . . . over and around us . 28.1
his l. still follows you . . 44.1
his l. remains the same . . 44.c
l. has banished every fear . 48.2
his l. my love kindles . . 92.2
in us his l. invested is . . 127.3
l. to the utmost . . . he gave . 130.4
bless me with his l. . . 144.2
right rewards, thy l. forgives . 146.3
races . . . his l. shall unite . 166.2
l. is victorious when Jesus . 166.4
come . . . where l. is beaming. 232.1
his l. intervening will pardon . 237.3
his the l. doth now entice . 249.2
thy l. . . . has broken . . . down 293.6
thy l. to me . . . can rid . . 297.4
l. lifted me 336.c
l. wrought the change . . 340.2
it was l. reached me . 342.1, c
l. that keeps . . . supplies . 342.2, 3
'tis there thy l. . . . appears . 368.2
the l. that found us . . 370.4
l. he so freely hath given . 373.4
l. that drew salvation's plan . 405.4
l. shall be the conqueror . 410.2
the joys thy l. has given. . 421.5
l. that pardons/cleanses/fills . 439.3
thy l. . . . is made known . 459.3
service which thy l. appoints . 485.4
while thy l. is left to me. . 498.5
all thy l. has done for me . 503.2
your l. to inspire me . . 506.4
the price thy l. has paid . . 513.2
thy l. attend me . . . 516.5
l. by loving deed expressed . 518.1
his l. laid hold on me . . 547.2
thy l. at last has conquered . 548.4
let thy l. my spirit cheer. . 563.5
yet shall thy l. uphold me . 618.3
deluge all my soul with l. . 620.4
l. our lives has sealed . . 692.1
let thy l. our will dictate. . 692.4
l. that claimeth lives . . 707.2
his l. in time past forbids . 712.3
l. beamed through . . . eyes . 855.4
l. has silenced all complaints . 926.1
thy l. sustaineth . . . 927.4
let thy l. remain . . . 958
his l. will ever fill . . . c194
O the l. that sought me . . c218

bring (1c), constrain, fill (2e), flow (2f), impart (c), inflame, make (3h), manifest (c), never (1b), out (b), prevail (b), reigns (1b), reveal (d), see (2b), shine (1c), show (1b), win (1c), work (1h)

b *by/through love*
b. almighty l. anointed . . 109.2
dies safely t. thy l. . . . 123.4
held . . . b. undying l. . . 126.1
b. the l. and pity . . . shown . 303.3
he will lift you b. his l. . . 336.3
b. the l. that never ceased 534.c, 3
interpreted b. l. . . . 567.3
my life surrounded is b. l. . 728.3
b. his l. o'ershaded . 889.1, c
lustred b. his l. . . . 896.3
brought us b. his l. . . 915.2

bind (1a)

c *in love*
God plans for you i. l. . . 44.c
much more . . . i. l. forgive . 50.c
yet i. l. he sought me . . 53.3
Jesus i. l. will lighten . . 186.3
still i. l. he calls . . . 225.1
i. l. and not in duty . . 242.4
gave i. l. of his . . . all . . 245.2
lost i. his l. 310.3
i. l., he lifted me . . . 339.3
i. l. he stooped to reach . 350.1
i. his l. died for me . . 395.3
he reigns i. l. . . . alone . . 541.4
safe i. thy l. 574.1
i. thy l. look down . . . 582.3
i. l. to bring . . . peace . . 702.3
blest Saviour, then i. l. . . 743.4
Jesus then i. l. is watching . 759.2
reigns i. l. for evermore . . 765.6

abide (2f), bind (1a), out (b)

4 *God's love described*
O wisest l. 18.3
O unexampled l. . . . 62.4
his l. is life to me . . . 65.3
watch of wondering l. . . 86.2
l. so torn with pain . . 131.3
l. for every sinner free . . 140.5
his l. . . . shall never die. . 142.1
his heavenly l. to me . . 180.4
l. of every love the best. . 182.3
the l. of God is broader . . 265.6
his is l. beyond a brother's . 377.1
none . . . find thy l. unheeding 456.3
thy l. is more than all to me . 486.2
all my riches is thy l. . . 497.4
a l. which cannot cease . . 545.1
new every morning is the l. . 668.1
how endless is thy l. . . 672.1
his all-discerning l. . . 738.2
l. that can never decay . . 808.1
his l. is new each morning . 854.1
sufficient is his l. . . . c120
his l. is like a rainbow . . c206

amazing, boundless (d), deathless, divine (d), dying (3b), eternal (2d), everlasting (g), great (2f), infinite (b), like (2f), matchless (b), mighty (1h), pardoning (b), perfect (2d, e), pure (2e), redeeming (c), strong (1e), tender (d), true (1e), unchanging (c), vast, wonderful (d), wondrous (c)

b *(possessive)*
fountains of goodness and l. . 8.2
a melody of l. . . . . 31.*
ministries of l. . . . 32.2
the glory of thy l. . . . 36.6
let l.'s sweet echo . . 51.3
the debt of l. I owe . . 105.4
the story of thy l. repeat. . 140.4
thy l.'s redemptive plan . . 167.3
the current of thy l. . . 182.1
earnest of l., and pledge . 207.3
he shows his prints of l. . 223.3
from the sunshine of l. . . 248.1
a message of l. . . . 273.3
whence . . . this waste of l. . 286.3
a sense of his l. . . . 318.3
a melody of l. . . 327.1, c
prove the delights of his l. . 397.4
led . . . to fountains of l. . 458.4
know that fellowship of l. . 465.1
wait l.'s bestowal . . . 493.2
the worth of l. can tell . . 497.4
freely flows at l.'s command . 520.3
into the light of his l. . . 535.3
given, in fulness of thy l. . 562.1
fountain of light and l. . . 651.1
a cross of l. and light . . 705.2
thy face of l. shines . . 741.2
a share in his l. . . . 794.2
l.'s sweet lesson to obey . 846.1
deep, sweet well of l. . . 896.2
greatest proof of his l. . . c121
gospel of l. . . . light . . c226

arms (1b), banner (b), cord (b), degree, depth (d), gift (2c), kingdom (1h), mystery (b, c), ocean (1c), power (4i), song (1b), throne (4b), whisper (b), wing (1c), wonder (1c)

c *John 15:13*
no man of greater l. . . 515.3
pay l.'s greatest price . . 922.3

d *Eph 3:19*
O l. that passeth knowledge . 299.2
l. surpassing understanding . 439.2
his l. passeth understanding . c212

e *1 John 4:18*
has his l. cast out . . . 243.2
my l. his fear shall quell . . 277.4
l. that is able to banish . . 443.3

5 *love and . . .*
sorrow and l. flow . . . such l. 136.3
his greatness and his l. . . 178.2
justice and his l. do blend . 269.2
l. and life and lasting joy . 547.c
thy presence and thy l. . . 560.4
thy l. and guardian care . . 721.5
l. and tender care . . . 856.*
my hope and l. . . . there . 880.3
your l. and joy to share . . 943.1
praising thy providence and l. 950
oil . . . l. for my fears . . c148

b *love and peace* *Gal 5:22*
l. and p. have come our way . 74.1
all is p. and perfect l. . . 125.c
thy reign of p. . . . and l. . 172.2
fruit of l. and joy and p. . 198.4
holy balm of p. and l. . . 200.2
I bring thee . . . p. and l.. . 229.4
more than life . . . l. and p. . 420.2
thou God of p. and l. . . 561.1
speak of its p. and its l. . . 904.2
grant our souls thy p. and l. . 942.4
gift of the Spirit is l. . . c46
p., the gift of God's l. . . c197

c *love and (power)* *2 Tim 1:7*
Spirit of . . . l. and p. . . 15.4

sing his p. and his l. . . . 16.1
I want the gift of . . . l. . . 214.1
God's l. and wondrous p. . 215.1
perfect in p., in l. . . . 220.3
Trinity, wisdom, l., might . 224.4
doubting thy great l. and p. . 409.5
Lord, in thy l. and thy p. . 437.4
light and l. and p. divine. . 445.4
by thy l.'s wondrous p. . . 469.4
fill me with thy l. and p.. . 474.4
being thou art of l. and p. . 509.3
his l. and p. can bless . . 560.3
O Trinity of l. and p. . 569.4
thy dear l., my healing p. . 729.1
p. and l. must still prevail . 744.2
Lord of life and l. and p.. . 789.1
l. is as great as his p. . . 962
gift of the Spirit is . . . l. and p. c46
held by the p. of a l. . . c48

faith (2d), grace (4a), light (4c), mercy (b), praise (3h), purity (b), truth (c)

6 *our response to love*
speak of . . . thy l., O Lord . 7.3
make but trial of his l. . . 21.4
we can't escape his l. . . 49.c
tell his l. to me . . . 65.2
lest I forget thy l. . . . 117.c
hide mine eyes from l. . . 131.3
dwell on his l. . . . 160.2
doubt no more his l. . . 249.3
wilt thou . . . l. requite . . 251.3
no one has claimed of his l. . 257.4
wondering at the l. . . 370.4
believe and his l. receive . 413.c
nor cared that we are l. . . 466.3
upon his l. I feast . . . 495.1
thy l. to tell . . . show . . 612.6
for ever faithful to thy l.. . 714.1
breathe to breathe thy l. . 720.3
publish . . . thy l. and . . . care 721.5
while we taste of his l. . . 808.3
thank . . . for all his l. . . 935.c
praising thy providence and l. 950

feel (2c), give (1n), know (3n), proclaim (c), prove (3d), see (3f), sing (3f)

7 *our love for God*
l. . . . with a constant mind . 5.4
how shall we show our l. . 15.1
only that I l. him too . . 48.3
I cannot help but l. him . . 65.2
l. him who . . . is yearning . 73.3
yet I l. thee, and adore . . 110.6
wounds make me l. thee . 111.3
never outlive my l. to thee . 123.3
we must l. him too . . 133.5
O l. above all earthly l. . . 135.4
my heart in l. goes out . . 138.2
to eternity, l. and adore . . 219.4
stoops to ask my l. . . . 307.2
I know I l. him . . . 323.2
I l. him for stooping . . 329.1
l. esteems it Heaven . . 333.3
him who merits all my l.. . 365.2
I want to l. him better . . 369.2
fill my soul with l. to thee . 445.2
fear and l. and serve aright . 466.5
ever l. and trust him . . 474.1
none do I l. like thee . . 486.2
my l. . . . no pain can take . 489.4
let me l. thee . . . . 503.*
let that l. . . . render thee . 503.1
we l. thee for the . . . worth . 515.2
I must l. thee 522.3
in l. my soul would bow. . 524.1
take my l., . . . I pour . . 525.6
thou, who callest forth our l. . 533.2
my law, my l., . . . sweet . 556.4
inspired by purest l. . . 581.1
my l. must bring its offering . 591.1
l. and grief . . . dividing . . 634.3
by the souls that l. him . . 682.3

because we l. him so . . 700.c
my l. for thee . . . confess . 719.1
may my l. to thee pure . . . be. 743.2
truth and person whom we l.. 748.3
in faithful l. remember . . 762.3
the one you l. the best . . 829.1
if I l. him, when I die . . 843.3
l. will be my only joy . . 846.2
bring him hearts that l. . . 849.2
my desire is now to l. him . 857.3
swift obedience answers l. . 867.2
lives . . . as tokens of our l. . 870.4
my hope and l. . . . are there 880.3
tokens of our deep . . . l. . 922.2
whose l. . . . designs to praise 944.1
teach me how to l. thee. . c105
I l. him better every day. . c169
can you wonder why . . . I l. . c211
O I l. him, yes, I l. . . . c216

b *love cross*
for the . . . l. of his c. . . 119.3
and I l. that old c. . . 124.1
we l. thee for that c. . . 515.2

c *love (Jesus)*
I l. thee, Lord Jesus . . 77.2
I l. thee, my Saviour . . 232.c
I l. the Christ who died . . 327.2
all who l. the Saviour, come . 338.1
I l. Jesus, hallelujah . . . I do . 338.c
my Jesus, I l. thee . . 357.1
thee, my Jesus, 'tis now . 357.*
unseen I l. the Saviour . . 370.2
would you know why I l. . 404.*
this is why I l. my Jesus. . 404.c
precious Jesus, O to l. . . 520.1
Christ is thy life . . . l. . . 718.3
l. . . . Christ's ways . . 816.3
who l. their redeemer . . 852.3
forward, l. Jesus alone . . 893.2

d *love [Lord]*
what shall I do my God to l. . 55.1
come, comrades...who l. the L. 312.1
prone to leave the God I l. . 313.5
come, ye that l. the Lord . 314.1
footsteps of the Lord he l. . 580.2
Lord, may l. and fear thee . 655.6
taught to l. the Lord . . 834.2
l. and serve the Lord below . 875.4

e *love name*
how I l. the Saviour's n. . 58.c
how I l. the n. of Jesus . . 63.c
I l. ... Saviour's n. ... of Jesus 67.3
I l. the n. of him . . . Jesus . 68.2
that n. I fondly l. . . . 68.3
a n. I love to hear . . . 69.1
O how I l. the Saviour's n. . 69.c
Jesus, the n. I l. so well . 69.3
I l. the sound of . . . n. . 360.c

f *love (other)*
may I l. thy precious word . 658.5
parents l. the sacred word . 661.3
for this flag our l. confess . 777.1
reach the land I l. . . . 877.2
how shall I l. that word . . 877.4
the Canaan that we l. . . 898.3
the reason they l. it so well . c202

g *no(t) love*
a world that l. not thee . . 135.2
sin of not l. thee . . . 296.2
we have not l. thee . . 466.3
some have never l. thee . 558.3
some have lost the l. . . 558.3

h *Luke 7:47*
l. I much? . . . forgiven . . 634.2

i *John 21:15*
poor sinner, l. thou me . 110.1, 5
you know I l. you . . . 294.*
he calls . . . that we l. him . 428.4
questioning: L. thou me? . 507.1
thou knowest I l. thee . . 507.c

j *1 John 4:19*
l. him who first l. me . . 846.*

best (2b), more (2d), serve (1f), song (1b), truth (e)

k *love to*
I l. its music to repeat . . 68.1
name I fondly l. to hear . . 68.3
I l. to sing its worth . . 69.1
I l. to hear . . . 69.1, 3
how I l. to be there . . 119.c
I l. to sing of . . . . 178.*
I l. to follow Jesus . . . 320.2
place where I l. to be . . 348.c
I l. to choose . . . my path . 606.2
makes me l. to fight . . 733.5
l. to hear the story . . . 840.1
stories . . . I l. to hear . . 848.1
we l. his works to do . . 851.5

8 *Christian love*
l. no barrier could confine . 5.1
l. until we l. 36.5
l. what thou dost l. . . 189.1
kindle a flame of . . . l. . . 199.1
from your l. my l. is learning . 206.3
with l. my heart keep pure . 416.2
l. that would anything do . 422.4
wear that pledge of l. . . 424.2
l. that cares . . . deep, strong 426.2
I in l. may be like thee . . 455.1
the smile of l. and beauty . 462.2
ask thee for a thoughtful l. . 485.2
a life of self-renouncing l. . 485.4
I would look up and . . . l. . 491.2
my l. his outpoured wine . 512.1
like thee in meekness, l. . 515.4
till all my life be l. . . . 516.3
clothe me with . . . l. . . 516.4
a heart whose l. engages . 522.2
l. with passion/principle . 522.3
l. with . . . heart . . . 522.3
burning l. is my need . . 527.c
with the Master's own l. . 527.2
let thy l. . . . o'erflow . . 533.2
may it be a life of l. . . 538.4
I sought for l. and . . . light . 541.1
souls impressed with . . . l. . 556.1
conforms not to thy l. . . 565.4
let all be wrought in l. . . 568.1
O may l. like thee . . . 568.3
the pure flame of l. . . 594.2
l. with every passion . . 607.3
let l. be first . . . last . . 620.4
deluge all my soul with l. . 620.4
softening gleam of l. . . 668.3
new strength and l. bestowed 675.2
thy l. let it . . . o'erpower . 720.1
with l. they keep . . . tryst . 878.5
l.'s unquenchable desire . 939.1
l. expressed in service . . c208

b *abide in love* *John 15:10*
out . . . to dwell in thy l.. . 300.3
in his l. a. . . . hiding . . 341.2
as I in your l. a. . . . 552.1
I would in thy l. a. . . . 627.1
in heavenly l. a. . . . 736.1
in his mighty l. a. . . . 759.c
let me in thy l. a. . . . 837.2

c *John 15:12*
how to l. each other . . 10.3
brother-l. binds man . . 10.4
teach us l.'s command . . 218.2
the whole of l.'s demands . 512.2
the law of l.'s demands . . 732.3

d *Col 2:2*
all who live in l. are thine . 10.3
in l. I share the joys. . . 375.3
binds our hearts in . . . l. . 660.1
unite our hearts in l. . . 661.4
one great fellowship of l. . 826.1
walk . . . in fellowship and l. . c143

e *love for (souls)*
fan my l. into a flame . . 205.2
tender in my l. for men . . 212.3
sinners yet demand my l. . 463.3
clear, winning word of l. . 519.2
l. for souls may ne'er be dead. 529.2
still the sinner l. . . . 568.3
a deep, burning l. for souls 649.1, c
lost and the outcast we l. . 687.2
hearts to l. the masses . . 704.3
l. them with a zeal . . . 720.5
ceaseless l. for men . . 796.4
l. that soul through me . . c79
l. I ask for . . . claim . . c83
a l. that feels for . . . world . c83

dying (3b), fill (2e), given (1n), impulse, more (2d), show (2b), work (1g)

9 *human love*
a *love for family, etc*
l. where l. is not returned . 50.2
great if someone l. me . . 544.2
l. that gazes . . . lasts . . 544.3
some we l. bear . . . burdens. 576.2
faces . . . which I have l. . 606.3
blest be the dear uniting l. . 659.1
l. fills every breast . . . 661.1
sweet when l. is there . . 663.1
l. at home . . . . 664.*
raise this child they l. . . 795.2
the l. that here surrounds . 795.3
what my l. should cherish . 842.2
to l. committing all their l. . 874.3
those we l. within the veil . 878.1
those I l. most and best . . 882.3
those I l. in the homeland . 895.3
friends . . . I have l. . . 906.3
many that we l. have left . 938.4
l. which knows no ending . 948.1

human (c), loved

b
what l. can compare . . 119.c
loved above all earthly l. . 135.4
l. grows cold . . . 172.5
l. divine, all l. excelling . 438.1
expel . . . each sinful l. . . 445.2
empty my heart of earthly l. . 480.1
l. of ease and . . . show. . 500.2
what l. with thine can vie . 515.3
never think . . . of other l. . 551.1
I l. to choose . . . path . 606.2
men . . . l. thee, praise thee not 683.2
to l. my sins 932.3

c *John 12:25*
l. life too much we lose it . 922.3

10 *love-*
be my l.-anointed King . . 122.4
the l.-light of Jesus' face . 848.2

loved *(adjective)*
fix in me his l. abode . . 214.3
his l. and his own . . . 852.1
rest from thy l. employ . . 890.1
our Father's l. abode . . 918.4

belovèd, one (2c)

loveliness
mars thy l. divine . . . 494.3
thy l. to see 547.4
transient gleam of l. . . 551.1
l. breaks on my sight . . 719.4

lovely-ier-iest
sunrise dyed the l. deeps . 103.2
the l. strain is this . . . 187.4
smile of Jesus' l. face . . 253.1
disclose thy l. face . . 412.2
all are l. in their time . . 494.1
life is l., free and good . . 544.1
l. than daylight . . . 632.1
pluck a l. garland there . . 658.1
old scenes, will l. be . . 668.3

b *Phil 4:8*
honest, just and l., too . . c56

lover
a *re Jesus*
l. of souls, from ill . . . 153.3
the l. of sinners adore . . 367.3
guide and helper, l. . . 510.c
l. of souls . . . victory . . 543.1
Jesus, tender l. of my soul . 600.1
Jesus, l. of my soul . . 737.1
Jesus, thou l. of souls . . c75

b *(human)*
must be a l. of the Lord . . 256.c
the love of l. 544.3
make me a l. of souls . . c75

loves see love (9b)

loving
1 *re divine*
l. wisdom of our God . . 18.2
how l. was his call . . . 94.2
thy l. heart, so rent . . 138.3
l. and tender from . . . birth . 175.1
a new and l. touch . . . 215.1
sin on his own l. heart . . 245.4
list to the l. call . . . 258.2
l. and kind art thou . . 296.4
heard his l. whisper . . 333.1
none other is so l. . . . 334.3
love by l. deed expressed . 518.1
live in his l. embrace . . 535.3
praise that l., living man . 544.5
l., forgiving, tender . . 623.2
thy l. hands will bless me . 631.4
thy l. hand doth thread . . 644.4
let me have thy l. mind . . 793.5
mine his l. promise . . 840.3

b *(with title)*
O l., living Lord . . . 36.4
my l. God to praise . . . 55.1
thou l., all-atoning Lamb . 140.3
'tis the l. Father calls . . 279.c
thy l. Spirit, Christ . . . 419.3
with all thy l. Spirit . . 520.2
precious, living, l. Lord . . 729.c
l. Jesus, gentle Lamb . . 793.3
to your l. heavenly Father . c4
Jesus, so patient, so l. . . c7
Jesus, he's l. and strong . c31

c *loving care*
I see his l. c. 334.2
grateful for thy l. c. . . 941.1

d *loving friend*
I've found a l. f. . . . 389.1
my unchanging, l. f. . . 504.3
l. F., we stand before . . 595.2

e *loving Saviour*
Jesus Christ, our l. S. . . 74.1
O l. S., take my heart . . 108.3
the S., gentle and l. . . 236.3
all a l. S. bore for thee . . 276.c
pass me not, O l. S. . . 301.1
l. S., . . . I bring the load . 421.3
O l. S., no dread of ill . . 726.1
leaning on the l. S.'s breast . 829.1
what a l. S. may . . . found . 835.1
of a l. S. ever near . . 835.c
where Jesus, l. S., waits . 872.3
O what a l. S. c194

arm (1b), kindness (b)

2 *re people*
faithful, l. service, too . . 336.2
every l. deed of mine . . 518.3
a child of l. lies . . . 544.3
stretch out a l. hand . . 612.3
touched by a l. hand . . 691.3
we bring with l. zeal . . 825.1
be thy l. child below . . 837.6
Jesus wants me to be l. . 844.2
to join their l. hands . . 949.2

b *loving heart*
give a pure and l. h. . . 466.3
a l., faithful h. . . . 475.4
Christ can fill the l. h. . . 545.3
Jesus, thou joy of l. h. . . 602.1

lovingly
l. he greets thee . . . 152.2
l. now he's waiting . . 255.2
thy truth I l. receive . . 407.1

low
the earth is not too l. . . 11.1
l. in the grave he lay . . 148.1
l. at his feet lay . . . 183.2
in accents meek and l. . . 299.3
kept l. by grace . . . 468.4
no one too . . . l. . . . 590.2
lost . . . the l. to raise . . 620.3
when sickness lays me l. . 709.3
when clouds hang l. . . 719.4
oft thy light burns l. . . 723.2
my heart may l. be laid . . 736.1
as I stoop to raise the l. . . 758.4
evening when lights are l. . c123

b *sweet and low*
a voice said, s. and l. . . 359.1
Jesus whispers s. and l. . 390.1

lower-st
to the l. child of man . . 439.2
let the l. lights . . . 478.c
we search the l. deeps . . 496.3
mercy . . . brought me l. . 548.3
all l. glories wane . . . 551.1
though least and l. . . 614.3
bending l., l. still . . . c35

lowing *(verb)*
the l. of the herds . . . 41.1
the cattle are l. . . . 77.2

lowly
1 *re people*
blessed are the meek and l. . 95.1
give us each a l. mind . . 193.4
at his feet l. bow . . . 248.3
with a l., contrite spirit . . 259.3
still to the l. soul . . 411.3
give us a . . . l. heart . . 411.4
a humble, l., . . . heart . . 444.3
a work of l. love to do . . 485.5
in l. paths of service . . 519.1
where l. spirits meet . . 648.1
then, l. kneeling, wait . . 674.1
a l. heart, that waits . . 839.4
l. we kneel in prayer . . 948.1

2 *re Jesus*
a *Zech 9:9*
to that l. manger bed . . 76.2
a l. cattle shed . . . 87.1
with the poor and . . . l.. . 87.2
watch the l. mother . . 87.3
how l., how gracious . . 92.2
of l. birth cam'st thou . . 101.2
in l. pomp ride on . . 150.2, 5
though l. thy lot . . . 175.1
from the l. manger . . 499.2

b *Matt 11:29*
Jesus l., meek and mild . . 259.2
in l. patience waiting . . 299.1
chooses out a l. way . . 398.1
l. paths our Lord has taken . 555.2
the meek and l. heart . . 555.4
like thee! l. in spirit . . 623.3
Christ, the l. Nazarene . . 776.3
not . . . like the l. Jesus. . c182

3 *(other)*
home, however l. . . . 663.1
l. cot or stately home . . 705.1
surround my l. grave . . 751.4

lowliness
a *Zech 9:9*
cam'st . . . in l. of thought . 174.2
to dwell in l. with men . . 411.2
b *Phil 2:3**
incense of l. 183.1, 5
clothe me with . . . l. . . 516.4
in l. I bend me . . . 635.2

loyal
thy l. peoples wait . . 171.1
thy l. servant I . . . 290.3
witness gives to l. hearts . 423.5
unswerving, l. . . . 574.4
keep us l. to our aim . . 863.5
l. service makes me free . 867.6

lure
the l. of strong desire . . 207.1
Satan . . . l. them . . . 885.2

lurk-ing
spare not one l. sin . . 494.3
deadly dangers l. . . . 801.2

lust
l. . . . shall flee thy face. . 172.3

lustre-d
adds more l. to the day . . 112.3
with l. shining more . . 196.5
dews of sorrow were l. . . 896.3

M

made see make

madly 19.3

madness 577.3

magnify *Luke 1:46**
fear . . . and laud and m. . 20.2
m. them all in me . . . 295.4
my risen Christ to m. . . 562.3

maid 701.4

mail 30.2

maim 789.4

maintain-ed
have I that ground m. . . 409.2
blood-bought right m. . . 563.4
m. the honour of his word . 735.1
a warfare to m. . . . 868.1
cause (1c)

majestic 657.2

majesty
ride on in m. . . . . 150.*
in aweful m. unfolds . . 871.4
b *Ps 93:1*
robed in dreadful m. . . 161.2
clothed in m. divine . . 875.2
c *Ps 145:12*
rise . . . in glorious m. . . 870.2
d *Jude 25*
to him all m. ascribe . . 56.2
all m. is thine . . . 171.3
his sovereign m. . . . see . 219.4
all might and m. . . . thine . 223.5
behold . . . majesty divine . 557.2
reach the m. on high . . 625.3

make-ing/made
1 *(general)*
the stars their courses m. . 171.2
need that m. us bold . . 198.5
which transgression has m. . 237.2
our guilt m. his Calvary . . 245.c
sin that m. it ache . . . 309.c
only m. us richer there . . 312.1
no change . . . m. any change 318.3
transaction so quickly was m. 371.2
sins that m. thee mourn . 442.4
judgments m. me quail . . 618.3
sleep . . . more vigorous m. . 671.4
no discouragement shall m. . 685.1
dread . . . m. my soul afraid . 726.1
habit m. us want to prove . 748.3
band m. my pulse fly . . 780.3
blood . . . m. the foe to fly . 807.2
strife m. thee . . . faint . . 816.2
m. tares or ripe wheat . . 928.3
all . . . m. it hard to say. . c95
b *passive*
m. ready and furnished . 289.3
seat was m. of . . . gold. . 590.1
for crops m. ripe . . . 936.2
2 *(people) make*
a *we make*
m. we thee our King . . 97.2
m. this hill our home . . 154.4
m. the . . . places smooth . 159.1
him my only portion m. . . 223.2
we m. his love too narrow . 265.5
no preparation can I m. . . 291.3
since I m. him my guide. . 376.3
trying now to m. the harbour. 478.3
now the sacrifice we m. . 481.3
hungered to m. a beginning . 553.1
would m. thy purpose mine . 566.3
kneeling . . . I m. my prayer . 605.1
contact I may m. . . . 613.2
help . . . m. more sacrifice . 619.4
m. our home the threshold . 663.3
fresh lips are m. . . . 677.4
to m. this life worthwhile . 706.3
one great Army m. . . 788.2
so we'll m. a thoroughfare . 815.3
I'm/he's going to m. my life 858.1, c
could we m. our doubts remove 898.3
m. Jesus King c220
b *make [vow]*
vows that now I m.. . . 482.3
fresh covenant to m. . . 534.3
covenant we this moment m.. 784.3
we our vows are m.. . . 788.1
pledges they're now m. . . 795.2
what promise are we m.. . 926.4
c *(others) make*
m. music for thy Lord . . 2.3
m. but trial of his love . . 21.4
m. . . . service your delight . 21.5
each . . . sweet music m.. . 43.1
m. the future, . . . present. . 158.3
m. no delay 235.1
m. the message clear . . 262.c
m. a full surrender . . . 343.3
m. friends of God's children . 458.1
come . . . m. a stand . . 798.2
m. salvation's story heard. . 832.c
boast (b), choice (b), haste (c), highway (a), know (5), ring (e), sure (b), surrender (b), wound (1b)
3 *God (makes)*
a *in creation* *Ps 121:2*
without our aid he did us m. . 3.2
m. us of clay 4.2
the Lord God m. them all. . 25.c
he m. . . . colours . . . wings. 25.1
m. . . . every one/all things 25.3, 4
filled the new-m. world . . 34.3
worlds thy hands have m. . 37.1
m. the atom's . . . forces. . 38.2
m. us more than nature's sons 38.5
hath m. Heaven and earth . 90.6
all its tribes were m. . . 167.2
Heaven and earth hath m. . 767.1
though m. quite sinless . . 785.3
all things . . . m. good . . 927.1
b *(general)*
he will m. it plain . . . 29.6
no crying he m. . . . 77.2
m. the nations prove . . 84.3
that m. a woman cry . . 91.1
thy prayer shall m. reply. . 122.3
m. of these days . . . sign. . 173.3
m. them his very own . . 179.3
Christ m. room for . . . souls . 266.2
to m. its waters sweet . . 510.3
nothing thou hast m. . . 568.3
Jesus m. our home a heaven . 663.1
m. human toil thine own. . 688.2
home eternal he has m. . . 711.3
each promise he has m. . . 723.1
defence . . . himself hath m. . 767.3
m. . . . place your temple. . 943.1
c *in lives*
m. thine abode in me . . 209.1
all that's wrong m. manifest . 446.1
m. me after thy will. . . 487.1
thyself . . . wilt m. my heaven. 562.1
m. thy demands on me . . 605.3
m. every tongue . . . flame . 609.2
m. . . . a quiet place. . . 615.1
m. . . . thy dwelling there. . 615.4
m. thy people hear . . . 626.1
m. us thy care. . . . 648.1
m. Calvary real . . . c81
atonement, blind (b), end (2b), fisher, haste (c), jewel (b), know (5a), peace (2l)
d *(passive—God the agent)*
a life m. up of praise . . 7.1
m. like him . . . rise. . . 143.5
hearts . . . m. fit temples. . 202.3
now m. willing to return. . 305.1
my soul was m. right . . 395.3
m. worthy by thy grace . . 461.4
m. into soldiers to fight . . 608.3
hearts are m. to bless thee . 642.3
story of our God-m. host. . 803.4
e *1 John 4:17*
my soul is m. perfect . . 436.4
f *(influence of divine qualities)*
thy wounds m. me love thee . 111.3
m. of weakness, might . . 197.3
salvation m. each burden light. 320.2
peace . . . m. fresh my heart . 358.3
m. my pathway bright . . 379.4
m. a saint of a sinner . . 471.c
name m. devils fly . . . 593.3
calm that m. . . . living psalm. 613.2
judgments m. me quail . . 618.3
m. a world of darkness shine. 657.3
m. his pathway bright . . 658.3
truth . . . m. the triumph. . 707.4
m. my earth . . . Heaven. . 729.4
faith . . . m. salvation sure . 733.4
faith will m. them all. . . 770.3
truth shall m. them flee . . 813.3
m. it live again . . . 827.1
m. for life's increase . . 827.4
fire that m. . . . heroes/willing. 830.3
g *mercy makes*
pleasure, by God's m. m. 227.1
tender m. m. thee room . 333.4
promise, by thy m. m. . . 419.2
h *love makes*
love m. him die . . . 323.2
Calvary-l. has m. the stair. . 369.3
l. which m. thee mine . . 475.c
his l. m. my Heaven. . . 535.4
eternal l. m. manifest . . 728.4
l. will m. . . . burden light. . 755.3
i *prayer makes*
p. m. . . . clouds withdraw . 646.2
p. m. . . . armour bright . . 646.3
p. will m. . . . a calm . . 663.3
4 *make (me)-noun*
heart vouchsafe to m. . . 55.5
m. us more than conquerors . 152.3
m. our hearts a . . . garden . 210.1
m. my heart a house . . 305.3
m. me his . . . guest. . . 373.2
m. us kings and priests . . 452.2
m. my heart his altar . . 495.2
m. me a vessel . . . 501.c
m. me a captive, Lord . . 508.1
m. me a blazing fire . . 521.2
m. me an heir 535.2
m. us warriors for ever . . 593.2
m. my life one blazing fire . 620.3
m. a garden there . . . 647.3
God m. my life . . . 838.*
he's going to m. my life. . 858.c
thy devoted servant m. me . 865.1
m. each heart a living stone . 941.2

m. me a lover of souls . . c75
m. me a channel . . . c84
m. my poor heart thy dwelling. c104

home (2e), temple (2b)

b *make me (verb)*
m. us love thee more . . 40.3
me to walk doth m. . . 54.2
m. the . . . heart to sing. . 177.2
m. all within me rejoice . . 318.2
m. the desert . . . bloom . 333.2
m. all the darkness depart . 371.1
m. my . . . conscience smart . 446.3
m. thy presence felt . . 531.2
m. thy people hear . . 626.1
touch . . . and m. me see . 650.3
m. me love to fight . . 733.5
m. my heart rejoice . . 740.3
m. me know . . . save . . 837.2
speak to m. me listen . . 862.3

c *make (adjective)*
m. me fit . . . dwelling . . 188.c
m. us fit to live or die . . 203.2
he m. me well . . . 330.2
m. my desire secure . . 416.2
quick . . . my conscience m. . 425.3
m. me worthy . . . 431.c
m. me quick to fight . . 446.4
m. us wise in knowing . . 466.1
Jesus m. me free indeed . 546.2
m. me blameless . . . 601.3
m. all our moments calm . 602.4
m. me aware of thee . . 613.*
m. me blest indeed . . 614.3
m. me ready 614.4
triumphant God will m. us . 702.1
hast m. us willing/free . . 707.3
m. us more earnest . . 933.4

d *make like*
m. us more l. Jesus . . 193.4
m. us l. thee 515.4
m. me more l. thee . . 584.3
m. me . . . what thou art . 793.3

e *make new* *2 Cor 5:17*
m. my heart anew . . 32.1, 3
change . . . and m. it n. . 257.2
he m. all things n. . . 267.3
your life . . . m. it anew. . 335.c
take my heart, but m. it n. . 492.2
who m. all things n. . . 749.3

f *make pure*
m. me crystal p. . . . 32.1
he m. my nature p. . . 45.2
that m. me p. within . . 113.1
m. and keep me p. . . 128.3
power to m. and keep me p. . 409.5
m. and keep me p. within . 737.4
to m. them p. in heart . . 791.3
cleanse . . . and m. me p. . 914.3

g *make (strong)*
m. me . . . s. to fight . . 188.3
to m. our weak hearts s. . 203.4
m. of my weakness might . 221.3
my heart and mind m. s. . 431.2
with holy valour m. me s. . 432.2
in thy love . . . m. me s.. . 437.4
m. weakness strength . . 490.2
grant me courage, m. me s. . 719.5
my Father, m. me s. . . 744.1
thine to m. us . . . s. . . 799.4
by blood and fire m. s. . . 821.3
m. me steadfast . . . s. . . 837.3

bold (b), brave (2b), clean (d), complete (b), free (1c), glad (b), good (3b), holy (3b), snow (c, d), whit, whole (2b-e)

h *make (thine)*
since he has m. us his . . 9.2
O m. me thine for ever . . 123.3
m. me . . . ever thine . . 445.4
with thy blessing m. us thine. 452.1
take my all and m. it thine . 460.3
for thy glory m. me thine. . 463.c

thy heart m. truly his . . 465.2
m. me Saviour, wholly thine . 474.3
till thou hast m. it thine . . 508.3
if thou wilt but m. it thine . 520.1
take my will and m. it thine . 525.5
m. . . . hearts thine own. . 604.4
m. us fully thine . . . 870.4

g *make own*
courage; m. it now our o. . 181.2
to m. his will my o. . . 732.3

maker *Isa 54:5*
our m. defender, redeemer . 16.5
declare their m.'s praise . 42.2
Christ, the mighty m., died . 105.3
stand before my m.'s face . 290.1
nor . . . see my m.'s face . 398.3
all things their m. praise . 494.1
my M. and my King . . 616.1
he is our m. . . . friend . . 785.6
God, our m., doth provide . 924.1
he only is the m. . . . 935.2

making *(n)* 51.1

man-men
1 *(re Jesus)* *(Acts 2:22)**
the right m. on our side . . 1.2
m. of God's own choosing . 1.2
pleased as m. . . . to dwell . 82.2
m. upon that weeping tree . 131.4
Son . . . as m. came down . 274.*
on earth a m. became . . 363.2
the power of God in m. . . 407.6
praise that loving . . . m. . 544.5
Christ, thou too art m. . . 558.4
m. who walked by Galilee . 618.2
O M. of Galilee . . . 628.*
the Son as m. is known . . 785.2
m. walked by Galilee . . 855.3
a young m. died . . . 855.4

b *man of sorrows* *Isa 53:3*
M. of s.! what a name . . 118.1
see the m. of s. now . . 147.1
O M. of s., praying . . 486.3

c *1 Tim 2:5*
mediator, the m. . . . Jesus . c156

son (1d)

2 *(re mankind)*
a *biblical*
as with gladness m. of old . 76.1
m. denied those hands . . 129.1
m. feared them so . . 129.2
nothing . . . that m. mocked . 245.3
let m. hurt him so . . . 274.2
Jesus was here among m. . 794.1
old m., meek and mild . . 839.2

wise (b)

b *general*
givest m. . . . light . . . 2.3
forbid that m.'s achievements 6.2
decideth the destiny of m. . 6.4
heard by listening m. . . 27.3
beast to brain of m. . . 38.3
reign . . . make m. free . . 63.2
no word of m. can . . . tell . 68.4
m.'s first heavenly state . 78.3
m. no more may die . . 82.3
let m. their songs employ . 84.2
peace to m. on earth . . 86.2
to m. the truth declarest . 97.4
drew near to dwell with m. . 102.1
bear with m. his . . . lot. . 102.1
freed m. from remorse . . 102.2
Christ . . . died for m. . . 105.3
still break to m. . . . bread . 129.3
wheresoever m. may move . 158.3
he died to make m. holy . 162.4
the breath of m. bestow . 171.2
to speak his love for m. . . 181.1
Holy Ghost to m. is given . 195.*
turns m. into heroes . . 197.3

lead m. to truth and joy . . 211.3
tender in my love for m. . 212.3
the measure of m.'s mind . 265.6
he taught m. . . . to smile . 274.c
why he tolerated m. . . 274.1
wherever m. is found . . 279.1
helper of m. in . . . need . 351.c
shared with m. . . . load . 398.3
brought it down to m. . . 405.4
dwell in lowliness with m. . 411.2
a way for m. to rise . . 414.4
the lowest child of m. . . 439.2
m. beholding must confess . 494.2
surpasses m.'s knowledge . 506.3
my life may guide m. . . 529.1
small the debts m. owe . . 572.3
fight to set m. free . . . 577.4
that we fail not m. . . 577.4
no boundary known unto m. 579.3
thou light of m. . . . 602.1
when m. . . . shall stand . 618.1
m. can triumph over death . 652.3
m. that nature . . . know . 656.3
to bring m. back . . . 680.2
today, calling to m. . . 680.3
Jesus calls for m. of war . 686.4
a voice to call m. . . . 706.3
until m. confess . . . 776.3
in ceaseless love for m. . . 796.4
m. shall cast aside . . . 827.2
land where m. is found . . 831.3
speaks through us to m. . 851.4
mysteries no m. beholds . 871.4
ere m. could reap . . . 923.1
m. the . . . fruits await . . 923.2
no m. will hunger . . . 927.4
m. drew near to see . . 939.2
direct m. to your throne . 943.3

c *all men*
have we a name for all m. . 71.3
all m. shall dwell . . . 166.2
all m. as brothers . . . 170.3
now flowing for all m. . . 298.1
to all m. I may prove . . 463.1
I may all m. surpass . . 530.1
salvation free to all m. . . 810.3
hearts of all m. . . . 827.4
when all m. . . . are free . 833.1
we, as all m., must obey . 874.2
all m. confessing . . . hand . 927.4
living that all m. . . . see . c59

d *angels and men*
a. and m. before him fall . 60.1
a. and m. be joined . . 62.1
sons of m. and a. say . . 143.1
m. and a. sing . . . 690.5
m. and a. then uniting . . 833.3

e *every man*
e. m. to his post . . . 703.4
grieved for e. child of m. . 855.4

f *hearts of men* *(Luke 21.26)*
the h. of humble m. . . . 36.2
sifting out the h. of m. . . 162.3
God can change the h. of m. 324.2
dwell within the h. of all m. . 827.4
m.'s h. grow faint . . . 864.1

g *God [and] man*
G. with m. is now residing . 75.2
peace . . . 'twixt m. and G. . 109.2
blessings G. on m. bestows . 257.3
G. and m. to reconcile . . 274.c
G. and m. in oneness . . 540.4
reconciled to G. and m. . 572.4
G. in m. can never fail . . 809.2
mediator 'twixt G. and m. . c156

h *souls of men*
power to gather s. of m. . 63.1
every fallen s. of m. . . 140.5
s. of m.! why will ye scatter . 265.1
the wandering s. of m. . . 526.1
for every s. of m. . . . 656.1

shame blight m.'s s. . . 789.4
by thee the s. of m. are fed . 934.2
i *Ex 10:11*
ye that are m. now serve . 699.2
j *John 3:3*
chronicles of twice-born m. . 774.2
k *John 10:18*
no m. can take it . . . 130.2
l *John 15:13*
no m. of greater love . . 515.3
fairer (b), fisher, form (b), goodwill, Jesus (8h), lame (b), see (3i)
3
a *men's virtues*
brother-love binds m. to m. . 10.4
the hearts of humble m.. . 36.2
m. can live for others . 50.2
m. . . . share/respond/feel . 50.3
blessèd are the m. of mercy . 95.2
the ministry of m. . . . 238.2
m. of grace have found . . 314.3
m. whose heart is set free . 372.2
like m. renewed . . . endued . 408.2
road that holy m. have trod . 583.1
noble army, m. and boys . 701.4
m. are wanted . . . of hope . 702.1
won by m. unarmed . . 705.4
mighty m. around us . . 804.2
fire that makes m. heroes . 830.3
m. in grace have grown . . 936.3
faith (2k)
b *men's weakness*
m. have wrought confusion . 6.4
a name to change m. . . 71.1
m., at war with m.. . . 83.2
hush . . . ye m. of strife. . 83.2
O love of God! O sin of m. . 121.5
the sins that m. enthrone . 129.2
O sin of m.! O love of God . 131.1
m. scorn thy sacred name . 172.5
m.'s puny judgment bar . . 185.3
unaided m. must fail . . 212.4
though m. crucify . . . 324.1
dying m. to save . . . 499.c
wayward m. to lead . . 528.3
m. rise in war . . . 529.3
ample grace for fallen m. . 656.2
m. die in darkness . . . 683.5
m. have sorely failed . . 706.1
m.'s darkness and loss . . 708.2
convincing m. of sin . . 730.3
to ruin m. in deed . . . 760.3
m. seldom hear his name . 832.1
many mighty m. are lost . 847.2
m. are thickly falling . . 864.2
m. is a weakling/no purpose . c210
sinful (c)
c *man as opposition*
whatever m. may say . . 334.1
from fear of m. . . . 401.2
let m. exclaim . . . 407.4
fear what m. may think . . 415.2
what m. think or say . . 437.4
let m. revile my name . . 526.2
m. heed...not...what are m. 683.2
I'll fear not what m. say. . 685.3
we own no m. as enemy . 705.1
whatever m. may say . . 782.2
fear not to lose m.'s favour . 805.3
in spite of m. and devils. . 810.1
though m. count thee poor . c249

mane 701.3

manfully 823.1

manger *Luke 2:7f*
voice from yonder m. . . 73.2
to that lowly m. bed . . 76.2
that m. rude and bare . . 76.3
away in a m. 77.1
from his poor m. . . . 78.3
laid her baby in a m. . . . 87.1
a m. his cradle 92.1
though laid in a m. . . . 92.2
and in a m. laid 93.4
cradled in a m. 97.2
Jesus was born in a m. . . 137.1
born in a m., so rude . . 175.1
from the lowly m. . . . follow. 499.2
baby in the m. laid . . . 829.c
asleep within a m. bed . . 855.1

manifest
m. thy mighty power . . 941.2
b *Mark 4:22*
all that's wrong make m. . 446.1
c *1 John 4:9*
to whom he m. his love . . 168.3
m. his pardoning favour . . 370.2
eternal love made m. . . 728.4

manifold
join . . . in m. witness . . 33.2
b *Neh 9:19*
know thy mercies m. . . 59.3

mankind
lose ourselves to save m. . 5.4
claims m. by grace divine . 30.4
love in saving lost m. . . 78.3
his blood m. hath bought . 90.6
all his sufferings for m. . . 191.1
live in him for lost m. . . 451.1
as a saviour of m. . . . 499.3
Lord and Father of m. . . 567.1
thy yearning pity for m. . . 594.1
what can I do to help m. . 706.2
our Saviour's giving to m. . 777.2
Satan has taught m. to sin . 885.2
b *all mankind*
it reaches all m. . . . 55.2
would all m. embrace . . 60.4
thou for all m. hast done . 62.4
is his gift to all m. . . . 74.3
I bring to you and all m.. . 93.2
all m. with me may prove . 140.5
love to thee and all m. . . 214.1
all m. let there be light . . 224.2
God hath bidden all m. . . 234.1
joyful news to all m. . . 249.1
all m. shall learn . . . 533.3
should tell to all m. . . 760.1
friend of all m. . . . 796.1
cord close-binding all m. . 826.2
Jesus died for all m. . . c22
Jesus (8h)

manna *Ex 16:15*; Rev 2:17**
m. to the hungry soul . . 58.2
with his m. . . . shall fill. . 344.3
day by day the m. fell . . 566.1
take the m. of today . . 566.2
feed . . . with m. sweet. . 612.2
true m. from on high . . 654.2
daily m. still provide you . 954.2

manner
fervent m. . . . praise . . 803.2
strange their word . . . m. . 939.2

mansion *John 14:2*
I rise to claim my m. . . 116.5
lives my m. to prepare . . 144.3
harps of gold and m. fair . 268.1
claim a m. there . . . 312.4
in Heaven you'll have a m. . 328.3
an heir to a m. . . . 354.3
in those m. sublime . . 371.3
a home, a m. fair . . . 811.c
with its m. of light . . . 883.3
the m. bright and blessèd . 892.1
marching up to m. bright . 902.1
each saint has a m. . . 905.3
b *mansions above*
rest in those m. a. us . . 139.3
leading homeward to m. a. . 247.2
kingdoms and m. a. . . 535.2
c *mansions of glory*
there are m. of g. prepared . 233.3
m. of G. and endless delight . 357.4
home to the m. of g. . . 808.4
there's a m. up in G. . . 899.c

mantle 16.3

many
1 *re people*
m. souls were won . . 198.3
m. said I'd run away . . 338.3
depths of m. a heart . . 612.4
in m. a soul, and mine . . 629.3
m. dying in sin everywhere . 708.4
m. dear children . . . there . 794.2
there are m. thousands . . 797.3
m. a thousand strong . . 815.1
m. choose the better part . 832.3
m. mighty men are lost . . 847.2
m. giants, great and tall . . 847.3
m. dear to my heart . . 886.4
m. that we loved have left . 938.4
m. found salvation free . . 939.2
reveal . . . to m. in this place. 946.3
so m. hearts are lonely/drear . c200
wonder (2c)
2 *re objects*
m. are the things . . . 52.1
m. thoughts . . . m. places . 119.1
by m. deeds of shame . . 172.5
m. a sorrow . . . m. a tear . 228.4
m. a conflict . . . doubt . . 293.3
faint . . . from m. a fall . . 337.3
pierced by m. a thorn . . 339.3
count your m. blessings . . 396.*
you have waited m. years . 433.1
m. the crushing defeats . . 437.1
days be few or m. . . . 477.3
weakened by m. a wound . 553.2
how m. fights I've lost . . 770.1
a flag of m. victories . . 774.1
m. kinds of darkness . . 841.3
too m. there must be . . 850.1
with m. dreams of fame . 860.4
sing we m. years of blessing . 939.1
b *many sins* *Luke 7:47*
your m. s. may be forgiven . 67.2
my s. they are m. . . . 298.2
my s. which were m. . . 394.2
their m. s. he will forgive . 814.1
Lord, my s. they are m. . . 883.2
c *Rev 19:12*
crown him with m. crowns . 156.1
danger (d), how (c)

map 30.3

mar-red
though they m. that image . 38.4
that suffering face so m. . 138.2
tears thy face have m. . . 299.2
in thy m. visage any grace . 353.1
everything that m. . . . 494.3

Marah *Ex. 15:23* . . . 510.3

march-ed-ing
1 *(God) marches*
he m. to victory . . . 130.3
the Christ is m. . . . 159.3
truth/day/God is m. on . . 162.*
2 *(we) march*
battalions now are m. . . 169.2
m. through Immanuel's . . 314.3

m. with bounding haste . 362.2
m. to meet the . . . King . 406.2
m. as to war . . . 690.1, c
sing our m. song . . . 700.*
our invading forces m. . . 705.2
his happy people m. . . 705.3
m. by the river of light . . 708.1
m. to the promised land . 765.1
one the m. in God begun . 765.5
m. forth to grand emprise . 799.2
God's soldier m. as to war . 801.1
we'll m. in his name . . 808.4
arm . . . and m. to fight . . 813.1
as . . . m. to Glory . . . 815.*
m. to the fray . . . 817.1
a day's m. nearer home . . 877.1
m. to Zion/together/to victory 901.*
we are m. home to Glory . 902.1
m. up the hillside . . . 903.1
m. on our journey . . . 903.2
keep on m. with . . . faith . c136
m. forth a company grand . c236
m. beneath the yellow . . c241

b *march along*
as we m. a. the way . . 367.c
against the foe to m. a. . . 432.2
Salvation Army is m. a. . . 681.*
we'll boldly m. a. . . . 775.2
to the happy land we'll m. a. . 807.1
cheerful m. right a. . . 813.3
as we gladly m. a. . . . 818.c
as we m. a. we'll shout . . 821.2
I'm a soldier . . . m. a. . . c229

c *march forward*
f. m. with blood and fire . 696.3
m. f. to the fight . . . 810.1
steadily f. m. . . . 814.c
go m. f. to the . . . land . . 817.3
m. ever f. 866.2

d *march on-ward*
ever singing, m. we o. . . 10.4
m. o. we go 698.2
o. we m. with the . . . fire . 700.c
m. o., salvation soldiers . . 810.1
m. o. in the light/through, etc 811.*
m. o.! we bring the jubilee . 815.c
m. o. bravely . . . 817.2
we are m. o. . . . . 818.*
we are m. o. our journey . 903.2
m. o., happy soldiers . . 905.4
keep a-m. o. . . . c153
m. o. bravely to victory . c228
we're m. o. together . . c244

victory (2d)

margin
on the m. of this river . . 471.4
the m. of that lone river . . 726.4
on the m. of the river . . 891.2

mark-ed
through the desert m. . . 159.1
m. out thine heir . . . 207.4
way is m. by love divine. . 400.1
light shall m. the road . . 442.6
m. for pureness . . . 531.2
garments . . . which m. out . 589.1
I want to be m. . . . 589.3
m. the way for me . . . 628.1
heart to m. and cheer . . 683.3
in paths he has m. . . 734.1
they m. the footsteps . . 879.4
m. each suppliant sigh . . 940.3

b *Gal 6:17*
the prophets' m. you bear . 95.3
hath he m. to lead me . . 228.2
grant . . . the m. of thy zeal . 484.1

marriage 949.1

mart
help you in life's busy m. . 664.3

office, field or m. . . . 688.3
in the home and in the m. . 832.3

martial
m. and mighty host . . 648.2
m. hosts assemble . . 803.1

martyrs
crown him, ye m. . . . 56.4
blessèd are the patient m. . 95.2
though as a m. die . . . 530.3
those m. bold and daring . 686.1

b *Acts 22:20*
the m. first 701.2

marvel-led
I m. how gently . . . 111.1
such a m. of wonder . . 395.2

marvellous *1 Peter 2:9*
dwell in his m. light . . 166.2
how m.! how wonderful . 179.c

Mary
a *Luke 1:27*
Christ is born of M. . . 86.2
M. was that mother mild . 87.1

b *Luke 10:39*
waiting, like attentive M. . 210.3

c *John 20:1*
lead me, like M. . . . 117.3

massed 905.4

masses 704.3

master
1 *re Jesus*
voc nc, but see blessed (3e)

b
your M. proclaim . . . 24.1
the M. surely heard . . 103.4
in my M.'s suffering . . 197.3
is he thy M. to be? . . 276.2
the M. of the sea heard . . 336.1
he's the M. of the sea . . 336.3
open and let the M. in . . 373.c
glad, because the M. said . 403.c
with the M. talking . . 430.3
the way the M. trod . . 462.2
all is in the M.'s hands . . 512.2
all my work is for the M. . 522.c
with the M.'s own love . . 527.2
learn more of your M. . . 564.4
I'll use my M. to serve . . 640.3
till the M. walketh along . 680.1
the M.'s call their choice . 680.2
the way the M. went . . 683.1
the M. praises . . . 683.2
in constancy follow the M. . 685.1
Christ, the royal M. . . 690.1
saw his M. in the sky . . 701.2
fight until the M. calls . 703.c
M.'s darkest battlefield . . 705.2
shown in the love of our M. . 739.1
the greeting of the M. . . 751.2
shout till the M. comes . . 807.3
the path that the M. trod . 811.1
the M., ready and kind . . 848.3
let us labour for the M. . . 907.3
nobly for their M. stood . 909.1
serve their M. . . . 909.2
sowing for the M. . . . 930.3
let the dear M. come in . . c18
in the M.'s footsteps . . c195

c *John 11:28*
the M. is come . . . 273.1

d *Lord and Master* *John 13:13*
as L. and M. of the whole . 480.3
I am thine, O L. and M. . . 510.c
O M., L., I come . . . 860.5

e *John 20:28*
gracious M. and my God . 64.2
joy (3c), will (1b)

2 *(other)*
all indicate a m. mind . . 27.2
m. o'er my sin . . . 303.4
power to m. wrong . . 432.2
until it m. find . . . 508.2

b
and the m.-builder calleth . 868.2

masterful 2.3

match
faith to m. our time . . 6.2
deeds must ever m. our creed 760.4
gospel that m. the hour . . c210

matchless
Jesus' name has m. worth . 63.2
the m. name of Jesus . 65.1, c
hail him as thy m. King . . 156.1
m. Jesus, break our bonds . 185.2
thy m. power is ever new . 559.3
weaver divine, thy m. skill . 644.1
what m. grace . . . 831.2

b *matchless love*
the wonders of his m. l. . 215.2
l., so wonderful, m. . . 319.1
O his m. boundless l. . . 418.c
enslave it with thy m. l. . . 508.2

matron 701.4

matter
no m. what you do . . 44.1
your colour will not m. . . 170.2
it doesn't m. now . . . 402.c
it does not m. who . . 814.c

May 318.1

maze 743.3

meadow
blossoming m. 10.2
bloom in every m. . . . 155.2
fair are the m. . . . 177.2
flowers fair the m. wear. . 850.2

meal 663.2

mean-ly
1 *(adjective)*
the poor and m. and lowly . 87.2
all m. wrapped . . . 93.4
the m. altar of my heart . . 199.1

2 *(verb)*
what m. that . . . cry . . 140.1
what he now m. to me . . 215.3
that m. me . . . . 403.*
if my grief m. . . . gain . . 729.3
with all its colours m. . . 779.2

b *(intend)*
I m. with Jesus . . . dwell . 275.4
I m. to shout salvation . . 338.5
while I've breath I m. . . 356.1
we m. to have the victory . 800.c
we m. to conquer wrong . 821.3
he had m. you should win . 893.2
step by step we m. to go . 901.1
the Army m. to lead . . 901.5

meaning
for its m. is sublime . . 63.1
is there a name for m. . . 71.2
there is m. in my word . . 463.1
unfolding its m. to me . . 553.1
love's m. to unfold . . 590.1
would you . . . know the m. . 783.1
now their m. found . . 894.2
man has no m. . . . c210

means *(n)* 15.5

measure
love . . . can never be m. . 47.3
peace . . . that knows no m. . 112.4
the m. of man's mind . . 265.6
none the love . . . can m. . 363.1
thine to m. all its windings . 510.1
salvation's full m. . . . 553.1
his grace has no m. . . 579.3
my hope I cannot m. . . 736.3
none can estimate their m. . 922.2
knows neither m. nor end . 962
b *Luke 6:38*
he gives me heavenly m. . 413.4
treasure in abundant m. . c249

measureless
O m. Might! 16.6
gave in love of his m. all. . 245.2
O m. depths of his grace . 535.3
unmeasured

meat
a *Ps 42:3*
my m. has been my tears . 762.1
b *John 6:27*
Christ is my m. . . . 346.4

mediator *1 Tim 2:5* . . c156

medicine
Christ is . . . my m. . . 346.4
the m. food 712.4

meek-ly
1 *(re Jesus)* *Matt 11:29*
thy face so m. and mild . . 88.5
holy, m., unspotted Lamb . 116.3
that m. head of thine . . 120.3
m. borne, that crown . . 126.2
bow thy m. head . . . 150.5
Jesus lowly, m. and mild . 259.2
in accents m. and low . . 299.3
with the mind, m. Lamb . 568.2
m. enduring . . . reproaches . 623.3
gentle . . ., m. and mild 793.1, 4
2 *(re people)* *Matt 5:5*
joy of all the m. 61.3
where m. souls will receive . 86.3
blessed are the m. . . . 95.1
m. their heritage possess . 198.4
with actions bold and m. . 212.1
a heart resigned, . . . m. . 444.2
with my spirit at its m. . . 528.2
the heart resigned and m. . 555.2
the m. and lowly heart . . 555.4
the old man, m. and mild . 839.2
young souls m. striving . . 849.2

meekness *Col 3:12**
make us like thee in m. . . 515.4
clothed upon with m. . . 584.2
b *2 Tim 2:25*
with m. to reprove . . 568.3

meet-met
1 *(adjective)*
m. it is for us to give . . 109.3
deal . . . as thou seest m. . 291.4
a temple m. for thee . . 411.4
temple m. for thy dwelling . 623.4
not m. that we . . . fear. . 772.3
a Kingdom m. for thee . . 827.3
b *Col 1:12*
sent down to make us m. . 195.4
2 *(verb) (God) meets-met*
hopes . . . m. in thee tonight. 86.1
to be m. by their Father. . 170.2
ready to m. you . . . 236.3
see, the Father m. him . . 550.1
come down to m. us here . 669.4
come down and m. us now . 784.4
b *meet-met (need)*
fire will m. our every n. . . 203.3
thou alone my n. canst m. . 292.1
he m. the n. of my heart . 371.1
begun to m. our n. . . 642.2
worked to m. our wants . 926.1
m. my n. just now . . . c86
c *Matt 28:9*
lo! Jesus m. thee . . . 152.2
3 *(general)*
love and sorrow m. . . 136.3
when care and sorrow m. me 343.2
could not m. my . . . desire . 379.3
to m. the glad . . . 485.2
only with failure I m. . . 553.2
all that I m. . . . my good . 712.4
need and . . . fulness m. . 741.4
may m. with runaways . . 806.2
m. both east . . . north . . 826.4
the people you may m. . . 829.2
nothing . . . m. the hunger . 830.1
supply which m. . . . need . 923.1
where joy and duty m. . . c40
b *meet (Jesus)*
I m. the good shepherd . . 111.1
languish thy descent to m. . 216.4
have m. with one who knows 311.2
Jesus my Saviour I m. . . 371.1
where all my wishes m. . . 556.4
with . . . pains they m. . . 558.1
teach me . . . m. thy gaze . 618.1
let my soul m. thee there . 647.1
I m. my Lord . . . 740.2
c *meet-met [opposition]*
armèd hosts to m. . . . 158.2
foes at every hand I m. . . 400.2
various hindrances we m. . 646.1
to m. the bold tempter . . 689.1
strong to m. the foe . . 698.2
they m. the . . . steel . . 701.3
nor shrink . . . dangers I m. . 734.1
m. and encounter the f. . . 734.3
if m. by Daniel's band . . 847.3
d *meet [in fellowship]*
we m. with one accord . . 196.2
by faith they m. . . . 573.3
here may we m., and talk . 590.4
we m. . . . to take/on earth . 603.3
where'er thy people m. . . 604.1
where lowly spirits m. . . 648.1
hope to m. again . . . 660.4
as in fellowship we m. . . 748.3
God be with you till we m. . 954.*
e *meet [in Heaven]* *1 Thess 4:17**
m. him by and by . . . 94.*
shall you . . . m. Jesus . . 94.c
to be m. by their Father. . 170.2
till for all thy glory m. . . 210.3
soon we hope to m. above . 239.4
as conqueror m. him there . 242.5
soon shall m. together . . 312.3
I'm bound to m. you . . 312.4
m. you in that . . . land . . 312.4
when my Lord I m. . . 375.3
marching to m. . . . King . 406.2
that we may m. in Heaven . 603.3
would not m. . . . judgment . 618.2
a friend to m. on . . . shore . 709.4
we shall m. on that . . . shore 900.c
we shall up in Glory m. . . 902.4
m. there with a . . . greeting . 908.2
till we m. at Jesus' feet. . 954.c
f *Amos 4:12*
prepare to m. your God . . 914.1

meeting
joyful will the m. be . . 235.c
my m. with Jesus to show . 553.1
saving power in this m. . . 608.1
salvation in this m. show . 608.2

mellow 40.1

melodious
of m. praises they sing . . 406.2
sing . . . the m. songs . . 900.2

melody *Eph 5:19**
a m. of love . . . . 31.*
to men . . . O wondrous m. . 72.6
a gladsome m. . . . 340.1
a m. in my heart today . . 340.c
he filled my heart with m. . 386.3
within my heart a m. . . 390.1
make my life into a m. . . 858.1
b
never . . . a sweeter m. . . 327.1

melt
m. the clouds of sin . . 10.1
m. the heart and . . . eye . 185.1
m. the hardness . . . 531.2
m. away and droop . . 559.4
as sunshine m. the snow . 705.4
break me, m. me . . . c53
b *2 Peter 3:10*
earth's foundations m. away . 746.5

member 157.3

memory
nor can the m. find . . 61.2
m. of deeds gone by . . 303.2
how sweet their m. still . . 442.3
take my m., mind and will . 492.2
take my m., mind and will . 520.2
flag of hallowed m. . . 774.2
written on God's m. . . 850.4
ever in my m. dwell . . c7

men see man

mending
save me from self-m. . . 430.1
m. their nets 680.1

mercies see mercy (i)

merciful
m. and mighty . . 220.1, 4
thou art m. and kind . . 576.3
Jesus is m. . . . will save . 691.c
Lord . . . mighty and m. . 714.2
b *Heb 2:17*
m. high priest . . . 880.3

mercy
with his m. surrounding . 19.4
all his m.'s store . . . 23.1
m. that hath loosed . . 23.4
praise your m. more . . 27.4
clouds . . . big with m. . . 29.3
is there a name for m. . . 71.2
m. calls you, break . . 75.4
m.'s gate open wide . . 126.1
m. is their plea . . . 129.c
since I. . . . m. found . . 140.4
m. is tenderly pleading . . 247.1
canst . . . forget the m. . . 250.3
he has m. and pardon . . 264.3
souls for m. plead . . . 269.2
depth of m. . . . reserved . 286.1
I plead by thy m. . . . 288.c
let thy m. light on me . . 295.2
fulness of m. . . . brought . 298.1
ocean of m. . . . I've stood . 298.5
his strong arm of m. . . 329.1
I see his hand of m. . . 334.1
pardon and m. bestowing . 383.3
wonderful message of m. . 384.3
the heart for m. craves . . 393.3
thy m.'s beams I see . . 412.3
now comprehend thy m. . . 454.5
in faith, thy m. claiming . 460.3

since I have known his m. . 536.3
m. moves the King . 555.2
by constant m. fed . 566.1
shed thy light of . . . m.. . 576.2
he addeth his m. . 579.1
m. thine own . . . delight . 601.3
on thy m. I rely . 627.2
m. drops . . . are falling . 637.c
word of m., giving succour . 655.5
m. shall unshaken stay . 746.1
m. is all that's written . 746.3
thy m. never dies . 746.4
go with your songs of m. . 830.2
sing about the m. . 835.2
thou hast m. to relieve us . 845.3
his m. doth expand . 896.2

b *mercy and love* *Jude 2*
to thy great . . . m. and l. . 33.2
l. and m. found me . 115.2
in his boundless l. and m. . 180.2
boundless l., unmeasured m. 225.4
echoes of m., whispers of l. . 310.2
O depths of l. and m. . 368.2
God in l. and m. found us . 722.2
to sing his l. and m. . 840.3
tokens of thy m. and l. . 870.1
I tell his l. and m. . c147

c *mercy and grace*
m. and g. abound . 384.2
m. . . . great, and g. . 405.c
the m. of thy g. . 590.4
for thy g. and tender m.. . 727.2
sing his m. and his g. . 892.1
for thy m. and thy g. . 937.1

d *mercy and peace* *1 Tim 1:2*
p. on earth, and m. mild . 82.1
speak of m. and of p. . 697.5

e *in mercy*
yet in m. take me in . 292.3
in m. think of me . 303.1
in his m. . . . bestow . 331.4
soul in m. to reclaim . 339.1
in m. let thy blessing . 470.3
in thy m. breathe upon me . 477.1
in thy m. heal us all . 558.5
in thy m. hear . . . prayer . 582.1
all . . . in m. given . 617.3
daily find in his m. . 724.1
for this in m. he gave . 831.1
if in m. thou wilt spare . 916.2
only let, in thy m. . c55

f *[God] in mercy*
Jesus, in his m., left . 52.3
God can in m. pardon . 186.4
in m. he will welcome . 225.c
Lord in m. tarries yet . 267.2
God in great m. pardoned . 347.c
God in . . . m. found us . 722.2

g *Ps 130:7*
for sinners there is m. . 188.3
there's m. with the Lord . 231.1
there's m. still for thee . 253.*
do not reject the m. . 255.c
there is m. with the Saviour . 265.4
may know there's m. still . 919.2
there is m. in Jesus . c23

h *Matt 5:7*
blessed are the men of m. . 95.2

i *mercy-ies of God* *Rom 12:1*
God's free m. streameth . 40.2
again, by God's abundant m.. 173.1
death thy endless m. seal . 199.4
pleasure, by God's m. made . 227.1
linger and heed not his m. . 264.2
a wideness in God's m. . 265.3
calls us; by thy m. . 428.5
thy faithful m. crown . 438.1
river of God's m. 462.1, 3
thank . . . for present m. . 552.1
in me thy m. move . 594.2
true thy m. are . 641.2
greater far . . . thy m. are . 642.2
God's m. holds . . . plan. . 723.2
m. shall on you descend . 920.4
our thanks for m. past . 950

new (d), rich (2c)

j *2 Cor 1:3*
Lord of m., love and truth . 159.1
coming to the Lord of m. . 470.2
beams our Father's m. . 478.1
Father of love . . . and of m.. 486.1
learning of our Father's m. . 595.2

k *Heb 4:16*
let me, at the throne of m. . 301.2

abundant (d), boundless (e), flow (2g), free (2c), goodness (c), make (3g), manifold (b), prove (3e), sake (1a), show (1c), stream (2c), sure (e), tender (e)

2 *mercy seat* *Ex 25:17**
ever seek the m. s. . 76.2
at the m. s. of God . 116.4
at the m. s. . . . kneel . 236.1
bring to the m. s. . 246.c
find peace at the m. s. . 246.3
there is a m. s. revealed. . 269.1
at the Father's m. s. . 278.2
I bow . . . at thy m. s. . 282.1
approach . . . the m. s. . 284.1
came to the m. s. pleading . 383.3
at the blest m. s. . 524.2
the m. s. . 573.1
long past the m. s. . 590.1
they behold the m. s. . 604.1
coming to the m. s. . 646.1
all at one m. s. . 648.1

merit
1 *re divine*
through the m. of his name . 63.c
thine all-sufficient m. . 79.4
by thy m. we find favour . 109.1
m. of thy grace claim me . 285.1
trusting only in thy m. . 301.3
m. my soul's best songs . 336.2
him who m. all my love . 365.2
through thy saving m. . 430.4

b *[Saviour's] merit*
to sing the S.'s m. . 109.3
all the S.'s dying m. . 191.1
won for us by Jesus' m. . 210.1
witnesser of Jesus' m. . 295.3
world through Jesus' m. . 622.2
to plead the S.'s m. . 783.3

2 *re human*
without m. or pretence . 595.2

merry . 830.1

message
hear again the m. ringing . 74.3
this m. as from God receive . 234.3
heed the gracious m. . 240.3
sweet is the m. today . 247.c
make the m. clear . 262.c
there is a m. . . . for us all . 270.1
we have a m. . . . from Jesus. 273.*
tell the m. all around . 393.1
Jesus came with m. clear . 398.2
gladly I accept the m. . 514.1
filled with m. from thee . 525.3
if love . . . seal not the m. . 530.1
let the glorious m. roll . 546.3
power . . . to speed the m. . 760.1
its m. is eternal . 781.1
a m. grand and true . 783.1
no difference in the m. . 824.4
may its m. be our guide . 856.3
may its m. . . . lead us . 856.4

b *hear message*
have you h. the m. . 242.1
h. the glad m. . 247.1
may this m. yet be h. . 463.1

c *message of . . .*
a m. of hope . . . love . 273.2, 3
wonderful m. of mercy . 384.3
m. of salvation . 655.2

messenger
the m. of old . 154.2
return sweet m. of rest . 442.4
m. proclaim . . . gospel . 945.3

Messiah *John 1:41**
now proclaim M.'s birth . 75.1
shall the true M. see . 161.2

met see meet

'mid see amid

midnight
through the m. sky . 38.1
it came upon the m. clear . 83.1
dark hath been the m. . 896.1

midst
victors in the m. of strife . 10.4
daily, in the m. of life . 142.3
the m. of common days . 618.1
in m. of mortal pain . 701.2

b *Matt 18:20*
thou in the m. of us . 603.1
there's Jesus in the m. . 664.3

c *Luke 24:36*
in our m. he's standing . 235.1

amid-st

midsummer . 318.1

might *(noun)*
1 *divine*
thou rulest in m. . 8.2
tell of his m. . 16.2
O measureless M. . 16.6
help . . . recognise your m. . 27.4
loosed . . . with Easter's m. . 30.4
with all-commanding m. . 34.3
shines in m. victorious . 40.2
is there a name for m. . 71.2
attests his royal m. . 126.2
Lord of truth and m. . 145.2
come in thy great m. . 172.4
his all-transforming m. . 178.3
now thy m. display . 188.1
m. and majesty are thine . 223.5
trusting Jesus and his m. . 352.1
trusting in his m. . 379.4
marvel of wonder and m. . 395.2
with full salvation m. . 431.2
glory and m. are beyond us . 506.1
whose m. burst . . . grave . 532.4
Christ would come in m. . 541.1
endeavour feel not thy m. . 635.3
m. divine . . . our stay . 702.2
saved by Jesus' m. . 803.3
by his m. restored . 803.4
whose m. must yet appear . 871.4
thou wast their . . . m. . 876.2

b *(for us)*
help us daily, by thy m. . 193.5
Lord . . . give the m. . 466.4
leaning on my Saviour's m. . 686.3
our strength . . . is thy m. . 692.4
fight . . . in his everlasting m.. 700.*
in the m. of Jehovah . . . go . 703.3
rejoicing in his m. . 818.1
strengthened by his m. . 866.c
arm us with holy m. . 870.3

power (4o), spirit (5d), wisdom (1e)

2 *(human)*
makes of weakness, m. . 197.3
make of my weakness m. . 221.3

weakness leaneth on his m. . 333.2
turns weakness into m. . . 830.3
sown in our weakness . . . m.. 931.c

b *with my might* (Deut 6:5)
shout with all my m. . 369.c
serve him with my m. . . 400.c
powers, with all thy m. . . 665.5
fight . . . with all thy m.. . 718.1
serve him with our m. . . 819.2
shout with all our m. . . 821.2

c *Zech 4:6*
it is not with m. . . . 527.3
not m., nor power . . . 581.2
dare not boast . . . in m. . 747.2

d
angry mob and Roman m. . 181.2
no foes shall stay his m. . 685.2
the Army soldier's m. . . 807.2

mighty
1 *re divine*
Christ, the m. maker . . 105.3
beginning was the m. Word . 141.1
the m. victor's brow . . 168.1
m. Lord, our hearts . . 201.2
so m. a defender . . . 345.4
such a m., m. King . . 402.c
holy courage, m., m. King . 499.3
m. Captain of the host . . 789.6

b *mighty God*
O M. God . . . . 39.1, c
they forget the m. God . . 559.2
m. God, thy . . . power . 559.3

c *mighty Saviour*
rejoices in this m. S. . . 341.3
Jesus, m. S., I trust . . 511.2
thou art a m. S. . . . 538.c

d *mighty Spirit*
m. moving of thy S. . . 192.1
m. S., dwell with me . . 212.4
pass me not, O m. S. . . 295.3
thy m. S. pour . . . 609.1

e
a m. fortress is our God . . 1.1
with a m. triumph . . . 148.c
ever by a m. hope . . . 212.4
my strong and m. tower . 344.2
m. wonders there I see . . 348.c
thy m. aid bestowing . . 448.4
m., wonder-working river . 471.c
shadow of a m. rock . . 476.1
most m. your working . . 506.1
weak, but thou art m. . . 578.1
thy m. comfort feel . . 603.4
a great, m. shower . . 608.1
bless thee for thy m. aid. . 642.3
hidden in its m. depths . . 658.2
heard this m. call . . . 700.1
a m. miracle of grace . . 858.c
m. signs and wonders . . 945.3

f *mighty arm* (Ps 89:13)
I have found a m. arm . . 311.3
may thy m. arm uphold them. 576.4
thy m. arm make bare . . 626.1

g *mighty deed*
Luke 24:19; 2 Cor 12:12
now the m. d. is done . . 107.4
the m. d. was done . . 304.2
let the m. d. be done . . 481.c

h *mighty love*
his l. is m. to compel . . 234.4
l. so m. and so true . . 336.2
his m. l., mighty to save . 364.c
m. l. that gave its all . . 741.1
in his m. l. abiding . . . 759.c
God's m. l. confess . . 833.3
like a m. sea . . . the l. . . c140

i *mighty power* *Eph 1:19**
deliver by thy m. p. . . 624.4
fill/convict . . . thy m. p. 638.2, 3
with m. p. my soul baptise . 649.3
strong . . . in his m. p. . . 695.2
Jehovah's m. p. . . . 822.2
manifest thy m. p. . . . 941.2
by his m. p. he holds me . c163

hand (1h), merciful (a), save (1h), sword (2b), work (1c)

2 *(general)*
join the m. chorus . . . 10.4
its m. energies fulfil . . 38.2
m. storms are on my head . 39.2
m. dread had seized . . 93.2
give the winds a m. voice . 393.4
m. gulf that God did span . 405.4
army, like a m. sea . . 550.c
for a m. revival we plead . 608.1
a m. revival is coming . . c63

ocean (1b), wind (1d)

b *re (people)*
wrestling on in m. prayer . 210.4
I myself would m. be...prevail 212.4
martial and m. host . . 648.2
like a m. army . . . Church . 690.3
captain of the m. throng . 698.c
lead our m. throng . . 700.2
m. men around us falling . 804.2
many m. men are lost . . 847.2
m. was their courage . . 866.1
faith, m. faith . . . c118

c *(re spiritual warfare)*
m. are your enemies . . 697.1
forth to the m. conflict . . 699.2
though m. the foe . . . 703.2
m. is the foe 787.3
m. are the tasks ahead . . 789.3
see the m. host advancing . 804.2
Hell's forces may be m. . . 810.2
in the m. conflict . . . 817.2
our foe may be m. . . . 820.3

d *Luke 1:52*
the m. have their day . . 6.4

mightier-st
in vain the m. powers . . 9.4
mighty works or m. name . 26.1

mild
all gentle thoughts and m. . 28.4
peace on earth, and mercy m. 82.1
m., he lays his glory by . . 82.3
Mary was that mother m. . 87.1
children all must be m. . . 87.3
by thy face so meek and m. . 88.5
infant, tender and m. . . 89.1
Jesus, so gentle and m. . 175.3
Jesus lowly, meek and m. . 259.2
gentle Jesus, meek and m. 793.1, 4
old man, meek and m. . . 839.2

milk see honey

milling 927.2

millions
m. there have been supplied . 239.3
m. have reached . . . m. more 275.1
while the heedless m. die . 696.1
help from the dying m. . . 702.2
m. who're drifting . . . 703.1
m. . . . into the Kingdom . 776.2
while m. sin-bound lie . . 780.2
m. wait, whose need . . 801.2
we'll let the m. know . . 821.c
where m. . . . have no hope . 832.2
hundreds and thousands, m. . 850.*

mind
1 *(re divine)*
all indicate a master m. . 27.2
dismissed you from his m. . 44.1
all thy m. declare . . . 210.4
unto his m. may reach . . 398.1
perceive the m. of God . . 656.3
heard with eager m. . . 871.2

b *Phil 2:5; 1 Peter 4:1*
let this m. be in us . . 174.3
that in me the m. of Christ . 451.1
in me this m. might be . . 451.3
arm me with the m. . . 568.2
m. that was in Christ . . 705.4
let me have thy loving m. . 793.5

2 *(human)*
our m. inspire . . . 20.3
wider than the human m. . 49.3
human m. can pity know . 50.1
keep and ponder in our m. . 78.3
seized their troubled m. . . 93.2
does sadness fill my m. . . 187.3
to every thankful m. . . 191.1
move . . . every m. . . 196.3
is your m. mixed up . . 244.2
the measure of man's m. . 265.6
any change in my m. . . 318.3
I . . . whose m. is dim . . 414.3
into the depths of m. . . 416.3
a willing m., a ready hand . 426.3
ask thee for a patient m. . 485.1
a m. to blend with . . . life . 485.3
I give you my m. . . . 506.3
train thou my m. . . . 529.2
I want a sober m. . . . 596.2
inhabitest the humble m. . 604.2
the wanderings of the m. . 619.2
take from my m. the stress . 647.2
fellowship of kindred m. . 660.1
our m. be set to hallow . . 668.2
have faith in God, my m. . 723.2
ensures for me an even m. . 728.1
powers of m. 833.2
pure . . . and clean my m. . 861.3
a wearied m. retaineth . . c72

b *with mind*
love . . . w. a constant m. . 5.4
w. a gladsome m. . . . 34.1
I come . . . w. quiet m. . 449.c
w. m. subdued . . . 566.5
w. confident and humble m. 744.3

c *mind and [heart]*
m. desiring truth and h. . . 27.5
for the h. and m.'s delight . 28.3
inform the m. and purify the h. 100.2
faith in my h. assures my m. . 176.3
moving . . . in our h. and m. . 192.1
my h. and m. make strong . 431.2
love with h. and m. . . 522.3
m. cannot show what the h. . 527.3
m., h. and voice . . . sing . 574.5
the same in m. and h. . . 659.5
with m. and hand and h. . 688.3
I rest, h., m. and soul . . 723.4
h. m. and will consecrating . 786.3

body (2g), will (2b)

d *Isa 26:3*
my m. upon thee . . . stayed. 513.1
whose m. is stayed on thee . c142

e *2 Tim 1:7*
gift . . . of a healthful m. . 214.1
health to the sick in m. . . 224.2
riches, healing of the m. . 293.4

give (1o) rightful (b)

3 *(phrases)*
covenant . . . ever kept in m.. 784.3
never m., go on . . . 805.*
let us bear in m. . . . 805.c
we don't m., for the trail . 903.1
never m. what lies before . c26
never m. what others do . c26

mine *(prep)* nc, but
a *Song 2.16*
if . . . he is m. for ever . . 53.1
he is m.! . . . . 388.*
I am his and he is m. . . 402.1
I am thine and thou art m. . 474.3

I am thine . . . thou art m. . 510.c
afford, for m. thou art . . 513.3
O to know that thou art m. . 520.1
I am his and he is m. . . 545.*
if thou, O Christ, art m. . . 565.4
shall say: This God is m. . 875.2
m., I know thou art m. . . c186
tells me . . . he is m. . . c191
2 *mine (noun)*
deep in unfathomable m. . 29.2
God of atom, God of m. . 30.1
thy word is like a . . . m. . 658.2
may I explore the m. . 658.5

mingle-d
sorrow and love flow m. . 136.3
m. with Heaven's gold . . 780.1

ministry
m. of love 32.2
through the m. of men . . 238.2
in thy m. committed . . 528.3

miracle
a m.! Yes, a m. . . . 215.c
I'm a m. of grace . . . 634.2
make my life into a m. . . 858.c
a mighty m. of grace . . 858.c
all that you need is a m. . c2

mire-y *Ps 40:2*
lifted me from the m. clay . 335.c
from sin's deep m. . . 401.2
hearts . . . go to the m. . . 704.1

mirror-ed
years are m. in his eyes . . 131.2
seeking to m. thy glory . . 786.2
m. of the Saviour's face. . 891.4

mirth 3.1

misery
I was sunk in m. . . . 328.1
in m. I walked alone . . 376.1
how much m. and blindness . 770.1
ye . . . who in m. languish . 905.2

misinterpret 790.2

miss-ed-ing
m. the blessings . . . 257.3
lest we m. thy . . . goal . . 577.3
m. thee, . . . should fall . . 726.2
we have m. the joy and grace. 748.1

mission
Christ's completed m. . . 173.2
there is m. in my living . . 463.1
for thy m. make me holy . 463.c
lost the sense of m. . . 463.2
souls are still my m. . . 463.3
help me see my m. plain . 528.4

mis-spent 379.2

mist
m. of doubt encompass me . 48.2
vanished like a m. . . . 399.1

mistake 309.c

mistrust 827.2

mite *Luke 21:2* 525.4

mixed
is your mind m. up . . 244.2
my gold be m. with dross . 522.1

mob 181.2

mock-ed-ing
fled and m. me as I wailed . 547.3
m. the cross and flame . . 701.3
b *Luke 22:63**
m. his anguish and pain . . 99.3
with m. scorn . . . 101.3
cruel thorns, the m. jeer. . 134.1
m. thus the . . . claim . . 147.3
men m. him and ... passed by 245.3
they scoffed and m. my God . 758.3

modern 834.1

molest 671.3

moment
loving . . . from m. of birth . 175.1
the m. fly apace . . . 255.3
the m. are few . . . 273.1
I live a m. at a time . . 385.4
peaceful, happy m. roll . . 387.c
m. flow in praising . . 521.3
take my m. and my days . 525.1
sweet the m. . . . 634.1
never a m. depart . . . 639.3
trusting as the m. fly . . 754.c
serving him m. by m. . . 844.4
its evils in a m. end . . 880.2
the m. you turn to the Lord . c2
God's m. for you . . . c106
b *each/every moment*
rest e. m. in the crucified . 417.2
sanctify e. m. fully . . . 463.c
now I'm trusting e. m. . . 549.3
e. m. to feel thy Spirit . . 589.4
make all our m. calm . . 602.4
e. m. watch and pray . . 667.3
blessings e. m. he crowns . 710.3
e. sacred m. spend . . 720.4
listening e. m. to . . . call . 757.4
e. m. to live for thee . . c33
c *that moment*
t. m. from Jesus a pardon . 22.2
ceasing t. m. from sinning . 553.1
t. m. the blessing . . 553.3
d *this moment*
thou dost t. m. come . . 208.3
feel t. very m. pardon . . 259.3
life at t. m. . . . 271.1, c
I'll start t. m. . . . 275.4
give thyself t. m. to him . 377.4
come t. very m. . . . 403.3
t. m. I know the blood . . 436.4
t. m. the work is complete . 454.3
at t. m. be clean . . . 459.2
from t. m., live or die . . 505.2
from t. m. rise . . . flame . 649.3
in t. glad m. . . . 692.3
covenant we t. m. make . 784.3
at t. m. we're rejoicing . . 795.1
t. m. I feel . . . afresh . . c92
t. m. I believe . . . c128

monarch
hath he diadem as m. . . 228.3
reach a m.'s throne . . 508.3

money *Isa 55:1* 240.4

month 925.4

mood 717.4

moon
thou silver m. 2.1
sun and m. bow down . . 17.4
our m. no more . . . withdrawn 275.2
no m. shall harm thee . . 767.3
b *Ps 148:3*
sun and m. and stars . . 28.2
sun, m. and stars . . . above . 33.2
sun, m. and stars forgot . 617.5

moonlight 177.3

moor 606.3

more
1 *(with adverb)*
m. sensibly within me live . 207.4
heart m. deeply bleed . . 586.3
I must m. closely dwell . . 618.c
life m. closely linked . . 618.2
himself m. fully know . . 634.4
help . . . live m. nearly . . 668.5
m. clearly would I realise . 717.2
2 *(with noun)*
humbly ask for m. . . . 23.1
m. lustre to the day . . 112.3
I pant for m. . . . 207.2
m. of their beauty see . . 258.1
yet there's room for m. . . 266.1
room for millions m. . . 275.1
m. to follow . . . . 418.*
one m. chain . . . riven . . 434.3
m. . . . if I had m. . . . 516.1
for m. of thy power . . . pray. 523.1
give me m. power . . . 523.3
less of self and m. of thee . 548.3
he sendeth m. strength . 579.1
help . . . make m. sacrifice . 619.4
m. holy living/thanksgiving . 622.3
ten thousand thousand m. . 629.3
as m. of Heaven . . . we see . 668.3
m. warriors are wanted . 684.1
m. heroes of faith . . . see . 684.4
his strength the m. is . . 685.2
still we get m. smiles . . 806.1
m. may thy salvation see . 919.1
b *more blessings*
b. m. than we can give . . 57.3
m. b. than . . . lost . . 160.4
b. m. than we can number . 938.2
c *more grace* *James 4:6*
m. g. for the good . . 265.4
he giveth m. grace . . 579.1
m. grace is wrought . . 615.4
d *more love* *John 21:15**
to l. and please thee m. . . 14.4
make us l. thee m. . . 40.3
for grace to l. thee m. . . 110.6
suffers . . . yet l. the m. . 142.4
saying: Christian, l. me m. . 428.3
l. him m. than these . . 428.4
m. and m. of l.'s supply . . 439.4
give me m. l., dear Lord . . 523.2
m. soul-saving love . . 609.1
hearts to l. him m. and m. . 704.1
e *more praise*
praise your mercy m. . . 27.4
I'll praise him m. and m. . 380.3
m. praise than I can give . 616.2
f *more than*
made us m. t. . . . sons . 38.5
m. t. I can . . . comprehend 52.3
justice . . . m. t. liberty . 265.3
m. t. life to me . . . 301.4
m. t. sufficient . . . grace . 319.2
m. t. life is Jesus . . 420.2
m. t. they can express . 560.3
m. t. thyself I cannot . . 565.3
m. t. human tongue . . 696.2
m. is he t. host . . . 728.4
I am m. to him t. guest . 728.4
g *more than all*
m. t. all, the heart . . 11.2
pleasure in his service m. . 399.1
m. t. all else . . . become . 451.4
thy love is m. t. all . . 486.2
our m. t. all we owe . . 533.2
m. t. all my lips . . . do . 591.2
m. t. all in thee I find . . 737.3
love him, m. t. all . . c216
h *2 Kings 6:16*
m. t. the foes 537.2
ask (2d), conqueror (2b), few (b)

3 *(with verb)*
m. and m. it spreads . . 165.2
lustre shining m. and m. . 196.5
I want to serve him m. . . 369.2
m. and m. thyself display . 412.4
see . . . desire thee m. . . 449.2
servant he became, yea m. . 451.2
peace I never knew b. . . 549.c
learn m. of your Master . . 564.4
baptise us m. and m. . . 575.1
as m. for thee we dare . . 642.3
prove still m. . . . prayer. . 642.3
m. enjoy them there . . 880.4
thy purpose m. may know . 919.3
m. receiving . . . m. to give . 921.2
gladly give thee m. and m. . 921.3
what must please thee m. . 925.5
trust and serve thee m. . . 926.3
what can I ask m. . . . c61

more (2d, e), much (c, d), once (4d), what (1d)

b *more like*
m. l. the heart of him . . 146.1
make us m. l. Jesus . . 193.4
m. and m. l. thee . . 584.1, 3
want to attain m. likeness . 589.2

4 *(with adjective)*
some m. convenient day . 226.1
m. full of grace than I . . 305.2
hardly m. favoured or blest . 373.2
m. glorious and bright . . 387.1
than gold . . . m. precious . 516.4
none m. blest than I . . 557.3
a place . . . m. sweet . . 573.2
m. sacred now is . . . hill . 590.1
with a step m. firm . . 614.2
his death . . . m. healing . . 634.4
sleep . . . m. vigorous make . 671.4
faith . . . m. blest reward . 748.4
the cup . . . not m. bitter . 758.2
be m. courageous still . . 782.3
wealth of God, m. bountiful . 796.2
a yet m. glorious day . . 876.5
m. deep I'll drink above . . 896.2
make us m. earnest . . 933.4

5
a *never/more*
n. m. alone, since thou . . 59.2
changeth n., n. m. . . 182.2
soul shall n. hunger m. . . 277.2
enter . . . leave us n. m.. . 299.3
over sin . . . n. m. grieve . 437.2
n. m. thy temples leave . . 438.2
n. m. stain my soul . . 502.3
n. m. our faith . . . dim . . 773.4
n. m. to dwell therein . . 783.4
they n. suffer m. . . . 911.6
n. m. to roam c10

b *no/any more*
faith desires n. m. . . . 26.4
God will plan for you n. m. . 44.2
that man n. m. may die . . 82.3
his hands n. m. were free . 129.1
he sets in blood n. m. . . 143.2
n. m. we tremble . . . 149.3
n. m. we doubt thee . . 152.3
rise and set n. m. . . . 160.1
fight . . . your God n. m. . 234.4
doubt n. m. his love . . 249.3
rise at once! delay n. m. . 267.3
n. m. shall darkness cloud . 277.4
I can hold out n. m. . . 307.4
where we shall part n. m. . 312.4
winters . . . are n. m. . . 318.4
sinking to rise n. m. . . 336.1
angels can do nothing m. . 367.3
I fear n. m. 375.1
Lord, I n. m. . . . blaspheme . 407.1
I will not grieve thee m.. . 409.5
haste . . . n. m. delay . . 412.2
come . . . n. m. to part . . 470.3
I can n. m. be careless . . 482.2
n. m. shall lead . . . astray . 509.2
n. m. to cause . . . grieve . 536.2
fear . . . mine n. m. . . 540.5
haunt my soul n. m. . . 551.2
thou canst give n. m. . . 565.3
I n. m. revere his name . . 592.2
thirst n. m. for drops . . 601.2
n. m. delaying . . . 702.3
he remembers sins n. m. . 724.c
up against me any m. . . 724.c
I'll hear n. m. . . . 724.c
we will n. m. . . . forsake . 784.3
till sin shall be n. m. . . 802.1
n. m. . . . aspect wear . . 925.3
leave them n. m. . . . c40
sail the wide sea n. m. . . c178

c *Isa 60:20*
sun . . . n. m. go down . . 275.2
moon n. m. . . . withdrawn . 275.2

d *sin no more* *John 8:11*
go in peace, s. n. m. . . 126.c
saved, to s. n. m. . . . 132.3
s. in mine n. m. . . . 290.1
bid me s. n. m. . . . 305.3
fearing and s. n. m. . . 454.1
n. m. lie down in s. . . 676.4
till we shall s. n. m. . . 915.3
in thy hand to s. n. m. . . c144
n. m. the servant of s. . . c157

e *Rev 3:12*
pillars, and go out n. m. . 533.5

f *Rev 21:4*
death and the curse . . . n. m. 160.4
spirits shall sorrow n. m. . 900.2

once (4d), remember (d), time (1h), war (1b), what (1d)

morn-ing
thou rising m. . . . rejoice . 2.2
the sunset, and the m. . . 25.2
through m. bright . . . 31.3
m. has broken 35.1
the m. light, the lily . . 42.2
our hearts rejoice this m. . 74.1
stay . . . until m. is nigh. . 77.2
salute the happy m. . . 78.1
born this happy m. . . 85.3
hail, thou ever-blessed m. . 88.c
the early dew of m. . . 98.2
welcome, happy m. . 155.1, c
thine own third m. . . 155.3
when m. gilds the skies . . 187.1
early in the m. our song . 220.1
it turns night to m. . . 237.2
look . . . thy m. shall rise . 332.3
dark and cheerless is the m. . 412.3
in my soul an Easter m. . . 520.5
with the m. . . . faces smile . 606.3
when purple m. breaketh . 632.1
pay thy m. sacrifice . . 665.1
each m. . . . God calls me . 666.4
when the m. wakens . . 673.4
abide . . . from m. till eve . 676.3
to thee our m. hymns . . 677.1
on Easter m. Jesus came . 855.5
the glad m. of my day . . 860.2
prayer in the m. . . . c114
in the m. when joybells . . c123
we'll sing in the m. . . c222

b *as morning*
once was bright as m. . . 123.1
as to each new-born m. . 632.2
disperse . . . as m. dew . . 665.4
as m. overwhelms . . 705.4

c *Ps 30:5*
m. of joy give . . . 183.4

d *Ps 139:9*
flying on the wings of m. . 776.1
if I take the wings of the m. . c134

new (d), sow (2c), star (d, f), watch (2b)

2 *re Heaven*
through the m. light . . 280.4
m. shall tearless be . . 621.3
at last, in that bright m. . 632.4
Heaven's m. breaks . . 670.5
one glorious m. . . . 888.1
wait till I see the m. . . 889.3
but aye the fadeless m. . . 895.1
the summer m. . . . m. awakes 896.1
m. breaks, eternal . . 907.1
that bright and cloudless m. . 907.2

morrow
sprung to life this m. . . 153.1
glorious unknown m. . . 948.3
the garden and the m. . . c14

mortal
of m. ills prevailing . . 1.1
this m. life also . . . 1.4
m., join the . . . chorus . 10.4
sweetest name on m. tongue 67.c
while m. sleep . . . 86.2
bow . . . to m. pain . . 150.5
the end of m. days . . 171.3
no m. so happy as I . . 318.2
resigned to m. ill . . . 532.3
passing m. understanding . 539.1
m. spirits tire and faint . . 559.2
in midst of m. pain . . 701.2
from the fret of m. years . 878.3
country far from m. sight . 880.1
a m. arrow pierced . . 890.2
timorous m. start . . . 898.2

Moses
a *Deut 3:27**
climb where M. stood . . 898.3

b *Matt 17:3*
where M. and Elijah stood . 154.2

c *Rev 15:3*
everlasting song of M. . . 880.4

most
a *(with adjective)*
m. blessèd, m. glorious . . 8.1
m. wonderful, m. sure . 18.1, 4
friends m. dear . . . 31.2
the gift m. wonderful . . 52.1
m. worthy of a sceptre . . 72.1
so, m. gracious Lord . . 76.1
offered gifts m. rare . . 76.3
make we . . . King m. dear . 97.2
the story m. precious . . 99.1
in this m. vital hour . . 198.5
health . . . m. vigorous . . 214.1
the m. distant land . . 243.3
heart's m. secret depths . 311.4
love m. true and strong . . 343.1
story m. precious . . . 384.1
m. impossible of all . . 407.2
once I thought m. worthy . 435.2
deed, m. gracious God . . 561.2
need . . . m. gracious Lord . 587.1
its m. holy learning . . 655.6
shed his blood m. precious . 805.3
youth's m. urgent call . . 869.2
m. by sin accurst . . . 919.2
m. aweful truth . . . 932.2

high (1b)

b *(with verb)*
things that charm me m. . 136.2
'tis thyself I covet m. . . 435.2
I'm humbled m. . . . 468.4
faith could m. have saved . 770.2
power should m. prevail . 770.2
all that m. we prize . . 774.1
happy m. of all to know. . 837.4
those I loved m. and best . 882.3
what thou m. desirest . . 935.3

c *(with adverb)*
m. wonderfully kind . . 265.6

something better m. surely . 298.4
thou m. surely nigh . . 717.3
promised God m. earnestly . 774.3

mother
dear m. earth 2.4
from our m.'s arms . . 12.1
as a m. stills her child . . 598.2
when m. of Salem . . 797.1
b *(mother of Jesus)*
a m. laid her baby . . . 87.1
Mary was that m. mild . . 87.1
love and watch the lowly m. . 87.3
round the virgin m. . . 89.1
gentle child of gentle m. . 97.1

motion
waves in angry m. . . 96.2
m. of a hidden fire . . 625.1

motive
blessed are the pure in m. . 95.2
m. beneath his control . . 458.4
with holy m. may . . . obey . 581.3
with every . . . m. scanned . 618.1
claims . . . my m., passions . 867.4
pure in m. and in thought . c56

motorway 30.2

motto
let our m. be: go on . . 805.c
our m. shall holiness be . 808.5
salvation is our m. . . 814.1

mould
m. me and make me . . 487.1
take me and m. me . . 501.c
m. the life I yield . . . 531.2
m. me, fill me . . . c53

mount-ain
1 *(literal)*
thy justice like m. . . . 8.2
field and forest, vale and m. . 10.2
the purple-headed m. . . 25.2
look down from lofty m. . 37.2
sheep on the lonely m. . . 88.2
steeper than the m. of time . 766.2
Calvary (c), Pisgah, plain (1b), quake, Zion
2 *(figurative)*
from barren m. . . . 159.5
steep was the m. . . . 388.2
lead me . . . up the m. . 429.1, c
or upon the m. steep . . 483.3
strayed far on the m. . . 740.1
flows from out the m. . . 762.2
climb up to the m. top . . c116
b *(sin)*
sins, although like a m. . . 232.2
sins of years rise m. high . 253.3
found me on sin's m. drear . 740.1
sins rose as high as a m. . c189
c *Matt 17:9*
thou bidst us leave the m. . 154.5
Christ of the m. . . . c98
d *Matt 17:20*
sink the m. to a plain . . 720.1
faith . . . m. to remove . . 733.1
faith . . . the m. move . . 756.5
e *Mark 13:14*
O escape to yonder m. . . 239.2
f *Luke 3:5; Isa 40:4*
as the m. are abased . . 159.2
cast down m. . . . 593.4
g *1 Cor 13:2*
faith . . . removing m. . . 530.2
3 *mount (verb)*
sometimes I m. . . . 468.1
though I m. the cross . . 489.2
I shall m. to the skies . . 543.4
m. aloft to thine abode . . 559.5
wing (f)

mountainside 711.1

mourn-er
let us look and m. . . . 121.1
we m. that e'er our hearts . 135.2
thy softened spirit m. . . 256.2
not without hope, I m. . . 305.1
sins that made thee m. . . 442.4
I m., I m. the sin . . . 448.2
pleasures lost I sadly m.. . 547.4
every m.'s sleep tonight. . 676.5
who m. their weakness . . 806.2
poor and those who m. . . 825.1
b *Matt 5:4; James 4:9*
tears of the m. be dried . . 364.3
they were m. here below . 879.2
c *Mark 16:10*
was m. by his disciples . . 96.4
tenderly m. and wept . . 117.2
friends who m. him dead . 855.5
d *Isa 60:20*
our days of m. ever gone . 275.2

mouth
thy m., O Lord, to me . . 407.5
God be in my m. . . . 953.1

move-d-ing
1 *(God) moves/is moved*
God m. in a . . . way . . 29.1
how swiftly didst thou m. . 62.4
m. with one impulse . . 196.3
rock which cannot m. . . 280.c
grace to me did freely m. . 307.2
mercy m. the King of Heaven. 555.2
in me thy mercies m. . . 594.2
on our . . . spirits m. . . 651.3
rock that naught can m. . 738.1
b *Acts 17:28*
live, dwell and m. in me . 516.3
c *2 Peter 1:21*
mighty m. of thy Spirit . . 192.1
m. by thee the prophets. . 651.2
know not how the Spirit m. . 730.3
water (1b)
2 *(we) move/are moved*
m. by true repentance . . 75.4
our hearts adoring m. . . 135.4
wheresoever men may m. . 158.3
while to his . . . throne I m. . 365.2
this alone my heart shall m. . 463.3
it cannot freely m. . . 508.2
the slow of heart to m. . . 519.2
who, as he onward m. . . 580.2
all with whom we m. . . 624.3
m. the Church of God . . 690.3
a heart that still m. . . 839.4
nightly pitch my m. tent . 877.1
he is summoned to m. . . 905.3
steady . . . the pilgrim m. . 911.1
we toward thine altar m. . 922.2
b *Ps 16:8**
from Jesus shall not m. . . 123.4
I shall not be m. . . . 710.2
c *Ps 121:3*
that thy foot be m. . . 767.2
d *Matt 9:36**
m. by thy divine compassion . 370.1
m. at the impulse . . . love . 525.2
his Spirit was m. . . . 527.1
except I am m. with compassion 527.c
how shall hearts m. . . 527.2
m. at the impulse of love . 786.4
mountain (2d)
3 *(other)*
years shall cease to m. . . 4.4
oceans m. at thy command . 171.2
seasons in fruitful order m. . 929.1

mown
among the new-m. hay . . 41.2
hay from the m. field . . 927.1

much
clouds ye so m. dread . . 29.3
spend m. time in secret . . 458.2
I have not m. to give . . 475.c
thou who hast done so m. . 488.1
there is m. to suffer/dare . 491.1
with m. condemnation . . 553.2
m. we need thy . . . care . 845.1
b *too much*
none can ever ask too m. . 563.2
loving life too m. . . . 922.3
c *Matt 6:30*
m. more to us . . . he gives . 935.2
d *Rom 5:10*
then how m. more . . . 50.c
m. more hath God in store . c44
forgive (1h), fruit (2b), how (c)

multiply-ied
a *Acts 12:24*
thy people . . . shall m. . . 629.2
b *2 Cor 9:10*
thou wilt use and m. . . 922.2
God is pledged to m. . . 923.3
c *1 Peter 1:2*
pardon there was m. . . 405.c
to m. trials he m. peace . . 579.1

multitude
lo, the m. were fed . . . 5.1
m. are dying and sinking . 482.2
m. are streaming downwards. 693.1
standard for the m. . . 774.4
to m. who struggle . . 830.2
there are m. in darkness. . 868.3

murmur
never a m. . . . frown . . 388.3
nor ever m. or repine . . 725.3
I will go without a m. . . 731.c
m. of self-will . . . 862.3

music
make m. for thy Lord . . 2.3
joyful m. lifts us . . . 10.4
may the m. of thanksgiving . 32.3
each . . . sweet m. make . 43.1
all m. but its own . . . 156.1
breathe into the m. . . 193.1
m. fills the balmy air . . 268.1
my heart is full of m. . . 369.1
m. in my soul today . . 387.2
there's m. in the air . . 664.2
Heaven's m. chimes . . 744.6
round the world with m. . 775.2
m. of church bell . . . 780.3
while salvation m. plays . 807.1
songs . . . and m. grand. . 873.2
never-ceasing m. rolls . . 887.5
notes of hallelujah m. . . 902.2
every note of m. . . . 943.3
fill the world with m. . . c220
with Jesus . . . there's m. . c220
the m. of the band . . . c230
b *[re name of Jesus]*
m. of thy name refresh . . 58.5
'tis m. in his ears . . . 62.3
m. in the sinner's ears . . 64.3
I love its m. to repeat . . 68.1
its m. dries the . . . tear. . 68.3
like m. in mine ear . . . 69.1
heavenly (e), ring (c), sphere, voice (1e)

must
1 *(God) must*
place . . . Saviour m. fill . 119.3
thou m. save . . . alone . . 302.2
Lord, this work m. do . . 581.2
whose might m. yet appear . 871.4
2 *(we) must*
he m. win the battle . . 1.2
church with psalms m. shout. 11.2
he . . . m. seek him . . 100.1
they m. bind them . . 129.2
we m. love him too . . 133.5
the vigil I m. keep . . . 176.2
the road that we m. take . 190.3
unaided man m. fail . . 212.4
thou m. his kingship own . 250.4
unless thou help . . . m. die . 291.1
m. speak their joys abroad . 314.1
sing I m., for Christ . . 346.1
I the summons m. obey . . 356.3
cross-bearing . . . m. share . 406.4
m. works . . . put away . . 408.1
light . . . in us m. glow . . 408.2
all I m. forsake . . . 434.2
men beholding m. confess . 494.2
it m. its crown resign . . 508.3
I m. more closely dwell . . 618.c
m. I not stem the flood . . 678.3
since I m. fight . . . 678.4
hard the battle ye m. fight . 697.1
Army to victory m. go . . 703.2
burden of shame he m. bear . 708.2
I m. feel his presence . . 731.1
the body m. keep . . . 739.2
deeds m. ever match . . 760.4
we m. repent . . . 785.4
we m. shine . . . 841.1, 3
his errands we m. run . . 851.2
all beauty we m. share . . 851.3
we, as all men, m. obey. . 874.2
souls . . . m. waken . . 875.3
m. all the world . . . know . 932.2
m. all . . . appear . . . 932.2
I really m. declare it . . c170
b *heart must*
the h. m. bear . . . part . . 11.2
your h. m. be kept pure . . 406.3
my h. m. yield its praise. . 591.1
this h. . . . m. beat . . . true . 779.2
c *must have*
I m. h. all things . . . 14.3
I m. h. the Saviour with me . 731.*
you m. h. your sins forgiven . 913.1
d *must be*
angel-choir m. b. . . . 70.c
children all m. b. mild . . 87.3
m. b. a lover of the Lord . 256.c
sacrifice . . . m. b. thy plea . 269.3
wonderful love it m. b. . . 289.1
blood m. b. my only hope. . 325.1
the river m. b. passed . . 325.4
how pure the soul m. b. . 414.1
chain m. yet b. riven . . 434.3
my steps m. b. . . . 449.c
what a life my life m. b. . 460.1
m. b. my life's ambition . 463.3
m. b. still my all in all . . 489.4
yea . . . my answer m. b. . 507.1
my life m. b. . . . bread . . 512.1
m. I b. carried . . . 678.2
the foe m. b. driven . . 681.2
m. b. on his side . . . 707.2
all m. b. well . . . 764.*
soldier m. courageous b. . 801.2
too many there m. b. . . 850.1
what m. it b. to b. there . 904.*
your garments m. b. white . 914.1
e *must not*
it m. n. suffer loss . . 699.1
m. n. God's plan frustrate . 801.2
you m. n. despair . . 817.2
prevail (d)
3 *(general)*
hate . . . m. yield to Jesus . 63.2
it m. be near, not far . . 335.3
'tis religion m. supply . . 464.2
love m. rule me . . . 522.3
love m. bring its offering . 591.1
trust m. face its trial . . 717.5
thy . . . love m. still prevail . 744.2
faith m. surely fail . . . 780.2
the sun m. set . . . 874.2
it m. abide alone . . . 923.3
what m. please thee more . 925.5
fruit they m. bear . . . 928.1
m. . . . its character give . 928.2

mutual 660.3

myrrh *Matt 2:11* . . . 90.5

myself nc, but see
consecrate, give (2g)

mysterious 29.1

mystery *Eph 1:9**
all above me m. I see . . 52.1
the cross in m. veiling . . 126.3
I cannot pierce the m. . . 131.3
angels would the m. scan . 439.2
m. no man beholds . . 871.4
m. their explanation . . 894.2
b
adore the m. of love . . 78.1
to know the m. of his love . 168.5
c *1 Cor 13:2*
wisdom lighting all m. . . 530.2

mystic
for the m. harmony . . 28.3
a little place of m. grace . 615.3
only faith, in m. flight . . 766.2

N

nail *John 20:25*
the cross where they n. him . 99.3
the hands my pride has n. . 122.1
held, not by n. . . . 126.1
was it for me, the n. . . 134.1
pierced and n. him . . 161.2
unto him who was n. . . 271.1
n. there by sins of mine . 326.2
by cruel n. were torn . . 339.3
point to the print of the n. . 364.1
the cross where they n. him . c89
know . . . print of the n.. . c248
b *Col 2:14*
n. my affections to the cross. 453.2
they are n. to the cross . . c24

naked 414.3

name
1 *(re divinity)*
Lord Sabaoth his n. . . 1.2
publish . . . wonderful n. . 24.1
mighty works or mightier n. . 26.1
let us blaze his n. abroad . 34.2
what thy healing n. . . 59.1
thy n. is joined with mine . 59.2
I may but gasp his n. . . 60.6
his n. the sinner hears . . 62.3
the honours of thy n. . . 64.2
the dearest/matchless n. 65.1, c
his n. dispels my guilt . . 67.4
dearest n. of n. to me . . 70.c
n. of all-redeeming love . . 70.4
say, is there a n. . . . 71.*
ring with thy belovèd n.. . 81.4
man of sorrows! what a n. . 118.1
a sacrifice of nobler n. . . 120.2
grants his n. to know . . 168.3
the Lord is his n. . . 183.1, 5
to our redeemer's n. . . 217.3
help us thy n. to sing . . 219.1
plead thy gracious n. . . 284.5
grace and glory of thy n. . 353.3
need lays hold upon thy n. . 456.3
mankind shall learn thy n. . 533.3
by thy conquering n. . . 543.1
I may extol thy n. . . . 574.3
no more revere his n. . . 592.2
thy n. makes devils fly . . 593.3
thy n. salvation is . . . life . 603.2
exert the virtue of thy n. . 629.1
blush to speak his n. . . 678.1
till thy n. . . . they share . 708.3
I know his n. . . . my trust . 735.2
have never heard his n. . . 797.3
men seldom hear his n. . . 832.1
hosanna to his n. . . . 853.1
the wonder of his n. . . 869.3
here inscribe thy n. . . 944.1
sacred to thine eternal n. . 946.2
b *name of Jesus*
the n. all-victorious of J. . 24.1
hail the power of J.'s n. . 56.1
how sweet the n. of J. . . 58.1
J., the n. high over all . . 60.1
J., the n. to sinners . . 60.2
bless the sound of J.' n. . 62.1
never fades the n. of J., etc . 63.*
J.! the n. that charms . . 64.3
the matchless n. of J. . 65.1, c
take the n. of J. . . . 66.*
I love the n. of J. . . . 67.3
the precious n. of J. . . 67.4
J.! O how sweet the n. . 68.'*
J., the n. I love so well . 69.3
beauty/rapture, etc in the n. . 70.*
no other n. but J. . . . 71.c
at the n. of J. 141.1
what is the n. of J. . . . 276.4
fast hold on J.' n. . . . 290.1
a Saviour, and J. his n. . . 319.3
love the sound of J.' n. . . 360.c
saved through J.' n. . . . 360.2
what a Heaven in J.' n. . . 367.2
precious . . . sound of J.' n. . 370.3
can in J.' n. believe . . . 407.1
where J.' n. is sweet . . 661.2
in the n. of Christ . . . 694.2
the n. of J. is a tower . . 714.3
wholly lean on J.' n. . . 745.1
the conquering n. of J. . . 787.3
in J.' n. . . . we bring . . 796.1
sang the praise of J.' n. . 834.1
J.' n. upon their lips . . 874.3
thy n., O J. . . . blessed . 876.1
sound the praise of J.'s n. . c27
hail the power of J.' n. . c175
c *Saviour's name*
I love the S.'s n. . . . 58.c
I love the blessèd S.'s n. . 67.3
O how I love the S.'s n.. . 69.c
Jesus is the S.'s n. . . 127.c
did we esteem the S.'s n. . 135.2
known the S.'s great n. . . 763.4
telling of the S.'s n. . . 869.3
d *Ex 20:7*
God's n. hold in reverence. . 823.2
e *Song 1:3*
his n. yields . . . perfume . 318.2
f *Matt 1:23*
by n. Immanuel . . . 72.4
g *Matt 6:9*
thy will . . . thy n. adored . 526.3
all hallowed be thy n. . . 624.1
h *through name* *John 20:31*
t. the merits of his n. . . 63.c
t. his n. . . . justice reign . 63.2
life is given t. thy n. . . 109.1
we have life in his n. . . 351.3
saved t. Jesus' n. . . . 360.2
t. the all-prevailing n. . . 481.4
in the all-prevailing n. . . 791.2
filled . . . t. his n. . . 808.3
i *[call on] name* *Acts 2:21*
offer . . . call upon his n. . 23.5
they who believe on his n. . 248.4
the n. whereon I cry . . 456.4
that . . . called upon thy n. . 674.2
all who will c. on his n. . 687.3
j *Acts 4:12*
the n. to sinners given . . 60.2
no other n. but Jesus . . 67.4
salvation in his n. . . . 869.3
other (1c)
k *Phil 2:10*
at the n. of Jesus bowing . 66.4
at the n. . . . every knee. . 141.1
humbled . . . to receive a n. . 141.3
n. to which all . . . bow . . 174.4
outward lips confess the n. . 496.2
all other n. above . . . 496.2
l *in name*
assembled in thy n. . . . 581.1
us . . . assembled in thy n. . 603.1
forth in thy n. . . . I go . . 667.1
in the n. of Jehovah will go . 703.1
in thy n. our flag . . . flies . 774.1
in the conquering n. . . . go . 787.3
fearless in thy n. we go . . 789.2
in . . . n. we'll triumph . . 804.3
we'll march in his n. . . 808.4
in his n. unsheathe . . 864.3
forth in God's great n. . . c238
m *fight in name*
in the n. of Christ . . . f.. . 694.2
in the n. of the King . . . f. . 820.4
we will f. in the n. . . . 820.5
in his n . we f. . . . 866.c
n *Ps 89:16*
delight shall be in thy n.. . 372.3
dear (2d), everlasting (h), extol, glorify (1c), glorious (1d), glory (2b, 5c), great (2g), holy (2c), love (7e), music (b), other (1f), power (4j), praise (3t), precious (c), proclaim (d), sacred (c), sake (1b), sanctify (c), sign (b), sound (c), sweet (3b), trust (4c)
2 *(re people)*
our n. are on his heart . . 9.4
he knows you by your n. . 44.c
God speaks your n. . . 267.2
over . . . promise write my n.. 303.4
let men revile my n. . . 526.2
someone . . . calls my n. . 544.2
speak to me by n. . . . 614.2
then will he own my . . . n. . 735.4
let his (her) n. appear . . 792.3
yet their n. are written . . 850.4
b *Isa 56:5*
their n. an everlasting n. . 168.4
c *John 10:3*
calling me by my own n. . c6
hand (1f) new (f) write (c)
3 *name-d (verb)*
as his own child he has n. me. 330.3
blessings, n. them . . . 396.*
as Christians truly n. . . 688.4
he whom Jesus n. . . . 707.2

narrow
we make his love too n. . 265.5
till I cross the n. sea . . 585.4
death, like a n. sea . . 898.1
to cross this n. sea . . 898.2
b *narrow way* *Matt 7:14*
keep us in the n. w. . . 76.4
when I'm in the w. so n. . 320.3
along life's n. w. . . . 334.c
there . . . found the n. w. . 366.3
far from the n. w. . . . 386.1
there's a n. w., and straight . 462.1
back to the n. w. . . . 691.4
as you tread the n. w. . . 790.2
seek the n. w. . . . 836.2
upward on the n. w. . . 859.3
the path is very n. . . . c205
fighting on the n. w. . . c227

nation
ye n. bow with . . . joy . . 4.1
to weary, hopeless n. . . 63.2
makes the n. prove . . 84.3
bid the n. see . . . 155.4
Jesus' love the n. fires . . 165.1
joy to the n. 166.1
n. feel . . . the thrill . . 173.3
the ransomed n. bow . . 223.3
no n. owns my soul . . 362.1
let the n. now rejoice . . 393.4
pour upon the n. . . . 682.2
kings and n. come and go . 799.1
this word it reaches n. . . 824.2
when the n. live together . 833.1
b *all nations*
all n. great and small . . 56.2

to you and all the n. . . 78.2
joyful, all ye n., rise . . 82.1
cross through all the n. . . 158.3
it flows for all n. free . . 252.3
all the n. we shall win . . 593.4
with peace all the n. . . 708.3
when flown o'er all the n. . 777.1
tell . . . n. all around . . 809.1
to the cross . . . all n. . . 810.c
the people of all n. . . 856.2

c *each/every nation*
age to age e. n. grows . 146.1
saints of e. n. . . . bow . . 185.4
we will e. n. call . . . 243.4
for the hope of e. n. . . 381.2
through e. land and n. . . 540.1
roll through e. n. . . . 546.3
sing and conquer e. n. . . 696.3
for e. tribe and n. . . 781.2
sins of e. tribe and n. . . 783.2
with salvation for e. n. . . 800.3
out of e. n. 803.4
won't lay . . . till e. n. . . 822.1
salvation to e. n. . . . carry . 822.c
till e. n. shall hear . . . 828.2
e. blood-bought n. . . 828.4
in e. n. fix thy throne . . 945.4

d *[Lord] of nations*
Saviour, Lord of the n. . . 177.4
O thou God of every n. . . 622.1
Lord of all n. 957

desire (1), heal (1e)

native
shall I whose n. sphere . . 414.3
trust their n. strength . . 559.4
Christian's n. air . . . 625.5
to bloom in n. bower . . 838.2

nativity 101.1

nature
1 *(re world)*
join with all n. . . . 33.2
more than n.'s sons to be . 38.5
all n. sings and . . . rings . 42.1
Heaven and n. sing . . . 84.1
the whole realm of n. . . 136.4
bids n. smile anew . . 494.2
now the powers of n. . . 875.3
all n. doth agree . . . c121

b *Lord of nature*
great L. of n., shaping . . 38.5
L. of all n. 177.1

2 *(human nature)*
he makes my n. pure . . 45.2
purifying all my n. . . . 201.4
refine the evil n. . . . 324.2
whole n. fill with joy . . 408.4
all my emptied n. fill . . 520.2
make all evil n. good . . 593.4
the judge, our n. wearing . 875.2
n. of seeds we now sow . 928.2
all my n. refine . . . c77

night (2c)

3 *(divine nature)*
thus are shown two n. . . 785.2
his n. is compassion . . 854.2
thou didst bind two n. . . 949.2

b *2 Peter 1:4*
thy n. . . . Lord, impart . . 444.5
with thy n. make us good . 452.2
plant thy n. in my heart . . 601.3
only as we thy n. wear . . 656.3
men that n. truly know . . 656.3
thy name and thy n. . . 708.3
let me now thy n. know . . c96

naught see nothing

nay
will he say me n. . . . 228.6
n. but I yield 307.4
n. in all things . . . 554.2
will not say thee n. . . 563.1
soul to whom the Lord said n. c87

Nazarene *Matt 2:23*
presence of Jesus the N. . 179.1
Christ, the lowly N. . . 776.3

Nazareth *Luke 2:51** . . . 855.2

near-nigh
1 *(general)*
until morning is n. . . . 77.2
angels bending n. the earth . 83.1
the last . . . strife is n. . . 150.4
angels are lingering n. . . 226.2
when no one else is n. . . 256.2
so n. to the Kingdom . . 263.*
when . . . the reef is n. . . 280.2
with this I venture n. . . 284.2
must be n., not far away . 335.3
a pain to feel it n. . . . 425.1
awake . . . when sin is n. . 425.3
looks . . . when sin is n.. . 596.3
abide . . . when night is n. . 676.3
when defeat seems . . . n. . 713.3
victory is n. 804.1
the world is ever n. . . 862.2
the darkness . . . draws n. . 874.2
home of my soul, how n. . 877.2
harvest home draws n. . . 926.4

b *foe near*
when our f. are n. us . . 655.2
see, the f. is n. . . . 698.1
my f. are ever n. me . . 862.2

blessed (2g), far (f)

2 *(God near us)* *Ps 34:18**
and still he is n. . . . 24.2
great physician now is n. . 67.1
yet we believe thee n. . . 198.1
the glory lingers n. . . 320.3
know thou wilt be n. me . 325.4
search . . . find thee n. . . 449.2
faith to know thee n. . . 466.2
few, but thou art n. . . 604.4
let me know . . . art n. . . 618.1
thy captain is n. . . . 689.3
when I sense thee n. . . 717.3
art thou most surely n. . . 717.3
his arms are n. . . . 718.4
feel his presence n. me . . 731.1
although thou art so n. . . 749.2
conscious you are very n. . 795.1
but our help is n. . . . 804.4
in thee . . . cometh n. . . 871.4

b *(with title)*
God is n. thee . . . 225.c
God is coming very n. . . 259.1
have you felt the Saviour n. . 418.2
remembering that God was n. 466.2
if my Lord is n. . . . 483.2
begone . . . my Saviour is n. . 712.1
peace with my Lord so n. . 768.3
believing, Jesus is n. . . 773.c
God's ever n. you . . . 773.3
Lord is n. when foes . . 798.3
sad when my Lord is n. . . c191

c *always/ever near*
were he a. thus n. . . 318.2
just the time . . . a. n. . . 334.1
knowing thee for e. n. . . 630.3
by day, art e. n. . . . 742.3
God's e. n. you . . . 773.3
his presence e. n. . . 814.2
our captain, e. n. . . . 818.3
in conflict he a. is n. . . 820.3
a loving Saviour e. n. . . 835.c
he is e. n. 836.3
a. n. from first . . . 938.2
e. n. to bless and cheer . c154
lives . . . he's e. n. . . c167

d *when near*
w. in the storm he is n. . 467.4
the time w. thou . . . n. . 523.4
days w. thou . . . wast n. . 557.3
lose . . . w. thou art n. . 587.2
safe w. thou art n. . . 627.2

e *if/while near*
not night i. thou be n. . . 676.1
Jesus, w. thou art so n. . 770.4
confidence w. he is n. . c132

f *(request)*
all our life be n. us . . . 12.2
Father, be thou n. . . . 40.3
be n. me, Lord Jesus . . 77.3
n. me, Lord, when dying . 123.4
dayspring . . . be n. . . 412.1
only want to have thee n. . 415.4
stay thou n. by . . . 587.2
be n. us in temptation's . . 624.4
come n. and bless us . . 676.6
Jesus, be n. to us . . . 955

bring (1k), draw (1d)

3 *(us near God)*
keep us to thy presence n. . 97.3
so n. to the Kingdom . . 263.*
with this I venture n. . . 284.2
sheltered n. thy side . . 284.4
dwell in safety n. him . . 377.3
n. thee I will be . . . 499.2
the promise calls me n. . . 560.1
evermore be n. thee . . 655.6
keep us so n. to him . . 773.4
just to be n. the dear Lord . 906.1

cross (2e), draw (2b)

4 *near (verb)*
even when I n. the river. . 350.3
when at last I n. the shore . 598.3

nearer
n. come, and teach us . . 193.2
every effort brings me n. . 369.2
to lift me n. Heaven . . 421.5
O for a n. walk . . . 445.3
dear Saviour, draw n. . . 513.c
I long to be n. to thee . . 521.1
draw me n. 585.c
n., my God, to thee . . 617.*
bring us daily n. God . . 668.4
the day is drawing n. . . 696.1
while the n. waters roll . . 737.1
a day's march n. home . . 877.1
bring me n. to thee . . c45

nearest 909.1

nearly 668.5

nearness 632.2

'neath see beneath

neck 701.3

need
1 *(God) needs*
Just where he n. me . . 706.c
Christ has n. of . . . soldiers . 787.2

2 *(others) need*
tell out thy n. . . . 225.4
the world's great n. I see . 482.1
if I am blind to human n. . 518.2
spirits n. thy care . . . 702.3
help mankind in n. . . 706.2
n. of the lost I can see . . 708.4
never yet forsook at n. . . 738.3
knows all you n. . . . 773.3
mankind in n. and woe . . 777.2
millions . . . n. is great . . 801.2
all have n. of . . . salvation . 824.1
meets a country's n. . . 923.1
thy creatures' daily n. . . 933.2
all that you n. is . . . c2

O how you'll n. him . . c11
the world/souls . . . n. us . c239

3 *(we) need*

a *(general)*
the n. that makes us bold . 198.5
we greatly n. thee . 213.3
I speak to thee my n. . . 290.2
interpreting its n. . . . 325.3
only my n. lays hold . . 456.3
I come with my n. . . . 488.c
my growing n. revealed . 534.1
greatly I n. the Saviour . 553.3
strength for daily n. . . 566.2
the n. is all my own . . 571.2
draw forth the cry of n. . 586.3
I n. thee every hour . 587.1
come for my n. in Jesus . 631.1
heart of our Army's n. . . 648.1
to tell my n., I know not . c82
the answer to my n. . . c151

b *(specific)*
strength we n. to obey . . 192.2
gild . . . with the light we n. . 193.3
the . . . faith and fire I n. . 440.2
burning love is my n. . . 527.c
Lord, show me what I n. . 588.4
thy saving power . . . we n. . 608.1
I need thy keen appraisal . 618.2
I n. thy love . . . to fill . 620.2
showers of blessing we n. . 637.c
I n. thy presence . . . 670.3
revival is our present n. . 760.2
much we n. thy . . . care . 845.1
hearts n. joyful songs . . 926.1

c *all [I] need*
all I have n. . . . provided . 33.c
all you n. . . . surely give . 73.2
down to answer all my n. . 91.3
all I n. to cleanse . . . 344.1
furnished with all that I n. . 553.4
knowest all its truest n. . 614.3
in all n. to Jesus go . . 634.4
in the love . . . all I n. . . 740.c
Jesus is all I n. . . c180/181

d *Heb 4:16*
just the time I n. him . . 334.1
helper . . . time of n. . . 351.c
grace for every time of n. . 539.2
grace beyond all n. . . 555.2
where . . . go in time of n. . 791.1

e *need never*
thou n. n. die . . . 271.4
I n. n. retreat . . . 366.5
n. n. rise again . . . 471.3
n. n. have a fear . . . 824.3
we n. n. be sorry . . . 899.1

f *need not*
n. no star to guide . . . 76.4
n. they no created light . . 76.5
n. n. one be left behind . 234.1
none n. perish . . . 239.3
n. n. fear a disappointment . 246.3
whosoever . . . n. n. delay . 279.2
thou n. n. fear . . . 320.3
hearts n. n. despair . . 363.4
I n. no other guide . . . 374.2
no words shall n. be . . 421.4
none n. fail . . . to claim. . 456.3
I n. n. fall 754.2

deep (3d), every (c), find (2e), great (2h), meet (2b), supply (2b)

needful
he'll give me n. grace . . 45.3
weary ones in n. hour . . 612.5
all n. weapons there . . 658.4
hast n. blessings . . . sent . 921.2

one (4b)

needless
what n. pain we bear . . 645.1

caused thy n. fear . . . 721.4
never . . . a n. care . . 917.3

needy
a n. sinner at thy feet . . 282.1
with Jesus, n. soul . . 333.4
n. souls . . . my mission . 463.3
my n. soul to fill . . . 586.3
poor and n. am I . . . 641.1

neglect-ed
no task for thee n. . . . 934.3

b *Heb 2:3*
salvation still n. . . . 913.2

neighbour
share my n.'s hardship . . 706.2
may serve my n. best . . 838.4
with our n. we may be fed . 927.2

neither
n. silver nor gold . . . 883.1
n. sighing nor anguish . . 905.2
fearing n. clouds . . . 930.2
knows n. measure nor end . 962

b *Rom 8:38*
n. life nor death can part . 444.3
n. pain nor tribulation . . 554.1
n. death, nor life . . . 554.3
n. peril nor the sword . . 555.1
n. life nor death can pluck . 723.3

nest 675.3

nets *Mark 1:18* . . . 680.*

nerve
n. my faint endeavour . . 345.3
n. me for the fight . . . 499.4

ne(v)er

1 *(re divinity)*
he n. from us will part . . 9.4
age to age it n. ends . . 55.2
it n. passed by one . . 55.3
n. fades the name of Jesus . 63.1
n. raised to seek . . . own . 129.2
shall n. lose its power . . 132.3
n. burst his . . . prison . . 153.c
shall n. call retreat . . . 162.3
arise, and n. set . . . 172.6
friendship . . . n. depart . . 273.2
n. will run dry . . . 312.2
n. a murmur and n. a frown . 388.3
thou n. saidst: No . . . 436.3
the Lord will n. hear . . 588.3
O n., Lord, depart . . . 597.3
throne shall n. . . . pass . . 677.5
n. bring them up . . . 724.c
n. let me fall 727.6
his sight is n. dim . . . 736.2
saints . . . n. be denied . . 763.2
n. cause . . . needless care . 917.3
glory n. hence depart . . 945.4
n. a prayer . . . soul c87

b *love never*
God's l. . . . n. be measured . 47.3
his l. . . . n. dies . . . 49.3
l. in death shall n. die . . 142.1
l. . . . n. swerving . . . 276.3
thy l. doth n. waver . . 538.c
l. . . . bends . . . n. dies. . 544.3
l. that lives . . . subsiding n. . 631.2
thy l. hath n. left us . . 938.3
his l. . . . can n. fade away . c207
l. that n. will end . . . c251

c *Heb 13:5*
he n. leaves me lonely . . c36

cease (c, d), change (1a), fail (1c, e), forsake (1), leave (1c, d), slumber (2a), waver

2 *(re ourselves)*
let me n., n. outlive . . 123.3
from God may n. depart . 190.2
who n. knew our God . . 314.1
see his face . . . n. sin . . 314.2
it n. knows an ending . . 328.2
I n. will despair . . . 334.2
I'll n. be the same again. . 376.c
n. praised the Lord before . 380.3
I n. would regard . . . 395.1
my bliss shall n. end . . 464.4
a n.-dying soul to save . . 472.1
follow thee, deny thee n. . 490.c
n. wept for thee . . . 547.4
shall n. think or dream . . 551.1
n. be a stranger there . . 556.5
fire . . . n. will die out . . 609.3
n. a moment depart . . 639.3
should n. be discouraged . 645.2
determined . . . n. to yield . 686.c
fight and n. give o'er . . 686.4
from thee n. . . . sever . . 693.2
prove the traitor n. . . 704.2
what my eyes have n. seen . 713.2
nor ever murmur or repine . 725.3
we n. will throw off . . 784.4
we n. will give in . . . 800.*
we n. will be driven . . 800.2
from his duties n. flee . . 801.2
yet we will n. fear . . . 814.2
shall we n. learn the truth . 827.3
n. from him roam . . . c154
n. let the old flag fall . . c243

doubt (c), fall (2d), fear (3f), forget (1b), joy (3b), leave (2a), need (3e), retreat (1), thirst (2d), tire

3 *(general)*
hate shall n. divide us . . 97.5
there is n. a . . . . 186.*
n. was a sweeter melody . 327.1
they have n., n. known . . 414.2
the world can n. fill . . 442.3
Satan n. shall prevail . . 532.2
Christless eyes have n. seen . 545.2
works . . . can n. buy them . 555.4
some have n. loved thee . 558.3
the world has n. known . . 564.2
pleasure that can n. cloy . 607.3
prayer is n. silent . . . 677.3
ear hath n. heard . . . 682.3
it n. outweighs . . . excludes . 758.1
n. heard of that . . . home . 794.3
have n. heard his name . . 797.3
n. disappointed turn away . 824.c
now n. laugh at all . . . 830.1
fruits that n. fail . . . 887.3
n.-ceasing music rolls . . 887.5
death will n. sever . . . 891.4
n.-withering flowers . . 898.1
joys will end, no n. . . . 899.2
song which n. hath an ending 934.4

b *(advice)*
be n. wanting there . . 699.3
shirk it n. 750.3
press on then, n. despair . 773.4
stand . . . and n. yield . . 809.3
yet n. be discouraged . . 810.2
the battle n. give o'er . . 812.2
n. think the victory won. . 812.3
in the . . . conflict n. yield . 817.2

4

a *can/could never*
passing time c. n. extol . . 70.1
joy that c. alter n. . . . 73.3
I can n. repay the debt . . 105.4
I c. n. remove a stain . . 292.5
his riches n. c. be told . . 356.2
my portion n. c. decay . . 356.2
tongue c. n. express . . 367.1
we n. c. prove the delights . 397.4
c. I n. be free . . . 459.1
before I n. c. see . . . 459.3

as we should but n. c. . . 544.5
gates c. n. . . . prevail . . 690.4
love that c. n. decay . . 808.1

b *may never*
sun m. n. rise . . . 251.2
I m. n. more grieve . . 437.2
I m. n. more stain . . 502.3
love . . . m. n. be dead . . 529.2
that tears m. n. flow . . 586.2
m. we n. waver . . . 866.c

c *[there is] never*
there is n. a . . . . . . 186.*
n. a burden . . . n. a friend . 246.c
n. a story so wondrous . . 384.2
earth has n. a spot . . . 663.1
n. a prayer/soul/sin c87

mind (3), more (5a), once (4b)

nevermore see more (5a)

new
sweet the rain's n. fall . . 35.2
re-creation of the n. day . 35.3
every day it's n. . . . 49.3
the n. and living way . . 113.2
eyes, n. faith receiving . . 123.4
n. words impart . . . 211.1
a n. and loving touch . . 215.1
as the light of n. hope . . 245.1
n. desires which . . . burn . 256.1
story so old, but so n. . . 319.c
washed white and garments n. 335.1
live in Christ's n. day . . 408.1
a revelation n. . . . 571.2
sharing in the n. communion . 595.3
n. power I want . . . 620.1
shining n. chance to live . 666.1
n. treasures still . . . 668.2
n. strength . . . bestowed . 675.2
filled with n. desire . . 788.1
this n. and living way . . 789.6
build a glad n. world . . 827.4
with each n. test . . . 874.1
praise be thy n. employ . . 890.5
let me dedicate this n. year . 916.1
n. vows for war we blend . 933.3
a n. touch of power . . c97
waiting n. visions to see . c103
yet joyous and n. . . . c106

b *new-*
filled the n.-made world . . 34.3
among the n.-mown hay . 41.2
life has a n.-found theme . c173
a n.-found intention . . c173

c *ever new*
the song for e. n. . . . 7.3
grace for e. n. . . . 223.3
power is e. n. . . . 559.3
story to us is e. n. . . 828.1
e. n. that joy will be . . 846.2

d *Lam 3:23*
n. mercies I see . . . 33.c
n. every morning . . . 668.1
every evening n. . . . 672.1
love is n. each morning . . 854.1
mercies n. and never-failing . 938.2

e *new heart* *Ezek 36:26**
change the h. and make it n. . 257.2
true, my h.'s quite n. . . 375.2
within me a n. h. create . . 436.3
take my h., but make it n. . 492.2

f *new name* *Rev 3:12*
my n. name is thine . . 59.2
write thy n. name . . . best n. . 444.5

g *new song* *Rev 5:9**
the s. for ever n. . . . 7.3
n. s. do now his lips employ . 62.3
sing the n. eternal s. . . 69.4
this n. s. thy creation . . 166.5
taught the glad n. s. . . 326.4
I'll sing the glad n. s. . . 375.3

my n. glad s. I raise . . 741.2
heart is a glad n. s. . . c157

creation (b), Jerusalem (c), life (2k), make (4e), things (1e)

new-born
Christ, the n. King . . . 75.1
welcome Christ . . . n. King . 79.c
glory to the n. King . . 82.1
my n. soul found breath . . 343.1
as to each n. morning . . 632.2
n. souls, whose days . . 825.3

newness *Rom 6:4* . . 589.4

news
go! Cry the n. . . . 127.c
hark! the gospel n. . . 239.1
bear the n. to every land . 393.1
I'll shout the n. . . . 401.3
spread the glorious n. . . 499.4
blessèd n. to proclaim . . 523.2
the n. proclaim . . . 831.1
this is good n. . . . c210

b *joyful news*
what your j. n. today . . 88.2
j. n. to all mankind . . . 249.1
spread the j. n. . . . 279.1

next
in this world and the n. . . 12.2
who'll be the n. . . . 278.*
one day . . . the n. deceive . 377.1
the n. the victor's song . . 699.4
are they n. the throne . . 909.2
if ere this time n. year . . 933.4

nigh
1 see near
2 *(nearly)*
the burden n. o'ercame . . 59.1

night
1 *(literal)*
a *(specific)*
that n. revealed and told . 72.2
my heart this n. rejoices . 73.1
o'er your flocks by n. . . 75.2
that n. in the long ago . . 80.1
o'er their flocks by n. . . 80.2
watched at dead of n. . . 88.3
silent n.! holy n.! . . . 89.*
on a cold winter's n. . . 90.1
watched their flocks by n. . 93.1
when the . . . n. had paled . 145.2

b *(general)*
watch that ends the n. . . 13.4
clothed in shades of n. . . 107.2
never a n. so long . . . 186.1
stars at n. do kindle . . 486.2
each n.-time . . . starlight . 666.4
glory to thee . . . this n. . . 671.1
if in the n. I . . . lie. . . 671.3
n. is drawing nigh . . . 673.1
through the coming n. . . 674.3
it is not n. if . . . near . . 676.1
abide . . . when n. is nigh . 676.3
morning overwhelms the n. . 705.4
shelter from the n.'s alarm . 740.1
when the n. may fall . . 740.3
harm thee in the silent n. . 767.3
n. with him is never n. . . 772.4
days . . . n. of strain . . 833.2

c *as night*
gloom fell deep a. n. . . 330.1
path be dark a. n. . . . 716.*
like a candle . . . in the n. . 841.1

2 *(figurative)*
anthems thrilled the n. . . 5.2
chaseth the horrors of n. . . 19.4
in the n. his dear name . . 63.3
not leave us in the n. . . 135.3
thy glory fills the n. . . 154.1
promise quenched in n. . . 267.1
out of my . . . sorrow and n. . 300.1
out of the depth of my n. . 378.1
fling off the n. . . . 408.1
sons of ignorance and n. . 414.5
sky by the n. be o'ercast . 537.3
the n. is dark 606.1
till the n. is gone . . . 606.3
all through the n. . . . 635.3
rise upon our n. . . . 669.1
leave behind the n. . . 682.2
face its trial in the n. . . 717.5
n. soon end in joyous day . 721.2
through the n. of doubt . . 765.1
fearless through the n. . . 765.2
though it be . . . n. . . 772.3
the n. draws near . . . 874.2
sowing . . . in the solemn n. . 931.1
gone is all my n. . . . c191
souls who dwell in . . . n. . c236

b *night [of sin]*
did I wander in s.'s n. . . 379.1
dark the n. of s. . . . 478.2
chase the dark n. of s. . . 602.4
s.'s dark n. be past . . 802.4

c *nature's night*
for the soul in n.'s n. . . 230.2
bound in sin and n.'s n. . . 283.3
brood o'er our n.'s n. . . 651.3

d *Job 35:10*
songs in the n. he giveth . 358.2

e *Rev 21:25*
we shall escape from n. . . 809.4
scatters n. away . . . 887.4
wait till the n. is o'er . . 889.3
no n. in the homeland . . 895.1
day excludes the n. . . 898.1

dark (2f), day (5b), shade (d), turn (1b)

nightfall 628.3

nightly
n. burned . . . star . . . 80.3
n. pitch my moving tent . 877.1

noble-r-st
turn my dreams to n. action . 32.2
your sweetest, n. lays . . 109.3
a sacrifice of n. name . . 120.2
then in a n., sweeter song . 132.5
n. and upright and true . . 679.1
a n. army, men and boys . 701.4
sound a n. call . . . 827.2
going to tread the n. way . 858.2
n. deeds and worthy strife . 867.3
follow . . . where n. hearts . 944.2

nobly
song they n. taught us . . 158.2
saints who n. fought of old . 876.3
n. for their Master stood . 909.1

nod 41.2

noise
hush the n., ye men . . 83.2
this day the n. of battle . . 699.4
the n. of earthly strife . . 884.3

none/no one
1 *(re people)*
n. ever will 119.3
to n. who ask . . . denied . 121.6
n. will ask what they . . 170.1
there is n. beside thee . . 220.3
need not one be left . . 234.1
no other one to hear . . 246.2
blessèd Lord refuses n. . . 251.4
when n. else is nigh . . 256.2
n. has ever trusted/claimed . 257.4
n. who seek him . . . ignores . 270.2
n. now to me is dearer . . 399.1

n. need fail . . . to claim. . 456.3
n. do I love like thee . 486.2
that n. may be denied . . 521.2
n. more blest than I . . 557.3
n. too sinful, or too low . . 590.2
n. . . . shall o'erthrow . . 799.1
n. will on himself depend . 799.3
n. else to be my guide . . 857.2
n. escape from his sight . . 893.1
not a friend . . . not one. . c182
there's n. like Jesus . . c207
n. appalling us . . . c239
b *none can*
n. c. be too vile/dark . . 232.3
n. c. perish there . . 284.1
n. c. quench . . . desire . 351.c
joy which n. c. hinder . . 352.2
n. . . . c. measure/tell . . . 363.1
heart in heart, n. c. part . 420.1
n. c. cry . . . unheeding . 456.3
n. c. pluck me . 468.3
n. c. forgive . . . console 486.1, 3
our union n. c. sever . . 495.2
n. but Christ c. satisfy . . 547.c
n. c. ever ask too much . 563.2
power that n. c. tell . . 591.1
joy that n. c. take away . 601.2
n. c. overthrow . . 707.4
n. c. estimate . . . measure . 922.2
deny (d), nothing (c), other (1e, f), perish (b)
2 *(general)*
all of self and n. of thee. . 548.1
n. of self and all of thee. . 548.4
soul finds happiness in n. . 556.3
gives, but borrows n. . . 657.2
other refuge have I n. . . 737.2

noon
has passed away at n. . . 98.2
at the n. of the day . . 611.2
prayer . . . at n. . . . c114

noonday
conscience as the n. clear . 665.2
brighter than the n. sun . . 909.1
sowing . . . by the n. glare . 931.1

noontide
when the n. is high . . 351.1
burning of the n. heat . . 476.1
sowing in the n. . . 930.1
we'll sing in the n. . . . c222

nor nc, but
a *life nor death* *Rom 8:38*
I. n. d. shall break . . 534.3
neither d., n. I. . . . 554.3
height, n. depth . . . 554.4
nor I., n. d. can part . . 659.5
I. n. d. can pluck . . . 723.3
death (2f, g), neither (b)

north
star drew near to the n.-west. 90.4
to the n., south, east . . 243.4
the n., the south are one . 362.3
from n. to south . . . unfurled. 779.1
in him no (meet) south . . . n.826.1, 4
love the best in the n., south. c230
desert or the star-lit n. . . c238

note
sweetest n. in seraph song . 67.c
theme its n. are weaving . 70.c
above the rest this n. . . 144.c
n. of triumph winging . . 803.1
sweetest n. of . . . music . 902.2
hope cheers him . . . n. . . 911.4
sweetest n. in all our songs . 925.5
every n. of music . . . 943.3

nothing/naught/nought
n. changeth thee . . . 8.3
n. on this earth . . . as sure . 49.1
Heaven and earth of n. . . 90.6
life is n. without thee . . 152.3
spake a world from n. . . 165.3
there's n. so precious . . 273.2
n. of good . . . done . . 306.3
n. that I have my own . . 345.2
angels can do n. more . . 367.3
forgetting in n. . . . to seek . 458.1
n. . . . thou didst not give . 532.1
n. of dark tomorrow . . 540.5
n. thou hast made . . 568.3
n. of our own we claim . . 648.2
n. know beside/desire/esteem 659.3
labour on, 'tis not for n. . 683.2
n. changes here . . . 736.1
n. seems hopeful . . . glad . 773.1
building comes to n. . . 827.3
n. we hold . . . keep . . 922.3
in n. is wanting . . 956
peace . . . n. to fear . . c196
b *[let] nothing*
let n. draw me back . . 59.4
let n. of sin remain . . . 218.1
let n. unholy remain . . 436.2
let n. your spirit dismay . . 537.3
may n. my way encumber . 766.3
let n. disturb . . . affright . 956
c *nothing/none but*
n. b. his loved ones know . 61.4
n. b. thy presence . . 91.2
n. b. Zion's children . . 157.3
n. b. thy blood can save . 292.*
n. b. the blood of Jesus . 306.*
n. b. good . . . betide thee . 377.4
n. b. the soul . . . 406.4
n. . . . desire b. . . . love . 480.5
n. can forgive b. thee . . 486.1
n. b. thy favour . . . 503.c
n. b. blest content . . 551.2
n. b. calm is found . . 752.3
n. keep b. that we give . 922.3
d *nothing but [Christ]*
n. b. Christ could help . . 336.c
n. b. Christ can satisfy . . 547.c
n. b. God is near . . 625.2
n. esteem, b. Jesus . . 659.3
e *nothing can*
n. . . . c. avail . . . 91.2
n. c. for sin atone . . 306.3
ties which n. c. sever . . 345.1
n. less c. be enough . . 549.3
n. c. I achieve . . . attain . 605.2
n. c. I lack 736.2
rock which n. c. move . . 738.1
n. then could stain . . 786.1
f *Lam 1:12*
is it n. to you . . . 245.*
g *1 Cor 13:3*
all my best works are n. . 416.3
or my work is n. worth . . 522.3
sacrifices profit me n. . . 530.3
h *1 Cor 1:28*
bring to n. the things . . 163.2
bring (2f), destroy (b), else (b), fear (3g), hard (c), lack (c), less (b), set (e), withhold

nought see nothing

nourished 159.4

now nc, but see
here, just (2c)

Nowell
N. sing all we may . . 72.c
the first N. 90.1
N., born is the King . . 90.c

number-ed
wake the dead in n. . . 153.2
give blessings without n. . 575.1
we rely not on our n. . . 722.3
sins of years are all n. . 893.1
more than we can n. . . 938.2

numberless
n. blessings each moment . 710.3
b *Rev 20:8*
n. as the sands . . . 908.1

O

oath *Heb 6:17*
I on his o. depend . . . 223.4
his o., his covenant . . 745.3

obedience
with gold of o. . . . 183.1, 5
give our hearts to thy o. . 428.5
the pathway of joyful o. . 501.2
in joyful o. . . . to fulfil . . 506.2
in o. to thy call . . . 532.1
with o. glad and steady . . 614.4
how swift o. answers love . 867.2

obedient
mild, o., good as he . . 87.3
I'll be o. to thy call . . 108.3
o. to thy welcome call . . 422.1
give me an o. heart . . 793.5
o. and resigned to thee . . 839.5

obey-ed-ing
strength we needed to o. . 192.2
who . . . helps me to o.. . 204.1
heed now . . . and o. . . 235.3
dost thou o.? he says . . 276.4
I the summons must o. . . 356.3
happy . . . the Saviour o. . 367.1
what could I do but o. . . 378.3
my heart shall o. . 422.c/589.c
o., I am blest 475.1
my heart . . . now thee o. . 490.2
seek . . . the grace to o. . 501.3
o. thee I will ever . . . 502.c
only thee, resolved to o. . 509.2
I will o. at all cost . . . 513.c
called . . . I gladly o. . . 543.2
o. when Jesus calls . . 575.2
impulse of his will o. . . 581.3
to the front! thy Lord o. . 702.3
who'll the war cry o. . . 703.2
'tis mine to o. 712.2
they are happy who o. . . 772.4
we o. divine commands . . 785.5
we are eager to o. . . . 789.2
to o. thee first of all . . 839.3
love's sweet lesson to o. . 846.1
gladly then shall I o. . . 865.2
o. thy Lord's command . . 923.3
let youth o. your calling . . 943.3
your Spirit be o. . . . 943.4

b *obey voice*
the v. of God o. . . . 433.1
be free . . . v. of God o.. . 471.4
hear thy v. . . . and I'll o. . 502.1
speak . . . I thy v. will o.. . 523.1
must o. the v. inaudible . . 874.2

c *obey word*
hasten now, his w. o. . . 241.c
we o. thy w. to go . . . 500.2
sworn . . . your w. to o. . 506.5
speak but the w. . . . will o. . 507.3

d *trust and obey*
t. a. o. . . . . 397.*
let us t. a. still o. . . 772.1
keep on believing, t. a. o. . c63

e *obey [will]* *Matt 8:27*
waves . . . did his w. o. . 96.2
billows his w. o. . . . 336.3
raging waves o. thy w. . . 598.2
whom winds and seas o. . 715.2
the winds and waves o. him . 935.2

f *Luke 2:51*
he would honour and o. . 87.3

g *John 10:4, 27*
all who their shepherd o. . 639.1

call (1e), trumpet (a)

object
heart on this o. be set . . 608.2
guards the o. of her care . 722.4
one the o. of their journey . 765.4
he is the o. of our praise. . 785.1

obscure-d-ing
no longing . . . o. the path . 5.3
gloom that once o. his day . 277.4
Saviour's face o. . . . 369.1
no dark clouds . . . o. . . 394.3

observing 788.2

obstruct 285.2

obtain-ed
redemption can be o. by you . 413.2
to o. a pure heart . . . 469.2
eternal life may o. . . . 523.2
which . . . I've failed to o. . 610.2
thus o. that inward calm . 613.2
till thou o. the crown . . 812.3
till we the crown o. . . 915.3

occupy 615.4

ocean
o.-depth of happy rest . . 10.3
beyond the o.'s line . . 27.1
o. move at thy command . 171.2
boundless as o. tide . . 224.4
free as the o. . . . 383.2
echo back, ye o. waves . . 393.2
stilled . . . o. that tossed . 402.2
boundless o., I would cast . 439.1
canst hush the o. wild . . 598.2
that in thine o. depths . . 621.1
there to an o. fulness . . 896.2
out in the o. divine . . c137

b *mighty ocean*
rolling as a m. o. . . . 182.1
boundless as the m. o. . . 230.1
come, m. o., and roll . . 298.3
who bidd'st the m. o. deep . 569.1

c *ocean [of love]*
'tis an o. vast of blessing . 182.3
full o. of . . . l. . . . 239.4
deep o. of l. . . . mercy 298.1, 5
I'll bathe in its full o. . . 368.1
thou art l.'s unfathomed o. . 452.4
gaze on the o. of l. . . 542.1
till in the o. of thy l. . . 676.6

odds 774.2

offences *Matt 13:41* . . 924.3

offend 853.1

offender
the vilest o. 22.2
I'm a pardoned o. . . . 724.c

offer-ed-ing
1 *(God) offers*
salvation . . . he o. free . . 46.1
full salvation is o. today. . 233.1
I have rest and peace to o. . 240.1
'tis o. . . . o. without price . 240.4
Saviour who o. peace . . 247.2
a pardon o. thee . . . 250.1
rejecting o. grace . . . 253.1
mercy he freely o. thee . . 255.c
o. pardon and peace to all . 258.3
salvation he o. to thee . . 260.c
took of the o. of grace . . 371.2
my Lord has o. his grace . 403.2
the priceless gift is o. . . 403.3
full salvation is o. here . . 413.2
to take . . . the gifts it o. . 415.3
the life which he o. . . 553.1
thy . . . will which o. life . 568.2
if this o. be rejected . . 913.2

2 *(we) offer*
humbly o. Christ their bread . 5.1
as they o. gifts most rare . 76.3
o. there in his presence . . 90.5
how can I o. thee less . . 457.c
o. each thought and deed . 493.1
what shall we o. . . . 533.1
hear the prayer we o. . . 570.1
we o. thee this temple . . 575.2
as o. to the living God . . 588.2
o. all my works to thee . . 667.2
o. him . . . devotion . . 777.4
o. to the King . . . 849.*
who will o. them today . . 868.2
all that we sincerely o. . . 922.2
accept the gifts we o. . . 935.3
accept the gift we o. . . 943.1

b *Heb 13:15*
o. the sacrifice of praise. . 23.5
o. the tribute of praise . . 900.3
praise and thanksgiving . . . o. 927.1

offering *(noun)*
1 *(by Jesus)* *Eph 5:2*
an o. and a sacrifice . . 414.4
no sacrificial o. . . . 870.2

2 *(by people)*
crown the o. now we pray . 203.4
our whole soul an o. be . 217.3
soul and body as an o. . . 470.3
consecrated o. . . . 511.1
consume my humble o. . . 511.3
God, what o. shall I give . 516.1
some o. bring thee now . . 524.1
o. and thanksgivings . . 921.1
this o. we have made . . 943.4

b *[bring] offering* *Ps 96:8*
these are the o. to lay . . 183.3
my love must bring its o. . 591.1
bring an o. to the altar . . 920.1
we bring thank o. . . . 936.1

accept (b)

office 688.3

officers 622.4

offspring *Rev 22:16* . . 82.2

oft-en
wrong seems o. so strong . 42.3
if . . . hearts are o. tender . 50.1
if men will o. share . . 50.3
foolish o. I strayed . . . 53.3
tell me the story o. . . . 98.2
o. longing I've stood . . 298.5
tempted, o. grow weary . 316.2
o. I've proved this . . . 320.3
sorrow's path I o. tread . . 337.4
o.-times weak and wayward . 341.2
o. with Jesus walking . . 430.3
o. has caused . . . grief . . 433.2
speak o. with thy Lord . . 458.1
o. I serve with weak . . 534.2
I o. say my prayers . . 588.1
o. I've pressed . . . throng . 610.2
o. found relief . . . escaped . 633.1
what peace we o. forfeit . 645.1
wishes to be o. there . . 646.1

o. for each other flows . . 660.3
o. in secluded ways . . 705.3
o. in the pleasant place . . 717.5
o. thy light burns low . . 723.2
O Lord, how o. . . . defeated . 747.1
o., therefore, we delay . . 748.2
o. have I heard . . . voice . 749.1
o. our trust . . . o. our hopes . 750.1
o. Satan's arrows wound . 806.1
though o. cast down . . 823.3
o. repeat before the throne . 877.4
o. when I'm sad . . . 881.1
o. are its glories . . . 904.1
our spirit o. grieves . . 930.3
o. toil seems dreary . . 934.3

b *Matt 23:37*
how o. would I gather . . 331.2

oil

a *Ps 23:5*
thou dost with o. anoint . 54.4

b *Isa 61:3; Heb 1:9*
sheds the o. of gladness . 573.2
o. for my woundings . . c148

old

tell me the o., o. story . 98.1,c
tell me the same o. story . 98.4
o. rugged cross . . 124.*
o. companions, fare you well . 275.4
story so o., but so new . . 319.c
not let o. bitterness depart . 572.2
the o. prophetic fire . . 651.1
o. friends, o. scenes . . 668.3
o. man, meek and mild . . 839.2
cross o. Jordan's tide . . 884.*
to the Jews o. Canaan . . 898.2
that o., o. story is true . . c202
roll the o. chariot along . . c224
keep the o. flag flying . . c242
never let the o. flag fall . . c243

b *dear old*
flag of the d. o. Army . . 779.c
leave the d. o. flag . . . 780.*
all about the d. o. book . . 829.1
back to the d. o. wells . . c40
d. o. Army flag . . . drum . c230
ranks of the d. o. Army . . c237

c *of old*
power hath founded o. o. . 16.3
with gladness men o. o. . 76.1
that glorious song o. o. . . 83.1
the messengers o. o. . . 154.2
God, that moved o. o. . . 202.1
Spirit . . . come as o. o. . 218.1
as o. o. apostles heard it . 428.2
like Abraham o. o. . . 763.3
saints o. o. obeyed . . 789.5
that sweet story o. o. . . 794.1
come, as thou didst o. o. . 827.2
nobly fought o. o. . . 876.3

things (1e), well (1a), young (b, c)

Olivet *Acts 1:12** . . . 496.5

omission 425.4

omnipotent *Rev 19:6*
he lives o. to save . . . 144.1
my gracious, o. hand . . 653.2
I'll trust his o. arm . . . 734.2
planted by o. hand . . 766.1

once

1 *(general)*
if o. thy pure waters . . 298.4
women's eyes, o. merry . 830.1
our warfare o. begun . . 869.4

2 *(re Jesus)*
o., in royal David's city . . 87.1
thou o. despisèd Jesus . . 109.1
o. was bright as morn . . 123.1
O. . . . Christ led forth . . 129.1
head that o. was crowned . 168.1
lives who o. was dead . . 249.4
o. despised, rejected . . 347.3
o. wandered on earth . . 354.2
thou wast o. a little child . 793.4
o. the King of Glory . . 840.1
o. a child like me . . . 840.2
that grace, o. given . . 940.4

b *Rom 6:10**
for me, and o. for all . . 131.4
o. he died . . . to save . . 143.4
o. lifted up to die . . . 590.2

c *once [slain]*
sacred head o. wounded . 123.1
Christ, that o. was slain . . 153.c
o. for favoured sinners s. . 161.1
in thy o. opened fount . . 421.1
who for me o. was slain . . 473.1
who for sinners o. was slain . 790.2

3 *(re people)*
hearts that o. were made . 202.3
o. has Jesus known . . . walked 267.1
gloom that o. obscured . . 277.4
o. my heart was poor . . 311.1
o. so sick at heart . . . 311.2
I o. was an outcast . . 354.3
robes were o. all stained . 359.1
o. I heard a sound . . . 373.1
o. I was far in sin . . . 374.1
o. in misery I walked . . 376.1
am I what o. I was . . 409.2
stubborn o. was my will . 422.2
o. I thought . . . did boast . 435.2
hours I o. enjoyed . . . 442.3
blindness o. I sacrificed . . 449.1
o. I thought I walked . . 549.1
places o. so rough . . . 549.3
a freeman, o. a slave . . 571.4
shall make him o. relent . . 685.1
o. were comrades . . . 878.1
o. they were mourners . . 879.2
o. the sword/fight/loss . . 894.2

blind (b), lost (3b)

4

a *at once*
creation sprang a. o. . . 141.2
come, then, a. o. . . . 246.3
rise a. o.! delay no more . 267.3
a. o. . . . iniquities roll . . 271.3
take with rejoicing . . . a. o. . 271.4
will join a. o. the fight . . 686.3
their wants a. o. remove . 909.3

b *never once*
n. o. they ceased . . . 158.1
n. o. hast thou forsaken . 762.3
n. o. forgotten be . . . 865.3

c *once again*
yet o. a., by . . . mercy . . 173.1
think o. a., he's with us . . 235.3
taught men o. a. to smile . 274.c
o. a. I seek thy face . . 305.2
o. a., the fount of life . . 456.1
visit my soul o. a. . . . 610.1
here o. a. . . . pressing . . 610.2
sing of his love o. a. . . 808.1
speak o. a., Lord . . . c100

d *once more*
o. m. I have reachèd . . 298.5
bid me be thy child o. m. . 303.1
flame o. m. brought nigh . 440.3
come o. m. to thee . . 448.2
o. m. 'tis eventide . . . 558.2
rise and to try o. m. . . 666.4
will vibrate o. m. . . . 691.3
bid me, but in vain, o. m. . 780.1
he's knocking o. m. . . c18

one

1 *(re divinity)*
the o. eternal God . . . 12.3
freely with that blessèd O. . 15.3
O bright eternal O. . . . 36.1
his dear anointed O. . . 106.4
the o. so holy, so divine . . 108.1
the sinless o. deride . . 121.3
come to me, saith o. . . 228.1
Christ, the blessèd o., gives . 258.2
look at the crucified o. . . 271.1, c
o. who knows my case . . 311.2
till o. draws near . . . 351.c
o. there is above all . . 377.1
blood of the crucified o. . 392.c
the holy o. is waiting . . 410.1
blood of the crucified o. . 427.2
risen O., enthroned . . 435.1
O thou life-giving o. . . 448.1
very dying form of o. . . 476.2
o. who can pardon iniquity . 724.2
God . . . is o. who cares . . 732.1
there's o. in every trial . . 750.1
the o. almighty Father . . 765.6
the o. you love the best . . 829.1
their o. true light . . . 876.2
o. God and o. mediator . . c156

three (a)

2 *(re people)*
so wide it never passed by o. . 55.3
o. bowed in shame . . 129.3
never a wandering o. . . 186.4
can find o. humble heart . 200.4
rest, thou labouring o. . . 240.1
if o. should ask of me . . 323.3
he can cheer o. in grief . . 329.2
lay down, thou weary o. . 332.1
thirsty o., stoop down . . 332.2
o. among the . . . throng . 514.4
as o. with vows to keep . . 522.2
to seeking o. made known . 539.1
may feed the hungering o. . 612.2
weary o. in needful hour . 612.5
weep o'er the erring o. . . 691.1
o., so vile as I . . . 709.1
to faithful o. are given . . 761.4
o. great Army make . . 788.2
pardon claim, O guilty o. . 831.4
o. of his heralds . . . 848.4
all the pure o. . . . bright o. . 852.2
ye heart-burdened o. . . 905.2
his chosen o. shall gather . 907.2
for me, the guilty o. . . c211

b *one and all*
to sinners, o. a. a. . . . 94.2
help us o. a. a. . . . 698.3

c *[loved] one*
with my belovèd o. . . . 7.2
none but his l. o. know . . 61.4
watcheth o'er his l. o. . . 182.2
there are l. o. I know . . 392.3
keep our l. o. . . ., distant . 582.1
with l. o. far away . . . 752.4

each (2b), everyone, little (d), lost (3c), none, thousand (c)

3 *(to imply unity)* *(John 17:21)*
earth and Heaven be o. . . 42.3
all their joys are o. . . . 57.1
whole creation join in o. . 57.4
o. with a world . . . 135.2
I will o. will 189.2
o. impulse/soul/feeling . . 196.3
we are o. for evermore . . 330.c
the north, the south are o. . 362.3
needful . . . o. with thee . . 565.1
we, as o., implore thee . . 643.1
at o. mercy seat, o. plea . 648.1
still are o. at heart . . . 659.1
joined in o. spirit . . . 659.2
o. their wish/prayer/rest . 661.1
all o. body we . . . 690.3
o. in hope/doctrine/charity . 690.3
o. in our aim to vanquish . 692.2
o. the light/object/strain . . . . 765.*
o. in holiness . . . faith . . . 769.3

they and we are o. . . 788.2
o. great fellowship . . 826.1
praise . . . and rest are o. . 878.5
share o. with another . . 927.3
be o. with us in purpose. . 943.1
divinely joined in o. . . 948.1
o. in our faith/hope/fight . c226

b *Gal 3:28*
o. in Christ, the King . . 705.2
Christly souls are o. in him . 826.4
in thee be o. . . . . 947.*

accord (b), faith (4b), hope (3d)

4 *(re objects)*
o. little word shall fell . . 1.3
born of the o. light . . . 35.3
o. thing reliable . . . 49.2
without o. plea . . . 293.1
rid . . . of o. dark blot . . 293.2
the stair a very wide o. . . 369.3
o. doubt should I allow . . 385.2
name them o. by o. . 396.1, c
o. more chain must yet . . 434.3
life . . . is o. of liberty . . 485.4
spare not o. lurking sin . . 494.3
serving Christ my o. desire . 522.3
there's o. way . . . obtain . 523.2
o. transient gleam . . . 551.1
o. that in calm repose . . 574.1
my life o. blazing fire . . 620.3
o. thing secures us . . 763.1
sad o. or bright o. . . . 848.5
o. golden dawning . . . morning 888.1
not . . . left o. treasure . . c55
if o. dark thought . . . c72
reward will be a grand o. . c237

b *Luke 10:42*
thou my o. thing needful. . 497.2
the o. thing needful . . 565.1

c *John 9:25*
this o. thing I know. . . 341.1
this o. thing I know. . . 347.*

d *[only] one*
only o. song I can sing . . 323.4
o. wish alone, God's will. . 536.3
only o. intention . . . c48
only o. flag for me . . . c241

day (4j)

oneness *John 17:21** . . 540.4

only nc, but

a *Mark 5:36*
o. trust him now . . . 231.c
trusting o. in thy merit . . 301.3
o. trust and obey . . . 397.5
o. believe, and . . . see . . 718.4

b *only Christ*
Jesus, o. Saviour . . . 258.3
Jesus . . . o. living way . . 279.2
o. C. is heard . . . 444.2
see . . . o. C. in me . . 479.3
C. o., always . . . in me . 487.4
o. like Jesus I long to be. . c68

c *not only*
n. o. share, but bear . . 421.3
n. o. . . . on that . . . day . 618.1
n. o. under summer skies . 717.2
n. o. when I sense thee . . 717.3
n. . . . those who o. start . 806.3
n. the rich . . . o. . . . 824.2

alone (e), one (4d)

onward
on my o. course . . . 345.3
yet o. I haste 355.5
as he o. moves . . . 580.2
while earth rolls o. . . . 677.2
bear it o. 697.2
o. to conquer the world . . 802.c
o. comes our . . . commander. 804.4
lay aside . . . o. pressing. . 805.1
when o. . . . they trace . . 949.3

b *go onward*
praise him as ye o. go . . 381.1
happy, as o. I go . . . 394.4
o. goes the pilgrim band. . 765.1
o. we go, the world . . 802.2

c *lead onward*
l. o., beaming bright . . 76.1
l. o., leading homeward . . 182.1
l. us o. faithfully . . . 769.1
l. o. through the darkness . 777.1
l. me o., upward . . . 842.4

fight (2f), march (2d)

d *(as command)*
o.! 'tis our Lord's command . 393.1
o., Christian soldiers . 690.1, c
o. then, ye people . . . 690.5
courage! o. 693.3
o., forward, shout aloud. . 698.c
o. in the cause of Jesus. . 776.1
o.! each success repeating . 778.3
o. to the prize . . . 892.4

open-ed-ing
each little flower that o.. . 25.1
swept from the o. plain . . 103.4
through an o. grave . . 130.3
for me, that o. tomb . . 134.2
who o. his bosom . . . 298.7
o. thine arms and take me . 305.2
I o. up my Bible . . . 403.1
in the o. air . . . prepare . 818.2
the o. ear, O Lord . . . 839.3
since the Army o. fire . . 939.1
out in the o. I walk. . . c157

b *open hearts*
Lord, our h. are o. . . . 201.2
h. are o. to receive thee. . 213.3
o. and let the Master in . . 373.c
if our h. are o. . . . 943.2

c *open [fountain]* *Zech 13:1*
the f. o. in his side . . . 121.4
the Lord will o. f. . . . 159.5
wounds of Christ are o. . . 237.c
living f. see, o. . . . 261.3
crimson tide o. for me . . 364.1
in thy once o. f. . . . 421.1
f. which to o. Christ . . 439.3
o. the f. from above . . 533.2
lo! the f. o. wide . . . 540.1
o. thou the crystal f. . . 578.2
lead them to thy o. side . 720.5

d *open [gates]* *Ps 118:19**
o. the life g. 22.1
o. is the g. of Heaven . . 109.2
mercy's g. o. wide . . . 126.1
Christ hath o. Paradise . . 143.3
he the door hath o. wide. . 165.3
fling o. wide the golden g. . 167.1
o. thus the paths of peace . 242.2
now the door is o. . . . 279.2
reach the o. door . . . 400.3
thine to fling an o. door . . 510.2
Heaven's g. to o. wide . . 843.2
the g. will o. wide . . . 884.*
the pearly g. will o. . . 892.4

door (2b, d), eye (2e), wide (c), window

opening *(adjective)*
dies at the o. day . . . 13.5
o. veil reveals the way . . 125.2
with o. light and evening. . 925.4

oppose-ing
in vain . . . o. . . . . 9.*
the world will o. you . . 233.2
fighting . . . o. the wrong . 681.1
strength to strength o. . . 699.2
all the arts of Hell o. . . 747.1
though all the world o. . . 814.2
storms that would . . . o. . c127

opposing *(adjective)*
smiling amid o. legions . . 686.2
a strong, o. band . . . 810.2

oppressed
weary heart, o. with sin . . 229.*
every soul by sin o. . . 231.1
peace to the sad and o. . . 247.2
heavy-laden, sore o. . . 261.2
serve the helpless and o. . 518.2
o. with various ills . . . 558.2
fear shall o. them . . . 813.3
the hungry and o. . . . 830.1
o. by my load c135

oppression 172.3

orbs 230.2

orchard 927.1

ordain
Jesus . . . me re-o.. . . 294.1
when thou didst me o. . . 409.4
if thy command o. . . . 629.2
what the Lord o. . . . 755.2

order-ed
before the hills in o. . . 13.3
called o. and delight . . 36.1
all the heavenly o. . . . 141.2
seasons in fruitful o. . . 929.1

b *Ps 37:23**
calmly o. the whole . . 479.3
let our o. lives confess . . 567.4
calm and o. all my days . . 630.2
o. all my steps aright . . 641.3
leave God to o. all . . . 738.1

ordinance 27.5

other

1
o. things may alter . . 49.2
singing upon the o. side . . 278.4
o. love save thine . . . 551.1
when o. helpers fail . . 670.1
when o. friendships cease . 709.2
help you some o. to win . 823.1
reach the o. side . . . 902.3
over on the o. shore . . 907.1
will be then in o. care . . 941.3

b *other [souls]*
o. s., refreshed and fed . . 512.1
o. lives to bring . . . 707.1
o. lives to win . . . 755.1
o. s. to free 788.c
o. s. draw nigh to thee . . c104

c *all other*
Jesus, good above a. o. . 97.1
when a. o. lights fade . . 237.2
one there is above a. o. . . 377.1
a. o. names above . . 496.2
a. o. joy is but an echo . . 711.1
a. o. ground . . . sand . . 745.c
above a. o. . . . pray . . 792.2
cast aside a. o. gods . . 827.2

d *each other*
teach us how to love e. o. . 10.3
feel e. o.'s sadness . . . tears 50.3
often for e. o. flows . . 660.3
help e. o. . . . cross to bear . 662.1
help us to build e. o. up. . 662.2
e. the o.'s joy/burden . . 663.3
kindred souls e. o. greet . 873.3
see e. o.'s face . . . 915.1
help e. gave the o. . . . 938.3

e *no/none other*
n. o. argument/plea . . 60.c
n. o. help is found . . 62.2
n. o. can take it . . . 119.3
n. o. place . . . one to hear . 246.2

n. o. fount I know . 306.c
n. o. is so loving . . 334.3
I need n. o. guide . 374.2
n. o. way to be happy . . 397.c
I ask n. o. sunshine . 476.3
wants to have n. o. will . 480.2
n. o. light . . . could see . 490.1
know n. o. will but thine . 509.2
n. o. dare I follow . 529.1
n. o. can I claim . . . 556.4
n. o. voice can speak . . 731.2
o. refuge have I n. . 737.2
n. o. ruler will we own . . 747.3

f *no other name* *Acts 4:12*
no o. n. is given . . . 62.2
no o. n. but Jesus . . . 67.4
there's no o. n. but 71.c
no o. good enough . . 133.4
no o. n., however high . . 269.3
I can come no o. way . . 292.4
no o. n. for me . . . 547.c

friend (1b)

2 *others*
men can live for o. . . . 50.2
while o. thou art calling . 301.1, c
o. may reject the weakling . 324.2
o., taught the glad new song 326.4
let o. boast of . . . gold . 356.2
joy of getting o. to climb . 369.3
one . . . above all o. . 377.1
the pearl which o. spurn . 407.5
only bring the power to o. . 435.3
that I may be used for o. . 435.c
that o. I may bless . . 475.2
o. fight to win the prize . . 678.2
hearts that can for o. feel . 704.2
friend when o. friendships . 709.2
if my grief means o.' gain . 729.3
seeing you, as o. have . . 748.1
heart will always o. brighten . 805.2
helpeth o. to be strong . . 838.3
o. for him to win . . . 857.3
living thy life for o. . 870.2
never mind what o. do . . c26
send to o. some blessing . c59

b *Matthew 27:42*
o. he saved . . 130.*
suffer, o. to save . . 623.3

ought
I'll praise thee as I o. . . 58.4
am I what I o. to be . 409.c
we have not . . . as we o. . 466.*
make me what I o. to be . 477.c
send me where I o. to go . 531.3
send us where we o. to go . 622.2
furnish all we o. to ask . 668.4
show me what I o. to do . 837.1

say (2b)

out of
condemns you o. o. hand . 44.3
take . . . o. o. his care . . 49.c
light came o. o. darkness . 94.1
o. o. the Father's heart . . 114.1
to die o. o. Christ . . . 263.3
o. o. my bondage . . . . 300.*
o. o. the angry waves . . 336.3
o. o. my/your darkness . . . . 378.*
glory . . . I'm o. o. Hell . . 380.1
keeps me o. o. . . . love. . 440.2
drive . . . from o. my soul . 440.2
o. o. his infinite riches . . 579.3
o. o. my stony griefs . . 617.4
forward, o. o. error . . 682.2
its end far o. o. sight . 716.1
save . . . o. o. the fire . . 720.2
o. o. the darkness hears . 740.3
flows from o. the mountain . 762.2
o. o. every nation . . . 803.4
o. o. darkness into light . . c4
brought me o. o. darkness . c160

b *out of love*
I serve thee o. o. l. . . 205.3
o. o. l. and compassion 289.1, c
thou didst suffer o. o. l. . 538.1

c *Rev 7:14*
o. o. great tribulation . . 170.3
o. o. trial brought . . . 466.5
o. o. great distress . . 909.2

d *2 Tim 3:11*
o. o. all . . . brought us . . 915.2

outburst 151.2

outcast *Isa 56:8**
by thee the o. . . . sought . 174.2
I once was an o. . . . 354.3
lost and the o. we love . . 687.2
to the o. and forlorn . . 697.5

outcrying 288.3

outcome 510.4

outlive 123.3

outpoured-ing
through atoning blood o. . 135.1
with grief, my soul o. . . 303.1
my love his o. wine . . 512.1
our gifts our hearts o. . . 922.1

outside
o. the fast-closed door . . 299.1
o. the land of promise . . 433.1
I'm not o. thy . . . care . . 761.2

outspread *Deut 32:11* . . 200.2

outstay 869.1

outstretched
those hands o. to bless . . 129.1
with arms o. in love . . 181.3
my o. hands to Heaven . . 208.4
under his o. wings . . . 227.c
stands with his o. hands . 260.c

outward
mind to blend with o. life . 485.3
our o. lips confess . . . 496.2
shall our o. work begin . . 863.2

outweigh
happiness . . . o. the toil . 399.3
it ne'er o. his grace . . 758.1

over/o'er
1 *preposition* nc, but
a *over all*
kingdom . . . rules o. all. . 24.1
streameth o. all the world . 40.2
the name high o. all . . 60.1
o. all victorious . . . 219.1
o. all . . . shall reign . . 362.1
God is o. all 396.3
abides, o. all prevailing . . 539.3
o. all the hills and dales . . 884.3
o. all these . . . plains . . 887.4

b *over there*
a palace for me o. t. . . 354.4
dwell in that land o. t. . . 406.4
think of the home etc o. t. . 886.*

land (2b)

2 *(adverb) (to mean finished)*
sorrow and pain all o. . . 45.3
the sun's eclipse is o. . . 143.2
the strife is o. . . . 151.1
my Father's wrath is o. . . 361.3
now the storm is o. . . 375.1
pilgrimage on earth is o. . 400.3
wrestlings be o. . . . 454.1
now that my struggles are o.. 457.3

when the toils . . . are o. . 500.3
till life be o. . . . 635.1, 3
now the day is o. . . . 673.1
when life's . . . race is o. . 709.4
wait till the night is o. . . 889.3
conflicts and dangers are o. . 894.1
strife and sorrow o. . . . 894.c
when all of life is o. . . 907.3
when . . . our journey's o. . 938.4

fighting (b), labour (c)

b *over and over*
grieved thee o. and o. . . 213.3
sing it o. and o. again . . 262.c
o. and o. . . . mighty sea . c140

overborne 825.1

o'erbound 246.1

o(v)ercast
sky by the night be o. . . 537.3
let us not be o. . . . 769.2

o'erclouded 433.1

overcom-ing
we shall o. at length . . 9.1
the burden nigh o. . . 59.1
loving kindness o. and won . 338.2
health that o. disease . . 631.2
ye may o. through Christ . 695.5
o. daily with . . . sword . . 757.3

b *Rev 3:21*
to him that o., a crown . . 699.4
to him that o. . . . crown . 823.3

c *John 16:33*
Christ has o. the world . . 5.5

d *1 John 5:4*
I o. the world . . . 495.3
the world o. by . . . grace . 640.5
thou shalt o. the world . . 799.4
victory that o. the world . c117

o'erfilled-ing
a cup o., a table spread . . 512.1
deeper joy, comes o. . . 711.1

overflow-ing
thankful, o. praise . . . 5.1
his heart the blood o. . . 348.3
his praise each heart o. . . 381.1
love that fills to o. . . 439.3
let it now my heart o. . . 455.1
thy blessing fill and o. . . 470.3
let thy love our souls o. . . 533.2
birds with . . . songs o. . . 545.2
all my soul o. . . . 546.1
until my very heart o. . . 612.6
rise . . . and my soul o. . . 647.c
hearts o. with compassion . 704.2

b *Isa 43:2*
waves your bark o. . . 280.2
grief shall not thee o. . . 653.3

cup (a)

o'erhead c238

overjoyed 348.2

o'erladen 534.2

overpast 882.2

o'erpower 720.1

over-ruling 644.c

o'ershade/shadow
may thy grace and peace o. . 576.4
beneath thy wings o. . . 632.3
there by his love o. . . 889.1

over-spread 892.2

o'ertake
death shall o. me . . . 751.4
b (*Gal 6:1*)
the woes of life o. me . . 112.2

o(v)erthrow-ing-n
strongholds it now o. . . 165.2
burn in me, my idols o. . 448.4
fighting for his o. . . . 532.2
Satan's kingdom o. . . 622.2
Satan's power to o. . . 687.1
legions of darkness o. . . 689.2
so truth shall sin o. . . 705.4
none can o. 707.4
shall they be o. . . . 762.2
none thine empire shall o. . 799.1
a cunning foe to o. . . 801.1
Saviour-King has sin o. . . 829.2

o(v)erwhelm-ed
o. at his almighty grace . . 223.3
when floods o. my safety . 628.3
as morning o. the night . . 705.4

owe
we o. thee thankfulness . . 15.2
debt of love I o. . . . 105.4
think how much we o. him . 377.2
our more than all we o. . . 533.2
small the debts men o. to us . 572.3
to thee my all I o. . . . 616.1
give . . . the life I o. . . 621.1
love I feel and o. . . . 846.4

own
1 (*verb—to mean possess*)
no nation o. my soul . . 362.1
no place on earth I o. . . 362.2
no other can I claim or o. . 556.4
2 (*verb—to mean recognise*)
a (*God*) *owns* [*Matt 10:32*]
he o. me for his child . . 106.5
o. us thy people still . . 648.3
o. my worthless name . . 735.4
o. us in that day as thine . 875.2
b (*we*) *own*
shall I fear to o. him . . 94.3
for my Lord and God I o. . 116.3
o. his title, praise . . . 147.3
will the Saviour then o. . . 169.1
barrenness rejoice to o. . . 217.4
till all thy truth I o. . . . 221.3
thou must his kingship o. . 250.4
I . . . o. thee conqueror . . 307.4
now I gladly o. him . . . 405.3
o. thy darkness passed away . 465.3
all I have thou shalt o. . . 473.2
o. the limit of . . . endeavour . 501.3
I o. thy lawful claim . . 509.1
o. my weakness . . . 605.1
heart shall o. thy sway . . 636.3
creatures o. thy sway . . 677.5
fear to o. his cause . . 678.1
we o. no man as enemy . . 705.1
my helplessness I o. . . 717.1
not ashamed to o. my Lord . 735.1
no other ruler will we o. . . 747.3
I o. his power . . . claim. . 867.1

3 (*adjective—general*)
all music but its o. . . . 156.1
its o. appointed limits . . 569.1
dare not trust your o. . . 699.3
do thine o. part faithfully . 738.3
accepting burdens not his o. . 801.2
b *all (its) own*
language all its o. making . 51.1
charms all their o. . . . 119.1
c *1 Cor 13:5*
never . . . seek . . . their o. . 129.2
love seeketh not her o. . . 530.c

4 (*adjective—re divinity*)
from his o. altar brought . 20.3
thy o. dear presence . . 33.3
for his o. name's sake . . 54.2
thine o. eternal Spirit . . 79.4
his o. redeeming love . . 87.5
thine o. secret stair . . 91.3
thine o. third morning . . 155.3
the Kingdom for thine o. . 161.4
no tears for his o. griefs. . 179.2
made them his very o. . . 179.3
sin on his o. loving heart . 245.4
take from thine o. hand . . 415.3
righteousness, his o. reward . 461.3
have thine o. way . . . 487.*
his o. best evidence . . 496.4
shalt have thine o. way . . 507.3
with the Master's o. love . 527.2
gift of God unto his o. . . 539.1
thine o. supreme delight . 601.3
give thine o. sweet rest . . 612.5
thine o. boundless store . 646.4
thine o. almighty wings . . 671.1
making human toil thine o. . 688.2
the King's o. army . . . 707.4
by his o. hand he leadeth . 725.c
thine o. right hand . . . 741.3
in thine o. sweet way . . 837.1
every race his o. . . . 866.3
for his o. pattern given . . 879.5
with his o. sweet comfort . c113
b *Christ's own*
we have C.'s o. promise . 690.4
C.'s o. banner leads . . 702.2
with C.'s o. bride . . . 949.4
c *God's own*
man of G.'s o. choosing . . 1.2
G. is his o. interpreter . . 29.6
gift . . . from G.'s o. hand . 52.1
G.'s o. word . . . sealed . 126.3
G.'s o. pardon . . . yours . 270.2
light of G.'s o. presence . 765.3
G.'s o. trumpeters . . . 868.1
let G. have his o. again . 920.2
come to G.'s o. temple . . 924.1
world is G.'s o. field . . 924.2
d *Rev 1:5**
apply thine o. blood . . 436.2
since his o. blood . . . spilt . 560.2
with thine o. life-blood . . 707.3
hath shed his o. blood . . 771.2
e *Rom 8:32*
expects his o. anointed Son . 150.4
my Father's o. Son . . 354.2
f (*ourselves as God's*) *John 13:1*
take possession of thine o. . 55.5
draws near his o. today . . 102.3
accept me . . . as thine o. . 108.3
formed . . . his o. abode. . 157.1
shall have his o. again . . 169.c
as his o. child . . . named . 330.3
the bliss of thine o. . . 372.4
his o. happy guest . . . 373.2
thine o. I will give thee . . 473.1
thine o. I am . . . give back . 492.3
take it for thine o. . . . 504.1
guard thou thine o. . . 516.2
my heart, it is thine o. . . 525.5
marked for thine o. . . 589.3
thousand hearts thine o. . 604.4
he claimed me for his o. . 730.1
chose us for his o. . . 738.2
seal him (her) as your o. . 792.3
his loved and his o. . . 852.*
as I am, thine o. to be . . 860.1
seal us thine o., we pray . 870.3
God resides among his o. . 909.2
keep us evermore thine o. . 937.4
make me thine o., Lord . . c85
he will remember his o. . . c122
g *all thine/his own*
all h. o. to keep . . . 130.2
to call them all h. o. . . 182.2
soul is all t. o. . . . 208.3
all t. o. I now restore . . 504.2
glory shall be all t. o. . . 626.3
a temple all t. o. . . . 941.2
image (a), restore (b), self (1b)
5 (*adjective—re ourselves*)
may no longing of our o. . 5.3
false limits of our o. . . 265.5
claim the crown . . . my o. . 283.4
no wisdom of my o. . . 325.2
naught . . . my o. I call . . 345.2
on my o. belovèd's arm . . 430.3
in my o. life is shown . . 435.3
my o. worthlessness . . 476.2
God and Heaven . . . my o. . 498.2
my will is not my o. . . 508.3
the need is all my o. . . 571.2
shatter my o. design . . 605.2
blind my o. 635.2
no strength of our o. . . 763.4
when my o. resources fail . 770.2
make them all my o. . . 770.3
their lives our o. inspire . . 939.1
b *1 Cor 6:19*
I would not be my o. . . 421.6
thy life and not my o. . . 479.1
my will is not my o. . . 508.3
not my o. . . . . 514.*
not my o., my Father's will . 566.4
naught of our o. we claim . 648.2
make (4h), strength (3b)

P

pace
swift . . . to stay the p. . . 861.4
with steady p. the pilgrim . 911.1

page
gild its holy p. . . . 193.3
beyond the sacred p. I seek . 650.1
here within its p. found . . 656.1
glory gilds the sacred p. . 657.2
that its p. might forthtell . 856.1
p. so fair . . . white and fair . 883.*

paid—see pay

pain
1 *(divine)*
his cup of p. and grief . . 5.3
mocking his anguish and p. . 99.3
grief and p. weighed down . 123.1
thine the deadly p. . . 123.2
love so torn with p. . . 131.3
what p. he had to bear . . 133.2
of thy death and p. . . 138.1
bow . . . to mortal p. . . 150.5
all my grief and p. . . 229.3
for me who caused his p. . 283.1
bearer of all p. . . . 628.2
p. and death to bear . . 835.2
scene . . . of bitter p. . . 848.5
2 *(human)*
blessing, p. and pleasure . 112.4
come, bring thy . . . p. . . 126.4
unmoved by human p. . . 142.3
helps me bear the p. . . 204.2
that p. and death defies . . 214.1
who is careless of our . . . p. 238.2
heed now the outcrying p. . 288.3
filled my heart with p. . . 390.2
or do I feel it p. . . . 409.4
then p. is sweet . . . 424.1
p. to feel it near . . . 425.1
light some p. is bringing in . 434.4
p. shall not hinder . . . 473.2
my love . . . no p. can take . 489.4
p. thy smile should win . . 503.1
welcome p. 526.2
my weariness brings p. . . 528.2
neither p. nor tribulation . 554.1
with what divers p. . . 558.1
fear and hunger, p. . . 576.2
rest, and p. is sweet . . 636.2
design may cause me p. . 644.3
what needless p. we bear . 645.1
it gives us inward p. . . 660.4
triumphant over p. . . . 701.1
in midst of mortal p. . . 701.2
ease which comes . . . after p. 719.3
what . . . are loss and p. . 729.3
sins that bring you p. . . 806.3
through fear or p. . . . 816.4
not from . . . p. or care . . 916.1
gift which costs you p. . . 920.2
fears nor p. nor death . . 948.2
b *joy and pain*
snow or sunshine, j. or p. . 544.2
I need thee . . . in j. or p. . 587.3
O j. . . . through p. . . 621.3
grant me in p. or gladness . 635.2
3 *no pain* *Rev 21:4*
sorrow and p. all o'er . . 45.3
toil . . . p. shall cease . . 453.4
toil and p. . . . be free . . 660.5
hope soars beyond . . . p. . 744.6
away from . . . doubt and p. . 872.2
p. of death are past . . 890.4
no p. in the homeland . . 895.1
pleasures banish p. . . 898.1
grief (2c), toil (1c)
4 *(pains of judgment) Rev 16:10, 11*
doomed . . . to endless p. . 75.4
eternal joy or lasting p. . . 785.6
5 *(verb)*
may the least omission p. . 425.4

painful
by thy p. agony . . . 140.3
though p. at present . . 712.4
pleasing or p. . . . 917.2

paint
p. the land 925.2
p. the wayside flower . . 935.2

palace
p. a toy . . . prisons . . . p. . 318.3
they're building a p. . . 354.4
home in the p. of God . . 886.2
for a p. and crown . . . c189

pale
how p. art thou . . . 123.1
when the . . . night had p. . 145.2
stars grow p. . . . 873.4

Palestine 142.2

palm
a *Isa 49:16*
my name's on the p. . . c125
b *John 12:13*
with p. . . . strowed . . 150.1
branch of the p. tree . . 848.4
c *Rev 7:9*
the crown . . . and the p. . 406.3
not for crown and p. . . 707.2
a victor's p. . . . 811.c
victor's p. for you . . . 899.2
there's a p. of victory . . 912.c

paltry 630.1

pang 771.3

pant-ing *Ps 42:1*
I p. for more . . . 207.2
now our p. souls inspire . 210.2
as p. the hart . . . so p. . 448.1
my heart, it p. for thee . . 453.1
as p. the hart . . . so longs . 557.1
my spirit p. for thee . . 650.1
as the hart that p. . . . 762.2

Paradise *Rev 2:7**
Christ hath opened P. . . 143.3
fair flowers of P. . . 156.3
hath P. found . . . 355.3
turns the key of P. . . 733.2
before thee in endless P. . 949.4

pardon
1 *(human)* *(Acts 7:60)*
with p. on his tongue . . 701.2
2 *(divine)*
a *(with title)*
God can in mercy p. . . 186.4
King of Glory offers p. . . 250.1
if you want p. then ask . . 270.2
God's own p. shall be yours . 270.2
the Lord has p. me . . 317.c
God in great mercy p. . . 347.c
sinner, but Jesus p. me . . 368.4
Lord has p. all my sin . . 380.3
Jesus spoke a p. free . . 402.2
freely Jesus p. me . . . 403.2
b *(general)* *(Isa 55:7)**
that moment . . . a p. . . 22.2
love of God that p. me . . 52.c
no other name brings p. . . 71.c
is there a name for p. . . 71.3
p. is the Father's will . . 127.c
engraving p. on my heart . 207.3
sign our uncontested p. . . 210.1
love intervening will p. . . 237.3
longing for p. today . . 247.1
canst thou leave his p. . . 250.3
feel this very moment p. . 259.3
before his throne, for p. . . 269.2
for p. at thy mercy seat . . 282.1
p. . . . blood hath brought . 287.2
welcome, p., cleanse . . 293.5
a free and p. slave . . 303.4
for my p. this my plea . . 306.2
thy righteousness, thy p. . 325.1
p. a rebel like me . . . 331.*
his p. I might claim . . 363.2
p. and mercy bestowing . . 383.3
graciously he p. me . . 386.2
for he p. me I know . . 389.c
p. there was multiplied . . 405.c
what a price my p. bought . 503.2
thou hast p. even me . . 538.3
how can your p. reach . . 572.2
p. thou dost provide, p. . . 605.1
thus provided, p., guided . 607.3
p. he gives unto all . . 687.3
they are p. for ever . . 724.c
I'm a p. offender . . . 724.c
I am trusting thee for p. . 727.2
that we might p. win . . 785.3
that he might p. bring . . 798.1
of his p. he . . . will assure . 819.2
p. is . . . then p. claim . . 831.4
there's p. for all . . . c23
he writes the p. on my heart . c128
p., the past behind me . . c152
c *pardon and peace*
p. for sin and a p. . . 33.3
p. and p. and heavenly joys . 214.2
I bring thee p., p. and love . 229.4
offer p. and p. to all . . 258.3
yes, he gave me p. and p. . 391.c
if you want p. . . . p. . . 427.1
it speaks of power, p., p. . c241
d *speak pardon*
O p.-s. blood . . . 290.3
grace . . . can p. s. . . 297.5
my Jesus s. a p. free . . 402.2
find (2p), iniquity (c), purchase, seal (d), sin (1c), transgression (b)

pardoner 600.1

pardoning *(adjective)*
his p. voice I hear . . . 106.5
saves by his p. blood . . 245.4
manifests his p. favour . . 370.2
turn them to a p. God . . 720.2
the word of a p. God . . 724.3
b *pardoning love*
Christ drew near with p. l. . 102.2
his p. l. receivèd . . . 381.3
showered upon me his p. l. . 388.3
the p. l. of Jesus . . . flows . 833.1

parents
brother, sister, p., child . . 28.4
p. of eternity . . . 452.4
p. hold him dear . . . 661.2
p. love the sacred word . . 661.3
our first p. strayed . . 785.3

these p., for your blessing . 795.1
p., teachers 834.3

part
1 *(noun)*
no p. of day or night . . 7.4
bear the largest p. . . 11.2
knows . . . bears my p. . . 68.2
battalions . . . will have p. . 169.2
want boldness, take p. . . 427.3
God will fulfil in every p. . 723.1
to take a soldier's p. . . 776.3
called upon its p. to play . 869.2
b *do part*
d. thine own p. faithfully . 738.3
give my heart . . . d. my p. . 830.c
may I humbly d. my p. . . c79
c *Luke 10:42*
to . . . secure the good p. . 469.2
choose the better p. . . 497.2
the bright and better p. . 664.3
God . . . give the better p. . 806.3
many choose the better p. . 832.3
d *(re self)*
in every p. with praise . . 7.*
this earthly p. of me . 189.3
is there p. of you . . . 244.1
nor hold back . . . any p. . 422.1
Lord, through every p. . . 430.4
let not self hold any p. . . 643.3
scatter . . . through every p. . c50
till every p. be clean . . c72
2 *part-ed-ing*
he ne'er from us will p. . . 9.4
where we shall p. no more . 312.4
seeking from my sin to p. . 348.1
heart in heart, none can p. . 420.1
life nor death can p. . . 444.3
dear Lord, no more to p. . 470.3
from treasures to p. . . 507.2
will not let us p. . . . 659.1
nor life, nor death can p. . 659.5
when we asunder p. . . 660.4
sea . . . still p. me . . . 749.2
how . . . p. from thee . . 874.2
p. with thy best . . . 923.3
b *(Rom 8:39)*
no sin . . . p. my Lord . . 447.4
who the Lord and me shall p. 545.3
c *Matt 27:35*
his purple robe is p. . . 126.2
d *part with all*
a. unlike thee now I p. . . 108.3
p. w. a. that's wrong . . 431.2
thou . . . w. a. didst p. . 475.4
I p. w. a. 513.1
Lord, w. my a. I p. . . 523.c
from a. . . . I will p. . . 543.2

parting
our p. hymn of praise . . 674.1
there is no p. there . . 881.c

partake
all p. the glorious bliss . . 165.1
shall constantly p. . . . 277.3
may of endless life p. . . 665.3

partaker
p. of the fall 56.3
b *Phil 1:7*
p. of the Saviour's grace . 659.5

partner 110.5

pass
1 *(God) passes*
completeness where his feet p. 35.2
I hear him p. 42.2
lately p. the Son of God. . 59.1
the days that he p. . . 99.2
when from death he p. . . 141.3
as he p., every land . . 159.5
soon will p. God's day . . 241.4
p. o'er my soul . . . 296.4
to p. the threshold . . . 299.1
p. me through the cleansing . 430.1
p. me . . . sterner cleansing . 522.1
thy sacred word is p. . . 714.2
b *Luke 18:37*
he did not p. me by . . 45.1
it never p. by one . . . 55.3
or it had p. by me . . . 55.3
as he p. by me I knelt . . 111.1
God cannot p. . . . by . . 127.3
Jesus is p. this way . . 247.1
p. me not . . . Father/Spirit 295.2, 3
p. me not . . . do not p. me by 301.*
Saviour only p. by . . 459.2
while the Spirit p. by . . 460.*
the Prince . . . is now p. . 542.4
King of Glory p. . . . 876.5
2 *(general)*
a garden, p. fair . . . 145.1
no clouds e'er p. along . . 268.2
the river must be p. . . 325.4
when the lifeboat p. . . 375.1
then the gloom had all p. . 395.3
I p. contented by . . . 461.2
p. the word along . . . 698.c
p. through tribulation . . 764.2
what conflicts we have p. . 915.2
all things are p. . . . 956
I let the storms p. o'er me . c145
b *Matt 27:39*
with the crowd we p. thee . 135.2
men mocked him and . . . p. by 245.3
while I p. my Saviour by . 547.2
c *Phil 4:7*
p. understanding is . . . love . 52.3
O love that p. knowledge . 299.2
peace that p. all understanding 304.3
p. mortal understanding . 539.1
peace which p. knowledge . 759.3
his love p. understanding . c212
d *pass away*
as his spirit p. a. . . 96.3
dew of morning has p. a. . 98.2
p. from this dark world a. . 356.3
own thy darkness p. a. . 465.3
its glories p. a. . . . 670.2
thy throne . . . p. a. . . 677.5
time for enlisting is p. a. . 681.4
stars grow pale and p. a. . 873.4
we p. a. from sight . . 938.4
let sin and error p. a. . . 942.4
it hath not p. a. . . . 949.1
life will p. a. c249
e *Matt 24:35*
word . . . shall not p. a. . 6.4
not till Heaven p. a. . . 228.6
past (2), thing (1e)

passage
fighting my p. to Heaven . 137.5
though a p. seem denied . 772.2
p. through a desert lies . . 911.2
to fight our p. through . . 912.2

passer-by 753.1

passing *(adj)*
my p. soul deliver . . . 153.3
light seems poor and p. . . 435.2
trifles of the p. hour . . 466.1
love of ease and p. show . 500.2
presence every p. hour . . 670.3
the p. gains of earth . . 796.3
b *passing time*
nor is dimmed by p. t. . . 63.1
p. t. can ne'er extol . . 70.1
after the p. of t. . . . 371.3
the gift of p. t. . . . 475.3
the t. for enlisting is p. . 681.4
above the things of p. t. . 729.4

passion
1 *(of Christ)* *Acts 1:3*
cross and p. on the tree . 140.3
dear tokens of his p. . . 161.3
true Recorder of his p. . . 191.2
thy cross and p. prize . . 432.3
p. and death on the tree. . 639.2
b
all his wonderful p. . . c77
2 *(of people)*
my thoughts, my p. fill . . 208.2
the pulse of p. stir again. . 211.2
free from your p. . . . 281.2
my p. are strong . . . 298.3
release that latent p. . . 463.3
love with p. 522.3
where the fires of p. roll. . 630.2
dark p. subdue . . . 823.1
by restless p. tossed . . 825.2
above the storms of p. . . 862.3
my motives, p., thoughts . 867.4
b *all/every passion*
from all earthly p. free . . 210.3
cast every evil p. out . . 432.2
all the evil p. slay . . . 481.2
with every p. blending . . 607.3
all the p. of my soul . . c32

passport 176.4

past
1 *(noun)*
dim p. and present clear . 31.2
fulfiller of the p. . . . 154.3
the p. o'er me creeping . . 237.1
dark . . . the p. has been . 292.3
pressing through the p. . 415.1
p. was long forgiven . . 434.3
sinful and black . . . the p. . 437.1
p. is under the blood . . 542.c
in the p. too unbelieving . 713.2
the things of the p. . . 928.1
the p. behind me . . . c152
a *all the past*
a. the guilty p. . . . away . 188.1
a. my p. is known . . . 285.3
a. the p. with its chances . 893.2
shine through a. the p. . . 938.2
2 *(adjective)*
our help in ages p. . . 13.1, 6
when earthly things are p. . 76.4
labour ended, Jordan p. . 228.5
when life's storms are p. . 280.4
p. defeats would bid . . 285.2
at last, all dangers p. . . 375.3
pardons p. transgression . 439.3
trust till the danger is p.. . 537.3
for all p. transgression . . 539.2
remember not p. years . . 606.2
storm of life is p. . . . 627.3
all your conflicts p. . . 695.5
friend when earth is p. . . 709.4
his love in time p. . . . 712.3
storm of life be p. . . . 737.1
trusting . . . earth be p. . . 754.4
sin's dark night be p. . . 802.4
in times that are p. . . 820.2
its joys as soon are p. . . 880.2
pains of death are p. . . 890.4
every chance will soon be p. . 913.2
thanks for mercies p. . . 950.1
for all that is p. . . . 962
till at last, fighting p. . . c154
harvest (2b), long (4a)
3 *(preposition)*
p. the reach . . . judgment bar 185.3
far p. my busy hands . . 416.3

pasture *Ps 23:2/John 10:9*
the verdant p. grow . . . 53.2
lie in p. green . . . 54.1
in my p. feed . . . 277.4
not for ever in green p. . . 570.2
p. I languish to find . . . 639.1
green p. are before me . . 736.3
b *Ezek 34:14*
in thy pleasant p. feed us . 845.1

path-way
obscure the p. . . . shown . 5.3
who the heavenly p. leave . 262.1
shadowed my p. for years . 288.1
lighting our p. from day . . 316.1
shining along our p. . . 316.c
I can see a p. through . . 320.3
on my p. his light . . 347.3
day by day this p. smooths . 358.3
snares beset my p. below . 389.1
no . . . doubt . . . p. obscure 394.3
round my p. the rays . . 400.1
rough . . . my p. may be . 473.3
though the p. be strewed . 502.2
thank you . . . for sunlit p. . 552.2
temptations my p. beset . 553.2
lowly p. . . . has taken . . 555.2
smooth and pleasant p. . 586.1
or from thy p. depart . . 597.2
brighten my p. . . . 628.1
when . . . thy p. shall lie. . 653.4
p. are smooth for . . . feet . 664.2
shadows on the earthly p. . 711.2
though thy p. be dark . . 716.*
star upon our p. abiding . 716.2
Christ is the p. . . . 718.2
in p. he has marked . . 734.1
though the p. be dim . . 740.2
nor clearly see the p. . . 748.2
praying, if the p. be drear . 754.3
the thorns in my p. . . 758.2
when your p. seems hid. . 759.2
find your p. is rough . . 805.1
find . . . your p. easy . . 817.c
my p. trace . . . 858.c
nor wander from the p. . . 862.1
the same p. to Heaven . . 879.5
walk this pilgrim p. . . 892.2
strew the p. with . . . light . 938.2
shadows . . . crossed our p. . 938.3
the hallowed p. they trace . 949.3
the p. is very narrow . . c205
b *path of*
the silent p. of earth . . 7.2
the p. of duty 320.c; 462.*; 868.c
wandered . . . the p. of sin . 391.1
in lowly p. of service . . 519.1
the p. of the cross . . . 522.1
the p. of consecration . . 534.1
the p. of prayer . . . trod . 625.6
as it falls on p. of woe . . 758.4
from the p. of sin and shame. 790.2
c *path of life* *Ps 16:11*
lead us in those p. o. l. . . 217.2
p. o. l. is plainly shown . . 656.1
my p. to l. is free . . 736.3
when l.'s p. runs steep . . 739.2
each perplexing p. of l. . . 918.3
d *Ps 23:3*
within the p. o. righteousness 54.2
lead us in those p. . . . 217.2
lead me into the p. o. truth . 857.1
e *Ps 27:11*
o'er a p. plain . . . 80.3
when p. are plain . . . 947.2
f *Ps 119:105*
our p. when wont to stray . 654.1
g *path of peace*
opening thus the p. o. p. . 242.2
'tis a p. o. peace and joy . 462.2
bright (1b), choose (2b), dark (2g), tread (c)

pathless 937.3

patience
in lowly p. waiting . . 299.1
clothe me with wisdom, p. . 516.4
teach me thy p. . . . 519.3
with passion and with p. . 522.3
p. helps to bear the cross . 555.3
give faith to fight with p. . 575.3
p. too, with understanding . 795.2
long p. follows toil . . . 923.2
fruit of the Spirit is p. . . c46
wait (2b)

patient
blessed are the p. martyrs . 95.2
I ask thee for a p. mind . . 485.1
strong and, ah! so p. . . 548.3
thou my p. spirit guide . . 596.4
holy . . . p. and brave . . 623.3
of p. hope . . . 948.2
p. endurance attaineth . . 956
Jesus, so p., so loving . . c7

patient-ly
cross . . . endured so p. . 515.2
love suffereth p. . . . 530.c
p. win them 691.4
who p. bears his cross . . 701.1
help me p. to bear pain . . 837.5
b
I waited long and p. . . 229.2
p. Jesus is waiting . . 264.1
so p. to wait 299.2
wait (2b)

pattern *(1 Tim 1:16)*
the p. be divine . . . 44.2
he is our childhood's p. . . 87.4
their p. and their King . . 411.2
him who my p. shall be . . 443.4
planned the p. of my ways . 644.1
thread the p. for my good . 644.4
for his own p. given . . 879.5

pavilioned 16.1

pay-ing/paid
1 *(God) pays*
p. sin's fearful cost . . 335.2
b *pay price*
to p. the p. of sin . . 133.4
blood which p. the p. . . 249.2
the p. thy love has p. . . 513.2
p. love's greatest p. . . 922.3
debt (b), ransom (b)
2 *(we) pay*
p. thy morning sacrifice . 665.1
our tuneful tribute p. . . 869.1
be the cheerful homage p. . 925.4
vow (c)

peace
1 *(general)*
in p. of home . . . 31.2
p. shall over all the earth . 83.3
where is thy reign of p. . . 172.2
with p. all the nations . . 708.3
p. in our time 827.1, 4
sweet p. and harmony . . 833.1
2 *(spiritual peace)*
have we a name for p. . . 71.1
p. . . . knows no measure . 112.4
give the . . . conscience p. . 120.1
p., the seal of sin forgiven . 210.4
would you like some p. . . 244.2
p. to the . . . oppressed . . 247.2
our crown of p. is gone . . 268.4
p. of thy sheltering fold . . 300.4
Jesus came with p. to me . 379.c
I would bring p. . . . 529.3
Heaven's p. . . . God's will . 539.3
p. my Saviour gives, p. . . 549.c
p. with every care . . . 551.3
confess the beauty of thy p. . 567.4
can p. afford 587.1
streams of pure . . . p. . . 601.2
call into thy fold of p. . . 630.2
what p. we often forfeit. . 645.1
this is the day of p. . . 669.3
thy p. our spirits fill . . 669.3
wait thy word of p. . . 674.1
call . . . thine eternal p. . . 674.4
in the days of p. . . . 711.3
p. be my reward . . . 717.6
for p. which follows . . 719.3
his word wrought p. . . 730.2
Jesus whispers p. within . 752.1
p. which comes with trusting 790.3
p. within my soul . . . c131
p. is mine . . . naught to fear. c196
b *peace and . . .*
power and p. combined . . 202.2
rest and p. to offer . . 240.1
p. and happiness ensure . 277.3
longed for solace and p. . 351.3
the sweet comfort and p. . 367.1
perfect hope and p. . . 423.3
p. and safety my reward . 556.5
p. and refreshment knows . 574.1
p. and gentleness abound . 664.1
what a blessèdness . . . p. . 768.1
good through p. or strife . 874.3
with plenty and with p. . . 929.2
dwell . . . confidence and p. . c143
joy (2g), love (5b), mercy (d), pardon (2c), rest (2b), righteousness (c)
c *peace and life* *Rom 8:6*
'tis l. and health and p. . . 64.3
my p., my l., my comfort . 207.3
our l. and p. to bring . . 411.2
name is l. and health and p. . 603.2
l. . . . and p. possessing . 634.1
its words are p. and l. . . 830.2
d *peace comes*
love and p. have c. . . 74.1
c. Heaven's p. to me . . 539.1
over its waves . . . c. p. . 542.1
p. which c. with trusting . 790.3
e *Matt 5:9*
blessed are the p. designers . 95.2
f *Matt 8:26*
turneth their fury to p. . . 19.3
p. amid the tempest's roar . 330.c
p., be still in all . . . 390.1
g *peace on earth* *Luke 2:14*
goodwill . . . and p. o. e. . 72.6
p. in endless flow . . . 74.2
in the highest: p. o. e. . . 80.c
p. o. e., and mercy mild . 82.1
p. o. the e. . . . goodwill . 83.1
p. shall over all the e. . . 83.3
p. to men o. e. . . . 86.2
angels singing p. o. e. . . 88.3
and to the e. be p. . . 93.6
p. and good tidings to e. . 99.1
h *go in peace* *Luke 7:50*
go on your way i. p. . . 67.2
go i. p., sin no more . . 126.c
whispered: go i. p. . . 366.4
i *Rom 5:1*
can give me p. with God . 297.2
my p. is made with God . 317.c
cease, I have p. . . . 379.4
I've wondrous p. . . . 413.4
at p. with God . . . 536.*
till I rest in p. with thee . . 585.4
I . . . at p. may be . . . 671.2
j *Rom 15:33*
crown him the Lord of p. . 156.3
thou God of p. and love . . 561.1
Spirit of p., my Comforter . 647.1

k *Eph 2:14*
this is all my . . . p. . . 306.4
l *[make] peace* *Eph 2:15*
p. is m. 'twixt man . . 109.2
broken p. might be restored . 135.1
my p. is m. with God . . 317.c
finding our p. restored . . c112
m *Phil 4:7*
p. of Christ makes fresh. . 358.3
p. of the Lord . . . laid . . 739.1
n *Col 1:2*
grace and p. o'ershadow . 576.4
belong (d), bestow (d), blessed (2e), bring (1g), destroy (b), fill (2g), find (2k), fruit (2e), give (1p), grant (c), have (2c), heavenly (f), inward (b), kingdom (h), multiply (c), pass (2c), path (g), perfect (2f), prince (1b), still (2b), sweet (3c)
3 *peace in Heaven*
his end untroubled p. . . 580.3
whisper thy p. to my soul . 771.3
welcome day of lasting p. . 813.4
his soul is found in p. . . 890.4
welcomes . . . to eternal p. . 894.1
our souls arrive in p. . . 918.4

peaceful
p. homes and healthful days . 15.2
wings of p. love . . . 217.5
far from the p. shore . . 336.1
p., happy moments roll . . 387.c
p. hours I once enjoyed . . 442.3
'twixt me and the p. rest . 598.3
the p. shores of Galilee . . 680.1
all is p., bright and fair . . 872.1

Peacemaker 529.3

peal-ing
p. over hill and dell . . 187.2
p. forth the anthem . . 550.c
like thunder grandly p. . . 802.3

pearl
a *Matt 13:46*
fairest . . . p. of great price . 175.c
p. of greatest price . . 346.1
p. which others spurn . . 407.5
b *1 Tim 2:9*
gold and p. more precious . 516.4

pearly *Rev 21:21*
I reach those p. gates . . 368.3
beyond the p. gate . . 780.4
bright and p. gates . . 872.3
the p. gates will open . . 892.4
p. gates are wide . . . 901.3

peculiar 160.5

peep 673.2

pen
tongue nor p. can show . 61.4
beyond the poet's p. . . 171.3

penalty 188.1

penetrating 201.2

penitence
in p. we come to thee . . 131.4
as . . . they in p. bow . . 175.3
kneeling in p. . . . 605.1
all in p. may bow . . 638.3

penitent
while as a p. I stand . . 120.3
hope of the p. . . . 236.2
to the p. and weak . . 555.2
the p. child to receive . . 691.2

penny 850.1

pent 877.1

Pentecost *Acts 2:1*
as on the day of P. . . 196.1
not at P. alone . . . 198.3
we want another P. . . 203.1
leads us back to P. . . 783.3

pentecostal
confer thy p. power . . 198.5
send a p. rain . . . 205.2
we wait the p. powers . . 216.1
cleanse . . . with p. flood . 218.3
God of p. fame . . . 447.3
fearing to p. daring . . 830.3
fill . . . with thy p. grace. . 941.2

people
1 *(general)*
all p. that . . . dwell . . 3.1
all thy p.'s consolation . . 79.2
born thy p. to deliver . . 79.3
Jesus, for thy p. dying . . 97.3
all thy p. are forgiven . . 109.2
p. . . . of every tongue . . 160.2
God wills for his p. . . 410.1
buses, towns and p. . . 544.1
grant to thy p. all . . . 561.3
all kingdoms and all p. . . 824.4
to all the p.—peace . 827.1, 4
the p. you may meet . . 829.2
for your p. everywhere . . 856.*
the p. of all nations . . 856.2
blessing reach every p. . . 927.4
b *Isa 40:1*
nor comfort a p. . . . 527.3
2 *(people of God)*
*Jer 31:33; Heb 8:10**
ye p. of his choice . . . 20.1
let the p. rejoice . . . 22.c
blessèd are ye, O my p. . 95.3
his p.'s hope . . . wealth . 168.6
loyal p. wait in faith . . 171.1
come, and thy p. bless . . 219.2
through his p. . . . close. . 238.1
look unto me, ye p. . . 272.3
shame on us, Christian p. . 299.1
p. that can be joyful . . 372.2
on thy p. pour thy power . 577.1
where'er thy p. meet . . 604.1
let thy p. be . . . aware . . 613.3
make thy p. hear . . . 626.1
thy p., saved below . . 629.2
to thy p. join . . . more . . 629.3
place of thy p.'s abode . . 639.2
we the p. of thy host . . 643.1
let not thy p. boast . . 648.2
own us thy p. still . . . 648.3
onward then, ye p. . . 690.5
thy p. ever would we be. . 692.1
a p. called . . . to fight . . 692.2
sometimes his happy p. . . 705.3
happy p. 722.1
o'er his ransomed p. shed . 765.3
sanctify . . . by thy p. here . 769.2
thy p. still are fed . . . 918.1
from thy thankful p. . . 921.3
come, ye thankful p. . . 924.1
gather thou thy p. in . . 924.4
O Lord, regard thy p. . . 944.1
when thy p. seek . . . 945.2
at thy p.'s prayer . . . 946.1
stay with thy p. . . . c98
b *Luke 4:18*
born to set thy p. free . . 79.1
should set thy p. free . . 101.3
came to set his p. free . . 274.c
he came to set his p. free . 468.c
c *Ps 106:48*
sound from his p. again . . 19.5
d *Ps 116:14*
vows . . . before his p. pay . 23.3

perceive
shall p. the mind of God . . 656.3
with eye and hand p. . . 748.3

perennial 601.2

perfect
1 *(re divinity)*
O perfect Life . . . 948.2
2
p. redemption, the purchase . 22.2
each p. gift of thine . . 28.5
p. life of thine eternity . . 189.4
your p. plan discerning . . 206.2
p. submission . . . 310.2, 3
complete . . . thy p. plan . 398.4
holy and pure and p. here . 407.5
to p. health restore . . 419.6
the power of p. cleansing . 432.1
p. and right, and pure . . 444.4
p. in the land of light . . 466.5
thy p. salvation to see . . 469.1
p. cleansing gaining . . 471.3
in him p. friendship . . 553.4
for a p. consecration . . 584.3
thy p. likeness to wear . . 623.1
p., present cleansing . . 757.5
p. is the grace . . . 764.1
O for a p. trust . . . 770.c
p. service . . . p. joy . . 788.3
p. deliverance and joy . . 808.2
b *perfect day* *Pro 4:18*
more unto the p. d. . . 196.5
shining to the p. d. . . 412.4
in which is p. d. . . . 465.3
thy glory to the p. d. . . 516.2
c *perfect holiness* *2 Cor 7:1*
the land of p. h. . . . 419.4
to p. h. and love . . 419.6
Spirit of p. h. . . . 441.2
d *perfect love* *1 John 4:12, 17-18*
all is peace and p. l. . . 125.c
joy and p. l. impart . . 210.4
p. in power, in l. . . . 220.3
thou God of p. l. . . . 221.1
to p. holiness and l. . . 419.6
calls . . . to p. faith and l. . 423.3
nothing less than p. l. . . 433.c
my soul is made p. in l. . . 436.4
glory in thy p. l. . . . 438.2
Christ of pure and p. l. . . 440.1
fill my soul with p. l. . . 441.c
Spirit of p. l. . . . 441.2
let p. l. apply the test . . 446.1
all, in p. l. renewed . . 533.5
guide into thy p. l. . . 596.4
rejoice in hope of p. l. . . 603.5
p. l. and friendship reign . 660.5
thy p. l. it claims to share . 742.1
O p. L. . . . transcending . 948.1
e *perfect (verb)*
waiting to p. within you . 410.1
p. us in love 662.2
love p. what it begins . . 741.4
p. them in love . . . 756.5
f *perfect peace* *Isa 26:3*
p. joy and p. p. are mine . 188.4
longing p. p. to win . . 227.2
in p. p. he keeps my soul . 317.3
I have p. p. within . . . 375.1
to p. hope and p. . . . 423.3
give me thy p. p. . . . 450.3
keep . . . my soul in p. p. . 513.2
O this full and p. p. . . 545.1
filled my soul with p. p. . . 549.2
grant me . . . thy p. p. . . 635.2
peace, p. p. . . . . 751.*
peace, p. p., in this . . 752.*
calls us to Heaven's p. p. . 752.7

thou wilt keep him in p. p. . c142

g *perfect rest*
the glory of that p. r. . 141.4
fit us for p. r. above . 668.5
in the love . . . is p. r. . 740.c
just to trust . . . is p. r. . 755.2
in him find p. r. . 828.3

h *perfect victory*
how to fight and win p. v. . 205.3
and give . . . p. v. 468.c, 2
win p. v. over sin . 819.3

i *perfect will* *Rom 12:2*
ready for all thy p. w. . 199.4
work on in me thy p. w. . 446.4
knowing now thy p. w. . 878.3
do thy p. w. below . 919.3

charity, way (1b)

perfectly
I am p. blessed . 367.4
p. restored in thee . 438.3

b *Matt 14:36*
blood . . . makes p. whole . 273.3
I long to be p. whole . 436.1

perform-ing
moves . . . his wonders to p. 29.1

b *Ps 61:8*
Lord, our vow p. . 788.c

c *Phil 1:6*
he will p. . 712.1

perfume . 318.2

peril
those in p. on the sea . 569.*
climbed . . . through p. . 701.4
p. of the winding way . 740.2
one the conflict . . . the p. . 765.5
life's p. thick confound . 954.3

b *Rom 8:35*
neither p. nor the sword . 555.1

perish
dominions rise and p. 6.4
evil shall p. . 173.c
p. self in thy pure fire . 194.2
your honours p. in a day . 356.2
p. every fond ambition . 498.2
crowns and thrones may p. . 690.4
when thy . . . hopes have p. . 753.3

b *[none] perish* *John 3:16*
dying, shall not p. . 73.4
none need p. . 239.3
none can p. there . 284.1
Jesus died that none might p. 363.4

why (1c), wither (b)

perishing . 691.*

perpetual
p. blessings . . . p. songs . 672.3
they keep p. tryst . 878.5

b *Jer 50:5*
in a p. covenant join . 784.1

perplex-ity *2 Cor 4:8*
guide us when p. 12.2
in p. we halt and linger . 711.2
each p. path of life . 918.3

persecution
a *Matt 5:10*
they who suffer p. 95.3

b *Rom 8:35*
p., want nor sword . 554.1
not distress or p. . 555.1

persevere *(Eph 6:18)*
give us grace to p. 97.1

and with joy we'll p. 97.5
strive and p. . 817.1

persistent . 192.3

person
God in three p. 220.1, 4
want . . . to be a better p. . 244.1
truth and p. whom we love . 748.3

persuade-d
a *Acts 26:28*
almost p. . 226.*

b *2 Tim 1:12*
am p. that he is able . 730.c

pervadeth . 517.3

perverse
p. and foolish . . . strayed 53.3
p., stubborn . . . my will. . 422.2

petition
large p. with thee bring . 563.2
our p. now presenting . 576.3
thy wings shall my p. bear . 633.2

phantom . 630.1

physician *Matt 9:12* 67.1

physics 30.3

pieces
tear Hell's throne to p. 800.3
foes . . . are dashed to p. . 864.4

pierce-d
I cannot p. the mystery . 131.3
though . . . dart should p. . 532.2
whose eagle eye could p. . 701.2
oft Satan's arrows . . . p. . 806.1
mortal arrow p. his frame . 890.2

b *Ps 22:16; John 19:34*
thorns his forehead p. 96.3
round his p. feet . 156.3
p. and nailed him . 161.2
p. on his beautiful brow . 331.1, c
his brow was p. . 339.3

c *Zech 12:10; John 19:37*
him, whom we have p. . 121.1
look on him we p. . 191.4
guilt . . . p. his hands . 245.c
hand my cruel sins had p. . 917.4

d *Heb 4:12*
p. the gloom of sin . 412.4

Pilate *Matt 27:2** . 137.3

pilgrim *Heb 11:13**
the lamp to p. given . 176.4
p. through this . . . land. . 578.1
to be a p. . 685.*
like to a p. . 740.2
onward goes the p. band . 765.1
I will be a p. . 859.3
steady pace the p. moves . 911.1

b *pilgrim way*
shine . . . on our p. way. 40.4
radiance . . . on our p. way . 711.2
sweet to walk in this p. w. . 768.2
we walk this p. pathway . 892.2

pilgrimage
all our earthly p. . 249.4
when life's p. . . . is o'er . 400.3
short is my p. . 882.2
through this weary p. . 918.1

pillar
a *Ex 13:21*
let the fiery, cloudy p. . 578.2

p. of fire . . . radiant cloud . 654.3
burns the fiery p. . 682.1

c *Rev 3:12*
in the temple . . . as p. . 533.5

pilot
Jesus, Saviour, p. me . 598.1, 2
fear not, I will p. thee . 598.3
p. of souls, I trust . 628.4
I can see my p.'s face . c131
I have a p. who guides . c132
Jesus, Saviour, p. me . c141

pine
1 *(noun)*
straightness of the p. trees . 32.2

2 *(verb)*
why do I languish and p. . 318.4
no longer . . . I p. . 364.2
my thirsty soul doth p. . 557.2
my spirit p. in poverty . 631.3
for closer communion I p. . 639.1

pining . 356.3

Pisgah *Deut 3:27* . 633.3

piston . 30.1

pitch . 877.1

pitiful
he answered our p. call . 245.2

b *Jas 5:11*
thou art p. and kind . 793.5

pity-d-ing
1 *(human)*
human minds can p. know . 50.1
let the world deride or p. . 157.3
snatch them in p. from sin . 691.1

2 *(divine)* *(Ps 103:13)**
amazing p., grace unknown . 105.2
his p. eye is dimmed . 121.2
thy p. without end . 123.3
our weakness, p., see . 200.7
God in p. lingers still . 251.3
by . . . p. thou hast shown . 303.3
in his p. unmeasured . 329.3
he p. my plight . 388.2
love that sees and p. me . 456.4
Saviour's p. plead in vain . 548.1
yearning p. for mankind . 594.1
Jesus p. our case . 687.3
proof . . . of heavenly p. . 777.2
p. my simplicity . 793.1

place
1 *(general)*
state again takes p. 78.3
the p. where Jesus lay . 90.4
many p. attract me . 119.1
the p. of all p. . 119.1
make the rugged p. smooth . 159.1
in earth's darkest p. . 224.3
no changes of season or p. . 318.3
no p. on earth I own . 362.2
a p. in that Kingdom . 392.4
the p. once so rough . 549.3
remains nor p. nor time . 556.2
while p. we seek . . . shun . 556.3
set our feet on lofty p. . 577.4
stablish our p. . 648.3
leave no unguarded p. . 695.3
the front! your p. is there . 702.1
grant me no resting p. . 723.4
holding fast its p. . 750.2
give a little child a p. . 793.2
although the p. be small . 838.2
earth . . . is not my p. . 880.1
accorded in Heaven a p. . 906.2
let no ill power find p. . 949.3
the sweetest p. of all . c116
there's a p. for you . c153

a p. for every warrior . . c237
b *every place*
conquer e. p. and time . 142.2
present, Lord, in e. p. . 517.3
e. p. is hallowed ground . 604.1
c *have place*
each has a p. . . . 850.3
treasures . . . h. no p. . 861.5
all h. their p. . . . 867.5
d *in my place*
in m. p. condemned . . 118.2
to bear in m. p. . . . shame . 319.3
in love . . . he took m. p. . 341.3
crooked, pleasant (b), time (1c), waste (b)
2
no other p. to leave . . 246.2
give him . . . rightful p. . . 249.3
p. where night . . . day . . 257.c
in him a resting-p. . . . 332.1
the p. where I love to be . 348.c
shadow for my abiding-p. . 476.3
soul has found a resting-p. . 536.c
wonderful p. called Calvary . c29
here is the p. c67
dwelling (b), hide (e)
3 *(the heart)*
there's a p. in my heart . . 119.3
not a p. . . . in the heart. . 241.2
a fixed abiding-p. may find . 451.1
for thyself prepare the p. . 480.1
make in my heart a quiet p. . 615.1
a little p. of . . . grace . . 615.3
come, occupy my silent p. . 615.4
b *Isa 51:3*
redeem its desert p. . . 647.3
4 *(Heaven)*
the p. where he is gone . . 87.5
highest p. that Heaven affords 168.2
in that thrice happy p. . . 195.4
is there a p. in the sky . . 289.3
in Heaven we take our p. . 438.3
a p., I dare believe . . . 536.2
show me that happiest p. . 639.2
p. of thy people's abode . 639.2
appoint my soul a p. . 735.4
I seek my p. in Heaven . . 880.1
I'd like to take my p. . . 884.1
O wondrous p. . . . 888.2
accorded in Heaven a p. . 906.2
b *prepare a place* *John 14:2*
journeyed . . . a p. to p. . 739.3
beautiful p. . . . gone to p. . 794.2
he'll p. for us a p. . . 892.1
to p. us a dwelling-p. . . 900.1
5 *(worship)*
a p. where Jesus sheds . 573.2
a p. than all . . . more sweet. 573.2
every p. is hallowed ground . 604.1
in this p. . . . made to bless . 642.3
come . . . the p. of prayer . 836.1
make of this p. . . . temple . 943.1
now consecrate this p. . . 946.1
reveal . . . to many in this p. 946.3
b *Acts 2:1*
meet . . . in our appointed p. 196.2
come . . . and fill the p. . . 216.2
come fill this p. . . . 643.2
Holy Spirit, fill this p. . . 941.2
holy (2d), secret (f)
6 *(place-d—verb)*
thy gracious hands . . . p. . 362.2
p. within thy . . . sight . . 414.1
if thy seal is p. on me . . 460.1
p. me on the highway . . 463.1
p. upon the sacred ark . . 590.1
my Lord has p. me . . 706.c
p. thy hand upon me . . 762.3
his hands had been p. . . 794.1

p. talents on thine altar . . 863.4
we p. on his great love . . 940.1
we p. this stone . . . 942.2
p. thy power within, Lord . c109

plagued 266.3

plain
1 *(noun)*
it descends to the p. . . 16.4
rocks, hills and p. repeat . 84.2
swept from the open p. . . 103.4
met . . . just now on the p. . 111.1
come with us to the p. . . 154.5
supply the p. below . . 159.5
come the p. and...mountainside 711.1
to beautify the p. . . . 923.1
with us here in the p. . . c126
b *Zech 4:7*
sink the mountain to a p. . 720.1
c *(re Heaven)*
shades . . . to p. of light. . 339.c
to gain the topmost p. . . 766.3
those wide extended p. . . 887.4
2 *(adjective)*
it's clear and p. . . . 49.2
the message clear and p. . 262.c
trust . . . his word is p. . . 262.2
way . . . is straight and p. . 275.3
see my mission p. . . . 528.4
b *Pro 15:19*
he will make it p. . . . 29.6
path (e)

plainly
tell me p.: Jesus lives . . 420.3
p., that my will shall bow . 446.3
path . . . is p. shown . . 656.1
so that all may p. see . . 777.4

plan-ned-ing
1 *(human)*
searching the p. designed . 416.3
sanguine hopes have p. . . 566.3
time . . . to think and p.. . 871.1
2 *(divine)*
thy hand still holds the p. . 6.4
your age-long p. . . . 38.3
God p. for you in love . . 44.c
my very steps are p. . . 48.2
love p. our life's course . . 51.c
who is it p. the route . . 204.1
your perfect p. discerning . 206.2
he p. to answer . . . prayers . 238.1
showed me what he had p. . 376.c
complete . . . thy perfect p. . 398.4
all thou art p. for me . . 501.3
shaping a p. divine . . 605.2
skill hath p. . . . my ways . 644.1
thy over-ruling p. I see . . 644.c
mercy holds a wiser p. . . 723.2
days . . . have all been p. . 732.c
must not God's p. frustrate . 801.2
p. our life . . . Saviour . . 863.1
with thy p. before us . . 863.5
I'll bless the heart that p. . 896.3
b *plan of [redemption]*
thy love's redemptive p. . 167.3
love . . . drew salvation's p. . 405.4
fuller know redemption's p. . 439.2
God p. redemption's grace . 590.1
depth of his salvation p. . 656.2
redemption's wondrous p.831.c; 952

plane
circles, p. and arcs . . 27.2
now on a higher p. . . 339.3
skilled at the p. . . . 611.2
a higher p. . . . found . . c80

planet 850.3

plant-ed
he p. his footsteps . . 29.1
p. holy fear in every heart . 190.2
p. thy nature in my heart . 601.3
p. by omnipotent hand . . 766.1
p. my feet on higher ground . c80

play
Eden saw p. 35.3
among the winds at p. . . 41.1
worthily in work and p. . . 675.2
while salvation music p. . 807.1
p. the music, p. . . . 807.1
at home, at school, at p. . 844.1
at home, at school, at p. . 849.3
youth . . . its part to p. . . 869.2
golden harps . . . p. . 902.1, 2

plea
we want no other p. . . 60.c
his love has a p. . . . 114.3
this shall be all my p. . . 116.5
mercy is their p. . . . 129.c
for my p. is heard . . . 188.4
sacrifice . . . be thy p. . . 269.3
promise is my only p. . . 284.2
my only p. Christ died . . 291.c
as I am, without one p. . . 293.1
yet is this still my p. . . 296.1
for my pardon, this my p. . 306.2
my glory and my p. . . 325.1
then I'll put in this p. . . 368.3
if faith but brings the p.. . 423.5
by faith put in my p. . . 562.2
one p. to share . . . 648.1
power my p. c93

plead-ed-ing
1 *(God) pleads*
his precious blood to p. . . 106.2
they strongly p. for me . . 106.3
forgive! I hear thee p. . . 122.3
their effectual p. . . . 129.c
your Saviour's p. cease . . 241.4
mercy is tenderly p. . . 247.1
while he's waiting, p. . . 250.c
come to the Saviour now p. . 263.1
let me hear thy tender p. . 463.2
he was sent to p. . . . 783.3
let . . . thy p. be heard . . c55
b *ever pleads* *Heb 7:25*
e. doth for sinners p. . . 116.4
hear me p. evermore . 229.1, c
he p. still for thee . . . c19
c *[Jesus] pleads*
J. is p., O list . . . 248.4
while J. is p., come . . 263.3
tarry when J. is p. . . 264.2
O J., thou art p. . . . 299.3
d *plead in vain*
not p. with thee in vain . . 229.3
long thou hast p. in vain . 473.1
p. in vain, and proudly . . 548.1
cause (1d)
2 *(we) plead*
for fire we p. 203.3
guilty souls for mercy p. . 269.2
p. thy gracious name . . 284.5
I p. by thy mercy, O save . 288.c
I have no right to p. . . 290.1
thy throne, a p. soul . . 303.3
came to the mercy seat p . . 383.3
hear my p., Lord . . . 441.c
as though by right of p. . . 456.3
hark to this p. of mine . . 457.1
for thy service, fit me, I p. . 488.c
mercy seat, p. for me . . 524.2
p. fresh covenant to make . 534.3
while I p. each . . . promise . 584.c
for a mighty revival we p. . 608.1
while I am p., pour out . . 623.4
for the showers we p. . . 637.c

before thy promise we could p. 642.2
p. with them earnestly/gently 691.2
p. for strength sufficient . 740.2
why . . . slow to p. . . 770.3
we for our children p. . . 791.1
Jesus, hear my humble p. . c74

pleasant
the p. summer sun . . 25.3
December's as p. as May . 318.1
easy, smooth and p. path . 586.1
then O how p. . . . 712.4
showing how p. and happy . 844.2
in thy p. pastures feed . . 845.1
b *Ps 16:6*
so often in the p. place . . 717.5

please-d-ing
1 *(general)*
the baits of p. ill . . . 596.2
p. or painful 917.2
in my life p. be . . . c85
2 *please God*
to love and p. thee more . 14.4
follows where he p. . . 197.2
p. him your chief concern . 343.3
naught, p. they not thee . 416.3
mind intent on p. thee . . 485.1
carried, Lord, to p. thee . . 503.1
in every way try to p. him . 844.1
try our best to p. him . . 849.3
these . . . my King may p. . 867.4
what must p. thee more. . 925.5
b *Matt 3:17*
thou art well p. to hear . . 784.4
c *Col 1:19*
p. as man . . . to dwell . . 82.2
d *Heb 13:16*
well p. in thy sight . . . 441.3

pleasure
1 *(earthly)*
blessing, pain and p. . . 112.4
fading is the worldling's p. . 157.3
heart has found its p. vain . 225.2
room for p. . . . business . 241.2
no thirsting for life's p. . . 320.1
p. sought, dearly bought . 379.1
he calls, in cares and p. . . 428.4
honour, p., and what else . 480.4
p. and wealth . . . no more . 509.2
p. lost I sadly mourned . . 547.4
Lord, in p. or woe . . . 904.4
b *earth's pleasures*
e.'s p. . . . dearly bought . 267.2
worldly p. all forsaken . . 474.2
farewell to worldly p. . . 502.3
e.'s p. . . . no longer allure . 640.4
e. p. we'll forsake . . . 912.2
c *Heb 11:25*
all the p. of sin I resign . . 357.1
2 *(spiritual)* *Ps 16:11**
lasting p., by . . . mercy made 227.1
go . . . where p. never dies . 266.c
drink endless p. in . . . 314.2
true p. abound . . . 355.3
what p. to our ears . . 382.1
p. in his service . . . 399.*
mine is the service of p.. . 457.3
sweetest p. while we live . 464.1
p. that can never cloy . . 607.3
who can tell the p.. . . 655.4
fields where p. never dies . 818.4
we find p. in the Army . . 869.1
p. banish pain . . . 898.1
river (2g)
3 *(divine)*
'tis the Father's p. . . . 141.1
all to his p. resigned . . 318.3
thy p. henceforth to fulfil . 422.2

b *Luke 12:32*
hope, by thy good p. . . 313.2
confirms his good p. . . 712.3

pledge
1 *(God) pledges*
love, and p. of Heaven . . 207.3
wear that p. of love . . 424.2
God is p. to multiply . . 923.3
2 *(we) pledge*
p. again my willing heart . 591.3
p. a fresh allegiance . . 777.4
the p. they're now making . 795.2
p. our faith . . . to hold . . 799.1
broken p. uncovered . . 893.1

plenteous *Ps 103:8*
so p. in grace . . . 372.1
O Lord, thy p. grace . . 415.3
p. grace with thee is found . 737.4

plenty
p. . . . unfailing store . . 277.2
he crowns . . . with p. . . 929.2

plied 688.2

plight 388.2

plough 935.1

pluck
p. the fairest flower . . 145.3
everyone who seeks may p. . 658.1
b *Zech 3:2*
p. me thence . . . 350.1
p. as brands from burning . 803.3
c *John 10:28,29*
none can p. me . . . 468.3
who shall p. him from . . . hands 555.1
life nor death can p. . . 723.3

plumb 858.3

plummet
Isaiah 28:17; Amos 7:7,8 . 446.2

plunge-d
p. beneath that flood . . 132.1
p. now into the . . . flood . 231.2
I p. 'neath the waters . . 298.6
p. into the fountain . . 309.1
p. in today 315.4
I p. in the crimson tide . . 364.1
p. in the fountain . . . 427.2
p. beneath thy . . . blood . 450.4
p. in the . . . wave . . . 535.c
with faith I p. me in this sea . 746.3

poet 171.3

point
1 *(noun)*
a p. my good . . . 207.2
life has p. and purpose . . 376.3
p. where all my wishes meet . 556.4
2 *(verb)*
help me p. the lost . . . 188.3
p. to the print . . . 364.1
would p. me to doom . . 437.3
my fearful heart p. back . . 440.3
p. poor sinners . . . 583.4
p. the way to holiness . . 656.2
p. me to the skies . . . 670.5
who p. the clouds . . . 715.2
p. them unto the Saviour . 790.2
may thousands . . . p. here . 946.4

pointless 376.3

poison 842.2

pole
sways from p. to p. . . 156.3
rolling on from p. to p. . . 230.1

pollution *2 Peter 2:20* . . 445.2

pomp
in lowly p. ride on . . 150.2, 5
his boasted p. and show . 157.3

ponder
p. anew what . . . can do . 19.2
yet deeper do I p. . . . 94.3
as I p. alone 119.1
when I p. o'er the story . . 770.1
as I p. his sweet grace . . c187
b *Luke 2:19*
O may we keep and p. . . 78.3

poor
1 *(re divinity)*
from his p. manger . . 78.3
so p. was he then . . . 92.1
homeless, rejected and p. . 99.2
2 *(literal)* *(Luke 4:18)*
p. and mean and lowly . . 87.2
certain p. shepherds . . 90.1
by thee . . . p. were sought . 174.2
bring salvation to the p. . 819.2
the p. and broken-hearted . 824.3
b *rich and poor*
both the r. and the p. . . 170.1
r. and p., for bond and free . 261.3
r. and p. as well . . . 814.c
tell the r. and p. . . . 829.2
3 *(spiritual)*
p. though I be, and weak . 7.3
p. lisping . . . tongue . . 132.5
slenderness of the p. wealth . 183.3
thou my p. treasure take . 285.1
pardon p. rebels like you . 331.2
treasures, p. and dim . . 420.2
in thy light seems p. . . 435.2
some p. . . . seaman . . 478.c, 3
p. and needy am I . . . 641.1
in some p. wandering child . 676.4
tell the p. wanderer . . 691.4
p. and those who mourn . 825.1
p. and sinful though we be . 845.3
p., unworthy me . . . c109
though men count thee p. . c249
enrich, spirit (6e)
b *poor heart*
once my h. was p. . . 311.1
my p. h. he sought and won . 335.1
take my p. h. . . . 424.2
Christ takes . . . my p. h. . 447.4
for my p. longing h. . . 448.3
my h. is weak and p. . . 508.2
shine into this p. h. . . 754.2
make my p. h. thy dwelling . c104
c *poor sinner*
say, p. s., lov'st thou . 110.1, 5
save a p. s. like me . . 137.*
now, p. s., look to him . . 239.1
p. s., harden not . . . 251.1
go . . . p. s. to save . . 321.3
p. s. of all kinds . . . 331.4
canst thou not save a p. s. . 543.1
point p. s. to . . . blood . . 583.4
can a p. s. come to Jesus . c8
save a p. s. like me . . c217
calling, p. s., to you . . c230
d *poor soul*
p., trembling s., he'll make . 253.c
mayst find, p. sin-sick s. . 253.2
p. . . . fainting s. . . . 254.2
made room for such p. s. . 266.2
love to the p. sinbound s. . 273.3
they bind my p. s. . . . 298.3
cast thy p. s. . . . 315.4
down my p. s. to redeem . 323.2
if so p. a s. as I . . . 492.1
rich in goods and p. in s. . 577.3
save p. s. out of the fire . 720.2

poorest
wandered on earth as the p. . 354.2
the p. child may bring . . 849.2

poppy 41.2

portal
flung wide life's p. . . 130.3
from Heaven's high p. . . 151.4
heavenly p. . . . ring . . 184.3

portent 176.4

portion *Ps 119:57**
how happy is our p. here . 43.3
him my only p. make . . 223.2
what my p. here . . . 228.4
Christ . . . shall be our p. 239.4
p. of that living bread . . 277.2
having for my p. Jesus . . 352.2
my p. never can decay . . 356.2
earth's salvation p. . . 452.4
sweet our p. . . . 722.1, 3
his (her) p. through the years 795.3
our chosen God and p. . . 918.5

portioned 485.1

possess-ed-ing
1 *(general)*
fears p. me 337.3
treasures long my heart p. 460.2
by evil power p. . . . 590.3
this hope p. me . . . c107
2 *(God) possesses*
of my Saviour p. . . . 367.4
heart, by my Saviour p. . 454.1
come and thy temple p. . 457.c
my ways and thoughts p. . 470.3
p. it thou, who hast . . 480.3
only thou p. the whole . . 497.1
thou thine own, p. it . . 516.2
thou shalt all my soul p.. . 615.2
till the world is p. . . . 684.4
hearts p. with dying love . 704.4
who God p. 956
my life p. c84
3 *(we) possess*
they the Kingdom shall p. . 95.1
the meek their heritage p. . 198.4
every virtue we p. . . . 200.6
I'm p. of a hope . . . 394.3
all the glories I p. . . . 406.c
the talents I p. . . . 475.2
rich am I such wealth p.. . 536.1
p. inward peace . . . 580.1
yet p. every blessing . . 607.1
life and health . . . p. . . 634.1
each the other's joy p. . . 663.3
humbly I may p. . . . 666.2
hearts p. love's . . . desire . 939.1
b *Deut 1:8**
the servant to p. the land . 419.4
p. the promised rest . . 879.4

possession
distribute all my p. . . . 530.3
with such treasure in p. . . 539.2
land where my p. lie . . 887.1
b *take possession*
t. p. of thine own . . . 55.5
t. p. of my breast . . . 214.3
t. p. of my breast . . . 563.4

possible *Mark 9:23* . . . 407.*

post
keep me faithful at my p. . 432.3
from my p. . . . not shrink . 686.3
from the battle's p. to take . 702.1
every man to his p. . . 703.4
how can I quit my p. . . 780.2

potent 129.3

potter *Isa 64:8*
thou art the p. . . . 487.1
as the p. handles the clay . 501.c

pour-ed-ing
1 *(God) pours*
thy pure radiance p. . . 40.3
they p. effectual prayers . 106.3
p. out his life for me . . 131.1
p. out his limitless life . . 245.2
opened . . . to p. out this sea. 298.7
p. on me . . . flood. . . 440.4
p. the balm . . . that heals . 457.2
p. . . . wisdom's loving ray . 682.2
p. his tenderness . . . 777.2
in autumn richly p. . . 925.3
b *Mal 3:10*
thy . . . blessings p. . . 940.3
c *pour Spirit Joel 2:28; Acts 2:17*
will surely p. all the S. . . 165.4
p. thy S. into this . . . breast. 201.c
p. in thy S.'s pure light . . 457.1
p. out thy Holy S. . . 575.1
on thy people p. thy power . 577.1
p. the S. from above . . 581.3
p. out thy S., a great . . 608.1
thy mighty S. p. . . . 609.1
p. out thy S., fill . . . 623.4
p. out thy S. while we wait . 692.4
O p. it in my soul . . . c91
2 *(we) pour*
p. contempt on . . . pride . 136.1
p. out thy . . . deep grief . 225.4
Lord, I p. at thy feet . . 525.6
we p. our ardent prayers . 660.2
p. out cries and tears . . 879.2
b *Ps 42:4*
I would p. out my soul . . 762.1

poverty
in deepest p. or wealth . . 356.3
my spirit pines in p. . . 631.3

power
1 *(general)*
the world of p. is thine . . 30.1
its wisdom, fame and p. . 223.2
prove the p. of prayer . . 604.3
now the p. of nature . . 875.3
2 *power of evil/death*
his craft and p. are great . 1.1
word above all earthly p. . 1.4
p. of death have done . . 151.2
temptations lose their p. . 587.2
foil the tempter's p. . . 670.3
with the p. of Hell contend . 694.2
their art and p. employing . 696.2
stronger than the p. of Hell . 751.3
vanquished death and . . . p.. 752.6
let no ill p. find place . . 949.3
bondage and p. of wrong . c157
b *power of sin*
the p. of cancelled s. . . 64.4
save us from . . . p. of s. . 230.4
cleanse me from its . . . p. . 302.1
where reigned the p. of s. . 423.4
saved from the p. of s. . . 431.4
from the guilt and p. of s. . 540.3
battle 'gainst the p. of s. . 700.1
redeemed us from the p. of s. 755.1
free from the p. of s. . . 857.3
free from the p. of s. . . c152
c *Rom 8:38*
in vain the mightiest p. . . 9.4
what p. my soul can sever . 345.4
principalities nor p. . . 554.3
p. to separate us . . . 554.4
no p. on earth . . . sever. . 854.3
d *Col 1:13*
no p. of darkness me molest . 671.3
tread all the p. of darkness . 695.6
evil (d), Hell, Satan (c)
3 *(human power)*
idle hours, mis-spent p. . . 379.2
take my soul and body's p. . 492.2
may speak with soothing p. . 612.5
restored to life and p. . . 668.1
I yield my p. 672.3
p. of mind, and . . . purpose . 833.2
though my p. are small . . 859.c
b *all [my] powers*
with a. our ransomed p. . . 20.4
let a. my p. . . . feel . . 207.4
quicken a. my drooping p. . 412.2
may it a. my p. engage . . 472.2
I a. my p. present . . . 526.3
let a. my p. . . . aspire . . 616.3
a. my p. . . . may unite . . 665.5
quickens a. my drowsy p. . 672.2
a. my p. to thee surrender . 865.1
a. my will and a. my p. . . c32
gospel that claims a. our p. . c210
c *every power*
take . . . use e. p. . . . 525.4
teach us . . . to use each p. . 656.4
e. ransomed p. engaging . 693.1
e. p. . . . engaging . . 702.2
might (2c)
4 *(divine power)*
his sovereign p. . . . made us. 4.2
thy p. hath founded of old . 16.3
sound his p. abroad . . 26.2
hands full of p. to raise . . 129.3
in the seat of p. enthrone . 147.2
whose p. a sceptre sways . 156.3
all the wonders of thy p. . 171.2
his triumphant p. I'll tell . . 180.3
perfect in p., in love . . 220.3
strength, O God of p. . . 526.4
matchless p. is ever new . 559.3
his p. no boundary . . 579.3
gentle p. of righteousness . 705.3
creator's p. to bless . . 871.1
for all thy p. has done . . 936.2
source (b)
b *(power shown in people)*
p. into strengthless souls . 60.3
seeking p. to send us . . 197.1
p. to walk the world . . 203.3
p. within our lives remain . 211.2
p. to conquer inbred sin . . 214.1
own thy fertilising p. . . 217.4
p. that can change . . 257.2
thy p. alone . . . bondage break 297.5
rise . . . and thy p. defy. . 303.2
p. is found by those . . 324.4
weakness will be p. . . 325.2
his p. can fashion lives . . 335.3
I thought that no p. . . 395.2
wonderful is his p. . . . 406.c
p. will . . . desires destroy . 408.4
I walked in p. with thee . . 409.2
to Jesus for the cleansing p. . 417.1
I believe thy p. the same . 419.5
p. to do the Master's will . 433.3
only bring the p. to others . 435.3
thy p. cannot fail . . . 459.2
let thy p. my soul refine. . 460.3
quicken . . . with thy p. . . 493.2
I part . . . thy p. to gain. . 513.1
p. to make me whole . . 513.2
for more of thy p. . . . pray . 523.1
lives thy p. proclaim . . 533.3
a p. within reveal . . . help . 571.3
with p., Lord, enter in . . 575.2
on thy people pour thy p. . 577.1
the p. of grace divine . . 585.2
thy p. ever present . . 589.4
a p. that none can tell . . 591.1

spring up . . . in heavenly p. . 601.2
so long thy p. hath blest . 606.3
new p. I want . 620.1
p. that dwells in thee . 620.2
p. shall conquer every foe . 620.2
I show thy p. to every foe . 620.3
with thy p. baptise us . 622.1
fill us with abundant p. . 622.3
send the p. . 643.c
p. to lift my head . 713.1
I am trusting thee for p.. . 727.5
his p. my sufficiency . 734.2
mercy's full p. . . . prove . 746.5
p. did dwell to speed . 760.1
the Lord is our p. . 763.4
his p. should most prevail . 770.2
if thy p. is not restricted. . 770.3
with triumphant p. abound . 815.2
thy p. alone can break . 827.1
I own his p. . 867.1
boast of his redeeming p. . 915.3
thy p. has worked to meet . 926.1
you in p. come down . 943.2
in thy p. let them roll . c78
p. divine . . . be it mine . c93
p. thy promise . . . plea . c93
let thy p. descend upon me . c93
make known thy p. . c98
place thy p. within, Lord . c109
the p. that sets us free . c199
it speaks of p., pardon . c241

c *all power*
descend with all thy p. . 196.1
in all thy quickening p. . 213.2
with all thy gracious p. . 217.1
all the p. of the cross . 800.3

d *power and . . .*
enfold you in its light and p. . 141.5
the p. and peace combined . 202.2
source of life and p. . 213.1
thy wisdom and thy p. . 415.3
floods of salvation and p. . 608.3
thy p. and goodness here . 945.1
grace (4b), guilt (b), love (5c), presence (d)

e *power to save*
I'll sing thy p. to s.. . 132.5
risen Lord with p. to s. . 134.3
a p. that s. and recreates . 135.3
to preach thy p. to s. . 303.4
such wondrous p. to s. . 741.1
thy p. doth s. me . 741.4
shouting Jesus' p. to s. . 910.1

f *power to keep*
boundless is his p. to k.. . 230.4
doubting p. to k. . 257.2
p. to k. me spotless . 303.c
k. every hour by thy . . . p. . 469.4

g *power of [Jesus]*
the S.'s p. will yet prevail . 149.3
J.' p. has set me free . 389.2
S., in thy p. draw near . 434.1
give up . . . through J.' p. . 784.2
through J.' p. conquer . 835.3
shouting J.' p. to save . 910.1

h *power of blood*
extol the p. of Jesus' b.. . 56.4
b. shall never lose its p.. . 132.3
p. in the b. of Calvary . 257.c
there's p. in the b. . 281.*
its p. has touched my soul . 434.5

i *power of love*
his l.'s constraining p. . 234.4
thy l.'s wondrous p. . 469.4
held by the p. of a l. . c48

j *power of name*
all hail the p. of Jesus' n. . 56.1
in his n. there's p. . 63.1
is there a n. for p. . 71.3
by the p. of his great n.. . 945.3
all hail the p. of Jesus' n. . c175

k *Rom 15:13, 19*
by the Holy Ghost's p. . 608.1
for thy p., O Holy Ghost . 643.1
Spirit (5e)

l *Matt 6:13*
men . . . whose p. was thine. 5.1
thine is the p. O Lord . 171.2
thine is the p. and mine . 456.4
thine is the Kingdom . . . p. . 951

m *all power* *Matt 28:18*
all p. to him is given . 345.3
p., all p., surely is thine . 487.3
Lord of all p., I give you. . 506.2
all p. is here and round . 744.5

n *power of God* *2 Cor 13:4*
by the p. of God eternal . 96.4
Christ, the p. of God in man . 407.6
a heart that by God's p.. . 415.5
brings the p. of God within . 733.6
p. from God is very sure . 760.2

o *power of [might]* *Eph 6:10*
ever kept by the p. of his m.. 321.1
strong in the p. of his m. . 322.4
the p. of grace divine . 584.2
armed with the p. of his m . . 679.3

p *resurrection power* *Phil 3:10*
mine for ever with r. p. . 495.2
in thy risen p. . 599.1

q *Spirit of power* *2 Tim 1:7*
I want the gift of p. . 214.1
show thyself, O God of p. . 504.3
Trinity of love and p. . 569.4
God of . . . grace and p.. . 576.1
gift of the Spirit is . . . p. . c46

r *word of power* *Heb 1:3*
speak the word of p. . 295.3

s *receive power* *Rev 5:12, 13*
all glory and p. . 24.3
worthy to r. . . . p. divine . 57.3
p. . . . worthy to r. . 109.3
I shall his p. adore . 223.4
praise and p. . . . to the Lamb. 696.c

t *power and glory* *Rev 11:17*
take . . . thy p. and reign . 150.5
take the p. and g. . 161.4
take thy p. and reign . 167.3
p. and g. unto the Lord . 184.3
p. unto God belongs . 724.1

almighty (b), display (b), divine (e), doubt (d), feel (2d), fill (2h), give (1q), greatness (b), hide (f), keep (3e), mighty (1i), pentecostal, sanctifying, saving (c), show (1d, 2c), touch (1e), wondrous (d)

powerful
shall acclaim his p. hand . 159.5
all-p. as the wind . 200.3
give us still thy p. aid . 202.3
p. stamp I long to feel . 214.4
hold me with thy p. hand . 578.1

praise-d-ing
1 *(worldly)*
wealth and p. no more . 509.2
men . . . p. thee not . 683.2
look not for reward or p. . 816.3

2 *(praise from God)*
the Master p. . 683.2
enough . . . if he shall p. . 683.3
you can gain eternal p. . 806.2

3 *(praise of God)*
morn, in p. rejoice . 2.2
his p. forth tell . 3.1
thankful, overflowing p. . 5.1
in every part with p. . 7.*
centre of unbroken p. . 10.2
we owe thee . . . p. . 15.2
girded with p. . 16.1
in the depth be p. . 18.1, 4
p. your mercy more . 27.4
p. for the singing...sweetness 35.1,2
p. with elation...every morning 35.3
swell the psalm of p. . 40.1
declare their maker's p. . 42.2
help to chant . . . p. . 109.3
all be prayer and p. . 156.3
unto thy greater p. . 163.2
spread his p. from shore . 182.2
humble prayer and fervent p.. 199.2
fill our hearts with . . . p. . 201.2
help us to p. . 219.1
eternal p. be . 219.4
majesty . . . and endless p. . 223.5
spent in promoting his p. . 298.7
I will p . thee . . . begin . 370.1
to thee the p. belongs . 382.3
our anthem of praise . 392.4
pray and p. thee . 438.2
long shall my p. ascend . 454.5
sole business be thy p. . 516.5
p. proclaiming in song . 537.4
p. that loving . . . man . 544.5
heart was tuned to p. . 557.3
in deeper reverence, p. . 567.1
free our hearts to . . . p. . 577.2
heart must yield its p. . 591.1
thee, whom angels p. . 592.1
bright with thy p. . 617.4
thine too the p. . 624.5
spread thy p. . 629.2
p. is wont to rise . 661.3
p. shall sanctify our rest. . 677.1
nor dies the strain of p. . 677.3
quiver at the shout of p. . 690.2
care evokes my p. . 728.3
shall make thy p. known . 762.2
he is the object of our p. . 785.1
eager to express our p. . 795.1
inspired with hope and p. . 825.3
I know he hears my p. . 840.3
praise and work . . . are one . 878.5
leader claims our p. . 879.5
p. never die . 887.5
p. voicing in . . . rejoicing . 888.2
p. be thy new employ . 890.5
loud let his p. ring . 897.1
fruit unto his p. . 924.2
p. and thanksgiving . . . offer. 927.1
we'll lift thy p. higher . 936.2
thine eternal goodness p. . 939.5
music be for your p. alone . 943.3
her gates to tell thy p. . 944.1
with saints and angels p. . 950

b *let praise*
let cheerful p. fill . 365.2
let his p. . . . o'erflow . 381.1
let them flow in . . . p. . 525.1
let our p. ascend . 803.2
loud let his p. ring . 897.1

c *set forth praise* *Ps 51:15**
I now set forth thy p. . 290.3
worthily set forth his p. . 533.1

d *Ps 63:5*
not for the lip of p. alone . 7.1
my lips thine eager p. . 353.3
thy p. our lips employ . 925.1

e *[sacrifice] of praise* *Heb 13:15*
offer the s. of p. . 23.5
raise this our s. of p. . 28.*
renders up the s. of p. . 762.3
offer the tribute of p. . 900.3
to thee bring s. of p. . 934.1

f *all praise*
all p. we would render . 8.4
all p. and thanks to God. . 12.3
to thee all p. and glory . 15.1
all p. to thee be given . 15.5
all p. to thee, for thou . 174.1
Lord . . . to you be all p.. . 506.1
all p. to thee, who . . . kept . 665.3

thine be all the p. . . . 741.3
all p. belongs . . . to thee . 926.1

g *Neh 9:5*
though high above all p. . 20.2

h *praise and love*
learns his . . . justice, l. and p. 142.5
to pray and p. and l. . . 196.4
l. and p. to Christ belong . 370.4
today . . . hope and p. and l.. 387.3
lost in wonder, l. and p.. . 438.3
fill our hearts with l. and p. . 576.4
may they l. and . . . p. thee . 582.4
wake dead souls to l. and p. . 669.5

i *praise and glory* *Phil 1:11*
to thee all p. and g. be . . 15.1
thy p. and g. shall not fail . 156.4
thine is the g. . . . the p. . 171.3
g. and honour, p. . . . 177.4
g. and p. to Jesus give . . 915.1

j *praise Father*
p. p. the F. 2.5
we p. thee, heavenly F. . 192.c
p. F., Son . . . 665.6/959
we p. thee, heavenly F. . 870.1

k *praise God*
p. with us the G. of grace . 17.4
the p. of my G. . . . employ . 21.1
my loving G. to p. . . . 55.1
p. and joy to G. . . . 74.1
p. sing to G., the King . . 86.2
throng of angels, p. G. . 93.5
G. be p. for all . . . 169.2
p. G., I believe . . . 222.*
the G. of Abraham p. . 223.1, 2
p. G. for what he's done . 380.1
p. G. through Jesus . . 408.5
a heart to p. my G. . . 444.1
wonderful . . . to p. my G. . 583.3
to G. be the p. . . . 640.2
p. G. . . . blessings flow 665.6/959
shout . . . the p. of our G. . 782.1
sing p. to our G. and King . 809.1
p. G.! 'tis whosoever . . 824.2
p. for all to G. be given . 834.2
O triune G., p. be . . . 958
p. G., I'm saved . . . 960
all the world p. to G. . . c226

l *praise him*
O p. h. alleluia . . . . 2.*
p. h.! p. . . . . . 17.*
p. h. for his grace . . . same . 17.2
O my soul, p. h. . . . 19.1
p. h. in glad adoration . . 19.1
p. h.! p. h.! Jesus . . 184.*
p. h. through eternity . . 380.c
now I'll p. h. . . . more . 380.3
p. h. as ye onward go . . 381.1
how wonderful to p. h. . 583.3
p. h., all creatures . 665.6/959
let us p. h., every one . . 769.1
till we p. h. again . . 808.1
we'll p. h. for all . . . 962

m *praise Jesus*
p. him! p. him! J. . . 184.*
may J. Christ be p. . . 187.*
we in J.' p. shall join . 880.4
glory and p. to J. give . 915.1
again in J.' p. we join . 915.1

n *praise King*
p., my soul, the K. . . 17.1
p. the everlasting K. . . 17.1
p. sing to God, the K. . . 86.2
let us sing: p. to our K. . 166.c
ring with p. to our K. . . 798.1
sing p. to our God and K. . 809.1
sing p. of our . . . K. . . c243

o *praise Lamb*
hallelujah, p. the L. . . 278.3
p. and power to the L. . 696.c
we'll p. the L. for ever . 899.2

p *praise Lord*
p. to the L., ... 19.*
p. ye the L., hallelujah . 20.c
p. the L., let . . . rejoice . 22.c
p. the L., for he is kind . 34.1
sing p. to our heavenly L. . 90.6
day is coming, p. the L. . 169.c
p. the L. with me . . 360.1
I never p. the L. before . 380.3
p. ye the L. . . . 381.*
glad p. to Christ, my L. . 574.5
p. ye the L., hallelujah . 695.c
p. the L. in . . . homes . 807.3
we will ever p. the L. . . 807.3
p. the L., 'tis whosoever . 824.c
p. the L.! From earthly . 894.1
we p. thee, L., with heart . 936.1
hallelujah, p. the L. . . c221

q *Ps 100:4*
enter then his gates with p. . 3.3
fill thy courts with . . . p. . 4.3

r *Ps 148:1*
p. to the holiest . . 18.1, 4

s *Ps 150:6*
all . . . come now with p. . 19.5
all things their maker p. . 494.1

t *praise name*
p., laud and bless his n. . 3.3
thy great n. we p. . . 8.1
sing the p. of his n. . . 63.3
proclaim its worthy p. . . 68.c
p. the n. of Jesus . . 68.4
own his title, p. his n. . 147.3
works shall p. thy n. . . 220.4
songs to p. his n. . . 275.2
next to p. his n. . . 278.3
p. his n., he lifted me . 339.c
saved me, O p. his dear n. . 371.2
p. ye his holy n. . . 383.c
cause thy n. to p. . . 620.3
we will p. his n. . . 818.1
sang the p. of Jesus' n. . 834.1
we p. thy n., Lord Jesus . 870.2
sound the p. of Jesus' n. . c27
p. his n., he has ransomed . c157
I'll p. his dear n. . . . c217

u *praise redeemer*
sing my great r.'s p. . . 64.1
I will p. my dear r. . . 180.3
proclaiming our great r.'s p. . 853.3

v *praise Saviour*
sons of God, your S. p. . 165.3
p. my S. all the day long . 310.c
what shall I do my S. to p. . 372.1
glorious S., thee I p. . 741.2
we'll shout our S.'s p. . . 815.c
shout the S.'s p. evermore . 819.3
join to sing the S.'s p. . 834.1
I'm going to p. my S. . . 858.1

w *praise Spirit*
p. the Spirit, Three in One . 2.5
we p. thee, Holy Spirit . 870.3

x *praise thee*
I'll p. thee as I ought . . 58.4
p. thee as long . . . breath . 357.3
I will p. thee, . . . begin . 370.1
I p. and adore you for all . 506.4
moments flow in p. thee . 521.3

bring (2g), fill (2i), garment (a), give (2f), holiest, hymn (b), more (2e), ring (d), shout (b), show (2d), sing (3g), song (1c), sound (d), work (1b)

praising *(adj)* 7.1

pray-ed-ing
1 *(Jesus) prays* *Luke 22:42; 23:34*
Jesus p. in Gethsemane . 96.3
the Father hears him p. . 106.4
in the garden he p. . . 137.2
sinners, he p. for you . . 140.1
he p.: Not my will . . . 179.2
Man of sorrows, p. . . 486.3
heard him p.: Forgive . 548.2
drawing closer as thou p. . 595.3

2 *(general)*
give us hearts . . . to p.. . 196.4
at such times we p. . . 316.2
striving and p. with tears . 321.2
where'er I speak . . . or p. . 356.4
there I learnt to p. . . . 366.3
from ever fearing to . . . p. . 437.4
p. that Christ would come . 541.1
he himself has bid thee p . 563.1
do I ever p. 588.1
not ever thus, nor p. . . 606.2
help us to p. 608.2
small time to think or p. . 675.1
wrestle and fight and p. . 695.6
sing, p. and swerve not . 738.3
p. through every toil . . 744.3
p., fighting, serving . . 788.2
learning how to p. . . 869.1
in steadfast faith p. on . 916.3
on all who p. . . . pour . 940.3
dying sinners p. to live . 945.2
p. and waiting . . . to see . c103

b *as/while [we] pray*
reach us as we p. . . . 173.2
praise thee . . . as we p. . 192.c
bring my sins . . . as I p. . 420.3
speak while . . . I p. 422.c; 589.c
as I labour and p. . . . 527.3
hear us while we p. . . 575.c
live more nearly as we p. . 668.5
now hear me while I p. . . 743.1
as we kneel to p. . . . 787.1
hear us as we p. . . . 787.c
give ear . . . each as we p. . 955
while I bow to p. to thee . c33
while I p. I shall find . . c166

c *when we pray*
prompt us when we . . . p. . 193.2
he heard me when I p. . . 348.1
burdens lifted when I p. . 719.2
hear us when we p. . . 845.2

d *Acts 7:60*
he p. for them . . . 701.2

e *1 Thess 5:17*
p. . . . without ceasing . . 438.2

f *Jas 5:13*
p., if the path be drear . . 754.3

behold (f), hear (1e), teach (1h), watch (2e)

3 (actual prayers)
a *(by a group)*
descend to us, we p. . . 86.4
for thy coming we p. . . 166.5
we p. thee, Lord, arise . . 172.4
grant us, we p. . . . greater . 173.3
to crown the offering . . . we p. 203.4
speak out thy will we p.. . 209.3
wake us, we p., to . . . life . 211.2
hear us, we humbly p. . . 224.1
heavenly Father, now we p. . 576.2
we claim, and p. for grace . 581.1
give us, we p. . . . . . 611.*
we would p. to serve . . 688.1
Saviour and Lord, we p. . 692.1
do thou assist, we . . . p. . 747.2
give us faith, . . . we p.. . 769.c
we p. thou wilt richly bless . 769.3
earnestly we p. . . . 792.2
we p. that you will grant . 795.2
seal us thine own, we p. . 870.3
we p. for thy presence here . 941.1
be present here we p. . . 943.1
p. for these before thee . . 947.1
Spirit of God, O hear us p. . c101

b *(by individuals)*
love me, I p. 77.3
I p., take all . . . away . . 140.3

I p. thee dwell within me . 221.3
as I am . . . I p. . . 285.1
in childlike faith I p. . 285.2
as I am, O hear me p. . 292.4
now to be pure I p. . 296.3
I p. that I may know thee . 435.1
weary, help me I p. . 487.3
kneeling . . . Lord, I am p. . 501.1
for more of thy power . . . p.. 523.1
my all-in-all, I p. . 565.2
I am p., blessèd Saviour . 584.*
love bestowed, Master, I p. . 675.2
I p. that when the trumpet . 774.3
in deep submission, I p. . 786.c
take thou my life . . . I p. . 786.c
seal me I p. . c68
a channel of blessing I p. . c84
p. and waiting . . . to see . c103

prayer
1 *(of Jesus)*
thy p. shall make reply . 122.3
path of p. thyself hast trod . 625.6
2 *(human)*
a *(general)*
breathe . . . name in p. . 66.2
all be p. and praise . 156.3
alike at work and p. . 187.1
humble p. and . . . praise . 199.2
p. rise from hearts . 226.2
lift thy heart in earnest p. . 253.3
not thy tears . . . or p. . 271.3
coming to the God of p. . 470.2
for the p. you granted . 552.3
by the energy of p. . 566.5
who speaks to God in p. . 580.1
a p. of words alone . 588.2
whose p. are not sincere . 588.3
the open door of p. . 595.1
prove the power of p. . 604.3
found of those in p. . 619.1
p. is . . . . 625.*
looks up to thee in p. . 632.3
sweet hour of p. . 633.*
prove . . . strength of p. . 642.3
everything to God in p. . 645.1
take it to the Lord in p. . 645.*
knows the worth of p. . 646.1
where . . . one their p. . 661.1
home where p. is heard . 661.3
gleam of love and p. . 668.3
this is the day of p. . 669.4
the voice of p. . 677.3
men of hope and . . . p.. . 702.1
to his footstool in p. . 794.2
to the place of p. . 836.1
p. gently lifts me . c94
whisper a p. . c114
p. changes things . c114
p. sustaining us . c239
b *(united prayer)*
our p. repeat the . . . cry . 127.3
wrestling on in mighty p. . 210.4
hear the p. we offer . 570.1
not for ease that p. . 570.1
we pour our ardent p. . 660.2
our p. for him (her) continue . 795.3
our p. . . . we sing . 796.1
our p., we now present . 918.2
our humble p. implore . 918.5
at thy people's p. . 946.1
lowly we kneel in p. . 948.1
c *(personal prayer)*
yea, every bygone p. . 91.3
not all my p. and sighs . 297.2
some song . . . or p. . 524.2
my constant p. shall be . 584.3
when I kneel in p. . 585.3
I often say my p. . 588.1
this sums up my p. . 589.5
kneeling . . . I make my p. . 605.1
talk with thee in p. . 615.3
grant me this, my earnest p. . 618.c
my constant longing and p. . 623.1
I cry to thee my p. . 647.1
by p. let me wrestle . 712.1
this alone shall be my p. . 916.1
d *1 Thess 5:17*
in never-ceasing p. . 714.4
e *Jas 5:16*
they pour effectual p. . 106.3
we bring with fervent p.. . 825.2
answer (1b, c), attend (b), hear (1f), house (d), instant (b), make (3i), prevail (c), restrain (b), watch (2f)

prayerfulness . 183.2

praying *(adj)*
to p. souls he . . . grants . 560.3
the childlike p. love . 720.1
ye happy p. band . 912.1

preach-ing *Acts 10:42.**
p. him to all . 60.6
p. the gospel of redemption . 158.3
p. his gospel to my heart . 191.2
charging me to p. . 303.4
ordain to p. thy word . 409.4
p. the gospel unto all . 700.1
let me live to p. thy word . 720.4
b *1 Cor 1:23*
p. Christ to a dying world . 811.4

preacher *Rom 10:14* . 527.2

precept
in his p. I run . 321.1
p. and promises afford . 657.1

precious
the story most p. . 99.1
p. Lamb by God appointed . 109.2
thy p. death and life . 140.3
pardon p., sure, complete . 259.3
there's nothing so p. . 273.2
bow at his p. feet . 278.2
O p. is the flow . 306.c
p. did that grace appear . 308.2
what a p. hiding-place . 341.c
from his p. hand I received . 371.3
this is the story most p.. . 384.1
at thy p. feet I lay . 447.2
proved this p. river . 471.3
bearing . . . p. tidings . 500.2
p. Jesus, O to love thee. . 520.1
how p. . . . is the love . 520.4
thank you . . . for p. comfort. 552.3
thy p. bleeding side . 585.c
p. things thou dost impart . 612.4
p. reviving again . 637.2
p. treasure . 652.1, 4
would the p. time redeem . 720.3
p. words of redeeming grace . 724.1
p., living, loving Lord . 729.c
behold the p. light . 819.1
jewels, p. jewels . 852.1
men the p. fruits await . 923.2
Calvary, so dear . . . so p. c7
to its p. principles . c241
b *precious blood* *1 Peter 1:19*
his p. b. to plead . 106.2
he sheds his p. b. . 107.1
p. b. my Saviour spilt . 108.c
Lord, I believe thy p. b. . 116.4
there he shed his p. b. . 128.1
dying Lamb, thy p. b. . 132.3
saved by his p. b. . 133.3
Jesus shed his p. b. . 231.2
p. b. of the Lamb . 281.c
interposed his p. b. . 313.3
p. b. . . . my only hope . 325.1
save me by his p. b. . 347.1
his p. b. he gave to redeem . 349.3
with his p. b. he bought us . 377.2
cleansing in thy p. b. . 423.1
p. b. does purge . 440.4
plunge beneath thy p. b. . 450.4
salvation through the p. b. . 504.c
washed by thy p. b. . 511.4
sinners to the p. b. . 583.4
whose p. b. . . . flows . 638.1
victory . . . through the p. b.. 702.c
p. is the b. that healed . 764.1
kept by his p. b. . 782.1
shed his b. most p. . 805.3
while the p. b. is flowing . c8
his p. b. salvation brought . c30
O the b., the p. b. . c149
p. b. . . . cleanses . c192
c *precious name*
p. n., O how sweet . 66.c
O the p. n. of Jesus . 66.3
delights to hear the p. n. . 67.4
the p. n. of Jesus . 68.1
how p. is . . . Jesus' n. . 370.3
exalt thy p. n. . 626.2
p. n. of him who died . 678.c
d *precious promise* *2 Peter 1:4*
thy p. p. were given . 216.1
thank you for your p. p.. . 552.3
while I plead each p. p. . 584.c
p. p. God hath given . 753.1
e *precious Saviour*
p., S., we are coming . 201.1
the love of my p. S. . 342.*
what a p. S. . 347.3
wholly thine, p. S. . 469.4
p. S., thou hast saved . 499.1
p. S., still our refuge . 645.3
f *precious soul*
p. s. are dying . 499.4
a p. s. is born again . 550.3
g *precious word*
dare believe thy p. w. . 638.2
may I love thy p. w. . 658.5
p. w.s of . . . grace . 724.1
h *Ps 72:14*
they are p. in thy sight . 576.4
we are p. in his sight . 722.2
i *1 Peter 1:7*
than gold . . . more p. far . 516.4
fountain (2c)

preparation . 291.3

prepare-d-ing
temple of my soul p. . 207.1
p. me for gain or for loss . 288.2
these p. us for the sight. . 414.5
p. with him to go or stay . 451.3
thy servant, Lord, p. . 472.3
for thyself p. the place . 480.1
come, my soul, thy suit p. . 563.1
my simple upright heart p. . 568.1
a spirit still p. . 596.3
for wholehearted service p. . 679.2
he shall p. thy way . 715.2
thine Army, Lord, p. . 774.4
tremble and p. to flee . 803.1
our Army we p. . 818.2
at his look, p. to flee . 875.3
for Heaven our spirits p. . 904.4
beauty . . . my Lord doth p. . c148
b *glories prepared* *1 Cor 2:9*
glories p. for our sight . 406.1
glories hath our God p. . 682.3
c *prepare to [meet]* *Amos 4:12*
p. to see thy face . 466.5
p. to meet your God . 914.1
for the harvest, O p. . 932.2
d *prepare [place]* *John 14:2*
he lives my mansion to p. . 144.3
glory p. in the skies . 233.3
for our use thy folds p. . 845.1

the Heaven p. for me . 880.1
the Lord my soul p. . 887.5
mansion, p. and all furnished . 905.3
home he has gone to p.. . c251

e *prepare [way]* *Matt 3:3*
every heart p. a throne . 81.1
every heart p. him room . 84.1
p. the way before him . 159.1
p. my heart for him . 448.4
thy wisdom shall the way p. . 744.4

place (4b), table

presence
his p. we have . 24.2
in thy p. rest . 61.1
offered there in his p. . 90.5
nought but thy p. . . . avail . 91.2
keep us to thy p. near . 97.3
I stand amazed in the p. . 179.1
to loose thy living p. . 181.4
fix thy sacred p. there . 207.1
calm thy sweet p. bestows . 209.1
my p. shall dispel . 277.4
promise your p. . 294.3
his p. disperses my gloom . 318.2
in his blessèd p. live . 336.2
appear in the p. of God . 372.3
feast . . . with his p. dear . 373.4
sing for joy in his p. . 392.2
Lord, we thy p. seek . 411.4
I want thy constant p. . 455.4
thy p. . . . coldly sought. . 466.3
in his p. daily live . 474.1
in thy p. humbly I bow . 487.2
how gracious his p. can be . 553.4
bestow, thy p. and thy love . 560.4
let thy p. be their light . 582.2
lead us to his holy p. . 595.1
thy promised p. claim . 603.1
whose p. is balm . 611.4
I need thy p. . 670.3
glory of the Saviour's p. . 711.3
his p. my steps shall attend . 734.1
in his p. blest . 740.c
whose p. keeps me pure . 742.3
the light of God's own p. . 765.3
let your guiding p. . 792.3
his p. ever near . 814.2
for thy p. here this day . 941.1
the glory of your p. . 943.2

b *presence cheer*
thy own dear p. to c. . 33.3
soul-c.ing p. restore . 318.4
does his blessèd p. c. . 418.2
your p. to c. me . 506.4

c *presence fill*
let thy sacred p. f. . 480.2
house still let thy p. f. . 516.3
be it with thy p. f. . 945.1
thy p. . . . f. all the realms . 946.1

d *presence and power*
p. and thy p. were shown . 198.3
thy p. and thy p. enfold . 534.c, 3
realise thy p. and thy p.. . 717.2

e *Ps 23:5*
in p. of my foes . 54.4

f *Heb 9:24*
the p. of his Son . 106.4
in the Father's p. Advocate . 347.2

feel (2e), fulness (c), secret (d)

present
1 *(noun)*
a *(gift)*
a p. far too small . 136.4

b *(time)*
dim past and p. clear . 31.2
make the future in the p. . 158.3
to serve the p. age . 472.2
though painful at p. . 712.4
safely to the p. day . 938.1
the p. shows God's mercy . c166

2 *(adjective)*
p. he is in all our woes . 127.2
p. everlasting Heaven . 210.4
salvation, full, p. and free . 454.4
p., Lord, in every place . 517.3
p. though the conflict . 539.3
thank you . . . for p. mercies . 552.1
p. we know thou art . 603.4
my earth a p. Heaven . 729.4
he will evermore be p. . 732.3
perfect, p. cleansing . 757.5
revival is our p. need . 760.2
be p. here we pray . 943.1
be p., gracious Saviour . 949.2

b *Ps 46:1*
a p. help is he . 496.5
p. grace and joys above . 940.1

c *Rom 8:38*
nor things p. . 554.3

d *Luke 5:17*
power ever p. to heal . 589.4

3 *(verb)*
when faith p. her claim . 198.2
our petitions now p. . 576.3
our prayers, we now p. . 918.2

b *present [bodies]* *Rom 12:1*
I now p. my body . 482.3
my will I here p. thee . 504.2
I all my powers p. . 526.3
health and talents p. . 786.3

faultless

preserve-d *Ps 121:7*
Jehovah shall p. thy going . 767.4
p. by power divine . 915.1

preserver *Job 7:20* . 785.1

preside . 190.1

press-ed-ing
so, my unworthiness p. . 553.3
thorn-crown p. thy brow . 586.2
ours to p. the battle here . 799.4

b *[cares] press* *2 Cor 1:8*
by Satan sorely p. . 284.3
temptations here . . . p. . 385.3
though my burdens p. me . 391.2
aid when heavy burdens p. . 719.1
hosts of sin are p. hard . 812.1
though trials may p. us . c122

c *[throng] press* *Luke 8:45*
with the crowd that p. . 129.1
weary . . . of the p. and t. . 564.1
often I've p. through the t. . 610.2
to thy feet I am p. . 610.2
p. through the t. . 681.2
by thronging duties p. . 752.2

d *pressed down* *Luke 6:38*
p. down and running o'er . 413.4
p. down and running o'er . 609.1

e *Phil 3:14*
p. on and bearing up . 212.4
I'm p. on toward the goal . 309.2
p. through the past . 415.1
p. on to find my Saviour . 470.2
p. on, never doubting . 689.3
p. on towards my home . 761.4
let us p. on then . 773.4
lay aside . . . onward p.. . 805.1
p. t'wards the prize . 818.4
may I p. on cheerily . 837.5

pretence . 595.2

prevail-ed-ing
of mortal ills p. . 1.1
strive and should p. . 18.3
not for long the grave p. . 145.2
power will yet p. . 149.3
goodness o'er my sin p. . 391.2
through the all-p. name . 481.4
your enemies almost p. . 537.2
he abides, o'er all p. . 539.3
friend who will p. . 709.2
I shall p. . 757.2
his power should most p. . 770.2
in thy strength we shall p. . 789.3
in the all-p. name, we ask . 791.2
through the blood . . . p. . 809.2
storm the kingdom, but p. . 816.2

b *love prevail*
thy l. has p. . 473.4
let that l., in power p. . 503.1
l. still p. . 530.c
power and l. must still p. . 744.2

c *prayer prevail*
through p. I shall p. . 366.5
my p. has p. . 436.4
p. of my heart does p. . 459.2
those who in p. p. . 642.3
grace that I, by p. p. . 762.3

d *must prevail*
our cause we know m. p. . 698.2
words which thou . . . m. p. 727.5
fight, and I m. p. . 877.3

e *Ps 129:2*
let the foe not p. . 641.3
my foes shall not p. . 762.2

f *Matt 16:18*
Satan never shall p. . 532.2
gates of hell can never . . . p.. 690.4

g *Acts 19:20*
ever mighty to p. . 165.2
mighty so as to p. . 212.4
word . . . will surely p. . 712.2

prevenient . 762.1

prevent
let no evil thing p. me . 504.2
p. the sun from shining . 854.1

prey
death cannot keep his p. . 148.3
beasts of p. come not . 268.3

price
redemption . . . such a p. . 507.2
treasures . . . countless p. . 668.2
secured at such a p. . 944.2

bought (a), money, pay (1b)

priceless
the p. gift is offered . 403.3
O what a p. treasure . 413.4

pride
p. . . . shall ne'er divide us . 97.5
the hands my p. has nailed . 122.1
weapons of my sinful p. . 122.4
bind, by p. and unbelief . 129.3
by their p. enslaved . 130.1
contempt on all my p. . 136.1
rolling in fullest p. . 224.4
free from your passion and p. 281.2
out of unrest and . . . p. . 300.3
years I spent in . . . p. . 405.1
I hate my p. . 415.2
approach to feel of p. . 425.2
bend our p. to thy control . 577.3
p. ruled my will . 606.2
evil tempers, p. . 783.4

b *self and pride*
s. and p. subduing . 430.2
all . . . s.-seeking and p. . 443.1
works . . . the s., the p.. . 448.4
farewell to s. and p. . 502.3
broken my selfish p. . 605.1
my p. and s. . . . cure . 914.3

priest
1 *(Christ)* *Acts 3:22; Heb 3:1*
crown him! . . . p. and King . 184.3
he is my prophet, p. . . 356.1
my merciful high p. . . 880.3
2 *(man)*
a *1 Sam 1:9; 3:2*
the p. of Israel, slept . . 839.2
b *Rev 1:6*
make us kings and p. . . 452.3
to be a king and p. . . 495.1

primal 949.1

Prince
1 *(Christ)*
the P. of Glory died . . 136.1
glorious P. of Life . . . 152.3
b *Prince of Peace* *Isaiah 9:6*
glad hosannas, P. of P. . 81.4
Heaven-born P. of P. . . 82.3
behold him . . . P. of P. . 108.1
by thy dying, P. of P. . 185.2
Christ of Glory, P. of P. . 479.1
P. of my p. . . . passing . 542.4
c *Acts 5:31*
thou P. and Saviour, come . 167.3
2 *John 16:11*
the p. of darkness grim . . 1.3

principalities *Rom 8:38* . . 554.3

principle
I want a p. within . . . 425.1
love with p. and fire . . 522.3
to its precious p. be true . c241

print *John 20:20*
he shows his p. of love . . 223.3
in his feet . . . are wound-p. 228.2
point to the p. . . . 364.1
know him by the p. . . c248

prison-ed
burst his three-day p. . . 153.c
loose the souls long p. . . 155.4
p. would palaces prove . . 318.3

prisoner *Luke 4:18*
the p.'s fetters breaks . . 60.3
he sets the p. free . . 64.4
comes, the p. to release. . 81.2
the p. leaps to lose . . 160.3
him who sets the p. free . 400.3

privilege
what a p. to carry . . . 645.1
I count it a p. here . . . c172

prize
1 *(noun)* *Phil 3:14*
thou our p. wilt be . . . 61.5
soul's eternal p. . . . 266.c
thy beauty be my chosen p. . 449.3
gain the everlasting p. . . 633.3
others fight to win the p. . 678.2
Christ is . . . the p.. . . 718.2
p. . . . is endless life . . 813.2
pressing t'wards the p. . . 818.4
onward to the p. before us . 892.4
2 *(verb)*
cross and passion p. . . 432.3
all that most we p. . . 774.1

problem
'mid the p. that distress . 759.1
p. of life . . . may assail. . c151

proceed 772.2

proclaim-ed-ing
my whole being may p. . . 7.1
my God, I will p. . . . 23.5
servants . . . your Master p. . 24.1
p. . . . how great thou art . 37.4
assist me to p. 64.2
let all saints p. 68.c
p. Messiah's birth . . . 75.1
thy welcome shall p. . . 81.4
with the angelic host p. . . 82.1
p. the holy birth . . . 86.2
p. thy conquering arm . . 100.3
p. thy royal degree . . . 101.2
p. that a Saviour was born 137.1, c
bow . . . his glory p. . 183.1, 5
hear the glad message p. . 247.1
here p., before thy face . . 415.3
each day p. the Christ . . 494.3
thy blessèd news to p. . . 523.2
our lives thy power p. . . 533.3
his praises p. in song . . 537.4
p. it loud and long . . . 700.3
p. God sitteth . . . 721.3
joyous tidings we p. . . 789.4
the news p. 831.1
p. . . . wondrous plan . 831.c; 952
should we fail p. . . . 853.3
his saving grace p. . . 869.3
youth p. its fight begun . . 869.4
when thy messengers p. . 945.3
b *proclaim [liberty]* *Isa 61:1*
to bind . . . their l. p. . . 832.1
freedom we p. . . . 866.2
p. my l. and washing . . c219
c *proclaim love*
be his l. in Christ p. . . 20.4
then I will thy l. p. . . . 58.5
his wonderful l. p. . . . 184.1
gladly his l. p. . . . 383.c
to p. thy wondrous l. . . 463.1
his boundless l. p. . . . 880.4
d *proclaim name* *Ex 33:19*
p. . . . hosannas to his name. 160.2
p. . . . glorious name . . 940.2
e *proclaim truth*
his saving t. p. . . . 60.5
so vast a t. p. to me . . 134.2
heralds here thy t. p. . . 946.2

proclamation c226

prodigal *[Luke 15:12 f]*
God's love to a p. race . . 119.2
my p. wanderings and shame 288.3
I come as the p. came . . 288.3

profane 480.3

profit
their p. and their joy . . 168.5
whether it be p. . . . loss . 352.3
sacrifices p. me nothing . . 530.3
b *Mark 8:36*
no p. canst thou gain . . 715.4

proffer 371.2

progress
no p. I truly had gained . . 553.3
or halt the p. of the years . 854.2

prolong
the echo shall p. . . . 7.4
earth p. the joyful strain. . 160.5
loud hallelujahs p. . . . 537.4

promise
1 *(false promise)*
its p. quenched in night . . 267.1
2 *(man's promises)*
I p. God most earnestly . . 774.3
p. in this sacred hour . . 784.2
Jesus, I have p. . . 862.1, 4
what p. are we making thee . 926.4
3 *(God's promise)*
his p. our spirits cheer . . 43.3
p. of things to be . . . 154.3
lo! the p. of a shower . . 165.4
show . . . thy p. sign . . 167.3
when comes the p. time . 172.3
boundless . . . p. of Jesus . 230.2
wonderful love he has p. . 264.3
the p. is secure . . . 279.3
thy p. is my only plea . . 284.2
p. your presence . . . 294.3
that p.: Whosoever will . 359.2
while his p. tells . . . 373.4
gift that thou hast p. me . 415.1
with tears his p. . . . repeat . 420.3
to thy p. I'm clinging . . 434.4
on thy p. . . . I lean . . 437.1
'tis the p. of his word . . 554.4
the p. calls me near . . 560.1
day by day, the p. reads . 566.2
feel the p. is not vain . . 621.3
this is the p. of love . . 637.1
before thy p. we could plead . 642.2
p. afford a . . . light . . 657.1
we have Christ's own p. . 690.4
we're trusting in the p. . . 700.3
firm . . . his p. stands . . 735.3
let this p. ring . . . 753.2
in his p. confiding . . . 759.c
he p. we should see . . 769.1
a p. he has given . . . 824.1
mine his loving p. . . . 840.3
thou hast p. to receive . . 845.3
Jesus, thou hast p. . . 862.4
thy p. is written . . . 883.2
prove . . . for he has p. . . 920.4
still his p., unbroken . . 939.4
power thy p. c93
faith . . . the p. sees . . c118
his p. is true c122
b *every promise*
over e. p. write my name . 303.4
e. p. is fulfilled . . . 423.5
by e. p. thou hast made. . 513.2
e. p. is true c130
c *promise of [grace]*
the sweet p. of his g. . . 26.2
we wait the p. g. . . . 216.2
by all the p. of g. . . 619.1
trust his rich p. of g. . . 738.3
d *promise of God*
to every . . . the p. of G. . 22.2
'tis the p. of G. . . . 392.1
the p. of G. are sure . . 755.*
standing on the p. of G. . 757.*
built upon G.'s p. sure . . 833.3
e *Acts 1:4*
claim the Father's p. mine . 208.4
p. of our heavenly Father . 213.1
f *(Acts 2:33)**
wait the p. of our Lord . . 196.2
from whom the p. came . . 198.2
draw near, O p. Comforter . 198.5
give us the p. Holy Ghost . 203.1
attend the p. Comforter . 214.2
g *Acts 13:23*
fulfilled his p. word . . 78.2
the Saviour p. long . . 81.1
p. from eternal years . . 88.1
h *Acts 2:39*
the p. is for you . . . 403.3
the p. is for me . . . 596.4
i *2 Cor 1:20*
all his p. embrace . . . 23.2
speaks all the p. . . . 26.3
all the p. of Jesus . . . 324.4
all the p. are mine . . . 481.4
by all the p. of grace . . 619.1
all the p. of God are sure . 755.c
j *Heb 4:1*
possesses the p. rest . . 879.4

k *Jas 1:12*
I'll win the p. crown . . 678.c
fit us for the p. crown . . 937.4
l *2 Peter 1:4*
lays hold of thy great p. . 201.3
m *1 John 2:25*
the life which he p. . . 553.4
believe (d), claim (2c), fail (1b), fulfil (d), give (1r), land (1c), receive (2h), stand (3e), sure (f)

promoting 298.7

prompt 193.2

prone 313.5

proof
the p. is Jesus . . . 270.3
Calvary is p. enough . . 324.1
p. supreme of . . . pity . . 777.2
p. of final victory . . . 777.4
greatest p. of his love . . c121

prophet
p. long ago foretold . . 72.4
by p. bards foretold . . 83.3
b *Matt 5:12*
the p.'s marks . . . blessings . 95.3
c *2 Peter 1:21*
moved by thee the p. wrote . 651.2
priest (1)

prophetic 651.1

proportion 453.4

prospect
sweet p. . . . lost all . . 318.1
what p. now I see . . . 460.1
p. droop and die . . . 761.1
beautiful p., converse . . 873.3

prosper 19.2

prostrate
let angels p. fall . . . 56.1
falling p. at his feet . . 66.4

protect-eth-ed-ing
p. them wheresoe'er . . 569.4
God, who comforts and p. me 583.3
its light . . . our way p. . . 655.3
thus p. . . . we boldly dare . 722.4
our captain . . . will p. us . 818.3
'neath his wings p. hide. . 954.2

protection
safely kept by thy p. . . 504.1
tender love, divine p. . . 938.2

proud
like earth's p. empires . . 677.5
foe . . . p. and strong . . 813.3
p. to serve their leader . . 866.1
p. to tell of . . . b. . . . c199

proudly
in vain, and p. answered . 548.1
p. we salute the colours. . 777.1
her standard p. flies . . 799.2

prove-d-ing
1 *(general)*
prisons would palaces p. . 318.3
p. by love's test . . . 507.1
scenes alike engaging p. . 556.1
what best for each will p. . 715.5
war . . . may p. distressing . 805.1
2 *(we) prove*
my life may p. . . . 205.3
may p. there is mission . . 463.1
my devotion to p. . . 493.3
p. the traitor never . . 704.2
p. a friend indeed . . . 706.2
p. for ever faithful . . . 714.1
on them my labours p. . . 720.3
habit makes us want to p. . 748.3
chances of p. . . . true . . 773.2
p. how swift obedience . . 867.2
sing and you will p. . . c201
b *Ps 17:3*
search, p. my heart . . 453.1
3 *prove God*
p. the beauty of thy house . 36.6
breadth and height to p. . 55.1
p. the gift unspeakable . . 55.4
p. the glories of . . . his love . 84.3
I've p. this to be true . . 320.3
in my yesterdays I p. them . 324.4
I've p. he is mighty . . 329.c
known and p. him long . . 343.1
this I shall p. 355.6
thy cleansing grace to p. . 440.1
p. this precious river . . 471.3
here we come to p. . . 603.2
p. the power of prayer . . 604.3
p. his death . . . healing . . 634.4
p. . . . strength of prayer . 642.3
all thy goodness p. . . 646.4
let us thine influence p. . . 651.1
the trusting soul shall p.. . 718.3
always p. sufficient . . 732.3
power my sufficiency p. . 734.2
p. the promises of God . . 755.1
thy gracious riches to p. . 786.4
delights we shall p. . . 905.4
b *Mal 3:10*
p. the Lord, for he . . . 920.4
c *(God) proves*
Christ who p. he loved us . 554.2
he p. by word and deed . . 555.2
p. thy greater things . . 769.2
d *prove love*
p. . . . strength of his l. . 126.4
p. thy sovereign . . . l. . 140.5
p. the delights of his l. . . 397.4
love our wakening . . . p. . 668.1
p. his unchangeable l. . . 734.2
e *prove mercy*
urge them his m. to p. . 687.2
m.'s full power I . . . p. . 746.5
all his m. p. c138
fulness (b)

provide-d-ing
thy hand hath p. . . . 33.c
boundless cleansing to p. . 126.1
best of blessings he'll p. . 377.4
didst p. by thy death . . 543.1
pardon thou dost p. . . 605.1
thus p., pardoned, guided . 607.3
'tis his to p. 712.2
boundless mercy will p. . . 718.3
the laws it will p. . . . 856.3
p. a robe and crown . . 891.3
raiment fit p. 918.3
p. food for thy children . . 927.3
daily manna still p. you . . 954.2
grace thou hast p. me . . c62
b
Jesus p. a rest . . . 139.3
strength . . . Lord will p. . 691.4
the Lord will p. . . . 763.1
God, our maker, doth p. . 924.1
c *Gen 22:8*
God will p. for sacrifice . . 668.2

provided 170.1

providence
behind a frowning p. . . 29.4
praising thy p. and love . . 950.1
his p. has led me . . . c147

providential 761.2

provoke-d
long p. him to his face . . 286.2
p. my hope or fear . . . 880.2

psalm
church with p. must shout . 11.2
swell the p. of praise . . 40.1
out of distress to . . . p.. . 300.2
makes of life a living p. . . 613.2
raise the warrior p. . . 707.2

publish-ing *Mark 1:45**
p. abroad his . . . name . . 24.1
p. the sinner's friend . . 720.4
p. with our latest breath. . 721.5

pull *2 Cor 10:4* 696.c

pulse
the p. of passion stir . . 211.2
call of band make my p.. . 780.3

punishment 108.1

puny 185.3

purchase-d *Acts 20:28**
redemption, the p. of blood . 22.2
p. there my pardon free . . 125.1
with his blood he p. me . . 180.c
p. of our dying Lord . . 216.2
Jesus p. on the tree . . 230.3
heir of salvation, p. of God . 310.1
p. my salvation, brought . 347.1
p. my pardon on . . . tree . 357.2
thou hast p. all for me . . 421.5
to p. a full salvation . . 427.1

pure
1 *(re divinity)*
p. Father of light . . . 8.4
so p. yet he has borne . . 108.2
p. as thou art p. . . . 431.4
Redeemer, p. as thou art . 623.c
b
thy p. radiance pour . . 40.3
perish self in thy p. fire . . 194.2
p. flame of the Spirit . . 443.3
sin appear in thy p. ray . . 446.1
thy Spirit's p. light . . . 457.1
streams of p. . . . peace . 601.2
cherished, true and p. . . 941.3
spread thy p. wing . . 949.3
c *Rev 22:1*
its waters are p. . . . 252.2
who seeks . . . that fountain p. 277.3
if once thy p. waters . . 298.4
I've tasted life's p. river . . 320.1
delight (2c)
2 *(re people)*
recreate me p. . . . crystal p.. 32.1
ever . . . p. and strong . . 32.3
p. and free from . . . alloy . 76.3
for all the p. and blest . . 139.3
I stand both p. and free . . 176.1
like Jesus, gentle, p. . . 193.4
now to be p. I pray . . 296.3
bliss of the p. . . . 364.3
holy and p. and perfect . . 407.5
how p. the soul must be . 414.1
till spotless all and p. . . 423.2
where we may be p. . . 429.1
p. and spotless let us be. . 438.3
speak me p. within . . 450.3
what to do to be p. . . 459.1
I would be p.- . . . 491.1
may I arise p. and fresh . . 673.4
teach me to be p. . . . 837.1
p. and holy . . . might be . 840.2
all the p. ones . . . 852.2
p. be my tongue . . . 861.3

p. as thou wouldst have . 863.3
the land of the p. . . . 905.1
wholesome grain and p. . 924.2

b *pure [desire]*
receive . . . first p. vow . . 5.4
craving into p. d. . . . 197.2
with purpose p. and deep . 534.3
p. and fervent heart-d. . 620.3

c *pure [heart]* *Matt 5:8*
blessed are the p. in motive . 95.2
until my h. is pure . . 189.2
when . . . h. are p. and free . 235.c
your h. must be kept p. . . 406.3
blest are the p. in h. . 411.1
chooseth the p. in h. . . 411.3
give us a p. and lowly h. . 411.4
with love my h. keep p. . . 416.2
a h. that is true . . . p. . 422.4
a h. . . . p. and good . . 444.4
give a p. and loving h. . . 466.3
to obtain a p. h. . . . 469.2
where the p. in h. may dwell . 591.1
hallelujah! to the h. that's p. . 755.c
grace to make them p. in h. . 791.3
such as from a p. h. flows . 910.3

d *pure joy*
swell with p. seraphic j. . 164.5
p. j. of the Eden above . 905.4
p. are the j. within . . c152

e *pure love*
highest strength, all p. l. . 202.2
with compassion p. . . 212.3
l. of God so p. . . 295.4
p., unbounded l. thou art . 438.1
Christ of p. and perfect l. . 440.1
thy p. l. within my breast . 480.5
inspired by p. l. to thee . . 581.1
be the p. flame of l. . . 594.2
may my l. to thee p. . . . be 743.2
a l. that's p. and clean . 779.2

f *Phil 4:8*
p. in motive and in thought . c56

keep (3h), make (4f)

3 *(other)*
flowing water, p. and clear . 2.3
receive . . . first p. vow . . 5.4
infant's slumbers, p. and light. 676.5

pureness 531.2

purer-st
p. and higher . . . our wonder 22.3
song of p. beauty . . . 70.c
Jesus is p. . . . shines p. 177.2, 3
strength, all p. love . . 202.2
his is beauty, p. rarest . 343.1

p. light shall mark . . . 442.6
in p. lives thy service . . 567.1
inspired by p. love . . 581.1
seat was made of p. gold . 590.1
p. word . . . may be heard . 867.4

purge-d *Ps 51:7**
p. our deepest stains . . 121.4
when he had p. our stains . 164.2
p. from every spot . . . 262.3
p. the dark halls . . . 416.1
p. and keep from . . . stain . 440.4
all offences p. away . . 924.3

b *purge hearts*
fire, and p. our h. . . . 217.3
Spirit divine, p. thou our h. . 218.2
p. my h. with holy fire . . 479.2

c *Heb 1:3*
p. thou my sin away . . 296.3

purify-d-ing *Titus 2:14**
thou only . . . p. the heart . 100.2
p. all my nature . . 201.4
Tongue of flame, come, p. . 211.2
O bliss of the p. . . . 364.*
p. from sinful dross . . 452.3
p. from inbred sin . . . 783.4
with each new test, are p. . 874.1
there, for ever p. . . . 924.4

purity
emblem of p. . . . good . . 175.2
Spirit of p. and grace . . 200.7
fragrance of p. . . . 383.1
if you want p., walk . . 427.3
Jesus, thy p. bestow . . 432.1
I want thy spotless p. . . 455.2
keeping my heart in p. . . 455.5
blue . . . of inward p. . . 777.3
the flag of p. 779.1
wonderful passion and p. . c77
it speaks of . . . peace and p.. c241

b *purity and love*
thy reign of . . . p. and l. . 172.2
in power, in l. and p. . . 220.3
clothe me with . . . l. . . . p. . 516.4

purple
the p.-headed mountain . 25.2
when p. morning breaketh . 632.1

b *John 19:2*
his p. robe is parted . . 126.2

purpose
1 *(divine)*
his p. will ripen fast . . 29.5
fulfil the p. of thy death . . 138.1

by God's eternal p. . . 174.4
in its p. ne'er swerving . . 276.3
his p. daily learn . . . 343.3
would make thy p. mine . 566.3
thy p. more may know . . 919.3

2 *(human)*
given a p. and a way . . 36.4
life has point and p. . . 376.3
my life's p. claimed . . 484.3
if my p. have altered . . 522.1
in heart, with p. pure . . 534.3
eyes my inmost p. see . . 667.2
each yearning p. . . . 682.2
cause shall every p. sway . 692.5
powers . . . strength of p. . 833.2
standing by a p. true . . 847.1
dare to have a p. firm . . 847.c
be one with us in p. . . 943.1
man has . . . no p. . . . c210

purposeful-less
empty, p. and worthless . 399.2
I follow a p. aim c173

pursue-d-ing
humble beast p. his road . 150.1
me who him to death p.. . 283.1
henceforth thy will p. . . 534.3
rejoices to p. the steps . . 657.4
my daily labour to p. . . 667.1
he (she) will choose them to p. 795.2

b *pursue way* *Ps 34.14**
I still my w. p. . . . 361.3
we'll p. our w. . . . 599.3

pursuits
fond p. I all give o'er . . 509.2
whate'er p. my time employ . 517.2

put
p. within my heart a melody . 327.2
I'll p. in this plea . . . 368.3
beneath my feet he's p. . . 401.2
p. a cheerful courage on . 559.1
by faith p. in my plea . . 562.2
p. off this robe of flesh . . 633.3
nor . . . p. my soul to shame . 735.2
p. his arm unfailing round . 954.3
he'll p. things right . . c22

b *(Gal 3:27)*
thy comeliness p. upon me . 589.2

c *Eph 6:11*
arise, and p. your armour on . 695.1
p. on salvation armour . . 699.3

flight (b), trust (3c), work (3b)

pylon 30.1

Q

quail
thy judgments make me q. 618.3
flesh and blood would q. . 749.3
warrior, faint or q. . . . 816.2

quake *Nah 1:5* . . . 107.3

quell-ed
fears to q., wrongs to right . 126.2
he all his foes shall q. . . 164.5
love his fear shall q. . . 277.4
to q. my flaming heart . . 303.2
struggles are q. . . . 416.4

quench-ed
its promise q. in night . . 267.1
my thirst was q. . . . 332.2
none can q. . . . desire . . 351.c
q. the kindling fire . . 425.2
q. the brands in . . . blood . 720.2
b *1 Thess 5:19*
nor let us q. . . . light . . 202.4
c *Isa 42:3*
flax God will not q. . . 269.2

quenchless 145.1

quest
like him in this blest q. . . 51.3
life is a q. 351.2
be this my only q. . . . 571.4
a pressing, absorbing q. . 666.3
turn . . . into an active q. . 858.3

question-ing
Lord, answer these q. . . 289.4
while I every q. sing . . 409.1
Lord, thou art q. . . . 507.1
q. cries do not cease . . 527.2
the Lord will q. . . . 666.3
I would be humbly q. . . 871.3

quick-er
hands q. to soothe . . 129.2
friend so q. to hear . . 246.2
q. as the apple of an eye . 425.3
q. to fight for thee . . 446.4
human hands were q. to feed. 518.1
q.-discerning eye . . . 596.3
nor hast thou . . . a q. ear . 717.3
a q. yet lasting choice . . 749.1
q. to hear each whisper . . 839.3

quicken-ed *Eph 2:1, 5**
with my q. ears I hear . . 48.2
since thou hast q. me . . 353.4
q. all my drooping powers . 412.2
q. each inner wish . . 493.2
thus with q. footsteps . . 599.3
q. our hearts . . . 608.1
q. all my drowsy powers . 672.2
q. sense and . . . joy . . 878.3
q. into life the seed . . 926.2

quickening *(adj)*
all may hear the q. sound . 140.4
come in all thy q. power . 213.2
thine eye diffused a q. ray . 283.3
may thy q. voice . . . remove. 603.5
let us feel its q. power . . 638.1
send forth thy q. breath . 669.5
q. joy or burdening care . 947.4
b *Ps 119:50*
the q. word of God . . 26.2
c *1 Cor 15:45*
in me a q. Spirit be . . 140.2
Holy Ghost, all-q. fire . . 207.1
Spirit's q. grace . . . 791.3

quickly
q. did his will obey . . . 96.2
sad days have q. sped . . 151.3
q. arise and away . . . 248.4
transaction so q. was made . 371.2
his smile q. drives it away . 397.2
b *come quickly* *Rev 22:20*
come q., gracious Lord . . 55.5
come q. from above . . 444.5
come q. and abide . . . 587.3
rend the heavens, come q. . 604.4
even so, Lord, q. come . . 924.4

quiet
the q. rooms of time . . 7.2
God speaks . . . by q. ways . 31.3
the q. waters by . . . 54.1
come to thee with q. mind . 449.c
doubts . . . in q. trust . . 551.2
in my q. strength . . . strong . 564.1
in this q. evening hour . . 576.1
make . . . a q. place . . 615.1
in the q. Temple heard . . 871.2
q. brave endurance . . 948.2

quietly *Lam 3:26* . 210.3

quietness *Isa 30:15*
drop thy still dews of q.. . 567.4
little shrine of q. . . . 615.2
grace is wrought in q. . . 615.4
then q. and confidence . . 717.6

quit
how can I q. my post . . 780.2
foe shall q. the field . . 813.3

quite
it sounds q. incredible . . 49.1
q. sure of salvation . . 364.2
true, my heart's q. new . . 375.2
washed in his blood q. white . 402.1
light will darken q. . . . 551.1
to help me q. through . . 712.3
serve God q. as well . . 780.3
though made q. sinless . . 785.3
make my heart q. clean . . c13

quiver 690.2

R

race
1 *(people)*
to our r. so freely given . . 28.5
to save a fallen r. . . . 62.4
atoned for all our r. . . 106.2
God's love to a prodigal r. . 119.2
r. long severed . . . 166.2
grace for a fallen r. . . 341.3
spurning not our sinful r. . 500.1
for all the r. expanding . . 539.1
to cleanse our fallen r. . . 590.2
Jesus . . . died for our r. . 687.3
lost and sinning r. . . . 777.2
whate'er your r. may be . . 826.3
God of their succeeding r. . 918.2
b *every race*
from every tribe and e. r. . 170.3
we are of e. class and r. . 705.2
declared in Christ for e. r. . 760.2
e. r. his own 866.3
Adam
2 *(life)*
see . . . the ending of the r. . 389.3
when I have . . . won the r. . 583.5
life's short r. is o'er . . 709.4
hinder in the r. . . . 816.1
goal of earth's strait r. . . 878.2
b *[run] the race* *Heb 12:1*
joined the heavenly r. . . 366.3
free soul may r. the r. . . 449.3
and r. the heavenly r. . . 559.1
r. the straight r. . . . 718.2
running in the heavenly r. . 861.4
saints whose r. is r. . . 939.3

radiance
thy pure r. pour . . . 40.3
the r. streaming . . . 112.3
joy's r. throw . . . 329.2
celestial r. from afar . . 711.2
beams with r. divine . . 868.3
show forth thy r. glorious . c102

Radiancy 412.4

radiant
face in r. vision dawns . . 353.1
r. cloud by day . . . 654.3
I catch its r. glory . . . 726.3
r. is the way before thee . 776.1
marching on . . . r. fields . 818.4
views the r. shore . . . 911.5

radiate c61

rage-d-ing
his r. we can endure . . . 1.3
elements . . . madly are r. . 19.3
Satan will r. 233.2
though the conflict r. . . 539.3
calm amid its r. . . . 569.2
r. waves obey thy will . . 598.2
rouse thee! war is r. . . 693.1
to the front! the fight is r. . 702.2
foes of God around us r. . 778.1
fierce and long . . . r. . . 804.4
fiercely it r. 813.2
b *[tempests] rage*
fire and t. r. 5.4
when the storms . . . r. . . 249.4
safe . . . though t. r. . . 574.1
though the t. . . . r. . . 751.3
what though the t. r. . . 882.2

rail
1 *(noun)*
Lord of cable . . . of r. . . 30.2
2 *(verb)* *Mark 15:29*
r. they against him . . . 130.1

raiment
a *Matt 6:28*
r. fit provide 918.3
b *Matt 28:3*
angels in bright r. . . . 152.1
c *Luke 23:34*
thy r. all over . . . dyed . . 111.2
d *Rev 3:5*
in sparkling r. bright . . 167.1

rain
distils in the . . . r. . . . 16.4
sweet the r.'s new fall . . 35.2
send a pentecostal r. . . 205.2
rainbow through the r. . . 621.3
you can't stop r. . . . 854.1
storm and r. . . . it lies . . 923.2
in r. and snow and sun . . 926.2
soft refreshing r. . . . 935.1
in sunshine, in r. . . . same . c207
b *1 Kings 18:41*
sound of abundance of r. . 637.2

rainbow
r. span the heavens high . 39.2
I trace the r. 621.3
his love is like a r. . . c206

raise-d-ing
1 *(God) raises*
born to r. the sons . . . 82.3
never r. to seek . . . 129.2
r. my sinking heart . . 303.1
healing . . . r. the fallen . . 724.1
r. the fallen, cheer . . . 737.3
Army . . . God is r. . . . 822.1
b *Matt 11:5*
power to r. . . . the dead . 129.3
your power to r. the dead . 748.2
c *Eph 2:6**
r. us to thy . . . throne . . 79.4
will r. our bodies too . . 149.3
r. to life again . . . 155.4
r. in Christ to life . . . 540.4
2 *(we) raise, in praise*
Father, unto thee we r. . . 28.*
the birds their carols r. . . 42.2
r. your joys . . . high . . 143.1
conspire to r. the sound . 382.2
to thy dear name we r. . . 674.1
loud your anthems r. . . 690.2
r. the warrior psalm . . 707.2
we'll r. the joyful cry . . 813.4
would their hosannas r. . 853.3
r. the . . . harvest home . 924.4
your hallelujahs r. . . . 929.1
our hearts we r. . . . 934.1
our witness would we r. . 944.1
b *raise song*
eternal God, our s. we r. . . 5.1
as s. of happiness I r. . . 134.3
r. the s. they nobly taught . 158.2
some s. to r., or prayer . . 524.2
my new glad s. I r. . . . 741.2
my sweetest songs I'll r. . 840.3
r. their s. of saving grace . 891.4
r. . . . a s. of praise . . 919.1
r. the s. of harvest home . 924.1
c *raise voice*
high as . . . our voices r. . . 4.3
whose sweet v. are r. . . 392.3
in glad song my v. to r. . . 613.1
now our v. r. 836.c
r. heart and v. now to thee . 939.5
our v. . . . r. the Three in One 940.2
determined my v. I'll r. . . c194
Bethel, Ebenezer
3 *(general)*
let the valleys all be r. . . 159.2
a cross that r. me . . . 617.1
the low to r. 620.3
as I stoop to r. the low . . 758.4
as they r. this child . . 795.2
to r. the corn 925.2
these walls we r. . . . 946.2
they nailed him . . . r. high . c89
b *raise [banner]*
r. the . . . standard higher . 696.3
r. your banner in the sky . 697.2
r. the standard high . . 698.1
we'll r. our banner h. . . 810.1

rally
r. round the banner . . 698.c
around our colours . . . r. . 775.1
r. round . . . standard . . 818.2

rampant 789.4

rampart 799.2

ran see run

random 868.3

ranging 707.4

ranks
all r. of creatures . . . 141.4
devil's r. deserted . . . 309.2
we'll fill the r. 700.2
come and join our r. . . 818.c
go from the r. below . . 894.c
fight in the r. c230
in the Army r. are we . . c236
r. of the dear old Army . . c237
in the r. of truth . . . c238

ransom-ed *Matt 20:28**
for he became my r. . . . 65.2
Immanuel . . . r. Israel . . 72.4
Jesus came down my r. to be. 114.1
the seal of my r. . . . 119.c
died to r., thee from sin . . 229.3
Saviour hath a r. found . . 253.1
from my sins has r. me . . 404.1
glory to God, he has r. me . c157
b *paid ransom*
he p. the r. for me . . . 99.3
by death our r. he has p. . 108.2
how . . . he was a r. p. . . 829.c
c *[gave] ransom* *1 Tim 2:6*
he the r. freely g. . . . 180.2
he g. his life to r. . . . 349.1
who g. himself a r. . . . c156

ransomed *(adjective)* *(Isa 35:10)**
r. healed, restored . . . 17.1
with all our r. powers . . 20.4
till the r. hosts in Heaven . 63.3
nor let that r. sinner die . . 106.3
to his r. worshippers . . 161.3
armies of the r. saints . . 167.1
when with the r. in Glory . 179.4
the r. nations bow . . . 223.3
next to join with the r. . . 278.4
r. servant, I restore . . . 505.2
one among the r. throng . 514.4

'tis the r. army . . . 550.c
born anew, a r. child . . 550.2
every r. power engaging . 693.1
o'er his r. people shed . . 765.3
shall join the r. throng . . 828.4
r. sinners of all kinds . . 893.3
r. in Glory we see . . . 908.1
when the r. host we see . 908.c

b *all the ransomed*
all his r. home to bring . . 118.5
till all the r. host . . . 132.3
all the r. shall gather . . 169.1

c *ransomed soul*
my r. s. he leadeth . . 53.2
bring our r. s. at last . . 76.4
r. s. . . . all for thee . . 524.4
bear me safe . . . a r. s. . 743.4

rapture
our r. when Jesus we see . 22.3
r. in the name of Jesus . . 70.4
angels with r. announce it . 139.1
with what r. gaze we . . 161.3
throbs of its r. reach us . . 173.2
sing with holy r. . . . 259.4
out of despair into r. . . 300.3
visions of r. burst . . . 310.2
Jesus saved me! O the r. . 350.1
soul . . . r. shall shout . . 364.4
tell its r. all abroad . . . 365.1
in loud r. . . . ring . . . 543.4
I sing in my r. . . . 710.3
await the heights of r. . . 711.3
abiding, r. divine . . . c36

raptured
bells my r. soul are calling . 39.4
till my r. soul shall find . . 115.c
my r. soul can only sing . 405.3

rapturous
singing the r. chorus . . 139.3
in r. songs to praise . . 275.2
abound in the r. sound . . 355.3
r. height of . . . delight . . 367.4
r. heights of his love . . 535.3
O the r. bliss to know . . 540.2
what r. songs are mine . . 726.3
transporting, r. scene . . 887.2

rare-st
offered gifts most r. . . 76.3
his is beauty, purest, r. . . 343.1
jewels rich and r. . . . 658.2
each gift of beauty r. . . 833.2

rather 295.2

ratified
promise r. by grace . . 760.2
the covenant is r. . . . 785.4

rave 280.2

ray
earth . . . reflect thy r. . . 10.2
rejoices in the mellow r. . 40.1
sun's last r. are fading . . 63.3
flung a quenchless r. . . 145.1
sheds not its glorious r. . . 224.1
diffused a quickening r. . . 283.3
lights . . . with sunshine r. . 316.c
bright r. come beaming . . 316.2
Heaven's r. falls today . . 379.4
the r. of glory shine . . 400.1
appear in thy pure r. . . 446.1
sends a shining r. . . . 519.4
restores its borrowed r. . . 621.2
wisdom's loving r. . . . 682.2
truth's unsullied r. . . . 697.4
brighter r. may shine . . 916.2
summer r. with vigour . . 925.2
labour ends with sunset r. . 934.3

cheering r. . . . to dim . . c166
r. of Heaven shine . . . c176

b *ray of light*
did the l. r. seem to say. . 103.2
withholds his r. of l. . . 107.2
a thousand r. of l. . . . 658.3
low, no r. of l. . . . 719.4
we see no r. of l. . . . 772.3

reach-ed-ing
1 *(God) reaches* *(2 Cor 10:13)**
it r. all mankind . . . 55.2
the hand of Jesus r. me. . 176.3
blood has r. me . 313.c; 520.c
strong arm . . . did r. me . 329.1
love r. me . . . . 342.*
in love he stooped to r. . . 350.1
so tender that it r. . . . 439.2
how can your pardon r. . . 572.2
this word it r. nations . . 824.2
blessing r. every people . . 927.4

2 *(general)*
r. the way we dream . . 27.6
stars that r. eternity . . 52.c
throbs of its rapture r. us . 173.2
past the r. of all despising . 185.3
once more I have r. . . 298.5
I unto his mind may r. . . 398.1
vainly aspire to r. . . . 456.2
r. a monarch's throne . . 508.3
r. out for the blessing . . 553.3
when we r. the end . . 579.2
r. the hidden depths . . 612.4
sublimest strains that r. . . 625.3
hills that . . . r. the skies. . 766.1
till hosannas r. the skies. . 834.3

b *Phil 3:13*
r. out faith's hand . . . 413.2
after thee my heart is r. . . 434.1
heights . . . I may not r. . . 585.4

c *reach [Heaven]*
when we r. the Glory land . 94.c
I r. the golden strand . . 115.4
millions have r. . . . shore . 275.1
shall safely r. the goal . . 344.2
I r. those pearly gates . . 368.3
feet shall r. the open door . 400.3
r. the glory . . . well done . 628.4
when I r. the margin . . 726.4
r. Heaven just as surely . . 780.3
faints to r. the land . . 877.2
I shall r. home at last . . 882.2
we r. the shining river . . 891.3
when we r. the other side . 902.3
r. fair Canaan's land . . 912.1
r. first their . . . end . . 938.4

read
to r. the secrets . . . 38.1
I have r. his . . . sentence . 162.2
shine . . . the book we r. . 193.3
no other friend can r. . . 325.3
in my heart I r. it so . . 359.3
heart I cannot r. . . . 421.2
all . . . thou canst r. . . 507.c
day by day, the promise r. . 566.2
chart, wherein we r. . . 654.2
I have r. of men of faith . 686.1
taught to r. his word . . 834.2
God our thought is r. . . 836.3
I may r. with childlike . . 839.5
r. it, and following . . . 856.2

b *read story*
as I r. the s. . . . 94.1
I r. the wondrous s. . . 123.2
when I r. that sweet s. . . 794.1

readily 348.2

ready
someone is r. . . . waiting . 278.1
snares are r. for my feet . 400.2

r., steady, pass the word . 698.c
into the r. ground to die . 923.1

b *ready to [forgive]* *Ps 86:5*
r. to meet you . . . 236.3
waiting, and r. to forgive . 255.2
Master, r. and kind . . 848.3

c *Luke 14:17*
all things . . . are r. . . 234.2
made r. and furnished . . 289.3

d *Titus 3:1*
r. for all . . . will . . . 199.4
ever r. for service I am . . 321.4
a r. hand to do . . . 426.3
r. for service whene'er . . 443.2
to serve thee I am r. . . 482.3
Lord, see me r. . . . 501.2
speak: and make me r. . . 614.4
r. . . . thy will to see . . c99

real
when all that now is r. . . 39.4
r. contentment has . . . laws . 244.3
make Calvary r. to me . . c81
r. life is beginning . . . c106

realise-ing
wider than . . . mind can r. . 49.3
r. Jesus and his smile . . 352.1
by thy torments r. . . 503.2
r. for ever . . . fruits . . 633.3
more clearly would I r. . . 717.2

reality
ever a bright r. . . . 455.5
thine in blest r. . . . 649.4
a living, bright r. . . . c90

really
if you would r. be . . . 98.3
no one . . . r. cares . . 238.1
I r. must declare it . . c170

realm
1 *(general)*
the whole r. of nature . . 136.4
r. of every tongue . . . 160.2
thy r. enfolds the universe . 171.1
a r. deserted 885.3
all the r. of space . . . 946.1

2
a *(Heaven)*
cease, as in the r. above . 172.2
lead to r. on high . . . 590.2
r. beyond the sky . . . 654.2
r. where sorrows cease . . 697.5
can see the r. beyond it . . 766.2
r. of fadeless day . . . 888.1
the r. of the blest . . . 904.1
thousands in the r. of day . 946.4
together on to the r. above . c195

b *realms of Glory*
angels from the r. of G. . 75.1
Jesus left the r. of G. . . 363.2
r. of endless g. . . . 381.1
when . . . r. of G. won . . 500.3
soon we in r. of G. . . 828.4

reap-ing
hearts to help him with the r.. 704.3
wider fields our comrades r. . 922.1
ere man could r. . . . 923.1

b *Gal 6:9*
we shall r. . . . the harvest . 500.3

c *Rev 14:16*
waiting for . . . time of r. . 930.1
soon the r. time will come . 932.c

reaper
the r.'s sickle . . . 926.3

b *Matt 13:30*
when God sends his r. . . 928.2
till the r. come . . . 931.3

c *Gal 6:9*
salvation r. we will be . 936.3
r. return with . . . sheaves . 936.4

rear . 942.2

reason
surpassing my r. . 119.2
that's the r. I can say . c1
found out the r. . c202
this is the r. we sing . c220

reassure-ing
thy r. voice to hear . 644.3
speak to r. me . 862.3

rebel
a guilty r. I . 45.1
God's life for r. given . 113.3
wilt thou as r. defy him . 276.2
pardon . . . r. like me/you . 331.*
each rising r. thought . 445.1
r. sinner's doom . 652.4
to a world of r. dying . 693.2

reborn *(John 3:3)* . 656.4

rebuff . 324.1

recall-ed
r. us when . . . astray . 192.3
Jesus r. me . 294.1

receive-d-ing
1 *(God) receives*
r. again our . . . vow . 5.4
wounds . . . r. on Calvary . 106.3
humbled . . . to r. a name . 141.3
words and thoughts r. . 492.1
into thy blessed hands r. . 720.4

b *receive us* *Rom 15:7*
his loving arms r. us . 66.3
if I ask him to r. me . 228.6
just as I am, thou wilt r. . 293.5
as thou art thou dost, r. . 303.4
thou wilt surely r. . 437.2
in Heaven with thee r. me . 635.1
the penitent child to r. . 691.2
r. and bless our child . 796.4
for I will r. them . 797.2
thou hast promised to r. . 845.3

c *Acts 7:59*
soul and flesh r. . 516.1
then my spotless soul r. . 597.4
r. my soul at last . 737.1

d *Rev 4:11; 5:12*
r. the glory due . 7.3
Jesus is worthy to r. . 57.3
thou art worthy to r. . 109.3
sinner (d)

2 *(we) receive*
earth r. her frame . 13.3
that moment . . . a pardon r. . 22.2
let earth r. her King . 84.1
eyes, new faith r. . 123.4
shepherds with wonder r. . 139.1
the sprinkled blood r. . 191.4
by heart r. and . . . blessed . 211.1
this message . . . from God r. . 234.3
you may r. it . 257.2
now the gift I r. . 322.2
strength the sinner r. . 348.3
favour divine I've r. . 367.2
his pardoning love r. . 381.3
thy truth I lovingly r. . 407.1
dare you . . . his love r. . 413.c
in faith, I r. salvation . 454.4
mine the faith r. cleansing . 456.4
life immortal I r. . 546.1
r. more than we sought . 642.1
we've r. the royal command . 702.2
dare thy word r. . 714.2
faith, which whosoe'er r. . 756.4
seed sown . . . life r. . 936.4
daily strength to r. . c33
I'm believing and r. . c42
new life r. . c176

b *receive blessing* *Ps 24:5*
waiting to r. thy b. . 201.1
thou shalt r. a b. . 255.c
b. supernal . . . I r. . 371.3
b. by faith I r. . 436.4
b. . . . humble saints r. . 461.3

c *receive grace* *John 1:16*
g. I will with thanks r. . 23.2
all r. the g. atoning . 191.4
of his g. have you r. . 418.1
let us all thy g. r. . 438.2
I do the heavenly g. r. . 447.4
g. my sightless eyes r. . 547.4
his fulness to r., and g. . 659.4
and now his g. r. . 785.6

d *John 1:12*
meek souls will r. him . 86.3
hearts are open to r. thee . 213.3
persuaded Christ to r. . 226.1
make haste to r. him . 273.1
invites you . . . to r. him. . 273.4

e *receive joy* *John 16:24*
what j. I r. . 367.2
for sorrow . . . j. shall r. . 372.4
light and j. r. . 655.1

f *John 20:22*
his Spirit I'm r. . 413.3

g *Acts 20:35*
love is giving and r. . 544.4
more and more r. . . . give . 921.2

h *Gal 3:14*
r. the promise of his word . 760.1
the promise now we may r. . 760.3

i *Jas 1:12*
I'll r. a crown of life . 222.c
sight (2e), wage (2b)

recess . 325.3

recite . 16.4

reckon-ed *(Rom 8:18)**
not r. it loss . 119.3
poor wealth . . . r. as thine . 183.3
r. all things . . . loss . 694.1
gladly r. all things loss . 915.3
r. on me following thee . c49

reclaim-ed
from sin's bondage to r. . 114.1
ruined sinners to r. . 118.1
eager to r. . 129.3
my soul in mercy to r. . 339.1
r. from sin's dark ways . 825.3

reclined . 639.1

reclothe *(Mark 5:15)* . 567.1

recognise
help us to r. your might . 27.4
Jesus always r. . 920.3

recompense . 145.3

reconcile-d-ing *Eph 2:16**
God and sinners r. . 82.1
my God is r. . 106.5
wilt thou not be r. . 259.2
God and man to r. . 274.c
r. us to God . 532.3
wanderer now is r. . 550.2
r. to God and man . 572.4

record
the r. of my sins repeat . 303.1
we his great name r. . 533.1
ways of God its lines r. . 656.1
cast my r. of sinfulness . c190

Recorder *1 John 5:7* . 191.2

recount . 655.4

recreate
with thy Spirit r. me . 32.1
power that saves and r. . 135.3
r. a deep compassion . 463.3

re-creation . 35.3

red
there blossoms r. . 621.4
blood-r. banner streams . 701.1
r. reveals . . . Calvary . 777.2

b *Isa 1:18*
though they be r. . 272.1
my sin was r. like crimson . 386.3
blood-red crimson tells . 783.2
blue

redeem-ed-ing
Jesus, mighty to r. . 165.3
the whole world r. . 298.1
so good to r. . 372.1
Jesus has died to r. us . 384.1
show me love that shall r. . 429.3
to r. and make you holy . 433.c
to be r. from sin . 447.2
since the Lord r. us . 755.1
r. at countless cost . 825.2
when r. by his side . c248

b *redeem soul*
for s. r. . 15.5
thou didst r. my s. . 138.4
my poor s. to r. . 323.2
flow through my s. r. . 647.3
died for me, my s. r. . 884.2

c *redeem [by blood]*
Rom 5:9; 1 Peter 1:18,19
precious b. r. me . 325.1
b. he gave to r. . 349.3
those r. by the b. . 392.2
who r. me by his b. . 514.1
he r. me, he r. me . c150

d *redeem time* *Eph 5:16*
would the precious t. r. . 720.3
r. the t. at thy command . 747.3

redeemer
a *(vocative)*
all hail, r., hail . 156.4
O Christ, my soul's r. . 221.2
my gracious r., my Saviour . 357.1
my r. from all sin . 370.1
I'll follow thee, . . . r. . 490.c
how precious, dear r. . 520.4
Jesus, our r., hear . 937.1

b *(general)*
light of our r.'s victory . 173.1
sing of my r. . 180.*
offering be to our r.'s name . 217.3
come to thy only r. . 247.2
love . . . in the r. we see. . 383.2
where our r. died . 413.1
such a r. as mine . 710.3
children who love their r. . 852.3
thou art my r., friend . 859.1
at last we behold our r. . 908.4
O what a r. is Jesus . c219

c *redeemer lives* *Job 19:25*
our great r. l. still . 5.5
know that my r. l. . 144.1, 4
we know that our r. l. . 146.3
I know that my r. l. 149.c/714.c
Heaven . . . my r. to know . 367.3

d *Isa 54.5*
our maker, defender, r. . 16.5
blessed (3f), great (1c), praise (3u)

redeeming *(adj)*
trust in his r. blood . . . 133.5
on thy r. wing . . . 224.2
boast of his r. power . . 915.3

b *redeeming grace*
God of all-r. g. 23.5
O all-r. g. 62.4
brings . . . r. g. to me . 129.c
g. so r. . . . pardon . . 237.3
words of r. g. . . . 724.1
round the world r. g. . 775.3
while r. g. is flowing . . 893.c
Jesus . . . for his r. g. . . 915.1

c *redeeming love*
depth of all-r. l. 55.4
name of all-r. l. . . . 70.4
through his own r. l. . . 87.5
all-r. l. . . . to plead . . 106.2
r. l. has been my theme . 132.4
l.'s r. work is done . . 143.2
we will sing r. l. . . . 367.c
spread a feast of r. l. . . 373.2
I may know r. l. . . . 385.1
courts . . . with r. l. . . 873.2
love, r. l., I see . . . c29

redemption
we have r. found . . . 43.2
r.'s happy dawn . . . 88.c
that wonderful r. . . . 98.2
we . . . our r. see . . . 154.3
preach the gospel of r. . . 158.3
chorus of free r. . . . 278.3
my r. cost . . . price . . 507.2
by thy grand r. . . . 707.c
sweet r. story . . . 828.1
r.'s endless song . . . 828.4

b *Eph 1:7/Col 1:14*
r., the purchase of blood . 22.2
r. by his death I find . . 46.2
r. through the blood . . 222.c
complete blood-bought r. . 413.2
for your r. . . . slain . . 885.4

plan (2b)

redemptive 167.3

re-design 44.2

reed
a *Isa 42:3/Matt 12:20*
nor will he break . . . r. . . 269.2

b *Matt 27:29*
that sceptre-r. discarded . 126.2

reef 280.2

refine-ing
r. the evil nature . . . 324.2
remain if thou r. . . . 416.2
love that shall redeem, r. . 429.3
wash . . . r. its dross . . 453.2
let thy power my soul r. . 460.3
thought and deed for r. . . 493.1
come, Saviour, and r. . . 494.3
design . . . thy gold to r.. . 653.4
all my nature r. . . . c77

b *Mal 3:2*
cleanse, thou r. Flame . . 416.2
r. fire, go through . . . c50

reflect-ed-ing
earth and heaven r. . . . 10.2
a cross r. there . . . 103.1
ever r. his goodness . . 844.3

reflex 455.2

refrain c226

refresh-ing *(Acts 3:19)*
r. my soul in death . . . 58.5
like spring's r. shower . . 213.2
thirsty land r. 295.1
soul-r. view of Jesus . . 442.2
daily r. by . . . dews . . 443.2
may drink and find r. . . 462.3
other souls, r. and fed . . 512.1
thee, and thy r. grace . . 557.1
give r. showers . . . 626.3
there shall be seasons r.. . 637.1
grant to us now a r. . . 637.3
hast r. me while I slept . 665.3
soft r. rain 935.1

refreshment
peace and r. knows . . 574.1
truly knows a heart's r. . . 580.1
find my soul's r. there . . 644.c

refuge *(Ps 46:1)**
the Lord our r. is . . . 9.2
there is r. from despair . . 257.1
while to that r. clinging . . 358.2
thou the r. of my soul . . 627.2
Saviour, still our r. . . . 645.3
Lord, in thee is r. . . . 713.1
other r. have I none . . 737.2
Jesus, my heart's deep r. . 889.3

b *find refuge*
r. find in him today . . 239.2
I have found a r. . . . 341.1
in . . . side a r. find . . 521.2
r. from my foes I find . . 728.1
find a r. from our foes . . 747.1
may the lost find r. . . 943.3

flee (2b)

refuse
our blessèd Lord r. none . 251.4
let those r. to sing . . . 314.1
ask, for I cannot r. . . 528.4
I'll not r. 605.3
nor any gleam of light r. . 871.3
r. the wrong c210

b *Heb 12:25*
shall we r. to hear him . . 121.3

regard-ed
ne'er would r. the salvation . 395.1

b
hath r. my helpless estate . 771.2
O Lord, r. thy people . . 944.1

regions
sweeping all the r. . . . 540.3
bright and sunny r. . . . 686.2
worldwide are the r. . . 803.2

registered 865.3

regret 551.2

reign-ed-ing
1 *(God) reigns*
Son and him who r. . . . 12.3
God who r. enthroned . . 72.6
who r. enthroned above . 223.1
almighty Father r. in love . 765.6
where thy will r. . . . 927.4

b *[love] reigns*
Father-love is r. o'er us . . 10.4
l. and friendship r. . . . 660.5
l. to all will r. . . . 661.4
where l. alone can r. . . 855.3

c *1 Cor 15:25**
joy . . . the Saviour r. . . 84.2
Saviour with the Father r. . 142.3
Jesus the Saviour r. . . 164.2
who r. in light above . . 465.1
Jesus' r. has now begun . 500.3
now as King he r. . . . 853.2
he that . . . doth r. . . . 909.3
Christ . . . is come to r.. . . c27

d *reign for ever* *Rev 11:15*
lives f. e. . . . to r. . . . 148.c
Jesus . . . r. f. e. . . . 184.3
now he is r. f. e. . . . 354.2
God, the Son, forever r. . 887.4

e *shall reign*
r. again to make men . . 63.2
his r. s. know no end . . 156.3
Christ . . . s. r. as King . . 158.c
Jesus s. r. where'er . . 160.1
God appears on earth to r. . 161.1
King who is coming to r. . 166.1
our Saviour-King s. r. . . 169.c
where is thy r. of peace . . 172.2
righteousness s. r. . . . 173.c
right s. r. 185.2
o'er all he yet s. r. . . 362.1
till our King . . . s. r. . . 816.4
o'er his Kingdom r. . . 828.4
o'er the kingdoms he s. r. . 833.2
while as King . . . he r. . . 908.4
Christ s. r., echo . . . c226

f *reign (in hearts)*
born to r. in us for ever . . 79.3
in . . . hearts to rule and r. . 138.1
blessings . . . where'er he r. . 160.3
within my conscience r. . . 194.3
wherever thou dost r. . . 198.4
r. thou within . . . 208.1
come and r. over us . . 219.1
if you want Jesus to r. . . 427.2
where Jesus r. alone . . 444.2
my Lord who r. supreme . 447.4
Christ . . . to r. . . . 541.*
without a rival r. . . . 563.4
r. . . . O r. over me. . . 957
r., O r., my Saviour . . . c51

power (4t)

2 *(man) reigns*
deathless it shall r. . . 508.2

b *2 Tim 2:12; Rev 22:5*
they r. with him above . . 168.5
in that land of Glory r. . . 268.4
would you r. with the King . 406.4
r. with thee above . . . 560.4
must fight if I would r. . . 678.4
at last go home to r. . . 686.2
he . . . shall r. eternally . . 699.4
above the sun r., r. for aye . 897.3
saints immortal r. . . . 898.1
r. with the sons of God . . c249

3 *(evil) reigns* *Rom 5:21*
where r. the power of sin . 423.4
where strife was r. . . . 539.2
sinks the r. of darkness . . 776.2
where evil r. 801.1

reinforcements 804.1

reject-ed-ing
r. offered grace . . . 253.1
do not r. the mercy . . 255.c
do not r. him and forfeit. . 273.4
others may r. the weakling . 324.2
r. the gift no longer . . 410.2
unwashed hearts are r. . . 893.1
if this offer be r. . . . 913.2

b *Isa 53:3*
homeless, r. and poor . . 99.2
once despised, r. . . . 347.3

rejoice-d-ing
rising morn, in praise r. . . 2.2
come ye before him and r. . 3.1
in whom his world r. . . 12.1
everything r. 40.1
believing souls, r. go . . 46.4
in freedom I r. . . . 48.2
believing, we r. to feel . . 120.5
the dying thief r. . . . 132.2
r., the Lord is King . . 164.1
r. in God sent down . . 195.*

they who believe . . . shall r. . 248.4
take with r. . 271.4
makes all within me r. . 318.2
in liberty r. . 324.3
r., r., O Christian . 334.3
now I hear thee and r. . 353.2
live r. every day . 365.c
the host of Heaven r. . 381.1
r. at last, I was sure . 395.3
where I r. to see . 403.1
the soldier of Jesus r. . 406.1
the faith that will r. . 733.2
at this moment we're r. . 795.1
r. in the blood . 814.3
r. in his might . 818.1
so will I r. to show . 846.4
r. with us, our brother . 927.3
r. the earth with . . . day . 942.4
he'll send you r. c31

b *hearts rejoice*
shall my fainting h. r. . 26.4
bid their h. r. . 62.5
all my h. this night r. . 73.1
all our h. r. this morning . 74.1
my h. shall r., Lord Jesus . 101.c
let every h. leap . . . and r. . 235.2
well may this glowing h. r. . 365.1
stay, and bid my h. r. . 636.3
calm . . . make my h. r. . 740.3

c *let . . . rejoice*
let the people r. . 22.c
let us r., the fight is won . 146.1
let every heart . . . r. . 235.2
let the nations now r. . 393.4

d *rejoice (in Heaven)*
a great day of r. . 169.1
trembling or r. . 250.4
angels in their songs r. . 625.4
around the . . . throne r. . 701.4
one the gladness of r. . 765.6
what a day of r. . 892.c

e *Isa 35:1*
the desert lands r. . 583.2

f *Ps 126:6*
we shall come r. . 930.1
bring . . . offerings and r. . 936.1

g *Luke 1:47*
how my soul r. . 341.3
my soul r. to pursue . 657.4

h *Luke 15:5, 6*
and home r. brought me . 53.3
come and r. with me . 311.*

i *Rom 5:2*
believing souls, r. go . 46.4
r. in glorious hope . 164.6
r. in hope of . . . love . 603.5

j *Phil 4:4*
call us to r. in thee . 10.2
r.; again I say, r. . 164.c

k *1 Peter 1:6*
great our r. through Jesus . 22.3

barrenness, glad (i), say (2c)

rejoicingly . 570.2

rejoin . 819.3

rekindle *(Luke 12:49)* . 209.*

release-d-ing
deliverance and r. . 71.1
from our fears . . . r. us . 79.1
comes, the prisoners to r. . 81.2
didst suffer to r. us . 109.1
break our bonds and give r. . 185.2
he fought for your r. . 242.2
Christ r. me . 391.2
wilt thou not my soul r. . 450.3
r. that latent passion . 463.3
my spirit he r. . 495.3
love has paid for my r. . 513.2
I was instantly r. . 539.2
renew, r. from sin . 562.2
fortress and my soul's r. . 631.2
comrade has found r. . 894.1

relent . 685.1

reliable . 49.2

reliant . 869.4

relief
compass all thy soul's r. . 129.3
let me . . . find a sweet r. . 301.2
finding complete r. . 383.3
soul has often found r. . 633.1
my r. will surely appear . 712.1

relieve-d *(Isa 1:17)**
wilt . . . cleanse, r. . 293.5
grace my fears r. . 308.2
thou hast mercy to r. us . 845.3

religion . 464.1, 2

relinquish . 249.1

rely-d-ing
on God's word r. . 222.1
help . . . on thyself r. . 472.4
on thy mercy I r. . 627.2
live, on thee r. . 692.3
thou on the Lord r. . 715.3
we r. not on our numbers . 722.3
unwavering faith shall r. . 734.1
my steadfast soul r. . 746.4
on our Father's love r. . 764.3
each upon his Lord r. . 799.3
yea, all on him r. . 828.3
if I by faith . . . r. . c120

remain
refuge . . . ever will r. . 9.2
his love r. the same . 44.c
victory r. with love . 121.5
yet we may not r. . 154.5
power within our lives r. . 211.2
let naught of sin r. . 218.1
though sharp the sting r. . 267.1
anchor drift or firm r. . 280.1
standards that r. . 324.3
self only may r. . 416.2
let nothing unholy r. . 436.2
rooted my weakness r. . 553.3
r. nor place nor time . 556.2
to go or r. . 640.3
church . . . constant will r. . 690.4
my soul's anchor may r. . 746.1
nor spot of guilt r. . 746.2
on this ground will I r. . 746.5
constant will r. . 750.1
why longer in your sin r. . 885.4
blocks of stone r. . 943.2
Father, let thy love r. . 958
a trace of sin r. . c72

b *John 15:16*
these flourish and r. . 198.4
let our gracious fruit r. . 533.4

remedy . 98.2

remember-ed-ing
r.! I'm the sinner . 98.3
dear Lord, r. me . 105.c
yet will I r. thee . 110.3
when I r. that day . 169.3
r. all my grief and pain . 229.3
O r. . . . Jesus dying . 276.c
r. that God was nigh . 466.2
in life's tempest just r. . 663.3
in faithful love r. thee . 762.3
help me to r. thee . 837.4
r. you're sowing . 928.3
r. God is not far away . c115
he will r. his own . c122

b *Ps 25:7*
r. not past years . 606.2

c *Luke 23:42*
O Lord, r. me . 105.c

d *Jer 31:34/Heb 8:12*
r. them no more . 272.3
he r. them no more . 724.c
my sins are r. no more . c188
never to be r. any more . c190

remembrance . 944.1

remembrancer *John 14:26* . 191.3

remind . 788.2

remorse
freed men from r. . 102.2
bitter the tears of r. . 298.2
torn by r. and grief . 383.3
dread r. and vain desire . 885.3

remote-st
tell to earth's r. bound . 43.2
not a distant God, r. . 238.2

remotely . 142.3

remove-ing
to feel the curse r. . 120.5
the sting of death r. . 126.1
all fear of want r. . 157.2
I can ne'er r. a stain . 292.5
till with joy I r. . 355.6
r. every stain . 436.2
r. everything that mars . 494.3
though all thy gifts r. . 562.1
our bodies may far off r. . 659.1
fear and distrust r. . 743.4
let me joyfully r. . 880.4
we make our doubts r. . 898.3
all their wants at once r. . 909.3

b *remove sin*
r. all his s. . 348.3
entirely all my s. r. . 419.6
s.'s disease . . . r. . 441.2
r. this load of s. . 563.3
whole of s. r. . 568.1
death of s. r. . 603.5

c *Matt 17:20/1 Cor 13:2*
faith . . . r. mountains . 530.2
which can r. . . . mountain . 720.1
great mountains to r. . 733.1

d *Col 1:23*
nor from my hope r. . 596.4

rend-ing/rent
the r. tomb proclaims . 100.3
heart, so r. and torn . 138.3
fetters thou art r. . 593.3
the storms of trial r. . 595.3
glad voices r. the sky . 807.3

b *Isa 64:1*
r. the heavens, come . 604.4

c *Matt 27:51*
the rocks do r. . 107.3
'mid r. rocks . 125.2
lightnings r. the skies . 126.3
shall r. the veil . 877.4

render
see the care . . . dost r. . 39.1
r. thee my life . 503.1
r. up my sword . 508.1

b *1 Thess 3:9*
all praise we would r. . 8.4
what shall I r. to my God . 23.1
r. up the sacrifice . 762.3
we only r. the tribute . 853.3

we would r. thanks to thee . 941.1
to thee we r. our thanks . 950.1

renew-ed-ing
Lord . . . shaping and r. . . 38.5
O soul-r. grace . 290.3
when I am all r. . 407.6
like men r. . 408.2
true comeliness r. . 494.2
in perfect love r. . 533.5
restore, r., release . 562.2
almighty to r. . 596.1
lives r. and souls reborn . 656.4
r. it boldly every day . 812.2
r. my will from day to day . c95
b *renew [heart]* *Ps 51:9*
beseeching for a heart-r. 434.1
a h. in every thought r. . 444.4
who only can our hearts r. . 581.2
hearts r. by grace divine. . 704.2
we would be r. within . 863.2
c *renew [vow]*
each vow r. . 534.3
let me my covenant r. . 618.3
I my vows to thee r. . 665.4
each faithful vow now r. . 786.2
we our vows r. . 787.4
d *Ps 103:5*
he r. my youth . 373.3
e *renew [strength]* *Isa 40:31*
our failing s. r. . 669.2
God will your courage r. . 679.1
soul shall her vigour r. . 734.2
he . . . our s. will r. . 823.3
they that wait . . . r. their s. . c66
f *Titus 3:5*
save me by r. . 430.2

renounce-ing *2 Cor 4:2*
r. . . . thy stubborn will . 251.3
r. every idol . 263.1
I r. the cursèd thing . 448.2
a life of self-r. love . 485.4
r. every worldly thing . 517.4
I want . . . a self-r. will . 596.2

renown
a child of high r. . 72.1
for thy sake to win r. . 860.5

rent see rend

re-ordain . 294.1

repair
to Jesus I r. . 187.1
the ruins of my soul r. . 305.3
let me to thy throne r. . 556.5
where soldiers may r. . 658.4
with singing I r. . 880.3

repay-aid
Saviour, I can ne'er r. . 105.4
thousandfold r. . 167.2
toil he doth richly r. . 397.3
the toils of life r. . 892.3

repeat
I love its music to r. . 68.1
r. the sounding joy . 84.2
he heard the waves r. . 103.3
our prayers r. the . . . cry . 127.3
story of thy love r. . 140.4
acts of faith and love r. . 199.4
the record of my sins r. . 303.1
the story r. . 367.3
his promise still r. . 420.3
trust, and still r. . 749.3
onward! each success r. . 778.3
oft r. before the throne . 877.4

repel . 480.4

repent *(Mark 1:15)**
r., believe, be born again . 275.3
we must r. . 785.4

repentance
your r. he'll ignore . 44.2
sinners moved by true r. . 75.4
b *Heb 12:17*
tears of r. will not save . 269.3
it is not thy tears of r. . 271.3

repentant . 708.2

repine-ing
men exclaim and fiends r. . 407.4
nor ever murmur or r. . 725.3
no sad r. . 888.2

reply-d-ing
worthy . . . our hearts r. . 57.2
thy prayer shall make r. . 122.3
thou earth, r. . 143.1
from depth to height r. . 187.4
faith is heard r. . 222.1
say, is thy heart r. . 276.2
amen, my soul r. . 312.4

report *Phil 4:8* . c56

repose
what can shake thy sure r. . 157.1
one that in calm r. . 574.1
knows . . . a soul's r. . 580.1
r. beneath thy wings . 632.3
soul . . . leaned for r. . 653.5
may my soul on thee r. . 671.4
weary calm and sweet r. . 673.3
found in Jesus calm r. . 910.3

reproach *Heb 13:13**
shame and r. gladly bear . 124.3
my highest glory his r. . 451.4
hail r. and welcome pain . 526.2
enduring cruel r. . 623.3
with us r. to dare . 825.4

reprove-ing
with meekness to r. . 568.3
b *John 16:8*
sins r., wants revealing . 893.c

request
gift from me . . . r. . 475.1
b *Phil 4:6*
our r. to thee we brought . 642.1

require
I r. a draught . 351.c
whate'er my future may r. . 385.4
this, only this, do I r. . 480.5
all I r. to cleanse me . 647.3
conflicts which faith will r. . 734.3
for every rule of life r. . 785.1

requite *Deut 32:6** . 251.3

rescue-d
r. us from all our foes . 17.3
to the r. came . 18.2
he, to r. me from danger . 313.3
seaman you may r. . 478.c
send me to the r. . 482.1
yes, a soul is r. . 550.2
to the r. we go . 687.1
r. the perishing . 691.*
only shall by him be r. . 824.2
it is grace that r. me . c164

research . 30.3

resemblance . 589.2

resemble . 88.5

resentment . 572.4

reserve-d
mercy still r. for me . 286.1
good or ill may be r. . 730.4
with no r. . 860.2

reside-ing
God with man is now r. . 75.2
gives . . . Spirit to r. . 195.1
that which in the heart r. . 494.1
I long to r. . 639.1
God r. among his own . 909.2
come and in me r. . c102

residue *Isa 38:10*
my r. of days . 505.1
I yield my r. of days . 644.1

resign-ed-ing
1
or winter from r. . 854.1
2
pleasures of sin I r. . 357.1
a heart r., submissive . 444.2
it must its crown r. . 508.3
r. to mortal ill . 532.3
the heart r. and meek . 555.2
teach me to r. . 565.4
faith, obedient and r. . 839.5
I that life to thee r. . 865.2
b *all resigned*
all to his pleasure r. . 318.3
to thee I all r. . 509.3
all . . . to thy wisdom I r. . 566.3
c *resign will*
now is my will r. . 416.4
my will . . . to r. . 509.2
I yielded, my will to r. . 553.3
I am to thy will r. . 729.2
our wills to thee r. . 870.4

resistance . 815.3

resistless . 540.3

resolve-d
my best r. I only break . 291.3
to Christ . . . r. to live . 480.4
only thee, r. to obey . 509.2
r. the whole of love's . 512.2
only thee, r. to know . 667.1

resound-ing
sweet echo in you be r. . 51.3
hearest the songs that r. . 263.2
through the world r. . 693.c
song of angels r. . 894.1

resources
you give such rich r. . 38.2
the end of our hoarded r. . 579.2
my r. would fail . 641.3
its last r., shall seal . 742.2
when my own r. fail . 770.2

respite . 302.2

resplendent . 781.1

respond . 50.3

rest-ing
1 *(God) rests*
heart wherein to r. . 200.4
in me delight to r. . 207.1
his sacred form would r. . 663.2
b *2 Cor 12:9*
let thy blessing r. on me. . 474.4
like a dove may r. on me . 584.1
fancy his blessing r. on me . 848.2
bid thy cloud of glory r. . 942.1

2 *(spiritual rest)*
ocean-depth of happy r. . 10.3
charm their griefs to r. . . 21.2
and in thy presence r. . . 61.1
Jesus provides a r. . . 139.3
my flesh in hope shall r. . 153.2
to triumph and r. . . . 170.3
a haven sweet of r. . . 182.3
God, our final r. . . . 190.3
that leads you into r. . . 231.3
I come to thee for r. . . 284.3
r. 'neath his . . . wing . . 390.3
do you r. each moment . . 417.2
there only can I r. . . . 450.2
a r. upon the way . . . 476.1
with what a r. of bliss . . 545.3
Lord, I come to thee for r. . 563.4
Master, and his r. in Heaven . 564.4
thy r., thy joy . . . share. . 612.7
until I r. . . . the captive. . 723.4
keep . . . in ways of r. . . 728.2
here is my hope . . . my r. . 746.3
the will of Jesus . . . is r. . 752.2
abundant peace and r. . . 761.2
blessèd r. of my soul . . 771.4
know the sweetness of his r.. 819.2
now the r. and fame . . 894.2
sigh for the blessing of r. . 900.2
in the haven of r. . . . c178

b *peace and rest*
I have r. and p. to offer . . 240.1
joy, p. and r. 541.3
till I r. in p. with thee . . 585.4
'twixt me and the peaceful r.. 598.3
abundant p. and r. . . . 761.2
r. and p. of the homeland . 895.3

c *[eternal] rest*
weary find eternal r. . . 160.3
return . . . to her e. r. . . 307.1
in ceaseless r. I roam . . 362.3
this r. is everlasting . . 413.4
eternal inward r. . . . 431.3
shall find in thee e. r. . . 940.4

d *Ps 37.7*
I r. on love divine . . . 297.6
I r. in thine . . . power . . 714.3
soul, r. thou in God . . 729.2
I r. on his . . . grace . . 745.2
r. in my Saviour as my all . 757.4

e *rest in word*
we r. on the unbroken w. . 198.2
I have r. in his w. . . 322.2
I r. upon thy w. . . . 596.4
r. . . . upon his holy w. . 698.1

f *rest [for ever]*
calling, to lasting r. . . 39.4
and then to r. for ever . . 345.3
I'll r. for evermore . . . 374.3
r. with thee . . . for evermore. 635.1
how sweet to r. for ever . 676.2
I shall for ever r. . . . 882.3
for ever in sweetest r. . . c94

g *rest above*
r. in those mansions a. . . 139.3
my glorious r. a. . . . 182.1
fit us for perfect r. a. . . 668.5

h *no rest*
without r. in my breast . . 379.3
no r. . . . when from thee . 448.3
I sighed for r. . . . 547.2

i *at rest* *Ps 55:6*
coming be at r. . . . 228.1
submission, all is at r. . . 310.3
loving, is at r. . . . 420.1
let thy heart be at r. . . 739.*
let him (her) lie at r.. . . 792.1
where . . . friends are at r. . 886.3

j *Song 1:7*
there only, I covet to r. . . 639.3
sweet to r. here with thee . c37

k *Mark 6:31*
come . . . apart and r. . . 564.1

l *Matt 11:28*
I have r. . . . to offer . . 240.1
come unto me and r. . . 332.1

m *Heb 4:11*
blessèd r. from inbred sin . 46.3
entered into r. . . . 551.3
possess the promised r. . . 879.4

n *Rev 14:13*
from their labours r. . . 876.1
r. from thy loved employ . . 890.1
r. in thy Saviour's joy . . 890.5

find (2m, n), give (1s), heavenly (g), land (1d), perfect (2g), repose, soul (2j), sweet (3d), weary (d)

3 *(remainder)*
above the r. this note . . 144.c
heard, but tell the r. . . 243.4
hallelujah! the r. of my days . 298.7
I'll spend . . . r. of my days . 422.2
give up all the r. . . . 480.5
leave the r. with God . . 750.3

4 *(general)*
I r. me in the thought . . 42.1
r. in heavenly peace . . 89.1
it took its r. 90.4
submissive r. . . . will . . 208.2
my r. a stone . . . 617.2
labour is r. 636.2
dreams disturb my r. . . 671.3
praise shall sanctify our r. . 677.1
the sun that bids us r. . . 677.4
don't fall out and r. . . 817.c
the weak may r. . . . 838.4
fighting nor r. . . . 864.c
work and r. are one . . 878.5

b *Ex 23:12*
O Sabbath r. by Galilee . . 567.3
this is the day of r. . . 669.2

c *Rev 4:8*
r. not now by day or night . 677.2

restful 574.1

resting *(adj)* *Isa 32:18*
I found in him a r.-place . 332.1
soul has found a r.-place . 536.c
grant me no r. place . . 723.4

restless
still this r. heart . . . 194.4
life's wild, r. sea . . . 428.1
why r., why cast down . . 557.4
bound the r. wave . . . 569.1
r. spirits yearn for thee . . 602.3
thy r. heart keep still . . 738.2
by r. passions tossed . . 825.2

restore-d-ing
ransomed, healed, r. . . 17.1
wealth of Heaven . . . r. . . 70.4
broken peace might be r. . 135.1
Jesus can r. his work . . 267.3
my heart r. its . . . ray . . 621.2
to cleanse me and r. . . 647.3
r. to life and power . . 668.1
thy . . . word r. the light. . 672.2
feelings . . . grace can r. . 691.3
by his might r. . . . 803.4
all finding our peace r. . . c112

b *restore own*
thine o. I now r. . . . 504.2
I r. to thee thy o. . . 505.2
thine o. we now r. thee . 870.4

c *restore soul* *Ps 23:3**
my s. he doth r. again . . 54.2
he r. my s., he renews . . 373.3
to perfect health r. my s. . 419.6

d *restore [joy]* *Ps 51:12*
my fallen spirit to r. . . 305.3

soul-cheering presence r. . 318.4
salvation, perfectly r. . . 438.3
r., renew, release . . . 562.2
my comfort to r. . . . 565.3
waters . . . your spirit r.. . c40

e *Acts 1:6*
till his Kingdom is r. . . 868.3

restrain *(Ps 76:10)*
only thy terrors, Lord, r. . 526.2

b
r. prayer, we cease to fight . 646.3

restricted 770.3

resurrection
glory of his r. share . . 907.2

b *Phil 3:10*
mine . . . with r. power . . 495.2

retain
his freshness shall r. . . 277.3
since the Lord r. his love . 853.2
a wearied mind r. . . . c72

retire 567.5

retold 774.2

retrace 581.4

retreat-ing
1
shall never call r. . . . 162.3
I never need r. . . . 366.5
no r., Hell defeating . . 702.c
never from the foe r. . . 778.3

2
a calm, a sure r. . . . 573.1

retrieve
who hath r. our loss . . 78.3
our loss of Eden to r. . . 140.2

return-ed-ing
1 *(God) returns*
from death r. . . . to keep . 130.2
from the fight r. . . . 147.1
greets . . . her r. King . . 155.2
suddenly r., and never . . 438.2
r., O holy dove, r. . . . 442.4

2 *(general)*
where love is not r. . . 50.2
day r. with thee . . . 155.4
trembling to its source r. . 199.2
joyless is the day's r. . . 412.3
all I r. thee, who gave . . 454.3
let there be no more r. . . 529.2
help us each r. day . . . 532.3
fresh from converse . . . r. . 564.4
r., sweet hour of prayer . . 633.1
delay its sure r. . . . 854.2
yielded in r. for toil . . 933.1
reapers r. with . . . sheaves . 936.4

b *Isa 55:7*
he will welcome thy r. . . 225.c
r., O wanderer, r. . . . 256.1
O r. ye unto God . . . 272.2
now made willing to r. . . 305.1
shall my soul r. again . . 307.1
hope for a happy r. . . 388.2
joy today for the soul r. . . 550.1
r. from his ways . . . 625.4

reunited 146.2

reveal-ed-ing
that night r. and told . . 72.2
my heart r. 102.4
opening veil r. the way . . 125.2
now r. his great salvation . 191.2

now our cancelled sin r. . . 210.2
to us r. our emptiness . 217.2
ready . . . his grace to r.. . 236.3
there is a mercy seat r. . 269.1
by his sorrow joy r. . 402.3
seemeth thee good r. 422.c; 589.c
that I may r. thy beauty . . 435.c
r. each crooked place . 446.2
thine the sealing and r. . 510.4
a power within r. . 571.3
the Lord will come, r. . 591.1
r. God's sword to everyone . 705.2
to Hannah's son r. . 839.2
sins reproving, wants r. . 893.c

b
to my heart thyself r. . 207.2
in Christ r. God himself . 232.1
but, O thyself r. . 603.4
talk with me . . . thyself r. . 636.1
r. I see the Lord . 650.3
r. Jesus through the word . 730.3

c *[come] reveal*
Holy Spirit, come r. . 434.2
let me love thee, come r. . 503.2
come down, r. the things . 756.1
come, O come to me r. . c74

d *reveal love*
cross r. . . . actions of l.. . 114.2
O Love, r. on earth . 449.1
come, then . . . r. thy l. . 581.3
red r. the love of Calvary . 777.2
come and r. a Saviour's l. . 946.3

e *light reveals*
kind is the l. that r. . 457.2
let the l. now falling r. . 502.1
growing l. . . . need r. . 534.1
l. your cross r. . 572.3

f *Isa 40:5/1 Peter 4:13*
God's great glory now r. . 159.2
to r. Heaven's glory . 835.2

g *Gal 1:16*
would thy life in mine r.. . 212.1

revealer
r. of the right . 221.3
r. of the truth . 870.3

revelation
grant us . . . greater r. . 173.3
O the glorious r. . 540.2
thank you for each r. . 552.1
a r. new . 571.2
let them be thy r. . 863.3

revere . 592.2

reverence
at thy feet in r. bow . 185.4
in deeper r., praise . 567.1
God's name hold in r. . 823.2

reverently . 90.5

review . 712.3

revile *Matt 5:11*
when the sons of earth r. . 95.3
let men r. my name . 526.2

revival
for a mighty r. we plead . 608.1
send a r. from above . 609.1
r. is our present need . 760.2
a mighty r. is coming . c63

revive-ing
greets with life r. . 155.2
my soul r., and now I live . 332.2
the source of r. power . 488.c

b *Ps 85:6*
r. our longing eyes . 172.4
r. us again . 355.c
precious r. again . 637.2

c *Hab 3:2*
to r. thy work afresh . 201.c
r. thy work, O Lord . 626.*

revoke . 75.4

revolution . 203.2

reward
not thirst for earth's r. . 5.3
thy right r. . 146.3
to do his will my best r.. . 451.4
my faith r. . 461.c
righteousness, his own r. . 461.3
peace and safety my r. . 556.5
faith . . . wilt thou r. . 613.2
peace be my r. . 717.6
grace as my shield and r. . 734.3
faith has . . . blest r. . 748.4
your r. shall be victory . 813.2
look not for r. or praise . 816.3

b *Isa 40:10**
Jesus comes! R. is with him . 159.2

c *Matt 5:12*
great is your r. in Heaven . 95.3
Christ our great r. . 803.c
r. will be a grand one . c237

rich-es
1 *(secular)*
with r. gifts to greet him . 92.1
which r. cannot buy . 277.2
nor adorning, r. and gay . 320.1
my Father is r. in houses . 354.1
counting the r. of earth . 427.4
r. in goods . 577.3
not the r. or learned . 824.2
r. may bring their wealth . 849.1
Lord, I care not for r. . 883.1
reap the r. supply . 923.1
the harvest r. and great . 923.2

poor (2b)

2 *(spiritual)*
a *(ours)*
give such r. resources . 38.2
how r. is my condition . 498.2
how r. am I . . . possessing . 536.1
r. to all intents of bliss . 565.4

b *(God's)*
compose so r. a crown . 136.3
r. the trophies Jesus brings . 147.2
by thy r. fellowship . 209.2
r. blessings to bestow . 231.2
love of love . . . r. and free . 250.1
blood of Christ so r. . 295.4
redeeming, so r. and so free . 298.1
fountain, so r. and sweet . 315.4
living waters r. and free . 439.1
thy Spirit's r. treasure . 457.3
r. truth that surpasses . 506.3
r. promises in me fulfil . 587.4
moments, r. in blessing . 634.1
jewels r. and rare . 658.2
trust his r. promises . 738.3
r. the trophies to be won . 776.1
r. tokens of thy mercy . 870.1
r. fruits of holiness . 936.3
Christ to me, so r. . c146

c *Eph 2:4*
in thy mercy, r. and free. . 538.3

d *rich [grace]* *Eph 2:7*
God's r. g. was granted . 52.2
see the r. of his g. . 60.4
g. for all is r. . 239.1
feasting on the r. of his g. . 390.3
offered his g. so r. . 403.2
and thy g., so r. . 470.1
may thy r. g. impart . 743.2
matchless g., how r. . 831.2
no place beside the r. . 861.5

e *riches* *Eph 3:8*
sight, r., healing . 293.4
my Father is r. . 354.1
his r. never can be told . 356.2
r. eternal . . . supernal . 371.3
all my r. is thy love. . 497.4
out of his infinite r. . 579.3
whose r. I cannot guess. . 666.2
thy gracious r. to prove . 786.4
going to taste the r. . 858.3

richer-est
r. blood than they . 120.2
r. gain I count but loss . 136.1
will only make us r. . 312.1
streams of r. worth . 312.2
yields the r. perfume . 318.2
I've found a r. treasure . 320.1
ever deeper, r. growing . 539.1
its flow may r., fuller be . 621.1
than r. gifts without them . 849.3

richly
so r. he poured out . 245.2
toil he doth r. repay . 397.3
dear Saviour, r. bless us . 575.1
every comrade . . . r. bless . 769.3
hand in autumn r. pours . 925.3

b *Col 3:16*
the word r. in us dwell . 533.4

richness . 777.2

rid
waiting not to r. my soul . 293.2
can r. me of . . . unrest . 297.4

ride-rode
r. upon the storm . 29.1

b *(Zech 9:9)*
r. on, r. on in majesty . 150.*
in lowly pomp r. on to die 150.2, 5
as he r. along . 853.1

rift . 142.4

right
1 *(re divinity)*
thy r. rewards . 146.3
Holy Spirit, r. divine . 194.3
blood-bought r. maintain . 563.4
his r. to rule each day . 867.1

b *Ezek 21:27*
give him his r. . 24.3
thou, who hast the r. . 480.3

c *by right*
place . . . his by r. . 168.2
glory that of r. was thine . 174.1
feel by r. they're thine . 475.3
to thee by every r. . 925.5
all praise belongs by r. . 926.1

2 *(re people)*
theirs the earth by r. . 95.1
as their r. thy righteousness . 372.3
he will make good his r.. . 685.2
Christ thy r. . 718.1

b *no right*
I have no r. to plead . 290.1
dare not ask . . . by r. . 456.3
selfish ends . . . no r. . 702.1

3 *(general)*
stand . . . for thy r. . 181.2
r. shall reign . 185.2
daily . . . choose the r. . 193.5
revealer of the r. . 221.3
might to establish the r.. . 527.3
in the conflict for r. . 537.2
fighting for r. . 681.1
join the fight for the r. . 700.*
the war for truth and r. . 777.1
conflict . . . for the r. . 813.1
choosing the r. . c210

b *God and right*
valiant for G. and the r. . 679.1
fight for G. and r. . . 798.3
battle for G. and the r. . 820.4
the field for G. and r. . . c243
c *do right*
to ever d. the r. . . . 203.3
live and d. the r. . . . 431.2
that all I d. is r. . . 441.3
hearts to . . . d. the r. . . 704.c
trust in God and d. the r. . 716.*
battle (3), cause (1b)
4 *(adjective/adverb)*
the r. man on our side . . 1.2
stay r. over the place . . 90.4
sought . . . set thee r. . . 110.2
the inward witness r. . . 113.1
lead us r. 202.4
sound the tidings r. along . 249.1
my soul was made r. . . 395.3
he came r. down to me . . 398.c
perfect and r., and pure . . 444.4
growing r. amid the weeds . 552.2
marching r. along . . . 813.3
he'll put things r. . . . c22
go r. back to . . . wells . . c40
r. into my heart . . . c64
I want to live r. . . . c71
b *Matt 5:29*
as dear as a r. eye . . . 481.3
c *right hand*
the joys at his r. h. . . 223.2
the saints at his r. h. . . 747.3
after death at thy r. h. . . 917.5
d *Ps 16:8*
set at my r. h. . . . 667.2
be thou at my r. h. . . 877.3
e *Ps 121:5*
thy defence on thy r. h. . . 767.3
f *Isa 41:10*
thine own r. h. doth keep . 741.3
g *Rom 8:34*
there at God's r. h. . . 45.2
he sits at God's r. h. . . 164.4
5 *(verb)*
Son of man, to r. my lot. . 91.2
wrongs to r. 126.2

righteous
read his r. sentence . . 162.2
all my Saviour's r. will . . 419.1
sufferers in his r. cause . . 909.1
b *Ps 23:3*
paths . . . all the r. go . . 217.2

righteousness *(Phil 3:9)**
his glorious r. I show . . 60.5
the glories of his r. . . 84.3
Jesus, thy blood and r. . . 116.1
r. shall reign 173.c
this is all my r. . . . 306.4
r. claim; thy r. wearing . . 372.3
by contrast with true r. . . 446.2
r., his own reward . . . 461.3
with r. we . . . conquer . . 821.3
peace . . . built in r. . . 827.1
b *righteousness divine*
r. d. and Christ . . . mine . 214.2
clothed in r. d. . . . 283.4
King of r. d. 452.1
c *Rom 14:17*
his Kingdom . . . peace, r. . 195.2
flag . . . for peace and r. . 777.1
d *1 Cor 1:30*
Jesus, thy r., lives . . . 271.4
e *Gal 5:5*
whence my hope of r. . . 290.2
thy r. . . . my only hope. . 325.1
my hope . . . blood and r. . 745.1

f *Eph 5:9*
gentle power of r. . . . 705.3
for truth and r. and thee. . 860.3
holiness (d), path (d), sun (1b)

rightful
give him now his r. place . 249.3
b *Mark 5:15*
reclothe . . . our r. mind. . 567.1

ring-ing/rang
now with joy is r. . . . 73.1
hear . . . the message r.. . 74.3
go! r. the earth . . . 127.c
tender call r. out . . . 131.4
the vault of Heaven r. . . 147.2
round . . . world let it r. . 158.2
r. of a thousand harps . . 167.2
loud with hosannas r. . . 184.3
as joyously it r. . . . 187.2
heard the message r. . . 242.1
there r. a melody . . . 327.c
the courts of Heaven r. . . 327.3
how the loud harps r. . . 550.c
victory's r. cheer . . . 713.3
let this promise r. . . . 753.2
loud r. the clarion call . . 781.3
its echoes, loudly r. . . 802.2
let the story r. out . . . 829.3
a voice divine r. through . 839.1
voices . . . r. in my ears. . 895.2
hills with joy are r. . . 934.1
there are joybells r. . . c153
b
their holy war cry r. . . 158.1
I'll send the r. cry along . 356.4
to the front! the cry is r.. . 702.1
louder r. out the cry . . 703.3
sound the r. cry . . . 813.1
c *[music] rings*
round me r. the m. . . 42.1
heavens . . . with their m. r. . 80.1
heavenly m. r. . . . 227.3
song of cheer is r. clear . . 340.1
I hear the m. r. . . . 358.1
there's a song that's r. . . 389.*
make the world with m. r. . 809.1
d *[praise] rings*
homes with p. r. . . . 142.1
to the heavens our p. r. . 700.3
let his p. r. 757.1
loud let his p. r. . . . 897.1
e *make ring*
m. the heavenly arches r. . 312.3
I'll make Heaven r. . . 543.4
shout and sing, m. Heaven r.. 798.1
make the world with music r.. 809.1
make . . . hallelujahs r. . . 821.1
make earth and Heaven r. . 940.2
arch, bell

ripe-n
r. fruits in the garden . . 25.3
purposes will r. fast . . 29.5
full sheaves of r. grain . . 923.1
crops made r. 936.2
b *Rev 14:15**
r. souls we wish to be . . 926.4
r. wheat for the garner . . 928.3

ripple 252.1

rise-ing-n/rose
1 *(general)*
dominions r. and perish . . 6.4
r. on every side . . . 159.4
let every creature r. . . . 160.5
sins of years r. . . . high. . 253.3
on the r. tide 280.3
memories . . . r. within me . 303.2
thy morn shall r. . . . 332.3

in my breast r. 379.3
not a shadow can r. . . 397.2
subdue each r. . . . thought . 445.1
need never r. again . . 471.3
higher still, and r. higher . 546.1
one into a thousand r. . . 629.2
r. the glorious thought . . 632.4
O r., Immanuel's tide . . 647.c
where secret rivers r. . . 648.3
kingdoms r. and wane . . 690.4
let courage r. 699.2
hills that r. to . . . skies . . 766.1
kingdoms r. and fall . . 799.1
scene that r. to my sight . 887.2
gloomy thoughts that r. . . 898.3
my sins r. as high . . . c189
b *rise [to God]*
a hundred anthems r. . . 163.3
our song shall r. to thee. . 220.1
prayers r. from hearts . . 226.2
ever let there r. to thee . . 569.4
our faint desires to r. . . 604.3
praise is wont to r. . . 661.3
yet higher r. 834.3
c *(sun) rise*
thou r. morn 2.2
before the r. s. . . . 13.4
afar, his r. s. . . . 145.1
till s. shall r. . . . 160.1
s. may never r. . . . 251.2
greets the r. of the s. . . 776.1
2 *(Jesus) rises*
r. upon our night . . . 669.1
r. to all eternity . . . 737.4
b *1 Cor 15:4*
he r. again, and he lives. . 125.c
on the third day he r. . . 137.4
in vain forbids his r. . . 143.3
the heart of him who r. . . 146.1
for us he r. 149.2
r. glorious from the dead . 151.3
r. from the tomb . . . 152.2
r., O buried Lord . . . 155.3
r. victorious in the strife . 156.2
r. . . . to bring us freedom . 242.c
he r. and now lives . . 687.3
to r. again triumphant . . 870.2
up from the grave he r. . . 884.2
r., he justified . . . c185
c *2 Cor 5:15**
who died, and r. on high . 156.2
who lived and died and r. . 445.3
arose
d *risen* *1 Cor 15:20**
the r. Son of God . . . 46.2
glory to the r. Lamb . . 67.3
r. Master, death defying . 97.3
glory to our r. head . . 151.3
r., conquering Son . . 152.1, c
I serve a r. Saviour . . 334.1
r. One, enthroned on high . 435.1
stand . . . in thy r. power . 599.1
warriors of the r. King . . 696.3
know you r. from the grave . 748.1
e *Christ risen* *Luke 24:34*
a r. Lord with power . . 134.3
C. the Lord is r. . . . 143.1
C. is r. from the grave . . 242.1
my r. C. to magnify . . 562.3
healing (1b)
3 *(we) rise*
r. to adore the mystery . . 78.1
all ye nations, r. . . . 82.1
like him we r. . . . 143.5
r. at once! delay no more . 267.3
sinking to r. no more . . 336.1
men r. in war . . . 529.3
but I long to r. . . . 585.1
r. a living flame . . . 649.3
shake off . . . joyful r. . . 665.1

God calls me to r. . . . 666.4
r. and fight for Christ . 799.2
we're r. every day . . 810.3
r. up, O youth . . 864.1
r. then . . . unsheathe . 864.3
r. by faith's . . . wings . 916.2
b *bid rise*
b. me r. a free . . . slave . 303.4
b. my spirit r. again . 618.3
b. me r. on . . . wings . 749.1
c *Luke 5:28*
I r., went . . . followed thee . 283.3
mine to r. when . . . call me . 510.1
r. up and follow thee . 567.2
d *Eph 5:14*
I r. from . . . sepulchre . 353.4
awake and r. . . . 408.2, 4
I r. to life divine . . 520.5
e *Col 3:1*
r. with him to things above . 146.2
shall r. and live again . 512.3
r. now with thee, my Lord . 513.3
r. to be hid in thy breast. . 639.3
f *rise [to heaven]*
from the dust of death I r. . 116.5
from earth I r. . . . 223.2
yea, and before we r. . 314.2
a way for man to r. . 414.4
comrades . . . shout as I r. . 543.4
put off this robe . . . and r. . 633.3
the saints triumphant r. . 876.5
to r. within the veil . 879.1
guilty souls r. alone . 893.1
to the home of gladness . . . r. 949.4
dead (2d)

rival 563.4

riven
from thy r. side . . . 302.1
drew me to his r. side . 348.1
one more chain . . . be r. . 434.3
every bond is r. . . . 546.2

river
1 *(natural)*
the r. running by . . . 25.2
b *Eccl 1:7*
flow back the r. . . . 509.3
2 *(figurative)* *(Rev 22:1)*
faint while such a r. . 157.2
r. shall begin to flow . 159.5
r. of delight . . . ever flow . 344.3
flows the wonderful r. . 384.3
the blood, O wondrous r. . 434.5
the r. of God's mercy . 462.1
there flows a wondrous r. . 471.1
where secret r. rise . 648.3
march by the r. of light . 708.1
crystal r. and . . . strand . 873.1
side of the r. of light . 886.1
fields . . . r. of delight . 887.2
shall we gather at the r.. . 891.1
stand by the beautiful r. . 908.3
where flows the crystal r. . 934.4
while I to the r. go . . c42
b *(death)*
beyond the r. . . . 115.c, 4
since Jesus crossed the r. . 153.3
when I cross the r.. . 309.3
the r. must be passed . 325.4
death's dark, swelling r.. . 338.5
when I near the r. . . 350.3
in Heaven . . . beyond the r. . 536.2
death's swelling r. . . 902.3
margin
c *(grace)*
grace is flowing like a r.. . 239.3
all the r. of thy grace . 303.4
from the r. of his grace . 314.2
r. of God's grace 320.c/462.c/868.c
r. of grace are abounding . 383.1
d *Isa 43:2*
the r. of grief . . . 653.3
e *Rev 22:1f*
stream is the r. of life . 252.3
tasted life's pure r. . 320.1
f *Isa 66:12*
when peace like a r. . 771.1
g *Ps 36:8*
where r. of pleasure I see . 710.1
like (1b)

road
the r. to life 38.5
thy footprints on my r. . . 59.1
on the r. beside me . . 59.2
on the r. thy wheels are not . 91.2
hymn of Calvary's r. . . 103.3
beast pursues his r. . . 150.1
desert mark his r. . . 159.1
the treacherous r. . . 176.3
r. that we must take . . 190.3
long is the r. 351.1
to shine upon the r. . . 442.1
light shall mark the r. . . 442.6
strait and thorny r. . . 559.2
nor tire along the . . . r.. . 559.5
with God along the r. . . 583.1
r. to bring us . . . nearer. . 668.4
walking life's toilsome r. . 675.2
ruin's ghastly r. . . 696.2
let the r. be long . . 716.1
when the r. . . . is rough . 805.c
I can tread the r. of life . . 857.2
a r. of high adventure . . 868.1
to travel an unending r. . . 885.2
the broad r. of folly . . 905.1
when alone on the r. . . c135
on the r. of happiness . . c195

roam
wilt thou r. farther . . . 248.1
bid thee no longer r. . . 250.5
in ceaseless rest I r. . . 362.3
forgive if I should r. . . 675.3
though his feet may r. . . 740.3
glorified ever shall r. . . 872.c
absent from him I r. . . 877.1
never more to r. . . . c10
abide, never from him r. . c154

roar
when the breakers r. . . 280.2
amid the tempest's r. . . 330.c
loud and angry billows r. . 478.2
blow, or thunders r. . . 526.4
fearful breakers r. . . 598.3
storm may r. without me . 736.1
lion

robe-ed
whose r. is the light . . 16.2
angels in r. of light . . 117.2
faring forth in r. of light . . 145.2
r. in dreadful majesty . . 161.2
r. in . . . garb of spring . . 177.2
r. his thoughts . . . 398.1
put off this r. of flesh . . 633.3
bright r. of gold . . . 934.1
b *Rev 6:11**
provided . . . r. are clean . 170.1
heir to a . . . r. and crown . 354.3
my r. were once all stained . 359.1
you may long for the r. . . 406.3
provide a r. and crown . . 891.3
a r. for each to wear . . 899.1
there's a spotless r. . . 902.c
r. which the glorified wear . 904.2
c *[white] robes* *Rev 7:13*
wear a spotless r. . . . 389.3
where the w. r. are seen . 429.1
in r. of light arrayed . . 701.4
r. in their garments of w. . 708.1
a r. of w., a crown . . . 811.c
r. in their garments of w. . 886.1
a r. for each to wear . 899.1
saints are r. in w. . . . 902.1
r. of w. and harps of glory . 902.5
d *washed robes* *Rev 7:14*
I've w. my r. in . . . blood . 359.c
their r. are w. as white . . 359.4
their r. surely blood-w. . . 893.3
w. their r. by faith below . 909.2
purple (b) white (c)

rock
1 *(re divinity)*
a *Ps 18:2*
be our r., our shield . . 622.3
lie at the foot of the r. . . 639.3
thou wast their r. . . . 876.2
b *rock of ages* *Isa 26:4*
on the r. of ages founded . 157.1
r. of ages, cleft for me . . 302.*
founded on the r. of ages . 833.3
firm on the r. of ages . . 889.3
r. of strength . . . our stay . 937.3
c *Matt 7:24*
the r. on which I build . . 58.3
he our r., our hope . . 184.2
fastened to the r. . . . 280.c
r. that naught can move . 738.1
on Christ, the solid r. . . 745.c
2 *(general)*
thought of r. and trees . . 42.1
r., hills and plains repeat . 84.2
from r. and tempest . . 569.4
hiding r. and . . . shoal . . 598.1
b *as/like rock*
firm as a r. . . . stand . . 4.4
like thy r. of . . . grandeur . 32.1
firm as a r., and sure . . 574.4
like a r. 'midst . . . billows . 750.2
c *Ex 33:22*
in the r. I'm hiding . . . 341.2
hideth . . . cleft of the r.. 710.1, c
d *Ps 40:2*
stand firm on the r. . . 612.3
e *Isa 32:2*
a cool shading r. . . . 288.4
shadow of a mighty r. . . 476.1
in the shadow of the r. . . 614.2
f *Luke 8:6*
sowing the seed on the r. . 931.2
rend (c)

rocket 30.2

rocky 887.3

rod
fear no threatening r. . . 95.2
power of Satan's r. . . 113.2
bow me to the r. . . . 305.1
hand still holds the r. . . 446.3
b *Ps 23:4*
r. and staff my comfort . . 53.4
r. and staff me comfort . . 54.3
protects me with his r. . . 583.3
with thine unerring r. . . 762.2
chastening, iron (b)

rode see ride

roll-ed-ing
1 *(noun)*
more heroes . . . on the r. . 684.4
the r. is called . . . 907.*
2 *(verb)*
voice that r. the stars . . 26.3

weight of iniquities r. . . . 271.3
every care on him to r. . . 344.1
glorious message r. . . . nation 546.3
fires of passion r. . . . 630.2
Army chariot r. . . . 775.1
never-ceasing music r. . . 887.5
r. the old chariot along . . c224

b (re time)
when r. years shall cease . 4.4
like an ever-r. stream . . 13.5
while endless ages r. . . 43.4
r. two thousand years . . 83.2
while . . . happy moments r. . 387.c
while eternal ages r. . . 514.2
while earth r. onward . . 677.2
r. seasons . . . move . . 929.1
singing . . . years r. on . . c147

c *(re water)*
r. as a mighty ocean . . 182.1
r. in fullest pride . . . 224.4
r. on from pole to pole . . 230.1
where its bright waves r. . 252.2
salvation like a river r. . . 254.2
Jordan's r. tide . . . 278.4
come, r. over me . . . 298.*
sorrow's waves . . . r. . . 317.3
though the waves r. high . 325.4
r. o'er my soul each day . 375.2
waft it on the r. tide . . 393.2
unknown waves before me r. 598.1
the nearer waters r. . . 737.1
stream shall o'er me r. . . 743.4
Jordan above me shall r. . 771.3
tell . . . how r. the sea . . 848.3
while Jordan r. between . 898.2
let them r. over me . . c78
comes . . . r. over me . . c140

billow, stone (2c), thunder (a)

d *roll away*
from my heart . . . r. a. . 309.1
the burden r. a. . . . 333.1
my heavy burden r. a. 340.1, c
r. a. at Calvary . . . 340.3
burden . . . heart r. a. . . 395.c
from me my burden did r. . 467.3
never . . . cannot r. a. . . c87
burden . . . he r. it a. . . c159
burden of my heart r. a. . c198

Roman 181.2

roof 728.3

room
quiet r. of time 7.2
r. for pleasure . . . business . 241.2
at the cross there's r. . . 261.*
r. for the lame . . . for thee . 266.2
Christ made r. 266.2
r. for . . . souls/sinners . 266.2,3
sure I am . . . r. for me . . 266.4
I have no r. to boast . . 468.4
r. to deny ourselves . . 668.4
there is r. for them all . . 794.3
r. in Jesus' side . . . 821.c
no r. for sadness . . . 899.3
r. at the cross . . . c21
there for me is r., Lord . . c109

b *yet room*
y. there is r. . . . for thee . 101.4
y. there's r. for more . . 266.1
r. for millions more . . 275.1
y. . . . mercy makes thee r. . 333.4

c *room [for Jesus]*
every heart prepare him r. . 84.1
r. in my heart 101.*/282.c/444.c
have you any r. for Jesus . 241.1
r. for Jesus, King . . . 241.c
r. and time now give . . 241.4

d *Luke 2:7*
found no r. 101.1

root-ed
r. my weakness remained . 553.3

b *Eph 3:17*
keep pure, r. in thee . . 416.2

rose
1 (*verb*—see rise)
2 *(noun)*
thank you . . . for wayside r.. 552.3
Sharon

rough-er
though r. be the fighting . 233.3
r. and steep . . . my pathway. 473.3
places once so r. . . . 549.3
thank you, too, for byways r. 552.2
find your path is r. . . 805.1
road we tread is r. . . . 805.c

b *rough way* *(Luke 3:5)*
r. and thorny be the w. . 453.4
w. may seem r. . . . 523.4
the w. is r., the fighting . c227

round
1 *(noun)*
each day is a r. of duty . . 666.3
the trivial r. 668.4
2 (*preposition—see around)*

rouse
r. from the slumber of sin . 373.1
soldier, r. thee . . . 693.1
r., then, soldiers . . . 698.c

rout-ing
all Hell's legions r. . . 609.3
r. the foe in fear . . . 686.4
hosts of Hell we're r. . . 693.3

route 204.1

rove
guide me, or I blindly r. . 630.1
while here o'er earth I r. . 636.1
mine, to call me when I r. . 652.2
where the glorified r. . . 905.2

royal
r. David's city 87.1
proclaiming thy r. degree . 101.2
attests his r. might . . 126.2
shall be thy r. throne . . 525.5
Christ, the r. Master . . 690.1
lift high his r. banner . . 699.1
received the r. command . 702.2
David's r. Son 853.2
lead them to his r. throne . 866.3
bearers of a r. proclamation . c226

b *Isa 62:3*
bring forth the r. diadem . 56.1
a r. diadem adorns . . . 168.1

rubies *(Pro 3:15)** . . . 354.1

rude
that manger r. and bare . . 76.3
shame and scoffing r. . . 118.2
so r. was thy cot . . . 175.1
chaos dark and r. . . . 569.3

rugged
old r. cross . . . . 124.*
that r. cross . . . for me. . 134.1
make the r. places smooth . 159.1
the steep and r. pathway . 570.2
r. are the heights . . . 641.1
from Calvary's r. cross . . 700.2
life's r. way 761.1
Calvary's r. tree . . . c19

ruin-ed
world . . . r. by the fall . . 46.1
r. sinners to reclaim . . 118.1
out of the depths of r. . . 300.4
in the r. of my life . . . 376.2
on the brink of r. fell . . 380.1
r.'s ghastly road . . . 696.2
have sought to r. man . . 760.3
a darkened r. lay . . . 890.3

b
the r. of my soul repair . . 305.3

rule-d-ing
1 *(human)*
pride r. my will . . . 606.2
simple r. and . . . guiding . 716.2
what though thou r. not . 721.3
for every r. of life . . . 785.1
2 *(divine)*
thou r. in might 8.2
God r. on high . . . 24.2
he r. the world with truth . 84.3
r. through all the worlds. . 104.6
r. o'er earth and Heaven . 164.3
thy r., O Christ, begin . . 172.1
thy over-r. plan I see . . 644.c
God . . . r. all things well . 721.3
faithful I stand in r. . . 744.5
his right to r. each day . . 867.1

b *rule in hearts* *Col 3:15**
r. in all our h. . . . 79.4
in blood-washed h. to r.. . 138.1
now r. in every h. . . 219.3
love must r. me . . . 522.3
r. my life supremely . . 591.3
where love alone can . . . r. . 855.3

c *Ps 103:19*
kingdom . . . r. over all . . 24.1

ruler
God is the r. yet . . . 42.3
no other r. will we own . . 747.3

run/ran
the river r. by . . . 25.2
successive journeys r. . . 160.1
that never will r. dry . . 312.2
I r. with delight . . . 321.1
many said I'd r. away . . 338.3
r. in self-chosen ways . . 422.2
r. not before him . . . 458.3
disciples turned and r. . . 544.5
everlasting circles r. . . 559.3
daily stage of duty r. . . 665.1
life's pathway r. steep . . 739.2
swift should r. . . . 842.2
his errands we must r. . . 851.2
he laughed and r. . . . 855.2
while eternal ages r. . . 890.5
on, then, to Glory r. . . 897.3

course (b), press (d), race (2b), swiftly (c), weary (f)

runaways 806.2

rung see ring

running *(adj)* 32.1

rush
what r. of hallelujahs . . 167.2
the world r. on . . . 458.2
I'll . . . r. to the field . . 686.c

rushing *(adj)*
thou r. wind . . . so strong . 2.2
fording the torrent so r. . . 388.1
wind (1d)

rustling
the r. of the trees . . . 41.1
in the r. grass . . . 42.2

ruthless 268.3

S

Sabaoth *Rom 9:29* . . 1.2

Sabbath 567.3

sacred
nations bow with s. joy . . 4.1
the s. gains of toil . . . 5.2
the s. cup of saving grace . 23.2
with yonder s. throng . . 56.5
they chant this s. lay . . 72.5
s. Infant, all divine . . 88.4
the light of s. story . 112.1, 5
from that s. hill . . . 126.c
s. hands of Jesus . . . 129.c
glory crowns thy s. brow . 185.4
kindle a flame of s. love . 199.1
fix thy s. presence there . 207.1
thy s. witness bear . . 219.3
have you seen the s. beauty . 242.4
let thy s. presence fill . . 480.2
here . . . in this s. hour . . 488.c
hear . . . the s. vow . . 504.2
I touch thy s. garment . . 520.3
engaged in his s. employment 553.4
souls impressed with s. love . 556.1
placed upon the s. ark . . 590.1
more s. now is Calvary's hill . 590.1
at this s. mercy seat . . 590.4
the springs of s. service . 591.1
this shall be the s. gleam . 591.3
all s. to thyself . . . 615.2
s. in the fireside warm . . 663.1
his s. form would rest . . 663.2
every s. moment spend . . 720.4
kneel beside thy s. cross . 729.1
promise in this s. hour . . 784.2
s. and indwelt by thee . . 786.1
s. arms of Jesus . . . 792.3
heap on his s. altar . . 929.3
s. to thine eternal name . . 946.2
b *(re Bible)*
beyond the s. page . . 650.1
unseal the s. book . . 651.2
glory gilds the s. page . . 657.2
c *sacred name*
to bless the s. n. . . . 57.4
men scorn thy s. n. . . 172.5
I bow and bless the s. n. . 223.1
d *sacred word*
set forth within the s. w. . 656.1
parents love the s. w. . 661.3
thy s. w. is passed . . 714.2
with eager mind, the s. w. . 871.2
ark, fire (2b), flame (2b), head (1b)

sacredness 7.4

sacrifice
1 *(divine)* *Heb 9.26**
s. in my behalf appears . . 106.1
a s. of nobler name . . 120.2
Jesus dies, a willing s. . 126.3
to see the approaching s. . 150.3
his the glorious s. . . 249.2
s. that Jesus gave . . . 269.3
an offering and a s. . . 414.4
Christ's s. availed . . . 706.1
make known . . . the s. of God 830.2
2 *(human)*
I s. them to his blood . . 136.2
who is it calls to s.. . . 204.2
by your s. adore him . . 242.5
I s. thy gifts for dross . . 449.1
gladly I s. their charms . . 461.2
now the s. we make . . 481.3
a s. to God 511.4
my s. profit me nothing . . 530.3
help me to make more s. . 619.4
rise to pay thy morning s. . 665.1
God will provide for s. . . 668.2
bless our s. 921.1
gain is found through s. . 922.3
shrink from s. . . . 944.2
b *complete sacrifice*
love asks a s. c. . . . 128.2
make the s. c. . . . 199.4
make your s. c. . . . 920.1
c *living sacrifice* *Rom 12:1*
l., dying, s. 452.3
my body a l. s. . . . 482.3
a holy, l. s. 516.1
praise (3e)

sacrificial
pluck . . . in the s. hour . . 145.3
purge . . . like s. flame . . 217.3
in this s. hour . . . dedicate . 789.1

sad
with s. and wondering eyes . 150.3
s., s., that bitter wail . . 226.3
are you somewhat s. . . 244.3
offers peace to the s. . . 247.2
set my s. heart free . . 282.2
weary and worn and s. . . 332.1
came . . . bound and s. . . 348.2
self-sufficient but s. . . 376.1
sometimes joyful . . . s. . 549.1
some are sick . . . sad . 558.3
away, s. doubt . . . 746.3
all is despairing . . . s. . . 773.1
s. . . . are fully blest . . 828.3
rich and poor, the s. . . 829.2
that comforteth the s. . . 838.3
s. ones or bright ones . . 848.5
oft when I'm s. . . . 881.1
no s. repining . . . 888.2
how can I be s. . . . c191
b *Luke 24:17*
s., they thought . . . done . 145.1
three s. days . . . sped . . 151.3

sadly
I confess to thee s. . . 296.3
pleasures . . . I s. mourned . 547.4

sadness
melt the clouds of . . . s. . . 10.1
if men can feel . . . s. . . 50.3
he feeleth for our s. . . 87.4
does s. fill my mind . . 187.3
for sorrow and s. I joy . . 372.4
with my heart so full of s. . 470.1
in sunshine or in s. . . 503.3
bid s. and sorrow depart . 537.1
my spirit pines in . . . s.. . 631.3
when faint . . . with s. . . 635.2
Jesus . . . dispelled the s. . 663.2
O banish s. 724.2
there'll be no s. . . . 888.c
will be no room for s. . . 899.3
bring s. to your heart . . c139
gladness for s. . . . c148

safe-ly
dies s. through thy love . . 123.4
anchor s. by the . . . shore . 280.4
s. to arrive at home . . 313.2
now s. am I 336.1
s. reach the goal . . . 344.2
s. 'neath the shelter . . 517.4
s. in thy love 574.1
s. when by thy side/nigh 627.1, 2
home s. in thy breast . . 675.3
s. shalt thou go on . . 715.3
s. in the dark day . . . till . 724.3
s. is such confiding . . 736.1
bear me s. above . . . 743.4
in Jesus' keeping we are s. . 752.4
s. shalt thou be . . . 767.2
s. and secure from all . . 768.c
feeling s. and blest . . 792.1
s. in the arms of Jesus . . 889.*
s. . . . in the sunlight . . 894.2
till s. landed there . . . 901.3
s. on that beautiful shore . 906.1
all is s. gathered in . . . 924.1
in Jesus I'm s. evermore . c178
b *bring safe*
b. us s. through Jordan . . 152.3
grace has b. me s. thus far . 308.3
b. me s. to Heaven . . 345.3
to his fold he s. b. us . . 377.2
through sleep . . . s. b. . . 668.1
will b. you s. through . 790.1, c
thou hast b. us s. . . . 938.1
c *guide safe*
g. lonely . . . seamen s. . . 63.3
he lives to g. me s. . . 144.3
s. to Glory he will g. thee . 377.4
s. into the haven g. . . 737.1
Spirit shall g. us s. home . 962
d *lead safe*
by his hand I'm s. l. . . 337.4
will l. me s. in the path . . 483.3
direct and s. l. . . . 561.2
Shepherd . . . l. me s. there . 641.3
keep (3g), land (3)

safest 716.2

safety
to him for s. flee . . . 253.3
peace and s. my reward. . 556.5
my s. thou wilt be . . . 628.3
s. for my trembling soul . . 713.1
for s. we hide . . . 763.4
in this alone your s. lies . 885.1
b *Ps 4:8*
dwell in s. near him . . 377.3

said see say

sail
clouds that s. in heaven . . 2.2
nor on the sea thy s. . . 91.2
I s. straight on . . . 628.4
s. through stormy seas . . 678.2
I s. the wide seas no more . c178

saint
1 *(past)*
thy s. have dwelt secure . 13.2
s. before the altar . . . 75.3
where the s. have trod . . 690.3
twelve valiant s. . . . 701.3
s. of old obeyed the call . 789.5
way the s. have trod . . 858.2
those warrior s. . . . 858.2
fed by s. unnumbered . . 869.3
fight as the s. . . . of old . 876.3
s. whose race is run . . 939.3
b *Jude 3*
to s. by Jesus given . . 733.2
2 *(present)*
s. with his mercy surrounding 19.4
fear him, ye s. 21.5
ye fearful s. . . . courage . 29.3

to his s. makes known . . 46.3
let all s. proclaim . . . 68.c
no s. . . . worth can tell. . 69.3
look, ye s.! the sight . . 147.1
s. like him shall die . . 149.2
s. of every nation . . . bow . 185.4
all the s. get home . . 312.3
s. of God, lift up . . . 381.1
where the s. can see . . 429.1
humble s. receive . . . 461.3
that feeds . . . every s. . . 559.2
sees the weakest s. . . 646.3
sound, with all thy s. . . 651.4
how firm . . . ye s. . . 653.1
his s. . . . ne'er be denied . 763.2
walls . . . the s. surround . 809.3
sing your songs, ye s. . . 809.4
me, of s. the least . . . 880.3
each s. has a mansion . . 905.3
to love . . . a s. appear . . 932.3
s. whose race is run . . 939.3
striving s. find grace . . 943.3
s. show forth thy praise . 946.2

b *saint/sinner*
convert . . . sinner to a s. . 290.2
make a s. of a sinner . . 471.c
sinners changed to s. . . 919.2

comprehend (b)

3 *(in Heaven)*
lives for ever with his s. . 148.c
armies of the ransomed s. . 167.1
all the s. adore thee . . 220.2
sing it with the s. . . . 337.c
with the s. will sing . . 368.4
s. above . . . more favoured . 373.2
s. in true happiness gaze . 639.2
with the s. at thy . . . hand . 747.3
for all the s. who . . . rest . 876.1
s. triumphant rise . . . 876.5
see the s. above . . . 879.1
land . . . the s.s' delight . 880.1
s. all immortal and fair . . 886.1
gather with the s. . . . 891.c
s. whom death . . . sever . 891.4
s. in glory stand . . . 897.1
where s. immortal reign . . 898.1
s. are robed in white . . 902.1
God doth in his s. delight . 909.2
his s. for ever feed . . . 909.3
where s. abide for ever . . 934.4
with his true s. alone . . 940.1

b *saints and angels*
s. and a. crowd around him . 147.3
a. and s. are singing . . 383.c
s. and a. . . . will sing . . 543.4
with s. and a. praising . . 950

inheritance, thousand (2d)

sake
1 *sake of Jesus*
s. of that dear name . . 127.4
for thy mercy's s. . . . 291.3
thy truth and mercy's s. . 305.3
for the Kingdom's s. . . 788.2
for thy s. . . . lose . . 796.3
for his s. fear not to lose . 805.3
for thy s. to win renown . 860.5

b *Ps 23:3*
for his own name's s. . . 54.2

c *dear sake*
sins for thy d. s. . . . 285.1
leaving all for his d. s. . . 428.2
give, for his d. s. . . . 512.2
meet on earth for thy d. s. . 603.3
bearing shame for his d. s. . 777.3

d *[Jesus'] sake*
sing with us, for Jesus' s. . 43.1
for the s. of the Christ . . 119.3
our blessed Saviour's s. . 481.3
to me, for Jesus' s. impart . 601.3

2 *our sake*
Jesus suffers for our s. . . 107.3
for the lost world's s. . . 482.3
sinner, 'twas for thy s. . . c19

sale 244.3

Salem 797.1

salt *Matthew 5:13* . . . 682.2

salute
s. the happy morn . . . 78.1
we s. our King . . . 692.3
proudly we s. the colours . 777.1

salvation
1 *(noun)*
safely to s.'s shore . . 63.3
he lives for our s. . . . 96.4
take s., take it now . . 240.1
do you his s. know . . 243.1
is not this s. grand . . 243.3
s. he offers to thee . . 260.c
before I found s. . . . 309.1
I abide in his s. . . . 330.c
he lives s. to impart . . 334.c
purchased my s. . . . 347.1
quite sure of s. I sing . . 364.2
he has bought for us s. . 381.2
s.! o the joyful sound . . 382.1
ne'er would regard the s. . 395.1
love that drew s.'s plan . 405.4
God wills . . . uttermost s. . 410.1
s.! s.! O tell to all . . . 410.3
self-s. will not do . . . 430.1
earth's s. portion . . . 452.4
I look for thy s. . . . 511.2
s.'s full measure to know . 553.1
my succour and s., Lord . 596.4
thy s. in this meeting show . 608.2
message of s. 655.2
faith . . . makes s. sure . . 733.4
whence . . . my s. come . . 767.1
bright emblem of s. . . 781.1
with s. for every nation . . 800.3
s. is our motto . . . song . 814.1
s. makes us free . . . 815.c
there's s. for the world . . 821.*
his s. to every nation . . 822.c
s.! shout/sing/speak s. . . 828.*
make s.'s story heard . . 832.c
sing in Glory s.'s story . . 888.3
yes, there's s. for you . . c20
glory, honour and s. . . c27

b *Ps 118:14*
he is thy health and s. . . 19.1
and his s. ours . . . 20.4
still Christ is my s. . . 361.3

c *Ps 25:5**
thou God of my s. . . . 370.1
thou God of full s. . . 452.1

d *Acts 4:12*
by which we can s. have . 62.2
s. in the name of Jesus . . 70.2
thy name s. is . . . 603.2
s. in his name . . . 869.3

e *Heb 5:9*
our hope of eternal s. . . 184.2
sunlight . . . of his eternal s. . 894.2

f *Rev 7:10*
ascribing s. to Jesus . . 24.2

g *[God's] salvation*
G.'s s. wrought . . . 174.2
G.'s great, free, full s. . . 413.2
seeking for G.'s full s. . . 553.2
crimson tells of G.'s s. . 783.2
all have need of G.'s s. . 824.1

Army (1a), boundless (f), bring (1h), free (2d), full (1h, j), gain (e), give (1t), great (2i), have (2d), heir (b), joy (2b), neglect (b), see (3g), seek (2e), shout (c), song (1d), visit (b), wall (b), wrought (d)

2 *(adjective)*
s. banner of love . 382.c/782.c
the depth of his s. plan . . 656.2
put on s. armour . . . 699.3
while s. music plays . . 807.1
girding on s. armour . . 869.4
s. reapers we will be . . 936.3

soldier (f)

same
to endless years the s. . . 13.3
thy fulness is the s. . . 14.2
still the s. as ever . . . 17.2
his love remains the s. . . 44.c
love of God is just the s. . 49.2
may that s. grace inspire . 760.1
he will do the s. for you. . 790.1
to all kingdoms . . . the s. . 824.4
seeking the s. Saviour . . c112
love for me is still the s.. . c175

b *1 Cor 12:6*
self-s. voice . . . self-s. way . 680.3
seeking the self-s. Lord . . c112

c *Heb 13:8*
Jesus! every day the s. . . 68.c
he is just the s. today . . 96.*
lives, eternally the s. . . 144.4
I believe thy power the s. . 419.5
the s. thy grace and truth . 419.5
touch, thy power . . . the s. . 628.2
in every age the s. . . . 629.1
yesterday . . . Jesus is the s.. 750.c
he's the s. today . . . c163
affections are always the s. . c207

2 *(general)*
light of that s. star . . . 90.3
tell me the s. old story . . 98.4
we are not the s. . . . 215.c
I'll never be the s. again. . 376.c
the s. path to Heaven . . 879.5

b *Rom 12:16*
the s. in mind and heart. . 659.5

Samuel *1 Sam 3:4f* . 839.3-5

sanctify-d-ing
by the cross are s. . . . 112.4
captain did appear to s. . . 163.3
come, O Spirit, come to s. . 188.2
O Spirit . . . may we be s. . 196.6
s. what should'st be thine . 211.3
come, as thou didst, to s. . 218.1
s. me now . . . . . 440.*
s. each moment fully . . 463.c
both to save and s. . . 479.3
all my actions s. . . . 492.1
s. me with the fire . . . 493.c
s. each human feeling . . 528.c
unless love doth s. . . 530.3
God himself has s. them . 555.4
let thy teaching s. . . . 582.5
s. . . . thy deepest distress . 653.3
thy praise shall s. our rest . 677.1
honest labour s. . . . 688.2
shall seal and s. . . . 742.2
let s. elation 828.1
with each emotion s. . . 861.2
blessed by God, are s. . . 874.1
then s. . . . this offering . 943.4

b *1 Thess 5:23*
wholly s. and seal us . . 195.3
accepted, s. in thee . . 287.3
to s. you/me wholly . . 410.*
we may be wholly s. . . 785.5
s. the whole c50

c *Ezek 36:23*
s. thy name, O Lord . . 769.2

altar (c)

sanctifying *(adj)*
s. power bestow . . . 531.3
promises afford a s. light . 657.1
send the s. power . . . c51

sanctuary 728.2

sand
ripple o'er golden s. . . 252.1
from sinking s. he lifted . . 339.c
other ground is sinking s. . 745.c
many, like the s. . . . 883.2
the s. of time are sinking . 896.1
s. of the seashore . . 908.1, c

sang see sing

sanguine 566.3

sapphire *Ezek 1:26* . . 150.4

Satan
in vain does S. then oppose . 9.1
S. is vanquished . . . 166.5
S.'s work destroy . . . 195.2
S. will rage 233.2
by S. sorely pressed . . 284.3
S. dismayed . . . doth flee . 323.5
S. tempt me sore . . . 344.2
S. never shall prevail . . 532.2
S. trembles when he sees . 646.3
oft S.'s arrows wound . . 806.1
o'er sin and S. . . . victory . 814.3
let not S.'s fiercest strife . 816.2
S. has taught . . . to sin. . 885.2
S. the tares 932.1

b *(Luke 13:16)*
in S.'s bondage held . . 81.2
bound with S.'s chain . . 155.4
bound by S.'s cruel fetters . 328.1
from all the bondage of S. . 608.3

c *power of Satan* *Acts 26:18*
p. of S.'s rod . . . 113.2
thence from S.'s p. . . 350.1
S.'s p. shall fall . . . 499.4
S.'s p. to overthrow . . 687.1
won from S.'s p. . . . 774.2

bruise (c), host (5a), kingdom (2)

satellite 30.2

satisfy-d-ing
may I with this be s. . . 14.2
Jesus . . . shall be s. . . 42.3
he alone can s. . . . 343.c
s. my deepest longings . . 531.3
none but Christ can s. . . 547.c
the bread that s. for ever . 631.2
I am s. to know . . . 758.c
sufficient . . . love to s. . . c120
I'm s. with Jesus here . . c174

b *Ps 107:9**
s. my spirit's yearning . . 206.1
my soul is s. 320.1
s. our soul's desire . . 481.c
thy favour my soul can s. . 503.c
s. my soul this hour . . 729.1

save-d-ing
1 *(God) saves*
move to s. a fallen race . . 62.4
love in s. lost mankind . . 78.3
hurt thee in s. thy sheep . 111.2
ransomed host of God be s. . 132.3
power that s. and recreates . 135.3
mercies yearn to s.. . . 135.4
ever lives to s. . . . 149.1
fills and s. us higher . . 197.2
tears . . . will not s. . . 269.3
thou must s. . . . alone . 302.2
that we may be s. . . . 319.c
here to s. and bless . . 434.2
thou through life shalt s. . 714.4
s. from earth to Heaven . 733.2

b *Jesus saves*
nothing . . . today J. s. . 245.4
J. . . . s. and keeps . . 258.3
very Christ can s. thy soul . 266.3
glory, J. s. me . 313.c/520.c
J. s. me and keeps me . 315.3
J. completely s. . . . 336.3
joy . . . for J. has s. me . 349.3
J. s. me . . . rapture/wonder 350.*
J. s. me now . . . 385.*
Jesus s. . . . . 393.*
I now can sing: J. s. . . 401.*
J. is merciful . . . will s. . 691.c
the Lord is s. souls . . 775.1
I believe J. s. . . . 808.c
J. s. me, s. me now . . c69
J. s., s. me now . . c183

c *came to save* *Luke 19:10*
Jesus c. the world t. s. . . 62.2
whom Jesus c. t. s. . . 98.3
c. t. succour, help and s. . 104.5
for those he c. t. s. . . 156.2
Jesus c. t. s. me . . . 347.1
Saviour of men c. . . . t. s. . 527.1
t. s. the world . . . c. . . 831.1
Lord c. down t. s. me . . 840.1
the Lord c. down t. s. me . c204

d *saved by blood*
s. b. his precious b. . . 133.3
s. b. his pardoning b. . . 245.4
nothing but thy b. can s. . 292.*
s., blessedly s., b. the b. . 321.*
b. of Jesus fully s. . . 404.2
whose b. was spilt to s. . 532.4
his b. doth s. the soul . . 798.1

e *(personal testimony)*
s., to serve him eternally . 114.2
my lost estate to s. . . 180.2
gav'st thy Son to s. me . . 221.1
s. a wretch like me . . 308.1
I am s., I am s. . . . 322.1
washed, and so was s. . . 348.1
he will still be s. me . . 350.3
s. from every fear . . . 352.2
s. through Jesus' name . . 360.2
he s. me, O praise . . 371.2
he s. me every day . . 374.2
the day Christ s. me . . 401.1
he's s., I'm believing . . 413.3
when most I'm s. . . . 468.4
I know thou dost s. me . . 473.4
not my own, but s. . . 514.1
I feel 'tis s. me . . . 546.3
thy people, s. below . . 629.2
the truth that s. me . . 650.2
all hail, I'm s. . . . 694.c
he has s. us gloriously . . 769.1
faith could most have s. me . 770.2
s. us, set us free . . . 788.1
s. by Jesus' might . . . 803.3
we're an Army s. . . . 821.3
praise God, I'm s. . . . 960
dying, he s. me . . . c185
he gave all to s. us. . . c213

f *(exhortation)*
he will s. you now . . . 231.c
Jesus lives to help and s. . 242.1
nothing . . . today Jesus s. . 245.4
thou wouldst be s. . . 251.*
O be s. 259.c
look unto him and be s. . . 271.1
be s. today 336.3
you may be s. c30

g *(request)*
O s. such just now . . . 175.3
Jesus, s. me now . . . 282.1
O s. me, dear Lord . . 288.c
s. me for thy mercy's sake . 291.3
Jesus, s. me through 430.1
s. me to the uttermost . . 430.c
both to s. and sanctify . . 479.3
s. this very hour . . . 562.2
thou art going to s. . . 608.3
s. . . . this very hour . 638.2, 3
s. us from our fear . . . 769.2
know that thou canst s. . 837.2

h *[mighty] to save* *Isa 63:1*
on high, almighty to s. . . 24.2
lives omnipotent to s. . . 144.1
Jesus is m. to s. . . . 249.*
call of the m. to s. . . 298.6
he is m. to s. 322.3
proved he is m. to s. . . 329.c
m. love, m. to s. . . . 364.c
triumph . . . in the m. to s. . 364.4
for thou art almighty to s. . 454.3
he's m. to s. . . . . 467.*
yes, Jesus is m. to s. . . 535.c
Father, strong to s. . . 569.1
tell them of Jesus, the m. to s. 691.1
King is the m. to s. . . 820.3

deliver (b)

i *save from sin* *Matt 1:21*
s. from the burden of s.. . 166.4
s. us from . . . power of s. . 230.4
wondrously s. from s. . . 315.2
fountain that s. from s. . . 315.3
through temptations s. . . 430.2
s. from the power of s. . . 431.4
s. from the guilt . . . of s. . 629.3
so wondrously s. from . . . s.. 640.1
s. me . . . from sinning and s. 640.2
s. from all s. 681.3
the faith that s. from s. . 733.6
power doth s. me . . . 741.4

j *save world* *John 3:17; 12:47*
s. the w. from . . . blight . 30.4
Jesus came the w. to s. . 62.2
to live a dying w. to s. . . 203.4
s. the w. . . . Jesus' merit . 622.2
to s. a lost w. . . . 687.3
God is s. the w. . . . 774.c
all the w. to s. . . . go . 821.c
God is raising now to s.. . 822.1
to s. the w. . . . came . . 831.1
greatest gift the w. to s. . 861.1

k *Acts 2:21/Rom 10:13*
s. those that . . . call . . 602.2
called on him to s. . . 701.2
s. whoe'er on Jesus call . 756.5

l *save sinners* *1 Tim 1:15*
s. whom Jesus came to s. . 98.3
to s. a poor s. like me . . 137.*
a s. s. by grace . . . 266.4
something worth s. in s. . 319.1
forward, poor s. to s. . . 321.3
poor s. of all kinds he s.. . 331.4
canst thou not s. a poor s. . 543.1
end in s. s. weary . . . 802.4
dangers braving, s. s. . . 819.c
for s. s., for victories . . 919.1
so to s. a poor s. . . . c217

m *save souls* *James 1:21*
once he died our s. to s. . 143.4
he who died our s. to s. . 149.3
s. shall be s. 166.4
life gave, thy s. to s. . . 260.2
Christ can s. thy s. . . 266.3
can s. this guilty s. . . 297.1
a never-dying s. to s. . . 472.1
thou hast s. my s. . . . 499.1
seek and to s. the s. . . 527.1
no immortal s. to s. . . 592.3
give me more s.-s. love . 609.1
s.-s. truth inspire . . . 609.2
s. poor s. out of the fire . 720.2
the Lord is s. s. . . . 775.1
his blood doth s. the s. . 798.1
God stoops . . . s. to s. . 885.4
the s. he died to s. . . 929.3
more earnest s. to s. . . 933.4

die (2f), grace (2o), keep (3f), other (2b), power (4e), seek (3b), uttermost

2 *(we) save* *(Jude 23)*
lose ourselves to s. 5.4
you may rescue, you may s. 478.c
earnestly seeking to s. 484.1
dying men to s. 499.c
love engages . . . s. the sheep 522.2
with cries, . . . tears, to s. 526.1
willing to suffer, others to s. 623.3
hearts to help him s. 704.3
the universe to s. 775.3

b *save lost* *Matt 18:11*
seeks and s. the lost 197.2
to help us s. the l. 783.3
forward go the l. to s. 814.2
dying I may help to s. 859.2
chosen . . . l. ones to s. c225

save (1m)

3 *(except)*
s. that which . . . resides 494.1
other love s. thine 551.1
s. the sight of thee 600.2
unarmed, s. with the mind 705.4
naught . . . s. by surrender 922.3

b *Gal 6:14*
nothing . . . s. the cross 107.5
forbid . . . s. in the death 136.2

saved *(noun)*
s. of earth shall gather 907.1
s. of the ages 908.2

saving *(adj)*
his s. truth proclaim 60.5
take . . . in s. faith 122.3
s. strength to show 155.3
through thy s. merit 430.4
give me more soul-s. love 609.1
soul-s. truth inspire 609.2
the s. sign display 697.4
know not how this s. faith 730.2

b *saving grace*
sacred cup of s. g. 23.2
I want to tell of s. g. 335.2
thy s. g. to claim 456.3
confess the s. g. of God 494.2
work . . . by his s. g. 769.1
they his s. g. proclaim 869.3
raise their song of s. g. 891.4

c *saving power*
s. p., this very hour 304.c
show forth thy s. p. 562.2
s. p. in this meeting 608.1

Saviour see Jesus
as a s. of mankind 499.3

saw see see

say-ing/said
1 *(God) says*
a *(with title)*
look . . . s. the Lord 272.3
who comes . . . Saviour s. 277.*
words my Lord would s. 398.1
glad, because the Master s. 403.c
Jesus now s.: Come up 910.4
God shall s.: Well done 912.3
Jesus s.: He who comes c16
to whom the Lord s. nay c87

b *(general)*
come, to me, s. one 228.1
the Comforter, tenderly s. 236.2
he s.: Follow me 276.4
s., by thy Spirit divine 289.4
wept over sinners . . . s. 331.2
s.: Christian, follow me 428.1
s.: Christian, love me more 428.3
thou never s.: No 436.3
s. they serve you best 518.2
nor power, thyself hast s. 581.2
wonderful . . . to hear him s. 583.1
when thou s. . . .: Be still 598.2
may I hear thee s. to me. 598.3
what hast thou to s. to me 614.1
what more can he s. 653.1
s. to all who seek 724.1
his kind look when he s. 794.1
sweetly smiled and kindly s. 797.1
the book s.: Whosoever 824.3
hands are wanted, hear him s. 868.2
he will s.: Come near 875.4

c *[voice] says*
s. our God's inspiring v. 95.3
let thy v. call me home, s. 101.4
I heard the v. of Jesus s. 332.*
until a v. s., sweet 359.1
I heard his v. unto me s. 490.2
he hears a v. which s. 911.3

d *John 2:5*
what he s. we will do 397.5

e *Rev 22:17*
tenderly s.: Come 235.1, 3
the bride and Spirit s. 261.3

f *(angels) say*
a host . . . which s. 72.3
Nowell the angel did s. 90.1
fear not! s. he 93.2
sons of men and angels s. 143.1

nay, word (1i)

2 *(we) say*
age to age shall s. 155.1, c
seems now some soul to s. 226.1
why not come and s. 255.4
a better world, they s. 268.1
could I hear some sinner s. 275.4
then is it anywhere s. 289.2
s., when the death-dew 357.3
I do not doubt, nor . . . s. 359.3
now I s.: Blessèd Master 373.1
would you not like . . . to s. 388.4
s. to sinners far and wide 393.2
but s. . . . thy will 410.2
s. there's naught to do 482.2
true it is to s. 494.1
souls who are bound may s. 523.3
my wistful heart s. 548.2
all that ye have s. 564.3
to live the words we s. 572.1
I often s. my prayers 588.1
go with the words I s. 588.1
not feeling what I s. 588.4
faith that s., yes 608.2
all I may think . . . or s. 665.5
hearts to s.: Thy will 704.2
what can I s. to cheer 706.1
hard . . . to s: Thy will 729.3
the kindly words you s. 790.2
let us s. . . . never mind. 805.3
shall s.: This God 875.2
takes . . . and smiling s. 911.2
that's the reason I can s. c1
just now as I s. to thee c33
now makes it hard to s. c95
fulness of joy I can s. c159

b *Ex 4:12; Luke 12:12*
what we ought to s. 193.2
and what I ought to s. 204.1

c *Phil 4:4*
now we can rejoice to s. 43.2
rejoice; again, I s. 164.c
each rejoicing s. 946.4

d
living, whatever men may s. 334.1
many s. I'd run away 338.3
care of what men think or s. 437.4
I'll fear not what men s. 685.3
they s. the fighting 780.2
they s. I can a Christian be 780.3
cry, whatever men may s. 782.2

3 *(interjection)*
s., is there a name 71.*
s., ye holy shepherds, s. 88.2
s., poor sinner, lov'st thou 110.1, 5
s., would'st thou bind 129.3
s., weary heart 229.*
s., are you weary? 257.1
s., is thy heart replying 276.2
s. why do I languish 318.4
s., do you wonder 388.4
s., are you weak 467.2
in the fight, s., does 805.1
O s., will you go 905.*

4 *(figurative)*
the light rays seem to s. 103.2
God is love, the cross is s. 324.1

scaffold 6.3

scale 510.2

scan-ned
the fiery heavens s. 27.3
s. his work in vain 29.6
would the mystery s. 439.2
s. the very wounds 558.4
thought and motive s. 618.1
eyes may s. the . . . height 766.2

scar-red
hands that were s. 129.2
those glorious s. 161.3
lo! that hand is s. 299.2

scarce-ly
I s. can take it in 37.3
I can s. dare to think 399.2
battles lost or s. won 466.4
beautiful . . . will s. seem 551.1

scarlet *Isa 1:18*
deep were the s. stains 176.1
though as s. be the stains 249.2
though your sins be as s. 272.1
though your sins be as s. 883.2

scatter-ed-ing
s. all their guilty fear 60.2
s. garments strowed 150.1
s. fear and gloom 152.2
s. full and free 295.1
s. all my unbelief 412.4
s. night away 887.4
sower's s. seed 926.2
plough the fields, and s. 935.1
s. thy life c50
s. a little sunshine c200

b *Matt 9:36*
will ye s. like a crowd 265.1

c *Luke 1:51*
hosts to meet and s. 158.2
s. the foe from the field 820.2

scene
changing s. of life 21.1
bring its s. before me 115.3
all s. alike engaging 556.1
s. where spirits blend 573.3
to see the distant s. 606.1
old s., will lovelier be 668.3
s. of deepest gloom 725.2
s. by the wayside 848.1
that s., in the garden 848.5
transporting, rapturous s. 887.2

scented 41.2

sceptre *(Heb 1:8)**
worthy of a s. . . . a crown 72.1
that s.-reed discarded 126.2
whose power a s. sways 156.3
from his s. shall spring 166.2
'neath thy s. . . . bending 593.3
but now the s. 894.2

scheming 693.1

school
home, at s., at play 844.1; 849.3

science
which we by s. trace . . 27.2
Lord of s. 30.3
the state or s. . . . 688.1

scoff-ed-ing *(2 Pet 3:3)*
bearing shame and s. rude . 118.2
they s. and mocked my God . 758.3
foes may s. 790.2

scorn-ed
with mocking s. . . . 101.3
sore abuse and s. . . . 123.1
s. or wealth divide . . . 142.4
men s. thy sacred name . . 172.5
s. him and left him to die . 245.3
hosts . . . s. thy Christ . . 577.2
the s. . . . may be daring . 758.3

scornfully 123.1

Scripture *(2 Tim 3:16)**
S.'s living words . . . 656.2
Father has inspired the S. . 785.1

sea
1 *(literal)*
meadow, flashing s. . . 10.2
cast, like a mantle, the s. . 16.3
lost them . . . above the s. . 41.1
thought of . . . skies and s. . 42.1
nor on the s. thy sail . . 91.2
born across the s. . . . 162.4
sing, ye islands of the s.. . 393.2
deeper than the deepest s. . 548.4
those in peril on the s. . . 569.*
lands beyond the s. . 832.c, 2
flows from s. to s. . . . 833.1
tales of the s. 848.1
b *earth and sea*
O Lord of Heaven and e. and s. 15.1
beyond the e., beyond the s. . 31.4
let e. and s. and sky . . 187.4
praise . . . in e. and . . . s. . 220.4
in e., or on the s. . . . 556.1
Lord of Heaven and e. and s. . 941.1
c *as/like sea*
love is as deep as the s.. . 47.1
it's as deep as the s. . . 49.c
like the wideness of the s. . 265.3
like the s. billows roll . . 394.c
army, like a mighty s. . . 550.c
sorrows like s.-billows . . 771.1
like the sands of the s. . . 883.2
death, like a narrow s. . . 898.1
over, like a mighty s. . . c140
d *[Galilee]*
the Master of the s. . . 336.1
beside the Syrian s. . . 567.2
the loaves beside the s. . . 650.1
by the silvery s. . . . 680.1
e *Matt 8:26*
Sovereign of the s. . . 598.2
stayed the tossing s. . . 628.3
whom winds and s. obey . . 715.2
how rolled the s. . . . 848.3
footsteps (b) land (2b) river (1b)
walk (1c)
2 *(figurative)*
a *(salvation)*
thou great crimson s. . . 298.2
reachèd this soul-cleansing s. 298.5
s. of boundless salvation . 298.7
wisdom's deepest, clearest s. 452.4
a never-ebbing s. . . . 496.1
I plunge me in this s. . . 746.3
the s. of forgetfulness . . c190
b *(difficulty)*
calm this tossing s. . . . 194.4
he's the Master of the s. . 336.3
life's wild, restless s. . . 428.1
life's tempestuous s. . . 598.1
the world's tempestuous s. . 607.1
wrestlers with the troubled s. 612.3
sail through stormy s. . . 678.2
o'er troubled s. . . . 725.2
a storm-tossed s. of care . 749.2
though the s. be deep . . 772.2
over the s. . . . pilot me . . c141
I sail the wide s. no more . c178
c *(death)*
till I cross the narrow s. . . 585.4
death, like a narrow s. . . 898.1
shrink to cross this . . . s. . 898.2
d *(Rev 4:6)*
around the glassy s. . . 220.2
gathered by the crystal s. . 337.c
over the jasper s. . . . 889.1
e *Mic 7:19*
the s. of forgetfulness . . c190

seashore *Hosea 1:10* . 908.1, c

seal-ed-ing
our sign and s. of victory . 163.4
thy endless mercies s. . . 199.4
bond that s. my vows . . 365.2
did my dedication s. . . 463.2
if love impassioned s. not . 530.1
from Eli's sense was s. . . 839.2
b *Eph 1:13, 4:30**
the s. of my ransom . . 119.c
word, by blood is s. . . 126.3
s. us to that day . . . 195.3
s. of my sin . . . forgiven . 207.3
stamp thyself the s. . . 207.4
s. us heirs of . . . salvation . 210.2
the sure, the certain s. . . 214.4
take and s. it . . . courts. . 313.5
erring, and he s. me . . 330.2
s. thou my breast . . . 424.2
for ever s. my breast . . 450.2
if thy s. is placed on me. . 460.1
let my heart be s. . . . 460.c
s. me ever thine . . . 521.1
s. me just now thy servant . 523.1
without his anointing and s. . 527.2
take . . . my calling s. . . 529.3
the heart that thou hast s. . 531.1
s. us within thy will . . 648.3
love our lives has s. . . 692.1
shall s. and sanctify . . 742.2
the grace that s. us . . 764.1
s. him (her) as your own . 792.3
s. thine image on my heart . 865.3
s. us thine own . . . 870.3
c *seal by Spirit* *Eph 1:13*
now s. me by thy Spirit . . 511.4
since his Spirit s. us . . 755.1
s. by thy Spirit, eternally . c52
Holy Spirit, s. me . . . c68
d *seal [pardon]*
reveal, with pardon s. . . 102.4
s. my pardon with his blood . 118.2
on the cross he s. my pardon. 180.c
peace, the s. of sin forgiven . 210.4
rose for me, my pardon s. . 884.2
e *Matt 27:66*
vain the stone . . . the s. . 143.3
vainly they s. the dead . . 148.2
f *Rev 7:3*
thy s. in my forehead . . 589.3

sealing *(noun)*
thine the s. and revealing . 510.4
s. again is all the s. . . 591.3
place thy hand . . . for my s.. 762.3

seaman
guiding lonely . . . s. . . 63.3
poor . . . s. 478.c, 3

search
1 *(we) search*
I s. his face and find . . 449.2
in vain we s. . . . deeps . . 496.3
2 *(God) searches*
s. the plan designed . . 416.3
b *Ps 139:23; Rom 8:27*
now s. me and try me . . 454.2
s. me and try me, Master . 487.2
c *search heart* *Psalm 139:23*
s., prove my h. . . . 453.1
s. now my h. . . . 457.1
Saviour, s. my h. today . 618.c
s. these h. before thee . 643.2

searcher 658.2

searching *(adjective)*
like s. eyes 27.3
placed within thy s. sight . 414.1
'neath the s. light . . . 434.3
to whose all -s. sight . . 453.1
thy kind but s. eye . . 522.2
thy kind but s. glance . . 558.4

season
no changes of s. or place . 318.3
in s. of distress . . . 633.1
s. and months and weeks . 925.4
the rolling s. 929.1
b *Isa 50:4*
a word in s. as from thee . 612.5
c *Ezek 34:26*
there shall be a s. refreshing . 637.1
d *(1 Peter 1:6)*
humbled for a s. . . . 141.3
for a s. slumber . . . 153.2

seasoned 799.3

seat
in the s. of power enthrone . 147.2
he took his s. above . . 164.2
fix in every heart thy s. . . 216.4
b *(Luke 13:29)*
grant us each a s. . . . 195.4
judgment (c) mercy (2)

seated 93.1

secluded 705.3

second
a s. Adam to the fight . . 18.2
born to give them s. birth . 82.3

secret
s. thoughts have stirred . 36.2
read the s. of your work . 38.1
down thine own s. stair . 91.3
from a s. armoury . . . 176.2
that silent, s. thought . . 517.2
the s. of victory I found . . 553.2
my s. fortress . . . 631.2
the stress of s. fear . . 647.2
where s. rivers rise . . 648.3
s. hopes have perished . . 753.3
I've found the s. of success . 806.1
deep s. of the flower . . 871.2
b *Ps 19:12*
deed and s. thought . . 287.2
c *Ps 25:14*
thy s. to me . . . made known. 372.4
s. of the Lord is theirs . . 411.1
tell me thy s. 519.1
Lord . . . revealing all the s. . 591.1

d *Ps 31:20*
in the s. of thy presence. 591.1, c
e *Ps 44:21*
I have no s. unknown . 294.2
heart's most s. depths . 311.4
my s. heart is taught . 485.4
surveys thy s. thoughts . 665.2
f *Ps 91:1*
dwell within the s. place . 728.1
g *Matt 6:6*
spend much time in s. . 458.2

secure-d
thy saints have dwelt s.. . 13.2
in him I am s. . 45.2
the promise is s. . 279.3
make my desire s. . 416.2
kept by thy grace s. . 431.4
to . . . s. the good part . 469.2
victory is s. . 707.4
happy, in his love s. . 722.1
in his strength s. we are. . 722.3
s. what I've committed . 735.3
one thing s. us . 763.1
safe and s. from all alarms . 768.c
we shall stand firm and s. . 833.3
s. at such a price . 944.2

securely . 954.1

see-ing/saw/seen
1 *(general)*
Eden s. play . 35.3
to s. the . . . sacrifice . 150.3
henceforth may s. some work 524.3
Satan trembles when he s. . 646.3
b *(literal)*
he gave us eyes to s. them . 25.4
I s. the stars, I hear . 37.1
s. the care thou . . . render . 39.1
they s. a host on high . 72.3
still we s. thee lie . 86.1
lookèd up and s. a star . 90.2
shepherds came thither to s. . 137.1
s. his kind look . 794.1
s. the flag . . . blood and fire 822.1
I s. forsaken children/hungry 830.1
kind to all I s. . 844.2
flowers fair . . . for all to s. . 850.2
s. the sights that dazzle . 862.2
away from all we . . . s.. . 874.2
s. each other's face . 915.1
I s. it in the heaven . c121
c *(passive)*
near the cross I would be s. . 138.4
trees shall now be s. . 159.4
Father can be s. in . . . Son 324.1
whitest robes are s. . 429.1
rays of light are s. . 658.3
a stain may yet be s. . c72
beauty of Jesus be s. . c77
d *Acts 7:56*
s. his Master in the sky . 701.2
2 *(God) sees*
could he s. a cross . 103.1
our weakness, pitying, s. . 200.7
s. this waiting host . 203.1
s. us on thy altar lay . 203.4
who is it s. me when I fall . 204.2
he s. thy softened spirit . 256.2
all my future thou canst s. . 285.3
deal . . . as thou s. meet . 291.4
Jesus, s. me at thy feet . 292.1
s. my heart, Lord, torn . 292.2
s. my sorrow . . . tears . 294.1
he s. my deep dismay . 386.2
s. how my soul desireth. . 420.4
thou s. I patiently wait . 436.3
s. me at thy footstool . 440.1
Lord, s. me ready . 501.2
thou s. . . . I willing am . 509.1
always to s. and hear . 742.3
Jesus s. them ere they fled . 797.1
well he s. and knows it . 841.2
looks . . . to s. us shine. . 841.2
b *love sees*
love that could s. . 319.1
love that s. and pities me . 456.4
thy ceaseless love s. all . 715.5
3 *(people) see*
hope can s. fulfilled . 39.4
above me mystery I s. . 52.1
seal of my ransom . . . I s. . 119.c
we s. thy Kingdom come . 154.4
more of their beauty s. . 258.1
for my cleansing this I s. . 306.2
I can s. a pathway . 320.3
things in the Bible I s. . 323.1
I s. the blue above it . 358.3
I s. the cleansing flow . 366.c
I first s. the light . 395.*
when death's flood I s. . 401.3
myself I want to s. . 409.1
here a deeper truth I s. . 434.3
crushing defeats I have s. . 437.1
blood for my cleansing I s. . 454.4
what prospects now I s. . 460.1
world's great need I s. . 482.1
I do not fear to s. . 485.1
worth which . . . we s. . 515.2
help me s. my mission . 528.4
I s. the treasure . 541.2
s. the tempter fly . 596.3
every sight I s. . 600.2
thy way at last I s.. . 605.3
I do not ask to s. . 606.1
I loved to s. . . . path . 606.2
with eyes that s. anew . 618.3
thy over-ruling plan I s. . 644.c
touch my eyes and make me s. 650.3
more of Heaven . . . we s. . 668.3
decay in all around I s. . 670.2
heroes of faith . . . we shall s. 684.4
need of the lost I can s.. . 708.4
rivers of pleasure I s. . 710.1
whatever lot I s. . 725.3
s. . . . shining lights of home. 740.3
vaster than the world has s. . 776.3
all may plainly s. . 777.4
what troubles we have s. . 915.2
s. what fruit we bear . 926.4
fruits of holiness we s. . 936.3
men drew near to s. . 939.2
open mine eyes to s. victory . c.81
ready, my God, thy will to s.. c99
waiting new visions to s. . c103
here we s. the golden glow . c153
b *see [God]*
we s. thee now appear . 36.3
I s. thy footprints . 59.1
veiled . . . the Godhead s. . 82.2
his cross and sorrow s. . 94.3
my soul looks back to s. . 120.4
s. but did not feel, thee die . 135.2
bid the nations s. . 155.4
shall the true Messiah s. . 161.2
s. him in the watch-fires . 162.2
I now have s. his greatness . 215.2
have you s. the . . . beauty . 242.4
s. the crucified . . . brow . 243.1
I s. his hand of mercy . 334.1
I s. his loving care . 334.2
I s. all I need . 344.1
mighty wonders there I s. . 348.c
I s. thee now, desire thee . 449.2
where'er thy steps I s. . 453.3
let me s. thy . . . hand . 463.2
when I s. . . . brightness . 470.1
s. the very dying form . 476.2
thy loveliness to s. . 547.4
to tell as I have s. . 591.3
glad when . . . smile we s. . 602.3
shall I s. thy footprints . 628.1
we long to s. your face . 748.1
we shall s. you, soon . 748.1
promises I now can s. . 757.5
summoned . . . wrath to s. . 875.3
the whole world might s. . c89
c *see [Lord]*
on the cross my L. I s. . 326.2
s. my L. they vanished . 399.1
when first I s. the L. . 442.2
his Saviour s. . 580.2
in thy book . . . s. the L. . 650.3
d *see goodness* *Ps 27:13*
his g. I have s. . 495.2
thy g., Lord, we s. . 926.1
e *Ps 36:9; Zech 13:1*
rejoiced to s. that fountain . 132.2
now we s. thy light . 185.3
now a living fountain s. . 261.3
shall s. my light upon him . 277.4
let me s. the light . 374.1
saints can s. the fountain . 429.1
in thy light I s. the fountain . 429.c
give us light thy truth to s. . 466.1
thy Kingdom of light may s. . c236
f *see [love]*
new mercies I s. . 33.c
love . . . than ever I s. . 99.3
love . . . in the redeemer we s. 383.2
mercy's beams I s. . 412.3
let me s. thy love . 503.2
s. in Jesus all the grace . 856.4
love, redeeming love, I s. . c29
his love and grace I've s. . c173
g *see [salvation]* *Luke 3:6**
our redemption s. . 154.3
mine eyes have s. the glory . 162.1
thou shalt my s. s. . 275.3
deliverance I s. . 298.3
let us s. thy great s. . 438.3
thy perfect s. to s. . 469.1
his s. we shall s. . 822.3
more may thy s. s. . 919.1
h *John 1:50*
s. even greater things . 769.1, 3
i *Matt 5:16*
day when men shall s. . 135.4
his likeness shall s. . 458.2
s. Christ . . . in me 479.1, 3
till all shall s. Christ . 487.4
men may s. the works I do . 518.3
world shall always s. Christ . 793.6
that men may s. thyself . c72
beauty of Jesus be s. in me . c77
j *faith sees* *Heb 11:1*
by f. I s. the stream . 132.4
by f. they s. and know . 359.4
f. . . . can Jehovah s. . 733.3
only f. . . . can s. the realms . 766.2
mighty f., the promise s. . c118
k *see [that]*
help us to s. 'tis only . 8.4
until, by faith, they s. . 359.4
my Lord, I could s. . . . died . 395.3
where I rejoiced to s. . 403.1
my heart, I seem to s. . 415.3
believe, and thou shalt s. . 718.4
give us eyes to s. . 756.2
l *not/cannot see*
far future I c. s. . 294.3
when Jesus no longer I s. . 318.1
I could n. s., but Jesus . 449.1
before I never could s. . 459.3
I s. no joy that turns . 489.2
where I c. s. I'll trust . 489.4
no other light . . . could s. . 490.1
Christless eyes . . . never s. . 545.2
no fairer charm I s. . 565.1
way before I c. s. . 717.1
the days I c. s. . 732.c
which yet I have n. s. . 736.3
nor clearly s. the path . 748.2

when we c. s. our way . . 772.1
though we s. no ray . . 772.3

m 1 Peter 1:8
what if thy form we c. s. . 558.2
though I c. s. him . . 840.3
we could n. s. thy form . 938.3

n Ex 33:20
thy glory may not s. . . 220.3

as (b), blind (b), face (2d, f), faith (3b), glory (4i), help (1l)

4
a *(exclamation)*
s., amid the winter's snow . 88.1
s. the Lamb of God appears . 88.1
s., the . . . wise men bring . 89.2
O sinner, s., for you . . 108.2
s., from his head . . 136.3
s., the streams of . . . waters. 157.2
s. how great a flame . 165.1
s. the Saviour stands . 260.c, 2
s.! helpless I cling . . . 454.2
s., the Father meets him . 550.1
s., the foe is nigh . . . 698.1

b *(imperative)*
draw near and s. . . . die . 107.1
s. him lifted up . . . 107.3
s. the man of sorrows now . 147.1
cry to Zion: S. thy God . . 159.2
s. ye not the cloud arise . 165.4
sinner, s. yon light . . . 260.1
s. the cause in Jesus' face . 286.3
s. what God hath done . . 396.c
s. the cleansing current . . 540.2
s. his banners go . . . 690.1
s. the foe before us falling . 693.3
s. the brazen hosts of Hell . 696.2
s. the millions who're drifting 703.1
s. the signal/host/banner . 804.*
s. the judge, . . . wearing . 875.2
s. the Kingdom I bestow . 875.4
s. him honoured . . . 894.1

taste (b)

5 *see in Heaven*
a *(see Jesus)*
rapture, when Jesus we s. . 22.3
when I s. thee as thou art . 58.4
eyes at last shall s. him . . 87.5
may we in glory s. . . . 219.4
we're going to s. . . . Lamb . 275.2
s. thee on thy . . . throne . 302.4
serve . . . till thee I s. . . 571.4
s. him and hear him above . 794.2
I shall s. Jesus . . . joy . . 881.2
when we all s. Jesus . . 892.c
Jesus, and . . . friends, we'll s. 912.3

b *(see Heaven)*
s. the courts of God . . 59.4
the soldiers of Jesus shall s. . 289.3
s. the Canaan that we love . 898.3
the city we shall s. . . . 901.2
s. the living fountains . . 902.4
Kingdom soon shall s. . . 932.4

c *(other)*
I shall s. the bliss . . . 372.4
when death's flood I s. . . 401.3
s. the saints above . . 879.1
friends I shall s. . . . 881.2
end of my journey I s. . . 886.4
wait till I s. the morning . . 889.3
ransomed in Glory we s. . 908.1
the ransomed host we s. . 908.c
s. all the saved of the ages . 908.2

d Matt 5:8
shall s the face of God . . 95.2
for they shall s. our God. . 411.1

face (2e, f), King (2b), stand (1b)

seeing *(adjective)*
sight of the all-s. eyes . . 459.1
God's all-s. eye surveys . . 665.2

seed
1 *(natural)*
there fell the tiny s. . . 923.1
after the s. is sown . . 923.2
scattered s. has grown . . 926.2
quickened into life the s. . 926.2
scatter the good s. . . 935.1
the s. time and the harvest . 935.3

2 *(figurative)* see sow

seek-ing/sought
1 *(God) seeks*
yet in love he s. me . . 53.3
s. thee wandering . . . 110.2
by thee . . . poor were s. . 174.2
the earth first you s. . . 175.2
Jesus s. me . . . stranger . 313.3
poor heart he s. and won . 335.1
in the wilderness he s. us . 377.2
wandering and weary he s. us 384.2
the Saviour s. and found 386.1, c
he came a-s., he pitied . . 388.2
O Joy that s. me . . . 621.3
love for help is s. . . . 921.3
Jesus s. me in tenderness . c171
O the love that s. me . . c218

b Matt 18:12, 13
Saviour came s. his sheep . 388.1
loving me, s. me, finding . 388.c
as thou hast s. . . . 612.1
s. us when we go astray . 845.2

c Luke 19:10
came to s. and to save . . 527.1

2 *(we) seek [spiritual]*
as we s. for vaster truth. . 27.4
s. until we know . . . 36.5
ever s. the mercy seat . . 76.2
to s. for a King . . . 90.3
when wise men came s. . . 92.1
thou art not far to s. . . 198.2
s. . . . beautiful stream . . 252.c
s. that consecrated spot . 261.2
who s. in faith . . . 277.3
s. from my sin to part . . 348.1
light . . . long I had s. . . 394.1
Lord, we thy presence s. . 411.4
while I s. for favour . . 420.3
here to s. thy healing . . 434.2
presence we have coldly s. . 466.3
before thy cross I'm s. . . 502.1
now at thy cross I s. . . 502.c
thus I s. the path . . . 534.1
one wish alone . . . I s. . . 536.3
s. the healing of thy cross . 590.4
life that only s. thy ways . 618.2
'tis all I wish to s. . . . 636.4
received more than we s. . 642.1
nor s. . . . to understand . 644.2
let us s. the heavenly balm . 663.3
s. the things before us . . 682.1
s. a shelter from . . . alarm . 740.1
s. the comfort of . . . hand . 740.2
s. to mirror thy glory . . 786.2
s. the narrow way . . . 836.2
I s. my place in Heaven . . 880.1
here s. the truth . . . 942.3

b *seek [God]* Isa 55:6*
who would the Father s. . 100.1
none who s. him Christ ignores 270.2
hope of all who s. him . . 334.3
those who have s. thee . . 436.3
we are come to s. the Father. 595.1
I s. thee, Lord . . . 650.1
lift . . . hearts to s. thee. . 669.4
earnestly s. him below . . 794.2
we're all s. the same . . c112

c *seek blessing*
s. today the Father's b. . . 433.3
forgetting . . . his b. to s. . 458.1
I s. the b. from the Lord. . 461.3
as I s. for that b. divine . . 493.2

d *seek joy*
s. the j. at his . . . hand. . 223.2
are you s. j. . . . 227.1
s. for j. but only sorrow . 257.3
the j., I s. so long . . 547.1

e *seek salvation*
all who will s. his s. . . 329.3
s. just now a full s. . . 433.1
in s. for God's full s. . . 553.2
s. salvation while you may . 885.1
turn to the Lord and s. s. . c27

f *seek [strength]*
we s. thy courage . . . 181.2
s. power to send us faster . 197.1
power is found . . . who s. it. 324.4
humbly I s. . . . the grace . 501.3
I s. for love and s. . . 541.1
Lord, we s. thy s. . . 576.3
s. the Spirit's . . . grace. . 791.3

g *seek/find* Matt 7:7, 8
how good to those who s. . 61.3
all who s. shall surely f. . . 249.1
those who s. . . . sure to f. . 270.2
power is f. by those who s. . 324.4
the hope of all who s. him . 334.3
him it s., and f., . . . blest . 420.1
to them that s. thee . . . good 602.2
where'er they s. thee . . 604.1
everyone who s. may pluck . 658.1
s.! and you're sure to f. . . c5
I have s. . . . f. my hiding-place c164

h Jer 29:13
s. with all their heart . . 806.3

all (3a), early (b), face (2g), own (3c)

3 *(we) seek*
a *(wrong seeking)*
s. in human wisdom . . 6.2
pleasures s., dearly bought . 379.1
vainly I s. a cure . . . 456.2
all I've s. or hoped . . . 498.2
while place we s. . . . 556.3
thoughts that s. forbidden . 630.2
s. a lighter cross . . . 780.1
s. not worldly ease . . 816.3

b *(seek others)* Luke 19:10
earnestly s. to save . . 484.1
some wanderer s. and won . 524.3
constrain to s. . . . souls . 526.1
so let me s. . . . children . 612.1
s. the wandering sinner . 623.2

lost (2b)

4 *(other)*
birds . . . s. their nest . . 675.3

b (1 Peter 5:8)
doth s. to work us woe . . 1.1
s. my soul to claim . . 724.3
powers of evil long have s. . 760.3

seeker 249.3

seeking
1 *(noun)*
life is a s. 351.2
evil, self-s. and pride . . 443.1

2 *(adjective)* Lam 3:25
no s. soul should be denied . 303.3
to s. ones made known . . 539.1
never a s. soul . . . nay . . c87

seem-ed
wrong s. oft so strong . . 42.3
light rays s. to say . . . 103.2
foe s. fierce and strong . . 169.3
evil forces s. . . . the sway . 171.1
s. now some soul to say . 226.1
when all else s. dreary . . 316.1
all the way s. gloomy . . 316.c
it s. I want to love/serve . 369.2
does the cross s. heavy . . 396.2
a weary journey s. . . 400.1

my heart, I s. to see . . 415.3
in thy light s. poor . . . 435.2
way may s. rough . . . 523.4
scarce s. beautiful again . 551.1
cross will then s. light . . 551.3
life s. as brief as blest . . 551.3
time . . . s. all no more . . 573.4
defeat s. strangely near . . 713.3
tasks of life s. hard . . 744.1
darkness s. to veil . . . 745.2
your path s. hid . . . 759.2
a passage s. denied . . 772.2
nothing s. hopeful . . . 773.1
work s. hard and dry . . 837.5
often toil s. dreary . . . 934.3
good s. turned to ill . . 947.3
b *Matt 11:26*
what s. thee good . 422.c/589.c
as best may s. to thee . . 917.2

seeming *(adjective)* . . . 719.3

seemly 3.3

seize-d
mighty dread had s. . . . 93.2
despair or doubt would s. us . 722.1
that death can s. upon . . 774.3
crown . . . we shall s. . . 808.5
kingdom of Satan we'll s. . 820.4

seldom 832.1

self
1 *(re divinity)*
thy blissful s. impart . . 210.1
draw me to thy dear s. . . 726.2
b *1 Peter 2:24*
his own s. he gave me . . 345.2
same (1b)
2 *(re people)*
thine are all, and s. is loss . 181.3
s. now crucify 188.2
perish s. in thy pure fire . 194.2
s. and shame unheeding . 242.3
your better s. deplores . . 244.1
chains of s.-indulgence . 257.3
s.-sufficient but sad . . 376.1
s. only may remain . . 416.2
feet ran in s.-chosen ways . 422.2
s.-mending; s.-salvation . 430.1
from s. I am not free . . 434.3
a life of s.-renouncing love . 485.4
all of s. and . . . . . 548.*
a s.-renouncing will . . 596.2
to die to s. each day . . 619.3
let not s. hold any part . . 643.3
s. nor earth . . . shall sever . 693.2
fight that s. may die . . 705.3
s.-consuming care . . . 715.4
the murmurs of s.-will . . 862.3
dead to s., we truly live . . 922.3
b *1 John 1:8*
I, s.-deceiving, felt stronger . 553.2
c *self and [sin]*
from sin and s. and shame . 447.3
destroy . . . sin, the s. . . 448.4
all s. and sin deliver . . 452.2
my sinful s. my only shame . 476.3
freedom from s. . . . sin . 541.2
of s. and sin swept bare . 615.3
in spite of s. and sin . . 749.2
d *deny self* *Matt 16:24*
with him and s.-denial . . 495.3
give me a s.-denying soul . 619.2
ours a life of s.-denial . . 787.4
join with us in s.-denial . . 920.c
Christ of s.-denial . . . 921.1
this, our time of s.-denial . 922.1
pride (b)

selfish
burn out every s. thought . 205.2
burn my every s. claim . . 415.4
all s. aims I flee . . . 461.c
sever from s. ambition . . 501.1
s. aims do we forsake . . 532.1
our wanton s. gladness . . 577.3
broken my s. pride . . 605.1
s. ends . . . claim no right . 702.1

selfishness
divided by s. and guile . . 6.3
greed and s. are free . . 833.1

semblance 200.2

send-ing-t
1 *(God) sends*
daily s. forth new life . . 63.1
s. this fire on me . . . 197.3
s. the fire . . . . . 203.*
s. a pentecostal rain . . 205.2
living water, Jesus, s. . . 282.3
hallelujah, s. the glory . . 355.c
s. a great salvation flood . 452.2
he s. more strength . . 579.1
s. thy grace 582.5
s. a great salvation flood . 593.4
all that thou s. me . . . 617.3
s. them upon us, O Lord . 637.3
s. the power, s. it . . . 643.c
s. forth thy . . . breath . 669.5
all-discerning love, hath s. . 738.2
when God s. his reapers . 928.2
he s. the snow in winter . 935.1
s. a new touch . . . s. it now. c97
b *send [from above]*
it was s. from Heaven a. . 327.1
s. thy Spirit from a. . . 445.4
s. a revival from a. . . 609.1
s. from the Saviour a. . 637.1
baby . . . s. from Heaven a. 935.c
All . . . are s. from Heaven a. 935.c
c *send blessings*
his b. he will s. . . . 920.4
needful b. in abundance s. . 921.2
Lord, s. to others some b. . c59
d *send [me]* *Isa 6:8*
power to s. us faster . . 197.1
s. by my Lord . . . I call . 234.2
where he s. we will go . . 397.5
s. me singing on my way . 401.1
O s. me to the rescue . . 482.1
here . . . Lord, s. me . 482.1, c
s. me where I ought to go . 531.3
s. us in the field to fight. . 593.2
s. us where we ought to go . 622.2
s. us forth . . . to show . . 760.4
s. us, Lord, into the fray . 789.2
s. me . . . where thou wilt s.. 865.2
he'll s. you rejoicing . . c31
e *John 3:17*
s. him to die 37.3
f *1 Peter 1:12*
God s. down from Heaven . 195.*
s. down to make us meet . 195.4
Holy Ghost s. down . . 216.1
the gift of God, s. free . . 240.4
God has s. his glorious light . 408.1
s. thy Spirit from above . 445.4
s. down thy likeness . . 516.4
O s. thy Spirit, Lord . . 650.3
s. to plead the . . . merit . 783.3
light (4f)
2 *(we) send*
s. the blessèd tidings . . 279.1, c
I'll s. the ringing cry . . 356.4
s. a gleam across the wave . 478.c
we'll s. the call for mercy . 802.3
we'll s. the cry along . . 814.1

3 *(other)*
hope that s. a shining ray . 519.4
hurts that hate can s. . . 544.4

sense
we s. a power divine . . 27.1
linking s. to sound . . . 28.3
judge not . . . by feeble s. . 29.4
a s. of his love . . . 318.3
lost the s. of mission . . 463.2
s. of sorrow over sin . . 496.4
wish and s. keeping . . . clean 540.3
let s. be dumb . . . 567.5
time and s. seem . . . no more 573.4
not only when I s. thee . . 717.3
from Eli's s. was sealed . . 839.2
quickened s. and . . . joy . 878.3
shame and s. of sin . . c157

sensibility 425.1

sensibly 207.4

sensitive 209.3

sent see send

sentence *(2 Cor 1:9)*
justice now revokes the s. . 75.4
I have read his righteous s. . 162.2
work out God's s. upon us . 928.1

sentenced *(Luke 23:24)* . . 137.3

separate-d
for ever s. from God . . 885.2
b *Rom 8:35, 39*
who shall dare to s. us . . 554.1
shall have power to s. us . 554.4
c *2 Cor 6:17*
s. from sin, . . . choose . . 212.5
from evil s. 495.1

sepulchre 353.4

sequence 30.3

seraph-ic-im
sweetest note in s. song . 67.c
thus spake the s. . . . 93.5
swell with pure s. joy . . 164.5
cherubim and s. . . . 220.2

serene
calm and s. my frame . . 442.6
if on life s. and fair . . 916.2

servant
1 *(divine)* *Isa 42:1*
who wast a s. 174.3
the suffering s. he became . 451.2
servant of my s.-Lord . . 451.4
2 *(human)*
ye s. of God . . . proclaim . 24.1
from . . . sting thy s. free . 151.5
take his s. up 164.6
reside in all his s. here . . 195.1
thy loyal s. I 290.3
God gives his willing s. . . 324.4
thy s. to possess the land . 419.4
s. of my servant-Lord . . 451.4
thy s., Lord, prepare . . 472.3
see me ready thy s. to be . 501.2
thy ransomed s., I restore . 505.2
seal me just now thy s. . . 523.1
grant that thy s. may be. . 527.3
to hide . . . thy s.'s eyes . 676.1
thy devoted s. make me . 865.1
the vale . . . his s. tread . 874.3
for ever thy s. to be . . c49
thy s. I'll be c103
b *1 Sam 3:9*
speak: thy s. heareth . . 614.1
c *Matt 8:8*
thy s. shall be healèd . . 456.1

d *Matt 10:25*
the s. as his Lord shall be . 407.5
should not the s. . . . still . 683.1

e *Matt 25:21*
s. of God, well done . . 890.1

f *John 12:26*
there shall thy s. be . . 862.4

g *Rom 6:18*
no more the s. of sin to be . c157

serve-d-ing
1 *(we) serve*
to s. your holy will . . 38.2
saved, to s. him eternally . 114.2
sin of not s. thee . . . 296.2
I'll s. him every day . . 326.1
I want to s. him more . . 369.2
as I s. him here . . . 373.4
s. him with my might . . 400.c
s. thee as thy hosts above . 438.2
there . . . to stand and s. . 461.4
to s. thee I am ready . . 482.3
how can I better s. thee. . 488.1
that I may s. thee worthily . 488.3
s. thee with . . . compassion . 493.3
every hour I'll s. thee . . 499.1
they s. you best who s.. . 518.2
s. with weak . . . hands. . 534.2
freedom to s. I crave . . 571.4
know thee, then to s. thee . 591.3
we will s. thee day and night. 593.2
to s. him joyfully . . . 706.c
praying, fighting, s. . . 788.2
as to s. him you aspire . . 790.3
s. thee all my happy days . 793.6
s. him with our might . . 819.2
s. him moment by moment . 844.4
s. beneath his banner . . 853.2
all who s. you well . . 856.1
s. thee all my days . . 861.1
s. thee to the end . 862.1, 4
proud to s. their leader . . 866.1
all . . . s. his will . . . 867.5
forged through s. him . . 874.1
trusting, s. every day . . 892.3
our lives to s. . . . 925.5
we'll trust and s. thee more . 926.3
labour we bring to s. thee . 927.2
inspire our hearts to s. thee . 944.2
teach me how to s. thee . c105

b *(with title)*
I s. a risen Saviour . . . 334.1
I'm s. such a mighty . . . King 402.c
live or die to s. my God . . 505.2
s. Christ my one desire . . 522.3
use my Master to s. . . 640.3
s. my God when I awake . 671.4
who will s. the King . . 707.1
the God I s. is one . . 732.1
s. God quite as well . . 780.3
who s. my Father as a son . 826.3
joy is found in s. Jesus . 857.1, c

c *Ps 100:2*
him s. with mirth . . . 3.1

d *Matt 4:10*
to s. my God alone . . 505.2
to s. but thee . . . 571.4
thee will we s. . . . alone . 747.3

e *Acts 13:36*
to s. the present age . . 472.2

f *Gal 5:13*
let me love him, s. him . . 94.3
s. thee out of love . . 205.3
s. and love thee best of all . 428.5
fear and love and s. aright . 466.5
let me love thee . . . s. thee . 591.c
ever s., ever free, loving . 846.4
loved and s. the Lord below . 875.4

g *serve [in Heaven]* *Rev 7:15*
see thy face and s. thee . 466.5
they s. thee still . . . 878.3

s. their Master day and night . 909.2

h *not serve*
sin of not s. thee . . . 296.2
we have not s. thee . . 466.4

below (b), best (2c), fear (3h), man (2i), singleness

2 *(other)*
may s. me while on earth . 932.3

service
his s. your delight . . . 21.5
lead us in s. 181.1
life in my s. be spending . 276.4
ever ready for s. I am . . 321.4
faithful, loving s., too . . 336.2
pleasure in his s. . . . 399.*
ready for s. whene'er . . 443.2
mine is the s. of pleasure . 457.3
s. which thy love appoints . 485.4
claim me for thy s. . . 492.1
your s. is song . . . 506.2
sworn in glad s. . . . 506.5
to be used in joyful s. . . 514.3
fill me . . . for s., Lord . . 521.1
forbid me not thy s. . . 522.1
s. with our Lord to take . . 532.1
called to thy s. . . . 543.2
in purer lives thy s. find . . 567.1
so that with willing s. . . 574.3
consecrate . . . to thy s. . 585.2
springs of sacred s. . . 591.1
for wholehearted s. prepare . 679.2
in my s. fight and die . . 694.4
perfect s. giving . . . 788.3
his s. is the golden cord . 826.2
in s. bold 861.3
to thy s. set apart . . . 865.3
the splendour of his s. . . 868.1
in the Army there is s. . . 869.2
equip for joyful s. . . . 870.3
lives be cleansed for s. . . 943.4
be to thy s. devoted . . c52
my s. blessing . . . c84
love expressed in s. . . c208
his s. calling us . . . c239

b *service [free]*
for s. sets me free . . . 178.1
lowly paths of s. free . . 519.1
freedom in s. I would find . 744.3
thy loyal s. makes me free . 867.6

c *Eph 6:7*
would you do s. for Jesus . 281.4

cord (a), fit (b)

set-ting
you, who s. the ordinance . 27.5
sought thee . . . s. thee right. 110.2
s. the kingdoms on a blaze . 165.1
arise, and never s. . . . 172.6
it s. my spirit . . . aflame. . 360.c
s. thou my zeal aflame . . 574.3
let every heart . . . be s.. . 608.2
s. us all on fire . . . 609.2
our mind be s. to hallow . 668.2

b *set forth*
I now s. f. thy praise . . 290.3
worthily s. f. his praise . . 533.1
s. f. within the sacred word . 656.1

c *[sun] set*
he s. in blood no more . . 143.2
s. shall rise and s. no more . 160.1
know we that the s. must s. 874.2
dawn till s. s. . . . 907.3

d *Mark 1:32*
at even, ere the sun was s. . 558.1

e *Acts 4:11*
those who s. at naught . . 161.2

f *(Luke 9:51)*
I'm going to s. my face . . 858.2

apart (b), feet (1c), free (1d-f), heart (4e), liberty (b), right (4d)

2 *(noun)*
a special s. of laws . . 244.3

settled 478.2

sevenfold *(Rev 4:5)*
his s. graces shower . . 15.4
quench thy s. light . . 202.4

sever-ed
s. now in Heaven . . . dwell . 146.2
races long s. . . . unite . . 166.2
he died from sin to s. . . 413.1
'tis the blood . . . can s.. . 434.5
longing to s. 501.1
from all that's wrong to s. . 502.c

b *(Rom 8:38, 39)*
ties which naught can s. . 345.1
what power my soul can s. . 345.4
no power of evil can s. . . 349.1
our union none can s. . . 495.2
who the child of God shall s. 555.1
nor earth . . . shall s. . . 693.2
no power . . . heart can s. . 854.3
no sin can s. a fellowship . 888.3
death will never s. . . . 891.4

severe 820.3

shackled 303.1

shade-ing-shadow
the fearful s. of loss . . 145.2
the gathering s. bid thee . 250.5
s. my pathway for years. . 288.1
sunshine or s. . . . 294.3
when the s. gathered o'er me. 330.1
not a s.-cloud . . . obscuring . 369.1
s. dispelling, with joy . . 371.1
out of the s. of sorrow . . 378.1
not a s. can rise . . . 397.2
no fearful s. shall wear . . 465.4
earth's deepening s. descend. 595.3
s. of the evening steal . . 673.1
where the s. deepest lie. . 697.4
s. on the earthly pathway . 711.2
comfort where the s. are . 711.2
beneath thy s. enrolled . . 774.2
s. of the life-giving tree . . 908.3
opening light and evening s. . 925.4
sowing in the s. . . . 930.2
s. deep have crossed . . 938.3

b *shadows fall*
when s. f. with evening . 31.3
dark s. were f. . . . 237.1
softly the s. f. . . . 675.1
evening while s. f. . . 675.c
when s. f. and dark . . 719.4
the s. of life are f. . . 753.4
valley, where the s. f. . . c116

c *shadow of cross*
walk . . . with its s. o'er me . 115.3
in the s. of the cross . . 145.1
beneath the s. of the cross . 427.c
I take, O cross, thy s. . . 476.3
tarry in the s. of the cross . 493.c
the cross, and its s. come . 916.3

d *shades of night*
clothed in s. of night . . 107.2
from s. of night to plains . 339.c
triumph o'er the s. of n.. . 412.1

e *Ps 17:8*
under the s. of thy throne . 13.2
with the s. of thy wing . . 737.2

f *Ps 23:4*
death s. us and ours . . 752.6
'tis the s. of the valley . . 903.3

g *Ps 121:5*
thy changeless s. . . . 767.3

h *Song 2:17*
when . . . s. flee . . 632.1, 4

earth's vain s. flee . . . 670.5
where no s. intervene . . 878.2
dark s. flee away . . . 888.1
not a s., not a sigh. . . 892.2
i *Isa 32:2*
a cool s. rock . . . 288.4
the s. of a mighty rock . . 476.1
in the s. of the rock . . 614.2
cleft of the rock that s. . . 710.c
j *Jas 1:17*
there is no s. of turning . . 33.1

shake-n-ing/shook
s. off thy guilty fears . . 106.1
s. the trembling gates . . 165.2
s. off dull sloth . . . 665.1
s. the slumber . . . eyes. . 696.1
s. the vast creation . . 875.1
b *Luke 6:48*
what can s. thy sure repose . 157.1
can s. my inmost calm . . 358.2
no tempest can my courage s. 489.4
all Hell . . . endeavour to s. . 653.5
c *Matt 24:29*
the powers of nature, s. . 875.3

sham 446.2

shame
1 *(divine)*
bearing s. and scoffing . . 118.2
thy s. and grief he bore . . 126.c
thy grief and s. . . . 140.3
though s. and death to him . 168.6
bore for me in grief and s. . 451.2
b *shame/cross* *Heb 12:2*
die for me on a c. of s. . 114.1
his c. of s. . . . our hope . 121.4
emblem of suffering and s. . 124.1
s. and reproach gladly bear . 124.3
the c., with all its s. . . 168.4
his c. s. speaks our s. . . 245.c
to bear the c. and s. . . 284.5
love thee for that c. of s. . 515.2
no c. . . . I fear no s. . . 526.2
first the c. . . . bearing s. . 777.3
glory for the c. and s. . 894.2
2 *(human)*
I fall in s. upon my knees . 122.1
laid . . . on one bowed in s. . 129.3
with our s. we shunned . . 135.3
by many deeds of s. . . 172.5
my prodigal wanderings and s. 288.3
s. on us, Christian people . 299.1
s., thrice s. upon us . . 299.1
came in my darkness and s. . 395.1
lifted me from s. . . . 403.2
the s. . . . that I hate . . 422.3
sinful self my only s. . . 476.3
wounds that s. would hide . 558.4
blush, be this my s. . . 592.2
burden of s. he must bear . 708.2
fear not s. or loss . . . 866.3
b *sin and shame*
when all was s. and s. . . 18.2
when I came . . . my s. and s. 52.2
bearer of our s. and s. . . 109.1
heavy load of s. and s. . . 127.4
s.'s darkness and s. . . 319.3
the depths of s. and s. . . 339.1
my s. and curse and s. . . 360.2
from s. and self and s. set free 447.3
s. my s. has brought . . 503.2
lips from s., . . . from s. . 674.2
s. is rampant, fear and s. . 789.4
paths of s. and s. . . 790.2
the haunts of s. and s. . . 832.1
free from the s. . . . sense of s. c157
c *sorrow and shame*
s., self and s. unheeding . 242.3
with s. and s. we open . . 299.3
lifted me up from s. and s. . 349.2
s., fear and s. . . . no more . 540.5
O the bitter s. and s. . . 548.1
d *Rom 9:33**
nor . . . put my soul to s. . 735.2
guilt (c)
3 *(verb)* *(Luke 19:40)*
s. our wanton . . . gladness . 577.3
stones cry s. 724.2
stones, our silence s. . . 853.3

shameful
such s. punishment . . 108.1
out of my s. failure . . 300.2

shape-ing
surely thou art s. all things . 6.2
Lord . . . s. and renewing . 38.5
s. a plan divine . . . 605.2

shapeless 36.1

share-d-ing
1 *(God) shares*
he s. in our gladness . . 87.4
thoughts and hopes thou s. . 97.4
came to s. our human life . 181.1
knows . . . your burden s. . 238.c
s. with men their heavy load . 398.3
not only s., but bear . . 421.3
for ever s. . . . whole . . 496.1
will all our sorrows s. . . 645.2
dost all our burdens s. . . 827.4
b
where Jesus knelt to s. . . 567.3
2 *(we) share with God*
glory for ever I'll s.. . . 124.3
s. their leader's victory . . 149.2
when I die be thou my s. . 477.4
it is joy to s. thy sorrow. . 502.2
Lord, let me s. that grace . 512.3
s. in the new communion . 595.3
may I thy consolation s. . 633.3
one day to be s. . . . 682.3
hearts to s. . . . the weeping. 704.3
till . . . thy nature they s. . 708.3
who the Father's kindness s.. 722.3
that I should s. his sanctuary. 728.2
love it claims to s. . . . 742.1
ask for a s. in his love . . 794.2
will you not s. it too . . 851.5
glory of his resurrection s. . 907.2
b *share [cross]*
thy cup of grief to s. . . 117.4
thy suffering bids me s.. . 138.3
in my Master's suffering s. . 197.3
in his cross-bearing . . . s. . 406.4
cross we gladly learn to s. . 818.2
to s. thy cross . . . choice . c108
privilege here his cross to s. . c172
c *share joy*
in love I s. the j. . . . 375.3
thy j., thy glory s. . . 612.7
your love and j. to s. . . 943.1
3 (we) share *with others*
often s. their gladness . . 50.3
the prophets' blessings s. . 95.3
s. in the gladness of all . . 372.4
not a sorrow we s.. . . 397.3
other souls . . . may s. . . 512.1
s. that wondrous heritage . 613.3
bread . . . I long to s. . . 631.4
one plea to s. 648.1
we s. our mutual woes . . 660.3
the other's burden s. . . 663.3
hasten their burdens to s. . 679.2
hearts to s. the . . . fight . 704.c
s. my neighbour's hardship . 706.2
teach us faithfully to s. . . 796.2
with us the work to s. . . 825.4
all beauty we must s. . . 851.3
s. the virtue of the wise. . 871.3
that fuller life to s. . . . 880.4
we did life's troubles s. . . 899.1
wisdom . . . teaches us to s.. 927.3
work . . . we gladly s. . . 941.3
whate'er in life . . . their s. . 947.4
I want to s. it c170

Sharon *Song 2:1*
my Christ is S.'s rose . . 346.3
sweet rose of S. . . . c54

sharp-er
though s. the sting . . 267.1
thorns . . . are not s. . . 758.2
keep your weapons s. . . 809.2

shatter 605.2

she
s. only touched . . . . . 304.*
as (s.) grows in knowledge . 792.3
(s.) will choose them . . 795.2
as (s.) learns earth's joys. . 795.3
may (s.) early choose to heed. 796.3
full stature (s.) is grown. . 796.4

sheaves
full s. of ripened grain . . 923.1
golden s. of harvest . . 929.3
b *Ps 126.6*
bringing in the s. . . 930.1, c
return with golden s. . . 936.4

shed
1 *(noun)*
a lowly cattle s. . . . 87.1
2 *(verb)*
star s. its beams around. . 115.2
balm of peace . . . to s.. . 200.2
s. not its glorious ray . . 224.1
glory he s. on our way . . 397.1
s. the oil of gladness . . 573.2
s. thou thy freshening dew . 669.2
b *shed blood* *John 19:34*
he s. his precious b. . . 107.1
precious b. . . . s. . . 116.4
on the cross he s. his b.. . 125.c
there he s. . . . b. . . 128.*
on the cross he s. his b.. . 132.c
for Jesus s. his . . . b. . . 231.2
since his b. for thee was s. . 249.4
thy Saviour's b. was s. . . 253.2
on him then who s. it . . 271.3
but that thy b. was s. for me. 293.1
thy b. s. so freely . . . 469.2
thou hast s. thy b. for me . 498.c
by the b. which thou didst s.. 534.c
b. . . . was s. to cleanse. . 590.2
hath s. his own b. . . . 771.2
for you did s. his b. . . 805.3
by the b. my Saviour s. . . c150
c *shed light*
who . . . s. his light . . 19.4
see my light upon him s. . 277.4
Christ his l. on you will s. . 408.4
s. thy l. of hope and mercy . 576.2
s. o'er the world thy holy l. . 602.4
so shall our l. be s. abroad . 688.4
l. . . . o'er his . . . people s. . 765.3
d *Rom 5:5*
s. it in my heart abroad . . 214.4

sheep
1 *(literal)* *(Luke 2:8)*
have ye left your s. . . 88.2
lay keeping their s. . . 90.1
2 *(figurative)*
a *Ps 79:13*
for his s. he doth us take . 3.2

b *Isa 53:6*
when like wandering s. . . . 4.2
crowd of frightened s. . . 265.1
found the s. that went astray. 337.2
I was the s. . . . wandered . 388.1
still straying s. to be led. . 527.1

c *John 10:11, 16*
hurt thee in saving thy s. . 111.2
shepherd, dying for his s. . 130.2
Saviour came seeking his s. . 388.1
engages . . . to save the s. . 522.2
s. for whom . . . shepherd died 720.5
with his s. securely fold . . 954.1

shelter-ed-ing
his s. was a stable . . . 87.2
I s. from such agonies . . 122.2
that, s. near thy side . . 284.4
the peace of thy s. fold . . 300.4
close s. in thy bleeding side . 424.3
home's a s. from the storm . 663.1
s. 'neath his holy roof . . 728.3
seeking a s. from . . . alarm . 740.1
in your care and s. . . . 792.1

b *Ps 61:3*
s. from the stormy blast. . 13.1
he . . . is my shield and s. . 341.1

c *(Ps 17:8)*
with s. wings outspread. . 200.2
he will s. you under . . . wings 227.c
peace . . . under his s. wings. 227.2
resting 'neath his s. wing . 390.3
safe 'neath the s. of thy wing. 517.4

shepherd
1 *(divine)* *(Ps 23:1)**
the Lord our s. is . . . 9.3
the King of love my s. is. . 53.1
the Lord's my s. . . . 54.1
my s. divine 111.3
was there ever kindest s. . 265.2
we lose the tender s. . . 265.5
the careful s.'s hands . . 555.1
be companion, friend and s. . 576.1
s. hear my prayer . . . 641.*
my s. is beside me . . . 736.2

b *Isa 40:11*
like a s., Jesus will guard . 184.1
where the s. leads . . . 614.2
s., lead me there . . . 641.3
like a s. lead us . . . 845.1

c *good shepherd* *John 10:11-16*
good s., may I sing . . 53.5
I met the good s. just now . 111.1
O s., good s. . . . 111.2, 3
he was the s., dying . . 130.2
thou S. of Israel, and mine . 639.1
for whom their s. died . . 720.5
I'll be a s. to these lambs . 797.2
tell them of the s. . . . 829.3

Israel (b)

2 *shepherds* *Luke 2:8*
these tidings s. heard . . 72.2
the s. joyful sped . . . 72.5
angels, s. . . . worshipped . 74.2
s. in the field abiding . . 75.2
to the watchful s. it was told. 78.2
song that the s. heard . . 80.2
say, ye holy s., say . . 88.2
certain poor s. in fields . . 90.1
while s. watched . . . 93.1
at whose feet the s. fall . . 104.1
the s. came thither . . 137.1
s. with wonder receive it . 139.1
s. came to worship him . . 855.1

b
comfort of the s.'s arm . . 740.1

shield *Ps 33:20**
our s. and defender . . 16.1
my s. and hiding-place . . 58.3
as a s. from every snare. . 66.2
my s. and tower . . . 223.2
be thou my s. . . . 284.4
he . . . is my s. and shelter . 341.1
he's my s., . . . prepares . 373.3
s. when darts are hurled . 495.3
s. in danger's hour . . 569.4
still my strength and s. . . 578.2
be our rock, our s. . . 622.3
he'll take and s. thee . . 645.3
hand stretched forth to s. . 764.1
s. this baby small . . . 792.2
he's your guide and s. . . 817.2
s. me with thy mighty hand . 837.3
s. my soul from sin . . 862.2

b *Eph 6:16*
the Lord's sword and s. . . 684.3
helmet and s., and a sword . 689.1
s. and banner bright . . 698.2
his grace as my s. and reward 734.3
forward with the sword and s. 809.3
take your s. and sword . . 817.3
with s. and banner bright . 818.1

sun (1a)

shifting 324.3

shine/shone
1 *(God) shines*
it s. in the light . . . 16.4
s. in might victorious . . 40.2
light of light, s. o'er us . . 40.4
he s. in all that's fair . . 42.2
yonder s. the infant light . 75.2
s. the everlasting light . . 86.1
Jesus s. brighter . . . purer . 177.3
s. thou on the book . . 193.3
light s. clear and bright . . 260.1
s. along our pathway . . 316.c
s. when all the way . . 316.c
the rays of glory s. . . 400.1
light to s. upon the road . 442.1
s. on my soul from Heaven . 446.1
s. from your word . . 506.3
yonder s. the light . . 641.3
may light upon me s. . . 658.5
s. through the gloom . . 670.5
s. upon them from above . 797.3
the light may never s. . . 868.3
mercies . . . brightly s. . . 938.2
the rays of Heaven s. . . c176

b *[ever] shine*
dear name s. . . . evermore . 63.3
ever the light . . . s. before us 173.1
ever s. till our faith. . . 230.2
here let thy light for ever s. . 516.3
s. one eternal day . . . 887.4

c *love shine*
with the l. that s. from it . 119.c
the light of his l. s. . . 758.4
l. sun is s. 888.2

d *Isa 60:1*
s. the glory of the Lord . . 555.1
whose glory s. . . . 592.1

e *Luke 2:9*
glory s. around . . . 93.1

f *2 Cor 4:6*
that . . . thy grace might s. . 174.1
light of life, within us s.. . 452.1
into my heart let them s. . 457.1
that light hath on thee s. . 465.3
O that they may s. in me . 555.3
if thou within us s. . . 651.4
brightly doth his Spirit s. . 754.2
God hath s. in our hearts . c158

face (2h)

2 *(we) shine* *Matt 5:16; Phil 2:15*
here shall in thine image s. . 407.4
may your love translucent s. . 518.3
in those garments to s. . . 589.1
in this dark world to s. . . 649.4
that in thine image s. . . 704.4
Jesus bids us s. . . . 841.*
to s. for him each day . . 844.1
always s. for him . . . 844.3

b *Matt 13:43*
bright s. as the sun . . 308.4
then we'll s. and shout . . 312.3
and then in Glory s. . . 560.5
they shall s. in their beauty . 852.c
crown will s. the brighter . 899.1
s. like the sun for ever . . 932.4

light (5b) perfect (2b)

3 *(other)*
star, s. in the east . . . 90.2
the . . . sun s. but dim . . 318.1
flowers with . . . beauties s. . 545.2
no light may s. . . . 761.1
prevent the sun from s. . . 854.1
at the s. of the river . . 891.4
brighter rays may s. . . 916.2
summer rays with vigour s. . 925.2
ten thousand charms . . . s. . c167

b *Ps 139:12*
darkness s. as the light . . 453.1
makes a world of darkness s.. 657.3
darkness changed to s. day . 719.2

shining
a *(adjective)*
every s. constellation . . 38.1
appeared a s. throng . . 93.5
with the s. host above . . 367.c
the robes bright and s. . . 406.3
hope that sends a s. ray. . 519.4
a s. new chance to live . . 666.1
to take his s. sword 701.c; 705.c
darkness changed to s. day . 719.2
s. lights of home . . . 740.3
crystal rivers and s. strand . 873.1
ere we reach the s. river. . 891.3

b *(noun)*
I trust the s. of thy face. . 762.1

ship 375.c

shipwrecked *(1 Tim 1:19)* . 63.3

shirk
do your duty, s. it never . 750.3
lonely work he cannot s. . 801.2

shivering 898.2

shoal 598.1

shops 544.1

shore
1 *(literal)*
spread . . . from s. to s.. . 182.2
free from care on any s.. . 556.2
peaceful s. of Galilee . . 680.1
numberless as the sands of the s. 908.c

b *Zech 9:10*
Kingdom stretch from s. to s. 160.1

2 *(figurative—Heaven)*
reached that blissful s. . . 275.1
safe by the heavenly s. . . 280.4
when . . . I near the s. . . 598.3
a friend . . . on Heaven's s. . 709.4
rejoicing on the far . . . s. . 765.6
break on the golden s. . . 889.3
fright us from the s. . . 898.3
gather . . . on the other s. . 907.1
toward the blissful s. . . 911.1
views the radiant s. . . 911.5

b *beautiful shore*
landed safe on that b. s. . 881.2
meet/sing on that b. s. . 900.c, 2
safe on that b. s. . . . 906.1

Canaan

3 *(figurative—other)*
safely to salvation's s. . . 63.3
far from the peaceful s. . . 336.1
far away from s. . . . 375.1
lights along the s. . . . 478.*
soldier on an alien s. . . 801.1

shoreline c137

short
s. as the watch . . . 13.4
this s.-enduring world . . 480.4
when ended life's s. day . 643.4
life's s. race is o'er . . 709.4
s. is my pilgrimage . . 882.2
b *Isa 59:1**
nor s. thine arm . . . 604.4

shortly 233.3

shoulder
s. to s. we stand . . . 702.c
b *Luke 15:5*
on his s. gently laid . . 53.3
on his s. . . . did lay . . 388.1

shout-ed-ing
church with psalms must s. . 11.2
with s. of acclamation . . 37.4
s. through the sky . . . 137.5
let s. of holy joy outburst . 151.2
I want to s. to all . . . 215.3
s., s. the sound . . . 279.1
soul . . . s. o'er the grave . 364.4
we'll all s. hallelujah . . 367.c
s. with all my might . . 369.c
I'll s. the news . . . 401.3
if you want liberty, s. . . 427.3
kindred will s. as I rise . 543.4
quiver at the s. of praise. . 690.2
I hear the warriors s. . . 693.3
glow, as they joyfully s. . 703.4
faith s. in triumph . . . 744.6
we hope to die s. . . . 763.5
we'll s. our battle cry . . 798.3
they s. their battle cry . . 799.2
loud hosannas s. . . . 807.1
how the anxious s. it . . 815.2
s. for joy 818.c
s. with all our might . . 821.2
tell it out with a s. . . . 829.c
s. for Daniel's band . . 847.4
s. Jesus' power to save. . 910.1
what a glorious s. there'll be . 912.3
angels s. the harvest home . 932.c
s. of exultation . . . 934.1
s. the harvest home . . 936.*
b *shout praises*
s. our Saviour's p. . . . 815.c
we'll s. the Saviour's p. . 819.3
you'll s. the p. c223
c *shout salvation*
then I mean to s. s. . . . 338.5
s. s. full and free . . . 393.4
s. aloud s. 815.1
salvation! s. s. . . . 828.1, 4
d *shout/sing*
we'll shine and s. and s. . 312.3
that is why I s. and s. . . 390.3
glory . . . I will s. and s. . 757.1
come, s. and s. 798.1
we will s. . . . we will s. . 807.3
s. and s. till the Master . 807.3
we'll s. and s. the victory . 892.c
I want to s. it . . . s. it . . c170
aloud

show-ed-ing/shown
1 *(God) shows*
s. me the tomb . . . 117.2, 3
saving strength to s. . . 155.3
s. . . . thy promised sign . 167.3
the favour he s. . . . 397.4
Lord, thy goodness s. . . 409.c
O the grace the Father s. . 418.3
will he not s. to the hearts . 527.2
redemption's grace to s. . 590.1
through thy life . . . is s.. . 595.1
Lord, thy salvation . . . s. . 608.2
s. me that happiest place . 639.2
s. me the truth concealed . 650.3
to s. by living faith . . 652.3
path of life is plainly s. . . 656.1
excellence hast s. . . . 688.2
s., where earthly forces fail . 744.2
thus are s. two natures . . 785.2
presence in his (her) life be s. 792.3
in . . . sun is s. thy hand . 926.2
b *show love*
l. and pity thou hast s. . 303.3
l. for all the world is s. . 324.1
Jesus . . . now s. me l. . 429.3
mine, to s. a Saviour's l. . 652.2
Father is s. in the l. . . 739.1
to s. his l. to everyone . 851.1
c *show mercy* *(Ex 20:6)**
forget the mercy . . . he's s. . 250.3
present s. God's mercy . . c166
d *show power* *(Ps 111:6)**
presence and thy p. were s. . 198.3
the p. of perfect cleansing s. . 432.1
s. forth thy p. 435.c
s. thy p. in me . . . 435.c
p. to others which . . . is s. . 435.3
his p. . . . shall be s. . . 459.3
s. forth thy saving p. . . 562.2
till his p. to everyone is s. . 829.2
e *show thyself*
O s. t. to me 123.4
s. t. to me, I cry . . 435.1, c
s. t., O God of power . . 504.3
s. t. beyond the grave . . 714.4
s. t. a God of love . . . 797.3
f *show [way]*
the path by Jesus s. . . . 5.3
s. the new and living w. . 113.2
the living w. is s. . . . 221.3
he's s. us the w. . . . 235.1
the Saviour s. the w. . . 700.2
cannot fail the w. to s. . . 772.1
Saviour has s. me the w. . 881.1
face (2i)
g *show how*
to keep . . . thou'lt s. me h. . 440.3
only s. me h. faulty . . 459.2
s. me h. to win . . . 531.3
Saviour is s. h. gracious . 553.4
to s. h. pure and holy . . 840.2
h *show what*
s. me w. to be 204.3
s. me w. he planned . . 376.c
s. w. thou art . . . 446.2
s. w. . . . never could see . 459.3
Lord, s. me w. I need . . 588.4
s. me w. I ought to do . 837.1
s. me w. . . . should cherish 842.2
i *John 20:20*
he s. his prints of love . . 223.3
s. his wounds . . . hands . 286.4
you do not s. your hands . 748.4
j *Ex 33:18; Mark 9:2*
s. us thy glory, Christ . . c98
face (2i)
2 *(we) show*
human hands compassion s. . 50.1
his . . . righteousness I s. . 60.5
nor tongue nor pen can s. . 61.4
fruits of truth . . . s. . . 408.2
may it be s. 'tis thy life . 479.1
s. forth the living word . . 494.2
to . . . world thee I may s. . 521.2
the mind cannot s. . . . 527.3
my meeting with Jesus to s. . 553.1
grant us grace to s. . . . 624.3
my colours I'll s. . . . 684.2
our colours boldly s. . . 821.c
s. Christ in loving kindness . 830.2
s. how pleasant and happy . 844.2
my life thy beauty s. . . c96
his glory s., I'm . . . growing. c176
singing we go, our joy to s. . c220
b *show love*
how shall we s. our l. to thee. 15.1
life that s. the Father-l. . 218.3
thy l., thy beauty s. . . 656.3
send us forth thy l. to s.. . 760.4
in ceaseless l. for men be s. . 796.4
rejoice to s. all the l. . . 846.4
c *show power*
that I may s. forth thy p. . 435.c
I s. thy p. to every foe . . 620.3
the p. of the cross we'll s. . 800.3
till his p. to everyone is s. . 829.2
d *show praise* *Ps 51:15*
thy love to tell, thy p. to s. . 612.6
and s. his p. below . . 659.2
I shall then s. forth thy p. 793.6
saints s. forth thy p. . . 946.2
3 *(others) show*
let them his glory also s. . 2.4
s. me that scene . . . 848.5
witnesses s. the same path . 879.5
4 *(noun)*
all his boasted pomp and s. . 157.3
fleeting is its glittering s. . 470.1
love of ease and passing s. . 500.2
without love 'tis empty s. . 530.2
earthly things are paltry s. . 630.1

shower
sevenfold graces s. . . . 15.4
spring's refreshing s. . . 213.2
s. . . . his pardoning love . 388.3
as a thirsty land for s. . 412.2
a great, mighty s. . . . 608.1
give refreshing s. . . . 626.3
b *Ezek 34:26*
lo! the promise of a s. . . 165.4
I hear of s. of blessing . . . 295.*
there shall be s. of blessing . 637.*
in copious s. . . . blessings . 940.3

shrine
offerings to lay on his s.. . 183.3
thy hallowed s. . . . 516.3
my heart the Spirit's s. . . 540.4
little s. of quietness . . 615.2
grant . . . worship at thy s. . 624.5
rang through the . . . s. . . 839.1

shrink-ing
it s. not but . . . delight . . 414.1
who shall dream of s. . . 682.1
from my post I will not s. . 686.3
nor s. from the dangers . . 734.1
timorous mortals . . . s. . . 898.2
forbid that we . . . s. . . 944.2

shrouding 916.3

shun-ned
with our shame we s. . . 135.3
friends may s. me . . . 498.4
no cross I s. 526.2
while place . . . we s. . . 556.3
s. evil companions . . . 823.2
what, too, it should s. . . 842.2

shut
s. his glories in . . . 105.3
b *Rev 3:7*
Hell may strive to s. . . . 533.4

sick *(Matt 8:16)*
health to the s. in mind . . 224.2
are you s. of wars . . . 244.2
I, once so s. at heart . . 311.2
s. was I, he made me well . 330.2
some are s. . . . sad . . 558.3
watch by the s. . . . 676.5
the sad, the s., the dying . 828.3
b *Matt 8:16*
they bring all the s. . . 104.3
the s. . . . around thee lay . 558.1
c *sin-sick*
find, poor sin-s. soul . . 253.2
tell every sin-s. soul . . 384.3
the sin-s. soul . . . wearied . 590.3
sin-s. and sorrow-worn . . 825.1
heal (c)

sickle
sword shall be s. . . . 166.3
b *Rev 14:15**
reaper's s. work has found . 926.3

sickness
out of my s. 300.1
in pining s. or in health . . 356.3
when s. lays me low . . 709.3

side
1 *(general)*
thief hangs on each s. . . 108.1
s. by s. with bitter loss . . 145.1
shall rise on every s. . . 159.4
who will leave the world's s. . 707.1
march together, s. by s. . 901.3
b *at our side*
the right man on our s. . . 1.2
stay by my s. until morning . 77.2
with Jesus at my s. . . 374.2
he is ever by my s., I know . 389.1
treasure with Jesus at my s. . 502.3
Father, be thou at our s. . 570.3
die in darkness at your s. . 683.5
with Christ on our s. . . 763.5
mighty power is on our s. . 822.2
tread . . . with Jesus by my s. 857.2
if thou art by my s. . . 862.1
Jesus, be by our s. . . 955
c *Heaven*
singing upon the other s. . 278.4
land me safe on Canaan's s. . 578.3
by the s. of the river . . 886.1
when we reach the other s. . 902.3
d *Ex 32:26*
the Lord's s. . . . . 707.*
2 *(Jesus' side)*
room at my s. for thee . . 101.4
sheltered near thy s. . . 284.4
as to his s. she stole . . 304.1
or we'll walk by his s. . . 397.5
daily by the Saviour's s. . 417.2
bliss at thy s. evermore . . 457.3
while keeping at thy s. . . 485.3
keep them . . . at thy s. . 582.2
never let me leave thy s. . 597.2
I am safe when by thy s. . 627.1
there is room in Jesus' s. . 821.c
safe by thy dear s. . . . 837.2
there, at my Saviour's s. . 882.3
when redeemed by his s. . c248
abide (2b)
b *[wounded] side* *John 19:34*
what is this w. . . . in thy s. . 111.2
fountain opened in his s. . 121.4
from the Saviour's w. s. . 239.3
from his s. flowed the blood . 260.1
from his s. flowed . . . blood . 271.2
from thy riven s. . . . 302.1
drew me to his riven s. . . 348.1
blood that flows from his s. . 427.c
s. be cleft in vain . . . 440.4
streams from . . . w. s. . 540.1
concealed in the cleft of thy s. 639.3
lead them to thy open s. . 720.5
blood flowed from his s. . 783.2
there is room in Jesus' s. . 821.c
those wounds in his . . . s. . c89
c *bleeding side*
behold his b. . . . s. . . 107.2
sheltered in thy b. s. . . 424.3
in thy b. s. a refuge find. . 521.2
to thy precious b. s. . . 585.c
d *hands and side* *John 20:20*
behold his bleeding h. and s. . 107.2
behold his h. and s. . . 156.4
in his feet and h. . . . his s. . 228.2
do not show your h. and s. . 748.4
3 *(verb)*
him who with us s. . . . 1.4

sift *(Amos 9:9)** . . . 162.3

sigh-ed-ing
weary and s. for rest . . 247.2
not all my prayers and s. . 297.2
for direction I s. . . . 376.3
blinded eyes, weary s. . . 379.1
not a s. nor a tear can abide . 397.2
I s. for rest and happiness . 547.2
s. to think of happier days . 557.3
breathe out . . . my last s. . 589.5
prayer is the burden of a s. . 625.2
nor s., nor dread . . . 874.3
I'm s. for the homeland . . 895.1
summer morn I've s. for. . 896.1
mark each suppliant s. . . 940.3
b *hear sigh*
he h. thy humble s. . . 256.2
God h. thy s. . . . 721.1
c *Isa 35:10*
sorrow and s. to cease . . 427.1
not a shadow, not a s. . . 892.2
sorrow no more, not a s. . 900.2
neither s. nor anguish . . 905.2

sight
1 *(re divinity)*
within thy searching s. . . 414.1
to whose all-searching s. . 453.1
his s. is never dim . . . 736.2
none escape from his s. . . 893.1
b *in his sight*
as a jewel in his s. . . . 330.3
adore . . . dwell in thy s. . 357.4
to be pure in the s. . . 459.1
we stand united in thy s. . 692.2
walking in your captain's s. . 695.4
and in his s. appear . . 915.1
stand in thy s. for evermore . 934.3
in his s. for evermore . . c233
c *Ps 90:4*
thousand ages in thy s. . . 13.4
d *Hos 6:2*
as in thy s. to live . . . 472.3
I shall live in thy s. . . . 543.3
e *Col 1:22; 1 Thess 5:23*
unspotted . . . in thy s. . . 422.4
make me blameless in thy s. . 601.3
pleasing (2d), precious (h)
2 *(re humanity)*
linking sense to . . . s. . . 28.3
nightly burned in their s. . 80.3
sprang at once to s. . . 141.2
the s. is glorious . . . 147.1
what joy the s. affords . . 147.4
wake my spirit, clear my s. . 194.1
thy long deluded s. . . 251.2
s., riches, healing . . . 293.4
visions . . . burst on my s. . 310.2
had a s. of Heaven . . 366.1
salvation held up to my s. . 395.1
glories prepared for our s. . 406.1
these prepare us for the s. . 414.5
Jesus brings me s. of thee . 449.1
hide not the worst from my s. 457.1
by the s. of Calvary . . 503.2
every s. . . . save the s. of thee 600.2
at the s. put off . . . flesh . 633.3
brings the truth to s. . . 657.1
loveliness breaks on my s. . 719.4
I see the s. that dazzle . . 862.2
rises to my s. . . . 887.2
what a (wonderful) s. . 908.1, c
b *give sight*
'twas there he g. me s. . . 374.1
s. for my blindness g. . . 488.3
to my eyes the s. is g. . . 729.4
c *faith/sight* *2 Cor 5:7*
till our f. is changed to s. . 230.2
till . . . f. in s. shall end . . 504.3
till our f. be s. . . . 682.3
our f. depends on s. . . 717.5
live by f. and not by s. . . 770.4
walking by f. and not by s. . 947.2
d *Luke 4:18*
bring . . . healing and s. . 224.2
s. to the inly blind . . . 224.2
e *John 9:11*
by faith, I received my s. . 395.c
f *[no] sight*
worlds beyond our s. . . 27.5
s. was gone and fears . . 337.3
veiled from my s. . . . 398.3
armies, just hid from your s. . 537.2
its end far out of s. . . 716.1
path seems hid from s. . . 759.2
beyond our keenest s. . . 871.4
country far from mortal s. . 880.1
we pass away from s. . . 938.4

sightless 547.4

sign
this shall be the s. . . . 93.3
our s. and seal of victory . 163.4
s. our uncontested pardon . 210.1
at the s. of triumph . . 690.2
the saving s. display . . 697.4
blue, the s. of holy living . 777.3
cross, it is thy battle s. . . 864.2
b *Isa 55:13*
make . . . an everlasting s. . 173.3
his name and s. who bear . 299.1
beneath his name and s. . 512.1
c *Matt 24:30*
show . . . thy promised s. . 167.3
d *Acts 4:30*
mighty s. and wonders done . 945.3

signal . . . . . 804.1, c

signature 214.4

signify . . . . . 274.*

silence-d
lives to s. all my fears . . 144.2
share with thee the s. . . 567.3
rang through the s. . . 839.1
our s. shaming . . . 853.3
thy love has s. all . . . 926.1

silent
the s. paths of earth . . . 7.2
s. as light 8.2
the s. stars go by . . . 86.1
s. night . . . . . 89.*
s. and still I stand . . . 131.1
tongue lies s. in the grave . 132.5
your heart be cold and s. . 241.4
that s., secret thought . . 517.2
my tongue be s., cold . . 573.5

occupy my s. place . . 615.4
voice of prayer is never s. . 677.3
if we were s. . . . stones cry . 724.2
harm thee in the s. night . 767.3
in s. worship I confess . 871.1
borders of the s. grave . . 910.1

silently
how s. . . . the gift . . 86.3
love worketh s. . . . 530.c
s. now I wait for thee . . c99

silver-y
s. moon with softer gleam . 2.1
s. and gold, his coffers . . 354.1
take my s. and my gold . . 525.4
mending . . . by the s. sea . 680.1
riches, neither s. nor gold . 883.1
dashing up its s. spray . . 891.2

simple-st
a message, a s. message . 270.1
in s. trust like theirs . . 567.2
the s. form of speech . . 625.3
s. rule and safest guiding . 716.2
my s. tongue fails to express. 728.4
Lord, accept these s. tokens . 922.2
b *simple [heart]* *Ps 19:7**
my s. upright h. prepare . 568.1
turn with s., childlike h. . . 654.5
imparted to the s.-h. . . 655.4
all my s. soul devour . . 720.1

simplicity 793.1

simply
tell me the story s. . . 98.1
s. to thy cross I cling . . 302.3
s. trusting every day . . 754.1

sin
1 a
cast out our s., and enter . 86.4
O love . . . O s. of man . . 121.5
the wounds my s. decrees . 122.1
strong to smite the s. . . 129.2
O s. of man! O love of God . 131.1
let naught of s. remain . . 218.1
oppressed with s. . . . 229.*
every soul by s. oppressed . 231.1
leave your s. and come . . 267.3
s. demand that I should die . 282.2
s. of not loving . . . serving . 296.2
infinite s. 296.2
O s. that hath no equal . . 299.2
out of my s. and into thyself . 300.1
be of s. the double cure . . 302.1
s. are under the blood . . 317.*
nailed there by s. of mine . 326.2
tell . . . of s. washed white . 335.1
at last my s. I learned . . 405.2
the s. I cannot count . . 421.1
awake . . . when s. is nigh . 425.3
let s. appear in thy . . . ray . 446.1
no s. shall ever . . . part. . 447.4
s. that drove thee from me . 448.2
by grace, and not by s. . . 468.4
spare not one lurking s. . . 494.3
rest, and hatred of s. . . 541.3
wage the war with s. . . 575.2
looks . . . when s. is near . 596.3
of s. the sinner convict . . 608.1
disperse my s. as . . . dew . 665.4
our aim to vanquish s. . . 692.2
s. is our challenged foe . . 705.1
truth shall s. o'erthrow . . 705.4
think of the s. everywhere . 708.2
false and full of s. I am . . 737.3
my s. are swallowed up . . 746.2
to drive s. from our land . 798.2
goes where s. is found . . 801.1
s. shall fly before us . . 815.3

yielding is s. 823.1
King has s. o'erthrown . . 829.2
s. to full fruition brought . 885.3
hand my cruel s. had pierced. 917.4
whose lives . . . by s. accurst. 919.2
to love my s. 932.3
b *come with sin*
c. with all thy s. . . . 232.2
c. with thy s. . . . lowly bow 248.3
Jesus is calling, c. with thy s.. c9
c *pardon sin*
p. for s. and a peace . . 33.3
freed . . . p. all my s. . . 361.1
the Lord has p. all my s. . 380.3
in . . . agony my s. are p. . 486.3
p. of my s. 600.1
p. every s., Lord . . . c109
d *every sin*
e. s. on him was laid . . 108.2
leaving e. s. 197.1
blood to wash my e. s. . . 303.c
from e. s. to deliver . . 384.3
from e. s. set free . . . 415.1
keep . . . from e. s. . . 767.4
pardon e. s., Lord . . . c109
e. s. had to go c198
e *all [my] sin* *1 John 1:7*
a. our s. on thee were laid . 109.2
a. my s. . . . laid upon thee . 119.c
burning a. my dross and s. . 201.4
from a. s.'s impurity . . 230.3
come with a. thy s. . . 232.2
even me with a. my s. . . 262.3
a. my s. I brought him . . 333.1
blood that can a. s. erase . 335.2
pardoned a. my s. . . . 361.1
my redeemer from a. s. . . 370.1
here, where a. s. depart . . 383.3
a. s. expose to Christ . . 408.3
entirely a. my s. remove . . 419.6
from a. the s. . . . have wept. 437.2
when from a. s. . . . freed . 457.2
a. my s. in thee to hide . . 486.1
I bring thee a. my s. . . 486.1
saved from a. s. . . . song . 681.3
grace to cover a. my s. . . 737.4
bring . . . with a. their s. . 814.c
a. defiling taint of s. . . 867.2
s. of years are a. numbered . 893.1
f *no sin*
s. and woe are done away . 268.1
till s. shall be no more . . 802.1
no s. can sever a fellowship . 888.3
s. cannot harm me there . . 889.2
no s. in the homeland . . 895.2
abound (b), against (b), bear (1e), bring (2h), cancelled, carry (1c), cleanse (c), confess (2c), conquer (2e), cover (c), deep (3e), destroy (d), forgive (1g), give (3c), hate (1a), hide (c), inbred, lay (2b), many (2b), purge (c), remove (b), take (1f), wash (3a, b)
2 *sin and . . .*
clouds of s. and sadness . 10.1
the woes of s. and strife . 83.2
redeem . . . s. and dark despair 138.4
master o'er my s., the world . 303.4
more full of grace . . . I of s.. 305.2
o'er s. and uncleanness...stand 364.1
wrecked by s. and strife. . 390.2
conquer over Hell and s. . 532.2
from s. and despair . . 535.2
snatch...from s. and the grave 691.1
turn from s. and folly . . 704.4
soars beyond death, pain and s. 744.6
let s. and error pass away . 942.4
s. and weakness . . . lost . c94
death (3d), fear (2g), grief (2d), self (2c), shame (2b), sorrow (2c), uncleanness

3
a *for sin*
his life an atonement for s. . 22.1
God's remedy for s. . . . 98.2
for s. that I have done . . 105.2
interceding . . . for your s. . 242.3
for thy s. . . . slaughter led . 253.2
for my s. . . . slain . . . 746.1
atone (a), die (2b), suffer (2d)
b *from sin*
every soul from s. awake . 43.1
separate from s., I would . 212.5
died to ransom thee from s. . 229.3
a step from s. to grace . . 255.3
from my s. I've liberation . 328.1
seeking from my s. to part . 348.1
liberty I claimed from my s. . 348.2
from s. that . . . woe . . 401.2
from s.'s deep mire . . 401.2
from my s. has ransomed me. 404.1
blood from s. can sever . . 434.5
from all the guilt of my s. . 437.1
to be redeemed from s. . . 447.2
no escape from the s. . . 459.1
renew, release from s. . . 562.2
from s. defend us . . . 845.2
shield my soul from s. . . 862.2
cease (e), cleanse (c), free (1f, h), freedom (b), keep (3o), save (1i)
c *in sin*
not left i. s. to stray . . 135.3
his gifts i. s. . . . squandered. 225.1
fast bound i. s. . . . 283.3
stooping, i. s. when I fell . 329.1
once I was far i. s. . . 374.1
no more lie down i. s. . . 676.4
many dying i. s. . . . 708.4
why longer i. your s. remain . 885.4
deep (3e)
d *over sin*
their victory o. s. . . . 102.2
victory he giveth o. s. . . 180.3
perfect victory o. s. . . 205.3
goodness o. my s. prevailed 391.2
o. s. I may never . . . grieve . 437.2
sense of sorrow o. s. . . 496.4
conquer o. Hell and s. . . 532.2
love will triumph o. s. . . 760.2
o. sin and Satan . . . victory . 814.3
win perfect victory o. s. . 819.3
4 *(possessive)*
in this world of s. . . . 86.3
from s. bondage to reclaim . 114.1
s. debt to pay . . . 126.1
to pay the price of s. . . 133.4
what depth of . . . grief and s. 135.1
s. wounds to lave . . . 135.4
s. strongholds . . . o'erthrows 165.2
break . . . the tyrannies of s.. 172.1
gentle voice: O heart of s. . 229.1
the joys of s. are flown . . 267.1
ease this weight of s. . . 297.3
the record of my s. repeat . 303.1
paid s. fearful cost . . 335.2
snapped s. fetters . . . 347.c
when s. tempests blow . . 347.2
lost in s. degradation . . 349.2
rise from s. dark sepulchre . 353.4
roused from the slumber of s. 373.1
wandered...in the paths of s. 391.1
from s. deep mire . . . 401.2
thraldom of indwelling s. . 459.1
from s. foul corruption . . 499.1
stray into the toils of s. . . 747.2
in this dark world of s. . . 752.1
s. sorrows to dispel . . . c7
bearer, burden (2d), darkness (2h), end (2b), hold (3b), host (5a), hostility, load (b), mountain (2b), night (2b), pleasure (1c), power (2b), servant (2g), slave (b), stain (c), trace, way (3d)

5
a *Isa 1:18*
though your s. be as scarlet . 272.1
my s. was red like crimson . 386.3
though your s. be as scarlet . 883.2
b *Isa 38:17*
my s. behind him cast . 366.2
c *Luke 11:4*
forgive our s. as we forgive . 572.1
d *John 16:8*
convincing men of s. . 730.3
s. reproving . 893.c
e *Rom 6:14*
freedom here from s. dominion 433.3
commit (c), dead (2c), go (3d), many (2b), more (5d), remember (d), under (c)
6 *sin-*
s.-forgiving Saviour . 257.4
flowed the s.-cleansing blood 271.2
no s.-cursed thing . . . allow . 440.2
plunge in the s.-cleansing wave 535.c
each s.-burdened soul knows. 708.3
sick (c), sinbound, stain (c)
7 *(verb)*
though we have s. . . . mercy 264.3
never, never s. . 314.2
nor s. in deed or word . 407.4
saving from s. and sin . 640.1
taught mankind to s. . 885.2
keep (3o), more (5d)

sinning *(adj)*
be wise the s. soul to win . 683.6
for a lost and s. race . 777.2

sinbearer
forsaken, our s. he . 130.4
there as the bearer of s. . 271.2
thou wonderful s. . 448.1

sin-bound
love to the poor s. soul . 273.3
power to save to s. souls . 303.4
free each s. slave . 775.2
while millions s. lie . 780.2

since
s. Jesus crossed the river . 153.3
s. I have been converted . 309.2
s. first I learned to love . 358.3
s. I made him my guide . 376.3
s. Jesus came into my heart . 394.*
s. I have known his mercy . 536.3
s. I know, as now I know . 545.2
s. I learned to trust him . 549.c
s. our requests . . . we brought 642.1
and s. he found me . 706.c
s. the Lord redeemed us . 755.1
s. his Spirit sealed us . 755.1
yet, s. we have known . 763.4
s. we assembled last . 915.2
s. the Army opened fire . 939.1
b *ever since*
e. s. by faith I saw . 132.4
fighting for God e. s. . 321.3
e. s. his kindness drew me . 343.1
I came, and e. s. I know. . 359.2
which I have loved long s. . 606.3
(*since* to mean *because,* nc)

sincere
draw near, with heart s. . 260.3
love that is true and s. . 443.3
whose prayers are not s. . 588.3
soul's s. desire uttered . 625.1
come with hearts s. . 836.3
with hearts s., we pray . 941.1
converse (b)

sincerely . 922.2

sincerity . 212.2

sinful
weapons of my s. pride . 122.4
I came to him so s. . 403.2
s. and black . . . past . 437.1
expel . . . each s. love . 445.2
purify from s. dross . 452.3
s. self my only shame . 476.3
spurning not our s. race . 500.1
rescued from his s. way . 550.2
no one too s. . 590.2
from every s. stain . 629.2
the slaves of s. bondage . 776.2
I am both weak and s. . 840.1
poor and s. though we be . 845.3
b *sinful heart*
to s. h. which knew him not . 102.1
s. though my h. may be . 295.2
before my s. h. was stirred . 339.2
refine this s. h. of mine . 494.3
c *sinful man*
though the eye of s. m. . 220.3
Christ receiveth s. m. . 262.*
a s. m. ashamed of thee . 592.1
d *sinful souls*
to the weary s. s. . 230.1
s., thirsting, fainting s. . 254.2

sinful/est . 262.2

sinfulness
s. before him flee . 63.2
my record of s. . c190

sing-ing-sang
1 *(inanimate) sings*
O hark to what it s. . 187.2
s. ye islands of the sea . 393.2
bird (b), vale (c)
2 *(sing in Heaven)*
in Canaan we will s. again . 43.4
there for ever may we s. . 76.5
s., all ye citizens . 85.2
s. the rapturous chorus . 139.3
s. the wonders of his grace . 223.4
s. upon the other side . 278.4
with the angels I will s. . 327.3
s. it with the saints . 337.c
I'll s. with the . . . crown . 357.4
with the saints will s. . 368.4
s. for joy in his presence . 392.2
go to s. among the angels . 840.3
they'll s. their welcome home 879.c
O how they sweetly s. . 897.1
s. on that beautiful shore . 900.2
songs of victory s. . 901.4
there are glad songs s. . c153
b *angels sing* *Rev 5:9**
stars and a. s. around thee . 10.2
ye, who s. creation's story . 75.1
when . . . her choirs shall s. . 101.4
have you heard the a. s. . 242.1
s. with holy rapture . 259.4
the a. s. a glorious song. . 326.5
a. and saints are s. . 383.c
a. their welcome will s. . 543.4
glory, how the a. s. . 550.c
men and a. s. . 690.5
c *Luke 2:13*
their choirs are s. . 73.1
the song that the angels s. . 80.1
hark! the herald angels s. . 82.1
hear the a. sing . 83.*
s., choirs . . . in exultation . 85.2
angels s. peace on earth . 88.3
how the angels in chorus s. . 99.1
rang when the angels s.. . 101.2

d *new [song]* *Ps 33:3*
I'll s. the new eternal s. . 69.4
then anew this s. we'll s. . 118.5
n. s. thy creation shall s. . 166.5
I'll s. the glad new s. . 375.3
e *Rev 15:3*
s. the everlasting song . 880.4
3 *(we) sing*
great congregation . . . shall s. 24.2
then s. my soul . . . to thee . 37.c
nor voice can s. . 61.2
sweetest carol ever s. . 67.c
I love to s. its worth . 69.1
that we may live and s. . 151.5
our brave forefathers s. . 158.1
never . . . ceased to s. . 158.1
s. we the King . 166.1
when his triumph we s. . 166.3
I love to s. of the Saviour . 178.*
I will s. of my redeemer . 180.*
help us while we s. . 193.1
in the desert ways I s. . 194.5
help us thy name to s. . 219.1
s. all the time . 326.*
I'll s.: Jesus is mine . 326.3
'tis of Jesus I would s. . 343.2
while I've breath . . . s. . 356.1
where'er I speak, or s. . 356.4
Jesus . . . thee will I s. . 364.4
and s. the angel's song . 374.3
and I'm s., s., s. . 389.c
I now can s.: Jesus saves . 401.1
sent me s. on my way . 401.1
I'll s. it when . . . in eternity . 401.3
while Jesus is . . . I can s. . 402.c
raptured soul can only s. . 405.3
you may s. of the joys . 406.1
while I every question s. . 409.1
to walk, to weep, to s. . 415.5
from ever fearing to . . . s. . 437.4
s., . . . I shall conqueror be . 543.3
glad moment while we s. . 692.3
hark! converts are s. . 703.4
in every tongue we s. . 705.2
happy . . . s. all the day. . 811.c
onward, s. as we go . 818.c
Christ for the world, we s. . 825.*
while children's voices s. . 834.c
yes, I would s. . 848.4
children all stood s. . 853.1
s. aloud: Hosanna . 853.2
s. as we go, going home . 903.c
s. we many years of blessing. 939.1
the Three in One to s. . 940.2
s. Ebenezer as the years . c147
s. we go, our joy . . . we know c220
b *(ever) sing*
e. s., march we onward . 10.4
e. his praises s. . 336.2
wonder why always I s.. . 388.4
let me s. always, only . 525.3
heart and voice shall e. s. . 574.5
we will e. s. . . . salvation . 821.1
c *heart sings*
my h. bursts forth to s. . 39.c
makes the woeful h. to s. . 177.2
tune my h. to s. thy grace . 313.1
he set my h. a-s. . 342.c
my h. doth s. for joy . 346.1
mind, h. and voice . . . s. . 574.5
my h. attuned to s. . 583.3
prayer with thankful h. we s.. 796.1
s. with cheerful h. and voice . 911.1
my glad h., while it s. . 916.2
my h. s. whenever I think . c187
d *sing glory*
his g. now we s. . 156.2
s. . . . g. be to God . 326.c
go s. g. home . 338.5
still I may s.: all g. to God . 354.4
I s. in my rapture: O g. . 710.3
e *sing grace*
O s. of his g. . 16.2

s. the wonders of his g. . . 223.4
tune my heart to s. thy g. . 313.1
of his g. I s. 347.3
quite sure . . . I s. of his g. . 364.2
s. . . . of his wondrous g. . 835.3
s. his mercy and his g. . . 892.1

f *sing love*
gratefully s. . . . his l. . . 16.1
s. his dying l. . . . 120.5
to s. of his l. for me . . 179.4
s. the Saviour's dying l. . 275.1
s. of his mighty l. . . 364.c
we will s. redeeming l. . 367.c
let us s. of his l. once again . 808.1
to s. his l. and mercy . . 840.3
s. the wondrous l. of Jesus . 892.1
s. songs of l. and praise. . 929.1

g *sing praise*
adoration shall s. to thy p. . 16.6
who like thee his p. should s.. 17.1
in songs of p. my heart . . . s. 39.c
shepherd, may I s. thy p. . 53.5
s. the p. of his name . . 63.3
s. my great redeemer's p. . 64.1
p. s. to God, the King . . 86.2
s. p. to our heavenly Lord . 90.6
so I'll s. in songs of p. . . 266.4
s. hallelujah, praise . . 278.3
live daily his p. to s. . . 281.4
no less days to s. God's p. . 308.4
ever his praises s. . . . 336.2
melodious p. they s. . . 406.2
s. the p. of him . . . 557.4
ever s. glad p. to Christ . . 574.5
spread his fame, his p. s. . 696.3
while . . . we s. p. to our God. 809.1
s. the p. of Jesus' name. . 834.1
join to s. the Saviour's p. . 834.1
how shall we fit p. s. . . 938.1
till all the world p. . . . s.. . c226
march . . . while we s. the p.. c243

h *sing song*
a nobler, sweeter s. I'll s. . 132.5
only one s. I can s. . . 323.4
hear the s. I cannot s. . . 387.2
s. our marching s. . . 700.*
may sing the conqueror's s. . 719.5
sweet s. of triumph s. . . 761.3
s. s. of expectation . . 765.1
s. . . . with loud joyful s. . 807.1
s. your s., ye saints . . 809.4
s. s. of love 929.1
s. . . . s. of grateful love . 929.1
travel along, s. a song . . c26
I'm s. a glory s. . . . c175
s. a s. of happiness . . . c201
we'll s. . . . s. of . . . Zion . c222

i *sing story*
I will s. the wondrous s. . 180.2
I will s. the wondrous s. 337.1, c
s. the gospel s. . . . 801.c
s. the deathless s. . . 828.4
we'll s. . . . salvation's s. . 888.3

4 *(imperative)*
s. to the Lord with . . . voice. 3.1
awake, my voice, and s. . . 26.1
s. the sweet promise . . 26.2
s. with us, for Jesus' sake . 43.1
Nowell, s. all we may . . 72.c
s. through all Jerusalem . 88.c
toil on and s. 158.3
give thanks, and s. . . 164.1
s., O earth . . . proclaim . 184.1
s. them over again . . . 258.1
s. it o'er and o'er again . . 262.c
lift up your voice and s. . 334.3
s. above/softly/in triumph . 393.3
then s. for joy, and use . . 408.5
so s. about it, as we can . 544.1
s. our marching song . . 700.*
s., pray, and swerve not . 738.3
s. to God, with . . . songs . 807.1
s. your songs, ye saints . 809.4
s. it with a spirit . . . 815.1
s. it as our comrades s. it . 815.1
salvation! s. salvation . . . 828.2
children, s. for gladness 835.1, c
s. about the mercy/Heaven 835.2, 3
s. to the Lord . . . s. songs . 929.1
s. and you will prove . . c201

b *let [us] sing*
let all the world . . . s. . . 11.*
first let me hear . . . then s. . 31.4
let us all unite to s. . . 43.1
let us join our voices s. . . 74.*
with the angels let us s.. . 89.3
s. the Saviour's merits . . 109.3
let Christians s. . . . 142.1
let his Church . . . s. . . 152.2
come let us s.: praise . . 166.c
let those refuse to s. . . 314.1
let me s. always . . . 525.3
let us s. of his love. . . 808.1

c *sing [for joy]* *Ps 67:4*
my heart doth s. for j. . . 346.1
s. for j. in his presence . 392.2
hear us as with j. we s. . 532.4
j.-bursts of s. . . . 724.2
s. now for gladness . . 724.2
Children, s. for gladness 835.1, c
with what gladness . . . truly s. 859.1
I am s., for j. is springing . c176

d *Isa 26:19*
awake, my soul, and s. . . 156.1

e *Isa 49:13*
sing ye heavens . . . 143.1

f *Jas 5:13*
s., if my way be clear . . 754.3

shout (d)

singer 838.3

singing *(noun)*
praise for the s. . . . 35.1
my heart is full of s. . . 328.2
the world shall hear our s. . 802.2
hark! the sounds of s. . . 803.1
with s. I repair . . . 880.3

single
nor a s. grace impart . . 555.4
pure delight of a s. hour. . 585.3
do not leave me one s. day . 635.1

singleness *Eph 6:5**
since, in s. of aim, I part. . 513.1
serve with s. of heart . . 688.1

sink-ing-sunk
s., by dying love compelled . 307.4
when s. the soul, subdued . 632.3
s. the mountain to a plain . 720.1
when life s. apace . . 763.5
slowly s. the reign . . 776.2
sands of time are s. . . 896.1

b *Ps 69:2; Matt 14:30*
for thee, though s. . . 253.2
I was s. in degradation . . 309.1
I was s. in misery . . . 328.1
I was s. deep . . . rise no more 336.1
I was s. fast . . . 375.1
in despair my heart would s. . 399.2
dying and s. into Hell . . 482.2
I s. in life's alarms . . . 508.1
every soul s. deep in sin. . 700.2
he'll leave me . . . to s. . . 712.3

sinking *(adj)*
raise my s. heart . . . 303.1
from s. sand he lifted me . 339.c
other ground is s. sand . . 745.c

sinless *Heb 4:15*
dare we the s. one deride . 121.3
s. in thy holy eyes . . . 673.4
quite s., we believe . . 785.3

sinner
(vocative nc, but see come (4b)
name to s. dear . . . given . 60.2
his name the s. hears . . 62.3
God and s. reconciled . . 82.1
earnest his entreaty to s. . 94.2
nor let that . . . s. die . . 106.3
for ever doth for s. plead . 116.4
ruined s. to reclaim . . 118.1
'twere not for s. such as I . 122.2
were all for s.' gain . . 123.2
s. plunged beneath that flood 132.1
would Jesus have the s. die . 140.1
name from the lips of s. . 141.3
s. in derision crowned him . 147.3
light of the s. in ways . . 175.3
a s., condemned, unclean . 179.1
where for s. there is mercy . 188.3
still thou dost on s. fall . . 216.3
s. may relinquish wrong. . 249.1
welcome for the s. . . 265.4
a s. saved by grace . . 266.4
though we're s. every one . 268.4
for s. he waits . . . 273.1
could I hear some s. say. . 275.4
a needy s. at thy feet . . 282.1
kind . . . when s. call . . 296.4
die for s. like you . . 319.c
for s. condemned . . . 319.2
warning s. to flee . . . 321.4
he wept over s. one day. . 331.2
strength the s. receives . . 348.3
that can make the s. white . 348.3
a s. by choice . . . 354.3
when as a s. I came . . 371.2
s. to Jesus now clinging . 383.c
say to s. far and wide . . 393.2
leading weary s. to the cross. 399.3
s. yet demand my love . . 463.3
that s. around may feel . . 523.3
declaring Christ to the s. . 530.1
let thy blood, for s. spilt. . 563.3
still the s. love . . . 568.3
may the s. find thee . . 575.2
of sin the s. convict . . 608.1
seeking the wandering s. . 623.2
the contrite s.'s voice . . 625.4
thy love for a s. declare . . 639.2
the rebel s.'s doom . . 652.4
not to fight 'gainst the s. . 687.2
s. on the Saviour calling . 693.3
make the foulest s. clean . 700.2
we s. to Jesus shall bring . 820.1
the s.'s heart confound . . 875.1
dying s. pray to live . . 945.2
where the s. finds pardon . c67

b *every sinner*
welcome e. s. there . . 138.4
e. drooping s.'s ears . . 140.4
thy love for e. s. free . . 140.5
suited to e. s.'s case . . 254.1
e. s. may be free . . . 381.2
grace for e. s. free . . 533.3
blood for e. guilty s. . . 638.1
did for e. s. die . . . 756.2
salvation! for e. s. . . 781.2
bring s. of e. kind . . 814.c
salvation in e. s.'s ear . 828.3

c *slain for sinners*
world of lost s. was s. . . 124.1
once for favoured s. s. . . 161.1
thou Lamb for s. s. . . 167.3
who for s. once was s. . . 790.2

d *Luke 15:2*
s. Jesus will receive . . 262.1
there is welcome for the s. . 265.4
Jesus . . . will welcome s. . c17

e *Rom 5:8*
love the faithless s. still . . 305.2
the lover of s. adore . . 367.3
while we were s. he loved us. 384.2
thy love for a s. declare . . 639.2

chief (b), ear (3b), friend (1d), guilty (b), kind (1), lost (3d), poor (3c), saint (2b), save (1i)

sister
brothers and s., draw near . 19.1
human love, brother, s. . . 28.4
brother, s., child . . . 938.4

sit
we will s. at his feet . . 397.5
s. no longer idly by . . 696.1

b *Isa 42:7**
those who s. in darkness . 830.1

c *Luke 13:29*
s. down in the Kingdom of God 170.*

d *Col 3:1**
he s. at God's right hand . 164.4

throne (4g)

skies see sky

skill-ed
mines of never-failing s. . 29.2
let my hand forget her s. . 573.5
strong hands were s. . . 611.2
thy matchless s. hath planned 644.1
warriors lend their . . . s. . 799.3
claims . . . craftsman's s. . 867.5
to employ my every s. . . 871.1

sky-skies
1 *(literal)*
that brightens up the s. . . 25.2
that which built the s. . . 26.3
for the beauty of the s. . . 28.1
through the midnight s. . 38.1
flash across the darkening s. . 39.2
thought . . . of s. and seas . 42.1
it's as high as the s. . . 49.c
stars in the bright s. . . 77.1
'mid . . . darkening s. . . 125.2
lightnings rend the s. . . 126.3
sorrows darken all our s. . 127.1
darkness veiled the s. . . 128.4
rings out upon the s. . . 131.4
stands empty to the s. . . 142.1
when morning gilds the s. . 187.1
than glows in any earthly s. . 387.1
steal across the s. . . . 673.1
'neath the western s. . . 677.4
raise your banner in the s. . 697.2
saw his Master in the s.. . 701.2
rise to reach the s. . . . 766.1
my eyes look to the s. . . 766.3
signal waving in the s. . . 804.1
glad voices rend the s. . . 807.3
till hosannas reach the s. . 834.3
bowed beneath the s. . . 855.4
'neath darkening s. . . 923.2
when earthly s. are grey. . c206
blood and fire 'neath . . . s. . c240

b *beyond the sky*
read of realms b. the s. . . 654.2
crown b. the glowing s.. . 818.4
prepare for joys b. the s. . 887.5
their home b. the s. . . 907.2

c *earth and sky*
in Hell or e. or s. . . . 60.1
cross, 'twixt e. and s. . . 134.1
fills all the e. and s. . . 167.2
let e. and sea and s. . . 187.4
praise thy name in e. and s. . 220.4
thee, the Lord of e. and s. . 516.1
praise through e. and s. . 629.2
blood, through e. and s. . 746.2
to thee, O Lord of e. and s. . 933.1

2 *(figurative)*
drifting dark across the s. . 40.3
spreads along the s. . . 165.4
drive . . . clouds from my s. . 318.4
not a cloud in the s. . . 397.2
your s. . . . be o'ercast . . 537.3
cleaving the s. . . . 617.5
even through clouded s. . 648.3
not only under summer s. . 717.2
bright s. will soon be o'er . 736.3
darkened be the s. . . 761.1
above the s. is dark . . 805.1
clouds may over-spread the s. 892.2
when . . . s. are bright . . 947.2
clear are the s. above me . c152
God's blue s. o'erhead . . c238

b *(Heaven)*
look down from the s. . . 77.2
when the s. bent down . . 80.2
the triumph of the s. . . 82.1
claim my mansion in the s. . 116.5
shout through the s. . . 137.5
ours the cross . . . the s. . 143.5
wingèd squadrons of the s. . 150.3
glory prepared in the s. . . 233.3
no clouds . . . along that s. . 268.2
is there a place in the s.. . 289.3
bound to meet you in the s. . 312.4
my homestead in the s. . . 369.1
all the armies of the s. . . 382.2
whose glory fills the s. . . 412.1
fit it for the s. . . . 472.1
I shall mount to the s. . . 543.4
live but for the s. . . . 661.3
point me to the s. . . . 670.5
must I be carried to the s. . 678.2
to lead me to the s. . . 709.1
the s. . . . is our goal . . 771.4
to draw thee from the s. . 812.1

slain
for a world . . . was s. . . 124.1
which to open Christ was s. . 439.3
for thine enemies wast s. . 515.3
I'll boast the Saviour s. . . 592.4
to save a lost world . . . s. . 687.3
before the . . . foundation s. . 746.1
Saviour for me was s. . . 848.5
for your redemption . . . s. . 885.4
spilt when he was s. . . c25

b *Lamb slain* *Rev 13:8**
L. . . . was s. for us . . 57.2
Jesus, the L. that was s. . 166.1
thou L. for sinners s. . . 167.3
blood of the L. that was s. . 437.1
blood of the L. who was s. . 808.1
the L. that was s. . . . c193

once (2c) slay

slake 277.3

slaughter *Isa 53:7*
as a lamb to cruel s. led. . 253.2
thou wast to the s. led . . 538.2

slave
rise . . . pardoned s. . . 303.4
s. of myself 456.2
a freeman, once a s. . . 571.4

b *slave [of sin]*
why . . . a s. to s. . . . 468.1
s. of s. to bring . . . 499.3
s. of s. and degradation . 702.3
free each s.-bound s. . . 775.2
s. of sinful bondage . . 776.2

slavery 433.2

slay-slain
a king to s. their foes . . 91.1
beasts on Jewish altars s. . 120.1
all the evil passions s. . . 481.2

strength thy foes to s. . . 575.3
my sins to s. 749.3

sleep-ing/slept
1 *(literal)*
thy deep and dreamless s. . 86.1
while mortals s. . . . 86.2
be there at our s. . . . 611.4
refreshed me while I s. . . 665.3
through s. and darkness . 668.1
ere I s., at peace may be . 671.2
sweet s. . . . vigorous make . 671.4
Guardian of my s. hours . 672.2
every mourner's s. tonight . 676.5

b *1 Sam 3:3*
priest of Israel, s. . . . 839.2

c *Matt 8:24*
amid its rage didst s. . . 569.2

2 *(figurative)*
guarded thee whilst thou s. . 117.2

slumber (2a), wake (2b)

sleepless 671.3

slenderness 183.3

slight-ed-ing
ungrateful was I to s. . . 114.3
his grace I long have s. . . 361.1
though they are s. him . . 691.2

sloth *(Heb 6:12)*
shake off dull s. . . . 665.1
cast s. away 683.4

slow
s. are my hands to work. . 488.2
my faith so small, so s. . . 742.1
why should I be s. to plead . 770.3

b *Neh 9:17**
s. to chide 17.2

c *Luke 24:25*
the s. of heart to move . . 519.2

slowly
tell me the story s. . . 98.2
s. they led him . . . 129.1
my heart has s. trusted . . 713.2
s. sinks the reign . . . 776.2

slumber
1 *(literal)*
sinks the soul . . . to s. . . 632.3
like infant's s., pure . . 676.5

2 *(figurative)* *Ps 121:4*
our Father never s. . . 722.3
no careless s. . . . close. . 767.2
he s. ne'er who keepeth . 767.2

b *(1 Thess 5:6)**
roused from the s. of sin . 373.1
stirred the s. chords again . 390.2
to waste your time in s. . 686.4
shake the s. from your eyes . 696.1
away from earthly s. . . 766.3

c *(1 Thess 4:14)**
and for a season s. . . 153.2

small
a present far too s. . . 136.4
what I've done . . . is s.. . 489.3
s. as it is, 'tis all . . 516.1
how s. the debts men owe . 572.3
s. time to think or pray . . 675.1
my strength of s. avail . . 780.2
shield this baby s. . . . 792.2
although the place be s. . 838.2
you in your s. corner . . 841.*
though my powers are s. . 859.c
ere from this s. house . . 905.3

b *great and small*
givest, to both g. and s. . 8.3
all creatures g. and s. . . 25.c

all nations g. and s. . . 56.2
here let all, g. and s. . . 73.3
conflict, whether g. or s. . 396.3
strength be g. or s. . . 477.3
halt, the blind, the g., the s. . 590.3
c *1 Kings 19:12*
still s. voice of calm . . 567.5
d *Isa 16:14*
s. and feeble was his day . 165.2
e *(Matt 6:30)**
my faith, though s. . . . reward 613.2
my faith so s., so slow . . 742.1
my faith still s., but sure . 742.3
even when my faith is s. . 754.1

smart 446.3

smile-d-ing
1 *(God) smiles*
tears and s. like us he knew . 87.4
to gild . . . with his s. . . 333.2
Jesus s. and loves me too . 338.c
realising Jesus and his s. . 352.1
his s. . . . drives it away. . 397.2
now thy s. is on me . . 459.3
while thou shalt s. upon me . 498.4
their pain thy s. should win . 503.1
how couldst thou s. on me . 507.2
glad when thy . . . s. we see. 602.3
his s. of approval . . . gain . 640.3
win my Father's s. . . . 706.3
in joy . . . s. doth afford. . 734.2
sweetly s., and kindly said . 797.1
s. to hear their song . . 853.1
just a s. from my Saviour . 906.3
'neath my Saviour's s. . . c196
b *[face] smile*
he hides a s. f. . . . 29.4
s. of Jesus' lovely f. . . 253.1
lifted . . . the s. of his f. . 364.2
when Jesus shows his s. f. 387.c
always looking on his s. f. . 390.3
there Jesus shows a s. f. . 560.1
God s. through his . . . f. . 855.2
2 *(we) smile*
he taught men . . . to s.. . 274.c
sometimes all s. . . . 468.1
meet the glad with . . . s. . 485.2
mine to s. in . . . failure . . 510.3
there's a s. on every face . 664.1
s. amid opposing legions . 686.2
I s. at the storm . . . 712.1
we're going to s. . . . 801.c
still we get more s. . . 806.1
follow Jesus . . . and s.. . 817.c
takes his staff, and s. says . 911.2
3 *(other)*
mayest s. at all thy foes . 157.1
where no verdure ever s. . 159.3
the s. of love and beauty . 462.2
bids nature s. anew . . 494.2
the world may always s. . 586.2
those angel faces s. . . 606.3

smiling see smile (1b)

smite-smote
hands strong to s. the sins . 129.2
s. and spare not . . . 446.3
b *Ps 121:6*
no sun . . . shall ever s.. . 767.3
c *Ex 7:20*
s. death's . . . wave before you 954.4

smitten 476.2

smoking *(Isa 42:3; Matt 12:20)* 269.2

smooth
it s. all its furrows . . . 237.2
day by day this pathway s. . 358.3
s. and pleasant path . . 586.1
paths are s. for little feet . 664.2

b *Luke 3:5*
make the rugged places s. . 159.1

smote see smite

snap-ped
my Jesus will s. . . . fetter . 273.3
s. sin's fetters . . . 347.c

snare *1 Tim 3:7**
as a shield from every s.. . 66.2
through many . . . toils and s.. 308.3
tempter's s. beset my path . 389.1
what though s. are ready . 400.2
oft escaped the tempter's s. . 633.1

snatch
to s. them from . . . grave . 526.1
s. them in pity . . . 691.1
to s. these from . . . Hell . 720.2
seek not . . . ease to s. . . 816.3

snow
amid the winter's s. . . 88.1
s. or sunshine . . . 544.2
as sunshine melts the s.. . 705.4
in rain and s. and sun . . 926.2
he sends the s. in winter . 935.1
b *Isa 1:18*
will make them like s. . . 883.2
c *white as snow*
it washes w. as s. . . . 128.1
wash and keep me w. as s. . 205.1
flood that washes w. as s. . 231.2
shall be as w. as s.. . . 272.1
flow that makes me w. as s.. 306.c
cleansed my heart as w. as s.. 347.1
can make the sinner w. as s.. 348.3
making me as w. as s. . . 350.2
I'll make them w. as s. . . 359.*
flow that washes w. as s. . 366.c
blood doth cleanse as w. as s. 401.3
he has washed me w. as s. . 404.c
are they w. as s. . . . 417.c
a heart as w. as s. . . . 426.1
aglow to be washed w. as s.469.1, c
make our soldiers w. as s. . 622.2
blood of Jesus cleanses w. . 798.*
forgive, and wash them w. as s. 814.*
blood that washes w. as s. . 909.2
garments must be w. as s. . 914.1
washed as w. as driven s. . c168
washing me w. as s. . . c219
d *whiter than snow* *Ps 51:7*
w., yes w. than s. . . . 281.3
I am w. than s. . . . 322.3
I shall be w. than s. . 436.1, c
a heart . . . w. than s. . . 443.c
I shall be w. than s. . . 459.c
w. than s., Lord, wash me . 487.2
blood washes w. than s. . 535.c
makes my heart w. than s. . 535.4
w. than the driven s. . . 540.2
his blood makes me w. than s. 808.c
cleansing w. than the . . . s. . c42
drive (c)

so *(conjugation)* nc, but
a *so [that]*
s. t. with willing service . 574.3
s. t. in full accord . . . 574.5
s. t. wherever I may go . 620.4
s. t. all may plainly see . 777.4
s. we may Jesus gain . . 915.3
s. t., rejoicing with us . . 927.3
s. t., if . . . next year . . 933.4
2 *(so with adjective)* nc, but see amazing, deep, gentle, glad, great (2f), mild
3 *(so with adverb)* nc, but
a *so [much]*
clouds ye s. m. dread . 29.3

men feared them s. . . 129.2
thou who hast done s. m. . 488.1
because we love him so. . 700.c
why it is I love him s. . . c211
b *John 3:16*
s. loved he the world . . 22.1
all because he loved me s. . 134.c
him, who loves me now so well 345.4
tell how he loved us s. . . 384.1
just because he loved me s. . 389.c
didst die, loving me s. . . 443.c
that God s. loved the world . 828.2
my Father loves me s. . . 837.4
because (a) long (4c) well (2f)

soar-ing
mountains high s. above . 8.2
as our spaceships s. . . 27.4
Lord of s. satellite . . 30.2
like the birds that s. . . 32.3
s. we now where Christ. . 143.5
I s. to worlds unknown . . 302.4
on eagle wings we s. . . 573.4
hope s. beyond death . . 744.6

sober *1 Peter 1:13** . . . 596.2

soft-er-st
silver moon with s. beam . 2.1
s. and sweet, doth entreat . 73.2
s. as the breath of even. . 200.5
with s. breathings stir . . 202.4
heaven above is s. blue . . 545.2
s. dews of kindly sleep . . 676.2
attends the s. prayer . . 715.4
s. refreshing rain . . . 935.1

soften-ed-ing
he sees thy s. spirit . . 256.2
love will s. every sorrow . 503.3
till daylight s. into even . . 564.4
some s. gleam of love . . 668.3
winters, s. by thy care . . 925.3

softly
tell me the story s.. . . 98.3
s. . . . Jesus is calling . . 264.1
sing it s. through the gloom . 393.3
whisper s. in your heart . 664.3
s. the shadows fall . . 675.1

soil
bursts from the furrowed s. . 923.2
seed in the fertile s. . . 931.2
fruits thy generous s. . . 933.1

sojourn *Heb 11:9* . . 880.2

solace
a s. here I find . . . 187.3
longed for, s. and peace. . 351.3
my hope, my s. . . . 356.4
my s. in thy grief is found . 486.3
thou wilt find a s. there . . 645.3

sold 161.2

soldier *(2 Tim 2:3, 4)*
s., give thanks, and sing . 164.1
he will lead his s. forth . . 312.2
I'm a s. bound . . . going home 338.1
God is with us, we're his s. . 381.3
while I am a s. here . . 563.5
made into s. to fight . . 608.3
make our s. white as snow . 622.2
bless our s. 622.4
makes the s.'s armour bright . 646.3
where s. may repair . . 658.4
his blood and fire s. . . 684.2
can I not a s. be . . . 686.1
a valiant s. be . . . 686.4
O s., awake 689.1
onward, Christian s. . . 690.*

s., rouse thee 693.1
rouse, then s., rally . 698.c
every s. who fears not . 703.1
his s. I would be . . . 774.3
our s. will be brave . . . wave. 775.1
glad to take a s.'s part . 776.3
keep us . . . faithful s. . 787.c
need of dauntless s. . 787.2
on to the conflict, s. . 813.1
will give his s. victory . 814.3
valiant s., marching/fighting . 817.*
join our ranks as s. . 818.c
I call to arms the s. . 830.2
home of the s. . . 873.*
bidding a s. . . . cease . 894.1
march on, happy s. . 905.4
that s. may be trained . 919.3
we as faithful s. keep . 922.1
I am a s., glory . . . washed . c229
b *Army soldiers*
fire, is the A. s.'s might . 807.2
we're s. in the A. . . 810.c
we're the s. of the A. . 822.1
s. in the A. 866.c
c *soldiers of the cross*
am I a s. of the c. . . 678.1
s. fighting round the c. . 694.1
s. of the c., arise . . 697.1
stand . . . ye s. of the c. . 699.1
s. of the c., be strong . 816.4
his warriors, s. of the c. . 866.3
ye valiant s. of the c. . 912.1
I want to be a s. of the c. . c231
s. of the c. are faring forth . c238
d *soldier of [Jesus]*
the s. of J. shall see . 289.3
s. of the heavenly King . 314.1
the s. of J. rejoices . 406.1
s. of J., be valiant . 681.c
s. of Christ, arise . . 695.1
s. of King J. . . 866.1, c
s. of Christ, well done . 890.5
the Lord's true faithful s. . 894.c
e *God's soldier*
G. is with us, we're his s. . 381.3
s. of our G., arise . 696.1
G. is keeping his s. . 800.1
G.'s s. . . . . . . 801.*
f *salvation soldier*
a s. s. . . . Jesus/glory I'll be 684.1, 3
s. s., fighting on . . 782.3
march on, s. s. . . 810.1
every true s. s. . . 902.4
g *true soldier*
a s. t., a s. who . . 801.1
may thy s., faithful, t. . 876.3
the Lord's t. faithful s. . 894.c
every t. salvation s. . 902.4
be a s. brave and t. . c228
s., brave-hearted and t. . c231
try again thy t. s. to be . c235
h *John 19:23*
parted 'mong the s. . . 126.2
i *2 Tim 2:4*
chosen to be a s. . . . c225
choose (1d)

sole-ly
devoted s. to thy will . 516.3
s. business be thy praise . 516.5
in thy s. glory may unite . 665.5

solemn
world in s. stillness lay . 83.1
soon in s. loneness . 325.4
hear in this s. evening hour . 558.5
fresh and s. splendour . 632.2
when, in s. covenant . 774.3
who hears our s. vow . 784.4
may this s. consecration . 865.3
sowing . . . in the s. night . 931.1
a moment so s. . . . c106

solemnise 638.3

solid
s. joys and lasting treasure . 157.3
s. comfort when we die . 464.2
on Christ, the s. rock . 745.c

sombre 644.2

some
1 *(pronoun)*
s. have heard, but tell . 243.4
s. of self and s. of thee . 548.2
s. are sick . . . lost the love . 558.3
s. we love . . . have wandered 576.2
s. would try to crush us . 810.3
s. may bring . . . health . 849.1
2 *(adjective)*
begin . . . s. heavenly theme . 26.1
kindled in s. hearts . 165.1
seems now s. soul to say . 226.1
would you like s. peace . 244.2
could I hear s. sinner say . 275.4
let s. showers fall on me . 295.1
light s. pain is bringing . 434.4
s. poor fainting . . . seaman 478.c, 3
s. clear, winning word . 519.2
s. offering/song/work . . . 524.*
s. softening gleam . . 668.3
s. poor wandering child . 676.4
help you s. other to win . 823.1
do s. witnessing for Jesus . 832.c
send to others s. blessing . c59
lay s. soul upon my heart . c79
b *some day*
exchange it s. d. for a crown . 124.c
he'll call me s. d. . . 124.3
s. d. I'll cross . . . the gates . 884.*
s. glad, sweet d. . . . 884.c

somebody/one
s. cares . . . knows . 238.c
s. is ready, s. is waiting . 278.1
s.'s life . . . s.'s care . 384.c
great if s. loves me . 544.2

something
feel s. better . . . must be . 298.4
s. worth saving . . 319.1
s. for thee . . . . 524.*
s. lives in every hue . 545.2

sometimes
if s. men can live/give/treat . 50.2
do you s., feel . . 238.1
s. we're tempted . . 316.2
path that's s. thorny . 462.1
s. the way be stony . 462.2
s. I mount . . . s. all frown . 468.1
s. . . . way may seem rough . 523.4
s. trusting . . . s. sad . 549.1
s. his happy people march . 705.3
s. 'mid scenes . . . bowers . 725.2
s. . . . the trail is a-winding . 903.1

somewhat 244.3

somewhere 186.1

son
1 *(divine)*
he gave us his S. . . . 22.1
come . . . through Jesus the S. 22.c
rejoicing through Jesus the S. 22.3
God's love brought his S. 47.2, 3
the presence of his S. . 106.4
risen, conquering S. . 152.1, c
pardon, through Jesus . . . S. 186.4
on Jesus, his S., will believe . 392.1
I believe on the S. . . 392.c
will of his glorious S. . 654.4
supplies through his eternal S. 695.1
mind . . . in Christ, the S. . 705.4
the S. as man is known . . 785.2
here let your S. be honoured . 943.4
b *(in Trinity)*
praise the Father . . . S. . . 2.5
the S. and him who reigns . 12.3
I believe in God the S. . 222.c
hail Father, S. and Holy Ghost 223.5
from the Father and the S. . 481.1
praise Father S. . . 665.6; 959
with God the Father dwell...S. 785.2
the Father, S. and Spirit . 833.3
Father, S. and Spirit, raising . 939.5
O Father . . . S. . . . Spirit . 958
c *Son of God*
the risen S. of G. . . 46.2
lately passed the S. of G. . 59.1
what a name for the S. of G. 118.1
of G. and man the S. . 177.1, 4
S. of G., with him to be . 180.4
S. of G.! Thy cross . . 185.1
S. of G. as man came down 274.*
thy power alone, O S. of G. . 297.5
when I think of G.'s S. . 319.3
can be seen in G. the S. . 324.1
dear S. of G. and . . . man . 398.4
thou S. of G. most high . 590.3
the S. of G. goes forth . 701.1
we follow Jesus, S. of G. . 705.1
with the conquering S. of G. 819.c
G., the S., forever reigns . 887.4
d *Son of man* *Matt 9:6*
O S. of m., to right my lot . 91.2
tree whereon the S. of m. . 131.1
thou of God and m. the S. . 177.1
S. of God and S. of m. . . 177.4
dear S. of God and S. of m. . 398.4
e *John 3:16*
spare thine only S. . . 15.3
he gave us his S. . . . 22.1
teach us in your only S. . 27.6
God gave his S. for me . 45.1
he should give his S. to die . 48.c
gav'st thy S. to save me . 221.1
beloved (b), David, dear (2f), own (4e), spare (c), virgin
2 *(human)*
bears all its s. away . . 13.5
more than nature's s. to be . 38.5
s. of men and angels say . 143.1
all the s. of want . . 160.3
the s. of ignorance . 414.5
fairer than the s. of men . 497.3
to Hannah's s. revealed . 839.2
foremost of the s. of light . 909.1
thy s., from earth apart . 942.3
b *sons of earth*
born to raise the s. of e. . 82.3
when the s. of e. revile you . 95.3
till s. of e. are s. of God. . 181.1
c *son of God John 1:12/1 John 3:1**
S. of G., . . . praise . . 165.3
till s. of earth are s. of G. . 181.1
s. of G., . . . trifles leaving . 693.c
forward, O ye s. of G. . 696.2
who serves my Father as a s.. 826.3
reign with the s. of G. . . c249
d *2 Cor 6:18*
well supply thy s. . . 157.2

sonship *(Rom 8:16)* . . 207.3

song
1 *(present)*
crowd . . . with thankful s. . 4.3
turned into a s. . . . 7.4
a s. of purest-beauty . . 70.c
every voice a s. . . . 81.1
this is our s. . . . 166.c
my s. shall ever be . . 179.c
will somewhere find a s. . 186.1
our s. shall rise to thee . 220.1

hearest the s. that resound 263.2
this is my story . . . s. 310.c
let our s. abound 314.3
this shall my s. in eternity 323.4
but not a s. like mine 326.5
merits my soul's best s. 336.2
a s. of cheer is ringing 340.1
life flows on in endless s. 358.1
s. that's ringing 389.*
the s., and the crown 406.3
let this be my s. 437.4
your service is s. 506.2
saved from all sin . . . s. 681.3
love . . . the theme of our s. 700.c
pleasant the conqueror's s. 712.4
rapturous s. are mine 726.3
with music and with s. 775.2
we'll have another s. 815.1
awake, happy s. 818.c
our universal battle s. 821.3
go with your s. of mercy 830.2
tell the world in s. 835.1
there in s. unbroken 835.3
make my life a little s. 838.3
the s. that they breathe 886.2
melodious s. of the blest 900.2
the s. of the blood-washed 904.2
thine shall be the s. 926.2
blessèd is that harvest s. 934.4
strange their word, their s. 939.2
life's a happy s. c201
life is a s. when you walk c215
I love the songsters' s. c230

b *song of love*
the l. s. which they bring 83.2
my s. shall be, l. for him. 400.3
sing s. of l. and praise 929.1
a s. of grateful l. 929.1
sing a s. of l. c201
sing . . . the s. of his l. c222

c *song of praise* *Ps 28:7*
in s. of p. my heart bursts 39.c
now be the s. of p. begun 151.1
we join our s. of . . . p. 173.1
so I'll sing in s. of p. 266.4
in rapturous s. to p. 275.2
call for s. of loudest p. 313.1
his p. proclaiming in s. 537.4
s. of p. I will ever give 578.3
demand perpetual s. of p. 672.3
with loud joyful s. of p. 807.1
thank him . . . in a s. of p. 836.c
demand successive s. of p. 925.4
sing s. of love and p. 929.1
O then with s. of p. 940.2

d *songs of salvation*
s. of s. are sounding 383.1
s. is our s. 814.1
in the morning the s. of s. c222

e *song of triumph*
the t. s. of life 10.4
let our s. his t. tell 149.1
raised in the t. s. 392.3
blend . . . in the t. s. 690.5
greet them with this t.-s. 744.1
sweet s. of t. sing 761.3
then to swell the t. s. 799.4
s. t. and music 873.2
steals . . . the distant t. s. 876.4

f *songs of victory*
this our s. of v. 393.4
the next the victor's s. 699.4
marching to s. of v. 901.2
s. of v., sing 901.4

g *all songs*
this a. my s. shall be 368.1
Jesus shall be a. our s. 381.3
still a. my s. shall be 617.1, 5
sweetest note in a. our s. 925.5
goodness has been a. my s. c147

h *Ps 118:14*
he shall be our s. 9.1
God is our strength and s. 20.4
if thou art my . . . s. 318.4
my solace, and my s. 356.4
Jesus shall be all our s. 381.3
Jesus is my light and s. 400.*

i *Isa 35:10; Rev 5:9*
join in the everlasting s. 56.5
be this th'eternal s. 187.5
this my ceaseless s. 360.4
redemption's endless s. 828.4
blending in s. unending 888.1
unceasing s. of gladness 899.3

deliverance (b), employ (2), give (1u), glad (f), glorious (2g), hear (1g), join (d), joyful (d), Lamb (2g), new (g), night (2d), raise (2b), sing (3h), sweet (3e), swell (2b)

2 *(song of angels)*
sweetest note in seraph s. 67.c
s. that the a. sang 80.1
s. that the shepherds heard 80.2
love s. which they bring 83.2
s. which now the a. sing 83.3
addressed their joyful s. 93.5
the s. of the a. band 94.c
a. descend with s. again 160.5
sing the a.'s s. 374.3
a. in their s. rejoice 625.4
when the s. of a. wake me 751.4
borne in a s. to me 889.1
the s. of a. resounding 894.1

glorious (2g)

3 *(other)*
God speaks . . . in bird and s. 31.1
Master surely heard the s. 103.4

songsters c230

soon
1 *re life*
I forget so s. 98.2
finds s. the joys . . . flown 267.1
s. as my all I ventured 361.2
thou s. shalt be fitted 458.4
flowers s. will be asleep. 673.2
bright skies will s. be o'er 736.3

2 *re Kingdom*
shalt see my glory s. 110.5
s. the desert will be glad 159.3
s. shall hear . . . voice 164.c
s. our coming King 347.3
s. shall have our colours 775.c
s. o'er every land and sea 810.3
s. . . . conflict cease, . . . dawn 813.4
Kingdom s. shall see 932.4

3 *re Heaven*
s. I shall see his face 45.3
s. we hope to meet above 239.4
we s. shall meet together 312.3
secret . . . s. be made known 372.4
s. end in joyous day 721.2
see you, s. or late 748.1
s. we shall escape 809.4
s. we in realms of Glory 828.4
I'll s. be at home 886.4
s. will the Lord . . . prepare 887.5
s. his beauty . . . pearly gates 892.4
s. shall we joyfully know 904.4
s. . . . delights we shall prove. 905.4
yes, s. we'll be massed 905.4

4 *re death*
s. that voice will cease 240.3
s. will pass . . . grace . . . cold 241.4
s. the day is coming 250.4
s. in solemn loneness 325.4
struggles s. shall cease 752.7
its joys as s. are past 880.2
blast s. will be overpast 882.2
grave you'll s. be lying 913.1
chance will s. be past 913.2
s. the reaping time 932.c

soothe-ing
it s. his sorrows 58.1
hands quick to s. 129.2
gentle s. of thy Spirit 192.1
it s. all life's sorrows 237.2
can s. thy troubled breast 261.2
s. and hush and calm it 325.3
s. the hurt with . . . balm 479.2
to s. and sympathise 485.2
words that s. and heal 529.3
may speak with s. power 612.5

sore
1 *(adjective)*
gaze upon thy s. distress 122.2
with s. abuse and scorn. 123.1
this s. bondage 297.5
s. temptations may beset 399.3
O by temptations s. 571.3

2 *sore-ly (adverb)*
the wolves have s. hurt 111.2
art thou s. distressed 228.1
heavy-laden, s. oppressed 261.2
by Satan s. pressed 284.3
I was wearied s. 311.3
Satan tempt me s. 344.2
my burden pressed me s. 391.2
I struggled s. 490.1
soul, though wearied s. 590.3
where men have s. failed 706.1
the s. stricken soul of life 827.1
when tempted s. to worry c145

sorrow
1 *(divine)*
his cross and s. see 94.3
for this thy dying s. 123.3
his s. darken all our skies 127.1
s. and love . . . meet 136.3
speak his s. ended 155.2
by his s. joy revealed 402.3
it is joy to share thy s. 502.2
in s. bowed beneath the skies 855.4
I think of all his s. c14

b *bore sorrows* *Isa 53:3*
Jesus, who our s. b. 97.4
tell of the s. he b. 99.2
thine the s. b. for me 122.1
acquainted with s. was he 137.2
Jesus who b. our s. 184.2
held our s. in embrace 242.4
our s. and suffering to share 245.1
he . . . all my s. b. 344.2
by s. that he b. 571.3

c *Lam 1:12*
no s. . . . like the s. he bore 245.3

man (1b)

2 *(human)*
it soothes his s., heals 58.1
bids our s. cease 64.3
child of s. and of woe 66.1
s. hides beneath her wings 145.3
comfort thy s. and answer 183.2
hear thy tale of s. 225.c
many a s., many a labour 228.4
earth has no s. 236.*
come, cast in thy s. 237.3
a heart o'erbound by s. 246.1
its s. all too keen 267.2
seeing my s. . . . my tears 294.1
out of my bondage, s. 300.1
when s.'s waves . . . roll 317.3
s.'s path I often tread 337.4
in s. he's my comfort 344.1
s. filled my . . . heart 363.3
out of the shadows of s. 378.1
not a s. we share 397.3
s. on my heart may fall 399.3
I bring the s. laid on me 421.4
when in my s. he found me 467.3
coming with my heart of s. 470.2
sense of s. over sin 496.4

love will soften every s.. . 503.3
bid sadness and s. depart . 537.1
our world so filled with s. . 576.2
when in s., when in danger . 582.3
bid the fears and s. . . . depart 599.2
who will all our s. share. . 645.2
our balm in s. . . . 674.4
to cheer a world of s. . . 706.1
wipe s.'s tears away . . 743.3
my s. to subdue . . . 749.3
peace, with s. surging round . 752.3
sing through days of s. . . 764.3
s. like sea-billows roll . . 771.1
though . . . through s. . . 805.2
sin-sick and s.-worn . . 825.1
it stanches s.'s tear . . 828.3
in the underworld of s. . . 832.1
trials and s. ... meaning found 894.2
aye the dews of s.. . . . 896.3
your s. shall cease . . . c31
not in s. to defeat me . . c166

b *[life's] sorrows*
all earth's s. . . . disappearing. 169.1
it soothes all life's s. . . 237.2
out of earth's s. . . . 300.2
life's s. lose their sting . . 503.1
Jesus is in all life's s. . . 750.2

c *sorrow and sin*
from s. and s. free . . 69.4
bring thy s., thy s. . . 126.4
away with s. and s. . . 153.1
all earth's s. and its s. . . 169.1
he took my s. and s. . . 179.3
liberty from s., fear and s. . 441.1
'mid earth's s. and s. . . 529.1
I see the s. and s. . . 830.1
abound: s. and want and s. . 841.3
when, from s. and s. free . 897.2
freedom from s., from s. . 904.3
free from s., free from s. . 924.4
gave s.'s s. to dispel . . c7

d *no sorrow in Heaven* *Rev 21:4*
from sin and s. free . . 69.4
all earth's s. . . . disappearing. 169.1
s. vanquished, labour ended . 228.5
for s. . . . joy shall receive . 372.4
realms where s. cease . . 697.5
there'll be no s. . . . 881.c
away from my s. and care . 886.3
no s. in God's tomorrow . 888.c
free from the blight of s. . 889.2
labour and s. cease . . 890.4
strife and s. over . . 894.c
there will be no s. there. . 899.3
our spirits shall s. no more . 900.2
freedom from sin, from s. . 904.3
from s. and trials are free . 908.2
shall all their s. chase . . 909.3
free from s., free from sin . 924.4
there'll be no s. there . . c250

care (3d), doubt (g), joy (2h), pain (3a), shame (2c), sigh (c)

sorrowing
bring all the sick and s. . . 104.3
s. heart . . . find rest . . 364.3

sorry 899.1

sought see seek

soul
1 *vocative—my soul*
arise, my s., arise . . . 106.1
hark, my s.! it is the Lord . 110.1
be swift, my s., to answer . 162.3
approach my s., the mercy seat 284.1
my s., ask what thou wilt . 560.2
come, my s., thy suit prepare. 563.1
have faith in God, my s.. . 723.3
my helpless s., rest thou . 729.2
hark, hark, my s. . . . 802.1
my s. be on thy guard . . 812.1
awake (b, e)

b *other souls*
believing s. rejoicing go . . 46.4
fearful s. discard thy fears . 249.3
come, thirsty s. . . . 254.3
s. of men! why . . . scatter . 265.1
trembling s., dispel thy fear . 269.1
leave it all . . . needy s.. . 333.4
s. in danger, look above. . 336.3
O s., consider and be wise . 885.1

c *Ps 42:5*
why cast down, my s. . . 557.4

d *Ps 103:1*
praise, my s., the King . . 17.1
O my s., praise him. . . 19.1

2 *my soul*
then sings my s. . . . to thee. 37.c
with grace our s. enduing . 38.5
in . . . hands my s. I trust . 48.1
refresh my s. in death . . 58.5
how it thrills our s. . . 66.3
how my s. delights to hear . 67.4
in nothing else my s. shall glory 107.5
my s. looks back to see. . 120.4
love . . . for my s. he gave . 130.4
love . . . demands my s.. . 136.4
waiting not to rid my s. . 293.2
wash thou my s. this day . 296.3
pass o'er my s. . . . 296.4
my s. outpouring . . . 303.1
they would leave my s. . . 303.2
when shall my s. return . . 307.1
amen, amen, my s. replies . 312.4
Satan, dismayed, from my s. 323.5
my s. revived . . . 332.2
my s. in mercy to reclaim . 339.1
with my s. . . . 'tis well. . 339.4
he's the fairest . . . to my s. . 344.1
what power my s. can sever . 345.4
gave his life to ransom my s.. 349.1
joy floods my s. . . . 349.3
no nation owns my s. . . 362.1
flow rolls o'er my s. . . 375.2
floods of joy o'er my s. . 394.c
my s. was lost . . . 402.2
by his stripes my s. was healed 402.3
thou my s. sustained . . 409.2
visit, then this s. . . . 412.4
my s. I cast 415.1
doubts that have darkened my s. 422.3
its power has touched my s. . 434.5
from my s. break every fetter. 439.4
drive . . . from out my s. . 440.2
set my s. at liberty. . . 446.4
my s. doth follow on . . 448.1
thou whom my s. adoreth . 448.3
wilt thou not my s. release . 450.3
my s. . . . draws nigh . . 454.2
with hope my s. is swelling . 460.1
let thy power my s. refine . 460.3
tempt . . . my s. repels . . 480.4
close...would my s. ever keep 483.3
no joy that turns my s. . . 489.2
grace our s. sufficing . . 500.2
never more stain my s. . . 502.3
I, believing, trust my s. . . 514.2
now . . . thou hast my s. . 516.2
in love my s. would bow . 524.1
my s. . . . fulness would prove 535.3
my s. has found a resting place 536.c
glory came thrilling my s. . 542.3
in thee my s. hath found . 547.1
ghosts . . . shall haunt my s.. 551.2
so longs my s., O Lord . 557.1
our s. shall drink . . . supply . 559.4
our s. shall fly . . . 559.5
take from our s. the strain . 567.4
comes down our s. to greet . 573.4
then yield up my s. . . 589.5
come, invade my s. . . 613.1
my s. . . . found relief . . 633.1
flow through my s. . . 647.3
my s. . . . supply . . . 671.3
he hideth my s. in . . . rock 710.1, c
my s. . . . faithfully commend. 714.4
seeking my s. to claim . . 724.3
my s. doth climb . . . 729.4
my s. shall fear no ill . . 731.c
keeps my s. alive . . . 733.6
my s. . . . vigour renew . . 734.2
nor . . . put my s. to shame . 735.2
appoint my s. a place . . 735.4
my s. doth triumph . . 741.3
all around my s. gives way . 745.3
I would pour out my s. . . 762.1
my s. has called upon thee . 762.2
lo! my s. . . . kneeling . . 762.3
it is well with my s. . . 771.*
held our s. in thrall . . 827.2
give to my s. . . . fire . . 830.3
shield my s. from sin . . 862.2
soon . . . my s. prepare . . 887.5
my s. I leave . . . to thy care. 917.1
our s. arrive in peace . . 918.4
grant our s. thy peace . . 942.4
illuminate my s. . . . c50
care my s. would flurry . . c145
brings the glory to my s. . c170

aspire, baptise, cleanse (e), feed (b), free (1b, d-f), hold (1b), inspire (c), keep (3k), overflow (a), pant, redeem (b), rejoice (g), restore (c), satisfy (b)

b *passive*
my s. is now united . . 361.1
my s. was made right . . 395.3
my s. was healed . . . 402.3
on thee . . . my s. is stayed . 419.2
my s. is made perfect . . 436.4
the s. kept clean . . . 541.3
no dread...make my s. afraid 726.1

c *let soul*
l. our whole s. an offering . 217.3
there l. my s. be blest . . 431.3
l. my s. look up . . . 585.2
l. my s. meet thee there . 647.1

d *(with adjective)*
stir our wayward s. . . 202.4
fill this empty s. of mine . 206.1
fill our spotless s. with God . 210.1
kneel . . . a pleading s. . . 303.3
my newborn s. found breath . 343.1
not stir my lifeless s. . . 353.4
my s. is full of joy . . . 402.c
a struggling s. for life . . 415.2
pain my well-instructed s. . 425.4
a s. on fire . . . baptised. . 426.3
divide this consecrated s. . 480.3
lead my captive s. astray . 509.2
bid our inmost s. rejoice. . 603.5
give me a self-denying s. . 619.2
my steadfast s. relies . . 746.4
young s. meekly striving . 849.2
as ripened s. we wish . . 926.4

burdened (b), faint (c), hungry, longing (1c), lost (3e), poor (3d), precious (f), ransomed (c), seeking (2), sinbound, sinful (d), thirsty (a), trembling (b), waiting, whole (1d)

e *all my soul*
a. our s. we bow . . . 424.4
a. m. s. o'erflowing . . 546.1
shall a. m. s. possess . . 615.2
deluge a. m. s. . . . 620.4
a. m. simple s. devour . . 720.1
a. m. s. with zeal . . . 733.5
body (2g)

f *fill my soul*
f. this empty s. of mine . . 206.1
f. our spotless s. with God . 210.1
f. m. s. with joy . . . 309.c
m. s. f. with rapture . . 364.4

Glory f. m. s. . . . 371.c
f. m. s. with perfect love . 441.c
f. m. s. with love to thee . 445.2
thought shall f. m. s. . 517.2
f. m. s. with perfect peace . 549.2
m. needy s. to f. . . . 586.3
his love will ever f. m. s. . c194

g *in/within my soul*
breathe in our s. . . . 211.3
in my s. are blending . . 222.3
joy and gladness in my s. . 309.2
finds an echo in my s. . . 358.1
sunshine/music . . . in my s. . 387.*
I have light in my s. . . 394.1
for ever to live in my s. . . 436.1
darkness brought into my s. . 448.2
in my s. an Easter morning . 520.5
I feel it in my s. . . . 562.3
knowledge...into my s. convey 565.2
depths within our s. . . 572.4
hear . . . love within my s. . 600.3
in many a s., and mine . . 629.3
pour it in my s. . . . c91
there is peace within my s. . c131

h *on my soul*
glory is dawning o. m. s. . 98.4
dawn upon this s. of mine . 194.1
falls today o. m. s. . . 379.4
shine o. m. s. from Heaven . 446.1
fire, descending . . . upon m. s. 511.3
here o. our s. descend . . 590.4
if o. m. s. a trace . . . c72
new touch . . . o. m. s., Lord c97

i *Ps 34:2*
my s. shall make her boast . 468.4

j *Ps 37:7*
my s. can rest in nothing . 446.4
when shall my s. . . . rest . 454.1
may my s. on thee repose . 671.4
until I rest . . . mind and s. . 723.4
my helpless s., rest thou . 729.2
blessèd rest of my s. . . 771.4
sweetly my s. shall rest . . 889.1

k *heart/soul* *Matt 22:37*
bless . . . with h. and s.. . 20.1
loving touch upon my h. and s. 215.1
until I rest, h. mind and s. . 723.4
my h. and s., are there . . 880.3

3 *your/thy*
compass all t. s.'s relief . 129.3
afar . . . t. s. has strayed . 225.1
his love . . . will pardon t. s. . 237.3
will y. bow y. s. . . . 242.5
no other name . . . bring t. s. 269.3
do not . . . forfeit y. s. . 273.4
want Jesus . . . in y. s. . 427.2
be calm in t. s. . . . 458.4
doom y. unrepenting s. . 885.2
keep the touch . . . on y. s. . c76
glory gets into y. s. . . c223

b *Ps 121:7*
every evil . . . keep thy s. . 767.4

4 *soul—the etc*
one s., one feeling breathe . 196.3
how pure t. s. must be . . 414.1
t. s. finds happiness in none 556.3
rich in goods and poor in s. . 577.3
knows . . . a s.'s repose. . 580.1
prayer is t. s.'s . . . desire . 625.1
when sinks t. s. . . . 632.3
when t. s. waketh . . 632.4
no weakness of t. s. . . 695.3
sorely stricken s. of life . . 827.1
man has . . . no s. . . . c210

b
power into strengthless s. . 60.3
joy that bears t. s. above . 70.4
t. wounded s. to cure . . 81.3
where meek s. will receive . 86.3
loose the s. long prisoned . 155.4
only faithful s. can hear . . 214.2
seems now some s. to say . 226.1
t. s. in nature's night . . 230.2
another s. forgiven . . 259.4
ten thousand thousand s. . 266.1
room for such poor s. . . 266.2
when guilty s. . . . plead. . 269.2
that s. will I supply . . 277.2
that s. shall never hunger . 277.2
gifts for s. distressed . . 287.1
still to t. lowly s. . . . 411.3
fountain . . . for t. s. unclean 417.3
needy s. are still my mission . 463.3
to t. s. it is the giver . . 471.1
t. s. who were lost . . 527.1
witnessing from soul to s. . 546.3
joy today for a s. . . . 550.1
yes, a s. is rescued . . 550.2
engaging prove to s. impressed 556.1
to praying s. . . . grants . . 560.3
s. shall be truly converted . 608.3
to t. hopeless s. make known 620.2
engage t. waiting s. to bless 633.2
that s. . . . never forsake . 653.5
lives renewed and s. reborn . 656.4
wake dead s. to love . . 669.5
blood-bought s. destroying . 696.2
t. trusting s. shall prove . 718.3
t. coward's s. may frighten . 805.2
t. s. about to die . . . 819.1
t. new-born s., whose days . 825.3
all Christly s. are one . . 826.4
kindred s. each other greet . 873.3
s. in sin's deep sleep . . 875.3
s. in darkness . . . calling . 922.1
lay some s. upon my heart . c79
love that s. through me . . c79
s. are needing us . . . c239

c
who would . . . their s. unite . 251.4
with gladness filled her s. . 304.3
their s. is Christ's abode. . 411.1
his s. is found in peace . . 890.4

d *soul that/who*
for s. w. led in deed . . 5.2
the s. t. now are starting . 169.2
the s. t. is trusting Jesus . 186.1
the s. t. once has walked . 267.1
s. w. are bound . . . 523.3
the s. w. were lost . . 527.1
s. t. . . . leaned for repose . 653.5
by the s. t. love him . . 682.3
the s. t. trusted him . . 738.3
the s. w. dwell in darkness . c236

e *Lev 17:11*
e'en for my s., was shed . 116.4
blood that atones for the s. . 271.3
no wound hath the s. . . 364.3
for my s. . . . blood was spilt. 403.1

each (2c) every (d) man (2h) other (1b) save (1m) sick (c) win (2d)

5 *(possessive)*
re Jesus
thou my s.'s glory . . . 177.1
thou guest of the s. . . 209.1
Christ, my s. redeemer . . 221.2
thou the refuge of my s. . 627.2
pilot of s., I trust . . . 628.4
sun of my s. 676.1
thou hast the guarding of my s. 717.4
still my s. defender . . 762.1
thou Guardian of my s. . . 862.3

b *(general)*
the s. enduring worth . . 181.4
the temple of my s. prepare . 207.1
fill every chamber of my s. . 208.2
the s. eternal prize . . . 266.c
from whence my s. distress . 290.2
the ruins of my s. repair. . 305.3
merits my s.'s best songs . 336.2
cure for my s.'s ailing . . 456.2
my s.'s greatest longing . 493.1
every feeling of my s. . . 503.1
let the yearning of my s. . 630.2
fortress and my s. release . 631.2
find my s. refreshment . . 644.c
bread of our s., . . . feed . 654.2
meet the hunger of my s. . 830.1
home of my s., how near . 877.2
all the passion of my s. . . c32

anchor, desire (2b), lover

6 *soul-*
s.-renewing grace . . . 290.3
reachèd this s.-cleansing sea . 298.5
s.-cheering presence restore . 318.4
that s.-transporting hour . 350.1
s.-cleansing blood of the Lamb 417.c
the s.-refreshing view of Jesus 442.2
give me more s.-saving love . 609.1
s.-saving truth inspire . . 609.2
create s.-thirst for thee . . 626.2

sound-ed-ing
let the amen s. 19.5
s. his power abroad . . . 26.2
linking sense to s. . . . 28.3
it s. quite incredible . . 49.1
Jesus, transporting s. . . 62.2
hark the glad s. . . . 81.1
s. through all the worlds . 223.3
the gospel news is s. . . 239.1
s. the tidings right along . 249.1
s. this word of grace . . 262.1
shout, shout the s. . . 279.1
grace! how sweet the s.. . 308.1
word with heavenly s. . . 319.2
abound in the rapturous s. . 355.3
once I heard a s. . . . 373.1
conspire to raise the s. . . 382.2
songs of salvation are s. . 383.1
s. . . . the depths of love . 651.4
voices have a kindly s. . . 664.1
let the gospel s. . . . 693.c
s. the battle cry . . . 698.1
long s. the cry . . . 703.1
hark! the s. of singing . . 803.1
s. the ringing cry . . . 813.1
s. a nobler call . . . 827.2
the call has s. . . . 894.1

b *joyful sound* *(Ps 89:15)*
repeat the s. joy . . . 84.2
O j. s.! O glorious hour . 149.1
who hears the j. s. . . 254.1
salvation! O the j. s. . . 382.1
we have heard the j. s. . . 393.1
the dumb s. j. cry . . . 590.3
when they hear the j. s.. . 815.2

c *sound [of name]*
sweet the n. of Jesus s.. . . 58.1
a sweeter s. than thy blest n.. 61.2
bless the s. of Jesus' n.. . 62.1
it s. like music in mine ear . 69.1
dance at the s. of his n.. . 355.2
I love the s. of Jesus' n.. . 360.c
precious is the s. of Jesus' n.. 370.3
we will s. his n. abroad . . 939.4

d *sound praise*
fill thy courts with s. p. . . 4.3
p. and joy to God we're s. . 74.1
s. his p.! Jesus who bore . 184.2
its p. s. and give . . . glory . 831.3
s. out the p. everywhere . 835.c
s. the p. of Jesus' n. . . c27

e *sound trumpet*
he has s. forth the t. . . 162.3
God's t. is s.: To arms . . 684.1
God's own trumpeters are s. . 868.1

f *hear sound*
all may h. the quickening s. . 140.4
who h. the joyful s. . . 254.1
whosoever h.! shout . . . the s. 279.1
once I h. a s. 373.1
we have h. the joyful s. . . 393.1
when they h. the joyful s. . 815.2
the tempting s. I h. . . 862.2

g *sound voice*
Jehovah's v. doth s. . 253.1
day by day his sweet v. s. . 428.1
insistent s. the v. divine . 864.2
h *Acts 2:2*
O S. of rushing . . . wind . 211.2
abundance (b), brass (b), trumpet (a, b), uncertain

source
s. of victory and joy . 113.3
the s. of all grace . 119.2
trembling to its s. return . 199.2
S. of life, live . . . in me. . 516.3
s. of calm unfailing . 539.3
s. of . . . prophetic fire . 651.1
eternal s. of every joy . 925.1
b *source of power*
s. of life and p. . 213.1
s. of reviving p. . 488.c
the true s. of p . c210

south see north

sovereign
his s. power, without our aid. 4.2
works his s. will . 29.2
depth of s. grace . 55.1
s. grace to all extends . 55.2
thy s., everlasting love . 140.5
s. majesty, may we . . . see . 219.4
throne of s. grace . 269.1
a s. balm for every wound . 382.1
fulfil thy s. counsel . 526.3
s. Lord, we bow . 576.3
s. word restores the light . 672.2
b *(with title)*
and did my s. die . 105.1
wondrous S. of the sea . 598.2

sow-ing-n
1 *(literal)*
after the seed is s. . 923.2
harvest of s. field . 927.1
s. or tilling . 927.2
2 *(figurative)*
though in loneliness we s. . 145.3
seeds now we are s. 928.1, 2
the nature of seeds we now s. 928.2
remember you're s. . 928.3
s. in the morning . . . . 930.*
s. the seed by the . . . . 931.*
b *Ps 126:5*
s. . . . tear-drops start . 931.3
s. in hope, till . . . come. . 931.3
seed s. with tears . 936.4
c *Eccl 11:6*
in the morning s. thy seed . 923.3
s. in the morning . 930.1
d *Matt 13:24, 25*
wheat and tares together s. . 924.2
the sower came to s. . 932.1
e *2 Cor 9:10*
seed for his Kingdom s. . . 923.3

sower
the s.'s scattered seed . 926.2
b *Matt 13:3*
in which the s. came to sow . 932.1

space
whose canopy s. . 16.2
dwellers all in time and s. . 17.4
boundaries of endless s. . 52.c
transcending time and s. . 71.2
content to fill a little s. . . 485.3
glorious eye pervadeth s. . 517.3
way out in s. . . 850.3
fill all the realms of s. . 946.1
Lord of all . . . worlds and s. . 957

spaceship . 27.4

spacious . 382.2

space see speak

span
rainbows s. the heavens high. 39.2
mighty gulf that God did s. . 405.4

spare
he tends and s. us . 17.3
me, the chief of sinners, s. . 286.1
world's bidders have to s. . 796.2
take my life, or s. it . 865.2
ask that thou shouldst s. . 916.1
if in mercy thou wilt s. . . 916.2
b *Isa 30:14*
O smite and s. not . . 446.3
search . . . do not s. it . . 457.1
s. not one lurking sin . 494.3
c *Rom 8:32*
didst not s. . . . Son . 15.3
God, his Son not s. . 37.3

spark . 165.1

sparkled-ing
sunrise . . . s. in his hair. . 103.2
in s. raiment bright . 167.1
issues from the s. throne . 312.2

sparrow
hundreds of s. . 850.1
b *Matt 10:29, 31*
eye is on the s. . c139

speak-ing/spoke-n/spake
voice . . . s. all the promises . 26.3
he s. to me everywhere . . 42.2
power into . . . souls he s. . 60.3
s., the . . . heart to cheer . 67.1
who s. a world from naught . 165.3
made flesh to s. his love. . 181.1
s. of Heaven . 200.5
here s. the Comforter . 236.2
now it s., and s. to thee. . 240.3
listen, belovèd, he s. . 542.4
when he s. . . . lands rejoice . 583.2
from thy lips his word is s. . 595.1
hear thee inly s. . 636.4
he s. through us to men. . 851.4
s. the faithfulness of God . 939.4
b *God speaks*
G. s. to us in . . . . . 31.*
G. s. your name . 267.2
G. s., who cannot lie . 385.2
G. was s. through him . 855.3
c *Jesus speaks*
J. s., and s. to thee . 110.1
my J. s. a pardon free . 402.2
only Christ is heard to s. . 444.2
when J. s. . . . is clear . 449.2
J. s., dissension ceased . 539.2
d *(request)*
O Voice . . . s. thou to me . 31.4
s. to my heart of Calvary . 125.c
s. to calm this tossing sea . 194.4
s. to our hearts today . 209.3
O s. while before thee 422.c; 589.c
let me hear thy voice now s. . 502.1
O s., and I will heed . 502.1
s., Saviour, s. . 502.c
s., Lord, and I . . . will obey . 523.1
s. and make me fully whole . 528.c
s. and tell me now . 534.2
s. through the earthquake . 567.5
Lord, s. to me, that I . 612.1
Master, s. . 614.*
s. with the voice that wakes . 626.1
s. . . . and let me feel . 636.1
s. again and bid me come . 749.2
let me hear thee s. . 862.3
s. to reassure . . . make me . 862.3
s. once again, Lord . c100
e *speak [will]*
s. out thy w. we pray . 209.3
then s. thy w., whate'er . 475.1
s. all thy w., dear Lord . 490.2
s. out thy wishes . 513.c
f *(John 15:3)*
s. the word of power to me . 295.3
the blessèd word was s. . 363.3
enter and s. me pure . 450.3
it is done, the word is s. . 520.4
from thy lips his word is s. . 595.1
the word he has s. . 712.2
g *1 Sam 3:9*
Master, s: thy servant . 614.1
pardon (2d) refuse (b) word (1i)
2 *(we) speak*
a *to God*
only s., and he will hear. . 261.1
I s. to thee my need . 290.2
while I s. to thee . 409.c
s. oft with thy Lord . 458.1
he walks . . . who s. to God . 580.1
why not s. my every need . 770.3
b *to others*
the common words I s. . . 7.2
let all my being s. of thee . 7.3
of a day long past we s.. . 198.2
would for Christ . . . s. . 212.1
s. my Lord's sincerity . 212.2
soldiers . . . must s. . 314.1
I could not s. . 353.3
made . . . the dumb to s. . 353.5
touch . . . that we may s. . 581.4
give power to s. . 609.3
Lord, s. . . . that I may s. . 612.1
may s. with soothing power . 612.5
blush to s. his name . 678.1
s. of mercy and of peace . 697.5
I'll s. the word of comfort . 706.1
salvation! s. salvation . 828.3
we s. of the realms/peace etc. . . 904.*
may every word here s. . 943.3
c *speak and*
work and s. and think . 199.3
where'er I s., or sing . 356.4
from ever fearing to s., sing . 437.4
all I think or s. or do . 492.2
in all I think, or s., or do. . 667.1
d *Matt 10:19*
tells me when to s. . 204.1
glorious (2h) prophet (c)
3 *(other)*
blackbird has s. . 35.1
thus s. the seraph . 93.5
s. his sorrows ended . 155.2
his cross s. our shame . 245.c
voices of evening call, s. . 675.1
no other voice can s. . 731.2
s. of inward purity . 777.3
it s. of grace divine . 781.2
her walls to s. salvation . . 944.1
it s. of power, pardon . c241

speaking *(noun)* . 953

spear *John 19:34*
was it for me . . . the s.. . 134.1
thorn, the crown, the s. . 368.2

special
contentment has a s. set . 244.3
no s. graces . 294.2

speech
robes . . . in childlike s. . . 398.1
the simplest form of s. . 625.3
uttered thought or s. . 682.3

speed-ing/sped
all the world of s. is thine . 30.2
joyful s. to Bethlehem . . 72.5
with joyful steps they s.. . 76.2
s. the day when men . . . see. 135.4
three sad days have quickly s. 151.3
s. the cross . . . victories . 158.3
s. us to labour . . . 173.2
s. forth thy flight . . . 224.3
time is now s. . . . 273.1
s. the war 'gainst sin . . 622.4
s., s. thy work . . . 683.4
power . . . to s. the message. 760.1

spell 693.1

spend-ing-t
gladly be s. in promoting . 298.7
eternal day of glory s. . . 309.3
mis-s. powers stained . . 379.2
years I s. in vanity . . . 405.1
s. all the rest of my days . 422.2
s. much time in secret . . 458.2
for thy truth . . . s.. . . 526.3
before thy throne I s. . . 585.3
before the cross I s. . . 634.1
every sacred moment s.. . 720.4
every treasure s. . . . c48

b *spend life*
s. my life for thee alone . . 108.3
henceforth my l. may be s. . 205.2
life in my service be s. . . 276.4

c *2 Cor 12:15*
labour on, s. and be s. . . 683.1
to s., and to be s. . . . 720.3

sphere
the music of the s.. . . . 27.3
rings the music of the s.. . 42.1
whose native s. is dark . . 414.3

spilt
blood my Saviour s. . . . 108.c
for us his blood was s. . . 108.2
yet for me thy blood was s. . 291.2
the Saviour's blood was s. . 403.1
blood so freely s. for me . 444.1
whose blood was s. to save . 532.4
'twas for me thy blood was s. 538.2
own blood for thee he s. . 560.2
thy blood, for sinners s.. . 563.3
the blood he s. . . . brings . c25

Spirit
1 *Holy Spirit/Ghost*
vocative nc, but see
gentle (b) mighty (1d)

a *Spirit come*
H. S., c., O c. 188.c
c., O S., c. to sanctify . . 188.2
c., gracious S., . . . dove . 190.1
c., thou everlasting S. . . 191.1
c., H. G., all-quickening . 207.1
c., H. G., all sacred fire . 208.1
c., H. S., thou guest . . . 209.*
c., thou all-inspiring S. . 210.1
c., H. G., and fill . . . 216.2
O c., great S., c. . . . 217.1
c., great S., c., make . . 218.c
H. S., c. revealing all . . 434.2
c., H. G., thy mighty aid . 448.4
c., thou burning S., c. . . 481.1
c., O c. great S., c. . . 481.c
c., O S., take control . . 630.2
c., H. G., our hearts . . 651.1
c., H. G., for moved . . 651.2
few on whom the S. came . 701.3
H. S., c. upon us . . . 787.1
c., H. S., and abide . . c62

b *Spirit divine*
S. d., attend our prayers . 217.1
S. d., come as of old . . 218.*
say, by thy S. d. . . . 289.4
O thou S. d., all my nature . c77
illumine me, S. d. c99

2 *(general)*
praise the S., Three in One . 2.5
with thy S. recreate me . 32.1
keep me ever by thy S. . . 32.3
S.'s true illumination . . 38.1
his S. turned our night . . 43.2
chiding/stirring of thy S. 192.2, 3
gives the Comforter, his S. . 195.1
give us the promised H. G. 203.1
by heart received and S. . 211.1
like thy S., gladly given . . 211.3
I believe in the H. S. . . 222.c
when willing, the S. came in . 321.2
all would hear the H. S. . 324.3
dead, his S. gave me life . 330.2
the H. S. entered . . . 361.2
his kind S. did yearn . . 388.2
the S. will come . . . has come410.1, 3
a H. S.'s energies . . . 414.4
now let thy S. bring me in . 419.4
the S. makes me clean . . 447.4
pour in thy S.'s pure light . 457.1
with thy S.'s rich treasure . 457.3
while the S. passes by . . 460.*
his S. only can bestow . . 465.1
taught by your S. . . . 506.3
his S. was moved . . . 527.1
my heart the S.'s shrine . 540.4
thy S. . . . this work must do. 581.2
by the H. G. . . . inflame . 626.2
if the H. S. bless . . . 652.3
defend us with thy S. . . 685.3
brightly doth his S. shine . 754.2
listening . . . to the S.'s call . 757.4
Saviour's blood, the H. G. . 779.2
yellow, emblem of the S. . 783.3
sanctified, kept by the S. . 785.5
your S. be obeyed . . . 943.4
his S. helping me . . . c107

b *Luke 23:46*
as his s. passed away . . 96.3

c *John 16:14*
the H. S. makes him known . 102.3

d *Rom 8:16; 1 John 5:8*
his S. answers to the blood . 106.4
let the H. S. witness . . 474.3
his S. answers to the blood . c129

e *Heb 9:14*
by thine own eternal S. . . 79.4
come, thou everlasting S. . 191.1
eternal S., heavenly dove . 946.3

born (1d), Father (1c)

3 *Spirit of . . .*
a *Rom 8:9*
the S. of the Lord in me . 204.c
thy loving S., Christ, alone . 419.3
the spirit of Immanuel . . c91
sweet S. of Christ . . c104

b *Spirit of God*
God's H. S. came . . . 215.c
God's H. S. with mine doth agree 323.3
S. of our God, descending . 607.3
S. of God, thou art . . 631.1
S. of God, O hear us pray . c101

c *Gen 1:2*
S. of God, that moved of old. 202.1
O H. S., who didst brood . 569.3

d *Spirit of grace* *Zech 12:10*
come, gracious S. . . . dove . 190.1
the S. of all g. . . . 196.2
S. of purity and g. . . 200.7
gracious S., dwell with me . 212.1
the S.'s quickening g. . . 791.3

e *Spirit of power/love* *2 Tim 1:7*
S. of life and l. and p. . . 15.4
pour all the S. of his l. . 165.4
ne'er from us depart, S. of p.. 219.3
S. of truth and l. . . . 224.3
S. of power within . . . 441.1
S. of health . . . perfect l. . 441.2
S. of eternal l., guide me . 630.1
S. of l., come . . . residing . c102

f *Spirit of truth* *John 14:17*
H. S., t. divine, dawn . . 194.1
S. of t., be thou . . . guide . 196.6
S. of t. and love . . . 224.3
H. S., revealer of the t. . 870.3

adopt, burn (1b), faith (2o), holiness (e), living (3c)

4
a *Spirit [dwell] Rom 8:9; 1 Cor 3:16*
S., d. with me . . . 212.*
abide, O gentle S. . . . 221.3
how d. thy S. in me . . 527.c
thy S. indwelling my heart . 589.4
in me thy S. d. . . . 594.2

b *Spirit fall* *Acts 10:44*
let thy S. f. on me . . 205.1
may your S. f. upon him (her) 795.3

c *give Spirit* *Luke 11:13*
H. G. to man is g. . . 195.*
now thy S. g. . . . 575.c
bestow, thy S. and thyself . 601.1
thy S. g. to me . . . c37

d *Gal 5:18*
thus led by his S. . . . 458.4

anoint (c), baptise (b), breathe (b), drink (f), fill (2j), guide (g), loving (1b), pour (1c), quickening (c), receive (2f), seal (c), send (1f), strive (c), water (1b)

5
a *Matt 3:16*
S. like a dove may rest . . 584.1

b *Acts 2:3*
the S.'s hallowed fire . . 379.3
the pure flame of the S.. . 443.3

c *Gal 5:22*
H. S. truth/love/right . . . 194.*
S. whose fruit is love . . 561.1
now the fruit of the S. is . c46

d *Rom 15:19*
H. S., now thy might . . 188.1
with the S.'s power endued . 408.2
arm me with the S.'s might . 516.5
by thy H. S.'s power . . 538.3
clothed us with the S.'s might 593.2
quicken . . . the H. G.'s power 608.1
may feel thy S.'s power . 613.1
marching on in the S.'s might 811.3

born (d), bride, dower, gift (2e), sword (2e)

6 *human spirit*
seek . . . our s. to sustain . 6.2
dew upon the s. falling . . 70.3
wake my s., clear my sight . 194.1
satisfy my s.'s yearning . . 206.1
falling, my s. appalling . . 237.1
adorning the s. with joy . . 237.2
he sees thy softened s. . . 256.2
long my imprisoned s. lay . 283.3
can make my s. whole . . 297.1
the s.'s strange . . . longings. 325.3
Godward our s. aspire . . 351.2
sets my s. all in a flame. . 360.c
my s.'s deep desire . . 379.3
on my naked s. bear . . 414.3
make my s. free . . . 441.c
my s. he releases . . . 495.3
thou hast my s. . . . 516.2
still shall my s. cleave . . 517.3
touch my s. again . . . 527.3
let nothing your s. dismay . 537.3
over its waves to my s. . . 542.1
grant . . . my s.'s longing . 548.4
even when my s. bleeds . 552.2

cares sweep o'er my s. . . 583.2
a s. still prepared . . . 596.3
my patient s. guide . . 596.4
our restless s. yearn . . 602.3
bid my s. rise again . . 618.3
hungering . . . may our s. be . 626.2
my s. pines in poverty . . 631.3
my s. to Calvary bear . . 639.2
my s. aspires to the things . 640.4
my s. pants for thee . . 650.1
on our disordered s. move . 651.3
it lifts my drooping s. up . 714.1
then my s. faints . . . 877.2
his s., with a bound . . 890.3
grace our s. will deliver . . 891.3
our s. shall sorrow no more . 900.2
for Heaven our s. prepare . 904.4
our s. often grieves . . 930.3
problems . . . s. may assail . c151

b *fill spirit*
he f. my s. with gladness . 178.1
with thyself my s. f. . . 665.4
thy peace our s. f. . . 669.3

c *[wounded] spirit* *Ps 51:17*
makes the w. s. whole . . 58.2
heal my w., broken. s. . . 301.3
w. s. need thy care . . 702.3

d *1 Thess 5:23*
through my flesh and s. . . 430.4
take my body, s., soul . . 497.1
my body, soul and s. . . . I give 511.1
my s., soul and flesh receive . 516.1
body, soul and s., all . . 532.1

cheer (b), contrite (c), free (1e), restore (d)

e *Matt 5:3*
blessèd are the poor in s. . 95.1
humble in s. I kneel . . 513.c
with my s. at its meekest . 528.2
like thee! lowly in s. . . 623.3
where lowly s. meet . . 648.1

f *(other)*
help, ye bright angelic s. . 109.3
the s. that surround thy throne 414.2
mortal s. tire and faint . . 559.2
a scene where s. blend . . 573.3
may young, eager s. . . 575.2
joined in one s. to our head . 659.2
sing it with a s. . . . 815.1
with a grateful s. . . . 836.c

spite
in s. of his foes . . . 137.4
s. of fears, pride ruled . . 606.2
in s. of self and sin . . . 749.2
in s. of men and devils . . 810.1

splendid
caught the vision s. . . 833.1
s. goal of earth's . . . race . 878.2

splendour
only the s. of light hideth . 8.4
pavilioned in s. 16.1
that wheels in s. . . . 38.1
love is touched with s. . . 50.1
s. of its clear unfolding . . 70.1
ancient s. fling 83.3
from Heaven's s. . . . sought . 175.2
solemn s. still is given . . 632.2
for the s. of his service . . 868.1
in life's early s. c213

spoil
no clouds can s. . . . 728.3
thorns will s. 931.2

spoke-n see speak

spot
seek that consecrated s. . 261.2
blessed is the s. to me . . 348.2
earth has ne'er a s. so fair . 663.1

b *2 Peter 3:14*
purged from every s. . . 262.3
blood can cleanse each s. . 293.2
take every s. of sin away. . 432.1
nor s. of guilt remains . . 746.2

spotless
1 *(re divinity)*
bore it s. to the last . . 141.3
I want thy s. purity . . 455.2

Lamb (2c)

2 *(re people)* *(2 Peter 3:14)*
fill our s. souls with God . . 210.1
power to keep me s. . . 303.c
wear a s. robe . . . 389.3
must be kept pure and s. . 406.3
holy life, s. and free . . 416.1
are your garments s. . . 417.c
fully cleanse till s. all . . 423.2
pure and s. let us be . . 438.3
than in a s. holiness . . 446.4
then my s. soul receive . . 597.4
help me to live a s. life . . 649.2
thou hast made . . . s. here . 662.3
there's a s. robe for you . . 902.c

spray 891.2

spread
s. their branches . . . 159.4
more it s. and grows . . 165.2
now it s. along the skies . . 165.4
gloom has s. 225.2
may it s. on every hand . . 243.3
shows his wounds, and s. . 286.4
s. a feast of redeeming love . 373.2
a table s. 512.1
s. the feast today . . . 550.3
vice destroy or virtue s. . . 581.2
griefs around me s. . . 743.3
s. their glory o'er me . . 766.1
clouds may over-s. the sky . 892.2
where golden fields s. far . 934.4

b *spread [gospel]*
s. . . . honours of thy name . 64.2
s. abroad the victor's fame . 147.3
s. his praise from shore . . 182.2
s. the joyful news . . . 279.1
to s. thy light wherever . . 426.3
help me s. the . . . news. . 499.4
our lives will s. your peace . 572.4
s. thy praise through earth . 629.2
s. the tidings everywhere . 835.1

c *spread wings*
Deut 32:11; Matt 23:27
come . . . and s. thy w. . . 217.5
s. his w., and hides us . . 722.4
O s. thy covering w. . . 918.4
s. thy pure w. o'er them . . 949.3

curtain fame (b) *outspread*

spring
1 *(season)*
summer and winter, and s. . 33.2
clothes herself for s. . . 155.2
robed in the . . . garb of s. . 177.2
like s.'s refreshing shower . 213.2
into the s. of his care . 378.2, 4
you can't stop s. . . . 854.1
everlasting s. abides . . 898.1
flowery s. at thy command . 925.2

2 *(general)*
like thy s. and . . . waters . 32.1
the s. of all my comfort . . 301.4
it has no s. of action . . 508.2
guard my first s. . . . 665.4

3 *(verb)*
s. fresh from the Word . . 35.1
s. in completeness . . . 35.2
creation s. at once to sight . 141.2
crucified, hath s. to life . . 153.1
truth from his sceptre shall s. . 166.2
truth . . . shall s. to flower . 656.4
purpose s. to . . . birth . . 682.2
joy-bursts . . . gaily are s. . 724.2
our gladness or woe will s. . 928.2
the deserts bloom and s. . 929.2
truth from Heaven that s. . 942.3
singing, for joy is s. . . . c176

b *Num 21:17*
well-s. of the joy of living . 10.3
s., O well, for ever s. . . 194.5
s. up, O Well, in . . . power . 601.2
s. thou up within my heart . 737.4

c *Isa 58:8*
thy health's eternal s. . . 557.4

d *Isa 58:11; John 4:14*
living waters, s. from . . . love 157.2
s. with living water flows . 254.3
a deep, celestial s. . . . 254.4
the precious fountain s. . 348.3
a fountain ever s. . . . 358.3
fount of life . . . upward s. . 456.1
s. up and flowing forth . . 522.3
thee, the ever-flowing s. . 559.4
the s. of sacred service . . 591.1
heart's deep fountains . . 749.1
to the s. that flows . . 762.2

e *Ps 87:7*
the s. of all my comfort . . 301.4
constant goodness is the s. . 616.1
in whom my s. are found . 647.1

sprinkle-d *Heb 12:24; 1 Pet 1:2*
s. now the throne of grace . 106.2
besprinkle

spurn-ed-ing
give where gifts are s. . . 50.2
I s. his grace . . . 380.2
trembled at the law I'd s. . 405.2
pearl which others s. . . 407.5
s. not our sinful race . . 500.1
s. . . . world's enticing . . 500.2
s. today the voice divine . 676.4
they s. or misinterpret . . 790.2
earth's allurement s. . . 803.3

spurring 192.3

squadrons 150.3

squandered 225.1

stable
his shelter was a s. . . 87.2
found in a s. the Saviour . 92.1
in a s. born our brother . . 97.1

stablish see establish

staff
God make my life a . . . s. . 838.4

b *Mark 6:8*
he takes his s., and . . . says . 911.2

ride/rode (b)

stage 665.1

stain-ed
or wash away our s. . . 120.1
purge our deepest s. away . 121.4
lose all their guilty s. . . 132.1
when he had purged our s. . 164.2
as scarlet be the s. . . 249.2
blood can wash away the s. . 253.3
I can ne'er remove a s. . . 292.5
s. with guilt 303.1
very deeply s. within . . 336.1
I hope the s. are washed away 359.3
mis-spent powers s. my heart 379.2
wash out its s. . . . 453.2

in your s., why still delay . 471.4
washing s. of condemnation . 540.2
naught . . . s. my commission 786.1
blackest s. brought to light . 893.1
a s. may yet be seen . . c72

b *every stain*
purged from e. . . . s. . . 262.3
we may be cleansed from e. s. 268.4
from e. s. made clean . . 415.1
apply . . . remove e. s. . . 436.2
love that cleanses e. s. . . 439.3
purge and keep from e. s. . 440.4
saved . . . from e. sinful s. . 629.2

c *stain/sin*
the scarlet s. of s. . . 176.1
s.'s deep crimson s. lay . 237.1
s. s. are lost in . . . flow . 281.3
s. with the s. . . . wrought . 287.2
my s. . . . many, their s. . 298.2
robes were once all s. with s.. 359.1
all my s. s. vanished . . 389.2
with s. of s. upon me . . 403.1
garments that are s. with s. . 417.3
look on this s.-s. heart . . 440.1
make my s.-s. conscience smart 446.3
never more s. . . . with s. . 502.3
from all s. of s. set free . . 536.1
freedom from s.'s hidden s. . 610.3
saved . . . from every sinful s.. 629.2

b *blood-stained*
it is the b.-s. mercy seat. . 573.2
lift the b.-s. banner high . 696.1
the b.-s. flag 779.1

stair
thine own secret s. . . 91.3
climbing up the golden s. . 369.c
love has made the s. . . . wide 369.3

stalking 847.3

stall
his cradle was a s. . . . 87.2
who is he in yonder s. . . 104.1

stammering 132.5

stamp-ed
you . . . have s. your image . 38.4
deeper s. thyself the seal . 207.4
powerful s. I long to feel . 214.4
s. thine own image deep . 623.c

stanch 828.3

stand-ing/stood
1 *(God) stands*
my surety s. 106.1
in my place condemned he s. 118.2
but we behold thee s. . . 163.4
dared to s. on trial alone . 181.2
in our midst he's s. today . 235.1
I found a friend to s. by me . 376.2
Jesus, s. among us . . 599.1
he is s. with us here . . c126

b *Acts 7:56*
I see my Saviour s. . . 45.2
see the Saviour s. . . 260.c, 2
there for me the Saviour s. . 286.4
there my exalted Saviour s. . 880.3

c *Rev 3:20*
behold me s. at the door 229.1, c
s. outside the fast-closed door 299.1
shame . . . to keep him s. . 299.1

2 *(general)*
before the hills in order s. . 13.3
love s. the test . . . 51.*
s. a lowly cattle shed . . 87.1
s. a old rugged cross . . 124.1
his cross s. empty . . . 142.1
where Moses and Elijah s. . 154.2
oft longing I've s. . . 298.5
in the ruins of my life I s. . 376.2
when by myself I s. . . 508.1
beyond . . . his winepress s. . 512.2
I s. all bewildered . . . 542.1
starlight s. watch . . . 666.4
his cross for ever s. . . 723.3
by divine appointment they s. 766.1
human feet s. on it . . 766.2
on the highest summit I'll s. . 766.3
s. for peace and righteousness 777.1
yellow s. for fire . . . 777.3
hear how the children s. . 848.2
the children all s. singing . 853.1
shall with glory s. fulfilled . 868.2
firmly . . . foundation s. . 873.4
danger and sorrow s. . . 882.1
why will you doubting s. . 897.2
s. dressed in living green . 898.2
so to the Jews old Canaan s. 898.2
death s. at the door . . 911.4
the valleys s. so thick . . 934.1
kingdom (1b), truth (d)

3 *(spiritual)*
faith is s. trial . . . 6.3
I s. both pure and free . . 176.1
s. unflinching for thy right . 181.2
s. by his cross . . . 352.3
o'er sin . . . exulting I s.. . 364.1
in the ruins . . . I s. . . 376.2
more than conqueror shall s. . 468.3
when by myself I s. . . 508.1
it only s. unbent . . . 508.3
fruit . . . that will s. . . 538.5
for ever s. on its guard . . 596.3
while I s. firm . . . 612.3
I'll . . . cause thee to s. . . 653.2
I'll s. for Christ . . . 687.c
we s. united in thy sight. . 692.2
shoulder to shoulder we s. . 702.c
faithful I s. in rule . . . 744.5
on Christ . . . I s. . . . 745.c
join our band, and make a s. . 798.2
we shall s. firm and secure . 833.3
s. by a purpose true . . 847.1
daring not to s. . . . 847.2
uphold . . . and I shall s. . 877.3
nobly for their Master s.. . 909.1
boldly have s. amid . . . fire . 910.4
under the flag we s. . . c226

b *(imperative)*
s. like the brave . 684.c/689.*
s. firm every one . . . 698.1
s. up, s. up for Jesus . . 699.*
s. in his strength alone . . 699.3
for Jesus boldly s. . . 810.2

c *Rom 5:2*
through . . . grace I shall s. . 437.3
by Jesus' grace we s. . . 781.3

d *stand alone*
I cannot s. a. . . . 325.2
God's soldier has to s. a. . 801.2
when all a. I s. . . . 837.3
dare to s. a. 847.c

e *stand on promises*
firm . . . his p. s. . . . 735.3
upon thy p. I s. . . . 741.3
s. on the p. . . . . 757.*
for ever his p. shall s. . . c125

f *2 Cor 1:24*
s. in faith, thy mercy . . 460.3
the f. in which he s. . . 555.1
let me s. by faith . . . c80

g *Eph 6:13*
s. and to the end endure . 574.4
s. complete at last . . 695.5

h *stand [in worship]*
while as a penitent I s. . . 120.3
silent and still I s. . . . 131.1
while in thy light I s. . . 415.3
there in thy strength to s. . 461.4
s. in the temple of our God . 533.5
we s. to bless thee . . 674.1

i *stand [in Heaven]*
my comrades beckoning s. . 780.4
the angels will s. . . . 879.c
on Jordan's . . . banks I s. . 887.1
where saints in glory s. . . 897.1
when we s. by the . . . river . 908.3
when on Jordan's bank he s. 911.5

j *stand [before God]*
bold shall I s. 116.2
while as a penitent I s. . . 120.3
I s. amazed in the presence . 179.1
s. all condemned b. G. . . 245.4
I s. b. my maker's face . . 290.1
Friend, we s. b. thee . . 595.2
host, s. here b. thee . . 643.1
they may s. b. thy face . . 791.3
when you s. in the light . . 893.*
s. in thy sight for evermore . 934.3
when redeemed . . . I shall s.. c248
bless (2b), complete (c), ground (2b), liberty (c), take (3c), throne (3c)

standard
1 *(principle)*
there are s. that remain . . 324.3
2 *(flag)*
beneath thy s. still . . . 692.5
raise the glorious s. higher . 696.3
raise the s. high . . . 698.1
round his s. ranging . . 707.4
a s. for the multitude . . 774.4
'neath our s., we're engaging 778.1
faith her s. proudly flies . . 799.2
rally round our blessèd s. . 818.2

standing 371.2

star
who holds the countless s. . 6.1
s. and angels sing . . . 10.2
the voice that rolls the s. . 26.3
I see the s., I hear . . . 37.1
higher than the s. . . . 52.c
the s. in the bright sky . . 77.1
the silent s. go by . . . 86.1
s. upon their way . . . 141.2
the s. their courses make . 171.2
the s. at night do kindle . . 486.2
sun, moon and s. forgot . 617.5
s. begin to peep . . . 673.2
there's a s. to guide . . 716.*
s. upon our path abiding . 716.2
yellow s. and red and blue . 779.c
s. grow pale and pass away . 873.4
he lights the evening s. . . 935.2
desert or the s.-lit north . . c238

b *Ps 148:3*
sun and moon and s. of light . 28.2
sun, moon and s. . . . above . 33.2

c *Rev 22:5*
where they need no s. . . 76.4

d *Job 38:7; Rev 22:16*
which the morning stars began 10.4
O morning s., together . . 86.2
brighter than the morning s. . 185.3
brighter than the morning s. . 516.4
coming with the morning s. . 641.2
like the s. of the morning . 852.c

e *Matt 2:2*
hail the s. that from far . . 73.3
did the guiding s. behold . 76.1
a glorious guiding s. . . 80.3
guiding s., lend thy light . 89.2
wondrous s., lend thy light . 89.3
they lookèd up and saw a s. . 90.2
by the light of that same s. . 90.3
to follow the s. wherever . 90.3
this s. drew near . . . 90.4
rich gifts . . . led by a s.. . 92.1

f *Rev 22:16*
there the bright and morning s. 115.2
arise, O morning S. . . 172.6
Jesus, bright s. of the earth . 175.1
found in him my s. . 332.3
he's . . . bright and morning s. 344.c
day-s., in my heart appear . 412.1
thou art . . . s. at eventide . 486.1
guide us, Bright and Morning S. 937.2

starlight-lit
beyond the s. universe . . 27.1
each night-time the . . . s. . 666.4

starry
all the twinkling s. host . . 177.3
boundless as the s. heavens . 230.2
thy word is like a s. host . 658.3
to wear a s. crown . . . c247

start-ed-ing
souls that now are s. . . 169.2
I'll s. this moment . . . 275.4
tears at times may s. . . 326.3
in the glorious fight to s. . 338.2
s. for the crown . . . 366.2
with every day that s. . . 724.2
unto those who only s. . . 806.3
will s. the world along . . 815.1
he s. up to hear . . . 890.2
timorous mortals s. . . 898.2
sowing . . . tear-drops s. . 931.3

state
man's first heavenly s. . . 78.3
rise to that immortal s. . . 314.2
I ask no higher s. . . . 441.4
the s. or science . . . 688.1
continuance in this s. . . 785.5
b *Phil 4:11*
in whatever worldly s. . . 916.1

stately 705.1

station 147.4

stature *(Luke 2:52)* . . . 796.4

stay
1 *(re God)*
a *(noun)* *Ps 18:18*
in trouble he's my s. . . 344.1
the Lord is my s. . . . 467.4
be their strength and s. . . 582.4
our anchor and our s. . . 654.3
my guide and s. can be . . 670.3
our s. in strife . . . 674.4
might divine shall be our s. . 702.2
rock . . . be thou our s. . . 937.3
trusting . . . surest s. . . c119
he's a helper and a s. . . c126
b *hope and stay*
our help, our h., . . . our s. . 43.3
he is my h. and s. . . 374.2
he then is all my h. and s. . 745.3
c *(verb)*
and s. by my side . . . 77.2
Holy Spirit, s. with me . . 206.c
s. thou near by . . . 587.2
s. with and strengthen me . 628.c
s. the tossing sea . . . 628.3
my God, vouchsafe to s. . 636.3
mercy shall unshaken s. . . 746.1
my tears to s. . . . 749.3
Jesus loves me! He will s. . 843.3
O Spirit, s. to comfort me . 958
s. with thy people, hallow . c98
d *ever stay*
s. close by me for e. . . 77.3
within my heart for e. s. . 432.1
O Jesus, e. with us s. . . 602.4
2 *(re people)*
past defeats would bid me s.. 285.2
s. no longer on the threshold . 433.2
from thee no longer can I s. . 450.1
with him to go or s. . . 451.3
teach . . . wayward feet to s.. 519.2
'tis equal joy to go or s.. . 556.3
beneath thy standard . . . s. . 692.5
in his dwelling-place I s. . 728.2
with you we will firmly s. . 748.2
still the waves or s. the winds. 854.1
swift . . . to s. the pace. . 861.4
with departed friends to s. . 902.2
don't s. in the valley . . c116
don't s. behind . . . c228
b *ever stay*
with him to e. s. . . 495.3
life which shall for e. s. . 601.2
c *Eccl 11:6*
at eve s. not thy hand . . 923.3
d *Isa 26:3*
s. in thy tranquillity . . 194.4
on him my every hope I s. . 400.2
on thee . . . my soul is s. . 419.2
my mind upon thee . . . is s. . 513.1
on thee my feeble steps I s. . 597.1
all my trust on thee is s.. . 737.2
whose mind is s. on thee . c142
3 *(other)*
there it did both stop and s. . 90.4
I know it's there to s. . . 327.2
no foes shall s. his might . 685.2

stead 108.2

steadfast
give me a s. mind . . . 574.4
fix on his work thy s. eye . 715.3
thy s. truth declare . . 721.5
on this my s. soul relies . . 746.4
s., wise and strong . . 837.3
b *Heb 6:19*
anchor . . . s. and sure . . 280.c
hope that is s. and sure . . 394.3
look up with a s. hope . . 585.2
c *Col 2:5*
in s. faith pray on . . . 916.3
charity and s. faith . . 948.2

steadily 814.c

steady
with obedience glad and s. . 614.4
ready, s., pass the word . 698.c
with s. pace the pilgrim . . 911.1

steal/stole
as to his side she s. . . 304.1
how to s. the bitter . . 333.2
shadows . . . s. across the sky 673.1
s. on the ear 876.4

steam 30.1

steel
God of concrete, God of s. . 30.1
though as s. the . . . chains . 249.2
tyrant's brandished s. . . 701.3

steep
a *(verb)*
wearied eyelids gently s. . 676.2
b *(noun)*
throng up the s. of light . . 167.1
climb the s. and cross . . 393.1
loath . . . to conquer the s. . 488.2
may not climb the heavenly s. 496.3
c *(adjective)*
on the lonely mountain s. . 88.2
s. was the mountain . . 388.2
s., too, my pathway . . 473.3
or upon the mountain s. . 483.3
the s. and rugged pathway . 570.2
rugged are the heights, and s. 641.1
they climbed the s. ascent . 701.4
however s. the way . . 719.5
when life's pathway runs s. . 739.2
s. than the mountains . . 766.2

stem
how to s. the tides . . . 303.2
must I not s. the flood . . 678.3

step-ping
1 *(re Jesus)* *1 Peter 2:21*
tread in his s., assisted . . 78.3
in Jesus' s. my s. must be . 449.c
where'er thy s. I see . . 453.3
in thy s. I will follow . . 473.c
s. of him I love . . . 657.4
teach me, Lord, thy s. . . 846.3
in his s. we follow . . . 866.c
2 *(re people)*
with joyful s. they sped . . 76.2
only a s. to Jesus . . . 255.*
a s. from sin to grace . . 255.3
let no foe your s. arrest . . 433.3
in Jesus' s. my s. must be . 449.c
leading s. by s. to thee . . 510.1
wandering to retrace their s. . 581.4
on thee my feeble s. I stay . 597.1
one s. enough for me . . 606.1
with a s. more firm . . 614.2
way appear s. unto Heaven . 617.3
I dare s. out to thee . . 628.3
s. and voices joined . . 682.1
I dare not take one s. . . 726.1
presence my s. shall attend . 734.1
s. fearless through the night . 765.2
keep in s. all the time . . 817.*
s. by s., O lead me onward . 842.4
s. by s. we mean to go . . 901.1
s. on together in the ranks . c238
b *Ps 37:23**
my very s. are planned . . 48.2
order all my s. aright . . 641.3
c *every step*
in e. s. be fellowship . . 7.4
o'er every . . . s. preside. . 190.1
in e. s. his hand doth lead . 317.4
guide (1e)

stern-er-st
pass me through a s. cleansing 522.1
s. disciples drove them back . 797.1
facing up to s. fact. . . 863.4
s. affliction clouds his face . 911.4

still-ed
1 *(adjective)*
how s. we see thee lie . . 86.1
silent and s. I stand. . . 131.1
drop thy s. dews . . . 567.4
my tongue be . . . cold and s.. 573.5
accents clear and s. . . 862.3
b *Ps 46:10*
waiting yielded and s. . . 487.1
restless heart keep s. . . 738.2
small (c), water (3a)
2 *(verb)*
where joys are never s. . . 39.4
our Babel s. 211.1
as a mother s. her child . . 598.2
b *peace, be still* *Mark 4:39*
s. this restless heart . . 194.4
I am with thee; p., be s.. . 390.1
he s. by his power the ocean. 402.2
in him, life's storms are s. . 539.3
when thou sayest . . .: be s. . 598.2
who s. the waves and stayed. 628.3
waves of strife be s. . . 669.3
you can't . . . s. the waves . 854.1
3 *(other)* nc, but
grant . . . s. greater revelations 173.3
speak . . . wishes s. clearer . 513.c

s. small voice of calm . . 567.5
but sweeter s., to wake . . 632.3
prove s. more the strength . 642.3
my faith s. small, but sure . 742.3

stillness 83.1

sting
sorrows lose their s. . . 503.1
though sharp the s. remain . 267.1
d *sting of death* *1 Cor 15:55*
the s. of d. remove . . 126.1
where, O d., is now thy s. . 143.4
from d.'s dread s. . . . free . 151.5
d. has lost its s. . . . 152.2
no terrors, and d. hath no s. . 166.4
the s. of d. has been destroyed 375.2
where is d.'s s. . . . 670.4
d. has lost its s. . . . 894.1

stir-red-ing
the tender s. of thy Spirit. . 192.3
s. them with an inward grace. 202.1
with softest breathings s. . 202.4
the pulse of passion s. again . 211.2
I could not s. my . . . soul . 353.4
s. the slumbering chords. . 390.2
now I am s. to wonder . . 529.3
mighty winds are s. . . 864.1
b *2 Tim 1:6*
still s. up thy gift in me . . 199.3
c *stir hearts*
thoughts have s. the h. . . 36.2
their h. were s. . . . 80.2
many thoughts s. my h. . . 119.1
before my sinful h. was s. . 339.2
s. my h.'s deep fountain. . 749.1

stock 662.2

stole see steal

stone
1 *Eph 2:20**
Christ is our corner-s. . . 940.1
2
worship gods of s. . . . 588.2
we place this s. . . . 942.2
blocks of s. remain . . . 943.2
this s. to thee in faith . . 945.1
b *Gen 28:18*
my rest a s. 617.2
c *Matt 28:2**
vain the s., the watch . . 143.3
angels rolled the s. away. . 145.2
angels rolled the s. away . . 152.1
d *Luke 19:40*
then would the s. cry shame . 724.2
the s., our silence shaming . 853.3
e *1 Peter 2:5*
make each heart a living s. . 941.2

stony
sometimes the way be s.. . 462.2
b *Gen 28:18*
out of my s. griefs . . . 617.4

stood see stand

stoop-ed-ing
1 *(God) stoops*
s. to set my . . . spirit free . 303.1
s. to ask my love . . . 307.2
I love him for s. . . . 329.1
when in love he s. to reach . 350.1
God s. from Heaven . . 885.4
2 *(we) stoop*
s. down and drink and live . 332.2
s. to worldly happiness . 497.3
e'en as I s. to drink . . 547.3
s. to help the dying . . 702.3
as I s. to raise the low . . 758.4

stop-ped
have you ever s. to think . 49.1
it did both s. and stay . . 90.4
you can't s. God . . . . 854.*

store-d
a *(divine)*
for all his mercy's s. . . 23.1
boundless s. of grace . . 58.3
plenty from the unfailing s. . 277.2
of love, a boundless s. . . 311.1
supply us from thy s. . . 575.1
thine own boundless s. . . 646.4
blessings from thy boundless s. 676.5
grace is boundless in its s. . 741.2
much more hath God in s. . c44
b *(human)*
a drop my s. 207.2
my time, my s., my talents . 482.1
'tis all my s. 516.1
I pour . . . its treasure-s. . 525.6
we have exhausted our s. . 579.2
thou hast my . . . s. . . c144
c *(other)*
the earth with its s. . . 16.3
vain world's golden s. . . 428.3
a s. of created beauty . . 666.2
all our coasts abundant s. . 925.3
d *(verb)*
grapes of wrath are s. . . 162.1
my earthen vessel is s. . . 457.3
fruitful ears to s. . . . 924.3
with thankfulness we s. . 926.3

storehouse
birds without barn or s. . 763.2
b *Mal 3:10*
bring your tithes into the s. . 920.1

storm
1 *(literal)*
dark . . . on the wings of the s. 16.2
rides upon the s. . . . 29.1
mighty s. are on my head . 39.2
through s. and rain . . 923.2
ere the winter's s. begin. . 924.1
2 *(figurative)* *(Mark 4:37)*
when the s. around . . . rage . 249.4
when the s. tides lift . . 280.1
now the s. is o'er . . . 375.1
when in the s. he is near . 467.4
where the s. are sweeping . 483.2
while the s. of trial rend. . 595.3
when the s. are o'er us . . 655.3
shelter from the s. . . 663.1
s. of deep affliction . . 663.3
amid the tempest and the s. . 687.c
I smile at the s. . . . 712.1
waves and clouds and s. . 721.2
the s. I face would threaten . 732.1
s. may roar without me . . 736.1
waves and s. go o'er my head 746.4
alas! a s.-tossed sea . . 749.2
in spite of self . . . and s. . 749.2
howling s. of doubt . . 757.2
the s. . . . may surround me . 758.1
the s. cannot hide . . . face . 758.c
in the s. sweet songs . . 761.3
above the s. of passion . . 862.3
we have trembled in the s. . 938.3
s. that would my way oppose c127
pilot's face in every s. . . c131
I let the s. pass o'er me . . c145
b *storms of life*
anchor hold in the s. of l. . 280.1
when l.'s s. are past . . 280.4
out of l.'s s. 300.2
l.'s s. are stilled . . . 539.3
when the s. of l. is past. . 627.3
till the s. of l. be past . . 737.1
calm (b)
3 *(verb)*
s. the forts of darkness . . 696.c
hell's dominions s. . . 788.c
s. the kingdom, but prevail . 816.2

stormy
shelter from the s. blast . 13.1
through all the s. blast . . 334.2
when the s. billows roll . . 627.2
sail through s. seas . . 678.2
in every high and s. gale . 745.2
trusting through a s. way . 754.1
sky is dark and s. . . . 805.1
on Jordan's s. banks I stand . 887.1
o'er the wild s. deep . . c178
b *Ps 148:8*
every s. wind that blows . 573.1
s. winds fulfil thy will . . 947.3

story
1 *(re Jesus)*
all the angels told the s. . 74.2
let us hear again the s. . . 74.3
do you know the s. . . 80.3
have you ever heard the s. . 96.1
the ever-thrilling s. . . 96.3
tell me the old, old s. . . 98.*
tell me the s. of Jesus . 99.1, c
love in that s. so tender. . 99.3
where'er . . . I'll tell the s. . 107.5
the s. of thy love repeat. . 140.4
fall . . . and the s. repeat . 367.3
this is the s. most precious . 384.1
O tell to all the s. . . 410.3
let the s. ring out loud . 829.3
let us make known the s. . 831.3
make salvation's s. heard . 832.c
I love to hear the s. . . 840.1
tell me the s. of Jesus . . 848.1
so that they be s. of Jesus . 848.5
may its dark s. ever . . . dwell. c7
that old, old s. is true . . c202
his lifetime s. c212
telling out the s. . . . c231
b *wonderful story*
w. s. of love . . . . 139.*
this w. s. so old, but so new. 319.c
tell out the w. s. . . . 384.1
w. s. of Jesus . . . 384.3
read (b) sing (3i) sweet (3f)
wondrous (e)
2 *(re people)*
God is near thee, tell thy s. . 225.c
this is my s. . . . song . . 310.c
tell not half the s. . . . 333.4
come and hear me tell my s. . 338.1
the s. of my life's defeat. . 770.1
tell the s. saved by grace . c245
3 *(other)*
tells its own s.—love . . 51.1
ye, who sang creation's s. . 75.1
all the light of sacred s. . 112.1, 5
now fulfil thy Church's s. . 577.1
beset him . . . with dismal s.. 685.2

straight
I sail s. on 628.4
take your weakness s. to Jesus 790.1
b *(Matt 7:13)**
the way to Heaven is s. . . 275.3
a narrow way, and s. . . 462.1
run the s. race . . . 718.2
strait

straightness 32.2

straightway
joyful sped to Bethlehem s. . 72.5
b *Mark 5:29*
s. she was whole . . . 304.1

strain
1 *(music)*
shall be our loudest s. . . 43.4
beneath the angel-s. . . 83.2
wake the immortal s. . . 139.1
earth prolong the joyful s. . 160.5
conquer, lift up the s. . . 173.c
the loveliest s. is this . . 187.4
angels chant the s. . . 253.3
swell . . . triumphant s. . . 550.3
prayer the sublimest s. . . 625.3
nor dies the s. of praise . . 677.3
one the s. that lips . . 765.5
burning s. are telling . . 802.1
s. of all its holy throng . . 934.4
2 *(effort)*
helps me take the s. . . 204.2
and the cables s. . . . 280.1
bear the s. of toil . . . 519.1
take from our souls the s. . 567.4
peace which follows after s. . 719.3
days of labour, nights of s. . 833.2
let him ease the . . . s. . . c126

strait-s
1 *(adjective)* *Matt 7:13*
'tis a s. and thorny road. . 559.2
goal of earth's s. race . . 878.2
2 *(noun)*
anchor hold . . . s. of fear . 280.2

strand
till I reach the golden s. . . 115.4
rivers and shining s. . . 873.1
stand on the hallelujah s. . 879.c

strange-ly
that s. expiring cry . . 140.1
spirit's s., deep longings . 325.3
when defeat seems s. near . 713.3
s. their word, their song. . 939.2

stranger
1 *(re Jesus)*
on earth though a s. . . 92.2
living as a homeless s. . . 97.2
2 *(re people)*
never be a s. there . . . 556.5
s. to the living word . . 697.3
b *Matt 25:35*
I was to God a s. . . . 361.1
c *Eph 2:12*
sought me when a s. . . 313.3
I once was . . . a s. on earth. 354.3
d *1 Peter 2:11*
though we are s. . . . 763.3
a s. in the world below . . 880.2
I'm but a s. here . . . 882.1

stray-ed-ing
perverse . . . oft I s. . . 53.3
not left in sin to s. . . . 135.3
will not let me s. . . . 204.1
from God thy soul has s. . 225.1
light of the s. . . . 236.2
lest my feet should s. . . 342.2
lead me, lest I s. . . 627.1, c
our path when wont to s. . 654.1
nor let me ever s. . . . 743.3
in our blindness we . . . s. . 747.2
our first parents s. . . 785.3
suffer not our feet to s. . . 789.6
b *Isa 53:6*
like wandering sheep we s. . 4.2
still s. sheep to be led . . 527.1
like to a lamb . . . s. . . 740.1

stream-ed-ing
1 *(general)*
like an ever-rolling s. . . 13.5
all created s. are dried . . 14.2
it s. from the hills . . . 16.4
willows watch by crystal s. . 39.3
pants the hart for cooling s. . 557.1
gently down the s. of time . 627.c
while the multitudes are s. . 693.1
his blood-red banner s. afar . 701.1
death's cold, sullen s. . . 743.4
its crimson glory s. . . 783.1
not Jordan's s. . . . 898.3
2 *(salvation)* *Ps 46:4; Zech 13:1*
where s. of living water . . 53.2
the cleansing s. does flow . 128.1
since by faith I saw the s. . 132.4
see, the s. of living waters . 157.2
his blood for thee s. . . 237.3
the beautiful s. . . . 252.*
s. that from the fountain . 277.3
living s. of richest worth . 312.2
drank of that life-giving s. . 332.2
Calvary's s. is flowing . . 413.c
s. through every land . . 540.1
s. an endless crimson tide . 540.1
s. of pure perennial peace . 601.2
s. from the fount of . . . grace 654.1
flows a s. to make . . . clean. 700.2
shall hear of Calvary's s. . 828.2
the s. on earth I've tasted . 896.2
beside the crystal s. . . 901.4
the cleansing s. is flowing . c221
b *streams [of light]*
from the cross the radiance s. 112.3
within thy l., now s. . . 221.3
come . . . where l. is s. 232.1, 3
l. and the glory shall s. . 233.1
c *streams of mercy*
God's free m. s. . . 40.2
s. of m. are abounding . 239.1
s. of boundless m. flow . 261.4
s. of m., never ceasing . 313.1
whence all the s. of m. flow . 601.3
desert (1b), gushing, healing (b)

street
1 *(on earth)*
in thy dark s. shineth . . 86.1
let s. and homes . . . ring . 142.1
laughter echoes in the s. . 664.2
in the hall and in the s. . . 829.2
2 *(in Heaven)* *Rev 21:21*
we shall tread the s. . . 892.4
s. are bright and fair . . 901.3
to tread the golden s. . . 902.4

strength
1 *(divine)*
saving s. to show . . . 155.3
all highest s. 202.2
hand of s., and . . . grace . 762.1
b *Isa 26:4*
Rock of s., be thou our stay . 937.3
c *Rev 5:12**
s. and honour give . . 184.1
2 *(given to man)*
prove all the s. of his love . 126.4
a song of deliverance . . . of s. 186.c
the s. we needed to obey . 192.2
for s. to ever do the right . 203.3
the s. the sinner receives . 348.3
thou dost my s. assure . . 423.2
life and s. do thence derive . 424.3
on thy s., O God, I lean . . 489.3
I sought for love and s. . . 541.1
feeds the s. of every saint . 559.2
s. that we may ever live. . 570.1
Lord, we seek thy s. . . 576.3
he sendeth more s. . . 579.1
inspire my soul with s. . . 616.3
new power I want, and s. . 620.1
s. to conquer every foe . . 620.1
let s. divine abound . . 624.4
new s. and love bestowed . 675.2
s . . . the Lord will provide . 691.4
our s. for warfare . . . might . 692.4
s. to s. oppose . . . 699.2
for s. to tread a lonely way . 719.2
thy all-sufficient s. . . . 738.1
s. to my fainting heart . . 743.2
there is s. in knowing Jesus . 759.1
s. and wisdom from above . 795.2
in our Saviour s. enough . 805.c
the s. that came from thee . 938.3
b *is strength* *Ps 46:1**
Jehovah is our s. . . . 9.1
God is our s. and song . . 20.4
our help, our hope, our s. . 43.3
my peace, my s., my joy . 346.4
be thou my s. . . . my all. . 468.3
be thou still my s. . . . 578.2
be their s. and stay . . 582.4
Jesus, my s., my hope . . 596.1
Christ is thy s. . . . 718.1
my s., my light, my Saviour . c181
c *by/in strength*
there in thy s. to stand . . 461.4
in thy s. I'm bound to conquer 477.4
in his s. we shall conquer . 687.4
strong in the s. . . . 695.1
stand in his s. alone . . 699.3
in his s. secure we are . . 722.3
by thy s. . . . overthrown . 762.2
in thy s. we shall prevail. . 789.3
s. by which all toil . . . 942.1
d *Ps 71:16*
who in the s. of Jesus . . 695.2
I'll go in the s. of the Lord . 734.*
fight in the s. of the King . 820.1
in Jesus' s. we'll undertake . 912.2
determined in thy s. to go . 933.3
e *[daily] strength* *Deut 33:25*
s. for today 33.3
s. proportion to my d. . . 453.4
I ask thee for the daily s. . 485.3
daily s. for daily needs . . 566.2
he giveth me s. as my day . 710.2
daily s. to receive . . . c33
f *Ps 84:7*
from s. to s. go on . . . 695.6
g *Isa 30:15*
in my quiet s. . . . strong . 564.1
quietness . . . shall be my s. . 717.6
h *2 Tim 2:1*
Lord, in the s. of grace . . 505.1
give (1v), renew (e), sufficient (b)
3 *(human)*
my heart, my s. . . . are his . 345.2
no s. is mine, I know . . 385.3
should my s. be great . . 477.3
such as trust their native s. . 559.4
our failing s. renew . . 669.2
his s. the more is . . . 685.2
all my s. exert . . . 720.5
though s. and health . . . gone 746.4
my s. of small avail . . 780.2
warriors lend their s. . . 799.3
s. of purpose . . . 833.2
what s. and health I have . 838.4
some bring s. and health . 849.1
b *own strength*
did we in our own s. confide . 1.2
little s. to call my own . . 489.3
not in my own s. . . . accomplish 501.3
c *2 Cor 12:9*
if my s. is at its weakest. . 528.2
fail (2b), goodness (b), weakness (c, d)
4 *(other)*
your s. is tried . . . 121.5

s. belongs to gentleness . 198.4
saved from the . . . s. of sin . 629.3
prove . . . the s. of prayer . 642.3
s. to s. oppose . . . 699.2

strengthen-ed *Isa 41:10*
I'll s. thee, help thee . . 653.2
b *Col 1:11*
the grace of Jesus s. me . 176.2
s. us to fight . . . 197.3
he supports and s. me . . 404.3
never failed to s. me . . 521.3
s. all who fight . . . 576.1
power of prayer to s. faith . 604.3
O s. me, that while I stand . 612.3
stay with and s. me . . 628.c
he will s. you within . . 790.1
comfort, s. and keep you . 823.c
s. by the cords of service . 833.3
s. by his might . . . 866.c

strengthless 60.3

stress
take . . . strain and s. . . 567.4
take . . . s. of secret fear . 647.2

stretch-ed-ing
1 *(God) stretches*
his Kingdom s. from shore . 160.1
b *Acts 4:30; Rom 10:21*
hands . . . s. upon a tree . 129.c
s. out thy hand, O God . . 173.3
strong arm was s. to me . 379.c
strong the hand s. forth . . 764.1
outstretched
2 *(we) stretch*
I may s. out a loving hand . 612.3
b *Ps 88:9; Matt 12:13*
up to thee my hands are s. . 434.1
empty hands I'm s. to thee . 435.1
now I s. forth my hand . . 437.3
we s. our hands to thee . . 481.1
fearless s. my eager hand . 520.3
s. out their hands to thee . 533.3

strew-strow-ed
scattered garments s. . . 150.1
path be s. with thorns . . 502.2
blessings . . . s. the path . 938.2

stricken
enchain the sorely s. soul . 827.1
frontiers of a s. world . . 864.4

strict 472.3

strife *(Gal 5:20)**
his cup of pain and . . . s. . 5.3
souls . . . from ways of s. . 63.1
with the woes of sin and s. . 83.2
O hush . . . ye men of s. . 83.2
aid us in thy s. 152.3
rose victorious in the s. . . 156.2
all that genders inward s. . 211.2
clouds unfold their wings of s. 280.1
as I am, so tired of s. . . 285.2
when a-wearied of the s. . 330.2
all the tumult and the s. . . 358.1
wrecked by sin and s. . . 390.2
sing above the toil and s. . 393.3
he has borne the s.. . . 402.3
in the desert and the s. . . 499.2
fear and hunger, pain and s. . 576.2
may conquer in the s. . . 582.5
our stay in s. 674.4
awake, for the s. is at hand . 689.1
through the battle and the s. . 731.3
if the s. should . . . grow . 805.2
deadly is the s. 813.2
struggle with crime . . . and s. 830.2
noble deeds and worthy s. . 867.3
all counted good through . . . s. 874.3
b *strife [ended]*
the s. is o'er 151.1
where s. was reigning . . 539.2
the waves of s. be still . . 669.3
the s. will not be long . . 699.4
when the s. on earth is done . 819.3
when all men from s. . . . free 833.1
above the waves of earthly s. 872.1
s. and sorrow over . . . 894.c
calms all earthly s. . . . 948.3
c *'mid strife*
victors in the midst of s.. . 10.4
faint amid the s. 70.3
unbent amid the clashing s. . 508.3
fame amid the worldly s. . 791.2
amidst the noise of . . . s. . 884.3
fierce (c)

strike
I s. those golden strings. . 368.4
s. for truth a telling blow . 801.1
by and by we'll s. the valley . 903.3

strings
I strike those golden s. . . 368.4
swept across the broken s. . 390.2

stripes *Isa 53:5*
by his s. we are healed . . 126.3
by the s. which wounded thee 151.5
by his s. my soul was healed. 402.3

strive-n-ing
in vain you s. to drown . . 267.2
s. in vain to look gay . . 318.1
after s. and praying . . 321.2
I cease from my s. . . . 410.2
s. to shut, but s. in vain. . 533.4
till all our s. cease . . . 567.4
wash . . . dust of earthly s. . 647.2
b *Luke 13:24**
our s. would be losing . . 1.2
I s. to climb the ladder . . 369.2
Saviour, in my daily s. . . 463.1
s. to be approved of God . 688.4
faith . . . for victory s. . . 733.6
daily s. to lead them . . 790.2
s. when . . . called . . . to cast. 816.1
do not give in but s. . . 817.1
s. to walk in holy ways . . 849.2
s. till the foes of God . . 864.4
my earnest s. after truth . 867.5
the faithful who have s.. . 939.3
the s. saint find grace . . 943.3
c *Gen 6:3*
s. afresh . . . prevail . . 18.3
while the Holy Spirit's s. . c8

strong
1 *(re divinity)*
every word of grace is s. . 26.3
s. Friend of sinners, hear . 282.2
so s. to deliver, so good. . 372.1
Jesus is s. to deliver . . 467.c
eternal Father, s. to save . 569.1
s. Deliverer 578.2
our Saviour s. and true . . 828.1
they are weak, but he is s. . 843.1
come along, for Jesus is s. . c3
Jesus, he's loving and s. . c31
b
grace of God so s. . . . 295.4
tender mercy . . . sweet and s. 548.3
firm in thy s. control . . 571.1
thy power . . . s., changeless. 571.3
c *strong arm*
his s. a. of mercy . . . 329.1
tell . . . of God's s. a. . . 335.2
his s. a. was stretched . . 379.c
by faith on his s. a. rely . c120
d *strong hand* *(Ps 89:13)*
in his s. h. . . . I trust . . 48.1
h. s. to smite the sins . . 129.2
whose s. h. were skilled . 611.2
s. the h. stretched forth . 764.1
thy h. unfailing, s. . . 926.2
e *strong love*
faithful, s. as death . . 110.4
l. unbounded . . . deep and s. 184.2
l. most true and s. . . 343.1
l. . . . s. than death . . 383.2
a deep, s. l. that answers . 426.2
bound . . . by l.'s s. cord . 757.3
your s. l. and tender care . 856.1
tower (1c)
2 *strong [in God]*
recreate me . . . s. and true/sure 32.1, 3
s. and fair and fruitful too . 159.4
I would be s. 491.1
s. shall be my hand . . 508.1
soldiers . . . be valiant and s.. 681.c
s. to meet the foe . . . 698.2
foot it . . . s. or weary . . 716.1
I want an even, s. desire . 720.2
legions, valiant, free and s. . 803.2
helpeth others to be s. . . 838.3
just as I am, young, s. . . 860.3
arms are s., Hallelujah . . 876.4
compassion deep and s. . c208
b *strong heart*
s. of h., toil on . . . 158.3
make our weak h. s. and brave 203.4
faltering h. may now be s. . 249.1
s. in h., with purpose pure . 534.3
c *strong faith* *Rom 4:20*
keeps f. sweet and s. . . 519.3
s. in f., with mind subdued . 566.5
rise on f.'s s. wings . . 749.1
d *strong/[weak]* *Heb 11:34**
to make our w. hearts s. . 203.4
faltering hearts may now be s. 249.1
I was w., I am s. . . . 322.4
weakling . . . can be s. . . 324.2
weakling, but he can be s. . c210
e *be strong* *2 Tim 2:1*
in my quiet strength . . . be s.. 564.1
firm . . . and s. in thee . . 612.3
be s. in the grace of the Lord. 679.*
s. in the strength . . . 695.1
s. in the Lord of hosts . . 695.2
soldiers of the cross, be s. . 816.4
f *2 Cor 12:10*
my weakness is s. . . . 506.2
make (4g)
3 *strong [wrong]*
wrong seems oft so s. . . 42.3
s. were the bonds of fault . 176.1
my passions are s. . . . 298.3
God's enemies s. . . . 687.4
a s. opposing band . . 810.2
field, though proud and s. . 813.3
foe (i)
4 *(other)*
wind that art so s. . . . 2.2
echo clear and s. . . . 32.3
lure of s. desire . . . 207.1
many a thousand s. . . 815.1

stronger
God is s. than his foes . . 9.*
self-deceiving, felt s. . . 553.2
s. than fear of death . . 724.3
peace, s. than . . . Hell . . 751.3
wiser, s., still becoming . . 842.4

stronghold *(2 Cor 10:4)* . . 165.2

strongly 106.3

strowed see strew

struggle-d-ing
just as I am, a s. soul . . 415.2
s. are quelled . . . 416.4
my s. and wrestlings be o'er . 454.1
some poor . . . s. seaman . 478.c
I s. sore, I s. vainly. . . 490.1
I s. and wrestled to win it . 542.2
multitudes who s. with crime 830.2
Jesus knows all about our s. . c182
b *struggles [cease]*
bade my s. cease . . . 366.4
s. cease, I have peace . . 379.4
now that my s. are o'er . . 457.3
when I had ceased from my s. 542.2
earth's s. soon shall c. . . 752.7
from earthly s. . . . release . 894.1

stubborn
renounce . . . thy s. will. . 251.3
s. once was my will . . 422.2
Lord, bend this s. heart . . 445.1
subdue . . . the s. heart. . 638.3
bend its s. will . . . 782.3

studied 855.2

stumble *1 Peter 2:8**
if e'er I disown you I s. . . 506.5
courage, brother, do not s. . 716.*

sturdy 855.2

subdue-d-ing
1 *(Phil 3:21)**
there let him s. all . . . 141.5
to teach, convince, s. . . 200.3
s. each rising . . . thought . 445.1
s. . . . the stubborn heart . 638.3
my sorrows to s. . . . 749.3
b
self and pride s. . . . 430.2
strong in faith, with mind s. . 566.5
the soul, s. by toil . . . 632.3
foes all s. 813.4
dark passions s. . . . 823.1

subjection *(1 Cor 9:27)* . . 415.5

sublime-st
for its meaning is s. . . 63.1
came to earth with gifts s. . 74.1
bowed before the child s. . 74.2
gathers round its head s. 112.1, 5
there in those mansions s. . 371.3
way . . . to that s. abode . 414.4
prayer the s. strains . . 625.3
guest . . . O thought s. . . 728.1

submission *(Jas 4:7)**
perfect s. 310.2, 3
in deep s. I pray . . . 786.c
in true s., bring all . . . 864.3

submissive
s. rests my cheerful will. . 208.2
a heart resigned, s., meek . 444.2
winds and waves s. heard . 569.2

submit 164.4

subside-ing
all doubts . . . trust s. . . 551.2
bid my anxious fears s. . . 578.3
love that lives . . . s. never . 631.2

subtle 773.1

succeed-ing
trusting . . . you'll surely s. . 773.3
eternal calm s. the storm . 911.6
God of their s. race . . 918.2

success
give thy word s. . . . 219.2

each s. repeating . . . 778.3
I've found the secret of s. . 806.1
crown our labours with s. . 833.3
s. and joy to make me bold . 860.4

successive
doth his s. journeys run . 160.1
demand s. songs of praise . 925.4

succour *Heb 2:18**
all who on his s. trust . . 21.3
who is he . . . comes to s. . 104.5
for my s. flying . . . 123.4
s. . . . come from thee . . 596.4
giving s. to the living . . 655.5

such
1 *(re people)*
not for sinners s. as I . . 122.2
O save s. just now . . 175.3
s., O Lord, am I . . . 284.2
guilty sinners, s. as I . . 284.5
s. as trust their . . . strength . 559.4
s. ever bring thee . . . 604.2
for s. our Saviour came . . 789.4
s. as from a pure heart . . 910.3
b *Matt 19:14*
of s. is the Kingdom . . 794.2
2 *(re things)*
you give s. rich resources . 38.2
cannot comprehend s. love . 48.1
s. shameful punishment . 108.1
are s. the wounds . . 122.1
I shelter from s. agonies . 122.2
s. wondrous, dying love . 128.2
did e'er s. love and sorrow . 136.3
at s. times I feel . . . 169.3
made room for s. poor souls . 266.2
I've had s. joy and gladness . 309.2
thoughts of s. amazing bliss . 314.2
for sunshine at s. times . . 316.2
at s. tremendous cost . . 325.1
rich . . . s. wealth possessing. 536.1
with s. treasure . . . 539.2
s. changeful feelings had . 549.1
with s. light feet the years . 551.3
s. happiness . . . fails . . 728.4
unworthy of s. grace . . 730.1
safe is s. confiding . . 736.1
s. blessings from thy . . . hand 918.5
sinner . . . sowing s. seed . 928.3
s. wondrous grace . . . provided c62
b *Matt 9:8*
his grace and power are s. . 563.2
thine is s. wondrous power . 741.1
in their lives s. power . . 760.1
c *Acts 3:6*
s. as I have I give . . . 475.2
s. as I have, Lord, I give. . c103
3 *such a . . .*
a *(people)*
for s. a worm as I . . . 105.1
found . . . O s. a friend . . 345.1
serving s. a mighty . . . King . 402.c
I've found s. a . . . Saviour . c155
b *(other)*
down to s. a world . . 88.4
faint while s. a river . . 157.2
s. a marvel of wonder . . 395.2
cost thee s. a price . . 507.2
s. a bright display . . . 657.3
s. a full salvation . . . 764.2
secured at s. a price . . 944.2

suddenly
s. a voice divine rang . . 839.1
b *Mal 3:1*
s. the Lord, descending . . 75:3
s. return, and never . . 438.2

suffer-ed-ing
1 *(to mean 'allow')*
nor s. him to die in vain . . 234.3
s. me to leave thee never . 865.3
b *Ps 121.3*
he will not s. . . . moved . 767.2
s. not our feet to stray . . 789.6
c *Matt 19:14*
s. me to come to thee . . 793.1
s. little children to come. . 797.1
2 *(God) suffers ('endures')*
he freely s. in our stead . . 108.2
thou didst s. to release us . 109.1
he s. still, yet loves . . 142.4
on the cruel cross he s. . . 180.1
Christ has s. on the tree . 239.1
I have heard how he s. . . 289.2
my Saviour s. on the tree . 360.1
thou didst s. out of love. . 538.1
s. my soul to set free . . 543.1
love that s., hoped . . 544.5
Christ s., we believe . . 785.3
b *suffer for*
while Jesus s. for our sake . 107.3
he hung and s. there . . 133.2
languished and s. for me . 289.2
one who s. there for me . 476.2
for you on the cross Jesus s. c20
on Calvary's tree he s. . . c161
c *suffer and die*
cried, when he s. and d. . 137.3
and s. and d. alone . . 179.3
for our sins he s. and . . . d. . 184.2
d *1 Peter 3:18*
for sins . . . he s. on the tree. 105.2
for our sins he s. and bled . 184.2
3 *(we) suffer ('endure')*
the world has s. long . . 83.2
nor s. a defeat . . . 366.5
all, to s., live or die . . 448.c
there is much to s. . . 491.1
willing to s., others to save . 623.3
gives the courage to s. . . 830.3
valiantly they s. . . . 866.1
b *1 Cor 3:15*
count it gain to s. loss . . 489.2
it must not s. loss . . . 699.1
c *1 Cor 13:4*
love s. patiently . . . 530.c
love that s., hoped . . 544.5
d *2 Tim 2:12**
they s....reign with him above 168.5
to s. and triumph with thee . 639.2
to s. and triumph I'll go . . 734.3
e *(Rev 7:16)*
they never s. more . . 911.6
justly persecution (a)

sufferers 909.1

suffering *(noun)*
1 *(divine)* *Heb 2:10*
weapons . . . broken by thy s. 122.4
the emblem of s. and shame . 124.1
all his s. for mankind . . 191.1
his cross of s. I behold . . 420.4
thy s. brought thee victory . 586.2
make known the s. of the cross 830.2
'twas the s. of Jesus . . c209
b *1 Peter 4:13**
thy s. bids me share . . 138.3
in my Master's s. sharing . 197.3
s. of the cross I . . . bear . 499.2
2 *(human)*
recompense for s. . . . 145.3
s. that I can't explain . . 544.2
by s. and temptation . . . tried 822.2
b
all our . . . s. to share . . 245.1

3 *(adjective)*
that s. face so marred for me 138.2
shining from his s. face . . 242.4
O s. Saviour, now to thee . 421.4
the s. servant he became . 451.2
follow thee, s. redeemer . 490.c
beamed through his s. eyes . 855.4

suffice-eth
grace our souls s. . . . 500.2
surrender alone will s. . . 507.2
less . . . will not s.. . . . 565.3
alone God s. 956

sufficiency *(2 Cor 3:5)* . . . 734.2

sufficient
self-s. but sad 376.1
b *2 Cor 12:9*
s. is thine arm alone . . 13.2
God's love is s. for me . . 47.*
by thine all-s. merit . . 79.4
more than s. God's grace . 319.2
my grace all-s. . . . supply . 653.4
Lord has always proved s. . 732.3
thy all-s. strength . . . 738.1
pleading for strength s. . . 740.2
s. is thy grace from day . 761.1
thy blood . . . is s. for me . 883.2
s. is his love to satisfy . . c120

suggest
direct, control, s. . . . 665.5
heavenly blue s. . . . 783.4

suit *(noun)* 563.1

suited 254.1

sullen 743.4

sums 589.5

summer
pleasant s. sun 25.3
s. and winter, and springtime. 33.2
when s. winds...are breathing 39.3
s. suns are glowing . . . 40.1
my s. would last . . . year . 318.2
thank you for the fruitful s. . 552.2
not only under s. skies . . 717.2
the s. morn I've sighed for . 896.1
s. rays with vigour shine . 925.2
in winter, in s. . . . the same . c207

summit 766.3

summon-ed
1 *(God) summons*
when I the s. must obey . 356.3
when I am s. to thee . . 484.3
how the s. will . . . confound 875.1
s. now his wrath to see . . 875.3
the heavenly s. came . . 890.2
s. home! . . . sounded . . 894.1
from . . . house he is s. . . 905.3
2 *(other)*
s. all, at Jesus' call . . 693.c
evil . . . s. its legions forth . 864.1

sun
1 *(figurative, re divinity)*
a *sun [and shield]* *Ps 84:11*
he is our s. and s. . . . 43.3
thou art my s. and my song . 318.4
in him my star, my s. . . 332.3
my s. and my s. . . . 410.3
be thou the s. that draws . 486.2
s. of my soul 676.1
b *Mal 4:2*
S. of righteousness . . . 82.3
he is the S. of righteousness . 346.2
S. of righteousness arise . 412.1
S. of righteousness arising . 452.3
c *Isa 60:20; Rev 21:33*
s. which goes not down . 76.5
our s. . . . no more go down . 275.2
love's s. is shining . . 888.2
2 *(natural)*
burning s. with golden beam . 2.1
night before the rising s. . 13.4
s. and moon bow down . . 17.4
the pleasant summer s. . 25.3
he the golden-tressèd s. . 34.4
summer s. are glowing . . 40.1
s.'s last rays are fading . . 63.3
tomorrow's s. may never rise. 251.2
builder of s. and the cross . 288.2
midsummer s. shines but dim. 318.1
awake, my soul, and with the s. 665.1
the s. that bids us rest . 677.4
greets the rising of the s. . 776.1
prevent the s. from shining . 854.1
bright above the s. reign . 897.3
in rain and snow and s. . . 926.2
b *(comparisons)*
hail thee as the s. above. . 10.1
face and garments, like the s.. 154.1
like a mist before the s. . . 399.1
majestic, like the s. . . 657.2
brighter than the noonday s. . 909.1
c *Ps 72:5*
reign where'er the s. . . 160.1
d *Ps 136:8*
the golden-tressèd s. . . 34.4
e *Matt 27:45*
s. in darkness hide . . . 105.3
s. withholds his rays . . 107.2
the s.'s eclipse is o'er . . 143.2
f *Mark 16:2*
afar, his rising s. . . . 145.1
moon (b), set (c, d), shine (1c), smite (b)
3 *(figurative)*
when the s. of bliss . . 112.3
the s. is always bright . . 320.c
walk...with our faces to the s. 462.3
the s. gone down . . . 617.2
ere/when the s. goes down . 913.*

sunbeam . . . . . 844.*

sundered 573.3

sunk see sink

sunlight
like thy . . . waves in s.. . 32.2
mine is the s. 35.3
flowers . . . in the s. beams . 39.3
without the s. of thy face . 726.3
ever in the s. gleaming . . 894.2

sunlit
new fall s. from Heaven . 35.2
a s. heart 426.1
thank you . . . for s. pathways 552.2

sunny 686.2

sunrise
when s. dyed the . . . deeps . 103.2
his tent, at s. 890.3

sunset
the s. and the morning . . 25.2
labour ends with s. ray . . 934.3

sunshine-ing
1 *(natural)*
fair is the s. 177.3
snow or s., joy or pain . . 544.2
as s. melts the snow . . 705.4
the breezes and the s. . . 935.1
in s., in rain . . . the same . c207
2 *(figurative)*
why from the s. of love . . 248.1
bright s. shall . . . gild . . 277.1
s. or shadows? I cannot tell . 294.3
God is our s. 316.1
into his s. day . . . 378.3
there is s. in my soul . 387.1, c
no other s. than the s. . . 476.3
for in s. or in sadness . . 503.3
that in thy s.'s blaze . . 621.2
there's s. on the hearth . . 664.2
through cloud and s. . . 670.3
the days of . . . golden s. . 711.3
the tempest and the s. . . 731.3
through s. or . . . tempest wild 741.1
sowing in the s. . . . 930.2
travel along in the s. . . c26
clouds will change to s. . c115
live in God's s. c116
through cloud and s. . . . trust c132
scatter a little s. . . . c200

sunward 10.4

supernal
come we to the joy s. . . 185.2
riches . . . and blessings s. . 371.3
each day is a gift s. . . 666.1
with gifts of grace s. . . 934.2

suppliant
God cannot pass a s. by. . 127.3
mark each s. sigh . . . 940.3

supplicant *(Phil 4:6)** . . 613.2

supply-d-ing
1 *(noun)* *Phil 1:19*
more and more of love's s. . 439.4
shall drink a fresh s. . . 559.4
grace . . . shall be thy s. . 653.4
ere man could reap the . . . s.. 923.1
come and drink a full s. . c16
2 *(verb)*
Lord . . . thy grace s. . . 97.3
thy flowing wounds s. . . 132.4
well s. thy sons and daughters 157.2
s. the plains below . . 159.5
millions there have been s. . 239.3
that soul will I s. . . . 277.2
'tis religion must s. . . 464.2
Lord, s. me from above . . 538.4
s. us from thy store . . 575.1
word of life, s. comfort . . 655.5
with heavenly thoughts s. . 671.3
the strength which God s. . 695.1
b *supply need* *Phil 4:19*
his full hand s. their n. . . 34.5
and he s. my every n. . . 317.4
it is love s. my every n. . . 342.3
we will find our n. s. . . 462.1
have their deepest n. s. . . 471.2
s. each daily n. . . . 561.2
all my n. just now s. . . 620.1
every day . . . s. all my n. . 727.4
Jesus every n. s. . . . 764.3
God can . . . my every n. s. . c120
c *supply wants*
our w. s., and none deny . 50.c
in him all my w. are s. . . 535.4
his fulness my w. shall s. . 734.1
provide for our w. to be s. . 924.1

support-ed
he s. and strengthens me . 404.3
let thy hand s. me still . . 453.3
thus s., even I . . . 630.3
toil . . . s. by thy word . . 678.4
near with grace to s. . . 689.3
still s. and comfort me . . 737.2
s. me in the 'whelming flood . 745.3

supreme-ly
find the life s. 27.6
till under thy s. control . . 208.2
at whose s. command . . 223.2
my Lord who reigns s. . . 447.4
shall rule my life s. . . 591.3
mercy, thine own s. delight . 601.3
proof s. of heavenly pity . 777.2

sure
lo! his doom is s. . . . 1.3
most s. in all his ways . 18.1, 4
to know thy favour s. . . 26.4
trace . . . the s. unfolding . 38.3
nothing . . . is as s. and certain 49.1
where is the s. . . . seal . . 214.4
hope . . . advocate s. . . 236.2
pardon, precious, s., complete 259.3
calm, s. haven of his breast . 333.3
fix the intention s. . . . 416.2
no spring of action s. . . 508.2
a calm, a s. retreat . . . 573.1
my s., unerring light . . 597.1
the victory's s. . . . 700.3
his s. trust and tender care . 715.1
sweet our portion is and s. . 722.1
faith still small, but s. . . 742.3
power from God is very s. . 760.2
delay its s. returning . . 854.2
s., will the harvest be . . 931.c
b *2 Tim 1:10*
make me strong and s. . . 32.1
makes the triumph s. . . 707.4
faith . . . makes salvation s. . 733.4
I would make s. of Heaven . 883.1
c *2 Tim 2:19*
shake thy s. repose . . 157.1
firm as a rock, and s. . . 574.4
thee, the s. foundation . . 944.1
d *sure [hope]* *Heb 6:19*
the soul steadfast and s. . 280.c
h. that is steadfast and s. . 394.3
s. my soul's anchor . . 746.1
e *sure mercies* *Isa 55:3**
his m. is for ever s. . . . 3.4
m. . . . ever s. . . . . 34.*
f *sure [promise]* *Rom 4:16*
thy word is s. . . . 642.3
the p. of God are s. . . 755.*
the p. . . . s. for all . . 760.3
word is s., thy p. . . 761.3
built upon God's p. s. . . 833.3
unending . . . p. are s. . . 870.1
g *we/l sure*
s. I am there's room . . 266.4
quite s. of salvation I sing . 364.2
I was s. that my soul . . 395.3
we're s. to have victory . . 800.1
I know . . . I'm s. he will . c120
h *sure to*
unbelief is s. to err . . . 29.6
almost is s. to fail . . . 226.3
who seek . . . s. to find him . 270.2
a future in Heaven for s. . 371.3
seek! and you're s. to find . c5
we're s. to win c240
i *(adverb)*
his grace will s. allow . . 385.4
s. it still will lead me on . . 606.3
defence

surely
Lord, s. thou art shaping . . 6.2
s. is his gift of grace . . 52.1
all you need I will s. give . 73.2
Master s. heard the song . 103.4
the Lord will s. pour . . 165.4
he will s. give you rest . . 231.1
all who seek shall s. find . 249.1
something better...s. would be 298.4
a hope that will s. endure . 371.3
that is s. theirs alone . . 414.2
the fire doth s. burn . . 415.4
thou wilt s. receive . . 437.2
s. now thy smile is on me . 459.3
s. I shall never fall . . . 468.3
changes that will s. come . 485.1
all power, s. is thine . . 487.3
I know thou s. must be still . 489.4
salvation . . . shall s. come . 596.4
light . . . so s. thou wilt be . 628.1
for my relief will s. appear . 712.1
the word . . . will s. prevail . 712.2
art thou most s. nigh . . 717.3
hath s. died for me . . 756.2
trusting . . . s. succeed . . 773.3
my faith must s. fail . . 780.2
reach Heaven just as s. . . 780.3
he will s. be with you . . 790.c
s. he shall lead us . . . 803.3
is s. kin to me . . . 826.3
peace s. based . . . 827.1
this I s. know . . . 840.1
s. thou dost know . . . 842.3
he will s. keep me . . . 857.3
the Lord will s. build . . 868.2
robes s. blood-washed . . 893.3
s. he will care for you . . c139
b *Ps 23:6*
s. his goodness and mercy . 19.2
goodness . . . shall s. follow me 54.5
c *Isa 53.4*
s. on him our sins are laid . 121.3

surest c119

surety
a crown in very s. . . . 228.3
b *Heb 7:22*
before the throne my s. . . 106.1

surge-ing
go s. through that heart . . 131.2
while the s. rave . . . 280.2
peace, with sorrows s. round. 752.3

surpass-ing
s. my reason but winning . 119.2
love s. understanding . . 439.2
truth that s. man's knowledge 506.3
I may all men s. . . . 530.1

surprise-d
s. you what the Lord . 396.1, c
can I be s. to fall . . . 770.2
I, at last, with glad s. . . 871.3

surrender-ed
time and talents I s. . . 201.3
s.! reject . . . no longer . . 410.2
waiting until I s. . . . 457.2
all to Jesus I s. . . . 474.*
dear Lord, I do s. . . . 482.1
I s. all to obey thy call . . 482.c
I will s. the dearest . . 507.c
utmost s. alone will suffice . 507.2
all my powers to thee s.. . 865.1
naught we hold save by s. . 922.3
b *full surrender*
come then, make a f. s. . . 343.3
I will s. f. 413.3
my will shall bow in f. s. . 446.3
Lord, I make a f. s. . . 504.1

surround-ed-ing
all thy works with joy s.. . 10.2
saints with his mercy s. . . 19.4
how scornfully s. . . . 123.1
with salvation's walls s.. . 157.1
by floods and flames s. . . 361.3
though darkness s. you . . 537.3
when evil shall s. . . . 624.4
foes may s. us . . . 681.2
his glorious cross s. . . 693.c
though Satan's hosts s. . . 722.2
my life s. is by love . . 728.3
peace, shall s. my . . . grave . 751.4
the storm . . . may s. me . 758.1
feel weakest, dangers s. . 773.1
may the love that here s. . 795.3
walls of fire the saints s. . 809.3
hosts of Hell . . . s. us . . 822.2
b *surround throne*
while ye s. his t. . . . 314.1
the spirits that s. thy t. . . 414.2

survey
when I s. the wondrous cross 136.1
God's all-seeing eye s. . . 665.2

surviving 630.3

sustain-ing-eth
seek . . . our spirit to s. . . 6.2
empower us to s. our cross . 211.3
s. the burden of the . . . vine. 512.3
firm to s., the . . . cross. . 596.2
though the loss s. . . . 930.3
prayer s. us c239
b *(Ps 55:22)*
his love s. us in thy will . . 5.5
thou my soul s. . . . 409.2
thank you . . . for grace s. . 552.1
anchor shall my soul s. . . 746.5
with the tree of life s. . . 909.3
thy love s., fruitful . . . 927.4

sustenance 631.3

swallowed *(1 Cor 15:54)* . . 746.2

swathing *(Luke 2:7)* . . . 93.4

sway
whose power a sceptre s. . 156.3
seem . . . to hold the s. . . 171.1
hold . . . absolute s. . . 487.4
heart shall own thy s. . . 636.3
thy creatures own thy s. . 677.5
shall every purpose s. . . 692.5
come beneath the s. of Christ 700.3
our flag shall have the s. . 810.3

sweat
wipe from your brow the s. . 564.1
blood (2b)

sweep-ing-t
s. from the open plain . . 103.4
that s. away the power . . 113.2
s. up to Glory . . . 344.3
Jesus s. across the . . . strings 390.2
by the blood-current s. . . 437.2
where the storms are s. . . 483.2
s. all the regions deep . . 540.3
cares s. o'er my spirit . . 583.2
we are s. through the land . 819.1
s. on to win 819.3
s. through the earth . . 827.2
s. through the gates . . 910.c
s. o'er . . . stormy deep . . c178
b *Matt 12:44*
of self and sin s. bare . . 615.3

sweet-est
1 *(noun)*
taste the s. of Jesus' word . 312.1
my love, life's only s. . . 556.4
2 *(re divinity)*
laid down his s. head . . 77.1
in thy s. humility . . . 88.5
came s. influence to impart . 200.4
calm thy s. presence bestows 209.1
his entreaty, kind and s. . 246.3
half so gentle, half so s. . 265.2
s. messenger of rest . . 442.4

warm, s., tender, even yet . 496.5
tender mercy . . . s. and strong 548.3
I long to feel thy s. touch . 610.1
ever in thine own s. way . 837.1
s. Rose of Sharon . . . c54
s. Spirit of Christ . . . c104
as I ponder his s. grace . . c187

3 *(general)*
the s. promise of his grace . 26.2
s. will be the flower . . 29.5
s. the rain's new fall . . 35.2
love's s. echo . . . resounding 51.3
s. chiming bells . . . 79.c
joy the s. assurance gives . 144.4
their fragrance ever s. . . 156.3
whene'er the s. church bell . 187.2
with compassion pure and s. . 212.3
s. is the message today . . 247.c
find a s. relief . . . 301.2
s. prospects . . . s. flowers . 318.1
then in fellowship s. . . 397.5
then pain is s., and life . . 424.1
how s. their memory still . 442.3
my chief delight his s. employ 451.3
work that keeps faith s. . . 519.3
feed . . . ones with manna s. . 612.2
glory of thy s. well done. . 628.4
s. the taste of earthly gain . 631.3
dawns the s. consciousness . 632.1
s. hour of prayer . . . 633.*
s. the moments, rich . . 634.1
labour is rest, and pain is s. . 636.2
home is s. when love . . 663.1
faces at the door are s. . . 664.2
with s. sleep . . . close . . 671.4
the world is fair and s. . . 711.1
each s. Ebenezer . . . 712.3
the bitter is s. . . . 712.4
s. our portion . . . 722.1, 3
this life of trust . . . how s. . 741.4
how s. to walk . . . this . . . way 768.2
a s. unmurmuring faith . . 839.5
love's s. lesson . . . 846.1
beautiful prospect, converse s. 873.3
some glad, s. day . . . 884.c
fellowship as blest, so s. . 888.3
the fair, s. morn, awakes . 896.1
Calvary, so dear, so s. . . c7

b *sweet name*
how s. the n. of Jesus . . 58.1
precious n. O how s. . . 66.c
the n. of Jesus is so s. . . 68.*
where Jesus' n. is s. . . 661.2

c *sweet peace*
waits . . . s. p. to bestow . 331.4
never express the s. . . . p. . 367.1
perfect p., fresh and s. . . 751.2
live together in s. p. . . 833.1
s. p., wonderful gift . . c197

d *sweet [rest]*
'tis a haven s. of r. . . 182.3
give thine own s. r. to me . 612.5
s. the repose . . . o'ershading. 632.3
give . . . calm and s. repose . 673.3
how s. to r. for ever . . 676.2
'tis s. to r. here . . . c37

e *sweet [song]*
each . . . s. music make. . 43.1
the s. though far-off hymn . 358.1

f *sweet story*
the s. most precious, s. . . 99.1
you can tell out the s. s. . 384.*
when I read that s. s. . . 794.1
the s. redemption s. . . 828.1

g *sweet voice* *Song 2:14*
s. angel v. 73.1
hark! a v. . . . soft and s. . 73.2
s. than music his v. . . 318.2
a v. said, s. and low . . 359.1
whose s. v. are raised . . 392.3
day by day his s. v. . . 428.1

h *sweet [water]*
its w. are pure and s. . . 252.2
this fountain, so rich and s. . 315.4
where the . . . s. w. flow . 483.1
the deep, s. well of love. . 896.2
wells where the w. are s. . c40

i *Ex 15:25*
thine to make its waters s. . 510.3

j *Ps 119:103*
s. are all thy words . . 353.2

accord (a), by and by, comfort (1b), communion, field (2b), lesson, low (b), note

sweeter
s. far thy face to see . . 61.1
s. sound than thy blest name 61.2
in a nobler, s. song . . 132.5
never was a s. melody . . 327.1
s. than human devotion . . 383.2
earth around is s. green . . 545.2
than all besides more s. . . 573.2
s. still, to . . . find thee . . 632.3
s. lesson cannot be . . 846.1
fuller, s. is that life . . . 878.4

sweet (3b-g)

sweetest
this shall be our s. song . . 43.4
s. note/name/carol ever sung . 67.c
the s. name on earth . . 69.1
bring your s., noblest lays . 109.3
dwell . . . with s. song . . 160.2
assurance I find s. rest . . 323.5
s. name I know . . . 390.c
s. joy I find in leading . . 399.3
s. pleasures while we live . 464.1
my s. thought henceforth . 517.4
themes for the s. songs . . 724.1
dare not trust the s. frame . 745.1
s. songs of triumph sing . 761.3
s. and brightest and best . 794.3
my s. songs I'll raise . . 840.3
the s. note in all our songs . 925.5
'tis the s. place of all . . c116

sweet (3b-g)

sweeten 604.3

sweetly
s. distils in the dew . . 16.4
hear the birds sing s. . . 37.2
come as the dew, and s. bless 217.4
s. echo the Saviour's call . 258.3
how s. Jesus whispers . . 320.3
what can s. be enjoyed . . 375.2
Jesus . . . s. smiled . . 797.1
s. my soul shall rest . . 889.1, c
how they s. sing: worthy . 897.1

sweetness
praise for the s. . . . 35.2
with s. fills my breast . . 61.1
lost all their s. to me . . 318.1
come in thy s. . . . 623.c
know the s. of his rest . . 819.2
sing in s. for your King . . 835.c

swell-ing
1 *(general)*
bosom s. with . . . joy . . 164.5
s. the hosts that . . . go. . 169.2
with hope my soul is s. . . 460.1
warmth to s. the grain . . 935.1

2 *swell [sound]*
s. the psalm of praise . . 40.1
let its praises ever s. . . 68.4
this note shall s. . . . 144.c
s. the triumph of his train . 161.1
who'll s. the chorus . . 278.3
angels, s. the . . . strain. . 550.3
we'll s. the . . . salvation theme 901.4
march to s. the . . . chorus . 902.2

b *swell song*
s. the s. of the angel band . 94.c
to s. the triumph s. . . 799.4
what warlike s. are s. . . 802.1
all unite to s. the s. . . 834.3

3 *swell-ing* *Jer 12:5*
tides that round me s. . . 303.2
to death's dark, s. river . . 338.5
from every s. tide of woes . 573.1
death's deep and s. flood . 583.5
fields beyond the s. flood . 898.2
across death's s. river . . 902.3

swerve-ing *(1 Tim 1:6)*
love in its purpose ne'er s. . 276.3
s. not from his ways . . 738.3

swift
s. to bless 17.2
his terrible s. sword . . 162.1
be s., my soul, to answer him 162.3
let them be s. and beautiful . 525.2
s. as the eagle cuts the air . 559.5
your hands s. to welcome . 611.3
s. to its close ebbs out . . 670.2
s. be my feet to stay . . 861.4

swift-ly
how s. didst thou move . . 62.4
ease which comes s. . . 719.3
how s. obedience answers love 867.2
your time is s. flying . . 913.1

b *Ps 147:15*
now the word doth s. run . 165.2

c *Prov 6:18*
for . . . flowers s. should run. 842.2

swing
s. wide the door . . . 227.*
s. your heart's door . . . open. 241.c

sword
1 *secular*

a *Isa 2:4; Mic 4:3*
s. shall be sickle . . . 166.3

b *Rom 8:35*
persecution, want nor s. . 554.1
neither peril nor the s. . . 555.1

2 *(figurative)*
force me to render up my s. . 508.1
for the altar or the s. . . 769.2
in his name unsheathe thy s. 864.3

b *Ps 45:3*
gird on thy mighty s. . . 219.2

c *Matt 10:34*
his terrible swift s. . . 162.1

d *sword of God*
wonderful . . . wield his s. . 583.4
with the s. of G. in hand . 686.2
to take his shining s. 701.c/705.c
his s. of truth in my hand . 734.3
gleams a consecrated s. . 799.2
with the s. of G. in hand . 819.1
once the s., . . . now the sceptre 894.2

e *sword of Spirit* *Eph 6:17*
help by the S.'s s. . . 561.4
unsheathed the S.'s s. . . 697.6
overcoming . . . with the S.'s s. 757.3
arm you with the S.'s s. . 813.1
with the s. of the S. . . 820.1
s. of the S. we'll wield . . 820.2

f *Heb 4:12*
S.'s two-edged s. . . 609.3
thy word my trusty s. . . 658.6

shield (b)

sworn
s. in glad service 506.5
b *(Luke 1:73)*
thy mouth . . . to me hath s.. 407.5
c *Heb 6:13*
he by himself hath s. . . 223.4

symbol 486.2

sympathise-ing
the s. Jesus 67.1
heart . . . to soothe and s. . 485.2
flows the s. tear . . . 660.3

symphony 858.1

Syrian *(Matthew 4:24)* . . 567.2

T

table *(Ps 23:5)*
my t. thou hast furnishèd . 54.4
he my t. prepares . . . 373.3
cup o'erfilled, a t. spread . 512.1

tableland c80

taint-ed
men, the t. and defiled . . 274.1
defiling t. of sin . . . 867.2

take-n-ing/took
1 *(God) takes*
a *(with name or title)*
Jesus t. the highest station . 147.4
Jesus from my heart did t. . 309.c
till Jesus t. me in . . . 361.1
but Jesus t. me in . . . 374.1
Christ t. the whole . . . heart. 447.4
lowly paths our Lord has t. . 555.2
b *(general)*
t. thy throne, O crucified . 122.4
to sanctify, to t. command . 163.3
he t. his seat above . 164.2
and wants to t. control . . 204.3
t. me to thee up on high . 318.4
there . . . he t. my place . 341.3
t. thy plummet . . . line . . 446.2
t. thy kingdom . . . crown . 532.4
come . . . t. control . . 630.2
when he t. the trail . . 903.2
shall t. his harvest home . 924.3
t. us through the darkness . 938.4
c *take [care]*
I'm certain he'll t. c. . . . 684.2
thou t. heed to all . . . need . 933.2
God will t. c. of you . . c124
d *Job 23:10*
he knows the way he t. . . 736.2
e *take [away]*
he all my griefs has t. . . 344.2
then my burden t. from me . 379.c
t. . . . stress of secret fear . 647.2
he t. my burden a. . 710.2
t. all my guilt a. . . . 743.1
he'll t. it a. c31
t. a. all that now . . . hard . c95
f *take sin* *John 1:29*
died to t. away my s. . . 37.3
Christ . . . t. all our s. away . 120.2
t. all, t. all my s. away . . 140.3
he t. my s. and sorrows . 179.3
the Lamb shall t. my s. away. 407.3
t. every spot of s. away. . 432.1
t. all my s. away . . 450.1, c
wash . . . t. all my s. away . c111
home (3d) power (4t)
2 *(God) takes us*
for his sheep he doth us t. . 3.2
t. me, Jesus, I am thine . 128.3
he will t. the sinfulest . 262.2
canst thou . . . treasure t. . 285.1
t. me, I can trust my all . . 285.3
t. me as I am . . . 291.*
I know thou wilt t. me . . 473.1
t. me, Jesus, t. me now. . 474.2
t. my undivided being . . 477.2
t. my . . . powers, t. my memory 492.2
t. my body, spirit, soul . . 497.1
t. me and mould me . . 501.c
claim it, t. it for thine own . 504.1
t. my . . . affection, t. . . . will. 520.2
t. my life/hand/voice . . . . 525.*
t. me, and my calling seal . 529.3
t. thou the helm . . . 628.4
in his arms he'll t. . . . thee . 645.3
t. this little child 792.1
t. me now, Lord Jesus, t. me. 865.1
b *take in* *(Matt 25:43)*
yet in mercy t. me in . . 292.3
open thine arms and t. me in. 305.2
till Jesus t. me in . . . 361.1
the captain t. me in . . 375.1
he will t. them in . . . 814.c
c *take all*
t. my all and make it thine . 460.3
t. all there is . . . t. what . 605.3
Jesus, t. them all . . . 859.c
d *take hand*
Saviour, t. my h. . . . 303.2
t. my h., and let them move . 525.2
t. thou my h. and guide me.635.1, 3
t. my h. and ever keep me . 842.1
Lord . . . t. thou my h. . . 861.4
e *take heart*
loving Saviour, t. my h. . 108.3
here's my h., Lord, t. . . 313.5
t. my poor h. and let it be . 424.2
Christ t. the whole . . . h. . 447.4
t. my h., but make it new . 492.2
t. my h. for ever . . . 503.c
O t. this h. of mine . . . seal . 521.1
t. my h., it is thine own . . 525.5
life (4c), possession (b)
3 *(people) take*
from mine example comfort t. 21.2
saints, fresh courage t. . . 29.3
t. ourselves out of his care . 49.c
t. the name of Jesus . 66.1, 2
no other can t. it . . . 119.3
the road that we must t. . 190.3
helps me t. the strain . . 204.2
then why not t. it now . . 255.1
when I t. him at his word . 339.2
t. the world, but . . . Jesus . 343.c
doubt him not, but t. his word 385.2
t. part in the fight . . . 427.3
in Heaven we t. our place . 438.3
my hand . . . t. hold of thee . 450.4
t. time to be holy . . . 458.*
service with our Lord to t. . 532.1
joy that none can t. away . 601.2
going t. thee to their home . 604.2
t. it to the Lord in prayer . 645.*
t. up the torch . . . 683.5
t. heed and beware . . 689.2
t. the field for Jesus . . 696.1
t. his shining sword 701.c; 705.c
I dare not t. one step . . 726.1
my faith t. hold of thee . . 742.2
glad to t. a soldier's part . 776.3
t. your weakness . . . to Jesus 790.1
t. your shield and sword . 817.3
then to t. my victor's crown . 860.5
I'd like to t. my place . 884.1
he t. his staff, and smiling . 911.2
t. Jesus to all the world. . c22
we've t. the field for God . c243
b *take cross* *(Matt 16:24)*
t. up thy c. and follow me . 275.3
t. the c. . . . need'st not fear. 320.3
I t., O c., thy shadow . . 476.3
t. up thy c. and follow me . 490.*
Jesus, I my c. have t. . . 498.1
bold to t. up . . . consecrated c. 596.2
that bravely t. the c. . . 619.3
let us t. up the c. . . . 915.3
c *take stand*
fire that t. its s. for Jesus . 197.2
I fain would t. my s. . . 476.1
I, like them, will t. my s. . 686.2
in the Army . . . we've t. our s. 687.1
in the cause . . . t. your s. . 817.3
we will t. our s. . . . 866.2
'neath the flag . . . t. our s. . c236
d *take way*
thence my w. I t. . . . 512.2
ere . . . our w. we t. . . 676.6
Lord, as we t. our chosen w.. 688.1
e *Ex 20:7*
nor t. it in vain . . . 823.2
f *take in*
I scarce can t. it in . . . 37.3
that I may t. it in . . . 98.2
g *take [from God]*
I'll t. the gifts . . . bestowed . 23.1
I t. the grace that flows . . 122.3
t. salvation . . . now . . 240.*
t. with rejoicing from Jesus . 271.4
come and t. thy crown . . 352.3
t. of the offer of grace . . 371.2
heart . . . has failed to t. . 415.3
believe and t. the blessing . 433.c
t. the manna of today . . 566.2
we meet, the grace to t. . 603.3
t. every virtue . . . grace. . 695.3
content to t. whate'er . . 738.2
e'en now, it t. by force . . 742.2
glory . . . from his hands shall t. 777.3
t. . . . his glorious commission 864.3
force (1b), freely (2c), man (2k), morning (1d)
4 *(other)*
first . . . state again t. place . 78.3
o'er Bethlehem it t. its rest . 90.4
e'en if life be t. . . . 222.2
and t. their flight . . . 224.1
my love . . . no pain can t. . 489.4
no right . . . to t. us . . 702.1

tale
hear thy t. of sorrow . . 225.c
t. of the sea 848.1

talent *(Matt 25:15)*
t. are few 294.2
the t. I possess . . . 475.2
be my t. two or fifty . . 477.3
each t. and grace thine . . 589.3
my t., gifts and graces . . 720.4
placing t. on thine altar . . 863.4
b *time and talent*
t. and t. I surrender . . 201.3
my t., my store, my t. . . 482.1
not my own; my t., my t. . 514.3
t., health and t. presenting . 786.3
give our t., bring . . . t. . . 833.2
life and t. and t. . . . 859.c
bring your t. and . . . t. . . 920.2
t. and t., day by day . . c34

talk-ed-ing
1 *(God) talks* *(Luke 24:32)*
he walks . . . and he t. with me 334.c
t. with me, Lord . . . 636.1
he t. about a Kingdom fair . 855.3
I hear him t. 884.3
2 *(people) talk*
in sweet communion t. . . 59.3
I am walking and t. with Jesus 321.1
they are t. of Jesus' grace . 372.2
you may t. of the harps . . 406.2
with the Master t. . . . 430.3
wonderful . . . to t. with God. 583.2
here may we meet, and t. . 590.4
t. with thee in prayer . . 615.3

when I t. with Jesus . . c113
t. with Jesus, work for Jesus. c215

tall 847.3

tare *Matt 13:24-30, 36-43*
wheat and t. together sown . 924.2
in the fire the t. to cast . 924.3
make t. or ripe wheat . 928.3
Satan, the t. 932.1
to grow . . . and be a t.. . 932.3
t. and wheat together grow . 932.3

tarry
the Lord in mercy t. yet . . 267.2
b *(Luke 24:29)**
give us quietly to t. . . 210.3
t. with me at the cross . . 348.c
as I t. in the shadow . . 493.c
c *Acts 22:16*
do not t., come to Jesus . 239.2
wanderer, t. not . . . 261.2
why should we t. . . . 264.2

task
his grace for every t. . 44.c, 3
full equipment for the t.. . 324.4
obedience your t. to fulfil . 506.2
the common t. . . . 668.4
fishermen toiled at their t. . 680.1
when my t. . . . is done . . 725.4
when t. of life seem hard . 744.1
mighty are the t. ahead . . 789.3
my daily t. shalt thou assign . 867.6
no t. for thee neglected . . 934.3
give (1w)

taste-d
bud may have a bitter t.. . 29.5
sweet the t. of earthly gain . 631.3
b *Ps 34:8*
t. and see the riches . . 60.4
c *1 Peter 2:3*
man may t. the grace . 140.5
had a t. of Heaven . . . 243.2
t. the sweets of Jesus' word. 312.1
t. life's pure river . . . 320.1
but this is the t. . . . 355.5
while we t. of his love . . 808.3
I'm going to t. the riches . 858.3
streams on earth I've t. . . 896.2
d *John 8:52*
before we t. of death . . 154.4
e *Heb 2:9*
Jesus t. death for me . . 107.5
that Jesus t. death for me . 360.4

tasteless 318.1

taught see teach

teach-ing/taught
1 *(God) teaches*
great things he hath t. us . 22.3
how he t. the . . . doctors . 96.1
he t. men . . . to smile . . 274.c
grace that t. my heart . . 308.2
t. me how to watch and pray. 365.c
heart is t. the truth . . 485.4
you t. us, Lord, to pray . . 572.1
wilt t. my yearning heart . 586.3
mine, to t. me what I am . 652.1
he will t. you what to do . 664.3
thou hast t. me to know. . 771.1
we are t. to love . . . read/way 834.2
wisdom . . . t. us to share . 927.3
b *John 14:26; 16:8-15*
to t., convince, subdue . . 200.3
is t. by your Spirit . . . 506.3
Spirit . . . thou hast t. me . 545.1

c *(request)*
t. us in your only Son . . 27.6
t. us . . . in all we use . . 38.2
t. O t. us . . . to resemble thee 88.5
t. us to feel thy greatness . 181.4
t. us love's command . . 218.2
t. me . . . feet to stay . . 519.2
t. me thy patience . . . 519.3
t. thy word and . . . will. . 531.1
t. me to live by faith . . 560.5
O t. me to resign . . . 565.4
t. us when we worship . . 575.2
t. us, guide us as we follow . 595.2
t. me the happy art . . 597.3
t. our faint desires to rise . 604.3
t. me, Lord, that I may t. . 612.4
t. me . . . to meet thy gaze . 618.1
t. me to love thy truth . . 650.2
so t. us . . . to use each power 656.4
t. me on thy arm to lean. . 713.2
t. us faithfully to share . 796.2
t. the little children . . 797.3
t. me to be pure and true . 837.1
Saviour, t. me day by day . 846.1
t. me . . . thy steps to know . 846.3
Jesu, Master, t. me now . 871.3
d *teach how*
t. us h. to love 10.3
t. me h. to fight and win . 205.3
t. me h. to give thee . . 221.2
he t. me h. to watch . . 365.c
t. us h. to gain by loss . . 452.3
t. us h. to fight . . . 787.2
t. me h. to grow in goodness 842.3
t. me h. to love/pray/serve . c105
e *Ps 143:10*
need thee . . . t. me thy will . 587.4
t. me to do thy will . . 649.2
f *Ps 144:1*
t. my hands to fight . . 568.1
t. us how to fight . . . 787.2
t. our hands to war . . c236
g *Isa 2:3**
t. me thy ways . . . 861.1
h *Luke 11:1*
you t. us, Lord, to pray . . 572.1
t. me how to pray . . . 588.4
Lord, t. us how to pray . . 625.6
Lord, t. me how to pray . c82
t. me how to pray . . . c105
i *Luke 12:12*
t. us what we ought to say . 193.2
2 *(other)*
raise the song they nobly t. . 158.2
others, t. the glad new song . 326.4
t. me, Lord, that I may t. . 612.4
truth all time has t. . . 827.3

teachers 834.3

teaching *(noun)*
let thy t. sanctify . . 582.5
to its heavenly t. turn . . 654.5

tear-tore-n
he t. the bars away . . 148.3
I've all my idols t. . . 344.2
help me to t. it . . 442.5
we'll t. Hell's throne . . 800.3
b *passive (torn)*
love so t. with pain . . 131.3
heart, so rent and t. . . 138.3
see my heart . . . t. with grief. 292.2
my heart was t. by fears. . 330.1
hands by cruel nails were t. . 339.3
t. by remorse and grief . . 383.3
lives now t. asunder . . 529.3

tear *(noun)*
1 *(divine)*
t. and smiles . . . he knew . 87.4

no t. for his own griefs . . 179.2
caused him bitter t. . . 250.2
t. thy face have marred . . 299.2
2 *(human)*
sacred gains of toil and t. . 5.2
freed men from . . . t. . . 102.2
the Saviour asks no t. . . 131.2
many a labour, many a t. . 228.4
not all my prayers . . . and t.. 297.2
bitter the t. of remorse . . 298.2
striving and praying with t. . 321.2
though t. at times may start . 326.3
my eyes were dimmed with t. 330.1
I was drowning in t. . . 376.2
not a sigh nor a t. . . . 397.2
with its hopes . . . and its t. . 420.1
with t. his promise . . . repeat 420.3
with t., two wonders I confess 476.2
I bring thee all my t. . . 486.3
with cries, entreaties, t.. . 526.1
laurels are bedewed with t. . 564.3
ills . . . t. no bitterness . . 670.4
my sins so slay, my t. to stay. 749.3
we get more smiles than t. . 806.1
it stanches sorrow's t. . . 828.3
poured out cries and t. . . 879.2
only a few more t. . . . 889.2
my eyes are filled with t. . 895.2
laughter for t. . . . c148
b *Ps 56:8*
God . . . counts thy t. . . 721.1
c *Luke 7:38*
wash them with my t. . . 140.4
with my t. . . . bathe . . 634.3
d *Rev 7:17*
from all temptation, t. . . 872.2
no t. within their eyes . . 878.5
there will be no t. . . . 881.c
dry, fall (3b), flow (1b), meat (a), repentance (b), sow (2b), wipe
3 *(other)*
daily fret and t. . . . 129.2

tear-drop
no t. glisten in the eye . . 268.2
gild the t. with his smile. . 333.2
while the t. start . . . 931.3

tearfulness 183.4

tearless *(Rev 7:17)* . . . 621.3

tedious 318.1

telescope 27.3

tell-ing/told
1 *(God) tells*
t. me of a Saviour's love . 69.2
t. me I am born of God 106.4; c129
Father . . . t. of his love. . 323.1
he t. me every care . . . roll . 344.1
while his promise t. . . 373.4
t. my homecoming to Heaven 388.3
he doth t. me plainly . . 420.3
t. me the truth, I will bear . 457.1
t. me thy secret . . . 519.1
t. thy will, Lord . . . 531.1
speak and t. me now . . 534.2
it t. thy love to me . . . 585.1
t. me all thou findest . . 618.c
things . . . ask him to t. me . 848.1
t. me . . . name written there. 883.1
Saviour t. me I am his . . c191
b *[angels] tell*
what a. tongue can t. . . 55.4
'twas by an a. t. them . . 72.2
all the a. t. the story . . 74.2
to . . . shepherds it was t. . 78.2
the great glad tidings t. . . 86.4
t. us of a Saviour's birth. . 88.3
story which a. voices t. . 840.1

c *[Bible] tells*
to t. me whence I came . . 652.1
to t. of joys to come . . 652.4
the B. t. us so . . . 814.1
for the B. t. me so . . 843.1

d *John 16:14*
who is it t. me what/when . 204.1

2 *(people) tell*
a *tell God*
t. out thy need . . . 225.4
here t. your anguish . . 236.1
t. the burden of thy heart . 261.1
t. it in thy Saviour's ear . 261.1
t. my true complaint . . 290.2
all I am t. I thee . . 296.3
wants my heart is t. . . 460.1
t. me all that you have said . 564.3
t. thee how all praise . . 926.1
to t. my need . . . c82
story (2)

b *tell others*
his praise forth t. . . . 3.1
O t. of his might . . . 16.2
lips that we might t. . . 25.4
t. of his . . . faithfulness . 26.2
t. to earth's . . . bound . 43.2
t. his love to me . . . 65.2
so glad to t. you . . 96.1, 2
t. how the angels in chorus . 99.1
our songs his triumph t. . 149.1
let hymns . . . triumph t. . 151.4
triumphant power I'll t. . . 180.3
t. of his excellent greatness . 184.c
some have heard, but t. . 243.4
t. him thou hast died . . 284.4
how could I t. . . . 323.3
when I just t. him . . . 323.5
I will t. you what induced . 338.2
t. its rapture all abroad . . 365.1
with joy I am t. . . . 371.1
I t. you: I'm glad . . . 376.1
t. it where'er . . . . . 384.*
that my life may t. for thee . 488.1
to t. as I have seen . . 591.3
thy love to t., thy praise. . 612.6
t. to all thy blessed will . . 620.2
will all thy goodness t. . . 622.4
t. them of Jesus, the mighty . 691.1
t. the poor wanderer . . 691.4
t. how for me . . . availed . 706.1
t. of what thou art . . . 741.2
speed the message they . . . t. 760.1
we t. to all the world . . 798.2
t. with no uncertain sound . 809.1
t. them in the east . . . . 829.*
t. the world, O t. . . . 832.c
t. the world in song . . 835.1
to t. of his great love . . 851.4
t. of the Saviour's name . 869.3
they shall come forth to t. . 893.3
let us t. of all . . . care . . 907.3
triumphs . . . yet been t. . c44
t. the world . . . cleansing . c47
I t. his love and mercy . . c147
t. of his wonderful love . . c217

c *Mark 5:19*
I want to t. . . . . . 335.*
I want to t. you all about it . c170

d *tell me*
t. me the old, old story . . 98.*
t. me the story of Jesus. . 99.*
t. it to me again . . . 139.1
I've been t. of a Heaven. . 289.3
t. me not of heavy crosses . 320.2
they t. me he wept . . 331.2
t. me what to do 459.1
t. me in . . . wonder . . 848.3

e *[can/not] tell*
no word of man can ever t. . 68.4
no saint . . . worth can t. . 69.3
we cannot t. what pains . 133.2
no tongue has ever t. . . 171.2
shadows? I cannot t. . . 294.3
take my hand, I cannot t. . 303.2
how or why, I cannot t. . . 339.4
his riches never can be t. . 356.2
none its depths can ever t. . 363.1
the grief I cannot t. . . 421.4
who the worth of love can t. . 497.4
glory . . . beyond us to t. . 506.1
power that none can t. . . 591.1
who can t. the pleasure . . 655.4
more than human tongue can t. 696.2
a joy no tongue can t. . . 759.3
loved me, I cannot t. why . c161
around (a), story (1a, 2), tidings (b)

3 *(other)*
t. its own story . . . 51.1
flag . . . t. of victory . . 779.1
it t. of full salvation . . 783.c
crimson t. of . . . salvation . 783.2
those burning strains are t. . 802.1
her gates to t. thy praise . 944.1

telling *(adj)* 801.1

temper-ed
1
my t. are fitful . . . 298.3
evil t., pride . . . 783.4
pride . . . t. cure . . . 914.3
2
with calm and t. zeal . . 568.2
the t. of my trust . . 717.5
t. every wind that blows . c127

tempest
when t. their warfare . . 19.3
then no t. shall appal . . 285.3
peace amid the t.'s roar . . 330.c
when sin's t. blow . . . 347.2
through the t. . . . calm . . 430.3
in the t. he hides me . . 467.4
no t. can my courage shake . 489.4
t. on my heart was falling . 490.1
from rock and t., fire . . 569.4
where the t. is loud . . 641.2
in life's t. . . . remember. . 663.3
amid the t. and the storm . 687.c
too unbelieving 'midst the t. . 713.2
through the t. . . . sunshine . 731.3
while the t. still is high . . 737.1
keep . . . through t. wild . 741.1
t. may sweep o'er . . . deep . c178
b *tempest-tossed* *Isa 54:11*
upon life's billows you are t.-t. 396.1
some poor seaman, t.-t. . 478.3
t. the boat in a t. . . . 848.3
rage (b)

tempestuous
over life's t. sea . . . 598.1
o'er the world's t. sea . . 607.1

temple
1 *(place)*
not in the t. crowd alone . 7.2
we offer thee this t. . . 575.2
as in thy t. I give praise . . 613.1
come to God's own t., come . 924.1
while in thy t. we appear . 925.1
make of this place your t. . 943.1
this t., Lord, we build . . 945.1
b *1 Sam 3:3*
t. courts were dark . . 839.1
watch the t. child . . . kept . 839.2
c *Mal 3:1*
in his t. shall appear . . 75.3
never more thy t. leave . . 438.2
d *Luke 2:46*
in the T. far away . . . 96.1
in the quiet T. heard . . 871.2
2 *(figurative)* *1 Cor 3:16**
the t. of the crucified . . 121.6
fit t. for thy grace . . . 202.3
the t. of my soul prepare . 207.1
fill this earthly t. now . . 208.1
let me thy t. be . . . 209.1
t. of indwelling God . . 214.3
a t. meet for thee . . . 411.4
never more thy t. leave . . 438.2
come and thy t. possess . 457.c
he keeps his t. clean . . 495.2
I would be thy holy t. . . 786.1
living stone in a t. . . 941.2
b *make temple*
my heart thy t. m. . . 285.1
my heart thy t. m. . . . 502.2
m. me a t. meet . . . 623.4
m. of this place your t. . 943.1
c *Rev 3:12*
stand in the t. of our God . 533.5

tempt-ed-ing
1 *(re Jesus)* *Matt 4:1*
he was tried and was t. . . 99.2
thou hast been troubled, t. . 558.4
2 *(re people)*
sometimes we're t. . . 316.2
Satan t. me sore . . . 344.2
when I am t. . . . my song . 437.4
t. as ye will 480.4
speak to guard the t. . . 581.4
when t. . . . parents strayed . 785.3
when I'm t. to do wrong . 837.3
the t. sounds I hear . . 862.2
when t. to forsake his God . 911.3
when t. sore to worry . . c145
t., I can feel his power . . c154

temptation
if t. round you gather . . 66.2
in t.'s desert a . . . rock. . 288.4
now tossed with t. . . 298.4
fierce t. try my heart . . 326.3
I have victory in t. . . . 330.c
in t. he's . . . mighty tower . 344.2
t. here upon me press . . 385.3
sore t. may beset me . . 399.3
amid t., he supports . . . me . 404.3
through t., save from sin . 430.2
t. my pathway beset . . 553.2
by t. sore . . . victory . . 571.3
t. lose their power . . . 587.2
have we trials and t. . . 645.2
when t. almost win three . 753.2
subtle t., troubles abound . 773.1
when t. fierce assail . . 789.3
suffering and t. . . . tried . 822.2
yield not to t. . . . 823.1
give victory in t. . . . 870.3
from all t., tears and care . 872.2
when I'm sad and t. arise . 881.1
safe from the world's t. . . 889.2
there's . . . no t. there . . 895.2
freedom from . . . t. and care. 904.3
b *hour of temptation*
crown him . . . in t.'s h. . 141.5
in t.'s threatening h. . . 576.3
be near us in t.'s h. . . 624.4
in t.'s darkest h. . . . 790.c

tempter *(1 Thess 3:5)*
though the t.'s snares beset . 389.1
sees the t. fly . . . 596.3
oft escaped the t.'s snares . 633.1
foil the t.'s power . . . 670.3
to meet the bold t., go . . 689.1
crushed by the t. . . . 691.3
break the t.'s spell . . . 693.1

ten see thousand (2a)

tend
Father-like he t. and spares . 17.3
bliss to which I t. . . . 880.2

tender
holy infant, t. and mild . . 89.1
his t. touch can heal . . 126.4
loving and t. from . . . birth . 175.1
the t. stirring of thy Spirit . 192.3
his t. last farewell . . . 200.1
t. Spirit, dwell with me . . 212.3
we lose the t. shepherd . . 265.5
with t. hand he lifted me . 339.c
gain this friend so t. . . 343.3
so kind, so true and t. . . 345.4
what a t., compassionate friend 371.1
yet so t. that it reaches . . 439.2
Jesus, thy wounding is t. . 457.2
let me hear thy t. pleading . 463.2
warm, sweet, t., even yet . 496.5
come, O Lord, with t. healing 528.c
wounds thy t. hands had healed 534.1
no t. voice like thine . . 587.1
nothing less will keep me t. . 591.2
Jesus, t. lover of my soul . 600.1
loving, forgiving, t. . . 623.2
thy t. touch now we implore . 675.c
oft . . . heard thy t. voice . 749.1
b *tender care*
children in thy t. c. . . 77.3
can a woman's t. c. cease . 110.3
sure trust and t. c. . . 715.1
much we need thy t. c. . 845.1
your . . . love and t. c. . 856.*
praise . . . for all thy t. c. . 870.1
his t. c. is everything . . c212
c *tender heart* *Eph 4:32*
if human h. are often t. . 50.1
t. h. were waiting . . . 663.2
while our h. are t. . . . 853.3
while my h. is t. . . . 865.1
h. glowing and t. . . . c213
d *tender [love]*
what a t. l. was thine . . 88.4
how t. his compassion . . 94.2
l. in that story so t. . . 99.3
t. in my l. for men . . 212.3
l. . . . so t. that it reaches . 439.2
l., so great and t. . . 504.1
t. l., divine protection . 938.2
assurance of t. charity . . 948.2
e *tender mercy* *Luke 1:78**
thy m. how t. 16.5
as m.'s t. call rings out . 131.4
his t. m. makes thee room . 333.4
day by day his t. m. . . 548.3
thy grace and t. m. . . 727.2

tenderest 673.3

tenderly
t. mourned and wept . . 117.2
t. saying: Come . . . 235.1
his accents t. say . . . 235.3
Comforter, t. saying . . 236.2
mercy is t. pleading . . 247.1
t. calling thee home . . . today 248.1, c
softly and t. Jesus is calling 264.1, c
Jesus watches, O so t. . . 341.2

tenderness
truth . . . love in its t. . . 183.3
and his t. rebuff . . . 324.1
poured his t. and grace . . 777.2
Jesus sought me in t. . . c171

tent
a t. or a cottage . . . 354.4
nightly pitch my moving t. . 877.1
t. . . . a darkened ruin lay . 890.3

terrible
this t. bondage within . . 459.1
b *(Song 6:4)**
his t. swift sword . . . 162.1

terror
nor fear the t. of our age . 5.4
Hell hath no t. . . . 166.4
only thy t., Lord, restrain . 526.2
chasing far the gloom and t. . 765.3

test
love stands the t. . . . 51.*
let . . . love apply the t. . . 446.1
value is proved by love's t. . 507.1
ask . . . my devotion to t. . 507.c
t. the heart . . . sealed . . 531.1
t. my faith through doubt . 644.3
with each new t. . . . purified. 874.1
help us . . . to t. ourselves . 926.4

testify 869.3

thank-s
no t. to them abideth . . 1.4
we t. thee for the . . . years . 5.2
cup . . . with t. receive . . 23.2
t. never-ceasing . . . 24.3
what language . . . to t. thee. 123.3
t. thee, heavenly Father . . 192.c
O 'tis of t. deserving . . 276.3
we t. thee we find . . . grace. 288.4
where I knelt to t. him . . 348.2
t. you, Lord, for . . . 552.*
for answered prayer we t. . 576.4
t. . . . for answered prayer . 642.1
t. thee that . . . heard . . 642.2
everlasting t. be thine . . 657.3
we t. thee that thy Church . 677.2
I t. thee for the . . . hope . 714.1
I t. thee, Lord . . . 719.*
t. you all our days . . . 795.1
t. him for his goodness . . 836.c
for your holy book we t. you . 856.*
for those we love . . . t. thee. 878.1
t. thee that thou takest heed . 933.2
heartfelt t. to thee ascend . 933.3
we t. thee then, O Father . 935.3
we t. thee for our birthright . 944.2
b *2 Chron 29:31**
we bring t. offerings . . 936.1
c *give thanks to God* *Heb 13:15*
now t. we all our God . . 12.1
all praise and t. . . . be given 12.3
soldiers, give t., and sing . 164.1
give t. to God on high . . 223.5
t. God! 'tis true . . . 375.2
give t. for everything . . 408.5
then t. the Lord . . . 935.c
everything (b), render (b)

thankful *(Ps 100:4)*
crowd thy gates with t. songs 4.3
t., overflowing praise . . 5.1
bring to every t. mind . . 191.1
give me a t. mind . . . 574.5
we'll bring him t. praise . 849.2
from thy t. people . . . 921.3
come, ye t. people, come . 924.1
b *thankful hearts*
drink with t. h. . . . 254.3
prayer with t. h. . . . 796.1
raise with t. h. a song . . 919.1
t. h. need joyful songs . . 926.1
our humble, t. h. . . . 935.3

thankfulness
we owe thee t. and praise . 15.2
join our song of t. . . . 173.1
with t. we store . . . 926.3
hear our song of t. . . . 937.1

thanksgiving
may the music of t. echo . 32.3
with t. we adore thee . . 576.4
give the Army more t. . . 622.3
t. thou wilt not despise . . 921.1

praise and t. . . . we offer . 927.1
on this t. day . . . 934.2

theirs
the secret of the Lord is t. . 411.1
that is surely t. alone . . 414.2
in simple trust like t. . . 567.2
contented . . . wounds be t. . 774.2
that t. may be the love . . 948.1

theme
begin . . . some heavenly t. . 26.1
Jesus is the wondrous t. . 70.c
this my constant t. shall be . 107.5
redeeming love has been my t. 132.4
their everlasting t. . . . 168.6
a t. that thrills all creation . 178.2
'twill be my endless t. . . 327.3
this all my t. shall be . . 368.4
Saviour's love will be the t. . 700.c
t. for the sweetest songs . 724.1
was e'er so grand a t. . . 828.2
beautiful t., the courts above. 873.2
swell the great salvation t. . 901.4
life has a new-found t. . . c173

themselves 685.2

thence
plucked me t. . . . 350.1
life . . . do t. derive . . 424.3
t. my way I take . . . 512.2
from t. my help is coming . 766.2

therefore
t. will not say thee nay . . 563.1
so often, t., we delay . . 748.2
t. are they next the throne . 909.2

therein 615.1

thick-est-ly
t. darkness broodeth yet . 172.6
lights time's t. gloom . . 683.5
men are t. falling . . . 864.2
valleys . . . t. with corn . . 934.1
life's perils t. confound . . 954.3

thief *(Luke 23:39)*
a t. hangs on each side . . 108.1
the dying t. rejoiced to see . 132.2
who saved the dying t. . . 266.3

thin 358.3

thine nc, but
a *I am thine/his* *Song 2:16*
Lord, if indeed I am t. . . 318.4
I am his, and he is mine. . 345.*
my God, I am t. . . . 355.1
all things are mine since I am his 358.3
I am his whate'er befall . . 399.2
living, dying, t. to be . . 470.3
I'm t., O blessèd Jesus . . 511.4
no longer mine, but t. I am . 516.2
the world may know I'm t. . 538.5
I am t., O Lord . . . 585.1
by thy grace I will be t. . . c10
cloudy or fine . . . I am t. . c49
b *we are thine*
t. w. will die . . . live . . 424.4
Saviour, w. are t. . . . 707.c
bought us, t. w. are . . 845.1
t.; do thou befriend us . . 845.2
ever (a) mine (1a) own (4g) wholly

thing-s
1
these t. I know . . . 6.3
other t. may alter . . . 49.2
many . . . t. I cannot understand 52.1
cam'st a little baby t. . . 91.1
promise of t. to be . . . 154.3

wicked t. . . . come not there. 268.3
the impossible shall be . . 407.3
a faithless, wandering t. . 421.2
the best t. I know . . . below. 451.c
t. of earth have filled . . 466.1
I may teach the precious t. . 612.4
the t. which endure . . 640.4
t. deemed impossible I dare . 744.4
t. I would ask him to tell . 848.1
the t. of the past will work . 928.1
he'll put t. right . . . c22
prayer changes t. . . . c114
the t. I love the best . . c230

b *1 Cor 1:27, 28*
we were that foolish t. . . 163.2
bring to naught the t. . . 163.2

c *1 Cor 2:10*
reveal the t. of God . . 756.1

d *2 Cor 4:18*
unseen t. above . . . 98.1
still to t. eternal look . . 667.3

e *2 Cor 5:17/Rev 21:5*
he maketh all t. new . . 267.3
when old t. passed away . 366.1
old t. have passed away . 375.2
who maketh all t. new . . 749.3

f *things above* *Col 3:1*
rise with him to t. a. . . 146.2
set my heart on t. a . . 630.1
seek the t. before us . . 682.1
above the t. of passing time . 729.4

g *true things* *Phil 4:8*
unto the true t. . . . aspire . 351.2
whatsoever t. are true . . c56

belong (d), cursed, do (2b, c), earthly (c), evil (c), glorious (2h), greater (c), one (4b, c), present (2c), renounce, think (2e), wonderful (e)

2 *all things*
a. t. their creator bless . . 2.5
shaping a. t. to thy design . 6.2
a. the vain t. that charm . 136.2
choose and cherish a. t. . 212.5
a. t. are possible . . . 407.3
I a. t. forgo . . . 436.2
a. the t. I held so dear . . 460.2
a. t. their maker praise . . 494.1
myself in a. t. to deny . . 509.1
my will in a. t. to resign . . 509.2
though I may a. t. know . 530.2
in a. t. to depend . . 597.3
that, having a. t. done . . 695.5
he filleth . . . a. t. . . . 929.2
a. t. are passing . . . 956
endurance attaineth to a. t. . 956

b *Isa 44:24**
whose hands a. t. created . 6.1
a. t. bright . . . wise . . 25.c
who has made a. t. well. . 25.4
a. t. living he doth feed . . 34.5
a. t. living thou madest . . 927.1
maker of a. t. near . . 935.2
for a. t. bright and good . 935.3

c *John 16:15*
all t. are mine . . . 358.3

d *Rom 8:37*
in all t. that may hurt . . 554.2

e *Eph 4:15*
let us in all t. grow . . . 662.3

abound (c), bear (2c), possible, ready (c), reckon, things (1e), well (2c)

think-ing/thought
1 *(God) thinks*
still in mercy t. of me . . 303.1
Lord . . . yet he t. of me. . 341.2

2 *(people) think*
don't t. that you have left . 44.1
don't t. . . . he despairs . . 44.c
don't t. that . . . he'll ignore . 44.2
don't t. that God will fail . 44.3
have you ever stopped to t. . 49.1
they t. his day was done . 145.1
t. once again 235.3
dost thou e'er t. . . . 276.1
I t. that the saints above . 373.2
t. how much we owe him . 377.2
in my blindness I t. . . 395.2
discouraged, t. all is lost . 396.1
I can scarcely dare to t. . . 399.2
fear what men may t. . . 415.2
not what I'm t. to be . . 415.2
all that . . . t. most worthy . 435.2
once I t. I walked . . . 549.1
sigh to t. of happier days . 557.3
t. of the sin everywhere . 708.2
love . . . forbids me to t. . 712.3
bids us t. of Christ . . . 783.2
I t., when I read . . . 794.1
ne'er t. the victory won . . 812.3
t. of the home/friends . 886.1, 2
let me t. how thy dear Son . 916.3
God be in my . . . t. . . 953
I t. of all his sorrow . . c14

b *when I think*
w. I t. how God . . . 37.3
w. we t. to find . . . way . 192.2
I am amazed w. I t. . . 319.*
w. I t. of the homeland . . 895.2
whenever I t. of Jesus . . c187
w. I t. of what he's done . c211

c *think and/or*
desire to work . . . and t. . 199.3
the care of what men t. or say 437.4
all I t. or speak or do . . 492.2
I shall never t. or dream . 551.1
all I may t., or do, or say . 665.5
know in all I t., or speak . 667.1
small time to t. or pray . . 675.1
time . . . to t. and plan . . 871.1
by wishing and t. . . . 928.3

d *Eph 3:20*
greater far than we can t. . 642.2

e *Phil 4:8*
t. on these things . . . c56

thought

third *(Luke 24:21)**
on the t. day he rose . . 137.4
'tis thine own t. morning . 155.3

thirst-ing
1 *(re Jesus)* *John 19:28)*
lips with t. are dried . . 121.2

2 *(re people)*
not t. for earth's reward. . 5.3
no t. for life's pleasure . . 320.1

b
flows their t. to assuage. . 157.2
alone his t. can slake . . 277.3
my t. was quenched . . 332.2
I t., thou wounded Lamb . 424.1
I t. thy . . . grace to prove . 440.1
with anxious . . . t. I come . 447.1
create soul-t. for thee . . 626.2

c *Matt 5:6*
blessed they who t. . . 95.1

d *John 4:14; Rev 7:16*
shall never t. again . . 277.3
drink, and t. no more . . 601.2
shall never, never t. again . c16

thirsty *Ps 42:2; (Jn 7:37)*
poor sinful, t., fainting souls . 254.2
t. souls, your wants disclose . 254.3
t. one, stoop down . . 332.2
my t. soul doth pine . . 557.2

b *thirsty land* *Ps 63:1*
hangs o'er all the t. l. . . 165.4
showers, the t. l. refreshing . 295.1
as a t. l. for showers . . 412.2
shadows a dry, t. l. . . 710.c

thither
his praise may t. fly . . 11.1
shepherds came t. to see . 137.1
free to all who t. go . . 261.4

thorn
path be stewed with t. . . 502.2
even for the t. beside . . 552.3
the t. in my path . . . 758.2

b *Isa 55:13*
where t. have flourished . 159.4

c *Matt 13:7*
sowing . . . the t. will spoil . 931.2

d *crown of thorns* *Matt 27:29*
cruel t. his forehead . . 96.3
with c. of t., they bore . . 101.3
a c. of t. he'll wear . . 103.2
forget thy t.-crowned brow . 117.1
with t., thine only crown . 123.1
that c. of cruel t. . . . 126.2
the cruel t. . . . mocking jeer . 134.1
or t. compose so rich a c. . 136.3
head that once was c. with t. 168.1
c. in very surety, but of t. . 228.3
I bore the cruel t. for thee . 229.2
seen his t.-crowned brow . 243.1
t. thy brow encircle . . 299.2
the t. they were pierced. 331.1, c
pierced by many a t. . . 339.3
love thee for wearing the t. . 357.2
the t., the c. the spear . . 368.2
a c. of t., a heavy cross . 451.2
a t.-c. pressed thy brow . 586.2

thorny
found sin's way is t. . . 225.2
path be dark and t. . . 391.3
if rough and t. be the way . 453.4
a path that's sometimes t. . 462.1
a path, though t., bright . 465.5
'tis a strait and t. road . . 559.2
find your path is . . . t. . . 805.1

thorough 459.1

thoroughfare . . . 815.3

thought *(noun)*
1 *(divine)*
thy secret t. have stirred . 36.2
cam'st . . . in lowliness of t. . 174.2
robes his t. in childlike . . 398.1

2 *(human)*
a *(general)*
through my t. and . . . heart . 430.4
behold we give our t. . . 515.1
t. and wish . . . keeping now. 540.3
surveys thy secret t. . . 665.2
my first springs of t. . . 665.4
nor of these hath uttered t. . 682.3
balance t. before the act . 863.4

b *(positive thoughts)*
wing to Heaven our t. . . 20.3
for all gentle t. and mild . 28.4
lift my t. above . . . 32.2
I rest me in the t. of rocks . 42.1
Jesus, the very t. of thee . 61.1
many t. stir my heart . . 119.1
but the t. of all t. . . . 119.1
blessed t.! for every one . 261.4
you strive to drown the t. . 267.2
t. of such amazing bliss . . 314.2
one t. shall fill my soul . . 517.2
that silent, secret t. . . 517.2
my sweetest t. henceforth . 517.4
kindling t. and glowing word . 612.6
with my waking t. bright . 617.4
shall rise the glorious t. . . 632.4
restored to life . . . and t. . 668.1

with heavenly t. supply . . 671.3
my last t.: how sweet . . 676.2
the t. comes back to me . 686.1
he leadeth me! O blessèd t. . 725.1
guest of God! O t. sublime . 728.1
I blend my wakening t. . . 871.2
beautiful t., though earth . 873.4
you may be saved, O glorious t. c30
and with my t. in tune . . c72

c *(negative thoughts)*
ill t. can die 41.2
cold my warmest t. . . 58.4
are your t. in turmoil . 244.2
purge the dark halls of t. . 416.1
subdue each . . . rebel t. . 445.1
things of earth have filled our t. 466.1
t. that seek forbidden ways . 630.2
no distracting t. within . . 630.3
where God is not! O aweful t. 885.3
those gloomy t. that rise . 898.3
if one dark t. . . . retaineth . c72

d *all my thoughts*
all our t. . . . thou sharest . 97.4
fill all my t., my passions . 208.2
all my ways and t. possessing. 470.3
all my words and t. receive . 492.1
let all my t. unite . . . 516.5

e *each/every thought* *2 Cor 10:5*
o'er e. t. and step preside . 190.1
e. t. of holiness, are his . . 200.6
burn out e. selfish t. . . 205.2
clean in e. wish and t. . . 415.5
a heart in e. t. renewed . . 444.4
subdue e. rising, rebel t. . 445.1
hallow e. t., let all within . 453.2
let e. trembling t. be gone . 559.1
control my e. t. . . . 568.1
e. power and t. engaging . 702.2

f *Ps 139:2*
God our t. is reading . . 836.3

g *Isa 55:8*
far above thy t. . . . 721.4
all human t. transcending . 948.1

deed (c, d) motive

thoughtful
I ask thee for a t. love . . 485.2
be t. for all who are weak . 679.2
be t. and earnest . . . 823.2

thoughtless 261.3

thousand
all earth's t. voices . . 40.1
O for a t. tongues . . . 64.1
two t. years of wrong . . 83.2
ringing of a t. harps . . 167.2
fairest of t., and pearl . . 175.c
grieved him by a t. falls . . 286.2
t. have in Christ believèd . 381.3
make a t. hearts thine own . 604.4
a t. rays of light . . . 658.3
the strain that lips of t. . . 765.5
memories a t. times retold . 774.2
emblem of a t. battles . . 777.1
t. and t. who wander and fall. 794.3
there are many t. . . . 797.3
souls, by t. humbly kneeling . 802.3
with a t. bands and a t. drums 807.3
sang it many a t. strong . 815.1
there are hundreds . . . t. . 850.*
louder than a t. thunders . 875.1
may t. in the realms of day . 946.4

b *Ps 90:4*
a t. ages in thy sight . . 13.4

c *Isa 60:22*
one into a t. rise . . . 629.2

2 *ten thousand*
earth, with her t. t. tongues . 4.3
blessings . . . with t. t. beside. 33.3
when we've been there t t years 308.4
through t. t. battles . . 684.2
its t. t. delights . . . prove . 905.4
t. t. charms around him shine. c167

b *Ps 91:7*
t. t. foes arise . . . 812.1

c *Song 5:10*
he's the fairest of t. t. . 344.1, c

d *Rev 5:11*
t. t. thousand are their tongues 57.1
t. t. saints attending . . 161.1
t. t. time t. t. 167.1
t. t. thousand souls there are 266.1
join t. t. thousand more . 629.3

thousandfold 167.2

thrall-dom
the t. of evil is broken . . 410.3
t. of indwelling sin . . . 459.1
have held our souls in t. . 827.2

thread 644.4

threaten-ing
should t. to undo us . . 1.3
when the clouds are t. . . 39.2
they shall fear no t. rod . . 95.2
temptation's t. hour . . 576.3
storms . . . t. to confound me 732.1
many dangers t. us all . . 792.2
smite death's t. wave . . 954.4
dangers may t. . . . c132

three
a *(re divinity)*
the Spirit, T. in One . . 2.5
to the great One in T. . . 219.4
God in t. persons . . 220.1, 4
blessèd Godhead, T. in One . 222.c
holy and blessèd T. . . 224.4
Holy Spirit, T. in One . . 785.2
the T. in One to sing . . 940.2

b
t. wise men came . . . 90.3
entered in those wise men t. . 90.5
the t. sad days have . . . sped 151.3
burst his t.-day prison . . 153.c

threefold 776.1

threshold
pass the t. o'er . . . 299.1
stay no longer on the t. . 433.2
t. of the city bright . . 663.3

threw see throw

thrice
t. welcome in our heart . . 213.1
t. shame upon us . . . 299.1
t. blessèd is that harvest . 934.4

happy (1d)

thrill-ed-ing
loud anthems t. the night . 5.2
t. our souls with joy . . 66.3
filling me, t. me . . . 114.c
feel . . . the t. of life divine . 173.3
a theme that t. all creation . 178.2
glory came t. my soul . . 542.3

thrilling *(adj)*
the ever-t. story, how he died 96.3
not hear the t. music . . 353.2

thrive 51.2

throb-bing
t. of its rapture reach us. . 173.2
this t. heart forget to beat . 573.5

throes 127.2

throne
1 *(general)*
t. and dominations . . 141.2
reach a monarch's t. . . 508.3
crowns and t. may perish . 690.4
tear Hell's t. to pieces . . 800.3

2 *(the heart)*
make thine everlasting t. . 55.5
let every heart prepare a t. . 81.1
his t. . . . the pure in heart . 411.3
tear it from thy t. . . . 442.5
my great redeemer's t. . . 444.2
exchange thy t. for . . . heart. 448.3
it shall be thy royal t. . . 525.5
my heart his t. . . . 541.4

3 *(judgment)* *Ps 9:7; Rom 14:10*
the judge upon the t. . . 265.5
see thee on thy j. t. . . 302.4
his great j. t. . . . 893.*
to his t. you'll have to go . 914.1

b *before throne*
b. Jehovah's aweful t. . . 4.1
backslider, fall b. his t. . . 269.2
boldly . . . kneel b. thy t. . 303.3
b. thy t., I here confess . . 489.3
that b. thy t. I spend . . 585.3
I bend me b. thy t. . . . 635.2
humbly at thy t. we bow. . 638.2
oft repeat b. the t. . . 877.4
we should b. thy t. appear . 933.4
we kneel in prayer b. thy t. . 948.1

c *stand before throne*
b. the t. my surety s. . . 106.1
when men b. thy t. shall s. . 618.1
b. his t. we'll s. complete . 888.3
when we s. b. his t. . . 899.2
prepare . . . to s. b. thy t. . 914.*

4 *throne of God*
under the shadow of thy t. . 13.2
he came from a t. . . . 92.2
thou didst leave thy t. . . 101.1
he who from his t. rules. . 104.6
take thy t., O Crucified . . 122.4
to the t. of Godhead . . 141.4
watcheth . . . from the t. . 182.2
coming, dear Jesus, to thy t. 368.3
from thy t. again come down. 532.4
thy t. shall never . . . pass . 677.5
firm as his t. his promise . 735.3
Jesus . . . he is on the t. . 752.5
lead them to his royal t. . 866.3
honoured at the t. of glory . 894.1
that on the t. doth reign. . 909.3
direct men to your t. . . 943.3
in every nation fix thy t. . 945.4

b *throne of love*
before the t. of l. . . 305.1
everlasting t. of l. . . 711.1

c *Heb 4:16*
bold I approach th'eternal t. . 283.4
let me at the t. of mercy . 301.2
to his blessèd t. I move . . 365.2
let me to thy t. repair . . 556.5

grace (3b)

d *Rev 3:21*
partner of my t. shalt be. . 110.5
all the treasures of his t.. . 770.3

e *Rev 5:6*
the Lamb upon his t. . . 156.1

f *Rev 5:7*
with angels round the t.. . 57.1
spirits that surround thy t. . 414.2

g *Rev 7:10*
him that sits upon the t.. . 57.4
Father on his sapphire t. . 150.4
God sitteth on the t. . . 721.3
God is still on the t. . . c122

h *Rev 7:15*
while ye surround his t. . . 314.1
around the Saviour's t. . . 701.4
therefore are they next the t.. 909.2

i *Rev 22:1*
flows from the t. of Jehovah . 252.2
issues from the sparkling t. . 312.2
flows from the t. of God . 471.c
flowing by the t. of God. 891.1, c

eternal (2e), Father (2g), glorious (2i), leave (1a), surround (b)

throned
not t. above, remotely high . 142.3
t. where glory dwelleth . . 896.3

enthroned

throng-ed-ing
(general)
a shining t. of angels . . 93.5
unperceived amid the t. . 370.4

b *(the saved)*
triumph with the heavenly t. . 43.4
with yonder sacred t. . . 56.5
with all the blood-bought t. . 69.4
ransomed saints t. . . . steeps 167.1
loved ones . . . that heavenly t. 392.3
one among the ransomed t. . 514.4
captain of the mighty t. . 698.c
shout with the happy t. . 807.1
strains of all its holy t. . . 934.4

c *join throng*
I'll j. the blood-washed t. . 374.3
I j. the blood-washed t. . . 375.3
we have j. the happy t. . . 381.3
j. our happy t. . . . 690.5
j. the ransomed t. . . . 828.4

press (c)

thronging *(adj)* 752.2

through nc, but
a *through and through*
thrilling me t. and t. . . 114.c
Jesus, save me t. and t.. 430.1, 2
blood and fire, t. and t. . . 779.c

throughout
a *(time)*
shall not fail t. eternity . . 156.4
undisturbed, t. the ages . 539.3
t. eternity, I am his . . 545.3
peace t. our early life . . . 674.4
t. my length of days . . 762.3
t. unending ages . . . sure . 870.1
t. their life . . . joined . . 948.1

b *(space)*
thy power t. the universe . 37.1

c *throughout [world]* *Mark 14:9*
t. the w. its breadth . . 55.3
shout aloud t. the land . . 782.1
t. the whole wide earth . . 826.1

throw-n/threw
a *(God) throws*
he can . . . joy's radiance t. . 329.2
t. his loving arms around . 337.2
his arm around me t. . . 731.1
arm had been t. around me . 794.1

b *(we) throw*
all that hinders . . . t. aside . 188.c
all my weakness I t. . . 507.3
t. off the bondage . . 693.3
never will t. off his fear . . 784.4

thunder
deep t.-clouds form . . 16.2
through t., fire and calm . 36.2
I hear the rolling t. . 37.1
when t. roll 39.2
deep t. roll 126.3
winds may blow, or t. roar . 526.4
breaking like the t. . . 529.3
though t. roll and darkened . 761.1
like t. grandly pealing . . 802.3

b *Rev 14:2*
louder than a thousand t. . 875.1

thus
for t. is was, is now . . 12.3
t., when the best . . . decaying 51.2
worthy . . . to be exalted t. . 57.2
t. to come from . . . bliss 88.4
t. spake the seraph . . . addressed 93.5
mocking t. the . . . claim . 147.3
is it t., O Christ eternal . 185.2
opening t. the paths of peace 242.2
wilt thou t. his love requite . 251.3
brought me safe t. far . . 308.3
were he always t. nigh . . 318.2
and t. he bound me to him . 345.1
t. grief-laden did I wander . 379.1
t. reveal each crooked place . 446.2
t. led by his Spirit . . 458.4
t. my all to thee to give . . 504.3
t. I sought the path . . 534.1
t. with quickened footsteps . 599.3
I was not ever t. 606.2
t. provided, pardoned . . 607.3
t. obtain that inward calm . 613.2
t. supported, even I . . 630.3
t. shall Heaven indeed begin . 630.3
only t. that souls are won . 683.4
t. protected . . . boldly dare . 722.4
t. are shown two natures . 785.2
from God (and t. the world) . 785.3
t. would I be . . . devoted . c52

thyself nc, but see
give (1j), reveal (b), show (1e)

tide
1 *(literal)*
boundless as ocean t. . . 224.4
waft it on the rolling t. . . 393.2
hold the t. that's going out . 854.2

2 *(figurative—death, problem)*
Jordan's rolling t. . . . 278.4
when the storm t. lift . . 280.1
on the rising t. . . . 280.3
how to stem the t. . . 303.2
swelling t. of woes . . 573.1
I'll cross old Jordan's t. . 884.*

3 *(salvation)* *(Rev 22:1)*
for cleansing to Calvary's t. . 281.2
the t. is now flowing . . 298.6
plunge in the crimson t. . . 364.1
kept . . . by Calvary's t.. . 443.1
endless crimson t. . . 540.1
O rise, Immanuel's t. . . 647.c
crystal t. for ever flowing . 891.1
where the full t. flow . . c137

tidings
sound the t. right along . . 249.1
let the angels bear the t. . 259.4
send the blessed t. . 279.1, c
bearing t., precious t. . . 500.2
joyous t. we proclaim . . 789.4
sing out the t. glorious . . 828.2
spread the t. everywhere . 835.1

b *tell tidings* *(Isa 40:9)*
the great glad t. t. . . 86.4
glorious t. of Jesus to t. . 329.1
t. the joyful t. . . . 550.3
t. the gospel t. . . . 832.2

c *Luke 2:10*
these t. shepherds heard . 72.2
joyful t. first begun . . 78.1
I bring good t. . . . 78.2
the great glad t. tell . . 86.4
t. of great joy I bring . . 93.2
peace and good t. to earth . 99.1

tie
joined . . . by every human t.. 59.2
closely twine those t. . . 345.1
blest be the t. that binds . 660.1

tight 809.2

tilling *(verb)*
sowing or t. 927.2

time
1 *(general)*
the quiet rooms of t. . . 7.2
t., like an ever-rolling stream . 13.5
late in t. behold him come . 82.2
towering o'er . . . t. . 112.1, 5
room and t. now give . . 241.4
t. is now speeding . . 273.1
I live a moment at a t. . . 385.4
take t. to be holy . . . 458.*
spend much t. in secret . . 458.2
all are lovely in their t. . . 494.1
whate'er pursuits my t. employ 517.2
gently down the stream of t. . 627.c
each night-t. . . . starlight . 666.4
small t. to think or pray . . 675.1
lights t.'s thickest gloom . 683.5
vain 'tis to waste your t. . 686.4
he my host . . . through t. . 728.1
the mountains of t. . . 766.2
t. but deepens their delights . 799.3
shall t. itself outstay . . 869.1
t.'s wild wintry blast . . 882.2
the sands of t. are sinking . 896.1
my web of t. he wove . . 896.3
your t. is swiftly flying . . 913.1

any (b) passing (b)

b *time and [eternity]*
through t. and in e. . . 107.5
not for . . . t. alone, but for e. 349.c
thine for t., and thine for aye 643.4
gathered in t. or e. . . . 931.c

c *time and [place]*
dwellers all in t. and space . 17.4
transcending t. and space . 71.2
conquer every p. and t. . . 142.2
to me remains nor p. nor t. 556.2
not t., nor p. . . . part . 659.5
t. and p. to think . . . 871.1

d *all time*
through a. t. abide . . 112.4
I forget a. t. and toil . . 636.2
the truth a. t. has taught . 827.3

e *all the time*
singing all the t. . . . 326.*
sounding joyfully all the t. . 383.1
Jesus saves me all the t. . 385.c
I live with Jesus all the t. . 402.1
keep in step all the t. . . 817.*
you'll be happy all the t. . c116
God is with us all the t. . . c123

f *harvest time* *Gen 8:22*
at h. t. our eyes behold . . 923.1
help us at this h. t. . . 926.4
the seed t. and the h. . . 935.3

g *2 Cor 6:2*
today is t. accepted . . 241.3
this is the t. . . . be wise. . 251.2

h *Rev 10:6*
t. and sense . . . no more . 573.4
t. shall be no more . . . 907.1

need (3d), reap (c), redeem (d), talent (b)

2 *(specific)*
faith to match our t. . . . 6.2
in any t. of trouble . . . 98.3
when comes the promised t. . 172.3
t. of . . . completed mission . 173.2
t. when thou wilt be near . 523.4
that a t. could ever be . . 548.1

let this t. of worship . . 599.1
his love in t. past . . . 712.3
wait thou his t. . . . 721.2
joys of that glorious t. . . 794.3
peace in our t. . . 827.1, 4
if ere this t. next year . . 933.4

3 *times*
his truth at all t. . . . stood . 3.4
ten thousand t. . . . 167.1
oft-t. weak and wayward . 341.2
a thousand t. retold . . 774.2
we have conquered in t. . 820.2

b *Ps 31:15*
Lord, my t. are in thy hand . 566.3
my t. are in thy hand . . 917.*

c *at times*
though at t. they feared . . 158.1
feel at t. . . . downhearted . 169.3
at such t. I find . . . 169.3
for the sunshine at such t. . 316.2
tears at t. may start . . 326.3
mine eye at t. can see . . 476.2
my heart at t. . . . crowded . 534.2
at t. uncertainly, we tread . 711.2
at t. 'tis hard for flesh . 729.3
the war at t. . . . distressing . 805.1
soul, how near at t. . . 877.2

timeless 449.3

timid 744.2

timorous 898.2

tiny
he made their t. wings . . 25.1
t. hands and downy head . 855.1
there fell the t. seed . . 923.1

tire
mortal spirits t. and faint . 559.2
nor t. along the . . . road . 559.5
work for victory, never t. . 696.3
blood and fire . . . never t. . 703.c
the faith which never t. . . 765.4
fight, nor will we t. . . 774.c

tired
are you t. of fighting . . 244.2
as I am, so t. of strife . . 285.2

tissue 38.3

tithe *(Mal 3:10)* . . . 920.1

title 147.3

today
still is ours t. 12.1
strength for t. and . . . hope . 33.3
everything is changing . . . t.. 49.2
be born in us t. . . . 86.4
what your joyful news t. . 88.2
when Christ draws near . . . t.. 102.3
Hell t. is vanquished . 155.1, c
Heaven is won t. . . 155.1, c
thy . . . gift t. we claim . . 203.1
walk thou/speak . . . t. . 209.2, 3
salvation is offered t. . . 233.1
here in our midst . . . t. . . 235.1
he's with us t. . . . 235.3
refuge find in him t. . . 239.2
t. is time accepted . . . 241.3
nothing . . . that t. Jesus saves 245.4
longing for pardon t. . . 247.1
sweet is the message t. . . 247.c
let the . . . grace claim me t.. 285.1
plunge in t. 315.4
I believe them for t. . . 324.4
he's in the world t. . . 334.1
Christ Jesus lives t. . . 334.c
be saved t. 336.3
in the fight I am t. . . . 338.3
a melody in my heart t. . . 340.c
Heaven's ray falls t. . . 379.4
sunshine/music/gladness . . . t. 387.*
he is waiting to be this t. . 388.4
ringing in my heart t. . . 389.*
seek t. the . . . blessing . . 433.3
try me, Master, t. . . . 487.2
use me t. 501.c
Christ 'midst the crowd of t. . 527.2
there is joy t. . . . 550.1
spread the feast t. . . 550.3
take the manna of t. . . 566.2
bless us here t. . . . 575.c
I ask t. that grace . . . 586.1
Lord, here t. my great need . 610.1
search my heart t. . . 618.c
O that t. they might fall . . 637.4
t. have you done your best . 666.3
let there be light t. . . 669.1
bring . . . fruit of t. . . 675.2
spurned t. the voice divine . 676.4
just as true t. 700.1
stand your ground, t. . . 750.3
that same grace inspire t. . 760.1
accept my offering t. . . 786.c
Jesus rose t. 836.2
for those who work t. . . 856.2
men's hearts grow faint . . . t. 864.1
who will offer them t. . . 868.2
with ours t. are blending . 934.4
you may be saved t. . . c30
a channel of blessing t. . . c84
Jesus can cheer me t. . . c207

b *call today* *Heb 3:13*
still he doth c. t. . . . 139.2
Jesus is . . . c. t. . . . 248.*
if we heed the c. t. . . . 869.2

c *come today*
c. to my heart t. . . . 209.1
almost persuaded, c. . . . t. . 226.2
thoughtless sinner, c. t. . 261.3
so c. to the fountain t. . 331.4
who will c. and wash t. . 359.4

d *Ps 95:7; Heb 3:7*
hear him t. 248.4
self-same voice is heard t. . 680.3

e *same today* *Heb 13:8*
he is just the s. t. . . . 96.*
yesterday, t. . . . the s. . 750.c
he's the s. t. as yesterday . c163

together
t. proclaim the holy birth . 86.2
t. let us look and mourn . 121.1
soon shall meet t. there . 312.3
t. every hour . . . 495.2
bound brave hearts t. . . 593.2
when the nations live t. . 833.1
march t. side by side . . 901.3
we're journeying t. . . c195
stepping on t. in the ranks . c238
we're marching on t. . . c244

tare

toil
1 *(noun)*
stray into the t. of sin . . 747.2

b *(work)*
the sacred gains of t. . . 5.2
above the . . . t. of wrong . 31.1
through many dangers, t. . 308.3
above the t. and strife . . 393.3
our t. he doth richly repay . 397.3
outweighs the t. and loss . 399.3
turned from home and t. . 428.2
days of t. and hours of ease . 428.4
in the t. and conflicts . . 499.3
when the t. of life are over . 500.3
bear the strain of t. . . 519.1
sweat and dust of t. . . 564.1
subdued by t. to slumber . 632.3
day with its t. is done . . 675.c
through the t. and fight . 682.1
no t. for him . . . in vain . 683.3
by making human t. thine own 688.2
praying through every t. . 744.3
t. of my work . . . lighter . 758.4
claims . . . my joys, my t. . 867.5
for t. and grief, or joy . . 874.1
one glimpse . . . t. of life repay 892.3
long patience follows t. . 923.2
yielded in return for t. . . 933.1
often t. seems dreary . . 934.3
strength . . . t. is blest . . 942.1

c *toil and pain*
till t. . . . and p. shall cease . 453.4
from sorrow, t. and p. . . . free 660.5
I'll bear the t., endure the p. . 678.4
through peril, t. and p. . . 701.4
bear p. and hardship, t. . 837.5

d *Gen 41:51*
I forget all time and t. . . 636.2

2 *(verb)*
strong of heart, t. on . . 158.3
for thee to t., . . . fight . . 466.4
t. on, faint not . . . 683.6

b *Luke 5:5*
the fishermen t. . . 680.1, 2

toiling *(adj)* 297.1

toilsome 675.2

token
dear t. of his passion . . 161.3
there were t. of his light . 330.1
for every t. of thy care . . 642.1
I have a t. in the blood . . 724.3
rich t. of thy mercy . . 870.1
yield thee as t. of our love . 870.4
accept these simple t. . . 922.2

told see tell

tolerated 274.1

toll
the death-bell will t. . . 237.3
each day its heavy t. demands 534.2

tomb
out of the . . . dread of the t.. 300.4
sing in triumph o'er the t. . 393.3
the t. no fearful shade . . 465.4
a hope to cheer the t. . . 683.5

b *Matt 28:2, 6*
the rending t. proclaims . . 100.3
show me the t. . . . empty t. 117.2, 3
was it for me, that opened t. 134.2
risen from the t. . . . 152.2

tomorrow
bright hope for t. . . . 33.3
wait not till t. . . . 237.3
t. you may call in vain . . 241.3
t.'s sun may never rise . . 251.2
joy . . . comes with t. . . 473.3
the hope of my t. . . . 529.1
knows naught of dark t. . 540.5
we expect a bright t. . . 764.3
strife may fiercer grow t. . 805.2
we may build a grand t. . 869.2
no sorrow in God's t. . . 888.c
don't you let the troubles of t. c139

tone
life's common looks and t. . 7.2
with earnest t. and grave . 98.3
in living echoes of thy t. . 612.1

tongue
with her ten thousand t. . 4.3
what t. can recite . . . 16.4
my heart and t. employ . . 21.1

begin, my t., some . . . theme 26.1
nor t. nor pen can show. . 61.4
O for a thousand t. . . 64.1
his songs our t. employ . . 66.3
sweetest name on mortal t. . 67.c
this poor . . . stammering t. . 132.5
no t. has ever told . . . 171.2
t. can never express . . 367.1
dwell upon our t. . . . 382.3
no t. can e'er express . . 406.c
my t. be silent, cold . . 573.5
more than human t. can tell . 696.2
with pardon on his t. . . 701.2
my simple t. fails to express . 728.4
a joy no t. can tell . . 759.3
pure be my t. 861.3

b *every tongue*
e. t. a living flame . . 609.2
with living fire touch e. t. . 942.3

c *Phil 2:11*
e. t. confess him . . . 141.1
let e. t. confess . . . 174.5

d *Rev 5:9*
people and realms of every t.. 160.2
in every t. we sing . . . 705.2

e *tongues of fire* *Acts 2:3*
give us hearts and t. of f. . 196.4
no cloven t. of f. appear . 198.1
came in t. of living flame . 200.3
O T. of flame, come . . 211.2

f *tongue of angels*
what a. t. can tell . . 55.4
thousand are their t. . . 57.1

tonight
met in thee t. . . . 86.1
saved, why not t. . . 251.*
for whom we pray t. . . 576.4
be every mourner's sleep t. . 676.5
are you coming home t. . c4

too
1
the heavens are not t. high . 11.1
the earth is not t. low . . 11.1
costing me t. dear . . 98.4
none can be t. vile/dark . . 232.3
we make his love t. narrow . 265.5
pleasures are t. dearly bought 267.2
its sorrows all t. keen . . 267.2
it is not yet t. late . . 267.2
nothing is t. hard for thee . 407.2
thou canst not be t. bold . 560.2
no one t. sinful . . . blind . 590.2
in the past t. unbelieving . 713.2
the fighting is t. hard . . 780.2
nor count the cost t. dear . 798.3
far (h) long (4d) much (b)

b *Ps 38:4*
the burden is t. great . . 421.1

2 *('also')*
only that I love him t. . . 48.3
we must love him t. . . 133.5
will raise our bodies t. . . 149.3
fair and fruitful t. . . . 159.4
as viewless t. . . . 200.3
assist you to conquer them t. 233.2
faithful, loving service, t. . 336.2
Jesus smiles and loves me t.. 338.c
rough and steep, t. . . 473.3
left my Saviour t. . . . 498.3
thank you, t., for . . . mercies 552.1
thank you, t., for byways . 552.2
Christ, thou t. art man . . 558.4
and his example t. . . . 580.2
thine t. the praise . . . 624.5
I t. would weave . . . 644.4
we t. will follow . . . 776.3
but of glory, t. . . . 787.4
patience t., with understanding 795.2
that we t. may guide . . 796.2
and by your actions t. . . 829.c
children, t., of modern days . 834.1
what, t., it should shun . . 842.2
we, t., would bring . . 849.1
they, t., shall be the Lord's . 853.3
laughed and ran and studied t. 855.2
honest, just and lovely, t. . c56
bring sadness . . . and burdens t. c139

b *you too*
thou, t., shalt be free . . 304.c
whosoever means you, t. . 403.3
will you not share it t. . . 851.5

took see take

tool 688.2

top c116

topmost 766.3

torch
yield my flickering t. . . 621.2
take up the t. . . . that light . 683.5
the t. of youth, uplifted . . 868.3

tore see tear

torment 503.2

torn see tear

torrent
fording the t. 388.1
o'er crag and t. . . . 606.3

toss-ed-ing *(Matt 8:24)*
speak to calm this t. sea . 194.4
t. about with . . . doubt . 293.3
now t. with temptation . . 298.4
lost, on the breakers t. . . 375.1
stilled . . . the ocean that t. . 402.2
whelm our t. bark . . . 654.3
storm-t. sea of care . . 749.2
by restless passions t. . . 825.2

b *Matt 8:24, 14:24*
t. on the waves of Galilee . 96.2
stayed the t. sea . . . 628.3
tempest (b)

touch-ed
1 *(God) touches*
God who t. earth . . 32.1, 3
his tender t. can heal . . 126.4
t. by the wonder . . . 138.2
he t. us and filled us . . 215.c
his t. will full salvation . . 267.3
power has t. my soul . . 434.5
t. me and heal me . . . 487.3
let thy t. now descend . . 493.1
thou hast t. me . . . 528.3
t. me with thy . . . hand. . 531.1
thy tender t. now we implore 675.c
t. my life into beauty . . c37
keep the t. of God . . c76

b *feel touch*
I've f. a new and loving t. . 215.1
I long to f. thy sweet t. . . 610.1
grant me to f. thy t. again . 644.3

c *Is 6:7*
to t. our lips 20.3
as t. with living flame . . 353.3
t. my lips with living coal . 528.c
with lips now t. by thee. . 561.4
O t. our lips, that we . . 581.4
t. us with the living coal. . 609.3
with living fire t. . . . 942.3
t. my lips with a coal . . c97

d *touch again*
t. my spirit a. 527.3
Healer, t. me a. . . . 610.*
another t., I ask another . 628.2
to feel thy t. a. . . . 644.3
O t. me a., Lord . . . c92

e *touch/power*
thy t. has still its ancient p. . 558.5
thy t., thy p. . . . the same . 628.2
send a new t. of p. . . c97

f *Matt 9:29*
that he may t. my eyes . . 650.3

2 *(other)*
if human love is t. . . . 50.1
t., their harps of gold . . 83.1
cool waters t. his feet . . 103.3
I'm t. the wave . . . 298.6
the t. of aught unreal . . 409.3
t. by a loving hand . . . 691.3
garment (b)

tough
also for the winters t. . . 552.2
fighting may be t. . . 805.c
way is rough, the fighting t. . c227

toward
cease t. the child . . . 110.3
pressing on t. the goal . . 309.2
moves t. the blissful shore . 911.1
we t. thine altar move . . 922.2

tower
rampart, t. and wall . . 799.2

b *Ps 48:12*
its t. with glory . . . 905.3

c *Ps 61:3*
my shield and t. . . . 223.2
my strong and mighty t. . 344.2
our rock, our shield, our t. . 622.3
the name of Jesus is a t. . 714.3
this our strong t. . . . 763.4

towering
rocks of t. grandeur . . 32.1
t. o'er the wrecks of time 112.1, 5

town
O little t. of Bethlehem . . 86.1
to you, in David's t. . . 93.3
shops and buses, t. and people 544.1

toy
a palace a t. would appear . 318.3
hollow joys, worldly t. . . 379.3

trace-d
which we by science t. . . 27.2
help us to t. . . . plan . . 38.3
t. we the babe . . . 78.3
burn up every t. of sin . . 203.2
I t. the rainbow . . . 621.3
lamp . . . whereby we t. . 654.1
I can t. to unbelief . . 770.1
fill me . . . pathway t. . . 858.c
hallowed path they t. . . 949.3
a t. of sin remaineth . . c72

track
by the Calvary t. . . . 59.4
not drive me from the t. . 440.3

traffic 615.1

trail . . . . . . 903.*

train
1 *(noun)* *(Isa 6:1)*
the triumph of his t. . . 161.1
with healing in thy t. . . 218.1
who follows in his t. . . 701.*
the t. of thy dear Son . . 799.1
Jesus and his t. . . . 815.3

2 *(verb)*
t. thou my mind . . . 529.2
soldiers . . . t. to fight . . 919.3

traitor 704.2

trample-ing
he is t. out the vintage . . 162.1
t. down and casts behind . 596.2

tranquillity 194.4

transaction
the great t.'s done . . . 365.3
the t. so quickly was made . 371.2

transcended-ing
t. time and space . . . 71.2
earthly joys, t., fade . . 711.3
all human thought t. . . 948.1

transfigure *(Matt 17:2)* . 162.4

transformation 324.2

transforming 178.3

transgression
what can his t. be . . . 108.1
mine was the t. . . . 123.2
wounds which t. has made . 237.2
b *Ps 32:1*
he'll forgive your t. . . 272.3
he has pardoned my t. . . 404.c
love that pardons past t. . 439.3
pardon for all past t. . . 539.2
c *Isa 53:5*
he was wounded for my t. . 137.2
for my t. he has borne . . 402.3

transient
nor visit as a t. guest . . 214.3
one t. gleam of loveliness . 551.1
ends life's t. dream . . 743.4

translate-ing
writing, guarding and t. . 856.1
b *Col 1:13*
t. me to eternal bliss . . 441.4

translucent 518.3

transport-ing
Jesus, t. sound 62.2
that soul-t. hour . . . 350.1
this t. all divine . . . 545.1
bright, t., rapturous scene . 887.2

travel-ing
we're t. home to Heaven . 275.1
promise . . . t. with me . . 294.3
t. an unending road . . 885.2
t. along in the sunshine . . c26

traveller
a way for t. to Heaven . . 36.4
brook by the t.'s way . . 654.1
seen, to guide the t. . . 658.3

travelling *(adj)*
till t. days are done . . 332.3
when t. days are over . . 892.2
when our t. days are done . 899.*

treacherous
the t. road may wind . . 176.3
hiding rocks and t. shoal . 598.1

tread-ing/trod
when I t. the verge . . 578.3
thou didst t. this earth . . 607.2
how could earth be t. . . 654.4
t. where the saints have t. . 690.3
t. all the powers . . . down . 695.6
at times uncertainly, we t. . 711.2
life's dark maze I t. . . 743.3
where they t. so valiantly . 789.5
the vale . . . his servants t. . 874.3
before us the journey have t. . 886.2
bright angel feet have t. . 891.1
we shall t. the streets . . 892.4
march to t. the golden street . 902.4
boldly the heroes t. . . . c238
b *tread [in steps]*
t. in his steps, assisted . . 78.3
in all thy footsteps t. . . 568.3
still in Jesus' footsteps t. . 659.2
marked the footsteps that he t. 879.4
c *tread path/way*
appear along the p. we t. . 36.3
t. the p. of darkness . . 155.3
walking in the p. he t. . . 330.3
sorrow's p. I often t. . . 337.4
while we t. this p. of duty . 462.1
safely in the p. . . . t. . . 483.3
t. the p. of joyful obedience . 501.2
p. . . . thou hast bid me t. . 529.2
p. may we t. rejoicingly . . 570.2
p. of prayer thyself hast t. . 625.6
brightening all the p. we t. . 765.3
up the p. that the Master t. . 811.1
thy chosen p. to t. . . . 944.2
the p. I t. is bringing . . c45
d *tread way*
when he t. the w. before you. 242.2
I've t. the w. before thee . 320.3
the w. the Master t. . . 462.2
w. . . . not the servant t. it . 683.1
strength to t. a lonely w. . 719.2
as you t. the narrow w. . . 790.2
noble w. the saints have t. . 858.2
e *tread road*
you help us t. . . . the r. . 38.5
r. that holy men have t. . 583.1
when the r. we t. is rough . 805.c
I can t. the r. of life . . 857.2
f *Rev 19:15*
thou who hast the winepress t. 532.3

treasure
1 *(earthly)*
forfeit all of earth's t. . . 623.1
earth's pleasures and t. . . 640.4
t. of earth . . . no place . . 861.5
2 *(personal)*
canst thou my poor t. take . 285.1
I lay my t. down . . . 415.4
faded are its t., poor . . 420.2
t. long my heart possessing . 460.2
unwilling from t. to part . . 507.2
I pour . . . its t.-store . . 525.6
dearest t. to him bring . . 777.4
we, too, would bring our t. . 849.*
all my life and t. . . . 859.1
bring your best . . . dearest t. . 920.2
every t. spending . . . c48
not . . . left one t., dear Lord. c55
thou hast my t. and my store. c144
b *Matt 2:11*
all our costliest t. bring . . 76.3
3 *(spiritual)*
with the t. of his grace . . 81.3
solid joys and lasting t. . . 157.3
Jesus, what t. you brought . 175.2
my t. and my all thou art . 207.3
I've found a richer t. . . 320.1
none can estimate the t. . 363.1
O what a priceless t. . . 413.4
how wondrous is my t. . . 502.3
with such t. in possession . 539.2
I saw the t. I might win . . 541.2
precious t., thou art mine 652.1, 4
who recount the t. . . . 655.4
each day is a golden t. . . 666.2
new t. still of countless . . 668.2
my Saviour has my t. . . 736.3
all the t. of his throne . . 770.3
turning leisure into t. . . 869.1
b *Matt 6:20*
his t. is on high . . . 277.1
laid up their t. above . . 367.1
I no t. had in Heaven . . 379.2
all my t. is above . . . 497.4
lay up t. in Heaven . . . c249
c *2 Cor 4:7*
with thy Spirit's rich t. . . 457.3
let thy t., excelling . . . c65
4 *(verb)*
t. up his bright designs . . 29.2

treasury
a never-failing t. . . . 58.3
found a t. of love . . . 311.1
b *Luke 21:1*
cast it in God's t. . . . 920.3

treat
sometimes t. their foes . . 50.2
will ye t. me so . . . 299.3

tree
1 *(natural)*
flourish as leaves on the t. . 8.3
hill and vale and t. . . . 28.2
straightness of the pine t. . 32.2
birds sing sweetly in the t. . 37.2
and rustling of the t. . . 41.1
the thought of rocks and t. . 42.1
a branch of the palm t. . . 848.4
fruits from t. and ground . 926.3
2 *(figurative)*
t. shall now be seen to grow . 159.4
on t. immortal grow . . 887.3
b *tree of life* *Rev 2:7; 22:2*
my Christ, he is the t. of l. . 346.3
where the t. of l. does grow . 374.c
shade of the l.-giving t. . . 908.3
with the t. of l. sustain . . 909.3
c *tree/cross* *(Acts 5:30)*
he suffered on the t. . . 105.2
behold him now on yonder t. . 108.1
led him to the t. . . . 129.1
stretched upon a t. . . . 129.c
that weeping t. . . . 131.1, 4
why hangs . . . on yonder t. . 140.1
cross and passion on the t. . 140.3
nailed him to the t. . . 161.2
Jesus purchased on the t. . 230.3
Christ has suffered on the t. . 239.1
nailed him to the t. . . 271.1
how he on the t. gained . . 276.1
laid down his life on the t. . 331.1
by faith I saw him on the t. . 333.1
Saviour suffered on the t. . 360.1
blood . . . shed upon the t. . c150
d *die on tree*
love let him d. on the t. . . 47.3
how he d. upon the t. . . 96.3
on yonder t. d. in grief . . 104.4
lo, he d. upon the t. . . 108.2
room . . . by d. on the t.. . 266.2
remember Jesus d. on the t. . 276.c
languished and d. on the t. . 289.2
love made him d. on the t. . 323.2
to Jesus who d. on the t. . 427.1
by thy death on the t. . . 543.1
proved . . . by his d. on the t.. 554.2
thy passion and death on the t. 639.2
him who d. upon the t. . . 809.4
living . . . then d. on the t. . 870.2
accursed, Calvary (d), hang (d)

tremble-d-ing
we t. not for him . . . 1.3
no more we t. at the grave . 149.3
alone, t. or rejoicing . . 250.4
then I t. at the law . . . 405.2
fire that t. in the breast . . 625.1
we have t. in the storm . . 938.3

b *Phil 2:12*
t. to its source return . . 199.2
c *Mark 5:33*
she came in fear and t. . . 304.2
d *Jas 2:19*
Satan t. when he sees . . 646.3
Hell's battalions t. . . 803.1

trembling *(adj)*
t. gates of Hell 165.2
t. hearts need not despair . 363.4
every t. thought be gone . 559.1
my t. feet should fall . . 726.2
lifts its t. hands . . . violent . 742.2
t. followers as well . . 893.3
b *trembling soul*
near the cross, a t. s. . . 115.2
poor t. s., he'll make thee . 253.c
t. s., dispel thy fear . . 269.1
safety for my t. s. . . . 713.1

tremendous 325.1

trespasses *(Matt 6:14)* . . 624.3

tressèd 34.4

trial
1
make but t. of his love . . 21.4
dared to stand on t. . . 181.2
2
their t. and their labours . 275.1
our troubles and our t. . . 312.1
we, out of t. brought . . 466.5
gives full strength for t. . 495.3
to multiplied t. . . . 579.1
while the storms of t. rend . 595.3
have we t. and temptations . 645.2
with thee thy t. to bless . 653.3
though our t. be great . . 687.4
face its t. in the night . . 717.5
there's one in every t. . . 750.1
peace, in each t. . . . 751.2
though t. should come . . 771.2
only a few more t. . . . 889.2
t. and sorrows . . . meaning . 894.2
t. without and within . . 904.3
when all my . . . t. are o'er . 906.1
from sorrows and t. are free . 908.2
though t. may press . . c122
though t. beset me . . c125
b *1 Peter 1:7*
faith is standing t. . . . 6.3
c *1 Peter 4:12*
when through fiery t. . . 653.4

tribe
let every kindred, every t. . 56.2
all the t. hosanna cry . . 150.1
the t. of Adam boast . . 160.4
all its t. were made . . 167.2
from every t. and . . . race . 170.3
salvation . . . for every t. . 781.2
sins of every t. and nation . 783.2

tribulation
a *Rom 8:35*
neither pain nor t. . . . 554.1
for in days of t. . . . 555.1
b *Rev 7:14*
out of great t. 170.3
though we pass through t. . 764.2

tribute
to his feet thy t. bring . . 17.1
Heaven its t. brings . . 171.1
render the t. of our words . 853.3
we our tuneful t. pay . . 869.1
offer the t. of praise . . 900.3

tried see try

trifle
are you a t. weary . . . 244.1
t. of the passing hour . . 466.1
earth's t. leaving . . . 693.c

trim *(Matt 25:7)* . . . 478.3

Trinity
three persons, blessèd T. 220.1, 4
blessèd Three, glorious T. . 224.4
T. of love and power . . 569.4
blest T. above . . . 870.4
holy, blessèd T. . . . 939.5

trip 375.c

triumph
1 *(divine)* *(Col 2:15)*
congregation his t. shall sing . 24.2
the t. of his grace . . . 64.1
Christ will t. over wrong. . 74.3
join the t. of the skies . . 82.1
his t. over death assured . 102.2
arose, with a mighty t. . . 148.c
thy t. now begin . . . 150.2
now is the victor's t. won . 151.1
let hymns . . . his t. tell . 151.4
hymns of t. sing . . . 152.2
hail his t. now . . . 155.2
who t. o'er the grave . . 156.2
swell the t. of his train . . 161.1
when his t. we sing . . 166.3
bespeaks the t. nigh . . 167.2
t. o'er the shades of night . 412.1
grace shall t. over sin . . 468.2
through thy t. I claim . . 543.1
he t. every hour . . . 705.3
long our Saviour t. here . . 942.2
song (1e)
2 *(human)* *(2 Cor 2:14)*
I t. and adore 14.4
we'll t. with the . . . throng . 43.4
raise your joys and t. high . 143.1
t. with their King . . . 149.2
sing and t. evermore . . 164.1
out of great tribulation to t. . 170.3
in thy cross we t. now . . 185.4
shout . . . and t. in death . 364.4
gives t. in answer to prayers . 373.3
sing in t. o'er the tomb . . 393.3
my days fresh t. win . . 413.4
to suffer and t. with thee . 639.2
man can t. over death . . 652.3
I t. still if thou abide . . 670.4
at the sign of t. . . . 690.2
to suffer and t. I'll go . . 734.3
my soul doth t. in thy word . 741.3
notes of t. winging . . 803.1
in our leader's name we'll t. . 804.3
tread the road . . . in t. . . 857.2
their t. to his death . . 879.3
greater t. than . . . been told . c44
b *triumph [of good]*
his truth to t. through us . 1.3
love will t., love will dare . 503.3
trust that t. over wrong . . 519.3
hope will t. over loss . . 555.3
truth . . . makes the t. sure . 707.4
trust that brings the t. . . 713.3
faith shouts in t. . . . 744.6
love will t. over sin . . . 760.2
3 *(evil)*
when the godless do t. . . 19.4
shall he a further t. win . . 885.2

triumphant
come . . . joyful and t. . . 85.1
yet was t. at last . . . 99.2
bore it up t. 141.4
he lives t. o'er the grave . 144.1
life t.! Alleluia . . . 146.1
hark, those loud t. chords . 147.4
his t. power I'll tell . . 180.3
the whole t. host . . . 223.5
raised in the t. song . . 392.3
swell the glad, t. strain . . 550.3
t. over pain 701.1
for t. God will make us . . 702.1
faith t. 713.3
with t. power abound . . 815.2
to rise again t. . . . 870.2
songs t. and music grand . 873.2
the saints t. rise . . . 876.5

triumphantly
when the winds t. swept . 103.4
with the saints . . . t. appear . 747.3
a flag . . . t. appears . . 774.1

triune 958

trivial 668.4

trod see tread

trophies
my t. at last I lay down . . 124.c
rich the t. Jesus brings . . 147.2
t. won from Satan's power . 774.2
rich the t. to be won . . 776.1

trouble
1 *(noun)*
in t. and in joy 21.1
fighting and t. arise . . 233.3
our t. and our trials here . 312.1
is there t. anywhere . . 645.2
leave me . . . in t. to sink . 712.3
though t. assail . . . 763.1
t. abound, nothing . . . hopeful 773.1
we did life's t. share . . 899.1
what t. we have seen . . 915.2
don't let the t. of tomorrow . c139
b *Ps 46:1*
to thee in every t. flee . . 14.1
in t. he's my stay . . . 344.1
c *2 Cor 1:4*
in any time of t. . . . 98.3
2 *troubled*
seized their t. mind . . . 93.2
soothe the t. brow of care . 129.2
how thy heart is t. . . . 259.1
t. with much condemnation . 553.2
thou hast been t. . . . 558.4
wrestlers with the t. sea. . 612.3
o'er t. sea 725.2
over life's t. sea . . . c141
b *troubled breast*
calms the t. breast . . . 58.2
soothe thy t. breast . . 261.2
weary brain and t. breast . 669.2

true
1
the true life of all . . . 8.3
with t. adoration shall sing . 16.6
moved by t. repentance . . 75.4
t. wisdom can impart . . 100.2
him, their t. creator . . 155.1
shall the t. Messiah see . 161.2
t. Recorder of his passion . 191.2
all who trust him find him t. . 335.3
so kind, so t. and tender . 345.4
contrast with t. righteousness 446.2
t. comeliness renew . . 494.2
saints in t. happiness gaze . 639.2
t. thy mercies are . . . 641.2
t. manna from on high . . 654.2
Jehovah . . . thy keeper t. . 767.3
a message grand and t. . . 783.1
our Saviour strong and t. . 828.1
standing by a purpose t. . 847.1
first, in t. submission . . 864.3
cherished, t. and pure . . 941.3
his promise is t. . . . c122

every promise is t. . . . c130
that old, old story is t. . . c202
t. happiness . . . holiness . c208
the t. source of power . . c210
just a t. devotion . . . c213

b *true and living*
Jesus is the t. . . . l. way . 279.2
the t. and l. word . . . 561.4
be our t. and l. way . . 937.3

c *true heart*
give me a h. that is t. . . 422.4
a h. that's t. and clean . . 426.1
contrite h., believing, t. . 444.3
h. that beat t. ever . . . 704.2
in him shall t. h. everywhere . 826.2

d *true [light]* *John 1:9*
Spirit's t. illumination . . 38.1
Christ, the t., the only l. . 412.1
in the darkness . . . one t. l. . 876.2

e *true love*
from a love so t. and deep . 265.1
love so mighty and so t. . 336.2
his is love most t. . . . 343.1
love that is t. and sincere . 443.3
for love so t. and changeless . 938.1

faithful (1d), soldier (g), thing (1g), witness (1e)

2 *true [to]*
pure and strong and t. . 32.1, 3
live a life that's t. . . . 257.2
I would be t. 491.1
nothing less will keep me t. . 591.2
be noble and upright and t. . 679.1
t. to our colours, we'll fight . 681.3
proving that you are t. . . 773.2
I'll be t. . . . t. to my Saviour. 778.c
be . . . kind-hearted and t. . 823.2
teach me to be pure and t. . 837.1
make me t. and brave . . 859.2
let us then be t. and faithful . 892.3
there's a welcome for the t. . 899.2
with his t. saints alone . . 940.1
every t. believer . . . 943.4
soldier . . . brave-hearted and t. c231
I'll be t. . . . only t. to thee . c234
if to Jesus you'll be t. . . c237
comrades, let us be t. . . c239
comrades, we will be t. . . c239
to its . . . principles be t. . c241

b *ever true*
to . . . cross I will e. be t. . 124.3
hearts that beat t. e. . . 704.2
must beat for e. t. . . . 779.2
will for e. be held t. . . 795.2
e. t. to the Army and God . 820.5
keep us t. for e. . . . c244

3 *it is true*
incredible, and yet it's t. . 49.1
it's t., this wonderful story . 319.c
I've proved this to be t. . . 320.3
'tis t. that poor sinners . . 331.4
'tis t., my heart's quite new . 375.2
this may be t. 467.2
'tis t. . . . no room to boast . 468.4
yet t. it is to say . . . 494.1
t., 'tis a strait . . . road . . 559.2
command . . . is just as t. today 700.1

b *(other)*
all that is not t. . . . 141.5
tell my t. complaint . . . 290.2
t. pleasures abound . . . 355.3
longings for the t. and good . 760.3
for ever be held t. . . . 795.2

truest 614.3

truly
offender who t. believes . . 22.2
t. adorning the spirit . . 237.2
no one t. knows you . . 238.1
t. feel love's . . . embrace . 269.1

only as I t. know . . . t. known 435.3
thy heart made t. his . . 465.2
no progress I t. had gained . 553.3
he t. knows . . . refreshment . 580.1
Lord, to see thee t. . . . 591.3
souls shall be t. converted . 608.3
when thy voice is t. heard . 614.4
men that nature t. know . . 656.3
as Christians t. named . . 688.4
God our way will t. lead . . 760.4
their sins confessing t. . . 831.4
Jesus . . . I can t. sing . . 859.1
yes, we t. have begun . . 869.4
dead to self, we t. live . . 922.3

trump-et
sounded forth the t. . . . 162.3
our t. are awake . . . 163.1
God's t. is sounding . . 684.1
the t. call obey . . . 699.2
youth obeys her t. call . . 799.2
while the t. blend . . . 803.2
hear the t. blow . . . 804.3

b *1 Cor 15:52; 1 Thess 4:16*
till t. from east to west . . 153.2
the t. of God shall sound . 164.c
O t. of the angel . . . 771.4
pray that when the t. calls . 774.3
hark the t.'s aweful sound . 875.1
when the t. of the Lord . . 907.1

voice (3c)

trumpeter 868.1

trust-ed-ing
1 *(God) trusts*
love that suffered . . . t. . 544.5
his sure t. and tender care . 715.1

2 *(we) trust—general*
t. for our trembling . . . 183.4
no one has ever t. unavailing . 257.4
wondrous peace through t. . 413.4
perfect hope and peace and t. 423.3
keeping my t. through . . . day 484.2
I cannot see I'll t. . . . 489.4
t. that triumphs . . . 519.3
t. till the danger is past . . 537.3
sometimes t. . . . doubting . 549.1
now I'm t. every moment . 549.3
in quiet t. subside . . . 551.2
hearts to t. through gain . 704.3
my heart has slowly t. . . 713.2
t. that brings the triumph . 713.3
the temper of my t. must face 717.5
t. and be unafraid . . . 723.1
I still can t. and . . . follow . 732.2
t. his rich promises . . 738.3
this life of t., how glad . . 741.4
t. through a stormy way . . 754.1
t. as the moments/days go by 754.c
and t., in all dangers . . 763.3
peace which comes with t. . 790.3
t., serving every day . . 892.3
fully t. in . . . fray . . . stay . c119
t. when dark clouds appear . c196

b *fight and trust*
t. and f. till life's . . . day . 543.2
keep us f., t. calmly . . 593.1
I'll f. and t. . . . repeat . . 749.3

c *simple trust*
in s. t. like theirs . . . 567.2
s. t. every day . . . 754.1

d *trust [self]*
in . . . hands my soul I t. . 48.1
take me, I can t. my all . . 285.3
I, believing, t. my soul . . 514.2
content to t. my way to thee. 644.c

childlike, obey (d)

3 *trust [God]* *Ps 37:3**
in thee do we t. . . . 16.5
I'll t. but in thee . . . 232.c

in him we t. when . . . dreary. 316.1
faith can firmly t. him . . 333.3
all who t. him find him true . 335.3
t. thee for a perfect cure . 419.5
we t. thee for the fire . . 481.c
since I learned to t. him . . 549.c
t. thou in me 571.1
I will t. thee, all my life . . 713.1
I am t. thee . . . . . 727.*
all my t. on thee is stayed . 737.2
I stand, t. in thee . . . 741.3
I dare to t. in thee . . . 749.3
t. him whate'er befall . . 754.c
t. him while life/till earth . 754.4
just to t. and follow him. . 755.2
I'll t. in thee . . . . 761.*
yes . . . I will t. thee . . 770.4
t. in him . . . succeed . . 773.3
t. him in your youth . . 836.4
we'll t. and serve thee more . 926.3
then, t. thee completely . . 947.3
t. him for all that's to come . 962
deliver all who t. in him . . c12
I am t., Lord, in thee . . c69
through cloud . . . I t. him . c132
t. thee ever c144

b *trust Jesus*
the soul that is t. J. . . 186.1
t. in J. . . . I am blest . . 323.5
now and ever t. J. . . . 352.1
I'm t. in J. for all . . . 542.c
happy we who trust in J. . 722.1
I am t. thee, Lord J. . 727.1, 6
J., I t. in thee . . . 741.1
t. J., that is all . . . 754.*
a perfect t. in the Lord . . 770.c
you will find that t. J. . . 790.3
t. in J., he's your guide . . 817.2
fully t. J. . . . alone . . c119

c *put trust* *Ps 7:1*
those who p. their t. . . 100.3
in thee . . . I p. my t. . . 714.2
we'll p. our t. in God . . 822.3
in thee . . . do I p. my t. . c73

d *trust God* *1 Tim 4:10**
t. in the God of hosts . . 700.2
t. in God and do the right . 716.*
who t. in God's . . . love . . 738.1
we'll put our t. in God . . 822.3
I'll t. my Father in Heaven . c133

e *[ever] trust*
hoping, t. ever . . . 115.4
now and ever t. Jesus . . 352.1
I will ever love and t. . . 474.1
help me . . . for ever to t. . 523.4
I am t. thee for ever . . 727.6
firm . . . ever my t. shall be . 889.3
I'll always t. in thee . . 917.5
t. thee ever, doubting . . c144

4 *trust (qualities)*
all who on his succour t. . 21.3
I t. the all-creating voice . 26.4
t. in his redeeming blood . 133.5
walking . . . t. in his might . 379.4
t. in thy sure defence . . 595.2
I t. thy guiding hand . . 628.4
in the strength of Jesus t. . 695.2
we're t. in the promise . . 700.3
I'll t. his omnipotent arm . 734.2
I t. the shining of thy face . 762.1
learn to t. for our bread . . 763.2
lean . . . t. in his love . . c138
t. in the cleansing flood . c149

b *trust grace*
t. him for his g. . . . 29.4
fully t. in his g. . . . 417.1
believe . . . t. his g. . . 633.2
for thy g. . . . t. now . . 727.2
t. his rich promises of g. . 738.3
when we t. his g. . . . 750.2

c *trust name*
I t. fully in his n. 52.2
t. in his n. alone 70.2
sinful but t. in his n. . . . 403.2
I t. in thy great n. 415.4
I t. in thy great n. 511.2
t. in that almighty n. . . . 562.2
his n. is all my t. 735.2

d *trust word* *Ps 119:42*
rest by t. in his word . . 231.1
t. him, for his w. is plain . 262.2
still t. in his word 458.3
boldly t. God's great word . 760.4
I t. thy word, O come . . . c88

5 *(false trust)*
sin of not t. thee 296.2
if I my t. betray 472.4
such as t. their . . . strength . 559.4
ye dare not t. your own . . 699.3
I dare not t. . . . frame . . 745.1
our t. has known betrayal . 750.1
want of faith to t. 770.1
I have t. least of all . . . 770.2

b *(other)*
there are those who t. me . 491.1

trusted *(adj)* 753.2, 4

trusting *(adj)* 718.3

trustful-ly
your burden cast, t. coming . 236.3
give me a t. mind 574.2

trusty 658.6

truth
willed his t. to triumph . . . 1.3
t. is on the scaffold . . . 6.3
they, who in his t. confide . 21.4
as we seek for vaster t. . . 27.4
given us minds desiring t. . 27.5
follow t. as he knew t. . . 27.6
all the world of t. is thine . 30.3
t. and justice reign again . 63.2
the t. declarest . . . t. to hear. 97.4
grant us . . . that t. to keep . 100.4
the Lord of t. and might . 145.2
his t. is marching on . . 162.1, c
justice and t. . . . shall spring. 166.2
lead men to t. and joy . . 211.3
till all thy t. I own . . . 221.3
no more thy t. blaspheme . 407.1
thy t. I lovingly receive . . 407.1
fruits of t. and goodness show 408.2
to thy t. my heart incline . 429.3
here a deeper t. I see . . 434.3
let holy t. condemn . . . 446.2
tell me the t., I will bear it . 457.1
rich t. that surpasses . . 506.3
for thy t. they may be spent . 526.3
soul-saving t. inspire . . 609.2
show me the t. concealed . 650.3
unlock the t. 651.2
who its t. believeth . . . 655.1
the t., of all our hopes . . 656.1
how shall we that t. declare . 656.3
brings the t. to sight . . 657.1
t. shall sin o'erthrow . . 705.4
t. and person whom we love . 748.3
the war for t. and right . . 777.1
strike for t. a telling blow . 801.1
t. be your watchword . . . 813.1
shall we never learn the t. . 827.3
wiser . . . becoming in thy t. . 842.4
earnest strivings after t. . 867.5
thy t. . . . thy works declare . 926.3
most aweful t., and is it so . 932.2
to thy great t. these walls . 942.2
here seek the t. from Heaven. 942.3

b *grace and truth* *John 1:14*
its beauty, t. and g. . . . 27.2
rules the world with t. and g.. 84.3
O Jesus, full of t. and g. . 305.2
for thy t. and mercy's sake . 305.3
the same thy g. and t. endure. 419.5
t. and g. shall spring . . 656.4
gentle power of . . . t. and g.. 705.3
thou art full of t. and g. . 737.3

c *truth and love*
Lord of mercy, l. and t. . . 159.1
the God of t. and l. . . . 164.2
t. in its beauty, and l. . . 183.3
Spirit of t. and l. 224.3
bearers of thy l. and t. . . 863.1

d *truth [endure]* *Ps 100:5**
God's t. abideth still . . . 1.4
his t. at all times . . . stood . 3.4
firm as a rock thy t. . . . 4.4
thy t. unchanged . . . stood . 602.2
his t. unchanging . . . sure . 707.4
thy everlasting t., Father . 715.5
thy steadfast t. declare . . 721.5
ages shall their t. endure . 755.c

e *Zech 8:19*
teach me to love thy t. . . 650.2

f *John 8:32*
the t. that makes . . . free . 485.4
the t. . . . made me free. . 529.1
the t. we dimly knew . . . 572.3
light . . . ours his t. to know . 760.4
t. shall make them flee . . 813.3

g *way, truth, life* *John 14:6*
thou art the t. . . . 100.2, 4
Yes, Jesus is the t., the w. . 231.3
thou art the t. and thou . . 529.1
united . . . life, t. and w. . 561.3
Jesus, my t., my w. . . . 597.1
the life, the t., the w. . . 625.6
you are the t., the l., the w. . 748.2
into the paths of t. . . . 857.1

h *2 Tim 2:15*
thy holy word the t. . . . 650.2
learn the words of t. . . . 836.4

desire (2d), faithfulness (b), light (4f), proclaim (e), righteousness (f), Spirit (3f)

i *(possessive)*
war with the foes of t. . . 373.3
carry t.'s unsullied ray . . 697.4
the heights of t. . . . calling . 711.2
his sword of t. in my hand . 734.3
into the paths of t. . . . 857.1
till t.'s full influence . . . 942.4
together in the ranks of t. . c238

j *truths*
how grand the t. 802.1
t. that are hidden 839.5

truthful
t. Spirit, dwell . . . would t. be 212.2
have I a t. heart 409.3

try-ied-ing
1 *(God) tries*
how he was t. 99.2
your strength is t. 121.5
thou hast been troubled . . . t. 558.4

2 *(we) try/are tried*
a *('test')*
temptations t. my heart . 326.3
by suffering . . . we are t. . 822.2

b *1 Peter 1:7*
the day that t. by fire . . 522.c

search (b)

c *('attempt')*
t. his works to do . . . 133.5
t. again and again . . . 467.2
t. now to make the harbour . 478.3
t. and scale the barrier . . 510.2
I t. the broken cisterns . . 547.3
infant lips can t. 625.3
rise and to t. once more . 666.4
the world's illusions t. . . 780.1
to beat us they've been t. . 800.1
some would t. to crush us . 810.3
t. to follow his footsteps . 840.2
in every way t. to please . 844.1
I can if I but t. 844.4
t. our best to please him . 849.3
I'll t. again . . . soldier to be . c235
why don't you t. c237

tryst
with death there's a t. . . 739.2
they keep perpetual t. . . 878.5

tumult
through all the t. . . . 358.1
Jesus calls us; o'er the t. . 428.1
bid its angry t. cease . . 569.3

tune-d
t. my heart to sing . . . 313.1
I'll t. my harp 368.4
every heart was t. to praise . 557.3
in t. with thy divinity . . . c72
keep your heart in t. . . . c114
your heart's in t. with him . c215

tuneful 869.1

turmoil
are your thoughts in t. . . 244.2
t. without, within 615.1

turn-ed-ing
1 *(God) turns*
t. their fury to peace . . . 19.3
t. my dreams to . . . action . 32.2
he cannot t. away . . . his Son 106.4
he t. his dying eyes . . . 107.4
fire that t. men into heroes . 197.3
he will not t. thee away. . 248.2
he t. with: Daughter . . . 304.3
Lord, turn my . . . heart to thee 445.3
t. not from me c85

b *Acts 26:18*
his Spirit t. our night to day . 43.2
he t. their Hell to Heaven . 60.2
it t. night to morning . . 237.2
where night is t. to day . . 257.c
t. our darkness and fears . 316.2
my night was t. to day . . 371.c
t. all my night into . . . light . 467.3
bid darkness t. to day . . 743.3
t. weakness into might . . 830.3
he has t. the . . . night to day. c1
night will t. to day . . . c115

2 *(general)*
care be t. into a song . . . 7.4
nothing . . . t. my heart . . 59.4
to your will my will is t. . . 206.c
t. from home and toil . . 428.2
when disciples t. and ran . 544.5
he walks . . . who t. his face. 580.3
to its heavenly teaching t. . 654.5
but t. not thy back . . . 689.2
hearts that t. from sin . . 704.4
loss now t. to gain . . . 719.3
t. them to a pardoning God . 720.2
that t. the key of Paradise . 733.2
to the hills I'll t. again . . 766.3
I'm going to t. my life . . 858.3
t. leisure into treasure . . 869.1
t. all my gain to loss . . 916.3
good seems t. to ill . . . 947.3

b *turn to [Lord]* *Hos 14:2**
t. to Jesus, bid him enter . 227.2
imploring t. to Calvary . . 405.2
from them to thee I t. . . 415.4
we t. unfilled to thee . . 602.1
and t. to thee again . . . 827.2
let us early t. to thee . . 845.3
O Lord . . . I t. to thee . . 867.6

the moment you t. to the Lord c2
t. to the Lord and seek . . c27

c *Gal 4:9*
no joy that t. my soul . . 489.2
do not let me t. again . . 497.3
no want shall t. me back . 736.2

d *turn away* *Heb 12:25*
almost persuaded, t. not away 226.2
known and t. away again . 267.1
never disappointed t. away . 824.c
don't t. him away . . . c11

anger (b), light (4i), upside

turning *(n) James 1:17* . . 33.1

twain *(Matt 27:51)* . . . 877.4

twelve *John 6:70** . . . 701.3

twice-born 774.2

twine 345.1

twinkling 177.3

'twixt
peace . . . 't. man and God . 109.2
cross, 't. earth and sky . . 134.1
't. me and the peaceful rest . 598.3
choice 't. . . . joys and thee . 749.1
one mediator 't. God and man c156
between

two
t. thousand years of wrong . 83.2
t. wonders I confess . . 476.2
be my talents t. or fifty . . 477.3
thus are shown t. natures . 785.2
they're t. a penny . . . 850.1
thou didst bind t. natures . 949.2

b *Heb 4:12*
Spirit's t.-edged sword . . 609.3

tyranny 172.1

tyrant 701.3

U

unaccompanied 412.3

unafraid
trust and be u. . . . 723.1
following . . . ever u. . . 859.3

unaided 212.4

unarmed 705.4

unavailing 257.4

unaverted 618.1

unbeclouded . . . 898.3

unbelief
blind u. is sure to err . . 29.6
bind, by pride and u. . . 129.3
though plagued with u. . 266.3
scatter all my u. . . . 412.4
hindered by your u. . . 433.2
begone, u. 712.1
I can trace to u. . . . 770.1
b *Mark 9:24*
kneeling . . . help my u. . 301.2

unbelieving
in the past too u. . . . 713.2
b *(Mark 9:24)*
help my heart, so u. . . 503.2

unbent 508.3

unblameable *Col 1:22** . . 455.3

unborrowed 154.1

unbounded
love u., wonderful . . 184.2
pure, u. love thou art . . 438.1

unbroken
centre of u. praise . . 10.2
the u. word of Jesus . . 198.2
u. faith to keep . . . 534.3
there in songs u. . . . 835.3
his promises, u., speak . 939.4

unceasing
with u. war grown wise . 799.3
u. songs of gladness . . 899.3

uncertain *1 Cor 14:8* . . 809.1

uncertainly *1 Cor 9:26* . . 711.2

unchangeable
prove his u. love . . . 734.2
our faithful, u. friend . . 962

unchanged-ing
my u. choice is made . . 356.1
b *(Mal 3:6)*
eternal God, u. 6.1
promises . . . u. in every way. 324.4
my u., loving friend . . 504.3
truth u. hath ever stood . 602.2
truth u. makes the triumph . 707.4
I rest on his u. grace . . 745.2
peace, still u. 751.3
my great u. friend . . . c163
c *unchanging love*
mine is an u. l. . . . 110.4
l., u., calls thee home . . 250.5
l., u. l., abounds . . . 254.4
who trusts in God's u. l. . 738.1

unclean *Isa 6:5**
a sinner, condemned, u. . 179.1
flowing for the soul u. . . 417.3

uncleanness *Zech 13:1* . . 364.1

unclouded
with bright, u. eyes . . 855.5
his glory u. we see . . . 908.4

unconfined
grace . . . immense and u. . 55.2
soul, enlarged and u. . . 619.2

unconsuming 885.3

uncontested 210.1

uncovered 893.1

uncreated 414.3

undaunted 687.4

under
u. the shadow of thy throne . 13.2
not only u. summer skies . 717.2
hand in hand u. the flag . c226
b *Ruth 2:12; Luke 13:34*
shelter you u. . . . wings 227.c, 2
gather you u. my wing . . 331.2
c *Rom 3:9*
why are you still u. sin . . 467.1
blood (2e), control (b), law (c)

undergo 155.3

underneath *Deut 33:27* . . 182.1

understand
don't think . . . fail to u. . 44.3
many . . . things I cannot u. . 52.1
make us to u. thy . . . will . 218.2
and that no one u. . . . 238.1
although I may not u. . . 437.3
nor seek thy will to u. . . 644.2
until thy will be u. . . . 644.4
one who cares and u. . . 732.1
he u. you, knows . . . need . 773.3
may we u. the wisdom . . 856.3

understanding *(noun)*
a *1 John 5:20**
patience, too, with u. . . 795.2
Jesus, grant us u. . . . 922.3
God be . . . in my u. . . 953
b *Phil 4:7*
passing u. is his . . . love . 52.3
peace that passeth all u. . 304.3
love surpassing u. . . . 439.2
passing mortal u. . . . 539.1
peace, far beyond all u. . 751.1
his love passeth u. . . . c212

undertake-took *(Isa 38:14)*
Jesus u. my cause . . . 380.2
u. to fight our passage . . 912.2

underworld 832.1

undimmed 799.1

undismayed *(Jos 1:9)* . . 721.1

undisturbed 539.3

undivided 477.2

undo-ne
darkness . . . death u. . . 146.1
alas, the duties left u. . . 466.4
b *Isa 6:5*
should threaten to u. us . . 1.3
gav'st him for a world u. . 15.3

undying 126.1

unending
peace and joy u. . . . 222.3
happiness and peace u. . . 857.c
throughout u. ages . . 870.1
to travel an u. road . . 885.2
voices blending in song u. . 888.1

unerring
my sure, u. light . . . 597.1
lead . . . with thine u. rod . 762.2

unexampled 62.4

unexpressed 625.1

unfailing
u. friend and guide . . 257.4
plenty from the u. store . 277.2
Jesus, source of calm u. . 539.3
thy loving-kindness so u. . 762.3
thy hand u., strong . . 926.2
put his arm u. round you . 954.3

unfaltering 297.6

unfathomed-able
deep in u. mines . . . 29.2
thou art love's u. ocean . 452.4

unfeeling 238.2

unfilled 602.1

unflinching 181.2

unfold-ing
day by day u. blessings . . 2.4
hearts u. like flowers . . 10.1
purposes . . . u. every hour . 29.5
the sure u. of your . . . plan . 38.3
splendour of its clear u. . 70.1
our guilt and shame u. . . 185.1
clouds u. their wings . . 280.1
u. its meaning to me . . 553.1
love's meaning to u. . . 590.1
all the world u. the glory . 656.4
in aweful majesty u. . . 871.4
blessings as the days u. . c44

unforgiving *(Matt 6:15)* . . 572.2

unfurl-ed
cheerful banners are u. . . 5.5
banner . . . everywhere u. . 40.2
let it float there wide u. . 697.2
be the banner still u. . . 697.6
keep every flag u. . . . 775.c
u. by every breeze . . . 779.1
u. the Army banner . . 781.1
fight beneath our flag u. . 782.1
with banner wide u. . . 798.2
banners u. to the breeze . 808.5
on with the flag u. . . . 811.4
with our banners u. . . 820.4
flag of blood and fire u. . 822.1
let this banner be u. . . 829.*
with flag u., tell it out . 829.c
with blood and fire u. . . 901.5
flying in every land u. . . c242
to the end . . . our flag's u. . c243

ungrateful 114.3

unguarded 695.3

unhasting 8.2

unheard 614.3

unheeding
self and shame u. . . . 242.3
can . . . find thy love u.. . 456.3

unhindered 774.1

unholy 436.2

union 495.2

unite-d-ing
1 *(with Christ)*
who would . . . their souls u.. 251.4
my soul is now u. to Christ . 361.1
u. to thee I shall be . 459.3
harmony, u. . . . with thee . 561.3
b *Ps 86:11*
let all my thoughts u. . . 516.5
in thy sole glory may u. . 665.5
2 *(with each other)*
let us all u. to sing . . . 43.1
races . . . his love shall u. . 166.2
with thy children I u. . . 613.3
blest be the dear u. love. . 659.1
u. our hearts in love . . 661.4
we stand u. in thy sight. . 692.2
'gainst the host of Hell u. . 778.2
men and angels then u. . 833.3
all u. to swell the song . . 834.3
they, with u. breath . . 879.3
b
though . . . foes all u. . . 763.1
all the hosts of Hell are u. . 800.1

universal
hail, thou u. Saviour . . 109.1
great God of u. love . . 140.2
Jesus, give . . . u. liberty . 593.1
this . . . our u. battle song . 821.3

universe
beyond the starlit u. . . 27.1
gave the u. its birth . . 30.4
throughout the u. displayed . 37.1
thy realm enfolds the u. . 171.1
the u. to save . . . 775.3
the grandeur of the u. . . 871.4

unknown
amazing pity, grace u. . . 105.2
leave his pardon still u. . 250.3
thy love u. has broken . 293.6
no secrets u. to you . . 294.2
when I soar to worlds u. . 302.4
bliss till now u. . . . 547.1
u. waves before me roll . . 598.1
a pilgrim in an u. land . 740.2
peace, our future all u. . 752.5
the glorious u. morrow . . 948.3

unless
u. thou help me I must die . 291.1
u. love doth sanctify . . 530.3
u. my sustenance . . . in thee. 631.3
u. it die it must abide . . 923.3

unlike 108.3

unlimited 49.3

unlock
he only could u. the gate . 133.4
u. the truth, thyself the key . 651.2

unloved 135.3

unmeasured
vast, u., boundless, free . 182.1
boundless love, u. mercy . 225.4
in his pity u. 329.3
u. grace for a fallen race . 341.3
comfort for u. days to be . 350.3

unmoved
u. by human pains . . 142.3
u. by Jesus' wondrous love . 379.2

unmurmuring 839.5

unnumbered
serve him against u. foes . 699.2
b *(Rev 7:9)*
fed by saints u. . . . 869.3

unpardoned 292.2

unperceived 370.4

unquenchable 939.1

unquestioning 503.3

unreal 409.3

unrenewed 268.3

unrepenting 885.2

unrest-ing
u., unhasting, and silent . 8.2
rid me of this dark u. . . 297.4
out of u. and . . . pride . . 300.3

unrighteousness
a *Rom 1:18*
I am all u. 737.3
b *1 John 1:9*
covered is my u. . . . 746.2

unseal-ed
fount of life u. . . . 456.1
u. the sacred book . . 651.2

unsearchable *Eph 3:8* . . 497.4

unseen
story of u. things above . . 98.1
b *(1 Peter 1:8)*
though u., I love . . . 370.2

unshaken
confidence u. 222.2
whose mercy shall u. stay . 746.1

unsheathe
still u. the Spirit's sword . 697.6
in his name u. thy sword . 864.3

unsleeping 677.2

unsought *(Luke 19:10)* . . 135.3

unspeakable
a *2 Cor 9:15*
prove the gift u. . . . 55.4
b *1 Peter 1:8*
cry, with joy u. . . . 756.3

unspoken
sing 'mid bliss u. . . . 835.3
when elate with joy u. . . 939.4

unspotted
a *(1 Peter 1:19)*
holy, meek, u. Lamb . . 116.3
b *James 1:27*
keep us from the world u. . 210.3
u. and pure in thy sight . . 422.4

unsullied 697.4

unswerving *(1 Tim 1:6)*
u., loyal, I would stand . . 574.4
our deep, u. love . . . 922.2

untired 453.3

untold
its store of wonders u. . . 16.3
out of the depths of ruin u. . 300.4
he has riches u. . . . 354.1
a victor's palm, a joy u. . . 811.c
u. glories linger there . . 873.1

untouched *(Heb 4:15)* 142.3

untroubled 580.3

untrue 498.3

unveil *(2 Cor 3:14)* . . . 102.4

unversed 163.2

unwashed
hearts u. in Jesus' blood . 268.3
u. hearts are rejected . . 893.1

unwavering *(Jas 1:6)* . . 734.1

unwilling
u. to give up thy sin . . 263.2
u. from treasures to part . 507.2

unworthiness *(Luke 15:19)* . 553.3

unworthy *(Luke 15:19)*
I, u., kneel before thee . . 528.1
why, u. of such grace . . 730.1
poor u. me, even me . . c109

upborne *(Ex 19:4)* . . . 223.4

uphold-eld *(Ps 37:24)*
u. by my gracious . . . hand . 653.2
b *(Ps 51:12)*
may thy mighty arm u. them . 576.4
yet shall thy love u. me . . 618.3
thy grace u. me . . . 741.4
u. thou me . . . I shall stand . 877.3
counsels guide, u. you . . 954.1

uplift-ed-ing
then, the veil u. . . . 40.3
standard . . . u. everywhere . 774.4
in each hand u. high . . 799.2
the torch of youth, u. . . 868.3

upright
let me u. be 32.2
his life u., his end . . . peace. 580.3
be noble and u. and true . 679.1
b *Ps 32:11*
all ye that are u. in heart. . 537.1
my simple u. heart prepare . 568.1

uprising *(Ps 139:2)* . . . 668.1

upside *(Acts 17:6)* . . . 801.c

upward
angels bear the tidings u. . 259.4
u. for aye . . . like a dove . 300.3
as on wings . . . I u. fly. . 369.1
fount of life . . . u. spring . 456.1
u. I fly 617.5
the u. glancing of an eye . 625.2
faith again is u. led . . 711.2
u., Christward, homeward . 776.2
lead me onward, u. . . 842.4
thou wilt lead me u. . . 859.3
march u. with our band . . 901.1
help . . . on the u. way . . c166

urge
u. us on our way 173.2
u. us on, and keep us thine . 202.3
u. them his mercy to prove . 687.2
when we u. his claims . . 832.3

urgent
u., insistent . . . voice divine . 864.2
youth's most u. call . . 869.2

use-d-ing
1 *(God) uses* *(2 Tim 2:21)*
thou didst choose and u. . 163.2
I love you, u. me again . . 294.1
that I may be u. for others . 435.c
fill me, and u. me today . 501.c
to be u. in joyful service . 514.3
u. every power as thou . 525.4
go where thou canst u. me . 528.4
few the gifts . . . thou canst u. 605.3
O u. me, Lord, u. even me . 612.7
he u. us each day . . . 851.1
u. them as . . . love demands. 861.4
thou wilt u. and multiply . 922.2
thou canst u. me every day . c60
that God may u. me . . c71
Lord, wilt thou u. me. . . c103
2 *(we) use*
resources, in all we u. . . 38.2
sing for joy, and u. each day . 408.5
teach us . . . to u. each power 656.4
let us u. the grace divine . 784.1
for our u. thy folds prepare . 845.1
my various energies to u. . 871.3
b *1 Cor 7:21*
my freedom I'll u. . . . to serve 640.3

useless 298.2, 4

utmost *(Heb 7:25)*
may I to the u. prove . . 55.4
love to the u. . . . he gave . 130.4
to prove thine u. will . . 419.2
u. surrender alone . . . suffice 507.2
beyond thy u. wants . . 560.3

utter-ed
desire, u. or unexpressed . 625.1
nor of these hath u. thought . 682.3
b *Ps 66:14*
more than all my lips may u. . 591.2

utterance *Acts 2:4** . . . 522.3

uttermost *Heb 7:25*
from the u., to the u. . . 249.c
and saves unto the u. . . 335.2
God wills . . . u. salvation . 410.1
to the u. he saves . . . 413.c
save me to the u. . . . 430.c
saved to the u. . . . 521.3
which saves us to the u. . 915.3

V

vain
the v. things that charm . 136.2
found its pleasures v. . . 225.2
all that I can do is v. . . 292.5
v. wanderings cease . . 351.3
the v. world's . . . store. . 428.3
ghosts of v. regret . . . 551.2
all besides is v. endeavour . 555.4
come . . . or life is v. . . 587.3
nor is the boasting v. . . 592.4
feel the promise is not v. . 621.3
earth's v. shadows flee . . 670.5
v. . . . waste your time . . 686.4
oft our hopes were v. . . 750.1
remorse and v. desire . . 885.3
b *[in] vain*
in v. . . . oppose, for God . 9.*
scan his work in v. . . 29.6
v. the stone, the watch . . 143.3
death in v. forbids . . . 143.3
you may call in v. . . . 241.3
in v. you strive to drown . 267.2
fields strive in v. . . . 318.1
in v. my fearful heart . . 440.3
in v. we search . . . deeps . 496.3
strive to shut, . . . in v. . . 533.4
no toil . . . be in v. . . 683.3
they bid me, but in v. . . 780.1
resistance is in v. . . . 815.3
c *Ps 127:1*
without thee . . . labours in v. 605.2
our work is all in v. . . 943.2
d *1 Cor 15:2, 14*
our faith had been in v. . . 153.c
e *Gal 2:21*
nor suffer . . . die in v. . . 234.3
thy side be cleft in v. . . 440.4
plead (1d), take (3e)

vainly
v. they watch . . . seal . . 148.2
v. I seek a cure . . . aspire . 456.2
I struggled sore . . . v. . . 490.1

vale-valley
forest, v. and mountain . . 10.2
hill and v. and tree . . . 28.2
over hill and v. the birds. . 39.3
send . . . tidings over v.. . 279.c
over the hills and the v. . . 637.2
hills, and brooks and v. . . 887.3
don't stay in the v. . . c116
b *vale [of death]* *Ps 23:4*
in death's dark v. . . . 53.4
walk in death's dark v. . . 54.3
in death's dark v. . . . no fear. 523.4
as through the v. I go . . 709.3
the v. . . . his servants tread . 874.3
v. . . . with milk and honey flow 887.3
'tis the shadow of the v. . 903.3
c *Ps 65:13*
the v. laugh and sing . . 929.2
the v. . . . they are singing . 934.1
d *Isa 40:4*
let the v. all be raised . . 159.2
lift up v., cast down . . 593.4
lily

valiant *(Heb 11:34)*
be v. for God and the right . 679.1
soldiers of Jesus, be v. . . 681.c
he who would v. be . . 685.1
you . . . v. soldier be . . 686.4
twelve v. saints . . . 701.3
legions, v., free . . . 803.2
v. and cheerful, marching . 813.3
v. soldier, marching . . . . 817.*
ye v. soldiers of the cross . 912.1
led by v. hearts . . . 939.1

valiantly *(Heb 11:34)*
where they trod so v. . . 789.5
v. they suffered . . . 866.1

valley see vale

valour
holy v. make me strong . 432.2
it calls to deeds of v. . . 781.2
deeds of v. we'll do . . c239

value
a world of shifting v. . . 324.3
love's v. is proved . . . 507.1

vanguard 787.2

vanish-ed
all my sin stains v. . . . 389.2
I saw my Lord they v. . . 399.1
fear shall v. in the fight . . 702.1
human hopes may v. . . c143

vanity
years I spent in v. . . . 405.1
to leave earth's v. . . . 461.1

vanquish-ed
to v. sin and death . . . 134.c
Hell today is v. . . . 155.1, c
Satan is v. 166.5
sorrow v., labour ended . . 228.5
one in our aim to v. sin . . 692.2
till every foe is v. . . . 699.1
love at last shall v. hate . . 705.4
Jesus has v. death . . 752.6

vanquisher 669.5

varied/varies
in their v. ways . . . 494.1
it v. with the wind . . . 508.2
v. the workings of thy hand . 644.2
the v. way . . . we journey . 711.1
my v. energies . . . 871.3

various
oppressed with v. ills . . 558.2
v. hindrances we meet . . 646.1

vast-er
v. as eternity thy love . . 4.4
as we seek for v. truth . . 27.4
so v. a truth proclaims . . 134.2
deep love of Jesus, v. . . 182.1
'tis an ocean v. of blessing . 182.3
v. the curse 243.4
Jesus, how v. thy love . . 368.1
v. than the world has seen . 776.3
shakes the v. creation . . 875.1

vault 147.2

veil-ed-ing
angels . . . all v. their sight . 8.4
then, the v. uplifting . . 40.3
though thou v. thy light . . 40.4
the cross in mystery v. . . 126.3
darkness v. the sky . . 128.4
v. from my sight . . . abode . 398.3
though . . . my future is v. . 473.4
till the v. be lifted . . . 682.3
though the future is v. . . 739.2
draw . . . the v., to show. . 744.2
darkness seems to v. . . 745.2
v. the future 937.2
b *Matt 27:51*
opening v. reveals . . . 125.2
rend the v. in twain . . 877.4
c *Heb 6:19*
anchor holds within the v. . 280.3
within the heavenly v. . . 733.4
holds within the v. . . . 745.2
those we love within the v. . 878.1
to rise within the v. . . 879.1
d *Heb 10:20*
v. in flesh the Godhead . . 82.2

vein 132.1

venomed 532.2

venture-d
with this I v. nigh . . . 284.2
soon as my all I v. . . 361.2

verdant 53.2

verdict 522.2

verdure 159.3

verge
from the v. of Hell . . 330.2
tread the v. of Jordan . . 578.3
snatch these from the v. . 720.2

very
a *(with adj/adv)*
God is coming v. near . . 259.1
glory . . . I know v. well . 323.3
v. deeply stained within . 336.1
the stair a v. wide one . . 369.3
I am so v. glad . . . 403.c
power from God is v. sure . 760.2
conscious you are v. near . 795.1
your all is v. little . . . 920.3
the path is v. narrow . . c205
b *(with noun)*
my v. steps are planned . 48.2
Jesus, the v. thought . . 61.1
our all, this v. day . . . 203.4
a crown in v. surety . . 228.3
canst feel this v. moment . 259.3
that v. Christ can save . . 266.3
is to come this v. moment . 403.3
the v. dying form of one . 476.2
till life's v. end . . . 491.c
can scan the v. wounds . 558.4
until my v. heart o'erflow . 612.6
hour (f)

vessel
with Christ in the v. . . 712.1
b *2 Cor 4:7*
my earthen v. is stored . . 457.3
make me a v. fit . . . 501.c
fill the e. vessel . . . c65

vibrate 691.3

vice 581.2

victim 696.2

victor
1 *(divine)*
crowns become the v.'s. . 147.1

spread . . . the v.'s fame . 147.3
he arose a v. . . . 148.c
now is the v.'s triumph . . 151.1
adorns the . . . v.'s brow . 168.1

2 *(human)*
v. in the midst of strife . . 10.4
I through him can v. be . . 134.2
let the v. in 167.1
v.'s crown will gain . . 686.2
the next the v.'s song . . 699.4
a v.'s palm, a joy untold . 811.c
to take my v.'s crown . . 860.5
win . . . the v.'s crown . . 876.3
there's a v.'s palm for you . 899.2
through thee may v. be . . 919.3

victorious
almighty, v., . . . we praise . 8.1
the name all-v. of Jesus . 24.1
shines in might v. . . . 40.2
brought it back v. . . . 141.3
from the fight returned v. . 147.1
rose v. in the strife. . . 156.2
love is v. when Jesus . . 166.4
Christ, who rose v. . . 181.4
Christ . . . over the world v. . 184.3
all-glorious, o'er all v. . . 219.1
let me v. be in death . . 560.5
v. voices . . . ever sing . . 821.1
till Christ shall be v. . . 828.2

victory
1 *(divine)*
at thy coming to v. . . 101.4
share their leader's v. . . 149.2
the v. is thine alone . . 163.1
light of our redeemer's v. . 173.1
suffering brought thee v. . 586.2
as thine the v. . . . 741.3
they claim the v. God's . 774.2
shout aloud the v. . . . 835.2

2 *(human)*
'tis life and v. . . . 62.3
the source of v. and joy . . 113.3
our sign and seal of v. . . 163.4
laurels of v. are waiting . . 233.3
there is v. in Jesus . . 433.1
there's v. for me . . . 468.c
there's v. within . . . 541.3
v. for me . . . . 543.*
the secret of v. I found . . 553.2
your v. and your failures . 564.3
greater v. every hour . . 622.3
v. will be your delight . . 679.3
fierce . . . but v. will come . 681.4
on then . . . on to v. . . 690.2
work for v. 696.3
from v. unto v. . . . 699.1
the v.'s sure 700.3
v. for me through . . . blood . 702.c
v. is secure 707.4
v. through the blood . . 750.3
above feeling, v.'s there . 773.4
a flag of many v. . . . 774.1
proof of final v. . . . 777.4
tells of v. 779.1
hosts he leads to v. . . 790.1
flushed with v. . . . 803.1
v. is nigh 804.1
our v. in the fight . . . 807.2
v. waits us on the field . . 809.3
the day of v.'s coming . . 810.*
v.'s mine . . . Christ within . 811.2
v., v., v. . . . . 813.*
on to v. grand . . . 847.4
whence their v. came . . 879.3
sing and shout the v. . . 892.c
there's a palm of v. . . 912.c
open mine eyes to see v. . c81
march on bravely to v. . . c228

b *go to victory*
the hosts that to v. g. . . 169.2
Army to v. must g. . . 703.2
we to v. g. 787.3
go on, g. on to v. . . . 805.c

c *have victory*
I h. v. in temptation . . 330.c
we shall h. the v. . . 593.1
we're sure to h. v. . . 800.1
we mean to h. the v. . . 800.c

d *march to victory*
he m. to v. 130.3
m. to songs of v. . . . 901.2
we m. to v. grand . . . 901.5
we'll m. to v. c243

e *victory/love*
v. remains with l. . . . 121.5
a captive to l.'s v. . . . 122.4
speed the v. of l. . . . 158.3

f *win victory*
battle's fought, the v.'s w. . 107.4
endless is the v. . . . w.. 152.1, c
v. we would w. . . . 197.1
and every v. w. . . . his . 200.6
w. perfect v. over sin . . 205.3
would you . . . a v. w. . . 281.1
sharing . . . when the v. is w.. 595.3
when the . . . v. w. . . 698.3
Heaven's v. are w. . . 705.4
by thy grace the v.'s w. . . 725.4
hold until v. is w. . . . 799.1
ne'er think the v. w. . . 812.3
w. perfect v. over sin . . 819.3
and the final v's w. . . 819.3
each v. will help . . . to w. . 823.1
serve . . . till v. is w. . . 853.2
battle fought, the v. w. . . 890.1
tell . . . of the v. w. . . 893.3
our v. are all w. . . . 899.c
sinners saved, for v. w. . . 919.1

g *victory [over death]* *1 Cor 15:55*
where's thy v. . . . grave . 143.4
the final v. over death . . 171.3
where, grave, thy v. . . 670.4
in . . . grave there is v. . . 684.3
the grave its v. . . . 894.1

h *give victory* *1 Cor 15:57*
how the v. he g. . . . 180.3
shout . . . Christ g. v. . . 215.3
g. you the v. again . . 233.c
and he g. me v. . . . 389.2
Jesus g. me v. . . . 404.4
g. me full v. every day . . 432.1
and g. them perfect v. . . 468.c
who loves me . . . g. v. . 571.3
Jesus g. the v., fight . . 694.3
g. v. in the fight . . . 770.4
g. the Army joy and v. . . 807.2
he will g. his soldiers v. . . 814.3
g. v. in temptation . . 870.3

i *1 John 5:4*
faith . . . into v.'s . . . cheer . 713.3
faith that . . . for v. strive . 733.6
thine, O faith, the v. . . 799.4
faith is the v. O glorious v. . c117

day (3h), perfect (2h), sin (3d), song (1f)

vie-ing
with them will still be v.. . 370.3
what love with thine can v. . 515.3

view
to human v. displayed . . 93.4
crown . . . shall v. . . 233.3
with Glory in my v. . . 361.3
soul-refreshing v. . . . 442.2
keeping . . . ever in his v. . 580.2
I v. my home 633.3
glory breaks upon my v. . 657.4
when . . . death is in v. . . 763.5
there to v. the . . . land . . 766.3
display for all to v. . . 781.1
the highest aims in v. . . 801.1
v. the landscape o'er . . 898.3
v. the radiant shore . . 911.5
Heaven appears in v. . . 912.2

viewless 200.3

vigil 176.2

vigour
soul shall her v. renew . . 734.2
summer rays with v. shine . 925.2

vigorous
v. when the body dies . . 214.1
me more v. make . . . 671.4

vile-st
v. offender who . . . believes. 22.2
guilty, v. and helpless we . 118.3
I, as v. as he, washed . . 132.2
none can be too v. . . 232.3
coming weak and v. . . 423.2
is this v. world a friend . . 678.3
bliss that one, so v. as I . 709.1
he the v. will assure . . 819.2
bring the v. . . . worst . . 919.2

vileness 423.2

village 544.1

vindicate 568.2

vine
deep secrets of the . . . v. . 871.2
cheer the v. 925.2

b *John 15:1*
Christ, the living v. . . 361.1
burden of the fruitful v. . 512.3

c *John 15:4*
as the branches from the v. . c176

vintage 162.1

violent 742.2

virgin *Isa 7:14; Matt 1:23*
God . . . and the virgin's Son. 78.1
offspring of a v.'s womb . 82.2
round the v. mother . . 89.1

virtue
1 *(Divine)*
forgiven through the v. . . 109.2
I love to sing of his v. . . 178.3
exert the v. of thy name . 629.1

b *Mark 5:30*
from him v. had healed her . 304.2
v., like a healing fountain . 520.3

2 *(human)*
all v. confounding . . 19.4
every v. we possess . . 200.6
vice destroy or v. spread . 581.2
take every v., every grace . 695.3
may share the v. of the wise . 871.3

visage *Isa 52:14*
how does that v. languish . 123.1
not see in thy marred v. . 353.1

visible 156.4

vision
clear to faith's v. . . . 114.2
might we hold the v. bright . 154.4
bursting on our v. . . 173.2
v. of rapture burst on . . 310.2
in radiant v. dawns . . 353.1
O V. clear! O Voice . . 398.4
then to faith's v. . . . 455.5
we have caught the v. . . 833.1

b *Acts 2:17*
waiting new v. to see . . c103

visit
nor v. as a . . . guest . 214.3
come, with me v. Calvary . 413.1
b *Ps 106:4*
v., then, this soul . . . 412.4
v. us with thy salvation . . 438.1
wilt thou not v. my soul. . 610.1

vital
in this most v. hour . . 198.5
the Christian's v. breath. . 625.5

voice
1 *(Divine)*
the v. that rolls the stars . 26.3
thy v. commanded light . 36.1
a v. from yonder manger . 73.2
at his v. creation sprang . 141.2
pleading . . . with gentle v. . 229.1
O list to his v. . . . 248.4
if they listen to his v. . . 324.3
may thy quickening v. . . 603.5
longing for thy v. . . . 614.1
echo to thy v. . . . 636.3
when thy v. shall bid . . 674.4
choose to heed thy v. . . 796.3
the v. that breathed . . 949.1
b *voice calls*
let thy v. c. me home . . 101.4
c. you with his . . . v. . . 227.3
the v. of Jesus c. . . . 240.1
soon that v. will cease . . 240.3
thy welcome v. that c. me . 423.1
a v. so gently c. . . . 490.1
thy tender v. which c. . . 749.1
deep . . . another v. is c. . 864.2
v. inaudible . . . that c. . . 874.2
c *voice of Jesus*
O hear the v. of J. . 67.1, 2
hark! the v. of J. . . 240.1
I heard the v. of J. . . 332.*
trump . . . v. of the Lord . 771.4
d *voice divine*
O V. d., speak thou to me . 31.4
charmed to confess the v. d. . 365.3
v. d., those accents . . 398.2
O Vision . . . V. d. . . . 398.4
spurned today the v. d. . . 676.4
suddenly a v. d. rang . . 839.1
insistent sounds the v. d. . 864.2
e *music of voice*
I hear the m. of his v. . . 48.2
sweeter than m. his v. . . 318.2
the thrilling m. of thy v. . . 353.2
at the last the m. of his v. . 740.3
I'll hear the m. of his v. . . 884.c
hear (2d), obey (b), say (1c), small (c), sound (g), sweet (3g)
2 *(voice of angels)*
hear . . . sweetest a. v. . 73.1
the a. herald's v. . . . 78.2
the v. of the a. bright . . 80.2
story which a. v. tell . . 840.1
'tis the v. of a. . . . 889.1
b *1 Thess 4:16*
hear the archangel's v. . . 164.c
v. that wakes the dead . . 626.1
O trump . . . v. of the Lord . 771.4
3 *(human)*
sing . . . with cheerful v. . 3.1
where holy v. chime . . 7.2
awake, my v., and sing . . 26.1
nor v. can sing . . . 61.2
let us join our v. . . . 74.*
every v. a song . . . 81.1
bless . . . with cheerful v. . 120.5
infant v. shall proclaim . . 160.2
take my v., and let me sing . 525.3
the contrite sinner's v. . . 625.4
v. have a kindly sound . . 664.1
steps and v. joined . . 682.1
blend with ours your v. . . 690.5
I'll be a v. to call . . . 706.3
no other v. can speak . . 731.2
till glad v. rend the sky . . 807.3
with victorious v. . . . sing . 821.1
while children's v. sing . . 834.c
our v. blending in song . . 888.1
the v. of the homeland . . 895.2
b *hearts and voices*
with h. and hands and v. . 12.1
bless . . . with h. and . . . v. . 20.1
mind, h. and v. . . . ever sing. 574.5
while with h. and v. we sing . 809.1
sings with cheerful h. and v. . 911.1
with joyful h. and v. . . . raise 929.1
praise . . . with h. and v. . 936.1
raising h. and v. now . . 939.5
c *trumpet voice* *Isa 58:1*
O for a t. v. 62.5
acclaim . . . with t. and v. . 537.4
with a t. v. we'll let . . 821.c
tell it with a clarion v. . . 829.3
lift (2d), raise (2c)
4 *(other)*
ye lights . . . find a v. . . 2.2
all earth's thousand v. . . 40.1
give the winds a mighty v. . 393.4
no tender v. like thine . . 587.1
v. of evening call . . . 675.1
the v. of prayer . . . 677.3
let the v. of hope be heard . 697.3
6 *(verb)*
v. in its giving . . . 51.1
our praises v. . . . 888.2

void
have left an aching v. . . 442.3
b *Gen 1:2*
from the shapeless v. . . 36.1

vouchsafe
my longing heart v. to make . 55.5
then, my God, v. to stay . 636.3
since the Lord v. to lead . 772.2

vow
receive again our . . . pure v. 5.4
happy bond that seals my v. 365.2
what the world may do or v. 402.c
all the outcome of my v. . 510.4
as one with v. to keep . . 522.2
my heart fulfil its v. . . 524.1
when . . . my v. were given . 534.1
grieved . . . ill-kept v. . . 534.2
faithful I stand in . . . v. . 744.5
we our v. are making . . 788.1
all, our v. observing . . 788.2
our v. . . . we now present . 918.2
new v. for war we blend . 933.3
closely knit in holy v. . . 947.1
b *hear vow* *Ps 61:5*
h. . . . v. that now I make . 482.3
h. this hour the sacred v. . 504.2
who h. our solemn v. . . 784.4
c *pay vows* *Ps 116:14*
my v. . . . before his people p. 23.3
life to give, my v. to p. . . 860.2
perform (b), renew (c)

W

waft 393.2

wage-ed-ing
1 *(verb)*
tempests . . . warfare are w.. 19.3
w. the war with sin . . 575.2
fiends are battle w. . 693.1
battle we are w. . . 778.1
war 'gainst Hell we're w. . 787.3
2 *(noun)*
worked for hireling w. . . 522.2
b *John 4:36*
receiving heavenly w. here . 352.2

wail-ed-ing
sad, that bitter w. . . 226.3
mocked me as I w. . . 547.3
b *Rev 1:7*
deeply w. . . . Messiah see . 161.2

wait-ed-ing
1 *(God) waits* *Isa 30:18**
a *(with title)*
Christ is w., fulness . . 227.1
here w. the Saviour, gentle . 236.3
Jesus is w. . . . w. today . 248.3
Jesus is w. to welcome . . 263.2
Jesus now is w. . . . 836.1
Jesus, loving Saviour, w. . 872.3
the Father w. over the way . 900.1
b *(general)*
w. the coming day . . 148.1
while he's w., pleading . . 250.c
for thy heart he's w. . . 250.2
thy soul he w. to free . . 253.1
come, he w. for thee . . 255.c
lovingly now he's w. . . 255.2
for sinners he w. . . . 273.1
w. so long . . . to set free . 276.3
in lowly patience w. . . 299.1
he w. in his mercy . . . 331.4
he is w. to be this today. . 388.4
the holy one is w. . . . 410.1
w. until I surrender . . 457.2
w. to answer prayer . . 560.1
still he is w. . . . receive. . 691.2
patiently (b)
2 *(we) wait*
near the cross I'll . . . w. . 115.4
thy loyal peoples w. . . 171.1
w. to receive thy blessing . 201.1
w., like attentive Mary . . 210.3
is there a heart that is w. . 247.1
someone is ready . . . w. . 278.1
watching and w., looking . 310.3
w. to prove thine . . . will . 419.2
you have w. many years . 433.1
while I'm w. in faith . . 457.1
now behold me w. . . 477.1
while I am w. yielded . . 487.1
I'm w. for the fire . . . 511.c
work and w. the verdict . 522.2
we w. beside thee . . . 595.3
w. for thy gracious word . 614.1
w. for thee, sweet hour . . 633.2
tender hearts were w. . . 663.2
w. thy word of peace . . 674.1
slaves of sin . . . w. . . 702.3
w. thou his time . . . 721.2
w. in cheerful hope . . 738.2
w. till thou . . . shall seal . 742.2
in your company we'll w. . 748.1
millions w. 801.2
a lowly heart, that w. . . 839.4
many dear . . . are w. . . 886.4
let me w. with patience . . 889.3
w. till the night . . . I see . 889.3
w. for the harvest . . . 930.1
they w. to give us welcome . 938.4
I am w. and thou art coming . c86
silently now I w. for thee . c99
w. new visions to see . . c103
b *Ps 37:7; 2 Thess 3:5*
thou seest I patiently w.. . 436.3
grant me patience to w.. . 493.2
let me w. with patience . . 889.3
c *Isa 40:31*
men who w. on thy word . 36.2
for him on whom I w. . . 485.5
give me on thee to w. . . 596.1
confidence and w. on the Lord 717.6
they that w. upon the Lord . c66
d *Acts 1:4*
w. the promise of our Lord . 196.2
Holy Ghost, on thee we w. . 198.1
in sweet accord we w. . . 211.1
w. the pentecostal powers . 216.1
calmly we w. the . . . grace . 216.2
pour out . . . while we w. . 692.4
e *1 Cor 1:7*
for thy coming we w. . . 771.4
f
w. not till tomorrow . . 237.3
just as I am, and w. not . 293.2
I cannot, cannot w. . . 780.4
3 *(other)*
hosts of angels w. . . . 130.3
the blessing w. for us . . 145.3
laurels of victory are w. . . 233.3
life and death are w. . . 333.4
victory w. us on the field . 809.3

waiting *(adj)*
on each w. soul confer . . 198.5
see this w. host . . . 203.1
let every w. heart . . . feel . 603.4
engage the w. soul to bless . 633.2
solemnise each w. heart . 638.3

wake-n-ing
1 *(natural)*
be there at our w. . . 611.1
when the bird w. . . . 632.1
our w. and uprising prove . 668.1
when the morning w. . . 673.4
bless us when we w. . . 676.6
the sun . . . is w. . . . 677.4
no fears can w. . . . nights . 728.3
I blend my w. thought . . 871.2
2 *(spiritual)*
w. the immortal strain . . 139.1
w. my spirit, clear my sight . 194.1
w. us . . . to larger life . . 211.2
I w.; the dungeon flamed . 283.3
lips thine eager praises w. . 353.3
with my w. thoughts bright . 617.4
thy life in mine is w. . . 631.4
w. dead souls to love . . 669.5
w. by kindness . . . 691.3
his wisdom ever w. . . 736.2
w. and watch . . . 816.3
b *Eph 5:14*
souls in . . . sleep must w. . 875.3
3 *(wake from death)*
w. the dead in number . . 153.2
voice that w. the dead . . 626.1
w. and find thee there . . 632.3
when I from d. shall w. . . 665.3
when the songs of angels w.. 751.4
b *Psalm 139:18*
when the soul w. . . . 632.4
awake

walk-ed-ing
1 *(God) walks*
w. . . . in life's way . . . today. 209.2
he w. with me and talks . 334.c
a friend to w. with me . . 376.1
w. thou through life . . 628.c
he will w. with me . . 736.3
all the way . . . w. with me . c110
drew near and w. with me . c135
b *(literal)*
the man who w. by Galilee . 618.2
till the Master w. . . . 680.1
a young man w. by Galilee . 855.3
c *Matt 14:25*
how he w. upon the sea . 96.2
who w. on the foaming deep . 569.2
2 *(we) walk*
me to w. doth make . . 54.2
beside thee as I w. . . 59.3
help me w. from day to day . 115.3
w. in the path he trod . . 330.3
or we'll w. by his side . . 397.5
to w., to weep, to sing . . 415.5
let us w. this path . . . 462.3
w. in his footsteps . . . 483.1
I w. in your freedom . . 506.5
have I ceased from w. . . 534.2
w. where Christ would lead . 619.4
w. life's toilsome road . . 675.2
w. in your captain's sight . 695.4
that . . . I may w. boldly. . 867.3
we will w. and worship ever . 891.2
we delight to w. c195
b *(walk alone)*
once in misery I w. a. . . 376.1
I dare not w. a. . . . 717.1
for I dare not w. a. . . 731.1
c *walk with God* *(Gen 5:24)**
O for a closer w. with G. . 442.1
so shall my w. be close . . 442.6
a humbler/holier . . . w. . 445.*
he w. with G. who . . . . 580.*
how wonderful . . . w. with G. 583.1
wonderful to w. with G. . c143
d *walk with Jesus*
soul that once has w. . . 267.1
w. and talking w. J. . . 321.1
when we w. w. the Lord . 397.1
w. in power with thee . . 409.2
all who w. with thee . . 429.3
oft w. J. w. 430.3
Master, let me w. with thee . 519.1
once I thought I w. with J. . 549.1
as we w. with thee abroad . 656.3
w. w. thee to Heaven . . 667.4
I will w. with him . . . 736.2
he knows . . . I will w. . . 740.2
w. each hour w. J. . . c152
out in the open I w. w. . . c157
a song when you w. w. J. . c215
w. w. J. all the way . . c231
e *walk with Saviour*
w. with my S., trusting . . 379.4
are you w. daily by the S. . 417.2
w. with my S., heart in h. . 420.1
w. with my S. in garments . 640.4
f *walk in light* *1 John 1:7/Isa 2:5*
forth to w. in light . . . 330.3
in that l. of life I'll w. . . 332.3
living . . . w. in the l. . . 352.1

their joy is to w. in the l.. . 372.2
w. . . . in the l. of his word . 397.1
purity, w. in the l. . . . 427.3
let us w. in the l. . . . 464.c
w. in the l. . . . . . 465.*
cleansed . . . w. in the l.. . 543.3
out in the open I w. . . c157

g *Ps 23:4*
yea, though I w. 54.3
w. through the valley . . 903.3

h *Isa 40:31*
shall w. and not faint . . c66

i *Jer 7:23**
only w. in his way . . . 739.1
to w. in this pilgrim way. . 768.2
let him (her) w. your way. . 792.2
striving to w. in holy ways . 849.2
while we w. this . . . pathway. 892.2

j *walk by faith* *2 Cor 5:7*
I'll w. by faith . . . to bear . 761.2
w. by f. and not by sight . 947.2

k *Eph 4:1*
have I w. worthily . . . 675.2

l *Col 2:6*
may we ever w. in him . . 659.3

white (b)

wall
without a city w. . . . 133.1
within these hallowed w. . 575.2
within no w. confined . . 604.2
high o'er . . . tower and w. . 799.2
these w. we rear . . . 942.2
these w. we raise . . . 946.2

b *Isa 60:18*
salvation's w. surrounded . 157.1
her w. to speak salvation . 944.1

c *wall of fire* *Zech 2:5*
a w. of f. about me . . 344.3
w. of f. . . . surround . . 809.3
a w. of f. around us . . 814.2

d *Rev 21:18*
till within the jasper w. . . 754.4

wander-ed-ing
through . . . glades I w.. . 37.2

b *(Heb 11:37, 38)*
once w. on earth . . . 354.2

c *(spiritual)*
sought thee w., set thee . 110.2
from Heaven . . . have w. . 225.1
a heart that has w. . . 247.1
w. from a love so true . . 265.1
weary of w. from my God . 305.1
from my Saviour w. far . . 309.1
w. from the fold of God . 313.3
prone to w., Lord . . . 313.5
I was w., and he found me . 330.2
after I'd w. in darkness . . 371.1
thus grief-laden did I w. . 379.1
when I was w. far away. . 386.c
the sheep that had w. away . 388.1
though I w. far from Jesus . 391.1
some have w. from the way . 576.2
lest haply I should w. . . 726.2
thousands who w. and fall . 794.3
nor w. from the pathway . 862.1
I was w. in the wilderness . c171

wanderer
O w., come 226.2
w., knowing not the smile . 253.1
return, O w., return . . 256.1
haste thee, w., tarry not . 261.2
Father calls the w. home . 279.c
gently calling: w., come in . 391.1
some w. sought and won . 524.3
w. now is reconciled . . 550.2
though like a w. . . . 617.2
compel the w. to come in . 683.6
tell the poor w. 691.4
ye w. from God . . . 905.1

wandering
1 *(noun)*
my prodigal w. and shame . 288.3
vain w. cease 351.3
I have ceased from my w. . 394.2
the w. of my will . . . 425.2
in our w. be our guide . . 570.3
control the w. of the mind . 619.2
till all our w. cease . . 918.4
through the avenues of w. . c6

2 *(adjective)*
like w. sheep we strayed . 4.2
there is never a w. one . . 186.4
bind my w. heart to thee . 313.4
w. and weary he sought us . 384.2
a faithless, w. thing . . 421.2
turn my w. heart to thee . 445.3
seek the w. souls of men . 526.1
welcoming his . . . w. child . 550.1
guide the w. to retrace . . 581.4
I may lead the w. . . . feet . 612.2
seeking the w. sinner . . 623.2
some poor w. child of thine . 676.4
shall direct thy w. feet . . 715.2
shall lead the . . . w. home . 802.2
our w. footsteps guide . . 918.3

wane
cause our faith to w. . . 6.2
all lower glories w. . . 551.1
kingdoms rise and w. . . 690.4

want-ed-ing
1 *(desire)*
a *(God) wants*
nor w., nor wasting . . 8.2
w. to take control . . . 204.3
your Saviour w. to be . . 336.3
Jesus w. me . . . . 844.*

b *(we) want*
we w. no other plea . . 60.c
we w. another Pentecost . 203.1
'tis fire we w. . . . 203.3
what you will I w. to be. . 206.c
I w. the gift of power . . 214.1
I w. to shout to all . . 215.3
if you w. it—it's yours . . 244.*
do you w. deliverance . . 257.1
if you w. pardon . . . ask . 270.2
I w. to tell . . . . . 335.*
I w. to love . . . serve him . 369.2
myself I w. to see . . . 409.1
I w. to answer thee . . 409.1
I only w. to have thee . . 415.4
I w. a principle within . . 425.1
I w. the first approach . . 425.2
I w., dear Lord, a heart . . 426.*
If you w. pardon . . . 427.*
I w. thee for ever to live. . 436.1
I w. my life . . . like thine . 440.1
I w. the witness, Lord . . 441.3
Saviour, I w. . . . . . 455.*
which w. . . . no other will . 480.2
all I w. I find in thee . . 517.4
I w. that adorning . . . 589.*
I w. a sober mind . . . 596.2
I w. a godly fear . . . 596.3
new power I w. . . . 620.1
I w. in this dark world . . 649.4
I w. . . . desire . . . zeal. . 720.2
I w. the faith of God . . 733.1
I w. the faith that wears . 733.3
I w. the faith that fires . . 733.5
thou . . . art all I w. . . 737.3
habit makes us w. to prove . 748.3
we w. henceforth our lives 933.1, 2
I w. to live right . . . c71
I w. to sing it . . . tell you . c170
we w. to fill the world . . c220
I w. to be a soldier . . c231

c *wanted*
more warriors are w. . . 684.1
in the conflict men are w. . 702.1
w., hearts . . . . . 704.*
hands are w. . . . 868.2

2 *(lack)*
come . . . your w. disclose . 254.3
all your w. and wounds . 254.4
out of my w. 300.1
w. my heart is telling . . 460.1
persecution, w. nor sword . 554.1
make all my w. . . . known . 633.1
the homes of w. and woe . 697.3
be never w. there . . . 699.3
no w. shall turn me back . 736.2
our inmost w. are known . 738.2
all for w. of faith . . . 770.1
crime and w. and strife . . 830.2
sin and w. and sorrow . . 841.3
sins reproving, w. revealing . 893.c

b *Ps 23:1*
my shepherd; I'll not w.. . 54.1

c *Ps 34:9, 10*
your w. shall be his care. . 21.5
all fear of w. remove . . 157.2
the sons of w. are blest . . 160.3
beyond thy utmost w. . . 560.3
sees all thy children's w. . 715.5
all their w. . . . remove . . 909.3
worked to meet our w. . . 926.1

d *Jas 1:4*
in nothing is w. . . . 956

supply (2c)

wanton *(Jas 5:5)* . . . 577.3

war
1 *(military)*
man, at w. with man . . 83.2
every insult, rift and w. . . 142.4
that w. may cease . . . 156.3
men rise in w. . . . 529.3

b *Isa 2:4*
time that w. . . . no more . 172.3

2 *(spiritual warfare)*
in the w. delighting . . . 309.2
so now to . . . work, to w. . 345.3
in the holy w. . . . 373.3
equip me for the w. . . 568.1
wage the w. with sin . . 575.2
speed the w. 'gainst sin . 622.4
warriors . . . help on the w. . 684.1
the w. will go on . . . 684.4
Jesus calls for men of w. . 686.4
marching as to w. . . 690.1, c
rouse thee! w. is raging . . 693.1
Son . . . goes forth to w. . 701.1
to the w.! to the w. . . 703.*
as to the w. we go . . 705.1
w. for truth and right . . 777.1
'tis a w. 'gainst Hell . . 787.3
with unceasing w. . . . wise . 799.3
till the w. shall end . . 799.3
soldier marches as to w. . 801.1
strains . . . of that great w. . 802.1
w. at times . . . distressing . 805.1
watch and w. through fear . 816.4
until thy w. is won . . . 864.c
glorious w. is won . . . 869.4
new vows for w. we blend . 933.3
filled with . . . w. for thee . 933.3
arm us . . . for the w. . . 937.2
we're in this w. to fight . . c243

b *Ps 144.1*
teach our hands to w. . . c236

cry (4d)

3 *(internal war)*
are you sick of w. . . . 244.2
w. without and fears within . 284.3

warfare
tempests their w. are waging. 19.3
in this w. I fight 321.4
first commenced my w. 338.3
our w.'s the Lord's 687.4
our strength for w. 692.4
in this w. . . . delighting. 778.2
w. may be hard and fierce 806.1
a w. to maintain 868.1
our w. once begun 869.4
the w. long 876.4
b *Ps 46:9; Isa 40:2*
ended is thy w. 352.3
w. and the conflict cease 813.4
life's long w. closed 890.4
soldier his w. cease 894.1

warlike 802.1

warring *(adj)*
thy children's w. madness 577.3
long and w. years 774.1

warm-est
cold my w. thought 58.4
love's w. embrace 269.1
of God's . . . w. embrace 335.2
w. my heart 412.3
w., sweet, tender . . . he 496.5
my w., best affection 520.2
sacred in the fireside w. 663.1
my love to thee pure, w. 743.2

warmth
givest . . . w. and light 2.3
w. to swell the grain 935.1

warning *(Matt 3:7)* 321.4

warriors
like a w. I shall come 338.5
made us w. for ever 593.2
more w. are wanted 684.1
I hear the w. shouting 693.3
w. of the risen King 696.3
raise the w. psalm 707.2
w. lend their strength 799.3
make thee, w., faint 816.2
they may all be w. bold 829.3
those w. saints 858.2
I will be a w., fighting 859.2
we will be his w. 866.3
welcomes a w. 894.1
a place for every w. c237

wash-ed-ing
1 *(general)*
there by faith I w. 348.1
all may be w. and forgiven 535.1
for all who are w. 794.2
healing for all who will w. 808.2
tear (2c)
2 *(request)*
w. us in the . . . blood 210.1
w. me, . . . or I die. 302.3
w. out its stain 453.2
w. the world in . . . fountain 593.4
w. from my hands the dust 647.2
b *wash /cleanse* *Psalm 51:2*
come and w. and make you clean 232.2
w. thou my soul . . . make clean 296.3
w. me, cleanse me 423.c
w. . . . and cleanse my soul 493.c
let the waves w. . . . cleanse. c78
w. me and cleanse me c111
c *2 Kings 5:10*
go, w., I'll make them 359.1
d *John 13:8, 9*
w. . . . till every part c72
3 *wash away sin/stain*
Acts 22:16; Rev 1:5
or w. a. our s. 120.1
I. . . . w. all my s. a. 132.2
guilty past is w. a. 188.1
come and w. your s. a. 239.2
fount where s. are w. a. 257.c
can my s. . . . be w. a. 285.1
what can w. a. my s. 306.1
he w. all a. s. of years 321.2
for he w. my s. a. 327.2
of s. w. white 335.1
hope the s. are w. a. 359.3
who will come and w. today 359.4
till all their s. are w. a. 359.4
when Jesus w. my s. a. 365.c
my s. were w. a. 371.c
he w. it all a. 386.3
s. . . . many are all w. a. 394.2
when I've no s. to w. a. 592.3
when he w. my s. a. 798.c
Jesus . . . w. my s. a. 811.c
he will w. a. my s. 843.2
he can w. your s. a. 893.c
who can w. away my s. c13
I know my s. are w. a. c149
b *blood washes sins/stains*
Rev 1:5, 7:14
his b. has w. our s. a. 43.2
it is the b. that w. white. 113.1
w. us in the atoning b. 210.1
heard of the b. which can w. 237.1
b. can w. away the s. 253.3
b. to w. my every s. a. 303.c
born . . . w. in his b. 310.1
be w. in the b. of the Lamb 321.4
I am w. in Jesus' b. 326.5
w. my robes in Jesus' b. 359.c
w. in the b. of the . . . one 392.c
know I am w. in his b. 402.1
are you w. in the b. 417.*
pray that his b. will w. 420.3
w. . . . in thy b. 423.c
w. me in thy cleansing b. 424.1
w. in the b. of the . . . one 427.2
w. our garments in thy b. 452.2
w. me in the b. of the Lamb 459.c
w. by thy precious b. 511.4
his b. w. whiter than snow 535.c
rejoicing in the b. that w. 814.3
who has w. us in his b. 819.c
b. that w. white as snow 909.2
w. in the b. of the Lamb. 910.*
chosen . . . w. in his b. c225
a soldier, w. in his b. c229
c *wash white* *Ps 51:7*
it is the blood that w. w. 113.1
of sins w. w. and garments 335.1
w. in his blood quite w. 402.1
w. stains . . . w. 540.2
blood (3b), robe (d), snow (c, d)

washing *(noun)* 436.2

waste-d-ing
nor wanting, nor w. 8.2
whence to me this w. 286.3
gold will w. and wear away 356.2
the w. of my winter 378.2, 4
vain 'tis to w. your time 686.4
b *Isa 52:9*
places w. and wild 159.3
c *(Luke 15:13)*
w. years, doubts and fears 379.2

watch-ed-ing
1 *(God) watches*
w. the lowly mother 87.3
w. o'er his loved ones 182.2
w. . . . from the throne 182.2
Jesus is . . . w. for you 264.1
Jesus w., O so tenderly 341.2
w. by the sick 676.5
he it is who w. o'er me 732.2
Jesus then in love is w. 759.2
above thee w. 767.4
w. o'er us all the way 938.1
2 *(people) watch*
w. long in hope and fear 75.3
near the cross I'll w. 115.4
w. and waiting, looking 310.3
so now to w., to work 345.3
eager eyes are w., longing 478.2
through constant w., wise 485.2
w. and war through fear 816.4
his w. the temple child 839.2
or w. at thy gates 839.4
many . . . waiting and w. 886.4
b *Ps 130.6*
I w. as for the morning 448.3
w. for the dawning 599.3
c *Matt 26:40*
wake and w. 816.3
d *Luke 2:8*
while w. o'er their fold 72.2
w. o'er your flocks 75.2
as they w. o'er their flocks 80.2
as we w. at dead of night 88.3
while shepherds w. 93.1
e *watch and pray* *Matt 26:41*
for which we w. . . . we p. 335.3
taught me how to w. and p. 365.c
help me to w. and p. 472.4
every moment w. and p. 667.3
keep w. and p. 683.6
w. and fight and p. 812.2
w. and we're p. 819.1
Gen 32:24-31
wrestle, w. and p. c76
f *Eph 6:18*
w. unto prayer 596.3
walking . . . w. unto prayer 695.4
put on . . . w. unto prayer 699.3
g *[angels] watch*
a. keep their w. 86.2
where the a. are w. 883.3
3 *(other)*
branching willows w. 39.3
seen him in the w.-fires 162.2
pillar . . . through w. dark 654.3
starlight stands w. 666.4
Church . . . w. is keeping 677.2
b *Ps 90:4*
short as the w. that ends 13.4
c *Matt 27:66*
vain the stone, the w. 143.3
vainly they w. his bed 148.2

watchers 753.2

watchful
ever w. is his care 722.3
w. care and . . . kindness 938.2
b *Luke 2:8*
then to the w. shepherds 78.2

watchword
w. at the gates of death. 625.5
forward! be our w. 682.1
truth be your w. 813.1

water
1 *(literal)*
flowing w., pure and clear 2.3
whirlwinds and w. 19.3
like thy . . . running w. 32.1
cool w. touched his feet 103.3
on land and on w. . . . show 684.2
b *Gen 1:2*
the w.' darkened face 202.1
move on the w.' face 224.3
2 *(death and difficulty)*
when the w. cold chill 280.3
from the w. lifted me 336.1

where . . . dark w. flow . . 483.2
light may flash across its w. . 726.4
while the nearer w. roll . . 737.1

b *Ps 69:14*
through the deep w. I call . 653.3

3 *(spiritual life)*
a *Ps 23:2*
the quiet w. by . . . 54.1
where still w. flow . . . 341.1
by w. still 725.2

b *Jer 2:13*
ah! the w. failed . . . 547.3

c *John 4:10*
long for the w., and cry . . 351.1
draught of the w. of life. . 351.c
Christ is the w. of life . . 351.c

d *John 19:34*
let the w. and the blood. . 302.1

e *[living] water* *John 4:10, 7:38*
streams of l. w. flow . . 53.2
see, the streams of l. w.. . 157.2
spring with l. w. flows . . 254.3
the l. w., Jesus, send . . 282.3
I freely give the l. w. . . 332.2
where the l. w. flow . . 374.c
l. w. rich and free . . . 439.1
that l. w. now bestow . . 601.1
land where l. w. flow . . 818.c
the w. of the old wells . . c40

f *(Rev 22:1)*
its w. gleam . . . are pure 252.1, 2
its w. so free are flowing . 252.c
balm . . . in its w. is found . 252.3
come to the w. . . . 257.3
thy w. can cleanse me . . 298.2
if once thy pure w. . . 298.4
I plunge 'neath the w. . . 298.6
life-giving w. are flowing . 383.1
where healing w. flow . . 590.1
come unto the healing w. 647.1, c
when the w. flow . . . appear. 647.2

sweet (3h)

watered *(passive)*
a *Ps 65:9*
w. by God's . . . hand . . 935.1

b *Isa 58:11*
make our hearts a w. garden . 210.1

wave
1 *(literal)*
like thy dancing w. . . 32.2
he heard the w. repeat . . 103.3
wind upon the w. beneath . 196.3
cross the w. 393.1
hath bound the restless w. . 569.1
or still the w. 854.1
winds and w. obey him . . 935.2

2 *(death)*
e'en death's cold w. . . 725.4
every w. like crystal . . 726.4
Jesus will the w. divide . . 902.3
these beside the chilly w. . 910.1
death's threatening w. . . 954.4

3 *(difficulty)*
the angry w. . . . o'erflow . 280.2
when sorrow's w. . . . roll . 317.3
though the w. roll high . . 325.4
out of the angry w. . . 336.3
a gleam across the w. . . 478.c
unknown w. before me roll . 598.1
when w. would whelm . . 654.3
through w. and clouds . . 721.2
the w. of earthly strife . . 872.1

b *Matt 8:24, 14:24*
disciples tossing on the w. . 96.2
the w. in angry motion . . 96.2
winds and w. submissive . 569.2
raging w. obey thy will . . 598.2

thee who stilled the w. . . 628.3
the w. of strife be still . . 669.3
upon the w. to thee . . 749.2

c *Ps 42:7*
though w. and storms go . 746.4
though thy w. . . . gone o'er . 762.1

4 *(spiritual life)*
where its bright w. roll . . 252.2
I'm touching the w. . . 298.6
all ills its w. deliver. . . 471.2
the sin-cleansing w. . . 535.c
over its w. to my spirit . . 542.1
heart its w. are cleansing . c42
let the w. wash . . . cleanse . c78
beneath its w. I am going . c221

5 *(verb)*
take up the torch and w. it . 683.5
'neath our colours w. . . 774.c
w., soldiers . . . keep w.. . 775.*
w. a message grand . . 783.1
our flag shall w. for ever . 800.1
see the signal w. . . 804.1
see the . . . banner w. . . 804.3
w. a branch 848.4

waver-ing *Heb 10:23**
thy love doth never w. . . 538.c
lead the . . . w. feet . . 612.2
battalions never shall w. . 800.2
should a comrade w. . . 805.3
may we never w. . . . 866.c

way
1 *(Divine)*
thy being and thy w. . . 7.1
moves in a mysterious w. . 29.1
grant us that w. to know . 100.4
it wins its widening w. . . 165.2
in Jesus' w. go on . . 312.1
drew me back into his w. . 337.2
have thine own w., Lord . 487.*
most wondrous your w. . 506.1
thou shalt have . . . w. . . 507.3
scorn . . . assail his w. . . 577.2
all the secrets of his w. . . 591.1
thy w. . . . I see . . . choose . 605.3
that only seeks thy w. . . 618.2
the w. he shall choose . . 640.3
the w. of God . . . record . 656.1
loved to wend his w. . . 663.2
back to the Father's w. . . 680.2
the w. the Master went . . 683.1
his w. is best, you see . . 732.c
swerve not from his w. . . 738.3
let him (her) walk your w. . 792.2
love . . . Christ's w. . . 816.3
in thine own sweet w. . . 837.1
the w. which thou didst go . 846.3
in his w. I may walk . . 867.3
King . . . passes on his w. . 876.5

b *Ps 18:30*
I thy perfect w. may see. . 455.3

c *Ps 37:23*
I delight in his w. . . . 640.2

d *Ps 145:17*
most sure in all his w. . 18.1, 4
good in all thy w. . . . 576.4

e *John 14:6*
in Jesus . . . a w. . . . 36.4
thou art the w. . . 100.1, 4
Jesus is the truth, the w. . 231.3
there's one w. . . . 523.2
thou art the w., none other . 529.1
thee, life, truth and w. . . 561.3
Jesus, my truth, my w. . . 597.1
the life, the truth, the w. . 625.6
you are the truth . . . the w. . 748.2
Christ, the life and w. . . 760.1

f *living way* *Heb 10:20*
shows the new and l. w. . 113.2
the l. w. is shown . . . 221.3

the true, the only l. w. . . 279.2
from this new and l. w. . . 789.6
be our true and l. w. . . 937.3

know (1c), narrow (b), teach (1g), walk (2i)

2 *(life in general)*
unfoldest blessings on our w. 2.4
every winding of the w. . 7.4
hath blessed us on our w. . 12.1
light and love upon my w. . 112.3
urge us on our w. . . . 173.2
we hesitated on the w. . . 192.3
no more . . . cloud his w. . 277.4
fears obstruct my w. . . 285.2
he brightens our w. . . 316.1
the w. grows brighter . . 340.3
as we march along the w. . 367.c
glory he sheds on our w. . 397.1
walk by his side in the w. . 397.5
sent me singing on my w. . 401.1
'tis a blessed w. and holy . 462.2
sometimes the w. be stony . 462.2
the w. that leads to God . 462.2
that is flowing by the w. . 462.3
a rest upon the w. . . 476.1
walk . . . to the end of the w. 506.5
in the homeward w. . . 519.2
the future's broadening w. . 519.4
whichever w. my course . 536.3
my w. has brighter grown . 549.c
meets him out upon the w. . 550.1
your blessing on my w. . . 552.1
God to guide my w. . . 556.3
do we ask our w. to be . . 570.2
there let my w. appear . . 617.3
which mark the w. for me . 628.1
content to trust my w. . . 644.c
brook by the traveller's w. . 654.1
our w. protecteth . . . 655.3
peace upon our homeward w. 674.2
he shall prepare thy w. . . 715.2
the w. before I cannot see . 717.1
perils of a winding w. . . 740.2
through a stormy w. . . 754.1
singing, if my w. be clear . 754.3
not knowing our w. . . 763.3
may naught my w. encumber 766.3
peace . . . attendeth my w. . 771.1
when we cannot see our w. . 772.1
radiant is the w. before . . 776.1
be the guardian of our w. . 845.2
only do thou guide my w. . 865.2
once were comrades of our w. 878.1
the storms . . . my w. oppose c127
help . . . on the upward w. . c166

choose (2b), commit (a), dark (2h), know (3h), lead (3g), life (6b), light (7b), long (2b), pilgrim (b), prepare (e), pursue (b), rough (b), show (1f), take (3d), tread (d)

b *all the way*
will be with us a. the w.. . 43.3
when a. the w. seems gloomy 316.c
a. the w. is marked by love . 400.1
a. the w. to Glory . . . 430.c
be thou with us a. the w. . 532.3
keep me fighting a. the w. . 586.1
Light that followest a. my w.. 621.2
gently lead me a. the w.. . 627.1
leave God to order a. thy w. . 738.1
a. the w. from earth . 753.1, c
joyful/victory a. the w. . 807.1, 2
follow Jesus a. the w. . . 817.c
close beside me a. the w. . 843.3
watching o'er us a. the w. . 938.1
go with him . . . a. the w. . c57
a. the w. from earth . . c110
trusting Jesus a. the w.. . c119
take care . . . o'er a. the w. . c124
following Jesus a. the w. . c206
walking with Jesus a. the w.. c231

c *way [to Heaven]*
go on your w. in peace . 67.2
the w. to Heaven's joys . 125.2
w. to Heaven is straight . 275.3
lights our w. up to Glory . 316.c
I am on my way to Heaven . 360.3
w. to that city of light . 406.1

3 *(manner, conduct)*
to reach the w. we dream . 27.6
to find an easier w. . 192.2
the w. to bring me back . 305.3
what w. could be found . 319.2
he chooses out a lowly w. 398.1
a. w. for man to rise . 414.4
the w. of my choosing . 501.2
there's one w. . . . obtain . 523.2
wandered from the w. . 576.2
cares to find an easier w. . 619.3
point the w. to holiness . 656.2
believing, this is the w. . 773.c
the w. to every blessedness . 806.1
taught the w. to Heaven . 834.2

b *ways*
speaks . . . by quiet w. . 31.3
gather . . . from w. of strife . 63.1
my fancied w. why . . . heed. 91.3
unversed in worldly w. . 163.2
in w. dark and wild . 175.3
in the desert w. I sing . 194.5
ran in self-chosen w. . 422.2
all my w. . . . possessing . 470.3
in their varied w. . 494.1
forgive our foolish w. . 567.1
all the traffic of the w. . 615.1
seek forbidden w. . 630.2
planned the pattern of my w.. 644.1
often in secluded w. . 705.3
keep my feet in w. of rest . 728.2
weary w. or golden days . 730.4
God to order all thy w. . 738.1
linger o'er familiar w. . 874.1

c *in every way*
reliable in e. w. . 49.2
unchanged in e. w. . 324.4
in e. w. try to please him . 844.1
in e. kind of w. . 851.1
help in e. w. we can . 851.2

d *way of sin*
found s.'s w. is thorny . 225.2
rescued from his sinful w. . 550.2
returning from his w. . 625.4
s.'s dark w. forsaking . 788.1
reclaimed from s.'s dark w. . 825.3

e *Psalm 139:3*
surveys thy . . . words and w. 665.2

f *1 Cor 12:31*
end of . . . w. is love . 146.2
learning the better w. . 529.2
love's the greatest w. . 544.4

g *no way*
I can come no other w. . 292.4
no other w. to be happy . 397.c
hearts to know no w. . 704.4

forsake (2c) know (1c) truth (g)
wisdom (1b)

4 *(in phrases)*
love . . . have come our w. . 74.1
stars upon their w. . 141.2
Jesus is passing this w. . 247.1
Master walketh along that w. 680.1
calling . . . self-same w.. . 680.3
all around . . . gives w. . 745.3
do not . . . falter by the w. . 817.1
w. out in space . 850.3
Father waits over the w. . 900.1
coming this w. . . . revival . c63

b *Acts 24:25*
go, Spirit, go thy w. . 226.1

clear (1)

wayside
thank you . . . for w. roses . 552.3
scenes by the w. . 848.1
sowing the seed by the w. . 931.2
he paints the w. flower . 935.2

wayward
stir our w. souls . 202.4
oft-times weak and w. . 341.2
the w. feet to stay . 519.2
w. men to lead to Heaven . 528.3
the w. and the lost . 825.2

weak
poor though I be, and w. . 7.3
w. is the effort of my heart . 58.4
my love is w. and faint . 110.6
oft-times w. and wayward . 341.2
though coming w. and vile . 423.2
faltering and w. my labour . 488.1
I feel how w. I am . 489.1
my heart is w. and poor . 508.2
serve with w. . . . hands . 534.2
to the penitent and w. . 555.2
I am w., but thou . 578.1
though my w. endeavour . 635.3
are we w. and heavy-laden . 645.3
my faith at best is w. . 731.2
my faith so w., so faint . 742.2
I am both w. and sinful . 840.1

b *Rom 14:1*
help those who are w. . 458.1
speak to . . . help the w. . 581.4
for all who are w. . 679.2
whereon the w. may rest . 838.4

c *weak and helpless*
he was little, w. and h. . 87.4
I am w. and . . . h. . 98.1
say, are you w., are you h. . 467.2
so w. I am, and h. . 726.1

strong (2d)

weakened . 553.2

weakest
to redeem the w. believer . 372.1
when he sees the w. saint . 646.3
when you feel w. . 773.1
how the w. conquer . 815.2

b *2 Cor 12:9*
if my strength is at its w. . 528.2

weakling
others may reject the w. . 324.2
man is a w. . c210

weakness
our w., pitying, see . 200.7
I know my w. . 491.2
how rooted my w. remained . 553.3
keep them, in their w. . 582.2
thou who knowest all my w. . 584.c
owning my w. . 605.1
all our w. thou dost know . 607.2
Jesus knows our every w. . 645.2
no w. of the soul . 695.3
w. left behind . 788.3
take your w. . . . to Jesus . 790.1
mourn their w. . 806.2
in our w. and distress . 937.3
my sin and w. . . . are lost . c94

b *1 Cor 15:43*
sown in our w. . 931.c

c *weakness [strength]* *2 Cor 12:9*
works through w. wrought . 5.2
w. will be power . 325.2
w. leaneth on his might . 333.2
strength for my w., Lord . 488.3
my w. is strong . 506.2
back on thy strength all my w. 507.3
our strength in hours of w. . 570.3

d *Heb 11:34*
fire . . . makes of w., might . 197.3
make of my w. might . 221.3
make w. strength . 490.2
turns w. into might . 830.3

wealth
all the w. of Heaven . 70.4
his people's w. . 168.6
slenderness of the poor w. . 183.3
my want and into thy w. . 300.1
Christ . . . glory and my w. . 346.4
holdeth the w. of the world . 354.1
w., honour, pleasure . 480.4
pleasure and w. and praise . 509.2
rich . . . such w. possessing . 536.1
to share the w. of God . 796.2
rich may bring their w. . 849.1

b *wealth or . . .*
colour, scorn or w. divide . 142.4
in deepest poverty or w. . 356.3
works or w. can never buy . 555.4
ask . . . not w. or fame . 791.2
we have no w. or learning . 849.1

weapons
lay thy w. down . 352.3
all needful w. there . 658.4
faithfully your w. wield . 694.5
keep your w. sharp . 809.2

b *2 Cor 10:4*
w. of my sinful pride . 122.4
lay all carnal w. down 701.c; 705.c

wear-ing
gold will . . . w. away . 356.2
thy righteousness w. . 372.3
w. that pledge of love . 424.2
no fearful shade shall w. . 465.4
thy seal . . . to w. . 589.3
thy perfect likeness to w. . 623.1
as we thy nature w. . 656.3
I want the faith that w. . 733.3
flowers fair the meadows w. . 850.2
the judge, our nature w. . 875.2
their barren aspect w. . 925.3

b *wear [crown]*
w. a c. with Jesus . 67.2
a c. of thorns he'll w. . 103.2
the next a c. to w. . 278.1
love thee for w. the thorns . 357.2
in Heaven I a c. shall w. . 499.2
now the c. of life are w. . 686.1
w. the c. before thy face . 698.3

c *wear robe*
w. a spotless r. . 389.3
r. for each to w. . 899.1
r. which the glorified w. . 904.2

weariness . 528.2

weary
to w., hopeless nations . 63.2
for I am weak and w. . 98.1
art thou w. . . . languid . 228.1
are you a trifle w. . 244.1
say, are you w. . 257.1
ye who are w., come home . 264.c
w. of wandering . 305.1
I was w. sore . 311.3
a-w. of the strife . 330.2
lay down, thou w. one . 332.1
came . . . w. and worn and sad 332.1
blinded eyes, w. sighs . 379.1
wandering and w. he sought 384.2
leading w. sinners . 399.3
life a w. journey seem . 400.1
the load that w. me . 421.3
w. I am of inbred sin . 450.3
wounded and w., help me . 487.3
his w., wandering child . 550.1
I shall forget the w. days . 551.2

w. . . . of the press . . 564.1
to w. ones in needful hour . 612.5
w. brain and troubled breast . 669.2
Jesus, give the w. . . . repose 673.3
w. eyelids gently steep . . 676.2
to the w. and the worn . . 697.5
foot it . . . strong or w. . . 716.1
w. ways or golden days . . 730.4
far and a-w. . . . may roam . 740.3
to the w. passer-by . . 753.1
end in saving sinners w. . 802.4
through this w. pilgrimage . 918.1
a w. mind retaineth . . c72

b *weary heart*
say, w. h., oppressed . . 229.*
is there a h. . . . w. . . 247.2
hope to the w. of h. . . 273.2
though my h. grows w. . . 334.2
does your h. grow w. . . 805.1

c *weary soul* *Jer 31:25*
love . . . to the w. sinful s. . 230.1
sweet to the w. s. . . 252.2
s. that are w. faint . . 351.1
with my faint, w. s. . . 469.1
soul, though w. sore . . 590.3
I rest my w. s. in thee . . 621.1

d *weary/[rest]* *Isa 28:12*
and to the w. rest . . . 58.2
the w. find eternal rest . . 160.3
w. and sighing for rest . . 247.2
Jesus is calling the w. to r. . 248.2
I rest my w. soul in thee . 621.1
a rest for all the w. . . 899.2
rest comes for the w. . . 934.3

e *grow weary*
thou hast g. w. . . . 225.2
often g. w. 316.2
though my heart g. w. . . 334.2
does your heart g. w. . . 805.1

f *Isa 40:31*
run and not be w. . . . c66

g *Gal 6:9*
nor w. in the conflict . . 781.3

h *Heb 12:3*
dreary, faint and w. . . 607.2

land (2d)

weave-ing/wove
theme its notes are w. . . 70.c
I too would w. . . . 644.4
my web of time he w. . . 896.3

weaver 644.1

web 896.3

wedding 949.1

weeds 552.2

weeks 925.4

weep-ing/wept
1 *(Jesus) weeps* *Luke 19:41*
they tell me he w. . . . 331.2

2 *(people) weep*
will for lost sinners w. . . 205.3
when I was w. . . . 237.1
bitter the tears . . . I w. . . 298.2
but useless is w. . . . 298.2
to walk, to w., to sing . . 415.5
sins over which I have w. . 437.2
still eyes that w. . . . 527.1
never w. for thee . . . 547.4
w. o'er the erring one . . 691.1
hearts to share . . . the w. . 704.3

b *Ps 126:6*
go then, though with w. . 930.3

c *Luke 23:28*
w. not for me, he cries . . 131.2

d *John 20:11*
tenderly mourned and w. . 117.2

e *Rom 12:15*
wipe the w. eyes . . . 485.2

f *(Rev 21:4)*
there will be no . . . w. . . 899.3

3
that w. tree . . . 131.1, 4

weigh-ed
with grief and pain w. down . 123.1
life w. down by care . . 246.1

weight
never a w. of woe . . . 186.2
thy w. of iniquities roll . . 271.3
thy work . . . ease this w. . 297.3
ills have no w. . . . 670.4
not for w. of glory . . 707.2

weighted
w. down with care . . 257.1

welcome
a *(from Jesus)*
he will w. thy return . . 225.c
souls are freely w. here . . 254.2
Jesus is waiting to w. thee . 263.2
there is w. for the sinner . 265.4
thou wilt . . . w., pardon . 293.5
obedient to thy w. call . . 422.1
I hear thy w. voice . . 423.1
w. his weary . . . child . . 550.1
your hands swift to w. . . 611.3
to bid these children w. . . 797.3
Jesus . . . will w. sinners . c17

b *(to Jesus)*
how they ring to w. Christ . 79.c
thy w. shall proclaim . . 81.4
as they w. his birth . . 99.1
gladly we w. thee . . . 175.c
we bid thee w. . . . thrice w. . 213.1
bid him w., for . . . peace . 227.c
bid him w. . . . your choice . 227.3

c *[in Heaven]*
to be met . . . and w. . . 170.2
hear the w. from the King . 389.3
angels their w. shall sing . 543.4
Saviour shall w. us home . 808.4
sing their w. home . . 879.c
w. a warrior to . . . peace . 894.1
there's a w. for the true . 899.2
he will bid us w. . . . 930.3
they wait to give us w. . . 938.4

d *(other)*
w. every sinner there . . 138.4
w., happy morning . . 155.1, c
hail reproach . . . w. pain . 526.2
the w. day of . . . peace. . 813.4

welcomed *(adj)* 423.4

well
1 *(noun)*
a *(Gen 26:18)*
go back to the old w. . . c40

b *(Isa 12:3)*
a w. of joy within . . . 413.4
deep, sweet w. of love . . 896.2

c *John 4:11*
the w. is deep, and I . . 351.c

spring (3b)

2 *(adverb)*
w. our feeble frame . . 17.3
w. might the sun . . . hide . 105.3
w. supply thy sons . . 157.2
glory . . . I know very w. . 323.3
sick . . . he made me w. . 330.2
I know 'tis w. . . . 339.4
w. may this glowing heart . 365.1
finish w. what we've begun . 462.3
never loved thee w. . . 558.3
to learn this lesson w. . . 566.1
to fight w. for thee . . 608.3
he can w. secure . . . 735.3
it is w. with my soul . 771.1, c
w. he sees and knows it. . 841.2
all who served you w. . . 856.1
w. may thy praise . . . employ 925.1

b *all well*
a. shall be w., friends . . 146.2
a. shall be w. in . . . peace . 166.3
I love you, a. will be w. . . 294.3
hear him whisper: a. is w. . 759.3
a. will be/is/must be w. . 764.*
a.'s w., a.'s w. . . . 960

c *Mark 7:37*
has made a. things w. . . 25.4
Jesus hath done a. things w. 144.c
he . . . hath done a. things w. 329.1
ruleth a. things w. . . . 721.3

d *as well*
you, too, a. w. as me . . 403.3
I may a. w. kneel down . . 588.2
the night a. w. as the day . 773.c
serve God quite a. w. . . 780.3

e *(also)*
bless our officers a. w. . . 622.4
rich and poor a. w. . . 814.c
trembling followers a. w. . 893.3

f *so well*
sweet the name I love s. w. . 68.4
the name I love s. w. . . 69.3
who loves me now s. w. . 345.4
thou knowest all s. w. . . 421.4
fight s. w. begun . . . 939.3
reason they love it s. w. . c202

f *well-*
my w.-instructed soul . . 425.4
win the w.-fought day . . 695.6
in the w.-fought fight . . 876.2

h *Matt 3:17*
Christ, his w. belovèd Son . 335.1

i *Heb 13:21*
w. pleasing in thy sight . . 441.3
if thou art w. pleased . . 784.4

j *well done* *Matt 25:21**
hear the Lord's: W. d. . . 222.c
the Saviour's glad w. d. . 500.3
glory of thy sweet w. d. . 628.4
earn the King's: W. d. . . 869.4
servant of God, w. d. . . 890.1
soldier of Christ, w. d. . . 890.5
God shall say: W. d. . . 912.3

farewell

wend-ing
and w. on to Glory . . 368.1
Jesus loved to w. his way . 663.2
as the birds homeward w. . 675.3

went see go

wept see weep

west
drew near to the north-w. . 90.4
. . . they shall come from the w. 170.*

east

western 677.4

wet 35.2

what nc, but
a *(as a question)*
w. is this wound . . . 111.2
w. means that . . . cry . . 140.1
w. my portion here . . 228.4
w. hath he at last . . . 228.5
w. has thy heart decided . 255.3

w. dost thou lack 263.1
w. keepeth thee back . . 263.1
w. does this signify . . 274.*
my Christ, w. shall I call . 346.5
w. love with thine can vie . 515.3
w. offering shall I give . . 516.1
w. to me . . . joys/sight . . 600.2
w. hast thou to say . . 614.1
w. are men 683.2
w. to me are loss and pain . 729.3
w. shall we children bring . 849.1
w. will then become of thee . 875.3
w. hope have you . . . 885.4
w. shall the harvest be . . 931.*
w. shall the answer be . . c28
w. have we to give . . c213
b *what can*
w. tongue c. recite . . 16.4
w. angel tongue c. tell . . 55.4
w. c. his transgression be . 108.1
w. love c. compare . . 119.c
w. c. shake . . . repose . 157.1
w. c. wash away . . . keep . 306.1
w. way could be found . . 319.2
w. power my soul c. sever . 345.4
w. love with thine c. vie . 515.3
w. else c. he withhold . . 560.2
w. . . . c. foil the tempter's . 670.3
w. c. I ask more c61
c *what if/though*
w. t. the saints . . . die . . 149.2
w. t. this earthly house . . 149.3
w. t. the treacherous road . 176.3
w. t. my joys . . . die . . 358.2
w. t. foes . . . snares . . 400.2
w. t. in the conflict . . 537.2
w. i. thy form we cannot see. 558.2
w. i. strength should fail . 586.3
w. i. dark and lonely days . 586.3
w. t. thou rulest not . . 721.3
w. t. I cannot know . . 732.2
w. t. the tempest rage . . 882.2
d *what more*
w. can I covet m. . . . 361.3
w. m. can he say . . . 653.1
w. can I ask m. c61
e *what might*
w. you m. have been . . 267.2
all the 'w. m. have been' . 893.2
do (1g), else (c), Jesus (10), and index to song book

what(so)ever
secure, w. I endure . . 45.2
w. I can be give to him . . 212.5
to do w. I know . . . 426.3
w. it cost 440.2
w. that idol be . . . 442.5
speak thy will, w. it be . . 475.1
w. pursuits my time employ . 517.2
life is great! W. happens . 544.2
w. conforms not to thy love . 565.4
w. I am I bring . . . 631.4
w. thy . . . grace hath given . 667.4
w. my cross may be . . 678.c
w. thy danger take heed . 689.2
w. I do, where'er I be . . 725.1
w. your race may be . . 826.3
my times . . . w. they may be. 917.2
grant, O Lord, w. may be . 941.3
w. in life . . . their share. . 947.4
b *Phil 4:11*
in w. estate 485.5
content, w. lot I see . . 725.3
take w. his gracious will. . 738.2
in w. worldly state . . 916.1
befall, betide, future (b), lot, say (1d), thing (1g)

wheat *Matt 13:25*
w. and tares together sown . 924.2
make tares or ripe w. . . 928.3
Jesus the w. 932.1
grow with w. and be a tare . 932.3
tares and w. together grow . 932.3

wheel
God of piston and of w. . 30.1
Lord . . . w. in splendour . 38.1
on the road thy w. are not . 91.2
b *Jer 18:3*
clay on the w. am I . . 416.4

whelm-ing *(Ps 124:4)**
would w. our tossing bark . 654.3
in the w. flood . . . 745.3

when *nc, but*
a *(as question)*
w. shall all hatred cease . 172.2
w. comes the promised time . 172.3
w. shall I hear . . . voice . 214.2
w. shall thy love constrain . 307.1
w. shall my soul return . . 307.1
w. shall I know . . . thee mine 447.1
w. shall my soul . . . rest . 454.1
w. shall we know...be perfect 466.5
w. shall I come . . . waters . 647.1

whence
cross, from w. a fountain . 232.2
w. to me this waste . . 286.3
from w. my soul's distress . 290.2
w. my hope of righteousness 290.2
love only knoweth w. it came 496.2
w. the healing stream . . 578.2
w. all the . . . mercy flow . 601.3
spring w. all my blessings . 616.1
to tell me w. I came . . 652.1
w. . . . salvation come . . 767.1
w. have come these legions . 803.2
ask them w. their victory . 879.3
w. have come these fields . 923.1

whene(v)er
w. the sweet church bell . 187.2
service w. he shall choose . 443.2
w. I blush . . . my shame . 592.2
w. I think of Jesus . . c187

where nc, but
a *(as question)*
w. could we hide . . . 49.c
w. . . . thy sting/victory . 143.4
w. is thy reign of peace . 172.2
w. is the . . . certain seal . 214.4
w. shall I thy praise begin . 370.1
w. are now those doubts . 399.1
w. is the blessedness/view . 442.2
w. is death's sting . . 670.4
w. would the cross be . . 773.2
w. shall we go in . . . need . 791.1

whereby 654.1

where(so)ever
w. men may move . . 158.3
Jesus shall reign w. the sun . 160.1
blessings . . . w. he reigns . 160.3
w. thou dost reign . . 198.4
come . . . w. ye languish . 236.1
sinner, w. thou art . . 261.1
news w. man is found . . 279.1
w. I speak, or sing . . 356.4
w. thy steps I see . . 453.3
w. in the world I am . . 485.5
w. they dwell . . . in thee . 556.1
w. thy children are . . 576.1
Jesus, w. thy people meet . 604.1
w. they seek thee . . . 604.1
w. he holds dominion . . 696.c
fight w. wrong is found . 705.1
whate'er I do, w. I be . . 725.1
w. he may guide me . . 736.2
witnessing . . . w. you may be 832.c
Heaven to me w. I be . . c172
b *wherever [go]*
take it then w. you go . . 66.1
follow the star w. it went . 90.3
w. I go I'll tell the story . . 107.5
tell it w. you go . . . 384.1
shout the news w. I go . . 401.3
spread thy light w. I may go . 426.3
burning w. I go . . . 447.3
w. thou goest to follow . . 509.1
a blazing fire w. I go . . 521.2
protect them w. they go . 569.4
w. I may go . . . . 620.*
know, w. I may go . . 686.c
flame . . . w. I may go . . 838.1
lot

wherefore
w. have ye left your sheep . 88.2
w., by God's . . . purpose . 174.4
w. to thee I all resign . . 509.3
w. in never-ceasing prayer . 714.4

wherein
humble heart w. to rest . . 200.4
w. I walked in power . . 409.2
chart, w. we read . . . 654.2
ground w. . . . anchor . . 746.1

whereon
w. the Saviour . . . was born. 78.1
tree w. the Son of man . . 131.1
the name w. I cry . . . 456.4
bread . . . w. we feed . . 654.2
staff w. the weak may rest . 838.4

wherewith 512.3

whether
w. it be profit . . . loss . . 352.3
conflict, w. great or small . 396.3
w. in the desert . . . c238

whichever 536.3

while/st nc, but
a *(noun)*
in darkness living all the w. . 253.1
with me, in me all the w. . 352.1
don't . . . rest for a w. . . 817.c
b *while you may* *(Heb 3:13)*
come to Jesus w. y. m. . 239.2
bid him enter w. y. m. . . 241.c
open, enter w. y. m. . . 279.2
seek salvation w. y. m. . 885.1
pray (2b)

whirlwinds *(Nahum 1:3)* . . 19.3

whisper-ed
1 *(human)*
faintest w. of my heart . . 48.1
hear the w. of your prayers . 238.c
w. words and longing eyes . 544.3
lower, while I w. . . . 548.3
w. a prayer c114
2 *(divine)*
how sweetly Jesus w. . . 320.3
near me and w.: It is I . . 325.4
he w.: Go in peace . . 366.4
Jesus w. sweet and low. . 390.1
attend the w. of thy grace . 636.4
w. softly in your heart . . 664.3
he can w. words of comfort . 731.2
blood of Jesus w. peace . 752.1
hear him w.: All is well . . 759.3
thou wilt w. thy peace . . 771.3
hear each w. of thy word . 839.3
bright angels w.: Come . 911.5
w., O so kind c36
b *whisper love*
mercy, w. of l. . . . 310.2
heard his l. w. . . . 333.1
hear thy w. l. . . . 600.3

whit *John 7:23*
thou every w. made whole . 520.4
bade me be every w. whole . 542.3
be every w. made whole . 562.3

white
morning light, the lily w. . 42.2
the black, the w., the dark . 170.2
on the pages w. and fair . 883.c
b *walk in white* *Rev 3:4*
power to w. the world in w. . 203.3
w. in w. . . . worthy . 431.c
w. . . . in garments of w. . 640.4
daily w. with thee in w.. . 919.3
c *Rev 3:5*
who are these arrayed in w. . 909.1
garment (e), harvest (2e), robe (c), snow (c, d), wash (3c)

whiter-st *Rev 7:13*
where the w. robes are seen . 429.1
our robes will be the w.. . 899.1

who nc, but
a *(as question)*
w. would not fear . . . name . 20.2
w. is he . . . . . 104.*
w. can faint while . . . river . 157.2
w. is it tells/gives/shows . 204.*
w.'ll be the next . . 278.*
this joy, w. can express . . 328.2
w. will come and wash . . 359.4
w. can tell . . . recount . . 655.4
w. like thyself . . . can be . 670.3
w. shall dream of shrinking . 682.1
w. follows in . . . train . 701.*
w.'ll the war cry obey . 703.2
w.'ll enlist in this Army . . 703.3
w. will be his helpers . 707.1
w. will leave . . . face the foe. 707.1
w.'ll fight for the Lord . 708.1, c
w. will heed . . . command . 868.1
w. will offer them today. . 868.2
w. will journey . . . with me . 881.3
w. can give you hope . 885.4
w. will come and go . 887.c
b *Ex 32:26*
w. is on the Lord's side . . 707.1
c *Isaiah 6:8*
w. . . . Jehovah will go . 703.1, 3
w. for him will go . . 707.1
d *Rev 7:13*
w. are these arrayed . 909.1
w. are these beside . . . wave. 910.1
e *Romans 8:35*
w. shall dare to separate . 554.1
w. the child . . . shall sever . 555.1
charge (d), like (2e)

who(so)ever *John 3:16; Rev 22:17*
w. heareth! shout . . . 279.1
w. will may come . . . 279.*
w. has found it . . 355.3
that promise: W. will . 359.2
w. will may come . . . . 403.*
faith, which w. receives. . 756.4
saves w. on Jesus calls . . 756.5
it is written: W. . . . . 824.*
hope for w. will . . 919.2

whole
1 *(entire)*
my w. being may proclaim . 7.1
the w. triumphant host . . 223.5
tell not half . . . the w. . . 333.4
your w. nature fill . . 408.4
the w. of sin's disease . . 441.2
calmly ordering the w. . . 479.3
Lord and Master of the w. . 480.3
trust . . . the w. of the day . 484.2
ever shared, for ever w. . 496.1
I bring my w. affection . . 504.1
the w. of love's demands . 512.2
possess it w. . . . 516.2
the w. of sin remove . . 568.1
fortify the w. . . . 695.3
for my w. life, I come . . 860.4
not a fragment, but the w. . c32
b *Rom 8:22*
the w. creation join . . 57.4
were the w. realm of nature . 136.4
c *whole heart*
yield thee the w. of my h. . 422.1
Christ takes the w. of . . . h.. 447.4
yield thee the w. of my h. . 543.2
d *whole [soul]* *1 Thess 5:23*
let our w. s. an offering be . 217.3
only thou possess the w. . 497.1
sanctify the w. . . . c50
e *whole world* *1 John 2:2**
the w. w. redeeming . . 298.1
the w. wide w. shall come . 700.3
atoning for a w. w.'s sin . 785.3
Christ for the w. wide w. . 829.*
that the w. w. might see . c89
f *Isa 54:5*
the w. wide earth . . 826.1, 4
2 *(sound)*
banish, and bid me be w. . 422.3
plunge . . . you shall be w. . 427.2
I long to be perfectly w.. . 436.1
bade me be w. . . . 467.3
b *make whole*
it m. the wounded spirit w. . 58.2
descend and m. me w. . . 215.1
m. guilty sinners w. . 230.1
soul, he'll m. thee w. . 253.c
blood . . . m. perfectly w. . 273.3
can m. my spirit w. . 297.1
cleansing the soul, m. it w. . 329.c
healed my disease and m. me w. 380.2
come and m. me w. . 419.6
which m. the wounded w. . 425.4
here and now it m. me w. . 434.5
cleanse and m. me w. . . 511.3
claim the power to m. me w.. 513.2
Lord Jesus, m. me w. . . 723.4
doth cleanse and m. it w. . 798.1
c *make fully whole*
in . . . love to be m. f. w. . 273.4
all I need to . . . m. me f. w. 344.1
come . . . to be m. f. w. . 448.2
weary soul to be m. f. w. . 469.1
saved . . . m. me f. w. . . 499.1
speak and m. me f. w. . . 528.c
d *Matt 9:22*
straightway she was w. . 304.1
faith hath made thee w. . 304.3
e *Acts 9:34*
Jesus m. thee w. . . 98.4
Christ can m. you w. . . 232.3
the Saviour m. me w. . . 371.c
Jesus can m. them w. . . 384.3
whit

wholehearted 679.2

wholesome 924.2

wholly
I am thine, w. thine . . 128.3
till I am w. thine . . . 189.3
w. to thyself devoted . . 210.3
to be thine, w. thine . . 469.4
life shall be w. for thee . . 473.4
make me, Saviour, w. thine . 474.3
claimed w. for thee . . 484.3
w. thine . . . to be/to live . 509.1
from this day be w. thine . 743.1
w. lean on Jesus' name . . 745.1
we would be w. thine . . c101
sanctify (b)

whosoever see whoever

why
a *(as question)*
for w.? The Lord . . . is good. 3.4
w. should'st thou heed . . 91.3
w. should Christ be crucified 108.1
w. hangs he then on . . . tree 140.1
w. . . . wilt thou roam . 248.1
w. should we tarry/linger . 264.2
w. will ye scatter/wander . 265.1
w. was he there as . . . sin . 271.2
w. from his side . . . blood . 271.2
yet w. should I fear . . 303.3
w. do I languish and pine . 318.4
w. are my winters so long . 318.4
cottage, w. should I care . 354.4
w. should we distrust . 377.3
w. then one doubt . . . allow. 385.2
w. should life . . . seem. . 400.1
w. . . . my cross a burden . 400.1
w. are you doubting . . . still. 467.1
w. should I be a slave . 468.1
w. still delay 471.4
w. restless, w. cast down . 557.4
w. should I doubt . . . 732.3
w. should I be slow to plead . 770.3
when he calls us, w. delay . 772.4
w. longer in your sin remain . 885.4
w. will you doubting stand . 897.2
w. still delay 897.2
w. should I doubt or fear . 917.3
b *why not?*
saved, w. n. tonight . . 251.*
w. n. take it now . . . 255.1
w. n. come and say . . 255.4
w. n. now be free for ever . 471.4
w. n. speak my every need . 770.3
w. don't you try . . . c237
c *Eze 18:31*
w. perish, . . . sinner, w. . 107.1
will ye perish, w. . . . 693.2
d *(general)*
w. I long to be like Jesus . 94.2
that is w. I shout and sing . 390.3
know w. I love Jesus . . 404.*
this is w. I love . . . 404.c
all is known, and that is w. . 522.2
w. God's wondrous grace . 730.1
nor w. . . . he claimed me . 730.1
loved me, I cannot tell w. . c161
that's w. I'm singing . . c175
how (d), wonder (2b)

wicked 268.3

wide
love is as w. as creation. . 47.2
w. as infinity; so w. . . 55.3
his arms extended w. . . 107.2
the stair a very w. one . . 369.3
deep, 'tis full, 'tis w. . . 413.1
wave it w. 683.5
float there w. unfurled . . 697.2
sea be deep and w. . . 772.2
with banner w. unfurled . 798.2
those w. extended plains . 887.4
I sail the w. sea no more . c178
b *wide [world]*
w. as the w. . . . command . 4.4
it's as w. as the w. . . 49.c
upon a w.-w. cross . . 127.2
round the w. w. . . . ring . 158.2
a w.-w. jubilee . . . 593.1
the whole w. w. shall come . 700.3
w. is fair . . . and w. . . 711.1
w.-w. battlefield . . 774.1
ww. are the regions . 803.2
round the w., w. w. . . 814.1
the whole w. earth . 826.1, 4
Christ for the whole w. w. . 829.*

c *[open] wide*
mercy's gate o. w. . . 126.1
flung w. life's portals . . 130.3
the door hath o. w. . 165.3
o. w. the golden gates . . 167.1
swing w. the door . . . 227.*
fountain, o. w. . . . 540.1
Heaven's gate to o. w. . . 843.2
the gates will o. w. . . 884.*
the pearly gates are w. . . 901.3
o. your heart's door w. . . c15
far (g)

widely
w. as his mercy flows . . 17.3
your heart's door w. open . 241.c
w. the doors now I fling. . 457.c

wideness 265.3

widening 165.2

wider
w. than the human mind . 49.3
fit me for yet w. service . 531.4
w. fields our comrades reap . 922.1

wield
wonderful . . . w. his sword . 583.4
w. the Spirit's . . . sword . 609.3
faithfully your weapons w. . 694.5
sword of the Spirit . . . w. . 820.2

wild
places waste and w. . . 159.3
light . . . ways dark and w. . 175.3
while . . . w. winds blow . 280.2
life's w., restless sea . . 428.1
soul returning from the w. . 550.1
for w. confusion, peace . 569.3
canst hush the ocean w. . 598.2
through tempest w. . . 741.1
time's w. wintry blast . . 882.2
o'er the w. stormy deep . c178

wilderness
found me in the dreary w. . 340.2
in the w. he sought us . . 377.2
a home within the w. . . 476.1
in the pathless w. . . 937.3
I was wandering in the w. . c171
b *Isa 35:6*
in life's w. . . . thy gardens . 288.4
c *Matt 4:1*
fasting in the w. . . . 104.2

wilful 433.2

will
1 *(Divine)*
love sustains us in thy w. . 5.5
works his sovereign w. . . 29.2
to serve your holy w. . . 38.2
the beauty of your w. . . 38.4
let his w. enfold you . . 141.5
let thy w. . . . be wrought . 205.2
to your w. my w. is turning . 206.c
make his w. your choice . 227.3
my Saviour's righteous w. . 419.1
prove thine utmost w. . . 419.2
according to thy w. . . 441.3
thy w. to find . . . 449.c
make me after thy w. . . 487.1
devoted solely to thy w.. . 516.3
tell thy w., Lord . . . 531.1
henceforth thy w. pursuing . 534.3
vindicate thy gracious w. . 568.2
the impulse of his w. obey . 581.3
within the fabric of thy w. . 644.1
seek thy w. to understand . 644.2
until thy w. be understood . 644.4
seal us within thy w. . . 648.3
w. of his glorious Son . . 654.4
let thy love thy w. dictate . 692.4
I am to thy w. resigned . . 729.2
to make his w. my own . . 732.3
whate'er his gracious w. . 738.2
thy w. and wish . . . the best. 761.2
when his w. is your desire . 790.3
surely based upon thy w. . 827.1
the breathing of thy w. . . 839.4
all . . . serve his w.. . . 867.5
Father, if 'tis thy w. . . 877.3
where thy w. reigneth . . 927.4
ready . . . thy w. to see. . c99
b *do will* *(Eph 6:6)**
just to d. his w. entirely . 343.3
I . . . d. his blessèd w. . . 344.3
live to d. his w. . . . 391.3
while we d. his good w. . 397.1
d. my Saviour's w. . . 413.3
to d. the Master's w. . . 433.3
d. the w. of God . . . 451.c
to d. his w. my . . . reward . 451.4
to d. my Master's w. . . 472.2
to know and d. thy w. . . 586.3
on earth to d. thy w. . . 624.2
hourly, I may d. thy w. . . 628.2
teach me to d. thy w. . . 649.2
joy to d. the Father's w. . 683.1
to d. the w. of Jesus . . 752.2
early let us d. thy w. . . 845.4
let me d. thy w., or bear . 865.2
d. thy perfect w. below . . 919.3
just to d. my Master's w. . c35
best to d. thy holy w. . . c72
c *will done* *Matt 6:10; 26:42*
and yet: thy w. be d. . . 362.3
all his w. from being d. . 399.1
thy w. shall be d. . . 410.2
thy only w. be d. . . 509.3
thy w. be d., thy name . 526.3
God's w. be d. . . . 536.3
Father, let thy w. be d. . 595.3
help us . . . to d. thy w. . 624.2
hard . . . to say: Thy w. . 729.3
thy w. be d. . . . . 744.*
hard to say: Thy w. be d. . c95
d *Ps 40:8*
w. of God be all my joy . . 451.3
I shall delight in thy w. . . 457.2
I joy in his w. 640.2
e *Matt 26:39*
he prayed: Not my w. . . 179.2
hearts to say: Thy w. . . 704.2
f *John 6:38*
not my own, my Father's w. . 566.4
g *Col 1:9*
I may know the w. of God . 451.1
know no other w. but thine . 509.2
to know and do thy w. . . 586.3
I would know no w. . . 865.2
blessed (2f), Father (2h), fulfil (e), God (3e), obey (e), perfect (2i), speak (1e), teach (1e)
2 *(human)*
until with thee I w. one w. . 189.2
to your w. my w. is turning . 206.c
rests my cheerful w. . . 208.2
the wandering of my w. . . 425.2
all my w. conform to thine . 445.1
that my w. shall bow . . 446.3
let thy grace my w. incline . 460.3
wants to have no other w. . 480.2
my w. I here present thee . 504.2
I give you my w. . . . 506.2
my w. is not my own . . 508.3
take my w., and make it. . 525.5
my w. is the w. of my God . 542.c
conform my w. to thine . . 560.5
to have no w. but thine . . 584.2
my w. be lost in thine . . 585.2
a self-renouncing w. . . 596.2
pride ruled my w. . . . 606.2
the murmurs of self-w. . . 002.3
he claims my w. . . . 867.2
renew my w. from day to day. c95
b *will and . . .*
all my body, mind and w. . 188.2
give thee my body . . . and w. 221.2
now we lay . . . mind and w.. 481.2
take my memory, mind and w. 492.2
take my memory, mind and w. 520.2
springs of thought and w. . 665.4
mind and w. consecrating . 786.3
his claim on heart and w. . 867.1
heart and w. . . . are thine . 867.6
body, intellect and w. . . 871.1
all my w. and all my powers . c32
blend (b), resign (c), stubborn
3 *(verb)*
a *(God) wills*
what you w. I want to be . 206.c
make me what thou w. . . 291.2
ask what you w. . . . 294.2
ask what thou w. . . . test . 507.c
die if thou shouldst w. . . 532.3
just as thou w. and when . 612.7
lead me where he w. . . 731.c
b *1 Thess 4:3*
God hath w. his truth . . 1.3
God w. for his people . . 410.1
he w. that I should holy be . 419.1
God w., indeed, this . . 760.3
c *(we) will*
with thee I w. one will . . 189.2
my soul, ask what thou w. . 560.2
d *(other)*
tempt as ye w. 480.4
who(so)ever

willing
1 *(re divinity)*
his w. hands and feet . . 121.2
Jesus dies, a w. sacrifice . 126.3
our Saviour w. dies . . 131.4
gracious, w. guest . . 200.4
he is w. to aid you . . 823.c
much he was w. to bear . c24
2 *(general)*
may we with w. feet . . 76.2
may I be w. . . . to bear. . 117.4
now made w. to return . . 305.1
when w., the Spirit came in . 321.2
God gives his w. servant . 324.4
I w. am . . . to follow thee . 509.1
with w. service . . . 574.3
w. to suffer 623.3
thou hast made us w. . . 707.3
fire that makes me w. . . 830.3
b *willing heart* *Ex 35:5*
pledged again my w. h. . 591.3
thy w. h. to mark . . 683.3
follow as with w. h. . . 776.3
c *1 Chron 28:9*
a w. mind, a ready hand . 426.3

willows 39.3

win/won
1 *(God) wins*
rejoice, the fight is w. . . 146.1
the victor's triumph w. . 151.1
Heaven is w. today . . 155.1, c
it w. its widening way . . 165.2
w. for us by Jesus' merit . 210.1
death your life might w. . 242.3
Jesus, thou hast w. us . . 788.1
his eternal glory w. . . 916.3
b *win heart*
surpassing . . . w. my heart . 119.2
my poor h. he sought and w. 335.1
overcame and w. my h. . . 338.2
who hast died my h. to w. . 370.1

dying love has w. my h.. . c174
broke my heart, w. my h. . c209

c *love wins*
l. w. in the garden . . 51.c
w. them to him by l. . . 94.2
thy l. had w. me . . 534.1
l. must w. 744.6
by l. that we might . . . w. . 785.3
dying l. has w. . . . c174

2 *(we) win*
he conquered, we shall w. . 5.5
that life to w. . . . 100.4
great the conquests to be w.. 158.2
longing perfect peace to w. . 227.2
my days fresh triumphs w. . 413.4
the realms of Glory w. . . 500.3
pain thy smile should w. . 503.1
the treasure I might w. . . 541.2
I . . . wrestled to w. it . . 542.2
fought . . . and w. the race . 583.5
until, the harbour w. . . 628.4
or Heaven itself be w. . . 654.4
through grace I'll w. . . 678.c
others fight to w. . . 678.2
stand . . . w. the field . . 694.5
w. my Father's smile . . 706.3
rich the trophies to be w. . 776.1
the prize that you shall w. . 813.2
I believe we shall w. . . 820.c
we shall w. with the fire. . 820.5
for thy sake to w. renown . 860.5
until thy war is w. . . 864.c
till this . . . war is w. . . 869.4
they have w. to . . . day. . 878.1
he had meant you should w. . 893.2
when Heaven at last is w. . 912.3
the last great conflict w. . 939.3
you shall win . . . friend. . c146
we're sure to w. . . . c240

b *win the day*
we shall w. the day . . 693.3
w. the well-fought day . . 695.6
we're bound to w. the day . 782.2
but we shall w. the day . . c227

c *win the fight*
rejoice, the f. is w. . . 146.1
we who f. . . . shall w. . 532.2
power to w. the f. . . 541.1
I shall w. in the f. . . 543.3

d *win [souls]* *Prov 11:30*
many s. were w. . . . 198.3
spent in w. s. for thee . . 205.2
some wanderer sought and w. 524.3
how to w. the lost ones . 531.3
how hardly s. are . . . w. . 564.3
all the nations we shall w. . 593.4
captives to Jesus we'll w. . 687.1
patiently w. them . . . 691.4
other lives to w. . . . 755.1
others for him to w. . . 857.3
do my part to w. that s. . c79

e *win world*
forward . . . w. the w. . . 696.3
we'll . . . w. the w. . . 800.3
w. the w. for Jesus . . c136

battle (1d), crown (2b), victory (2f)

3 *(other)*
when temptations almost w. . 753.2
shall he . . . triumph w. . . 885.2

wind
1 *(noun)*
it varies with the w. . . 508.2

b
thou rushing w. 2.2
the cold w. in the winter . 25.3
in w. that drift the clouds . 31.1
when summer w. . . . breathing 39.3
among the w. at play . . 41.1
when the w. . . . swept. . 103.4
while . . . wild w. blow . . 280.2
though the w. may blow . 341.1
give the w. a mighty voice . 393.4
then w. may blow . . . 526.4
give to the w. thy fears . . 721.1
or . . . stay the w. . . . 854.1
tempers every w. that blows . c127

c *Matt 8:26*
w. and waves submissive . 569.2
whom w. and seas obey . 715.2
chided . . . hushed the w. . 848.3
the w. and waves obey him . 935.2

d *Acts 2:2*
like mighty rushing w. . . 196.3
no rushing, mighty w. . . 198.1
all-powerful as the w. . . 200.3
rushing of the mighty w. . 202.2
sound of rushing, mighty w. . 211.2
come as a mighty rushing w. 216.3
mighty w. are stirring . . 864.1

earthquake, stormy (b)

2 *(verb)*
treacherous road may w. . 176.3

winding
every w. of the way . . 7.4
thine to measure all its w. . 510.1
perils of the w. way . . 740.2
the w. trail . . . . 903.*

window *(Mal 3:10)* . . 920.4

wine 512.1

winepress *Isa 63:3; Rev 19:15*
beyond the brook his w. . 512.2
thou who hast the w. trod . 532.3

wing
1 *(noun)*
he made their tiny w. . . 25.1
angels with bright w. . . 268.1
clouds unfold their w. . . 280.1
each may be a w. to lift. . 421.5
if on joyful w. . . . 617.5
thy w. . . . petition bear. . 633.2

b *wings of faith*
on w. of . . . f. I upward fly . 369.1
rise on f.'s strong w. . . 749.1
give me the w. of f. . . 879.1
rise by f.'s exultant w. . 916.2

c *wings of love*
the w. of peaceful l. . . 217.5
as on w. of l. . . . fly . . 369.1
on w. of l. our souls . . 559.5
on the w. of l. we'll fly . 819.1

d *Ps 17:8*
beneath her w. recompense . 145.3
under his outstretched w. . 227.c
peace . . . sheltering w.. . 227.2
'neath his sheltering w. . . 390.3
'neath the shelter of thy w. . 517.4
repose beneath thy w. . . 632.3
beneath . . . almighty w. . 671.1
with the shadow of thy w. . 737.2
while hiding 'neath thy w. . 761.3
'neath his w. . . . hide you . 954.2

e *Ps 104:3*
on the w. of the storm . . 16.2

f *Ex 19:4; Isa 40:31*
on eagle's w. upborne . . 223.4
on eagle w. we soar . . 573.4
mount up with w. . . . c66

g *Matt 23:37*
gather you under my w.. . 331.2
gathers, spreads his w. . . 722.4

dove (b), heal (1b), morning (1d), outspread, spread (c)

2 *(verb)*
w. to Heaven our thought . 20.3
w. your flight 75.1
w. my feet and filled . . 534.1
w. my words 612.4
notes of triumph w. . . 803.1
up to Glory w. our flight . 809.4

wingèd *(adj)* 150.3

winning *(adj)* 519.2

winter
the cold wind in the w. . . 25.3
summer and w. . . . harvest . 33.2
see, amid the w.'s snow. . 88.1
on a cold w.'s night . . 90.1
why are my w. so long . . 318.4
w. and clouds are no more . 318.4
out of the wastes of . . . w. 378.2, 4
also for the w. tough . . 552.2
or w. from resigning . . 854.1
ere the w. storms begin . . 924.1
w., softened by thy care . 925.3
nor w.'s chilling breeze . . 930.2
he sends the snow in w. . 935.1
in w., in summer . . . same . c207

wintry 882.2

wipe-d *Isa 25:8; Rev 7:17*
w. from mine eyes the tear . 48.1
lives to w. away my tears . 144.2
w. away your tears . . 243.2
my tears are w. away . . 326.1
he w. away my tears . . 366.4
who will w. away my tears . 470.2
w. the weeping eyes . . 485.2
no tears to w. . . . 592.3
all tears are w. away . . 627.3
w. sorrow's tears away . . 743.3
for he will w. away all tears . 888.c
w. the tears from . . . face . 909.3

wisdom
1 *(divine)*
loving w. of our God . . 18.2
true w. can impart . . 100.2
freedom . . . w. increase . 166.3
w.'s deepest, clearest sea . 452.4
nor learned thy w. . . 466.1
Lord of all w. . . . 506.3
clothe me with w. . . 516.4
to thy w. I resign . . 566.3
grant us w. . . . courage . 577.*
my w. and my guide . . 597.2
learn the w. it imparts . . 654.5
w.'s loving ray . . . 682.2
his w. shall guard me . . 734.2
his w. ever waketh . . 736.2
w. shall the way prepare . 744.4
may we understand the w. . 856.3
thy w. guiding . . . 927.3
of light and w. the fount . c98

b *Prov 4:11*
in w.'s ways proved . . 910.2

c *wisdom and power* *1 Cor 1:24*
thy w. and thy p. . . . 415.3
God of w., grace and p.. . 576.1

d *Jas 3:17*
inspire with w. from above . 196.4
I want thy w. from above . 455.3
strength and w. from above . 795.2

e *wisdom and might* *Rev 5:12*
all w. and m. . . . 24.3
Trinity, w., love, m. . . 224.4
God of w., love and m. . 498.4
God is your w. . . . m. . . 773.3

2 *(human)*
with w. kind and clear . . 212.2
no w. of my own . . . 325.2
though I have w. . . . 530.2
urge his claims with w. . . 832.3

b *1 Cor 3:19**
or seek in human w. . . 6.2

its w., fame and power . . 223.2
not boast . . . in human w. . 747.2

wise
things w. and wonderful . 25.c
by thine all-w. command . 39.1
he lives, my w. . . . friend . 144.3
O then, be w. . . . 251.2
so w. a Counsellor . . . 345.4
w. in knowing thee . . 466.1
through . . . watching, w. . 485.2
with . . . war grown w. . . 799.3
make me steadfast, w. . . 837.3
w. may bring their learning . 849.1
share the virtue of the w. . 871.3
b *wise men* *Matt 2:1*
w. m. worshipped . . 74.2
story that the w. m. . . 80.3
eastern w. m. bring gifts . 89.2
three w. m. came . . 90.3
entered in those w. m. . 90.5
when w. m. came seeking . 92.1
the w. and holy m. . . 96.1
c *Prov 11:30*
be w. the . . . soul to win . 683.6
d *Matt 11:25*
with the w. to give rest . . 527.3
truths . . . hidden from the w. 839.5
e *1 Tim 1:17*
God only w. 8.1
consider (b)

wiser-st
O w. love 18.3
mercy holds a w. plan . . 723.2
w., stronger, . . . becoming . 842.4

wish-es
1 *(noun)*
in every w. and thought . 415.5
w. and feeling brought . . 416.1
quicken each inner w. . . 493.2
speak out thy w. . . . 513.c
one w. alone, God's will . 536.3
thought and w. and senses . 540.3
where all my w. meet . . 556.4
do the w. of my heart go . 588.1
all my wants and w. known . 633.1
one their w. . . . prayer . . 661.1
thy will and w. . . . best . 761.2
2 *(verb)*
w. that you were happy . 244.3
nothing to w. or to fear . . 318.2
'tis all I w. to seek . . . 636.4
I would not w. to know . 644.2
w. to be often there . . 646.1
I w. that his hands . . 794.1
w. you'd gone forward . . 893.2
if you w. to go to Heaven . 913.1
I w. them there . . . 917.1
ripened souls we w. to be . 926.4
by w. and thinking . . 928.3

wistful
my w. heart said faintly . 548.2
cast a w. eye . . . 887.1

withdraw-n
prayer makes . . . cloud w. . 646.2
though every comfort be w. . 746.4
b *Isa 60:20*
moon no more will be w. . 275.2

wither-ed-ing
never-w. flowers . . . 898.1
b *Ps 90:6**
we . . . w. and perish . . 8.3
c *Joel 1:12*
though joys be w. all . . 746.4

withhold-eld
the sun w. his rays . . 107.2

the breath of man . . . w. . 171.2
clay . . . am I, nothing w. . 416.4
nothing from his altar I w. . 420.4
so long w. by me . . . 482.1
nor should I aught w. . . 524.1
not a mite would I w. . . 525.4
naught to w. from thee . . 861.1
b *Ps 84:11*
what else can he w. . . 560.2

within nc, but
a *2 Cor 7:5*
war without and fears w. . 284.3
fightings w. and fears . . 293.3
all without and all w. . . 431.4
foes without and foes w. . 468.1
turmoils without, w. . . 615.1
conflict, without and w. . 640.2
trials without and w. . . 904.3
fightings without and fears w. 915.2
b *Ps 103:1*
makes all w. me rejoice . . 318.2

without
1
thy pity w. end . . . 123.3
believe on him w. delay . . 231.3
as I am, w. one plea . . 293.1
not w. hope, I mourn . - . 305.1
yet loves me w. end . . 311.4
come, w. delaying . . 348.3
w. rest, in my breast . . 379.3
joy w. alloy 391.c
come to him w. delay . . 433.1
love w. a limit . . . 439.1
there are souls w. bread. . 527.1
w. his anointing and seal . 527.2
w. love 'tis empty show . 530.2
w. a rival reign . . . 563.4
like them, w. a word . . 567.2
give blessings w. number . 575.1
words w. the heart . . 588.3
w. merit or pretence . . 595.2
w. a hope to cheer . . 683.5
w. committing sin . . . 714.2
I will go w. a murmur . . 731.c
the birds w. barn . . . 763.2
give him worship w. end . 785.6
richest gifts w. them . . 849.3
join us then w. delay . . 869.2
b *without [God]*
life is dark w. thee . . . 40.4
I could not live w. him . . 65.3
life is naught w. thee . . 152.3
I could not do w. thee . . 325.*
what . . . life w. him . . 399.2
not worth living w. him . . 420.2
he that w. thee builds . . 605.2
w. thee how could earth . 654.4
w. thee I cannot live . . 676.3
w. thee I dare not die . . 676.3
w. the sunlight of thy face . 726.3
w. God as architect . . 827.3
aid (b), cease (d), fear (3h), money
2 *(outside)*
w. a city wall . . . 133.1
the storm may roar w. me . 736.1
within

withstood 286.2

witness-er
1 *(Divine)*
a *(to Jesus)* *Heb 10:15*
thou W. of his dying . . 191.3
W. of Jesus' merit . . 295.3
b *(to us)*
w. thou hast died for me . 140.2
with . . . light thy w. bear . 207.4
thy sacred w. bear . . . 219.3
he the w. gives . . . 423.5
let the Holy Spirit w. . . 474.3

c *1 John 5:8*
w. with the blood . . . 756.1
d *1 John 5:10*
keeps the inward w. right . 113.1
not darken his w. within . 166.4
constantly w. Jesus loves . 323.3
I want the w., Lord . . 441.3
his w. is within . . . 496.4
the w. in himself he hath . 756.4
e *Rev 3:14*
true w. of my sonship . . 207.3
2 *(general)*
join . . . in manifold w. . . 33.2
w. for Jesus, I am fully his . 352.c
w. here that Jesus saves . 385.1
w., from all sin set free . . 407.6
thy faithful w. will I be . . 526.4
w. from soul to soul . . 546.3
let me thy w. live . . . 597.4
thy blood-besprinkled w. . 629.1
to work or to w. . . . 640.3
w. where the dawning glows. 776.1
we are w. for Jesus . . 832.*
do some w. for Jesus . . 832.c
there is w. in the Army . . 869.3
our w. would we raise . . 944.1
I w. that I'm born again . . c173
b *Heb 12:1*
the long cloud of w. . . 879.5

woe
a *(divine)*
eye is dimmed with w. . . 121.2
thou didst feel . . . w. . . 607.2
drink his cup of w. . . 701.1
b *(general)*
doth seek to work us w. . . 1.1
child of sorrow and of w. . 66.1
flee from w. and danger. . 73.2
w. of sin and strife. . . 83.2
w. of life o'ertake me . . 112.2
present . . . in all our w.. . 127.2
to vanquish sin . . . and w. . 134.c
joy, for all its former w. . . 167.2
never a weight of w. . . 186.2
our emptiness and w. . . 217.2
sin and w. are done away . 268.1
all my sins . . . and my w. . 333.1
the bitter from life's w. . . 333.2
my soul . . . filled full of w. . 348.1
filled my life with w. . . 401.2
Christ, our w. dispel . . 558.3
every swelling tide of w. . 573.1
so by my w. to be nearer . 617.4
healing . . . for human w. . 638.1
we share our mutual w. . . 660.3
homes of want and w. . . 697.3
to Hell's endless w. . . 703.1
days of joy, or days of w. . 711.3
as it falls on paths of w.. . 758.4
mankind in need and w. . . 777.2
nor can its happiness or w. . 880.2
in pleasure or w. . . . prepare. 904.4
who in affliction's w. . . 910.3
gladness or w. will spring . 928.2
bearing all my w. . . . c219

woeful 177.2

woke see wake (2a)

wolves *(John 10:12)*
the w. have sore hurt thee . 111.2
w. devour thy fold . . . 172.5

woman
that made a w. cry . . 91.1
fall from w.'s eyes . . 830.1
b *Isa 49:15*
can a w.'s tender care . . 110.3

womb 82.2

won see win

wonder-s
1 *(divine)*
its store of w. untold . . 16.3
his w. to perform . . 29.1
his hand the w. wrought . 42.1
mighty w. there I see . 348.c
Jesus saves me! O the w. . 350.2
such a marvel of w. . . 395.2
two w. I confess . . 476.2
give us a day of w. . 575.1
O w. of w., to God . 640.2
day of w. . . . 875.1
w. of w., I shall be there . c251
b *wonder of*
of all the w. of thy power . 171.2
the w. of his name . . 869.3
c *wonder of love*
glories . . . w. of his l. . 84.3
the w. of his matchless l. . 215.2
what a w. that Jesus l. . 323.4
the w. of his glorious l. . 476.2
d *wonder-working* *Dan 6:27**
there's a w.-w. power . 257.c
power, w.-w. power . 281.c
mighty, w.-w. river . 471.c
thy w.-w. blessings pour . 940.3
e *Heb 2:4**
by mighty signs and w. . 945.3
grace (3c)
2 *(human)*
our w. . . . when Jesus we see 22.3
when I in awesome w. . . 37.1
kneel in awe and w. . . 73.3
shepherds with w. receive it . 139.1
w. how he could love me . 179.1
can you w. that I want . 335.*
w. at the love that found . 370.4
lost in w., love . . . 438.3
now I am stirred to w. . 529.3
all bewildered with w. . 542.1
routing the foe in . . . w. . 686.4
can I w. I have faltered . 770.2
tell me, in accents of w. . 848.3
w., men drew near to see . 939.2
b *wonder why*
gaze and w. w. Jesus died . 94.3
we w. w. . . . . 274.*
do you w. w. I always sing . 388.4
can you w. w. it is . . c211
c *Ps 71:7*
I'm a w. unto many . 338.4

wonderful
in all his words most w.. . 18.1
all things wise and w. . . 25.c
the gift most w. . . . 52.1
that w. redemption . . 98.2
for w. peace he brings . 227.c
w. words of life . . . 258.*
w. power in the blood . 281.*
thy w., life-giving flood . 298.5
love wrought the change so w. 340.2
what a w., w. day . . 371.1
because of that w. day . 371.3
w. message of mercy . 384.3
still flows the w. river . 384.3
on that w., w. day . . 386.*
what a w. change . . . wrought 394.1
w. is the peace . . . power . 406.c
thou w. sin-bearer . . 448.1
how w. it is/'twill be . 583.*
w. Healer, touch me again . 610.*
his friendship is so w. . 851.5
what a w. sight . . 908.*
w. place called Calvary . . c29
by thy w. power . . . c39
all his w. passion . . c77
'tis w. to know/walk/dwell . c143
joy, joy, w. joy . . . c184
w. gift from above . . . peace c197
w. home he has gone . . c251
b *wonderful [Jesus]*
w., w. J., in the heart . . 186.c
a w. Saviour is J. . . 329.c
my w., w. Saviour . . 342.*
a w. Saviour is J. . . 710.1, 2
I've found such a w. Saviour . c155
O what a w. Saviour . . c156
this w. Saviour, he's mine . c162
won my heart; w. J. . . c209
for you and me; w. J. . . c214
w. Saviour, w. friend . . c251
c *Isa 9:6*
publish . . . his w. name. . 24.1
d *wonderful love*
God's l. to me is w. . . 48.*
w. that he should give . . 48.c
O it was/is w. l. . . . 114.*
w. story of l. . . . 139.*
how w. is my Saviour's l. . 179.c
his w. l. proclaim . . 184.1
l. unbounded, w., deep . . 184.2
w. l. he has promised . . 264.3
a w. l. it must be . . 289.1
God's l., so w., matchless . 319.1
I'll tell of his w. l. . . c217
w. l. that never will end . c251
e
w. things in the Bible . . 323.1
story (1b)

wonderfully 265.6

wondrous
tell of his w. faithfulness . 26.2
Jesus is the w. theme . . 70.c
O w. melody . . . 72.6
all his w. childhood . . 87.3
we saw a w. light . . 88.3
w. star, lend thy light . . 89.3
a w. attraction for me . 124.2
when I survey the w. cross . 136.1
with his w. voice . . 227.3
w. Deliverer . . . 257.4
the cross has w. glory . . 320.3
when w. words . . . say. . 398.1
w. peace through trusting . 413.4
the blood, O w. river . . 434.5
there flows a w. river . . 471.1
how w. is my treasure . . 502.3
most w. your ways . . 506.1
w. change, . . . victory . 541.3
w. Sovereign of the sea . . 598.2
to share that w. heritage . 613.3
thy w. doings heard . . 677.4
redemption's w. plan . . 831.c
city . . . so w. fair . . 833.2
Jesus dwells; O w. place . 888.2
redemption's w. plan . . 952
the w. light of God . . c160
b *wondrous gift*
the w. g. is given . . 86.3
thy w. g., O Lord . . 742.1
build, with all thy w. g. . 827.3
what w. g. are in my care . 871.1
c *wondrous love*
O w. l. . . . . . 45.*
'twas l., 'twas w. l. . . 46.c
God's w. l. in saving . . 78.3
thy w. l. has conquered . 108.3
what w., w. l. . . . dying l. . 128.2
my redeemer and his w. l. . 180.1
Jesus died, O w. l. . . 242.c
O w. l. . . . . 243.*
l. of l. so w. . . . 250.1
what w. l. 253.2
great compassion and of w. l. 272.2
O w. l., to bleed and die . 284.5
w. l. . . . I receive . . 322.2
w. l. reached me . . 342.c
O what w. l. . . . 347.2
unmoved by Jesus' w. l. . 379.2
w. l. without a limit . . 439.1
to proclaim thy w. l. . . 463.1
thy w. l. declare . . 524.2
I'm happy in his w. l. . . 811.c
riches of his w. l. . . 858.3
sing the w. l. of Jesus . . 892.1
tell of all his w. l. . . 907.3
d *wondrous power*
felt God's love and w. p. . 215.1
by thy love's w. power . . 469.4
to sing his w. power . . 583.3
thine is such w. p. to save . 741.1
all thy w. p. flowing . . c60
e *wondrous story*
'tis the Lord! O w. s. . . 104.c
I read the w. s. . . . 123.2
I will sing the w. s. . . 180.2
w. s. of the Lamb . . 326.4
I will sing the w. s. . 337.1, c
how w. is the s. . . . 363.2
never a s. so w. . . . 384.2
O the w. s. . . . . 546.*
w., w. s. 803.4
f *Psalm 72:18*
who w. things hath done . 12.1
grace (3c)

wondrously
so w., saved from sin . . 315.2
w. saving from sinning . . 640.1

wont
our path when w. to stray . 654.1
b *Acts 16:13*
praise is w. to rise . . . 661.3

wood-lands
when through the w. . . 37.2
fairer the w. 177.2
farmland, field and w. . . 544.1
blossom and w. . . . 927.1

woo-ed-ing
he w. and won them . . 94.2
w. them to God again . . 212.3
w. us to Heaven . . . 258.2
how hardly souls are w.. . 564.3

wool *Isa 1:18* . . . 272.1

word
1 *(divine)*
a *John 1:1*
fresh from the W. . . . 35.1
O W. invisible, we see thee . 36.3
was the mighty W. . . 141.1
God's Word made flesh . . 181.1
w. of God and inward light . 194.1
come, thou incarnate W. . 219.2
dies with thee, O W. divine . 512.3
pants for thee, O living W. . 650.1
b *word of God* *(Rev 19:13)**
quickening w. of G. . . 26.2
'tis the w. of G.'s love . . 119.2
G.'s own w. . . . sealed . 126.3
on G.'s w. relying . . 222.1
by G.'s w. . . . I learned . 405.2
the w. of G. can never fail . 407.3
w. of the ever-living G. . 654.4
the w. of a pardoning G. . 724.3
by the living w. of G. . . 757.2
trusted G.'s great w. . . 760.4
so the w. of G. declares . 932.1
I believe in the w. of G. . c130
c *(general)*
one little w. shall fell him . 1.3
that w. above all . . . powers. 1.4
all his w. most wonderful 18.1, 4
w. of Bible 30.3
men who waited on thy w. . 36.2

thy w. alone true wisdom 100.2
his w. dispel the darkness . 126.4
Jesus' w. is glorified . 165.3
new w. impart that echo . 211.1
here in his w. he's shown . 235.1
the sweets of Jesus' w.. . 312.1
w. with heavenly sound. . 319.2
glorious gospel w. declares . 385.1
take his w., and Jesus . 385.2
when wondrous w. . . . say . 398.1
through thy w. . . . stand . 437.3
view of Jesus and his w. . 442.2
thy w. is clear . . . 449.2
helpless I cling to thy w. . 454.2
feed on his w. . . . 458.1
shines from your w. . . 506.3
teach thy w. . . . Lord . 531.1
'tis the promise of his w. . 554.4
from thy lips his w. . 595.1
speak thy conquering w. . 609.3
give power unto thy w. . 626.3
now honour thy w. . 637.3
more . . . thy w. declares . 642.1
concealed within thy w.. . 650.3
laid . . . in his excellent w. . 653.1
Lord, thy w. abideth . 655.*
Spirit breathes upon the w. . 657.1
thy w. is like . . . 658.*
w. restores the light . 672.2
wait thy w. of peace . 674.1
supported by thy w. . 678.4
w. he has spoken . . 712.2
sacred w. is passed . 714.2
who dare thy w. receive. . 714.2
w. with . . . comfort fraught . 725.1
revealing . . . through the w.. 730.3
whisper w. of comfort . 731.2
the honour of his w. . 735.1
triumph in thy w. . . 741.3
the promise of his w. . 760.1
his (her) devotion to thy w. . 796.4
this w. it reaches nations . 824.2
its w. are peace and life. . 830.2
taught to read his w. . 834.2
each whisper of thy w. . 839.3
w. full of kindness . . 848.2
the grace your w. imparts . 856.4
life . . . is in that w. . 877.1
how shall I love that w. . 877.4
thy w., from error free . 941.3

d *hear word*
thy Saviour, h. his w. . 110.1
w. chaos and darkness h. . 224.1
I h. thy w., my Saviour . 562.3
w. . . . waves submissive h. . 569.2

e *living word* *1 Peter 1:23*
camest . . . with the l. w. . 101.3
brought to me the l. w. . 398.2
shows forth the l. w. . 494.2
the true and l. w. . 561.4
for thee, O l. W. . . 650.1
the Scriptures' l. w. . 656.2
strangers to the l. w. . 697.3
by the l. w. of God . 757.2

f *at word*
at his w. Hell disappears . 243.2
I took him at his w. . 339.2
at thy w. they gave up all . 789.5

g *Isa 40:8*
w. cannot be broken . 157.1
w. Hell disappears . . 243.2
the w. . . . can never fail . 407.3
thy w. is sure . . 642.3
thy w. is sure . . 761.3

h *Isa 55:11*
no w. . . . fruitless fall . 558.5

i *Matt 8:8*
say but the w. . . 456.1
speak but the w. . . 507.3

j *John 17:17*
thy holy w. the truth . 650.2

abide (i), according, believe (c), cast (h), dwell (3b), every (e), faithful (1c), flesh (d), fulfil (1f), give (1y), glorify (1d), grace (3d), gracious (2c), holy (2b), increase (d), life (2d, g), light (4g), obey (c), power (4r), preach (a), precious (g), rest (2e), sacred (d), speak (1f), sweet (3j), swiftly (b), trust (4d)

2 *(human)*
praise in the common w. . 7.2
no w. of man can ever tell . 68.4
w. that help and heal . 212.1
can't express by w. alone . 215.3
no w. shall needed be . 421.4
there is meaning in my w. . 463.1
my w. and thoughts receive . 492.1
some clear, winning w. . 519.2
ease aching hearts with w. . 529.3
whispered w. . . . 544.3
without a w. rise up . 567.2
guide my w. aright . 568.1
grace to live the w. we say . 572.1
go with the w. I say . 588.1
a prayer of w. alone . 588.2
w. without the heart . 588.3
wing my w. 612.4
kindling thought and glowing w. 612.6
surveys . . . thy w. and ways. 665.2
thought or speech a w. . 682.3
pass the w. along . . 698.c
speak the w. of comfort. . 706.1
w. which thou . . . give . . 727.5
misinterpret . . . w. you say . 790.2
the tribute of our w. . 853.3
my lips, that purest w. . 867.4
strange their w. . . 939.2
may every w. here spoken . 943.3

deed (d), season (b)

work-ed-ing
1 *(divine)*
w. his sovereign will . 29.2
scan his w. in vain . 29.6
read the secrets of your w. . 38.1
care thou to thy w. . . 39.1
when he first the w. begun . 165.2
worthy is the w. of him . 165.3
let thy w. in me be done . 188.c
thy w. . . . all the earth . 198.3
Jesus can restore his w. . 267.3
thy w. alone . . . can ease . 297.3
saved by the w. he has done. 319.c
confirms the blessèd w. . 423.4
w. on in me thy . . . will. . 446.4
thy w. to do, thy help . 581.1
varied the w. of thy hand . 644.2
fix on his w. thy . . . eye. . 715.3
Master whose w. . . . known. 739.1
what a w. the Lord has done. 769.1
thy power has w. to meet . 926.1
the harvest is thy w. . 926.2
thy truth . . . thy w. declare . 926.3

b *Ps 145:10*
all thy w. . . . surround thee . 10.2
all his w. adore . . 155.1
all thy w. shall praise . 220.4

c *mighty works* *Mark 6:5*
for m. w. . . . wrought . . 5.2
m. w. or mightier name . 26.1
most m. your w. . . 506.1

d *John 14:12*
try his w. to do . . 133.5

e *Phil 1:6*
the w. is complete . . 454.3
finish . . . this w. of thine . 531.4

f *work of grace* *(Rom 11:6)*
when the w. of g. is done . 110.5
then be the w. of g. begun . 251.4
what thy g. shall w. in me . 287.3
deepen in me thy w. of g. . 649.2

g *work of love*
l.'s redeeming w. is done . 143.2
l.'s atoning w. is done . . 261.4
l. w. silently 530.c

h *Gal 5:6*
faith that w. by love . 733.1

begin (1b), consider (a), do (2d), revive (c), wonder (1d), wrought (b)

2 *(human)*
who doth prosper thy w. . 19.2
w. and receiving . . . wages . 352.2
w. with little fervour . 466.4
w. for thee . . . 484.*
a w. of lowly l. to do . 485.5
slow are my hands to w. . 488.2
w. that keeps faith sweet . 519.3
have I w. for hireling wages . 522.2
I can w. and wait . . 522.2
some w. of l. begun . 524.3
finished my w. . . . mount . 543.4
w. till daylight softens . 564.4
speed thy w. . . . 683.4
w. for victory . . . 696.3
lonely w. he cannot shirk . 801.2
w. till Jesus calls . . 818.*
with us the w. to share . 825.4
when my w. seems hard . 837.5
for those who w. today . 856.2
our outward w. begin . 863.2
our w. on earth is done . 907.3
we would w. with thee . 927.2
filled up with grateful w. . 933.2
w. . . . we gladly share . 941.3
w. for Jesus . . . c215

b *work and . . .*
alike at w. and prayer . 187.1
heart's desire to w. and speak 199.3
now to watch, to w., to war . 345.3
to w. or to witness . 640.3
worthily in w. and play . 675.2
both to w. and play . . . fight. 869.1
praise and w. . . . are one . 878.5
filled with both w. and war . 933.3

c *all my work*
a. m. best w. are naught . 416.3
of a. m. w. . . . the aim. . 516.5
a. m. w. is for the Master . 522.c
let a. m. w. . . . wrought . 568.1
offer a. m. w. to thee . 667.2
a. our w., confirmed . 863.3

d *Matt 5:16*
men may see the w. I do . 518.3

e *Gal 5:6*
the faith that w. by love. . 733.1

f *not of works* *Eph 2:9*
nor yet good w. . . . atone . 269.3
not by the w. that we do . 319.c
or my w. is nothing worth . 522.3
w. . . . can never buy . 555.4
failure every w. of mine . 555.4
our w. is all in vain . 943.2

g *Col 1:10*
fruitful in good w. for thee . 933.1

h *2 Tim 2:15*
of my w. . . . not ashamed . 484.3

do (1b), faith (2l), good (3c), work (1g), wrought (c)

3 *works of evil*
doth seek to w. us woe . . 1.1

b *Rom 13:12**
the w. of darkness fail . 198.4
w. of darkness put away . 408.1

c *1 John 3:8*
Satan's w. destroy . 195.2
destroy the w. of sin . 448.4

4 *(other)*
sickle w. has found . 926.3
will w. out God's sentence . 928.1

workers *(Matt 9:38)* . . 482.1

working *(adj)*
the Christ of w. days . . 618.2

workman *2 Tim 2:15* . . 688.4

works 688.3

world
1 *(general)*
in whom his w. rejoices . . 12.1
filled the new-made w. . . 34.3
this is my Father's w. . . 42.*
changing in the w. today . 49.2
throughout the w. . . . known 55.3
that the w. would taste . . 60.4
the w. in . . . stillness lay . 83.1
the w. has suffered long . 83.2
joy to the w. . . . . . 84.*
he rules the w. with truth . 84.3
his w.-embracing heart . . 127.2
a w.-wide cross . . . 127.2
who spake a w. from naught 165.3
over the w. victorious . . 184.3
power to walk the w. . . 203.3
through the w. . . . light . 224.4
why Christ came into the w. . 274.*
he's in the w. today . . 334.1
the wealth of the w. . . 354.1
the w. may ever see Christ . 479.3
the w.'s great need I see . 482.1
wherever in the w. . . 485.5
around me in the w. . . 489.2
w. so filled with sorrow . . 576.2
wash the w. in . . . fountain . 593.4
the w.'s tempestuous sea . 607.1
with the w., myself and thee. 671.2
through the w. our way . . 676.6
the w. shall be given . . 681.2
forth into the w.'s highway . 683.6
till the w. is possessed . . 684.4
vaster than the w. has seen . 776.3
the w. shall yet belong . . 782.3
fill the w. with glory . . 801.c
onward to conquer the w. . 802.c
till the w. is full of joy . . 807.3
joy to be had in this w. . . 808.2
make the w. with music ring . 809.1
as through the w. we go . 814.3
will start the w. along . . 815.1
the w. to his feet . . . bring . 820.5
w. with . . . ring . . . 821.1
there's salvation for the w. . 821.*
turn the w. from darkness . 821.2
Christ for the w. . . . we bring 825.*
build a glad, new w. . . 827.4
the w. for God . . . 830.*
tell the w., O tell the w.. . 832.c
a w. which is to be . . 833.1
tell the w. in song . . . 835.1
O beauteous w., how part . 874.2
before the w. confessed . 876.1
means to lead the w. . . 901.5
in this w. we suffer loss . 912.1
tell the w. . . . cleansing . c47
fill the w. with music . . c220
the w. is needing us . . c239
to the end of the w. . . c243

b *all the world*
let a. t. w. . . . sing . . 11.*
a. t. w. of power/speed . 30.*
streameth over a. t. w. . 40.2
a. t. w. may now go free . 128.4
if a. t. w. . . . may live . . 140.2
come, a. t. w. . . . 234.2
that a. t. w. might know . 261.4
love for a. t. w. is shown . 324.1
in a. t. w. around me . . 334.2
though a. t. w. forsake . 344.2
to a. t. w. I dare avow . . 440.4
leaving a. t. w. behind . 470.2
though a. t. w. forsake . 498.c
through a. t. w. her watch . 677.2
a. t. w. his Kingdom . . 866.3
a. t. w. is . . . field . . 924.2
must a. t. w. the harvest . 932.2
feels for a. t. w. . . . c83
more than a. t. w. beside . c216
till a. t. w. praises . . c226

c *Matt 24:14*
on a. t. w. to call . . . 62.5
send . . . tidings to a. t. w. . 279.1
a. t. w. may Jesus know . 500.2
as we to a. t. w. unfold . 656.4
through t. w. resounding . 693.c
command to go into t. w. . 700.1
we tell to a. t. w. . . 798.2
a. t. w. shall hear us . . 815.3
a. t. w. to save . . . 821.c
take Jesus to a. t. w. . . c22
a. t. w. there is cleansing . c47

d *Matt 5:14*
t. w. may know I'm thine . 538.5
t. w. shall always see . . 793.6
within t. w. to glow . . 838.1

e
from all ills in this w. . . 12.2

f *(Heaven)*
when that w.'s glory . . 98.4
there is a better w. . . 268.1

around (b), below (c), field (2c), foundation (c), Jesus (8g), kingdom (1i), light (2e), love (2i), save (1j), upside, whole (1e), wide (b), win (2e)

2 *[sinful] world* *Rom 3:19**
w. divided by selfishness . 6.3
gav'st him for a w. undone . 15.3
loved the w. of sinners . . 46.1
in this w. of sin . . . 86.3
to such a w. as this . . 88.4
for a w. of lost sinners . . 124.1
a fallen w. like this . . 414.2
for the lost w.'s sake . . 482.3
toiled . . . for the w. astray . 680.2
to a w. of rebels dying . . 693.2
o'er a faithless, fallen w. . 697.2
to cheer a w. of sorrow . . 706.1
strayed . . . (and thus the w.) 785.3
frontiers of a stricken w. . 864.4
a w. at random drifting . . 868.3

dying (3d)

b *dark world* *Eph 6:12*
in the w.'s d. ways . . 173.1
I am this d. w.'s light . . 332.3
pass from this d. w. . . 356.3
in this d. w. to shine . . 649.4
makes a world of d.ness . 657.3
the w.'s d. night . . 683.4
peace, in this d. w. of sin . 752.1
in the w. is d.ness . . 841.1
d.ness in this w. abound . 841.3

c *(worldly spirit)* *(1 Cor 2:12)**
this w., with demons filled . 1.3
best in this w. is decaying . 51.2
this w.'s empty glory . . 98.4
cross, so despised by the w. . 124.2
a w. that loves not thee. . 135.2
let the w. deride or pity . . 157.3
the w. will oppose you . . 233.2
master o'er my sin, the w. . 303.4
a w. of shifting values . . 324.3
take the w. but . . . Jesus . 343.c
what the w. may do or vow . 402.c
vain w.'s golden store . . 428.3
void the w. can never fill . 442.3
the w. rushes on . . . 458.2
the w.'s delight and cheer . 460.2
great the w.'s attractions . 461.2
empty is the w.'s enjoyment . 470.1
content to let the w. go by . 476.3
this short-enduring w. . . 480.4
let the w. despise . . . 498.3
spurning . . . w.'s enticing . 500.2
to lose the w. I can afford . 513.3
all the w. holds dear . . 564.2
converse...w. has never known 564.2
that the w. may . . . smile . 586.2
calls me from a w. of care . 633.1
is this vile w. a friend . . 678.3
leave the w.'s side . . 707.1
the w.'s illusions try . . 780.1
than this w.'s bidders have . 796.2
leave the w. behind us . . 836.2
the w. is ever near . . 862.2
safe from the w.'s temptations 889.2

d *John 15:18*
though . . . w. should hate us. 805.3
though all the w. oppose . 814.2

crucified (2a) overcome (c, d) unspotted (b)

worlds *Heb 1:2, 11:3*
w. beyond our sight . . . 27.5
consider all the w. . . . made. 37.1
rules through all the w. . 104.6
'midst flaming w. . . . 116.1
through all the w. above . 223.3
soar to w. unknown . . 302.4
to fairer w. on high . . 314.3
brighter w. above . . . 657.4
Lord of all nations, w. . . 957

hang (b)

worldling 157.3

worldly
unversed in w. ways . . 163.2
w. honours all forsaking . 320.2
hollow joys, w. toys . . 379.3
w. pleasures all forsaken . 474.2
stoop to w. happiness . . 497.3
farewell to w. pleasure . . 502.3
renouncing every w. thing . 517.4
ease and w. scheming . . 693.1
'twixt w. joys and thee . . 749.1
pride, and w. folly . . . 783.4
amid the w. strife . . . 791.2
seek not w. ease . . . 816.3
away from w. loss and gain . 872.2
in whatever w. state . . 916.1

worm *Ps 22:6* . . . 105.1

worn
weary and w. and sad . . 332.1
to the weary and the w. . 697.5
sin-sick and sorrow-w. . . 825.1

worry c145

worship
1 *(true)*
w. him in humbleness . . 2.5
w., honour, power . . 109.3
we w. thee, O Crucified . 135.1
and w. only thee . . . 442.5
teach us when we w. . . 575.2
let this time of w. . . . 599.1
grant us to w. at thy shrine . 624.5
there they w. him . . . 663.2
ere our w. cease . . . 674.1
give him w. without end . 785.6
with joyful hearts we w. . 795.1
we w. and adore thee . . 870.4
in silent w. I confess . . 871.1
we will walk and w. ever . 891.2
in this house may w. thee . 941.3

b *Ps 95:6**
come and w., w. Christ . . 75.*

c *Ps 96:9**
w. the Lord in the beauty 183.1, 5
I w. . . . in the light . . 640.5

d *Zech 14:16*
O w. the King, all glorious . 16.1

e *(at nativity)*
shepherds, wise men w. . 74.2
who was w. by the angels . 96.1
shepherds came to w. him . 855.1

2 *(false)*
w. of the vain world . . 428.3
w. gods of stone . . . 588.2

worshippers 161.3

worst
powers . . . have done their w. 151.2
the w. of Adam's race . . 266.4
hide not the w. . . . 457.1
help him save the w. . . 704.3
the vilest and the w. . . 919.2

worth
Jesus' name has matchless w. 63.2
I love to sing its w. . . 69.1
no saint . . . w. can tell . 69.3
the soul's enduring w. . . 181.4
streams of richest w. . . 312.2
something w. saving . . 319.1
it is not w. living . . . 420.2
who the w. of love can tell . 497.4
love thee for the . . . w.. . 515.2
or my work is nothing w. . 522.3
knows the w. of prayer . . 646.1

worthier
dwelling-place, and w. thee . 200.7
bring a w. gift to Heaven . 618.3

worthily
that I may serve thee w. . 488.3
w. set forth his praise . . 533.1
b *Eph 4:1**
have I walked w. . . . 675.2

worthless-ness
empty, purposeless and w. . 399.2
ah, how w. they appear . . 460.2
my own w. 476.2
will he own my w. name . 735.4

worthy
a *(re divinity)* *Rev 4:11, 5:12*
w. the Lamb that died . . 57.2
w. the Lamb . . . reply . . 57.2
Jesus is w. to receive . . 57.3
proclaim its w. praise . . 68.c
most w. of a sceptre . . 72.1
thou art w. to receive . . 109.3
w. is the work of him . . 165.3
sound . . .: W. the Lamb . 223.3
w. is our Saviour-King . . 897.1
b *(re humanity)* *Rev 3:4**
w. through his blood . . 431.c
made w. by thy grace . . 461.4
c *(other)*
once I thought most w. . 435.2
noble deeds and w. strife . 867.3

worthwhile 706.3

wound-ed
1 *(re divinity)*
five bleeding w. he bears . 106.3
thy w. they are deep . . 111.2
what is this w. . . . side. . 111.2
the w. my sin decrees . . 122.1
for me thy w. . . . intercede . 122.3
w. hands of Jesus . . . 129.c
thy flowing w. supply . . 132.4
those w., yet visible . . 156.4
in his feet . . . w.-prints . 228.2
from the Saviour's w. side . 239.3
stands with his w. hands . 260.2
shows his w. 286.4
in flowing w. appears . . 368.2
to those dear w. I flee . . 368.2
to dwell within thy w. . . 424.1
the Saviour's w. side . . 540.1
the w. of Jesus, for my sin . 746.1
still extends his w. hands . 880.3
b *wounds make*
thy w. m. me love thee . . 111.3
w. . . . were m. for thee . 237.c
w. . . . were m. as he died . c89
c *Isa 53:5*
sacred head once w. . . 123.1
w. for my transgressions . 137.2
the stripes which w. thee . 151.5
thou w. Lamb of God . . 424.1
2 *(re humanity)*
makes the w. spirit whole . 58.2
the w. soul to cure . . 81.3
sin's w. to lave . . . 135.4
a balm for each w. . . 252.3
all your wants and w. . . 254.4
no w. hath the soul . . 364.3
sovereign balm for every w. . 382.1
which makes the w. whole . 425.4
w. and weary, help me . . 487.3
weakened by many a w. . 553.2
scan the very w. . . . 558.4
cleanse thou the w. . . 647.2
w. spirits need thy care . . 702.3
contented . . . w. be theirs . 774.2
b *Ps 109:22*
here bring your w. hearts . 236.1
c *Ps 147:3*
it binds up the w. . . . 237.2
d *heal wounds* *Jer 30:17*
soothes . . . h. his w. . . 58.1
when bleeding h. thy w. . 110.2
h. my w., broken spirit . . 301.3
I was w. and he h. me . . 330.2
w. thy tender hands had h. . 534.1
healer of w. 628.2
that will the w. h. . . 704.2
h. the w. . . . the fallen . . 724.1
3 *(verb)*
Jesus, thy w. is tender . . 457.2
who shall w. or . . . pluck . 555.1
friends may w. you . . 790.2
Satan's arrows w. . . 806.1
oil for my w. c148

wove see weave

wrapped
w. in ease and . . . scheming. 693.1
b *Luke 2:7*
w. in swathing bands . . 93.4

wrath
his chariots of w. . . . 16.2
can my God his w. forbear . 286.1
my Father's w. is o'er . . 361.3
b *Matt 3:7*
flee from the w. . . . 321.4
c *Rev 6:17*
summoned . . . w. to see . 875.3
d *Rev 16:19**
where the grapes of w. . . 162.1

wreck-ed
towering o'er the w. . . 112.1, 5
all my life was w. . . . 390.2

wrestle-ed-ing
strugglings and w. be o'er . 454.1
struggled and w. to win it . 542.2
they w. hard, as we do now . 879.2
b *Gen 32:24*
w. on in mighty prayer . . 210.4
w. and fight and pray . . 695.6
by prayer let me w. . . 712.1
O w., watch and pray . . c76

wrestlers 612.3

wretch-ed
a *Rom 7:24*
that saved a w. like me . . 308.1
lead the w., lost . . . home . 802.2
b *Rev 3:17*
poor, w., blind . . . 293.4

write/written/wrote
my name is w. on his hands . 106.1
over every promise w. . . 303.4
prophets w. and spoke . . 651.2
mercy is all that's w. . . 746.3
so long as 'tis w. . . . 763.2
w. it on your banners . . 813.c
it is w.: Whosoever . . 824.1
w. on God's memory . . 850.4
w., guarding and translating . 856.1
thy promise is w. . . . 883.2
b *Jer 31:33; Heb 8:10*
w. on my heart every word . 99.1, c
w. . . . name upon my heart . 444.5
w. thy law upon my heart . 446.3
w. the pardon on my heart . c128
c Luke 10:20; Rev 21:27
find my name is w. there . 59.4
my name's w. down . . 354.3
is my name w. there . . 883.*
he w. my name down . . c189

wrong
the din and toil of w. . . 31.1
w. seems oft so strong . . 42.3
Christ will triumph over w. . 74.3
two thousand years of w. . 83.2
fears to quell, w. to right . 126.2
griefs for all our w. atone . 127.1
w. shall be ended . . . 166.2
sinners may relinquish w. . 249.1
they force me to w. . . 298.3
will w. desires destroy . . 408.4
Lord, if I am w. . . . 409.5
the power to master w. . . 432.2
trust that triumphs over w. . 519.3
heart that broods on w. . . 572.2
opposing the w. . . . 681.1
the powers of sin and w. . 700.1
wherever w. is found . . 705.1
where they combat w. . . 803.2
who forgives the w. . . 835.1
free from . . . power of w. . c157
life is not all w. . . . c201
refusing the w. . . . c210
b *conquer wrong*
what is w. to c. . . . 193.5
daily c. sin and w. . . . 816.4
we mean to c. w. . . . 821.3
c *do wrong*
them that did the w. . . 701.2
when I'm tempted to do w. . 837.3
d *all that's wrong*
part with all that's w. . . 431.2
all that's w. . . . manifest . 446.1
all that's w. to sever . . 502.c

wrought
men have w. confusion . . 6.4
his hand the wonders w. . 42.1
let thy will in me be w. . . 205.2
sins which I have w. . . 287.2
could have w. such a marvel . 395.2
thou hast w. its chain . . 508.2
grace is w. in quietness . . 615.4
believing . . . w. peace . . 730.2
b *wrought work* *Isa 26:12**
he alone the work hath w. . 165.3
work of faith hast w. . . 407.4
here let thy work be w. . . 416.1
fully he the work hath w. . 721.4
c *Heb 11:33**
works through weakness w. . 5.2
work with little fervour w. . 466.4
all my works . . . w. in love . 568.1
d *Eph 1:20*
God's salvation w. . . 174.2
he w. so great salvation. . 341.3
change (2b)

wrung 127.2

Y

yawning 151.4

year
rolling y. shall cease . . 4.4
thank thee for the fruitful y. . 5.2
our hope for y. to come . 13.1
two thousand y. of wrong . 83.2
with the ever-circling y. . 83.3
the y. of his labours . . 99.2
distant y. in Palestine . . 142.2
rise for every fighting y. . 163.3
waited, days and y. . . 250.2
shadowed my pathway for y. 288.1
joyless and useless for y. . 298.4
there ten thousand y. . . 308.4
I was saved y. ago . . . 321.2
y. are fleeting fast . . . 325.4
not . . . y. of time alone. . 349.c
wasted y., doubts and fears . 379.2
this through countless y. . 400.3
y. I spent in vanity . . . 405.1
you have waited many y. . 433.1
fears for future y. . . . 551.2
the y. will fleet . . . 551.3
goodness through the y. . 552.1
so shall added y. fulfil . . 566.4
remember not past y. . . 606.2
grave of y. gone by . . 753.3
long and warring y. . . 774.1
portion through the y. . . 795.3
halt the progress of the y. . 854.2
journey through the y. . . 874.1
from beyond the y. . . 874.2
the fret of mortal y. . . 878.3
dedicate this new y. . . 916.1
ere this time next y. . . 933.4
through another y. . . 937.1
many y. of blessing . . 939.1
the y. so gladly given . . 939.3
thine our y. . . . shall be. . 939.5
all through the y. . . . c147

b *sins of years*
though s. of y. rise . . 253.3
washed all away s. of y. . 321.2
s. of y. are all numbered . 893.1

c *all the years*
all the changing y. . . 6.1
hopes . . . of all the y. . . 86.1
all our broken y. . . . 131.2
summer . . . all the y. . . 318.2

d *endless/eternal years*
to e. y. the same . . . 13.3
will e. y. enrol . . . 70.1
promised from e. y. . . 88.1
while e. y. . . . run . . 559.3

crown (3b)

yearn-ing
a *(God) yearns*
him who with love is y. . . 73.3
thy . . . mercies y. to save . 135.4
his kind Spirit did y. . . 388.2
thy y. pity for mankind . . 594.1

b *(we) yearn*
satisfy my spirit's y. . . 206.1
in my breast rose the y. . . 379.3
I y. for them, not thee . . 547.2
thou wilt teach my y. heart . 586.3
restless spirits y. for thee . 602.3
all the y. of my heart . . 614.3
let the y. of my soul . . 630.2
each y. purpose springs . . 682.2

yellow
y. stands for fire . . . 777.3
fiery y., emblem . . . 783.3

blue

yesterday
I lost them y. 41.1
through the years of y. . . 552.1

b *Heb 13:8*
in my y. I proved them . . 324.4
y., today, forever . . . 750.c
the same today as y. . . c163

yet nc, but
a *not yet*
it is not y. too late . . 267.2
not y. my Saviour known . 720.3
God never y. forsook . . 738.3

b *Heb 2:8*
not y. we hail the day . . 163.4

c *(still)*
y. deeper do I ponder . . 94.3
wounds, y. visible above . 156.4
y. wider service . . . 531.4
higher and y. higher rise . 834.3
a y. more glorious day . . 876.5

room (b)

d *(re time)*
power will y. prevail . . 149.3
o'er all he y. shall reign . . 362.1
which y. I have not seen . 736.3
the world shall y. belong . 782.3
might must y. appear . . 871.4
generations y. to be . . 941.3
glories we may y. behold . c44
greater triumphs than . . . y. . c44

yield-ed-ing
1 *(God) yields* *(Matt 27:50)*
y. up the gift of life . . 5.3
who y. his life . . . 22.1
King . . . didst y. the glory . 174.1
his name y. . . . perfume . 318.2

2 *(we) yield*
when all to thee shall y.. . 163.4
lo, we y. thee adoration . . 185.4
heart must y. its praise . . 591.1
conquer, and never to y. . 686.c
stand . . . and never y. . . 809.3
in the . . . conflict never y. . 817.2
y. is sin 823.1

b *yield [to Christ]* *Rom 6:13-19*
I y. upon my knees . . 122.4
y. to his love's . . . power . 234.4
nay, but I y., I y. . . . 307.4
y. to Jesus crucified . . 343.3
Master, I y. to thee . . 416.4
waiting y. and still . . . 487.1
when I had fully y. . . 549.2
I y., my will to resign . . 553.3
y. up my soul to thy care . 589.5
y. my flickering torch . . 621.2
I y. my residue of days . . 644.1
I y. my powers . . . 672.3
y. to the law of love . . 732.3
y. . . . their contrite hearts . 802.3
I would y. that heart . . 865.1
y. gladly to thee . . . c55

c *yield all/whole*
I y. to thee my little all . . 108.3
I have y. my all . . . 119.3
I y. thee the whole . . . 422.1
y. thee up my all . . . 448.c
all . . . I y. to thee . . 524.4
I y. thee the whole . . . 543.2
gladly I y. thee my all . . 786.2

d *yield life*
take/mould the l. I . . . y. 531.1, 2
to thee our l. we gladly y. . 692.1
our lives we gladly y. thee . 870.4

3 *(other)*
hate at last must y. . . 63.2
the iron fetters y. . . . 81.2
y. to the Saviour's day . . 776.2

b *Heb 12:11*
fruit unto his praise to y. . 924.2
y. in return for toil . . . 933.1

yoke *Matt 11:30*
take his easy y. upon you . 343.3
to bear thy easy y.. . . 667.3

yon-der
with y. sacred throng . . 56.5
a voice from y. manger . . 73.2
let us hasten y. . . . 73.3
y. shines the infant light . 75.2
who is he in y. stall . . 104.1
who is ye on y. tree . . 104.4
behold him now on y. tree . 108.1
why hangs he . . . y. tree . 140.1
escape to y. mountain . . 239.2
sinner, see y. light . . 260.1
y. shines the light . . . 641.3
roll is called up y. . . . 907.*
in the blood of y. Lamb . . 909.2

yore
forget the . . . days of y. . 551.2
the evil days of y. . . . 724.c
fought in days of y. . . 866.1

young
proclaim their y. hosannas . 160.2
ever new, and ever y. . . 559.3
may y., eager spirits obey . 575.2
y. souls meekly striving . . 849.2
a y. man walked . . . died 855.3, 4
friend of the y. . . . 860.1
just as I am, y., strong . . 860.3

b *young/old*
tell it to the y. and . . . o. . 829.3
teachers, o. and y. . . 834.3

c *Acts 2:17*
the y., the o. inspire . . 196.4

youth
lasts when y. has faded . . 544.3
y. obeys her trumpet call . 799.2
upward into y. . . . 842.4
Lord of my y. . . . 861.*
call upon us in our y. . . 863.1
rise up/forward/arm . . . y. . 864.*
the brightness of my y. . . 867.5
the y. of every land . . 868.1
the torch of y., uplifted . . 868.3
claiming y.'s allegiance . . 868.3
y. is learning how to pray . 869.1
y. is called . . . urgent call . 869.2
y. proclaims its fight begun . 869.4
let y. obey your calling . . 943.3
courage . . . hope of y. . . c238

b *Ps 103:5*
he renews my y. . . . 373.3

c *Eccles 12:1*
trust him in your y. . . 836.4
the glad days of y. . . 857.1, c
these glad days of y. . . 870.3

youthful
let my y. heart be thine . . 865.1
y. hands to build my city . 868.2
in their y. days found . . 910.2

Z

zeal

1 *(divine)*

grant . . . the marks of thy z.. 484.1
would find thy z. . . . in me . 594.1
love . . . a z. like thine . . 720.5
his z. inspired their breast . 879.4

2 *(human)*

could my z. no respite know . 302.2
have I the z. I had . . . 409.4
Lord, give the z. . . . 466.4
lack in compassionate z. . 527.2
my earnest z. be found . . 568.2
with calm and tempered z. . 568.2
set thou my z. aflame . . 574.3
the fervour of my z. . . 594.2
a calmly fervent z. . . . 720.2
we bring with loving z. . . 825.1
nor did their z. offend . . 853.1

b *zeal [inspire]*

inspired my early z. . . 463.2
with z. inflame . . . host . 609.2
my soul with z. inspires . 733.5
courage and z. . . . inspire . 734.3
strength . . . my z. inspire . 743.2

Zion

a *(Jerusalem)*

when . . . to Z. Jesus came . 853.1

b *(Heaven)*

Z., city of our God . . 157.1
Saviour, if of Z.'s city . . 157.3
cry to Z.: see thy God . . 159.2
Z. beams with light . . 682.1

c *Ps 137:3*

we'll sing the songs of Z. . c222

d *Ps 149:2*

none but Z.'s children . . 157.3

e *Isa 24:23**

reigneth on Z.'s . . . hill . . 853.2
led on by Z.'s King . . 901.4

f *Isa 51:11*

to Z.'s happy land . 901.1, 5
we're marching to Z. . . 901.c

g *Amos 6:1*

too long at ease in Z. . . 482.2

Concordance of Scripture in songs

MANY sub-sections in the Concordance are headed by Scripture references, because the songs illustrate that particular text or draw on its language (*Authorised Version*). Those texts are assembled here in biblical order, and you are referred to the appropriate sections in the main Concordance, or occasionally to whole songs or verses which paraphrase or clearly refer to the text.

As in the main Concordance, the sign * indicates that the text is a well-known representative of others which could have been chosen. Words are bracketed when they do not actually appear in the *AV* text, or when the connection between songs and text is less marked.

Old Testament

Genesis
1:2 (chaos)* darken (b) darkness (1b) Spirit (3c) void (b) water (1b)
1:3 light (1b, 4e)
1:26 image (a)
2:7 form (b)
2:15 Eden*
3:15 bruise (c) head (3b)
3:19 (dust (a))
5:24 walk (2c)*
6:3 strive (c)
6:4 (giants)
6:7 destroy (e)
8:22 harvest (1) time (1f)
11:9 Babel
17:8 Canaan*
19:17 escape (b) look (2h)
22:8 provide (c)
26:18 (well (1a))
28:10 Jacob*
28:12 angel (c) descend (2b) ladder
28:17 gate (f)
28:18 stone (2b) stony (b)
28:19 Bethel*
32:24 watch (2e) wrestle (b)
32:26 let (1d)
32:30 face (2f)
41:51 forget (c)
46:30 alive (b)

Exodus
3:5 ground (1b)
3:6 Abraham (a)*
3:8 honey*
3:14 I AM
4:12 say (2b)
7:20 smite (c)
10:11 man (2i)
13:21 pillar (a)
14:21 divide (b)
15:23 drink (a) Marah
15:25 sweet (2i)
16:15 manna*
19:4 eagle
20:3 gods
20:6 (show (1c))
20:7 take (3e)
22:29 first (1b)*
23:12 rest (4b)
25:16 ark*
25:17 gold (1c) mercy (2)*
32:26 who (b)
33:18 show (1j)
33:19 proclaim (d)
33:20 see (3n)
33:22 cleft cover (b) rock (c)
34:5 cloud (1b)
35:5 willing (2b)

Leviticus
6:9, 13 altar (b) burn (2b)
8:35 charge (b)*
9:24 consume (b)
17:11 atone (b)* soul (4e)
25:9 jubilee

Numbers
6:24-26 face (2h) gracious (2d) keep (3i) lift (1c) *Song 961*
21:17 spring (3b)

Deuteronomy
1:8 possess (3b)*
3:27 Pisgah (Moses)*
6:5 might (2b)*
10:17 gods
13:17 cursed
17:8 plea
20:8 faint (2b)
21:23 accursed
32:2 distil
32:3 (ascribe)*
32:6 requite*
32:11 outspread spread (c)
33:25 strength (2e)
33:27 everlasting (b) underneath

Joshua
1:5 (fail) (1a)* forsake (1a)
1:7 courageous
1:9 dismay (undismayed)
3:8 Jordan*

Ruth
2:12 under (b)

1 Samuel
1:9 Eli* temple (1b)
1:20 Hannah*
2:9 feet (1b) keep (3j)
3:2 priest (2a) (slept)
3:3 lamp (b) sleep (1b) temple (b)
3:9 servant (2b) speak (1g)
7:12 Ebenezer hither
17:47 (Jesus (6c))

2 Samuel
7:14 chastening
22:35 see Psalm 144:1

1 Kings
8:27 Heaven (2b)
8:30 forgive (1b) Heaven (3c)
8:56 fail (1b)
18:21 halt (2b)
18:38 fire (2c)
18:41 abundance (b) rain (b)
18:44 cloud (1c) hand (2c) small (c)
19:12 earthquake fire (1b)

2 Kings
1:10 fire (2c) Heaven (2i)
5:10 wash (2c)
6:16 more (2h)

1 Chronicles
16:23-36 see Psalm 96:1-13
28:9 willing (2c)
29:5 consecrate*

2 Chronicles
16:8 rely*
29:31 thank (b)*
32:8 flesh (c)

Ezra
9:6 blush

Nehemiah
2:4 Heaven (4b)
9:5 bless (2b) blessing (e) praise (3g)
9:17 slow (b)*
9:19 manifold (b)
9:26 cast (h)

Job
7:20 preserver
10:8 hand (1c)
10:9 clay (b)
19:25 redeemer (c)
20:8 dream (b)
22:5 infinite (c) iniquity (a)
23:10 know (1c) take (d)
26:7 hang (b)
35:10 give (1u) night (d)
38:7 star (d)
42:6 abhorring

Psalms
4:3 apart (b)
4:8 safety (b)
5:5 hate (b) iniquity (b)
5:11 joyful (b)
7:1 trust (3c)
8:1 excellent*

8:3 consider (a)
9:7 throne (3)
10:14 help (1b)
10:16 (King (2m))*
14:3 good (1b) goodness (b)
16:6 pleasant (b)
16:8 move (2b)* right (4d)
16:9 glad (d)
16:11 fulness (c) path (c) pleasure (2)
17:1 ear (2b)
17:3 prove (1b)
17:8 hide (d) shadow (e) shelter (c) wings (d)
17:15 face (2c) likeness
18:2 rock (1a)
18:11 pavilioned
18:18 stay (1a)
18:30 way (1b)
19:7 simple (b)*
19:12 secret (b)
20:4 fulfil (b)
21:4 length (a)
22:6 worm
22:11 help (1c)*
22:15 dust (b)
22:16 pierce (b)
23 *Songs 53, 54*
23:1 shepherd (1a)* want (2b)
23:2 lie (3b) pasture water (3a)
23:3 lead (3i) path (d) restore* (c) righteous (b) sake (1b)
23:4 comfort (1c) death (2b) fear (2c) rod (b) shade (f) vale (b) walk (2h)
23:5 anoint (a) cup (a) table
23:6 dwell (2f) ever (c) follow (1b) goodness (c) house (b) oil (a) presence (e) surely (b)
24:1 fulness (d)
24:3 ascend (b)
24:4 hand (2d)
24:5 receive (2b)
24:7 King (2h)
24:10 host (2b)
25:5 salvation (1c)*
25:7 remember (b)
25:14 secret (c)
27:8 face (2g)
27:11 path (3e)
27:13 see (3d)
28:7 dance (b) song (1c)
29:11 give (1v)
30:5 morning (1c)
31:6 see Luke 23:46
31:15 time (3b)
31:20 secret (d)
32:1 cover (c) transgression (b)
32:7 compass (b) deliverance (b) hide (e)
32:8 eye (1b) guide (1a)
32:11 glad (i) upright (b)
33:3 sing (2d)
33:18 eye (1c)
33:20 shield (a)*
34:1 bless (2a)*
34:2 boast (b) soul (2i)
34:4 fear (2e)*
34:7 around (c)
34:8 taste (b)
34:9 fear (1a)* want (2c)
34:14 pursue (b)*
34:18 canticle (c) near (2a)
35:18 congregation*
36:7 kindness (b)* river (2g)
36:9 see (3e)
37:1 fret*
37:3 commit (a)
37:4 desire (2c)
37:5 trust (3)*
37:7 rest (2d) soul (2j) wait (2b)
37:23 guide (1e) order (b)* step (2b)* way (1c)
37:24 uphold (a)
37:37 end (2i)
38:4 burden (2b) go (3d) heavy (b) too (b)
38:13 dumb*
39:4 frail
39:12 cry (3b)
40:2 clay (c) feet (1c) mire rock (2d)
40:8 delight (2b)* will (1d)
42 *Songs 448, 557 and 762*
42:1 fountain (2d) heat long (1c)§ pant
42:2 living (3b)* thirsty
42:3 day (4k) meat (a)
42:4 pour (2b)
42:5 hope (4b)* soul (1c)
42:7 billow deep (2b) wave (3c)
42:11 health (b)
43 *Song 457*
43:3 bring (1m) hill (3c) lead (3j) light (4f)
44:21 secret (e)
45:2 fairer (b)
45:3 sword (2b)
46:1 help (d) present (2b) (refuge (a)*) strength (2b) trouble (b)
46:4 stream (2a)
46:9 warfare (b)
46:10 still (1b)
48:2 earth (2b) joy (1b) king (2b)
48:12 tower (b)
48:14 guide (1a)
51:2 wash (2b)
51:6 desire (2d)
51:7 purge* snow (d) wash (3c)
51:9 renew (b)
51:10 clean (b) create (b)
51:12 joy (2b) restore (d) (uphold (b))
51:15 praise (3c)* show (2d)
51:17 contrite (b) spirit (5c)
54:4 helper
55:5 fearfulness
55:6 dove (b) rest (2i)
55:22 burden (2c) (sustain) (b)
56:8 tear (2b)
57:7 fix (b)
61:1 attend (b)*
61:3 shelter (b) tower (c)
61:5 vow (b)
61:8 perform (b)
62:2 defence*
62:11 belong (b)
63:1 early (b) thirsty (b)
63:5 praise (3d)
63:8 hard (b)
65:9 watered (a)
65:11 crown (3b) fatness goodness (d)
65:12 hill (3d) leap (3b)
65:13 vale (c)
66:9 hold (1b)
66:14 utter (b)
67:4 sing (4c)
67:6 increase (b)
68:16 hill (2d) leap (b)
68:19 benefit*
69:2 sink (b)
69:14 water (2b)
69:34 earth (e)
71:7 wonder (2c)
71:16 strength (2d)

§Prayer Book Version

72:5 sun (2c)
72:14 precious (h)
72:18 wondrous (f)
72:19 glory (4d)
73:24 counsel (b) glory (3a)
73:25 desire (2a)* earth (3b) thank (3d)
73:26 fail (2c)
76:10 (restrain)
77:19 footstep (b)
78:20 gushing
79:13 sheep (2a)
80:1 Israel (b)
81:11 hearken
84:7 strength (2f)
84:11 glory (4f) sun (1a) withhold (b)
85:6 revive (b)
85:9 dwell (1e)
86:2 soul (3b)
86:5 ready (b)
86:11 unite (1b)
86:15 compassion (d) full (1e)
87:3 glorious (2h)
87:7 spring (3e)
88:9 stretch (2b)
89:2 ever (d)
89:13 (mighty) (1f) (strong) (1d)
89:15 (sound) (b)
89:16 name (1n)
90 *Song 13*
90:1 dwelling (b)
90:4 sight (1c) thousand (1b) watch (3b)
90:6 wither (b)*
91:1 almighty (c) dwell (2c) secret (f)
91:4 feathers
91:7 thousand (2b)
91:9 high (1b)*
91.11 angel (d) charge (c) feet (1f)
91:12 hand (1d)
92:4 glad (1b)
93:1 majesty (b)
95:6 worship (1b)*
95:7, 11 see Hebrews 3:8-11
96:4 great (1a)
96:8 due glory (4e) offering (2b)
96:9 beauty (1d) holiness (c) worship (1c)
99:5 footstool*
100 *Songs 3 and 4*
100:2 endure (b) serve (1c)
100:3, 5 God (5c) good (2b)
100:4 court (b) gate (b) praise (3q) thankful
100:5 endure (b) God (5c) good (2b) truth (d)
102:1 hear (1c)
102:25 founded (a)
103 *Song 17*
103:1 soul (1d) within (b)
103:3 disease (b)
103:5 renew (d) youth (b)
103:8 plenteous
103:11 highest (b)
103:13 like (2d) (pity (2))*
103:14 dust (a) know (1d)
103:19 rule (2c)
104 *Song 8*
104:2 light (3b)
104:2, 3 build (1d) chariot wing (e)
105:3 glory (2b) (5c)
106:4 visit (b)
106:48 people (2c)
107:5 faint (c) hungry
107:9 longing (2d) satisfy (b)*
107:16 iron (a)
107:29 see Matthew 8:26
107:30 haven

107:37 fruit (1b)
109:22 wound (2b)
110:7 head (2b)
111:6 (show) (1d)*
116:13 cup (b)
116:14 people (2d) vow (c)
118:14 salvation (1b) song (1h)
118:19 open (d)*
119:17 bountiful*
119:25 (according)*
119:32 enlarge (b)
119:36 incline*
119:42 trust (4d)
119:50 quickening (b)
119:57 portion*
119:103 sweet (3j)
119:105 feet (1d) lamp (c) light (4g) path (f)
119:117 hold (1c)
119:174 long (1d)
121 *Song 767*
121:1 come (7b) help (1e) hill (3e) lift (2c)
121:2 earth (1f) make (3a)*
121:3 feet (1e) move (2c) suffer (1b)
121:4 Israel (c) slumber (2a)
121:5 keeper (b) preserve right (4e) shade (a)
121:6 day (2k) smite (b)
121:7 preserve soul (3b)
121:8 come (2e) go (2j)
124:4 (whelming)*
126:3 do (2c) glad (a)
126:5 sow (2b)
126:6 bring (i) come (6b) rejoice (f) sheaves (b) weep (2b)
127:1 build (b) (building) except (b) house (c) labour (b) vain (c)
129:2 prevail (e)
130:1 depth (b)
130:6 watch (2b)
130:7 mercy (g)
132:9 clothe (c)
136 *Song 34*
137:3 Zion (c)
137:5 forget (1d)
139:2 thought (2f) (uprising)
139:3 way (3e)
139:9 morning (1d)
139:10 hand (1e)
139:12 alike (b) light (1c) shine (3b)
139:18 wake (3b)
139:23 search (2b, c)
140:12 cause (c)
143:10 teach (1e)
144:1 fight (2g) fingers teach (1f) war (b)
145:1 blessed (2d) ever (e)
145:10 work (1b)
145:12 glorious (2e) majesty (c)
145:14 fall (2b)
145:17 bountiful§ way (1d)
146:7 loose (b)
147:3 wound (2c)
147:15 swiftly (b)
148:1 height (b) holiest praise (3r)
148:3 moon (b)
148:6 establish (b)
148:8 stormy (b)
149:2 Zion (d)
150:2 greatness (a)
150:6 breath (2b) praise (3s)

Proverbs

3:6 direct
3:15 (rubies)*
3:17 path (g)
4:11 wisdom (1b)
4:18 perfect (2b)
4:26 aright (b)§
6:6 consider (b)
6:18 swift (c)
7:2 (apple) eye (2f)
8:25 hill (3f)
10:6 head (2c)
11:30 win (2d) wise (c)
15:19 plain (2b)
18:24 brother (b)

Ecclesiastes

1:7 river (1b)
11:6 eve (b) sow (2c) stay (2c)
12:1 evil (e) youth (c)

Song of Solomon

1:3 name (1e)
1:7 rest (2j)
2:1 lily Sharon
2:4 banner (b) (banquet)
2:14 sweet (3g)
2:16 (ever) (a) mine (a) (thine) (a)
2:17 break (e) shadow (h)
5:9 fairest (b)
5:10 thousand (2c)
6:4 (terrible) (b)*
8:6 death (2d)

Isaiah

1:16 clean (d)
1:17 (relieve)*
1:18 crimson (b) red (b) scarlet sin (5a) snow (b) wool
1:25 dross
2:3 teach (1g)*
2:4 sword (a) war (1b)
2:5 walk (2f)
4:4 burn (1b)
6:1 (train) (1)
6:5 unclean* undone (1b)
6:6 altar (d) coal fire (2d) (flame (2c))
6:7 touch (1c)
6:8 send (1d) who (c)
7:14 Immanuel virgin
9:2 see (3e)
9:6 born (2a) counsellor prince (1b)
12:2 Jehovah (b)
12:3 well (1b)
16:14 (feeble) small (d)
22:23 glorious (2i)
23:16 melody (b)
24:4 fade (b)
24:14 lift (2d)
24:23 Zion (e)*
25:4 distress (2a)
25:8 wipe (a)
26:1 bulwark
26:3 keep (3k) mind (2d) perfect (2f) stay (2d)
26:4 rock (1b)§ strength (1b)
26:12 wrought (b)*
26:19 sing (4d)
28:12 weary (d)
28:17 line (b) plummet
30:14 spare (b)
30:15 confidence (1b) quietness strength (2g)
30:18 wait (1b)*
30:19 gracious (2e)
32:2 land (2d) rock (2d) shadow (i)
32:18 resting
33:17 King (2b)
33:21 glorious (1c)
35:1 desert (1b) rejoice (e)
35:3 feeble
35:6 desert (1b) lame (b) leap (c) wilderness (a)
35:10 (ransomed (a)*) sighing (c) song (1i)
38:10 residue
38:14 (undertake)
38:17 sin (5b)
40:1 people (1b)
40:2 end (2j) warfare (b)
40:3 highway (a)
40:4 mountain (2f) valley (d)
40:5 reveal (f)
40:8 word (1g)
40:9 (tidings) (b)
40:10 reward (b)*
40:11 arm (1c) carry (1b) flock (a) gently (b) lead (3j) shepherd (1b)
40:21 hear (2f) know (3f)
40:22 curtain
40:31 *chorus 66* eagle faint renew (e) wait (2c) walk (2h) weary (f) wing (f)
41:10 dismay fear (3d) right (4f) *Song 653:2* strengthen (a)
42:1 servant (1)
42:3 break (f) bruised (a) flax quench (c) reed smoking
42:7 darkness (2b)* sit (b)
43:2 overflow (b) *Song 653.3*
44:24 thing (2b)*
45:2 brass (a)* crooked
45:22 look (2d)
45:23 see Phil 2:10
46:9 like (2e)
46:13 bring (1k)*
49:13 sing (2e)
49:15 forget (2b) forgetful woman (b)
49:16 hand (1f) palm (a)
50:4 season (b)
50:7 confound (b)*
51:3 garden (2) gladness (b) place (3b)
51:11 Zion (f)
51:22 cause (d)*
52:7 feet (1b)
52:9 waste (b)
52:10 bare (2a)
52:13 extol
52:14 visage
53:3 acquainted despise (b) grief (1a) man (1b) reject (b) sorrow (1b)
53:4 afflicted bear (1d) carry (1c) grief (2a) surely (c)
53:5 stripe transgression (c) wound (1c)
53:6 astray lay (2b) like (1a) sheep (2b) stray (b)
53:7 lamb (1b) slaughter
53:12 bear (1e)
54:5 maker redeemer (d) whole (1f)
54:11 tempest (b)
55:3 sure (e)*
55:4 commander leader (1)
55:6 seek (2b)*
55:7 forsake (2c) (pardon (2b)) return (2b)
55:8 thought (2g)
55:11 word (1h)
55:13 sign (b) thorn (b)
56:5 everlasting (h) name (2b)
56:8 outcast*
58:1 voice (3d)
58:6 band (3b)
58:8 spring (3c)
58:11 garden (2) spring (3d) watered (b)

§marginal reading

§marginal reading in *AV*

59:11 short (b)*
59:16 arm (1d)
60:1 shine (1d)
60:18 gate (c) wall (b)
60:19 everlasting (f) light (2d)
60:20 more (5c) mourn (d)
sun (1c) withdraw (b)
60:22 thousand (1c)
61:1 see Luke 4:18
bind (1b, 2) captive (b)
(captivity) liberty (b)
(prisoner) proclaim (b)
61:3 ashes beauty (1f)
garment (a) oil (b)
61:7 joy (3b)
62:3 diadem royal (b)
62:4 Beulah
63:1 almighty (d) save (1h)
63:3 winepress
64:1 rend (b)
64:8 potter
66:12 river (2f)

Jeremiah
2:13 cistern drink (b)
fountain (1f) water (3b)
7:23 walk (2i)*
8:20 harvest (2b)
8:22 balm
10:10 King (2f)
12:5 swell (3)
18:3 wheel (b)
18:4 clay (d)
23:3 fold (1c)
29:13 seek (2h)
30:17 (healer)* wound (2d)
31:3 (eternal (2d))
everlasting (g) law (d)
31:10 keep (3l)
31:25 weary (c)
31:33 heart (7g) law (d)
people (2a) write (b)
31:34 remember (d)
32:17 hard (c)
33:11 bring (2g)*
45:3 find (2n)
45:5 great (2j)
48:40 fly (b)
50:5 covenant (b)
perpetual (b)

Lamentations
1:12 nothing (f) sorrow (1c)
3:22 compassions (f) fail (1c)
3:23 faithfulness* new (d)
3:25 seeking (2)
3:26 quietly
3:41 lift (2e)

Ezekiel
1:26 sapphire
16:14 comliness
18:31 why (1c)
21:27 right (1b)
34:14 pasture (b)
34:26 season (c) shower (b)
36:23 great (2g) sanctify (c)
36:26 new (e)*

Daniel
2:44 kingdom (1b)
6:27 wonder (1d)*
7:9 ancient (b) garment (e)
9:24 end (2b)

Hosea
1:10 seashore
6:2 sight (1d)
6:3 follow (2h)
6:4 early (c)
11:4 cord (b) draw (1b)
13:14 destruction
14:2 graciously turn (2b)*
14:4 anger (b) backsliding
freely (1b)

Joel
1:12 wither (c)
2:28 see Acts 2:16-21

Amos
4:11 burn (3b)
4:12 meet (3f) prepare (c)
6:1 (ease (b)) Zion (g)
7:7, 8 line (b) plummet
9:9 (sift)*

Jonah
2:7 faint (c)
4:2 gracious (b)*

Micah
4:3 sword (1a)
7:18 iniquity (c)
7:19 sea (2e)

Nahum
1:3 whirlwind
1:5 quake
1:13 burst (1b)

Habakkuk
2:4 see Galatians 2:20
3:2 revive (c)
3:4 hide (f)

Haggai
2:7 desire (1a)

Zechariah
2:5 fire (2e) wall (c)
3:2 brands fire (3b) pluck (b)
4:6 might (2c)
4:7 plain (1b)
4:10 despise (c)
8:19 truth (e)
9:9 King (2c) (lowliness (a))
lowly (2a) (ride (b))
9:10 shore (1b)
12:10 look (2c) pierce (1c)
Spirit (3d)
13:1 fountain (2a) open (c)
see (3e) stream (2a)
uncleanness
14:9 King (2d)
14:16 worship (1d)

Malachi
3:1 suddenly (b) temple (c)
3:2 refine (b)
3:3 gold (1d)
3:6 change (1a)
(unchanged (b))
3:10 blessings (b) bring (3c)
pour (1b) prove (3b)
storehouse (tithe)
window
3:17 come (i) jewel (b)
4:2 arise (1b) heal (1b)
sun (1b)
4:5 dreadful

New Testament

(When the key word appears in the same context in other Gospels this is indicated by M., Mk., L. and J.)

Matthew
1:18 birth (1)
1:21 save (1i)
1:23 see Isaiah 7:14
God (1e) name (1f)
2:1 east (b) wise (b)
2:2 star (e)
2:11 frankincense gift (1b)
gold (1e) myrrh
treasure (2b)
2:23 Nazarene
3:3 Mk, L, prepare (e)
3:7 L, flee (1b) (warning)
wrath (b)
3:11 L, fire (2a)
3:12 garner
3:16 Mk, L, (descend (1c))
dove (a) Spirit (5a)
3:17 Mk, L, beloved (b)
please (2b) well (2h)
4:1, 2 Mk, L, (desert (1c))
tempt (1) wilderness (c)
4:2 Mk, L, fast (2)
4:10 serve (1d)
4:19 Mk, fisher follow (2f)
4:24 divers Syrian*
5:3-12 *Song 95*
5:3 blessèd (1d)
Kingdom (1c) spirit (6e)
5:4 comfortless mourn (b)
5:5 meek (2)
5:7 mercy (h)
5:8 pure (2c) see (5d)
5:9 call (2f) children (2c)
peace (2e)
5:11 revile
5:12 L, exceeding glad (h)
heaven (3e) prophet (a)
reward (c)
5:13 L, salt
5:14 world (1d)
5:16 glory (4e) light (5b)
see (3i) shine (2a)
work (2d)
5:29 eye (2g) right (4b)
6:6 secret (g)
6:8 L, know (1e)
6:9 L, Father (1d) name (1g)
Song 624
6:10 earth (3c) Kingdom (1d)
will (1c)
6:11 bread (b)
6:12 forgive (1c)
6:13 deliver (a) evil (b) glory (4h)
Kingdom (1e) power (4l)
6:14 Father (1d) (trespass)
6:15 (unforgiving)
6:20 lay (3b) treasure (3b)
6:26 L (bird (c))
6:28 (lily (b)) raiment (a) *Song 871.2*
6:30 much (c) (small (e))*
7:7 L, ask (2b) find (2d)
seek (2g)
7:8 L, knock (a)
7:11 Father (1e) gift (1c)

7:13 broad (b) gate (d) (straight) (b) strait (1)
7:14 narrow (b)
7:24 build (c) rock (1c)
7:25 founded (b)
8:8 L, servant (2c) word (1i)
8:12 darkness (2c)
8:16 (sick (a, b))
8:19 follow (2g)
8:24 Mk, L, sleep (1c) (toss (a, b)) wave (3b)
8:26 Mk, L, calm (b)* (peace (2f)) sea (1e) wind (1c)
8:27 Mk, L, obey (e)
9:6 Mk, L, Son (1d)
9:8 such (2b)
9:12 Mk, L, physician
9:20 Mk, L, garment (b) hem
9:22 comfort (1d) daughter (b) faith (1d) whole (2d)
9:29 touch (1f)
9:31 Mk, fame (b)*
9:36 Mk, compassion (e) move (2d)* scatter (b)
9:37 labourer
9:38 harvest (2c) (worker)
10:8 freely (2b) heal (1c)
10:16 harmless
10:19 speak (2d)
10:22 Mk, end (2k) endure (c)
10:25 servant (2d)
10:28 body (2b)
10:31 sparrow (b)
10:32 confess (1b) (own (2a))
10:34 sword (2c)
11:5 raise (1b)
11:12 force (1b)
11:15 hear (3d)*
11:19 L, friend (1d)
11:25 wise (d)
11:26 seem (b)
11:28 come (4c) give (1s) (labouring) laden (b) rest (2l)
11:29 find (2m) learn (b) lowly (b) meek (1)
11:30 light (8b) yoke
12:13 Mk, L, stretch (2b)
12:20 see Isaiah 42:3
12:44 sweep (b)
13:3 Mk, L, sower
13:7 thorn (c)
13:15 close (1b)
13:24 sow (2d)
13:25 tare wheat
13:30 cast (c) gather (c) grow (3c) reaper (b)
13:32 branch (b)
13:38 field (2c)
13:39 harvest (2d)
13:41 angel (e) offence
13:42 fire (3c) wail (b)
13:43 shine (2b)
13:46 pearl (a)
14:19 Mk, L, bless (1e)* bread (c) loaves
14:24 toss (b) wave (3b)
14:25 Mk, walk (1c)
14:30 sink (b)
14:36 perfectly (b)
15:29 Galilee
16:6 beware
16:18 gate (e) prevail (f)
16:24 Mk, L, deny (b) follow (2f) self (2d) (take (3b))
16:26 gain (d, f)
17:1f *Song 154*
17:2 L, face (2h) garment (c) (transfigure)
17:3 Moses (b)
17:4 good (3c)
17:9 mountain (2c)
17:20 Mk, mountain (2d) remove (c)
18:8 everlasting (c)
18:11 L, save (2b)
18:12 L, seek (1b)
18:20 midst (b)
18:23f *Song 572.3*
19:6 join (c)
19:13 Mk, L, children (1b)
19:14 come (2c) such (1b) suffer (1c)
19:20 Mk, L, lack (b)
19:26 Mk, L, impossible
19:27 Mk, L, forsake (2b)
19:29 inherit
20:11 heat (b)
20:12 day (2j) heat (h)
20:16 choose (1b) few (c)
20:22, 23Mk, cup (c) drink (c)
20:28 Mk, ransom (a)*
21:8 Mk, L, branch (c) garment (d)
21:9 hosanna (a)
21:15 children (1c) hosanna (a)
21:17 Mk, Bethany*
22:9 highway (b)
22:37 soul (2k)
23:12 (abased)
23:19 altar (c) gift (1d)
23:27 spread (c)
23:37 L, gather (b) oft (b) wing (g)
24:14 world (1c)
24:29 shake (c)
24:30 Mk, sign (c)
24:31 Mk, gather (c)
24:35 pass (2e)
25:7 lamp (d) (trim)
25:15 (talent)
25:21 joy (3c) servant (2e) well (2j)*
25:34 blessed (2g) kingdom (1f)
25:35 *Song 518.2* stranger (2b)
25:43 (take (2b))
26:28 shed (2b)*
26:35 Mk, deny (c)
26:36 Mk, Gethsemane
26:39 will (1e)
26:40 Mk, watch (2c)
26:41 watch (2e)
26:42 will (1c)
26:53 angel (f)
26:58 Mk, afar (b)
27:2 L, Pilate*
27:29 Mk, hail (b) King (2e) reed (b) thorn (d)
27:35 crucify (1b) part (2c)
27:39 pass (2b)
27:42 Mk, cannot (a) other (2b)
27:45 sun (2e)
27:46 forsake (1b)
27:50 yield (1)
27:51 rend (c) (twain) veil (b)
27:60 tomb
27:66 seal (e) watch (3c)
28:1 first (1c)
28:2 angel (g) stone (2c)* tomb (b)
28:3 raiment (b)
28:9 meet (2c)
28:18 power (4m)
28:19 Mk, go (2k) *Song 760.1*
28:20 end (2m) (ever (f)) lo (a) *Song 732.3*

Mark

1:15 (repent)*
1:18 net
1:24 know (3g)
1:32 even (1b) set (d)
1:45 blaze (b) publish*
2:7 forgive (1d)
4:22 manifest (b)
4:28 blade ear (1) full (1g)
4:37 (storm (2a))
4:39 still (2b)
5:4 fetter (b)
5:15 reclothe (rightful (b))
5:19 tell (2c)
5:25f *Song 304*
5:29 straightway (b)
5:30 virtue (1b)
5:33 fear (2b) tremble (c)
5:36 only (1a)
6:5 work (1c)
6:8 staff (b)
6:31 apart (c) rest (2k)
7:37 well (2c)
8:29 (Jesus (7b))
8:36 profit (b)
8:38 ashamed (a)
9:2 show (1j)
9:23 possible
9:24 help (1b) unbelief (b) (unbelieving (b))
9:41 belong (c)
10:14 forbid (b)
10:15 (childlike)
10:16 (arm (1e))
10:28 leave (2c)
11:22 faith (1e)*
12:34 kingdom (g)
13:14 mountain (2e)
14:9 throughout (c)
15:29 Galilee* rail (2)
16:2 sun (2f)
16:10 mourn (c)
16:15 gospel (b)*

Luke

1:14 gladness (b)*
1:27 Mary (a)
1:32 child (1)*
1:33 end (d)
1:46 magnify*
1:47 rejoice (g)
1:48 estate (b)
1:49 do (2c)
1:51 scatter (c)
1:52 mighty (2d)
1:53 (hungry)
1:73 (sworn (b))
1:74 fear (3h)
1:75 holiness (d)
1:78 dayspring high (3d) tender (e)*
1:79 guide (1f)
2:4 Bethlehem* line (c)
2:7 manger room (d) (swathling) wrapped (b)
2:8 abide (2c) field (1b) flock (b) (sheep (1)) shepherd (2a) watch (2d) watchful
2:9 afraid (b) glory (5b) shine (1e)
2:10 fear (3e) tidings (c)
2:11 city (1b) David
2:12 baby (a)*
2:13 angel (h) host (3b) sing (2c)
2:14 glory (5b) goodwill peace (g)
2:16 hasten (b)
2:19 ponder (b)
2:25 consolation
2:30 eye (2k)
2:32 glory (4i)
2:46 doctors temple (1d)
2:49 (business (b))
2:51 Nazareth* obey (f)
2:52 (stature)
3:5 mountain (2f) (rough (b)) smooth (b)
3:6 see (3g)*
4:18 Isaiah 61:1 broken (2b)* bruise (b) captive (b) (captivity) deliverance fetter (c) free (1d) heal (1d) liberty (b) people (2b) poor (2a) prisoner sight (2d)

4:22 gracious (2c)
5:4 launch (b)
5:5 toil (2b)
5:17 present (2d)
5:28 rise (3c)
6:35 (kind (2a))
6:38 measure (b) press (d)
6:48 shake (b)
7:38 kiss tear (2c)
7:47 forgive (1h) love (7h) many (2b)
7:50 peace (2h)
8:6 rock (2f)
8:45 press (c)
9:23 daily (b)
9:51 set (f)
10:18 fall (3c)
10:19 (hurt)
10:20 write (c)
10:39 Mary (b)
10:40 cumbered
10:42 choose (2c) good (3d) one (4b) part (1c)
11:1 teach (1h)
11:4 sin (5c)
11:13 Spirit (4c)
12:12 say (2b) teach (1i)
12:19 (goods)
12:24 barn
12:32 fear (3d) pleasure (3b)
12:33 fail (1d)
12:35 light (5c)
12:49 earth (3d) fire (2f) kindle (b) (rekindle)
13:12 infirmity
13:16 (Satan (b))
13:24 strive (b)*
13:29 come (1b) east (seat (b)) sit (c)
13:34 under (b)
14:10 higher (c)
14:13 feast
14:17 feast ready (c)
14:21 halt (1)
14:23 compel (b)
14:27 bear (2b)
14:28 cost (b)
15:2 sinner (d)
15:4 find (1b) lost (3b)
15:5, 6 come (4j) rejoice (h) shoulder (b)
15:7 joy (1e)
15:10 angel (i)
15:12 (prodigal) (f)
15:13 (waste (b))
15:19 (unworthiness) (unworthy)
15:20 *Song 550.1*
15:24 lost (3b)
16:14 (deride)
16:26 gulf
17:5 increase (c)
17:33 lose (b)
18:37 pass (b)
19:5 haste (c)
19:7 (guest)
19:10 lost (2b) save (1c) seek (1c, 3b) (unsought)
19:40 (shame (3)) stone (2d)
19:41 weep
19:42 belong (d) know (2d)
19:48 (hang (c))
21:1 treasury (b)
21:2 cast (b) mite
21:26 (man (2f))
21:34 care (2e)
22:19 bread (d)
22:29 (appoint (a))
22:30 eat
22:41 kneel (1)
22:42 pray (1)
22:44 agony blood (2b) fall (3d)
22:63 mock (b)*
23:24 (sentenced)
23:28 weep (2c)
23:33 (Calvary (a))
23:34 forgive (1e) know (2e) pray (1) raiment (c) *Song 131.4*
23:39 (thief)
23:41 justly
23:42 remember (c)
23:46 commend hand (1g) spirit (2b)
24:15 draw (1d) Jesus (2c)
24:17 sad (b)
24:19 mighty (1g)
24:21 (third)*
24:25 slow (c)
24:29 abide (1b) (tarry (b))*
24:32 (talk (1))
24:34 rise (2e)
24:36 midst (c)
24:49 endue

John

1:1 beginning (b) life (2d) Word (1a)
1:4 Life (2d, e)*
1:9 true (1d)
1:12 give (1q) receive (2d) son (2c)*
1:13 born (1c)
1:14 dwell (1b) flesh (d) full (1d) truth (b)
1:16 fulness (a) grace (2f) receive (2c)
1:18 bosom (1b) Father (2b)
1:29 behold (d) Lamb (2b) take (1f)
1:41 Messiah*
1:50 greater (c) see (3h)
2:5 say (1d)
3:3 born (1b) man (2j) (reborn)
3:8 born (1d)
3:14 lift (3b)
3:15 eternal (2c)
3:16 because (a) everlasting (e) (gift (2b)) life (2f) love (2i) perish (b) so (3b) Son (1e) whosoever
3:17 save (1j) send (1e)
3:19 light (4h)
4:10 (gift (2g)) give (1x) water (3c, e)
4:11 well (1c)
4:14 (come (4d)) drink (d) spring (3d) thirst (2d)
4:35 field (2d) harvest (2e)
4:36 wage (2b)
4:42 Jesus (8g)
5:30 Father (2h)
6:27 meat (b)
6:35 bread (e) hunger (b)
6:37 cast (m)
6:38 Heaven (2h) will (1f)
6:41 bread (f)
6:50 die (1f)
6:51 bread (g) live (3b)
6:68 go (2l) life (2g)
6:70 twelve*
7:23 whit
7:37 drink (d) (thirsty)
7:38 water (3e)
8:11 move (5d)
8:12 light (2e)
8:16 alone (d)
8:23 above (2e)
8:32 free (1c) truth (f)
8:36 free (1c) indeed (b)
8:51 death (1b) (die (1f))
8:52 taste (d)
8:58 I AM
9:4 day (2d)
9:11 sight (2e)
9:25 blind (b)* one (4c)
9:30 eye (2e)
10:3 name (2c)
10:7 door (2b)
10:9 enter (c) find (2j) pasture
10:10 (abundant (b))
10:11 sheep (2c) shepherd (1c)
10:12 hireling (wolves)
10:15 life (1c)
10:16 fold (b) sheep (2c)
10:18 man (2k)
10:27 obey (g)
10:28 give (1m) life (2h) pluck (c)
10:29 pluck (c)
10:35 break (g)
11:25 dead (2b) life (2i) live (2d)
11:28, 29call (1d) Master (c)
12:13 palm (b)
12:24 abide (2d) die (1g) fall (3e) ground (1c)
12:25 lose (c) love (9c)
12:26 honour (b) servant (2f)
13:1 end (e) own (4f)
13:8 wash (2d)
13:13 Master (1d)
13:23 bosom (1) lean (c)
14:2 Father (2e) gone (1b) mansion place (4b) prepare (d)
14:5 know (3h)
14:6 come (3b) Father (1f) life (1d) truth (g) way (1e)
14:9 Father (1g) *Song 100 and 718.2*
14:12 work (1d)
14:16 abide (1a) Comforter (1b) give (1f)
14:17 Spirit (3f)
14:18 leave (1c, d)
14:23 abode (a)
14:26 remembrancer teach (1b)
14:27 give (1p) leave (1b) *Song 751.2*
15:1 vine (b)
15:2 fruit (2b)
15:3 speak (1f)
15:4 abide (2e) branch (d) vine (1c)
15:7 ask (2c)
15:10 abide (2f) love (8b)
15:11 joy (2c, d)
15:12 love (8c)
15:13 friend (2c, 3c) greater (b) love (4c) man (2l)
15:15 call (1g) friend (2e)
15:16 fruit (2e) remain (b)
15:18 hate (c) world (2d)
15:26 Father (1h)
16:8 (convince) reprove (b) sin (5d) teach (1b)
16:11 Prince (2)
16:13 guide (a, g)
16:14 (Spirit (2c)) tell (1d)
16:15 thing (2c)
16:20 (joy (2h))
16:22 joy (2e) receive (2e)
16:24 joy (2d)
16:32 Father (1i)
16:33 overcome (c)
17:2 give (1m)
17:3 know (3k)
17:5 (glory (3b))
17:10 glorify (2a)
17:12 keep (3m)
17:17 word (1j)
17:21 (one (3a)) oneness*
17:24 glory (4j)
18:1 (brook (b)) garden (1b)
18:11 drink (c)
18:24 bind (4)
19:2 purple (b)
19:5 crown (1d)
19:17 bear (1c)
19:23 soldier (h)
19:28 thirst (1)

19:30 bow (1b) finish (b)
19:34 blood (2c) pierce (b) shed (2b) side (2b) spear water (2d)
19:37 see Zech. 12:10
19:41 garden (1c)
19:42 lay (2c)
20:1 Mary (c)
20:11 weep (d)
20:12 angel (j)
20:17 (ascended)
20:20 print show (1i) side (2d)
20:22 breathe (1b) receive (2f)
20:25 nail (a)
20:27 (believing (b)) faithless (b) hand (1a)*
20:28 Jesus (7c) Master (e)
20:31 life (2j) name (1h)
21:15 love (7i) more (2d)*
21:20 lean (1c)

Acts

1:3 passion (1)
1:4 promise (3e) wait (2d)
1:5 baptise (b)
1:6 restore (e)
1:11 (gaze)
1:12 Olivet*
2:1 accord (b) Pentecost place (5b)
2:2 fill (2j) (man (1a)) sound (1h) wind (1d)
2:3 appear (3b) cloven Spirit (5b) tongue (e)
2:4 spirit (5b) utterance*
2:17 pour (1c) vision (b) young (c)
2:21 call (2d) name (1i) save (1k)
2:22 man (1a)*
2:24 death (3b)*
2:33 (promise (3f))
3:6 such (2c)
3:13 (Father (3))
3:14 just (1b)
3:15 (life (5c))
3:19 (refresh)
3:22 (priest (1))
3:24 foretold
4:11 set (e)
4:12 name (1j) other (f) salvation (1d)
4:27 anoint (b) holy (1b)
4:30 do (3c) sign (d) stretch (1b)
4:31 assemble (b)
4:33 great (2e)
5:30 hang (d) (tree (2c))
5:31 Prince (1c)
5:39 fight (3)
6:1 (increase (d))
7:46 favour (b)*
7:56 see (1d) stand (1b)
7:59 receive (1c)
7:60 (pardon (1)) pray (2d)
8:16 fall (1a)*
9:11 behold (1f)
9:34 whole (2e)
10:36 Jesus (8e)
10:38 anoint (c)
10:42 judge (1)* preach (a)*
10:44 (Spirit (4b))
11:26 (Christian)
12:7 chain (b) fall (3f)
12:24 multiply (a)
13:23 promise (3g)
13:36 serve (1e)
16:9 come (4h) help (2c)
16:13 wont (b)
16:26 loose (b)
16:31 believe (c)
17:6 (upside)
17:24 (Jesus (8d))
17:27 (afar (c))
17:28 move (1b)
17:31 judgment (b)*
19:20 prevail (g)
20:11 weep (2d)
20:28 purchase*
20:32 grace (3d)
20:35 receive (2g)
22:16 tarry (c) wash (3a)
22:20 martyr (b)
24:25 go (2i) way (4b)
26:18 darkness (2d)* day (5b) light (4i) Satan (c) turn (1b)
26:28 almost (b) persuade (a)

Romans

1:4 holiness (e)
1:9 gospel (c)
1:16 ashamed (a)
1:17 see Galatians 2:20
1:18 unrighteousness (a)
2:7 immortal (b)
3:3 faith (2m)
3:9 under (c)
3:19 world (2a)*
3:24 free (2b) freely (1c)
3:28 faith (1b)*
4:7 cover (c)
4:16 sure (f)
4:20 strong (2c)
5:1 peace (2i)
5:2 hope (3e) rejoice (i) stand (3c)
5:5 abroad (c) shed (2d)
5:8 die (2g) sinner (e)
5:9 justify* redeem (c)
5:10 death (3c)* enemy (b) much (d)
5:11 atonement
5:12 death (3d)
5:14 Adam
5:18 gift (2d)
5:20 abound (b)*
5:21 death (3d) reign (3)
6:2 dead (2c)
6:4 life (2k) newness
6:5 likeness
6:6 destroy (d)
6:10 once (2b)*
6:13 yield (2b)
6:14 dominion (b) sin (5e)
6:15 grace (2g) law (c)
6:18 free (1f, h) servant (2g)
6:22 fruit (2d) holiness (f)
7:15 hate (1a)
7:24 wretched (1a)
8:1 condemnation
8:6 peace (2c)
8:9 dwell (1c) Spirit (3a, 4a)
8:11 body (2c)
8:12 debtor
8:15 (Abba)* adoption bondage (a)* Spirit (2d)
8:16 (sonship) Spirit (2d)
8:17 (glorify (2b))
8:18 (reckon)*
8:21 glorious (2f)
8:22 groan (b) whole (1b)
8:27 search (1b)
8:28 good (1c)
8:29 conform image (b)
8:32 freely (1d) own (4e) spare (c)
8:33 charge (d)
8:34 right (4g)
8:35-39 *Songs 554 and 555*
8:35 distress (2a) evil (d) peril (b) persecution (b) sword (b) tribulation (a)
8:37 conqueror (2b) thing (2d)
8:38 angel (k) death (2f) neither (b) nor (a) power (2c) present (2c) principalities sever (b)
8:39 depth (c) (part (2b)) separate (b) (sever (b))
9:21 clay (d)
9:29 Sabaoth
9:33 believe (f) (shame (2d))*
10:6 bring (2j)
10:7 deep (2c)
10:13 call (2d) save (1k)
10:14 preacher
10:21 stretch (1b)
11:6 (work (1f))
12:1 body (2d) holy (2e) mercy (i) present (3b) sacrifice (2c)
12:2 conform good (3f) perfect (2i)
12:9 cleave*
12:11 fervent (a)
12:12 instant (b)
12:15 *Song 663.2* weep (2e)
12:16 same (2b)
13:11 awake (b)
13:12 work (3b)
14:1 faith (2f) weak (b)
14:8 live (2e)
14:10 judgment (2c) throne (3)
14:11 see Phil 2:10
14:12 account*
14:17 joy (2g) Kingdom (1h) righteousness (c)
15:6 glorify (1a)
15:7 receive (1b)
15:11 laud
15:13 fill (2f) power (4k)
15:19 power (4k) Spirit (5d)
15:33 peace (2j)
16:20 bruise (c) feet (1g) (foe (c)) head (3b)

1 Corinthians

1:7 coming (1b) wait (2e)
1:8 confirm
1:9 faithful (1b)
1:23 preach (b)
1:24 (Jesus (7d)) wisdom (1c)
1:27 choose (1c) thing (1b)
1:28 (nothing (h))
1:30 righteousness (d)
2:2 crucify (1c) know (3i)
2:8 glory (4c)
2:9 eye (2h) hear (3f) heart (6e) prepare (b)
2:10 thing (1c)
2:12 (world (2c))*
2:14 foolish (b)
3:11 lay (2d)
3:15 suffer (3b)
3:16 Spirit (4a) temple (2a)*
3:19 wisdom (2b)*
6:19 own (5b)
6:20 (blood (2f)) bought (a)
7:21 use (2b)
7:22 freeman
9:24 prize see Phil 3:14
9:26 uncertainly
9:27 (subjection)
10:4 drink (e)
10:6 evil (c)
12:1 gift (2e)
12:6 same (1b)
12:13 bond (b) drink (f)
12:31 way (3f)
13:1f *Song 530*
13:1 charity love (1b)
13:2 faith (2n) know (3i) mountain (2g) mystery (c) remove (e)
13:3 nothing (g)
13:5 own (3c)
13:7 bear (2c)
13:8 (fail (1e))
13:12 know (3m)
13:13 greatest (b) hope (3b)

14:8 uncertain
14:33 (confusion)
15:2 vain (b)
15:3 die (2b)
15:4 arise (1c)* rise (2b)
15:10 bestow (b) grace (2h)
15:14 vain (d)
15:20 rise (2d)*
15:22 alive (c)
15:25 reign (1c)*
15:31 (die (1h))
15:43 weakness (b)
15:45 quickening (c)
15:49 image (c)
15:52 trumpet (b)
15:54 death (2h) (swallowed)
15:55 sting (b) victory (2g)
15:57 victory (2h)

2 Corinthians

1:3 comfort (1e) mercy (j)
1:4 trouble (c)
1:8 press (b)
1:9 (sentence)
1:12 (converse (b))
1:20 promise (3i)
1:24 stand (3f)
2:14 (triumph (2a))
3:3 living (3c)
3:5 (sufficiency)
3:6 life (2l)
3:14 (unveil)
3:18 glory (2c)
4:2 renounce
4:4 light (4j)
4:6 *chorus 158* give (1z) glory (4k) God (1f) knowledge (b) light (4k) shine (1f)
4:7 earthen treasure (3c) vessel (b)
4:8 despair (b) perplex
4:9 cast (k)
4:13 faith (2o)
4:15 abundant (c)
4:16 (inward (a))
4:18 look (2e) thing (1d)
5:1 earthly (b) eternal (2b) house (e)
5:6 (absent) body (2e)
5:7 sight (2c) walk (2j)
5:10 appear (2b)
5:14 constrain love (2d)
5:15 rise (2c)
5:17 (creation (b)) (make (4e)) thing (1e)
6:2 accept (c) time (1g)
6:17 separate (c)
6:18 son (2d)
7:1 perfect (2c)
7:5 fear (2c) within (1a)
8:9 (enrich)
9:7 cheerfully grudgingly
9:8 grace (2b)
9:10 (hope (3f)) multiply (b) sow (2e)
9:15 gift (2f) unspeakable (a)
10:1 gentle (1a)
10:4 carnal pull stronghold weapon (b)
10:5 thought (2e)
10:13 (reach (1))*
11:2 jealous
12:9 grace (2i) rest (1b) strength (3c) sufficient (b) (weakest (b)) weakness (c)
12:10 strong (2f)
12:12 mighty (1g)
12:15 spend (c)
13:4 power (4n)
13:14 communion grace (2j) (Father (1c))

Galatians

1:4 deliver (a)
1:15 grace (2n)
1:16 reveal (1g)
2:19 live (2j)
2:20 faith (2c) give (1j)* Jesus (8i) life (4h) (live (1d)) (live (2k))
2:21 die (2h) frustrate rain (e)
3:13 curse
3:14 receive (2h)
3:26 child (4b)*
3:27 (put (b))
3:28 free (1j)* one (3b)
4:9 turn (2c)
4:15 blessedness (b)
4:25 Jerusalem (b)
4:26 (born (1e))
4:27 barrenness
4:31 free (1k)
5:1 free (1c)* liberty (c)
5:5 righteousness (e)
5:6 work (2e)
5:13 serve (1f)
5:18 Spirit (4d)
5:20 (strife)*
5:22 fruit (2e) gentle (1b) gentleness joy (2g) love (5b) Spirit (5c)
5:24 affection (b)
6:1 (overtake) (b)
6:2 burden (1b, 2f) (law (b))
6:5 burden (1b) (work (1h))
6:9 reap (b) (reaper (c)) weary (g)
6:14 crucify (2) forbid (c) glory (2d) save (3b)
6:15 (creation (b))
6:17 (bear (2d)) mark (b)

Ephesians

1:3 blessing (f)
1:7 blood (2h) redemption (b)
1:9 mystery (1a)*
1:13 seal (b, c)*
1:14 earnest (1)*
1:18 know (2f)
1:19 greatness (b) mighty (1i)
1:20 wrought (d)
1:22 head (1c)*
2:1 quicken*
2:4 great (2f) rich (2c)
2:5 grace (2o) quicken*
2:6 raise (1c)*
2:7 rich (2d)
2:8 faith (1c) gift (2g)
2:9 boast (c) work (2f)
2:10 (form (c))
2:12 (alien) hope (3c) stranger (2c)
2:13 blood (2i)*
2:14 peace (2k)
2:15 peace (2l)
2:16 reconcile*
2:19 (citizen) household
2:20 corner (b)* stone (1)*
2:22 habitation
3:8 least (b)* rich (2e) unsearchable
3:15 family
3:16 (inner)
3:17 dwell (1c) grounded root (b)
3:18 breadth (broad) comprehend (b) depth (d) height (c) length (b)
3:19 fulness (a) know (3n) knowledge (c) love (4d)
3:20 abundantly (b) ask (2d) think (2d)
3:21 (ages (2c)) glory (5d)
4:1 walk (2k) (worthily (b)*)
4:4 body (2f) (calling*) hope (3d)
4:6 Father (1b)
4:8 captive (c)
4:11 gift (2h)
4:13 faith (4b)
4:15 grow (3d) thing (2e)
4:18 (blindness)* life (1e)
4:30 seal (1b)
4:32 tender (c)
5:2 offering (1)
5:9 fruit (2e) righteousness (f)
5:14 rise (3d) wake (2b)
5:16 redeem (d)
5:18 fill (2j)*
5:19 melody (a)*
6:5 singleness*
6:6 (will (1b))*
6:7 service (c)
6:10 power (4o)
6:11 armour put (c)
6:12 world (2b)
6:13 do (1d) stand (3g)
6:14 gird
6:15 feet (1h)
6:16 dart* shield (b)
6:17 hand (e) helmet sword (2e)
6:18 (persevere) watch (2f)

Philippians

1:6 begin (1b) perform (c) work (1e)
1:7 partaker (b)
1:11 praise (3i)
1:19 supply (1)
1:20 death (2g) 21 die (1b) expectation
1:21 gain (g) Jesus (5b) live (2e)
2:3 lowliness (b)*
2:5 mind (1b)
2:8 humble (2b)
2:9f exalt *Song 141*
2:10 bow (2d) exalt (c) name (1k)
2:11 confess (1b) Father (1j) Jesus (3f) tongue (c)
2:12 tremble (b)
2:15 shine (2a)
3:7 count (c) gain (d) (lose (d)) loss (c)
3:9 (righteousness (a))*
3:10 power (4p) resurrection (b)
3:12 (attain)*
3:13 reach (2b)
3:14 press (e) prize (1)
3:21 glorify (1b) subdue (1)
4:1 joy (1c)
4:4 rejoice (j) say (2c)
4:6 request (b) (supplicant)*
4:7 pass (2c) peace (2m) understanding (b)
4:8 *chorus 56* glorious (1f) thing (1g)
4:11 content (a) (estate (a)) (lot) state (b) whatever (b)
4:12 instructed
4:13 do (1e)
4:18 abound (c) have (2g)
4:19 supply (2b)

Colossians

1:2 peace (2n)
1:9 will (1g)
1:10 (fruitful) good (3e) work (2g)
1:11 strengthen (b)
1:12 inheritance meet (1b)
1:13 darkness (2e) dear (2f) power (2d) translate (b)
1:14 blood (2h) redemption (b)
1:19 please (2c)

1:22 sight (1e) (unblameable)*
1:23 remove (d)
1:25 fulfil (f)
2:2 love (8d)
2:5 stedfast (c)
2:6 walk (2l)
2:9 Godhead
2:14 nail (b)
2:15 (triumph (1))
2:19 band (3c) increase (e)
3:1 rise (3e) sit (d)* thing (1f)
3:3 hide (g)
3:4 appear (1a)* glory (3c)
3:11 all (4d, 6b)
3:12 humbleness meekness*
3:15 rule (2b)*
3:16 dwell (3b) richly (b)
3:17 deed (d)*
4:12 complete (c)
4:17 fulfil (c)

1 Thessalonians

2:13 cease (d)
2:19 hope (2a) joy (1d)
3:5 (tempter)
3:7 distress (2b)
3:9 render (b)
4:3 will (3b)
4:12 lack (c)
4:14 (slumber (2c))*
4:16 angel (1) archangel dead (2d) trumpet (b) voice (2b)
4:17 ever (g) (meet (3e))*
5:6 (slumber (2b))*
5:8 faith (2d)
5:10 live (3a)
5:17 pray (2e) prayer (2d)
5:18 everything (b)
5:19 quench (b)
5:21 fast (b)
5:23 body (2g) sanctify (b) sight (1e) spirit (6d) whole (1d)

2 Thessalonians

1:11 faith (2l) fulfil (e)
1:12 glorify (1c)
3:1 glorify (1d)
3:5 wait (2b)

1 Timothy

1:1 hope (2a)
1:2 mercy (d)
1:6 (swerve) (unswerving)
1:11 glorious (2d)
1:12 count (b)
1:15 chief (b) save (1l)
1:16 (pattern)
1:17 immortal (c) invisible* King (2f) wise (e)
1:19 (shipwrecked)
2:5 *chorus 156*
2:6 ransom (c)
2:9 pearl (b)
3:7 snare*
3:15 ground (2c)
4:7 exercise
4:10 Jesus (8h) trust (3d)
6:8 clothing food (b)
6:12 faith (2j) fight (3h) lay (3c) life (2m)

2 Timothy

1:5 persuade (b)
1:6 gift (2i) stir (b)
1:7 love (5c) mind (2e) power (4q) Spirit (3e)
1:10 bring (1e) (immortal (b)) immortality* sure (b)
1:12 commit (b) day (3i) know (3c) persuade (b) *Song 730.c*
2:1 grace (2k) (strength (2h)) strong (2e)
2:3 soldier (a)
2:4 choose (1d) soldier (i)
2:12 reign (2b) suffer (3d)*
2:13 deny (d)*
2:15 approve ashamed (b) truth (h) (work (2h)) workman
2:19 foundation (b) sure (c)
2:21 (use (1))
2:25 meekness (b)
3:11 out of (d)
3:16 (Scripture)*
3:17 furnished (b)
4:7 fight (2h, i) keep (2e)
4:8 lay (2e) (long (1e))

Titus

1:2 cannot (b) lie (1)
1:9 faithful (1c)
2:10 adorn (b) doctrine (b)
2:11 bring (1h)*
2:13 appearing hope (3g)
2:14 purify*
3:1 ready (d)
3:5 renew (f)

Hebrews

1:2 worlds
1:3 power (4r) purge (1c)
1:7 flame (2d)
1:8 (sceptre)
1:9 oil (b)
1:12 everlasting (d)
1:14 heir (b)*
2:3 great (2i) neglect (b)
2:4 wonder (1e)*
2:8 yet (b)
2:9 crown (1c) taste (e)
2:10 captain suffering (1a)
2:17 merciful (b)
2:18 succour*
3:1 priest (1)
3:2 appoint (b)
3:6 (firm)
3:7 to day (d)
3:8 harden
3:13 today (b) (while (b))
3:14 faith (2g)
4:1 promise (3j)
4:8 rest (4c)
4:11 enter (d)
4:12 edged sword (2f) pierce (d) two (b)
4:15 (sinless) (untouched)
4:16 bold (c) grace (2l, 3b) mercy (k) need (3d) throne (4c)
5:9 salvation (1e)
6:11 full (1f)
6:12 (sloth)
6:13 sworn (c)
6:17 oath
6:18 flee (2b)
6:19 anchor hope (3h) steadfast (b) sure (d) veil (c)
7:16 endless (b)
7:22 surety (b)
7:25 able (c) (Father (1k)) intercede (b) live (1c) plead (b) uttermost (utmost)
8:2 (pitch)
8:6 covenant (c)
8:10-12 see Jeremiah 31:33, 34
9:12 (beast (b)) blood (1b) holy (2d)*
9:14 Spirit (2e)
9:24 presence (f)
9:26 sacrifice (1)*
9:28 bear (1e) (bearer)
10:15 witness (1a)
10:20 veil (d) way (1f)
10:22 assurance (b)* draw (2b) full (2f)
10:23 faith (2h) waver*
10:32 illuminate*
11:1 evidence see (3j)
11:3 worlds
11:8 Abraham (b) know (3p)*
11:9 land (1c) sojourn
11:13 afar (d) earth (3e) embrace (b) faith (3b) pilgrim*
11:14 country (b)
11:16 (city (2a))*
11:25 pleasure (c)
11:33 lion wrought (c)*
11:34 strong (2d)* (valiant (a)) (valiantly) weakness (d)
11:37 (wander (b))
12:1 beset lay (3d) race (2b) witness (2b)
12.2 author endure (d) look (2f) shame (1b)
12:3 weary (h)
12:11 yield (3b)
12:17 repentance (b)
12:24 (besprinkled)* sprinkle
12:25 refuse (b) turn (2d)
12:28 godly fear (1b)
13:1 brotherly
13:5 see Joshua 1:5 leave (1c) never (1c) today (e)
13:8 same (1c) yesterday (b)
13:13 reproach*
13:15 offer (2b) praise (3e) thank (c)
13:16 please (2d)
13:21 well (2i)

James

1:6 ask (2e) (unwavering)
1:4 want
1:11 fade (b)
1:12 promise (3k) receive (2i)
1:14 entice*
1:17 above (2f) gift (2j) shade (j) turning
1:21 save (1m)
1:27 unspotted (b)
2:19 fear (4b) tremble (d)
3:5 fire (3d) kindle (c)
3:10 blessing (c) (cursing)
3:17 wisdom (1d)
4:6 give (1h) more (2c)
4:7 devil (b) fly (c) (submission)*
4:8 draw (1d)
4:9 mourn (b)
5:5 wanton
5:11 pitiful
5:13 pray (2f) sing (4f)
5:16 confess (2b) effectual fault (b) fervent (b) prayer (2e)

1 Peter

1:2 multiply (c) sprinkle
1:3 abundant (d)
1:4 fade (c) (fadeless)
1:5 keep (3e)
1:6 rejoice (k) (season (d))
1:7 fire (3e) gold (1f) precious (i) trial (2b) try (2b)
1:8 joy (2l) see (3m) (unseen (b)) unspeakable (b)
1:12 angel Heaven (2j) send (1f)
1:13 sober*
1:18 gold (1g) redeem (c)
1:19 Lamb (2c) precious (b) (unspotted (a))
1:23 abide (2i) word (1e)
2:3 gracious (c) taste (c)

2:4 stone (2e)
2:8 stumble*
2:9 marvellous light (4i)
2:11 stranger (2d)
2:21 example follow (d) step (1)
2:24 self (1b)
3:3 adorn (c)
3:13 harm
3:18 suffer (2d)
4:1 arm (3b) cease (e) mind (1b)
4:12 fiery (b) trial (2c)
4:13 reveal (f) suffering (1b)*
5:2 feed (d)* flock (a)*
5:4 crown (2c) fade (c) (fadeless) glory (2e)
5:5 clothe (b)
5:6 hand (1h)*
5:7 care (1a)
5:8 lion (seek (4b))
5:10 glory (2f)

2 Peter

1:3 divine (e)
1:4 give (1r) nature (3b) precious (d) promise (3l)
1:10 fall (2d)
1:19 daystar
1:21 move (1c) prophet (c)
2:20 pollution
3:3 (scoff)
3:10 earth (g) earthly (c) melt (b)
3:12 haste (d)
3:14 blameless spot (b) (spotless (2))
3:18 grow (3e)

1 John

1:1 life (2d)
1:3 fellowship (a)
1:5 darkness (2f) light (2b)
1:7 blood (2g, j) clean (c) cleanse (c) fellowship (b) sin (1e) walk (2g)
1:8 deceive (b) self (2b)
1:9 confess (2c) forgive (1g) just (1d) unrighteousness (b)
2:1 advocate
2:2 sound (n) whole (1e)*
2:17 abide (2g)
2:25 promise (3m)
3:1 bestow (c) (bestowal) Father (2f)* son (2c)*
3:2 (Jesus (9c))*
3:8 destroy (c) work (3c)
3:9 commit (c)
3:24 dwell (2d)*
4:8 love (2b)
4:9 live (2f) manifest (c)
4:12 perfect (2d)
4:17 bold (1d) make (3e) perfect (2d)
4:18 (banish (b)) cast (n) love (4e)
4:19 first (3b) love (7j)
5:4 overcome (d) victory (2i)
5:7 (Recorder)
5:8 Spirit (2d) witness (1c)
5:10 witness (1d)
5:14 (hear) (1f)
5:20 understanding (a)*
5:21 (idol)*

2 John

9 abide (2h)

Jude

2 mercy (b)
3 contend saint (1b)
23 (save (2a))
24 faultless keep (3o)
25 dominion (a) majesty (d)

Revelation

1:5 begotten dead (2e) first (3e) own (4d) wash (3a, b)
1:6 priest (2b)
1:7 cloud (1d) descend (1b) eye (2i) wail (b)
1:11 first (3d)
1:18 alive (d) death (3e) key (b)
2:5 fall (2e)
2:7 paradise* tree (2b)
2:10 crown (2d) faithful (2d) gain (b)
2:17 manna*
2:27 iron (b)
3:4 white (b) worthy (b)*
3:5 raiment (d) white (c)
3:7 shut (b)
3:8 door (2c)
3:12 more (5e) new (f) pillar (b) temple (2c)
3:14 faithful (1d) faithfulness witness (1e)
3:17 blind (c) wretched (b)
3:20 door (2d) knock (b) stand (1c)
3:21 grant (d) overcome (b) throne (4d)
4:4 gold (2b)*
4:5 (sevenfold)
4:6 crystal (b) glassy sea (2d)
4:8 almighty (e)* holy (1c) rest (4c)
4:10 cast (j)
4:11 Lamb (2e) receive (1d) worthy (a)
5:5 Judah
5:6 Lamb (2d) throne (4e)
5:7 throne (4f)
5:8 harp*
5:9 kindred (b) new (g)* sing (2b) song (1i) tongue (d)
5:11 angel (n)* thousand (2d)
5:12 blessing (g) glory (5e)* honour (c) Lamb (2e) power (4s) receive (1d) strength (1c) wisdom (e) worthy (b)
6:2 conquer (1a) conquering (a)
6:11 robe (b)*
6:16 wrath (c)
6:17 wrath (c)
7:3 seal (f)
7:9 palm (c) (unnumbered (b))
7:10 salvation (1f) throne (4c)
7:13 array (b) garment (e) robe (c) white who (d)
7:14 come (5b) great (2j) Lamb (2f) out (b) robe (d) tribulation (b)
7:15 serve (1g) throne (4h)
7:16 suffer (3e) thirst (2d)
7:17 eye (2j) fountain (2b) lead (3i) robe (d) (suffer (3e)) tear (2d) (tearless) wipe (a)
10:6 time (1h)
11:15 ever (h) Kingdom (1i) kingdom (3) reign (1d) *Song 782.3*
11:17 power (4t)
11:18 fear (1c)
12:10 accuser
12:11 (bleeding (b)) Lamb (2f)
13:8 foundation (c) slain (1b)*
14:2 thunder (b)
14:4 (follower (b))
14:13 labour (c) rest (2n)
14:15 ripe (b) sickle (b)*
14:16 reap (c)
15:3 Lamb (2g) Moses (c) sing (2e)
15:4 holy (1c)
16:10 pain (4)
16:14 great (2d)
16:19 wrath (d)*
19:1 alleluia hallelujah
19:6 omnipotent
19:12 many (2c)
19:13 (Word (1b))
19:14 army (2b)
19:15 tread (f) winepress
19:16 (Jesus (8f)) King (2j)
20:8 numberless (b)
20:11 earth (1h)
20:14 Hell (b)
21:2 bride Jerusalem (c)
21:4 death (3f) eye (2j) more (5f) pain (3a) sorrow (2d) (weep (2f))
21:5 thing (1e)
21:6 fountain (2e) freely (1d)
21:12 gate (f)
21:18 gold (2c) jasper* wall (d)
21:21 gold (2c) (pearly) street (2)
21:23 light (4l) sun (1c)
21:25 night (2e)
21:27 write
22:1 crystal (b) flow (2a) pure (1c) river (2a, e) throne (4i) (tide (3)) (water (3f))
22:2 heal (2e) leaves (4b) tree (2b)
22:3 curse
22:4 face (2e)
22:5 reign (2b) star (c)
22:16 offering star (d, f)
22:17 freely (2c) say (1e) whosoever
22:20 quickly (b)